The Concise Oxford
DICTIONARY OF
OPERA

THE CONCISE OXFORD
DICTIONARY OF
OPERA

Second edition

by
Harold Rosenthal
and
John Warrack

London
OXFORD UNIVERSITY PRESS
New York   Melbourne
1979

Oxford University Press, Walton Street, Oxford OX2 6DP

OXFORD LONDON GLASGOW NEW YORK
TORONTO MELBOURNE WELLINGTON
IBADAN NAIROBI DAR ES SALAAM CAPE TOWN
KUALA LUMPUR SINGAPORE JAKARTA HONG KONG TOKYO
DELHI BOMBAY CALCUTTA MADRAS KARACHI

ISBN 0 19 311318 X

Second edition © Harold Rosenthal and John Warrack

First published 1964
Second edition 1979

Set in Great Britain by G. A. Pindar & Son, Scarborough,
printed and bound at the Pitman Press, Bath

FOREWORD

Within seventy years of the emergence of opera as a distinctive art form in Florence around 1600, the wealth of new works had led to the first attempt at a catalogue. This was the celebrated *Drammaturgia*, a list of all dramatic works compiled in 1666 by Leone Allacci, a Chiot scholar who had become librarian of the Vatican in 1661. His work gradually found a number of successors; and they continue to increase. Not only catalogues, but guides, companions, collections of analyses and synopses, histories both general, national, and local – all these are published in what seems ever increasing abundance, to say nothing of the specialist literature on every aspect of operatic composition, theory, and performance. At the same time, the vast increase in musicological activity, stimulated by the large numbers of research students emerging from universities, has led to an enormous amount of information, hitherto remote and obscure of access, becoming widely available. Almost every country with a claim to a musical tradition has in recent years published or substantially enlarged its own national encyclopedia. We have drawn upon many of these works, as well as upon original scores, upon copious correspondence with scholars, archivists, and artists all over the world, and upon our own records and research. What we have had in mind is to provide the opera-goer with a concise but comprehensive work of reference – and perhaps also of some entertainment.

We have, naturally, been obliged to lean heavily on our distinguished predecessors in their various fields; but wherever possible, every fact has been checked against several authorities. Error is easily perpetuated from one reference work to another: it is never sufficient to suppose that because a date is given as, say, 1667 in six works of reference, the seventh (which has not copied a corrupt source) may not be right with 1676. Nor does the problem necessarily become less acute in more modern times: no fewer than five different birthdays for Mattia Battistini can be found in leading music encyclopedias published in the 1950s. We draw attention to these problems in sympathy, not rebuke: accuracy, the *raison d'être* of a reference book, is an elusive ideal, and any lexicographer who throws stones at his colleagues does so in full knowledge of the fragility of his own windows. In reworking our dictionary for the present second edition, we have gone over every entry in the light of new information published since the original edition of 1964; we have corrected errors and filled in gaps, hoping only to have taken one more step along the road towards a fair and accurate survey of the rich tradition of opera.

In preparing a second edition, we have also substantially enlarged the book. We have, for instance, greatly extended the coverage of the development of opera in all countries of the world. Under the country itself will be found a survey of the general artistic development of its national opera; under the various towns of that country, when they are important enough to warrant it, there is a more factual account of opera's establishment and growth there; while the major cities and towns are also sometimes given extra treatment in separate entries on the histories of their leading opera houses. A system of cross-references should help to direct the reader to entries containing further relevant information on a particular subject. A further guide is provided by a system of asterisks: an asterisk before a word indicates an entry that is relevant to the one being consulted. Thus under Italy, the reader is given a list of cities including Milan; under Milan, a list of opera houses including La Scala; and in the entry on La Scala, the name of Toscanini is asterisked since there is material in his entry relevant to the history of La Scala: it does not follow that every mention of Toscanini throughout the book carries an asterisk. We have also added to a number of entries a bibliographical reference: normally this is confined to one standard work on the subject for further information and reading, in the case of composers usually one including fuller work-lists than we can provide.

We have also extended the number of literary references, so as to provide a convenient check-list. Completeness is unattainable here, as elsewhere, but we have listed as many operas as we can on the works of important writers and on famous subjects (e.g. Don Juan). The demands of conciseness have prevented us from publishing complete lists of the operas setting the most popular subjects, such as Ariadne, Alexander, and Semiramide, since they run into three figures: but we have made an effort to compile full lists of the operas written on works by Shakespeare, Scott, and other writers to whom composers have most frequently turned. We have included rather a large proportion of singers, since most general works of reference tend, reasonably, to place the interpreter below the creator in importance; and we have now added a larger number from important operatic eras of the past, such as those of Imperial Russia or Parisian Grand Opera. As far as the past is concerned, we have tried to include a fuller selection of those whose artistry influenced composers and fellow performers, thus contributing to operatic history. Contemporary artists have presented more difficulty, but we have included a generous selection of those who have either already established themselves internationally, and about whom the opera-goer might wish to know, or who are likely to do so within the next few years. We have allowed ourselves to include a few who may not rank as international figures but are highly prized in their own country. Every reference book must face the challenge of why one subject is in, another out. We are well aware that different compilers would have chosen differently; our dictionary claims conciseness rather than completeness. It is no less obvious that every reference book becomes out of date as soon as it is published: we have had to make our closing date the autumn of 1978.

Though we have not made much use of abbreviations, except chiefly for the names of opera houses (see list on pp. xi–xii), there are a number of usages that require elucidation.

Dates of operas, unless otherwise explained, are of first production; we have normally added the composition date only when it antedates production by a significant number of years. We should have preferred to give composition dates in all cases, but they are so often undiscoverable that we have had to bow to consistency. Opera titles are normally in the original language (though there are exceptions here: we have not used Russian titles nor indeed the Cyrillic alphabet at all); the English translation in brackets is often literal rather than a suggestion for general use. When an opera is known in England only by an English title (e.g. *The Bartered Bride*) we give the original in brackets. In the singer entries, the seasons and appearances are only the most notable ones. We have used the conventional, if misleading, term 'created . . .' to mean 'first singer of . . .'.

Place-names have presented the usual problem. We have, with very few exceptions, given the name currently used in the country concerned: that is, Ljubljana (not Laibach), Oslo (not Christiania). We have given alternative names in brackets, though without explanation, which would usually involve a short historical essay. There are two natural exceptions to this rule. We follow normal English usage in writing Munich, Warsaw, Florence, etc., though we give the originals in brackets in their main entries (Ger., München; Pol., Warszawa; It., Firenze). And when a town has changed its own name, we give it according to how it was known at the time: thus it becomes possible for a stay-at-home composer to be born in St Petersburg, study in Petrograd, and die in Leningrad, though never for another to be born in Pressburg, study in Pozsony, and die in Bratislava. Cross-references help to clear up these matters. In the case of the Alsatian capital, we take the liberty of settling for Strasbourg.

It goes without saying that we spell all personal names as the owner would himself, complete with accents even when it is unlikely that many English readers are familiar with the effect of Latvian apostrophes or Hungarian double-acutes. Transliteration from Cyrillic (and to a lesser extent Greek) has been as difficult as always. Though basically we follow that approved by the School of Slavonic Studies, we do make certain deviations, preferring clarity and familiarity to total consistency (Tchaikovsky, not Chaykovsky). The Italian 'long i' is discarded (Barbaia, not Barbaja) except in initials: no one will look up Iommelli.

A certain number of brief synopses will be found. While it is obvious that we are not competing with Kobbé, Lubbock, and similar books, we felt that a reminder might be useful in the case of repertory operas; rarer works are given a sentence or two indicating the plot or at least the subject. We have not generally taken up space with the plots of stories very familiar from other contexts: there is no synopsis of Britten's *A Midsummer Night's Dream* since, despite the composer's special view of the work, the plot is Shakespeare's.

As regards dates, we retain the old-style English dates before the adoption of the Gregorian calendar in 1752; however, Russian dates, and those of other countries who retained the Julian calendar into modern times, are given in New Style.

We owe so much to so many kind and scholarly people that the problem of selection once again becomes troublesome. For advice, help, and information on specific subjects, we continue to be particularly indebted to Senhor A. F. de Almeida, Count Giacomo Antonini, Mr Jack Belsom, Dr Rosalia Bix, Sgr Rodolfo Celletti, Mr Eric Crozier, Mr Winton Dean, Dr Stana Djurić-Klajn, Dr Pavel Eckstein, Mr Peter Forster, M Paul Francy, Dr Alfred Frankenstein, Mr Frank Freudenthal, Sgr Giorgio Gualerzi, M Jacques Gheusi, Mr Bertil Hagmann, Mr Peter Heyworth, Dr Kurt Honolka, Mr Arthur Jacobs, Mr Michael Kennedy, Dr Desző Legány, Mr Mark Lubbock, Mr Richard Macnutt, Dr Carlo Marinelli, Mr William Marshall, Mr Julius Mattfeld, Dr Kornel Michałowski, Dr Carl Morey, Mr William Nazzaro, Dr Alena Němcová, Dr Henry Orlov, Mr Charles Pitt, Mr K. A. Pollak, Mr Georgi Polyanovsky, Mr Leo Riemens, Mr Lionel Salter, Sgr Claudio Sartori, Mr Max de Schauensee, Mr Gerhard Schepelern, Dr Horst Seeger, Mr Nicholas Slonimsky, Mr Patrick J. Smith, Mr Marius Sotropa, Mr Jani Strasser, Sgr Raffaele Vegeto, Mr William Weaver, Mr Joseph Wechsberg, Dr Joachim Wenzel, and M. Stéphane Wolff. We are also grateful to the archivists, Dramaturgs, and other officials of opera houses too numerous to name individually, whose help was invaluable in providing and checking information. To the patient staffs of the London Library and the British Library we continue to owe a debt for their tolerance of all our importunities and for their knowledge of many obscure sources of information. For the first edition, we were especially grateful to Mr Frank Merkling, Mr Andrew Porter, and Mr Robert Tuggle, all of whom read the entire typescript and made large numbers of useful suggestions; we are no less grateful now to the Earl of Harewood, who furnished us with lists of corrections and suggestions arising from that edition, and to Mr Charles Jahant, whose encyclopaedic knowledge of operatic facts, dates, details, and recherché lore was enthusiastically placed at our disposal.

We should also like to acknowledge the help provided by numerous correspondents from all over the world: many of them were previously unknown to us, and trouble to send in sometimes a single new fact.

London – Rievaulx   H.D.R.
December 1978   J.W.

BIBLIOGRAPHY

We have given under individual composers, singers, and opera houses a bibliographical mention of the standard work on the subject. To draw up even a summary list of the writings on the history, theory, and practice of opera is impossible in a brief space: the interested are directed to the bibliographies in the article *Oper* in the German encyclopaedia *Die Musik in Geschichte und Gegenwart*, and in the article *Opera* in *The New Grove Dictionary of Music and Musicians*. We may also mention the useful bibliographies attached to articles in the Italian *Enciclopedia dello Spettacolo*. Another excellent general bibliography may be found in the standard *A Short History of Opera* by Donald J. Grout (New York, 1947), and one of a more particular nature in Patrick J. Smith's study of the history of the opera libretto, *The Tenth Muse* (New York, 1970). However, we think it may be useful to give two short lists here, of catalogues of operas, and of books of synopses and analyses. Caution is advised in consulting some of the catalogues, particularly the earlier ones: a common fault is the inclusion of a number of titles that prove on investigation to be ballets or incidental music or other works that can hardly be described as operas.

CATALOGUES

L. Allacci: *Drammaturgia* (Rome, 1666; continuation by G. Pasquali, Venice, 1755)

L.-C. de Lavallière: *Ballets, opéras, et autres ouvrages lyriques* . . . (Paris, 1760, R/1967).

F. Clément and P. Larousse: *Dictionnaire lyrique, ou Histoire des Opéras* (Paris, 1867–9, four supplements to 1881; further supplements by A. Pougin, 1899 up to 1904).

T. Lajarte: *Bibliographie musicale du Théâtre de l'Opéra* (Paris, 1877–9).

C. Dassori: *Opere e operisti* (Genoa, 1903).

J. Towers: *Dictionary-Catalogue of Operas and Operettas* . . . (Morgantown, 1910, R/1967).

G. Albinati: *Piccolo dizionario di opere teatrali, oratori, cantate ecc.* (Milan, 1913).

R.-A. Mooser: *Opéras, intermezzos, ballets, cantates, oratorios joués en Russie durant le dix-huitième siècle* (Geneva, 1945, 2/1955).

A. Loewenberg: *Annals of Opera, 1597–1940* (Cambridge, 1943, 2/1955, 3/1978).

U. Manferrari: *Dizionario universale delle opere melodrammatiche* (Florence, 1954–5).

K. Michałowski: *Opery polskie* (Kraków, 1954).

A. Bauer: *Opern und Operetten in Wien* (Graz and Cologne, 1955).

W. Smith: *The Italian Opera and Contemporary Ballet in London, 1789–1820* (London, 1955).

J. Mattfeld: *A Handbook of American Operatic Premières* (Detroit, 1963).

Aldo Caselli: *Catalogo delle opere liriche pubblicate in Italia* (Florence, 1969).

C. Northouse: *Twentieth Century Opera in England and the United States* (Boston, 1976).

SYNOPSES AND ANALYSES

C. Annesley: *The Standard Operaglass* (London, rev. 1901).

Harewood, ed.: *Kobbé's Complete Opera Book* (London, 9/1976).

E. Newman: *Opera Nights* (London, 1943).

E. Newman: *Wagner Nights* (London, 1949).

W. Zentner and A. Würz: *Reclams Opern- und Operettenführer* (Stuttgart, 15/1951).

E. Newman: *More Opera Nights* (London, 1954).

R. Fellner: *Opera Themes and Plots* (London, 1958).

M. Lubbock: *The Complete Book of Light Opera* (London, 1962).

V. Pankratova and L. Polyakova: *Opernye libretto* (Moscow, 1970).

ABBREVIATIONS

OPERA HOUSES AND CONSERVATORIES

Barcelona	L.	Teatro Liceo
Berlin	D.	Deutsche Oper
	H.	Hofoper
	K.O.	Komische Oper
	S.O.	Staatsoper
	Sch.	Schauspielhaus
	Stä. O.	Städtische Oper
	V.	Volksoper
Brussels	La M.	Théâtre Royale de la Monnaie
Buenos Aires	C.	Teatro Colón
Florence	P.	Teatro alla Pergola
	C.	Teatro Comunale
Genoa	C.F.	Teatro Carlo Felice
Glyndebourne	Gly.	
Leningrad	K.	Kirov Theatre
(St Petersburg)	M.	Maryinsky Theatre
London	C.G.	Covent Garden
	Col.	Coliseum
	D.L.	Drury Lane
	G.S.M.	Guildhall School of Music
	Hm.	Haymarket
	H.M.'s	His (Her) Majesty's
	Ly.	Lyceum (English Opera House)
	R.A.H.	Royal Albert Hall
	R.C.M.	Royal College of Music
	R.F.H.	Royal Festival Hall
	St J's.	St. James's
	S.W.	Sadler's Wells
	T.C.M.	Trinity College
Manchester	R.M.C.M.	Royal Manchester College of Music
Milan	Sc.	Teatro alla Scala (La Scala)
	T.d.V.	Teatro dal Verme
	T.L.	Teatro Lirico
	T.N.	Teatro Nuovo
	T.R.D.	Teatro Regio Ducal
Moscow	B.	Bolshoy Teatr
	Z.	Zimin Teatr
Munich	N.	Hof- und Nationaltheater
	P.	Prinzregenttheater
Naples	S.B.	Teatro San Bartolomeo
	S.C.	Teatro San Carlo
	T.N.	Teatro Nuovo
New York	Ac. of M.	Academy of Music
	C.C.	City Center
	Met.	Metropolitan Opera House
	P.O.H.	Palmo's Opera House

Paris	B.P.	Bouffes-Parisiens
	Ch.É.	Théâtre des Champs-Élysées
	C.I.	Comédie-Italienne
	F.-P.	Fantaisies-Parisiennes
	O.	Opéra (Académie Royale de Musique)
	O.C.	Opéra-Comique
	T.I.	Théâtre-Italien
	T.S.B.	Théâtre Sarah Bernhardt
	T.L.	Théâtre-Lyrique
Philadelphia	Ac. of M.	Academy of Music
Prague	N.	Narodni Divadlo (National Theatre)
	Cz.	Czech Theatre
	P.	Prozátimní Divadlo (Provisional Theatre)
Rome	Ad.	Teatro Adriano
	Ap.	Teatro Apollo
	Arg.	Teatro Argentina
	C.	Teatro Costanzi
	R. (or O.)	Teatro Reale dell'Opera
St Petersburg (see Leningrad)		
Turin	T.R.	Teatro Regio
	V.E.	Teatro Vittorio Emanuele
Venice	F.	Teatro La Fenice
	S.B.	Teatro San Benedetto
	S.C.	Teatro San Cassiano
	S.G.Cr.	Teatro San Giovanni Crisostomo
	S.G.P.	Teatro Santi Giovanni e Paolo
	S.L.	Teatro Santa Lucia
	S.Sam.	Teatro San Samuele
Vienna	B.	Burgtheater
	J.	Theater in der Josephstadt
	Kä.	Kärntnertortheater
	L.	Theater in der Leopoldstadt
	S.O.	Staatsoper
	V.O.	Volksoper
	W.	Theater auf der Wieden (later Theater an der Wien)

NATIONALITIES AND LANGUAGES

Cz.	Czechoslovak	It.	Italian
Dan.	Danish	Yug.	Yugoslav
Flem.	Flemish	Lat.	Latin
Fr.	French	Pol.	Polish
Ger.	German	Port.	Portuguese
Gr.	Greek	Rom.	Romanian

MISCELLANEOUS

B.B.C.	British Broadcasting Corporation
B.N.O.C.	British National Opera Company
cap.	capacity
Carn.	Carnival (usually beginning 26 Dec. of previous year and lasting until Feb. or Mar.)
C.B.S.	Columbia Broadcasting System
C.R.	Carl Rosa Opera Company
cond.	conductor, conducted
E.N.O.	English National Opera
E.O.G.	English Opera Group
O.H.	Opera house
prod.	producer, produced
(R)	has made operatic gramophone record
T.	theatre
TV	television
rev.	revised
*	*see marked entry for further relevant information*

KEY TO VOCAL COMPASSES

c''' to c''''

c'' to b''

c' to b'

c to b

C to B

C_1 to B_1

A

Aachen (Fr. Aix-la-Chapelle). Town in North Rhine Westphalia, Germany. Companies from Holland, later France and Italy, visited the town in the 18th cent., and Johann Böhm's company brought *Die Entführung* and *Die Zauberflöte*; performances in the Komödienhaus auf dem Katschhof, built 1752 and one of the first civic theatres in Germany. In 1825 a fine new theatre was built by *Schinkel. A performance of Handel's *Deborah* in 1834 drew Chopin and Hiller from Paris (Mendelssohn came to part of a rehearsal). The town has long had a reputation as a springboard for young talent, and artists who worked there early in their careers include Leo Blech, Karajan, and Sawallisch. The present theatre (cap. 944) was opened 1951; Gabriel Chmura has been music director since 1974.

Abbado, Claudio (*b* Milan, 26 June 1933). Italian conductor. Studied Milan, Vienna with Swarowsky. Won Mitropoulos competition for conductors in 1963. Milan Sc., 1965, music director since 1968; London, C. G., 1968; Salzburg since 1965. One of the most gifted of the younger generation of Italian conductors, as at home with the works of Berg and Nono as with those of Rossini and Verdi. (R)

Abbey, Henry Eugene (*b* Akron, Ohio, 27 June 1846; *d* New York, 17 Oct. 1896). American impresario. First manager of the N.Y. Met (1883); lost nearly $500,000. Shared management with Grau and Schoeffel, 1891-6.

Abbott, Emma (*b* Chicago, 9 Dec. 1850; *d* Salt Lake City, 5 Jan. 1891). American soprano. Studied New York with Achille Errani and in Europe with Wartel, Sangiovanni, and Delle Sedie. Début London, C.G., 1876, Marie (*La Fille du régiment*) and N.Y., same role, 1877. Married Eugene Wetherell 1875; together promoted Emma Abbott English Grand Opera Company. Introduced 'specialities', such as popular ballads, into operas in which she appeared.

Abencérages, Les, ou L'Étendard de Grenade. Opera in 3 acts by Cherubini; text by V. J. Étienne de Jouy, after J. P. Florian's novel *Gonzalve de Cordove* (1791). Prod. Paris, O., 6 Apr. 1813, in the presence of Napoleon, with Branchou, J. Armand, Nourrit, Dérivis, Lavigne, Alexandre, Bertin. Revived Florence 1957. The plot tells of the disputed triumphs of Almansor, the last of the Moorish Abenceragi warriors, and his final overthrow at Granada in 1492.

Abigaille. Nabucco's daughter (sop.) in Verdi's *Nabucco*.

Abingdon. Town in Berkshire, England. Alan Kitching and his wife opened the Unicorn T. in 1959, with the first English stage performance for 225 years of Handel's *Orlando*. Its success led to an annual Handel opera in Kitching's own English translation. Works produced, many for the first time since Handel's day, have included *Partenope, Agrippina, Admetus, Poro, Amadigi, Flavio, Sosarme, Il pastor fido*, and *Arminio*. In the early years the performances were partly amateur, but by 1970 they had become almost fully professional. In 1972 a successful appeal for funds resulted in the Unicorn T. continuing two more seasons; performances by the company of *Lotario* were given at the 1976 City of London Festival, after which no further productions were planned.

Abonnement (*Fr* subscription). The term used in German and French opera houses for the various subscription series, the financial mainstay of the season. The subscribers are known in Germany as *Abonnenten*, in France as *abonnés*, in Italy as *abbonati*.

Ábrányi, Emil (*b* Budapest, 22 Sept. 1882). Hungarian composer, son of Emil (1851-1920), poet, librettist, and translator of many librettos into Hungarian, including *Tristan* and *Carmen*. Emil jun. has composed a number of operas, some to his father's texts. His works include *Monna Vanna* (1907), *Paolo és Francesca* (1907), *Don Quijote* (1917), and an opera on Bach, *A Tamás templom karnagya* (1947). Music director Cologne 1904-6, Hanover 1907-11, Budapest from 1911 in various theatres.

Abreise, Die (The Departure). *Musikalisches Lustspiel* in 1 act by D'Albert; text by Ferdinand von Sporck, after August von Steigentesch's drama. Prod. Frankfurt, 20 Oct. 1898; London, King's (Hammersmith), 3 Sept. 1925; Provo, Utah, 30 Oct. 1973. His most successful comic opera. A simple anecdote about the efforts of Trott (ten.) to encourage Gilfen (bar.) to depart on a journey, thus leaving Luise (sop.), Gilfen's neglected wife, free to receive his advances. Eventually it is Trott who is sent off, the jealousy aroused in Gilfen serving to renew his devotion to his wife.

Abscheulicher! Leonore's aria in Act 1 of Beethoven's *Fidelio*, in which she first rages against her husband's imprisoner Don Pizarro, and then prays for a rescue.

Abu Hassan. Singspiel in 1 act by Weber; text by Franz Karl Hiemer, after a tale in the *1,001 Nights* (added by Antoine Galland to the original collection; published 1712). Prod. Munich, 4 June 1811; London, D.L., trans. W. Dimond with music adapted by T. S. Cooke, 4 Apr. 1825; N.Y. (London version), 5 Nov. 1827. Abu Hassan (ten.) and his wife Fatime (sop.)

1

attempt to pay their creditors first by tempting Omar (bar.) with Fatime's charms so that he will pay their debts, then by obtaining money as benefit for each other's faked death. The Caliph's concern for them exposes the plot, but they are forgiven.

Académie de Musique. The name originally given to a number of French opera houses and companies, most celebratedly the Paris *Opéra.

Academy of Music, New York. Opera house which stood at the NE corner of Irving Place and 14th Street. Opened 2 Oct. 1854, with Grisi and Mario in *Norma*, succeeding the Astor Place Opera House. Home of all the New York Mapleson seasons and scene of the American débuts of Patti and Tietjens, and of the American premières of most Verdi operas, as well as *Rienzi, L'Africaine, Carmen, Roméo et Juliette*, and *Andrea Chénier*. Succeeded by the Metropolitan, 1883, as the leading New York opera house, but still used for opera until the turn of the century, when it became a theatre and then a cinema. Demolished 1925.

Ach, ich fühl's. Pamina's (sop.) aria in Act 2 of Mozart's *Die Zauberflöte*, lamenting Tamino's apparent indifference.

Acis and Galatea. Masque in 3 acts by Handel; text by John Gay, including adaptations of, or original work by, others including Pope and Dryden, after Ovid's *Metamorphoses,* XIII, 750-897. Probably written and performed at Cannons between 1718 and 1720; first complete public performance, Lincoln's Inn T., 26 Mar. 1731, with Rochetti, Wright, Leveridge; N.Y., Park T., 21 Nov. 1842. Galatea (sop.) alone among the nymphs and shepherds is sad, because Acis (ten.) is absent. He returns, followed by the giant Polyphemus (bass) who also loves Galatea. Polyphemus crushes Acis under a rock, and Acis is transformed into a spring. Other operas on the subject by Lully (1686), Stolzel (1715), Haydn (1790), Bianchi (1792), Naumann (1801), Hatton (1844), and Zarbo (1892).

Ackermann, Otto (*b* Bucharest, 18 Oct. 1909; *d* Berne, 9 Mar. 1960). Swiss conductor. Studied Bucharest and Berlin. When 15 conducted Royal Romanian Opera Company on tour. Düsseldorf 1928-32; Brno 1932-5; Berne 1935-47; guest conductor at leading Italian opera houses, Vienna, Paris, Brussels, Barcelona, 1946-53; Generalmusikdirektor, Cologne, 1953-8; Zurich 1958-60. (R)

Ackté (orig. Achté), **Aïno** (*b* Helsinki, 23 Apr. 1876; *d* Nummela, 8 Aug. 1944). Finnish soprano. Daughter of Lorenz Nikolai Achté, baritone and conductor, and Emmy Achté (Strömer), soprano. Studied with her mother and then Duvernoy in Paris. Début Paris, O.,

1897, Marguerite; Paris until 1904; N.Y., Met., 1904-6; London, C.G., 1907. First British Salome 1910. Had a voice of purity and power, an excellent dramatic instinct and stage presence. Director of the Finnish National Opera, 1938-9. Published two vols. of autobiography in 1925 and 1935, translated into Swedish and German. (R). Her sister, **Irma Tervani** (1887-1936), was for many years leading mezzosoprano, Dresden O. (R)

Adalgisa. Norma's confidante and rival (sop.) in Bellini's *Norma*.

Adam, Adolphe (*b* Paris, 24 July 1803; *d* Paris 3 May 1856). French composer. Overcoming strenuous parental opposition, he studied music first secretly and then at the Conservatoire. Boieldieu influenced him, steering his talents into the medium for which they were best suited, opéra comique. His fluency hindered success in more serious forms; but, as he said himself, 'my only aim is to write music which is transparent, easy to understand, and amusing to the public'. He wrote some 20 opéras comiques between 1829 and his death. The most enduringly successful has been *Le Postillon de Longjumeau* (1836), an agreeable and tuneful work whose delicacy of scoring at times suggests an almost Berliozian skill. Other works occasionally seen include *Si j'étais roi* (1852).
Bibl: A. Adam: *Souvenirs d'un musicien* (1857; 2/1871); A. Pougin: *Adolphe Adam* (1877).

Adam, Theo (*b* Dresden, 1 Aug. 1926). German bass-baritone. He sang in the Dresden Kreuzchor, and then studied with Rudolf Dietrich. Début, Dresden State Opera, 1949, Hermit in *Der Freischütz*. Bayreuth since 1952; Berlin, S.O. since 1957. Sang his first Wotan in 1963 since when he has performed the role in the leading European houses, including Bayreuth, and at N.Y., Met. As well as being one of the leading Wagner heroic baritones, has also sung with success as Don Giovanni, Pizarro, Boris Godunov, and Wozzeck. Has also produced opera at Berlin, S.O. (R)

Adamberger, Valentin (*b* Munich, 6 July 1743; *d* Vienna, 24 Aug. 1804). German tenor. Active in Vienna, also visiting Italy (under the name of Adamonti) and London. According to his friend Mozart, a singer 'of whom Germany may well be proud'. For him Mozart wrote the part of Belmonte, and Vogelsang in *Der Schauspieldirektor*.

Adami, Giuseppe (*b* Verona, 4 Feb. 1878; *d* Milan, 12 Oct. 1946). Italian librettist. Furnished Puccini with librettos for *La rondine, Il tabarro*, and (with Simoni) *Turandot*. Also wrote texts for operas by Vittadini and Zandonai.

Adams, Suzanne (*b* Cambridge, Mass., 28 Nov. 1872; *d* London, 5 Feb. 1953). American soprano. Studied Paris with Bouhy and Marchesi. Début Paris, O., 1895, Juliette. London, C.G., 1898 in the same role, which, like that of Marguerite, she studied with Gounod. Created Hero in Stanford's *Much Ado About Nothing* in 1904. N.Y., Met., 1899-1903. Married the cellist Leo Stein. His death in 1904 led to her early retirement from the stage. (R)

Added numbers. In days when the singer was more valued than the composer, separate songs were sometimes added purely as display items. Mozart wrote several arias for insertion into other composers' works, e.g. 'Mandina amabile' (K480) for Coltellini, Calvesi, and Mandini in Bianchi's *La villanella rapita.* A more familiar example is the Lesson Song, often substituted for Rossini's 'Contro un cor' in Act 2 of *Il barbiere di Siviglia.* For this many different pieces have been used, including arias prophetically produced from the future by various prima donnas, and even ballads. Melba used to have a piano wheeled on to the stage and turned the scene into a ballad concert, generally ending with 'Home, Sweet Home'.

Addio del passato. Violetta's (sop.) aria in Act 3 of Verdi's *La traviata.* After reading Germont's letter she bids farewell to her happy past with Alfredo.

Addio fiorito asil. Pinkerton's (ten.) aria in Act 2 of Puccini's *Madama Butterfly,* bidding farewell to the home where he has lived with Butterfly.

Addio senza rancor. Mimì's (sop.) aria bidding farewell to Rodolfo in Act 3 of Puccini's *La Bohème.*

Adelaide. Town in South Australia. Adelaide was long dependent on touring companies, and on occasional local enterprises such as an Intimate Opera Group. Performances were normally given in Her Majesty's T. But in 1970 the foundations were laid for a new Festival T. on the south bank of Torrens Lake; the project was over-subscribed by the public within a week; and the theatre (cap. 2,000) was opened in 1973. The smaller 635-seat theatre opened in 1974, as also did an open-air amphitheatre and an experimental theatre (cap. 380) called The Space. Opera performances are given in all auditoria. The New Opera S. Australia formed in 1974 has pursued an adventurous policy under the musical direction of Myer Fredman with productions of works by Weill, Janáček, and Britten as well as the more conventional repertory.

Adele. The maid (sop.) in J. Strauss's *Die Fledermaus.*

Adelphi Theatre, London. Four theatres of this name have occupied a site on the north side of the Strand since 1819. In 1831 the Lyceum's English Opera Company performed there; the C. R. Company gave occasional performances there in the 1870s and 1880s. The company of the Berlin K. O. appeared there in 1907, giving the first British performances of *Contes d'Hoffmann*; and short seasons were given there of *Sorochintsy Fair* in 1942 and of Italian opera in 1959.

Adieu, notre petite table. Manon's (sop.) aria in Act 2 of Massenet's opera, bidding farewell to the little table in the room she has shared with Des Grieux.

Adina. A wealthy and beautiful landowner, heroine (sop.) of Donizetti's *L'elisir d'amore.*

Adler, Kurt Herbert (*b* Vienna, 2 Apr. 1905). Austrian, now American, conductor and manager. After studying in Vienna and working with Max Reinhardt became one of Toscanini's assistants at Salzburg in 1936. Emigrated to America in 1938; chorus master and assistant cond. Chicago Opera, 1938-42. Joined the San Francisco Opera in 1943 in a similar capacity; later assistant to Gaetano Merola, the company's general manager. On Merola's death in 1953 appointed general director of the San Francisco Opera Association. Gradually lengthened the season from five weeks in 1953 to ten weeks in 1972, and greatly enlarged the repertory.

Adler, Peter Herman (*b* Jablonec, 2 Dec. 1899). Czech, now American, conductor. Studied Prague Conservatory. After holding various posts in Europe (Brno, Bremen, Kiev, Prague), went to America 1939, making his début (1940) in a concert in New York. Assisted Fritz Busch to launch the New Opera Company, N.Y., 1941, conducting *The Queen of Spades.* Director, Columbia Concerts Opera from 1944. Since 1949, Director, N.B.C. Television Opera; responsible for broadcasts of *Billy Budd, War and Peace, Der Rosenkavalier, The Carmelites,* and many others. Cond. première of Menotti's *Maria Golovin,* Brussels World Fair 1958. In 1969 founded the National Educational Television Opera, known as N.E.T., which gave the first U.S. performance of Janáček's *From the House of the Dead* in its first season. N.Y., Met., 1972-3.

Admeto, Re di Tessaglia. Opera in 3 acts by Handel; text an altered version by Haym or Rolli of an Italian libretto by Aurelio Aureli, *L'Antigone delusa da Alceste.* Prod. London, Hm., 31 Jan. 1727, with Bordoni and Cuzzoni. Revived Abingdon 1964.

Adriana Lecouvreur. Opera in 4 acts by Cilea; text by Arturo Colautti, from the drama *Adrienne Lecouvreur* (1849) by Scribe and Legouvé. Prod. Milan, T.L., 6 Nov. 1902, with Pandolfini, Caruso, De Luca, cond. Campanini;

London, C.G., 8 Nov. 1904, with Giachetti, Anselmi, Sammarco, cond. Campanini; New Orleans, 5 Jan. 1907, with Tarquini, Constantino, Fornari, cond. Conti. Tells of the famous actress Adriana (Adrienne) Lecouvreur (1692-1730) (sop.), of the Comédie Française, rival of Princess Bouillon (mezzo) for the love of Maurice de Saxe (ten.). She dies from inhaling the scent of a bunch of poisoned violets sent by the Princess. Michonnet (bar.), the stage-manager of the theatre, is also in love with Adriana. Other operas on the subject by Vera (1856), Benvenuto (1857), and Perosio (1889).

Aennchen. Agathe's cousin (sop.) in Weber's *Der Freischütz.*

Africaine, L'. Opera in 5 acts by Meyerbeer; text by Scribe. Prod. Paris, O., 28 Apr. 1865, with Marie Sass, Marie Battu, Naudin, Faure, cond. Haine; London, C.G., 22 July 1865 with Lucca, Fioretti, Wachtel, Graziani, cond Costa; N.Y. Ac. of M., 1 Dec. 1865, with Carozzi-Zucchi, Ortolani, Mazzoleni, Bellini, Antonucci, cond. Bergmann. Enormously popular in the 19th cent., the opera had nearly 60 performances during its first four seasons. Tells how Vasco da Gama (ten.) sails to find a new land beyond Africa, and is wrecked on the African coast. He returns to Portugal with two captives, Nelusko (bar.) and Selika (sop.) ('l'Africaine' of the title), with whom he has fallen in love. She finally sacrifices her life so that Vasco can marry his former love, Inez (sop.). A *zarzuela* by Manuel Fernandez Caballero, *El duo de la Africana* (1893), derives from the opera.

Agathe. Daughter (sop.) of Kuno, the Prince's head forester, in Weber's *Der Freischütz.*

Agnesi, Luigi (orig. Louis Ferdinand Leopold Agniez) (*b* Erpent, Namur, 17 July 1833; *d* London, 2 Feb. 1875). Belgian bass. Studied Brussels Conservatoire and Paris with Duprez. Member of Eugenio Merelli's Italian Company in Germany and Holland. Début Paris, T.I., 1864, Assur (*Semiramide*); London, H.M.'s, 1865. Famous for his Rossini singing.

Agnes von Hohenstaufen. Opera in 3 acts by Spontini; text by Ernst Raupach. Prod. Berlin, 12 June 1829 (the 1st act had already been given on 28 May 1827). Spontini's last opera. First 20th-cent. revival Florence, 14 May 1954, with Tebaldi, cond. Serafin. The plot tells of the love of Agnes (sop.), daughter of the Countess Ermengard, for Henry of Brunswick (ten.), son of the rebel Duke of Saxony, and describes the political intrigues by the Emperor Henry VI of Hohenstaufen (bass) and the French King (disguised as the Duke of Burgundy) (bar.), to prevent Agnes and Henry of Brunswick marrying. The action takes place in Mainz.

Agrippina. Opera in 3 acts by Handel; text by Vincenzo Grimani. Prod. Venice, S.G.Cr., 26

Dec. 1709, with Tesi, F. Boschi, Pellegrini, G. Boschi. Probably Handel's only opera produced in Italy during his three-year stay. Revived Halle 1943 with Dertil, cond. R. Kraus.

Aguiari, Lucrezia (*b* Ferrara, 1743; *d* Parma, 18 May 1783). Italian soprano. Also known, from her illegitimacy, as La Bastardella or La Bastardina. She studied singing in a convent with the Abbot Lambertini, making her début in Florence in 1764. In 1768 appointed court singer in Parma, and the same year created the leading soprano role in Paisiello's *Peleo e Teti* in Naples. In 1780 married Giuseppe Colla after having created leading roles in several of his operas, and retired. Mozart heard her sing in Parma in 1770, and said that she had 'a lovely voice, a flexible throat, and an incredibly high range', going on to quote a passage he heard her sing that ranges from C' to C'''. She was engaged for the Pantheon, London, in 1775 and 1776 to sing two songs at £100 a night.

Ägyptische Helena, Die (The Egyptian Helen). Opera in 2 acts by Strauss; text by Hugo von Hofmannsthal, after various classical legends. Prod. Dresden, 6 June 1928, with Rethberg, Maria Rajdl, Kurt Taucher, cond. Fritz Busch; N.Y., Met., 6 Nov. 1928, with Jeritza, Laubenthal, cond. Bodanzky. Originally conceived as an operetta. Revived (shortened) for the 1933 Salzburg Festival, and again by Clemens Krauss and Rudolf Hartmann, Munich, 1940.

Ah! fors' è lui. The Andantino opening to Violetta's (sop.) aria 'Sempre libera' in Act 1 of Verdi's *La traviata,* in which she asks herself if she is really falling in love.

Ah, fuyez, douce image. Des Grieux's (ten.) outburst in Saint-Sulpice in Act 3 of Massenet's *Manon,* when he tries in vain to drive the image of Manon from his mind.

Ah! non credea mirarti. Amina's (sop.) sleep-walking aria from the last act of Bellini's *La sonnambula,* which leads to the final rondo:

Ah! non giunge! which she sings as she awakens and sees her beloved Elvino beside her.

Ah sì, ben mio. Manrico's (ten.) aria to his beloved Leonora, consoling her as they shelter in a fortress, in Act 3 of Verdi's *Il trovatore.*

Aida. Opera in 4 acts by Verdi; text by Ghislanzoni from the French prose of Camille du Locle (1868), plot by August Mariette Bey. Prod. Cairo Opera House, 24 Dec. 1871, with Pozzoni, Grossi, Mongini, Medini, Costa, Steller, cond. Bottesini; Milan, Sc., 8 Feb. 1872, with Stolz, Waldmann, Fancelli, Pandolfini, Maini, cond. Verdi; N.Y., Ac. of M., 26 Nov. 1873, with Torriani, Cary, I. Campanini, Maurel; London, C.G., 22 June 1876, with Patti, S. Scalchi, Nicolini, Cotogni, Bagaggiolo, cond. Bevignani.

Aida was not, as is often supposed, written

for the opening of the Suez Canal (1869), nor commissioned by the Khedive of Egypt to open the new *Cairo Opera House the same year; Mariette did suggest his story to the Khedive to celebrate the opening of the Canal, but the synopsis did not reach Verdi until 1870. The Cairo Opera opened in 1869 with *Rigoletto*.

The action, which takes place in ancient Egypt, tells of the love of Radamès (ten.), the captain of the guard, for the slave girl Aida (sop.). She is the daughter of Amonasro (bar.), King of Ethiopia, who is captured by Radamès and the victorious Egyptian troops. Tricked into betraying military secrets, Radamès is condemned to be buried alive. He is joined in his tomb by Aida, who dies with him, while Amneris (mezzo), the King of Egypt's daughter, who has loved Radamès in vain, prays for him. *Bibl*: H. Busch (ed.): *Verdi's Aida* (1978).

Aiglon, L' (The Eaglet). Opera in 5 acts by Honegger (Acts 2-4) and Ibert (Acts 1 and 5); text by Henri Cain after Edmond Rostand's drama (1900). Prod. Monte Carlo, 11 Mar. 1937, with Fanny Heldy and Vanni-Marcoux. Announced for production in Naples in Feb. 1939 but cancelled on Mussolini's orders after the dress rehearsal. Revived Paris, O., 1952.

Ai nostri monti. The duet for Manrico (ten.) and Azucena (mezzo), in Act 4 of Verdi's *Il trovatore*, in which they console one another with memories of their homeland.

Air. See *Aria*.

Aix-en-Provence. Town in Provence, France. At the annual summer festival, founded by Gabriel Dussurget and André Bigonnet in 1948, operas are mostly performed in the fine open-air theatre (cap. 1,700), in the Archbishop's Palace designed by Cassandre, and occasionally elsewhere, e.g. at Les Baux (*Mireille*, 1954) and the Parc du Tholonet (*Carmen*, 1957). The Festival has given performances of Mozart, Rossini, Cimarosa, Rameau, Grétry, Gluck, Monteverdi, and Haydn, and during the 1950s introduced to a wider public Graziella Sciutti, Teresa Berganza, Teresa Stich-Randall, and Leopold Simoneau. During the 1960s the general standard of the performances, especially in Mozart, declined; public interest, however, was maintained by extending the repertory to include *Falstaff, Ariadne auf Naxos,* and *Pelléas et Mélisande*. With Bernard Lefort's appointment in 1973 the festival quickly recovered its high standards.

Aladdin. (1) Fairy opera in 3 acts by Bishop; text by G. Soane. Prod. London, D.L., 29 Apr. 1826, as a counter-attraction to Weber's *Oberon* at C.G. A failure, it had to be withdrawn. Weber was present at the first performance and noted a charming hunting chorus; but the audience greeted it by whistling the *Freischütz* hunting chorus for him. Bishop's major opera, though

containing spoken dialogue.

(2) Opera by Atterberg. Prod. Stockholm, 18 Mar. 1941. Other operas on the subject by Gyrowetz (1819), Wichtl (*c*.1840), Hornemann (1888), Rota (1968).

Albanese, Licia (*b* Bari, 22 July 1913). Italian, now American, soprano. Studied with Giuseppina Baldassare-Tedeschi. Winner from 300 contestants in a nation-wide competition sponsored by the Italian government at Bologna. She made her début at the Milan T.L. in April 1931 as Cio-Cio-San. London, C.G., 1937, Liù and Nannetta; N.Y., Met., 1940-66. Chosen by Toscanini for his broadcasts (also recorded) of *La Bohème* and *La traviata*. (R)

Albani, (Dame) **Emma** (orig. Marie Louise Cécile Lajeunesse) (*b* Chambly, nr Montreal, 1 Nov. 1847; *d* London, 3 Apr. 1930). Canadian soprano. Educated Montreal, then New York, where her singing in the choir of the Roman Catholic Cathedral so impressed the Bishop that he advised her father to let her take up music. Studied Paris with Duprez and subsequently Milan with Lamperti. Début Messina, 1870, Amina, adopting the name of Albani for professional purposes; London, C.G., 1872-96; N.Y., Met., 1890. First C.G. Mignon, Elsa, Elisabeth, Senta, Desdemona. Married Ernest Gye, son of C.G.'s director, and later manager of the theatre himself. Continued to sing in concerts until 1911 and then devoted herself to teaching.
Bibl: E. Albani: *Forty Years of Song* (1911).

Albania. During the Turkish occupation (1497-1912), Albania could not develop an operatic life. The first genuine Albanian national operas are *Mrika*, by P. Yakov, and *Rozafa*, by Michele Koliqi to a text by Andrea Zadêja (1890-1945) on the legendary foundation of Scutari Castle through the self-sacrifice of a beautiful girl. After the Second World War a National T. was founded in Tirana, with 45 actors, 60 dancers, a chorus of 85, an ensemble of solo singers, and an orchestra of 45. Performances began in the former cinema (cap. 600) built by the Italians. Works performed have mainly been Russian (e.g. *A Life for the Tsar* and Dargomyzhsky's *Rusalka*) or the most popular works in the international repertory (*La traviata, The Bartered Bride*). There have also been operatic settings of Giorgio Fishta's dramas by Martin Gjoka, operas by Zef Shestani and K. Trago, and an operetta, *The Dawn,* by Kristo Kono, a story of life on a collective farm with music based on folk song. A professional group was founded at the Migjeni T. in Shkoder (Scutari) in 1949, and there are others in Durrës (Durazzo) and Korcë.

Albéniz, Isaac (Manuel Francisco) (*b* Camprodón, 29 May 1860; *d* Cambô-les-Bains, 18 May 1909). Spanish composer. Though known

principally as a pianist-composer, Albéniz's pioneering work for Spanish music included the composition of operas and *zarzuelas*. In 1891 he signed a contract with the banker Francis Burdett Money-Coutts to set the latter's librettos, but the only successful work to result was *Pepita Jiménez* (1896). He had meanwhile produced *The Magic Opal* (text by Arthur Law) in London in 1893. The ambitious *King Arthur* trilogy, *Merlin, Lancelot,* and *Guinevere,* to Coutts's texts, was never performed. Of his *zarzuelas, San Antonio de Flórida* (1894) had some success.
Bibl: H. Collet: *Albéniz et Granados* (1926, 2/1948).

Alberich. The Nibelung (bass-bar.) of the title of Wagner's *Der Ring des Nibelungen,* whose renunciation of love and theft of the Rhinegold precipitates the events of the whole cycle. His name derives from Old High German and Middle High German *alp* or *alb* = elf, and Gothic *reiks* = ruler, also the source of the name *Oberon. In *The Ring,* he is the dark embodiment of this magic authority: in the answers to Mime's riddles in *Siegfried,* Wotan describes the Nibelungs as Schwarzalben and their ruler as Schwarz-alberich, the gods as Lichtalben and their ruler, himself, as Lichtalberich.

Albert, Eugen d' (orig. Francis Charles) (*b* Glasgow, 10 Apr. 1864; *d* Riga, 3 Mar. 1932). German pianist and composer of French descent and British birth. Studied at the National Training School in London. Early success as a pianist; later a pupil of Liszt in Vienna. Very active as an opera composer in Germany from 1893. Of his 20 operas only *Die Abreise* (1898) and *Tiefland* (1903) have endured, though *Flauto Solo* (1905) and *Die toten Augen* (1916) had a success when they appeared. *Tiefland,* a mixture of late German Romanticism and *verismo,* retains a slender hold on European repertories.
Bibl: W. Raupp: *Eugen d'Albert* (1930).

Albert Herring. Opera in 3 acts by Britten; text by Eric Crozier, after Maupassant's story *Le Rosier de Madame Husson* (1888). Prod. Gly., 20 June 1947 with Pears, Cross, cond. Britten; Tanglewood, Mass., 8 Aug. 1949. The plot turns on the attempts of a small Suffolk town to elect a May Queen and, in default of one of sufficient virtue being found, the choice of Albert Herring (ten.) as May King: he dismays the community by spending his prize money on a debauch, which nevertheless serves to liberate him from his domineering mother. The gallery of Suffolk characters includes the formidable Lady Billows (sop.).

Alboni, Marietta (orig. Maria Anna Marzia) (*b* Città di Castello, 6 Mar. 1823; *d* Ville d'Avray, 23 June 1894). Italian contralto. Studied with Ber-

tinotti. So impressed Rossini that he taught her the contralto roles in his operas. Début Bologna 1824, Climene in Pacini's *Saffo.* Engaged as leading contralto London, C.G. 1847, its first season as Royal Italian Opera, making début on opening night as Arsace (*Semiramide*). So enthusiastically received that she became the rival attraction to Jenny Lind at H.M.'s and her salary was raised from £500 to £2,000. In 1848 at C.G., Meyerbeer wrote for her the Page's aria in *Les Huguenots,* and the same year she agreed to sing the baritone role of Carlos in the first C. G. *Ernani* after the part had been turned down by both Tamburini and Ronconi. Continued to appear in London intermittently until 1858. Toured U.S. 1853; officially retired 1863, following her marriage to Count Pepoli, though she sang again in concerts and opera in France, Brussels, and elsewhere until 1872. Sang at Rossini's funeral with Patti. Her voice, a true contralto, ranged from g to g''. One of the greatest contraltos in operatic history.
Bibl: A. Pougin: *Marietta Alboni* (1912).

Alceste. Opera in 3 acts by Gluck; text by Calzabigi, after the tragedy by Euripides (438 BC). Prod. Vienna, B., 26 Dec. 1767, with Antonia Bernasconi, Tibaldi, Poggi; London, 30 Apr. 1795, with Giorgi-Banti, Kelly, Baghetti; N.Y., Wellesley College, 11 Mar. 1938. French version revised by Gluck, with text by L. du Roullet, prod. Paris, O., 23 Apr. 1776, with Levasseur, Legros, Gelin. The preface to the score, one of the key documents in the history of opera, embodies Gluck's view that opera should be not merely an elegant concert in costume but a form of music drama (text often reprinted, e.g. Eng. trans. in A. Einstein: *Gluck* (1936) and O. Strunk: *Source Readings in Music History* (1950)).
Other operas on the subject are by Lully (1674 – saluted by Mme. de Sévigné as 'un prodige de beauté'), Strungk (1680), Draghi (1699), Schürmann (1719), Handel (1734), Lampugnani (1745), Schweitzer (1773 – intended as the first step towards a German national opera), Gresnick (1786), Portogallo (1793), Staffa (1852), Gambaro (1882), Boughton (1922), and Wellesz (1924).

Alcina. Opera in 3 acts by Handel; text by Antonio Marchi, after Ariosto's *Orlando furioso* (1516). Prod. London, C.G., 16 Apr. 1735, with Carestini; Dallas, 16 Nov. 1970, with Sutherland. Frequently revived in modern times.

Alda (orig. Davies), **Frances** (*b* Christchurch, New Zealand, 31 May 1883; *d* Venice, 18 Sept. 1952). New Zealand soprano. Studied Paris, Mathilde Marchesi; début Paris, O.C., 1904, Manon. After appearances at Brussels, La M., London, C.G., and Milan, Sc. – where she met Toscanini, who became her life-long friend, and Gatti-Casazza, whom she later married – was engaged N.Y., Met., 1908, until 1929. Created Roxane in Damrosch's *Cyrano de Bergerac*, title role in Victor Herbert's *Madeleine*, and Cleopatra in Hadley's *Cleopatra's Night*. The first Louise at Sc., under Toscanini. Famed for her volatile temperament, professional quarrels, and many law cases. (R)

Bibl: F. Alda: *Men, Women and Tenors* (1937).

Aldeburgh Festival. Founded in 1948 by Benjamin Britten, Eric Crozier, and Peter Pears, devoted to music and the other arts, and held at Britten's home town of Aldeburgh, on the Suffolk coast. Britten's music and taste are the dominant features of the festival, which combines high quality with a pleasantly local, informal character. First performances have included Britten's *Let's Make an Opera* (1949), Berkeley's *A Dinner Engagement* (1954), Britten's *Noye's Fludde* (1958), *A Midsummer Night's Dream* (1960), all the 3 Church Parables, Williamson's *English Eccentrics* (1964), Walton's *The Bear* (1967), Birtwistle's *Punch & Judy* (1968), Crosse's *Purgatory* and *The Grace of Todd* (1969), Gardner's *The Visitors* (1972), Britten's *Death in Venice* (1973) and revised *Paul Bunyan* (1976). In 1969 the disused Maltings building at Snape was adapted as a second auditorium but burned down only hours after it had been officially opened by Queen Elizabeth II. Swiftly re-built, it was ready for use the following summer. Since then it has housed productions of *Idomeneo*, *The Rape of Lucretia*, *King Arthur* (Purcell), and the première of *Death in Venice*. In September 1970 an annual autumn season was instituted under the title Opera at the Maltings. After Britten's death in 1976 Mstislav Rostropovich became an artistic director of the festival.

Aleko. Opera in 1 act by Rakhmaninov; text by Vladimir Nemirovich-Danchenko, after Pushkin's poem *The Gypsies* (1824). Prod. Moscow, B., 27 Apr. 1893, with Korsov, Klementyev, Deysha-Sionitskaya, Vlasov, Shubina, cond. Altani; N.Y., Jolson's T., 11 Jan 1926, with La Touche, Saratovsky, Ignatiev; London, Collegiate T. 2 May 1972, with M. King, Robiczek, cond. Badacsonyi. The work was composed as a graduation exercise for three students of Arensky's composition class at the Moscow Conservatory; all set the same libretto, and with his setting Rakhmaninov graduated with the highest honours. Aleko (bass) has abandoned his settled life to wander with a group of gypsies. When his gypsy lover Zemfira (sop.) tires of him and plans to run off with a young gypsy (ten.), he kills her; the gypsies abandon him to his fate.

Alessandro. Opera in 3 acts by Handel; text by P. A. Rolli. Prod. London, Hm., 5 May 1726, with

Faustina Bordoni (making her début, as Rossane), Cuzzoni, Boschi, Senesino. Revived as *Roxana, or Alexander in India*, probably with additions by Lampugnani, King's, 15 Nov. 1743. Revived in German edition, Stuttgart 1959. Alexander the Great is the subject of over 100 operas, most to *Metastasio's libretto *Alessandro nell'Indie*.

Alessandro Stradella. Opera in 3 acts by Flotow; text by 'W. Friedrich' (Friedrich Wilhelm Riese) after a French *comédie mêlée de chants* by P.A.A. Pittaud de Forges and P. Duport, originally prod., with new airs by Flotow, in 1837. Prod. Hamburg, 30 Dec. 1844; London, D.L., in English with music arranged by Benedict, 6 June 1846; N.Y., 29 Nov. 1853. Set in Venice and Rome in about 1670, the opera tells of episodes in the life of the composer Stradella. At a Carnival, Stradella (ten.) abducts Leonore (sop.), ward of Bassi (bass), and carries her off to Rome. The lovers are pursued by Bassi's hired assassins, but first they and later Bassi himself are won over by Stradella and his art. Other operas on *Stradella's adventurous life by César Franck (1844, piano score only) and Sirico (1863).

Alfano, Franco (*b* Posilippo, 8 Mar. 1876; *d* San Remo, 27 Oct. 1954). Italian composer. Studied Naples with De Nardis and Serrao, then Leipzig with Jadassohn. His first operas, *Miranda* (1896) and *La fonte di Eschir* (1898) were soon forgotten, and his first success came with his Tolstoy opera *Risurezzione* (1904): rapidly taken up abroad, and a favourite work of Mary Garden's, this shows him beginning to move away from the *verismo* tradition. He developed a weightier and more personal vein in *L'ombra di Don Giovanni* (1914), which he refined in his next opera, *La leggenda di Sakuntala* (1921; score destroyed in war, rev. as *Sakuntala*, 1951). Accused over his Balzac opera *Madonna imperia* (1927) of having Frenchified Italian opera, he attempted a reconciliation with his Italian origins in *L'ultimo Lord* (1930), *Cyrano de Bergerac* (1936), and *Il Dottor Antonio* (1949). Also wrote radio opera, *Vesuvio* (1950).

Though a number of these operas have retained a hold on the Italian repertory, and have been appreciated for Alfano's excellent understanding of the voice, it is for his completion of Puccini's *Turandot* that he is best remembered. He had once planned an opera on the subject himself, and was chosen for the task by Toscanini, who conducted the opera's première without Alfano's ending on 25 Apr. 1925, adding it for the next performance. Enough was left in the sketches for Alfano to work them into complete shape; and though it has been objected that there is a perceptible break in style, no attempt has been made to improve upon Alfano's perfectly acceptable work.

Alfio. A teamster (bar.), husband of Lola, rival and eventually murderer of Turiddù in Mascagni's *Cavalleria rusticana*.

Alfonso. (1) Don Alfonso (bass), the cynical philosopher who proposes the wager that produces the plot of Mozart's *Così fan tutte*.

(2) Alfonso d'Este (bar.), Duke of Ferrara, in Donizetti's *Lucrezia Borgia*.

(3) Alfonso XI (bar.), King of Castile, in Donizetti's *La Favorite*.

Alfred. Rosalinde's tenor lover in Johann Strauss's *Die Fledermaus*.

Alfred the Great. King of England, 871-99. Operas on him are by Mayr (1818), Donizetti (1823: the semi-fictional plot includes a Danish general named Atkins), Wolfram (1826), Reuling (1840), Raff (1851), Bechtel (1880), Gatty (1930).

Alfredo. The younger Germont (ten.), Violetta's lover in Verdi's *La traviata*.

Alice. Ford's wife (sop.) in Verdi's *Falstaff*.

Allegra, Salvatore (*b* Palermo, 13 July 1898). Italian composer. Studied Palermo with Cilea and Favara. Though best known as an operetta composer, including of *La maschera nuda* (1925, on sketches left by Leoncavallo), he has also written the operas *Ave Maria* (1934), *I viandanti* (1936), *Il medico suo malgrado* (1938), and *Romulus* (1952).

Allegranti, Maddalena (*b* Florence, *c* 1750; *d* ? Ireland, *c* 1802). Italian soprano. Début Venice 1770; then studied Mannheim. Great success in Germany until 1778; London from 1781 to 1783. For some years then *prima donna buffa* at Dresden. Earlier in her career Burney had noted her 'pretty, unaffected manner'; while Mozart thought her far better than Ferraresi, though he added that this was not saying much. Casanova, who saw her in Bologna in 1771, found her both 'adorabile' and 'pericolosa'.

Allen, Thomas (*b* Seaham, Co. Durham, 10 Sept. 1944). British baritone. Studied London, R.C.M. with Hervey Alan. Gly. Chorus 1969. Début W.N.O. 1969, Figaro (Rossini) and regularly since. London, C.G. from 1971; Aldeburgh 1974, creating Valerio in *Voice of Ariadne*; Gly. since 1973 as Figaro, Guglielmo, Papageno, Forester in *Cunning Little Vixen*, and most successfully as Don Giovanni in 1977. Repertory also includes Count Almaviva, Belcore, Valentin, Billy Budd, and Pelléas. One of the finest baritones to have emerged in England in the post-war period, possessing a virile voice of beautiful quality, and first-rate acting ability. (R)

Allestimento (*It* preparation). The term used in Italy for the production of an opera, especially as it is announced in the **cartellone* outlining the season's plans. A *nuovo allestimento* is a new production of a repertory work.

Allin, Norman (*b* Ashton-under-Lyne, 19 Nov. 1884; *d* London, 27 Oct. 1973). English bass. Studied R.M.C.M. 1906-10, with John Acton and Francis Harford. Originally intended to teach, but after marriage in 1912 to the mezzo-soprano Edith Clegg concentrated on singing. Début with Beecham Company 1916, London, Aldwych, as Aged Hebrew (*Samson et Dalila*); graduated to King Mark, Dosifey, Méphistophélès, etc. C.G. début 1919, Konchak, later that year Gurnemanz. Leading bass and director of B.N.O.C. 1922-9. Bartolo in the opening performance, Gly. 1934; C. R. 1942-9. Professor, R.A.M. 1935-60 and R.M.C.M. 1938-42. One of England's finest basses. (R)

Almaviva. The Count, who, as a tenor, woos and wins Rosina in Rossini's *Il barbiere di Siviglia*; and, as a baritone, has to be taught a lesson for his infidelity to her in Mozart's *Le nozze di Figaro*.

Almaviva, ossia L'inutile precauzione. See *Barbiere di Siviglia, Il*.

Almira. Opera in 3 acts by Handel; text by Friedrich Feustking, after Pancieri's Italian libretto for Boniventi. Prod. Hamburg, 8 Jan. 1705. Handel's first opera, containing 41 German and 15 Italian airs. Other operas on the text by Boniventi (1691), Fedeli (1703), and Keiser (1706).

Altani, Ippolit (Karlovich) (*b* S. Ukraine, 27 May 1846; *d* Moscow, 17 Feb. 1919). Russian conductor. Studied St Petersburg with Zaremba and A. Rubinstein. Conducted Russian opera in Kiev, 1867-82, including the first provincial performance of an opera by Tchaikovsky (*Oprichnik*, 1874). Chief conductor Moscow, B., 1882-1906, including the premières of Tchaikovsky's *Mazeppa* (1884) and Rakhmaninov's *Aleko* (1893), and first Moscow performances of many important Russian operas, incl. *Boris Godunov* (1888), *Queen of Spades* (1891), and *Snow Maiden* (1893). Tchaikovsky had some lessons from him before conducting the première of *Cherevichki*.

Althouse, Paul (*b* Reading, Pa., 2 Dec. 1889; *d* New York, 6 Feb. 1954). American tenor. Début Hammerstein Opera N.Y. with Philadelphia Opera, 1911, as Faust. Met., 1913, Dmitry. Created roles in *Shanewis* (Cadman), *Madeleine* (Herbert), *Canterbury Pilgrims* (De Koven), *The Legend* (Breil). Studied in Europe, then re-engaged for Met. as Heldentenor 1934-40. Siegmund at Flagstad's Met. début as Sieglinde, first American Tristan there. After his retirement, his pupils included Richard Tucker, Eleanor Steber, and Irene Dalis. (R)

Alto (*It* high). A term for certain voices. The female alto is usually known as *contralto. The male alto is usually a bass voice singing *falsetto: it is thus not the same as *counter tenor. It is also one of the registers of the *castrato voice. The range is about from f to a''.

Alva, Luigi (*b* Lima, 10 Apr. 1927). Peruvian tenor. Studied Lima and Milan. Début Lima, 1949, in *zarzuela, Luisa Fernanda*. After a year at the Sc. school sang Paolino at the opening night of the Piccola Scala in December 1955; Edinburgh 1957; London, C.G., 1960, Almaviva, subsequently as Fenton and Ferando; N.Y., Met., since 1963. Has sung extensively in Europe including Holland, Gly., Aix, and Salzburg Festivals, where he is especially admired in Mozart and Rossini. Has also sung in several modern works by Malipiero, Chailly, and Mortari at the Piccola Scala. (R)

Alvarez, Albert (orig. Raymond Gourron) (*b* Bordeaux, 1861; *d* Nice, 26 Feb. 1933). French tenor. Studied in Paris with Martini. Début Ghent 1887, Faust; appearances in French provinces. Paris, O., 1892, Faust; London, C.G., 1893, Leicester in De Lara's *Amy Robsart*. N.Y., Met., 1899-1903. Created Nicias (*Thaïs*), Helion (De Lara's *Messaline*), and Aragui (*La Navarraise*). Possessed a robust voice coupled with fine physique and stage presence. (R)

Alvarez, Marguerite d' (orig. Marguerite Alvarez de Rocafuerte) (*b* Liverpool, ? 1886; *d* Alassio, 18 Oct. 1953). English contralto of Peruvian parentage. When 16 sang at a diplomatic reception in London. After three years' study in Brussels, début Rouen, 1904, Dalila. American début, N.Y., with Hammerstein Company, 1909, Fidès; London, London O.H. (Stoll), 1911, Queen (*Hérodiade*). Also sang at C.G., Chicago, and Boston. A highly emotional and dramatic artist who was hardly suited to the concert platform where she chose to spend the greater part of her career.
Bibl: M. d'Alvarez: *Forsaken Altars* (1954).

Alvaro. Don Alvaro (ten.), a Peruvian of Inca blood, hero of Verdi's *La forza del destino*.

Alvary, Max (orig. Maximilian Achenbach) (*b* Düsseldorf, 3 May 1856; *d* Gross-Tabarz, Thuringia, 7 Nov. 1898). German tenor. Son of painter Andreas Achenbach. Despite parental opposition studied with Stockhausen in Frankfurt and Lamperti in Milan. Début Weimar, 1879, Alessandro Stradella; N.Y., Met., 1885, Don José (opposite Lilli Lehmann, also making her American début), remaining with the company until 1889. First U.S. Loge, Siegfried, and Adolar. Sang Tristan and Tannhäuser, Bayreuth 1891, and in the first C.G. *Ring* under Mahler 1892, which was begun with *Siegfried* so that Alvary could make his début in his favourite role. Forced by illness to leave the

stage 1897. First singer to play Wagner heroes without a beard.

Alyabyev, Alexander (Alexandrovich) (*b* Tobolsk, 15 Aug. 1787; *d* Moscow, 6 Mar. 1851). Russian composer. Fought as a hussar against Napoleon in 1812; studied music in St Petersburg and left the army in 1823. His comic opera *Lunnaya noch* (The Moonlight Night) was comp. 1822 and prod. 1823; at the same time he wrote his song *Solovey* (The Nightingale), which became very popular and was often used by Patti, Viardot, and Sembrich for the Lesson Scene in Act 2 of Rossini's *Barbiere*. He settled in Moscow, and played an active part in the opening of the B. in 1825. He was banished from Moscow in 1828 partly for alleged murder, partly for his association with the Decembrists: he returned at the end of the 1830s after travels in the East and South of Russia. His operas include two Shakespeare works, *Burya* (The Tempest, comp. *c*1835) and *Volshebnaya Noch* (The Enchanted Night, comp. 1838-9, after *A Midsummer Night's Dream*), *Rybak i Rusalka* (The Fisherman and the Water Nymph, comp. 1841-3, prod. Moscow 1965), and *Ammalet-Bek* (comp. 1842-7). His knowledge of folk music, systematically acquired in exile, and his understanding of Oriental and Caucasian subjects were significant in the development of Russian opera in the years immediately preceding Glinka.
Bibl: B. Dobrokhotov: *Alexander Alyabyev* (1966).

Alzira. Opera in a prologue and 2 acts by Verdi; text by S. Cammarano, after Voltaire's tragedy *Alzire, ou Les Américains* (1730). Prod. Naples, S.C., 12 Aug. 1845, with Tadolini, Fraschini, Colette; N.Y., Carnegie Hall, 17 Jan. 1968, with Ross, Cecchele, Quilico, cond. Perlea; London, Collegiate T., 10 Feb. 1970, with Duval, Wilcock, cond. Badacsonyi. One of Verdi's rare failures: he later called it *brutto* (ugly). Revived Rome 1967, with Zeani, Cecchele, MacNeil, cond. Capuana. The Inca princess Alzira (sop.) was betrothed to Zamoro (ten.), but is forced into marriage with Gusman (bar.), the Spanish political governor. Zamoro, whom all believe to be dead, leads an unsuccessful rebellion against the Spaniards, and stabs Gusman during the wedding ceremony. Gusman forgives him as he dies.

Other operas on the subject by Zingarelli (1794), Roszisky (1794), Nicolini (1796), Manfroce (1810), and *pasticcio* by Nasolini and others (1796).

Amadis. Opera in a prologue and 5 acts by Lully; text by Quinault. Prod. Paris, O., 18 Jan. 1684. Parody by Romagnesi and Riccobini prod. Paris, Nouveau T.I., 1740. A sequel, *Amadis de Grèce*, was set by Destouches (1699). Other operas on the subject are by

Handel (London, Hm., 25 May 1715), Berton (1771), J.C. Bach (1779), Stengel (1798), and Massenet (comp. 1902, prod. Monte Carlo 1922).

Amahl and the Night Visitors. Opera in 1 act by Menotti; text by composer, after Bosch's painting *The Adoration of the Magi.* Prod. N.B.C. Television 24 Dec. 1951 (the first opera written for TV); stage prod., Indiana University, 21 Feb. 1952. It describes the reception of the Magi, on their way to Bethlehem, by a little crippled boy.

Amalia. An orphan (sop.), niece of Count Moor, in Verdi's *I masnadieri.*

Amato, Pasquale (*b* Naples, 21 Mar. 1878; *d* Long Island, New York, 12 Aug. 1942). Italian baritone. Début Naples, T. Bellini, 1900, Germont. London, C.G., 1904, with S. C. Company; but despite success never returned. N.Y., Met., 1908-21, where created Jack Rance in *La fanciulla del West,* Cyrano de Bergerac in Damrosch's opera, and Napoleon in Giordano's *Madame Sans-Gêne.* Retired owing to ill health and went to live in Italy, but returned to America in 1928; sang Germont at the N.Y. Hippodrome on the 25th anniversary of his American début. In 1935 appointed head of voice and opera at Louisiana University. (R)

Amelia. (1) Boccanegra's daughter Maria, brought up as Amelia Grimaldi (sop.), in Verdi's *Simon Boccanegra.*
(2) Wife (sop.) of Renato (Anckarstroem) and lover of Riccardo (Gustavus III) in Verdi's *Un ballo in maschera.*
(3) The heroine of Menotti's *Amelia goes to the Ball.*

Amfiparnasso, L'. *Comedia harmonica* by Vecchi, the second of his four madrigal comedies. Probably first sung in Modena in 1594; N.Y., French Institute, 13 Mar. 1933. Though attempts at staging have been made, this succession of five-part songs is a predecessor of opera rather than an early example. Dramatic continuity is given to a number of 16th-cent. vocal forms. The culmination of an Italian tradition of such works. Revived Florence Festival, 1933 and 1939.

Amfortas. The Keeper of the Grail (bar.) in Wagner's *Parsifal,* where he is the son of Titurel: his name may originally derive from his battle cry in other legends, 'Amor fortis' ('Love is strong').

Amico Fritz, L' (Friend Fritz). Opera in 3 acts by Mascagni; text by P. Suardon (N. Daspuro), after Erckmann-Chatrian's novel (1864). Prod. Rome, C., 31 Oct. 1891, with Calvé, Synnemberg, De Lucia, Lhérie, cond. Ferrari; London, C.G., 23 May 1892 with Calvé, G. Ravogli, De Lucia, Dufriche, cond. Bevignani; Philadelphia,

8 June 1892. A light pastoral comedy about the confirmed bachelor Fritz (ten.), a rich landowner; Rabbi David (bar.), the professional match-maker; and Suzel (sop.), the charming daughter of one of Fritz's tenants, with whom Fritz eventually falls in love. Also opera by Edwards (1893).

Amneris. The King of Egypt's daughter (mezzo) and Aida's rival for Radamès in Verdi's *Aida.*

Amonasro. The King of Ethiopia (bar.), Aida's father in Verdi's *Aida.*

Amore dei tre re, L' (The Love of the Three Kings). Opera in 3 acts by Montemezzi; text by Benelli, after his verse tragedy (1910). Prod. Milan, Sc., 10 Apr. 1913, with Villani, Ferrari-Fontana, Galeffi, De Angelis, cond. Serafin; N.Y., Met., 2 Jan. 1914, with Bori, Ferrari-Fontana, Amato, Didur, cond. Toscanini; London, C.G., 27 May 1914, with Edvina, Crimi, Cigada, Didur, cond. Moranzoni. Fiora (sop.) has been forced for political reasons to marry Manfredo (bar.), son of King Archibaldo (bass). While Manfredo is absent on a campaign, the old king murders his daughter-in-law for refusing to reveal the name of her lover, Avito (ten.). He poisons her lips hoping that Avito will come to see her body. Avito dies from kissing the poison, as does Manfredo, who cannot live without his wife.

Amsterdam. Capital of Holland. The first opera performed was *Le fatiche d'Ercole per Deianira* by P.A. Ziani, 31 Dec. 1680. Together with *De Triomfeerende Min* by Hacquart (written in 1679), this was given in a specially built theatre. Performances were then given in the Stadsschouwburg, in the Operahuis (where a German Jewish company played in 1784), and in the T.-Français (where a French company moved having previously performed in an inn). Some of these performances were in Dutch. In 1882 Angelo Neumann's Wagner Company gave *The Ring* in the Paleis voor Volksvlijt; and in 1883 the successful Wagner Vereeniging was founded: it gave many performances of operas by composers other than Wagner. There was also a resident Italian company, 1897-1942. During the German occupation the Municipal Opera Enterprise was formed (1941) and from this was developed, in 1946, De Nederlandsche Opera, which gave performances in Dutch in the Stadsschouwburg. The first company with that name had been founded in 1886, and eventually gave 200 performances a year not only in Amsterdam but in North Holland, Rotterdam, Utrecht, and Hilversum. In 1965 it was reorganized as the Nieuwe Nederlandse Opera under Maurice Huismann (also administrator of the Brussels La M.); this performs in other Dutch cities regularly. Huismann resigned in 1970. In 1973 Michael Gielen was music director, Götz Friedrich chief producer. Hans de Roo succeeded Huismann as administrator. An Opera Studio was formed in the 1974-5 season, to encourage young audiences and to give chamber opera in schools.

Am stillen Herd. Walther's (ten.) aria in Act 1 of Wagner's *Die Meistersinger,* telling the Masters where and from whom he learned to sing.

Ancona, Mario (*b* Livorno, 28 Feb. 1860; *d* Florence, 23 Feb. 1931). Italian baritone. A lawyer and diplomat before studying singing with G. Cima. Début Trieste, 1889, Scinda in *Le Roi de Lahore.* Brought to London by Lago for a scratch season at the Olympic T. Engaged by Augustus Harris for C.G. 1893, singing Tonio in first London *Pagliacci,* and in Stanford's *The Veiled Prophet.* London regularly until 1901. N.Y., Met., 1893-7, and Manhattan Opera 1906-7; Chicago until 1916. Retired shortly after and taught in Italy. (R)

Anders, Peter (*b* Essen, 1 July 1908; *d* Hamburg, 10 Sept. 1954). German tenor. Studied with Grenzebach and later Mysz-Gmeiner. Début Berlin, 1931 in Max Reinhardt's production of *La Belle Hélène.* Berlin, S.O., 1936-49 in the lighter lyric roles; especially successful as a Mozart singer. His voice then began to grow heavier, and in 1950 he sang Walther and Otello in Hamburg. British début 1950, Edinburgh Festival, Bacchus under Beecham, under whom he also sang Walther at C.G., 1951. One of the most intelligent and musical of German tenors. Died after a car accident. (R) *Bibl:* F. Pauli: *Peter Anders* (1963).

Andersen, Hans (*b* Odense, 2 Apr. 1805; *d* Copenhagen, 4 Aug. 1875). Danish writer. He is best known for his fairy tales (168 published 1835-72), but originally hoped to become an actor or singer and worked in the Royal T., Copenhagen. He also worked as librettist, adapting Scott for Bredal's *Bride of Lammermoor* (1832) and for his friend Weyse's *Festen paa Kenilworth* (1836), and Manzoni's *I promessi sposi* for Gläser's *Bryllupet ved Como Søen* (The Wedding on Lake Como, 1849), also writing the text of *Nøkken* (The Water-Sprites, 1853) for Gläser. Operas based on his fairy tales are as follows (alphabetical order):
The Cat and Mouse in Partnership: T. Chanler (*The Pot of Fat,* 1955).
The Cobbler of Delft: Bersa (1914).
The Emperor's New Clothes: Kjerulf (1888); J. Clokey (1924); Kósa (*A király palástja,* 1926); Høffding (1928); Wagner-Régeny (1928); R. Kubelík (1946); E.F. Burian (1947); D.S. Moore (1948); G. Ránki (*Pomádé király új ruhája,* radio 1950, prod. 1953); Simeone (1956); Jenni (1965); Novák (1969); Wood (1972); Glaser (1973).
The Garden of Paradise: Bruneau (1923); Němeček (*Rajská zahrada,* 1933).

Little Christina: Hartmann (1846); Leoni (1901).
The Little Mermaid: Maliszewski (*Syrena,* 1928); M. More (1951).
The Match Girl: Enna (1897); Veretti (1934).
The Mother: L. Moreau (*Myrialde,* 1912); J. Wood (1942); Vlad (1951); S. Hollingsworth (1954); Koppel (1965).
The Nightingale: Enna (1912); Stravinsky (1914); J. Clokey (1925); Irmler (1939); Schanazara (1947); D. Lamb (1954); B. Rogers (1955); Gallois-Montbrun (1959).
The Princess and the Swineherd: Poldini (*Csavargó és királyleány,* 1903); Reutter (1928).
The Princess on the Pea: Enna (1900); Toch (1927).
The Raven: Hartmann (1832).
The Shepherdess and the Sweep: J. Smith (1966).
The Snow Queen: Asafyev (1907); Gużewski (1907); Gerrish-Jones (1917); Gaboro (1952); Zanaboni (1955); K. Thies (1957).
The Ten Kisses: Sekles (1926).
The Tinderbox: Fougstedt (*Tulukset,* 1950).
The Travelling Companion: Stanford (1925); Hamerik (1946).

Anderson, Marian (*b* Philadelphia, 17 Feb. 1902). American contralto. Most of career a concert artist, but first Negro singer at Met. (Ulrica, 1955). (R)

Andrade, Francisco d' (*b* Lisbon, 11 Jan. 1859; *d* Berlin, 8 Feb. 1921). Portuguese baritone. Began as amateur, later studied with Miraglia and S. Ronconi. Début San Remo 1882, Amonasro; London, C.G., 1886, Rigoletto; returned there yearly until 1890. Berlin, H., 1906-19. Particularly remembered for his elegant portrayal of *Don Giovanni.* (R) His brother, Antonio d'Andrade, was a tenor (C.G. 1889-90). (R)

Andrea Chénier. Opera in 4 acts by Giordano; text by Illica. Prod. Milan, Sc., 28 Mar. 1896, with Carrera, Borgatti, Sammarco; N.Y., Ac. of M., 13 Nov. 1896; London, Camden Town Hall (in English), 16 Apr. 1903. Set in Paris just before and immediately after the French Revolution, the opera tells of the love of Madeleine de Coigny (sop.) for the poet Chénier (ten.). Gérard (bar.), former servant in the Coigny household, also loves Madeleine; he becomes an important figure in the revolution and writes an indictment against Chénier, who is condemned to death. Madeleine joins Chénier in the condemned cell and they go to the guillotine together.

Andreini (orig. Ramponi), **Virginia** (*b* Milan, 1 Jan. 1583; *d* Bologna, 1630). Italian soprano. Originally an actress in her husband's theatrical company. Chosen by Monteverdi to create the title-role in his *L'Arianna* in Mantua in 1608. Known as 'La Florinda'. Her husband, **Giovanni**

Battista Andreini (*b* Florence, 9 Feb. 1579; *d* Reggio Emilia, 8 June 1654) was the author of the *sacra rappresentazione*, La Maddalena, for which Monteverdi set the prologue. He published the librettos of several works during the early years on the 17th cent.

Andreozzi, Gaetano (*b* Aversa, 22 May 1755; *d* Paris, 21 or 24 Dec. 1826). Italian composer and singing teacher. Studied Naples (fellow pupils included Cimarosa, Giordani, and Zingarelli), also with his uncle, Jommelli, whence his nickname 'Jommellino'. After having various works performed, he visited Russia (?1784), returning to Italy in 1785. He married his pupil Anna de Santi, who sang in many of his operas; they later separated. Remarried in 1801, he continued a successful career as an opera composer, and made an abortive attempt to act as impresario in Naples in 1806. When Barbaia won the job, however, he devoted himself more to teaching, then being forced by poverty to move to Paris in search of pupils. His operas are Neapolitan in style, and are designed for virtuoso singers. The most successful was *La principessa filosofa* (1794).

Andrésen, Ivar (*b* Oslo, 27 July 1896; *d* Stockholm, 24 Nov. 1940). Norwegian bass. Début Stockholm, 1919, the King *(Aida)*. Dresden State Opera 1925-34; Berlin S. O. 1934-6; Bayreuth 1927-36; and was made a German Kammersänger. London, C.G., 1928-31, singing leading Wagner bass roles, as well as Sarastro, which he repeated at Gly. in 1935, and Osmin. N.Y., Met., 1930-2. He possessed a beautiful voice, noble in sound, and was a fine artist. (R)

Anelli, Angelo (pseud. Nicolò Liprandi and Marco Landi) (*b* Desenzano, 1 Nov. 1761; *d* Pavia, 9 Apr. 1820). Italian librettist. Attached to Milan, Sc. 1793-1817; an excellent comic librettist. His texts include *L'italiana in Algeri* (Mosca, 1808; Rossini, 1813) and *Ser Marcantonio* (Pavesi, 1810: the basis of the text for Donizetti's *Don Pasquale*). The many other composers for whom he wrote include Cimarosa, Coccia, Dussek, Gazzaniga, Guglielmi, Martín y Soler, Mayr, Paer, Pacini, Pavesi, and Zingarelli.

Anfossi, Pasquale (*b* Taggia, nr San Remo, 25 Apr. 1727; *d* Rome, Feb, 1797). Italian composer. Studied with Piccinni and Sacchini, and composed his first opera, *La serva spiritosa*, in 1763; but his first great success was *L'incognita perseguitata* (1773), written to the same text as Piccinni's. Among his 70-odd operas, *La finta giardiniera* (1774 – a year before Mozart's), *L'avaro* (1775), *La vera constanza* (1776), and *Il curioso indiscreto* (1777) won him much fame. Conducted the Italian opera in London, 1781-3.

Angeles, Victoria de los. See *Los Angeles, Victoria de.*

Angélique. Opera in 1 act by Ibert; text by Nino. Prod. Paris, T. Fémina, 28 Jan. 1927, with Bériza, Warneri, Ducros, Marvini, cond. Golschmann; N.Y., 44th St. T., 8 Nov. 1937, with Morel, Dolci, Ilosvay, Perulli, Chabay; London, Fortune T., 20 Feb. 1950, with Castle, D. Craig, T. Jones, Sale, Lawrence, cond. Renton. Boniface, the owner of a Paris china shop, is persuaded by his friend Charlot that the only way to rid himself of his shrewish wife Angélique is to put her up for sale.

Aniara. Opera in 2 acts by Blomdahl; text by Erik Lindegren, after Harry Martinson's epic poem (1956). Prod. Stockholm, 31 May 1959, with Hallin, Djellert, Vikström, Ulfung, Saedén, Tyrén, cond. Ehrling; Edinburgh Festival, same cast, 3 Sept. 1959; Montreal, Place des Arts, by Royal Swedish O., 31 May 1967. A space-craft carrying refugees from earth, devastated in an atomic war, is on its way to Mars. It is knocked off course, and must continue to fly in space for ever. A very successful work, produced in a number of other countries soon after its première.

Anitúa, Fanny (*b* Durango, 22 Jan. 1887; *d* Mexico City, 4 Apr. 1968). Mexican mezzo-soprano. Studied Rome. Début Rome, Nazionale, 1909, Orfeo. Milan, Sc., from 1910, where she sang Etra in the première of *Fedra* (Pizzetti), 1915; and was chosen by Toscanini to sing Orfeo and Azucena 1923-6. Sang regularly in Buenos Aires until 1937, and then taught singing in Mexico City. (R)

Ankara. Capital of Turkey. First permanent theatre opened in 1930 (Halk Evi, cap. 638). In 1934 Carl Ebert was invited to form a school of drama; this was established in 1939. Hindemith assisted him with the musical side of his productions. Opera was not properly organized until 1947, when the Devlet Tiyatrosu (State T.) opened; this had an opera section which began with the French and Italian repertory and in 1952 gave the first Turkish opera, Adnan Saygun's *Kerem*.

Anna Bolena. Opera in 2 acts by Donizetti; text by Romani. Prod. Milan, T. Carcano, 26 Dec. 1830, with Pasta, Orlandi, Rubini, F. Galli; London, H.M.'s, 8 July 1831, with Pasta, Rubini, Lablache; New Orleans, Nov. 1839, with J. Calvé, Bamberger. Frequently performed, with Grisi and Tietjens, but then not until revived at Barcelona, Liceo, 1948, with Scuderi, and Milan, Sc., 1957, with Callas. Loosely based on the well-known historical events, the plot tells how King Henry VIII (bass), in love with Jane Seymour (mezzo), wants to dispose of his wife Anne Boleyn (sop.). The return of Anne's former lover, Percy, Earl of Northumberland (ten.), affords the king the opportunity of accusing Anne of adultery, and she is tried and sentenced to death.

Annibale, Domenico (*b* Macerata, *c*1705; *d* ?Rome, 1779). Italian male soprano. After successes at Rome and Venice, and at Dresden in Hasse's operas, he was engaged by Handel for C.G. 1736-7, where he made his début in the title role of *Poro*. After further Handel performances he returned to Dresden, and eventually to Italy.

Ansaldo, Pericle (*b* Genoa, 1 Jan. 1889; *d* Rome, 29 Sept. 1969). Italian stage technician. Collaborated with his father, Giovanni Ansaldo, until the end of 1927. Responsible for the mechanical improvements and technical installation when the T. Costanzi became the T. Reale dell' Opera, Rome, 1927, and helped to adapt the Terme di Caracalla for opera. Installed new stage mechanism at the Verona Arena, 1948. Held appointments at Milan, Sc., the Colón (Buenos Aires), and the T. Municipale (Rio de Janeiro).

Ansani, Giovanni (*b* Rome, 11 Feb. 1744; *d* Florence, 15 July 1826). Italian tenor. With *Davide re-established the supremacy of the tenor in Italian opera after the age of the *castrato*. During the 1780s and 1790s sang in the leading Italian theatres and also in London (1782); much admired by Burney. Created roles in operas by Paisiello, Cimarosa, Anfossi, etc. Retired from stage 1795 and became a teacher; his pupils included Manuel Garcia and Lablache.

Anselmi, Giuseppe (*b* Catania, 17 Nov. 1876; *d* Zoagli, nr Genoa, 27 May 1929). Italian tenor. Studied violin and composition, then joined an operetta company touring Italy and the Near East. Heard by Giulio Ricordi who suggested that he study with Mancinelli. Début Athens, 1896, Turiddù; Italian début 1901; London, C.G., same year. Reappeared C.G. intermittently until 1909. Greatly admired in Buenos Aires, and appeared regularly in Warsaw, St Petersburg, and Madrid. Had a great affection for Madrid and left his heart to the theatrical museum there, where it is preserved. One of the foremost exponents of the art of *bel canto*, with a beautiful voice and a finished style. (R)

Ansermet, Ernest (*b* Vevey, 11 Nov. 1883; *d* Geneva, 20 Feb. 1969). Swiss conductor. Studied Lucerne, and became professor of mathematics. Then studied composition with Bloch and conducting with Mottl and Nikisch; made his début as an orchestral conductor in 1911. He conducted the first performance of *L'Histoire du soldat* (1918), *The Rape of Lucretia* (1946), and Frank Martin's *Der Sturm* (1956). His performances of *Pelléas et Mélisande, Boris Godunov*, and *Die Zauberflöte* in Hamburg, Geneva, and elsewhere during the latter years of his life were greatly admired. He wrote several books, essays, and articles on music and philosophy. (R)

Ansseau, Fernand (*b* Boussu-Bois, nr Mons, 6 Mar. 1890; *d* Brussels, 1 May 1972). Belgian tenor. Studied Brussels with Demest. Trained as a baritone for two years, as a tenor for three. Début Dijon, 1913, Jean (*Hérodiade*). Career interrupted by the war, but in 1918 sang at the reopening of Brussels, La M. London, C.G., 1919, and subsequently Paris, O.C., 1920 and 1921. Chicago 1923-8. Confined his career to Belgium and France from 1930, retiring at the height of his powers in Feb. 1939. Professor of Singing at the Brussels Conservatoire 1942-4. One of the finest tenors of the inter-war years. (R)

Antefatto (*It* antecedent fact). The device for explaining to an audience background facts or previous events which they must know in order to understand the plot from the start; it may be contained in a narration, as with *Il trovatore,* or printed as a prefatory paragraph to a libretto, as with some by Piave and Romani.
See also *Argomento*.

Antheil, George (*b* Trenton, 8 July 1900; *d* New York, 12 Feb. 1959). American composer. Studied with Sternberg and Bloch. His first opera, *Transatlantic* (1930), in which he used jazz rhythms, aroused some interest when produced in Frankfurt: its subject is a corrupt campaign for a Presidential election. Other stage works include *Helen Retires* (1934), *Volpone* (1953), and two 1-act operas, *The Brothers* (1954) and *The Wish* (1955).

Antigone. The daughter of Oedipus by his mother Jocasta. After Oedipus had put out his eyes, she accompanied him to Colonus, returning to Thebes in order to defy the tyrant Creon's ban on the burial of her brother. She was shut up in a cave, where she and her lover Haemon, Creon's son, killed themselves. Sophocles's tragedy (441 BC) has been the subject of some 30 operas, including works by Orlandini (1718), Zingarelli (1790), Honegger (1927, in an adaptation by Cocteau), Ghislanzoni (1929), Pallantio (1942), Liviabella (1942); and Orff (using Hölderlin's translation), prod. Salzburg, 9 Aug. 1949 with Fischer, Ilosvay, Zadek, Fehenberger, Haefliger, Uhde, Kusche, Greindl, cond. Fricsay; N.Y., Brooklyn Ac. of M., 21 Apr. 1968, with Borkh, Mannion, Lewis, Page, Alexander, cond. Scherman.

Antonia. The consumptive singer (sop.), one of Hoffmann's loves in Offenbach's *Les Contes d'Hoffmann.*

Antwerp (Fr. Anvers; Flem. Antwerpen). Town in Antwerpen, Belgium. Home of the Royal Flemish Opera, founded in 1893 by bass Hendrik Fontaine and opened on 3 Oct. that year with *Der Freischütz*. Performances were originally given in the Royal Dutch T., but since 1907 the Opera has had its own theatre (cap. 1,050), and the title Royal was granted to it in 1920. The company is subsidized by state, city, and province. All operas are sung in Flemish and over 300 artists are employed each season (end of Sept. to end of July). During the 1960s, under the direction of Renaat Verbruggen with Fritz Célis as music director, several important foreign works had their first Belgian performances there, e.g. *A Midsummer Night's Dream* (1962), *Capriccio* (1964), *The Nose* (1965), *The Whirlpool* (1968), and *Greek Passion* (1969). Performances of *Der Ring des Nibelungen* and *Parsifal* are a regular feature. The large repertory also includes works by Flemish composers, e.g. Jan Blockx and August de Boeck.

The Antwerp Chamber Opera, founded in 1960 to perform operas by Auber, Grétry, Mozart, Donizetti, etc., amalgamated with the Dutch Chamber Opera in 1971 to form the Flemish Chamber Opera with its headquarters at the Ring T.

Anvil. A percussion instrument, imitating a real anvil, used in Wagner's *Ring* and other works. Real anvils appear on the stage in Auber's *Le Maçon*, *Il trovatore*, *Benvenuto Cellini*, and *Philémon et Baucis*; an anvil is split by Siegfried in Act 1 of *Siegfried* with the newly forged sword Nothung.

Apollo et Hyacinthus, seu Hyacinthi Metamorphosis. Latin comedy in 1 act by Mozart; text by Rufinus Widl. Prod. Salzburg, 13 May 1767; London, Fortune T., 24 Jan. 1955. Not strictly an opera, but a prologue and nine musical numbers as intermezzo to Widl's *Clementia Croesi*.

Apostolescu, Nicu (*b* Brăila, 31 July 1896). Romanian tenor, formerly baritone. Studied Bucharest with Dimiter Popovici. Début Cluj, 1921, Amonasro. Sang baritone roles 1921-3; début as tenor 1923 (Radamès), while continuing to sing such roles as Scarpia and Rigoletto. Bucharest Opera as leading tenor 1926-44; sang in first Bucharest performances of *Parsifal*, *Tristan und Isolde*, *Tannhäuser* *Meistersinger*, and *Otello*. Otello in Italy 1928-30 (Venice, Bologna, Genoa, etc.). Considered the finest singing actor on the Romanian operatic stage of his day.

Appia, Adolphe (*b* Geneva, 1 Sept. 1862; *d* Lyon, 29 Feb. 1928). Swiss scenic artist and philosopher. Studied Paris, became a keen Wagnerian. Appalled by the visual aspect of what he saw at Bayreuth (especially *Parsifal* and *Tannhäuser*), which he considered at least half a century out of date, he made his first sketches for a production of *The Ring* in 1892, and then set out his ideas in two important

books: *La Mise-en-Scène du drame Wagnérien* (1895) and *Die Musik und die Inszenierung* (1899). He insisted that two-dimensional settings killed theatre: the only true form of theatre was *Wort-Ton Drama*. 'If man is three-dimensional, scenery must be three-dimensional.' Lighting was the most important element in production; light is 'the supreme scene painter, the interpreter, the most significant plastic medium on the stage'. Accordingly all his designs were grey, waiting for lighting to provide them with the necessary colours.

He was encouraged in his ideas by the Countess de Béarn; she built a house in the grounds of her Paris house for him, where, in 1903, he staged the Lillas Pastia scene from *Carmen* and scenes from Schumann's *Manfred*. In 1912 Wolf Döhrn invited him and Dalcroze to work in his theatre at Hellerau near Dresden, where in 1912 they produced Gluck's *Orfeo*. In 1923 Toscanini invited him to design *Tristan und Isolde* at Milan, Sc., which evoked much hostile reaction. In 1924 and 1925 embarked on a new *Ring* at Basel, but there the opposition to his then revolutionary ideas forced the theatre to abandon the project when it was only half-way through.

His theories, expressed in his many writings, and his designs influenced Gordon Craig, Stanislavsky, Max Reinhardt, Josef Svoboda, and especially Wieland Wagner at Bayreuth in the period after the Second World War. It has been rightly said that Appia and not Wagner is the father of modern opera staging.
Bibl: A. Appia: *La Musique et la mise-en-scène* (1963).

Aprile, Giuseppe (known as Sciroletto or Scirolino) (*b* Martina Franca, Taranto, 29 Oct. 1732; *d* Martina Franca, 11 Jan. 1813). Italian male contralto. Studied Naples with G. Sciroli, whence his nicknames. Début Naples, S.C., 1753 in small roles; began his international career in Parma in 1755. In 1756 engaged on Jommelli's suggestion for Stuttgart, where he remained for ten years, and where Schubart heard him and wrote: 'In him art and nature are marvellously combined; he sings with the purity of a bell up to E above the treble stave.' Referred to by Kelly in his *Memoirs*. From 1780 he taught singing: one of his pupils was Lady Hamilton.

Arabella. Opera in 3 acts by Richard Strauss; text by Hofmannsthal. Prod. Dresden, 1 July 1933, with Ursuleac, Bokor, Jerger, cond. Krauss; London, C.G., 17 May 1934, same artists; N.Y., Met., 10 Feb. 1955, with Steber, Gueden, London, cond. Kempe. Hofmannsthal's last Strauss libretto. The story concerns the efforts of the impoverished Count Waldner (bass) to make a profitable marriage for his daughter Arabella (sop.). A wealth of Viennese complications intervenes before she is happily betrothed to Mandryka (bar.), and her younger sister Zdenka (sop.) to Arabella's former admirer Matteo (ten.).

Araia, Francesco (*b* Naples, 25 June 1709; *d* ?Bologna, before 1770). Italian composer. The first of many Italian composers to serve the Russian Court, he arrived in Russia in 1735 and remained until 1759. His *La forza dell'amore e dell'odio* (The Power of Love and Hate, 1736) was given in St Petersburg in Italian, though Russian librettos were printed. This was followed by *Il finto Nino, overo La semiramide riconosciuta* (1737) and *Artaserse* (1738). *Tsefal i Prokris* (Cephalus and Procris, 1755) was the first opera in Russian, to a text by A.P. Sumarokov; it was sung by Russians, with court singers as chorus, but is essentially an opera seria with no Russian national colouring. His last Russian opera was *Alexander in India* (1775). Brief return visit to Russia in 1762.

Arangi-Lombardi, Giannina (*b* Marigliano, Naples, 20 June 1891; *d* Milan, 9 July 1951). Italian soprano. Studied with B. Carelli, Adelina Stehle, and Poli-Randaccio. Début as mezzo, Rome, C., 1920, Lola. Soprano from 1923. Milan, Sc., 1924-30 under Toscanini; chosen by Melba to tour Australia with her, 1928; sang in leading opera houses of Europe (not C.G.) and South America. Noted for her Lucrezia Borgia, La Vestale, Gioconda, and Aida. First Italian Ariadne. Taught at the Conservatorio Giuseppe Verdi, Milan, 1938-47, and in Ankara from then until shortly before her death. (R)

Archers, The. Opera in 3 acts by Benjamin Carr; text by W. Dunlap, on the William Tell story. Prod. N.Y., John St. T., by Old American Opera Company, 18 Apr. 1796. The first American opera of which parts of the music (two numbers) survive.

Archibaldo. The blind King of Altura (bass) in Montemezzi's *L'amore dei tre re*.

Archilei (orig. Concarini), **Vittoria** (*b* Rome, 1550; *d* Florence, *c*1618). Italian soprano and lutenist. Wife of the composer Antonio Archilei. For many years in the service of the Medici, and sang in many of the court musical entertainments, including the *intermezzi,* in the period just before the birth of opera; almost certainly participated in the early operas of Peri, Cavalieri, and Caccini. Known as 'La Romanina'.

Arditi, Luigi (*b* Crescentino, 22 July 1822; *d* Hove, 1 May 1903). Italian composer and conductor. Appeared in America, 1847-55; settled in London, and conducted regularly at H.M.'s and C.G., 1858-92. Conducted many touring companies, including those organized by Mapleson with Patti. Conducted first London performances of many operas, including *Faust,*

Der fliegende Holländer, Un ballo in maschera, I vespri siciliani, Mefistofele, Cavalleria rusticana, and *Hänsel und Gretel.* Remembered as the composer of the song 'Il Bacio'.
Bibl: L. Arditi: *My Reminiscences* (1896).

Ardon gl'incensi. The opening words of Lucia's Mad Scene in Donizetti's *Lucia di Lammermoor.*

Arensky, Anton (Stepanovich) (*b* Novgorod, 12 July 1861; *d* Terioki, 25 Feb. 1906). Russian composer and conductor. Studied St Petersburg with Zikke, Rimsky-Korsakov (helped to prepare the vocal score of *The Snow Maiden*), and Johannsen. He then moved to Moscow to teach; his pupils included Rakhmaninov and Skryabin. A close friend of Tchaikovsky; his first opera *A Dream on the Volga* (1891) has the same subject as *The Voyevoda.* Its great success was not matched by that of his second opera, *Rafael* (1894). His *Nal and Damayanti* (1904) has a text by Modest Tchaikovsky. His music shows Tchaikovsky's influence.

Argentina. For all its present riches, the operatic life of Argentina did not develop until the last third of the 19th century. The country was dependent on Italian singers visiting Buenos Aires. As in most countries, the first national operas treated local subjects (Inca stories and, to a lesser degree, popular tales of pampas life) in an Italianate style; later works drew upon folk melodies and national musical characteristics. The first important Argentinian opera was F. Hargreaves's *La gata blanca,* a work in an opera buffa vein that proved very influential. Arturo Berutti (1862-1938) won a popular success with his *Pampa* (1897, after the gaucho drama *Juan Moreira* by Juan José Podestá); his other works include *Yupanky* (1899), the very successful *Khryse* (1902), *Horrida nox* (1908), and *Los héroes* (1909), each in some way making use of indigenous Argentinian subjects and colouring. Panizza's *Aurora* (1908; with libretto by Illica) sought to reconcile folklore with *verismo* manner; other operas showing a strong European influence were by Gaito (*Shafras, Caio Petronio, Flor de Nieve*) and E. García Mansilla (a Rimsky-Korsakov pupil whose *Ivan* was premièred in St Petersburg).

P. de Rogatis's *Huemac* (1916) was the first work which really sought to make fully operatic use of Argentinian musical characteristics. The first local opera in Spanish was Felipe Boero's *Tucumán,* which won the first national opera competition in 1918. Many Argentinian operas now began to appear, including Boero's *Raquela* (1923), set on a pampas ranch, and his *El matrero* (1929), also set in the countryside and, for its effective use of local tunes and dances, regarded as one of the most important Argentinian operas. Other significant works were written by A.L. Schiuma (*Tabaré,* 1925), Gaito (*Ollantay,* 1926; *La sangre de las guitarras; Las virgenes del sol,* 1939), G. Gilardi (*Ilse,* 1923; *La leyenda del Urutaú,* 1934), De Rogatis (*Novia del Hereje,* 1935), R.H. Espoile (*Ciudad Roja,* 1936), and Arnaldo D'Esposito (*Lin-Candel,* 1941). These works use local subjects and music drawn either from Inca scales and rhythms or from folksong and dance. Parallel with this development went a movement that kept strong links with European opera: important works were written by C. López Buchardo (*El sueno del Alma,* 1914), Athos Palma (*Nazdah,* 1924), Rafael Peacan del Sar (*Chrysanthème,* 1927: a Puccinian work based on Pierre Loti and set in Japan), J.B. Massa (*La Magdalena,* a Biblical opera), Panizza (*Bizancio,* 1939: on a Byzantine subject) and J. J. Castro (*Proserpina y el extranjero,* 1951: Verdi prize opera, transferring classical legend to South America).

Outside Buenos Aires, the country has been largely dependent on touring opera, with few premières: exceptions are Massa's *L'Evaso* (1922) at Rosario, Enrique Casella's *Corimayo* (1926) and *Chasca* (1939) at Tucumán. Occasional seasons have been given at Rosario, Tucumán, Mendoza, Santa Fé, Córdoba, and Bahía Blanca, by companies based on Buenos Aires. At the T. Argentino of La Plata, the capital of the province of Buenos Aires, there have been regular seasons.

See also *Buenos Aires, Colón.*

Argomento (*It* argument). In 17th-cent. librettos, especially Venetian, the text was usually prefaced by an argument, or summary of events that had taken place before the opera story; sometimes this included a summary of the plot itself. See also *Antefatto.*

Aria (*It* air, from *Gr* and *Lat* aer, a term which came to mean a scheme or model, i.e. a melody which could be repeated with different words). The elaborated song-form of opera (and oratorio), for solo voice (occasionally two voices) with instrumental accompaniment. Its nature has changed substantially with the history of opera, reaching its high point of formality in the period *c*1650-1750 and then growing looser.

Originally the aria developed, from the recitative of the first operas, as a point of heightened expression or deepened contemplation, and had already acquired greater expressive weight and function in Monteverdi's last operas by comparison with his *Orfeo.* The early *ostinato aria* employed a *basso ostinato*: a classic example, which is also an early example of the *da capo aria,* is the final duet of Monteverdi's *Poppea.* Subdivisible into many detailed categories, the *aria col 'Da Capo'* was usually in three parts, with the second in the relative major or minor key and the third a

repeat of the first (to be ornamented by the singer).

This type was highly formalized by Alessandro Scarlatti, and used with great effect by Handel (it was normally for a solo singer, though Scarlatti has examples of an *aria a quattro* for four people). The *aria di sortita* (exit aria) was the most prominent form in *opera seria, and was sung by a character at the end of a scene just before leaving the stage. Already in common practice with *Zeno's librettos, it was brought to a fine art by *Metastasio. Rigidly applied rules demanded that no singer should have two arias consecutively, and that each principal must have five (all different in character). Arias chiefly concerned with expressive content included the *aria di carattere, aria di mezzo carattere* (usually more restrained in feeling), *aria di sentimento, aria di strepito, aria agitata, aria infuriata,* and *aria di imitazione* (in which voice and instruments vied with each other in imitating the sounds of nature). Arias chiefly for technical display included the *aria di bravura, aria di agilità, aria di portamento* (usually dignified with wide dynamic range, unornamented), and *aria cantabile* (gentle and sad, delicately ornamented). Arias more directly connected to the dramatic situation included the *aria di lamento* (or simply *lamento*) and *aria del sonno* (or sleep aria, sung to the sleeping beloved). Arias of more declamatory nature included the *aria parlante* and *aria declamata* (usually for expressing powerful or passionate sentiments). Arias concentrating on formal niceties included the *aria in rondò* (or simply *rondò*: a common five-part form was *a-b-a-c-a*) and *aria variata* (in the form of variations). There was also the elaborately accompanied *aria concertato* and the very rare *aria senza accompagnamento.* Miscellaneous categories included the *aria di baule* (or trunk aria, the favourite number which a singer carried in his luggage for introduction into whichever opera he sang) and the *aria del sorbetto* (or sorbet aria, the number assigned to a minor character, which gave the spectators the chance to retreat to enjoy an ice).

The above categories were usually assigned to principals and noble characters: those of humbler birth were normally confined to the *arietta* or *canzonetta.* The aria's two parts were properly, and by Metastasio very effectively, disposed into two contrasting thoughts, perhaps a simile drawn from nature to which a moral would be applied before the return of the first part, now elaborated by the singer. Though it became a suffocating convention, imposing a monotonous pattern on opera, at its best the formal aria of this period, *c*1650-1750, served to halt the plot and at well-judged points provide a moment of reflection before the character departed and the action resumed. A somewhat later feature, also formal but at the same time tending to break down the old rigidity, was the double aria: resulting from the desire of virtuoso singers to display their techniques, this consisted of two separate arias of contrasting character (perhaps dramatic and lyrical) which were brought together.

Of the smaller forms, the *arietta* was usually simpler, nearer to a song and neither lengthy nor difficult. In early French opera the *ariette* was a coloratura piece to Italian words, later (from *c*1750) an easy solo song in French forming part of a *comédie mêlée d'ariettes*: the more formal *air* was more elaborate, especially in the accompaniment. *Arioso*, or *recitativo arioso*, is recitative of a lyrical and expressive character, reconciling the expressiveness of aria with the declamatory freedom of recitative. In comic opera, particular types included the *aria di catalogo*, often very rapid in declamation and the predecessor of the *patter song: this involved a list of various items, perhaps of exotic places, or assorted grandees (Gazzaniga: *L'isola di Alcina*), or the goods in a shop (Goldoni's text for *Lo speziale*). The most famous example, which also slyly parodies the convention, is Leporello's catalogue of his master's lovers in *Don Giovanni* (copied by Da Ponte from Bertati's libretto for Gazzaniga's *Don Giovanni Tenorio*).

The subsequent history of the aria is one of continual loosening of form, though versions of the old Italian *da capo* have proved tenacious as the natural balance of the form has remained effective. Moreover, even when formal divisions had been totally dissolved, as above all in Wagner, the ancient dramatic instinct to balance narrative with reflection has shown in moments whose melodic distinctiveness and contemplative intensity suggest an equivalent of the aria: such in Wagner are Siegmund's 'Winterstürme' or Walther's 'Am stillen Herd'. Subsequently, renewed interest in classical procedures has naturally rekindled an interest in the more or less formal aria as capable of playing a functional role in modern opera.

Ariadne. Daughter of Minos and Pasiphae, who saved Theseus from the Minotaur's labyrinth by giving him a guide thread, and was later abandoned by him on Naxos. The first of nearly 50 surviving Ariadne operas is Monteverdi's once-famous *Arianna*, of which only the beautiful *lamento* is extant. Other operas on the subject are by Kusser (1692), Porpora (1714), Keiser (1722), Marcello (1727), Feo (1728), Handel (1734), Benda (1775 – a melodrama which Mozart thought 'really excellent'), Edelmann (1782), Winter (1796), Massenet (1906), Strauss (1912), Milhaud (1928), and Martinů (1961).

Ariadne auf Naxos (Ariadne on Naxos). Opera in 1 act, later with a scenic prelude, by Richard Strauss; text by Hofmannsthal. Originally to be given after Molière's *comédie-ballet*, *Le Bourgeois Gentilhomme* (1670), for which Strauss had written incidental music: in this form, prod. Stuttgart 25 Oct. 1912, with Jeritza, Siems, Jadlowker, cond. Strauss; London, H.M.'s, 27 May 1913, with Von der Osten, Bosetti, Marak, cond. Beecham. Second version, prod. Vienna, Court, 4 Oct. 1916, with Jeritza, Kurz, Lehmann, Környey, cond. Schalk; London, C.G., 27 May 1924, with Lehmann, Ivogün, Schumann, Niemann, cond. Alwin; Philadelphia, Civic Opera, 1 Nov. 1928, with Peterson, Boykin, Williams, House, cond. Smallens. The work's first form was impracticable, requiring both a theatrical and an operatic company for the same evening. The second version substitutes for Molière's play a prelude in which word is sent from the 'bourgeois gentilhomme', who has engaged an opera company and a *commedia dell'arte* troupe, that their entertainments must also take place simultaneously so as to be over in time for a fireworks display.

The opera tells of the enraged Composer (sop.) who is soothed first by the old Music Master (bass) then by Zerbinetta (sop.), leader of the rival group, and lastly by his faith in music. On her island, Ariadne (sop.) is the subject of much comment from the comedians. She sings of her longing for the kingdom of death, to which Zerbinetta replies by trying to convert her to a more flirtatious philosophy. When Bacchus (ten.) arrives, Ariadne greets him as Death, and there follows a long love duet. They ascend into the sky together, which Zerbinetta considers acceptance of her advice.

Ariane et Barbe-Bleue (Ariadne and Bluebeard). *Conte musical* in 3 acts by Dukas; text adapted from Maeterlinck's drama (1901), written with Dukas in mind. Prod. Paris, O.C., 10 May 1907, with Georgette Leblanc, Vieuille, cond. Ruhlmann; N.Y., 29 Mar. 1911, with Farrar, Rothier, cond. Toscanini; London, C.G., 20 Apr. 1937, with Lubin, Etcheverry, cond. Gaubert. Dukas's only opera, initially successful.

See also *Bluebeard*.

Arianna (Ariadne). Opera in 3 acts by Handel; text ? F. Colman, after P. Pariati's text *Arianna e Teseo* for Porpora (1714). Prod. London, King's, 26 Jan. 1734.

Arietta. See *Aria*.

Ariodant. Opera in 3 acts by Méhul; text by F. B. Hoffman, after Ariosto's poem *Orlando furioso* (1516). Prod. Paris, O.C., 11 Oct. 1799. Said to be Méhul's own favourite among his operas. See also *Orlando*.

Ariodante. Opera in 3 acts by Handel; text by A. Salvi, after Ariosto's poem *Orlando furioso* (1516). Prod. London, C.G., 8 Jan. 1735, with Strada, Negri, Young, Carestini, Beard, Waltz, Stoppelaer; N.Y., Carnegie Hall, 9 Mar. 1971, with Steffan, Wise, Caplan, Raskin, Stewart, Meredith, Solem, cond. Simon.
See also *Orlando*.

Arioso. See *Aria*.

Arkel. The aged, blind King of Allemonde (bass) in Debussy's *Pelléas et Mélisande*.

Arkhipova, Irina (Konstantinovna) (*b* Moscow, 2 Dec. 1925). Russian mezzo. After studying with Leonid Savransky, joined the Sverdlovsk Opera as a soloist (1954-6); won an award in the 1955 International Competition in Warsaw. In 1956 joined the Moscow B. Début as Carmen; sang the first B. performances of Nilovna (Khrennikov's *The Mother*), Princess Helen (*War and Peace*), Varvara (Shchedrin's *Not Love Alone*) and other new works, as well as Eboli, Amneris, Carmen, Azucena, and the classical Russian mezzo roles. In 1960 sang Carmen at the Naples S.C., and in 1965 visited the Milan Sc. with the B., singing Marfa (*Khovanshchina*) and Marina (*Boris*), roles she repeated the following year in Italian. She appeared in Montreal with the B. during EXPO 1967. San Francisco, 1972. C.G. 1975, Azucena. She possesses a rich, dramatic voice and an imposing stage presence. (R)

Arkor, André (*b* Liège, 23 Feb. 1901; *d* Liège Dec. 1971). Belgian tenor. Studied Liège with Malherbe and Seguin. Début Liège, 1924, Gérald in *Lakmé*, appearances at Ghent and Lyons. Leading tenor, Brussels, La M., 1930-42. Guest appearances at the Paris O.C. A distinguished Mozart singer. Director of the T. Royal, Liège, 1950-67. (R)

Arlecchino (Harlequin). Theatrical *capriccio* in 1 act by Busoni; text by composer. Prod. in the same bill as his *Turandot,* Zurich, 11 May 1917, with Wenck, Grunert, Moissi, cond. Busoni; London, B.B.C. broadcast, Jan. 1939, TV 12 Feb. 1939; N.Y., Carnegie Hall (semi-staged), 11 Oct. 1951; Gly., 25 June 1954, with Malbin, M. Dickie, Gerster, cond. Pritchard. Set in Bergamo in the 18th cent., this short work introduces such familiar *commedia dell'arte* figures as Harlequin (a speaking role), Columbine (sop.), Doctor Bombasto (bass), Leandro (ten.), etc. The four parts of the opera are called 'Harlequin as Rogue', 'Harlequin as Soldier', 'Harlequin as Husband', and 'Harlequin as Conqueror'.

Arlesiana, L' (The Girl from Arles). Opera in 3 acts (originally 4) by Cilea; text by Leopoldo Marenco, after Daudet's drama (1872). Prod. Milan, T.L., 27 Nov. 1897, with Ricci, De Paz, Caruso, cond. Zuccari. 3-act version, same theatre, 22 Oct. 1898; Philadelphia, 11 Jan.

1962; London, Camden Town Hall, by Philopera Circle, 17 May 1968, with Keetch, R. Remedios, cond. Manton. Federico (ten.) is in love with Rosa Mammai (mezzo), but discovers she is the mistress of Metifio (bar.), a muledriver; his family arrange that he marry his childhood sweetheart, Vivette (sop.). He kills himself on the eve of the wedding.

Arline. The daughter (sop.) of Count Arnheim in Balfe's *The Bohemian Girl*.

Arme Heinrich, Der (Poor Heinrich). Opera in 3 acts by Pfitzner; text by James Grun, after a medieval legend. Prod. Mainz, 2 Apr. 1895, with Cruvelli, Neumann, Heydrich, cond. Pfitzner.

Armenia. The first Armenian opera, by Tigran *Chukhadjian (1837-98) was *Arshak II* (1868, prod. 1945); this was a story of the liberation of Armenia in the 4th cent., composed on Italian models. Chukhadjian followed it with a series of lighter works, including *Arif* (1872) and *Kese-Kyokhva* (The Balding Elder, 1874), which used Armenian folk music; his operetta *Leblebidje* (The Chick Pea Seller, 1876), a satirical comedy, won a limited international success, and other works followed, including historical operas and a *féerie (semi-seria), Zemire* (1891). He directed an operetta company 1872-8. His example encouraged other Armenian composers, including Armen Tigranian (1879-1950), whose Romantic opera *Anush* (Alexandropolis, now Leninakan, 1912) made fuller use of local colour and customs.

The first Armenian ensembles were formed in the 1860s, giving performances of the Russian and international repertory as well as of the pioneer Armenian works; but only in the 1920s did a company begin giving regular performances touring Armenian and Russian towns. It was with this group, under S. Talyan, that many Armenian artists, including Alexander Melik-Pashayev, began their careers. In 1927 the Erevan Conservatory founded an opera class. New Armenian operas included *Seda* (1921) by Anushavan Ter-Gevondian (1887-1961), and *Almast* (1928, Moscow 1930) by Alexander Spendiarian (Spendiarov) (1871-1928), both on historical subjects. The first permanent Armenian company was formed in Erevan, from the conservatory class, in 1932 and began operations on the following 20 Jan. with *Almast*; it was named after Spendiarov. The theatre (cap. 1,200) was built in 1933. Among the Armenian composers encouraged to write for the new ensemble were Aro Stepanian (1897-1966) (the comedy *Khraby Nazar*, 1935, and *David Sasunsky*, 1936), Artemy Ayvazian (*b* 1902) (another comedy, *Taparnikos*, 1938), and Karo Zakarian (*Mardjan*, 1941), all on Armenian subjects and using folk music. A season of Armenian opera was given in Moscow in 1939.

The Spendiarov Opera and Ballet T. (cap. 1,130) opened in Erevan in 1940: works written for it include Tigranian's *David Bek* (1950) and Araratyan's *Tsar Hadjik* (comp. 1945), on patriotic themes. Many works came after the war, including Ter-Gevondian's children's opera *From the Sun's Rays* (1949) and Stepanian's *The Heroine* (1950) and *Nune*. A second Moscow season followed in 1956. Later Armenian operas include *Artsavaberd* (1957) by Andrey Babayev (1923-64), on the subject of collectivization in Armenia, *Sos i Barditer* (1957) by V. Tigranian, *Krusheniye* (The Ruin, 1968) by Armenian, *Skazka dlya Vzroslikh* (A story for Grown-Ups, 1970) by E. Arutunian. The repertory includes Russian and Armenian works, as does that of the Musical Comedy T. founded in 1942, and as well as Western classics the theatre has staged the first U.S.S.R. productions of *Oedipus rex* and *West Side Story* (both in 1963).

Armide. Opera in 5 acts by Gluck; text by Quinault, after Tasso's poem *Gerusalemme liberata* (1575). Prod. Paris, O., 23 Sept. 1777, with Levasseur, Legros, Gelin, Larrivée; London, C.G., 6 July 1906, with Bréval, Laffitte, Seveilhac, Crabbé, cond. Messager; N.Y., Met., 14 Nov. 1910, with Fremstad, Caruso, Amato, Gilly, cond. Toscanini. Among some 40 operas based on Tasso's poem are works by B. Ferrari (1639), Lully (1686), Handel (*Rinaldo,* 1711), Traetta (1761), Jommelli (1770), Salieri (1773), Mysliveček (1779), Haydn (1784), Häffner (*Renaud,* 1801), Righini (two 2-act operas, *Gerusalemme liberata* and *La Selva incantata,* 1803), Rossini (Naples, S.C., 11 Nov. 1817, with Colbran), and Dvořák (1904). Armida, a beautiful queen with supernatural powers, tries to win Rinaldo, but grows cooler by the time he begins to love her. When he is summoned away she sets her palace on fire and disappears.

Arminio. Opera in 3 acts by Handel; text by A. Salvi. Prod. London, C.G., 12 Jan. 1737. Revived Oldenburg (in German) 1963.

Arndt-Ober, Margaret. See *Ober, Margaret Arndt.*

Arne, Thomas (Augustine) (*b* London, 12 Mar. 1710; *d* London, 5 Mar. 1778). English composer. His first opera *Rosamond,* a resetting of a text by Addison, was well received in 1733. Other operas followed, and in 1738 his reputation was made with his music for Milton's *Comus.* Visited Ireland several times, producing operas there, and also became composer at D.L. and the Vauxhall Gardens. In 1760 moved to C.G., producing there his *Thomas and Sally.* Artaxerxes (1762), text translated from Metastasio, was set in Italian style with recitative replacing dialogue. There followed *Love in a Village* (1762) and *Olimpiade* (1764),

in which Metastasio was now set in Italian. Arne made distinctive contributions to 18th-cent. theatrical music, not least by the charm of some of his individual songs. His sister **Susanna** (1714-66), a singer and actress, married Theophilus Cibber; Handel wrote the part of Micah in *Samson* for her, and she sang in the first performance of *Messiah.* His son **Michael** (1740-86) was a singer and composer of stage works.

Arnold (Melcthal). A Swiss patriot (ten.) in love with the tyrant Gessler's daughter Mathilde in Rossini's *Guillaume Tell.*

Arnold, Samuel (*b* London, 10 Aug. 1740; *d* London, 22 Oct. 1802). English composer, organist, conductor, and editor. At the age of 23 became composer at C.G., adapting and writing music for the comic opera *The Maid of the Mill* (perf. 1765). He left some 50 stage pieces for London theatres.

Arnoldson, Sigrid (*b* Stockholm, 20 Mar. 1861; *d* Stockholm 7 Feb. 1943). Swedish soprano. Daughter of the tenor Oscar Arnoldson, with whom she studied. Later studied with Maurice Strakosch, who taught her several of his sister-in-law Patti's roles; then Berlin with Desirée Artôt-Padilla. Début Prague, 1885, Rosina. Engaged by Augustus Harris for his trial season of Italian opera, London, D.L., 1887; C.G. 1888 and 1892-4; N.Y., Met., 1893. Charlotte in first London *Werther.* Continued to sing until 1916, after which she taught in Vienna 1922-38 and later in Stockholm. Her voice encompassed three octaves, and as well as coloratura and lyric roles she sang Carmen. She married the impresario Maurice Fischof. (R)

Arnould, Sophie (Madeleine) (*b* Paris, 14 Feb. 1740; *d* Paris, 18 Oct. 1802). French soprano. Studied with Marie Fel and Hippolyte Clairon, and made her début at the Paris O. in 1757, remaining a member of the company for 20 years. Created the title-role of Gluck's *Iphigénie en Aulide* and Eurydice in his *Orphée,* and was also highly successful in the works of Rameau, Francoeur, and Monsigny. She possessed a fine though not large voice, and was a passionate actress. She lacked self-discipline both in her private life and as a singer, which resulted in a vocal decline before she was 40. She retired in 1788 with a state pension of 2,000 livres. Mme de Pompadour said of her, 'With such talents, you may become a princess.' Her wit and conversation made her much sought after in Parisian society. Pierné wrote a one-act opera, *Sophie Arnould* (1927), based on events in her life.
Bibl: B. Douglas: *The Memoires of Sophie Arnould, Actress and Wit* (1898); E. and J. De Goncourt: *Sophie Arnould d'après sa correspondence et ses mémoires* (1877).

Aroldo. See *Stiffelio.*

Arroyo, Martina (b New York, 2 Feb. 1940). American soprano. Studied at Hunter College and with Marinka Gurewich, making her professional début in the first U.S. performance of *Assassinio nella cattedrale* at Carnegie Hall, 1958. The same year won the Metropolitan Auditions of the Air and made her début as the Voice from Heaven in *Don Carlos*, N.Y., Met., March 1959. After singing small roles in New York she joined the Zurich Opera in 1963, and has appeared regularly as a guest artist all over Europe. She returned to the Met. to sing principal roles in 1965. London, C.G., since 1968. Her repertory includes Reiza, Norma, and the Verdi dramatic soprano roles. (R)

Artaxerxes. Opera in 3 acts by Arne; text by Metastasio, in composer's translation. Prod. London, C.G., 2 Feb. 1762 with Brent, Tenducci, Peretti, when riots ensued because of increased seat prices; N.Y., 31 Jan. 1828, with Hackett, Sharpe, Austin, Pearman, Horn. Metastasio's libretto was first set by Leonardo Vinci in 1730; among some 45 other operas on the subject are works by Hasse (also 1730), Gluck (1741 – his first opera), Graun (1743), Terradellas (1744), Jommelli (1749), Galuppi (1751), Paisiello (1765), Piccinni (1766), Sacchini (1788), Cimarosa (1781), Anfossi (1788), and Isouard (1795).

Artists in opera. Artists who appear in opera, or have operas based on their works, are as follows:
Fra Angelico: Hillemacher (1924).
Hieronymus Bosch: Menotti (*Amahl and the Night Visitors*, 1951).
Benvenuto Cellini: Berlioz (1838); Rossi (1845); Schlösser (1847); Lachner (1849); Diaz (19th cent.); Bozzano (1871); Saint-Saëns (*Ascanio*, 1890).
Dürer: Sonnenfeld (*Albrecht Dürer w Wenecji*, 19th cent.); Barravalle (1890); Baussnern (1901); Baselt (late 19th-early 20th cent.); Mraczek (*Herr Dürers Bild*, 1927).
Fragonard: Pierné (1934).
Gauguin: Elizalde (1948); Gardner (*The Moon and Sixpence*, 1957).
Goya: Barbieri (*Pan y toros*, 1864); Granados (*Goyescas*, 1916).
Matthias Grünewald: Hindemith (*Mathis der Maler*, 1938).
Hogarth: Stravinsky (*The Rake's Progress*, 1951).
Michelangelo: Isouard (1802); F. Ricci (1841); Buongiorno (1903); Alfred Mendelssohn (1964).
Rembrandt: Badings (*De Nachtwacht*, comp. 1943, prod. 1950); Klenau (1937).
Tilman Riemenschneider: Pászthory (1937).
Rubens: see Van Dyck.
Salvator Rosa: Rastrelli (1832); Bassi (1837); Bergson (c1850); Bianchi (1855);

Sobelewski (1859); Duprato (1861).
Andrea del Sarto: Baravalle (1890); Weingartner (*Meister Andrea*, 1920); M. Rosselli-Nissem (1931); Lesur (1969).
Karel Škreta: Bendl (1883).
Van Dyck: Villent-Bordogni (1845: includes a duet between Van Dyck and Rubens); Michel (*La Meunière de Saventham*, 1872); A. Müller (between 1875 and 1882).
Van Gogh: Nevit Kodalli (mid 20th cent.).
Velasquez: R. Strauss (*Friedenstag*, 1938).
Leonardo da Vinci: Wade (*The Pupil of Da Vinci*, 1839); Różycki (*Meduza*, 1912); Schillings (*Mona Lisa*, 1915); De Ninno (*Monna Lisa*,?).

Artôt, Désirée (Marguerite Joséphine Désirée Montagney) (b Paris, 21 July 1835; d Berlin, 3 Apr. 1907). Belgian mezzo-soprano, later soprano. Daughter of Jean Artôt, horn-player at Brussels, La M. Studied with M. Audran and Pauline Viardot. Engaged for Paris, O., on Meyerbeer's suggestion; début 1858 as Fidès. After appearances in Italy and Germany in mezzo roles, emerged as a soprano, and sang as such in London concerts 1859-60; H.M.'s 1863 as Marie (*Fille du régiment*), Violetta, and Adalgisa (then sung invariably by sopranos); C.G. 1864-6. On her visit to Russia in 1868 Tchaikovsky proposed marriage, but next year she married the Spanish baritone Mariano Padilla y Ramos (1842-1906), with whom she often sang thereafter. Their daughter **Lola Artôt de Padilla** (b Sèvres, 5 Oct. 1876; d Berlin, 12 Apr. 1933) was a pupil of her mother. Début 1904 Paris, O.C. After appearances at Berlin, K.O., joined Berlin H. 1909, singing there until 1927. The first Berlin Octavian. (R)

Arts Council of Great Britain. An independent body, working without any control by the Government. Its primary responsibility, as laid down in its Royal Charter (9 Aug. 1946), is 'to preserve and improve standards of performance in the various arts'. The Council makes grants to C.G., S.W., and other operatic organizations, professional and amateur. Its total grant from the treasury was initially £235,000; by 1976-7 this had risen to over £37,150,000 of which about one quarter goes to opera. The council's chairmen have been Lord Keynes, Sir Kenneth Clark, Lord Cottesloe, Lord Goodman, Patrick Gibson, and, since 1977, Kenneth Robinson.

Arundell, Dennis (b London, 22 July 1898). English actor, producer, author, and composer. Educated Tonbridge and Cambridge (Cyril Rootham and Stanford). Produced Rootham's *The Two Sisters*, Cambridge 1922, and first stage performance of *Semele*, Cambridge 1925. Other important Cambridge productions included *The Soldier's Tale* (1928), Honegger's *King David* (his own translation, 1929), and *The*

Fairy Queen (1931). After the war was responsible for a number of productions at S. W., including *The School for Fathers* (*I quatro rusteghi*) (1946), *Shvanda* (own translation, 1948), *Faust* (1949), *Tosca* (1949), *Kaťa Kabanová* (1951), *Werther* (1952), *The Consul* (1954), and *The Flying Dutchman* (1958). Collaborated with Sir Thomas Beecham in his 1951 production of *The Bohemian Girl* at C. G. and has produced several radio operas, including *A Tale of Two Cities* and *The Rake's Progress*. Abroad has worked at Helsinki and with the Elizabethan Opera Trust in Australia. Has composed two operas, *Ghost of Abel* and *A Midsummer Night's Dream*, and written three books, one on Purcell (1927), *The Critic at the Opera* (1957), and *The Story of Sadler's Wells* (1965, 2/1977).

Ascanio in Alba. *Serenata teatrale* in 2 acts by Mozart; text by G. Parini, perhaps after Count Claudio Stampa. Prod. Milan, T.R.D., 17 Oct. 1771 a day after Hasse's last opera, *Ruggiero*. It was then that Hasse is said to have observed, 'This boy will make us all be forgotten.'

Aschenbach. The writer (ten.) who is the central figure of Britten's *Death in Venice.*

Aschenbrödel. See *Cinderella.*

Assassinio nella cattedrale, L' (Murder in the Cathedral). Opera in 2 parts, with an intermezzo, by Pizzetti; text by composer, after A. Castelli's trans. of the dramatic poem by T.S. Eliot (1935). Prod. Milan, Sc., 1 Mar. 1958, with Rossi-Lemeni, cond. Gavazzeni; N.Y., Carnegie Hall, 17 Sept. 1958, concert perf., with Rossi-Lemeni, cond. Halasz; Coventry, by S.W., 12 June 1962, with Garrard, cond. Davis. The plot is based on the historical events leading to the assassination in Canterbury Cathedral of Thomas à Becket (bass), Archbishop of Canterbury, by four knights in the service of Henry II.

Astrua, Giovanna (*b* Graglia, nr Vercelli, *c* 1720; *d* Turin, 28 Oct. 1757). Italian soprano. Studied in Milan. Début Venice, 1739; after appearing in other Italian cities was engaged for the Court Opera, Berlin, 1746-56, where she created leading roles in operas by Benda and Graun. Especially famous for her singing of the bravura aria 'Mi paventi' in Graun's *Brittanico.*

Astuzie femminili, Le (Feminine Wiles). Opera in 2 acts by Cimarosa; text by Giovanni Palomba. Prod. Naples, Fondo, 16 Aug. 1794; London 21 Feb. 1804; N.Y., Town Hall, 31 Oct. 1966. According to the terms of her father's will, Bellina (sop.), the richest heiress in Rome, is to marry Giampolo (bass), an elderly merchant from Bergamo. Her tutor, Dr Romualdo (bass), although betrothed to Leonora (mezzo), Bellina's governess, also wants to marry the young girl. Bellina herself is in love with the young Filandro (ten.); they run off together and, returning disguised as Cossack officers, are successful in their ruse to get married.

Atalanta. Opera in 3 acts by Handel; text anon., after B. Valeriani's *La caccia in Etolia*. Prod. London, C.G., 23 May 1736 on occasion of the marriage of Frederick Prince of Wales (son of George II) to Princess Augusta of Saxe-Gotha, with Conti (Gizziello), Negri, Strada, Beard. Revived Hintlesham Festival, 1970. This *pièce d'occasion* tells of the love of the Atalanta, the princess huntress-nymph for the king shepherd Meleager. The opera ends with Mercury bringing Jupiter's greeting to the newlyweds, i.e. Prince Frederick and Princess Augusta.

Atanasov (Georgyev), **Georgy** (*b* Plovdiv, 18 May 1882; *d* Fasano, 17 Nov. 1931). Bulgarian composer. Studied privately, in Bucharest, and (1901-3) in Pesaro with Mascagni. Returning home, he worked as a bandmaster, then conducted the first opera performances in *Bulgaria. Known as The Maestro, he is regarded as the founder of Bulgarian opera. In his operas, which are still highly regarded in Bulgaria, he sought to confer technical maturity on the emergent local art by absorbing Italian influences and later, less successfully, those of Wagner and Strauss. These are the historical operas *Borislav* (1911), *Gergana* (1917), *Zapustyalata vodenitsa* (The Abandoned Mill, 1923), *Tsveta* (The Flower, 1925), *Kosara* (1927), and *Altsek* (1930); the first Bulgarian operetta, *Moralisti* (1916); and five children's operas, including *Za ptichky* (For the Birds, 1909), *Samodviskoto izvorche* (The Fountain of Samodiva, 1911), and *Zlatnoto momiche* (The Golden Girl, 1915).
Bibl: L. Sagayev: *Maestro Georgy Atanasov* (1960).

Athanael. The coenobite monk (bar.) who tries to save and then falls in love with Thaïs in Massenet's opera.

Athens (Gr. Athinai). Capital of Greece. Opera was first given by a visiting Italian company in 1840 (*Barbiere*); enthusiasm was so great that a ticket black market instantly developed. But though French operettas were performed in the summer theatre at Nea Phaleron in 1873, and there were some student performances in 1876, the first professional Greek company was not formed until 1888. After a successful performance of Donizetti's *Betly*, it toured Egypt, the Near East, France, and Romania with a repertory of Italian works and some by Karrer and Xyndas, but closed in 1890. In 1898 Dionysios Lavranga, with a group of amateurs, founded the Elliniko Melodrama, which opened at the T. Demotikon with *Bohème* in 1900 and toured Greece and Greek centres in the Levant. In 1933 Manolis Kalomiris founded the Ethnikos Melodramatikos Omilos (National Opera Company); this closed in 1935. Finally, a national company under the auspices of Ethnikon T. was formed in 1939, later moving to the Olympia T.: it opened in 1940 with *Fledermaus*. In 1944 the company became the Ethniki Lyriki Skini (National Lyric T.), under Kalomiris, opening with Samaras's *Rhea*.

After the war, the theatre was demolished and replaced with a modern building (cap. 900). The artistic director is Dimitri Chorafas, with the assistance of Arda Mandikian and Manos Hadjidakis. There is a permanent roster of 31 soloists, with a chorus of 65. The season runs from Oct. to May; the company then visits Salonika for a month, also sometimes playing in Patras, and returns to Athens for the festival in July. A good repertory and tradition have developed, and among many distinguished singers to have begun their careers there is Maria *Callas, for whom performances of *Medea* and *Norma* have been staged at Epidauros. Many internationally known Greek singers, such as Kostas Paskalis, Luisa Bosabalian, Teresa Stratas, and Tatiana Troyanos have been persuaded to appear again there.

Atherton, David (*b* Blackpool, 3 Jan. 1944). British conductor. Studied Cambridge and London Opera Centre. Début Cambridge, 1966, *Ariadne auf Naxos;* also perfs. of *Oberon* and *Béatrice et Benedict*. C.G. since 1967 first as répétiteur; conductor from 1968 (*Il trovatore*) in wide repertory including world première of Henze's *We Come to the River* (1976). Aldeburgh Festivals, conducting world premières of Birtwistle's *Punch and Judy* (1968) and Crosse's *Grace of Tod* (1969). (R)

Atlántida, L'. Scenic oratorio by Falla; text by composer, after Jacint Verdaguer's poem (1877). Prod. Milan, Sc., 18 June 1962, with Simionato, Stratas, Puglisi, Halley, cond. Schippers; N.Y., Philharmonic Hall (opening night), 29 Sept. 1962, with Farrell, Madeira, London, cond. Ansermet. An epic Spanish saga, telling how Atlantis is submerged by flood; how Spain is saved from Hercules; how Barcelona came into being; and how Columbus discovered the New World. Also *Atlantyda,* opera by Guzewski (comp. 1913-20, not prod.).

Atlantide, L'. Opera in 4 acts by Tomasi; text by F. Didelot, after Pierre Benoit's novel (1920). Prod. Mulhouse, 26 Feb. 1954. Antinea (mimed role), a maenad, rules the land of Atlantis. She lures two officers of the French Foreign Legion, a Lieutenant (ten.) and Captain (bass), to her domain, and they fall ardently in love with her. One she kills with a silver hammer, the other dies in the desert pursuing a phantom that is her double.

Atlantov, Vladimir (Andreyevich) (*b* Leningrad, 19 Feb. 1939). Russian tenor. Studied Leningrad, 1963, with Bolotin, having won 2nd

Glinka Prize, 1962. Début as soloist, Leningrad, K., 1963; worked as student artist, Milan, Sc., 1963-5. Tchaikovsky Prize, 1966; International Singers' prize, Sofia, 1967. Moscow, B., since 1967; guest appearances Milan, Vienna, Wiesbaden, etc. Repertory includes Vladimir, Hermann, Lensky, Don José, and Italian roles. Since 1977 has been singing baritone roles. (R)

Attaque du moulin, L' (The Attack on the Mill). Opera in 4 acts by Bruneau; text by Louis Gallet, after the story in Zola's *Soirées de Médan* (1880). Prod. Paris, O.C., 23 Nov. 1893, with Leblanc, Delna, Vergnet, cond. Danbé; London, C.G., 4 July 1894, with Nuovina, Delna, Cossira, cond. Flon; N.Y., New T., 8 Feb. 1910, with Noria, Delna, Clément, cond. Tango. The Miller Merlier's daughter Françoise is betrothed to a young Flemish peasant, Dominique; but their celebrations are interrupted by a recruiting party, causing Françoise's foster-mother Marcelline to denounce all war. Though Dominique is not in fact called up, when the mill is attacked he is seized by the Germans and condemned to be shot. When he escapes, the German captain demands Merlier's life in his stead; in order to save Dominique for his daughter, Merlier sacrifices himself deliberately.

Atterberg, Kurt (*b* Göteborg, 12 Dec. 1887; *d* Stockholm, 15 Feb. 1974). Swedish composer. His works, highly respected in Sweden, include five operas: *Härvard Harpolekare* (Härvard the Harper, 1919), *Bäckhästen* (The River Horse, 1925), *Fanal* (The Burning Land, 1934), *Aladdin* (1941), and *Stormen* (after *The Tempest,* 1949).

At the Boar's Head. Opera in 1 act by Holst; text by composer, after Shakespeare's dramas *Henry IV* Parts 1 and 2 (1597-8) with two Shakespeare sonnets. Prod. Manchester, by B.N.O.C., 3 Apr. 1925, with Constance Willis, T. Davies, Allin, cond. Sargent; N.Y., MacDowell Club, 16 Feb. 1935. The plot is closely derived from the Falstaff episodes in Shakespeare's Henry plays.

Attila. Opera in prologue and 3 acts by Verdi; text by Solera, after Zacharias Werner's drama *Attila, König der Hunnen* (1808). Prod. Venice, F., 17 Mar. 1846, with Sofia Loewe, C. Guasco, Marini, N. Constantini; London, H.M.'s, 14 Mar. 1848, with Cruvelli, Gardoni, Belletti, Cuzzoni; N.Y., 15 Apr. 1850, with Tedesco, Lorini, Corradi-Setti, L. Martinelli, cond. Bottesini. In 452 AD Attila (bass) has invaded Italy. Against his orders, a group of women including Odabella (sop.) has been saved; she swears vengeance upon him with the very sword he courteously grants her. Ezio (bar.) tries to bargain with Attila, offering him the world if he may retain Italy, but Attila rejects this. Odabella's lover Foresto (ten.) leads refugees into the islands of what is destined to become

Venice. He is reassured by Odabella that she still intends to destroy Attila, who is now disturbed by a dream which becomes reality when Pope Leo (bass) advances from Rome to appeal, successfully, to Attila to halt. In Act 2, Attila is saved by Odabella from being poisoned with a cup of wine at Foresto's hands; she wishes to keep vengeance to herself. Finally Attila appears, and accuses Ezio, Foresto, and Odabella of treachery. Odabella stabs him. Other operas on Attila (*c* 406-453), King of the Huns, are as follows: J. W. Franck (1682), Farinelli (1806), Generali (1807), Mosca (1818), Persiano (1827), F. Malipiero (*Ildegonda di Borgogna*, 1847, prod. four months before Verdi's and re-named to avoid confusion).

Auber, Daniel (-François-Esprit) (*b* Caen, 29 Jan. 1782; *d* Paris, 12-13 May 1871). French composer. Studied with Ladurner, and in 1805 produced a *comédie mêlée d'ariettes, L'Erreur d'un moment,* which encouraged Cherubini to take him as a pupil. His early opéras comiques were unsuccessful, but through Cherubini he worked with the librettist Planard on three operas, *Le Testament* (1819), *La Bergère châtelaine* (1820), and *Emma* (1821), of which the last two were successful. He then met Scribe, with whom he began a long and famous collaboration. Though influenced by Rossini in the works which immediately followed, including *Leicester* and *La Neige* (both 1823), he recovered a more French manner with what he described as an 'opéra français', *Léocadie* (1824), and still more with *Le Maçon* (1825), the first of his mature opéras comiques. In these, he was able to give his idiom an Italianate sparkle without forfeiting his French grace and lyricism: they include *Fiorella* (1826), *La Fiançée* (1829), *Fra Diavolo* (1830: his masterpiece in this vein), *Le Philtre* (1831), *La Marquise de Brinvilliers* (1831), *Le Serment* (1832), *Gustave III* (1833: an exceptionally vivid and original work), *Lestocq* (1834: a work also remarkable for some powerful chorus writing), *Le Cheval de bronze* (1835), *Le Domino noir* (1837), *Zanetta* (1840) and *Les Diamants de la couronne* (1841). Light, neatly composed, and elegant, the best of these works have a charm that is contained especially in lively dance rhythms, tuneful numbers, by turns witty and sentimental, and deft orchestral accompaniment.

However, *La Muette de Portici* (1828) stands out from this series as serious and political in content (Masaniello's revolution in Naples in 1647). It contains massive crowd scenes, vivid local colour, an extended harmonic range, and powerful orchestral and dramatic effects, and hence demands staging on the grandest scale. Such was its immediate effect that the Brussels première in 1830 touched off the Belgian revolt against the Dutch; and its longer-term artistic effect as a pioneer French grand opera was to inaugurate a style taken up by Rossini, Halévy, Meyerbeer, and Wagner himself, who was a great admirer of Auber and was influenced by *La Muette* in *Lohengrin.*

After about 1840, Auber's lighter style (which Wagner reproached for having grown ineffective , and compared to the work of a barber who lathers but forgets to shave) developed into a more lyrical manner, as in *La Part du Diable* (1843), *Haydée* (1847), and *Le Premier Jour de bonheur* (1868). He was Director of the Paris Conservatoire, 1842-70. Wagner wrote cordial and penetrating appreciations of him, and at his death Rossini, referring to his short stature, observed, 'Piccolo musico, ma grande musicista' ('A small musician, but a great music-maker').

Bibl: C. Malherbe: *Auber* (1911).

Auden, W(ystan) **H**(ugh) (*b* York, 21 Feb. 1907; *d* Vienna, 28 Sept. 1973). English, later American, poet. He wrote librettos for Britten's *Paul Bunyan* (N.Y., Columbia University, 1941), and, with Chester Kallman, Stravinsky's *The Rake's Progress* (1951), Henze's *Elegy for Young Lovers* (1960), and *The Bassarids* (1966), and Nabokov's *Love's Labour's Lost* (1973). Also with Kallman translated *Don Giovanni* and *Die Zauberflöte.*

Bibl: W. H. Auden: Essays in *The Dyer's Hand* (1963).

Audience. The audience is an integral part of an operatic performance, and its reaction to artists and to the work can make or mar a performance. Audience reaction can even colour a work's career, as with the disastrous premières of *Il barbiere di Siviglia, Norma, La traviata, Tannhäuser* (Paris version), and more recently Nono's *Intolleranza.* Demonstrations by a *claque or clique against the composer, individual artists, and conductors may be cited as instances of professional or semi-professional audience intervention. In days when opera was principally the pastime of the nobility, the audience regarded itself as no less important than events on the stage. The house lights were left on, so that ladies could quiz each other through their opera glasses, commenting upon their rivals' appearance and demeanour.

Audience participation in Italy is a source of great enjoyment, if not always to the performers, and Italians resent attempts by uninstructed visitors at obtaining silence during the music. The audience at La Scala (except for the noisy members of the first and second galleries) has a reputation among singers for 'sitting on its hands'. In Naples, however, the audience behaves as a large family outing, arriving late, chatting during tedious parts of the work, and purring with pleasure when a favourite singer neatly turns a phrase or produces a fine top note. Notoriously the hardest audience to please is at Parma, a town which is therefore much feared by singers. It is said that a tenor leaving by train the morning after a poor performance asked for his bags to be carried by a porter, who declined on artistic grounds.

German and Austrian audiences are far more serious, their demeanour sometimes approaching that of a church congregation. This is especially so at Bayreuth, where the slightest creak from the uncomfortable wooden seats is regarded as want of seriousness. English audiences continually surprise visiting singers by their warmth, though they can react sharply and vociferously when displeased. Americans are generally regarded as much more prodigal with their enthusiasm.

The largest opera audiences are to be found in the great open-air performances in Italy during the summer, e.g. at the Verona Arena. The smallest audience in operatic history was King Ludwig of Bavaria, who commanded private performances of Wagner in the National T. in Munich.

Audran, Edmond (*b* Lyons, 12 Apr. 1840; *d* Tierceville, 16 Aug. 1901). French composer. The most popular of his operettas was *La Mascotte* (1880), a success he never equalled despite considerable subsequent development and expansion of his style. *La Poupée* (1896) has been claimed as his masterpiece. His sole opera, *Photis* (1896), was never published, and has been forgotten.

Au fond du temple saint. The tenor-baritone duet for Nadir and Zurga in Scene 1 of Bizet's *Les Pêcheurs de perles*, in which they recall the beautiful Leïla they both once loved.

Aufstieg und Fall der Stadt Mahagonny (Rise and Fall of the City of Mahagonny). Opera in 3 acts by Weill; text by Brecht. Prod. Leipzig, 9 Mar. 1930, with Trummer, Fleischer, Zimmer, cond. Brecher (orig. prod. as a *Songspiel* [*sic*], Baden-Baden, 1927); N.Y., Town Hall, 23 Feb. 1952; London, S.W., 16 Jan. 1963, with Cantelo, Dowd, Te Wiata, cond. Davis; first full U.S. perf. N.Y., Anderson T., 28 Apr. 1970. Mahagonny is the city of material pleasure. Jenny and her colleagues move in, followed by Jimmy and his lumberjack friends on the spend; there develops a love affair between the two, based upon hard cash as well as affection. A hurricane threatens the city, but is miraculously deflected. Act 2 illustrates Gluttony, Love, Fighting, and Drinking, all carried on to excess and without restraint. Jimmy cannot pay for his drinks; tried according to Mahagonny's scale of values, he is sentenced to two days for indirect murder, four years for 'seduction, by means of money', and, for not paying his whisky bill, death.

Auftrittslied (*Ger* entry song). The aria in which a character introduces himself to the audience

either directly or by addressing another character, e.g. Papageno's 'Der Vogelfänger' in Mozart's *Die Zauberflöte*.

Augsburg. Town in Bavaria, Germany. In 1677-8, J. H. Kusser gave there his German operas *Medea*, *Julia*, and *Die unsträfliche Liebe*; and his lead was followed by J. G. Mayr, who in 1716 produced *Jakob und Lea*. The city was then largely dependent upon visiting Italian troupes, most notably that of Peruzzi. In 1803 Weber's *Peter Schmoll* was given there: Weber's half-brother Edmund was then conductor at the theatre, and the city had a good tradition of support for the arts. The Stadttheater (cap. 1,300) was opened in 1877, enlarged 1938-9; it was destroyed by bombs in 1944. The present theatre (cap. 1,010) was opened in 1956 with *Figaro*. Peter Ebert was Generalintendant 1968-73, Rudolf Stomberg from 1973. Istvan Kertesz was Generalmusikdirektor 1958-63. Among other premières were the first German *Battaglia di Legnano*, 1932, and a new German version of *Les Troyens* (only slightly cut), 1971. Open-air performances are given at the Rote Tor, which was inaugurated with *Fidelio*, 1930.

Austin, Frederic (*b* London, 30 Mar. 1872; *d* London, 10 Apr. 1952). English baritone. Studied under Charles Lunn. Début London, C.G., 1908, Gunther in the English *Ring* under Richter; then principal baritone, Beecham Company. Peachum in his new version of *The Beggar's Opera* (London, Lyric Hammersmith, 1920). Artistic Director of the B.N.O.C. 1924. General administrator of Beecham's Imperial League of Opera in the 1920s. Taught on retirement – pupils include Constance Shacklock. (R) His son **Richard** (*b* 26 Dec. 1903) has conducted with the C. R. and at S. W. Head of the opera department, R.C.M., from 1953. (R)

Austin, Sumner (*b* London, 24 Sept. 1888). English baritone. C. R. 1919, then sang with the O'Mara Opera Company. Valuable member of Old Vic Opera Company in the 1920s; S.W. until 1940, being particularly distinguished in Mozart. Produced several operas at S.W., including *The Travelling Companion*, *The Bartered Bride*, *Falstaff*, *Walküre*, *Don Carlos*, and *The Wreckers*. After the war taught at the G.S.M., and produced *Wozzeck* (1951) and *Tannhäuser* (1955) at C.G.

Austral (orig. Wilson), **Florence** (orig. Mary) (*b* Melbourne, 26 Apr. 1894; *d* Newcastle, N.S.W., 15 May 1968). As a child was known by her stepfather's name, Favaz. Scholarship, Melbourne Conservatory, 1914. Went to New York, 1918, for further study with Sibella and offered Met. contract, which she refused. Engaged by C.G. for the Grand Season of 1921 which was abandoned. Début 1922, Brünnhilde, B.N.O.C. Also Aida and Isolde with company, and

Brünnhilde during international seasons 1924, 1929, and 1933. Guest artist, S.W., 1937-9; appearances in Berlin, America, and her native Australia. (R)

Australia. Until after the Second World War, opera in Australia was mostly based on visiting companies. The first opera performance was of Bishop's *Clari* in 1834, by a local company. The next performance was ten years later: *Cenerentola,* given by the Dramatic Company (in which the only singer among the actors was Vincent Wallace's sister Wallace Bushelle). In 1845 Count Carandini, a political refugee from Italy, founded a company with his wife as prima donna and gave successful performances of *Freischütz, Fra Diavolo,* and some Italian operas. Between 1850 and 1860 the Anna Bishop Opera Company gave seasons in New South Wales and Victoria. Among companies active during these years were the Lyster Grand Opera Company, an American group that gave English-language performances until 1880; local singers were increasingly employed in their seasons. Other companies included the Montague Turner Company (1881-4) and that of Martin Simonson, who had toured a company in 1866 and in 1886-7 gave an enterprising season that included *Belisario* and *Roberto Devereux*: the latter group included some excellent Italian singers whose art set Australia an early high standard of vocalism. Other groups followed in the 1890s; 1900 saw the first performance of a work by Wagner, under the auspices of George Musgrove. A season of Italian opera by the J.C. Williamson Company followed in 1901, when Musgrove also toured with more German opera (including even parts of *The Ring*); these were polyglot performances, each singer using his own language.

In 1911 Nellie Melba, who had long wanted to take a company to her native land, joined Williamson in a tour with singers who included John McCormack, Eleanora de Cisneros, Scandiani, and Rosina Buckman in a catholic repertory. The Quinlan Opera Company came in 1912 with Beecham as one of the conductors; their success led to a return in the following year with a repertory that included the Australian première of *Die Meistersinger*. An Italian company visited the country in 1916; in 1921 Williamson formed a company of local artists; and in 1924, Melba was back, on a farewell tour, with Toti dal Monte and Dino Borgioli in her company. Melba helped to organize a further season in 1928 with a similar company now strengthened by, among other leading singers, Arangi-Lombardi, Merli, and John Brownlee. New standards of presentation were set in 1932 by the Imperial Grand Opera Company, which included Lina Pagliughi and Primo Montanari.

After the Second World War, further seasons were given by the Nevin Trust. Then in 1952, the two leading groups, the National T. Opera Company of Melbourne and the N.S.W. National Opera of Sydney, pooled their resources as the first step towards a national opera; each received a grant of £A5,000. Singers in these companies included Elizabeth Fretwell, Marie Collier, and Ronald Dowd. When rivalries developed, each company carried on its separate existence until the establishment of the Elizabethan Trust in 1954. In 1955 another Italian company visited Australia, and in that year Warwick Braithwaite assumed the artistic directorship of the Sydney company, resigning in mid-season because of managerial interference. With the arrival of Hugh Hunt, director of the Elizabethan Trust, it was announced that the Trust would not now take over the N.O.C. but a new company, under the Trust, would tour the Commonwealth. In 1955 also, the N.S.W. State Government launched a competition for the design of a new Sydney opera house, won by a Dane, Joern Utzon. In July 1956 the Trust launched its first season at Adelaide with a four-week season of Mozart operas, followed by a tour of the main cities lasting until February 1957. In December 1957, Karl Rankl was appointed music director of the Trust; he launched his first season in July 1958, but resigned in 1961. In 1965 Joan Sutherland toured with her own Sutherland-Williamson Company. The Trust was renamed the Australian Opera Company in 1969, with Carlo Felice Cillario as music director. Cillario resigned in 1971; he was succeeded by Edward Downes 1972-6, then by Richard Bonynge, from 1976. The new opera house at Sydney, the first in the country specially built for opera, opened in 1973.
See also *Adelaide, Melbourne, Sydney.*

Austria. See *Bregenz, Graz, Innsbruck, Klagenfurt, Salzburg, Vienna.*
See also *Germany.*

Avant de quitter ces lieux. Valentine's (bar.) aria in Act 2 of Gounod's *Faust*. Composed for the English production with Santley.

Ayrton, William (*b* London, 24 Feb. 1777; *d* London, 8 Mar. 1858). English writer on music and theatrical manager. As music director of the King's T. gave English premières of *Così fan tutte* (1811), *Zauberflöte* (1811), and *Don Giovanni* (1817). Critic of *The Morning Chronicle* (1813-26) and *The Examiner* (1837-51); with Clowes he edited the periodical *The Harmonicon* (1823-34).

Azerbaijan (Republic of U.S.S.R.). A primitive form of Azerbaijani opera known as *mugam,* basically a kind of staged song-cycle, has survived since the 4th or 5th cent. Baku's first theatre was opened in 1873, and visiting opera companies performed there. The first steps towards a formal musical theatre were taken at the turn of the century in Shusha and Baku with the staging of traditional dramas with music, including the popular *Leila and Medjnun*. This was set as the first true Azerbaijani opera (Baku, 1908) by Uzeir Hadjibeyov (1885-1948), and the work remains in the repertory; other operas of his include *Sheikh Senan* (1909), *Rustum and Sohrab* (1910) and what is regarded as the masterpiece of Azerbaijani opera, *Kyor-oglu* (The Blind Man's Son, 1937), as well as musical comedies (e.g. *Arshin mal alan* (The Travelling Salesman, 1913).

In May 1920 a state company was formed (Akhundov Opera and Ballet T.); the opera company became independent in 1924. For them, Glière wrote the first large-scale national opera, *Shekhsenem* (1934). Other operas given were by Abdul Muslim Mahomayev (1885-1937), whose *Shah Ismail* (1919) and especially *Nerghiz* (1935) have been very popular. The theatre built in 1910-11 was reconstructed in 1938 (cap. 1,281). In April 1938 a season of Azerbaijani opera was given in Moscow, including most of the above works. Further

operas followed in the war, including *Khozrov ve Sinu* (1942) by Niyazi (Taghizade) (*b* 1912) and *Maskarad* (1945) by Boris Zaidman (*b* 1908), with particular success attending *Vatan* (Fatherland, 1945) by Kara Karayev (*b* 1918). Post-war operas included *Nizami* (1948) by Afrasiyab Badalbeyli (*b* 1907) and the very succcessul *Sevil* (1953) by Fikret Amirov (*b* 1922). In those years the repertory widened to include French and Italian operas as well as the Russian works which began entering the repertory in the 1930s, and it has since widened further still. The Baku Opera and Ballet T. has separate Azerbaijani and Russian sections, as does the Musical Comedy T., founded in 1938.

Azione sacra (*It* sacred action). Italian term occasionally used for an opera on a religious subject, e.g. Refice's *Cecilia*.

Azione teatrale (*It* theatrical action). Italian 17th-cent. term for an opera or musical festival play.

Azucena. The gypsy (con.), Manrico's mother, in Verdi's *Il trovatore*.

B

Baccaloni, Salvatore (*b* Rome 14 Apr. 1900; *d* New York, 31 Dec. 1969). Italian bass. Boy soprano Sistine Chapel. Studied with Kaschmann. Début Rome, Ap., 1922, Bartolo (*Barbiere*). Engaged 1926 by Toscanini for Milan, Sc. where after three seasons in normal bass repertory he specialized in *buffo* roles. London C.G., 1928–9; Gly. 1936-9, Leporello, Bartolo; Osmin, Alfonso, and Pasquale (his greatest role). U.S. début Chicago, 1930; N.Y., Met., 1940–62. Appeared in every major opera house and was considered by many the greatest *buffo* since Lablache. (R)

Bacchus. See *Dionysos*.

Bach, Johann Christian (*b* Leipzig, 5 Sept. 1735; *d* London, 1 Jan. 1782). German composer. Youngest son of Johann Sebastian and Anna Magdalena Bach. Studied Berlin with his brother Emanuel. In Italy he produced *Artaserse* (Turin, 1761), *Catone in Utica* (Florence, 1761), and *Alessandro nell'Indie* (Naples, 1762). In London from 1762, produced *Orione* for the King's T. (Feb. 1763), a brilliant occasion attended by George III and Queen Charlotte; Burney remarked upon Bach's disuse of the *da capo* aria and the delicacy of his orchestral technique (which included the first appearance of clarinets in an English opera orchestra). *Zanaida* (May 1763) was almost as successful. His next true opera, *Adriano in Siria* (1765), was not so well received, but *Carattaco* (1767) restored his fortunes; he also made additions to Piccinni's *Olimpiade* and Gluck's *Orfeo*. In Mannheim produced *Temistocle* (1772) and **Lucio Silla* (1774), returning to London for the very successful *La clemenza di Scipione* (1778); for Paris he wrote *Amadis des Gaules* (1779). All are on tragic subjects, and the disposition of the public to opera buffa did not help him; nevertheless, his works, which imported some German characteristics into the fashionable Italian style, were admired by good judges apart from Burney. His brother **Johann Christoph** (1732-95) also wrote some successful operas, to texts by Herder and others. Their brother **Wilhelm Friedemann** (1710-84) is the subject of an opera by Graener (1931). Their father **Johann Sebastian** is the subject of an opera by Emil **Ábrányi (1947). *Bibl:* C. Terry: *John Christian Bach* (1929, 2/1967).

Bacquier, Gabriel (Augustin Raymond Théodore Louis) (*b* Béziers, 17 May 1924). French baritone. Studied Paris Conservatoire. Début Nice, 1950, in Landowski's *Le Fou,* with José

Beckmans's Compagne Lyrique Française. Brussels, La M., 1953-6; Paris, O.C., 1956, O. since 1958; Gly., 1962, Count Almaviva; London, C.G., since 1964 as Count Almaviva, Sir Richard Forth, Malatesta, and Scarpia; N.Y., Met., since 1964. Aix Festivals as Don Giovanni and Falstaff. Has developed into one of the most elegant and stylistic of present-day artists; a gifted actor and accomplished singer. (R)

Baden–Baden. Town in Baden-Württemberg, Germany. Early premières included Gounod's *Colombe* and Reyer's *Erostrate* (1860). The T. der Stadt (cap. 512) opened in 1862 with *Das Nachtlager von Granada*, and Berlioz's *Béatrice et Bénédict* had its première there in the same year. Pauline Viardot sang there 1864-6, and later settled in the town. Other premières have included Hindemith's *Hin und zurück*, Toch's *Die Prinzessin auf der Erbse*, and Milhaud's *L'Enlèvement d'Europe*, at the 1927 Chamber Music Festival.

Badescu, Dinu (Constantin) (*b* Craiova, 17 Oct. 1904). Romanian tenor, orig. baritone. Studied Bucharest with George Folescu. Début Cluj, 1931, Germont; second début same year as tenor, Lionel in *Martha*. Bucharest Opera 1934-61. Appearances in Italy 1938-9; Vienna, V., 1941-4, guest appearances in Berlin, Dresden etc.; Vienna, S.O., 1948; continued to appear until 1961 in U.S.S.R., Poland, and elsewhere in Eastern Europe. Much admired in Verdi repertory. (R)

Badini, Ernesto (*b* San Colombano al Lambro, 14 Sept. 1876; *d* Milan, 6 July 1937). Italian baritone. Studied Milan Conservatory and later studied *buffo* roles with Cesari. Début San Colombano 1895, Figaro (*Barbiere*). In 1908 he sang Beckmesser at the T. d. V., Milan, after which he decided to concentrate on character and *buffo* roles. Sang Ford at the Verdi celebrations, Parma 1913, under Toscanini, who then took him to Milan Sc. where he sang regularly until his death. C. G.'s first Schicchi, and sang regularly there until 1931. Also Salzburg and Florence Festivals. Created Plake in Wolf-Ferrari's *Sly* (1927) and roles in operas by Lozzi, Zandonai, and Mascagni. (R)

Bagnara, Francesco (*b* Vicenza, 1784; *d* Venice, 21 Oct. 1866). Italian scene painter. Studied Venice with the painter Giuseppe Borsatto, then worked at the F., 1810-20, S.M. *c*1812, S. B., and from 1820 again at the F. Painted over 1,100 sets, for the premières or Venetian premières of many works by e.g. Rossini, Bellini, and Donizetti. Also famous as a painter and garden designer.

Bahr-Mildenburg (Mildenburg von Bellschau), **Anna** (*b* Vienna, 29 Nov. 1872; *d* Vienna, 27 Jan. 1947). Austrian soprano. Studied Vienna with Papier, Hamburg with Pollini. Début Hamburg 1895, Brünnhilde. Soon became leading Wagner soprano. Bayreuth 1897 Kundry, and later Ortrud. London, C.G., 1906, Isolde and Elisabeth, and first London Klytemnestra 1910; Vienna 1908-17. After retirement taught in Munich, and 1921-6 stage director at Nationaltheater, but sang a final Klytemnestra, Augsburg, 1930. 1938 taught in Berlin. Married writer Hermann Bahr 1909, with whom she wrote *Bayreuth und das Wagner-Theater* (1910). (R)

Bailey, Norman (Stanley) (*b* Birmingham, 23 Mar. 1933). English baritone. Grew up in South Africa and Rhodesia; studied, and subsequently taught, in the music department of Rhodes University. Studied Vienna with Adolf Vogel, Julius Patzak, and Josef Witt. Début Vienna, 1959 in *Cambiale di matrimonio*. Linz 1960-3, Wuppertal 1963-4, Düsseldorf 1964-7. London, S.W., since 1967, début as Figaro (Mozart), then sang Hans Sachs in the memorable production of *Die Meistersinger* under Goodall; Wotan, Gunther, Pizarro, and Kutuzov in *War and Peace*. Has appeared in the Wagner repertory at C.G. and at Bayreuth. His Sachs, wise, human, and benevolent, and his Wotan, both magisterial and moving, display an inherent musicality and feeling for the text. (R)

Baker, (Dame) **Janet** (*b* York, 21 Aug. 1933). English mezzo. Studied London with Helene Isepp, and in 1956 won second prize in the Kathleen Ferrier Competition. Début 1956, Roza in Smetana's *The Secret*, Oxford University Opera Club. In 1959 sang Eduige in Handel's *Rodelinda* with the Handel Opera Society, the first of several Handel roles, including Irene in *Tamerlano*, and the title roles in *Ariodante* and *Orlando*. 1961-76 sang regularly with the English Opera Group, e.g. as Dido (Purcell), Lucretia, Nancy in *Albert Herring*, and Kate in *Owen Wingrave*. Has sung Dorabella, Octavian, and Berlioz's Dido for Scottish Opera. C. G. regularly since 1966, incl. Dido, Cressida, Idamante. She displays a special affinity for the music of Monteverdi and Cavalli, and was very successful as Poppea with S. W., Penelope in *Ulisse*, and Diana in *La Calisto* at Gly. Her repertory includes Vitellia in *La clemenza di Tito*, Maria Stuarda (Donizetti), and Charlotte (*Werther*). Her highly individual and beautiful voice, her warmth of personality, and her intelligent feeling for words, and a dramatic range which encompasses both tragic and comic roles, combine to make her one of the outstanding artists of the day. (R) *Bibl*: A. Blyth: *Janet Baker* (1973).

Baklanov, (orig. Bakkis), **Georgy** (Andreyevich) (*b* Riga, 4 Jan. 1881; *d* Basel, 6 Dec. 1938). Russian (orig. Latvian) baritone. Studied Kiev, and St Petersburg with Pryanishnikov. Début Kiev

1903, Amonasro. Moscow, B., 1905-9, e.g. in Rakhmaninov's *Miserly Knight* and *Francesca da Rimini*. London, C.G., 1910; Boston, 1916; Chicago, 1917-26. A singer with a powerful voice and dramatic personality, admired as the Demon, Prince Igor, Eugene Onegin, Rigoletto, and Scarpia; he also sang bass roles, incl. Ruslan and Méphistophélès. (R)

Balfe, Michael (*b* Dublin, 15 May 1808; *d* Rowney Abbey, Herts., 20 Oct. 1870). Irish composer and singer. Studied in Ireland and worked in various musical capacities before leaving for Italy, where he continued his studies, some under Filippo Galli. Début Paris, 1827, Rossini's Figaro; the composer expressed his approval. Principal baritone Palermo, 1829-30, where his first complete opera, *I rivali de se stessi*, was produced. Returning to London in 1835, he began his career as a composer of English operas with the very successful *The Siege of Rochelle* (D.L., 1835); he followed this with the almost equally successful *The Maid of Artois* (1837, for Malibran). He also sang Papageno in the first performance in English of *The Magic Flute*. Back in Paris by 1841, having failed in an attempt to establish English opera at the *Lyceum (Keolanthe, 1841), he continued his career there, returning to England for the greatest success of his 29 operas: *The Bohemian Girl* (1843). From 1857 to 1863 he was closely associated with the Pyne-Harrison project for an English national opera: his own chief success was *The Rose of Castile* (1857). He continued to travel, making two successful visits to Russia, before turning gentleman farmer and retiring to an estate in Hertfordshire. His melodies are often graceful and charming, and his gift for a memorable tune led him to place much importance on ballads in his operas, but he was little interested in the expression of character and had less flair for dramatic development. Nevertheless, he did write, in *Catherine Grey* (1837), the first English Romantic opera without spoken dialogue. Sir Thomas Beecham's revival of *The Bohemian Girl* at C.G. in 1951 was coolly received. *Bibl*: C. Kenny: *Memoir of Balfe* (1875).

Ballad opera. A popular form of English entertainment flourishing in the 18th cent., in which spoken dialogue alternated with musical numbers, usually fitting new words to old ballads, folk tunes, or (particularly in its later stages) melodies by different composers. Though developed from earlier theatrical practice, the genre may be dated from its most famous example, the Gay/Pepusch *The *Beggar's Opera* (1728). This was characteristic in its satire of contemporary politicians and of the excesses of the Italian opera and its prima donnas. Ballad opera resembled the contemporary French *opéra comique en vaudevilles* (including its occasional parody of serious operas); the translation into German of Charles Coffey's The Devil to Pay (1731) and its sequel The Merry Cobbler (1735) influenced the development of *Singspiel. After the first flood of ballad operas in 1728-35, which rapidly became so popular as to threaten the Italian opera (even of Handel) which they lampooned, the genre waned, to be revived in a somewhat modified manner with (generally) original tunes: a famous example is Arne's *Love in a Village. Most of the early ballad operas were produced at the Little Haymarket T. (where Gay had seen some opéras comiques en vau-devilles given by the *Théâtre de la Foire bet-ween 1720 and 1728), or at Lincoln's Inn Fields T. Modern operas making use of the genre include Vaughan Williams's Hugh the Drover, in which ballad-type songs are incorporated into a fully composed opera, and Weill's Die Dreigroschenoper, in which the numbers are introduced in a conscious imitation of the old form in general and The Beggar's Opera in particular.

Ballet in opera. Ballet was an integral part of the masque and other entertainments from which opera partly developed, and has survived in opera in various forms up to the present day. There are final dances in the earliest operas (Peri's and Caccini's Euridice, 1600, Monteverdi's Orfeo, 1607), and ballets occur in other 17th-cent. Italian operas: most elaborate of all was Cesti's Il *pomo d'oro (1667), which includes a ballet in each act and a triple ballet in the finale. In English opera, ballet survived from the masque and appeared in 17th-cent. opera, e.g. Purcell's Dido and Aeneas (1689). It also occurred in German opera of the 17th cent., and by the mid-18th cent. it appeared in Italian opera, in festive and other works. However, there and in Gluck's operas the influence was primarily French; and it is in France that ballet has played its most crucial, and often controversial, part in opera.

Lully fixed the tradition by incorporating into opera the ballet de cour, and by the end of the 17th cent. there had emerged a new form, *opéra-ballet. Rousseau (Dictionnaire de Musique, 1768) deplored the irrelevance of the opera ballets of his time. Ballet remained an essential feature of 19th-cent. French *grand opera, and the tradition of placing the ballet in the second act, in order to accommodate those subscribers who preferred to arrive having dined, was still rigid at the time of the Paris performances of Tannhäuser in 1861, so that only with great difficulty did Wagner succeed in flouting tradition and placing the obligatory ballet as the rewritten Venusberg scene opening the opera. Nevertheless, Wagner was not opposed to dance as one of the elements of music drama, and himself made dramatic use

of it in both Die Meistersinger (1868) and, more organically, Parsifal (1882). Verdi was also willing to incorporate ballets into his operas, even as late as Aida (1871) and Otello (1887). The Russians, with their special talent for dance and their orientation towards French art, have found a regular place for ballet in opera: a celebrated example is that of the Polovtsian Dances in Borodin's Prince Igor (1890), and almost all Tchaikovsky's operas include occasions for dancing. In the 20th cent., an organic place for dance occurs in e.g. Strauss's Salome (1905), Berg's Wozzeck (1925), Schoenberg's Moses und Aron (1932, prod. 1957), Britten's Gloriana (1953), and Tippett's The Midsummer Marriage (1955).

Balling, Michael (b Heidingsfeld am M., 27 Aug. 1866; d Darmstadt, 1 Sept. 1925). German conductor. Educated Würzburg. Viola player at Mainz, Schwerin, and then Bayreuth, where he became an assistant conductor 1896; conducted Parsifal, Tristan, and The Ring, 1904-25. Conducted The Ring in English for the Denhof Company in Edinburgh 1910, and Orfeo with Brema in London, Savoy. He founded the first school of music in Australia at Nelson in 1892. Succeeded Richter as conductor of Hallé 1912. From 1919 music director at Darmstadt. From 1912 editor of Breitkopf and Härtel's edition of Wagner.

Ballo in maschera, Un (A Masked Ball). Opera in 3 acts by Verdi; text by Somma, based on Scribe's text for Auber's Gustave III ou Le Bal masqué, in turn based on fact. Prod. Rome, Ap., 17 Feb. 1859, with Dejean, Scotti, Sbriscia, Fraschini, Giraldoni, cond. Angelini; N.Y., Ac. of M., 11 Feb. 1861; London, Ly., 15 June 1861, with Tietjens, Lemaire, Gassier, Giuglini, Delle Sedie, cond. Arditi. Riccardo or Gustavus III (ten.) is in love with Amelia (sop.), wife of his friend and secretary Renato or Anckerstroem (bar.). Ulrica or Mme Arvidson (mezzo) foretells Riccardo's death at the hand of a friend; this proves to be Renato, who mistakenly believes his wife has been false to him, and so joins in a plot to murder Riccardo at a masked ball. As he dies, Riccardo declares that Amelia is innocent, and forgives his enemies.

When Verdi first submitted his libretto to the San Carlo Theatre, Naples, the censor protested that the assassination of a king could not be shown on the stage, and demanded that Verdi adapt his music to a new libretto. Verdi refused, and left Naples. A Rome impresario offered to produce an altered version of the work; and so the locale was changed from 18th-cent. Stockholm to 17th-cent. Boston. Another version used at the Paris première (1861) set the story in Naples. The names of the leading characters are thus (in the order of setting, Stockholm, Boston, Naples): Gustavus III, Riccardo (Count of Warwick), Riccardo (Duke of

Olivares); Anckarstroem, Renato, Renato; Count Ribbing, Samuele, Armando; Count Horn, Tomaso, Angri; Mam'zelle Arvidson, Ulrica, Ulrica. The 'Stockholm' version has in recent years (C.G. 1952, Paris, 1958) begun to re-establish itself over the formerly popular 'Boston' version; and the production at the Stockholm Opera itself in 1958 was particularly accurate in details of the original events.

Baltimore. Town in Maryland, U.S.A. The Baltimore Civic Opera (founded in 1932), originally an opera workshop, became fully professional in 1950, and is under the artistic direction of Rosa Ponselle. Opera is also performed by the Chamber Opera Society of Baltimore and at the Opera Department of the Peabody Conservatory of Music under the direction of Robert Lawrence, who staged the first U.S. performances of Massenet's *Thérèse* and Malipiero's *Sette Canzoni* there in 1973.

Baltsa, Agnes (*b* Lefkas, 19 Nov. 1944). Greek mezzo-soprano. Studied Athens, Munich, and Frankfurt. Début Frankfurt, 1968, Cherubino. Frankfurt 1968-72; Berlin, D., since 1972. C.G. 1976; 1977 Cherubino; Houston 1971, Carmen; Vienna since 1976, Salzburg since 1977. Roles include Orpheus, Sextus, Dorabella, Dido (Berlioz), Herodias, Octavian, Composer, Rosina, and Cenerentola. (R)

Bampton, Rose (*b* Cleveland, 28 Nov. 1908). American soprano, orig. contralto. Studied Curtis Institute, Philadelphia, with Connell and Queena Mario. Début Chautauqua, 1928, Siebel. N.Y., Met., 1932, Laura (*Gioconda*). Sop. début 1935, Leonora (*Trovatore*), though continued to sing mezzo roles until 1937. Won warm praise as Donna Anna and Alceste, and in the 1940s successfully undertook several Wagner roles, including Kundry and Sieglinde. Remained at the Met. until 1950. (R) Her husband, **Wilfred Pelletier** (*b* Montreal, 1896), conducted at the Met. occasionally 1917-43, and helped to organize the Met. Auditions of the Air. (R)

Bánk bán. Opera in 3 acts by Erkel; text by Béni Egressy, after József Katona's tragedy (1814). Prod. Budapest, 9 Mar. 1861, with Hollósy, Ellinger, Telek, Koszegi, cond. Erkel; London, Collegiate T., 20 Feb. 1968, by University College Opera Society, with Louis, Bateman, Jenkins, Sadler, cond. Badacsonyi.

Banská Bystrica. Town in Czechoslovakia. Opera is given in the J. G. Tajovský T., normally about 3-4 times a week in the season, by a company of about 20 soloists. The company also tours the region.

Banti, Brigida Giorgi (*b* Crema, 1757; *d* Bologna, 18 Feb. 1806). Italian soprano. Began life as a street singer, and made her way to Paris singing at inns and cafés. Heard by De Vismes, director of the O. who engaged her after a brilliant audition; made her spectacular début there in 1776. Difficulties followed, owing to her carelessness and lack of training, though she later had considerable success in other countries, especially England (1779-1802). Her voice was said to have been pure, rich, and even throughout a wide range, with a beautiful *cantabile*; her acting ability and high spirits made her unfailingly popular. She appeared in several operas written specially for her by Paisiello, Zingarelli, Anfossi, and others. She married the dancer Zaccaria Banti in 1779. After Mrs Billington's return to London, Banti went back to Italy; she bequeathed her larynx, which was of great size, to the municipality of Bologna. Michael Kelly wrote of her that 'more perfect, more impassioned, more divine singing, perhaps was never heard'. Da Ponte, on the other hand, found her 'ignorant, stupid, and insolent'. Haydn composed his 'scena di Berenice' for her.
Bibl: G. Banti: *Vita di Brigida Banti* (1869).

Bantock, (Sir) **Granville** (*b* London, 7 Aug. 1868; *d* London, 16 Oct. 1946). English composer. Developed late, though already as a student he had written a 1-act opera *Caedmar* (1893). Took on various conducting posts while continuing to compose. In 1900 became principal of the Birmingham and Midland Institute School of Music; his mature works date from this period. He was attracted by oriental subjects and Hebridean folklore, and in 1924 produced, with Marjorie Kennedy-Fraser as librettist, *The Seal-Woman*. (R)
Bibl: M. Bantock: *Granville Bantock* (1972).

Baranović, Krešimir (*b* Šibenik, 25 July 1894; *d* Belgrade, 17 Sept. 1975). Yugoslav conductor and composer. Studied Zagreb, and Vienna (1912-14), and has held appointments as music director at the operas of Zagreb (1915-25), Belgrade (1927-9), and Bratislava (1945-6); at Zagreb introduced a wide new repertory, especially of Russian and Yugoslav opera, and gave the first performance there of *The Ring*. Professor at the Belgrade Conservatory from 1946. Has written two operas, *Striženo-košeno* (Shaven and Shorn, 1932), a national opera praised for its skilful use of folk music and its humorous situations, and the comic *Nevjesta od Cetingrada* (The Bride of Cetingrad, after the novel *Turci idu* (The Turks are Coming), comp. 1942, prod. 1951). (R)

Barbaia, Domenico (*b* Milan, 1778; *d* Posillipo, 19 Oct. 1841). Italian impresario. Started as a waiter (invented *barbaiata*, coffee or chocolate with a head of whipped cream); became director of the Naples S.C. and T.N. and other Royal opera houses (1809-40, with interruptions). Here he staged e.g. *La vestale* (1811, with his mistress, Colbran), and in 1815 brought Rossini to Naples with a 6-year contract to compose two operas a year. When the S. C. burnt down in Feb. 1816, Barbaia promptly rebuilt it and reopened it in Jan. 1817. Also obtained the concession of the Vienna Kä. and W. (1821-8). Here he organized brilliant seasons,introducing to Vienna Rossini and other Italian composers including Bellini and Mercadante, and commissioning *Euryanthe* from Weber. Also controlled the S. and the Canobbiana, Milan (1826-32). A man of sharp instincts,and artistic flair, he was quick to spot the talents of Rossini, Bellini, and Donizetti, and to find them effective employment; and his practical encouragement served to set on their careers these and other leading composers of the day. By introducing Spontini's *La Vestale* and Gluck's *Iphigénie en Aulide* to Naples, he began the Italian tradition of opera seria with orchestral recitative, such as Mayr's *Medea in Corinto* (1813) and Rossini's *Elisabetta, Regina d'Inghilterra* (1815). Appears in Auber's *La Sirène* (1844).

Barber, Samuel (*b* Westchester, 9 Mar. 1910). American composer. His first opera, *Vanessa*, with a libretto by Menotti, was prod. N.Y., Met., 1958, and his second, *Antony and Cleopatra*, opened the new Met. in 1966. Both are in a late-Romantic manner. (R)

Barbier, Jules (*b* Paris, 8 Mar. 1822; *d* Paris, 16 Jan. 1901). French librettist. Collaborated with Michel *Carré on many librettos, providing composers with texts which derived from many authors, including Goethe, Dante, and Shakespeare, but which formed the subjects into a conventionalized, often sentimentalized, version of the original that was exceedingly effective in the terms of most contemporary French opera. His librettos include those for Gounod's *Faust, Polyeucte, Philémon et Baucis*, and *Roméo et Juliette*, Meyerbeer's *Dinorah*, Thomas's *Mignon, Francesca de Rimini*, and *Hamlet*, and Offenbach's *Les Contes d'Hoffmann*. Their lighter side is shown in their text for Massé's *Les Noces de Jeannette*.

Barbier von Bagdad, Der (The Barber of Bagdad). Opera in 2 acts by Cornelius; text by composer, after *The Tale of the Tailor*, from *The 1,001 Nights*. Prod. Weimar, 15 Dec. 1858, with Milde, Wolf, Gaspari, Roth, cond. Liszt; N.Y., 3 Jan. 1890, with Traubmann, Kalisch, Fischer, cond. Damrosch; London, Savoy, 9 Dec. 1891, by R.C.M. students. Initially a failure owing to local intrigues against Liszt, whose departure from Weimar this occasioned; since Mottl's revision and revival (Karlsruhe, 1884) it has become popular. The plot turns on the efforts of Nureddin (ten.), abetted by the barber Abul Hassan Ali Ebn Bekar (bar.), to contrive a

meeting with Margiana (sop.), the Caliph's daughter. Despite Nureddin's imprisonment and near-suffocation in a chest, all is eventually resolved and the blessing of the Caliph (bar.) is obtained. Other operas on the subject are by H.C. Hataš (after 1780), André (1783), and Champein (n.d.).

Barbiere di Siviglia, Il (orig. *Almaviva, ossia L'inutile precauzione*) (The Barber of Seville; orig. Almaviva, or The Useless Precaution). Opera in 2 acts by Rossini; text by Sterbini, after *Beaumarchais's comedy (1775). Prod. Rome, Arg., 20. Feb. 1816, with Giorgi-Righetti (coloratura-mezzo, though the role has often been taken by a soprano), M. Garcia, Zamboni, cond. Rossini; London, Hm., 10 Mar. 1818, with Fodor, Garcia, Naldi; N.Y., Park T., 3 May 1819, in Bishop's version with Leesugg, Phillips, Spiller; N.Y., Park T., 29 Nov. 1825 (first Italian-language perf. in U.S.) with Maria Garcia (later Malibran) and her mother, father, and brother as Bertha, Almaviva, and Figaro. The first performance in Rome was one of the greatest fiascos in the history of opera. As Paisiello's opera (see below) enjoyed great popularity, the opera was originally entitled *Almaviva, ossia L'inutile precauzione*; the title *Il barbiere di Siviglia* was first used at Bologna in 1816. The overture had already been used by Rossini for *Aureliano in Palmira* (1813) and *Elisabetta, Regina d'Inghilterra* (1815). Count Almaviva (ten.) masquerading as Lindoro, a poor student, woos Rosina (mezzo), ward of old Doctor Bartolo (bass), who wants to marry her himself. The young lovers, helped by the wily Figaro (bar.), barber and factotum to Bartolo's household, successfully thwart all the old man's plots and elope together.

Barbiere di Siviglia, ossia L'inutile precauzione, Il. Opera in 4 acts by Paisiello; text by G. Petrosellini, after Beaumarchais's comedy (1775). Prod. St Petersburg, 26 Sept. 1782 in Italian, in Russian (trans. I. Vien), T. Dereviany, 27 Aug. 1790; London, Hm., 11 June. 1789, with Storace, Kelly, Benucci; New Orleans, T. Français, 10 Dec. 1805. Other operas on the subject are by Benda (1776), Elsperger (1783), Weigl (*Die betrogene Arglist*, 1783), Schulz (1786), Isouard (1796), Morlacchi (1816), Dall'Argine (1868), Graffigna (1879), Giménez and Nieto (*zarzuela*, 1901), Cassone (1922), and Torazza (1924).

Barbieri, Fedora (*b* Trieste, 4 June 1920). Italian mezzo. Studied with Toffolo and Giulia Tess. Début Florence, 1940, Fidalma. After appearances at all leading Italian opera houses, sang at Buenos Aires, Colón, 1947; C.G. 1950, with Milan Sc. Company as Quickly, 1957-8 as Azucena, Amneris, and Eboli, 1964 Quickly; N.Y., Met., 1950-4, 1956-7, 1967-8, making début on opening night of Bing's régime as

Eboli. In Italy much admired as Orfeo and Carmen. She has a repertory of more than 100 roles. (R)

Barbieri-Nini, Marianna (*b* Florence, *c* 1820; *d* Florence, 27 Nov. 1887). Italian soprano. Teachers included L. Barbieri, Pasta, and Vaccai. After a disastrous Milan Sc. début in *Belisario* (early 1840) and several other unfortunate appearances in which her very unattractive features distracted from her vocal gifts, she made a successful appearance at Florence 1840-1 as Lucrezia Borgia, wearing a mask throughout the first act and completely conquering the public by her voice alone. Considered one of the finest dramatic sopranos of her day and chosen by Verdi to create the leading soprano roles in his *I due foscari*, *Il corsaro*, and *Macbeth*. Retired in 1856 and taught. After the death of her first husband, Count Nini of Siena, she married the Viennese pianist Leopold Hackensöllner.
Bibl: L. Hackensöllner: *Le memorie di una cantatrice.*

Barbirolli, (Sir) **John** (*b* London, 2 Dec. 1899; *d* London, 29 June. 1970). English conductor of Italian parentage. Studied London, T.C.L. and R.A.M. Began career as cellist. Formed string orchestra in 1924: invited to join B.N.O.C. 1926. London, C.G., 1928, conducting *Butterfly* and *Bohème*. Music director C.G. English Company 1930. Conducted at C.G. until 1933 and again 1937 (*Tosca* and *Turandot*). Guest conductor S.W., Vienna S. O. 1946-7. Returned to C.G., Oct. 1951; guest conductor until 1954. In charge of new production of *Orfeo* with Ferrier, 1953, and *Tristan* when Fisher sang her first Isolde. After 15 years in the concert hall, he returned to opera, recording *Madama Butterfly* and *Otello*, and, in 1970, conducting *Aida* at the Rome Opera. (R)
Bibl: M. Kennedy: *Barbirolli, Conductor Laureate* (1971).

Barcarolle. The French, in international use, for the Italian *barcaruola* or *barcarola*, a boat-song, especially of the Venetian gondoliers. The rhythm, ostensibly imitating the motion of a gondola or other small boat, is a gentle 6/8 with alternating strong and weak beats. It has been used in opera by Hérold in *Zampa*, Auber in *Fra Diavolo* and *La Muette de Portici*, Donizetti in *Marino Faliero*, Verdi in *Un ballo in maschera*, and, most famously, Offenbach in *Les Contes d'Hoffmann*.

Barcelona. Town in Cataluña (Catalunya), Spain. (Names in Catalan form are given in brackets.) Opera was first given there at the T. de la Santa Cruz (Creu), opened in 1708 with Caldara's *Il più bel nome*. The first opera by a Catalan composer for the theatre was Durán's *Antigono* (1760). In 1838 a rival theatre was opened, the T. Montesión (T. Mont-Sion), and

the Santa Cruz changed its name to the T. Principal. In 1843 opera was given at the T. Nuevo (T. Nou), and four years later the T. Liceo (Gran T. del Liceu) (cap. 3,500) opened; this was built with money raised by the Liceo Filarmónico (Liceu Filharmónic), and designed by Miguel Garriga Roca (Miquel Girriga i Roca). In 1861 it was destroyed by fire; 1,000 shares were issued to raise funds to rebuild the theatre, and the descendants of the shareholders still own the Liceo with the permanent right to the individual ownership of a seat. The present house (cap. 3,000) was designed by José Oriol Mestres and opened on 20 Apr. 1862; by its charter it must give at least one Spanish opera a year. The first opera in Catalan, Goula's *A la Voreta del Mar* (On the Seashore) was given there in 1881 and extracts from Falla's *Atlántida* were heard there in 1961, before the opera's stage première in Milan. The theatre remained closed during the Spanish Civil War and did not re-open until 1942. Opera seasons are given yearly from Nov. until Mar., when French, German, Italian, and even Russian companies appear. Most great singers and conductors have appeared there.

Bardi, Giovanni, Count of Vernio (*b* Florence, 5 Feb. 1534; *d* Rome 1614 or 15). Italian writer and composer, in whose palace in Florence the *Camerata used to meet.

Bari. Town in Puglia, Italy. The T. Piccinni was inaugurated in 1854 with Donizetti's *Poliuto*. The T. Sediele, opened in the early 19th cent., was closed when it partly collapsed in 1835, and performances were given for a time in the grotesque T. La Zuppiera ('soup-tureen'), so named from its shape. But opera first found a permanent and worthy home in the T. Petruzzelli (named after two brothers who planned it) (cap. 4,000), inaugurated on 14 Feb. 1903 with *Les Huguenots*.
Bibl: A. Giovine: *Il Teatro Petruzzelli di Bari, 1903-1969* (1971).

Baritone (*Gr* βαρύτονος, heavy-tone). The middle category of natural male voice. Several subdivisions exist within opera houses: the commonest in general use (though seldom by composers in scores) are given below, with examples of roles and their approximate tessitura. These divisions often overlap, and do not correspond from country to country. In general, distinction is more by character than by tessitura, especially in France: thus the examples of the roles give a more useful indication of the different voices' quality than any attempted technical definition.

German: Spielbariton (Don Giovanni: A♭ – g'); Heldenbariton (Orestes in *Iphigénie en Tauride*: c – a♭'); hoher Bariton (Hans Heiling: c – a♭'); Kavalierbariton (the Count in *Capriccio*: c – a♭'). There is also the Bass-Bariton (Wotan, Sachs: A♭ – f).

The Italian baritono (Dandini: c – a♭') is not generally subdivided, though professionals may speak of baritono brillante and baritono cantante.

French: bariton (Escamillo: c – a♭'); bariton-Martin (Pelléas: c – a'). In early music (Lully to Rameau), basse-taille (G – f').

Barnaba. The Inquisition spy (bar.) in Ponchielli's *La Gioconda.*

Barnett, John (*b* Bedford, 15 July 1802; *d* Leckhampton, 16 Apr. 1890). English composer and singer of Prussian and Hungarian extraction (his father, Joseph Beer, was possibly a cousin of Meyerbeer). He appeared as a boy singer at the London Ly. (1813-18). Studied with William Horsley and Charles Horn; from 1826 he wrote incidental music for farces and other pieces. Became music director of the Olympic T. in 1832, but when Samuel Arnold reopened the Ly. as the English Opera House in 1834, he began to write operas for it. His 'romantic grand opera' *The Mountain Sylph* (1834) replaced dialogue with recitative and is continuously composed in freer forms than were known in England at the time. It ran for 100 nights, and long remained popular. Influenced by Weber, especially *Der Freischütz* and *Oberon*, it is in turn the immediate object of the satire of Sullivan's *Iolanthe.* Having quarrelled with Arnold, Barnett transferred to D. L. for *Fair Rosamond* (1837) and *Farinelli* (1839), which returned to ballad opera in style. After abortive attempts to form a permanent English Opera House at St J.'s (1838) and the Prince's T. (1840), he moved to Cheltenham as a singing teacher, and wrote no more operas. His daughters **Rosamund** and **Clara** became singers; of his brothers, **Joseph** was a singing teacher and father of J. F. Barnett, and **Zarah** wrote texts for some of his operas.

Barraud, Henry (*b* Bordeaux, 23 Apr. 1900). French composer. Studied Bordeaux, and Paris (incl. with Dukas). His operas are *La Farce de Maître Pathelin* (after a medieval play) (comp. 1937, prod. 1948); *Numance* (Salvador de Madariaga, after Cervantes) (comp. 1950, prod. 1955); the comic *Lavinia* (comp. 1958, prod. 1961); and a radio opera, *La Fée aux miettes* (1967).

Barrault, Jean-Louis (*b* Vésinet, 8 Sept. 1910). French actor and producer. Apart from his distinguished career in the theatre, he has produced opera and operetta, including *La Vie parisienne* in Paris and Cologne, *Faust* at the N.Y., Met., and *Wozzeck* at the Paris O.

Barrientos, Maria (*b* Barcelona, 10 Mar. 1883; *d* Ciboure, 8 Aug. 1946). Spanish soprano. Studied violin and piano Barcelona Conservatory, and then after only six months' vocal study made début at Barcelona as Marguerite

de Valois when 15. London, C.G., 1903; N.Y., Met., 1916-20, where she was the first Queen of Shemakha in 1918. *Puritani, Lakmé,* and *Sonnambula* were specially produced in N.Y. for her. (R)

Barsova (orig. Vladimirova), **Valeriya** (Vladimirovna) (*b* Astrakhan, 13 June 1892; *d* Sochi, 13 Dec. 1967). Russian soprano. Studied Moscow, with Masetti. Début Moscow, Z., 1917. Sang with Shalyapin in *Barbiere* in Petrograd; then Rosina at the Moscow B., where she remained until 1948. Sang in Stanislavsky's opera studio at the Moscow B., and at Nemirovich-Danchenko's Moscow Arts T. opera studio, 1920-4. Her most famous roles included Lyudmila, Queen of Shemakha, Snow Maiden, Gilda, Violetta, Butterfly, Musetta, Lakmé, and Manon. Taught Moscow Conservatory 1950-3. Had a light, agile voice and a brilliant coloratura technique. (R)

Barstow, Josephine (Clare) (*b* Sheffield, 27 Sept. 1940). English soprano. Studied Birmingham University, and after teaching English for two years joined Opera for All 1964. Début as Mimi. Further study London Opera Centre. London, S.W., 1967-8, Cherubino, Eurydice, Second Lady, Dew Fairy; W.N.O.C. since 1968. London, C.G., since 1969; created Denise in Tippett's *The Knot Garden,* Young Woman in Henze's *We Come to the River* (1976), and Gayle in *The Ice Break* (1977). S.W. (later E.N.O.) since 1972, creating Marguerite in Crosse's *Story of Vasco* (1974), Natasha in first English prod. of *War and Peace,* Jeanne in *The Devils of Loudun,* and Autonoe in *The Bassarids;* also very successful as Emilia Marty, Octavian, Salome, Violetta, and Elisabeth de Valois. Guest appearances Aix-en-Provence, Geneva, N.Y., Met. Repertory also includes Lady Macbeth, Jenůfa, and Alice Ford. Has a highly individual voice, which with her musical sensibility and dramatic gifts, combines to make her an outstanding singing actress. (R)

Bartered Bride, The (Cz. *Prodaná nevěsta;* lit. The Sold Bride). Opera in 3 acts by Smetana; text by Sabina. Prod. Prague, P., 30 May 1866, with Gayer von Ehrenburg, Polák, Hynek, Paleček, cond. Smetana; Chicago, Haymarket, 20 Aug. 1893 (amateur); London, D. L., 26 June 1895, in German by Ducal Court Opera of Saxe-Coburg and Gotha.

Smetana made five versions of the opera: No. 1 (virtually operetta), 2 acts, overture and 20 numbers, 2 perfs.; No. 2, 2 acts, omitting a duet and adding a ballet, 27 Oct. 1866, 13 perfs.; No. 3, 2 acts, alterations incl. new Beer Chorus and Polka, 29 Jan. 1869, 4 perfs.; No. 4, 3 acts, alterations incl. new Furiant and Skočna, 1 Jan. 1869, 9 perfs.; No. 5, 3 acts, with recitatives and minor alterations, 25 Sept. 1870. After initial failure, Smetana's most popular opera: 100th Prague performance 7 May 1882.

Mařenka (sop.) loves Jeník (ten.), but her parents have decided she must marry a man she has never seen, the son of Tobias Micha, as arranged by the marriage broker Kecal (bass). This unknown proves to be Vašek (ten.), a simpleton whom Mařenka persuades to have nothing to do with her. Meanwhile Kecal gives Jeník 300 crowns to renounce Mařenka if she will indeed marry Micha's son. Vašek falls for the circus dancer Esmeralda, but when Jeník arrives the bitter Mařenka decides she will after all marry Vašek – until it is revealed that Jeník has outwitted Kecal and the others, since he is himself Micha's son by a previous marriage and so can both marry Mařenka and keep the money.

Bartók, Béla (b Nagyszentmiklós, 25 Mar. 1881; d New York, 26 Sept. 1945). Hungarian composer. His large output includes only one opera, the early A kékszakállú herceg vára (Duke Bluebeard's Castle, comp. 1911, prod. 1918). Influenced on the one hand by Debussy (Pelléas) together with Poe and the French Romantics, on the other by Schoenberg (Erwartung) and Freud, the opera is an original and powerful piece of music drama, adapting the old Bluebeard legend as a symbolist handling of the theme of man's essential loneliness and woman's fatal inability to penetrate it. (R) Bibl: H. Stevens: The Life and Music of Béla Bartók (1953).

Bartoletti, Bruno (b Sesto Fiorentino, 10 June 1926). Italian conductor. Studied Florence, début there 1953, Rigoletto. Chicago Lyric Opera since 1957; music director, Rome, O., 1965-71. One of the most gifted Italian opera conductors. (R)

Bashkiria. Bashkir national opera began with the country's absorption into the U.S.S.R. in 1919, and the foundation of a Bashkir section at the Moscow Conservatory in 1932. Bashkir composers trained here included Halik Zaymov (b 1914), Zagir Ismailov (b1917) and Rauf Murtazin (b 1910). A Bashkir State Opera and Ballet T. was opened in Ufa in 1938, with nine young Moscow-trained Bashkir soloists: the first opera given was Paisiello's La molinara (in Bashkiri). The ensemble was enlarged in 1941.

The first primitive attempts at Bashkir operas date from the 1930s. In 1940, Khakmar by Muslim Valeyev (1888-1956) was staged; regarded as the first Bashkir opera, this is based on a contemporary folk subject and uses folk music. There followed historical operas by Anton Eichenwald (1875-1952) (Mergen, 1940), by Nikolay Chemberdji (1903-48) (Kargulas, The Swallow, 1941) and a collaboration between Zaymov and Antonio Spadavecchia (b 1907) on a folk tale, Ak Buzat (The White Stallion, 1942). After the war came Murtazin's Azat (1949), a story of the Civil War which won

much respect as evidence of a new maturity in Bashkir opera. Further works by Ismailov include the historical opera Salavat Yulayev (1955), the musical comedy Svoyachenitsa (The Sister-in-law, 1959), and Shaura (1963).

Basile Baroni, Adriana (b Posillipo, c 1580; d Rome, c 1640). Italian contralto. After successful appearances in Rome, Florence, and Naples, engaged by Monteverdi for Mantua in 1610; sang there until 1623. Monteverdi considered her voice and technique unsurpassed, and her artistry did much to help establish the new style of singing required for opera. Known as 'La Bella Adriana' because of her beauty. Her daughters **Leonora** (b Mantua, Dec. 1611; d Rome, Apr. 1670) and **Caterina** (b Mantua, c1620; d?) were both singers.

Basle (Ger. Basel, Fr. Bâle). Town in Switzerland. Opera was performed at the T. auf dem Blömlein, built 1834. The present Stadttheater (cap. 1,150) was opened on 20 Sept. 1909 with Tannhäuser. Honegger's Jeanne d'Arc au bûcher received its première there in 1938, Sutermeister's Titus Feuerfuchs in 1958, and The Consul its first European perf. in 1951.

Bass (It. basso, low). The lowest category of male voice,. Many subdivisions exist within opera houses: the commonest in general use (though seldom by composers in scores) are given below, with examples of roles and their approximate tessitura. These divisions often overlap, and do not correspond exactly from country to country. In general, distinction is more by character than by tessitura, especially in France: thus, the examples of the roles give a more useful indication of the different voices' quality than any attempted technical definition.

German: tiefer Bass (Sarastro: E – e); Bassbuffo or komischer Bass (Osmin: F – f); hoher Bass (Kaspar: G – f).

Italian: basso profondo (Ramfis: D – e); basso comico or basso-buffo (Bartolo, Basilio: F – f); basso cantante (Padre Guardiano: F – f).

French: basse-bouffe (Jupiter: F – f); basse de caractère (Méphistophélés: G – e); basse chantante or basse noble (Brogni: F – f). In early music (Lully to Rameau), basse-contre (E♭ – d').

Slavonic basses are able to achieve great depth, sometimes reaching G₁.

Bassarids, The. Opera seria, with intermezzo, in 1 act by Henze; text by W. H. Auden and Chester Kallman after The Bacchae of Euripides. Prod. Salzburg, 6 Aug. 1966 in a German translation by Maria Basse-Sporleder with Hallstein, Meyer, Little, Driscol, Melchert, Paskalis, Dooley, Lagger, cond. Dohnanyi; Santa Fe, 7 Aug. 1968, in the original English, with Caplan, Sarfaty, Mandac, Driscoll, Bressler, Reardon, Jamerson, Harrower, cond. Henze; London, B.B.C., 22 Sept. 1968 with Carlyle, Sarfaty, Watts, Young, Egerton, Bryn-Jones, Griffiths, cond. Downes; London, Col., 10 Oct. 1974, with Barstow, Pring, Brecknock, Herincx, prod. and cond. Henze. Another opera on the subject is Ghedini's *Le baccanti* (1948).

Bass-baritone. The male voice which combines, as in the part of Wotan, the qualities of *basso profondo* and *basso cantante*.

Basse-taille. The old French term for a tenor strong in the lower register, thus approximating to the modern *baritone with a range of G to f'; the true tenor was known as *haute-taille or haute-contre.

Bassi, Amedeo (*b* Florence, 20 July 1874; *d* Florence, 15 Jan. 1949). Italian tenor. Studied Florence with Pavesi. Début Castelfiorentino 1897, *Ruy Blas* (Marchetti). Chosen to sing Radamès at opening of Colón, Buenos Aires, 1908. N.Y., Manhattan Opera, 1906-8; London, C.G., 1907, first London Walther (*Loreley*), Frederico (*Germania*) (1907), and Dick Johnson (1911). Created Lionello in Mascagni's *Amica* (Monte Carlo 1905), and Angel Clare in D'Erlanger's *Tess* (Naples 1906). During Toscanini's régime at La Scala 1921-6 sang Loge, Parsifal, and Siegfried. Retired from stage 1926 and taught; his pupils included F. Tagliavini. (R)

Bassi, Carolina Manna (*b* Naples, 10 Jan. 1781; *d* Cremona, 12 Dec. 1862). Italian contralto. Daughter of Giovanni Bassi, a comic bass; with her brother Nicola she appeared in a company of *Raggazi Napoletani* founded by her father, at the Naples S.C. in 1789. One of the outstanding singers of her day, she created leading roles in Meyerbeer's *La semiramide riconosciuta, Margherita d'Anjou*, and *L'esule di Granata*, Rossini's *Bianca e Faliero*, and in works by Pacini and Mercadante. Retired from the stage in 1828, but continued to sing in concerts. Her brother **Nicola** (1767-1825), considered by Stendhal to be the best *buffo* bass of the day, sang in Paris and Milan. Another brother, **Adolfo**, was a composer and for some years director of the T. Nuovo, Trieste, where his five operas were produced.

Bassi, Luigi (*b* Pesaro, 5 Sept. 1766; *d* Dresden, 13 Sept. 1825). Italian baritone. Studied with Morandi; début Pesaro, 1799, in Anfossi's *Il curioso indiscreto*. After further study with Laschi, engaged for Prague, 1784-1806. Mozart, impressed by his Count in the first Prague *Figaro* (1786), wrote Don Giovanni for him (1787). After a period in Vienna, returned briefly to Prague before moving to Dresden in 1815. Here, his voice now feeble, he became producer at the Italian Opera; nevertheless, he gave a warm welcome to Weber and supported him in his difficulties with Morlacchi. Beethoven, who met him in Vienna in 1824 and 1825, referred to him in his conversation books

as 'il focoso italiano' (the fiery Italian).

Bastianini, Ettore (*b* Siena, 24 Sept. 1922; *d* Sirmione, 25 Jan. 1967). Italian baritone. Début (as bass) Ravenna 1945, Colline. While preparing Padre Guardiano in *Forza del destino* sang some of the tenor music of that opera, and decided to raise his voice to baritone. Second début Dec. 1951, Germont. N.Y., Met., 1953-60 and 1964-6. London, C.G., 1962; Milan, Sc.; Salzburg, etc. Sang role of Prince Andrey in first stage performance outside Russia of Prokofiev's *War and Peace* (Florence 1953). Greatly admired as a Verdi baritone. (R)

Bastien und Bastienne. Singspiel in 1 act by Mozart; text by F. W. Weiskern, after Favart's parody of Rousseau's *Le Devin du village* (1752). Prod. Vienna, in Anton Mesmer's garden theatre, Sept. 1768 – the only production for 122 years; London, Daly's, 26 Dec. 1894; N.Y., 26 Oct. 1916. Bastienne (sop.) believes herself forsaken by Bastien (ten.), and Colas (bass) is to help her win him back. He advises feigned indifference, also telling Bastien that Bastienne has grown cold towards him. The ruse succeeds: Bastien woos Bastienne ardently and all ends happily.

Battaglia di Legnano, La (The Battle of Legnano). Opera in 3 acts by Verdi; text by S. Cammarano, after Joseph Méry's drama, *La Bataille de Toulouse* (1828). Prod. Rome, Arg., 27 Jan. 1849, with Giuli-Borsi, Marchesi, Fraschini, Colini; Cardiff, 31 Oct. 1960 (as *The Battle*) with Harper, Ferendinos, Ronald Lewis, Alan, cond. Groves; N.Y., Amato T., 28 Feb. 1976. The work's celebration of the defeat of the Emperor Barbarossa by the armies of the Lombard League in 1176 alarmed the censor; it was also performed as *La sconfitta degli austriachi* (Parma, 1860), and, with altered names and places, as *L'assiedo di Arlem* (Barbarossa becoming the Duca d'Alba). The Cardiff performance transferred the action to Italy during the Nazi occupation. Arrigo (ten.), returning to Milan to join the forces of the Lombard League against Frederick Barbarossa (bass), finds that his fiancée, Lida (sop.), has married his friend Rolando (bar.). Rolando has Arrigo imprisoned, but the latter manages to escape and joins in the battle in which Frederick is killed.

Batti, batti, O bel Masetto. Zerlina's (sop.) aria in Act 1 of Mozart's *Don Giovanni*, in which she invites her lover's wrath but regains his heart.

Battistini, Mattia (*b* Contigliano, 27 Feb. 1856; *d* Contigliano, 7 Nov. 1928). Italian baritone. Studied law until 20, then turned to singing. Studied with Eugenio Terziani and Persichini in Rome. Début Rome, Arg., 1878, Alfonso (*Favorite*). London, C.G., 1883, Riccardo (*Puritani*), with little success; D.L. 1887, and not again in

London until 1905, by which time he had established himself as the greatest living Italian baritone. Possessed a high baritone of exceptional range (Massenet rewrote Werther for him), reaching a', and could sing florid music with great agility. Had a repertory of more than 80 operas, and continued to sing until he was over 70. Visited S. America, 1881, 1882, and 1889, with Tamagno, but never sang in U.S.A. Was highly esteemed in Russia and Poland. (R)

Bauermeister, Mathilde (*b* Hamburg, 1849; *d* Herne Bay, 15 Oct. 1926). German, later British, soprano. First appearance when 13, taken up by Tietjens who took charge of her musical education and sent her to the R.A.M., where she studied under Schira. Début Dublin, 1866; London, C.G., 1868, Siebel; sang there intermittently until 1885 and then every year from 1887 to 1905, when she made her farewell in a special matinée organized by Melba. Made 16 trips to America, first as a member of Mapleson's company and then at the Met. Sang more than 100 roles, most of them at C.G., including Aennchen (*Freischütz*), Magdalena, Mamma Lucia. In 1892 she saved a *Don Giovanni* performance by singing Elvira at a few hours' notice in place of the indisposed Sofia Ravogli.

Baylis, Lilian (*b* London, 9 May 1874; *d* London, 25 Nov. 1937). English musician and theatre manager. Daughter of Newton Baylis, a singer, and Liebe Cons, singer and pianist. Her aunt, Emma Cons, became lessee of the Royal Victorian Coffee Music-hall, known as the Old Vic, and invited her to manage it, which she did from 1898 to her death. She laid the foundations of a national English opera company, and, with Ninette de Valois, of a ballet company. In 1931 she reopened the London S.W. as the north London equivalent of the Old Vic, but after two seasons it became exclusively the home of the opera and ballet companies, the Old Vic being used for drama.
Bibl: H. Williams: *The Vic-Wells: The Work of Lilian Baylis* (1935).

Bayreuth. Town in Franconia, Germany. Once ruled by the sister of Frederick the Great; famous since 1876 as the home of the Richard Wagner Festivals.

The first theatrical performance was probably in 1662, on the occasion of the marriage of Princess Erdmuthe Sophie of Saxony to the Margrave: the *Ballett der Natur* and a Singspiel, *Sophia,* both by Siegmund von Birken, were performed on 30 Nov. In 1735, under the Margrave Frederick of Hohenzollern (who married Frederica Sophie Wilhelmine of Prussia, sister of Frederick the Great), a period of great artistic activity was inaugurated. The beautiful Baroque opera house, designed by Giuseppe and Carlo Bibiena, was opened in 1748 with Hass's *Ezio*; performances were also given in the open air at the Hermitage. Famous Italian singers appeared there, including Bordoni, Galletti, and Paganelli. After the death of Princess Sophie in 1758 artistic activity quickly declined; and with the death of the Margrave local musical activity was transferred to Ansbach, where the new Margrave resided. The Bavarian State Opera gives annual performances in the old opera house every spring.

Wagner had originally hoped to build his festival theatre in Munich under the patronage of King Ludwig II, and plans were drawn up by Gottfried Semper; but these had to be abandoned owing to various intrigues against Wagner and Ludwig in the Bavarian capital. In 1871 Wagner succeeded in persuading the Bayreuth authorities to provide the necessary land on which to build a theatre and a home ('Wahnfried'). The foundation-stone of the theatre was laid on 22 May 1872, when Wagner conducted Beethoven's 9th symphony in the local theatre with an orchestra consisting of many of Germany's leading musicians, among them Richter as timpanist.

The theatre (cap. 1,800), originally planned as a temporary structure, is mostly made of wood and brick, with an auditorium resembling a classical amphitheatre. It has superb acoustics, largely due to the innovation of a covered orchestra pit. The theatre opened on 13 Aug. 1876 with *Rheingold*, which launched the first complete *Ring* cycle ever to be given. Richter conducted and the singers included Materna, Unger, Niemann, Betz; Lilli and Marie Lehmann were two of the Rhinemaidens and Valkyries. The audience included Liszt, Grieg, Bruckner, Mahler, Tchaikovsky, Saint-Saëns, Nietzsche, Kaiser Wilhelm I, and Ludwig II. The first season lost more than £12,000 and there were no further performances until 1882, when *Parsifal* was given its première. From 1883 until 1908 Cosima Wagner was the director of the festivals; from 1908 to 1930 Siegfried Wagner; from 1931 to 1944 Winifred Wagner; from 1951 to 1966, Wieland and Wolfgang Wagner; from 1966, Wolfgang Wagner. The conductors have included, up to 1914, Richter, Levi, Mottl, Strauss, Siegfried Wagner, Seidl, Muck, Balling; up to 1944 Busch, Von Hoesslin, Elmendorff, Toscanini, Furtwängler, Strauss, Tietjen, De Sabata, Abendroth; and since 1951 Knappertsbusch, Karajan, Keilberth, Krauss, Jochum, Cluytens, Sawallisch, Kempe, Maazel, Stein, Varviso, Böhm, Leinsdorf, Boulez, and (the first Englishman) Colin Davis.

The greatest revolution in staging took place after the Second World War when Wagner's grandsons simplified the production, costumes, and settings, and purged the works of most of their naturalistic appurtenances and their Germanism, emphasizing instead their symbolism and universality.

In 1961 August Everding became the first outside producer to work at Bayreuth since the early 1950s; in collaboration with the designer Josef Svoboda he produced *Der fliegende Holländer*. In 1972 the East German Götz Friedrich produced a highly controversial and politically-angled *Tannhäuser*; and in 1976, Bayreuth's centennial year, there was an even more controversial production of *The Ring* by Patrice Chéreau, conducted by Boulez.
Bibl: G. Skelton: *Wagner at Bayreuth* (1965, 2/1976).

Beard, John (*b*? London, *c* 1717; *d* Hampton, 5 Feb. 1791). English tenor. One of the most famous English singers of his day, which was still dominated by the castratos. Début in Galliard's *Royal Chase*; also sang in a number of Handel performances at C.G., dividing his appearances between there and Drury Lane. A famous Macheath in various revivals of *The Beggar's Opera*. Succeeded Rich as manager of C.G. in 1761, resigning in 1767 chiefly on account of deafness. His voice was described as being powerful rather than sweet, but flexible and wide in range, a manly sound in comparison with the rival castratos; for him Handel wrote the tenor parts in *Samson*, *Judas Maccabaeus*, *Jephtha*, *Israel in Egypt*, *Hercules*, and *Belshazzar*.

Beatrice di Tenda. Opera in 2 acts by Bellini; text by Felice Romani. Prod. Venice, F., 16 Mar. 1833 with Pasta, Del Serre, Curioni, Cartagenova; London, King's T., 22 Mar. 1836 with Colleoni-Corti, Seguin, Winter, Cartagenova; New Orleans, Charles St. T., 5 Mar. 1842 with Ober-Rossi, Marozzi, Salvatori, Perozzi. First 20th-cent. revival Catania 1935, with Arangi-Lombardi. Beatrice (sop.), married to Filippo Visconti, Duke of Milan (bar.), is in love with Orombello (ten.). Orombello is loved in vain by Agnese (mezzo), with whom the Duke, having tired of Beatrice, is himself in love. Agnese betrays the lovers to the Duke and, although she later pleads with him to spare Beatrice's life, the Duke refuses, as Beatrice's followers have risen in revolt against him.

Béatrice et Bénédict. Opera in 2 acts by Berlioz; text by composer, after Shakespeare's comedy *Much Ado About Nothing* (1598-9). Prod. Baden-Baden, 9 Aug. 1862, with Charton-Demeur, Monrose; Glasgow, 24 Mar. 1936; Washington 3 June 1964, with Dussault, Porretta, Readon, cond. Callaway. Hero (sop.) looks forward to seeing Claudio (bar.) on his return from the wars, but the return of Bénédict (ten.) is sardonically greeted by Béatrice (sop.). Gradually the love beneath their banter is disclosed, and they agree to marry. Berlioz introduces the character of Somarone (bass), a pedantic Kapellmeister whose dull repeated fugue is a satire on pedantry in general and probably Cherubini in particular.

Beaumarchais, Pierre Augustin Caron de (*b* Paris, 24 Jan. 1732; *d* Paris 19 May 1799). French playwright and amateur musician. His fame rests upon the first two plays of the *Figaro* trilogy, *Le Barbier de Séville* (Comédie-Française, 1775) and *La Folle Journée, ou Le Mariage de Figaro* (1778; Comédie-Française, 1784). For the former he wrote some songs, possibly adapted from Spanish airs. The third play of the *Figaro* trilogy, *La Mère coupable* (T. du Marais, 1792) represents a return to the *larmoyant* style of his early plays, and tells how the Countess has a child by Cherubino and how Figaro saves his master from a swindling Irish infantry officer; it was seriously considered for an opera by Grétry.

As a librettist, Beaumarchais is known chiefly for *Tarare*, a 5-act opera with music by Salieri (it had been declined by Gluck) (Paris, O., 1787). The second edition of the libretto contains an interesting preface addressed 'Aux abonnés de l'Opéra, qui voudrait aimer l'opéra': it claims a greater importance for words (coupled with the comment that operatic music is apt to be too dense for them), discusses the legitimate subjects for librettos, and concludes by mentioning the collaboration with Salieri. Beaumarchais's colourful and versatile personality is sketched in his own Figaro.

Operas on his works are as follows:
Le Barbier de Séville (1775): F. Benda (1776); Paisiello (1782); Weigl (1783); Schulz (1786); Reinagle (1794); Isouard (1796); Rossini (1816); Dall'Argine (1868); Graffigna (1879); Niteo (1901); Cassone (1922); Torazza (1924).
La Folle Journée, ou Le Mariage de Figaro (1778, prod. 1784): Shield (1784); ?Persicchini (*c* 1782); Mozart (1786); version of Mozart by Tarchi (1789); Dittersdorf (1789); Portugal (1799); L. Ricci (1838).
La Mère coupable (1792): Milhaud (1966).
Other operas making use of the character of Figaro are by Paer (*Il nuovo Figaro*, 1794); Tost (*Figaro*, 1795); Morlacchi (*Il nuovo barbiere di Siviglia*, 1816); Carafa (*Les Deux Figaros*, 1827); L. Ricci (*Il nuovo Figaro*, 1832); Mercadante (*I due Figaro*, 1835); Speranza (*Les Deux Figaros*, 1838); C. Kreutzer (*Die beiden Figaro*, 1840); L. Rossi (*La figlia di Figaro*, 1846); Cagnoni (*Il testamento di Figaro*, 1848); Aimon (*Les Deux Figaros*, *c* 1850); G. Panizza (*I due Figaro*, n.d.); P. H. Allen (*La piccola Figaro*, 1931); Delmas (*La Conversion de Figaro*, 1931); Klebe (*Figaro lässt sich scheiden*, 1964). Also Massenet (*Chérubin*, 1905). Opera based on *Tarare* by Mayr (*Atyr*, 1814). Also operetta *Beaumarchais* by Cools (1931).

Bechi, Gino (*b* Florence, 16 Oct. 1913). Italian baritone. Began studies at 17 with Raoul Frazzi and then with De Giorgi. Début Empoli 1936, Germont. Became Italy's leading baritone and sang with great success at the Scala, Rome, Lisbon, South America, etc. His interpretations of Iago, Nabucco, Amonasro, Gérard, Hamlet, and other dramatic roles gained him a reputation which was not upheld when he sang Iago and Falstaff in London, C.G., with the Sc. Company in 1950. He returned to London (D.L.) to sing William Tell in 1958. Only U.S. appearances were in 1952. He created *Monte Ivnor* (Rocca) in 1939 and Alfano's *Don Juan de Mañara* in 1941. Retired 1965, since when he has taught. (R)

Beckmesser. The pedantic town clerk (bass), unsuccessful aspirant to Eva's hand, in Wagner's *Die Meistersinger von Nürnberg*.

Beecham, (Sir) **Thomas** (*b* St Helens, 29 Apr. 1879; *d* London, 8 Mar. 1961). English conductor. Son of Joseph Beecham, a wealthy industrialist and musical amateur. No formal musical education, but after Oxford travelled extensively abroad. Conductor of a small touring opera company 1902-4. Greatly interested in opera and influenced by *Maurel who had settled in London and had set up a private school there. In 1910, backed by his father, launched his first opera season at C.G., which opened with the first English *Elektra*, and included works by two other composers with whom Beecham became closely identified, Ethel Smyth's *The Wreckers* and Delius's *A Village Romeo and Juliet*. An autumn season that year lasted three months and introduced *Salome* to London. Beecham also introduced *Feuersnot*, *Ariadne auf Naxos*, and *Rosenkavalier* to London before the First World War. Responsible for the Russian opera seasons at D.L. in 1913 and 1914. During the First World War he financed and established the *Beecham Opera Company. In 1919 he found himself lessee of C.G. and in 1920, owing to financial difficulties, his company went into liquidation and he himself withdrew from operatic activity for nearly 12 years. Was able to return to C.G. in 1932, and from then until 1939 was its chief conductor, artistic director, and financier.

Appeared as guest conductor in Cologne, Munich, Hamburg, and Berlin during the inter-war years, and at the Met. and other American theatres 1941-4. After the war he conducted little opera in England, notable exceptions being *Ariadne auf Naxos* at Edinburgh 1950; *Meistersinger* and *The Bohemian Girl*, C.G. 1951; Delius's *Irmelin*, Oxford 1953; *Zémire et Azor*, Bath 1955; and a number of works for the B.B.C. In 1958 he conducted a series of Italian, French, and German operas at the T. Colón, Buenos Aires. Beecham's contribution to opera in England was inestimable. The tragedy is that he was never able to settle and build a permanently based organization after the demise of his war-time company. (R)

Bibl: C. Reid: *Thomas Beecham* (1961).

Beecham Opera Company. Although Sir Thomas Beecham organized an English Opéra Comique Company at Her Majesty's T. in 1910, and took over the Denhof Company in 1913, it was not until October 1915 that the permanent Beecham Company came into being with a short season at the Shaftesbury T., London, which included the production of Stanford's *The Critic* and Ethel Smyth's *The Boatswain's Mate*. In the spring of 1916 the company gave a season at the Aldwych T. in Manchester, when, according to Sir Thomas, the company 'evolved overnight from the chrysalis state of a smallish troupe of Opéra Comique dimensions into the full growth of a Grand Opera organization, with an enlarged quota of principals and an augmented chorus and orchestra'. Beecham had inherited the scenery used by the Diaghilev Company at Drury Lane in 1914 and left in England at the outbreak of war, and was so able to give performances of *Boris, Ivan the Terrible, Prince Igor*, etc.

The repertory further included a number of works by Wagner, the inclusion of which was attacked by the more reactionary press at that time; Playfair's classic productions of *Figaro, Così fan tutte*, and *Die Zauberflöte*; the stock Verdi works, including *Otello*, which had one of its greatest interpreters in Frank Mullings, and *Falstaff*. Beecham's singers included the best of an outstanding generation of British artists—Agnes Nicholls, Rosina Buckmann, Jeanne Brola, Edith Clegg, Désirée Ellinger, Edna Thornton, Miriam Licette, Mignon Nevada; Frederic Austin, Norman Allin, Maurice D'Oisly, Walter Hyde, Frank Mullings, Robert Parker, Robert Radford, Frederick Ranalow; and the conductors besides Beecham were Buesst, Coates, Harrison, Goossens (II and III), and Pitt.

The company continued to function until December 1920, when it was forced into liquidation after the débâcle of Beecham's International season at C.G. It was not allowed to die, however, and was organized into the *British National Opera Company.

Beethoven, Ludwig van (*b* Bonn, 15 or 16 Dec. 1770; *d* Vienna, 26 Mar. 1827). German composer. Beethoven's only completed opera, *Fidelio*, was the result of a commission from the T. an der Wien, and went through a number of revisions. Beginning as a setting of one of the popular escape stories of the period, this Singspiel is transformed by Beethoven's humane passion into an uneven but magnificent expression of faith in liberty and loathing of tyranny. The characters become universal symbols in the course of the opera; the opera itself has become a symbol of liberty, and has frequently been chosen to reopen opera houses after destruction or enforced closure by war. Beethoven also made sketches for *Vestas Feuer*, to a text by Schikaneder, and wrote some of a Witches' Chorus for *Macbeth*. He contemplated many other subjects, including *Faust*.

Beggar's Opera, The. Ballad opera in 3 acts arranged, adapted, and partly composed by Pepusch; text by John Gay. Prod. London, Lincoln's Inn Fields T., 29 Jan. 1728, with Fenton, Walker – run of 62 nights; N.Y., Nassau St. T., 3 Dec. 1750. The most famous and popular of all *ballad operas, it may have been suggested to Gay by a remark of Swift that an opera set in a prison 'would make an odd pretty sort of thing'. The purpose is doubly satirical, lampooning politicians (Walpole in Macheath) as well as famous singers (the notorious Bordoni – Cuzzoni battle during Bononcini's *Astianatte* on 6 June 1727 in the Polly–Lucy rivalry), and mocking the Italian opera conventions of the period – the prologue and the artificial happy ending among others. The work was revived almost every year from 1728 to 1886, when Sims Reeves sang Macheath.

The hero, Macheath (ten.), is the leader of a band of highwaymen. Betrayed by some of his women, he is removed to Newgate Gaol, in the charge of Lockit the gaoler (bar.). Lockit's daughter Lucy (sop.) and the fence Peachum's (bass) daughter Polly (sop.) jostle for his favour, and even protest that they will be hanged with him; but eventually the Beggar (spoken role) who has introduced the opera intervenes to achieve a happy ending.

The work's modern vogue dates from Frederic Austin's version given at the Lyric, Hammersmith, from 5 June 1920 for 1,463 nights (the longest run of any opera) with Nelis, Marquesita, Ranalow, Austin, cond. Goossens. Later versions have included Dent's (Birmingham, in a circus tent on a bomb site, 22 May 1944, by the Clarion Singers); Britten's, a recomposition so thorough as to amount to an original work (Cambridge, Arts, 24 May 1948, with Rose Hill, Evans, Pears, cond. Britten); Manfred Bukofzer's (N.Y., Brander Matthews T., 6 Apr. 1954, for Columbia University, with Polen, Bybell, Farrell, cond. Rhodes); Bliss's (for a film, 1953, with Laurence Olivier and Stanley Holloway singing as Macheath and Lockit, and singers doubling the actors including Leigh, Vyvyan, Coates, Cameron, Boyce). There have been other versions in different countries at different times, e.g. by Bucci (1950).
See also *Dreigroschenoper*.

Begnis, Giuseppe de, and **Giuseppe Ronzi de.**
See *De Begnis*.

Bei Männern. Duet in Act 1 of Mozart's *Die Zauberflöte* in which Pamina (sop.) and Papageno (bar.) sing of the joys and power of love.

Bel canto. (*It* beautiful singing). The traditional Italian art of singing in which beautiful tone, fine legato phrasing, and impeccable technique are emphasized, even if at the expense of the more dramatic style favoured in Germany. The term, an imprecise one, was probably first used in a volume of *ariette da camera* by Vaccai (before 1840). Bel canto flourished in various styles between the 17th and 19th cents. and is now in decline.

Belcore. The sergeant (bar.) in Donizetti's *L'elisir d'amore*.

Belgium, Under the Spanish domination of the 17th cent., French taste, especially for ballet, ruled the theatre. In 1681 the Académie de Musique was opened, and the first opera theatre, the T. de la Monnaie, followed in 1700. Few Belgian composers emerged at first in a tradition dominated by the French; opéra-comique was established with the occupation of Marshal Saxe in 1746. The first true Belgian opera was *Le Déguisement pastoral* (1759) by Pierre van Maldere. Other Belgian operas were written by the director of the Monnaie, Ignaz Vitzthumb (of Austrian origin). In Liège, Jean-Noël Hamal wrote 'opéras burless' in Liegois (see *Dialect in opera*); and from Liège emerged the greatest Belgian opera composer, *Grétry. In the 19th cent. an international repertory began to be heard in the principal cities of Belgium. In 1830, a famous performance of Auber's *La Muette de Portici* initiated a revolution. Two scholar-directors of the Académie were also composers, Fétis and Gevaert; another important figure was Albert *Grisar. A taste for grand opera developed, and respected works were written by *Franck (*Hulda, Ghisèle*) and Blockx (in Flemish). Paul Gilson (1865-1942) wrote *Prinses Zonneschijn* in Flemish, but drew upon an international musical language that included use of Leitmotiv; Jan Van der Eeden (1842-1913) was influenced by Italian *verismo*; Eugène Samuel-Holeman (1863-1944) was an Impressionist. Latterly a more flourishing, independent tradition of Belgian composers has developed.
See also *Antwerp, Brussels, Ghent, Liège*.

Belgrade. The opera theatre was founded in 1894, though opera had been given earlier. A visit from the Zagreb Opera in 1911 did much to encourage the foundation of a permanent company, but not until the winter of 1919-20 was one engaged and the composer Stanislav Binički (1872-1942) appointed director and conductor. He built up a repertory based on French and Italian popular favourites. The company developed especially in the decade 1924-34 under Stevan Hristić (1885-1948), who also founded the Belgrade Philharmonic. In his ten years, he engaged many foreign singers, especially Russian, and trained the first generation of Serbian singers. The repertory was extended to include many Slavonic classics, Russian, Czech, and Polish, as well as some Serbian operas. Many famous singers were invited as guests, including Shalyapin, Destinn, Marcel Journet, and others; and visits from the Sc. and the Paris O. C. encouraged an awareness of international standards. Between the wars the company made a visit to Frankfurt. The National T. was bombed in 1941, but during the German occupation some operatic life continued. In 1945 the first opera to be given in liberated Belgrade was *Eugene Onegin*; the enterprising and efficient director and conductor 1944-59 was Oskar Danon. The repertory was widened, and tours were undertaken, first to Switzerland in 1954, then to many other centres; a busy programme of recordings was also undertaken. The company maintains its position as one of international standing.

Belhomme, Hypolite (*b* Paris, 1854; *d* Nice, 16 Jan. 1923). French bass. Studied Paris Conservatoire; début Paris, O.C., 1879 as Baskir in *Lalla Roukh* (David). Sang at O.C. until 1886, and again 1891-1901, 1908-16; there he created Crespel (*Hoffmann*), the Bohemian in *Louise* and many other roles; also the first Paris Pistol and Benoit. Sang Kecal in first Brussels *Bartered Bride* (1905). (R)

Belisario. Opera seria in 3 acts by Donizetti; text by Cammarano after Jean-François Marmontel's drama *Bélisaire* (1776). Prod. Venice, F., 4 Feb. 1836 with Ungher, Vial, Pasini, Salvatori; London, 1 Apr. 1837 with Giannoni, De Angioli, Sgr. De Angioli, Inchiade; New Orleans, French Opera House, Apr. 1842 with Ober-Rossi, Bamberger, Perozzi, Salvatori.

Belisarius (ten.), general in the Emperor Justinian's army, returns in triumph to Constantinople after defeating the Bulgarians. His jealous wife Antonia (sop.), believing him guilty of their son's murder (and also because she is in love with Eutripio, Captain of the Imperial Guards), concocts evidence against him so that he is arrested for plotting against the life of the Emperor. He is blinded and sent into exile; but then is reunited with his son who, far from having been murdered, helps lead Justinian's troops to victory. Mortally wounded, Belisarius dies, but not before his wife has confessed. Other operas on the subject are by Philidor (1796), Saint-Lubin (*c* 1827), and Maurer (1830).

Bell Song. The name usually given to the soprano aria 'Où va la jeune Hindoue?' sung by Lakmé in Act 2 of Délibes's *Lakmé*.

Bella figlia dell'amore. Quartet in Act 3 of Verdi's *Rigoletto* for Gilda (sop.), Maddalena (mezzo), the Duke (ten.), and Rigoletto (bar.), in which the Duke woos Maddalena, while Rigoletto comforts the anguished Gilda with promises of retribution.

Belle Hélène, La (Fair Helen). Operetta in 3 acts by Offenbach; text by Meilhac and Halévy. Prod. Paris, Variétés, 17 Dec. 1864; London, Adelphi, 30 June 1866; Chicago, 14 Sept. 1867. A satirical version of the story of Helen of Troy which mocks the Second Empire by highlighting its preoccupation with sex and its generally lax morals.

Belle nuit, O nuit d'amour. *Barcarolle* for Giulietta (sop.) and Niklausse (mezzo) in Offenbach's *Les Contes d'Hoffmann*.

Belletti, Giovanni Battista (*b* Sarzana 17 Feb. 1813; *d* Sarzana, 27 Dec. 1890). Italian baritone. Début Stockholm 1837, Figaro (Rossini); there he had great successes with Jenny Lind in Meyerbeer and Donizetti roles. London début 1848, H.M.'s, as Carlo in *Ernani*. Toured U.S.A. with Lind and Benedict under Barnum. Generally considered one of the great baritones of the 19th cent.; especially admired in his Meyerbeer roles.

Bellezza, Vincenzo (*b* Bitonto, Bari, 17 Feb. 1888; *d* Rome, 8 Feb. 1964). Italian conductor. Trained Naples Conservatory. Début Naples, S.C., 1908, *Aida*. Conducted widely in Italy, and then was engaged at Buenos Aires, Colón. N.Y., Met., 1926-35; London, C.G., 1926-30 and 1935-6. Conducted Melba's Farewell (1926), first English *Turandot* (1927), and London débuts of Ponselle, Gigli, and other artists. Rome O. and other Italian theatres 1935-64. Returned London 1957, Stoll, and 1958, D.L. (R)

Bellincioni, Gemma (Cesira Matilde) (*b* Monza, 17 Aug. 1864; *d* Naples 23/4 Apr. 1950). Italian soprano. Daughter of Cesare Bellincioni, a bass-buffo, and the contralto Carlotta Soroldoni, with whom she studied. Début Naples, 1880, T. della Società Filarmonica in Dell'Orefice's *Il segreto della duchessa*. Sang widely in Europe and America. The first Santuzza (1890), Fedora (1898), and Italian Salome, London, H.M.'s, 1889, and C.G. 1895. Considered an outstanding Violetta by Verdi, who said 'she put new life into the old sinews'. She retired from the stage in 1911 and then taught in Berlin, Rome, Siena, finally Naples. Married the tenor **Roberto Stagno** (1840-1897), the original Turiddu. Their daughter **Bianca** (*b* Budapest, 23 Jan. 1888) studied with her mother; début Graz, 1913. (R)
Bibl: G. Bellincioni: *Io e il palcoscenico* (1920); B. Stagno-Bellincioni: *Roberto Stagno e Gemma Bellincioni* (1943).

Bellini, Vincenzo (*b* Catania, 3 Nov. 1801; *d* Puteaux, 23 Sept. 1835). Italian composer. Studied under Zingarelli at the San Sebastiano Conservatory, Naples. His student works, including an operetta and his first opera, *Adelson e Salvini* (1825; rev. recit. replacing dialogue, late 1820s, unprod.), displayed gifts for lyricism and flowing melodies which were to characterize all his compositions. *Adelson*, performed in the theatre attached to the conservatory, was heard by Barbaia, the impresario of both Milan Sc. and Naples S.C., who immediately commissioned an opera from Bellini for the latter theatre; this was *Bianca e Gernando* (1826; rev. as *Bianca e Fernando*, 1828), first performed before King Francis I. Barbaia immediately gave a second commission, this time for Milan Sc., which resulted in *Il pirata* (1827); its success was helped by Rubini's singing of the tenor role, specially composed for him, which broke away from the florid Rossini style then in vogue. *La straniera* (1829) and *Zaira* (1829) met with rather less success; but *I Capuleti e i Montecchi* (1830), as revivals in Italy have shown, contains some of the composer's most beautiful music. With *La sonnambula* and *Norma* (both 1831), Bellini's gifts reached maturity. The first work is a tenderly elegiac rustic idyll, the latter a lyric drama reaching tragic grandeur in its last act. It was much admired by Wagner, not least for Romani's libretto: 'Bellini is one of my predilections because his music is strongly felt and intimately bound up with the words.' *Norma* was followed by *Il fù ed il sarà* (1832, lost: prob. pasticcio by other hands) and *Beatrice di Tenda* (1833) which was not a success, though its revival at Palermo (1959), in a revised form by Gui, revealed many hidden treasures in a work that looked forward to Verdi. Bellini's last opera, *I Puritani* (1835), despite a poor libretto by Pepoli, triumphed because of its ravishing melodies. Overworked and weak in health, he fell ill while visiting a friend at Puteaux and died there of dysentery. He was buried at Paris, but his remains were removed to Catania in 1871.

Bellini's melodic form exercised a strong influence on a whole generation of musicians including Chopin and Berlioz. For a time his works were under a cloud, being considered weak in dramatic force, no more than display pieces for singers. But revivals in recent years with singers of the stature of Callas, Sutherland, and Simionato have resulted in their winning new appreciation.

Belloc-Giorgi, Teresa (orig. Maria Teresa Ottavia Faustina Trombetta) (*b* San Benigno Canavese, nr Turin, 2 July 1784; *d* San Giorgio Canavese, 13 May 1855). Italian mezzo of French parentage. Début Turin, 1801; Milan, Sc., 1804-24. She appeared in London under the name of Bellochi (1819) and was particularly successful as Tancredi. Rossini wrote roles for her in his *L'inganno felice*, and *La gazza ladra*. According to Stendhal, however, she had an 'ugly and coarse-grained voice'. She also created roles in Pacini's *La vestale* and Mercadante's *Elisa e Claudio*.

Belmonte. A Spanish nobleman, the hero (ten.) of Mozart's *Entführung aus dem Serail*.

Belorussia. Although opera was performed in Minsk as early as 1852, musical life was first organized in the 1920s; the first Belorussian opera was *Osvobozhdeniye truda* (Labour Liberated), written in 1923 by Nikolay Churkin (1869-1964). Attempts at staging operas in the 1920s led to the formation of opera classes in Minsk in 1930 and thence to the foundation in 1933 of the Belorussian National Opera and Ballet T. (Bolshoy T.). Starting with *Carmen* (25 May 1933) and a selection of Russian and Western classics, this developed a national repertory with, first, *Mikhas Podgorny* (1939) by Evgeny Tikotsky (*b* 1893), *U pushchakh Polesya* (In the Forests of Polesye, 1939) by Anatoly Bogatyryov (Bogatyrau) (*b* 1913), both on subjects concerning struggles for independence, and *Tsvetok schastya* (The Flower of Happiness, 1940) on a folk legend by Alexey Turenkov (1886-1958). The invasion halted progress, and the company was evacuated to Gorky and Kovrov, though two successful operas were written during the war years, Bogatyryov's *Nadezhda Durova* (1946) and Tikotsky's *Alesya* (1944). After the war followed *Kastus Kalinovsky* (1947) and *Pesnya o Schastye* (Song of Happiness, 1951) by Dmitry Lukas (*b* 1920), *Andrey Kostenya* (1947) by Nikolay Aladov (*b* 1890), *Masheka* (1945, prod. 1955) by Grigory Pukst (*b* 1900) and *Yasny rassvet* (Bright Dawn, 1958) by Turankov. Subsequent operatic development seems to have been less vigorous than in other republics. The company makes summer tours of the republic and its neighbours.

Benda, Jiří (Georg)**Antonín** (*b* Staré Benátky, 30 June 1722; *d* Köstritz, 6 Nov. 1795). Czech composer. He moved to Prussia, becoming Kapellmeister at Gotha. Here he produced a number of successful Singspiels, of which the most important is *Der Dorfjahrmarkt* (1775). At the age of 52, in 1775, he appeared as the master of a new form of stage music with his spoken 'duodramas' *Ariadne auf Naxos* and *Medea*, which greatly impressed a number of contemporaries, including Mozart. Other successful works, which have been revived in modern times, include the Singspiel, *Romeo und Julie* (1776), and the duodrama *Pygmalion* (1779). His nephew **Friedrich** (1745-1814) also wrote some operas, and Singspiels, including *Das Blumenmädchen* (1806); and his son **Friedrich Ludwig** (1752-92) wrote some songs, duets, and a chorus for a translation of *Le Barbier de Séville* for Dresden (1776) and Singspiels.

Bender, Paul (*b* Driedorf, 28 July 1875; *d* Munich, 25 Nov. 1947). German bass. Studied with Luise Ress and Baptist Hoffmann. Début Breslau, 1900, Hermit in *Freischütz*. Munich 1903-35; London, C.G., 1914 (first Amfortas in England) and 1924; N.Y., Met., 1922-7. Distinguished in Wagner and as Osmin, Sarastro, and Baron Ochs. Created Pope Pius V in *Palestrina*, and was first German Don Quichotte. Bavarian Kammersänger and teacher at Munich Music School till his death. His pupils included Josef Greindl and Hans Hopf. (R)

Bendl, Karel (*b* Prague, 16 Apr. 1839; *d* Prague, 20 Sept. 1897). Czech composer. Studied Prague Organ School, and gained conducting experience abroad, especially in Paris. Succeeding Smetana as conductor of the Hlahol Choral Society, he did much to enlarge the repertory (e.g. with works of the young Dvořák); and his understanding of voices shows in the operas he soon began writing. His Meyerbeerian *Lejla* (1868) impressed audiences, and in 1874 he joined the Provisional T. as second conductor; but his *Starý ženich* (The Old Bridegroom, comp. 1874) was too similar to *The Bartered Bride* and was therefore withheld by the composer until Smetana's death. After a period abroad, he settled again in Prague and wrote a *verismo* opera, *Černohorci* (The Montenegrins, 1881), a comedy also in the Smetana manner, *Karel Škréta* (1883), and a tragedy, *Dítě Tábora* (The Child of Tabor, 1888). A gifted and versatile musician, he was one of the most important Czech opera composers to emerge in Smetana's immediate wake.

Benedetti, Michele (*b* Loreto, 17 Oct. 1778; *d*?). Italian bass. In 1811 sang in first Italian perf. of *La vestale* in Naples, which became his artistic home; there he created Elmiro Barberigo in Rossini's *Otello* (1816), Idraste in *Armida* (1817), title-role in *Mosè* (1818), Ircano in *Ricciardo e Zoraide* (1818), Fenicio in *Ermione* (1819), Douglas d'Angus in *La donna del lago* (1819), and Leucippo in *Zelmira* (1822). London, 1822. Also appeared in first performances of operas by Mayr, Pacini, Mercadante, and Bellini (*Bianca e Fernando*). Stendhal gives a vivid description of his Moses.

Benedict, (Sir) Julius (*b* Stuttgart, 27 Nov. 1804; *d* London, 5 June 1885). German, later English, composer, conductor, teacher, writer, and pianist. Studied at Stuttgart and Weimar, where he met Weber; then became Weber's pupil and protégé. Weber took him to Vienna in 1823, where he was appointed conductor of the Kärntnerthor-T. In 1825 went to Naples and conducted at the S.C. and Fondo. Here his *Giacinto ed Ernesto* (1829) was found too German for Italian taste; it was followed by *I Portoghesi in Goa* (1830), which on its performance in Stuttgart was found too Italian for German taste. In 1834 he moved to Paris, where he met Malibran. At her suggestion visited London in 1835, and remained there until his death. Held appointments at D.L. (1838-48), the Ly. (from 1837), and H.M.'s (from 1852), and was active as one of the composers struggling to establish English opera. His own best known work is *The Lily of Killarney* (1862). Also active in the concert hall, conducting Jenny Lind's first oratorio appearance (*Elijah*, 1848) and directing most of her concerts in the U.S.A. Knighted in 1871. His music reflects the influence of Weber, and is skilfully written; but in unpropitious conditions, his operas were no more successful than those of his contemporaries.

Benefit. In the 18th and 19th cents. these were special performances, generally at the end of the season, the proceeds of which went to a certain composer, singer, or impresario. In Italian, a distinction is nowadays made between a *beneficenza*, in financial support of a person or organization, and a *beneficiata*, in which an important artist is given an evening in which to display his special talents, usually in a mixed programme. In our day, Benefit or charity performances of opera are given in aid of an organization or institution. These are very common in New York, where during the course of the season the Met. gives several Benefits, generally at increased prices.

Bennett, Richard Rodney (*b* Broadstairs, 29 Mar. 1936). English composer. His excellent craftsmanship and fluent capacity to provide music for different situations are shown in his four operas, *The Ledge* (1961), *The Mines of Sulphur* (1963), *Penny for a Song* (1968), and *Victory* (1970).

Benois, Alexandre (Alexander Nikolayevich) (*b* St Petersburg, 3 May 1870; *d* Paris, 9 Feb. 1960). Russian designer. Son of the architect Nikolay Benois and Camilla Cavos, a daughter of the architect Alberto Cavos (1801-63) who was in turn the son of Caterino *Cavos and helped in the rebuilding of the Moscow B. in 1853. After working with Bakst and other artists in Diaghilev's influential group *Mir Iskusstva* (The World of Art), Benois began to design for the Maryinsky Theatre (including *Götterdämmerung*, 1903). In 1908 Diaghilev engaged him to design *Boris Godunov* for his first Paris season. Also designed the sets for première of Stravinsky's *The Nightingale* (1914). Benois occasionally designed for opera during the 1920s (including *The Golden Cockerel*, Paris 1927), but he was mostly associated with the theatre and ballet until 1938, when he was invited to join his son Nicola (see below) at the Milan Sc. From then until 1957 he designed many operas, including *Faust*, *La traviata*, *Eugene Onegin*, and *Tosca*. He was an artist with a particular flair for the fantastic and spectacular, with a vivid sense of colour and design: *The Golden Cockerel* at Paris in 1927 was a classic example of his brilliant, essentially Russian talent. His niece **Nadia** (1894-1975) was a

ballet designer, and the mother of Peter Ustinov.
Bibl: A. Benois: *Memoirs* (trans. M. Budberg, 1964).

Benois, Nicola (Nikolay Alexandrovich) (*b* St Petersburg, 2 May 1901). Russian scenic designer, son of Alexandre Benois. Worked with his father in Russia, France, and England, mostly on ballet; then summoned to Milan Sc. by Toscanini in 1925 to design *Boris Godunov* and *Khovanshchina*. Has remained in Italy ever since, and from 1936 to 1970 was the Sc.'s chief designer. Has been responsible not only for Russian operas in the repertory but has designed the *Ring* and other German and Italian works. He also worked at the Rome O. and the Colón, Buenos Aires. His wife is the soprano Disma de Cecco.

Benucci, Francesco (or Pietro) (*b c*1745; *d* Florence, 5 Apr. 1824). Italian bass. After singing in Italy 1769-82, went to Vienna, where he was the first Figaro (1786) and Guglielmo in *Così fan tutte* (1790); also the Leporello of the revised *Don Giovanni* at Vienna in 1788. Less admired in London in his season as principal bass at the King's in 1788 than on the Continent.

Benvenuto Cellini. Opera in 2 acts by Berlioz; text by Léon de Wailly and August Barbier, after the autobiography of Benvenuto Cellini (1558-66; pubd. 1728). Prod. Paris, O., 10 Sept. 1838, with Dorus-Gras, Dérivis, Duprez, Stoltz, cond. Habeneck; London, C.G., 25 June 1853, with Julienne, Didiée, Tamberlik, Tagliafico, cond. Berlioz; Boston, 3 May 1975, with Wells, Vickers, Reardon, Beni, cond. Caldwell. Berlioz's first opera, initially a failure, though later championed by Liszt in performances at Weimar (from 20 Mar. 1852 in a revised 3-act version); the London première, in Queen Victoria's presence, also failed through engineered opposition, and Berlioz immediately withdrew the work.

Set in Rome in 1532, the opera is based on some events in the life of Benvenuto Cellini. Teresa (sop.), daughter of the Papal Treasurer Balducci (bass), plans to elope with Cellini (ten.), disguised as a friar, during the Roman Carnival, but their plan is overheard by Fieramosca (bar.), a sculptor also in love with Teresa. In the confusion of the Carnival, with Fieramosca also disguised as a friar, a fight develops in which Cellini kills Pompeo (bar.). Ascanio (mezzo), Cellini's apprentice, brings Teresa to Cellini's studio and Cardinal Salviati (bass) comes to demand by midnight a statue he has commissioned if Cellini is not to be handed over to the law for abduction and murder. Despite a strike organized by Fieramosca, Cellini, having thrown into the crucible every piece of precious metal he possesses, succeeds in casting his Perseus and thus earning a pardon.

Other operas on Cellini by L. Rossi (1845), Schlösser (1845), Lachner (1849), Kern (1854), Venzano (1870), Bozzano (1871), Orsini (1875), Diaz (1890), Tubi (1906), Courvoisier (1921).

Bérain, Jean (*b* St Mihiel, 28 Oct. 1637; *d* Paris, 25 Jan. 1711). French scenic designer. Succeeded Bigarini at the Salle des Machines, and as designer at the Paris O. In 1674 succeeded Gissey as designer to the King, and designed costumes and settings for many court spectacles. In 1680 he began a collaboration with Lully, providing designs for the premières of all Lully's operas produced in Paris, 1680-7. After Lully's death he worked with Desmaerts, Campra, and Destouches. André Tessier called him 'le grand créateur du pays d'opéra'. His costume designs for both opera and ballet are justly renowned and have become collectors' pieces.

Berenice. Opera in 3 acts by Handel; text by Antonio Salvi (first composed by Petri in 1709). Prod. London, C.G., 18 May 1737, with Strada, Gizziello, Annibale, Bertoli. Unsuccessful. There are some 20 other operas on the subject.

Berg, Alban (*b* Vienna, 9 Feb. 1885; *d* Vienna, 24 Dec. 1935). Austrian composer. Studied with Schoenberg, 1904-10, who exercised a deep influence on him and to whom *Lulu* is dedicated. *Wozzeck* (1925) and *Lulu* (unfinished, prod. 1937) are among the most powerful and original music dramas of this century, each expressing in its way Berg's profound compassion for the lowest in humanity. In *Wozzeck* this is for the materially underprivileged. Though the opera is fascinatingly constructed out of instrumental forms, such as suite, sonata, and rondo, Berg stresses that tenderness for the dregs of humanity, transcending the fate of the individual Wozzeck, should fill the listener's mind and not curiosity about the formal means. Unlike *Wozzeck*, *Lulu* is a dodecaphonic opera, with a musical form attached to each of the characters. These are entirely creatures of instinct, and it is for the tragic direction in which this takes them that Berg invites compassion. Lulu herself represents raw female sexuality and its destructive effect upon others. Musically *Lulu* rises to greater heights than *Wozzeck*, though the latter's more easily shared compassion has helped to make it one of the most successful of modern operas.
Bibl: M. Carner: *Alban Berg* (1975).

Berg, Natanael (*b* Stockholm, 9 Feb. 1879; *d* Stockholm, 14 Oct. 1957). Swedish composer. He had 5 operas produced in Stockholm, all with librettos by himself: *Leila*, after Byron's *The Giaour* (1912); *Engelbrekt* (1929); *Judith*, after Hebbel (1936); *Birgitta* (1942); and *Genoveva*, after Hebbel (1947).

Bergamo. Town in Lombardy, Italy. Opera was first given in 1786 when the T. Riccardi was inaugurated on 24 Aug. with Piccinni's *Didone*. The theatre burnt down in 1797, and was reopened in 1799. In the early years of the 19th cent. many important singers appeared there, including the locally-born Rubini and Donzelli, and great attention was given to the works of Simone Mayr; later Rossini was more popular. In 1897, after extensive rebuilding and on the centenary of the birth of Bergamo's most famous composer, Donizetti, it was renamed the T. Donizetti (cap. 2,000). The opening season included *La favorita, Lucia di Lammermoor*, and *Maria di Rohan*. Toscanini conducted the opening *Lucia*, but, dissatisfied with the standards and the public attitude, withdrew from the rest of the season. In 1937 the theatre was given a subsidiary title, the T. della Novità, and has pursued a policy of producing several new operas each season, including Ghedini's *Maria d' Alessandria* (1937), Barilli's *Medusa* (1938), Napoli's *Un curioso accidente* (1950), Tosatti's *Il sistema della dolcezza* (1951), Malipiero's *Il festino* and *Donna Urraca* (1954), Viozzi's *Allamistakeo* (1954), Hazon's *Requiem per Elisa* (1957), Ferrari's *Cappuccia o della liberta* (1958), Zanon's *La leggenda di Giulietta* (1969), and Sanzogno's *Boule de Suif* (1970). It has also revived Donizetti's *Rita, Anna Bolena, Maria di Rohan, Maria Stuarda, Giovedi Grasso, Pigmalione*, and *Belisario*. The Bergamo audience is generally considered, after that of Parma, the most difficult to please in Italy.
Bibl: G. Donati-Pettini: *Teatro Donizetti* (1930).

Berganza (orig. Vargas), **Teresa** (*b* Madrid, 16 Mar. 1935). Spanish mezzo-soprano. Studied with Lola Rodrigues Aragon. Début Aix-en-Provence 1957, Dorabella. Milan, Sc., 1957-8 and subsequently; Gly. 1958, Cherubino, 1959, Cenerentola; London, C.G., 1960, Rosina, 1963, Cherubino; Dallas, 1958, Isabella, and Neris (*Médée*). Edinburgh 1977, Carmen. A typically rich-voiced Spanish mezzo-soprano, and an excellent singer in florid music. (R)

Berger, Erna (*b* Dresden, 19 Oct. 1900). German soprano. Studied at Dresden with Heta Boeckel and Melita Hitzl. Début Dresden 1925, First Boy (*Zauberflöte*); Bayreuth 1929-31; Salzburg 1932, Blondchen, 1954-5, Zerlina; Berlin, S. O. 1930-2, 1934; London, C.G., 1934, 1935, 1938, and after the war (Queen of Night, Sophie, Gilda). Also appeared N.Y., Met., and continued to sing in opera in Germany and Austria until 1955, when she devoted herself to teaching. Her most successful pupil is Rita *Streich. Berger's voice retained its youthful freshness and girlish quality throughout her long career. (R)
Bibl: K. Höcher: *Erna Berger* (1961).

Bergknappen, Die (The Miners). Opera in 1 act by Ignaz Umlauff; text by P. Weidmann, Prod. Vienna, B., 17 Feb. 1778. First German Singspiel produced at the Burgtheater instituted by the Emperor Joseph. Other operas on the subject are by Hellwig (1820, after Körner), Oestrich (1839), and M. Hertz (*Gwarkowie*, 1880).

Berglund, Joel (Ingemar) (*b* Torsåker, 4 June 1903). Swedish bass-baritone. Studied with John Forsell, Stockholm Conservatory 1922-8. Début Stockholm 1928, Lothario (*Mignon*). Soon established himself as leading Wagner singer, and sang in Buenos Aires, Zurich, Vienna, and Chicago before the war as Sachs, Wotan, and Dutchman. Bayreuth, 1942, Dutchman. N.Y., Met., 1945-9. Director of Stockholm Royal Opera 1949-56; continued to make occasional appearances in opera until 1970. (R)

Bergonzi, Carlo (*b* Parma, 13 July 1924). Italian tenor, formerly baritone. Studied Parma with Grandini. Début Lecce 1948, Figaro (Rossini). Sang baritone roles for three years; then, after further period of study, second début Bari 1951, Chénier. London, Stoll, 1953, Alvaro; C.G. 1967 and subsequently; Chicago 1955; N.Y., Met., since 1956. Sings with taste and discretion, and is especially impressive in the Verdi repertory. (R)

Berkeley, (Sir) Lennox (*b* Oxford, 12 May 1903). English composer. He took up music seriously after leaving Oxford in 1926, and studied with Nadia Boulanger for six years. He did not write an opera until 1953, when he produced a full-scale 3-act setting of a libretto by Alan Pryce-Jones, *Nelson* (prod. S.W.). This was not a success, due in part to a lengthy plot with contrived situations. Berkeley turned next to Paul Dehn, who provided him with a libretto for a 1-act comic opera, *A Dinner Engagement* (Aldeburgh, 1954); it is a work of much dexterity and considerable comic appeal. His third opera, *Ruth* (1-act) with a libretto by Eric Crozier, was produced by the E.O.G. (London, Scala, 1956); his fourth, *The Castaway*, was also produced by the E.O.G. (Aldeburgh, 1967).

Berkshire Festival. An annual summer festival given at Tanglewood, Mass., and instituted by Serge Koussevitsky in 1937. The operatic contribution to the festival is generally provided by the opera department of the Berkshire Music Center under the direction of Boris Goldovsky. The American premières of *Peter Grimes, Albert Herring, Zaïde, Idomeneo*; revivals of *Il turco in Italia, Queen of Spades*; and the first performances of works by American composers – Mennini's *The Rope*, Bucci's *Tale for a Deaf Ear*, and Lukas Foss's *Griffelkin* – have been features of the festivals since 1947. Singers who were heard at Tanglewood in the early days of their careers include Mario Lanza,

James Pease, Mack Harrell, Frances Yeend, Leontyne Price, and Irene Jordan.

Berlin. Town in Germany, from 1871 until 1945 capital of united Germany, now capital of East Germany. Opera is now given principally in three theatres; in West Berlin at the Deutsche Oper, in East Berlin at the Staatsoper unter den Linden and the Komische Oper.

The first opera performances (of Italian works) were given in 1688, during the reign of Frederick I of Prussia. The first opera house, the Hofoper, opened only in Dec. 1742 in the reign of Frederick the Great with Graun's *Cleopatra e Cesare*. Opera began to develop chiefly under B.A. Weber from 1795; however, Singspiel was given in 1786. The influential Count Brühl directed the opera from 1815; he wanted Weber as music director, but was overruled, and Spontini held the position 1820-42. However the first opera at the Neues Schauspielhaus, Weber's *Der Freischütz* (1821), proved a national triumph, greatly encouraging the cause of German opera and, with the fame of Spontini's work, giving Berlin new importance as an operatic centre. The Königstädter-T. was inaugurated in 1824, becoming the Wallnertheater in 1851; here Italian opera was given, with performances by Sontag and Pasta. Meyerbeer was director in succession to Spontini from 1842, with Nicolai as one of the conductors; his *Lustigen Weiber von Windsor* was given its première in 1849. During this period, opera was also given at the Krolloper (1843), especially works by Lortzing, and the Friedrich-Wilhelmstädtisches-T. (from 1883 Deutsches T.) which was directed by Lortzing 1850-1. The Victoria-T. gave Italian opera with singers including Artôt and Patti. Berlin increasingly became a major centre of opera, especially German; high standards were attained under Weingartner (1891-8) and Strauss (1898-1918).

In 1919 Max von Schillings took over the Königliche Opera, and it was renamed the Staatsoper. He was succeeded by Heinz Tietjen (1925-43); the music directors were Blech (1918-23, 1926-37) sharing with Kleiber (1924-33), Furtwängler (1933-4), Krauss (1934-5) and from 1936 to 1943 Heger, Schüler, Egk, Karajan, and Elmendorff. Under Kleiber, premières were given of *Wozzeck* (1925) and works by Busoni, Janáček, Strauss, Stravinsky, and Křenek. Under the Nazis this adventurous policy was retarded. Kleiber returned for a short period after the war. Between 1918 and 1943, singers included Ivogün, Leider, Lemnitz, Ljungberg, Cebotari, Ursuleac, Anders, Bockelmann, Domgraf-Fassbänder, Lorenz, Schlusnus, and Roswaenge. At the end of the war, the theatre was destroyed and the company resumed activities under Ernst Legal at the Admiralspalast on 8 Sept. 1954 with Gluck's *Orpheus*. In 1954 Max Burghardt was appointed Intendant, and on 4 Sept. 1955 the Oper unter den Linden (cap. 1,450) reopened with *Meistersinger* under Konwitschny (music director until 1962). He was succeeded by Otmar Suitner.

In 1896 Kaiser Wilhelm II planned a new opera house for Berlin, and Kroll's T. in the Königsplatz was bought. After many delays building was planned to begin in 1914, but the war intervened; the new theatre finally opened in 1924. For a two-year period, from May 1926, while the Oper unter den Linden was being rebuilt, its company played at the Kroll Oper (which was officially renamed the Oper am Platz der Republik), alternating, from the autumn of 1927, with the Kroll's own independent company under the musical direction of *Klemperer and with Legal as Intendant. Under this joint direction, and when the Linden Oper's company returned to its own home, the Kroll became the leading experimental opera theatre in Europe. As well as Mozart and Verdi, the repertory included memorable productions of *Luisa Miller*, *The Kiss*, *La Périchole*, *Le Médécin malgré lui*, and then contemporary works including Hindemith's *Cardillac*, *Neues vom Tage*, *Hin und Zurück*, Křenek's *Leben des Orest*, *Der Diktator*, and *Das geheime Königreich*, Milhaud's *Le Pauvre Matelot* and *Angélique*, Schoenberg's *Erwartung* and *Die glückliche Hand*, Weill's *Der Jasager*, Stravinsky's *Oedipus Rex* and *Mavra*, and Janáček's *From the House of the Dead*. In addition to Klemperer the conductors were Zemlinsky, Fritz Zweig, and Rankl, and the singers included Novotna, Eisinger, Pauly, Krenn, Schützendorf, and Wittrisch. The theatre was closed in 1931, and in 1933 it became the home of the Reichstag.

The Städtische Oper (originally the Deutsches Opernhaus on the Bismarckstrasse, and sometimes known as the Charlottenburg Opera) was opened in Nov. 1912, cap. 2,100, Intendant Georg Hartmann. From 1925 to 1934 it reached a high artistic level, with Walter, Denzler, and Stiedry as its conductors, and Tietjen, Singer, and Ebert as Intendants. Singers included Ivogün, Lehmann, Reinhardt, Müller, Schöne, Nemeth, Onegin, Kipnis, and, Reinmar, and there were outstanding productions of *The Queen of Spades*, *Pelléas et Mélisande*, *Der Corregidor*, *Euryanthe*, and operas of Mozart and Verdi. During the Nazi régime, Wilhelm Rode, the baritone, was Intendant, and Goebbels its guiding spirit, as Goering was of the Staatsoper. Rother, Schmidt-Isserstedt, and Ludwig were its chief conductors. It was destroyed by bombs in 1944. After the war it reopened in the T. des Wests, former home of the Volksoper (cap. 1,529) with Bohnen as its Intendant; he was succeeded by Tietjen in 1948; and by Carl Ebert

1955-61. Leo Blech returned from exile to conduct, 1949-54. Fricsay was for a short time music director but resigned after a number of disagreements, and the conducting was shared between Richard Kraus, Arthur Rother, and guests. Singers included Elisabeth Grümmer, Lisa Otto, Helene Werth, Fischer-Dieskau, Beirer, Greindl, Haefliger, Konya, Neralic, and Suthaus. The rebuilt house on the Bismarckstrasse opened in 1961 with Gustav Sellner as Intendant and reverted to the name Deutsche Oper. Lorin Maazel was music director from 1965 to 1971. Egon Seefehlner became Intendant in 1972. Premières since the war include Henze's *König Hirsch* and *Der junge Lord*, Klebe's *Alkmene*, Dallapiccola's *Odysseus*, Blacher's *200,000 Taler*, Fortner's *Elisabeth Tudor*, and the first stage performance in Germany of *Moses und Aron*.

The Komische Oper, formerly the Scala T., opened in 1947 (cap. 1,338) and under Walter *Felsenstein became one of the most discussed opera houses in Europe. The brilliant productions of *The Cunning Little Vixen*, *Figaro, Zauberflöte, Falstaff, Hoffmann, Otello*, and *Carmen* have attracted opera-goers from all countries. Joachim Herz became Generalintendant in 1976.

Berlioz, Hector (*b* La Côte-St-André, 11 Dec. 1803; *d* Paris, 8 Mar. 1869). French composer. Almost all Berlioz's music was dramatic in conception, whether ostensibly a symphony (*Symphonie Fantastique*), a concerto (*Harold en Italie*), or one of his hybrids – the dramatic symphony *Roméo et Juliette*, the monodrama *Lélio* (significantly a sequel to the *Symphonie Fantastique*),and the *légende dramatique, La Damnation de Faust*. Though the latter has been staged, it is essentially not theatrical but a work for the imaginative listener in the concert hall.

Berlioz was first drawn to opera by the idea of setting episodes from the life of Benvenuto Cellini, whose autobiography he probably first read in 1831. Greatly attracted to a fellow-artist of heroic and Romantic individuality, he also sensed a kinship with Cellini's struggles to assert himself in the face of academicism and intrigue and to produce against all the odds a shining masterpiece. The project of a 2-act opéra comique was turned down by the O.C., and Berlioz cast the work instead for the O. *Benvenuto Cellini* (1838) is an uneven opera, showing signs of Berlioz's attempt to match the conventions of singers and of the O., but the brilliance and warmth of the music far outweigh these patches, and the Roman Carnival scene remains one of the most thrilling spectacles in all opera.

Faced with public neglect in the field of opera after the failure of *Cellini*, Berlioz found himself cut off from the medium into which his talents should naturally have flowed; thus when he made an opera out of Virgil, he took less account of practical considerations of performance in France. *Les Troyens* (comp. 1856-8; complete prod. 1890) is an opera on the largest scale, and triumphs over normal operatic considerations. It is an epic that embraces the spectacular and the lyrical, that combines startling originalities with a classical grandeur which looks back past Spontini to Gluck. Berlioz's love of Virgil was a typical Romantic paradox: there is the ache for a lost age of purity, balance, and order, yet equally a sense of identification with the heroes and heroines who act with Romantic urgency and passion. Though the work is constructed in a sequence of episodes, making no use of Leitmotiv, there is the connecting theme of the divine command that the Trojans (with their Reminiscence Motive of the Trojan March) shall found their new city of Rome; and this lends dramatic impetus and cohesion to all the skilfully contrasted scenes. With the understanding of 'open form' which he had acquired from his study of Shakespeare, Berlioz can include in his pattern all the familiar operatic devices together with dramatic orchestral tableaux (the Royal Hunt and Storm), a sequence of incidental entertainments (at Carthage), arias for minor characters that confer new emotional dimensions on the major theme (Hylas, the sentries), even a scene in which the central character is silent (Andromache, her presence accompanied by a grave clarinet obbligato). *Les Troyens* is one of the noblest monuments of operatic imagination in the history of the art.

It was as a rest after the exertions of *Les Troyens*, so Berlioz said, that the comedy *Béatrice et Bénédict* (1862) was written, as well as in tribute to Shakespeare. It includes some infelicities (the leaden parody of academicism in Somarone's repeated fugue), but there is in the musical handling of the subject a tenderness and ironic wit worthy of Shakespeare's own, justifying Berlioz's description of the opera as 'a caprice written with the point of a needle'. Its German successes, before the production of the second part of *Les Troyens* (the Carthage acts), gave Berlioz false hopes of a good reception for the greater work.

In 1847 Berlioz was invited by Jullien to become music director at *Drury Lane as part of an ill-fated attempt to found an English national opera.

Bibl: H. Berlioz: *Mémoires* (1865, pubd. 1870; trans. D. Cairns, 1969); J. Barzun: *Berlioz and the Romantic Century* (1951, 2/1969).

Bernacchi, Antonio Mario (*b* Bologna, ? 23 June 1685; *d* Bologna, Mar. 1756). Italian male contralto. Studied with Pistocchi and Ricieri. After appearances in Venice and Bologna went to London in 1716. In 1717 he sang Goffredo in revival of Handel's *Rinaldo*, a role previously sung by women contraltos and sopranos. Engaged in 1729 by Handel to replace Senesino, he created the title role in Handel's *Lotario*, and Arsace in *Partenope*. His compass was narrower than Senesino's (a-e'', with a single f'' in *Partenope*). He returned to Italy in 1730, and despite a vocal decline continued to sing until 1736. In 1737 he founded a school in Bologna, and his many pupils included Guarducci and Raaff.

Bernauerin, Die. 'Ein bairisches Stück' in 1 act by Orff; text by composer, in Bavarian dialect after an old Bavarian ballad on the historical story of Agnes Bernauer. Prod. Stuttgart, 15 June 1947, with composer's daughter Godela in title role, cond. B. Wetzelberger; Kansas City (University of Missouri), 21 Mar. 1968. Based closely on the original ballad, the story is one of love opposed and finally destroyed by demonic powers. Agnes Bernauerin, daughter of the owner of a public baths, marries a nobleman, Albrecht, but is accused of witchcraft and murdered. Taking much of its manner from a medieval mystery play, the work is essentially a spoken drama with music, becoming operatic chiefly in the love scene and the finale.

Berne (Ger. Bern). Town in Switzerland. Opera is performed at the Stadttheater (cap. 1,000), opened 25 Sept. 1903 with *Tannhäuser*.

Bernstein, Leonard (*b* Lawrence, Mass., 25 Aug. 1918). American composer and conductor. Educated Boston and Harvard. Studied composition with Edward Hill and Walter Piston; then conducting at Curtis Institute under Reiner. Koussevitzky's assistant Tanglewood 1942, where he directed the American première of *Peter Grimes* (1946); Rodzinski's in N.Y. 1943. Conducted his own *Trouble in Tahiti* at Brandeis University 1952 and N.Y., C.C. 1958, and the Visconti-Callas *Medea* and *Sonnambula* at Milan Sc. 1954 and 1955. N.Y., Met., 1964; Vienna S.O. 1966. He returned to the Met. in Sept. 1973 to conduct the new production of *Carmen*, which opened the first season after the Bing régime. (R)

Berry, Walter (*b* Vienna 8 Apr. 1929). Austrian bass-baritone. Studied Vienna Academy with Endré Koreh, Hermann Gallos, Hans Duhan, and Josef Witt. Début Vienna S.O. 1950; sang several small roles, then in 1953 Masetto and later Figaro, Leporello, Guglielmo, Wozzeck, Barak, and Ochs, and in the Italian repertory. Salzburg Festival since 1953; N.Y., Met. since 1966. London, R.F.H., with Vienna Opera 1954. C.G. 1976, Barak. (R)

Bersa, Blagoje (*b* Dubrovnik, 21 Dec. 1873; *d* Zagreb, 1 Jan. 1934). Yugoslav composer.

Studied Zagreb from 1893 with Zajc, Vienna 1896-9 with Fuchs and Epstein. A leading figure in Croatian music between 1900 and 1920, he gave a new lead to opera especially with *Oganj* (Fire; comp. to German text as *Der Eisenhammer* (The Iron Hammer), 1905-6; prod. 1911). Written in post-Wagnerian style, this is set in a factory and makes advanced use of music to represent machinery and its role in the life of the workers who use it. He also wrote *Jelka* (1896-1901, not prod.), on Italian models, and the comedy *Postolar od Delfta* (The Cobbler of Delft, 1914). His many pupils benefited from the new ideas, especially the enlarged awareness of German and Russian music, which he introduced into Croatian musical life. His brother **Vladimir** (1864-1927) wrote *Cvijeta* (1898) and *Andrija Čubranović* (1900). A third brother, Josip, sometimes acted as their librettist.

Bertati, Giovanni (*b* Martellago, 10 July 1735; *d* Venice, 1815). Italian librettist. His first text, for Tozzi's *La morte di Dimone* (1763), inaugurated a list of some 70, chiefly for Venice. Most of his librettos are comic, and show the influence of Goldoni, in some imitative texts and details and in their neat, rapid sense of theatre, though they are by no means void of independent and quite sharp social comment. His greatest success was his text for Cimarosa's *Il matrimonio segreto* (1792); and his version of *Don Giovanni* for Gazzaniga had a direct and specific influence on Da Ponte's for Mozart (for example in his characteristic love of *catalogue arias). He also wrote librettos for Galuppi, with whom he went to Vienna in about 1770, Guglielmi, Paisiello, Anfossi, Bianchi, Paer, Zingarelli, and others. He was Caesarean Poet, 1790-4.

Berton, Henri-Montan (*b* Paris, 17 Sept. 1767; *d* Paris, 22 Apr. 1844). French composer. Violinist at the O. from an early age. Studied with Sacchini. Début as composer with sacred drama at Concert Spirituel. Most famous for *Les Rigueurs du cloître* (1790), a pioneering example of *rescue opera from which *Fidelio* took its example; and for *Montano et Stéphanie* (1799) (popular in the first half of the 19th cent.), *Le Délire* (1799), and *Aline, reine de Golconde* (1803), a very successful work which even reached America. He was music director at the T. I., 1807-9, then chorus master at the O. After *Françoise de Foix* (1809) he began to lose his following and became embittered and reactionary. However, at its best, his music has melodic and harmonic enterprise, including a remarkable pioneering use of motive, and especially a feeling for instruments.

His son **Henri** (-François) (*b* Paris, 3 May 1784; *d* Paris, 19 July 1832) was also a composer, who wrote a number of light pieces of small originality, most successfully *Ninette à la* *cour* (1811) to a text by *Favart. Taught singing, Paris Conservatoire, 1821-7. His son **(Adolphe)** (1817-51) was a singer who had a modest career in France and Algiers.

Berton, Pierre-Montan (*b* Maubert-Fontaines, 7 Jan. 1727; *d* Paris, 14 May 1780). French bass, conductor, and composer. Father of the above. Début Paris, O., 1744, but immediately withdrew. Sang at Marseilles *c* 1746-8, then conducted at Bordeaux. Conductor, Paris, O., from 1755, greatly raising orchestral standards. He helped to introduce Gluck to Paris, but was best known for his arrangements of older works, e.g. by Rameau and Lully, to suit contemporary taste. Manager, O., with Trial, from 1767; director from 1770; in sole charge as director-general 1775-8.

Bertoni, Ferdinando Gasparo (*b* Salò, 15 Aug. 1725; *d* Desenzano, 1 Dec. 1813). Italian composer. He was the composer of some 50 operas, many of them to Metastasio texts. The best known was *Quinto Fabio* (1778), which led to his engagement at the King's T., London. Here he wrote many works which Burney noted, 'would please and soothe by their grace and facility, but not disturb an audience by enthusiastic turbulence'.

Bertram, Theodor (*b* Stuttgart, 12 Feb. 1869; *d* Bayreuth, 24 Nov. 1907). German baritone. Son of the baritone Heinrich Bertram (1825-1903) and soprano Marie Bertram-Mayer (1838-82). Studied with his father. Début Ulm, 1889, Hermit in *Freischütz*; after engagements in Hamburg and Berlin, joined Munich, H., 1893-1900. N.Y., Met., 1899-1901, Wagner repertory, Herr Fluth, and Pizarro; London, C.G., 1900, 1903, 1907, Wagner roles, Pizarro, and Fluth. Bayreuth 1901-6, where he was much admired by Cosima Wagner, especially as Wotan; also Amfortas there, and first Bayreuth Dutchman in 1901. After the death of his wife, the soprano Fanny Moran-Olden (1855-1905), he became increasingly depressed and eventually committed suicide. (R)

Berwald, Franz Adolf (*b* Stockholm, 23 July 1796; *d* Stockholm, 3 Apr. 1868). Swedish composer. Studied with his father Christian Berwald (1740-1825) and Dupuy, violinist of the Hovkapellet, which he then joined. He began composing seriously in 1817, beginning an opera *Gustaf Vasa* in 1827. In Berlin in 1829 he contemplated other operatic subjects, and began work on them, but his first completed stage works were operettas, *Jäg gar i kloster* (I Enter the Monastery, 1842) and *Modehandlershan* (The Modiste, 1845). Three operas followed: *Ein ländliches Verlobungsfest in Schweden* (A Swedish Country Betrothal, 1847: dedicated to Jenny Lind, who took part in the first performance of excerpts); *Estrella di Soria* (comp. 1840s; prod. 1862); and *Drott-*

ningen av Golconda (The Queen of Golconda, comp. 1864, prod. 1968).
Bibl: R. Layton: *Franz Berwald* (1959).

Besanzoni, Gabriella (*b* Rome, 20 Sept. 1888; *d* Rome, 8 July 1962). Italian mezzo-soprano. Studied with Alessandro Maggi and Hilde Brizzi. Originally a light soprano, she found her voice changing and became a contralto. Début Viterbo 1911, Adalgisa. Appeared at all leading Italian opera houses including Milan Sc. where she sang Orfeo and Carmen under Toscanini. N.Y., Met., 1919-20; Chicago and South America. Her last appearances were as Carmen at the Terme di Caracalla, Rome, in 1939. Well known for her Isabella and Cenerentola. (R).

Besch, Anthony (*b* London, 5 Feb. 1924). English producer. After early experience with the Oxford University Opera Club (*Idomeneo*, 1947), he worked with Carl Ebert at Glyndebourne 1951-5, and produced *Der Schauspieldirektor* there in 1957. Has successfully staged many operas for S.W. and later the E.N.O., Scottish O. and C.G. Produced the premières of Berkeley's *Castaway*, Birtwistle's *Punch and Judy*, Lutyens's *Time Off? Not a Ghost of a Chance*, as well as the first performances in England of *The Nose* and Ginastera's *Bomarzo*. His Mozart productions have won praise. He is a traditionalist in the best sense.

Besuch der Alten Dame, Der (The Visit of the Old Lady). Opera in 3 acts by Gottfried von Einem; text by Friedrich Dürrenmatt, after his drama of the same name. Prod. Vienna, S.O., 23 May 1971, with Christa Ludwig, Beirer, Waechter, Hotter, cond. Stein; San Francisco, 25 Oct. 1972, with Resnik, Cassilly, Wolansky, Yarnell, cond. Peress; Gly., 31 May 1973, with Meyer, Crofoot, Bell, Garrard, cond. Pritchard. The once impoverished Claire Zachanassian (mezzo) originally known as Klara Wäscher and now the richest woman in the world, returns to her home town of Güllen. She meets Alfred III (bar.), her former lover and father of her illegitimate child, and offers the town a billion if he is killed. This eventually happens; the cause of his death is declared to be heart-failure. Claire claims the body and gives the mayor the cheque she had promised. The people of Güllen express their happiness and satisfaction that justice has been done.

Bettelstudent, Der (The Beggar Student). Operetta in 3 acts by Millöcker; text by Zell and Genée. Prod. Vienna, W., 6 Dec. 1882, with Finaly, Schweighofer, Girardi; N.Y. 19 Oct. 1883 with Geistinger, Stebold, Schmitz, Friest, Schultze; London, Alhambra, 12 Apr. 1884, with Fanny Leslie, Mervin, Hood. Also operetta by Winter (1785), after Cervantes's *La cueva de Salamanca*, and Singspiel by Schenk (1796).

Bettoni, Vincenzo (*b* Meleganano, 1 July 1881; *d* Milan, 4 Nov. 1954). Italian bass. Début Pinerolo 1902, Silva. Well established in Italy before the First World War. Milan, Sc., 1905, 1926-40, especially in *buffo* roles. Gly. 1934, Don Alfonso; London, C.G., 1935, as Don Magnifico, Mustafà, Don Basilio, Colline, and Sam. Created Eziel in *Il Dibuk* (Rocca), Sc. 1934, and was the Gurnemanz in the first Barcelona performance of *Parsifal,* 1914. He appeared frequently with Conchita Supervia in the 1920s and 1930s in Rossini's operas. (R)

Betz, Franz (*b* Mainz, 19 Mar. 1835; *d* Berlin, 11 Aug. 1900). German baritone. Studied Karlsruhe. Début Hanover 1855, Herald (*Lohengrin*). Appeared as guest Berlin, H., 1859, as Don Carlos in *Ernani*, and was engaged on permanent contract, remaining a member of the ensemble until 1897. His roles there included Don Giovanni, Lysiart, Hans Heiling, William Tell, and Orestes (Gluck); also the first Berlin Falstaff. One of Wagner's most trusted singers, he created Hans Sachs in Munich in 1868, and the Wanderer in *Siegfried* at Bayreuth (1876), also singing Wotan in *Rheingold* and *Walküre* in the first Bayreuth *Ring*. He returned to Bayreuth in 1889 as Sachs and Kurwenal. Never sang in opera in England, or U.S.A., but appeared in London in 1882 singing at Crystal Palace and at a Richter concert. The *Musical Times* critic wrote of his 1889 performances that they were 'still without flaw'. His wife **Johanne Betz** (1837-1906) was a coloratura soprano, daughter of Philipp Jakob Düringer, director of the Berlin Schauspielhaus (1853-76), and author of a biography of Lortzing.

Bevignani, Enrico (*b* Naples, 29 Sept. 1841; *d* Naples, 29 Aug. 1903). Italian conductor and composer. Studied with Albanese and Lillo. Went to London 1863 as répétiteur at H.M.'s; then at C.G. 1869-87 and 1890-6 as conductor; N.Y., Met., 1894-1900, and appearances in Moscow and St Petersburg. Conducted first London *Aida* (1876), *Gioconda* (1883), *Amico Fritz* (1892), *Pagliacci* (1893), and Patti's last appearance at C.G. (1895).

Bianca und Giuseppe, oder Die Franzosen vor Nizza. Opera in 4 acts by Kittl; text by Richard Wagner, after Heinrich König's novel. Prod. Prague, 19 Feb. 1848. Wagner wrote the scenario in 1836 for himself, but did not use it; he revised it in 1842 for Reissiger, who did not use it either.

Bibiena. Italian family of scene designers and architects of the Baroque era, whose work was seen all over Europe, but especially in Parma and Vienna. The family name was Galli; Bibiena was added from their father's birthplace.

(1) **Ferdinando** (1657-1743) and (2) **Francesco** (1659-1739) studied at Bologna and with Rivani, one of Louis XIV's stage machinists at Versailles. Ferdinando was engaged by the Duke of Parma and worked in the T. Farnese; he then went with his brother to Vienna, where they were responsible for the décor for the court fêtes and theatrical performances. They were the first to exploit the *scena per angolo,* or diagonal perspective, which replaced central perspective of scene design, the great characteristic of the Baroque stage.

(3) **Alessandro** (1686-1748), son of (1). Spent most of his working life at Mannheim.

(4) **Giuseppe** (1696-1757). Son of (1). Designed the famous Margrave Opera House in Bayreuth. Was the first to use transparent scenery lit from behind.

(5) **Antonio** (1700-74). Son of (1) Designed the T. Comunale, Bologna.

(6) **Giovanni Maria** (*c*1704-69). Son of (1). Built a theatre in Lisbon.

(7) **Carlo** (1728-1827). Son of (4). Worked with his father at Bayreuth and also at Drottningholm, Sweden, where some of his designs are still extant.

The style of the Bibienas is so much alike that it is often difficult to distinguish between their work. Designs by one or other of the family were provided for operas by A. Scarlatti, Vivaldi, Caldara, and Gluck.

Bielefeld. Town in Westphalia, Germany. The Stadttheater (cap. 890) was built in 1904. Bernhard Conz has been music director since 1951. Among enterprising revivals was one of Weber's *Peter Schmoll* in 1955. In 1968 Friedelind Wagner staged *Lohengrin* there.

Bignens, Max (*b* Zurich, 9 June 1912). Swiss scenic designer. Studied in Zurich, Munich, Florence, and Paris. Resident designer Berne 1939-45, Basle 1945-51 and 1956-61, Munich, Gärtnerplatz T., 1951-6 and 1963-5, Darmstadt 1961-3. Since 1965 Cologne, with engagements in Frankfurt and the Bavarian State Opera. Designed the settings for the première of Zimmermann's *Soldaten* at Cologne, and for several productions at the Schwetzingen Festival.

Billington, Elizabeth (*b* London, *c*1765; *d* Venice, 25 Aug. 1818). English soprano. Daughter of Carl Weischel, first oboe at King's T. and a popular singer who was a favourite pupil of J. C. Bach. She studied with Bach and James Billington, a double-bass player and singing teacher, whom she married. Début Dublin 1783, Polly (*Beggar's Opera*). C.G. from 1786. Heard by King of Naples, 1794, who procured her an engagement at the San Carlo where she appeared in Bianchi's *Iñes de Castro,* specially written for her. Successful appearances all over Italy and at the King's, Haymarket, with the Italian Company, where she was the first English Vitellia (*Clemenza di Tito*) (1806). Greatly admired by the Prince of Wales, whose mistress she was said to have been. Mount Edgcumbe likened her voice to a flute or flageolet. Haydn wrote *L'Arianna abbandonata* for her.

Billy Budd. Opera in 4 acts by Britten; text by E.M. Forster and Eric Crozier, after Melville's unfinished story (1891). Prod. London, C.G., 1 Dec. 1951, with Pears, Uppman, Dalberg, cond. Britten; N.Y., N.B.C. Television, 19 Oct. 1952. New 2-act version broadcast 13 Nov. 1960, with Pears, J. Ward, Langdon, cond. Britten; prod. London, C.G., 9 Jan. 1964, with Lewis, Kerns, Robinson, cond. Solti; repeated in N.Y. 1966 by same cast and conductor. First U.S. stage performance of revised version Chicago, 6 Nov. 1970, with Lewis, Uppman, Evans, cond. Bartoletti.

The opera, which has no female roles, is set on a man-o'-war in Napoleonic times. It tells of the impressment of a young sailor, Billy (bar.), into service in the Navy: his natural goodness excites the resentment of the master-at-arms Claggart (bass), who falsely accuses him of treachery. Inhibited by his stammer, Billy lashes out at Claggart, who falls dead; and Billy is hanged from the yard-arm. The opera is told as a memory of distant events by Capt. Vere (ten.), who has proved unable to save Billy. Also opera by Ghedini (1949).

Bindernagel, Gertrud (*b* Magdeburg, 11 Jan. 1894; *d* Berlin, 3 Nov. 1932). Successful in Wagner roles. Berlin S.O. 1921-7, and Stä. O. 1930-2. After a performance in Berlin (Brünnhilde in *Siegfried*) she was shot by her jealous husband as she left the theatre. (R)

Bing, (Sir) Rudolf (*b* Vienna, 9 Jan. 1902). Manager and impresario. Studied Vienna. Manager of Viennese concert agency from 1923. Then held appointments at Darmstadt and Berlin under Carl Ebert who brought him to Gly. 1934. General Manager 1936, a position he held for ten years. In 1946 became a naturalized British subject and helped to found the Edinburgh Festival; director 1947-9. General Manager of the N.Y., Met., 1951-72. Knighted in 1971. Took silent role of Sir Edgar in N.Y. première of Henze's *The Young Lord*, 1973.
Bibl: R. Bing: *5,000 Nights at the Opera* (1972).

Birmingham. Town in Warwickshire, England. Despite the enterprise of Granville Bantock in putting on the English première of Gluck's *Iphigénie en Aulide*, the city was for long dependent on touring companies. A performance of Raybould's *The Sumida River* in 1916 was followed by the première of Messager's *Monsieur Beaucaire* in 1919 and then a series of productions at the Repertory T. from 1920, when Sir Barry Jackson mounted *Così fan tutte, The Immortal Hour, Don Pasquale, Il mat-*

rimonio segreto, Don Giovanni, The Boatswain's Mate, and the première of *Fête galante*. Local amateur companies have contributed – the Barfield Opera Company with a number of lesser-known 19th-cent. works as well as one new work, Margaret More's *The Mermaid* (1951); the Midland Music Makers with some enterprising productions, including *William Tell, Prince Igor, Les Huguenots, Les Troyens, Ivan the Terrible, Masaniello, I Lombardi, La gazza ladra, Mosè, The Jacobin,* and the British première of *Die Feen*.

The Barber Institute, part of Birmingham University, has also staged some important productions, including the British première of Rameau's *Hippolyte et Aricie* (1965) and Haydn's *Orfeo* (1967), as well as performances of Handel's *Admetus*, Haydn's *Paris and Helen*, and Bizet's *Jolie Fille de Perth*.

Birtwistle, Harrison (*b* Accrington, 15 July 1934). English composer. Studied Manchester, with Richard Hall, and R.A.M. In 1967, with Peter Maxwell Davies, he founded the Pierrot Players with the object of giving performances of works, initially Schoenberg's *Pierrot Lunaire*, that were more in the region of music theatre than concert pieces. His first opera, *Punch and Judy* (1968), is an exceedingly unconventional treatment of the old children's puppet show, cast in semi-expressionist manner and including a costumed orchestra by the stage and other devices to blur the operatic conventions. *Down by the Greenwood Side* (1969) is a macabre piece of cabaret-style music theatre. One of the most original and gifted of contemporary English composers.

Bishop, Anna (orig. Ann Riviere) (*b* London, 9 Jan. 1810; *d* New York, 18 Mar. 1884). English soprano. Studied piano with Moscheles and singing with Henry *Bishop, whom she married in 1831. Début in concert April 1831. Toured with the harpist Bochsa in 1839; on her return she appeared at an operatic concert in costume at H.M.'s, after which she eloped to the continent with Bochsa, avoiding France where there was a warrant out for his arrest. After successful concert appearances in Scandinavia, Russia, and Austria, made her Italian début at Verona in 1843 and was hailed as 'La restoratrice del vero canto'. She was engaged by command of the King of the Two Sicilies as *prima donna assoluta* in Naples for the S.C. and Fondo Theatres, where she appeared 327 times in 20 operas over a period of 27 months. Verdi heard her in *I due foscari*, but refused to have her in *Alzira*: when she was suggested to Donizetti for *Caterina Cornaro* he replied, 'No, for Christ's sake, not la Bishop! Are you joking?' Mercadante, however, wrote *Il Vascello di Gama* for her, and the Pope was so charmed by her singing of an air by Palestrina that he conferred on her the Ancient and Noble

Order of Saint Cecilia. She returned to England 1846 and sang at Drury Lane in Balfe's *Maid of Artois*. N.Y. début 1847, Linda; 1850 sang title role in first U.S. *Martha*. Bochsa died of dropsy in Sydney in 1856 and she married Martin Schulz, a diamond merchant in N.Y., and continued her career, making many concert tours, including visits to the Far East, India, Australia, etc. Her last public appearance was in N.Y. in April 1883; and she died there. She was said to have had a brilliant technique, but to be wanting in expression.

Bishop, (Sir) Henry (Rowley) (*b* London, 18 Nov. 1786; *d* London, 30 Apr. 1855). English composer and conductor. Started working as a music seller when only 13, published some songs, later studied with Bianchi. His first operatic work was *The Circassian Bride* (1809), and though this was destroyed its success, and that of other pieces, led to him being appointed music director at C.G., 1810-24. Here he adapted a number of foreign operas, e.g. *Don Giovanni, Figaro, Barbiere*, and *Fidelio*, mercilessly rewriting portions and introducing music of his own, as was then fashionable. Moving to D.L., he produced among many other works *Aladdin* (1826) as an attempted rival attraction to Weber's *Oberon* at C.G.; he was also music director at Vauxhall. Most of his works consist of numbers interpolated into a spoken play, and in many cases 'operas' credited to him include only a few numbers, or even a single number. Even *Aladdin*, his most substantial work, includes spoken dialogue. He married Ann Riviere (see above) in 1831; knighted 1842.
Bibl: R. Northcott: *The Life of Sir Henry Bishop* (1920).

Bispham, David (*b* Philadelphia, 5 Jan. 1857; *d* New York, 2 Oct. 1921). American baritone. Studied Florence with Vannuccini and Milan with Lamperti. First appearance London in concert, 1890; following year stage début English Opera House, Longueville, *La Basoche* (Messager); D.L., 1892, Kurwenal; C.G. 1892-1902; N.Y., Met., 1896-1903, where he appeared in the first U.S. performances of Paderewski's *Manru* and Smyth's *Der Wald*. Great advocate of opera in English. (R)
Bibl: D. Bispham: *A Quaker Singer's Recollections* (1920).

Bizet, Georges (*b* Paris, 25 Oct. 1838; *d* Bougival, nr Paris, 3 June 1875). French composer. Teachers at the Conservatoire included Gounod. His earliest operatic essays stand in the first period of composition he later disavowed; of them perhaps *Le Docteur Miracle* (comp. 1856) and *Don Procopio* (comp. 1858-9, prod. 1906) are the most promising, containing passages of true originality as well as competent imitations of the best models (Donizetti

and Rossini chief among them). *Ivan IV* (comp. 1862-3, prod. 1946) has languished, though parts of it are familiar from use in later works. The first important opera was *Les Pêcheurs de perles* (1863), which while more widely derivative is also of greater originality and freedom, with some ravishing passages of the finest Bizet. *La Jolie Fille de Perth* (comp. 1886, prod. 1867), though still eclectic, shows an impressive advance, with increased dramatic command now joining a vein of refined lyricism. *La Coupe du Roi de Thule* (1868, surviving only in fragments) is said to advance still further, strikingly anticipating *Carmen*. Bizet completed his father-in-law Halévy's *Noé*, unpromisingly; and then a brief but intense concentration on opéra comique with *Calendal* (comp. 1870), *Clarissa Harlowe* (comp. 1870-1), and *Griséldis* (comp. 1870-1) led to *Djamileh* (comp. 1871, prod. 1872). This failed chiefly because of Bizet's too original treatment of a poor libretto. A lost operetta and *Don Rodrigue* (comp. 1873), the surviving fragment of which does not impress, preceded his last and greatest work, *Carmen* (comp. 1873-4, prod. 1875). Here at last was the perfect libretto for him. He was at his fullest mastery; the characterization is superb, the progress of the drama magnificently portrayed in music of unprecedented strength and colour. *Carmen* is the greatest of all opéras comiques.
Bibl: W. Dean: *Georges Bizet* (1948, 2/1965).

Bjoner, Ingrid (*b* Kraakstad, 8 Nov. 1927). Norwegian soprano. Studied Frankfurt, and Wiesbaden with Paul Lohmann. Début Oslo Radio, 1956 as Third Norn and Gutrune in *Götterdämmerung* opposite Flagstad, who engaged her for Norwegian National Opera 1957, where she made her stage début as Donna Anna. Wuppertal, 1957-9; Düsseldorf, 1959-61; Munich since 1960, where she sang Empress in *Frau ohne Schatten* at reopening of National T., recreated Daphne, and sang Isolde at 10th anniversary of opera's première there. London, C.G., 1967 Senta, Sieglinde, Leonore; N.Y., Met., 1961-7; Bayreuth, 1960, Freia, Helmwige, Gutrune. Munich since 1961. As well as Wagner and Strauss, repertory includes Iphigénie, Vitellia, Selika, Turandot, and Verdi roles. A lyric-dramatic soprano of much power and beauty. (R)

Björling, Jussi (orig. Johan) (*b* Stora Tuna, 5 Feb. 1911; *d* Stockholm 9 Sept. 1960). Swedish tenor. Taught by father and first sang in public when six. Member of Björling Male Quartet with father and two brothers. Studied Royal Opera School, Stockholm, with John Forsell and Tullio Voghera. Début Stockholm 1930, Lamplighter in *Manon Lescaut*; sang there regularly until 1939. Vienna 1936; Chicago 1937; London, C.G., 1939 and not again until 1960; member of Met., N.Y., 1938-60 (except during war years). Sang Italian, French, and Russian repertory, but (except for Mozart) not German. Had a warm and appealing voice and sang with excellent taste. Married soprano Anna-Lisa Berg, 1935, with whom he sometimes appeared. (R) His brother Karl Gustaf, known as **Gösta** (b 21 Sept. 1912; d 10 Oct. 1957), studied with Carpi in Milan and Marcantoni in Rome; début Göteborg 1937, and sang in Stockholm from 1940 until his death. (R) *Bibl:* B. Hagman (ed.): *Jussi Björling* (1960).

Björling, Sigurd (b Stockholm, 2 Nov. 1907). Swedish baritone. Studied with Louis Condé 1928-30, Stockholm Conservatory 1933-4 and Royal Opera School 1934-6 with Torsten Lennartson. Début Stockholm 1934, Billy Jackrabbit in *La fanciulla del West.* Encouraged to study Wagner roles by Leo Blech. London, C.G., 1951, Kurwenal, Amfortas, and Wotan; Bayreuth 1951; N.Y., Met., 1952-3. Married to the soprano Edith Oldrup. No relation to Jussi. (R)

Blacher, Boris (b Newchang, China, 6 Jan. 1903; d Berlin, 30 Jan. 1975). German composer. Despite great difficulties he pursued his studies rigorously, and after 1945 became recognized as one of Germany's most important composers and teachers. His brilliant intellect applied itself to the problem of original dramatic music in a dance drama *Fest im Süden*, some ballets, a scenic oratorio *Romeo und Julia* (after Shakespeare), a dramatic oratorio *Der Grossinquisitor* (after Dostoyevsky), and six operas – *Fürstin Tarakanova* (1945), the chamber opera *Die Flut* (1947), *Die Nachtschwalbe* (1948), *Preussisches Märchen* (1952), *Abstract Oper No. 1* (1953), *Rosamunde Floris* (1960). Librettist, with *Einem, of the latter's *Dantons Tod* and *Der Prozess.*

Blachut, Beno (b Ostrava–Vítkovice, 14 June 1913). Czech tenor. Studied Prague 1935-9. Début Olomouc 1938, Jeník. Prague National T. since 1941. Especially distinguished in works of Smetana, Dvořák, and Janáček. (R)

Blamont, François Colin de (b Versailles, 22 Nov. 1690; d Versailles, 14 Feb. 1760). French composer. As Court composer produced various works upholding the traditions of French operatic style; reinforced his views with a pamphlet *Essai sur les goûts anciens et modernes de la musique française* (1754) which appeared at the height of the *Guerre des Bouffons.

Bland, Maria Theresa (b Italy, 1769 ; d London, 15 Jan. 1838). English singer. Born of Italian-Jewish parents named Romanzini, as which she first appeared in public, 1773. Member of D.L. Company 1786-1826, excelling in operas of Storace, Arnold, etc. Her son **Charles** was the first Oberon in Weber's opera at C. G., 1826; and another son, **James** (1798-1861), was a successful bass-buffo.

Bleat. Vocal device whereby a single note is quickly reiterated with varied pressure of the breath. Also known as Goat's Trill (Ger. *Bockstriller;* Fr. *chévrotement;* It. *trillo caprino;* Sp. *trino de cabra*). P.F. Tosi, in his famous and authoritative *Opinioni de' cantori antichi e moderni* (1723), observes that a trill is *caprino* if its two notes are less than a semitone apart, or if the trill is sung with unequal speed or force. Spohr (*Violinschule*, 1832) describes the *Bockstriller* as a trill at the unison. It occurs in Monteverdi; and Wagner demands it of the tailors (because of the legend they narrate) in *Meistersinger*, Act 3, sc. 2.

Blech, Leo (b Aachen, 21 Apr. 1871; d Berlin, 24 Aug. 1958). German conductor and composer. Studied Berlin with Bargiel and Rudorff, then Humperdinck. Conductor, Aachen 1893-9; Deutsches T. Prague, 1899-1906; Berlin Royal Opera 1906-23 (Generalmusikdirektor from 1913). Toured U.S.A. 1923 with ensemble from Stä. O. After a short absence in Vienna and elsewhere, returned to Berlin as joint Generalmusikdirektor with Erich *Kleiber of the S., his appointment being terminated in 1937 because of his Jewish descent. Riga 1937-41; Stockholm from 1924 as guest, and regularly 1941-7, where his Wagner performances were greatly admired. Returned to Berlin as conductor of the Stä. O. 1949. He celebrated his 80th birthday by conducting in Berlin his *Das war ich* (Dresden, 1902) and *Versiegelt* (Hamburg, 1908). (R)

Bliss, (Sir) Arthur (b London, 2 Aug. 1891; d London, 27 Mar. 1975). English composer and conductor. The dramatic nature of Bliss's music was first fully revealed in his brilliant ballet scores; he did not turn to opera until *The Olympians* (1949). Though J.B. Priestley provided him with an original and imaginative subject for a Romantic opera, the work did not make its promised impact despite some fine music (especially in Act 2). Bliss's second opera was *Tobias and the Angel* (text by Christopher Hassall: B.B.C. TV, 1960). (R)

Blitzstein, Marc (b Philadelphia, 2 Mar. 1905; d Martinique, 22 Jan. 1964). American composer. Studied with Ziloti, Boulanger, and Schoenberg, eventually abandoning his early experimental style because of his belief that music should readily communicate to the widest possible audience. Turning to the stage, he wrote a number of operas, among them *The Cradle Will Rock* (1937), *No for an Answer* (1940), and *Regina* (1949). He was also responsible for a version of Weill's *Dreigroschenoper* (1954).

Bloch, Ernest (b Geneva, 24 July 1880; d Portland, U.S.A., 15 July 1959). American composer of Swiss birth. His Jewish origins have had the largest emotional, and to some extent technical, influence on his style. His only opera is *Macbeth* (1910); written in a style owing something to *Pelléas* and to Dukas, it has been highly praised for its intelligent and often dramatic handling of the subject. (R)

Blockx, Jan (*b* Antwerp, 25 Jan. 1851; *d* Kapellenbos, nr Antwerp, 26 May 1912). Belgian composer. The most gifted Flemish composer of his day; wrote 8 operas in which his Romantic tendencies and his feeling for his native folklore are shown. They are: the 1-act comedy *Iets vergeten* (To Forget Something, 1876); the 4-act *Maître Martin* (1892); his first major work, the brilliantly successful *Herbergprinses* (The Princess of the Inn, 1896); the less successful 3-act *Thyl Uilenspiegel* (1900); the popular 3-act *De Bruid der zee* (The Bride of the Sea, 1901); *De Kapel* (The Chapel, 1903); and *Baldie* (1908, rev. 1912 as *Liefdelied*), which was intended to complete a triptych of works, with *Herbergprinses* and *De Bruid der Zee*, on Flemish national life, but did not match the success of its partners.
Bibl: F. Blockx: *Jan Blockx* (1943).

Blomdahl, Karl-Birger (*b* Växjö, 19 Oct. 1916; *d* Kungsängen, 16 June 1968). Swedish composer and conductor. Studied Stockholm with Rosenberg and Tor Mann. His first opera, *Aniara* (1958), made a great impression for its imaginative and technically resourceful use of modern methods, and was widely staged in the years following its première; it won the first Nordiska Radets Prize, 1965. His only other opera was *Herr von Hancken* (1965), a black comedy; he left an unfinished opera, *Sagan om den stora Datan.*

Blondchen (or **Blonde**) Constanze's maid (sop.) in Mozart's *Die Entführung aus dem Serail.*

Bloomington. Town in Indiana, U.S.A. The Opera School of the University, under the direction of Dean Bain, succeeded during the 1960s in attracting a distinguished teaching staff, including several retired singers, among them Margaret Harshaw, Virginia McWatters, Charles Kullman, and Marko Rothmüller, the producer Hans Busch, and the designer C.M. Cristini. The yearly opera production of the 1950s expanded into regular performances spread out over the whole academic year and open to the public, and included *L'incoronazione di Poppea, Deidamia, La pietra del paragone, Comte Ory, Rosenkavalier, Luisa Miller, The Carmelites,* and even *Die Walküre* and annual performances of *Parsifal.* The Indiana University Arts Centre (cap. 1,500) opened in Jan. 1972 with *Don Giovanni.*

Blow, John (*b* Newark, bapt. ? 23 Feb. 1649; *d* London, 1 Oct. 1708). English composer. *Venus and Adonis* (*c*1685), his only work for the stage, is an important predecessor of Purcell's *Dido*

and Aeneas, and has a claim to be the earliest true English opera.

Bluebeard, A character in Perrault's *Contes de ma mère l'oye* (Mother Goose's Tales, 1697), who attempted to kill his latest wife Fatima for unlocking the forbidden door behind which lay the the bodies of his previously murdered wives. Grétry's *Raoul Barbe-bleu* (1789) was the first of many Bluebeard operas, a number of which give the legend new interpretations. They include Offenbach's *Barbe-Bleue* (1940), Dukas's *Ariane et Barbe-Bleue* (1907), Bartók's *Duke Bluebeard's Castle* (1918), Rezniček's *Ritter Blaubart* (1920), and Frazzi's *L'Ottava moglie di Barbablù* (1940). According to some versions of the legend, Mélisande was one of Bluebeard's escaped wives, hence her traumatic state at the beginning of Debussy's opera. Limnander's *Château de la Barbe Bleue* (1851) is not connected with the legend.

Bluebeard's Castle See *Duke Bluebeard's Castle.*

Boatswain's Mate, The. Opera in 1 act by Ethel Smyth; text by composer, after W.W. Jacobs's story. Prod. London, Shaftesbury, 28 Jan. 1916, with Buckman, Roy, Pounds, Wynn, Ranalow, cond. Smyth. The composer's most successful opera.

Bocca chiusa (*It* closed mouth, i.e. humming). The technique has been employed for teaching purposes, to encourage the pupil to produce tone while conserving the breath, and Caruso used to study his roles by humming them before using the voice proper. The most famous use in opera is the Humming Chorus in Act 2 of Puccini's *Madama Butterfly.*

Bockelmann, Rudolf (*b* Bodenteich, nr Luneburg, 2 Apr. 1892; *d* Dresden, 9 Oct. 1958). German bass-baritone. Educated Celle and Leipzig, studied singing with Oscar Lassner 1920-3. Début Leipzig 1921, Herald (*Lohengrin*); Hamburg 1926-32; Berlin, S.O. 1932-45. Appeared regularly at Bayreuth 1928-42, and C.G. 1929-30 and 1934-8; Chicago Civic Opera 1930-2. An outstandingly fine Hans Sachs and Wotan. His Nazi sympathies prevented him from resuming his career after the war and apart from a few appearances in Hamburg and the German provinces he devoted his time to teaching. A German Kammersänger. (R)
Bibl: Berndt v. Wessling: *Verachtet mir die Meister nicht!* (1963).

Bockstriller. See *Bleat.*

Bodanzky, Artur (*b* Vienna, 16 Dec. 1877; *d* New York, 23 Nov. 1939). Austrian conductor. Studied Vienna Conservatory and later with Zemlinsky. Violinist at Vienna, H., and from 1902 to 1904 Mahler's assistant there. After appointments in Prague and Mannheim, he conducted the first performances of *Parsifal* in England at C.G. in 1914, and the following year succeeded Alfred Hertz as chief German conductor at the N.Y., Met:, which position he held till his death (except for the 1928-9 season). He prepared new editions of *Oberon*, *Fidelio*, and *Boccaccio* for New York. Wagnerians were always annoyed by the notorious 'Bodanzky cuts' in *The Ring* and other operas. (R)

Bogianckino, Massimo (*b* 10 Nov. 1922). Italian pianist and administrator. Studied Rome, Santa Cecilia, with Rossi, Casella, and Mortari. After a short career as a pianist, taught at the Carnegie Institute, Pittsburgh, and the Rossini Conservatory, Pesaro. Artistic director Accademia Filarmonica, Rome, 1960-3; artistic director Rome O., 1963-8; administrator and artistic director Spoleto Festival 1969-72; artistic director, Milan, Sc., 1972-5: Florence, C., from 1975. Wrote a study of the French and Italian theatres during the Baroque period and a monograph on Scarlatti.

Bohème, La (The Bohemian Girl). Opera in 4 acts by Puccini; text by Giacosa and Illica, after Henri Murger's novel *Scènes de la vie de Bohème* (serially, 1847-9). Prod. Turin, T.R., 1 Feb. 1896, with Cesira-Ferrani, Gorga, cond. Toscanini; Manchester 22 Apr. 1897, with Esty, Cunningham; Los Angeles 14 Oct. 1897, with Montanari, Agostini.

Also: opera in 4 acts by Leoncavallo; text by composer, after Murger. Prod. Venice, F., 6 May 1897, with Frandin, Storchio, cond. Pome; N.Y., Columbia University, 31 Jan. 1960, with Lo Monaco, Simeone, Polakoff, Ottaviano, cond. Robinson; London, Camden Town Hall, 12 May 1970, with Morgan, Cryer, Collins, Lyon, cond. Gover.

Puccini's opera was at first a comparative failure; only after its third production (Palermo, 1896) were its merits fully recognized. Leoncavallo's work, which keeps more strictly to the events and in some ways the characters of the novel, was then wholly overshadowed, but in recent years it has aroused new interest.

In Puccini's opera, the four Bohemians share a Paris attic; they are the poet Rodolfo (ten.), the painter Marcello (bar.), the musician Schaunard (bar.), and the philosopher Colline (bass). Rodolfo meets their neighbour Mimì (sop.) and they fall in love; at the same time Marcello recovers his old lover Musetta (sop.) from a wealthy admirer. But the relationship of both couples develops stormily, and the Bohemians resume their studio life. Mimì, dying of consumption, is brought in by Musetta: they try to save her, but it is too late. Also opera *La Petite Bohème* by Hirschmann (1905).

Bohemian Girl, The. Opera in 3 acts by Balfe; text by Alfred Bunn, after the ballet-pantomime *The Gypsy* by St Georges. Prod. London, D.L.,

27 Nov. 1843; N.Y., 1844. The plot, a confused tale of love, gypsies, mistaken identity, and false accusations, did not prevent the opera being very popular up to about 1930. Revived by Beecham, C.G. 1951.

Böhm, Karl (*b* Graz, 28 Aug. 1894). Austrian conductor. Originally studied law, then music at Graz Conservatory and Vienna. In 1917 coach at Graz, and then in 1918 second and 1920 first conductor; début 1917 *Trompeter von Säckingen*. Recommended by Karl Muck to Walter who engaged him for Munich in 1921. Generalmusikdirektor, Darmstadt 1927-31; Hamburg 1931-3; Dresden 1934-42; Vienna 1942-4, and Generalmusikdirektor of rebuilt house 1954; resigned a year later following criticism of his long absences abroad. London début with Dresden Company at C.G. 1936; returned 1977. N.Y., Met., from 1957. Regularly at Salzburg and Italian theatres. Bayreuth 1962-70. With Krauss, the leading Strauss conductor in the 1930s and 1940s, directing premières of *Daphne* and *Die schweigsame Frau*. Also distinguished in Mozart and the modern repertory, including *Wozzeck*. (R)

Böhme, Kurt (*b* Dresden 5 May 1908). German bass. Studied Dresden Conservatory with Kluge. Début Dresden 1930, Caspar; Dresden 1930-50; Munich since 1950. London, C.G., 1936 with Dresden Company, and 1956-70. N.Y., Met., 1954-7. Has sung all over Europe and in South America. An outstanding Baron Ochs, and highly regarded for his Wagner interpretations. (R)

Bohnen, Michael (*b* Cologne, 2 May 1887; Berlin, 26 Apr. 1965). German bass-baritone. Studied with Fritz Steinbach and Schulz-Dornburg. Début Düsseldorf 1910, Caspar; Wiesbaden 1912-13; Berlin, H. 1911, 1914, 1916-19. N.Y., Met., 1922-32; Berlin, Deutsches Opernhaus, 1933-45. Intendant of the Stä. O., Berlin, 1945-7. Also sang at Bayreuth in 1914 (Hunding and Daland); London, D.L., in the Beecham season that year as Ochs and Sarastro, and at Salzburg. His large voice, of extensive range, enabled him to cope with both bass and baritone roles. As a gifted and individual actor, he was attracted by roles that lay outside the normal repertory. While a member of the Met. sang Francesco in Schillings's *Mona Lisa* and Jonny in Křenek's *Jonny spielt auf*. (R)

Boieldieu, Adrien (orig. François-Adrien) (*b* Rouen, 16 Dec. 1775; *d* Jarcy, 8 Oct. 1834). French composer. Studied Rouen with Cordonnier and Broche. Success came at 18 with the opéra comique *La Fille coupable* (1793), followed by *Rosalie et Myrza* (1795). In Paris from 1796, produced a number of operas showing a fluent but imitative talent; the most famous was *Le Calife de Bagdad* (1800). He replied to

Cherubini's reproach, after a performance of this work, 'Are you not ashamed of such an undeserved success?', by offering himself as a pupil; and *Ma Tante Aurore* (1803) shows the benefits of this training. In 1804 he went to St Petersburg, succeeding Sarti as Court composer, and while there wrote about an opera a year, also greatly improving operatic standards, before returning to Paris in 1810. Quickly re-establishing his popularity, he continued it with *Jean de Paris* (1812). His masterpiece is *La Dame blanche* (1825). One of the most striking French Romantic operas of the decade, it owes something to Weber (who greatly admired it) and exercised an influence on Wagner especially in *Der fliegende Holländer* and *Lohengrin*. Wagner was also a great admirer of Boieldieu's next opera, *Les Deux nuits* (1829), whose chorus 'La belle nuit' was, as Berlioz pointed out, a source for the *Lohengrin* Bridal March. In both works, the traditions of earlier Romantic opera (e.g. Gaveston as a raging villain in the line of Dourlinsky, Pizarro, and Caspar) are turned to new expressive effect, especially by means of an individual vein of chromatic harmony and skilful orchestration; with them, Boieldieu reaches the peak of his achievement. His health, affected by his Russian years, then deteriorated into tuberculosis, and the 1830 revolution removed him from his official positions. His son by his second wife, the singer Jenny Philis-Bertin, was **Adrien-Louis-Victor Boieldieu** (1816-83), who studied with his father and had, with *Marguerite* (1838), a success that subsequent works did not maintain.

Bibl: G. Favre: *Boieldieu, sa vie et son oeuvre* (Paris, 1944-5).

Boito, Arrigo (orig. Enrico) (*b* Padua, 24 Feb. 1842; *d* Milan, 10 June 1918). Italian composer, librettist (sometimes as Tobia Gorrio), and critic. Son of an Italian painter and a Polish countess; studied Milan with Mazzucato, and there formed a lifelong friendship with Faccio. Together they went to Paris, where Boito first met Verdi, began to consider Faust and Nero as operatic subjects, and wrote the libretto for Faccio's *Amleto* (1862). Back in Milan, he associated himself with the artistic reform movement known as the Scapigliatura, and served under Garibaldi. In 1868 *Mefistofele* was performed at Milan, Sc.; it failed, partly through its length and the inadequacy of the performance. Depressed, Boito turned to writing librettos for other composers and to translating operas (incl. *Freischütz*, *Rienzi*, and *Ruslan and Lyudmila*). A revised version of *Mefistofele* was successful in 1875; further revisions were made and performed in 1876 and 1881.

The revision of *Simon Boccanegra* for revival in 1881 pleased the hitherto hostile Verdi, and led to work on *Otello* and hence to the friendship that Boito regarded as the most important event of his life; after *Falstaff* had followed, he began work on *King Lear* and even wrote part of the opening scene. Verdi had meanwhile urged Boito to continue his own musical career with *Nerone*; but he never completed it, and it was eventually posthumously performed in a version edited by Toscanini and Vincenzo Tommasini.

Boito's intelligence and skill as a librettist have been widely praised. He served many composers excellently, and furnished Verdi with the brilliant (though by no means flawless) text for *Otello* and the incomparable one for *Falstaff*: the occasional misjudgements in the tragedy, such as the distortion of the character of Iago, are absent from the comedy, in which Boito's verbal brilliance and elegant wit are supreme. His texts for his own two operas are ambitious, too much so for his own musical powers and his creative resolve, and the many revisions and procrastinations reveal his difficulty in realizing his lifelong vision of the conflicting attractions of virtue and evil. His own music is capable of grandeur, but it is a quality he has difficulty in sustaining and it frequently degenerates into mechanical gestures. As a critic, he was a keen but discriminating Wagnerian, latterly unenthusiastic, and champion of Meyerbeer and Verdi. Other librettos include *La falce* (Catalani) and *La gioconda* (Ponchielli).

Bibl: P. Nardi: *Vita di Arrigo Boito* (1942, 2/1944).

Bologna. Town in Emilia, Italy. The first opera to be heard there was Cavalieri's *La disperazione di Fileno* in 1600 at the T. da Casa Bantivoglio. The first public performance of opera was Giacobbi's *Andromeda* in 1610 at the T. del Publico, and the first public theatre was the T. Formigliari. Operas were also performed at the Marsigli (1710-1825) and the Malvezzi (1653-1745). The most famous prima donna of the period was Maria Maddalena *Musi, nicknamed La Mignatto (the leech). The present home of opera in Bologna is the T. Comunale, designed by Antonio Galli Bibiena; it opened in 1763 with Gluck's *Trionfo di Clelia*. The Comunale under Angelo Mariani, Martucci, and Toscanini championed Wagner's cause in Italy, and the first performances in Italy of *Fliegende Holländer, Lohengrin, Tannhäuser, Tristan und Isolde* and *Parsifal* were all given there. In 1871 the Comunale gave the first Italian *Don Carlos*, and in 1875 welcomed Boito's *Mefistofele* after its Scala fiasco. Since the World War II the Comunale's repertory has been one of the most adventurous in Italy.

Bibl: L. Trezzini: *Due secoli di vita musicale: storia del Teatro Comunale di Bologna 1763-1966* (1966).

Bolshakov, Nikolay (Arkadyevich) (*b* Kharkov, 23 Nov. 1874; *d* Leningrad, 20 June 1958). Russian tenor. Studied St Petersburg with Pryanishnikov. Début with Kharkov company, St Petersburg 1899. Member of the Maryinsky Company 1906-29; guest appearances London (1913), Paris, Berlin, Barcelona. Roles included Hermann, Lensky, Vaudémont (*Yolanta*), Don José, Faust, Pinkerton, Rienzi, the Finn (*Ruslan*), and other Russian roles. Taught Leningrad Conservatory 1923-53, professor from 1935. (R)

Bolshoy Theatre. See *Moscow*.

Bomarzo. Opera in 2 acts by Ginastera; text by Manuel Mujica Lainez, after his novel of the same name (1962). Prod. Opera Society of Washington, D.C., 19 May 1967 with Penagos, Simon, Turner, Novoa, Torigi, cond. Rudel; London, Col., 3 Nov. 1976, with Pring, Clark, Chard, cond. Lovett. The opera takes place in 16th-cent. Italy and tells in a series of flashbacks of the frustrations of the hunchback Duke of Bomarzo.

Bonci, Alesandro (*b* Cesena, 10 Feb. 1870; *d* Viterbo, 10 Aug. 1940). Italian tenor. Studied Pesaro, and Paris with Delle Sedie. Début Parma 1896, Fenton. Engagements all over Italy, including Sc., followed. London, C.G., 1900; N.Y., Manhattan Opera, 1906. Appeared intermittently at C.G. until 1908, and in America until 1925. Continued to sing in Italy until 1935. Was a singer of taste and refinement, greatly admired by Lilli Lehmann. At his best in Bellini, Rossini, and Donizetti. (R)

Bondeville, Emmanuel (*b* Rouen, 29 Oct. 1898). French composer. His Molière opera buffa, *L'École des maris* (1935) was popular in France; he followed this with a Flaubert opera, *Madame Bovary* (1951), and with *Antony and Cleopatra* (1972, based on Hugo's translation of Shakespeare). His intelligent appreciation of the operatic possibilities in such distinguished but widely contrasted authors has been highly praised in France, and his discreet but well-judged music found dramatically very effective. Director of the O. C. 1948-51, of the O. 1951-9.

Bondini, Marianna (*b* Dresden, 18 Oct. 1780; *d* Paris, 25 Oct. 1813). Italian soprano, daughter of the above. Studied Bologna with Sartorini. Début Paris, 1807; sang Susanna in the first performance in Italian of *Figaro* in Paris same year. Mentioned by Stendhal in his biographies of Haydn and Metastasio. Married the bass **Luigi Barilli** (1767-1824), who sang with her in Paris and was the manager of the Italian company at the Odéon.

Bondini, Pasquale (*b* ?; *d* Bruneck, Tyrol, 30 Oct. 1789). Italian bass. Director of the Italian Opera in Prague 1781-8. *Figaro* was performed there with tremendous success, to Mozart's great happiness, in Dec. 1786, as a result of which Bondini requested his next opera, *Don Giovanni*, and produced it there, 29 Oct. 1787. He married the soprano Caterina *Saporiti.

Boninsegna, Celestina (*b* Reggio Emilia, 26 Feb. 1877; *d* Milan, 14 Feb. 1947). Italian soprano. Without any formal vocal or musical study, made her début at Reggio Emilia when 15, Norina. Then went to Pesaro Conservatory; second début, Fano 1896, Gilda. Her voice was a dramatic soprano of great power and range, and her *mezza voce* singing and phrasing were much admired. London, C.G., autumn seasons 1904 and 1905, Aida, Leonora (*Trovatore*), and Amelia. N.Y., Met., 1906-7. After retiring from the stage she taught; pupils included Margherita Grandi. (R)

Bonn. Town in Westphalia, capital of West Germany. Travelling opera companies began visiting the town towards the end of the 17th cent. In 1745 there was a visit from Pietro Mingotti's troupe, under Locatelli, then in 1757 and 1764 from Angelo Mingotti's troupe. Beethoven's father organized Italian performances 1767-71, including *La serva padrona*, and both he and Beethoven's grandfather were involved in them. The theatre was opened in 1778. Neefe worked in the town, 1779, and the repertory included opera buffa and opéra comique as well as Singspiel. Opera is now given in the Stadttheater, opened 1965 (cap. 896).

Bononcini, Giovanni Battista (*b* Modena, 18 July 1670; *d* ?Vienna, 9 Aug. 1747). Italian composer. His first operatic ventures were in Rome, Vienna, and Milan; but in 1720 he arrived in London, where he was welcomed in high circles, receiving a salary from the Duke of Marlborough. Many of his operas were produced there before he returned to Vienna, where he apparently died in obscurity. He was a skilful musician who suffered by the comparison with Handel, and (it is said) from his own arrogant disposition. His operas did, however, satisfy the increasingly sentimental taste of the day. His brother **Antonio Maria Bononcini** (1677-1726) had an early success with *Camilla* (1696), and his many other works were popular in Italy in his own day.

Bonynge, Richard (*b* Epping, N.S.W., 29 Sept. 1930). Australian conductor. Studied Sydney and London, and originally planned to become a pianist. Début Vancouver 1963, *Faust*; London, C.G., from 1964; N.Y., Met., from 1970; also conducted extensively in Europe and USA. Music director, Australian O., 1975. Married to Joan *Sutherland; has specialized in the bel canto and French repertories. (R)

Bordeaux. Town in Gironde, France. Opera is first recorded in 1688, and French singers

began making regular appearances soon after. Francoeur's *Pirame et Thysbé* was given in 1729. In 1735 Mlle Dujardin built an opera house for her company in the Municipal Gardens, and in 1752 an Académie Royal de Musique was founded, with a company that included 10 soloists. The Grand T. Municipal, one of the finest opera houses in France, was opened in 1780 (cap. 1,158). The designer was Victor Louis. Damaged in the Revolution, it was restored in 1799. During the 19th cent. it increased in importance, and companies from Paris played there regularly. The theatre was modernized in 1938. Vanni Marcoux was director 1948-51. Premières in modern times include that of Bizet's *Ivan IV* (1951) and the first French *Mathis der Maler* (1963). During the 19th cent. there were also four flourishing operetta theatres. The Bordeaux Festival (founded 1950) includes opera.
Bibl: J. Latreyte: *Le Grand Théâtre de Bordeaux* (1977).

Bordogni, Giulio Marco (*b* Gazzaniga, 23 Jan. 1789; *d* Paris, 31 July 1856). Italian tenor. Studied with Mayr, début Milan, T. Re, 1813 in *Tancredi*. After appearances in other Milan theatres, including Sc., he settled in Paris in 1819, where he took part in the first French perfs. of Paer's *Agnese* and Mercadante's *Elisa e Claudio* and in the operas of Rossini. Admired by Cherubini, who appointed him Professor of singing at the Conservatoire in 1820. He retired from the stage in 1833 and continued to teach privately. His many pupils included Sontag, Cinti-Damoreau, and Mario.

Bordoni, Faustina (*b* Venice, c1695; *d* Venice, 4 Nov. 1781). Italian soprano. Studied with F. Gasperini and B. Marcello. A brilliant début in 1716 in Pollarolo's *Ariodante* led to her becoming known as 'The New Siren'. After her wide successes in Italy, Munich, and Vienna, Handel brought her to London in 1726, where she delighted all with her impeccable technique, intelligence, and delightful presence – all except Cuzzoni, with whom she had a famous quarrel (see *Beggar's Opera*) and with whom she sharply divided London's popular favour. She returned to Venice, where she married *Hasse. A fine portrait of her was painted by Rosalba Carriera. Opera on her, *Faustina Hasse* by Louis Schubert (1879).

Borgatti, Giuseppe (*b* Cento, 17 Mar. 1871; *d* Reno, Lago Maggiore, 18 Oct. 1950). Italian tenor. Studied Bologna. Début Castelfranco Veneto 1892, Faust. In 1896 created the title-role of *Andrea Chénier* at Milan, Sc., and three years later, after singing Lohengrin and Walther, was invited by Toscanini to sing Siegfried at Milan Sc. where he became Italy's finest Heldentenor. He sang widely in Europe and South America but did not appear at C.G.

or the N.Y. Met. Retired from the stage in 1914 owing to failing eyesight, but continued to sing in concerts until 1928. (R)

Borghi-Mamo, Adelaide (*b* Bologna, 9 Aug. 1826; *d* Bologna, 28 Sept. 1901). Italian mezzo-soprano. On the advice of Pasta and Donzelli studied for the stage with Festa. Début Urbino 1843, in Mercadante's *Il giuramento*. Sang with great success all over Europe including Paris (1854-60) and London (1860). Created roles in operas by Halévy, David, Mercadante, etc. Married tenor Michele Mamo 1849. Her daughter **Erminia** (1855-1941) was born in Paris, a few hours after her mother had sung Azucena in a perf. of *Trovatore*. She studied with her mother and was chosen by Boito to sing Margherita and Elena in the revised *Mefistofele* at Bologna 1875.

Borgioli, Armando (*b* Florence, 19 Mar. 1898; *d* nr Codogno, 20 Jan. 1945) Italian baritone. Début Milan, T. Carcano, 1925, Amonasro (*Aida*); London, C.G., 1927-39, and from 1931 to 1935 sang at the N.Y. Met. A famous Verdi baritone and Barnaba, Jack Rance, and Enrico. Killed in an air attack on a train taking him from Milan to Modena. (R)

Borgioli, Dino (*b* Florence, 15 Feb. 1891; *d* Florence 12 Sept. 1960). Italian tenor. Studied with Eugenio Giachetti at Florence. Début Milan, T. Corso, as Arturo in *I Puritani*, 1914. Engaged by Melba for her farewell tour of Australia. Début London, C.G., 1925 as Edgardo (*Lucia*). Regular visitor to C.G. until 1939, Gly., Salzburg, San Francisco, etc. Much admired as a Rossini and Mozart singer and for his elegance and good taste. In 1949 was appointed vocal director of the *New London Opera Company and produced for them *La Bohème* and *Il barbiere di Siviglia*. (R)

Bori, Lucrezia (orig. Lucrecia Borja y Gonzalez de Riancho) (*b* Valencia, 24 Dec. 1887; *d* New York, 14 May 1960). Spanish soprano. Educated in a convent, she did not begin her vocal training until she was 20 (Milan, under Vidal). Début Rome, T. Adriano, 1908, Micaëla. Sang with Caruso in Paris as Manon 1910; first Italian Octavian, Milan 1911; American début at the N.Y. Met. as Manon Lescaut 1912. Her career was threatened in 1915 by a throat operation, but after further study she was able to return to the stage, Monte Carlo 1919. Reappeared at the Met. in 1921 and remained a member of the company until her retirement in 1936. Considered one of the greatest stylists of her day. Never sang in England. (R)

Borisenko, Vera (orig. Veronica) (Ivanovna) (*b* Bolshaya Nemka, 16 Jan. 1918). Russian mezzo. Studied Minsk 1938-40; Kiev 1943, with Evtushenko. Sverdlovsk 1941-5; Kiev 1945-6; Moscow, B., from 1946 (except 1963-5). Roles

57

include Lyubava (*Sadko*), Lyubasha (*Tsar's Bride*), Marfa, Carmen. Has appeared in Austria and England. (R)

Boris Godunov. Opera in 4 acts, with a prologue, by Mussorgsky; text by composer, after Pushkin's drama *The Comedy of the Distress of the Muscovite State, of Tsar Boris, and of Grishka Otrepiev* (1826), and Karamzin's *History of the Russian Empire* (1829). Original version comp. 1868-9, rejected by St Petersburg Opera 1870. Three scenes of composer's revision (1871) prod. St Petersburg, charity perf., 17 Feb. 1873, with Petrov (as Varlaam), Komisarzhevsky, Platonova; whole opera (with further minor revisions) 8 Feb. 1874, with Melnikov as Boris and same cast, cond. Nápravník. Banned after 25 performances, revived after composer's death in Rimsky-Korsakov's first revised edition, St Petersburg 10 Dec 1896. Rimsky's second version (1906-8), prod. Paris, O., 19 May 1908; Moscow, B., 17 Oct. 1908; N.Y., Met., 19 Mar. 1913, with Didur, cond. Toscanini; London, D.L., 24 June 1913, with Shalyapin. Original version first performed abroad, London, S.W., 30 Sept. 1935, with Stear. This has 7 scenes – 4 from Pushkin, 2 devised by Mussorgsky from indications in the play , l developed from two separate scenes in it. Other versions by Meligailis (Riga, 1924) and Shostakovich (Leningrad, 4 Nov. 1959).
1. Boris (bass) has murdered the young Dmitry, heir to the throne, and is pretending to decline the crown himself. His agents incite the crowd to persuade him to 'relent'. 2. Though plagued by guilt, Boris goes to be crowned. 3. In his cell the old monk Pimen (bass) is concluding a history of Russia; with him is the novice Grigory (ten), who resolves to avenge Dmitry. 4. Grigory, who claims to be Dmitry, with two other friars, Varlaam (bass), and Missail (ten), reaches an inn on the Lithuanian border. Grigory is identified but escapes the pursuing soldiers. 5. To Boris in his rooms, word is brought by his councillor Shuisky (ten.) of the pretender in Lithuania. To reassure him on the death of Dmitry, Shuisky recounts the murder, which throws the guilt-racked Tsar into a state of hallucination. 6. Outside St Basil's Cathedral in Moscow the people begin to believe in the right of the false Dmitry. A Simpleton (ten.) robbed of a groat asks Boris to repeat his murder on the robbers; Boris prevents his arrest, and asks for prayer, but the Simpleton refuses and falls to mending his shoes with a song for poor Russia. 7. In the Council Hall an edict against the pretender is being read when Boris breaks in distraught and collapses dead.
In his second version Mussorgsky made considerable additions and alterations, and arranged the scenes as follows.
Prologue: 1 and 2. Act 1:3 and 4. Act2:5. Act 3

(recast): Scene 1 – Dmitry's lover Marina sits in her father's Polish castle dreaming of when she will rule Russia, and Rangoni (bass) pleads the Catholic cause; Scene 2 – Marina (mezzo) joins Dmitry in the gardens, and she persuades him not to give up his ambitions. Act 4:7 and an extra scene in the Kromy Forest, in which the people are in revolt against Boris; the pretender passes *en route* for Moscow, leaving the Simpleton singing sadly for Russia as in the now discarded 6. The order of these last two scenes is frequently reversed in order to allow the protagonist the final curtain; the counter argument holds the protagonist to be, in fact, the Russian people. A revival at C.G. 1958, with Christoff, used all these scenes, as did that at the Met. in 1957. Both reverted to the original orchestration. Also opera by Mattheson (1710).

Borkh, Inge (orig. Ingeborg Simon) (*b* Mannheim, 26 May 1917). Swiss soprano. Début Linz 1937, as actress. Two years later went to Italy to study singing with Muratti in Milan, and then at the Mozarteum, Salzburg. Début Lucerne 1940, Czipra (*Zigeunerbaron*). Engagements in Switzerland until 1952 when her performance of Magda Sorel caused a sensation and led to engagements in Germany (1952) and America (1953). Edinburgh 1952, Leonore; London, R.F.H; with Stuttgart Opera, 1955, Elektra; N.Y., Met., 1958; C.G, 1959, Salome; 1967 Dyer's wife in *Frau ohne Schatten.* Renowned for Lady Macbeth and Elektra. In 1977 began career as *chanteuse* and straight actress. (R)

Borodin, Alexander (Porfiryevich) (*b* St Petersburg, 12 Nov. 1833; *d* St Petersburg, 27 Feb. 1887). Russian composer. Borodin finished only one opera, a pastiche *The Bogatyrs* (1867); material from *The Tsar's Bride* was used in other works; the solitary Act 4 of *Mlada* (1872) has never been performed; his masterpiece, *Prince Igor* (1869-70, 1874-87), was prepared for publication by Rimsky-Korsakov and Glazunov and produced in 1890. If *Boris Godunov* is Russia's greatest operatic tragedy, *Prince Igor* (together with *A Life for the Tsar*) is her epic, filled with historical splendour, noble attitudes, lyrical outpourings, and the exhilarating clash of Russian patriotic feeling with the Oriental brilliance of the Polovtsians. *Bibl:* S. Dianin: *Borodin* (1955, Eng. trans., 1963).

Boronat, Olimpia (*b* Genoa, 1867; *d* Warsaw, 1934). Italian soprano. Studied in Milan and made her début in Genoa or Naples in 1885. After appearances in Spain, Portugal, and South America, was invited to appear at St Petersburg in 1894, where she became a great favourite. Married into the Polish aristocracy and abandoned the stage between 1896 and 1902. She then sang again in Russia, and in 1909 returned to sing in Italy after a long absence. She possessed a beautiful limpid voice, a flawless technique, and was a consummate musician. Her great roles were Rosina, Violetta, Elvira in *I Puritani,* and Ophélie in *Hamlet.* After retiring from the stage she established a school of singing in Warsaw. (R)

Borosini, Francesco (*b* Modena, *c*1690; *d* ?). Italian tenor. Best known for his successful appearances in Handel's operas in London, beginning with *Tamerlano* in 1724.

Bortnyansky, Dmitry (Stepanovich) (*b* Glukhanov, 1751; *d* St Petersburg, 10 Oct. 1825). Russian composer. Studied with Galuppi, whom he followed to Italy. His *Creonte* and *Alcide* were prod. Venice 1776, and *Quinto Fabio* Modena 1778. Back in Russia, he was responsible for bringing many new Russian singers to St Petersburg, and composed for the Grand Duke Paul (later Paul I) the French operas *Le Faucon* (The Falcon, 1786), *La Fête du seigneur* (The Lord's Feast, 1786 or -7), and *Le Fils rival* (The Rival Son, 1787). Though elegantly written, these lack any national colouring: like others of his day, Bortnyansky was concerned to learn from the best Italian models rather than found more than the beginnings of an original Russian school. His church music was edited by Tchaikovsky (1881).
Bibl: B. Dobrokhotov: *D. S. Bortnyansky* (1950).

Boschi, Giuseppe (*b* Viterbo, ? ; *d* ?). Italian bass, much admired for his Handel performances in London between 1719 and 1728.

Boston. Town in Mass., U.S.A. The first opera heard in Boston was *Love in a Village,* July 1769, given in a concert performance owing to the authorities having banned public stage performances in 1750. The first stage performance was *The Farmer* (a ballad opera) in July 1794. Opera in English was the rule up to the 1850s when touring companies began to visit the city. In 1855 Grisi and Mario sang in Boston for the first time, and in 1860 Patti sang the first Rosina of her career there. The Mapleson Company began to visit Boston in 1878 and Grau's French Company in 1879. During the 1880s and 1890s the Boston Ideal Opera Company, the Theodore Thomas American Company, and the Castle Square Company all gave seasons in Boston.

In November 1909 the Boston Opera Company, for which the Boston Opera House was specially built, began its short but spectacular career (516 perfs. of 51 operas) with *La gioconda* (Nordica in title role). Under the management of Henry Russell, who took the company to Paris in 1914, Boston enjoyed five magnificent seasons during which the company included Bori, Garden, Destinn, Melis, Georgette Leblanc, Dalmores, Clément, Mura-

tore, and Vanni Marcoux. Weingartner made his American début in 1912 conducting *Tristan.* The company collapsed through lack of funds in 1914. In 1915 and 1916 the Boston Grand Opera Company gave two seasons, with many of the singers of Russell's company. Then followed nine seasons organized by the Boston Opera Association, which brought the Chicago Opera each spring to Boston. Other local companies, which performed either at the Metropolitan T. or the Boston Opera House which was demolished in 1958, included the Fleck Grand Opera, the Boston Civic Opera, the Boston Grand Opera.

In 1946 Boris Goldovsky founded the New England Opera T. which gave the American première of *Les Troyens* in 1955. In 1958 the Opera Company of Boston was established under the musical and artistic direction of Sarah Caldwell. The company has given the first U.S. performance of *Moses und Aron,* Ginastera's *Montezuma,* and the original versions of *Boris Godunov* and *Macbeth.*
Bibl: Q. Eaton: *The Boston Opera Company* (1965).

Bouche fermée. See *Bocca chiusa.*

Boué, Geori. See *Bourdin.*

Bouffes-Parisiens. Theatre in Paris (cap. 820) opened on 5 May 1855 with Offenbach's *Les Deux aveugles.* Was the home of operetta and light opera by Offenbach, Hervé, Lecocq, Audran, and Messager. Still a boulevard theatre with an operetta tradition.

Bouffons, Guerre des. See *Guerre des Bouffons.*

Boughton, Rutland, (*b* Aylesbury, 23 Jan. 1878; *d* London, 24 Jan. 1960). English composer. His brave and systematic attempt to establish an English school of Wagnerian music drama was pursued with remarkable single-mindedness and energy; and though his 'Bayreuth' at Glastonbury did not, after many efforts, establish itself permanently, he at least won wide popularity with *The Immortal Hour* in London in 1922. His music has tunefulness and an individual imagination, though not on the Wagnerian scale he hoped; and his faith in his purpose, which like Wagner's was social as well as artistic, never wavered in the face of prolonged neglect. His operas include *The Birth of Arthur* (comp. 1907-9, prod. 1920), *Alkestis* (1922), *The Queen of Cornwall* (1924), and *The Lily Maid* (1934).
Bibl: M. Hurd: *Immortal Hour* (1962).

Bouhy, Jacques (Joseph André)(*b* Pepinster, 18 June 1848; *d* Paris, 29 Jan. 1929). Belgian baritone. Début Paris, O., 1871, Méphistophélès. Created Escamillo (1875). London, C.G., 1882. Director of N.Y. Conservatory 1885-9, and taught there 1904-7, then in Paris.

Bouilly, Jean-Nicolas (*b* La Coudraye, 23 Jan. 1763; *d* Paris, 14 Apr. 1842). French author and librettist. Member of the Committee for Public Instruction, friend of Mirabeau, and dedicated Jacobin. First emerged as a librettist with *Pierre le Grand* (1790) for Grétry, but his name is forever associated with the text for Gaveaux's *Léonore, ou L'Amour conjugal* (1798), which became after various vicissitudes the source of Beethoven's *Fidelio. However, the great success in his own time was the text for Cherubini's *Les *Deux journées* (1800), which Beethoven and Goethe regarded as the ideal opera libretto. It is a vivid and well-constructed piece of work, fundamentally expressing Bouilly's political beliefs in natural virtue and the perfectibility of man. Other composers who made use of his dramas, or his librettos, include Aimon, Auber, Berton, Boieldieu, Dalayrac, Gyrowetz, Isouard, Méhul, and Weigl.
Bibl: J.-N. Bouilly: *Mes récapitulations* (3 vols., Paris 1836-7).

Boulevard Solitude. Opera in 7 scenes by Henze; text by the composer and Grete Weil. Prod. Hanover, Landestheater, 17 Feb. 1952, with Clause, Zilliken, Buckow, cond. Schüler; London, S.W., 25 June 1962; with Cantelo, Carolan, Glossop, cond. Lovett; Santa Fe, 2 Aug. 1967, with Brooks, Driscoll, Fortune, cond. Baustian. In this modern setting of the Manon Lescaut story, Des Grieux (ten.) becomes a drug addict and is shot at the end of the opera by Manon (sop.).

Boulez, Pierre (*b* Montbrison, 25 Mar. 1925). French composer and conductor. Studied Paris with Messiaen and Leibowitz. In 1948 acted as conductor and composer for Jean-Louis Barrault's company. In 1965 conducted *Wozzeck* at the Paris O. Engaged in 1966 by Wieland Wagner to conduct *Parsifal* at Bayreuth and *Wozzeck* in Frankfurt. Conducted *Pelléas et Mélisande* at London C.G. in 1969 and 1972. Cond. centenary *Ring*, Bayreuth 1976. His controversial utterances on opera include his proposal that all opera houses should be blown up; but meanwhile he has continued to give distinguished performances in them. (R)

Bourdin, Roger (*b* Paris, 14 June 1900; *d* Paris, 14 Sept. 1973). French baritone. Studied Paris Conservatoire with Gresse and Isnardon. Début Paris, O.C., 1922, as Lescaut (Massenet). Member of O.C., and O. until late 1930s. London, C.G., 1930, Pelléas. Appearances in Italy, South America. Was married to the soprano **Geori Boué** (*b* 1918), who made her Paris début in 1939 as Mimì. (R)

Bovy, Vina (orig. Johanna Pauline Felicité Bovi van Overberghe) (*b* Ghent, 22 May 1900). Belgian soprano. Studied Ghent. Début Ghent 1918, Argentine in Poise's *Les Deux billets*.

After appearances in Brussels, Paris, South America, and Italy, was engaged in 1936 for the N.Y. Met., début as Violetta. Reappeared in the Belgian and French provinces after the war, and from 1947 until 1955 was director of the Royal Opera, Ghent. (R)
Bibl: J. Deleersnyder: *Vina Bovy* (1965).

Box. See *Palco.*

Braham (orig. Abraham), **John** (*b* London, 20 Mar. 1774; *d* London, 17 Feb. 1856). English tenor of Jewish parentage. Studied with Leoni; début when ten at C.G. in Benefit for his teacher. After his voice had broken he was taken up by a rich benefactor and became a teacher of the piano. In 1794 began to sing again, and in 1796 was engaged at D. L. by Storace. Was then engaged by the Italian Opera, and from 1798 to 1800 appeared in Italy with great success. In 1801 sang at C.G. for the first time, and then at the Ly. and King's T. Was considered without rival on the Italian stage, and was a renowned Handel singer. He often, as was the custom of the time, composed his own music for certain works in which he appeared. Sang Max in *Freischütz* in English in 1824, and created the role of Huon in *Oberon* (1826), for which he made Weber write him a different principal aria. In the 1830s his voice became lower and he sang Don Giovanni and William Tell at D. L. Toured America with little success 1840-2 and again in 1848; he made his last appearance in a concert in 1852.
Bibl: J. Mewburn Levien: *The Singing of John Braham* (1945).

Braithwaite, Nicholas (*b* London, 26 Aug. 1939). Son of Warwick Braithwaite. Assistant conductor, S.W. Opera from 1971; director of Glyndebourne Touring Opera from 1977.

Braithwaite, Warwick (*b* Dunedin, N.Z., 9 Jan. 1898; *d* London, 18 Jan. 1971). N.Z. conductor. Studied R.A.M. 1916-19. Conductor of O'Mara Company 1919-22, and later on musical staff of B.N.O.C. After appointments with the B.B.C., joined S.W. and was, with Lawrance Collingwood, responsible for many important productions there (1933-40), including the first performance by the company of *Fledermaus*, *Mastersingers*, *Fidelio*, and *Don Carlos*. Conducted London, C.G., 1950-2; music director of the *Welsh National Opera Company 1956-60; returned S.W. 1960-8. (R)

Brambilla. Famous Italian family of musicians. (1) **Paolo** (*b* Milan, 9 July 1787; *d* Milan, 1838) composed a number of operas including *Il carnevale di Venezia* (Turin, 1819) and 12 ballets for Milan Sc. He had five children, all singers: Annibale, Ulisse, Emilia, Erminia, and the best known:
(2) **Amalia** (*b* Milan; *d* Castellammare di Stabia, Aug. 1880), whose repertory included

Norma, Lucia, and Maria Padilla. She married the tenor G.B. Verger; their son was the baritone Napoleone Verger. There were five cousins, all sisters and all singers, as follows:

(3) **Marietta** (*b* Cassano d'Adda, 7 June 1807; *d* Milan, 6 Nov. 1875), contralto. Studied Milan with Secchi; début London, 1827, as Arsace. Milan, Sc., 1835-45, where she created Orsini (*Lucrezia Borgia*); Vienna, 1837-42, where she created Pierotto (*Linda di Chamounix*). Her range was g to g'.

(4) **Teresa** (*b* Cassano, 23 Oct. 1818; *d* Milan, 15 July 1895), soprano. Studied Milan; début 1831. Created Gilda and sang with success in Paris and St Petersburg. The three other sisters were Giuseppina, Annetta, and Laura. Their niece

(5) **Teresina** (*b* Cassano d'Adda, 15 Apr. 1845; *d* Vercelli, 1 July 1921) was a soprano. She studied with her aunts Marietta and Teresa. Début Odessa, 1863. Chosen by Ponchielli (whom she married in 1874) to sing Lucia in the new version of his *I promessi sposi* during the opening season of the T. Dal Verme, Milan. Her roles included Gioconda, Aida, and Elsa. She retired from the stage in 1889 and then taught in Geneva and Pesaro until 1911. Descendants of the family included Arturo, head of the costume department at Sc. in the 1950s; and the film actor Tullio Carminato, who appeared in films with Grace Moore.

Branchu (orig. Chevalier de Lavit), **Alexandrine Caroline** (*b* Cap Français, S. Domingo, 2 Nov. 1780; *d* Passy, 14 Oct. 1850). French soprano. Studied Paris Conservatoire with Garat. Début Paris, T. Feydeau, 1799; Paris, O., 1801-26, where she created leading roles in Cherubini's *Anacréon* and *Les Abencérages*. Considered the greatest French dramatic soprano of her day and highly praised for her performances of Gluck's Alcestis, Armida, and Iphigenia, and Piccinni's Dido. Married the ballet dancer Branchu in 1799 and retired from the stage in 1826.

Brandt, Marianne (orig. Marie Bischoff) (*b* Vienna, 12 Sept. 1842; *d* Vienna, 9 July 1921). Austrian mezzo-soprano. Studied with Frau Marschner and Viardot. Début Olomouc, 1867, Rachel; London, C.G., 1872, Leonore (*Fidelio*). Ten years later sang Brangäne in the first English *Tristan* at D.L.; in that same year sang Kundry in the second Bayreuth *Parsifal*. N.Y., Met., 1884-8. After 1890 settled in Vienna and taught singing. (R)

Brangäne. Isolde's attendant (mezzo) in Wagner's *Tristan und Isolde*.

Brannigan, Owen (*b* Annitsford, nr Newcastle, 10 Mar. 1908; *d* Annitsford, 10 May 1973). English bass. Studied G.S.M. Début Newcastle with S.W. 1943, Sarastro. S.W. 1944-9 and

1952-8. Created Swallow (*Peter Grimes*) 1945, Collatinus in *Rape of Lucretia*, 1946, Noye in *Noye's Fludde*, 1958, Bottom in *A Midsummer Night's Dream*, 1960. One of the best English buffo singers; possessed a voice of large size and excellent quality and a warm stage presence. (R)

Branzell, Karin (Maria) (*b* Stockholm, 24 Sept. 1891; *d* Altadena, Calif. 15 Dec. 1974). Swedish mezzo-soprano. Educated Stockholm, studied with Thelma Hofer and Enrico Rosati. Début Stockholm 1912, Prince Sarvilaka in D'Albert's *Izeyl*; N.Y. Met., 1924, Fricka, and remained there as leading mezzo until 1944; London, C.G., 1935-8. One of the finest mezzos of the inter-war years. (R)

Bratislava (Ger. Pressburg; Hung. Poszony). Town in Czechoslovakia. The opera company is, with Brno, second only to Prague in size and importance. Opera is given at the Slóvak National T. by a company of about 45 soloists. The theatre was substantially rebuilt and enlarged in 1972.

Brazil. The first theatres were built in the 18th cent. However, operatic life did not develop very fast until the transfer to Brazil of the Portuguese Court in the Peninsula War brought with it an encouragement of opera. The Opera Nacional was founded in 1857; its repertory included *zarzuela* and Brazilian opera as well as Italian opera. The first important Brazilian opera composer was Carlo Gomes (1836-1895); his works include *A Noite do castelo* (1861) and *Joana de Flandres* (1863). Moving to Milan, he studied further and absorbed Italian (especially Verdian) influences, and wrote *Il Guarany* (1870). His *Lo schiavo* (1889) was performed in Rio de Janeiro. Other significant Brazilian composers of the period included Joaquin de Macedo (*d* 1925) with *Tiradentes*; Leopoldo Miguez (1850-1902) with *Pelo amor!* and *Saldunes*; and Henrique Oswald (1854-1931), of Swiss origin, with *Croce d'oro*, *Le Fate*, and *Il Neo*. Others included Itiberê da Cunha (1848-1913); Alberto Nepomuceno (1864-1920), with *Artemis* (1898), *Abul* (1913), and *O Garatuja* (1904), which take a stand for Portuguese as a singing language; Francisco Braga (1868-1945) with *Jupira* (1900), *Anita Garibaldi* (1901), and *Contractador de diamantes* (1901); and O. Lorenzo Fernandez (1897-1948), with *Malazarte* (1931). The dominating and prolific Heitor Villa-Lobos (1887-1959) wrote *Izart* (1912), *Jésus* (1918), *Zoe* (1919), and *Malazarte* (1921), as well as the operettas *Madalena* (1948) and *Yerma* (1955). Opera is given chiefly at the T. Municipal, Rio de Janeiro, and the T. Municipal, São Paulo, mainly by visiting companies.
See *Rio de Janeiro*, *São Paulo*.

Break. The point at which the tone quality changes between different registers of the voice. •

Brecht, Bertolt (*b* Augsburg, 10 Feb. 1898; *d* Berlin, 15 Aug. 1956). German dramatist. he wrote the version of *The Beggar's Opera* known as *Die Dreigroschenoper* (1928) for Kurt *Weill, also the texts for *Happy End* (1929), *Mahagonny* (1930), *Der Jasager* (1930), and for Wagner-Régeny's *Persische Episode* (*Der Darmwäscher*) (1940-50). *The Trial of Lucullus* by Sessions (1947) and Dessau (1951) are based on his works, as is Cezar's *Galilieo Galilei* (1964).

Brecknock, John (*b* Long Eaton, 29 Nov. 1937). British tenor. Studied Birmingham with Frederick Sharp. S.W. 1966 (chorus), soloist from 1967, developing into leading tenor with E.N.O. in such roles as Almaviva, Count Ory, Belmonte, and Werther; created Vasco in Crosse's *Story of Vasco* (1974). Guest appearances C.G., Scottish Opera, Houston, N.Y., Met., etc. Repertory also includes Ottavio, Tamino, Edgardo, Fenton, and Anatoly (*War and Peace*). Has developed into one of the few British tenors capable of encompassing the high tessitura of the early 19th-cen. Italian repertory. (R)

Bregenz. Town in Vorarlberg, Austria. A summer open-air festival was inaugurated in 1956 in the specially constructed lakeside theatre (cap. 6,400). Artists from the Vienna S. O. take part in performances of Mozart operas and Austrian operettas, and Italians in works by 18th- and early 19th-cent. composers.

Brema, Marie (orig. Minny Fehrmann) (*b* Liverpool, 28 Feb. 1856; *d* Manchester, 22 Mar. 1925). English mezzo-soprano. Studied with Henschel. Stage début London, Shaftesbury T., 1891, Lola, in first English *Cavalleria rusticana*. Established herself as a Wagnerian and sang Ortrud, Fricka, and Kundry at Bayreuth 1894-7. Although a mezzo sang the *Götterdämmerung* Brünnhilde in Paris under Richter. Toured U.S.A. with Damrosch Company 1894-5, and at Met. 1895-6. Created Beatrice in Stanford's *Much Ado About Nothing*, C.G., 1901, and in 1910 organized an opera season of her own at the Savoy T., singing Orfeo in English. After leaving the stage she was for many years director of the opera class at the R.M.C.M.

Bremen. Town in Lower Saxony, Germany. An early *Faust* opera, I. Walter's *Doktor Faust*, had its first performance there, 1797. The former Staatstheater, scene of the première of Gurlitt's *Wozzeck* (1926), and the first performances in Germany of Dvořák's *Kate and the Devil* (1909) and Malipiero's *Antonio e Cleopatra* (1939), was destroyed during the Second World War. The première of

Mohaupt's *Die Bremer Statdtmusikanten* was given in 1949. The new T. am Goetheplatz (cap. 1,100) opened 27 Aug. 1950.

Brent, Charlotte (*b*? ; *d* London, 10 Apr. 1802). English soprano. Studied with Arne; début Dublin 1755. One of the most famous interpreters of Polly (*Beggar's Opera*) at C.G. and created the role of Mandane in Arne's *Artaxerxes* (1762). Particularly renowned as a Handel singer.

Brescia. Town in Lombardy, Italy. The first opera performed there was Ziani's *Tullo Ostilio*, inaugurating the T. degli Erranti in 1688. After several rebuildings, it was renamed the T. Grande (1811), opening with Mayr's *Ifigenia in Aulide* (27 Dec. 1810). The present auditorium, the fifth in two centuries, was designed by Girolamo Magnani, and was inaugurated in Aug. 1863 with *Il trovatore* and *Un ballo in maschera*. In 1894 the young Toscanini conducted *Manon*, *Puritani*, and *Traviata*, and it was there on 28 May 1904 that the revised *Madama Butterfly* scored its first success after the Scala fiasco three months earlier. Eva Turner sang her first Turandot in Italy there in 1926.

Breslau. See Wrocław.

Bréval, Lucienne (orig. Berthe Agnes Lisette Schilling) (*b* Männendorf, 4 Nov. 1869; *d* Neuilly-sur-Seine, 15 Aug. 1935). Swiss, then French, soprano. Studied Paris Conservatoire with Wartot. Début Paris, O., 1892, Selika; London, C.G., 1899; N.Y., Met., 1901. Created Grisélidis (Massenet), Ariane (Dukas), Pénélope (Fauré), and Lady Macbeth (Bloch). One of the greatest French singers of her day, equally at home in Rameau, Gluck, and Wagner. (R)

Brilioth, Helge (*b* Växjö, 7 May 1931). Swedish tenor, formerly baritone. Studied Royal Academy of Opera School, Stockholm, and subsequently Rome and Salzburg. Originally a pianist and organist, later turned to singing, making his début as a baritone at Drottningholm as Bartolo in Paisiello's *Barbiere di Siviglia*. After singing at Bielefeld 1962-4, where his roles included Germont, Posa, Ford, Beckmesser, and Orlofsky, returned to Stockholm for a further period of study and made a new début as a tenor in 1965 as Don José. Bayreuth 1969-71, Siegmund; Salzburg Easter Festival, 1970, Siegfried; C. G. since 1970 as Siegmund, Siegfried, Tristan, and Parsifal. Although his voice is not of the largest Heldentenor proportions, he is one of the best Wagner singers of the 1970s. (R)

Brindisi. From the Italian *far brindisi*, 'to drink one's health': a drinking song, e.g. Alfredo's and Violetta's 'Libiamo' in *La traviata*.

British Broadcasting Corporation. Opera came into the broadcasting programmes as early as 6 Jan. 1923, when 2LO relayed a B.N.O.C. performance of *Hansel and Gretel* from C.G. – this was the first broadcast from an opera house in Europe. Further B.N.O.C. broadcasts included *Figaro, Walküre,* and *Siegfried.* In Oct. 1923 the first studio opera was given, *Roméo et Juliette.* As well as broadcasts from C.G. and other theatres in the 1920s the B.B.C. began an ambitious series of studio performances under Percy Pitt which lasted from 1926 to 1930 and included *Le Roi d'Ys, Pelléas,* and *Louise,* as well as the more popular works in the repertory. From 1929 to 1931 the Labour government subsidized C.G. through the B.B.C. and there were many broadcasts from that theatre. Studio opera, however, ceased until 1937, when a Music Productions Unit was formed with Stanford Robinson as its music director. Between 1934 and 1939 the Corporation gave concert performances at the Queen's Hall of *Wozzeck, Lady Macbeth of the Mtsensk District,* and *Mathis der Maler.*

Since the establishment of the Third Programme, later Radio Three, more and more opera has been given on the B.B.C. There have been not only broadcasts from British opera houses, but also direct transmissions from the European summer festivals at Bayreuth, Salzburg, Munich, etc., and broadcasts of tapes made of studio performances in France, Germany, and Italy, often of works unfamiliar to the English listener. Studio opera in England has revived, and there have been many outstanding performances including *Tristan, Die Walküre, Les Troyens, La Jolie Fille de Perth, Elektra, Les Deux Journées,* all under Beecham, as well as numerous other works, familiar and unfamiliar, under distinguished conductors with leading British and foreign singers. During the summer Promenade Concert seasons, several complete performances of opera are given each year by Gly., C.G., and other operatic organizations. In 1972 a comprehensive survey of French opera was given, including many rare works and the first-ever complete performance of Verdi's original *Don Carlos* score.

British National Opera Company. Formed in 1922 by leading singers and musicians of the *Beecham Opera Company forced into liquidation Dec. 1920. Its Board of Directors included Robert Radford, Percy Pitt, Walter Hyde, Aylmer Buesst, Agnes Nicholls, and Norman Allin. Pitt was the company's first Artistic Director, succeeded by Frederic Austin. The company was launched at Bradford in Feb. 1922, and in May of that year gave performances of *The Ring, Parsifal, Tristan,* and other full-scale works, and included the leading British singers and conductors of the day in its

ranks. In the spring of 1924 it was prevented from giving its annual season at C.G. as the directors of the Royal Opera wished to restore international opera, and its subsequent London seasons were given at His Majesty's, where the first performance of *Hugh the Drover* was given that season. Other new works given by the company included Holst's *The Perfect Fool* (1923) and *At the Boar's Head* (1925).

Guest artists included Melba, Joseph Hislop, Dinh Gilly, and Edward Johnson, who appeared with the company during its C.G. seasons. By 1928 the company was in serious financial straits. It owed some £5,000, but had, during its last working year, paid more than £17,000 in entertainment tax. The company was taken over as the Covent Garden English Company in 1929, but survived as such only three seasons.

Britten, Benjamin (Lord Britten of Aldeburgh) (*b* Lowestoft, 22 Nov. 1913; *d* Aldeburgh, 4 Dec. 1976). English composer, conductor, and pianist. His early operetta *Paul Bunyan* (1941) was soon withdrawn, though some of the songs were revised and performed at Snape in the 1974 Aldeburgh Festival; it was then revived, Aldeburgh 1976. With his first major stage work, however, *Peter Grimes* (1945), he established himself as an opera composer of the first importance. Rooted in tradition, it is entirely original in its sharpness of invention and in the conception of the hero as what was to be the first of a series of 'outsider' figures in his art; and it reveals the deep sympathy for the victims of misunderstanding, horror of the destruction of innocence, and attachment to his native Suffolk seaboard that have always marked his work. In 1945, just as the war was over, a delighted England fastened upon *Grimes* as token that a major operatic talent was at last working on these shores.

However, largely owing to the uncomomic conditions of large-scale opera, Britten now turned to chamber opera, forming the *English Opera Group for the presentation of such works. *The Rape of Lucretia* (1946) was given at Glyndebourne, and shows more vividly than *Grimes* his mastery of simple means to an expressive end: the use of the 12-piece orchestra is resourceful and creative. From this tragedy he turned in *Albert Herring* (1947) to comedy (with an element of pathos). The transfer of a Maupassant story to a Suffolk setting rekindled Britten's ability to satirize, with simple musical strokes, local rural types in operatic terms. *Herring* is naturally faster than *Lucretia*, but also more intricate. Britten's ingenuity harnesses a wide range of musical devices to comic ends; the technique is still more assured, and with it comes a widening of expressive power.

For his next two stage works, Britten made use of unusual forms: Gay's *Beggar's Opera* (1948) was recomposed in terms that were delightfully apt; and *Let's Make an Opera* (1949) is in the first part a play rehearsing a cast of children and grown-ups for participation in the second, the opera *The Little Sweep*. Two years later, he gave further proof of his versatility with a realization of *Dido and Aeneas* (he was a profound admirer of Purcell, to whom he consciously owed much in his setting of the English language).

Also in 1951 there appeared Britten's first full-scale opera since *Grimes*, *Billy Budd*. Since the action takes place on a man-o'-war, the cast is all male; and this posed problems of texture and variety which were, with characteristic mastery, turned to advantage in creating an original atmosphere. The scoring is fascinating, drawing especially richly on woodwind and brass; thematically, the work was the most closely knit, and formally the most complex and subtle, of any opera Britten had yet composed.

The opera which followed was again large in scale: *Gloriana* (1953). Written for the Coronation of Queen Elizabeth II, it at first excited a good deal of non-musical hostility, chiefly on account of the libretto: this naturally drew the non-musicians' attention more closely than the music, which includes some splendid inventions, and recent revivals have proved the misguidedness of the initial resistance to a fine work.

In the chamber opera *The Turn of the Screw* (1954) the process of thematic integration is, for special expressive purposes, carried still further: the technique of using one principal theme which 'turns' in orchestral interludes is used as a metaphor of the drama, mirroring the inexorable turning of Henry James's screw.

Noyes Fludde (1958) was based on one of the Chester Miracle Plays, and is a marvel of composition with slender, even makeshift means set to positive emotional advantage. Boys' bugle classes and school recorder groups are used in the orchestra, children's voices on the stage (the work should be given in church).

A Midsummer Night's Dream (1960) was written with both chamber and large-scale performance in mind. Aided by a well-organized libretto (by himself with Peter Pears), Britten penetrated into the heart of the play and into the world of sleep that had long been another of his fascinations. Fairies, nobles, and rustics are skilfully characterized, and the music is made a strong symbol of how, through the action of the dream, the lovers shed their tensions and find each other, to wake to new happiness.

Britten followed up some of the ideas in *Noyes Fludde* and his experience of Japanese No plays with three 'Church Parables', *Curlew River* (1964), *The Burning Fiery Furnace* (1966), and *The Prodigal Son* (1968). Designed to be performed in church, and taking some of their ritual nature and their dramatic and instrumental techniques from No plays, they are nevertheless individual works that absorb the Japanese influence into a strong, extremely original form of drama that is at least as strongly rooted in early English religious music drama. *Curlew River*, which actually uses a Japanese story, *Sumidagawa* (see *Japan*), is not only the most Oriental but also the strictest of the three technically; having mastered these new disciplines, Britten clearly felt able to relax them in the other two, The common framework remains of a dramatic fiction of performance by a group of monks who arrive in the church singing a plainchant (which in different ways provides the musical material for each work), and having staged their morality, withdraw to the original chant.

A new set of special problems was presented when Britten was commissioned by the B.B.C. to write a T.V. opera. After careful study of the techniques available, he produced *Owen Wingrave* (1971), based like *The Turn of the Screw* on a Henry James story, and made into a libretto by Myfanwy Piper. The theme is one of pacifism, another of Britten's lifelong preoccupations; and though dramatically it is a one-sided statement of fervent belief rather than a consideration of the issues involved in pacifism, the work is most skilfully written and characteristically turns the limitations of television to positive advantage while seizing the opportunities presented by its special techniques (such as the ability to cross-fade between widely separated characters who nevertheless sing as part of the same musical gesture in a duet). The work has also been staged (C.G., 1973).

Myfanwy Piper was again the librettist for *Death in Venice* (1974), a setting of Thomas Mann's *Novelle* that draws on ballet for some of the sequences, and gives major roles to the central figure of Aschenbach (tenor) and to the ever-changing figure (baritone) that in various guises draws him towards his destruction.

Britten also made an edition (1951) of Holst's *The Wandering Scholar*. As a conductor, he largely confined himself to his own works in the opera house; but especially at the Aldeburgh Festival, and on tour in England and abroad, he directed brilliant performances of works in the English Opera Group's repertory. The originality and range of his contribution to opera is second to that of no composer in the 20th cent. (R)

Bibl: P. Howard: *The Operas of Benjamin Britten* (1969); E. White: *Benjamin Britten: His Life and Operas* (1970); P. Evans: *The Music of Benjamin Britten* (1979).

Brno (Ger. Brünn). Town in Czechoslovakia. The opera company is, with Bratislava, second only to Prague in size and importance. Opera was given from the 1730s by Italian companies, including those of Angelo and Pietro Mingotti, and Philippo Neri del Fantasia, in the Městské divadlo (Civic T.) situated in the Reduta Hall. Operas included Galuppi's *Argenide* (1733) and M. Luchini's *Vincislao* (1739), on the subject of King Václav II. In 1767 Tuček's Singspiel, *Zamilobaný ponocný* (The Nightwatchman in Love), was given in Czech; the first opera given in Czech was Méhul's *Joseph* (1839), followed by Škroup's *Dratenik* (The Tinker, 1840). In 1882 the new building of the German Stadttheater was opened (cap. 1,185), equipped with the first electric light in Central Europe. Czech opera was given in the Prozatímní Divadlo (Provisional T.), 1884-94, in Veveří Street; this was rebuilt in 1894, when its name was changed to Národní Divadlo (National T.). In 1918 the Czech theatre moved to the building of the German theatre. Opera is now given in the Janáček Opera House opened in 1965 (cap. 1,400). The repertory has been notable for its enterprise, and Brno retains a reputation for attention to contemporary works: it has given the premières of all Janáček's operas except *Mr Brouček;* in 1958 all Janáček's operas were given during the International Janáček Congress, and most of them keep their place in the repertory. There is a small opera studio, Komorní opera Miloše Wasserbauera (Miloš Wasserbauer Chamber Opera), built in 1957 by the Janáček Academy.

Bronskaya (orig. Hacke), **Evgeniya** (Adolfovna) (*b* St Petersburg, 1 Feb, 1888; *d* Leningrad, 12 Dec. 1953). Russian soprano. Studied with her mother, E. de Hacke, and in Milan with Teresa Arkel. Début Tiflis 1901. Kiev 1902-3; Moscow, Solodovnikov, 1905-6; 1907-10 sang chiefly abroad, e.g. in Italy, France, and U.S.A. (Boston O.C.) sometimes under her married name, Makarova; 1910-23 St Petersburg/Petrograd, Maryinsky. Taught Petrograd/Leningrad 1923-50. A brilliant coloratura, her repertory included Lucia, Gilda, Micaela, Musetta, Violetta, Marfa, Tatyana, Snow Maiden. (R)

Brouček, The Excursions of Mr. See *Excursions of Mr Brouček, The.*

Brouwenstijn, Gré (van Swol) (*b* Den Helder, 26 Aug. 1915). Dutch soprano. Studied Amsterdam Music Lyceum. Début Amsterdam 1940 as one of the Ladies in *Die Zauberflöte.* Joined the newly-formed Netherlands Opera in 1946, where her first success was as Tosca. London, C.G., Aida, 1951; appeared regularly in London in Verdi operas until 1964. Bayreuth 1954-6; Elisabeth, Gurune, Eva, Sieglinde; and Leonore in Wieland Wagner's Stuttgart *Fidelio.* South American début at the Colón, Buenos Aires, under Beecham, 1958; Gly. 1959; Chicago 1959. Gave her farewell performance in Amsterdam in 1971 in *Fidelio.* One of the most musically intelligent of post-war sopranos, with a warmly vibrant voice. (R)

Brownlee, John (*b* Geelong, 7 Jan. 1900; *d* N.Y., 10 Jan. 1969). Australian baritone. Studied first in Melbourne; heard by Melba who brought him to London. Début as Marcello in Acts 3 and 4 of *La Bohème* on the night of Melba's farewell, 8 June 1926. Then studied further with Dinh Gilly. Regular member of the Paris O. 1927-36, appearing also at C.G. Gly. 1935, sang Count Almaviva, Don Giovanni, and Don Alfonso there regularly until the war. He was a member of the N.Y. Met. 1937-58, and from 1957-69 was an excellent head of the opera department at the Manhattan School of Music. A finely schooled singer, with a pleasing if not brilliant voice. (R)

Bruch, Max (*b* Cologne, 6 Jan. 1838; *d* Friedenau, 2 Oct. 1926). German composer and conductor. Bruch's reputation rests upon his concert works rather than upon his 3 operas, which were never more than moderate successes: they are an operetta, *Scherz, List und Rache* (1858); *Die Loreley* (to a text by Giebel first written for Mendelssohn: 1863); and *Hermione* (after *The Winter's Tale,* 1872).

Bruneau, Alfred (*b* Paris, 3 Mar. 1857; *d* Paris, 15 June 1934). French composer and critic. His early, and to conservative listeners sensational, opera *Le Rêve* (1891) was based on Zola, to whom he turned for many of his later stage works. Its success was followed with the more mature *L'Attaque du moulin* (1893); and then 3 operas with Zola as librettist. *Messidor* (1897) suffered from the public opposition to Zola during the Dreyfus case; but *L'Ouragan* (1901) was a triumph, as was *L'Enfant Roi* (1905), a lighter piece despite its serious thesis on the importance of children in marriage. Zola died in 1902, mourned by Bruneau in *Lazare* (1903 unprod.), but his subjects continued to occupy the composer. Without being stylistically influenced by Wagner, Bruneau benefited French opera by his use of Wagnerian principles; his music serves its texts faithfully and seriously despite a certain intrusive crudity in its realism. He was also a gifted critic.
Bibl: A. Boschot: *La Vie et les oeuvres de Alfred Bruneau* (1937).

Brunette (*Fr* little brown one). A kind of song popular in the late 17th and early 18th cent. in which, from the Renaissance ideal of the 'petite brune' as simple and gentle, love is affirmed in tender rather than passionate terms. It was therefore usually simple melodically, perhaps a rondo in form and cast in a few verses; found in French opera from Lully to Rameau.

Brünn. See *Brno.*

Brünnhilde. A Valkyrie (sop.), Wotan's favourite daughter, in Wagner's *Die Walküre, Siegfried,* and *Götterdämmerung.*

Brunswick (Ger. Braunschweig). Town in Lower Saxony. The first opera house there was opened in 1690 in the Hagenmarkt with Kusser's *Cleopatra* and saw the first performances of a large number of German operas by Kusser, Keiser, Schürmann, Hasse, and others during the last half of the 17th and first half of the 18th cent. The former Landestheater was destroyed during the Second World War, and the present Staatstheater (cap. 1,370) was opened in 1948 with *Don Giovanni.*

Bruscantini, Sesto (*b* Porto Civitanova, 10 Dec. 1919). Italian baritone. Studied with Luigi Ricci in Rome. Début Civitanova 1946, Colline. Milan, Sc., from 1949. At Gly. 1951-6 established himself as a stylist in Mozart and Rossini; has sung buffo roles all over Europe. Chicago from 1961, when he began singing Verdi dramatic roles. Repertory of 108 roles. (R)

Brussels (Fr. Bruxelles, Flem. Brussel). Capital of Belgium. One of the earliest Flemish operas was Benoit's *Isa,* produced at the T. du Cirque in 1867. The principal home of opera Brussels is the T. Royal de La Monnaie, named after an *atelier monetaire* which occupied the site in the 17th cent. The present building (cap. 1,700) dates from 1856, but the first Monnaie was built in 1700. The theatre's most glorious period was between 1875 and 1889 under Lapissida, with Joseph Dupont as music director, when the premières of Massenet's *Hérodiade* (1881), Reyer's *Sigurd* (1884), Chabrier's *Gwendoline* (1886), and Godard's *Jocelyn* (1888), were given: the company included Sylva, Vergnet, Devries, Renard, Soulacroix, Devoyod, Fursch-Madi(er), Calvé, Caron, Litvinne, and Melba.

During the First World War the German government organized seasons by German companies; 1916-18 performances included *Rosenkavalier* conducted by Strauss with the three original Dresden sopranos, and *Der Ring des Nibelungen.* From 1918 to 1953 the theatre was under the direction of Corneil du Thorant; during this period premières included Milhaud's *Malheurs d'Orphée* (1926), Honegger's *Antigone* (1927), Prokofiev's *The Gambler* (1929) as well as the first performances in French of *Prince Igor, The Golden Cockerel, Turandot, Ariadne auf Naxos, I quatro rusteghi, Wozzeck, The Rape of Lucretia, Albert Herring, The Rake's Progress,* and *The Consul.* The company included, at various times, Mina Bolotine, Vina Bovy, Clara Clairebert, Fernand Ansseau, André d'Arkor, Joseph Rogatchewsky, and John Charles Thomas. From 1953 to 1959 the tenor Rogatchewsky was the director, and the

ensemble included Rita Gorr, Huberte Vecray, Gabriel Bacquier, Pierre Fleta, and Huc-Santana.

In 1959 Maurice Huismann became director. He dispensed with a large permanent ensemble and instead invited foreign companies to visit Brussels, engaging Belgian and French artists for specific operas. In 1963 the theatre was renamed the Opéra National, with André Vandernoot as musical director; it is also the home of Maurice Béjart's 'Ballet du XXe Siècle'.

Bibl: J. Salès: *Théâtre royale de da Monnaie, 1856–1970* (Brussels, 1971).

Bucharest (Rom. Bucureşti). Capital of Romania. Opera was first given by an Italian company in 1787. A German company directed by Johann Gerger came from Transylvania, a German-dominated area with a Mozart tradition, to play in Princess Ralu's theatre 'At the Red Fountain' in 1818, with a repertory of Rossini and Mozart (*Idomeneo*). Eduard Kriebig's company followed in 1823, the Fourreaux Company in 1831-2, Theodor Müller's in 1833 on its way home from Russia; artists of the latter remained to work in a theatre built by Momolo, including Ion Wachmann (1807-63), who had directed the company, 1831-3, and continued in the capital until 1835. The repertory was based on French and Italian works and on Mozart, together with Wachmann's *Braconierul* (The Poacher, 1833); 60 performances were given in 1833-4. Application was made for an Italian theatre in 1833, and this paved the way for a national theatre formed through the new Philharmonic Society. Further Italian companies came, from 1842. In 1852 the Teatrul Naţional opened under Wachmann (dir. 1852-8); the company alternated with an Italian group under Basilio Sansoni that had been given a state subsidy in 1843. Under a succession of artistic directors, opera flourished in a wealthy stratum of society that was keen to encourage Western culture; the repertory was primarily Italian.

A new departure was marked by the appointment in 1877 of George Stephănescu, who in the face of great difficulties kept opera active in the capital for many years: he founded Opera Română (1885-6), the Compania Lirică Română (1902-4). Romanian artists were still lower paid than the Italians, and this resulted in the closure of the Romanian company and the emigration of its best artists. Nevertheless, Stephănescu gave 31 performances between 1889 and 1891; from 1897 to 1901 another company occupied the theatre. At the T. National between 1901 and 1910 regular Italian seasons were given which, though uneven in standard, included among guest artists Tetrazzini, Litvinne, Battistini, Ruffo, and others of distinction. German seasons were also given (*Hol-*

länder and *Lohengrin,* 1910) and also French: these were languages in use among the upper classes, who were slower than musicians to appreciate that the similarity of Romanian to Italian made it an excellent language for opera (although the Italian composer Bimboni's *Haidoucul* (The Brigand) had been sung in its Romanian text by Italians as early as 1888).

During the war, progress was limited: during the German occupation the Dessau Opera visited for seasons, but local activity included a Student Opera that gave 63 performances in 1914-15, a company formed by the tenor Stefanescu-Cerna at the Blanduzia Garden (1915), the formation of the Gabrilescu Company and of another company at the Leon Popescu T. (1915), and of a company under the baritone Jean Atanasia (1916). Then in 1919 the Asociaţia Lirică Romîna Opera was formed under the direction of the composer Ion Nonna Otescu (1888-1940) and under the patronage of Queen Maria: the company opened with *Aida* at the Teatrul Naţional, and as well as giving much encouragement to local artists, drew distinguished singers (Slezak) and conductors (Weingartner, Nedbal). In 1921 this success led to the opera being made a state institution, Opera Română, and housed at the Lyric T., where the season opened with *Lohengrin* under Enescu; his successors included George Georgescu (1922-7) and Ionel Perlea (1929-30). In 1924, 11 of the best singers resigned in protest against the government's restrictive attitude, and in 1930 the company had to move to an unsuitable building and halve its singers' salaries. Nevertheless, a number of new Romanian operas were staged. Earthquake in 1940 and bombing in 1944 wrecked the old theatre. The new Opera (cap. 1,100) was opened in 1953 with *The Queen of Spades*.

Operetta, first given at the T. Momolo in 1850 and very popular, fell into a period of neglect between the wars when two revue companies dominated the Bucharest stage, but is now again well established in its own T. de Stat de Operetă.

Bibl: I. Masoff: *Istoria Teatrului Naţional din Bucureşti* (?1961).

Büchner, Georg (*b* Godelau, 17 Oct. 1813; *d* Zurich, 19 Feb. 1837). German dramatist. Operas based on his works are as follows.
Dantons Tod (1835): Einem (1947).
Woyzeck (1836, unfin.): Berg (1925), Gurlitt (1926), Pfister (1950).
Leonce und Lena (1836): Weismann (1925), Schwaen (1961).
Marie Tudor (after Hugo, 1836): Wagner-Regény (1935).

Buckman, Rosina (*b* Blenheim, N.Z., *c*1880; *d* London, 30 Dec. 1948). New Zealand soprano. Studied Birmingham and Midland School of Music. Début Wellington, 1906, in Hill's *A*

Moorish Maid. In Australia from 1909, and in 1911 joined the Melba Grand Opera Company. London, C.G., 1914; Beecham Company 1915-20; B.N.O.C. 1923. A famous Aida, Butterfly, and Isolde. Subsequently taught in London at the R.A.M. Married to the tenor Maurice d'Oisly. (R)

Budapest. Capital of Hungary (uniting in 1872 the towns of Buda and Pest). Regular opera performances were given in German from 1787, when the Castle T. opened, some also in Hungarian from 1793, the year of the first national opera, Chudy's *Pikkó Herceg* (Prince Pikkó). Most important foreign operas were performed soon after their local premières. A large German City T. opened in 1812 (with Beethoven's *König Stephan* and *Die Ruinen von Athen*); this burnt down in 1847. In 1837 the Pestí Magyar Szinház (Pest Hungarian T.) opened with *Il barbiere di Siviglia* (29 Aug.). This remained the country's most important musical theatre until 1884: the directors were Ferenc *Erkel (1838-74), Hans *Richter (1871-5), and Sándor Erkel (1875-84). The repertory was at first largely Italian, with Hungarian translations gradually supervening, and this helped to encourage the development of national opera. From the 1840s, Erkel's operas joined the repertory, and the theatre was quick to stage important foreign works as they appeared (with the major exception of Wagner's, resisted as far as possible by Erkel but pressed by Richter). It was a mature company of international standard that moved into the beautiful new Operház (Opera House) (cap. 1,310), opened on 27 Sept. 1884 with acts of *Lohengrin* and *Bank Bán*. Performances were also given in Buda Castle.

Mahler (1888-91) introduced much German opera; Nikisch (1893-5) added more Italian, French, and Hungarian works. After a slack period (1900-12), the company was revivified under Miklós Bánffi; despite the war and its aftermath, operatic life was re-established on a healthy basis, and, despite opposition, the works of Bartók and Kodály entered the repertory. With Miklós Radnai as Intendant (until his death in 1935) and Sergio Failoni conducting (1928-48), many other contemporary works followed. Damaged in the war, the Opera House re-opened on 15 Mar. 1945 and the repertory began to include more Russian works; the company was also much enlarged. The Director, 1946-56, was Aladár Tóth, who invited Klemperer to conduct opera for the first time in Europe since 1933. Performances are also given in the open air on Margaret Island and at the Zoo. Chamber operas are given on the Odry stage. The company also toured (1948-55) as a Csrdűlő Opera (Rolling Opera), visiting towns and industrial centres in a special train. Budapest has, virtually since its establishment as an operatic centre, been the cradle of all the greatest Hungarian singers and has drawn major artists from all over Europe to its stages. Important post-war conductors have included Janos Ferencsik, Ferenc Fricsay, and Otto *Klemperer (1947-50).

The city's second theatre opened in 1911 as the Népopera (People's Opera) (cap. 2,450). In 1917 it became the Városi Szinház (Civic T.) and a filial in 1951 of the Opera House; from 1925 it was privately owned and concentrated on operetta. Used as a cinema in the war, it reopened as a filial in 1951, and is known as the Erkel T. Operetta has also been given at the Pesti Népszinház (Pest People's T.), opened 1875; at the Budai Népszinház (Buda People's T.), 1861-4 and 1867-70; at the Kisfaludy Szinház, from 1897; at the Magyar Szinház (Hungarian T.), opened 1897; and especially at the Király Szinház (T. Royal), opened 1903.

Bibl: I. Balassa: *A hetvenőt éves M.Á. Operház 1884-1959* (1959).

Buenos Aires. At the beginning of the 19th cent., Buenos Aires had one small and simply constructed theatre, the Coliseo (1804, renamed the T. Argentino in 1838). The first operatic performances here were selections from Italian opera organized by Juan Picazzarri in 1813. From various visiting singers a regular company was formed, and gave the first complete opera, *Il barbiere*, in 1825. Disbanded by the Rosas dictatorship, the company was replaced by visiting groups, including a French ensemble which in 1831 gave works by Dalayrac and Mercadante in the recently (1828) constructed T. del Parque Argentino and in the Coliseo. Operatic selections were also given in the T. Principal de la Victoria (1838), and complete operas from 1848, when the company could boast a very effective team of both Italian and native singers and conductors. The repertory was entirely Italian, with Donizetti now the most popular composer. Two French companies were also formed in 1852 and 1854, both of which gave an almost exclusively French repertory; these two groups, though very different in quality, managed to win an increasingly loyal public. By 1854, 30 new productions were given in the city; and two years later *zarzuelas* were added to the repertory.

These successes led to the demand for a new and improved theatre; and the first T. Colón (cap. 2,500, with a special women's gallery) was duly opened on 25 Apr. 1857 with *La traviata*. This became the centre of the country's operatic life. The smaller T. de la Opéra was opened on 25 May 1872 with *Il trovatore*; it was demolished in 1935. From 1868 the Colón was directed by the powerful and influential Angelo Ferrari; though he ran a basically Italian repertory that included early performances of

works by Verdi, Ferrari also saw to it that the Colón reflected the general European operatic scene of the day, and even gave a number of premières of works by Marotta, A. Agostini, Cavalieri, and Torrens Boqué. In 1881 a visiting French company under Maurice Grau gave a season that included *Carmen*. At the same time the T. de la Opéra was widening its repertory to include more Italian works; both houses were by now of sufficient repute to attract the finest Italian singers of the day. The T. de la Victoria had meanwhile not ceased activity, and was responsible for the première of the first opera by an Argentinian composer, F. Hargreaves's *La gata bianca* (1877). At the T. Politeama local premières were given, including *Le Villi* (1886), *Der fliegende Holländer*, and *Roméo et Juliette* (1887), *Lakmé* (1888) and *Otello* (1888, a few days ahead of the Colón); one of the stars of the 1888 season was Patti.

After the destruction of the old Colón in 1889, the rebuilt T. de la Opéra became the city's operatic centre in a busy period; there were regular visits from major Italian singers and conductors (Campanini 1889 and from 1893, Mascheroni from 1894, Mugnone from 1898, Toscanini in 1901, 1903-4, and 1906), and the repertory was broadened to include more German and French and even Argentinian works, though little pre-19th-cent. opera was given.

On 25 May 1908 a performance of *Aida* opened the new T. Colón (cap. 2,487, with standing room for 1,000); in 1935 the administration passed into municipal hands. The long domination of Italian opera now finally began to give way to a truly international repertory that regularly included German, Spanish, and even Czech and Russian opera, though pre-classical opera never succeeded and even Mozart continued to be neglected. The first complete *Ring* was given in 1922 under Weingartner (with Lotte Lehmann). Moreover, the rapid expansion of the Colón's activities and its emergence as one of the world's great opera houses was reflected in the busy life of the smaller theatres of the capital: at the T. Coliseo, *Parsifal* was given as early as 1913, Mascagni conducted the première of his *Isabeau* (1911), and new Argentinian works were staged; new native operas were also given at the T. Politeama and a more limited and sporadic repertory at the T. Avenida, T. Odeón, and other smaller theatres. Buenos Aires remains the richest operatic city of the continent, and one capable of challenging the greatest European and North American cities in the excellence and diversity of its operatic life.

See also *Argentina, Colón.*

Buesst, Aylmer (*b* Melbourne, 28 Jan. 1883; *d* St Albans, 25 Jan. 1970). Australian conductor.

Studied Melbourne, Brussels, and London; and subsequently at Leipzig under Nikisch. After engagements at Breslau and Göritz came to England where he was engaged by the Moody-Manners (1914-16) and Beecham Companies (1918-20). One of the founders of the B.N.O.C. He married May Blyth, a soprano of that company. Particularly admired for his Wagner interpretations, and author of an excellent analysis of The Ring. (R)

Buffo (It buffoon, comedian: possibly derived from the Lat. bufo = toad, from the inflated gloves used for exchanging comic blows on the stage). In the theatre, a buffone is a comic actor; in opera, a buffo is a singer of comic roles, hence basso buffo. *Opera buffa is a term for comic opera.

Bühne (Ger stage or theatre). The term is also used in the plural for theatre, e.g. Städtische Bühnen = Civic T.

Bühnenfestspiel (Ger stage festival play). Wagner's term for Der Ring des Nibelungen, deriving from his wish to make the work's staging a special occasion.

Bühnenweihfestspiel (Ger stage consecration festival play). Wagner's term for Parsifal.

Bulgaria. Western art forms were first introduced mainly by foreign bandmasters, after Bulgaria was liberated from Turkish rule (1396-1878). The first Bulgarian orchestra was founded in Shumen in 1851 by a Hungarian, Mihály Shafran (1824-1905). His successor, Dobry Voynikov (1833-78), was compelled to emigrate to Romania, where he ran a small musical theatrical company. In 1890 the first Bulgarian dramatic and operatic company, the Dramatichesko-Operna Trupa, was founded in Sofia. Though two series of performances were given in 1891 and 1908, when representations were made to the authorities with a project for a national opera, it was not until 1910 that regular seasons were established. The first Bulgarian libretto, a translation of Lucrezia Borgia, was published in 1891. Despite the success of these seasons, the lack of practical assistance held up the development of opera; many Bulgarian singers went abroad to study, however, either to Italy, Austria, or Russia, and it was a group of these who in 1907 formed the Bulgarska Operna Druzhba (Bulgarian Operatic Association). Performances were given in the Naroden Teatar (National T.). The first opera sung in Bulgarian was Pagliacci (1909).

Meanwhile, in 1878, profiting by the country's new freedom, Emanuil Manolov (1860-1902) had left to study in Moscow. Back by 1886, he set himself the task of founding a modern Bulgarian art music on the basis of the country's rich folk song and dance tradition. He is the composer of the first attempt at a Bulgarian opera, Siromakhkinya (The Poor Woman,

1900); though it is unfinished, two acts were given by an amateur company in Kazanluk in Dec. 1900. It was completed through the efforts of the Operna Druzhba (prod. Sofia, 1910). School performances of opera had also begun at Shumen in 1909; but it was during the next decade that opera really began to spread to other Bulgarian towns, notably Varna, Plovdiv, and Ruse.

The next Bulgarian opera was Kamen i Tsena (The Stone Pyramid, 1911), with melodies by Ivan Ivanov (1862-1941), harmonized and scored by the Czech conductor Václav Kaucký (1857-1917) and prod. in Sofia. Next came Georgy *Atanasov's historical opera Borislav (1910) and Dimiter Hadjigeorgyev's (1873-1922) Takhin Begovitsa (The Wife of Takhir-Bek, 1911). 'Maestro' Atanasov is the most important creative figure of the early days of Bulgarian opera, of which he is honoured as the founder. Another important figure of these early years was Todor Hadjiev (1881-1956), who conducted most of the new operas.

In 1921 a new period opened with the establishment of Bulgarian opera on a more professional basis, under the direction of Moysey Zlatin (1882-1953), Atanasov, and Hadjiev. Prominent composers of opera and operetta between the wars included Pancho Vladigerov (b 1899) (Tsar Kaloyan, 1936); Veselin Stoyanov (b 1902), who studied in Vienna with Franz Schmidt and came for a time under Schoenberg's influence but, reverting to folk inspiration, wrote the comic Zhensko Tsarstvo (The Kingdom of Women, 1935) and the Flaubert opera Salammbô (1940); and Lyubomir Pipkov (b 1904), composer of Yaninite Devet Bratya (Jana's Nine Brothers, 1937), Momchil (1948) and Antigona 43 (1963). More companies were formed during the 1930s as opera rapidly gained in popularity, but there was no permanent opera outside Sofia until after the war. A new impetus was given to operatic life, and there are now five National Operas as well as companies at Vratsa (founded 1953, opened with Traviata 1954) and Burgas (founded and opened with Traviata, 1955) and subsidised amateur companies based on other towns (Shumen and Sliven) as well as about 30 other amateur groups that, with professional assistance, give short seasons in their own areas. Contemporary opera composers include Marin Goleminov (b 1908) (Ivaylo, 1958); Konstantin Ilyev (b 1924); Parashkev Hadjiev (b 1912) (son of Todor), author of six operas including Albena (Varna, 1962, and in E. Germany) and Maystory, 1966); and Boyan Ikonomov (b 1900).

In 1912 a professional operetta group was formed: this encouraged native operetta, which has become extremely popular and attracts a large following. Operetta composers include, as well as Atanasov, Asen Kara-

stoyanov (b 1893), composer of five operettas including *Mikhail Strogov* (1940), Yosif Tsankov (b 1911), composer of five operettas including *Juana* (1939), and the prolific Boris Levyev (b 1902).
See also *Plovdiv, Ruse, Sofia, Stara Zagora, Varna*.

Bibl: P. Staynov and others: *Entsiklopediya na balgarskata muzykalna kultura* (1967).

Bülow, Hans von (b Dresden, 8 Jan. 1830; d Cairo, 12 Feb 1894). German conductor and pianist. After early musical training he went to Leipzig University to study law, and to Berlin where he wrote for *Die Abendpost* (defending Liszt and Wagner). The first performance of *Lohengrin* at Weimar under Liszt so overwhelmed him that he threw up the law and went to Zurich to study with Wagner. In 1851 he studied the piano under Liszt, whose daughter Cosima he married in 1857. In 1864 he became chief conductor at the Royal Opera, Munich, conducting there the first performances of *Tristan* (1865) and *Meistersinger* (1868) of which he also made piano scores. When Cosima deserted him for Wagner in 1869 he left Munich and toured Europe. In 1878 he was appointed conductor at the Court T. Hanover, and in 1880 Court Music Director at Meiningen.

A brilliant pianist and one of the great virtuoso conductors of the day, he was also a man of difficult temperament. Nevertheless, he behaved nobly over Cosima's desertion and sent her a consoling message on Wagner's death; and his forceful personality exercised a strong influence on musicians of his time, including the young Richard Strauss.
Bibl: H. Reimann: *Hans von Bülow* (1909).

Bumbry, Grace (Melzia) (b St Louis, Missouri, 4 Jan. 1937). American mezzo-soprano. Studied Boston, Chicago, and Santa Barbara with Lotte Lehmann. Début Paris, O., 1960, Amneris; Basle 1960-4; Bayreuth 1961, Venus; C. G. since 1963 as Eboli, Amneris, Salome, Tosca; Salzburg 1964-5 Lady Macbeth, 1966-7 Carmen; Milan Sc. 1966 and subsequently; N.Y., Met., since 1965. Repertory includes Santuzza, Delilah, Azucena, Fricka, and Orpheus. Since 1970 has also sung soprano roles. Has a beautiful and vibrant voice and a powerful dramatic personality. (R)

Bungert, August (b Mühlheim o/Ruhr, 14 Mar. 1845; d Leutesdorf, 26 Oct. 1915). German composer. Studied Mühlheim with Kufferath, Cologne with Seiss and others, Paris with Bazin, later Berlin with Kiel. In 1889 he formed a friendship with Carmen Sylva, Queen of Romania, under whose patronage was formed in 1911 the Bungert-Bund, with a magazine *Der Bund*, dedicated to the advancement of Bungert's works. His first opera was the comedy *Die Studenten von Salamanca* (1884).

His Wagnerian ambitions, doomed to failure by his lack of Wagner's genius, included the intention of building a 'Bayreuth' at Bad Godesberg on the Rhine for the performance of his Homeric tetralogy *Die homerische Welt*: this embraced *Odysseus' Heimkehr* (1896), *Kirke* (1898), *Nausikaa* (1901), and *Odysseus' Tod* (1901).
Bibl: M. Chop: *August Bungert* (1915).

Bunn, Alfred (b London, 8 Apr. 1806 or 1807; d Boulogne, 20 Dec. 1860). English theatre manager and librettist. After being stage manager at D.L. and manager of the T. Royal, Birmingham, he became joint manager of D.L. and C.G. in 1833. Between 1833 and 1835 he was responsible for the London appearances of Malibran and Schröder-Devrient. In 1835 he paid Malibran £3,375 for 19 appearances at C.G. He provided bad librettos and translations for a number of operas. His cheeseparing measures of economy have become legendary, and artists often found themselves engaged to sing in both theatres on the same evening. It is recorded that during the 1834-5 season 'female dancers pattered from one house to the other six times during the evening, and underwent the operation of dressing and undressing no less than eight'.
Bibl: A. Bunn: *The Stage* (1840).

Buona figliuola, La (The Good Daughter). Properly, *La Cecchina, ossia La buona figliuola*. Opera in 3 acts by Piccinni; text by Goldoni, after Samuel Richardson's novel *Pamela, or Virtue Rewarded* (1740). Prod. Rome, T. delle Dame, 6 Feb. 1760, with Borghesi, Savi, De Cristofori, Lovattini, Casaccia; London, Hm., 25 Nov. 1766, with Guadagni, Savi, Lovattini, Morigi, Quercioli, Maggiori, Piatti, Michele. It has occasionally been revived in Italy since 1945. Piccinni's 18th opera and greatest success. The text had already been set by Dani (1756) and Perillo (1759). Piccinni's less successful sequel was *La buona figliuola maritata* (text by Goldoni), prod. Bologna 10 June 1761 (also set by Scolari, 1762); a further sequel, by Latilla, was *La buona figliuola supposta vedova* (text by Bianchi), prod. Venice, Carn. 1766.

Burghersh, (Lord) (John Fane) (b London, 3 Feb. 1784; d Wansford, 16 Oct. 1859). English composer and musical organizer, son of the 10th Earl of Westmorland (succeeded to the title in 1841). He devoted such time as he could spare from his busy military, political, and diplomatic career to music, founding and for many years acting as President of the R.A.M. His compositions, which he promoted during his autocratic reign at the R.A.M., included seven operas in the Italian manner he regarded as the only authentic musical style: performed, except for the first, at Florence, they include

Bajazette (1821), *Fedra* (1824), *Il torneo* (1829), and *L'assedio di Belgrado* (1830: English version, *Catherine*).

Burgstaller, Alois (*b* Holzkirchen, 27 Sept. 1871; *d* Gmünd, 19 Apr. 1945). German tenor. Studied with Bellwidt and Kniese. After singing small roles at Bayreuth, was heard there between 1896 and 1902 as Siegmund, Siegfried, Erik, and Parsifal. His singing of this latter role at the N.Y. Met. in 1903, before the copyright had expired, resulted in his banishment from Bayreuth. Remained at the Met. until 1909. (R)

Burgtheater (Theater bei der Hofburg). The predecessor in Vienna of the Opera House on the Ring, where all the important productions took place until 1869. It was the scene of the premières of Gluck's *Orfeo*, *Alceste*, and *Paride ed Elena*, of Mozart's *Entführung*, *Figaro*, *Così fan tutte*, of Cimarosa's *Il matrimonio segreto*, and of the first Viennese performances of *Lohengrin* and Cherubini's *Médée*. Now the State T. for spoken drama.

Burian, Karel (known more generally as Carl Burrian) (*b* Rousínov, nr Rakovník, 12 Jan. 1870; *d* Senomaty, 25 Sept. 1924). Czech tenor. Studied Brno and Prague with Wallerstein. Début Brno, Provisional T., 1891 as Jeník. After engagements in Reval, Aachen, Cologne, and Hanover, was at Hamburg 1898-1902, when he went to Dresden. London, C.G., 1904 and subsequently, as Tristan, Tannhäuser, Lohengrin, and Herod in *Salome*, which role he had created in Dresden in 1905. Arnold Bax wrote that Burrian was a 'horrifying Herod, slobbering with lust and apparently almost decomposing before our eyes'. (R)

His brother **Emil** (*b* Rakovník, 12 Dec. 1876; *d* Prague, 9 Sept. 1926) was a leading baritone at the Prague National T. (1906-26), and sang regularly in Germany. The latter's son **Emil František** (*b* Plzeň, 11 June 1904; *d* Prague, 9 Aug. 1959) was a composer and producer, remarkable for his work in avant-garde opera. He wrote much stage music, including 8 operas of which the most important is *Maryša* (1940).

Burkhard, Paul (*b* Zurich, 21 Dec. 1911; *d* Zurich, Sept. 1977). Swiss composer. Popular for his operettas, among them *Casanova in der Schweiz* (1943) and *Feuerwerk* (1950).

Burkhard, Willy (*b* Évilard-sur-Bienne, 17 Apr. 1900; *d* Zurich, 18 June 1955). Swiss composer. His opera *Die schwarze Spinne* (1948, rev. 1954) had a considerable success on its first production.

Burla (*It* joke). A term used colloquially in the 18th cent. for comic *intermezzi*, whence *burletta* and *burlettina*.

Burning Fiery Furnace, The. Church parable by Britten; text by William Plomer. Prod. Orford

Church, Suffolk, 9 June 1966, with Pears, Tear, Drake, Shirley-Quirk, Godfrey; Caramoor, N.Y., 25 June 1967, with Velis, Metcalf, Lankston, Berberian, Pierson. Based closely on the Biblical narrative in Daniel 3, the work tells how Nebuchadnezzar (ten.) is converted to the God of Shadrach, Meschach, and Abednego when they survive being thrown into the fiery furnace.

Burrowes, Norma (Elizabeth) (*b* Bangor, 24 Apr. 1944). Welsh soprano. Studied London, R.A.M. with Flora Nielsen, and later with Rupert Bruce-Lockhart. Début Gly. Touring Opera 1970, Zerlina; Gly. Festival 1975, *Cunning Little Vixen*. C.G. 1970 Fiakermilli, and subsequently Woodbird, Despina, Oscar; E.N.O. since 1971; Salzburg 1971-3 Blonde; Aix Festival 1977 Despina; Toronto 1977 Marie (*Fille du régiment*). Repertory also includes Zerlina, Susanna, Fiorilla (*Turco in Italia*), and Nannetta. (R)

Burrows, Stuart (*b* Pontypridd, 7 Feb. 1933). Welsh tenor. Originally schoolmaster, turned to singing after winning prize at 1954 National Elsteddfod. Début W.N.O. 1963, Ismaele (*Nabucco*). C.G. since 1967; San Francisco 1967 Tamino; N.Y., Met, since 1971; Salzburg 1970 Don Ottavio. Guest appearances Vienna, Paris, etc. Repertory includes Elvino, Ernesto, Faust, Des Grieux (Massenet), Lensky, Alfredo, and Fenton, as well as all leading Mozart tenor roles of which he is considered one of the best exponents in recent years. (R).

Bury, John (*b* Aberystwyth, 27 Jan. 1925). English designer. Educated London University. After working as chief designer for Joan Littlewood's T. and the Royal Shakespeare Company with Peter Hall, turned to opera; designed *Moses and Aaron*, *The Magic Flute*, and *Tristan and Isolde* for C.G., working with Peter Hall as producer; Gly. also with Hall, *La Calisto*, *Il ritorno d'Ulisse*, *Don Giovanni*, and *Le nozze di Figaro*. His designs for Cavalli and Monteverdi succeed in catching the Baroque spirit while making use of modern stage apparatus and techniques.

Buryat Mongolia. Formed as an autonomous republic of the U.S.S.R. in 1923, the region previously had little organized cultural life, though there flourished a primitive kind of sung and danced stage epic known as *ekhor*. In 1926 there were organized the first music courses, whose students travelled the region giving small quasi-operatic entertainments on a special railway carriage. The State T. was opened in the capital, Ulan-Ude, on 7 July 1932: the director was Pavel Berlinsky (*b* 1900), who also composed the first Buryat opera, *Bair* (1938). This was followed in 1940 by *Enkhe Bulat Bator* (Enkhe, the Hero of Steel), by Markian Frolov (1892-1944); both works were included in a Moscow season of Buryat works that year. In 1941 Berlinsky wrote a musical comedy, *Shchaste* (Happiness), but the work's success was inhibited by difficulties with local singers used to a native musical tradition of unison singing and a pentatonic scale. Nevertheless, Berlinsky managed to stage productions of *Eugene Onegin* and *Faust* (1943). After the war, many singers went to study in Moscow and Leningrad, and on their return they began to build up a repertory of Russian and Western classics; the composers Knipper and Ryauzov came to study the folklore and to compose, respectively, *Na Baykale* (On Lake Baykal) and *Medegmasha* (both 1948). In 1948 the opera group separated from the drama section, and in 1952 the theatre was reorganized in a new building as the Order of Lenin Opera and Ballet T. (cap. 718). In 1960 the company visited Moscow with a repertory that included *Prince Igor* (in Mongolian). Other Buryat operas include the comedy *Prodelky Dyady Morgon* (Uncle Morgon's Tricks, 1957) by Baudorzha Yampilov (*b* 1916) and *Probratimy* (Blood Brothers, 1958), on a 17th-cent. subject by Dandar Ayusheyev (*b* 1910), and *Chuvesny Klav* (The Miraculous Treasure, 1970) by Yampilov.

Busch, Fritz (*b* Siegen, Westphalia, 13 Mar. 1890; *d* London, 14 Sept. 1951). German conductor. Studied locally and then at Cologne under Steinbach. Appointed Riga 1909, Aachen 1912, Stuttgart 1918, where he became Generalmusikdirektor. Succeeded Reiner at Dresden 1922; under his leadership the Dresden Opera enjoyed one of its most glorious periods. His uncompromising attitude to Hitler caused him to leave Germany in 1933. He went first to Buenos Aires, where he conducted 1933-6 and 1941-5, and also came to establish the *Glyndebourne Opera with Carl Ebert in 1934, returning each year until the war, and again in 1950 and 1951. N.Y., Met., 1945-9, also appearances elsewhere in Europe and America. His Mozart was superb, and he was also an outstanding conductor of Wagner and verdi. (R) His son, **Hans Busch,** is a producer, and head of the opera department at Indiana University.
Bibl: F. Busch: *Aus dem leben eines Musikers* (1949; trans. 1953).

Busenello, Gian Francesco (*b* Venice, 24 Feb. 1598; *d* Legano, 27 Oct. 1659). Italian librettist. Son of a lawyer; spent most of his life in his native city as a lawyer himself, but was not very successful and became rather cynical. His sharp realism, combined with a vivid awareness of sex, made him an ideal librettist for Monteverdi; his greatest work is *L'incoronazione di Poppea* (1634). In this there is not only a sense of the stage, of the nature and powers of a composer, of verbal and syllabic

niceties, but above all an insight into human behaviour and the ability to view even the most culpable of characters with a degree of understanding backed by a wry tolerance and a sardonic humour – qualities which did much to enlarge the scope of the young art of opera. His other librettos are for Cavalli's *Gli amori d'Apollo e di Dafne* (1640), *Didone* (1641), *La prosperità infelice di Giulio Cesare dittatore* (1646), and *Statira* (1655); according to Livingston, he also wrote a libretto *La discesa d'Enea all'Inferno* (1640).
Bibl: A. Livingston: *La vita veneziana nelle opere di G. F. Busenello* (1913).

Bush, Alan (*b* London, 22 Dec. 1900). English composer. His sympathy with Communism has dictated his choice of operatic subjects. These include a children's operetta, *The Press Gang* (1946), *Wat Tyler* (1950), an operetta *The Spell* (1953), *The Men of Blackmoor* (1955), *Guyana Johnny* (1966), and *Joe Hill* (1970). His works have been particularly successful in East Germany, and are also admired even by those who cannot accept their dominantly political outlook.

Busoni, Ferruccio (*b* Empoli, 1 Apr. 1866; *d* Berlin, 27 July 1924). Italian composer and pianist. His four operas have won limited but enthusiastic appreciation in Germany, though never in Italy, and are occasionally revived, *Arlecchino* (1917) with conspicuous success at Gly. (1954). The others are *Die Brautwahl* (1912), *Turandot* (1917), and *Doktor Faust* (completed by Jarnach, prod. 1925), for which Busoni's great friend and champion E.J. Dent claimed nobility and beauty despite its austere vein.
Bibl: E. J. Dent: *Ferruccio Busoni* (1933).

Bussani, Francesco (*b* Rome, ? ; *d* ?,). Italian bass. Début Rome, 1763, in Guglielmi's *Contadine bizzare*; Vienna 1784-94, where he created Bartolo and Antonio in *Le nozze di Figaro*, Alfonso in *Così fan tutte*, and Geronimo in *Il matrimonio segreto*; also Masetto and the Commendatore in the first Vienna *Don Giovanni*. Married the soprano **Dorotea Sardi** in 1786; she created Cherubino, Despina, and Carolina, and sang in London in 1809.

Busser, Henri (*b* Toulouse, 16 Jan. 1872; *d.* Paris, 30 Dec. 1973). French conductor and composer. Studied Paris Conservatoire with Widor and Gounod. Début Paris, O.C., 1902, conducting *Le Roi d'Ys*. Responsible for revivals of *Iphigénie en Tauride*, *Orfeo*, and other works. Also conducted at the O., and was director of the O.C. 1939-41. Works include *Jane Grey* (1891), *Daphnis et Chloé* (1897), *Les Noces corinthiennes* (1922), and *Le Carrosse du Saint-Sacrement* (1948).

Butt, (Dame) Clara (*b* Southwick, Sussex, 1 Feb. 1873; *d* North Stoke, 23 Jan. 1936). English contralto. Studied with Rootham at Bristol and at the R.C.M., London, and subsequently with Bouhy and Gerster. In 1892 sang Orfeo in a student performance at the Lyceum T. Her whole career was devoted to the concert platform, but in 1920 she was persuaded by Beecham to sing Orfeo under his baton at C.G. (R)

Byelorussia. See *Belorussia.*

Byron, George Gordon (Lord) (*b* London, 22 Jan. 1788; *d* Missolonghi, 19 Apr. 1824). English poet. Operas on his works are as follows.

The Bride of Abydos (1813): Poniatowski (1845); A. Fell (1853); F. Saud (1858); T. Dubois (1864); Barthe (1865); Lebrun (1897).

The Corsair (1813): Pacini (1831); Schumann (1844, unfin.); Bronsart (1875); Marracino (1900).

The Giaour (1813); Bovery (1840); Hermann (1866); N. Berg (*Leila,* 1912); Delmas (1928).

Lara (1814): Ruolz (1835); Salvi (1843); Maillart (1864); Marsick (1929).

Parisina (1815): Donizetti (1833); Giribaldi (1878); Keurvels (1890); Veneziani (1901).

The Siege of Corinth (1816): A. Cahen (1890).

Manfred (1817): Petrella (1872); Bogatyryov (1926).

Don Juan (1819): Blaramberg (comp. 1902). Canto 2 (the Haidee episode): Polignac (1877); Fibich (*Hedy,* 1896).

Marino Faliero (1820): Donizetti (1835); Holstein (1877, unfin.); Freudenberg (1889).

Cain (1821): Delvincourt (*Lucifer,* 1949); Schmodtmann (1952); Lattuada (1957).

Heaven and Earth (1821): Glière (1900).

The Two Foscari (1821): Verdi (1844); Bogatyryov (1926).

Sardanapalus (1821): Litta (1844); Alany (1852); Joncières (1857); Maître (1870); Famintsyn (1875); Duvernoy (1882, prod. 1892); Grunenwald (1961).

Also operas *Lord Byron* by Giarda (1910) and V. Thomson (1972).

C

Cabaletta (also *cabbaletta, cavaletta*. From It. *cavatinetta,* dim. of *cavatina,* which in turn dim. of *cavata:* extraction). The term has several meanings. It is usually applied to a short aria of simple, reiterated rhythm, with repeats. Rossini, whose operas have many, told Clara Novello that the first statement should be sung as written; thereafter the singer could embellish as he pleased. Anne's cabaletta in Stravinsky's *The Rake's Progress* is of this type, though deviations from the score would hardly be encouraged. In the 19th cent. the term grew to mean the final section only of an aria in several parts, usually quick and brilliant but now actually written down. It has also been used to describe the first section of an aria; this would on its reappearance be varied and often with triplets in the accompaniment (this has suggested a derivation from *cavallo,* a horse, from the galloping movement). One of the earliest examples of the cabaletta is the aria 'Le belle immagini' in Gluck's *Paride ed Elena.* Famous cabalettas include 'Ah! non giunge' in *La sonnambula,* 'Sempre libera' in *La traviata,* and 'Di quella pira' in *Il trovatore.*

Caballé, Montserrat (*b* Barcelona, 12 Apr. 1933). Spanish soprano. Studied Barcelona with Eugenia Kemmeny and later with Napoleone Annovazzi and Conchita Badia. Début Basel, 1956, First Lady. Basel 1956-9; Bremen 1959-62; repertory at that time included Aida, Salome, Renata (*The Fiery Angel*), Ariadne, Tatyana, Eva, and Elisabeth (*Tannhäuser*). Milan, Sc., 1960, Flowermaiden; regularly there since 1969 in major roles, including Lucrezia Borgia, Maria Stuarda, Norma. Mexico 1964; Gly. 1965 as Countess Almaviva and Marschallin.; N.Y., Carnegie Hall, Lucrezia Borgia, 1965; has since become identified with the Bellini-Donizetti repertory. N.Y., Met., since 1965. London, C.G., Violetta, 1972; regularly since 1975. Repertory also includes Imogene in *Il pirata,* Elisabeth I in *Roberto Devereux,* Caterina Cornaro, Elisabeth de Valois, and Giovanna d'Arco. Has an almost faultless technique, a beautiful limpid voice, and intelligent musicianship. Married to the tenor Bernabé Marti (*b* Villaroyade la Sierra, 1934). (R)

Caccini, Francesca (*b* Florence, 18 Sept. 1587; *d* Lucca?, *c* 1640). Italian composer, singer, and instrumentalist, known as 'La Cecchina'. Daughter of Giulio Caccini (see below). Appeared in Florence and elsewhere in Italy, then in Paris in 1604 at the court of King Henry IV; participated in numerous productions in Florence 1608-15 as a singer, and also player on the clavicembalo, chitarrone, and lute. Encouraged by Buonarotti, she turned to composition. Her *Ballo delle zigane* was given at the Pitti Palace in Feb. 1615. She collaborated with Da Gagliano for *Il matrimonio di S. Agata* (1622). In 1625 the première of her ballet-opera *La liberazione di Ruggero dall'Isola d'Alcina* so impressed the visiting Prince Władisław Zygmunt that he was encouraged to import opera into *Poland. Her sister **Settimia** (1590-1640) sang at the Medici court, 1602; created Venus in Monteverdi's *Arianne* at Mantua in 1608. She married Alessandro Ghivizzani (1572-1632), also in the service of the Medici as maestro di capella, who sang in Monteverdi's *Mercurio e Marte* for the opening of the T. Farnese in 1628.

Caccini, Giulio (*b* Rome, *c* 1545; *d* Florence, 10 Dec. 1618). Italian singer and lutenist to the Duke of Tuscany, but famous as one of the first opera composers. By 1589 he was a member of the *Camerata. Following Vincenzo Galilei, he wrote music giving increased importance to the single voice; hence he has (wrongly) been called the inventor of monody. His recitatives sung to his own accompaniment led to dramatic scenas, and so towards opera. Some of his music was included in *Euridice* (1600) by his rival Peri, and he then also set Rinuccini's text complete. This was the first published opera. He also set the same writer's *Dafne* and contributed to *Il rapimento di Cefalo.* His arias and choruses for this are in his collection *Le nuove musiche* (1602), which marked the new change in style from polyphony to monody. Other important collections appeared. One of the first composers to use a figured bass.

Cadenza. Literally Italian for cadence, whence an elaborate flourish ornamenting a final cadence at any point in an aria. From a tonic chord in its second inversion, the singer extemporized using his vocal virtuosity. He would come to rest eventually on the dominant, which was played by the accompaniment with its succeeding tonic. The ternary form of the da capo aria allowed three cadenzas, the last displaying the singer's most brilliant acrobatics. The excesses of some singers were reproached by *Tosi in 1723. In the early 19th cent., singers studied harmony in order to prepare their own cadenzas for insertion into operas; the results frequently pleased audiences of admirers but enraged the composers, who proceeded to write cadenzas themselves. Sometimes special cadenzas were written for individual singers, e.g. Rossini's *Semiramide* cadenzas for Patti. Singers and voice teachers edited volumes of cadenzas, one of the most famous being Marchesi's *Variantes et points d'orgue,* which gives nine different cadenzas for 'Ah, fors'è lui' in *La traviata.*

Cafaro, Pasquale (b San Pietro in Galatina, 6 (or 16) Feb. 1706; d San Pietro, 23 (or 25) Oct. 1787). Italian composer. Studied Naples, Conservatorio della Pietà die Turchini, with Leo and later became second maestro. His operas, incl. *La disfatta di Dario* (1756) and *Creso* (1768), led a contemporary to compare him to a majestic and placid river; though they lack dramatic life, they give him a place in history as a connection between the second and third Neapolitan school.

Caffarelli (orig. Gaetano Majorano) (b Bitonto, 12 Apr. 1710; d Naples, 31 Jan. 1783). Italian male soprano. Discovered by Domenico Caffarelli, whose name he took. Studied with Porpora for 5 years, allegedly concentrating on studies: Porpora sent him on his way with the words, 'Go my son, I have nothing more to teach you. You are the greatest singer in Europe'. Début Rome, T.V., 1724 (when 14). After triumphs in Venice, Milan, and Bologna, Caffarelli settled again in Naples. Spent 6 months in London during 1738, singing in Handel's *Faramondo* and *Serse*, but was said then to have been in poor voice. From 1741 sang regularly at Naples, S.C., also travelling widely in Italy and receiving the highest salary then ever paid to a singer. Visited France 1753, giving private recitals to cheer the Dauphine during the last months of her pregnancy as well as appearing in concerts and opera in Paris. Said to have been the first singer to have introduced chromatic scales as embellishments in quick movements. A highly quarrelsome man, who had once been under house arrest and once imprisoned for his behaviour to other singers, he challenged the poet Ballot de Sauvot to a duel over the merits of French and Italian music, and wounded him. Later sang in Lisbon, surviving the famous earthquake of 1 Nov. 1755. Retiring to Italy, he bought a dukedom and two palaces with the huge fortune he had amassed. One of the most famous of all the great castratos (Bartolo refers to him in the Lesson Scene of *Barbiere*).

Cagliari. Capital of Sardinia. The first theatre, built partly of wood, opened in 1770 and was called Las Plasas or the T. Regio. Reconstructed in 1836, it reopened as the T. Civico with *Belisario*. First performances were given of several operas by Sardinian composers, including Gonella's *Ricciarda* and Dessy's *Don Martino d'Aragona*. The theatre was destroyed during an air-raid in 1943. Opera was also performed in the Teatro Diurno, which was renamed the T. Cerruti in 1859 and was demolished in 1895, and in the Politeama Regina Margherita, also destroyed during the Second World War. Performances are now given in the T. Massimo, and during the summer in the open air.

Cagnoni, Antonio (b Godiasco, 8 Feb. 1828; d Bergamo, 30 Apr. 1896). Italian composer. Studied Voghera and Milan, producing while still a student the highly successful *Don Bucefalo* (1847). In 1856 became maestro di cappella at Vigevano, in 1863 director of the Istituto Musicale in Novara, in 1886 maestro di cappella at S. Maria Maggiore in Bergamo. *Michele Perrin* (1864) shows an awareness of Wagner, but *Claudia* (1866) reverts to a simpler manner. He had greater success with *Papà Martin* (1871; prod. London, Ly., by C.R. Company, 1875 as *The Porter of Havre*), and especially with his last work, *Francesca da Rimini* (1878). In the latter he makes quite advanced use of Leitmotiv. Of his 19 operas, only *Re Lear* was unperformed.

Cahier, Mme Charles (orig. Sarah-Jane Layton Walker) (b Nashville, Tenn., 6 Jan. 1870; d Manhattan Beach, Cal., 15 Apr. 1951). American contralto. Studied Paris with Jean De Reszke. Début Nice 1904; leading contralto of the Vienna Opera 1907-11; N.Y., Met., 1911-13 as Azucena, Amneris, and Fricka. Taught at the Curtis Institute. Also known as Mrs Morris Black. (R)

Cairo. Capital of Egypt. The opera house, commissioned by Ismail Pasha at cost of 2 million Egyptian pounds, was built in less than 6 months from plans by Italian architects. This replaced the old Vice-Regal T. Opened 1 Nov. 1869 with *Rigoletto*. *Aida* was commissioned for the new theatre (not for its opening) and performed there on Christmas Eve 1871 at a cost of 150,000 Egyptian pounds. From 1869 to 1961 opera was given regularly by foreign artists, especially Italians, only orchestra and chorus being Egyptian. After the Second World War, German, Yugoslav, and other visiting ensembles performed there. In 1961 *The Merry Widow* was sung in Arabic by an Egyptian cast. A modern house designed by a German architect is planned to be built at Gizeh. In 1972 the mostly wooden theatre burnt down.

Calaf. A Tartar prince (ten.), hero of Puccini's *Turandot*.

Caldwell, Sarah (b Maryville, Missouri, 6 Mar. 1928). American producer and conductor. Studied Boston and staged first opera, Vaughan Williams's *Riders to the Sea,* at Tanglewood while still a student. Founded Boston Opera Company in 1957 and been its director ever since. Produced first U.S. perfs. of *Boris Godunov* in its original version, first full U.S. stage perf. of *The Trojans, Intolleranza, Moses and Aaron,* and *War and Peace.* N.Y. City Opera 1973, *The Young Lord* and *Ariadne auf Naxos.* Conducts most of her Boston productions. One of the few U.S. producers displaying a contemporary approach to opera, which she treats as music theatre. First woman conductor at N.Y. Met. (*La traviata*), 1976.

Calife de Bagdad, Le. Opera in 1 act by Boieldieu; text by Saint-Just, after an Oriental tale. Prod. Paris, O.C., 16 Sept. 1800, with Gavaudan, Dugazon, Elleviou, Bertin, Paulin; London, H.M.'s 11 May 1809; New Orleans, 2 Mar. 1806. Also opera by M. Garcia (1812).

Calisto, La. Opera by Cavalli; text by Giovanni Faustini, after Ovid's *Metamorphoses*, II, 401-507. Prod. Venice, T. San Apollinare, 1651; prob. then unprod. until Leppard version, Gly., 26 May 1970, with Cotrubas, Stadler, Baker, Bowman, Gottlieb, Trama, Davià, cond. Leppard; Cincinnati, University, 12 Apr. 1972. Destiny informs Nature and Eternity that Jove has decreed that Calisto (sop.) daughter of Lycaon, King of Pelasgia, should be added to the stars as one of the immortals. Jove (bass) descends to an earth laid waste, accompanied by Mercury (bar.) to help restore nature, only to discover that Calisto has become a nymph of Diana (mezzo). Calisto rejects his advances, so Jove disguises himself as Diana and tries to seduce her. Endymion (counter-ten.), in love with the real Diana, is taken captive by Pan (bass) and his shepherds, but eventually united with his beloved. Meanwhile Calisto, who has been changed into a little bear by Juno (sop.), is taken to Mount Olympus by Jove, now restored to his normal person; there she will shine eternally as Ursa Minor.

Callas (orig. Kalogeropoulou), **Maria** (Anna Cecilia Sofia) (*b* New York, 3 Dec. 1923; *d* Paris, 16 Sept. 1977). Greek soprano. Studied Athens with Elvira De Hidalgo. Début 1938, Santuzza. Verona Arena 1947, Gioconda; Milan, Sc., 1951-8 and again 1960-2, where she sang in revivals of *Norma*, *Medea*, *Anna Bolena*, *Il pirata*, *Poliuto*, etc.; London, C.G., 1952-3, 1957-9, 1964; Chicago 1954-6; N.Y., Met., 1957-8, 1965; Dallas 1958-9. Her range, technique, and style made her the first soprano since Lilli Lehmann to have sung both Isolde and Lucia, Brünnhilde and Violetta. Her highly individual voice and great dramatic and musical talent were responsible for the revival of works by Rossini, Bellini, and Donizetti. Her vocal technique, which was not flawless, her intelligent treatment of the text, and her dramatic intensity combined to make her the most controversial singer of the period 1951-64, after which for personal reasons she withdrew from public appearances, while continuing to make occasional recordings. In 1971-2 she held a series of master classes at the Juilliard School in New York, and in 1973, together with Di Stefano, produced *I vespri Siciliani* to open the rebuilt T. Regio, Turin. (R)
Bibl: J. Ardoin and G. Fitzgerald: *Callas* (1974); J. Ardoin: *The Callas Legacy* (1977).

Calunnia, La. Don Basilio's (bass) aria in Act 1, scene 2 of Rossini's *Il barbiere di Siviglia.*

Describes gleefully the growth of slander from a little breeze to a gale that can blast a man's reputation.

Calvé, Emma (orig. Rosa Noémie Emma Calvet de Roquer) (*b* Decazeville, 15 Aug. 1858; *d* Millau, 6 Jan. 1942). French soprano. Studied with Puget, Marchesi, and Laborde. Début Brussels, La M., 1882, Marguerite. Milan, Sc., and other Italian houses from 1886; London, C.G., 1892-1904; N.Y., Met., 1893-1904; Manhattan Opera 1907-9; Boston 1912; Nice 1914. Retired from stage 1914, but made occasional concert appearances until 1927. Created Suzel (*L'amico Fritz*), Anita (*La Navarraise*), and Massenet's Sapho. First. C.G. Santuzza, Suzel, Amy Robsart, Salome (*Hérodiade*). Her most famous role was Carmen. Reynaldo Hahn said 'She never betrayed the music; her singing was always of the most perfect beauty'. (R)
Bibl: E. Calvé: *Sous les ciels j'ai chanté* (1940).

Calzabigi, Ranieri de' (*b* Livorno, 23 Dec. 1714; *d* Naples, July 1795). Italian librettist. His librettos brought him in touch with Metastasio, an edition of whose works he published during a stay in Paris. Here he and his brother ran a lottery, with Casanova as partner and under the protection of Mme de Pompadour, before being expelled. He is famous as the author of three librettos for *Gluck, *Orfeo ed Euridice* (1762), *Alceste* (1767), and *Paride ed Elena* (1770). These constitute a reform, away from the exaggeration and artificiality of *opera seria*, in favour of simplicity and dramatic truth. As witness of a return both to the earliest opera and to the Greek ideal from which that had derived, he turned to the Orpheus story. There was also, in particular reaction to opera seria, an emphasis on the characters as human beings rather than stereotypes, and a renewed care for the natural declamation of poetry; music would thus play a role more closely connected to the drama than to the demands of singers. Calzabigi imposed these reforms upon himself as well as upon Gluck, for his verses are designed not as the vehicle of elaborate metaphors or conceits but as the direct, lyrical articulation of dramatic situations. This is seen at its purest in *Orfeo*; in the other operas, especially *Paride,* more concessions are made.
Bibl: G. Lazzeri: *La vita e l'opera litteraria di Ranieri Calzabigi* (1907).

Cambert, Robert (*b* Paris, *c*1628; *d* London, *c* Feb. 1677). French composer. Studied Paris with Chambonnières. With the Abbé Perrin, he wrote *La Pastorale d'Issy* (1659), claiming it as the 'première comédie françoise en musique' (it was in fact preceded by Michel de la Guerre's *Le Triomphe de l'amour* (1654-5)). It consists of 14 songs, linked by *ritornelli*, with an overture (music lost). Cambert and Perrin then collaborated, also in 1659, on *Ariane et Bacchus* (prologue and 5 acts; music lost). In 1669 they obtained the privilege for performing opera in French, and in 1670 rented the Salle du Jeu de Paume de la Bouteille, the ancestor of the *Paris Opéra, and the first attempt at permanent opera in *France. Here they performed *Pomone* (1671). But the backers retained all the profits, and Perrin was imprisoned for debt; Cambert went on to write *Les Peines et les plaisirs d'amour* (1672), reputedly a better work (as with *Pomone*, only the prologue and first act survive). When Lully took over in 1672, Cambert moved to London, where he founded a short-lived Royall Academy of Musick in Covent Garden, and saw some of his works staged. He was possibly murdered by his servant.

Bibl: L. de La Laurencie: *Les Créateurs de l'opéra français* (1930).

Cambiaggio, Carlo (*b* Milan, 12 Dec. 1798; *d* Milan, 13 Apr. 1880). Italian bass, manager, and librettist. Début Varallo, 1829, in Mercadante's *Elisa e Claudio*. Director T. Carcano, Milan, 1832-4, where he was greatly admired as Dulcamara. Venice 1836-46, as singer and manager; fulfilled similar functions in Rome, T.V., 1846 and Portugal 1837. Continued to sing until the 1860s. Said to have been an intelligent musician and gifted comic actor. Composed comic duets for himself and his wife, the soprano Antonia Ranieri. One of his texts was set by Ricci and inserted in *L'elisir d'amore*.

Cambiale di matrimonio, La (The Bill of Marriage). Opera in 1 act by Rossini; text by Rossi, after Camillo Federici's comedy (1790). Prod. Venice, T. San Moisè, 3 Nov. 1810, with Morandi, Ricci, Rafanelli, De Grecis; N.Y., 44th St. T., 8 Nov. 1937, with Morel, Ilosvay, Hollander, Zangheri, Perulli; London, S.W., 23 Apr. 1954 by T. dell'O. Comica, Rome. Rossini's first opera to be performed. The duet 'Dunque io son' later used in Act 1 of *Il barbiere di Siviglia*. Sir Tobias Mill (bass), an English merchant, has promised the hand of his daughter Fanny (sop.) to Slook (bar.), a Canadian merchant. Fanny, however, is in love with Edoardo (ten.), and Slook helps them outwit Tobias.

Cambridge. English university town. The Cambridge University Musical Society has done much for English opera (especially if one considers Handel a native composer), above all in the period 1902-41 under E.J. *Dent, who was lecturer at King's from 1902, and Professor of Music there from 1926. During this latter period the following works were performed: Purcell's *King Arthur* (1928), Honegger's *Le Roi David* (1929), Purcell's *The Fairy Queen* (1931), Handel's *Samson* (1932), *Susanna* (1935 and 1938), *The Choice of Hercules* (1935), Vaughan Williams's *The Poisoned Kiss* (1936), Handel's *Saul* (1937), and Purcell's *The Tempest* (1938).

Before these productions the most important event, which had a far-reaching effect on opera in English, was the 1911 production of *The Magic Flute*, in Dent's translation, with a cast that included Steuart Wilson and Clive Carey. This led to the long-overdue acceptance of Mozart's opera into the English repertory.

Productions in more recent years have included Handel's *Solomon* (1948), Cavalieri's *La rappresentazione di anima e di corpo* (1951), Monteverdi's *Orfeo* (1950), Tranchell's *The Mayor of Casterbridge* (1951), Handel's *Athalia* and Vaughan Williams's *Pilgrim's Progress* (1954). In 1954 the Cambridge University Opera Group was formed, largely in the hope of staging works less 'academic' than those chosen for the official university productions. It has performed Cimarosa's *Il matrimonio segreto* (1955), Stravinsky's *The Rake's Progress* and Vaughan Williams's *Sir John in Love* (1956), Honegger's *Jeanne au Bûcher* (1957), Orff's *Catulli Carmina* and Liebermann's *The School for Wives* (1958), *The Mayor of Casterbridge*, Berkeley's *A Dinner Engagement*, and Bizet's *Don Procopio* (1959). It was from the group's efforts in 1956 that the *New Opera Company sprang.

Cambridge Theatre, London. Opened in 1930; has given opera on several occasions including a run of *Hänsel und Gretel* in 1934, and a two-year unbroken series (1946–8) by Jay Pomeroy's New London Opera under the artistic direction of Dino Borgioli and with Alberto Erede as musical director; the repertory consisted of *Don Pasquale, Don Giovanni, Rigoletto, Falstaff, Barbiere di Siviglia, Bohème,* and *Tosca,* Artists included Grandi, Noni, Welitsch, Rothmüller, Stabile, and Martin Lawrence. In 1951 the first English performance of Menotti's *The Consul,* with the original New York cast, was given there.

Camden Festival. Annual arts festival organized by the London Borough of Camden; devotes much of its efforts to reviving long-neglected operas and giving first British (or London) performances of contemporary works. Originally known as the Camden Arts Festival and mounted its operatic performances in the old St Pancras Town Hall; since 1970 the performances have been given in the modern Collegiate T. in Gower Street (part of London University), though Delius's *Koanga* was produced at Sadler's Wells T. in 1972. Productions have included J. C. Smith's *Ulysses* (1963), Haydn's *Il mondo della luna* (1961), *L'infedeltà delusa, L'incontro improvviso* (1966), *La fedeltà premiata* (1971), Rossini's *La pietra del paragone* (1963), *Il turco in Italia* (1965), *Elisabetta, Regina d'Inghilterra* (1968), *La donna del lago* (1969), *Tancredi* (1971), Verdi's *Un giorno di regno* (1961), *I masnadieri* (1962), *Aroldo* (1964), *Il corsaro*

(1966), Donizetti's *Maria Stuarda* (1966), *Marino Faliero* (1967), *Torquato Tasso* (1974), Leoncavallo's *La Bohème* (1970), Cilea's *Adriana Lecouvreur* (1971), Smetana's *The Secret* (1972), Rakhmaninov's *Aleko* (1972), Massenet's *La Navaraise* (1972), Hindemith's *Mathis der Maler* (1974), and Meyerbeer's *L'Étoile du Nord.*

Camerata (*It* society). The group of poets, musicians, and others which met in the house of the Florentine noble Giovanni de' Bardi from the years before 1580, in that of Jacopo Corsi from 1592. Though not exclusively a musical gathering, it gave rise to the discussions and experiments which led to the emergence of the new form of musical drama that was opera. The leading members included Jacopo Corsi, Vincenzo Galilei (father of the astronomer), Piero Strozzi, *Peri, *Caccini, Emilio de' Cavalieri, and *Rinuccini.

Their aim was to restore music to the position they conceived it to have held in ancient Greek drama, one of close, functional participation. Some of their principles were anticipated by *liturgical music drama, but their intelligence and practicality were new; various experiments followed their discussions, e.g. the costumed performance by Caccini of a madrigal setting by Strozzi for the wedding of Francesco de' Medici in 1579, and Galilei's setting of the Lamentations of Jeremiah (1582) 'after the fashion of the Ancient Greeks'. In 1586 Bardi's comedy *L'amor fido* was performed, with music consisting of six sung interludes, and in 1588 Cavalieri's *Rappresentazione di anima e di corpo*, consisting of recitatives and short choruses: these are nearer oratorio (the latter work is usually regarded as the first) than opera. Caccini's *Le nuove musiche* (1601) laid the basis for the development of a true dramatic style in music; it contained airs and madrigals in a new monodic style with thoroughbass accompaniment. The title of his work has come to be applied to the music of the period that, in reaction to the polyphonic style, attempted to give words prime importance in a monodic style. From this tendency came the work generally held to be the first true opera, Peri's *Dafne* (1597). The music is lost, but probably, like the works which immediately followed it, consisted of extended recitatives carefully stressing the meaning of the words, with discreet instrumental accompaniment.

Cammarano, Salvatore (*b* Naples, 19 Mar. 1801; *d* Naples, 17 July 1852). Italian librettist. After having various dramas produced, made his début as a librettist with *La sposa* (1834) for Vignozzi. From 1835 he was house poet of the S.C., Naples. Befriended Donizetti and wrote the texts for *Lucia di Lammermoor* (1835), *Belisario* (1836), *Pia de' Tolomei* (1837),

Roberto Devereux (1837), and *Maria di Rudenz* (1838). For Verdi, wrote *Alzira* (1845), *La battaglia di Legnano* (1849), *Luisa Miller* (1849), and *Il trovatore* (1853). In all he wrote some 50 librettos, including 9 for Mercadante and 6 for Pacini. A careful and skilled craftsman, he was adept at fashioning an effective libretto in traditional vein that would gratify composer, audience, and even censor, though often a good deal of the distinctive quality of his original source was thereby lost. His brother **Luigi Cammarano** (*c*1800-1854) was a composer.

Campana sommersa, La (The Sunken Bell). Opera in 4 acts by Respighi; text by Guastalla, after Gerhard Hauptmann's 'fairy-drama' *Die versunkene Glocke* (1896). Prod. Hamburg, 18 Nov. 1927, with Callam, Graarud, Guttmann, cond. Wolff; N.Y., Met., 24 Nov. 1928, with Rethberg, Martinelli, De Luca, cond. Serafin. Heinrich, a bell-founder, falls under the spell of the fairy Rautendelein (sop.), and follows her to the mountains. He returns home on the death of his wife Magda (sop.), but cannot forget Rautendelein, and on his own deathbed he calls for her and she returns to him.

Campanello di notte, Il (The Night Bell). Also known as *Il campanello dello speziale* (The Chemist's Bell). Opera in 1 act by Donizetti; text by composer, after a vaudeville by Brunswick, Troin, and Lhérie, *La Sonnette de nuit*. Prod. Naples, T.N., 1 June 1836 with Schultz-Oldosi, Ronconi, Casaccia; London, Ly., 30 Nov. 1837; N.Y., Lyceum, 7 May 1917. Don Annibale Pistacchio (bass), an elderly apothecary, has married young Serafina (sop.). Her former lover Enrico (ten.) disrupts their wedding night by presenting himself in various disguises at the apothecary's door, ringing the night-bell (the Campanello of the title) and demanding that various prescriptions are dispensed by the unfortunate bridegroom.

Campanini, Cleofonte (*b* Parma, 1 Sept. 1860; *d* Chicago, 19 Dec. 1919). Italian conductor. Studied Parma Conservatory. Début Parma 1882, *Carmen*. Music staff N.Y., Met., 1883-4; N.Y., Ac. of M., 1888; Milan, Sc., 1903-6; London, C.G., 1904-12. Conducted premières of *Adriana Lecouvreur*, *Siberia*, and *Madama Butterfly*. Conducted first London *Madama Butterfly*, *Pelléas et Mélisande*, *La fanciulla del West*, and *I gioielli della Madonna*. Manhattan Opera 1906-9 (Artistic Director), Chicago 1910-19 (General Manager 1918-19). Married the soprano Eva Tetrazzini. One of the great opera conductors of his day.

Campanini, Italo (*b* Parma, 30 June 1845; *d* Parma, 22 Nov. 1896). Italian tenor, brother of above. Studied Parma Conservatory with G. Griffini and later with Lamperti in Milan. Début Parma, Gennaro in *Lucrezia Borgia*, 1863. First Italian Lohengrin, Bologna, 1871. London début, D.L., 1872, Gennaro (*Lucrezia Borgia*); regularly there until 1881. N.Y., Ac. of M., 1873. Faust at opening of Met. 1883 and member of company 1891-4. Also impresario, and brought his brother Cleofonte to N.Y. to conduct American première of *Otello*.

Campiello, Il (The Square). Opera in 3 acts by Wolf-Ferrari; text by Ghisalberti, after Goldoni's comedy (1756). Prod. Milan, Sc., 12 Feb. 1936, with Favero, Carosio, Tess, Baccaloni, cond. Marinuzzi. The action revolves around the lives of four families who live in a little square in Venice; in the climactic scene a street fight develops, in which two elderly mothers, sung by character tenors, participate.

Camporese, Violante (*b* Rome, 1785; *d* Rome, 1839). Italian soprano. An aristocrat and married to a nobleman (Giustiniani), she did not begin her career until 1815. Studied Paris with Crescentini. Milan, Sc., 1817-30 where she created Bianca in *Bianca e Faliero* (Rossini); London, Kings T., 1817-24. A fine Mozart singer; roles included Donna Anna, Dorabella, and Sextus (*La clemenza di Tito*). First London Donna Anna, Ninetta (*La gazza ladra*), and Desdemona (Rossini's *Otello*). Sang until 1829.

Campra, André (*b* Aix-en-Provence, 4 Dec. 1660; *d* Versailles, 14 June 1744). French composer of Italian descent. Started career as church composer and was director of music at Notre Dame, Paris, by the age of 34. Began writing operas in secret for fear of the Church's displeasure, though his attempts at pseudonymity were soon exposed. In 1700 left Notre Dame, and devoted himself to writing many stage works that won great popularity. Among the most successful was the first, *L'Europe galante* (opéra-ballet, 1697). *Les Fêtes vénitiennes* (1710) was revived at Aix, 1975. His works satisfied the current French taste for variety and ingenuity while showing marked originality and progressiveness, and his declared aim was to combine the best in French and Italian music. The most important French stage composer between Lully and Rameau: though he lacks the grandeur of the former or the eloquence of the latter, his music has an attractive melodic liveliness.
Bibl: M. Barthélemy: *André Campra* (1957).

Canada. On 14 Nov. 1606 an original masque devised by Marc Lescarbot and called *Le Théâtre de Neptune* was played from small boats in the harbour of Port Royal on the Bay of Fundy. But this enterprise had no immediate successors. Towards the end of the 18th cent. opera performances began in Halifax, Quebec, and Montreal, and early in the 19th cent. in Toronto. By the middle of the 18th cent. a regular circuit of the main towns of the provinces of Upper and Lower Canada (now Ontario and Quebec) was travelled by small touring companies, and by many famous soloists from England, Europe, and the United States who presented opera excerpts and concerts. From the 1850s full companies made regular visits to Montreal and Toronto and often to many smaller centres; by 1900 almost every town had some acquaintance with opera and the larger cities frequently saw a standard repertory, including Weber and Wagner.

Productions of local origin were sporadic, and permanent companies had no lasting success until the middle of the 20th cent. The most successful has been the Canadian Opera Company (1950), which in addition to its seasons in Toronto and visits to Ottawa has, since 1958, sent out a touring company which visits every inhabited area of Canada as well as many towns in the United States. Premières have included Harry *Somers's *Louis Riel* (1967) and many first performances in Canada. Herman Geiger-Torrel was director 1950-76; he has been succeeded by Lotfi Mansouri. Since 1968 the touring company has been accompanied by its own orchestra. In 1961 productions by the T. Lyrique de Nouvelle-France began in Quebec City. L'Opéra du Québec was set up in 1971 to consolidate operatic production in Quebec and Montreal as well as other centres in the Province, but ceased operations in May 1975. A similar co-operative venture was established in 1972 in western Canada by the Opera Associations of Vancouver, Edmonton, Calgary, and Winnipeg, all of which began the local production of opera on a regular schedule during the 1960s.

Notable summer productions have been by the Stratford Festival, the summer festival at the National Arts Centre in Ottawa, and the Guelph May Festival.

Of special importance has been the transmission of opera by the Canadian Broadcasting Corporation. In 1948 the C.B.C. Opera Company was formed to present Canadian performers in live studio productions of a wide range of standard, unfamiliar, and contemporary works. The C.B.C. has also commissioned several operas, including Willan's *Transit Through Fire* (1942) and *Deirdre* (1946), John Beckwith's *Night Blooming Cereus* (1959), Kelsey Jones's *Sam Slick* (1967), and Murray Adaskin's *Grant, Warden of the Plains* (1967). T.V. productions began in 1953 with *Don Giovanni*. C.B.C. radio also transmits throughout the country important opera productions from many cities in Canada as well as from Europe and the U.S.A.

Despite the absence of permanent companies, numerous operas and operettas have been written by composers in Canada from the early 19th cent. There have also been many outstanding Canadian performers, incl. the conductors Wilfred Pelletier and Mario Bernardi; the singers Emma Albani, Pauline

Donalda, Edward Johnson, and Raoul Jobin of an earlier era; and more recently Victor Braun, Maureen Forrester, Don Garrard, Louis Quilico, Joseph Rouleau, Léopold Simonèau, Teresa Stratas, and Jon Vickers. See also *Montreal, Toronto, Vancouver.*

Caniglia, Maria (*b* Naples, 5 May 1905). Italian soprano. Studied Naples with Roche. Début Turin 1930, Chrysothemis. Swiftly became leading Italian lyric-dramatic soprano of the 1930s, singing at Milan, Sc., 1930-43 and again until 1951. London, C.G., 1937, 1939, and 1950, with Sc. Company; N.Y., Met., 1938-9. Married Pino Donati 1939, director of Verona Arena and latterly of T. Comunale, Bologna, and artistic director of the Chicago Lyric Opera until his death in 1975. An admired Tosca and Adriana Lecouvreur. (R)

Canio. The leader (ten.) of the strolling players in Leoncavallo's *Pagliacci.*

Cantelli, Guido (*b* Novara, 27 Apr. 1920; *d* Paris (air-crash), 24 Nov. 1956). Italian conductor. Studied Milan Conservatory with Pedrollo and Ghedini. Début Novara 1943. Conducted the Milan Sc. orchestra in London 1950. Turned his attention to opera in 1956 when he conducted *Così fan tutte* at the Piccola Scala. The announcement of his appointment as music director of Sc. was made a few days before his death. (R)

Canterbury Pilgrims, The. (1) Opera in 3 acts by Stanford; text by G.A.A'Beckett, after Chaucer's poem (unfin., 1400). Prod. London, D.L., 28 Apr. 1884.
(2) Opera in 4 acts by De Koven; text by Percy Mackaye, after Chaucer. Prod. N.Y., Met., 8 Mar. 1917, with Mason, Sembach, cond. Bodanzky.

Cantilena. (*It* lullaby or sing-song). Orig. the part of a choral composition with the main tune, or a small piece for one voice. Now used to describe a smoothly flowing, melodious part, or to indicate that a passage should thus be performed.

Canzone. A word of Provençal origin (*canzo*) describing a certain style of song. It has had various other meanings; in operatic usage it came, by the 18th cent., to mean an actual song outside the dramatic situation, e.g. 'Voi che sapete' in *Le nozze di Figaro*. The diminutive Canzonetta usually describes a short, simple song.

Capecchi, Renato (*b* Cairo, 6 Nov. 1923). Italian baritone. Studied violin, and singing in Milan with Ubaldo Carrozzi. Début Reggio Emilia 1949 as Amonasro. Milan, Sc., since 1950; N.Y., Met., 1951-4; London, C.G., 1962 and 1973 as Melitone and Bartolo (Rossini); Aix and Edinburgh Festivals, as Don Giovanni, Malatesta,

Dandini. A versatile and distinguished singing-actor, he has created many roles in contemporary works including Ghedini's *Billy Budd* and *Lord Inferno,* Napoli's *Un curioso accidente,* and Malipiero's *La donna è mobile.* (R)

Čapek, Karel (*b* Malé Suatoňovice, Bohemia, 9 Jan. 1890; *d* Prague, 25 Dec. 1938). Czech novelist and dramatist. Operas on his works are as follows: *Věc Makropulos* (1922): Janáček (1926); *Krakatit* (1924): Berkovec (1961); *Kašlik* (1961); *Bila Nernoc* (1937); Andrašan (1968).

Capobianco, Tito. (*b* La Plata, Argentina, 28 Aug. 1931). Argentinian producer. After working in the Argentine and Mexico, he was appointed producer and technical director of the T. Colón, Buenos Aires, in 1959, a position he held until he went to the U.S.A. in 1962 as artistic director of the Cincinnatti Summer Opera. N.Y., City Opera since 1965: here his productions have included *Hoffmann, Giulio Cesare, Bomarzo, Don Rodrigo, Anna Bolena,* and *Maria Stuarda.* Berlin 1972; Paris 1973; Sydney 1974. Director San Diego Opera from 1977.

Capoul, Joseph-Amédée-Victor (*b* Toulouse, 27 Feb. 1839; *d* Pujaudran-du-Gers, 18 Feb. 1924). French tenor. Studied Paris. Début O.C. 1861, Daniel in Adam's *Le Chalet.* London, D.L., 1871-5; C.G., 1877-9; N.Y., Ac. of M., 1871-4; Met. 1883-4 and 1892. Created many roles in Paris, and was a fine Fra Diavolo and Roméo. Taught N.Y. 1892-9. Stage manager Paris, O., 1897-1905.

Cappuccilli, Piero (*b* Trieste, 9 Nov. 1929). Italian baritone. Studied with Luciano Donaggio. Début Milan, T. N., 1957, Tonio. Milan, Sc., since 1964; N.Y., Met., 1959-60; Chicago since 1969; London, C.G., 1967, Germont, 1974, Iago, 1975, Renato; 1976 Boccanegra (with Sc.). His repertory of almost 50 operas includes 16 by Verdi. (R)

Capriccio. Opera in 1 act by Richard Strauss; text by Clemens Krauss and composer. Prod. Munich 28 Oct. 1942, with Ursuleac, Ranczak, Hann, Hotter, cond. Krauss; London, C.G., by Bavarian State Opera, 22 Sept. 1953, with Cunitz, Töpper, Kusche, Schmitt-Walter, cond; N.Y., Juilliard, 2 Apr. 1954, with Davy, Mackenzie, Stewart, Rue, cond. Waldman. A dramatized conversation piece, set in Paris at the time of Gluck's operatic reforms, which discusses whether words, as personified by the poet Olivier (bar.), or music, as personified by the composer Flamand (ten.), are of greater importance in opera. Poet and musician are both in love with the Countess Madeleine (sop.), who promises to choose one or the other the following day. The subject, however, remains unresolved. The old Italian tag from which the work takes its text, *Prima la musica e poi le parole* (First the music and then the words) is also the title of an opera by Salieri (1786).

Capuana, Franco (*b* Fano, 29 Sept. 1894; *d* Naples, 10 Dec. 1969). Italian conductor. Studied Naples, with De Nardis. Début Naples, 1919, *Aida*. Milan, Sc., 1937-40, 1946-52 (from 1949 as music director. Conducted several world premières in Italy, including Alfano's *L'ultimo Lord* (Naples, 1930), Refice's *Margherita da Cortona* (Milan, 1937), and Ghedini's *La pulce d'oro* (Genoa, 1940), as well as first performances in Italy of Honegger's *Judith* (Naples, 1937), *Jenůfa* (Venice, 1941), and Hindemith's *Hin und zurück* (Rome, 1943); also important revivals of Cherubini's *Lodoïska* (Milan, 1950) and *Elisa* (Florence, 1960), and Verdi's *Oberto* (Milan, 1951) and *Alzira* (Rome, 1967). Conducted the first post-war operatic perf. at C.G., *La traviata* with the S.C. Company, 5 Sept. 1946, and perfs. by C.G., 1951-2. A specialist in the non-Italian repertory, notably Wagner and Strauss. Collapsed and died while conducting *Mosè* on the opening night of the 1969-70 season at the S.C., Naples. His sister **Maria Capuana** (1891-1955) was a well-known mezzo-soprano specializing in the Wagner repertory. (R)

Capuleti e i Montecchi, I (The Capulets and the Montagues). Opera in 4 parts by Bellini; text by Romani, after Shakespeare's tragedy *Romeo and Juliet* (*c*1595-7). Prod. Venice, F., 11 Mar. 1830, with Giuditta Grisi, Caradori-Allan, Bonfigli, Antoldi; London, 20 July 1833, with Pasta, Méric, de Landey, Donzelli, Galli; New Orleans 4 Apr. 1847, with Rossi, Pantanelli, Ceresina, Candi. Text originally set by Vaccai, whose last act was until 1895 substituted for Bellini's in Italy, following a lead given by Malibran. Bellini himself used parts of his unsuccessful *Zaira* (1829) in it. Revived Milan, Sc., 1960 in version by Abbado, using tenor Romeo.

Caradori-Allan (orig. de Munck), **Maria** (Caterina Rosalbina) (*b* Casa Palatina, Milan, 1800; *d* Surbiton, Surrey, 15 Oct. 1865). Alsatian soprano. Studied with her mother, whose name she assumed for professional purposes. Début London, King's T., 1822, Cherubino. Sang regularly in London until 1827 and again from 1834, mostly in concerts. Created Giulietta in Bellini's *I Capuleti e i Montecchi*. Her salary rose from £300 in 1822 to £1,200 in 1827. Also sang at Milan, Sc., and Paris, T.I.

Carafa (de Colobrano), **Michele Enrico** (*b* Naples, 17 Nov. 1787; *d* Paris, 27 July 1872). Italian composer. After serving in the army in Russia (1812) and elsewhere and being decorated for gallantry, devoted himself to music.

His first success was with *Gabriella di Vergy* (1816). In Naples formed a lifelong friendship with Rossini, to two of whose operas he contributed, *Adelaide di Borgogna* and *Mosè in Egitto*. From 1821 he had much success in Paris, especially with *Jeanne d'Arc* (1821), *Le Solitaire* (1822), *Le Valet de chambre* (1823), and particularly *Masaniello* (1827), the last despite Auber's work on the same subject; he also had some success with *Le nozze di Lammermoor* (1829), *La Prison d'Édimbourg* (1833), and finally *Thérèse* (1838). A French citizen from 1834; from 1837 member of Académie des Beaux-Arts, and a prominent member of Rossini's circle. Much influenced by Rossini (who said, 'He made the mistake of being born my contemporary'), and later also by Cherubini. Though excellently written, his operas lack melodic individuality. In 1860 Rossini asked him to reshape the French text of *Semiramide* from two into four acts and to compose the ballet music compulsory for the O.; and knowing Carafa to be old and impoverished, generously assigned to him all the rights.
Bibl: F. Bazin: *Notice sur la vie de M.C. de Carafa* (1873).

Caramoor. The estate of Walter and Lucie Bigelow Rosen in Katonah, N.Y., where an annual summer festival, established in 1946 and including opera, takes place. The festivals have included productions of *L'incoronazione di Poppea*, *Dido and Aeneas*, and as well as the first U.S. performances of Britten's *The Burning Fiery Furnace*, *Curlew River*, and *The Prodigal Son*. Julius Rudel was music director 1963-76.

Cardillac. Opera in 3 acts by Hindemith; text by Ferdinand Lion, after E.T.A. Hoffmann's story *Das Fräulein von Scuderi* (1818). Prod. Dresden, 9 Sept. 1926, with Claire Born, Grete Merrem-Nikisch, Max Hirzel, Robert Burg. Concert perf. in English, London, B.B.C., 18 Dec. 1936, with Eadie, Licette, McKenna, Fear, cond. Raybould. First stage version in England, New Opera Company, S.W., 11 Mar. 1970 with Pashley, Robson, Wakefield, Cameron, cond. Lovett; Santa Fe, 26 July 1967 with Yarick, Endich, Stewart, Reardon, cond. Craft. Revised version (new libretto by composer, score unchanged), Zurich 20 June 1952 with Hillebrecht, Müller-Bütow, Lichtegg, Brauer, cond. Reinshagen. Concerns a master jeweller, Cardillac (bar.), who murders his customers rather than part with his creations.
Also opera by Dautresme (1867).

Carelli, Emma (*b* Naples, 12 May 1877; *d* Montefiascone, 17 Aug. 1928). Italian soprano. Studied with her father, the composer Beniamino Carelli. Début Altamura 1895 in Mercadante's *Vestale*; Milan, Sc., 1899-1901, where she was the first Italian Tatyana. Married the impresario Walter Mocchi, who managed the Rome O. and the Colón, Buenos Aires, where Carelli regularly sang. She managed the Rome O. herself 1912-26. Made her last appearance in 1914 as Iris. Her greatest role was Zazà. (R)

Carey, Clive (*b* Hedingham, 30 May 1883 English baritone; *d* London, 30 Apr. 1968). English baritone later teacher and producer. Studied R.C.M. and under Jean de Reszke. Papageno in the famous Cambridge *Magic Flute* 1911. Old Vic Opera Company 1920, sang in and produced *Figaro, Don Giovanni, Magic Flute*. Professor of Singing, Adelaide 1924-8. Toured U.S.A. and Canada as Macheath (*Beggar's Opera*). Opera producer at S.W. 1933; Adelaide Conservatory 1939, and Melbourne 1943-5. Director S.W. 1945-6. Professor of singing and director of opera at R.C.M. 1946-53.

Carl Rosa Opera Company, Royal. English opera company founded by Karl August Nicolaus Rose, a German violinist from Hamburg who came to England in 1866. After the death of his wife, the soprano Euphrosyne Parepa, in 1874, Rosa (as he was now known) decided to devote his life to presenting opera in English. In Sept. 1875 the Carl Rosa Opera Company came into being with a performance of *The Marriage of Figaro* at the Princess's Theatre, London. Rosa became associated with Augustus Harris, manager of Drury Lane, and a prosperous 5 years followed (1883-8). Harris then took over Covent Garden, and in 1889 Rosa died. The company became a touring organization, giving only occasional London seasons.

In 1893 Queen Victoria conferred the title 'Royal' on the company following a performance at Balmoral Castle. From 1900 until 1916 the company was under the management of Alfred van Norden; and from 1916 until 1923 Arthur Winckworth and Mrs Carl Rosa (Rosa's second wife) were co-directors. After the First World War the company took over both the Harrison-Frewin and the Alan Turner companies. The former was under the management of H. B. Phillips, who in 1923 took over the direction of the Carl Rosa Company. At this time Phillips had two and sometimes three companies touring the provinces.

Phillips died in 1950 and his widow directed the company, with Arthur Hammond as music director, from then until 1957, when she was succeeded by H. Procter-Gregg. In 1953 the Arts Council made a grant of £20,000 to the company which was increased in stages to £61,000 for 1957-8. At the same time the Arts Council provided the funds for the purchase of the company from her. Internal differences between the board of directors and Procter-Gregg

led to the latter's resignation in 1958 and to the withdrawal of the Arts Council's subsidy. At the end of 1958 most of its personnel were taken over by Sadler's Wells, when Norman Tucker and his associates launched their new scheme of opera and operetta in London coupled with a greater amount of touring of the provinces. The company made an unsuccessful attempt to stage a come-back in 1960.

The company gave the first perf. in England of *Manon* (1885), *La Bohème* (1897), and *Andrea Chénier* (1903), and the premières of a number of British works, including Goring Thomas's *Esmeralda* (1883) and *Nadeshda* (1885), Stanford's *The Canterbury Pilgrims* (1884), and Lloyd's *John Socman* (1951).

Carmelites, The. See *Dialogues des Carmélites.*

Carmen. Opera in 4 acts by Bizet; text by Meilhac and Halévy, after Mérimée's *nouvelle* (1845). Prod. Paris, O.C., 3 Mar. 1875, with Galli-Marié, Chapuy, Lhérie, Bouhy, cond. Deloffre; Vienna 23 Oct. 1875 (in German, with recitatives by Guiraud replacing spoken dialogue); London, H.M.'s, 22 June 1878, with Hauk, Valleria, Campanini, Del Fuente, cond. Arditi; N.Y., Ac. of M., 23 Oct. 1878, with Hauk, Campanini. The first serious objection to the performance of *Carmen* with recitatives came from Saint-Saëns, who declared it nonsensical. Guiraud's version not only distorts the opera's true opéra-comique nature but removes essential information in the dialogue and dilutes some characters. Nevertheless, the restoration of the original to currency has been a slow process.

In Seville in 1820, Micaela (sop.) comes to find her friend Don José (ten.), a corporal under the command of Captain Zuniga (bass). But José is fascinated by the gipsy Carmen (mezzo), and when she is arrested after a fight he contrives her release. He is in turn arrested, but refuses to desert when he is later released; however, Carmen, though beginning to fall under the spell of the Toreador Escamillo (bar.), persuades him to flee with her and a group of smugglers. Following them, Escamillo fights with José, who is led away from the now bored and scornful Carmen by Micaela. Outside the Seville bullring, Carmen promises herself to Escamillo if he wins; but the dishevelled José appears, and stabs her as Escamillo emerges triumphantly with the crowd.

Carmina Burana (Songs of Benediktbeuren). Scenic cantata by Orff; text by composer and Michel Hofmann, later Wolfgang Schadewaldt, from poems in Latin, Old German, and Old French in a Latin codex of 13th-cent. songs in the monastery of Benediktbeuren (pubd. 1847). Prod. Frankfurt 8 June. 1937, with Ebers, Stern, cond. Wetzelsberger; San Francisco 3 Oct.

1958, with Malbin, Manton, cond. Ludwig; London, R.F.H., 26 Jan. 1960.

Carnicer (y Batlle), **Ramón** (b Tarrega, 24 Oct. 1789; d Madrid, 17 Mar. 1855). Spanish composer. Studied Barcelona, where in 1814 he formed an Italian company led by *Generali. Contributed inserted numbers to Italian operas; made his début as an opera composer with *Adele di Lusignano* (text by Romani, 1819) and then two other *semi-seria* works. Moved to Madrid in 1828 and produced four more operas to Romani texts, *Elena e Malvina* (1829), *Cristoforo Colombo* (1831), *Eufemio di Messina* (1832), and *Ismalia* (1838). He was the outstanding Spanish composer of opera, albeit Italian opera, in the early 19th cent.

Carnival. From the Lat. *carnem levare*: the putting away of meat as food. The period before Lent traditionally associated with festivity and licence. For operatic purposes, the season is usually dated from 26 December until the beginning of Lent in March or April, when especially in Italy in the 17th cent. new operas were produced. The celebrations differed widely in nature from country to country and from town to town. In Italy, the most licentious were in Rome, as Goethe distastefully observed, and are represented in Act 2 of Berlioz's *Benvenuto Cellini*; the most sumptuous were in Venice.

Caro nome. Gilda's (sop.) aria in Act 1, scene 2, of Verdi's *Rigoletto*, expressing her love for the 'student' Gualtier Maldé, who is in fact the Duke of Mantua.

Caron (orig. Meuniez), **Rose** (Lucille) (b Monderville, 17 Nov. 1857; d Paris, 9 Apr. 1930). French soprano. Studied Paris with Obin and Massol, and later with Sass. Début 1880 in concert; stage début Brussels 1883, Alice (*Robert le Diable*), where she created Brunehilde in Reyer's *Sigurd* (La M., 1884) and title-role in his *Salammbô* (1890), and the title-role in Godard's *Jocelyn* (1888). Paris, O., 1885-8 and 1890-5, and occasional appearances until 1908; here she was the first French Sieglinde and Desdemona. Professor of singing, Paris Conservatoire, 1902-8. (R)

Carosio, Margherita (b Genoa, 7 June 1908). Italian soprano. Début Novi Ligure 1924, Lucia. London, C.G., 1928, 1946, 1950. Milan, Sc., 1929, where she created Egloge in Mascagni's *Nerone*, 1935. Originally a light soubrette, she developed into a lyric soprano and returned to London as Violetta in the Naples S.C. 1946 season. (R)

Carré (orig. Giraud), **Marguerite** (b Cabourg, 16 Aug. 1880; d Paris, 26 Dec. 1947). French soprano. Daughter of the theatre director of Nantes where she made her début as Mimì, 1899. Paris, O.C., 1901, whose director, **Albert Carré**, she subsequently married, divorced in

1924, and remarried in 1929. Created 15 roles at the O.C. Also the first Paris Cio-Cio-San, Snegurochka, and Salud (*La vida breve*), and an outstanding Louise, Manon, and Mélisande. (R)

Carré, Michel (b Paris, 1819; d Argenteuil, 27 June 1872). French librettist. Furnished most of the leading French composers of the second half of the 19th cent. with librettos, including Meyerbeer (*Dinorah*), Gounod (*Mireille, Faust, Roméo et Juliette*, and five more), Bizet (*Pêcheurs de Perles*), Thomas (*Hamlet, Mignon*), Offenbach (*Contes d'Hoffmann*), often in collaboration with Jules *Barbier. Uncle of Albert Carré (see above). Sometimes wrote under the name of Jules Dubois.

Carreras, José Maria (b Barcelona, 5 Dec. 1946). Spanish tenor. Studied Barcelona with Jaime Francesco Puig. Début aged 10 as Trujaman in Falla's *Retablo de Maese Pedro*. Professional début Liceo, Barcelona, Flavio (*Norma*); soon singing Ismaele in *Nabucco* and Gennaro in *Lucrezia Borgia* opposite Caballé, who furthered his career. London July 1971 in concert perf. of *Maria Stuarda*; C.G., since 1974 as Alfredo, Nemorino, Rodolfo etc., and Oronte in first C.G. perf. of *I Lombardi*. N.Y., City Opera 1972; Met. from 1974; appearances also in Dallas, San Francisco, and other U.S. cities. Milan, Sc., 1975. A serious and highly gifted young artist with one of the most naturally beautiful tenor voices of the day. (R)

Carron (orig. Cox), **Arthur** (b Swindon, 12 Dec. 1900; d Swindon, 10 May 1967). British tenor. Début London, Old Vic., 1929; subsequently leading tenor there and S.W. until 1935; C.G. 1931, 1939. N.Y., Met., 1935-46 where he created Nolan in Damrosch's *The Man without a Country* (1937); also sang in Chicago, Cincinnati, Philadelphia, and South America. Returned to England, C.G., 1947-51. One of the best English dramatic tenors of the inter-war years, especially as Tannhäuser, Canio, and Otello.

Carte, Richard D'Oyly (b London, 3 May 1844; d London, 3 Apr. 1901). English impresario. He was the son of a music publisher and was originally destined for a musical career, but soon turned to the business side of music, first as manager of Patti, Mario, Gounod, and others, then as a theatre manager, introducing to England Lecoq's *Giroflé-Girofla* and Offenbach's *La Périchole* and *Whittington*. In 1875 he commissioned *Trial by Jury* from Gilbert and *Sullivan, and its great success led to his forming a company to continue to present works by them at the Opéra-Comique in London. He then built his own theatre, the Savoy, which opened with *Patience* in 1881. Here the Gilbert and Sullivan partnership flourished for ten uninterrupted years, to be resumed in 1893 with *Utopia Ltd* and 1896 with *The Grand Duke*. In 1891 Carte made an attempt to establish English Grand Opera and built the English Opera House (now the Palace Theatre) in Cambridge Circus, which opened with Sullivan's *Ivanhoe*. The venture was not a success. Carte introduced electric lighting into the theatre and abolished charges for programmes and cloakrooms. His theatrical enterprises were continued by his widow until her death in 1913, then by his sons, and now by his granddaughter Bridget.

Cartellone (*It* a large placard; hence a playbill). The term has come to mean the list of operas to be performed during the season. The *cartellone* does not include the names of artists appearing; they are listed under a separate heading, *elenco artistico*.

Caruso, Enrico (*b* Naples, 27 Feb. 1873; *d* Naples, 2 Aug. 1921). Italian tenor. Studied with Guglielmo Vergine and Vincenzo Lombardi. His début at the T.N. Naples 16 Nov. 1894, in *L'amico Francesco* (Morelli), led to engagements all over Italy. Created Maurizio (*Adriana Lecouvreur*) and Loris (*Fedora*). Appeared with Melba at Monte Carlo early in 1902. London, C.G., 1902, as Duke of Mantua, 1904-7, 1913-14. N.Y., Met., 1903-20, making more than 600 appearances in nearly 40 operas including Dick Johnson in the world première of *La fanciulla del West* and the first Metropolitan performances of *Armide* and *La forza del destino*.

Caruso possessed one of the most beautiful tenor voices the world has ever known. In his young days it was mellow, sumptuous, of baritone-like quality in its lower register, and until 1906 he sang with almost reckless abandon and gaiety. During the next stage of his vocal career he subtilized his art, and his phrasing and style became well-nigh impeccable. In 1908-9 he suffered a temporary vocal setback, and subsequently his voice darkened. But all who heard him sing at any stage in his career claim that no sound like it has been heard since. He was moreover a convincing actor, especially in such roles as Eleazar, Canio, and Vasco da Gama.

Caruso was perhaps the first true 'gramophone' tenor; he began recording in 1902 and made his last recordings in 1920. It is said that during his lifetime his royalties from records amounted to something between four and five hundred thousand pounds. From his many records perhaps his 'Una furtiva lagrima' (1904) and 'O Paradiso' (1910) represent operatic singing at its very greatest. His career came to an end on Christmas Eve 1920 when he was singing Eleazar in *La Juive* while suffering from acute pain which developed into bronchial pneumonia. The centenary of his birth was the occasion of world-wide celebrations in 1973. (R)
Bibl: D. Caruso: *Enrico Caruso, his Life and Death* (1945); T. R. Ybarra: *Caruso* (1953).

Carvalho (orig. Carvaille), **Léon** (*b* Port-Louis, France, 18 Jan. 1825; *d* Paris, 29 Dec. 1897). French impresario. Studied Paris Conservatoire and was a singer at the O.C. 1851-5, where he met Marie *Miolan whom he married in 1853. Director, T.L., 1856-8; then stage manager, O., and director, O.C., 1876-87. In the latter year the theatre was burned down and 131 people were killed; Carvalho was fined and imprisoned for negligence, but in 1891 after a successful appeal was reinstated in his former position.

Cary, Annie Louise (*b* Wayne, 22 Oct. 1841; *d* Norwalk, Conn., 3 Apr. 1921). American mezzo. Studied Boston, Milan with Giovanni Corsi, and Baden-Baden with Viardot. Début Copenhagen 1868, Azucena. After appearances in Stockholm, Hamburg, St Petersburg, appeared London, C.G., 1870 (as Louise Cari), Maffio Orsini in *Lucrezia Borgia*. Engaged by Strakosch for U.S.A., where she sang Amneris in first U.S. *Aida* and was the first American-born woman to sing a Wagner role – Ortrud in 1877. Greatly admired by Anton Rubinstein, who called her voice the most beautiful he had ever heard in the whole world. Retired from stage in 1881 following many cancellations due to serious vocal trouble.

Casaccia. Family of Italian buffo singers.
(1) **Giuseppe** (*b* Naples, 1714; *d* Naples, 1783). Début T. Fiorentini, Naples, 1749. Created Mengotto in Piccinni's *Buona figliuola* (Rome 1760), and noted for his performances in Paisiello. Sang for 34 years.
(2) **Antonio** (generally known as Casacciello) (*b* Naples, 1719; *d* Naples 22 Feb. 1793). Brother of above. Début Naples 1749 and sang there exclusively for 39 years in operas by Anfossi, Cimarosa, Guglielmi, Piccinni, and Paisiello.

Giuseppe's son **Filippo** (*b* 1751) sang buffo roles in the Italian provinces; Antonio's son **Carlo** (*b* Naples 1768) sang 1785-1827; his son **Raffaelle** (*d* Naples, 1852) sang in operas by Rossini and Donizetti; best known for his Don Checco in De Giosa's opera, which he sang for 96 consecutive performances in 1850. His son **Ferdinando** (*d* Naples, 1894), last of the family, sang from 1852 to 1890.

Casanova de Seingalt, Giovanni Jacopo (*b* Venice, 2 Apr. 1725; *d* Dux (Duchcov), 4 June 1798). Italian writer and adventurer. He was notorious for his amorous exploits, and his daring escape from the Piombi in Venice, and many other incidents are colourfully related in his 12 volumes of *Mémoires* (1791-8). Translated Rameau's *Zoroastre* for Dresden in

1752, and wrote the texts for many other works, some for the stage, with music; he also left a Utopian romance entitled *Icosaméron* in which there are thoughtful observations on the relationship of words and music in opera. He was a friend of Da Ponte, and may have been present at the first performance of *Don Giovanni*. Operas on his adventures are as follows: Lortzing (1841), Pulvermacher (1890), Eysler (early 20th cent.), Różycki (1923), Andreae (4 1-act operas, 1924), Pick-Mangiagalli (1929).

Casavola, Franco (*b* Mondugno, 13 July 1891; *d* Bari, 7 July 1955). Italian composer. An early adherent of Futurism, he wrote a number of works for the movement, turning later to traditional opera with greater general success: his operas include the 1-act comedy *Il gobbo del Califfo* (1929), *Astuzie d'amore* (1936), and *Salammbô* (1948).

Casazza, Elvira (*b* Ferrara, 15 Nov. 1887; *d* Milan, Jan. 1965). Italian mezzo-soprano. Début Varese, 1909. Milan, Sc., 1915-42; London, C.G., 1926, 1931. A favourite artist of Toscanini, famous for her Mistress Quickly. Created Debora in Pizzetti's *Debora e Jaële* (1922) and La Commandante in *I cavalieri di Ekebù* (1925). After 1948 taught singing, first at Pesaro, latterly in Rome. (R)

Caspar. An evil huntsman (bass) in Weber's *Der Freischütz*.

Casella, Alfredo (*b* Turin, 25 July 1883; *d* Rome, 5 Mar. 1947). Italian composer. Studied Paris, with Fauré; returned to Italy in 1915. He wrote three operas: *La donna serpente* (1932); the 1-act chamber opera *La favola d'Orfeo* (1932); and a 1-act mystery, *Il deserto tentato* (1937).

Cassilly, Richard (*b* Washington, D.C., 14 Dec. 1927). American tenor. Studied Baltimore, Peabody Institute. Début N.Y., Broadway T., 1955, Michele (*Saint of Bleecker Street*). After appearances with the New York City Opera, Chicago Opera, etc., made European début 1965, Geneva, as Raskolnikoff (Sutermeister). Hamburg State Opera since 1965; London, C.G. since 1968 as Laca, Grimes, Otello, Florestan, Siegmund, Tannhäuser. A very large man with impressive physique and voice, and a powerful actor. (R)

Casta Diva. Norma's (sop.) aria with chorus in Act 1 of Bellini's *Norma,* praying to the Moon for peace between Gaul and Rome.

Castagna, Bruna (*b* Bari, 15 Oct. 1905). Italian contralto. Début 1925 Mantua, Nurse (*Boris Godunov*). Milan, Sc., 1925-8, 1932-4. N.Y., Hippodrome, 1934; Met. 1935-45, where her Adalgisa, Laura, and Verdi roles were much admired. Her sister **Maria Castagna** (sometimes known as Maria Falliani) was also active

as a contralto in Italy and the U.S.A. in the 1920s and 1930s. (R)

Castellan (orig. Chastel), **Jeanne Anais** (*b* Beaujeu, Rhône, 26 Oct. 1819; *d* ?, ?). French soprano. Studied with Cinthie-Damoreau, Bordogni, and Nourrit at the Paris Conservatoire, where she gained first prize for singing 1836. Début Varese 1837 as Amina. After appearances in Italy and Austria, engaged for a Philharmonic Concert in London 1844. H.M.'s 1845-7; C.G. 1848-53. Created Bertha (*Le Prophète*); first C.G. Glicera (Gounod's *Sapho*), Cunegunda (Spohr's *Faust*), and Amazili (Spohr's *Jessonda*). New Orleans, 1843; Boston and N.Y., 1843-4; St Petersburg 1844-6.

Castelmary, Armand (Comte de Castan) (*b* Toulouse, 16 Aug. 1834; *d* New York, 10 Feb. 1897). French bass. Paris, O., 1863-70, where he created Don Diego in *L'Africaine* (1865), *Hamlet* (1868), and the Grand Inquisitor in *Don Carlos* (1867). London, C.G., 1889-96; N.Y., Met., 1893-7, but had already appeared in U.S.A. in 1870 with French Company in New Orleans, in 1879 with Strakosch's Company, and in 1890 with the Patti-Tamagno company. Repertory included Bertram in *Robert le diable*, Méphisthophélès in both Gounod's and Boito's operas. Collapsed and died during a performance of *Martha* at the Met. in which he was singing Sir Tristan. He was married for a time to the soprano Marie *Sasse.

Casti, Giovanni Battista (*b* Acquapendente, 29 Aug. 1724; *d* Paris, 5 Feb. 1803). Italian dramatist and librettist. He travelled widely, and visited Russia, where he wrote *Lo sposo burlato* (1779), and Vienna, where he wrote *Re Teodoro in Venezia* (1784), both for Paisiello. There followed works for Salieri, including *Prima la musica e poi le parole* (1785), a sharp satire on the low status of 18th-cent. librettists and the caprices of composers; it includes some glancing blows at Da Ponte. For Salieri he also wrote *Cublai, Gran Can de' Tartari* (1788, unprod.), and other works. He developed the *dramma eroicomico*, in which a famous historical character is presented in a laughable light, thus foreshadowing Offenbach. A skilled craftsman, with ·a cutting wit and a vein of melancholy, he deserved, in spite of his views, greater composers.

Castil-Blaze, François (*b* Cavaillon, 1 Dec. 1784; *d* Paris, 11 Dec. 1857). French writer on music and composer. His chief work is the 2-vol. *De l'Opéra en France* (1820), which discusses the suitability of words for music and the components of opera, also attacking theatre managers, critics, and translators. He was himself a critic (of the *Journal des Débats*, 1822-32) and a distinguished translator; but he was guilty of needlessly adapting foreign works and upsetting their proportions, not least by inserting numbers of his own. His version of Weber's *Der Freischütz* as *Robin des bois* (1824) caused the distress of the composer, and the rage of his successor on the *Débats,* Berlioz. He also included parts of *Euryanthe* (which he later translated, 1831) in a *pasticcio, La Forêt de Senart* (1826). Father of the critic Henri Blaze de Bury (1813-88).

Castle Gardens. A place of popular entertainment in New York in the middle of the last century, and the scene of performances by visiting foreign opera companies after the destruction of the Park T. in 1848. It was here that Grisi and Mario made their American débuts in *Lucrezia Borgia* in 1854.

Castor et Pollux. Opera in prologue and 5 acts by Rameau; text by Pierre Joseph Bernard. Prod. Paris, O., 24 Oct. 1737, with Pellisier, Tribou, Chassé, and rev. without prologue and new Act 1, 1754; Glasgow (amateur), 27 Apr. 1927; N.Y., Vassar College, 6 Mar. 1937. Revived Florence Festival, 1935, with Lubin, Villabella, Rouard, cond. Gaubert.

Pollux is the son of Jupiter and is immortal, Castor the son of Tyndareus and mortal. Castor has been killed, but when Pollux offers himself in Castor's place to Telaira, she is confused and insists instead that Jupiter must be persuaded to restore Castor to life. Jupiter agrees on condition that Pollux take his place in Hades, while also revealing to him the delights of the Heavenly Pleasures on Olympus. Pollux remains firm, but at the gates of Hades he is met by Phoebe, who loves him and tries to turn him back, while Telaira spurs him on. With Mercury's help, he enters Hades; Castor agrees to return to earth and to tell Telaira he cannot accept Pollux's sacrifice. But Jupiter intervenes to declare that both Castor and Pollux shall be taken up to Olympus; Telaira will follow; Phoebe is left, and kills herself. Other operas on the legend are by Bianchi (1780), Vogler (1791), Federici (1803), and Winter (1806).

Castrato (*It* castrated), or **Evirato** (*It* unmanned; the term *musico* was also current in the 17th cent). A male soprano or contralto whose unbroken voice has been artificially preserved by means of a surgical operation before puberty. The practice of systematically castrating boys so as to provide adult sopranos and contraltos was justified by the Roman Catholic Church interpreting an injunction of St Paul to the effect that women should keep silent in church (1. Cor. XIV, 34).

The voice thus produced was, compared to the female equivalent, stronger and more flexible, often voluptuous in tone, and capable of the utmost delicacy and brilliance, because the vocal chords were prevented from undergoing their normal process of thickening, which

renders them less agile as well as causing them to produce lower notes. The castratos' heyday was in Metastasian *opera seria;* they were less in demand for comic opera. They became a cardinal feature of the opera of the period, as much admired for their virtuosity as they were mocked and resented for their vanity and touchiness; they formed an operatic subculture whose true nature and merit it is difficult now to appreciate fully. Their virtuosity encouraged composers to write, both for individual singers and for the castrato voice in general, music of unparalleled brilliance, through which we can obtain some notion of what their powers must have been. However, these parts must in modern revivals be sung either by a counter-tenor, who has a crucially different timbre, by a woman, who adds to this difference the awkwardness of the different sex, or by transposing down for a true tenor, which inevitably distorts the balance of the music.

With the reforms of Gluck, the art of the castrato went into a decline that continued until the demands of dramatic truth in opera, coupled with those of humanity, eventually exterminated it. Castratos were still common in the early 19th cent., when Rossini composed *Aureliano in Palmira* for the last great castrato, *Velluti; but his anger at the singer's decoration of already elaborate music turned him away from castratos. The last composer of importance to write for the male soprano was Meyerbeer with *Il crociato in Egitto* (1824) for Velluti. Though Wagner was interested in the idea of obtaining Domenico Mustafà (1829-1912) for the part of the self-emasculated Klingsor, he eventually abandoned the idea. The last professional castrato (though he did not appear in opera) was Alessandro Moreschi (1858-1922), who made ten records in 1902-3. The modern breeches role, or *travesti* part, is a survival of the tradition.

Bibl: A. Heriot: *The Castrati in Opera* (1960).

Castro, Juan José (*b* Avellaneda, 7 Mar. 1895; *d* Buenos Aires, 3 Sept. 1968). Argentinian composer, conductor, pianist, and violinist. In 1951 he won the Verdi prize offered by Milan, Sc., for his opera *Proserpina e lo straniero* (1952). Also wrote the operas *La zapatera prodigiosa* (comp. 1943, prod. 1949) and *Bodas de sangre* (1956).

Catalani, Alfredo (*b* Lucca, 19 June 1854; *d* Milan, 7 Aug. 1893). Italian composer. Studied in Lucca and Paris, and in Milan under Bazzini, who introduced him to the reform movement Scapigliatura Lombarda: through this he first heard Wagner's music and also met Boito, who wrote the text of his first opera, *La falce* (1875). Subsequent operas included *Elda* (pubd. 1876, prod. 1880; rev. as *Loreley,* prod. 1890), *Dejanice* (1883), and the successful Romantic

opera *Edmea* (1886). His most famous work was *La Wally* (1852), a work championed by his friend Toscanini (who christened his daughter Wally). Though regarded with reserve by Verdi, and himself recognizing that he was in a weak position beside Verdi and Puccini in his publisher Ricordi's attentions, Catalani managed to achieve a personal style seen at its most clearly defined in *Wally*. He was reproached for Germanizing Italian music, partly because of the prominence he gave to the orchestra, e.g. in symphonic interludes; but his vocal writing is essentially Italian, and his real weakness is his proneness to accept Romantic subjects without being able to give his characters proper dramatic definition.
Bibl: A. Bonaccorsi: *Alfredo Catalani* (1942).

Catalani, Angelica (*b* Sinigaglia, 10 May 1780; *d* Paris, 12 June 1849). Italian soprano. Educated at a convent in Rome, but forced by her parents' reduced circumstances to take up singing. Studied with her father Antonio, and P. Morandi. Début Venice 1797, Lodoïska (Mayr); Milan, Sc., 1801; London 1806. The first London Susanna (*Figaro*) 1812. Manager of the T.I., Paris, 1814-17. Also appeared in Riga, Lemberg, Vilna, and Brno in 1820; and in Romania as Rosina, Angelina, and in other parts, 1821. Retired from the operatic stage 1821 and founded a school near Florence. One of the highest-paid prima donnas, receiving as much as 200 guineas for singing *Rule Britannia* or *God Save the King*. Married French diplomat Paul Valabrègue, who told Ebers, manager of the King's T. that all that was necessary for a successful opera season was 'ma femme, et quatre ou cinque poupées'.
Bibl: G. Radiciotti: *Angelica Catalani* (1924).

Catalogue Aria. A popular form of *aria in the 18th cent. consisting of a comically rapid enunciation of a list of items. One of the librettists who used it most effectively was *Bertati, whose *Don Giovanni* for Gazzaniga includes one listing the different classes of girls seduced by the hero. It was this which provided the model for Da Ponte, listing the girls by country, in his libretto *Don Giovanni*; and it is the aria sung by Leporello (bar.) in Act 1, scene 2, of Mozart's opera that is usually intended by the description Catalogue Aria.

Catania. Town in Sicily. Bellini's birthplace: the T. Massimo Bellini (cap. 2,000) was opened on 31 May 1890 with a performance of *Norma*. The theatre was modernized 1948-52, and gives a spring and autumn season annually. In Nov. 1951 the 150th anniversary of the birth of Bellini was celebrated there with gala performances of *Norma, Il pirata, I Puritani*, and *La sonnambula*.

Catel, Charles-Simon (*b* Laigle, 10 Jan. 1773; *d* Paris, 29 Nov. 1830). French composer and theorist. Studied Paris with Gossec. He joined the band of the Garde Nationale, also acting as répétiteur at the O. from 1792 and professor at the newly founded Conservatoire from 1795. His operas reflect the atmosphere of the Empire and of the emergent Romanticism, and include *Sémiramis* (1802), the grandiose and spectacular *Les Bayadères* (1810), and a fairy opera, *Zirphile et Fleur de Myrte* (1818). He also wrote six *opéras-comiques*, whose style is closer to that of 18th-cent. *opera buffa*, though *Wallace* (1817) is one of many contemporary works inspired by the Romantic fashion for Scotland. Catel sought to move away from the closed number opera and to develop character and situation by use of *Reminiscence Motive, large-scale harmonic design, and at times an almost symphonic development. At his best, he exemplifies the maximum variety and flexibility compatible with the pomp and visual grandeur of the Empire style.
Bibl: F. Hellouin and J. Picard: *Catel* (1910).

Caterina Cornaro. Opera in prologue and 2 acts by Donizetti; text by Giacomo Sacchero, after Vernoy de St Georges's libretto *La Reine de Chypre* for Halévy. Prod. Naples, S.C., 12 Jan. 1844, with Goldberg, Salvetti, Fraschini, Coletti, Arati. Concert perfs. London 1972, N.Y. 1973. Revived Naples, S.C., 1972 with Gencer, Aragall, Bruson, Clabassi, cond. Cillario. The wedding of Caterina (sop.), daughter of Andreas (bass), to a young Frenchman, Gerardo (ten.), is postponed when Mocenigo (bass) brings word that Lusignano, King of Cyprus (bass), wishes to marry her. After much intrigue, involving Lusignano being slowly poisoned by Mocenigo, Gerardo joins the Knights of the Cross to help Lusignano defend Cyprus against the Venetians. Lusignano is mortally wounded; as he dies he entrusts his people to Caterina's care. Gerardo then returns to Rhodes. (In a revised finale for the Parma production, Donizetti makes Lusignano inform Caterina that Gerardo has been killed in battle.)

Also operas on subject by Halévy (1841), Lachner (1841), Balfe (*The Daughter of St Mark*), and Pacini (1846).

Catherine the Great (Catherine II) (*b* Stettin, 2 May 1729; *d* St Petersburg, 10 Nov. 1796). Empress of Russia. Celebrated for, among other things, her encouragement of opera in Russia, she wrote some librettos herself. Besides her native German, she wrote (faultily, but expressively) in both Russian and French. She invited to Russia both Tartini and Galuppi, the first of a succession of Italians who were to stimulate and organize the Russian theatres and compose works for them; she also encouraged French opera. As an admirer of the Encylopedists, she favoured opéra-comique, with its social content and comment, though of a reactionary kind; and in this vein, though with little ear for the music then provided, she wrote a number of librettos. These consisted of a political propaganda piece, *The Beginnings of the Government of Oleg* (1786, music Pashkevich, Canobbio, Sarti), *Fevey* (1786, Pashkevich), *The Novgorod Bogatyr Boyeslayevich* (1786, Fomin), *The Brave and Bold Hero Akhrideyich* (1787, Vančura), *The Bogatyr Kosometovich* (1789, Solar), and *Fedul with his Children* (1791, Solar and Pashkevich).

Catulli Carmina. *Ludi scaenici* by Orff; Latin text, after Catullus, by composer. Prod. Leipzig 6 Nov. 1943, cond. Schmitz; Cambridge, Arts, 4 Mar. 1958, with Edmonds, Pullin, cond. Darlington. The work is divided into three sections; in the first the young boys and girls are reminded by their elders that Catullus died of love; in the second and third, the story of Catullus is told, including the desertion of Catullus by Lesbia in favour of Caelus. When Lesbia returns, Catullus rejects her.

Cavalieri, Emilio de' (*b* Rome, *c* 1550; *d* 11 Mar. 1602). Italian composer. A leading member of the *Camerata, he helped Peri and Caccini to develop the representative style that was to be the basis of the new art of opera. His most important work is the sacred drama *La rappresentazione di anima e di corpo* (1600), an important precursor of opera.

Cavalieri, Katharina (orig. Franziska Cavalier) (*b* Währing, 19 Feb. 1760; *d* Vienna, 30 June 1801). Austrian soprano. Studied with Salieri, who wrote several operas for her, and when barely 15 was engaged to sing at the Italian Opera in Vienna. Joined the German Opera founded by Emperor Joseph II 1776. Mozart composed Constanze (*Entführung*) and Mme Silberklang (*Schauspieldirektor*) for her, as well as Elvira's 'Mi tradì' in *Don Giovanni* for its Vienna première. He wrote that she was 'a singer of whom Germany might well be proud'.

Cavalieri, Lina (orig. Natalina) (*b* Viterbo, 25 Dec. 1874; *d* Florence, 7 Feb. 1944). Italian soprano. A child of poor parents, she sold programmes in the Rome O. and oranges to passers-by. In 1893 she sang in Paris cafés, in 1894 at the Folies-Bergère, and later at the Empire T. in London. Taken up by a Russian prince, Alexander Bariatinsky, she began musical studies in Paris. Début Lisbon, T. São Carlo, 1900, Nedda; audience protests at her second performance prevented the opera from being finished, after which she and Bariatinsky parted. Further studies in Milan with Marianli-Masi; second, and successful, début Naples, S.C., Mimì. After engagements in St Petersburg and Warsaw, she created L'Ensoleillad in Massenet's *Chérubin* at Monte Carlo (1905). N.Y., Met., 1906-8, where she was first U.S. Fedora and first Met. Manon Lescaut and Adriana Lecouvreur; also appeared with Manhattan and Chicago Companies. London, C.G.,

1908, Fedora, Manon Lescaut, Tosca; London Opera House, 1911, as Salomé in *Hérodiade* and Giulietta (*Hoffmann*).

One of the most beautiful women ever to have appeared in opera, she was much admired by the aristocracy and royalty; she boasted a string of pearls from the Tsar, a diamond-encrusted mother-of-pearl case from the Prince of Monaco, and other jewels valued at $3m. She was married four times, one of her husbands being the French tenor Lucien *Muratore; while married to him she made several films, including *Manon Lescaut*. She died during an air-raid on Florence during the Second World War; on her way to a shelter, she decided to return to her villa for her jewels. A film of her life, 'La donna più bella del mondo' (with Gina Lollobrigida) was made in 1957. (R) *Bibl:* L. Cavalieri: *Le mie verità* (1936).

Cavalieri di Ekebù, I (The Knights of Ekebù). Opera in 4 acts by Zandonai; text by A. Rossato, after Selma Lagerlöf's novel *Gösta Berlings saga* (1891). Prod. Milan, Sc., 7 Mar. 1925, with Fanelli, Casazza, Lo Giudice, Franci, Autori, cond. Toscanini.

Cavalleria rusticana (Rustic Chivalry). Opera in 1 act by Mascagni; text by G. Menasci and G. Targioni-Tozzetti, after G. Verga's drama (1884) based on his story (1880). Winner of the contest for a 1-act opera organized by Sonzogno in 1889. Prod. Rome, C., 17 May 1890, with Bellincioni, Stagno, Salassa, cond. Mugnone; Philadelphia, Grand Opera House, 9 Sept. 1891, with Kört-Kronold, Guille, Del Puente cond. Hinrichs; London, Shaftesbury T., 19 Oct. 1891, with Mariani, Vignas, Brambara, cond. Arditi. Santuzza (sop.), pregnant by Turiddu (ten.), is distraught when she finds he has deserted her in favour of the attractive young Lola (mezzo), wife of the village drover, Alfio (bar.). A final appeal to Turiddu by Santuzza to return to her is of no avail, and so she tells Alfio all that has happened. Alfio swears vengeance, challenges Turiddu to a duel, and kills him. The action takes place in a small Sicilian village on Easter morning; the famous Intermezzo is played between the two scenes of the opera, while the stage remains empty.

A sequel, *Silvio*, by Borch, comp. *c* 1898. Another opera on the subject by Gastaldon (*Mala Pasqua*, 1890).

Cavalli (orig. Calett Bruni), **Pier Francesco** (*b* Crema, 14 Feb. 1602; *d* Venice, 14 Jan. 1676). Italian composer. He sang at St Mark's as a boy under Monteverdi; then adopted the name of his patron Federico Cavalli. Later he was organist at St Mark's. His first opera was *Le nozze di Teti e di Peleo* (1639); thereafter he produced a new opera each year for the T. San Cassiano. *Ormindo* was written in 1644, *Giasone* (originally his most successful work) in 1649, *Calisto* in 1651. In 1660 he was persuaded by Mazarin to visit Paris to write *Ercole amante* (1662) for the wedding of Louis XIV, but on the Cardinal's death he fell prey to the scheming of Lully and returned disheartened to Venice, where he was made maestro di cappella of St Mark's.

Between 1639 and 1666 Cavalli wrote over 40 operas, a rate which is prodigious even though he had only to notate vocal line and bass and add indications of sinfonias and scoring; he did not write out in full the score, whose realization was left to the performers. He had to use many poor librettos, though he did also collaborate with *Busenello and Faustini. A gifted and ingenious melodist, he lacked Monteverdi's powerful and enterprising sense of human drama but could at his finest portray the emotions of his characters with great eloquence and beauty; and this mastery of free melody enabled him to compose long sections of his operas in which the freedom of movement between set aria, arioso, and recitative offers a comparison in this respect with Wagner.

The plots tend to be less diverse than their titles would indicate, and often return to the idea of two or more pairs of confused lovers whose adventures involve mistaken identity, elaborate misunderstandings, disguises, and other confusions, resolved in a last-minute recognition and happy ending; round these main characters are usually gathered secondary figures such as comic servants, loyal squires, frequently a *travesti* part for a tenor playing the grotesque role of a lecherous duenna. It is less in any serious emotion than in the entertainment value and occasional poignancy of the complications that the essence of the opera resides. New interest was aroused in Cavalli's works by the realizations and recompositions of *Ormindo* and *Calisto* by Raymond Leppard (Gly., 1967 and 1970).

Bibl: J. Glover: *Cavalli* (1978).

Cavaradossi. A painter (ten.), hero of Puccini's *Tosca.*

Cavata (*It* extraction, i.e. the drawing of tone from an instrument). In 18th-cent. opera the term was applied to short ariosos at the end of a long recitative: the melody is 'carved out' of the preceding music.

Cavatina (*It* dim of *cavata). In 18th- and 19th-cent opera, a short solo song, simple in style and lacking the da capo, often consisting of a short instrumental introduction to a single sentence or statement set to music. Examples are the Countess's 'Porgi amor' and, in more elaborately developed form, Figaro's 'Se vuol ballare' in *Le nozze di Figaro.* Later examples include Agathe's 'Und ob die Wolke' (*Freischütz*), Norma's 'Casta diva' (*Norma*), and Norina's 'So anch'io la vertù magica' (*Don Pasquale*); Verdi wrote many such numbers up to

Leonora's 'Tacea la notte placida' (*Trovatore*), after which he abandoned the description. The term is also used of a song-like air included as part of a long *scena* or accompanied recitative, and of a song-like piece of music, e.g. Raff's *Cavatina.*

Cavos, Caterino (*b* Venice, 30 Oct. 1775; *d* St Petersburg, 10 May 1840). Italian composer. His father Alberto played an important part in Venetian operatic life; he was in charge of La Fenice, and arranged the début there of Angelica Catalani. Caterino studied in Venice with Bianchi, and made his mark early as a composer of dramatic music. He travelled to Russia in 1798, and was made Director of the Imperial Theatres. Here he flung himself energetically into musical life as a conductor, composer, arranger, organizer, and singing teacher, playing the dominant part in the development of Russian operatic life in the first decades of the 19th cent. He was responsible for the Russian premières of *Der Freischütz* (1824), *Fra Diavolo, Robert le Diable,* and other works. His many pupils, some of whom formed the first generation of properly trained Russian singers, included Osip Petrov, Josephine Fodor-Mainvielle, and Anna Vorobyova. He was Kapellmeister of the Italian company (1828-31) and German and Russian companies (1832-40).

However, his real influence on Russian musical life was as a composer. From the first he took an interest in Russian subjects (having done so even while still in Italy), and beginning with a fairy opera, *The Invisible Prince* (1805), he wrote a number of works which set a fashion for later Russian opera in their use of folk and patriotic, and especially legendary and magical, subjects, and also in their reliance on the fantastic and spectacular in staging. These included the successful *Ilya Bogatyr* (1807) and *The Cossack Poet* (1812). But his major work is *Ivan Susanin* (1815), a *rescue opera with dialogue on the same subject as Glinka's *A Life for the Tsar* (though ending happily), which is typical of his skill in grafting Russian folk music and folk subjects onto the Italian stock as one of the first moves towards the growth of a national Russian opera. Two further operas were *Dobrynya Nikitich* (1818) and *The Firebird* (1823).

His wife, **Camilla Baglioni,** was a singer of comic parts. Of their sons, **Giovanni** was a respected conductor in St Petersburg; and **Alberto** (1801-63) was an architect who worked on theatre design, being responsible for rebuilding the Moscow B. after the fire of 1853 and also rebuilding the St Petersburg M. and Mikhaylovsky; he also wrote a *Traité de la construction des théâtres.* Alberto's daughter Camilla married Nikolay Benois; their son was Alexander *Benois.

Cebotari, Maria (*b* Kishinyov, 10 Feb. 1910; *d* Vienna, 9 June 1949). Bessarabian soprano. After singing in school and church choirs, joined a travelling company; then Moscow Arts T. Studied Berlin with Oskar Daniel. Début Dresden 1931, Mimì; remained member of company until 1936; Berlin 1934-44; Vienna 1946-9. London, C.G., 1936 (with Dresden Company – Susanna, Zerlina, and Sophie); returned with Vienna Opera 1947 (Countess, Donna Anna, Salome). Created Aminta in Strauss's *Schweigsame Frau* (1935), Julia in Sutermeister's *Romeo und Julia* (1940), Lucille in Einem's *Dantons Tod* (1947), and Iseut in Martin's *Le Vin herbé* (1948). A fine artist, with a beautiful fresh voice and charming stage appearance. (R)
Bibl: A. Mingotti: *Maria Cebotari* (1950).

Cecchi, Domenico (*b* Cortona, *c* 1650; *d* Cartona, 1717). Italian male soprano, known as Cortona. Début Bologna, 1672 in *Nino* (composer unknown). After engagements in Italy went to Munich in 1688; soon returned to Italy. Well known for his performance in Cardinal Ottoboni's *Colombo* in Rome; in 1707 created Flavio in Gasparini's *Flavio Anicio Olibrio* in Venice.

Cecchina, La. See *Buona figliuola La.*

Cecilia. *Azione sacra* in 3 acts by Refice; text by E. Mucci. Prod. Rome, T.R., 15 Feb. 1934, with Muzio; Buenos Aires, Colón, 4 Oct. 1934, with Muzio, based on the legend of Cecilia and Valerian, and of Cecilia's martyrdom.

Celeste Aida. Radamès's (ten.) aria praising Aida's beauty in Act 1 of Verdi's *Aida*.

Cellini, Benvenuto. See *Benvenuto Cellini*.

Cenerentola, La; ossia La bontà in trionfo (Cinderella). Opera in 2 acts by Rossini; text by Jacopo Ferretti after Étienne's text for Steibelt's opera. Prod. Rome, Valle, 25 Jan. 1817, with Giorgi-Righetti, Guglielmi, De Begnis, Verni; London, Hm., 8 Jan. 1817, with Teresa Belocchi; N.Y., Park T., 27 June 1826 by Garcia's company, with Malibran, Barbieri, Mme. Garcia, Milon, Garcia jun., Rosich, Angrisani. The plot follows the familiar fairy story by Perrault. Angelina (mezzo), known as Cinderella, is ill-treated by her father, Don Magnifico (bass) and her two step-sisters, Clorinda (mezzo) and Tisbe (sop.). The Prince Ramiro (ten.), in search of a wife, changes places with his valet Dandini (bar.), and falls in love with Angelina at first sight. Alidoro (bass), the Prince's tutor (the equivalent of the fairy godmother in the children's versions), helps Angelina to attend the ball at the palace. In place of the glass slipper there is a silver bracelet, by means of which the prince discovers the identity of Angelina and makes her his bride.
See also *Cinderella*.

Censorship in opera. Like the theatre, opera has come into conflict with the censorship in various countries. In England, religious subjects were long forbidden on the stage: Rossini's *Mosè* and Verdi's *Nabucco* appeared under different guises in Victorian times. *Samson et Dalila* was kept off the London stage until 1909; Massenet's *Hérodiade* appeared under the guise of *Salome* with the names of the characters changed, and Strauss's own *Salome* had to be altered for its Covent Garden première in 1910. In Italy and France political rather than moral censorship was responsible for the troubles attendant on the productions of *Nabucco*, *I Lombardi*, *Rigoletto*, *Un ballo in maschera*, and other works. Nazi Germany banned many operas for political and racial reasons, and there were similar bans in Italy and the U.S.S.R. Since the war the East German authorities have banned the original version of Dessau's *Lukullus* and Orff's *Antigone*, while Ginastera's *Bomarzo* was banned in Buenos Aires for 'moral' reasons; and the strict control over art in Communist countries suppresses many works.

Central City. Town in Colorado, U.S.A. The San Francisco Opera Company visited the town as early as the 1860s, with *La Grande Duchesse de Gérolstein*. The original Montana T. burnt down in 1874, and the Belvedere T. opened in 1875 on the second floor of a brick building. The Richings-Bernard Company gave *Trovatore*, *Martha*, and *Maritana* with success, and in 1877 a local group gave *The Bohemian Girl*. This proved so popular that subscriptions were raised for the Teller Opera House (cap. 500), opened in 1878. However, interest declined with the town's depopulation as the mining concerns withdrew. In 1932 a series of summer festivals began, concentrating on operetta and drama; the first opera was *The Bartered Bride* (1940). The festival was suspended 1942-5, and resumed 1946 with *Entführung* and *La traviata*. Other works heard there have included *The Ballad of Baby Doe* (première July 1956), *Italiana in Algeri*, *Martha*, and *La périchole*.

Cephalus and Procris. The classical legend, best known as told by Ovid (*Metamorphoses*, 7), describes how Cephalus tested Procris's virtue by disguising himself, and conquered her; in some versions, she fled but later effected a reconciliation by a similar trick on him. In the end, he killed her by accident when she was spying on his supposed rendezvous with a lover. The story has been set many times, e.g. by Grétry; text (3 acts) by Marmontel. Prod. Versailles 30 Dec. 1773 and Paris, O., 2 May 1775. Other operas by Caccini (*Il rapimento di Cefalo*, 1600), Hidalgo (*Celos aun del ayre matan*, the first Spanish opera, 1660), Krieger (1689), Elisabeth Laguerre (the first opera by a woman at the Paris O., 1694), Araia (a very early Russian opera, 1755), Bronner (1701), Batistin (1710), Gillers (1711), and Kerpen. See also *Così fan tutte*.

Cercar la nota (*It* to seek the note). The vocal habit of moving from a note by slightly anticipating the next one, either by linking two notes with a passing note or, more commonly, by touching on the second of two notes as a kind of light upbeat before it is properly sounded.

Cereni (*It* from *cero*, candle). From the 17th cent. to the early 19th cent. *cereni* librettos, hastily and inaccurately printed on poor paper, were often on sale outside the theatre for the use of patrons who wished to consult them by candlelight during the performance. Surviving examples are often stained with the wax drippings that gave them their name.

Cerquetti, Anita (*b* Montecòsaro, nr Macerata, 13 Apr. 1931). Italian soprano. Studied Perugia. Début Spoleto 1951, Aida. Chicago 1955; Milan, Sc., 1958. Quickly established herself as one of the finest Italian dramatic sopranos, her best roles being Norma, Abigaille, and Amelia. But after an operation in 1958 she quickly went into eclipse. (R)

Čert a Káča. See *Devil and Kate, The*.

Cervantes Saavedra, Miguel de (*b* Alcalá de Henares, bapt. 9 Oct. 1547; *d* Madrid, 23 Apr. 1616). Spanish writer. Operas on his works are as follows:

La Numancia (1582-7): J. H. van Eeden (1898); Barraud (1955)

Don Quixote (pt 1, 1605; pt 2, 1615): Sajon (1680); Förtsch (1690); Eccles (1684); Ève (1700); Gillier (*La Bagatelle*, 1712); F. B. Conti (1719); Feo (1726); Treu (1727); Caldara (1727); Ristori (1727); Silva (1733); Caldara (*Sancio Panza*, 1733); Boismortier (1743); Martini (1746); Holzbauer (1755); Piccinni (*Il curioso*, 1756); Telemann (1761); Philidor (*Sancho Pança*, 1762); Gherardeschi (*Il curioso indiscreto*, 1764); Paisiello (1769); Bernardini (1769); Piccinni (1770); Salieri (1770); Anfossi (*Il curioso indiscreto*, 1777); Beecke (1788); Gerl (1790); Hubaček (1791); Tarchi (1791); W. Müller (1802); Generali (1805); Mariani (1810); Seidel (1811); Bochsa (*Les Noces de Gamache*, 1815); Mercadante (*Les Noces de Gamache*, 1825); Garcia (1827); Mendelssohn (*Die Hochzeit des Camacho*, 1827); Mercadante (1829-30); Donizetti (*Il furioso all'isola de S. Domingo*, 1833); Rodwell (1833); Mazzucato (1836); Macfarren (1846); Clapisson (1847); Hervé (1848); Rispo (1859); Reparaz (*La venta encantada*, 1871); Caballero (*El loco de la Guardilla*, 1861); Arrieta (*La insula Barataria*, 1864); Reparaz (*Las bodas de Camacho*,

1866); E.-H.-A. Boulanger (1869); Planas (1871); Pessard (1874); Clay (1876); Weinzieri (1879); L. Ricci, jun. (1881); Neuendorf (1882); L. de Larra (*En un lugar de La Mancha*, 1887); Roth (1888); De Koven (1889); Santonja (1896); Jacques-Dalcroze (1897); Rauchenecker (1897); Kienzl (1898); Chapì (1902); Ferrán (*Las bodas de Camacho*, 1903); Kaufmann (1903); Legouix (*Le Gouvernement de Sancho Pança*, 1903); Barrera (*El carro de las cortes de Muerte*, 1907); Beer-Waldbrunn (1908); Besi (1908); Hervitt (1909); Heuberger (1910); Pasini (1910); Massenet (1910); Dall'Orso (1916); E. Ábrányí (1917); Falla (*El retablo de Maese Pedro*, 1923); Lévy (1930); Halffter (*Clavileño*, comp. 1936); Rodriguez Albert (1948); Frazzi (1952); Rivière (1961); Petrassi (1967); Halffter (1970).

Operas using the character of Don Quixote in a new context include: Leo (*Il fantastico*, 1743); Gomes (*Il nuovo Don Chischiotte*, 1748); F. Bianchi (*Il nuovo Don Chischiotte*, 1788); Champein (*Le Nouveau Don Quichotte*, 1789); Dittersdorf (*Don Quixote der Zweite*, 1795); Moniuszko (*Nowy Don Kiszot*, 1842); Hochberg (*Der neue Don Quixote*, 1861); Noskowski (*Nowy Don Kiszot*, 1890); Jarecki (*Nowy Don Kiszot*, comp. 1901).

Novelas ejemplares (1613): *El casamiento Engañoso*: Anfossi (*Il matrimonio per inganno*, 1779). *La fuerza de la sangre*: Auber (*Léocadie*, 1824). *La gitanilla*: Kaffka (*Die Zigeuner*, 1778); Balfe (*The Bohemian Girl*, 1843); Reparaz (1861); Garcia (1890); Gabrielson (*Gipsy Blonde*, 1934). *El celoso extremeño*: Barrera (1908); see also *El viejo celoso* (below). *Rinconete y Cortadillo*: Doncel (*La picaresca*, 1850). *La ilustre fregona*: Laparra (1931). *Ocho comedias y ocho entremeses nuevos* (1615): *La cueva de salamanca*: Winter (*Der Bettelstudent*, 1785); Gay (1908); Paumgartner (1923); Mojsisovics (*Der Zauberer*, 1920); Lattuada (*La caverna de Salamanca*, 1938). *El viejo celoso* (1615, after *El celoso extremeño*): Petrassi (*Il cordovano*, 1949). Also operas by Grétry (*À trompeur, trompeur et demi*, 1792); Henze (*Das Wundertheater*, 1949); Orff (*Astutuli*, 1953).

Operas on Cervantes himself are as follows: Foignet (*Michel Cervantes*, 1793); Lassen (*Le Captif*, 1865); Aceves (*El Manco de Lepanto*, 1867); J. Strauss (*Das Spitzenbuch der Königin*, 1880).

Česke Budějovice. Town in Czechoslovakia. Opera was formerly given in the S. Bohemian T. about 3-4 times a week in the season by a company of about 20 soloists. The company moved to a new theatre in 1972. It tours in the region.

Cesti, Pietro Antonio (*b* Arezzo, 5 Aug. 1623; *d* Florence, 14 Oct. 1669). Italian composer. Wrongly known as Marc'Antonio from a contraction of his later title of Marchese. Became a friar; later studied with Carissimi in Florence. His first operas, *Orontea* (1649) and *Cesare amante* (1651), established him as a leading composer of the day. He was later released from his vows, and led a busy and adventurous life that included a period as maestro di cappella to the Archduke Ferdinand of Austria. His most famous work was *Il *Pomo d'Oro* (1667). Cesti was, with Cavalli, the most important of the composers who followed up the original work of the *Camerata. His music is marked by lyricism and expressiveness, aided by an inventive use of dissonance.

Chabrier, (Alexis-) **Emmanuel** (*b* Ambert, Puy-de-Dôme, 18 Jan. 1841; *d* Paris, 13 Sept. 1894). French composer. Studied with Manuel Zaporta and began composing early. His parents insisted that he follow a legal career; he nevertheless managed to continue learning composition with Tarnowski, Semet, and Hignard. His interest in poetry led him to form friendships with, among others, Catulle Mendès and Villiers de l'Isle Adam, to whom he taught music, and Verlaine, who provided him with librettos of two operettas, *Fisch-Ton-Kan* (1863-4) and *Vaucochard et fils 1er* (1864), both unfinished. He was also a close friend of Manet, and his musical gifts as a pianist and improvizer won him the entry to Paris salons and friendships with Fauré, Chausson, Duparc, and D'Indy. He planned an opera, *Jean Hunyade* (1867, unfin.: fragments used in *Gwendoline* and *Briséis*). His vivid comic flair found expression in *L'Étoile* (1877) and *Une Éducation manquée* (1879), though their liveliness does not exclude tenderness and some harmonic adventurousness. Through Duparc, he came to admire Wagner, and the experience of hearing *Tristan und Isolde* in Munich led him to resign the government post he had occupied and dedicate himself to music in 1880. The first opera to follow was *Gwendoline* (1886, text by Mendès), set in medieval England and filled with vigorous battles and stirring love duets; it is Wagnerian in its use of Leitmotiv and in its extreme harmonic emancipation. He also composed quadrilles on themes from *Tristan*, in witty but appreciative vein; he was at this time a leading member of the group of French Wagnerians known as 'Le Petit Bayreuth'. He then produced an *opéra comique*, *Le Roi malgré lui* (1887), the piece in which his gifts for elegant melody and lively characterization are most fully displayed. He worked on *Briséis*, without succeeding in finishing it, and also left uncompleted an opéra comique, *Le Sabbat* (1877) and an opera, *Les Muscadins* (1880). *Bibl:* F. Robert: *Emmanuel Chabrier: L'homme et son oeuvre* (1969).

Chailly, Luciano (*b* Ferrara, 19 Jan. 1920). Italian composer, critic, and administrator.

Studied Bologna and Milan, and with Hindemith at Salzburg. Artistic director Milan, Sc. 1968-71. His operas include *Ferrovia sopra e levata* (Bergamo, 1957), *Una domanda di matrimonio* (Milan, 1957), *Markheim* (Spoleto, 1967) and *L'idiota*, based on Dostoyevsky (Rome, 1970). His son **Riccardo** (*b* Milan 20 Feb. 1953) studied in Milan and Siena, made his début as a conductor Milan, T.C. in 1973 in *Werther*; Chicago, 1974 *Madama Butterfly*; Milan, Sc. 1978 *Masnadieri*; C.G. 1978 *Don Pasquale*.

Chalabala, Zdeněk (*b* Uherské Hradiště (Moravia), 18 Apr. 1899; *d* Prague, 4 Mar. 1962). Czech conductor. Studied Brno, where from 1925 to 1936 he conducted at the Brno Opera. Prague, 1936-45; Ostrava 1945-9; Brno again 1949-52; Prague Opera 1953-62. Particularly distinguished in the Slavonic repertory. (R) His wife **Běla Rozumová** (*b* Přibam, 8 Feb. 1903), a coloratura soprano, made her début at Ljubljana (Mařenka), sang at Brno 1925-36, and since 1942 has taught at the Prague Conservatory.

Chaliapin. See *Shalyapin*.

Chamber opera. Since opera was born from the meetings of the Florentine *Camerata around 1600, chamber opera may be said to be its original form. It has now come to mean a short work cast on a small scale, generally with a few singers and instrumentalists, telling a simple story. Though strictly an *intermezzo*, Pergolesi's *La serva padrona* ranks as a chamber opera. An increasing number of modern composers have shown an interest in using smaller forces, partly in reaction to the full apparatus of traditional opera, partly for the creative possibilities, perhaps in the less formal context of what has become known as *music theatre. The *Intimate Opera Company was established in England; a pioneering enterprise was the formation of the *English Opera Group by Britten and others. In recent years a number of groups have found in the smaller scale of opera not only economy and convenience for touring and so forth, but a form of opera yielding rich creative results in its own right.

Champagne Aria. See *Finch' han dal vino*.

Chanson de la puce, La (The Song of the Flea). Méphistophélès's (bass or bar.) aria in the second part of Berlioz's *La Damnation de Faust*.

Chapí (y Lorente), **Ruperto** (*b* Villena, 27 Mar. 1851; *d* Madrid, 25 Mar. 1909). Spanish composer. Studied Madrid with Arrieta. His first zarzuela, *Abel y Caín* (1873) was followed by a period as a bandmaster; he then wrote a 1-act opera, *Las Naves de Cortés* (1874), whose success, with Tamberlik singing Cortes, won him a

:udy grant. He wrote more operas, but is
imous as the author of over 100 *zarzuelas* in
/hich he won particular success with the
iiddle and upper classes of Madrid.

harlotte. Werther's lover (mezzo) in Mas-
enet's *Werther.*

harlottenburg. See *Berlin.*

harpentier, Gustave (*b* Dieuze, 25 June 1860;
Paris, 18 Feb. 1956). French composer.
tudied with Massenet, and won the Prix de
ome with his *scène lyrique, Didon* (1887). His
iost famous work is the opera *Louise* (1900).
s success, partly for its startling realism and
beral social views, partly for its lyrical fluency,
/as as great as the failure of its sequel, *Julien*
i913). Charpentier also founded, in 1902, a
onservatoire Populaire Mimi Pinson, where
/orking girls such as his Louise could act and
ng and learn music and dancing.

harpentier, Marc-Antoine (*b* Paris, 1636
i1634); *d* Paris, 24 Feb. 1704). French com-
oser. Studied in Rome with Carissimi, and on
is return to Paris collaborated with Molière at
ie T.-Français. He wrote some 17 operas,
/hich had a considerable success and won the
omposer high respect even at a time when
ully's influence was supreme. *Médée* (1693)
/as, through the poor text, never the success it
romised to become; it contains some strong
nd original music.

harton-Demeur, Anne (Arsène) (*b* Saujon, 5
lar. 1824; *d* Paris, 30 Nov. 1892). French sop-
ano. Début Bordeaux 1842, Lucia. London,
.L., 1846; St James's T. 1849-50; H.M.'s 1852.
he first London Eudoxie (*La Juive*), Angèle (*Le
'omino noir*), Countess (*Comte Ory*),
atherine (*Les Diamants de la couronne*); sang
lso in first London performances of many
ther French works. Created Béatrice in Ber-
oz's *Béatrice et Bénedict* (1862) and Dido in
es Troyens à Carthage (1863). Sang at the
aris O. in the Berlioz festival 1870 with
hristine Nilsson. In 1871 sang Cassandre in
ie first performance (in concert) of *La Prise de
roie*. Married the flautist Demeur.

haucer, Geoffrey (*b* London, *c* 1340; *d*
ondon, 25 Oct. 1400). English poet. Operas on
is works are as follows:
roilus and Cressida (*c*1380-2): Walton (1954).
he Canterbury Tales (unfin., 1400): Stan-
ird (1884); De Koven (1917). *The Pardoner's
ale*: Sokolov (1961); E. Lubin (1966); J. Davis
i967); A. Ridout (1973). *The Nun's Priest's
ale*: J. Barthelson (1967). *The Knight's, Nun's
'riest's*, and *Pardoner's Tales*: Crosse (*The
Vheel of the World*, 1972).

hausson, Ernest (*b* Paris, 21 Jan. 1855; *d*
imay, 10 June 1899). French composer.
tudied law, later taking up music and

becoming a pupil of Franck. Never needing to
earn his living, he worked slowly, carefully, and
diffidently at composition. He wrote three
operas, which show a sensitive, if light,
response to Wagner. They are *Les Caprices de
Marianne* (1880), *Hélène* (1884), and (the only
one performed) *Le Roi Arthus* (1903).
Bibl: J. Gallois: *Ernest Chausson* (1967).

Chautauqua. City in N.Y. State. An annual
summer opera festival was inaugurated with
Martha in July 1929. All operas are sung in
English, and many young American artists
have had their first opportunities there. In 1954
the Ford Foundation made a special five-year
grant to the organization. The repertory strikes
a balance between popular works, and novelties including *Albert Herring, The Crucible, Le
donne curiose, The Devil and Daniel Webster,
Susannah*, and *Wuthering Heights.*

Che farò senza Euridice. Orfeo's (mezzo)
lament at the loss of his wife Euridice in Act 3
(Act 4 in some versions) of Gluck's *Orfeo ed
Euridice.*

Che gelida manina. Rodolfo's (ten.) aria to
Mimì in Act 1 of Puccini's *La Bohème*, with
which he makes his first approach to her. She
replies with 'Mi chiamano Mimì'.

Chekhov, Anton (Pavlovich) (*b* Taganrog, 29
Jan. 1860; *d* Badenweiler, 15 July 1904). Russian writer and dramatist. A lover of music, he
knew Tchaikovsky and dedicated a volume of
stories to him; a plan for their collaboration on
an opera on Lermontov's *Bela* came to
nothing. Operas on his works are as follows.
He Forgot! (1882): Prybik (?).
Surgery (1884): Ostroglazov (?); Ferroud
(1928).
On the Highway (1885): Nottara (*La drumul
mare*, 1934).
Romance with a Double-Bass (1886):
Dubensky (1916); Sauguet (1930); Bucchi
(1954).
The Witch (1886): Yanovsky (1916); Hoiby
(1958); Vlasov and Feré (radio 1961, prod.
1965).
Swan Song (1888): Chailly (1957).
The Bear (1888): Jirásek (1965); Walton (1967).
The Proposal (1889): Chailly (1957); Röttger
(1960); J. Wagner (1965); Bohác (1971).
The Marriage (1889): Ehrenberg (1916).
The Admiral: Andreoli (1960).
The Boor: Bucci (1949); Fink (1955); Argento
(1957); Kay (1960); Moss (1961).
The Box: C. Eakin (1961).
The Crisis: Chailly (1966).
The Seagull (1896): Vlad (1968); Pastieri
(1974).
The Sneeze: A. Mascagni (1956).

Chelard, Hippolyte (*b* Paris, 1 Feb. 1789; *d*
Weimar, 12 Feb. 1861). French composer.

Studied in Paris with Gossec and, after winning the Prix de Rome in 1811, in Italy, with Zingarelli and Paisiello among others. He produced his first opera, the comedy La casa da vendere, at Naples (1815). Back in Paris, he wrote Macbeth (1827; libretto by Rouget de Lisle), but it was withdrawn after five performances and Chelard left for Munich; here the work's success won him the post of Kapellmeister. Returning once more to Paris, he produced La Table et le logement (1829), which was unsuccessful; back again in Munich, he had further successes with Mitternacht (1831) and a German version of La Table (as Der Student) in 1832. In 1832-3 he conducted in London with a company that included Schröder-Devrient. His most celebrated and successful work was Die Hermannschlacht (1835). He also worked in Augsburg (1836), and as Kapellmeister in Weimar, preceding Liszt. Macbeth is in the French grand opera tradition, Mitternacht in that of the emergent German Romantic opera.

Ch'ella mi creda libero. Dick Johnson's (ten.) aria in Act 3 of Puccini's La fanciulla del West, in which he asks that Minnie should be told not that he is to be lynched, but he has been freed.

Chelsea Opera Group. A group formed by Colin Davis, David Cairns, and Stephen Gray in 1950 to give concert performances of Mozart's operas. It started in Oxford with a performance of Don Giovanni. The Group first appeared in London at St Pancras Town Hall, in 1953, with Fidelio. It has given performances of works by Berlioz, Verdi, and Wagner and has been an excellent training ground for several young British conductors (Davis, Sillem, Matheson, Nicholas Braithwaite, Norrington). Several singers of the Royal Opera and E.N.O. have tried out roles with the Group, e.g. Glossop sang his first Don Giovanni, Hammond-Stroud his first Beckmesser, Pauline Tinsley her first Forza Leonora. The Group performs regularly in London, Oxford, and Cambridge.

Chemnitz. See Karl-Marx-Stadt.

Che puro ciel. Orfeo's (mezzo) aria as he gazes on the beauties of the Elysian Fields in Gluck's Orfeo.

Cherevichki. See Vakula the Smith.

Cherubini, Luigi (b Florence, 8 or 14 Sept. 1760; d Paris, 15 Mar. 1842). Italian composer. Studied in Italy, producing at first church music and then an opera, Quinto Fabio (1780). He visited London in 1784, and then Paris. He had written 13 Italian operas by the time he established himself permanently in Paris in 1788; but with Démophon (1788) he broke away from this earlier vein and began developing the mature style that makes him a father figure of French Grand Opera in particular, and of Romantic opera in general. This manner was

first fully revealed in Lodoïska (1791), in whic there is a new, richer handling of the orchestra a more powerful and functional use c ensemble, a stronger sense of dramati motivation, and the emergence of certai character types that were to impress man subsequent composers: the villain Dourlinsky for instance, is an operatic ancestor of bot Beethoven's Pizarro and Weber's Kaspar.

Meanwhile, Cherubini had directed an Italia Opera in Paris; and in 1795 he joined the new founded Conservatoire as an Inspector c Studies. Other early traits of Romantic oper begin to emerge in the works that followed i these years, e.g. Élisa (1794): a particula contribution was Cherubini's use of natura forces to play a crucial part in the drama (a fir in Lodoïska, an avalanche in Élisa), as well a his more fully developed use of arias for secor dary characters. An equally important ingre dient for Romantic opera was the influence Rousseau, not only in the Swiss setting of Élis but in the handling of peasants or other simpl people as embodying qualities of the highes virtue. Élisa also introduced into operatic cu rency the so-called musique d'effet.

Médée (1797) is an elevated tragedy, nobl and rather cold; it is, none the less, an oper charged with forceful statements of passior remote from human reality though the charac ters, even Medea herself, may seem to b There is a strong contrast to Les Deux journée (1800), with its handling of simple character and its consequent use of smaller music forms such as the *arietta and *couple Bouilly's text was regarded by Beethoven a exemplary, and as a *resuce opera the wor profoundly influenced Fidelio: like the late Faniska (1806), another rescue opera, the wor includes simple, ballad-like interpolations in dark, dramatic plot, and makes rich use of th orchestra to carry the story and the emotions c the characters. Cherubini's methods her include a looser handling of set numbers, an even a suggestion of Leitmotiv. Above all, was Cherubini's success in embodying in novel operatic manner the idealization c simple life, in which servants or peasants a no longer comic figures or ingénus but huma figures proposing righteous moral sentiment that won him the admiration of both Bee hoven and Goethe.

Though he wrote a number of further opera (including the interesting and underrated Pin malione (1809), which actually uses Rous seau's text in an Italian version), and the bett known Les Abencérages (1813), Cherubir turned away from opera in his later years give his attention to sacred music. He wa greatly admired in Paris, but his career ther was not smooth: after a quarrel with Napoleor he went to Vienna with Faniska, returnin when the French occupied the city. He wa

director of the Conservatoire from 1821 to 1841. Though often derided – by Berlioz, among others – for his pedantry and for a distinct (and self-confessed) severity in his music, he was a master of technique, and at its finest his music possesses brilliance, purity, and originality. It is not only for his example as a founder of Romantic opera that his works deserve attention.
Bibl: B. Deane: *Cherubini* (1965).

Cherubino. Countess Almaviva's page (sop.) in Mozart's *Le nozze di Figaro.*

Chest voice. The lowest of the three main registers of the voice, the others being the 'middle' and the 'head'. So called because the tone of the lower notes in the singer's range, when using this voice, almost seems to go from the larynx into the chest. This method of production gives the richest notes, and is essential for strength and carrying power in the lower register. Garcia considered that the chest voice predominated in men, and it is favoured especially by Italians. Abuse of the chest voice, especially by Italian mezzo-sopranos, is also a common feature of present-day Italian singing.

Cheval de Bronze, Le (The Bronze Horse). Opera in 3 acts by Auber; text by Scribe. Prod. Paris, O.C., 23 Mar. 1835; London, C.G., 14 Dec. 1835; New Orleans 15 Apr. 1836, with St Clair, Heyman, Bailly.

Chezy (orig. von Klencke), **Helmina** (orig. Wilhelmine) **von** (*b* 26 Jan. 1783; *d* Geneva, 28 Jan. 1856). German poet and librettist. She is best known for her libretto for Weber's *Euryanthe,* an erratic piece of work which has always been held responsible for the opera's long period of neglect.

Chicago. Town in Illinois, U.S.A. The first opera given in Chicago was Bellini's *Sonnambula,* 29 July 1850. Two years later an Italian company gave a season of grand opera under the direction of Luigi Arditi, with Rosa de Vries as leading soprano. The first opera house in the city, the Crosby Opera House, was built in 1865, and destroyed by fire in 1871; and opera had no permanent home until 1889, when the Chicago Auditorium opened with *Roméo et Juliette;* from then until 1910 short seasons were given by visiting companies, including the Abbey and Grau, Damrosch, Savage, Mascagni, and Conried organizations.

In 1910 the Chicago Grand Opera Company was formed, consisting of elements of the recently disbanded Hammerstein Company, with Andreas Dippel as Artistic Director and Cleofonte Campanini as Music Director. Mary Garden, who sang Mélisande on the second evening (4 Nov. 1910), became the dominating figure of opera in Chicago. Not only did she sing there from 1910 to 1931, scoring special successes in the French repertory, but she was appointed General Director for the 1921-2 season, Campanini having died in 1919 and his successor Marinuzzi resigning after a year. Garden's sole season as Director, during which the world première of Prokofiev's *The Love of the Three Oranges* was given, resulted in a deficit of more than a million dollars.

From 1922 to 1930 the finances of the opera were guaranteed by a group headed by Samuel Insull, who also became President of the organization; it was then known as the Chicago Civic Opera Company. On 4 Nov. 1929 the new Civic Opera House (cap. 3,593) was opened, with a performance of *Aida,* but in 1932 the company was one of the casualties of the depression. Several European artists, including Lehmann, Leider, Olczewska, Kipnis, Turner, Tourel, and Kiepura, made their U.S. débuts during this period.

From 1933 to 1946 there were various attempts to put opera on a more or less permanent basis, first by Paul Longone (1933-9), then Fortune Gallo, assisted for a short period by Martinelli (1941-2), and Fausto Cleva (1944-6), none of which proved wholly successful. During these régimes, US débuts were made by Björling (1937), Masini (1938), Tagliavini (1946), and Tajo (1946). Martinelli sang his first Otello (1936) and only Tristan (1939). Then came seven years during which opera in Chicago was given only by visiting companies. Since 1954 the Chicago Lyric T. and its successor, the Lyric Opera of Chicago, under the management of Carol Fox, have given successful seasons with international artists including Callas, Nilsson, Simionato, Tebaldi, Del Monaco, Di Stefano, Christoff, and Gobbi. Bruno Bartoletti is the music director; Pino Donati wars artistic adviser until 1975. A new opera by Penderecki was commissioned for 1976 as part of the 200th anniversary of the founding of the U.S.A. but postponed until 1978.
Bibl: R. Davis: *Opera in Chicago* (1966).

Chi mi frena? The sextet sung by Lucia, Alisa, Edgardo, Arturo, Enrico, and Raimondo in Act 2 of Donizetti's *Lucia di Lammermoor.*

China. Chinese opera, commonly called Pekin opera, is a mixed genre that does not match the normal European notion of opera. It combines singing, recitation, playing, poetry, acting, dancing, mime, and even acrobatics, making minimal use of scenery or props and depending for production upon the individual actor's understanding of the tradition and his own part in it. There are broadly three types, the patriotic-hierarchical, the social-military, and the colloquial. Characters are generally divided into *sheng* (male roles), *tan* (female roles), *chou* (comedians), and *ching* (painted-face roles). Much well-understood ritual attaches to the movements and costumes, extending to the colours of the latter. Singing consists of a kind of heightened speech, not unlike *Sprechgesang*; the accompaniment is by up to eight Chinese instruments and does not accompany words but sets the mood and frames the action.

Chisholm, Erik (*b* Glasgow, 4 Jan. 1904; *d* Cape Town, 7 June 1965). Scottish conductor, composer, and critic. Studied in Glasgow, later with Tovey in Edinburgh. He conducted the C.R. 1933-4, and the Glasgow Grand Opera Society 1930-9; with the latter he performed *Benvenuto Cellini, Les Troyens, Idomeneo, La clemenza di Tito,* Dvořák's *Jakobín,* and many other then little known works. Prof. of Music, Univ. of Cape Town, 1945-65; here he also introduced rare operas, bringing to London in 1956-7 a season of South African works and giving the British première of Bartók's *Duke Bluebeard's Castle* (1957). His own 10 operas include *The Isle of Youth* (comp. 1941), *Simoon* (1953), and *The Inland Woman* (1953). He also worked as a critic, and published *The Operas of Leoš Janáček* (1971).

Chorley, Henry Fothergill (*b* Blackley Hurst, Lancs. 15 Dec. 1808; *d* London, 16 Feb. 1872). English critic and translator. Critic of *The Athenaeum* 1836-68, in whose pages he violently opposed Wagner and, in his early days, Verdi. Translated many foreign operas into English, including *Orfeo, Iphigénie en Tauride, Faust, Mireille,* and *Dinorah.* Wrote librettos for works by Wallace, Benedict, and Sullivan. His writings included *Music and Manners in France and Germany* (1841), *Handel Studies* (1859), and *Thirty Years' Musical Recollections* (1862, revised and edited by Ernest Newman).

Chorus. From the Greek χορός, a festive dance or those who performed it. The Attic drama first consisted of tales told by a single actor in the intervals of the dance; later the function of the chorus was to join in and comment upon the drama from the place before and below the stage known as the ορχήστρα (orchestra). This function passed, with modifications, into opera. For some time the chorus took little part in the actual drama, but supported it in ensembles that served also as a musical contrast. Gluck first made the chorus a vital part of the drama. From then on crowds of courtiers, nobles, guests, priests, citzens, boyars, slaves, prisoners, and so on thronged opera, sometimes joining in the arias (a famous instance is Norma's 'Casta diva'), but more often acting as a static point of repose, commenting on the action, summing it up, joining in usually to provide a bustle of activity parallel to it, and abetting the soloists rather than furthering it on their own. With Wagner the chorus assumed a still more dramatic role. No chorus appears in *The Ring* until the Gibichungs' entry in *Götterdämmerung,* but the citizens of Nuremberg are intrinsic to the plot of *Die Meistersinger.* Britten, while using the chorus as the main dramatic force pitted against the hero in *Peter Grimes,* places his Male and Female Chorus as soloists in *The Rape of Lucretia* outside the action physically as well as dramatically. A still more definite reversion to Greek method occurs, for obvious reasons, in Stravinsky's *Oedipus Rex.* In general the chorus today is involved in the drama more closely than ever before.

An opera chorus is normally divided into the conventional soprano, contralto, tenor, and bass (although 19th-cent. French choruses were usually simply S.T.B.), with the numbers varying according to requirements. It is maintained on the permanent staff of an opera house under the direction of a chorus-master. Additional choruses of children are sometimes needed (e.g. for the Urchins' Chorus in Act 1 of *Carmen*), and certain schools specialize in their provision.

Christiania. See *Oslo.*

Christie, John (*b* Eggesford, 14 Dec. 1882; *d* Glyndebourne, 4 July 1962). English organ builder and operatic amateur. Educated at Eton, where he was for a time a master, and Cambridge. Married the soprano Audrey *Mildmay 1931, and in 1934 founded the *Glyndebourne Opera at his country seat in Sussex, for the artistic achievements of which he was awarded the C.H. in 1955.
Bibl: W. Blunt: *John Christie of Glyndebourne* (1968).

Christoff, Boris (Kirilov), (*b* Sofia, 18 May 1914). Bulgarian bass. After taking a law degree, he joined the Gusla Choir, Sofia, as an amateur and was heard by King Boris, who provided funds for him to go to Rome to study with Stracciari. Further study Salzburg with Muratti. At end of war was in a displaced persons camp. Début in concert 1946; stage début Rome, Arg., 1946, Colline. Milan, Sc., since 1947. London, C.G., 1949-50, where he sang his first Boris, 1958-74 Philip, Fiesco, Boris, and with C.G. company at Edinburgh Festival, Don Basilio. San Francisco 1948-50; Chicago 1958-63. Equally at home in German, Italian, and Russian repertory. His roles include Rocco, King Mark, Gurnemanz, Hagen, Julius Caesar (Handel), Ivan Susanin, Khonchak, Dosifey, Xochubey (*Mazeppa*), and the leading Verdi bass roles. His voice, though not large, is firm and used with great dramatic skill, and he has a sensitive feeling for words. He is one of the great interpreters of Boris Godunov, and a fine King Philip. (R)

Christophe Colomb. Opera in 2 parts (27 scenes) by Milhaud; text by Claudel. Prod

Berlin, S.O., 5 May 1930, in German text by R. S. Hoffmann, with Reinhardt, Scheidl, cond. Kleiber. Concert perfs London, Queen's Hall, 16 Jan. 1937; N.Y., Carnegie Hall, 6 Nov. 1952, with Dow, Harrell, cond. Mitropoulos.

There are some 35 operas on Columbus, including by Ottoboni (*Il Colombo*, 1690, lost), Morlacchi (1828), Fioravanti (1829), Ricci (1829), Carnicer (1831), Bottesini (1847), Barbieri (1848), Franchetti (1892, celebrating the 400th anniversary of the discovery of America), Egk (1933 for radio, rev. 1942 for stage), Vasilenko (1933), and Schuller (1968).

Chrysothemis. Elektra's sister (sop.) in Strauss's *Elektra*.

Chukhadjian, Tigran (*b* Constantinople, 1837; *d* Constantinople, Feb. 1898). Armenian composer. Studied Constantinople with Mangioni, and in Milan. On his return home, he worked in various theatres, and then wrote the first Armenian national opera, *Arshak Erkrod* (Arshak II, 1868). Only excerpts were performed in his lifetime; the complete première (after rediscovery and revision of the score) took place in 1945. This work was followed by the comedy *Arif* (1872), another comedy, *Kyose kyokhva* (The Balding Elder, 1873), and then a third, *Leblebidji* (The Chick-Pea Seller, 1876; rev. 1943 as *Karine*); *Zemire* (1880) was a fairy opera semiseria. In these works, Chukhadjian was the first Armenian composer to reconcile Western operatic techniques with the characteristics of his native folk melody; the ardent nationalism of his work played a part in encouraging Armenians in their liberation movement against Turkey. The comedies show a feeling for Armenian local life and manners.

Church Parable. A term coined by Benjamin Britten for his *Curlew River*, The *Burning Fiery Furnace*, and The *Prodigal Son*, works which derive from the example of the No Plays of *Japan and in which a small group of singers and players presents the dramatic fiction of monks staging an opera on a moral subject to a church congregation.

Cibber (orig. Arnt), (Mrs) **Susanna** (*b* London, Feb. 1714; *d* London, 30 Jan. 1766). English singer (mezzo?) and actress. Probably trained by her brother Thomas Arne; début 1732. Sang and acted in many productions, including first performance of *Messiah* (Dublin 1742). Her singing of 'He was despised' moved Dr Delaney to exclaim, 'Woman, for this thy sins be forgiven thee!' Her voice was not of outstanding power or beauty in an age of great voices, though described as 'sweet' and 'plaintive'. But Handel admired her singing greatly, and she sang many of his works until 1746, when she devoted herself entirely to the stage.

Ciccimarra, Giuseppe (*b* Altamura, 22 May 1790; *d* Venice, 5 Dec. 1836). Italian tenor.

Generally considered one of the finest tenors at the time of Rossini. A regular member of the S.C., Naples, where he created Iago (1816), Goffredo in *Armida* (1817), Aronne in *Mosè* (1818), Ernesto in *Ricciardo e Zoraide* (1818), Pilade in *Erminione* (1819), and Condulmiero in *Maometto II* (1820). He retired from the stage in 1826 and taught singing (and the piano) in Vienna; his pupils included Joseph Tichatschek (the first Rienzi and Tannhäuser), Sofia Löwe, Clara Heinefetter, and Staudigl.

Cicéri, Pierre-Luc-Charles (*b* St-Cloud, 17 or 18 Aug. 1782; *d* St-Cléron, 22 Aug. 1868). French stage designer. Studied singing, later turning to painting and becoming an assistant at the Paris O. 1810; *Peintre du Roi*, 1825. His designs include those for *Le Comte Ory* (1828), *La Muette de Portici* (1829), *Guillaume Tell* (1829), and *Robert le Diable* (1833). The greatest French designer of his day, he opened up a new expressive range by his use of three-dimensional scenery and panoramic effects. His association with Louis *Daguerre was epoch-making, and set new standards of accuracy in historical detail and in grandeur of pictorial effect, matching and encouraging the grandiose ambitions of contemporary French *Grand Opera. For *La Muette* he designed a view of Vesuvius seen through a splendid palace, with woods and houses in the middle distance, for *Robert le Diable* a cloister, imitating that of Montfort l'Amaury, of which three sides were constructed. His earlier designs for the ballet *La Belle au bois dormant* (1825) pioneered the device of revolving drums turning a backcloth so as to produce an illusion of the characters on a journey. Cicéri's four pupils Despléchins, Diéterle, Séchan, and Feuchères further developed his work in the years 1833-48, specializing in outdoor scenes, transformations, and thrilling effects.

Cid, Le. Opera in 4 acts by Massenet; text by D'Ennery, Gallet, and Blau, after Corneille's drama (1637). Prod. Paris, O., 30 Nov. 1885, with Devries, J. and E. De Reszke, Plançon; New Orleans 23 Feb. 1890, with Dauriac, Beretta, Mary, Saint-Jean, Belleroy, Geoffrey, Rossi. Other operas on the character by Stuck (1715), Leo (1727), Sacchini (1764), Piccinni (1766), F. Bianchi (1773), Paisiello (1775), Roesler (1780), Farinelli (1802), Aiblinger (*Rodrigo et Zimène*, 1821), Savi (1834), Pacini (1853), Neeb (1857), Cornelius (1865), Boehme (1887).

Cielo e mar! Enzo's (ten.) aria praising the sky and sea in Act 2 of Ponchielli's *La Gioconda*.

Cigna, Gina (*b* Paris, 6 Mar. 1900). French-Italian soprano. Studied with Calvé, Darclée, Storchio, and Russ. She married the tenor Maurice Sens, and as Ginette Sens made her debut at Milan, Sc., 1927 (Freia). In 1929 she reverted to her own name; and from 1933 she was the leading Italian dramatic soprano, possessing a repertory of over 70 operas, and being particularly famous for her Gioconda and Turandot. London, C.G., 1933, 1936, 1937, 1939. N.Y., Met., 1936-8; San Francisco and Chicago. Resumed singing after war, but seriously injured in motor accident in 1948, and had to give up stage career. Since then has been teaching in Canada and Italy. (R)

Cikker, Ján (*b* Banská Bystrica, 29 July 1911). Czech (Slovak) composer. Studied composition Prague with Křička and Novák, conducting with Dědeček and in Vienna with Weingartner. Has taught and worked in the opera in Bratislava since 1939. His vivid post-Romantic idiom, which owes something to Bartók and Janáček as well as remaining loyal to the music of his native Slovakia, has found its fullest expression in a number of successful operas: *Juro Jánošík* (1954), *Beg Bajazid* (Prince Bajazid, 1957), *Mr Scrooge* (comp. 1954, prod. 1963), *Vzkriesenie* (Resurrection, after Tolstoy, 1962), *Das Spiel von Liebe und Tod* (1969), and *Coriolanus* (1973).

Cilea, Francesco (*b* Palmi, 23 July 1866; *d* Varazza, 20 Nov. 1950). Italian composer. Studied with Cesi and Serrao in Naples, where he produced his first opera, *Gina* (1889). The success of this led Sonzogno to commission the equally successful *La Tilda* (1892). His *L'Arlesiana* (1897) was less well received. 1896-1904, taught in Florence; and during this time he produced his most popular opera, *Adriana Lecouvreur* (1902). His last opera was *Gloria* (1907). His music is conspicuous for its charm and ingenuity rather than its dramatic urgency. *Bibl:* E. Moschino: *Sulle opere di Francesco Cilea* (1932).

Cimarosa, Domenico (*b* Aversa, 17 Dec. 1749; *d* Venice, 11 Jan. 1801). Italian composer. Studied Naples, where he produced his first operas. Until 1787, he was active both in Rome and Naples, becoming Paisiello's great rival: works of these years include *L'Italiana in Londra* (1778), *Il pittore parigino* (1781), *I due baroni di Rocca Azzurra* (1783; for the 1789 Vienna production Mozart wrote an aria), *Il marito disperato* (1785), and *L'impresario in angustie* (1786). For other Italian cities he wrote *Il convito* (1781), *L'olimpiade* (1784), and *Artaserse* (1784). In 1787-91 he directed the opera in St Petersburg, where he wrote *Cleopatra* (1789) and *La vergine del sole* (1789); but unable to endure the Russian climate, he moved to Vienna to succeed Salieri as Court Kapellmeister. Here it was that he wrote his most famous work, *Il matrimonio segreto* (1792); so successful was the first performance that the Emperor Leopold II had supper served to the cast and the performance repeated.

Returning to Naples in 1793 on Leopold's death (1792), he became maestro di cappella to the King: his operas of this period include *Le astuzie femminili* (1794) and the serious operas *Penelope* (1794) and *Gli Orazi ed i Curiazi* (1796). His openly expressed republican sympathies on the arrival of the French in Naples led to his imprisonment; on his release, he set off once more for Russia, but died in Venice on the way.

Though he wrote a large amount of music in all forms, including serious operas, Cimarosa's real talent lay in *opera buffa*. Here his fertile invention, his graceful and witty vocal writing, and his deft ear for orchestration, especially a rapidity of humour in ensembles, make him an ancestor of Rossini. In his own day, he was compared to Mozart, whose liveliness he can match, but whose depth of feeling and whose ability to construct long scenes lie far outside his range. Serious subjects brought out a more conventional vein in him. Opera on an incident in his life by Isouard, *Cimarosa* (1808). *Bibl:* M. T. Tibaldi: *Cimarosa e il suo tempo* (1939).

Cincinnati. Town in Ohio, U.S.A. Various opera companies played in the town during the last century, and many distinguished singers, including Patti, sang there. The musical tradition is German, and the May Festival choral and orchestral rather than operatic. But there is an annual summer season of open-air opera at the Zoological Gardens (founded in 1920) which has been predominantly Italian, though in more recent years Wagner and Strauss works have come into the repertory. Regarded as 'the cradle of American opera singers'. Artists who made either their operatic débuts there, or first appearances in roles for which they later became famous, have included James Melton, Jan Peerce, and Dorothy Kirsten. Since 1970 the company has been known as the Cincinnati Summer Opera, and has performed indoors in the rebuilt Music Hall.

Cinderella. The English name for the heroine of Charles Perrault's story *Cendrillon*, in his *Contes de ma mère l'oye* (1697), known in Italian as *Cenerentola, in German as Aschenbrödel. Operas on the story are by Laruette (1759), Isouard (1810), Steibelt (1810), Rossini (1817), Garcia (1826), C. T. Wagner (*Papelka*, 1861), Chéri (1866), Conradi (1868), Langer (1874), Rokošny (1885), Massenet (1899), Wolf-Ferrari (1900), Albini (*c* 1900), Forsyth (early 20th cent.), Blech (1905), Asafyev (1906), Buttykay (1912).

Cinti-Damoreau, Laure (orig. Laure Cinthie Montalant) (*b* Paris, 6 Feb. 1801; *d* Chantilly, 25 Feb. 1863). French soprano. Studied Paris Conservatoire with Bordogni and with Catalani, who suggested she Italianize her name to

Mlle Cinti. Début Paris, T.I., 1815, Paris O., 1826-8, and 1831-5, where she created leading soprano roles in Rossini's *L'assedio di Corinto, Mosè, Comte Ory,* and *Guillaume Tell,* and was the first Isabelle (*Robert le Diable*) and Elvira (*Muette de Portici*). At the O.C., 1837-43, she created leading roles in a number of Auber's works including *Le Domino noir.* London, Hm., 1822 and 1833. Toured U.S. 1843-4. Professor of singing at the Paris Conservatoire 1833-56. Married the tenor V.C. Damoreau. She wrote a *Méthode de Chant* (1849).

Cio-Cio-San. The Japanese name of Madama Butterfly, the heroine (sop.) of Puccini's opera.

Circe. In Greek mythology, especially as related in Homer's *Odyssey,* a sorceress living on the island of Æææ. When Odysseus visited her island, she turned his companions into swine, but was forced by Odysseus, who had eluded the spell, to release them. Odysseus stayed with her for a year. Most operas on her legend have as their subject the visits of Odysseus or of Telemachus, who had come in search of his father, and may therefore overlap with those dealing with these subjects: see also *Odysseus* and, especially *Telemachus.* Operas on the subject are as follows:
Freschi (1679); Pollarolo (*Circe abbandonata d'Ulisse,* 1692); Desmarets (1694); Boniventi (*Circe delusa,* 1711); Keiser (1734: his last opera); Astaritta (*Ulisse e Circe,* 1777); Albertini (*Circe und Ulysses,* 1786); Gazzaniga (1786); Winter (1788, unprod.); Paer (1792); Egk (1948).

Ciro in Babilonia (Cyrus in Babylon). Opera in 2 acts by Rossini; text by Francesco Aventi. Prod. Ferrara 14 Mar. 1812, with Marietta, Marcolini, Manfredini, Savinelli, and Fraschi. Among some 20 other operas on Cyrus are those by Cavalli (1654), Caldara (1736), Hasse (1751), and Agnesi (*Ciro in Armenia,* 1753; the most important work of one of the first woman opera composers).

Cisneros (orig. Broadfoot), **Eleanora de** (*b* New York, 1 Nov. 1878; *d* New York, 3 Feb, 1934). American mezzo-soprano. Studied with Muzio-Celli and Jean de Reszke. Début as Siebel, N.Y., American T., 1898 under name of Eleanor Francis. Sang as Eleanor Broadfoot, N.Y., Met., 1899-1900; after further study, second début as De Cisneros, Turin, 1902. London, C.G., 1904-6, appearing in first London *Adriana Lecouvreur* and *Andrea Chénier,* Manhattan Opera 1907-9; Melba Company (Australia) 1911. First Italian Countess in *Queen of Spades* (1906), and Klytemnestra (1909). Final appearance, Cleveland Stadium O., 1932. (R)

City Center of Music and Drama, New York. The home of the *New York City Opera, 1944-65, when it moved with the New York City Ballet to the State T., Lincoln Center.

Clapisson, (Antoine-) **Louis** (*b* Naples, 15 Sept. 1808; *d* Paris, 19 Mar. 1866). French composer. Son of a horn player at the Naples S.C.; studied in Bordeaux and in Paris with Habeneck, also playing the violin in opera orchestras. He had an early success with a comic opera, *La Figurante* (1838), which he followed up with a long succession of works which caught the taste of the Paris public. He defeated Berlioz in the election to a chair at the Institut by a large majority (to the indignation of Offenbach), and the appeal of his *Gibby-la-Cornemuse* (1846) was partly responsible for drawing audiences away from the première of *La Damnation de Faust.*

Claque (*Fr* smack, clap). A group engaged by a performer or impresario to applaud, show appreciation, demand encores, and do whatever they can as apparently ordinary members of the audience to encourage a favourable reception.

Hired support of a performer (or attack on a rival) is almost as old as human vanity and deceit, and is recorded in classical antiquity (e.g. by Suetonius of Nero's young supporters). There are records of organized applauders for early Venetian opera, of hired opposition bringing about the failure of an opera in Bologna in 1761, and of many similar occasions. The use of the term *claquer,* to applaud for money, seems to have been introduced with the first systematic use of hired applause in France in the 19th cent. In 1820 a claque agency was opened by a certain Sauton under the title *L'Assurance des succès dramatiques.* Acting under a *chef de claque* was a team of *claqueurs* known, from their traditional position under the chandelier in the Opéra, as the *chevaliers du lustre.* These included *tapageurs,* who applauded vigorously, *connaisseurs,* who added knowing exclamations of approval, *pleureurs* (or more often *pleureuses*), who used concealed smelling-salts to encourage tears of emotion, *bisseurs,* who called for encores, *chatouilleurs,* who sustained their neighbours with witty sallies or offers of sweets, *commissaires,* who held forth on the performance's merits in the intervals, and *chauffeurs,* who 'warmed up' the house before the performance and spread tales of fantastic triumphs afterwards. By the 1830s and 1840s the claque was playing a powerful part in French opera, and was made the subject of some vivid comments by Berlioz (in *À Travers chants* and especially the 7th Evening of *Les Soirées de l'orchestre*). According to Berlioz, the claque was hired by singers, not the management, who received payment in return for the assurance of a monopoly. He reports that the *claqueurs* were known as Romans, from the example of Nero, and in giving a lively, sardonic account of their activities he makes much play of their leader's 'Roman' name, Auguste. A late 19th-cent. tariff included plain applause, 5 francs; renewed applause, 15; expressions of horror, 5; murmurs of alarm, 15; groans, 12.50; guffaws, 5; cries of 'Oh, how funny' etc., 15. To ensure the accurate introduction of these effects, the *chef de claque* was invited to dress rehearsals and given the score to study.

The claque has long endured as an institution in Italy, a country where the drama of opera-going extends well beyond the footlights. Another tariff quoted in 1919 included applause for a gentleman's entry, 25 lire; for a lady, 15; ordinary applause, 10; insistent applause, 15-17, pro rata; interruptions with 'Bene!' or 'Bravo!', 5; a 'bis', 50; wild enthusiasm, a special sum to be arranged. Nowadays the usual practice is for the *capo di claque* to be paid a flat sum. The most famous claque in modern Italy has been that of La Scala, organized by Carmelo Alabiso (a former Toscanini tenor) and Antonio Carrara, 30-40 strong and including students, teachers, and even two barbers.

In England, the claque has not achieved the same status, though at Covent Garden in the 1890s Jean de Reszke was allowed *faveurs de claque*, free tickets for his admirers. It was probably introduced into America in 1910 when Gatti-Casazza allowed the tenor Bonci's valet, so it is said, to form a claque so as to save the failing production of *Armide*. A claque flourished at the Met. in the 1920s (led by Schol, an umbrella-maker). In 1954 Rudolf Bing cut the number of standing places, the traditional post of the claque, in order to restrain it; the *chef de claque* then was one John Bennett, who allowed his men only their tickets. Ezio Pinza used to pay them to leave him alone, a form of protection racket. Some singers have gone further and resorted to an 'anti-claque', hired to bring down a rival. They have even clashed: when a rival singer's fans tried to boo Maria Callas at Milan Sc., the claque responded so briskly that two people were sent to prison as a result of the ensuing brawl.

In Germany the claque has not flourished so greatly, but one of the most famous of all time was that commanded by Schostal in Vienna in the 1920s, and vividly described by a former member, Joseph Wechsberg, in *Looking for a Bluebird*. Like many claqueurs, Schostal prided himself on his artistic integrity in only applauding works to which he felt he could honestly lend his support. The Vienna claque is not alone in applauding, free of charge, for his artistry a singer who has declined to employ it. Conversely, the claque at Parma once refunded a tenor his money and booed his subsequent performances. It has always been the claim of *claqueurs* that they are encouragers of excellence, defenders of talent, and that they earn their fees as honestly as any publicity man and with more discrimination.

Clément, Edmond (Frédéric-Jean) (*b* Paris, 28 Mar. 1867; *d* Nice, 24 Feb. 1928). French tenor. Studied Paris with Warot. Début O.C., 1889, Vincent (*Mireille*); remained there as leading tenor until 1909 and created leading roles in many French operas including Bruneau's *L'Attaque du moulin* (1893) and Saint-Saëns's *Hélène* (1905); was the first Paris Fenton and Pinkerton. N.Y., Met., 1909-11; Boston 1911-13. One of the most elegant and stylish French singers of his day. (R)

Clemenza di Tito, La (The Clemency of Titus). Opera in 2 acts by Mozart; text by Metastasio, altered by Mazzolà. Prod. Prague, 6 Sept. 1791, with Fantozzi, Antonini, Baglioni; London, H.M.'s, 27 Mar. 1806 (the first Mozart opera in London, with a cast that included Billington and Braham); Tanglewood, 4 Aug. 1952, with Jordan, Flemming, Winston, Matheson, Lansee, Sharretts. Metastasio's text was also set by some 20 other composers, including Gluck (1752). The Emperor Titus (ten.) plans to marry Berenice, thus arousing the jealous rage of Vitellia (sop.); she urges Sextus (con.), who is in love with her, to lead a conspiracy against Titus. When Titus decides instead to marry Servilia (sop.), sister of Sextus, she tells him that she loves Annius (mezzo). Titus now resolves to marry Vitellia, who not knowing of this further change of plan initiates a conspiracy and the burning down of the Capitol. Titus escapes, but after further complications forgives Sextus and then Vitellia.

Cleopatra. Queen of Egypt (*b* 69B.C.; *d* 30B.C.). Lover of Caesar and of Antony. There are some 70 operas about her including Canazzi (1653), Cousser (1691), Mattheson (1704), Graun (1742), G. Scarlatti (1760), Danzi (1779), ?Kaffka (1779), Anfossi (1788), Cimarosa (1789), Nasolini (1791), F. Bianchi (1801), Weigl (1807), Paer (1808), Combi (1842), Freudenthal (1874), L. Rossi (1876), Pedrell (1878), Freudenberg (1882), Sayn-Wittgenstein-Berleburg (1883), Massé (1885), Benoît (1889), Morales (1891), Enna (1894), Yuferov (pubd. 1900), Massenet (1914), Hadley (1920), P. H. Allen (1921), O. Strauss (1923), Brand (c1930), Malipiero (1938), La Rosa Parodi (1938), Bondeville (1973). See also *Shakespeare* for settings of *Antony and Cleopatra* among the above.

Cleva, Fausto (*b* Trieste, 17 May 1902; *d* Athens, 6 Aug. 1971). Italian-American conductor. Assistant cond. N.Y., Met., 1920-1; chorus-master 1935-42; leading conductor of Italian repertory from 1950. Also conducted in Chicago (artistic director 1944-6), San Francisco, Cincinnati Summer Opera, and elsewhere in America. Died while conducting Gluck's *Orfeo* in the T. of Herodes Atticus. (R)

Cloches de Corneville, Les (The Bells of Corneville). Opera in 3 acts by Planquette; text by Clairville and Gabet. Prod. Paris, Folies-Dramatiques, 19 Apr. 1877; N.Y. 22 Oct. 1877; London, Folly T., 23 Feb. 1878. Planquette's most popular opera; at the end of a run of 461 performances the manager served the last audience with 2,000 rolls and free beer.

Cluj (Hung. Kolosvár; Ger. Klausenburg). Town in Romania, principal town of Transylvania. The first season was given in 1920 through the efforts of the composer Tiberiu Brediceanu and the director Constantin Pavel. The company prospered under the baritone Popovici-Bayreuth, and has introduced a number of new Romanian operas, including Brediceanu's *Seara Mare* (1924), Negrea's *Marin Pescarul* (1934) and Drăgoi's *Năpasta* (1928) and *Kir Ianulea* (1939). There is also an opera house giving performances in Hungarian.

Cluytens, André (*b* Antwerp, 26 Mar. 1905; *d* Paris 3 June 1967). Belgian conductor. Studied Antwerp. Antwerp Opera 1927-32; Lyons from 1935; Paris, O. and O.C., since 1947; Bayreuth 1955-8, 1965. Was a frequent guest Vienna and Italy. (R)

Coates, Albert (*b* St Petersburg, 23 Apr. 1882; *d* Cape Town, 11 Dec. 1953). Anglo-Russian conductor and composer. Originally in commerce in St Petersburg; began musical studies at Leipzig when 20. Appointed répétiteur at Leipzig by Nikisch with whom he studied 1904. Conducting appointments at Elberfeld, Dresden, and Mannheim followed. Chief conductor and artistic director of St Petersburg Opera 1909-17, and returned intermittently until 1934. London, C.G., 1914 and 1919-24; also *The Ring* with B.N.O.C. 1929 (*Boris* with Shalyapin), 1935-8. In 1936 organized Coates-Rosing Opera Company. Operas include *Samuel Pepys* (Munich 1929) and *Pickwick* (London, C.G., 1936). (R)

Coates, Edith (*b* Lincoln, 31 May 1908). English mezzo-soprano. Engaged for Old Vic Shakespeare Company 1924, but soon joined the opera company, first in the chorus, then in small solo parts, the first of which was Giovanna in *Rigoletto*. Leading mezzo-soprano S.W. 1931-46; C.G. 1937-9, 1947-63. Created Auntie (*Peter Grimes*), Mme Bardeau (*The Olympians*). The Countess in *The Queen of Spades* was one of her most striking roles. (R)

Coates, John (*b* Girlington, nr Bradford, 29 June 1865; *d* Northwood 16 Aug. 1941). English tenor. Originally a baritone, and sang Valentine as an amateur with C.R. without success; engaged by D'Oyly Carte Company 1894. Retired for a further period of study and emerged as tenor singing in light opera 1899-1900. London, C.G., 1901, Faust; created Claudio in Stanford's *Much Ado about Nothing*

the same year. Toured Germany 1902-7, and U.S.A. 1926-7. Later member of Moody-Manners and Beecham companies. One of the best British Tristans and Siegfrieds. (R)

Cobelli, Giuseppina (*b* Maderno, 1 Sept. 1898; *d* Salo, 10 Aug. 1948). Italian soprano. Studied Cologne with G. Benvenuti and at Hamburg. Début Piacenza 1924, Gioconda. Great success as Sieglinde, Milan, Sc., in the following year led to yearly appearances there in Wagner (her Isolde was much admired) and modern Italian works. Created leading roles in Respighi's *La fiamma* and Montemezzi's *La notte di Zoraima*. Forced to abandon her career in 1944 owing to deafness. (R)

Coburg. Town in Bavaria, Germany. The first opera performances were given in 1630 under Duke Johann Ernst, with Melchior Frank as music director. Performances were given in 1717 under C. C. Schweitzelsberger. In 1764 a Bühnenlokal was opened, and perfs. of *Entführung* and *Zauberflöte* were given. The operatic tradition developed in the early 19th cent. under L. Schneider, who had been recommended by Weber; a performance of *Der Freischütz* was given in 1823. The Herzogliche Coburg-Gothaische Hoftheater opened under A. Lübcke, 1827, the Landestheater (cap. 1,000) 1840 with Auber's *Le Lac des fées*. In 1858 Ernst II, Duke of Saxe-Coburg-Gotha's *Diana von Solange* was produced. Malipiero's *Mysterium Venedigs* was given its première in 1932.

Coccia, Carlo (*b* Naples, 14 Apr. 1782; *d* Novara, 13 Apr. 1873). Italian composer. Studied Naples with P. Casella, then Fenaroli, later Paisiello, who got him his first appointment (with the King of Naples). His first opera, *Il matrimonio per lette di cambio* (1807) was a failure, but with Paisiello's continued support he soon wrote *Il poeta fortunato*, which had a success in 1808. In Venice 1809-17, he developed his characteristic genre, *opera semi-seria*, of which the most successful example was *Clotilde* (1815). He was criticized for copying other men's music, and for the hastiness in his work that led to great unevenness; and the emergence of Rossini forced him to seek a new arena abroad, in Lisbon (1820-3) and London (1824-7). He conducted at the King's T., and in 1827 broke a six-year silence with *Maria Stuarda*. In the same year he returned to Italy, where he had further successes especially with *Caterina di Guisa* (1833). A period of further study, especially of German music, during his silence caused a change in style, but the new seriousness in his work did not help him to retain popularity as fashion turned in new directions. He was director of the Turin Conservatory, 1836-40. He gave up opera in 1841.

Bibl: G. Carotti: *Biografia di Carlo Coccia* (1873).

Cocteau, Jean (*b* Maisons-Laffitte, 5 July 1889; *d* Paris, 12 Oct. 1963). French writer and librettist. Collaborated with Honegger in *Antigone* and Stravinsky in *Oedipus Rex,* for which he also sometimes took the part of the narrator. Also provided librettos for Milhaud's *Le Pauvre matelot* and Poulenc's *La Voix humaine.* (R)

Colbran, Isabella (Angela) (*b* Madrid, 2 Feb. 1785; *d* Bologna, 7 Oct. 1845). Spanish soprano. Studied in Madrid with Pareja and Naples with Marinelli and Crescentini. Début Paris 1801; Milan, Sc., 1807; engaged by Domenico Barbaia, whose mistress she became, to sing at Naples 1811; and also became the *favorita* of the King of Naples. She deserted both in 1815 to live with Rossini, whom she married in 1822. For her he wrote *Elisabetta, Regina d'Inghilterra.* She also created the leading soprano roles in his *Otello, Armida, La donna del lago, Mosè, Semiramide,* and *Maometto II.* She was considered the finest dramatic coloratura soprano in Europe from 1801 to 1822, though her voice began to weaken after 1815. She composed 4 vols. of songs.

Coletti, Filippo (*b* Anagni, 11 May 1811; *d* Anagni, 13 June 1894). Italian baritone. Studied Naples with Alessandro Busti; début Naples. T. del Fondo, 1834 in *Il Turco in Italia.* During the next decade established himself as one of the leading exponents of Bellini and Donizetti, and from 1844, when he sang Carlo in *Ernani* in Venice, F., became one of the leading Verdi baritones, creating Gusmano in *Alzira* (1845) and Francesco in *I masnadieri* (1847). He was the first Rigoletto in Rome when the opera was given as *Viscardello,* and also a distinguished Luna, Germont, Boccanegra, and Doge in *Due Foscari,* in which role Chorley found him second only to Ronconi. He also created roles in operas by Pacini and Donizetti.

Colin. The hero (ten.) of Rousseau's *Le Devin du village.* From this role the term *colin* was used in French opera of the late 18th and early 19th cent. for a rustic lover, generally sentimental and tender.

Coliseum Theatre, London. Built by Sir Oswald Stoll in 1904; London's largest theatre (cap. 2,354) with the largest stage. In its days as a music hall, appearances by opera singers and ballet dancers were an important feature. In June 1913 a series of living tableaux of *Parsifal* was presented with Wagner's music arranged and conducted by Henry Wood. Sadler's Wells Opera first appeared there in April 1959 with productions of *Fledermaus* and *The Land of Smiles.* Since September 1969 it has been the home of the Sadler's Wells (now English National) Opera.

Colla voce (*It* with the voice). A direction to the instrumental part to follow the voice part carefully, usually in a passage where the rhythm is, or is likely to become, free. The phrase *colla parte* is also used.

Collier, Marie (*b* Ballarat, 16 Apr. 1926; *d* London, 7 Dec. 1971). Australian soprano. Studied Melbourne with Mme. Wielaert and Gertrude Johnson. Début Melbourne, Santuzza, 1954, followed by tour of Australia as Magda Sorel in *The Consul,* which she sang 70 times. Further study, Milan, with Ugo Benvenuti Giusti 1955-6. London, C.G., 1956 as Musetta and sang there regularly until her death; her roles included Marie in *Wozzeck,* Katerina Izmaylova, Hecuba in *King Priam,* Liù, Lisa, Cressida, Chrysothemis, Manon Lescaut, and Jenůfa. At Sadler's Wells she sang Káťa Kabanová, Minnie, Venus, Concepción, and Emilia Marty in *The Makropoulos Case.* San Francisco, Katerina Izmaylova, and Minnie 1965; Emilia Marty 1966; Woman in *Erwartung* 1968; N.Y., Met., 1967, where she created Christine Mannon in *Mourning Becomes Electra,* also 1967-8 and 1969-70 as Musetta and Santuzza. Never a flawless vocalist, she was nonetheless gifted with a vibrant and very individual voice and generous personality, which made her performances of Puccini and Janáček especially memorable. (R)

Colline. The philosopher (bass) of the four Bohemians in Puccini's *La Bohème.*

Collingwood, Lawrance (Arthur) (*b* London, 14 Mar. 1887). English conductor and composer. Choirboy at Westminster Abbey, then went to Russia and became Albert Coates's assistant at St Petersburg. Joined Old Vic in the 1920s; principal conductor S.W. 1940-6. His *Macbeth* had its first performance at S.W. in 1934; he also conducted there the first performance in England of *Tsar Saltan* (1933) and the original version of *Boris Godunov* (1935). (R)

Colmar. Town in Alsace Lorraine, France. The T. Municipal (cap. 750), designed by Boulanger, opened in 1849. From 1870 to 1919 performances were generally given by the Strasbourg Opera and touring companies; from 1919 to 1940 by the Strasbourg and Mulhouse companies. During the German occupation the theatre was modernized and a permanent opera company set up. Since 1972 Colmar, with Mulhouse and Strasbourg, is part of the *Opéra du Rhin.

Cologne (Ger. Köln). Town in North Rhine Westphalia, Germany. The first permanent theatre was built in 1822, with S. Ringelhardt as director until 1832. The company included Lortzing as singer and actor. The first local *Fidelio* was given in 1822. Under F. Hiller, the first local Wagner performances were given in 1853 (*Tannhäuser*) and 1855 (*Lohengrin*); Wagner himself conducted a subscription concert for Bayreuth in 1873 at Gürzenich. The new theatre was opened 1872, and enjoyed a good Wagner and Verdi tradition under Otto Lohse, Eugen Szenkar, Fritz Zaun, Otto Ackermann, and Wolfgang Sawallisch. The theatre's greatest years were 1917-24 under Otto Klemperer; this period included the premières of Korngold's *Die tote Stadt* (1920) and the first German *Káťa Kabanová* (1922). The theatre was bombed in 1943; the Grosses Haus (cap. 1,346) opened in 1957 with *Oberon*. Wolfgang Sawallisch was Generalmusikdirektor 1960-3, Istvan Kertesz 1964-73, John Pritchard since 1978. Premières since the war have included Henze's *Ein Landarzt* (1953), Fortner's *Bluthochzeit* (1957), and Zimmermann's *Die Soldaten* (1965); and the German premières of Prokofiev's *The Fiery Angel* (1960), Nono's *Intolleranza* (1962), and Britten's revised *Billy Budd* (1966).

Colón, Teatro, Buenos Aires. The leading opera house of South America. For many years it gave the old-fashioned type of international opera season (May to Sept.) with French, German, and Italian works sung in their original languages by leading foreign artists. The first Colón was opened in Apr. 1857 (cap. 2,500) with *La traviata* with Lorini and Tamberlik. Opera was performed there regularly until 1888 by Italian and French ensembles which included Bellincioni, Boronat, Fricci, Borghi-Mamo, Sanz, Battistini, De Lucia, Gayarré, Kaschmann, Stagno, Tamagno. In 1887 the old Colón was sold to the National Bank for 950,000 pesos to be used for the building of a new opera house. During the 20 years before the present theatre was built, opera was given at the T. de la Opera. The present building (cap. 2,487, 1,000 standing) opened on 25 May 1908 with *Aida*; the first season included Panizza's *Auroa*, commissioned by the government. Cesar Ciacchi was the manager until 1914 and under his direction Toscanini returned to Buenos Aires, where he had previously conducted some seasons at the T. de la Opera 1901-6. Toscanini's 1912 season included the first perfs. in S. America of *Ariane et Barbe-Bleue, Germania* and *Königskinder* by a company that included Bori, Matzenauer, Anselmi, Amato, De Luca, and De Angelis.

From 1915 to 1925 the seasons were directed by Walter *Mocchi; as well as bringing Italian and French artists to the Colón, he engaged Weingartner and a German ensemble including Lehmann, Wildbrunn, Schipper, etc. for the *Ring* and *Parsifal* in 1922. From 1926 to 1930 Ottavio Scotto (Muzio's husband) was the impresario. In 1931 the Colón became a municipal theatre with a general manager and artistic director. The 1931 season included several operas conducted by Klemperer (his last complete *Ring* in any opera house) and Ansermet.

Busch conducted regularly 1933-6 and 1941-5; Kleiber, 1937-41 and 1946-9; and Albert Wolff 1938-46.

After 1949, financial difficulties during the Perón regime resulted in a lowering of artistic standards; but after the 1955 revolution the theatre regained its former traditions. In 1958, the theatre's 50th anniversary, Beecham conducted memorable performances of *Zauberflöte, Fidelio, Otello, Carmen,* and *Samson et Dalila*. In 1967 six complete *Ring* cycles were given, conducted by Leitner, who had been a regular visitor since 1960, with Nilsson, Windgassen, and David Ward. The change of government in 1973 resulted in a complete upheaval of the Colón's administration and artistic policy. See also *Buenos Aires.*
Bibl: R. Casamano: *La historia del Teatro Colón* (1969).

Colonello, Attilio (*b* Milan, 9 Nov. 1930). Italian designer. Studied Milan with Gio Ponti and Ernesto Rogers. Designed *La traviata,* Florence Festival 1956; *Mefistofele,* Milan, Sc., 1958; and then frequently for productions in Rome, Palermo, Naples, etc., collaborating with Eduardo De Filippo, Margherita Wallmann, and Graf. Designed *Lucia di Lammermoor,* N.Y., Met., *Orfeo* at the Boboli Gardens, Florence (1957), Pizzetti's *Clitennestra* (Milan 1965), and *Luisa Miller* (Edinburgh Festival 1965).

Coloratura. (Not, as commonly supposed, an Italian word, but derived from the German *Koloratur.*) Coloratura of itself means elaborate ornamentation of melody; thus a coloratura soprano is one who specializes in this type of music, formerly known as *canto figurato,* distinguished by light, quick, agile runs and leaps and sparkling *fioriture* (which is the correct Italian word for flourishes or ornamentation).

Coltellini, Celeste (*b* Livorno, 26 Nov. 1760; *d* Capodimonte, nr Naples, 28 July 1828). Italian mezzo. Daughter of the poet and librettist Marco Coltellini (see below); studied with G. B. Mancini and G. Manzuoli. Milan, Sc., 1780; Naples, T. dei Fiorentini, from 1781, where she created Paisiello's *Nina.* Highly regarded as an interpreter of Paisiello, Mozart, Cimarosa, etc. and said to have excelled in the expression of sentiment. Her sister **Anna** sang with success in Naples, 1782-94.

Coltellini, Marco (*b* Livorno, 13 Oct. 1719; *d* St Petersburg, Nov. 1777). Italian poet and librettist. Father of above. Invited to Vienna, probably by Calzabigi, where he eventually succeeded Metastasio as Court Poet; but an indiscreet satire directed against Maria Teresa in 1772 led to his leaving Vienna for St Petersburg, where he became official librettist at the Imperial T. He wrote the librettos for Mozart's *Finta semplice,* Haydn's *L'infedeltà delusa,*

Gluck's *Telemaco,* and for operas by Traetta, Galuppi, Salieri, Sarti, Scarlatti, and Paisiello.

Combattimento di Tancredi e Clorinda, Il. Dramatic cantata by Monteverdi; text from Tasso's *Gerusalemme liberata,* Canto XII, vv. 52-68 (1575). Perf. Venice, Palazzo Mocenigo, Carn. 1624. Though not strictly an opera, the work is written *in genere rappresentativo* and was intended for performance by costumed actors and a singing narrator (Il Testo) during a musical evening after madrigals had been sung 'senza gesto' (without action): a dramatic convention is thus implied. Though this did not prove fruitful for the development of opera, in modern times there has been some re-awakening of interest in the musical and dramatic ideas which it embodies, and composers with a particular interest in *Music Theatre, e.g. Alexander Goehr, have turned to it for an example. Tancredi, a Christian knight, has fallen in love with Clorinda, a Saracen maiden. He pursues a Saracen in armour, who has burnt a Christian castle, and in single combat defeats his opponent. But when he agrees to give his fallen adversary Christian baptism, 'he' reveals 'his' identity as Clorinda.

Com'è gentil. Ernesto's (ten.) aria in Act 3 of Donizetti's *Don Pasquale,* which takes the form of a serenade.

Come scoglio. Fiordiligi's (sop.) aria in Act 1 of Mozart's *Così fan tutte* declaring that she will remain as firm as a rock against all temptations by her would-be seducer.

Come un bel dì di maggio. Chénier's (ten.) aria in Act 4 of Giordano's *Andrea Chénier,* sung while he awaits execution.

Comédie mêlée d'ariettes. A type of French comic opera, developing from the example of Italian buffo opera at the time of the *Guerre des Bouffons, consisting of a light romantic comedy into which were inserted songs. Under the influence of Rousseau and one of the first of them, *Le Devin du village,* they often included political and social comment. Examples include Gluck's *La Rencontre imprévue,* Philidor's *Tom Jones,* Monsigny's *Le Déserteur,* and Grétry's *Zémire et Azor.*

Comelli, Adelaide (orig. Adèle Chaumel) (*b*?; *d* Romano, 30 Jan. 1874). French mezzo. Studied Paris. In 1820 she married Rubini and continued to sing as Comelli-Rubini. Created Calbo in *Maometto II* and Argene in Rossini's cantata *La riconoscenza.* It is also thought she was the page in the première of *Elisabetta, Regina d'Inghilterra.* Stendhal says the Neapolitans delighted in building up her reputation in order to play her off against Colbran, and also suggests that Rossini was 'head over heels in love with her' before she married Rubini, and he Colbran.

Comic opera. A term sometimes loosely used in English for *opéra-comique,* which has precise applications, or for any musical comedy.

Comme autrefois. Leïla's (sop.) cavatina in Act 2 of Bizet's *Les Pêcheurs de perles.*

Commedia dell'Arte. A dramatic genre of unknown origin that flourished in Italy from the 16th cent. and had a strong influence on drama and hence on opera. It consisted of improvized comedy following a scenario, rather than a written dialogue, and making use of stock characters. The most important were the *zanni,* whose *lazzi* (slapstick routines) included acrobatics and gestures as well as dialogue: often comic servants, either dull-witted or shrewd, but always ready to introduce foolery into any situation, the *zanni* were the essence of the *commedia.* They include the foolish, agile Arlecchino (Harlequin), the cunning, agile Brighella, the cunning, cowardly Scapino, and among others Pedrolino, Scaramuccia, Pulcinella, Mezzetino, Coviello, and Burattino. There might also be an elderly parent or guardian, Pantalone, the *magnifico;* his pedantic, gullible crony Gratiano, the *dottore;* the swaggering Spanish captain; the love-lorn Inamorata, who was often named Isabella, Flaminia, Silvia, Valeria, or Olivetta; her servant or confidante, often named Colombina, sometimes Fioretta, Violetta, or Smeraldina; and the hero, often named Fortunio, Fulvio, and a variety of other names. Certain of these characters were traditionally associated with Italian cities: Pantalone was a Venetian merchant, the doctor Bolognese, Arlecchino and Brighella from Bergamo, Scaramuccia and Pulcinella from Naples. Most of the characters would be masked, except for the lovers, and all would be readily identifiable by traditional dress, such as Arlecchino's diamond-patterned motley, the doctor's black cape and hat, the clown's slack white costume with pom-poms down the front.

The plots of the *commedia dell'arte* were many and various – the confusions of disguise, mistaken identities, muddles between twins, a lover pretending to be a servant so as to win his girl from the clutches of a rich old man, a couple of unknown origin who turn out to be brother and sister, and many more. The virtuosity of the Italian troupes won the genre immense popularity, and spread its fame across Europe. It influenced many playwrights, including Shakespeare, and in France particularly Molière and Beaumarchais. Hence the influence passed into the plots of many operas, especially opera buffa, whether directly or indirectly. The characters appear in, for instance, Busoni's *Arlecchino,* Ethel Smyth's *Fantasio,* Strauss's *Ariadne auf Naxos,* and Mascagni's *Le maschere;* and there is the celebrated clash of reality with illusion by means of the *com-*

media dell'arte in Leoncavallo's *Pagliacci*. More crucially, the schematization of comic plots into types provided opera librettists and composers with a comic tradition which could be richly varied and refreshed: the plot of Rossini's *Il barbiere di Siviglia* is an outstanding instance of a pure *commedia dell'arte* plot given new vividness and wit; while more than traces survive into Mozart's *Figaro* without any diminishment of the characters' rich humanity.

Commedia per musica (*It* comedy for music). A term used in Italy in the 18th cent. for comic opera.

Como. Town in Lombardy, Italy. Opera is given in the spring. The T. Sociale (cap. 1,000) was opened in August 1813 with a performance of Portogallo's *Adriano in Siria*. Stendhal thought highly of the performances during the theatre's initial season, writing, 'C'est à Como qu'il faut aller pour jouir de la musique'. During the 1860 season *Garibaldi a Como* by the tenor M. Filiberti, who sang the title-role, was produced. After Milan Sc. was destroyed in 1943, the Sociale offered the company hospitality for part of the 1943-4 season.
Bibl: anon.: *Centocinquantanni di storia del Teatro Sociale di Como* (1964).

Competitions. From time to time competitions have been sponsored by various bodies for the composition of operas. Possibly the most famous was that (one of a series) organized by the publisher Edoardo Sonzogno for a 1-act opera in 1889; three prizes were awarded, one to Mascagni's *Cavalleria rusticana*. In more recent years there have been two important competitions: one organized by the Arts Council of Great Britain in 1950 for the Festival of Britain, and the other organized by Milan Sc. for the 1951 Verdi celebrations. The former resulted in four operas being awarded prizes: Arthur Benjamin's *The Tale of Two Cities*, Alan Bush's *Wat Tyler*, Berthold Goldschmidt's *Beatrice Cenci*, and Karl Rankl's *Deirdre of the Sorrows*. Benjamin's has been performed in Great Britain (and also in Metz). Bush's has been staged in Leipzig and Weimar, and has also been given by the B.B.C. at S.W. 1974. The Italian competition resulted in a Scala production of Castro's *Proserpina e lo straniero*, and one at the Naples S.C., of Jacopo Napoli's *Mas' Aniello*.
Vocal competitions are more frequent: the Metropolitan Auditions of the Air discovered Eleanor Steber and Leonard Warren; while in Europe, international vocal contests in Britain (e.g. the Queen's Prize, the Kathleen Ferrier Competition), Austria, Holland, Switzerland, and Italy, have helped many subsequently famous singers at the start of their careers.

Comprimario (*It* with the principal). A secondary or small-part artist or singer. Examples of comprimario roles are Spoletta, Goro, and the whole host of duennas and confidantes.

Comte Ory, Le (Count Ory). *Opera buffa* in 2 acts by Rossini; text by Scribe and Delestre Poirson, an expansion of a 1-act comedy (1817) after an alleged old Picard legend set down by Pierre-Antoine de la Place (1785). Prod. Paris, O., 20 Aug. 1828, with Cinthie-Damoreau, Nourrit, Dabadie, Levasseur, cond. Habeneck; in Italian, London, H.M.'s, 20 Feb. 1829, prob. for Rossini's 37th birthday with Montecillé, Castelli, Currioni, De Angalis, Galli, cond. Bochsa N.Y., 22 Aug. 1831, with St Clair, Paradol, Deschamps, Privat. The first of Rossini's two French operas and his penultimate stage work; it contains much of the music of *Il viaggio a Reims* with 12 additional numbers.
The Countess Adèle (sop.) is melancholy, her brother and the menfolk of the castle of Fourmoutier having left for the Crusades. Ragonde (con.), the Countess's companion, decides to consult the hermit – in reality the licentious Comte Ory (ten.), who has encamped at the castle gates and offers expert advice on amorous matters. He is aided in his exploits by his friend Raimbaud (bar.). Ory's tutor (bass) and his page Isolier (mezzo), who is in love with the Countess, arrive in search of Ory. Isolier's plan to enter the castle, disguised as a nun, so appeals to the Count that he and his followers disguise themselves in nun's habits, and lay siege both to the ladies in the castle and to the wine cellars. The return of the crusaders, just as matters are getting out of hand, results in Ory's and Isolier's defeat in their pursuit of the Countess.
Also opera by Miltitz (*c*1830).

Congiura (*It* plot, conspiracy). The name sometimes given to-scenes of conspiracy in Italian opera. Examples are 'Ad augusta!' in Part 3 of Verdi's *Ernani* and 'Dunque l'onta' in Act 3 of his *Un ballo in maschera*.

Connais-tu le pays? Mignon's (mezzo) aria in Act 1 of Thomas's *Mignon*, the famous 'Kennst du das Land?' of Goethe's original, trying to answer Wilhelm's questions about her origins.

Conried (orig. Cohn), **Heinrich** (*b* Bielitz, 13 Sept. 1848; *d* Meran, 27 Apr. 1909). German operatic impresario and manager. Began career as an actor in Vienna; after holding managerial positions in a number of German cities went to America in 1888. Succeeded Maurice *Grau as director the N.Y. Met. 1903, and also organized his own company. Resigned owing to ill health in 1908.

Consul, The. Opera in 3 acts by Gian-Carlo Menotti; text by composer. Prod. Philadelphia 1 Mar. 1950, with Neway, Powers, Lane, Marlo, MacNeil, Lishner, McKinley, cond. Engel; London, Cambridge T., 7 Feb. 1951, with similar cast, cond. Schippers. The action takes place in a nameless police state in Europe and depicts the efforts of Magda Sorel (sop.) to obtain a visa for herself and her husband, John (bar.), a revolutionary who is being pursued by the secret police. The Consul's Secretary (mezzo) frustrates all attempts to see the Consul, by giving out innumerable forms. John is eventually arrested and Magda commits suicide by gassing herself; as she dies, she sees in a dream her husband and all the people she has met at the Consulate who urge her to join them on the journey to Death whose frontiers are never barred.

Contes d'Hoffmann, Les (The Tales of Hoffmann). Opera in 3 acts by Offenbach; text by Barbier and Carré, founded on the stories *Der Sandmann, Geschichte vom verlorenen Spiegelbilde,* and *Rat Krespel* by E.T.A. Hoffmann. Revision, recitatives, and part of orchestration by Guiraud. Prod. Paris, O.C., 10 Feb. 1881, with Isaac, Ugalde, Talazac, Taskin; N.Y., 5th Avenue T., 16 Oct. 1882, with Dérivis, Betty, Maire, Mangé, Ducos; London, Adelphi T., 17 Apr. 1907, with Franzillo-Kauffmann, Nadolovitch, Hofbauer, cond. Cassirer.

Offenbach died during rehearsals of *Hoffmann,* and it was re-arranged (cutting the Giulietta act) by Guiraud for the première. Twelve years later the missing act was restored, but before the Antonia act. Correctly, the opera is largely with spoken dialogue, and in the order here given.

Prologue. Luther's wine-cellar in Nuremberg. Councillor Lindorf (bar.), who assumes during the course of the opera Hoffmann's evil genius (Coppelius, Dapertutto, Dr Miracle), bribes Andrès (ten.) to give up a letter from Stella, the prima donna, to Hoffmann (ten.) arranging a rendezvous. The students arrive and with them Hoffmann and his friend Niclausse (mezzo). Hoffmann is persuaded to tell the story of his three loves. Each act of the opera is one of his 'tales'.

Act 1. Hoffmann's first love was Olympia the doll, invented by Spalanzani (bar.) and Dr Coppelius (bass-bar.). Coppelius sells Hoffmann a pair of magic spectacles through which Olympia (sop.) appears human. At a party given by Spalanzani for his 'daughter's' coming-out, Hoffmann declares his love for Olympia, and dances with her. Coppelius, who has been swindled by Spalanzani, returns and smashes Olympia; Hoffmann discovers that his love is a doll.

Act 2. Hoffmann has now come back to Munich, where he has fallen in love with the frail young singer Antonia (sop.), daughter of Councillor Crespel (bass). Antonia is consumptive and has been forbidden to sing, but Dr Miracle (bass-bar.), by bringing her mother's picture to life, forces her to sing and thus brings about her death. For a second time Hoffmann

has lost his love.

Act 3. Hoffmann is in Venice, where he has met the beautiful courtesan Giulietta (mezzo). She is in the power of Dapertutto (bass-bar.), the magician, who wishes to procure Hoffmann's reflection (in other words, his soul). Giulietta finds no difficulty in fascinating Hoffmann and carrying out Dapertutto's wish; and Hoffmann, bereft of his shadow, tries to obtain the key to Giulietta's room from Schlemil (bass), whom he kills in a duel, only to find Giulietta drifting away in a gondola with the dwarf Pitichinaccio.

Epilogue. Back in Luther's tavern, the 'tales' are over. Hoffmann is drunk, and when Stella arrives it is Lindorf and not Hoffmann who leads her away.

Continuo. Abbrev. of *basso continuo.* In the scores of 17th- and 18th-cent. opera, the bass part accompanying *recitative, performed generally by harpsichord (often played by the conductor), sometimes also with cello.

Contralto (*It* against the alto, i.e. contrasting with the high voice). In German, Alt (the voice), Altistin (the singer). The lowest category of female (or artificial male) voice. Several subdivisions exist within opera houses: the two commonest in general use (though seldom by composers in scores) are given below, with examples of roles and their approximate *tessitura.* In general distinction is more by character than by *tessitura*: thus the examples of the roles give a more useful indication of the different voices' quality than any attempted technical definition.

German: dramatischer Alt (Erda: f-f''); komischer Alt (Frau Reich in *Die lustige Weiber von Windsor*: f-f'').

Italian and French contralto roles are not generally further subdivided into categories, and have a similar *tessitura* to the German.

See also *Castrato, Mezzo-soprano.*

Contratenor. See *Countertenor.*

Converse, Frederick (Shepherd) (*b* Newton, 5 Jan. 1871; *d* Westwood, 8 June 1940). American composer. Studied at Harvard, then Munich. *The Pipe of Desire* was produced at Boston in 1906, and in 1909 became the first American opera to be performed at the Met. His other operas are *The Sacrifice* (1911), *Sinbad the Sailor* (1913, unprod.), and *The Immigrants* (1914, unprod.).

Cook, Thomas Aynsley (*b* London, July 1831 or 1836; *d* Liverpool, 16 Feb. 1894). English bass. Originally boy soprano and trained by Hopkins at the City Temple; then studied with *Staudigl in Germany. After singing in several German theatres made British début at Manchester 1856. Member of Lucy Escott's National English Opera Company and the Pyne-Harrison Company. Carl Rosa Company from

1874. Devilshoof (*The Bohemian Girl*) was probably his most famous role. See also *Goossens*.

Cooke, Tom (*b* Dublin, 1782; *d* London, 26 Feb. 1848). Irish singer, composer, and instrumentalist. Sang in various stage works in Dublin and London; principal tenor, D.L., 1815-35, director from *c*1821. Produced his own *Oberon* in the same year as Weber's, in part rivalry and parody. Adapted many foreign operas, with substitutions of his own, including *Abu Hassan, La Dame blanche, La Muette de Portici,* and *La Juive*.

Cooper, Emil (Albertovich) (*b* Kherson, 13 Dec. 1877; *d* New York, 16. Nov. 1960). Russian conductor of English descent. Studied Odessa, Vienna, and Moscow, incl. with Taneyev and Nikisch. Début Odessa 1896. Kiev 1899-1906; Moscow, B. and Z., 1904. Cond. première of *The Golden Cockerel*, also London première, 1914. Cond. Russian seasons, Paris 1909-11. Left Russia in 1924, and after various engagements in Europe (incl. Riga), Chicago Opera 1929-32; N.Y., Met., 1944-50, where he introduced *Peter Grimes* and *Khovanshchina*. Also a distinguished Wagner conductor, directing first Russian performances of *Meistersinger* and *The Ring*. (R)

Copenhagen (Dan. Kjøbenhavn). Capital of Denmark. Opera was given in the mid-17th cent., including Caspar Förster's *Il Cadmo* (1663). Schindler's *Der vereinighte Götterstreit* (1689) was given at the Amalienborg T., which burned down during the performance, killing 180 people. Foreign companies began visiting the city from the mid-18th cent.: Italian and French opera was performed, and a German company under Keiser was at the Court T. 1721-3, giving the première of his *Ulysses* (1722) for Frederick IV's birthday. In 1749 Prince Christian's birth was celebrated with the première of Gluck's *La contesa dei numi*. After a period of decline owing to opposition from the King, on religious grounds, the opera was revived and Sarti was made director of the theatre (from 1772, the Kongelige T.).

One of the earliest operas produced at the National T. was Scalabrini's *Den belønnede kjaerlighed* (Love Rewarded, translated from *L'amor premiato*, 1758). Many Italian operas were given, and a singing school founded. J.A.P. Schulze was director 1787–95, F.L.A. Kunzen 1795-1817; Kunzen raised the standard and introduced many new works, especially foreign ones. The Swedish musician Johan Svendsen was director 1883-1908, during which period the Royal T. (cap. 1,300) was built. Carl *Nielsen, who succeeded him 1908-14, had begun his career as second violinist in the orchestra. Nielsen was succeeded by Georg Høeberg, who conducted the only complete

Ring given in the theatre. He resigned in 1931, and was succeeded by Johan Hye-Knudsen, who shared the conducting with Egisto Tango (restoring the Swedish setting of *Un ballo in maschera* among other enterprises). During the German occupation, *Porgy and Bess* received its first performances outside America (1943), but was then suppressed; there were also performances of other works banned in Nazi Germany. Since Tango's death in 1951, Hye-Knudsen and John Frandsen have shared the conducting, with guest appearances from Lamberto Gardelli and Wolfgang Rennert.

A second auditorium, the New Stage (cap. 1,091), was opened in 1931. There is also an operetta, Nörrelzo (cap. 1,141), renamed the Scala in 1954.

Bibl: G. Leicht and M. Hallar: *Det kongellge Teaters repertoire 1889-1975* (1977).

Copland, Aaron (*b* New York, 14 Nov. 1900). American composer. Studied with Wittgenstein and Rubin Goldmark, and with Boulanger in Paris. His first opera was *The Second Hurricane* (1937), a 'play opera' for high schools. *The Tender Land* (1954) is a pastoral drama set in the Mid-west during the depression years; its idiom is similar to that of *Appalachian Spring,* while the earlier opera uses Copland's more nervy, jazz-influenced manner. (R)

Copley, John (Michael) (*b* Birmingham, 12 June 1933). English producer. Studied National School of Opera, London, with Joan Cross. Appeared as the Apprentice in *Peter Grimes* at C.G, 1950. Stage manager, S.W.; produced *Il tabarro* there 1957. Resident producer C.G., where as well as reviving other producers' works, has staged successful productions himself of the Mozart repertory, Gluck's *Orfeo, La Bohème, L'elisir d'amore, Benvenuto Cellini* and *Ariadne auf Naxos,* and for E.N.O. *La traviata, Carmen, Il trovatore, Maria Stuarda, Der Rosenkavalier,* and *Werther.* Has also worked with Australian Opera, Dallas Opera, etc. His productions are marked by a high degree of invention, and he is very successful in getting singers to act in a natural manner.

Coq d'Or, Le. See *Golden Cockerel, The.*

Corder, Frederick (*b* London, 26 Jan. 1852; *d* London, 21 Aug. 1932). English conductor, composer, teacher, and translator. Studied R.A.M. and Cologne. His most successful opera was *Nordissa* (1887), performed by the C.R.; but with the death of Rosa and the collapse of Corder's hopes of taking part in a revival of English opera, he turned to teaching and translation. His pupils included Bantock, Bax, and Holbrooke; but he is best remembered now for the translations he made, together with his wife Henrietta, of Wagner's *Tristan,*

Meistersinger, and *The Ring.* He was concerned to match Wagner's alliterative *Stabreim, which he does ingeniously but often quaintly. These versions were performed at C.G. and elsewhere.

Corelli, Franco (Dario) (*b* Ancona, 8 Apr. 1921). Italian tenor. Studied Milan, Florence, Pesaro, Spoleto. Début Spoleto 1951, Don José; London, C.G., 1957, Cavaradossi; N.Y., Met., 1961, Manrico. Has sung regularly at Milan, Sc., since 1954, and has established himself as one of the leading Italian heroic tenors. Especially successful as Manrico, Dick Johnson, and Calaf. Married the soprano Loretta Di Lelio. (R)

Corena, Fernando (*b* Geneva, 22 Dec. 1916). Swiss-born bass of Turkish parentage. Originally intending to take holy orders, studied at Fribourg University. Began Geneva 1937-8; further encouraged by Vittorio Gui and studied in Milan with Enrico Romano. Zurich 1940-7; Trieste 1947, Varlaam. N.Y., Met., 1953, succeeding Salvatore Baccaloni as leading basso-buffo. Edinburgh Festival, Falstaff 1955, Pasquale 1963; London, C.G., 1960, Bartolo (*Barbiere*). (R)

Corfu (Gr. Kerkyra). Capital of the Ionian island of that name, which was subject to Venice 1386-1797. The island's first theatre was completed in 1691 – the Loggia, later T. San Giacomo. Financed from Venice, this was the first permanent theatre in the Levant, and seasons were given by visiting Italian companies in the 18th cent. The works of Spiridon Xyndas, Pavlos Karrer, and Spiro Samara were given here. In 1895 the Phoenix T. was opened; this ceased to be a theatre in 1945. The larger Demoticon T. opened in 1902, where Lavrangas's *Dido* (1909) and other Greek works were given; it was destroyed by shells in 1943.

Corneille, Pierre (*b* Rouen, 6 June 1606; *d* Paris, 1 Oct. 1684). French playwirght. Operas on his works are as follows:

Le Cid (1637): Pollarolo (*Flavio Bertarido,* 1706); Handel (*Flavio,* 1723); Sacchini (1769); Aiblinger (*Rodrigo und Zimene,* 1821); Schindelmeisser (*Der Rächer,* 1846); Gouvy (comp. 1863); Cornelius (1865); Massenet (1885); Wagenaar (1916).

Cinna (1640): Caldara (*La clemenza di Tito,* 1734); Hasse (*Tito Vespasiano,* 1735); Graun (1748); Portugal (1793); Asioli (1793); Paër (1795).

Horace (1640): Salieri (1786); Cimarosa (*Gli Orazi e i Curiazi,* 1796); Portugal (1798); Mercadante (*Orazi e Curiazi,* 1846).

Polyeucte (1643): Donizetti (1838); Gounod (1878).

La Mort de Pompé (1643): Graun (*Cesare e Cleopatra,* 1742).

Héraclius (1647): Ziani (1671).

Andromède (1647): Mattiali (*Perseo,* 1664);

Lully (*Persée,* 1682).

Théodore (1647): Papebrochio Fungoni (1738).

Nicomède (1651): Grossi (1677).

La Toison d'or (1660): Draghi (1678).

Sophonisbe (1663): Caldara (1708); Traetta (1761).

Attila (1667): Ziani (1672).

Psyché (1671): Locke (1675); Champein (early 19th cent).

Cornelius, Peter (*b* Mainz, 24 Dec. 1824; *d* Mainz, 26 Oct. 1874). German composer. After an attempt at an acting career, studied music and became a loyal friend of Liszt and Wagner. Liszt produced *Der Barbier von Bagdad* at Weimar (1858), but the organized opposition led to its withdrawal and to Liszt's resignation as court conductor. After his association with Wagner in Vienna he composed *Der Cid* (1865) then *Gunlöd* (1891). Almost alone of the New German School and its followers, Cornelius was concerned to give German comic opera greater maturity than he found in the works of for instance, Lortzing. In the entertaining *Barbier von Bagdad,* he shows an intelligent appreciation of how the example of Berlioz might be used to this end, and there are some influences of *Benvenuto Cellini;* but it is also a work of no little charm in its own right.

Cornelius, Peter (*b* Labjerggaard, 4 Jan. 1865; *d* Copenhagen, 25 Dec. 1934). Danish tenor. Studied in Copenhagen and Berlin. Début Copenhagen, as baritone, 1892, Escamillo; after further study, tenor début (again at Copenhagen) 1899, Steersman. Bayreuth 1906; London, C.G., 1907-14; chosen by Hans Richter to sing Siegfried in the English *Ring* performances of 1908 and 1909; continued to sing until 1922, after which he taught in Copenhagen. (R)

Bibl: C. Cornelius: *Peter Cornelius* (1925).

Corno di Bassetto. See Shaw, G. Bernard.

Corregidor, Der (The Mayor). Opera in 4 acts by Wolf; text by Rosa Mayreder, after Alarcón's story *El Sombrero de tres picos* (1874). Prod. Mannheim 7 June 1896, with Hohenleitner, Rüdiger, Krömer; London, R.A.M. (in English) 13 July 1934, with Dawes, Rodd, Davies, Der Prangnell, cond. Barbirolli; N.Y., Carnegie Hall 5 Jan. 1959 (concert), with Conner, Lipton, Kelley, Thompson, Gramm. Wolf's only opera.

Frasquita, the miller's wife (sop.), dismissing her husband Tio Lucas's (bar.) jealousy as groundless, uses the advances of the elderly Corregidor (ten.) to obtain a post for her nephew. When this is achieved the Corregidor arrives, soaked from having fallen into the mill stream; Frasquita defends herself with a musket. Tio Lucas has meanwhile been summoned to town by the Corregidor; he realises that this is a false errand, but passes Frasquita in the dark on his way home as she comes to

nd him. When Lucas finds the Corregidor
sleep in bed, he dresses in the old man's
othes; on waking the Corregidor is beaten by
e officers who have come from the town.
hen the Corregidor reaches his own house,
s own wife Mercedes (sop.) refuses him
dmission, pretending that she has mistaken
ucas for him. Lucas, taken for the murderer of
e Corregidor, is also beaten; and the opera
ds with everyone even.

Also opera by Zandonai (*La farsa amorosa*,
933).

orri. Italian, later English, family of musicians.
(1) **Domenico** (*b* Rome, 4 Oct. 1744; *d*
ndon, 22 May 1825). Italian singing teacher,
omposer, and publisher. Studied Naples with
orpora. His operas include *La raminga fedele*
770) and *The Travellers, or Music's Fascina-
on* (1806). He promoted performances in
dinburgh and London, where he established
mself as a publisher in Soho in 1790.

(2) **Sophia Giustina** (*b* Edinburgh, 1 May
775; *d* ?, after 1828). Anglo-Italian soprano.
aughter of above. Studied with her father and
evoted most of her life to the concert plat-
rm. Married Jan Ladislav Dusik (Dussek), and
s Sophia Dussek appeared at King's T. in 1808,
operas by Paisiello, Fioravanti, Nasolini, and
arti. Not to be confused with Josepha Dusek.

(3) **Fanny Corri-Paltoni** (*b* Edinburgh, 1801; *d*
. Anglo-Italian mezzo-soprano. Niece of (1).
tudied with Catalani. London, King's T., 1818-
, Countess Almaviva, Donna Anna,
orabella, Queen of Night, Ameniade in first
ndon *Tancredi*. Pursued a successful career
Germany, Italy, and Spain. Married the
nger Paltoni. Said to have possessed a voice
fine quality, with a brilliant shake.

Other members of the family include **Patrick
nthony** (1820-76), singer and conductor;
enry (1822-88), singer and conductor; **Haydn
r.,** (? 1842-77), baritone; **Ghita** (?–?), soprano
ith C.R.; and **Charles** (1861-1941), conductor,
om 1895 to 1935 chief conductor of the Old
c and later Vic-Wells Opera.

rsaro, Il (The Corsair). Opera in 4 acts by
rdi; text by Piave, after Byron's poem (1813).
od. Trieste 25 Oct. 1848, with Barbieri-Nini,
pazzini, Fraschini, De Bassini, Volpini;
ndon, Camden T., 15 Mar. 1966, with Tinsley,
nclair, Smith, Drake, cond. Head. Verdi's
ast successful opera. Corrado (ten.) is cap-
red leading an expedition against Pasha Seid
ar.). He is rescued by Gulnara (sop.), the
isha's favourite slave, who kills Seid. Gulnara
d Corrado return to the latter's island home
find Medora (sop.), Corrado's betrothed,
ing.

Other operas on the subject are by Pacini
831) and Arditi (1846).

rsi. Italian family of singers.

(1) **Giovanni** (*b* Verona 1822; *d* Monza, 4 Apr.
1890). Italian baritone. Début Milan, 1844, Dandini in *Cenerentola*. Milan, Sc., from 1847 and
Paris, T.I. Specially noted for his Rigoletto and
Doge (*Due foscari*), as well as in the Donizetti
repertory. Retired from stage 1870 and taught
in St Petersburg, later Milan.

(2) **Achille** (*b* Legnano, 1840; *d* Bologna, 15
Apr. 1906). Italian tenor, brother of above.
Début Milan, T. Carcano, 1859, *Lombardi*; Sc.
from 1860; successful in the Rossini repertory.
Retired 1882 and became a teacher; pupils
included his daughter Emilia and nephew
Antonio *Pini-Corsi.

(3) **Emilia** (*b* Lisbon, 21 Jan. 1870; *d* Bologna,
17 Sept. 1927). Italian soprano, daughter of
above. Début 1886 Bologna, Micaela. After successes as Lucia, Gilda, Rosina, turned to the
dramatic repertory and sang Manon Lescaut,
Gioconda, and Sieglinde. Retired from stage
1910 and taught in Milan and Bologna, where
her pupils included the tenors Ettore Cesa-
Bianchi and Angelo Minghetti.

Corsi, Jacopo (*b* Florence, 17 July 1561; *d* Florence, 1604). Italian musical amateur. It was in
his house that the *Camerata met, and in which
were first performed *Peri's *Dafne* and *Caccini's *Euridice*, probably with Corsi at the harpsichord. He composed two songs used in *Dafne*
by Peri, who was his pupil.

Cortis, Antonio (*b* Valencia, 12 Aug. 1891; *d*
Valencia, 2 Apr. 1952). Spanish tenor. Début
1915 as comprimario, then graduated to larger
roles. International career began in Rome,
1920. Chicago 1924-32; London, C.G., 1931,
Calaf. One of the best interpreters of Dick
Johnson (*La fanciulla del West*). Retired from
the stage while still at the height of his powers
in the mid-1930s. (R)

Cosa rara, Una. Opera in 2 acts by Martín y
Soler; text by Da Ponte, after Luis Velez de
Guevara's story *La luna della sierra*. Prod.
Vienna, B., 17 Nov. 1786; London, 10 Jan. 1789,
with Graziani, Elisabetta Borselli, Sgra Delicati,
Fausto Borselli, Forlivesi, Delicati, Fineschi,
Torregiani.

Lilla (sop.) has been promised by her brother
Tita (bass) as bride to Don Lisargo (bass), but
she is in love with Lubino (bar.), to whom she
remains faithful although also pursued by
Prince Giovanni (ten.) and his chamberlain,
Corrado (ten.). One of the great successes of its
day, the opera drew the Viennese public away
from *Figaro*, causing Mozart to quote a piece
from the Act 1 finale in the Supper Scene of
Don Giovanni with Leporello's comment,
'Bravi! *Cosa rara*!' Martín's use in the opera of a
mandoline had a clear influence on Mozart in
writing Don Giovanni's serenade. The opera
contains one of the first Viennese waltzes.
Adapted by Stephen Storace as *The Siege of*

Belgrade, 1791. Sequel, music by Schack, text by Schikaneder, *Der Fall ist noch weit seltener!*, prod. Vienna, W., 10 May 1790.

Così fan tutte (Women are like that). Opera in 2 acts by Mozart; text by Da Ponte, probably after Ariosto's *Orlando furioso*, Canto 43 (1516), perhaps in turn deriving from the story of *Cephalus and Procris in Ovid's *Metamorphoses.* Prod. Vienna, B., 26 Jan. 1790, with Del Bene, Villeneuve, D. Bussani, Calvesi, Benucci, F. Bussani; London, Hm., 9 May 1811, with Bertinotti-Radicati, Collini, Sgr and Sgra Cauvini, Tramezzani, Naldi; N.Y., Met., 24 Mar. 1922, with Easton, Peralta, Bori, Meader, De Luca, Didur. The supposed immorality of the plot led to many adaptations, often under different titles, in the 19th cent.

Act 1, Scene 1. A café in Naples. Two officers, Ferrando (ten.) and Guglielmo (bar.), wager the cynical Don Alfonso (bar.) that their respective lovers Fiordiligi (sop.) and Dorabella (sop.) will be faithful in their absence.

Scene 2. Don Alfonso tells the ladies of their lovers' impending departure on active service. Tears surround the soldiers' farewell.

Scene 3 introduces the maid Despina (sop.). The officers return disguised as Albanians, and having unsuccessfully wooed each other's lady, pretend to take poison. Despina, disguised as a doctor, magnetizes them to life, and they resume the attack.

Act 2 finds Guglielmo beginning to wear down his friend's lover Dorabella; Ferrando, more slowly, succeeds with Fiordiligi, and Despina (now a 'lawyer') prepares a double marriage contract. Word that the officers are returning sends the 'Albanians' packing, to return in their true guise pretending fury at their betrayal. Alfonso reveals the truth, thus allowing all to end happily.

Cossira (orig. Coussival), **Emile** (*b* Orthez, 1854; *d* Quebec, Feb. 1923). French tenor. Studied Bordeaux. Début Paris, O.C., 1883 Richard Coeur de Leon (Grétry); O. 1888-91, created title-role in Saint-Saëns's *Ascanio*. Tristan in the first perf. in French of Wagner's opera, Brussels 1894; first French Walther at Lyons, 1896. London, C.G., 1891, 1894, and 1900 as Faust, Roméo, Raoul, Don José. His wife **Emma,** mezzo-soprano, was the Magdalene in the Lyons *Meistersinger*. (R)

Cossotto, Fiorenza (*b* Crescentino, nr Vercelli, 22 Apr. 1935). Italian mezzo. Studied Turin with Paola della Torre. Début Milan, Sc., 1957, creating Sister Matilde in *Dialogues des Carmélites,* and has sung there regularly since. First major success as Leonora in *La favorita* (1961). London, C.G., 1959 as Neris in *Medée* and subsequently as Azucena, Eboli, Amneris. Chicago Lyric O. since 1964; N.Y., Met., since 1968. Generally considered the Italian suc-

cessor of Stignani and Simionato. Married t the bass Ivo Vinco (*b* 1928).(R)

Cossutta, Carlo (*b* Trieste, 8 May 1932). Italia tenor. Studied Buenos Aires. Début there 195 Alfredo. Colón from 1958, at first in small role created title role in Ginastera's *Don Rodrig* (1968). London, C.G., from 1964, Duke Mantua, Turiddu, Otello, Manrico, Gabrie Adorno, Don Carlos, and Cavaradossi. N.Y Met., from 1973; Paris, Milan, Sc., etc. At h best an exciting *tenore robusto*. (R)

Costa, Michael (Andrew Angus) (orig. Miche Andrea Agniello) (*b* Naples, 4 Feb. 1808; Hove, Sussex, 29 Apr. 1884). Italian compos and conductor of Spanish descent. Studie Naples. Settled in London and eventual became naturalized. Engaged as maestro piano at the King's T. 1830; director and co ductor there from 1833 to 1846, during whic period he brought the orchestra and ensemb to a state of efficiency hitherto unknown London. From 1846 conductor of the Philhar monic Society; 1847-69, music director of th newly opened Royal Italian Opera, C.(Knighted 1867. In 1871 he was again appointe to Her Majesty's Opera, and continued the until 1879. His operas include *Il delitto puni* (1826), *Il sospetto funesto* (1827), *Il carcere d degonda* (1829), *Malvina* (1829), *Malek Adh* (1837 with Grisi, Lablache), and *Don Carl* (1844).

Cotogni, Antonio (*b* Rome, 1 Aug. 1831; Rome, 15 Oct. 1918). Italian baritone. Studie with Fontemaggi. Début Rome, T. Metastasi 1852, Belcore (*L'elisir d'amore*). Milan, S from 1860. London, C.G., 1867, Valenti (*Faust*); member of company until 1889, bei the Enrico in *Lucia* on the night of Melba début 1888. St Petersburg 1893-6, and 'farewell' *Don Pasquale* in Feb. 1898. Had repertory of 127 roles. 1902 became a pr fessor of voice at Santa Cecilia, Rome. Famo singers who studied with him include Jean Reszke and Battistini, and among his pupils Rome were Lauri-Volpi, Gigli, and Stabile. (F

Cotrubas, Ileana (*b* Galaţi, 9 June 1939). Rom nian soprano. Joined Bucharest Opera ch dren's choir in 1948 and appeared in *Bohèm Tosca, Carmen,* etc. Studied singing wi Emanuel Elenescu at the Bucharest College Music and with Constantin Striescu at th Bucharest Conservatory. Début in Bucharest 1964, as Yniold, remaining there until 1966 a singing Blonde, Cherubino, Siebel. Won fi prize at 's-Hertogenbosch Internation Competition in Holland; further study Vien 1966. Brussels, La M., 1967 Constanze a Pamina; Salzburg, 1967, First Boy, 1969, Ba tienne; Gly. 1969, Mélisande, 1970 Calist Pamina; Frankfurt Opera 1968-71; London C. since 1971 as Tatyana, Susanna, Norina, V etta, Mélisande, Gilda, Micaela. Milan, Sc., 1974 Mimì. Chicago since 1973, Mimì, Norina, Violetta, Eurydice; Paris, O., 1974 Manon. Guest appearances Vienna, Berlin, etc. One of the most vocally and dramatically versatile artists to have emerged in the late 1960s; she is a gifted a tragic actress as a comedienne, and her voice is always used with taste and intelligence. (R)

Countertenor. A high male voice that uses naturally produced tone with a large degree of head resonance; not to be confused with male alto, castrato, or falsetto. Though covering the soprano or contralto range, it is essentially masculine in timbre – clean, penetrating, and flexible, with an almost instrumental purity. Popular from medieval times to about the 18th cent., the high countertenor has been revived in recent times with great success by Alfred Deller, Russell Oberlin, James Bowman, and others; the low countertenor, associated mostly with church music, seems now non-existent. Britten uses it to suggest a non-human quality for Oberon in his *Midsummer Night's Dream*.

Countess (Almaviva). The Count's wife (sop.) in Mozart's *Le nozze di Figaro*.

Coup de glotte (*Fr* stroke of the glottis). A method of attacking a note whereby the false vocal chords (two membranes above the true vocal chords) are closed and then quickly opened to release the tone. It should not be an abrupt release from pressure, when a sharp cough or click results, but a start of pressure from stopped breath.

Couplets. The French term, originally meaning 'stanzas', in general use in 18th- and 19th-cent. opera, operetta, and Singspiel for a strophic song, generally witty in character. Examples are found in Grétry, Auber (*Fra Diavolo*), and especially in operettas by Hervé, Offenbach, and Lecocq. In Germany the word is generally used in the singular, e.g. by Johann Strauss for the *couplet* in *Fledermaus*, 'Mein Herr, was dächten Sie von mir' and elsewhere, also by Millöcker, Lehár, Heuberger, Fall, and others.

Covent Garden. The name of three theatres that have occupied roughly the same site in Bow Street, London, since 1732. The site of the theatre had been church land (in fact a convent garden, hence its name).

The first theatre was opened by John Rich on Dec. 1732 with Congreve's *The Way of the World*; the first musical work heard there was *The Beggar's Opera*. The majority of events at Covent Garden during its first hundred years were of a dramatic rather than an operatic nature, though Handel's *Atalanta, Alcina,* and *Berenice* all had their first performances there. The theatre was destroyed by fire on 19 Sept. 1808.

The second theatre opened a year later. In 1826 Charles Kemble, the manager, invited Weber to compose a work for Covent Garden; this was *Oberon*. Events between 1833 and 1847 included Alfred Bunn's 1833 season with Malibran and Schröder-Devrient; the 1835 season when Malibran sang in *Sonnambula* and *Fidelio*; the artistically successful but financially disastrous seasons 1839-42 with Adelaide Kemble in *Norma* and other works; the German company that appeared in 1842; and the visit of the company from Brussels in 1845 when there were performances which Chorley called 'unmutilated and meritorious' of *Guillaume Tell, Les Huguenots,* and *La Muette de Portici*. In 1847 the theatre became the Royal Italian Opera, with a company which included a number of artists who had seceded from Her Majesty's T. with their music director *Costa. They began operations with Rossini's *Semiramide*. In 1851 Frederick Gye became the manager, a position he held until 1879. The second theatre was burnt down in 1856, and the present theatre opened on 15 May 1858 with Meyerbeer's *Les Huguenots*.

From 1858 until 1939, with the exception of an interruption during the First World War, opera was given every year during the London 'season', and virtually every artist of international repute appeared there. All operas were sung in Italian until the days of Augustus Harris (manager 1888-96), who introduced opera in the original language. Covent Garden became the Royal Opera in 1892, in which year Wagner came into his own there when Mahler and the Hamburg company gave the first Covent Garden *Ring*.

From Harris's death until 1924 the theatre was controlled by the Grand Opera Syndicate under various managers and music directors. Grau was in charge of both the N.Y. Met. and Covent Garden from 1897-1900; Messager directed both the Paris O.C. and C.G. from 1901 to 1904; and Percy Pitt, Richter, and the manager Neil Forsythe were in partial or full control until 1914.

Beecham first conducted there in 1910, and in a series of spring and autumn seasons introduced the major Strauss operas to London, as well as *A Village Romeo and Juliet* and *The Wreckers*. The theatre remained closed 1914-18, by which time Beecham was in command of London's operatic life. By the end of the 1920 season he had gone into voluntary liquidation and the B.N.O.C., which developed from Beecham's own English company, occupied Covent Garden for winter and summer seasons 1922-4. From 1924 to 1931 German opera under Bruno Walter prospered with the famous Wagner and Strauss performances with Leider, Lehmann, Schumann, Olczewska, Melchior, Schorr, Janssen, Kipnis, etc. Beecham returned in 1932 and became artistic adviser and then director until 1939. Those years included the Rossini performances with Supervia, Mozart with Lemnitz, Berger, Tauber etc., and more great Wagner performances under Beecham, Furtwängler, Reiner, and Weingartner, with Flagstad, Lubin, Thorborg, Bockelmann, and Weber. In November 1936 the Dresden State Opera paid a visit and Strauss conducted his *Ariadne*.

The theatre was used as a dance hall 1940-5, but in 1946 it reopened as the home of a permanent company with a government subsidy, paid through the Arts Council. Karl Rankl was music director 1946-51; Rafael Kubelík from 1955 to 1958; Georg Solti from 1961 to 1971; and Colin Davis from 1971. David Webster was general administrator from 1946 to 1970; John Tooley since 1970. Since the war several native operas have received world premières, including Britten's *Billy Budd* (1951) and *Gloriana* (1953), Walton's *Troilus and Cressida* (1954), Tippett's *The Midsummer Marriage*, (1955), *The Knot Garden* (1970), and *The Ice Break* (1977), and Peter Maxwell Davies's *Taverner* (1972). Also of importance were the staging of Berg's *Wozzeck* under Kleiber (1952), Janáček's *Jenůfa* (1956), and *The Trojans* (1957), both under Kubelík, Verdi's *Don Carlos* under Giulini (1958), *Fidelio* (1961) under Klemperer, *Tosca* (1964) with Callas and Gobbi, *Arabella* and *Moses und Aron* (1965) under Solti, *Pelléas et Mélisande* (1969) under Boulez, and the première of Henze's *We Come to the River* (1976). Following a successful Promenade Concert performance of *Boris Godunov* in August 1971 in collaboration with the B.B.C., the Opera House (in conjunction with the Midland Bank) has organized its own series since 1972. In 1976 Götz Friedrich was appointed Chief Producer.
Bibl: H. Rosenthal: *Two Centuries of Opera at Covent Garden* (1958).

Covered tone. The tone-quality produced when the singer's voice is pitched in the soft palate. It is gentler, more veiled in timbre, than open tone, and gives greater intensity and beauty to the transitional notes, i.e. c to e in the baritone and bass register, and f' to a' in the tenor and soprano range. It is also a help in reaching well-placed high notes and is sometimes employed by lyric voices singing dramatic arias or even dramatic roles, e.g. when a coloratura sopano sings Butterfly or a lyric baritone sings Rigoletto.

Cowen, (Sir) Frederic (Hymen) (orig. Hymen Frederick) (*b* Kingston, Jamaica, 29 Jan. 1852; *d* London, 6 Oct. 1935). English composer, conductor, and pianist. When only 8 he composed an operetta, *Garibaldi, or The Rival Patriots*, to a libretto by his 17-year-old sister. Studied with Goss and Benedict, later Leipzig with Moscheles and Reinecke. His first opera was *Pauline* (1876); later ones were *Thorgrim* (1890), *Signa* (1893), and *Harold* (1895). *Signa* was composed as a potential successor to Sullivan's *Ivanhoe* in D'Oyly Carte's project for an English National Opera; when the project failed, Cowen secured a production in Milan (T d.V., 1893), but there were only two performances owing to sharp dissensions (which nearly led to a duel between Boito and Son zogno), and the unfortunate opera was finally produced in a third version by Augustus Harris at C.G. in 1894.

Cox, Jean (*b* Gadsden, 16 Jan. 1932). American tenor. Studied at the University of Alabama, the New England Conservatory of Music, Boston, and Rome with Luigi Ricci. Début New England Opera T., Boston, 1951, Lensky. Spoleto, 1954, Rodolfo. Kiel, 1954-5, Brunswick 1955-9; Mannheim since 1959. Bayreuth 1956 as Steersman in *Fliegende Holländer*, and since 1967 Lohengrin, Parsifal, Walther, and Siegfried. Chicago, 1964, 1970, 1973 as Bacchus, Erik, and Siegfried. Repertory includes Steva in *Jenůfa*, Apollo in *Daphne*, Sergey in *Katerina Izmaylova* and the Cardinal in *Mathis der Maler*. One of the few convincing Siegfrieds of the 1970s. (R)

Cox, John (*b* Bristol, 12 Mar. 1935). British producer. Studied Oxford, where he produced the British stage première of *L'Enfant et les sortilèges* in 1958. Assistant to Rennert at Gly. 1959, returned there in 1970 and appointed director of productions 1972. S.W. since 1969; Frankfurt 1971; Australian Opera 1974; also a frequent visitor to Wexford. With Alexander Goehr was director of the Music Theatre Ensemble. Generally acknowledged as one of the most gifted of the younger British producers, with eye for vivid detail.

Crabbé, Armand (*b* Vandergoten, 23 Apr. 1883; *d* Brussels, 24 July 1947). Belgian baritone. Studied Brussels with Gilles, Desiré Demest 1902-4, and Milan with Cottone. Début Brussels, La M., 1904, Nightwatchman (*Meistersinger*); London, C.G., 1906-14. Returned after a long absence in 1937 as Gianni Schicchi. Also appeared in Chicago, Buenos Aires, and Milan Sc. Much admired as Beckmesser, Figaro (Rossini), and Mârouf, which part was specially transposed for him by Rabaud. Wrote *Conseil sur l'art du chant* (Brussels, 1931), and *L'art d'Orphée* (Brussels, 1933). (R)

Cracow. See *Kraków*.

Credo in un dio crudel. Iago's (bar.) aria in Act of Verdi's *Otello*, in which he expounds his belief in a cruel god who has fashioned him in his own likeness. Boito's most substantial and personal addition to the part in its derivation from Shakespeare.

Crescendo (*It* growing). Increasing in loudness

Now a basic part of music, the crescendo was once a controversial novelty. According to Burney, the first opera in which it was used seems to have been Terradellas's *Bellerofonte* (1747). This refutes the claim made by Mosca to have used it for the first time in his *I pretendi delusi* (1811). The innovation was, and still is, often credited to Rossini, with whom it bordered on a mannerism. His finest use of it is in *Barbiere* to suggest graphically the rising gale of slander in Don Basilio's 'La calunnia'.

Crescentini, Girolamo (*b* Urbino, 2 Feb. 1762; *d* Naples, 24 Apr. 1846). Italian male mezzo-soprano. Studied with Gibelli. Début Padua 1782 in Sarti's *Didone abbandonata*. Created Cherubini's Artaserse, Livorno (1783), Romeo in Zingarelli's *Giulietta e Romeo* (Milan, Sc. 1796), and sang in Cimarosa's *Gli Orazi e i Curiazi* (Venice 1796). His only London appearances in 1785 not successful, and he was replaced in mid-season by Tenducci. In 1803 he sang to inaugurate the new theatre at Piacenza; 1805 appointed professor of singing to the Imperial Family. Napoleon heard him sing in Vienna and was so impressed that he engaged him for Paris, 1806-12. Then Rome, and finally Naples Conservatory, where Isabella Colbran was one of his pupils.

Crespin, Régine (*b* Marseilles, 23 Feb. 1927). French soprano. Studied Paris with Cesbron-Viseur and Jouatte. Début Mulhouse, 1950, Elsa. Paris from 1951. Bayreuth 1958, Kundry; Gly. 1959, Marschallin; London, C.G., since 1960, Marschallin, Tosca, and Elsa. N.Y., Met., since 1962. Salzburg, Easter Festival 1967, Brünnhilde (*Walküre*). N.Y., Met., 1975-6 (Carmen). Since 1977 has been singing mezzo roles. Has established herself as one of the most sensitive and moving French singers of the day. An outstanding Marschallin. (R)

Crimi, Guilio (*b* Paterno, nr Catania, 10 May 1885; *d* Rome, 29 Oct. 1939). Italian tenor. Début Palermo, 1910, Manrico; London, C.G., 1914, Avito in first London *L'amore dei tre re*. N.Y., Met., 1918-22; created Luigi and Rinuccio in world premières of *Il tabarro* and *Gianni Schicchi*. Chicago 1916-18 and 1922-4. Returned to Italy and continued to sing in Milan and Rome until 1928. After his retirement taught: pupils include Gobbi. Was also creator of Paolo in Zandonai's *Francesca da Rimini* Turin 1914). (R)

Cristoforeanu, Florica (*b* Rîmnicu-Sărat, 16 Aug. 1887; *d* Rio de Janeiro, 1 March 1960). Romanian soprano. Studied Milan with Vaneri Filippi and Bordilla. Début Capodistria, 1908, Lucia, under name of Cristina Floreanu. From 1909 to 1919 a leading operetta singer in Bucharest and Milan, managing the Città di Milano company. In 1919 sang Magda in *La rondine* and Lodoletta, and in 1921 Cio-Cio-San

at Dal Verme, Milan, which marked the true beginning of her operatic career. Milan, Sc., 1927-32 where she created Mariola in *Fra Gherardo* under Toscanini; also sang Santuzza, Carmen, and Charlotte. Rome, T.R., 1928-34, where she created roles in operas by Malipiero and Persico. Toured South America; here her career continued until 1940, when she was forced to retire because of ill-health. Repertory also included Isolde, Kundry, Fedora, and Adriana Lecouvreur. (R)

Critic, The, or An Opera Rehearsal. Opera in 2 acts by Stanford; text by Lewis Cairns James, after Sheridan's comedy (1779). Prod. London, Shaftesbury, 14 Jan. 1916, with Hatchard, Maitland, Barrigar, Mullings, Heming, Langley, Ranalow, cond. Goossens (III).

Crociato in Egitto, II (The Crusader in Egypt). Opera in 2 acts by Meyerbeer; text by Rossi. Prod. Venice, F., 7 Mar. 1824, with Velluti; London, Hm., 3 June 1825, with Velluti and Malibran. The first Meyerbeer opera in London, and the last and most successful of his Italian works. Armando d'Orville (orig. castrato, later mezzo), a knight of Rhodes, is assumed dead in Egypt during the Sixth Crusade; but under the name of Elmireno, he has become the confidant of the Sultan Aladino (bass). He falls in love with Palmide (sop.), Aladino's daughter, and converts her to Christianity. Adriano (ten.), Armando's uncle, arrives to sue for peace, but Elmireno's true identity is discovered and he and the other captured Christians are sentenced to death. Armando, however, saves the Sultan's life after a plot to overthrow him; Armando and Palido are reunited, and a peace treaty is signed.

Cross, Joan (*b* London, 7 Sept. 1900). English soprano. Joined chorus of Old Vic 1924, soon graduating to small roles (First Lady, Cherubino) and then to leading ones. Principal soprano S.W. 1931-46; director of Opera Company 1943-5. C.G., 1931, 1934-5, 1947-54. One of the founder members of the English Opera Group 1945. Created Ellen Orford (*Peter Grimes*, 1945), Female Chorus (*Rape of Lucretia*, 1946), Lady Billows (*Albert Herring*, 1947), and Queen Elizabeth (*Gloriana*, 1953) – all by Britten. After 1955 she devoted herself to teaching, especially at the National School of Opera (formerly the Opera School) which she founded with Anne Wood in 1948. Has also produced opera for S.W. and C.G., as well as in Holland and Norway. One of the outstanding British operatic artists of the century, an artist of great warmth and intelligence. (R)

Crosse, Gordon (*b* Bury, 1 Dec. 1937). English composer. After studying at Oxford and researching into 15th-cent. music, studied composition with Petrassi in Rome. Though he has shown a particular interest in semi-dramatic works for children, notably *The Wheel of the World*, based on Chaucer's *The Canterbury Tales* (1972), he has also composed three operas. *Purgatory* (1966) is a very tautly written, intelligent, and atmospheric 1-act work based on W. B. Yeats's play; he added the rather less effective comedy *The Grace of Todd* as a companion piece (1969). His first full-length opera was *The Story of Vasco* (1974).

Crown Diamonds, The. See *Diamants de la couronne*.

Crozier, Eric (*b* London, 14 Nov. 1914). English writer and producer. With Benjamin Britten and John Piper, co-founder of the English Opera Group (1947). Librettist of Britten's *Albert Herring* and *Let's Make an Opera,* and (with E. M. Forster) *Billy Budd*; also of Berkeley's *Ruth.* Produced new English version of *The Bartered Bride* (made by Crozier and Joan Cross), S.W. 1943, and premières of *Peter Grimes,* S.W. 1945, and *The Rape of Lucretia,* Gly. 1946; also U.S. première of *Grimes,* Tanglewood 1946.

Cruvelli, Sofia (orig. Crüwell, Johanne Sophie Charlotte) (*b* Bielefeld, 29 Aug. 1824; *d* Nice, 6 Nov. 1907). German soprano. Studied Paris with Piermarini; later with Bordogni and Lamperti. Début Venice, 1847, Odabella (*Attila*). London, H.M.'s, 1848 Elvira and Abigaille; C.G. 1854 Donna Anna, Leonore, Desdemona (Rossini); Paris, T. I., 1851-3 as Elvira, Norma, Semiramide, Leonore; Paris, O., 1854-6, at salary of 100,000 francs, as Valentine, Rachel, Giulia and Hélène, which she created in Verdi's *Vêpres siciliennes.* Left stage after marriage to Comte Vigier in 1856. Generally considered one of the best Verdi sopranos of the mid-19th cent. Her sister, **Friederike Marie Crüwell** (1824-68), mezzo-soprano, studied with Roger and sang in France and Italy.

Cuba. The first opera heard in Cuba was based on Metastasio's libretto *Didone abbandonata* (1776: music unknown). The T. Coliseo, later renamed the T. Principal, was opened in Havana in 1803. The T. Tacon, opened in 1838, was for many years the home of visiting opera companies from Europe, especially French and Italian. It became the T. Nacional in 1915, and was inaugurated with *Aida* under Serafin. In 1920 Caruso sang there, receiving his highest fee ever, $90,000 for ten performances.

Despite plans for a national opera *Antonelli* by Manuel Samuell Robredo as early as 1839, set in Havana, the first Cuban opera was the 1-act *La Hija de Jefté* (1875) by Laureano Fuentes Matous; this was recomposed as the 3-act *Seila* (1917). Other Cuban opera composers have included Guillermo Tomás (1868-1933) (*Sakuntala*); Eduardo Sánchez de Fuentes (*Yumuri*, 1898; *El Náufrago*, 1901; *Kabelia*, 1942); and Gaspar Villate (1851-91), whose

operas are entirely Europeanized: among them are *Angelo, tirano de Padua* (1867), *Las primeras armas de Richelieu* (1871), and *Zelia* (1877), all prod. in Europe before Havana. An opera drawing on more specifically Cuban sources was *La Esclava* (1921) by J. M. Estévez. Operetta and *zarzuela* are also popular. See also *Havana*.

Cuénod, Hugues (*b* Coiseaux-sur-Bevey, 26 June 1902). Swiss tenor. Studied Lausanne, Basle, Vienna with Fr Singar-Burian. After teaching at the Geneva Conservatory, began career as singer in concerts. Stage début 1928 Paris, Ch.E., in *Jonny spielt auf.* U.S.A. 1929 in *Bitter Sweet.* Opera since 1943, when he sang in Geneva in *Fledermaus.* Milan, Sc., 1951. Gly. since 1954, London, C.G., 1954, 1956, 1958. Specializes in a number of selected roles including Sellem (*The Rake's Progress*), Basilio (*Figaro*), and the Astrologer (*Golden Cockerel*). An artist with a very individual style and stage manner, a singer of great intelligence and musicianship. (R)

Cui, César (Antonovich) (*b* Vilna, 18 Jan. 1835; *d* St Petersburg, 26 Mar. 1918). Russian composer and critic, of French descent. Studied with Moniuszko and in St Petersburg. With Balakirev founded the Russian nationalist group of composers known as the *moguchaya kuchka*, or 'mighty handful', from a phrase of Stasov's: the others were Borodin, Mussorgsky, and Rimsky-Korsakov. An enthusiastic, often sharp-tongued, worker for Russian national opera, he wrote a number of operas himself that won some success in their own day but that have not held the stage: *The Captive of the Caucasus* (comp. 1857-82, prod. 1883), *The Mandarin's Son* (1859), *William Ratcliff* (1869), *Angelo* (1876), *Le Flibustier* (1894), *The Saracen* (1899), *A Feast in Time o' Plague* (1901), *Mam'zelle Fifi* (1903), *Matteo Falcone* (1907), *The Captain's Daughter* (1911), and *Puss in Boots* (not prod.). He made a completion of Mussorgsky's *Sorochintsy Fair.*

Cunning Little Vixen, The (*Cz.: Příhody Lišky Bystroušky*). Opera in 3 acts by Janáček; text by composer, after Rudolf Těsnohlídek's verses for drawings by Stanislav Lolek, published serially in the Brno newspaper *Lidové Noviny* during 1920. Prod. Brno, 6 Nov. 1924, with Hrdličková, Snopková, Flögl, Pour, Pelc, cond. Neumann; London, S.W., 12 Mar. 1961, with Bronhill, Easton, cond. Davis; N.Y., Hunter College, 7 May 1964, with Killmer, Fiortito, cond. Bamberger.

Sharpears the vixen (sop.) is caught by the Forester (bar.) and kept as a pet. She laments her lot to the dog Lapák (mezzo or ten.), and having incited rebellion among the hens against their cock (sop.), she manages to escape. Having dispossessed the badger (bass) by fouling his lair, she settles in. In the world of men, the Priest (bass) is gloomy because he is to be transferred, the Forester is sighing for the mysterious girl Terynka, who has also fascinated the Schoolmaster (ten.); and though they play cards together in the inn, disorder threatens. They leave, rather drunk, and confused about the allure of Terynka; Sharpears watches them. She takes Goldenmane (sop. or ten.) as mate; they are married by the woodpecker. Harašta the poacher (bass) comes upon the fox family, and shoots Sharpears. Back in the inn, the Forester is sad that he cannot now find the vixen whose image haunts him; and the marriage of Terynka to Harašta does nothing to cheer the men up. They feel their ageing emphasized by the coming of spring. Alone in the woods, the Forester falls into a doze; waking, he observes the animals, among them a foxcub exactly like her mother, and taking new comfort from this vision of nature always renewing itself, he lies back at peace.

The German version by Max Brod goes to great pains to emphasize an identity between the men and animals (e.g. Priest and Badger), and between the Vixen and Terynka, which Janáček deliberately left oblique.

Curlew River. Church Parable in 1 act by Britten; text by William Plomer, after Jūro Motomasa's No play *Sumida-gawa* (early 15th cent.). Prod. Orford Parish Church, 13 June 1964, with Pears, Shirley-Quirk, Drake, Garrard; Katonah, N.Y., Caramoor Festival, 26 June 1966, with Velis, Clatworthy, Berberian. The first of Britten's 'church parables', it is cast in the dramatic metaphor of monks processing into church to enact a mystery play. This concerns the arrival of a Madwoman (ten.) at a ferry seeking her lost son, who proves to have died. She is ferried across the river, where like other travellers she pays respect to the shrine in his memory established on the other side.

Also opera by Raybould (1916).

Curtain Call. (It. *chiamata*; Ger. *Ruf*) The bow made by singers and conductor (and on special occasions producer, designer, and even chorus-master) at the end of a scene or act of an opera. The applause of the audience generally regulates the number of bows taken by artists; but see also *Claque*. In Italy the main curtain calls occur during the course of the evening, the audience generally leaving the theatre immediately after the final curtain; in England, on the other hand, the greatest enthusiasm is reserved for the calls at the end of the evening. At the Metropolitan, Rudolf Bing abolished solo curtain calls, though there were recalcitrant prima donnas. In German opera houses solo calls are rare. At Bayreuth until after the war there were no curtain calls, the curtain being raised just once to display the

final tableau; but more recently singers, conductor, and producer have been called at the end of the performance; there are now even curtain calls for *Parsifal.*

Curtin, Phyllis (Smith) (*b* Clarksburg, West Va., 3 Dec. 1922). American soprano. Studied Wellesley College, Mass., New York, and with Boris Goldovsky at Boston and Tanglewood. New England Opera T. 1946. N.Y., C.C., from 1953; Met. 1961. Vienna 1960. Created Cathy in Floyd's *Wuthering Heights* and title role in same composer's *Susannah*; first N.Y. Cressida in Walton's *Troilus and Cressida* and the three female roles in Einem's *The Trial.* Also successful as Salome, Mistress Ford, and in Mozart. (R)

Cuzzoni (Sandoni), **Francesca** (*b* Parma, *c*1700; *d* Bologna, 1770). Italian soprano. Daughter of the violinist Angelo Cuzzoni. Studied with Petronio Lanzi. Début Parma, 1716. After successes in Bologna and Venice, engaged in 1722 by Heidegger for King's T. at £2,000 a year; when she failed to arrive, Heidegger sent his second cembalist, Sandoni, to bring her to London, and on the journey she married him. London début creating Teofane in Handel's *Ottone* January 1723; also created several other Handel roles including Cleopatra (*Giulio Cesare,* 1724,), Asteria (*Tamerlano,* 1724), Rodelinda (1725), Lisaura (*Alessandro,* 1726). The engagement of Faustina *Bordoni in 1726 led to the celebrated public rivalry between the two, culminating in a brawl on stage during a performance of Bononcini's *Astianatte* in 1727. Left London for Venice, but returned in 1734, engaged by Porpora for Lincoln's Inn Fields; remained until 1737 and returned finally in 1750. Imprisoned for debt in Holland; returned to Bologna where she became a button-maker, and died in extreme poverty. Quantz described her voice as 'clear and agreeable soprano; a pure intonation, and a fine shake; her compass extended two octaves from C to c in alt'.

Cycle. In opera, the name given to a group of works telling a more or less consecutive story, but partly for reasons of length, partly for dramatic effect, separable and performable on different nights. The earliest operatic cycle is Sartorio's pair *La prosperità di Elio Seiano* and *La caduta di Elio Seiano,* both in 3 acts with text by Niccolò Minato (prod. Venice 1667). The best-known, and greatest, cycle remains Wagner's *Der *Ring des Nibelungen.* Upon this certain others were modelled, e.g. Bungert's *Homerische Welt* (based on the Odyssey) and Holbrooke's *The Cauldron of Annwyn.*

Cyrano de Bergerac. (1) Opera in 4 acts by Alfano; text by Henry Cain, after Rostand's drama (1891). Prod. Rome, T.R., 22 Jan. 1936, with Caniglia, Luccioni, cond. Serafin.

Cyrano (ten.), the poet-soldier, is disfigured

by a huge nose and is repulsive to women. He falls in love with the beautiful Roxane (sop.) and pays court to her through the mouth of Christian, who also loves her. Only when Cyrano is on his deathbed does Roxane learn the truth and realises that she really loves him.

(2) Opera in 4 acts by Damrosch; text by W. J. Henderson, after Rostand. Prod. N.Y., Met., 27 Feb. 1913, with Alda, Amato, cond. Hertz.

Czechoslovakia. Opera was first given in 1627, when Italian singers came from Mantua to Prague to perform a *commedia pastorale cantata* by G.B. Buonamente and Cesare Gonzaga for the Coronation of Ferdinand III. Italian opera was thereafter given on the Hradčany, the citadel of Prague, and in 1723 Fux's *Costanza e fortezza* was produced for the 4000 visitors to the Coronation of Charles VI. Later, Italian opera (including premières of Vivaldi's works and an opera written on a Czech mythological theme, *Praga nascente da Libussa e Primislao*) was given in a theatre built by Count František Špork in his Prague residence Na Poříčí. The expansion of Italian opera in the 18th cent. led to the building of theatres in nobles' castles, where opera was given by Italian companies augmented by domestic musicians. Important castle centres included Špork's Kuks, Český Krumlov, the Moravian castles of Holešov, Vyškov and Kroměříž, and Questenberg's Jaroměřice, where in about 1730 *L'Origine di Jaromeritz in Moravia,* by František Míča (1694-1744) was staged. This was the first opera to be given in a Czech translation from Italian. The Italian *opera buffa* and baroque dramas influenced the Hanatic operas (from the district of Haná), composed in Hanatic dialect by Alanus Plumlovský (1703-1759) and performed in the premonstratensian monastery of Hradiště from 1747 (*Pargamotéka*), also the *Opera de Rebellione Boëmica Rusticorum* (1775-7) by the East Bohemian teacher Jan Antoš (?–?) and *Opera Bohemica de Camino* by Karel Loos (1724–1772), written in Czech. The Italian companies of Denzio, Locatelli, Molinari, Angelo and Pietro Mingotti, Bondini, and Domenico Quardasoni visited Prague, also Brno, Olomouc, Opava, and spas in West Bohemia; in the second half of the 18th cent these were gradually replaced by German companies, producing Singspiels, *vaudevilles,* and plays using songs and dances in Czech and German. By now the standard had evidently fallen. The castle opera prods. died out during the first half of the 19th cent.; some were given in Náměšť, where works by Naumann, Gluck, and Handel were staged, mostly in German translations by Count Haugwitz and performed by his domestic musicians.

In 1783 Count Nostic's National T. opened; here Mozart conducted *Figaro,* and for it he wrote *Don Giovanni* and *La clemenza di Tito.* At

the same time an important contribution to German and Italian opera was made by expatriate Bohemians, including Jiří *Benda, Josef *Mysliveček, Florian Gassmann (1729-74), Leopold Koželuh (1747-1818), Pavel *Vranický, and Vojtěch *Jírovec. From 1813 to 1816 C.M. von Weber was Intendant in charge of a German company replacing the Italians; he substantially improved the company, raised orchestral and theatrical standards, and widened the repertory to include many of the French works that were to form the basis of German Romantic opera.

The new national consciousness had been stimulating efforts towards Czech Opera: a few Italian works were sung in Czech in the 1794-5 season, and Mozart's *Seraglio* was given in Czech in 1806, but Czech opera really dates from the work of František *Škroup. In 1824 he gave a perf., with Czech singers, of Weigl's *Die Schweizerfamilie,* and in 1826 came the first true Czech opera, *Dráteník* (The Tinker). Škroup wrote two more operas on Czech historical subjects, but neither won the success of *Dráteník.* Another historical subject, *Žižkův dub* (Žižka's Oak), was set by František Kott (1808-84), prod. Brno 1841 in German, 1842 in Czech, and by Jiří Macourek (1815-63), prod. Prague 1847.

It took *Smetana to recognize that a more mature method than a simple musical play using folk songs was demanded as a basis for the development of a true national opera. He was conductor of the Provisional T., 1868-74; he impressed his audiences with *Braniboři v Čechách* (The Brandenburgers in Bohemia, 1866), but won their hearts with *Prodaná nevěsta* (The Bartered Bride, 1866, rev. 1869, 1870). He further set an example of how to treat heroic as well as folk themes in a genuinely Czech idiom with *Dalibor* (1868). In the same year building commenced of the National T., intended as a symbol of the nation's independent spirit. Smetana's *Libuše* was produced at the theatre in June 1881 before the completion of the building, which shortly burned down. Of *Dvořák's operas (by which he set considerable store), only *Rusalka* has entered the international repertory; other of his works, especially *Čert a Káča* (The Devil and Kate, 1899) and *Jakobín* (The Jacobin, 1889), have remained in Czech repertories, but though wholly Czech in spirit and of much charm in their handling of history and legend, they lack Smetana's fundamentally dramatic qualities.

Smetana's immediate successor was *Fibich, who absorbed some Wagnerian influences into a Czech national idiom; others who successfully built upon Smetana's example included Vilém Blodek (1834-1874) with *V studni* (In the Well, 1867); Karel Bendl (1838-1897), with *Leila* (1867); Richard Rozkošný (1833-1913); Josef Nešvera (1842-1914); Karel

Šebor (1843-1903); and Karel Weiss (1862-1944). The first outstanding Czech conductor was Karel Kovařovic (1862-1920), who introduced *Rusalka* and was in charge of the National T., 1900-20. Here he introduced much French opera, Strauss, Mussorgsky, and more Wagner into the repertory, and warmly supported contemporary Czech opera. Of his own operas, the most successful was *Psohlavci* (The Dogheads, 1898).

Outstanding among composers of the period before the emergence of Janáček, however, was J.B. *Foerster, whose *Eva* made a great impression in 1899. By now, opera was well established in Czechoslovakia, and a flourishing, independent genre. Nevertheless, it held no interest for some of the leading composers: Suk wrote no operas, Novák few, though his *Lucerna* (The Lantern, 1923) is a striking piece. Work of greater significance came from Otakar *Ostrčil, who was influenced by Fibich and who had his greatest success with his Tolstoy opera *Honzovo království* (Johnny's Kingdom, 1934). Other good work in the fruitful period between 1900 and 1925, when 102 new Czech operas were given, was done by Otakar Zich (1879-1934) with *Malířský nápad* (The Painter's Whim, 1910) and later by Rudolf Karel (1880-1945) with *Smrt kmotřička* (Godmother Death, 1933). But the period is dominated by Leoš *Janáček, although *Jenůfa*, first performed in Brno in 1904, did not gain proper recognition until the Prague production of 1916. He is one of the great figures in the history of opera, and the first Czech composer completely to absorb what his country's musical background had to offer and to make of it a mature, modern, truthful, and flexible idiom at the service of profound human understanding. His greatest work was done between 1916 and his death in 1928.

He has somewhat overshadowed his successors. Alois *Hába experimented with microtonal music, notably in *Matka* (The Mother, 1931). Otakar Jeremiáš (1892-1962) made an interesting (and so far unique) attempt, *Bratři Karamazovi*, at setting *The Brothers Karamazov* (1928). Emil František Burian (1904-59), a many-sided man of the theatre, had a success with *Maryša* (1940). Jaromír *Weinberger had an international success with *Švanda dudák* (Shvanda the Bagpiper, 1927). But the most important figure to win international fame was Bohuslav *Martinů, a substantial part of whose work was done outside Czechoslovakia but who had a great local success with *Julietta* (1938).

Semi-independently, Slovak opera had been developing since the formation of the Czechoslovak state in 1918. The first Slovak opera composer is Ján Bella (*Kovač Wieland*) (Wieland the Smith), comp. 1890, to Wagner's subject). But the most significant has been Eugen

*Suchoň, whose *Krútňava* (The Whirlpool, 1949) has been widely staged, together with Ján *Cikker, whose most important work has been his Tolstoy opera *Vzkriesenie* (Resurrection, 1962). Later Czech opera composers include Iša Krejčí (1904-68), Jan Hanuš (*b* 1915), Jiří Pauer (*b* 1919), Václav Kašlík (*b* 1917; his Čapek opera *Krakatit* uses *musique concrète* and electronic music), Jan F. Fischer (*b* 1921), Pavel Bořkovec (1894-1972), Jarmil Burghauser (*b* 1921), Emil Hlobil (*b* 1901), Janáček's pupil Osvald Chlubna (1893-1971), Ilja Hurník (*b* 1922), Jiří Dvořáček (*b* 1928), Josef Berg (1927-71; he uses novel techniques in his chamber operas, e.g. *The Return of Ulysses*, 1967), and Václav Trojan (*b* 1907). Czech operatic life is one of the richest in the world, with full varied and balanced repertories in the twelve cities with permanent companies. See also *Banská Bystrica, Bratislava, Brno, České Budějovice, Košice, Liberec, Olomouc, Opava, Ostrava, Pizeň, Prague*, and *Ústí nad Labem*.

Czerwenka, Oscar (*b* Linz, 5 July 1924). Austrian bass. Début Graz 1947, Hermit (*Freischütz*). Vienna O., since 1951; Salzburg since 1953. Gly. 1959, Ochs; N.Y., Met., 1959. Has a repertory of more than 75 roles and is especially successful in buffo roles including Osmin, Kecal, and Ochs. (R)

D

Dabadie, Henri-Bernard (*b* Pau, 19 Jan. 1797; *d* Paris, May 1853). French baritone. Studied Paris Conservatoire. Début Paris, O., 1819 Cinna (*La Vestale*). Remained at O. until 1835, where he created Pharaon in *Moïse* (1827), Raimbaud in *Le Comte Ory* (1828), the title-role in *Guillaume Tell* (1829), and Belcore in Auber's *Le Philtre* (1831). In 1832 he created Belcore in *L'elisir d'amore* in Milan, not to Donizetti's satisfaction. He married the soprano **Louise Zulme Léroux** (*b* Boulogne, 4 Oct. 1796; *d* Paris, November 1877), who sang at the O. 1824-35, creating Sinaïde in *Moïse* and Jemmy in *Guillaume Tell*.

Dafne. Opera in a prologue and 6 scenes by Peri; text by Ottavio Rinuccini. Prod. in Jacopo Corsi's Florence house, probably Carnival 1597. The first opera. Music now lost. Also opera by Schütz, prod. Torgau, 23 Apr. 1627 to text by Martin Opitz after Ottavio Rinuccini. The earliest German opera; music lost. See also *Daphne*.

Daguerre, Louis-Jacques-Mandé (*b* Corneilles, 18 Nov. 1787; *d* Bry-sur-Marne, 10 July 1851). French physicist, painter, and scenic designer. Though more widely known as a pioneer of photography and inventor of the Daguerrotype (1839), he was also an influential scenic designer. After working in the theatre, he moved to the Opéra in 1822, where his first designs (with *Cicéri) were for Isouard's *Aladin*. At the Diorama, the theatre he opened also in 1822, he developed a number of new pictorial and mechanical effects, and he made use of these at the Opéra to support Cicéri in giving French Grand Opera a new scenic realism and splendour. He was largely responsible for banishing the old Italian system of *châssis*, or wings, with their denial of perspective and creation of a series of corridors; and his contribution to the heightened realism of Cicéri's sets included the creation of the illusion of moving clouds, perhaps covering and then revealing the moon, trees which cast shadows when the sun came out, and many similar devices. He was responsible for the installation of the panorama at the Opéra.

Daland. A Norwegian sea-captain (bass), father of Senta, in Wagner's *Der fliegende Holländer*.

Dalayrac (or D'Alayrac), **Nicolas** (*b* Muret, 8 June 1753; *d* Paris, 27 Nov. 1809). French composer. His opéras-comiques, of which he wrote 61 between 1781 and 1809, were enormously popular for their naïve, sentimental tunefulness throughout the Revolution and Empire.

His characteristically Romantic rescue subjects and his occasional musical originalities scarcely affected the essentially pretty, 'galant' atmosphere.

Dalibor. Opera in 3 acts by Smetana; text by Josef Wenzig, after the legend, translated from German into Czech by Ervín Špindler. Prod. Prague, Novoměstské T., on the occasion of the laying of the foundation stone of the National T., 16 May 1868, with Benevicová-Milcová, Ehrenberg, Lukes, Barcal, Lev, Šebesta, Paleček, cond. Smetana; Chicago, Sokol Hall, 13 Apr. 1924; Edinburgh, King's T., by Prague National T., 17 Aug. 1964, with Domaniská, Přibyl, cond. Krombholc. In Czechosolovakia the work has been regarded as a rescue opera with a significance for national liberty comparable to that of *Fidelio*.

Dalibor (ten.) has been captured by his enemies for his killing of the Burgrave in revenge for the slaying of his friend Zdeněk; the Burgrave's daughter Milada (sop.) begins to feel pity for him. She disguises herself as a boy, apprenticing herself to the gaoler Beneš (bass), and takes Dalibor's beloved violin to his dungeon. Dalibor's rescue is achieved, but Milada is wounded in the attempt, and dies in Dalibor's arms; he stabs himself.

Also opera by Knott (1846).

Dalila. The Philistine temptress (mezzo) in Saint-Saëns's *Samson et Dalila*.

Dallapiccola, Luigi (*b* Pisino, 3 Feb. 1904; *d* Florence, 19 Feb. 1975). Italian composer. Studied Florence. One of the leading dodecaphonist composers of his country, he successfully used the formal demands of the technique to give expression to an innate lyricism and love of the voice. *Vol di notte* (Night Flight, 1940), after St-Exupéry's *Vol de nuit*, is an ingenious attempt to put contemporary ideas and incidents on the operatic stage without severing connexions with tradition. *Il prigioniero* (The prisoner, 1950) is a more powerful work, with Dallapiccola's almost obsessive sympathy with prisoners finding strong expression in the Inquisition theme of Villiers de l'Isle Adam's *La Torture par espérance*. *Ulisse*, comp. 1959-68, was prod. Berlin 1968.

Dalla Rizza, Gilda (*b* Verona, 12 Oct. 1892; *d* Milan, 5 July 1975). Italian soprano. Studied Bologna with V. Ricci and Orefice. Début Bologna 1912 Charlotte (*Werther*). Her singing of Minnie brought her to the notice of Puccini, who wrote Magda for her in *La Rondine*: she created this role at Monte Carlo in 1917. The first Italian Lauretta and Angelica (Rome 1919); she sang these roles in London, C.G., 1920. Greatly admired by Toscanini, who engaged her for Milan Sc. from 1923; her Violetta was a great success. Created leading roles in *Anima allegra* (Vittadini), *Giulietta e Romeo* (Zandonai), *Palla de' Mozzi* (Marinuzzi) and *Il piccolo Marat* (Mascagni). First Italian Arabella. Retired 1939, but sang Angelica at Vicenza 1942 in the Puccini celebrations. Professor of singing, Venice Conservatory 1939-55: pupils included Elena Rizzieri. Married to the tenor Agostino Capuzzo (1889-1963). (R)

Dallas. Town in Texas, U.S.A. From Nov. 1957 it has, under Lawrence Kelly (general manager, *d* 1974) and Nicola Rescigno (music director, general manager from 1974), presented annual seasons with Callas, Berganza, Simoniato, Sutherland, Schwarzkopf, Bastianini, Taddei, Vickers etc., and with Zeffirelli as chief producer; the repertory has included *Alcina, Il barbiere, Don Giovanni, L'italiana in Algeri, Medea, La traviata.* More recent productions have included *Giulio Cesare, Anna Bolena, La Favorite, Macbeth, Aida, Fedora, Fidelio* (the company's first German opera, prod. in 1971), *Werther,* and *The Golden Cockerel.* U.S. débuts of Dernesch, Gwyneth Jones, and Olivero. Opera is performed in the Fair Park Music Hall (cap. 3,419).

Dalla sua pace. Ottavio's (ten.) aria in Act 1 of Mozart's *Don Giovanni,* declaring that his own joy or sorrow depends on that of Donna Anna.

Dal Monte, Toti (orig. Antonietta Meneghel) (*b* Mogliano Veneto, 27 June 1893; *d* Treviso, 25 Jan. 1975). Italian soprano. Piano studies interrupted by an injury, studied voice with Barbara Marchisio. Début Milan, Sc., 1916, Biancafiore (*Francesca da Rimini*). After a further period of study with Pini-Corsi, and appearances in the Italian provinces, sang in Beethoven's 9th Symphony at Turin under Toscanini, who engaged her to sing Gilda at Sc. in 1922. After this she decided to concentrate on the *soprano leggiero* repertory. Sang regularly in Milan, Rome, and Naples; Chicago from 1924 to 1928; N.Y., Met., 1924-5; London, C.G., 1925. One of the last Italian 'divas' to delight audiences in old-fashioned Patti-like concerts. Her voice was small, pure, and inclined to whiteness; its agility was remarkable. In the last years of her career she sang Mimì and Butterfly. She retired from the stage in 1943; then taught in Milan, Rome, Venice, and the U.S.S.R. Her pupils included Gianna d'Angelo and Dolores Wilson. (R)
Bibl: T. Dal Monte: *Una voce nel mondo* (1962).

Dalmorès, Charles (orig. Henry Alphonse Brin) (*b* Nancy, 31 Dec. 1871; *d* Hollywood, 6 Dec. 1939). French tenor. Début Lyon (as Charles Brin), 1899, Loge in concert perf. of *Rheingold*; stage début Rouen, Oct. 1899, Siegfried. Brussels, La M., 1900-6 London, C.G. 1904-5, 1909-11; N.Y., Manhattan Opera, 1906-10; subsequently with Chicago Opera. Famous for his Faust, Jean (*Le Jongleur de Notre Dame*), Julien, Pelléas, etc. Toured Germany and

Austria 1908-14 in Wagner. Devoted the latter part of his life to teaching. (R)

D'Alvarez, Marguerite. See *Alvarez, Marguerite d'*.

Dame Blanche, La (The White Lady). Opera in 3 acts by Boieldieu; text by Eugène Scribe, after Scott's novels *The Monastery* (1820) and *Guy Mannering* (1815). Prod. Paris, O.C., 10 Dec. 1825, with Rigaut, Boulanger, Desbrosses, Henry, Ponchard, Féréol, Frimin, Belnie; London, D.L., 9 Oct. 1826; N.Y., 24 Aug. 1827. Parody, *Die schwarze Frau,* by A. Müller (1826).

George Brown (ten.), an English officer, asks the Scottish farmer Dickson (ten.) for lodging, and tells them about his half-forgotten origins and his life as a soldier. Jenny (sop.), Dickson's wife, tells him that the neighbouring castle is to be sold since the owners are Jacobites who must flee to France: the farmers hope to combine to buy the castle, and Dickson has sworn to serve a mysterious white lady who is said to be in the castle. She has summoned Dickson, but George offers to go instead. In the castle Gaveston (bass), former steward, enters with his ward Anna (sop.), who has promised to reveal the family secret. George is admitted, and eventually is left alone. He falls into a doze, and sees the white lady: it is in fact Anna, who has recognized him as a young officer she once nursed, but she believes her to be a ghost. Next morning, at the sale of the castle, Anna approaches George, and on her instructions from the 'white lady' he outbids his rivals and buys the castle. Later, in the castle, he is led to the treasure hidden in the pedestal of the statue of the white lady by Anna, who has taken the statue's place: he turns out to be the rightful heir, and when Anna is unveiled they fall into one another's arms.

Damigella (*It* damsel, maid). Developing from the young servant or confidante of the **commedia dell'arte,* the *damigella* was in turn the ancestress of the **soubrette.* Usually pretty, impertinent, flirtatious, and considerably shrewder than many of the upper-class characters, she often took a crucial hand in the manipulation of the plot. A classic instance of the *damigella* is in Monteverdi's *Poppea,* where Ottavia's (unnamed) maidservant explains something of the nature of love to the agitated *valetto* (Ottavia's page), here providing a light interlude before the drama of Seneca's death.

Damnation de Faust, La. *Légende dramatique* in 4 parts by Berlioz; text by composer, after Goethe's *Faust,* pt 1 (1773-1808), in Gérard de Nerval's translation (1828 and 1840), including contributions from Almire Gandonnière. Completed 1846, incorporating *Huit Scènes de Faust* (1828) in altered form. Concert perf. Paris, O.C., 6 Dec. 1846, with Duflot-Maillard,

Roger, Hermann-Léon, cond. Berlioz. Prod. Monte Carlo, 18 Feb. 1893, with J. de Reszke, Renaud, cond. Jehin; Liverpool, 3 Feb. 1894, by C. R.; New Orleans (concert perf.), 1894, with Tylda, Devilliers, Devries, Gardoni, cond. Brunel.

There have been many subsequent attempts at staging a work that was not conceived for the theatre (though Berlioz had the intention of rewriting it for staging), e.g. by Béjart at the Paris O. in 1964 and by Geliot at the London Coliseum in 1969.

The plot makes use of episodes from Goethe, with Méphistophélès (bass) tempting Faust (ten.) to bargain his soul in exchange for renewed youth. Faust grows sated with the pleasures provided by Méphistophélès, which include drunken companionship in Auerbach's Cellar, military glory (Berlioz introduces his version of the Rakoczy March), Nature, and love for Marguerite (sop.), whom he betrays: finally he is borne off to Hell in a Ride to the Abyss, while Marguerite is saved.

D'amor sull' ali rosee. Leonora's (sop.) aria in Act 4 of Verdi's *Il trovatore*, in which she sings of her love for Manrico as she stands beneath the tower in which he is imprisoned.

Damrosch, Leopold (*b* Poznań, 22 Oct. 1832; *d* New York, 15 Feb. 1885). German conductor. He occupied an important place in the musical life of New York: after the financially disastrous first season of Italian opera at the Met. 1883-4, he was called upon to organize a German season there for 1884-5. He engaged a fine company of singers, and conducted every performance from 17 Nov. until 9 Feb., including the first American *Walküre*. He was succeeded on his death by his son **Walter** (*b* Breslau, 30 Jan. 1862; *d* New York, 22 Dec. 1950), a pupil of Bülow. Between 1885 and 1891 he directed the American premières of *Rienzi, Meistersinger, Tristan und Isolde, Rheingold, Siegfried, Götterdämmerung, Euryanthe, Queen of Sheba,* and *Barbier von Bagdad.* Formed his own opera company 1894 (see below), but returned to the Met. 1900-3. The rest of his life was spent in the concert and educational worlds. Composed 5 operas, *The Scarlet Letter* (1896), *The Dove of Peace* (1912), *Cyrano de Bergerac* (1913), *The Man Without a Country* (1937), and *The Opera Cloak* (1942). His brother **Frank** (*b* Breslau, 22 June 1869; *d* New York, 22 Oct. 1937) studied with his father and Moszkowski. Chorus master Met., N.Y., 1885-91.

Bibl: W. Damrosch: *My Musical Life* (1923, 2/1930).

Damrosch Opera Company. Formed and financed by Walter Damrosch in 1894, after successful concert performances at Carnegie Hall of *Walküre* and *Götterdämmerung.* Sing-

ers during first three seasons included Gadski, Sucher, Klafsky, Ternina, Brema, Alvary, Bispham, and Fischer. The first season resulted in a profit of more than $50,000 despite the heavy expenses of touring Wagner operas from coast to coast in America. In the spring of 1898 Melba intimated that she would like to join the company, and her manager, C.A. Ellis of Boston, became the company's business manager. The name of the organization was changed to the Damrosch-Ellis Company in N.Y., 1897, and its ranks included Melba, Calvé, and Lilli Lehmann. In 1899, owing to a mounting deficit, the company was disbanded.

Damse, Józef (*b* Sokołów, 26 Jan. 1789; *d* Rudno, 15 Dec. 1852). Polish composer. During a long career working in various capacities in the Warsaw theatre, he composed, arranged, or compiled a very large number of operas, operettas, and other musical pieces, including *Adolf i Julia* (1839), *Cecylia* (1841), *Indiana i Charlemagne* (1843), *Kontrabandzista* (1844 – not after Scott), *Pierwsza wyprawa mœodego Richelieu* (1844), and many other pieces.

Dance of the Apprentices. Dance by the Nuremberg apprentices and the girls from Fürth in the final scene of Wagner's *Die Meistersinger.*

Dance of the Blessed Spirits. Dance in Act 2 of Gluck's *Orfeo ed Euridice.*

Dance of the Comedians. Dance in Act 3 of Smetana's *The Bartered Bride* in which the clowns and dancers of the travelling circus are put through their paces.

Dance of the Hours. The entertainment put on by Alvise Badoero for his guests in Act 3 of Ponchielli's *La Gioconda,* in which the eternal struggle between darkness and light is symbolized.

Dance of the Seven Veils. Salome's dance before Herod in Strauss's *Salome,* before which he promises her anything: her choice is the head of John the Baptist. Sometimes performed by a dancer replacing the singer.

Dance of the Sylphs. Part of Faust's dream, properly known as Ballet of the Sylphs (*Ballet des sylphes*), in Berlioz's *Damnation de Faust,* as he sleeps on the banks of the Elbe.

Dance of the Tumblers. Dance of the *skomorokhi,* itinerant singers and dancers, before Tsar Berendey in Act 3 of Rimsky-Korsakov's *The Snow Maiden.*

Dance round the Golden Calf. Act 2, scene 3 of Schoenberg's *Moses und Aron,* in which the people indulge in an orgy at Aaron's instigation.

Dances, Polovtsian. See *Polovtsian Dances.*

Danco, Suzanne (*b* Brussels, 22 Jan. 1911). Belgian soprano. Studied in Prague with Fernando Carpi. Début Genoa 1941, Fiordiligi. Has sung extensively in Italy where she was the first Sc. Ellen Orford (1947); Marie in *Wozzeck* at Naples S.C. (1949). Edinburgh (with Gly.) 1948, Fiordiligi; London, C.G., 1951, Mimì; Gly., Donna Elvira. (R)

Dandini. Prince Ramiro's valet (bar.) in Rossini's *La cenerentola*.

D'Angeri, Anna (orig. Anna von Angermayer de Redernburg) (*b* Vienna, 14 Nov. 1853; *d* Trieste, 14 Dec. 1907). Austrian soprano. Studied Vienna with Marchesi. Début Mantua, 1872 Selika. Vienna, Hofoper, 1878-9; Milan, Sc., 1879-81; Verdi chose her for Amelia in the revised *Boccanegra* (1881); London, C.G., 1874-7, Selika; first London Ortrud and Venus. Retired in 1881 on her marriage to Vittorio Dalem, director of the T. Rossetti, Trieste.

D'Annunzio, Gabriele (Pescara, 12 Mar. 1863; *d* Gardone, 1 Mar. 1938). Italian writer. His multifarious activities included work in the musical world. He was editor (more in name than in fact) of the *Raccolta nazionale delle musiche italiane*, together with Malipiero, Casella, Pizzetti, and others; and the series of 36 volumes *I classici della musica italiana* (from 1917) included several operas. A qualified admirer of Wagner, he was opposed to *verismo* and sought to encourage classical and pre-classical Italian opera. During his military occupation of Fiume he drew up a constitution that included two sections giving a central importance to music in the life of the state, and he planned to build an arena for 10,000 spectators who would be admitted free of charge to musical events. Music, especially the operas of Wagner, Verdi, Monteverdi, and Marcello, plays an important part in his creative writing. He wrote the libretto of *Parisina* for Mascagni and of *Fedra* for Pizzeti, with whom he formed a close artistic association. Operas on his works are as follows:

Francesca da Rimini (1901): Zandonai (1914).
La figlia di Jorio (1904): Franchetti (1906); Pizzetti (1954).
La fiaccola sotto il moggio (1905): Pizzetti (*Gigliola*, unfin.).
Il sogno d'un tramonto (1905): Malipiero (unprod., 1913).
La nave (1908): Montemezzi (1918).
Fedra (1909): Pizzetti (1915).
Parisina (1913): Mascagni (1913).
Bibl: A. Casella and others: *Gabriele D'Annunzio e la musica* (1939).

Danon, Oskar (*b* Sarajevo, 7 Feb. 1913). Yugoslav conductor. Studied Prague. Music Director Belgrade Opera 1945-63, director of opera, Belgrade Conservatory, 1963-70. Chicago 1962. Edinburgh Festival, 1962. (R)

Dante Alighieri (*b* Florence, May 1265; *d* Ravenna, 14 Sep. 1321). Italian poet. Operas based on his *La divina commedia* (*c*1307-21?) are as follows.

L'Inferno. The Francesca da Rimini episode, V. 116-142: Carlini (1825); Mercadante (1828); Generali (1829); Staffa (1831); Fournier-Gorre (1832); Aspri (1835); Borgatta (1837); Morlacchi (unfin., 1839); Devasini (1841); Canetti (1843); Brancaccio (1844); Marcarini (1871); Goetz (1877); Moscuzza (1877); Cagnoni (1878); Thomas (1882); Nápravník (1902); Rakhmaninov (1906); Mancinelli (1907); Emil Ábrányi (1912); Zandonai (1914); Henried.
The Gianni Schicchi reference, XXX.32-3: Puccini (1918).
The Ugolino episode, XXXIII: Dittersdorf (1796).

Operas on Dante himself are by Carrer (*Dante e Beatrice,* 1852); Philpot (*Dante and Beatrice,* 1889); Godard (*Dante,* 1890); Foulds ('concert opera' *The Vision of Dante,* 1904); Gastaldon (*Il sonetto di Dante,* 1909); Nouguès (*Dante,* 1931).

Dantons Tod (Danton's Death). Opera in 2 parts by Einem; text by the composer and Blacher after Büchner's drama (1835). Prod. Salzburg 6 Aug. 1947 with Cebotari, Patzak, Schoeffler cond. Fricsay; N.Y., City Opera, 9 Mar. 1966, with Grant, Lampi, Dupree, Reardon, Beattie, cond. Märzendorfer. Danton (bar.), disillusioned by the French Revolution, makes impassioned speeches against it and is arrested by Robespierre (ten.) and sentenced to death by the revolutionary tribunal. The mob greets his public execution with singing and dancing.

Danzig. See *Gdańsk.*

Dapertutto. The evil sorcerer (bar.) in the Giulietta episode in Offenbach's *Les Contes d'Hoffmann.*

Daphne. (1) In classical mythology, the daughter of the Thessalian river-god Peneus, who narrowly escaped the pursuing Apollo by being changed into a laurel-tree: see Ovid, *Metamorphoses* I, 453-567. Operas on her legend include some of the first written, and are as follows: Jacopo Corsi (undated and incomplete, two fragments extant); Peri (1597); Caccini (lost, perhaps prod. 1600); Gagliano (1608); Schütz (1627; the first German opera, music lost); Ariosti (1696); Aldrovandini (1696); A. Scarlatti (1700); Astorga (1709); Mulé (1928).

(2) Opera in 1 act by Richard Strauss; text by Josef Gregor, after the classical legend. Prod. Dresden 15 Oct. 1938, with Teschemacher, Ralf, Kremer, cond. Böhm (in a double bill with *Friedenstag*); Santa Fe 29 July 1964, with Stahlman, Shirley, Petersen, cond. Crosby.

Daphne (sop.), daughter of Peneios (bass) and Gaea (mezzo), falls in love with Apollo (ten.), who comes down to earth disguised as a shepherd, but refuses to yield to him. Leukippos (ten.), a shepherd who is in love with Daphne, also tries to win her love. He is killed by Apollo, who reveals himself as a god and turns Daphne into a laurel bush.

Da Ponte, Lorenzo (orig. Emanuele Conegliano) (*b* Ceneda, 10 Mar. 1749; *d* New York, 17 Aug. 1838). Italian poet and librettist. First studied for the priesthood, but later settled in Vienna as court poet to Joseph II. Famous for the librettos he wrote for Mozart, *Le nozze di Figaro, Don Giovanni,* and *Così fan tutte*. He left the city on the Emperor's death in 1790, being out of favour with Leopold II. From 1793 he worked at London, D.L., but had to leave England secretly; he reached America in 1805. From 1826 to 1837 he held a chair in Italian at Columbia University and also wrote his entertaining, Casanova-esque autobiography. In 1825 he and Manuel Garcia were among the first to give opera in the U.S.A., and in 1833 he was responsible for the establishment of the Italian Opera House in New York. He wrote 36 librettos in all.
Bibl: L. Da Ponte: *Memorie* (4 vols, 1823-7, 2/1829, Eng. trans. 1929); A. FitzLyon: *The Libertine Librettist* (1955).

Darclée, Hariclea (orig. Haricly Hartulary) (*b* Braila, 10 June 1860; *d* Bucharest, 10 Jan. 1939). Romanian soprano. Studied Bucharest, and Paris with Faure. Début Paris, O., 1888, Marguerite. Success dated from Feb. 1889, when she replaced Patti at the O. as Juliette. Milan, Sc., from 1890, where she created La Wally (1892); N.Y., with little success, 1896. In Rome created Iris and Tosca. Successful as Valentine, Elisabeth (Buenos Aires 1897, 1903, 1909), Manon Lescaut, and in the *bel canto* operas of Bellini and Donizetti. Considered by the Italians to be vocally similar to Lilli Lehmann. Her vocal decline began in 1905, and though rich when she retired from the stage in 1918, she was forced to spend her declining years in the Verdi Home in Milan, and died penniless in Bucharest. (R) Her son **Ion Hartulary-Darclée** (*b* Paris, 7 July 1886; *d* Bucharest, 2 Apr. 1969) studied in Paris with Leroux and Widor, and in Milan with Amedeo and Victor de Sabata. He conducted in Italy, France, Switzerland, and Spain, 1915-30. His operas are *Jaretiera* (1909), *Capriciu antic* (1911), *Amorul mascat* (1913), *Anonima Potin* (1916), *La Signorina Sans-Façon* (1920), *Marjery* (1927), *Zig-Zag* (1928), *Operetta* (1929), *Atlantic-City* (1930).

Dardanus. *Tragédie* in 5 acts by Rameau; text by Leclerc de la Bruyère. Prod. Paris., O., 19

Nov. 1739. Teucer is at war with Dardanus, son of Jupiter, and has promised to marry his daughter Iphise to Antenor, a neighbouring king. With the help of the magician Ismenor, Dardanus meets Iphise; the reveal their love for each other. He is saved from being killed through the intervention of Venus; and other gods join him. A monster is sent to ravage Teucer's coasts, but Dardanus now comes to his enemy's aid and destroys the monster just as it is attacking Teucer. Peace is made between them, and Dardanus and Iphise are united. Other operas on the subject are by Stamitz (1770) and Sacchini (1784).

Dargomyzhsky, Alexander (*b* Dargomyzh, 14 Feb. 1813; *d* St Petersburg, 17 Jan. 1869). Russian composer. Born on his father's estate, he moved to St Petersburg in 1817 and made an early success as pianist and composer. His first opera was *Esmeralda* (comp. 1840, prod. 1847), a work in grand opera vein acknowledging the best French models (especially that of Auber). *Rusalka* (1856) took further a few hints in *Esmeralda* of his interest in melodic recitative. Its failure temporarily discouraged him, but later, impelled by the desire among Balakirev's disciples for a new Russian idiom, he completed his last opera *The Stone Guest* (1872), in which the characters express themselves in 'mezzo-recitative'. This pays the closest attention, in short, irregular phrases, to the inflection of Pushkin's words, with the orchestra in its turn subordinate to the voice. Though embodying a radical reform, *The Stone Guest* remains little more than a historical curiosity through Dargomyzhsky's inability to match his theories with music of sufficient worth.
Bibl: A. Dargomyzhsky (ed. N. Findeyzen): *Avtobiografiya* (1921).

Darmstadt. Town in Hesse-Darmstadt, Germany. Its musical traditions date back to the mid-16th cent. Under Grand Duke Ludwig I, a Ducal T. was built in 1810, and in 1819 the Grosses Haus (cap. 1,370) was opened. Verdi's *Vêpres siciliennes* and *Don Carlos* had their first German performances there in 1857 and 1868, and Gounod's *Faust* and *Reine de Saba* in 1861 and 1863. In 1919 the theatre came under the control of Hesse, with Gustav Hartung as Intendant, followed by Ernst Legal and Carl Ebert. Karl Böhm was music director 1927-31. The theatre was destroyed in 1944. From December 1945 to 1972 performances were given first in the Orangerie and then in the Stadthalle; Gustav Rudolf Sellner was Intendant, 1951-60. The new Grosses Haus (cap. 956) opened in 1972 with *Fidelio*. Prokofiev's *The Gambler* and Honegger's and Ibert's *L'Aiglon* had their first German performances in 1956 and 1968.

Daudet, Alphonse (*b* Nîmes, 13 May 1840; *d* Paris, 16 Dec. 1897). French writer. Operas on his works are as follows:
L'Arlésienne (1872): Cilea (1897).
Sapho (1884): Massenet (1897).
Tartarin sur les alpes (1885): Pessard (1888).

Dauvergne (D'Auvergne), **Antoine** (*b* Moulins, 3 Oct. 1713; *d* Lyons, 23 Feb. 1797). French composer. He arranged and composed a number of operas, of which the most famous is *Les Troquers* (1753): this is historically important as the first French work on the model of the Italian intermezzo, using recitative instead of dialogue. He also wrote *La Coquette trompée* (1753), *Énée et Lavinie* (1758), *Hercule mourant* (1761), and *Pyrrhus et Polyxène* (1763).

David. Hans Sachs's apprentice (ten.) in Wagner's *Die Meistersinger von Nürnberg*.

David. Opera in 5 acts by Milhaud; text by Lunel. Commissioned by Koussevitsky Foundation. Prod. (concert version in Hebrew) Jerusalem, 1 June 1954 for 3,000th anniversary of foundation of Jerusalem. First stage perf. Milan, Sc. 2 Jan. 1955 with Pobbe, Ratti, Gardino, Colzani, Rossi-Lemeni, Tajo, cond. Sanzogno; Hollywood Bowl, 22 Sept. 1956 with Nelli, Dixon, Presnell, Harrell, Tozzi, cond. Solomon. The opera is based on the events chronicled in the chapters 1 and 2 of the Book of Samuel.

David, Félicien (*b* Cadenet, 13 Apr. 1810; *d* St Germain-en-Laye, 29 Aug. 1876). French composer. He espoused Saint-Simonism, and when the sect was dispersed in 1832 left for the Orient. Here he found inspiration for his 'Oriental' works, among which are the operas *La Perle du Brésil* (1851), *Herculanum* (1859), *Lalla Roukh* (1862), and *Le Saphir* (1865). He also stimulated more distinguished contemporaries, including Gounod, Bizet, and especially Delibes, in their Oriental operas. His delicate, tuneful music was greatly admired by Bizet, whose most immediate successor he was.
Bibl: R. Brancour: *Félicien David* (1911).

David, Giacomo (*b* Presezzo, nr Bergamo, 1750; *d* Bergamo, 31 Dec. 1830). Italian tenor. Studied Naples. Début Milan, 1773. Sang at the opening performances of the T. Nuovo, Trieste (1801), and the Carcano, Milan (1803). Milan, Sc., 1782-3, 1799-1800, 1802-3, and 1806-8 in works by Mayr, Portogallo, Cimarosa, Sarti, etc. London 1791, but only in concert. Considered by Mount-Edgcumbe, who heard him in Naples, to be excellent in opera. His pupils included his son, Giovanni (see below), and Andrea Nozzari.

David, Giovanni (*b* Naples, 15 Sept. 1790; *d* St Petersburg, 1864). Italian tenor. Son of above; studied with his father. Début Siena, 1808, in

Adelaide di Gueschino. Milan, Sc., 1814, where he created Narciso in Rossini's *Il Turco in Italia*. Subsequently Rossini wrote parts for him in *Otello*, *La donna del lago*, and other works. Appeared in London in 1818 and 1831. Sang until 1839, when his voice began to fade. He subsequently became manager of the opera house in St Petersburg. He had a range of three octaves. Stendhal considered him the finest tenor of his generation. His daughter **Giuseppina** (1821-1907) sang in Rome and St Petersburg, and his nephew **Giacomo Antonio** sang at the T. Valle in 1837.

Davies, Ben(jamin) (*b* Pontardawe, nr Swansea, 6 Jan. 1858; *d* Bath, 28 Mar. 1943). Welsh tenor. Début Birmingham 1881, Thaddeus (*Bohemian Girl*). Sang with C. R. and D'Oyly Carte's Royal English Opera, creating the title role in Sullivan's *Ivanhoe* (1891). Sang Faust at C.G. 1892, and the title role in Cowen's *Signa* there in 1894. (R)

Davies, Cecilia (*b* London, *c*1750; *d* London, 3 July 1836). English soprano. Appeared in Dublin 1763-4, and in 1767 in London. Sang in Vienna, where with her sister Marianne taught Maria Theresa's daughters to sing and act. Appeared in Milan with great success in 1771, then Naples and Florence, where she created Sacchini's *Armida*. Christened by the Italians 'L'Inglesina' and considered superior to any Italian singer except Gabrielli, whom she 'even rivalled in neatness of execution' (Mount-Edgecumbe). Returned to London 1773 and 1777.

Davies, Peter Maxwell, see *Maxwell Davies, Peter*.

Davies, Ryland (*b* Cwm, Ebbw Vale, 9 Feb. 1943). Welsh tenor. Studied R.M.C.M. Gly. chorus 1964, and was first winner of the John Christie Award; début W.N.O. 1964 Almaviva; Scottish Opera 1966 Fenton; Gly. Touring Opera 1967 Nemorino, and Festival since 1968. C.G. since 1969; Salzburg 1970; San Francisco 1970 and N.Y., Met. 1975. Repertory also includes Belmonte, Ferrando, Ottavio, Ernesto, Hylas (*Trojans*), and Lensky. Possesses a pleasing light tenor voice heard to best advantage in smaller theatres. Married to the mezzo-soprano Anne Howells. (R)

Davies, Tudor (*b* Cymmer, 12 Nov. 1892; *d* London, 2 Apr. 1958). Welsh tenor. Joined B.N.O.C. at its inception; C.G. début as Rodolfo on opening night of its first London season. Remained with the company several seasons, creating Hugh the Drover (1924) and leading roles in Holst's *At the Boar's Head* and Smyth's *Fête Galante*. Philadelphia, Civic Opera, 1928, Lohengrin. Leading tenor Old Vic and S.W. 1931-41, and C. R. 1941-6. Sang in first S.W. perf. of Benjamin's *The Devil Take Her*, *The*

Snow Maiden, and *Don Carlos.* His voice, originally fresh and warm, was affected by singing roles (like Florestan and Manrico) that were too heavy for him. (R)

Davis, Colin (*b* Weybridge, 25 Sept. 1927). English conductor. Studied clarinet R.C.M.; début R.F.H. as ballet cond., 1952, after engagements with Kalmar Orchestra and Chelsea Opera Group. After appointment with B.B.C. Scottish Orch., engaged at S.W. 1959, music director 1961-5. C.G. début 1966; music director from 1971. Has appeared at Gly., N.Y. Met., and widely elsewhere. A gifted and lively musician, with a special feeling for Mozart, Berlioz, Britten, Stravinsky, Tippett, and more recently Wagner. (R)

Davydov, Stepan (Ivanovich) (*b* ?1777; *d* Moscow, 22 May 1825). Russian composer. Studied with Sarti. Kapellmeister in St Petersburg 1800-4 and 1806-10; also taught singing in Moscow. He is best known for his work on **Lesta, dneprovskaya rusalka* (Lesta, the Dnepr water spirit). Basically a Singspiel, taken over from Kauer's *Das *Donauweibchen,* the work was reworked and added to by Davydov; making use of both town and country songs, he gave it an original Russian flavour and at the same time a distinctive Romantic colouring. He is one of the most important figures in Russian opera before Glinka (who knew *Lesta* and may have been influenced by it).

De Amicis. Italian family of singers.
1) **Antonio Domenico** (*b* Fermo, *c*1716; *d* ?). Italian bass. Appeared in Dublin with company which he took over from Antonio Minelli in 1761. He married the soprano Rosalba Baldacci (*b* Atri, *c*1716; *d* ?).

(2) **De Amicis Buonsollazzi, Anna Lucia** (*b* Naples, 1733; *d* Naples, 1816). Daughter of the above. Studied with her father. Début Bologna, 1755, in Galuppi's *La calamità dei cuori.* Was the favourite singer of J.C. Bach in London (1763). Heard by Mozart in Mainz, Venice, and Naples; he wrote Giunia for her in *Lucio Silla,* which she created in Milan (1772). Leopold Mozart wrote of her that 'she sings and acts like an angel'. Was the first singer to introduce staccato divisions in singing; according to Burney, her voice went up to E♭'''. She retired in 1779. Her elder sister Marianna and her brother Gaetano (*b* Naples, 1746) were also singers.

De Angelis, Nazareno (*b* Rome, 17 Nov. 1881; *d* Rome, 14 Dec. 1962). Italian bass. Sang as boy in Sistine Chapel Choir. Début 1903, Acquila, Il Podestà (*Linda di Chamounix*). Sang in all leading Italian theatres until 1959, and with Chicago Opera 1910-11 and 1915-20. Considered one of the greatest Italian basses of his day; created Archibaldo in *L'amore dei tre re,* and particularly renowned for his Mefistofele, Mosè, Zaccaria, and his Wagner interpretations. Retired 1939. (R)

Death in Venice. Opera in 2 acts by Britten; text by Myfanwy Piper, after Thomas Mann's story *Der Tod in Venedig* (1911). Prod. Snape, 16 June 1973, with Pears, Shirley-Quirk, Bowman, Bergsma, Huguenin, choreography Ashton, prod. Graham, cond. Bedford; N.Y., Met., 18 Oct. 1974, with Pears, Shirley-Quirk, cond. Bedford.

The plot closely follows the original story. Aschenbach (ten.), a famous writer, leaves Germany for Venice, where he succumbs to the allure of a boy, Tadzio (dancer), who represents the Dionysiac side of his character which has hitherto suppressed too far beneath a cool Apollonian view of life. He tries to leave the cholera-stricken city, but is frustrated by an accident to his luggage, and returns to indulge his solitary and self-devouring obsession. Watching Tadzio playing on the beach with other boys, he collapses and dies. The opera is cast in scenes connected by interludes, and makes prominent use of dance; the roles of the figures (such as an Elderly Fop) who contribute to Aschenbach's downfall are all taken by the same baritone.

De Bassini (orig Bassi), **Achille** (*b* Milan 5 May 1819; *d* Cavadei Tirreni, 3 July 1881). Italian baritone. Studied with Perelli; début *c*1837, Voghera, in *Belisario* and *Norma.* Rome, 1844, created Francisco in *I due Foscari,* a role he repeated at Milan Sc. where he also sang Tell, Figaro, Carlo in *Ernani.* Created Corsaro (Trieste, 1848), Miller in *Luisa Miller* (Naples, 1849), Melitone in *Forza* (St Petersburg 1862) (Verdi had also hoped that he would create Rigoletto). London, C.G. 1859, Germont, Luna, etc. His wife **Rita** (Gabriella) **Gabussi** (*b* Bologna, *c*1815; *d* Naples, 26 Jan. 1891), made her début in Milan as Rosina in 1830. Sang at most of the leading Italian theatres including Milan Sc. and Naples S. C., where she created the title role in Mercadante's *Medea* (1851), but her voice was already in decline and she retired soon after. Their son **Alberto** (*b* Florence, 14 July 1847; *d* ?) made his début in Venice in *Belisario* in 1869, and then specialized in the French repertory 1880-90; he became a baritone, went to the U.S.A. in 1898 with the Royal Italian Grand Opera Company, and then taught singing.

De Begnis, Giuseppe (*b* Lugo, Romagna, 1793; *d* N.Y., Aug. 1849). Italian bass. Début Modena 1813 in Pavesi's *Ser Marcantonio.* Developed into leading buffo of his day, and as such engaged by Rossini in 1817 to create Dandini in *La Cenerentola.* Sang London 1821-7 – début as Geronio (*Il Turco in Italia*) with his wife Giuseppina as Fiorilla. 1823-4 directed opera season at Bath, and 1834-7 in Dublin, where he had first sung in 1829.

De Begnis, Giuseppina Ronzi (*b* Paris 11 Jan.

800; *d* Florence, 7 June 1853). Italian soprano, wife of above. Studied with Garat. Début Florence, 1815. More successful in London and Naples than in Paris, though even there her Donna Anna was considered the finest ever heard, and the best until Sontag. Excelled, however, in light roles. Created roles in five Donizetti operas, *Fausta, Sancia di Castiglia, Maria Stuarda, Gemma di Vergy,* and *Roberto Devereux.* Retired on death of her husband.

Debora e Jaële. Opera in 3 acts by Pizzetti; text by composer, after Judges xvi. Prod. Milan, Sc., 16 Dec. 1922, with Tess, Casazza, Pinza, cond. Toscanini. Jaële (sop.) is accused by the Hebrews of friendship with their enemy, Sisera (ten.). Debora (mezzo) promises them victory and persuades Jaële to go to the enemy's camp and kill Sisera; but when the moment comes, Jaële cannot bring herself to do this. The Hebrews launch a successful battle and Sisera seeks refuge with Debora, who kills him to save him from more horrible tortures at the hands of his captors.

Debrecen. Town in eastern Hungary. Touring companies first performed there in 1799, and the first permanent company was formed in 1860. The Csokonai T. (cap. 698) opened in 1865. The present company was formed in 1952, and tours the region.

Debussy, (Achille) **Claude** (*b* St-Germain-en-Laye, 22 Aug. 1862; *d* Paris, 25 Mar. 1918). French composer. Despite plans for operas on the subject of Tristram and Yseult and on *As You Like It,* as well as on works by Heine and by Poe (who deeply influenced him), Debussy's only opera is *Pelléas et Mélisande* (1902). This remains one of the most original operas in the history of music, where it occupies a pivotal place. Wagnerian in its use of the orchestra to carry most of the emotion (especially with the interludes later incorporated), it is also anti-Wagnerian in its reticence with a story of love, jealousy, and murder. Though based on Maeterlinck's deliberately vague Symbolist drama and making subtle use of the symbol of Mélisande's long golden hair and the theme of men's blindness, its clarity of declamation looks forward to a new directness in expression. *Pelléas* is a masterpiece inhabiting a unique and haunting world of its own creation, and its allusive twilight atmosphere continues to fascinate by reason of the inventiveness with which Debussy realizes the shadowy emotions in music. Maeterlinck violently opposed the opera and even threatened Debussy with assault when the role of Mélisande was taken away from his wife, Georgette Leblanc, and given to Mary Garden by Carré, director of the Opéra-Comique. He did not find it hard to arouse hostility; but *Pelléas* has long since been accepted as a master-

piece. Part of one of the two versions drafted of *La Chute de la Maison Usher* was reconstructed by W. Harwood and perf. New Haven, Feb. 1977.

Bibl: E. Lockspeiser: *Debussy* (2 vols., 1962-5).

Decembrists, The. Opera in 4 acts by Shaporin; text by Vsevolod Rozhdestvensky, using verses by A.N. Tolstoy and based on the historical events of the rising of December 1825. Prod. Moscow, B., 23 June 1953, with Ivanov, Pirogov, Petrov, Selivanov, Verbitskaya, Pokrovskaya, Kositsina, cond. Melik-Pashayev. Also opera by Vasily Zolotaryov (1925; rev. as *Kondraty Ryleyev,* 1957).

De Fabritiis, Oliviero (*b* Rome, 13 June 1902). Italian conductor. Studied Rome with Setaccioli and Refice. Début Rome, T. Adriano, 1920. Rome, T.R., 1934-61, conductor and artistic secretary 1934-43. Conducted first opera perf. at the Terme di Caracalla (*Lucia*) in 1937, and first perf. of *Simon Boccanegra* at C.G. London, 1965. Guest appearances all over Europe. (R)

De Falla, Manuel. See *Falla, Manuel de.*

De Grecis, Nicola (*b* Rome 1773; *d* ?). Italian bass. Début Rome, 1795. From 1805 to 1826 often at Milan, Sc.; Venice, San Moise; Rome, Valle. Created Slook (*Cambiale di matrimonio*), Blansac (*Scala di seta*), Gaudenzio (*Signor Bruschino*). Repertory included buffo roles in operas by Mayr, Nicolini, Paer, Pavesi, etc.

Deh, vieni alla finestra. Don Giovanni's (bar.) serenade to Elvira's maid in Act 2 of Mozart's *Don Giovanni,* in which he sings to his own mandolin accompaniment (often played pizzicato on a violin).

Deh, vieni non tardar. Susanna's (sop.) aria in Act 4 of Mozart's *Figaro* in which she expresses her love for Figaro.

Deidamia. Opera in 3 acts by Handel; text by P. Rolli. Prod. London, Hm., 10 Jan. 1740, with Adreoni, Francescina, Edwards; Hartford, 25 Feb. 1959. Handel's last opera; originally unsuccessful, being given for 3 nights only. Other operas on the subject are by Campra (1735), Maréchal (1893), and Rasse (1906).

De Lara (orig. Cohen), **Isidore** (*b* London, 9 Aug. 1858; *d* Paris, 2 Sept. 1935). English composer. Trained Milan Conservatory where he studied composition under Mazzucato, and in Paris under Lalo. Maurel suggested that he should change his cantata *The Light of Asia* into an opera, which was performed under its Italian title *La luce dell'Asia* at C.G. 1892. His *Amy Robsart* was performed three the following year. Other operas that enjoyed a limited success were *Messaline* (1899) and *Naïl* (1912). His compositions owe much to Massenet and Saint-Saëns. He constantly campaigned for the establishment of a permanent British Opera.

Delibes, Léo (b St-Germain-du-Val, 21 Feb. 1836; d Paris, 16 Jan. 1891). French composer. Studied Paris, with Adam and others. Accompanist at the T. L. 1853. His first stage work was the operetta *Deux sous de charbon*, for the T. Folies-Nouvelles (1855); his first opera was *Maître Griffard*, for the T. L. (1857). In 1863 he became accompanist at the O. then second chorus-master under Massé (1865-72). This turned his interest from operettas, with which he won popularity, to the ballet; he won fame with *Sylvia* and *Coppélia*. But opera drew him back, and he wrote three works for the Opéra-Comique, *Le Roi l'a dit* (1873), *Jean de Nivelle* (1880), and the famous *Lakmé* (1883). In keeping with the current vogue for the 'mysterious' East, an *opéra comique* tradition refreshed by the Romantic poets' fascination, and stimulated further by the example of Félicien *David, Delibes set his tale of the English lieutenant and the Indian girl Lakmé with a wealth of delightful mock-Oriental melody. It is chiefly for the charming tunefulness and the decorative scoring that *Lakmé* and the ballets retain an appeal which led Tchaikovsky, who learnt much from them, to prefer Delibes to both Brahms and Wagner.
Bibl: H. de Curzon: *Léo Delibes* (1927).

Delius, Frederick (b Bradford, 29 Jan. 1862; d Grez-sur-Loing, 10 June 1934). English composer. Delius's operas belong to the earlier part of his career. The most successful has been *A Village Romeo and Juliet* (1900-1, prod. 1907). *Irmelin* (1890-2) was first produced in 1953 in Oxford by Beecham, to whose enthusiasm is also due the English production, at C.G. in 1935, of *Koanga* (1895-7, prod. 1904). Delius's other operas are almost entirely known through excerpts. They are *The Magic Fountain* (1893, unprod.; B.B.C. 1977), *Margot-la-rouge* (1902., unprod.), and *Fennimore and Gerda* (1908-10, prod. 1919).
Bibl: A. Hutchings: *Delius* (1948).

Della Casa, Lisa (b Burgdorf, nr Berne, 2 Feb. 1919). Swiss soprano. Began vocal training when 15 in Zurich with Margarete Haeser, who was her only teacher. Début Solothurn-Biel 1941, Butterfly; Zurich, Stadttheater, 1943-50; Salzburg 1947, Zdenka; Gly. 1951, Countess (*Figaro*), and later that year Munich as Sophie and in her most famous role, Arabella, which she sang in London, 1953 and 1965; Vienna, S.O., 1952-74; N.Y., Met., 1953-68. Outstanding in the Strauss repertory, having graduated from Sophie through Oktavian to the Marschallin, which role she sang for the opening of the new Salzburg Festspielhaus in 1960. Retired 1974. She was able to spin out Strauss's vocal line with controlled legato, and was also an admirable Mozart singer. (R)
Bibl: D. Debeljević: *Ein Leben mit Lisa della Casa* (1975).

Delle Sedie, Enrico (b Livorno, 17 June 1822; c Paris, 28 Nov. 1907). Italian baritone. Studied with Galeffi and Persanola. Début Pistoia 1851 Nabucco. Sang all over Europe with great success. First London Renato. Despite his great style, musicianship, and dramatic talents, his vocal limitations earned him the nickname of 'l baritono senza voce'. Invited by Auber to accept a professorship at the Paris Conservatoire, where he taught 1867-71; then privately with his wife Margherita Tizzoni (dParis 1888).
Bibl: E. Delle Sedie: *L'Art Lyrique* (1874); *Riflessioni sulle cause della decadenza della scuola di canto in Italia* (1881); and *Estetica de canto e dell'arte melodramatica* (4 vols. 1885).

Dello Joio (orig. Dello Ioio), **Norman** (b New York, 24 Jan. 1913). American composer Studied with Hindemith. His operas are *The Triumph of St Joan* (1950), *The Ruby* (1955), *The Trial at Rouen* (1956), and *Blood Moor* (1961). (R)

Delmas, Jean-François (b Lyons, 14 Apr. 1861; d Saint-Alban de Monthel, 29 Sept. 1933). French bass-baritone. Studied Paris Conservatoire with Bussine and Obin. Début Paris, O., 1886, St Bris; between then and 1927 he sang and created more than 50 roles there including parts in *Salammbô* (Reyer), *Ariane et Barbe Bleue, Thaïs,* and *Monna Vanna*. The first French Wotan, Hagen, and Gurnemanz, and the first Paris Hans Sachs. (R)

Del Monaco, Mario (b Florence, 27 July 1915). Italian tenor. Studied Pesaro with Melocchi. Sang (non-professionally) T. Beniamino Gigli Mondaldo, at age of 13, in Massenet's *Nar cisse*. When 20 invited by Serafin to compete for a place in the studio attached to the T dell'Opera, Rome, and gained the place from 80 competitors. After six months decided to rely on personal study and gramophone records of the great singers of the past. Début Pesaro 1939, Turiddu, London. C.G., with San Carlo, 1946, returned 1962 as Otello, probably his finest role. San Francisco 1950; N.Y., Met. 1951-9, where he was exceedingly popular in the Verdi repertory and as Andrea Chénier Possessed a thrilling natural voice of enor mous power and great dramatic intensity. (R)

Delna (orig. Ledan), **Marie** (b Meudon, nr Paris 3 Apr. 1875; d Paris, 23 July 1932). French con tralto. Studied Paris with Laborde and Savary Début Paris, O.C., 1892, Dido. After five years a the O.C. went to the O., where she was leading contralto, 1898-1901. Milan, T.L., 1898-1900 Retired temporarily after her marriage in 1903 reappeared 1908, and continued to sing until her retirement in 1922. She was the first Paris Charlotte and Mistress Quickly. London, C.G. 1894; N.Y., Met., 1909-10. (R)

De los Angeles, Victoria. See *Los Angeles, Victoria de.*

Del Prato, Vicenzo (*b* Imola, 5 May 1756; *d* Munich, *c*1828). Italian male soprano. Studied with Gibelli. Début 1772 Fano. After singing in Italy, was engaged for Stuttgart, 1779, and 1780-1805 in Munich where he created Idamante in *Idomeneo*. Mozart called him 'mio molto amato castrato'.

De Luca, Giuseppe (*b* Rome, 25 Dec. 1876; *d* New York, 26 Aug. 1950). Italian baritone. Studied Rome with Persichini and Cotogni. Début Piacenza 1897, Valentine. Created Michonnet in *Adriana Lecouvreur*, Milan, T.L., 1902. Engaged Milan Sc. for 1903-4 and during his initial season created Sharpless, and Gleby in Giordano's *Siberia*. London, C.G., 1907, 1910, and a solitary appearance as Figaro (Rossini), 1935; N.Y., Met., 1915-35 and 1939-40. During his period in N.Y. made more than 700 appearances in 80 different operas, creating Paquiro in *Goyescas* (1917) and Gianni Schicchi (1918). In Nov. 1947 celebrated his Golden Jubilee as a singer in a special concert in N.Y.; spent the rest of his life as teacher at Juilliard School. His classic phrasing, effortless style, and immaculately produced voice marked him out as one of the finest exponents of bel canto of this century. When 70 could still sing Rigoletto and Sharpless. (R)

De Lucia, Fernando (*b* Naples, 11 Oct. 1860; *d* Naples, 21 Feb. 1925). Italian tenor. Studied Naples. Début Naples, 1885, Faust. London, D.L., 1887, C.G. 1892-6, 1900, where he was the first London Fritz, Canio, and Cavaradossi, and the first C.G. Turiddu. N.Y., Met., 1893-4. In Italy he created Amico Fritz. A highly accomplished singer and master of bel canto, renowned for his singing of Rossini, Bellini, and Verdi. Retired from stage 1917, but sang Stradella's 'Pietà, Signore' at Caruso's funeral in 1921. He taught in Naples, where his pupils included Nemeth, Pederzini, and Thill. (R)

De Lussan, Zélie (*b* New York, 21 Dec. 1861; *d* London, 18 Dec. 1949). American soprano. Trained by her mother; début in concert when 16. Stage début Boston 1886, Arline. Engaged by Augustus Harris for his first C.G. season, 1888, and sang Carmen. During her career appeared in this role over 1,000 times with nearly 60 Don Josés. C.R., 1890-1910; N.Y., Met., 1894-5 and 1898-1900. A famous Zerlina, Mignon, Cherubino, and Nedda. (R)

De Méric (orig. Bonnaud), **Joséphine** (*b* Strasbourg,?; *d* ?). French soprano. London, King's T., where she was the first London Adalgisa and Giulietta (*Capuletti*), both opposite Pasta; also sang Donna Elvira to Schröder-Devrient's Donna Anna. She sang in Italy as Giuseppina Demery and married the tenor A. Timoleone.

She is not to be confused with Henriette *Méric-Lalande, nor the latter's daughter, who sang at C.G., 1849-50, as Mlle de Méric.

De' miei bollenti spiriti. Alfredo's (ten.) aria which opens Act 2 of Verdi's *La traviata*, and in which he sings of his happiness with Violetta.

Demon, The. Opera in 3 acts by Anton Rubinstein; text by Pavel Viskovatov, after Lermontov's poem (1841). Prod. St Petersburg, M., 25 Jan. 1875, with Krutikova, Petrov, Raab, Komissarzhevsky, Melnikov, cond. Nápravník; London, C.G., 21 June 1881, with Albani, Lassalle, E. De Reszke, the first Russian opera in London, and when given in 1888 the first opera to be sung in Russian in London; prob. Boston 1891 by Hebrew Opera Company, also New York 1903.

Demougeot, Marcelle (orig. Jeanne Marguerite Marcelle Decorne) (*b* Dijon, 18 June 1871; *d* Paris, 24 Nov. 1931). French soprano. Studied Dijon and Paris. Début Paris, O., 1902 Donna Elvira. Sang there regularly until 1925. Created title role in Saint-Saëns's *Dejanire,* Monte Carlo 1911. First *Rheingold* and *Walküre* Fricka at the O., 1909; later the leading French Wagner soprano of her generation, singing Brünnhilde, Venus, Elisabeth, and Kundry with great success. (R)

De Muro, Bernardo (*b* Tempio Pausania, 3 Nov. 1881; *d* Rome, 27 Oct. 1955). Italian tenor. Studied Rome and with Sbriscia and A. Martino. Début Rome 1910, Turiddu. Milan, Sc., 1911, Folco (*Isabeau*), 1912 Don Carlos. Guest appearances in Europe, South America and towards the end of his career with minor companies in U.S.A. After retiring from stage in 1943, taught singing in New York. (R) *Bibl:* B. de Muro: *Quand' ero Folco* (1955).

Demuth, Leopold (orig. Leopold Pokorný) (*b* Brno, 2 Nov. 1861; *d* Czernowitz (Chernovtsy), 4 Mar. 1910). Austrian baritone. Studied Vienna with Joseph Gänsbacher. Début Halle 1889, Hans Heiling. Leipzig, 1891-6, Hamburg, 1896-8. Engaged by Mahler for Vienna 1898, remaining there until his death. Bayreuth 1899 Hans Sachs and Gunther; died from a heart attack while giving a concert. Gramophone records reveal a most beautiful baritone voice and refined musical style. (R)

Denhof Opera Company. Formed in 1910 by Ernst Denhof, a German-born musician living in Edinburgh, to give performances of *The Ring* in English in the provinces. The first series, under Balling, was followed in 1911 by appearances in Leeds, Manchester, and Glasgow, and in 1912 in Hull, Leeds, Liverpool, Manchester, and Glasgow. By this time the repertory had been enlarged to include *Elektra* (first performance in English), *Orfeo, Fliegende Holländer, Tristan,* and *Meistersinger*. In 1913, *Pelléas,*

Rosenkavalier (both for the first time in English), and *Zauberflöte* were added, but by then the company was making a heavy loss. After two weeks in Birmingham and one in Manchester the company had lost £4,000. Beecham, who was one of the conductors, took it over; and many of its personnel, which included Marie Brema, Gleeson-White, Caroline Hatchard, Agnes Nicholls, Walter Hyde, Frederic Ranalow, Frederic Austin, and Robert Radford, soon became associated with Beecham's own opera company.

Denmark. Opera was first produced in Denmark in the mid-17th cent., and attempts were made to initiate Danish opera with librettos by N. H. Bredal set by Sarti; however, these and others were virtually Italian works. The most important composers of the 18th cent. who tried to establish Danish opera were J. E. Hartmann (1726-93) and F. L. A. Kunzen (1761-1817), whose *Holger Danske* (1789, after Wieland's *Oberon*) won respect. The German J. A. P. Schulz (1747-1800) attempted a form of Danish Singspiel based on the popular French *opéra-comique*; he had some success with *Host-geldet* (The Harvest Festival, 1790) and *Peters Bryllup* (Peter's Wedding, 1793). Romanticism was slow to make its force felt in the struggling young tradition, but it is apparent in some of the six operas written by C. E. F. Weyse (1774-1842); these include some to texts by Oehlenschläger and Hans Andersen (*Festen paa Kenilworh,* after Scott, 1836). The influence of Cherubini, and through him Weber, shows in the operas of D. F. R. Kuhlau (1786-1832).

But the real influence of Romanticism is revealed in the work of J. P. E. Hartmann (1808-1900; grandson of J. E. Hartmann). He collaborated with Oehlenschläger on *Korsarerne* (The Corsairs, 1835) and with Hans Andersen on *Liden Kirsten* (Little Kristina, 1846). Niels Gade wrote the somewhat Mendelssohnian *Mariotta* (1850), and Peter Heise (1830-79) *Drot og Marsk* (King and Marshal, 1878) in which suggestions of Wagner are heard; Berlioz is suggested in Asger Hamerik's (1843-1923) *La vendetta* (1870). Folklore and folk music are drawn upon by Peter Lange-Müller (1850-1926) in *Vikingeblod* (The Blood of the Vikings, 1900); a more eclectic composer was August Enna (1860-1939). The dominating talent of the later period, however, was Carl *Nielsen. Modern composers who have contributed to a distinctive Danish operatic tradition include Knudaage Riisager (*b* 1897) with *Susanne* (1950), Finn Høffding (*b* 1899), Ebbe Hamerik (1898-1951) with *Stepan* (1924), and Vagn Holmboe (*b* 1909) with *Fanden og Børgemesteren* (The Devil and the Burgomaster, 1940).
See also *Copenhagen.*

De Nobili, Lila (*b* Lugano, 3 Sept. 1916). Italian designer. Studied Paris and Rome. Collaborated with Visconti for the famous Callas *Traviata* at Milan Sc., 1965 and with Zeffirelli for the London C.G. *Rigoletto,* 1964.

Dent, E(dward) **J**(oseph) (*b* Ribston, 16 July 1876; *d* London, 22 Aug. 1957). English scholar and teacher. His influence upon English operatic life, and its relationship to the European scene, is incalculable. His translations of Mozart's operas set a new standard: if idiosyncratic, their wit, fluency, and singability were unsurpassed in their day, and they quickly became integral. His production of *The Magic Flute* at Cambridge in 1911 set in motion the reappraisal of Mozart in England; he also arranged and produced several early English operas, especially those of Purcell, and apart from his reworking of *The *Beggar's Opera* did some original composition. His study of *Mozart's Operas* (1913) is a masterpiece of knowledge and shrewd scholarship; other important books were *Alessandro Scarlatti* (1905), *The Foundations of English Opera* (1928), and *Ferruccio Busoni* (1935). A series of his lectures was reprinted as *The Rise of Romantic Opera* (ed. W. Dean, 1976). He also contributed widely to journals of every description; while his immense store of learning was ever at the disposal of younger and less wise men.

Denzler, Robert (*b* Zurich, 19 Mar. 1892; *d* Zurich, 25 Aug. 1972). Swiss conductor. Pupil of Andreae at Zurich, further training at Bayreuth and Cologne. Music director, Zurich Opera, 1915-27 and 1934-47. During the latter period he directed world premières of *Lulu* (1937) and *Mathis der Maler* (1938). (R)

De Paolis, Alessio (*b* Rome, 5 Apr. 1893; *d* N.Y. 9 Mar. 1964). Italian tenor. Studied Rome, Santa Cecilia, with Di Pietro. Début Bologna 1919, Duke of Mantua. Sang Fenton on the opening night of Toscanini's new régime at Sc. 1921. After several seasons there and with other Italian theatres as leading lyric tenor, turned in 1932 to character roles, and developed into one of the outstanding comprimario singers of the day. As such he sang at the Metropolitan 1938-64. (R)

Depuis le jour. Louise's (sop.) aria in Act 3 of Charpentier's *Louise,* recalling the day when first she yielded to Julien.

Dereims, Étienne (*b* Montpellier, 26 Apr. 1845; *d* Paris, Apr. 1904). French tenor. After appearances in French provinces engaged Paris, O. 1879, where he created Don Gomes in Saint-Saëns's *Henri VIII* (1883) and Gauthier in Ferrier's *Tabarin* (1885); was also the Opéra's first Duke of Mantua (1885). Married to the soprano Jeanne *Devries.

De Reszke, Édouard (orig. Edward) (*b* Warsaw, 22 Dec. 1853; *d* Garnek, 25 May 1917). Polish bass, brother of Jean (see below). Studied Warsaw with Ciaffei and Italy with Steller and Coletti. Engaged by Escudier for Paris, and accepted by Verdi as the King in Paris première of *Aida* (1876), in which role he made his début under the composer's baton. Milan, Sc., 1879-81, where he created Ruben in Ponchielli's *Il figliuol prodigo* and Gilberto in Gomez's *Maria Tudor*; also sang Fiesco in revised *Boccanegra*. In Turin created the King in Catalani's *Elda*. London, C.G., 1880; Chicago 1891, With his brother Jean was a key member of the Paris, Met., and C.G. companies during the last decade of the century. Sang Méphistophélès in the 500th *Faust* at the O. (1887) with Jean in the title role; was a distinguished Saint-Bris, Frère Laurent, and Leporello. Later in his career he assumed with equal success Wagner roles, first in Italian, then in German, including Sachs, King Mark, and Hagen. Left the stage in 1903, and after an unsuccessful attempt to teach in London (1906-8) and then in Warsaw retired to his estate in Poland, where after the outbreak of war in 1914 he lived in extreme poverty and seclusion, first in the cellar of his house and then in a cave. His voice was of great volume and richness, and he was able to sing rapid passages with consummate ease. His great height and imposing stage presence, coupled with a powerful dramatic personality, made him one of the greatest basses in the history of opera. (R)

De Reszke, Jean (orig. Jan Mieczysław) (*b* Warsaw, 14 Jan. 1850; *d* Nice, 3 Apr. 1925). Polish tenor, brother of Edouard (above). Studied with Ciaffei and then Cotogni in Milan. Début as baritone (as Giovanni de Reschi) Turin 1874, Alfonso. London, D.L., same year in same role and as Don Giovanni and Valentine. Two years later sang in Paris, still as a baritone. His brother, convinced he was a tenor, suggested he study with Sbriglia, and after a period with that teacher made his tenor début in 1879 in Madrid in the title role of *Robert le Diable*, with little success. For the next 5 years only sang in concerts, but in 1884 was persuaded by Maurel and Massenet to sing John the Baptist in *Hérodiade* at its Paris première, which he did with great success. This led to Massenet completing his *Le Cid* with De Reszke in mind; sang in the world première the following year. In 1887 sang Radamès on the opening night in Augustus Harris's first Grand Opera season at D.L.; C.G. début 1888, Vasco da Gama. Returned to London nearly every year until 1900, as Roméo, Raoul, Faust, and later Lohengrin, Walther, Tristan, and Siegfried. N.Y., Met., 1891-1901, after which he sang only once more, Canio (his only appearance in the role), in Paris (Dec. 1902).

A revival of *Orfeo* with him in the tenor role was suggested, and he even rehearsed for a revival of Reyer's *Sigurd*. Spent the rest of his life teaching, first in Paris and then in Nice. His many pupils included Edvina, Saltzman-Stevens, Sayão, Teyte, and Steuart Wilson. His voice was one of exceptional beauty, which he coloured with great skill. His musicianship and phrasing were considered impeccable, and his personal charm and dramatic ability made him one of the greatest tenors of all time. His sister **Joséphine** (orig. Józefina) **de Reszke** (*b* Warsaw, 4 June 1855; *d* Warsaw, 22 Feb. 1891), soprano, studied in St Petersburg and made her début in Venice in 1874 in *Il Guarany*. Paris, O., 1875-84, where she created Sita in *Le Roi de Lahore*, and sang with much success as Rachel, Selika, Valentine, etc. She retired in 1884 at the height of her career to marry Baron Leopold de Kronenberg.
Bibl: C. Leiser: *Jean de Reszke and the Great Days of Opera* (1934).

Dérivis, Henri Etienne (*b* Albi 2 Aug. 1780; *d* Livry (Seine et Oise) 1 Feb. 1856). French bass. Début Paris, O., 1803 Sarastro in the arrangement of *Die Zauberflöte* known as *Les Mystères d'Isis*; remained at O. until 1828, creating leading bass roles in Spontini's *La Vestale, Fernand Cortez*, and *Olympie*; in Cherubini's *Les Abencérages*, Méhul's *Les Amazones*, and Mahomet II in Rossini's *Le Siège de Corinthe*. Possessed a powerful bass voice, but said to have been only a mediocre actor.

Dérivis, Prosper (*b* Paris, 28 Oct. 1808; *d* Paris, 11 Feb. 1880). French bass, son of above. Studied Paris with Pellegrini and Nourrit. Début Paris, O., 1831, remaining there for 10 years and creating De Nevers in *Les Huguenots*, Balducci in *Benvenuto Cellini*, Félix in *Les Martyrs*, and other roles. Milan, Sc. 1842-3 where he created Zaccaria in *Nabucco* and Pagano in *I Lombardi*. Vienna, K., 1842, where he created the Prefect in *Linda di Chamounix*. Retired from stage 1857 and taught singing at the Paris Conservatoire. Considered with *Lavasseur the best French bass of his day.

D'Erlanger, Frédéric (*b* Paris, 29 May 1868; *d* London, 23 Apr. 1943). English composer of French and German descent. Studied Paris with Anselm Ehmant. His *Inès Mendo* was given at C.G. in 1897, when the composer's name appeared as Ferd. Regnal; his *Tess* followed in 1909, with Destinn, Zenatello, and Sammarco in the cast. A banker by profession, he gave much financial support to C.G. and for many years was one of its directors.

Dermota, Anton (*b* Kropa, 4 June 1910). Yugoslav tenor. Studied Ljubljana and Vienna. Début Cluj, 1934; Vienna since 1936. Regularly at Salzburg. Sang with Vienna Company at C.G., 1947 (Ottavio, Ferrando, and Narraboth).

It is as a Mozart tenor that he is most renowned. Since 1966 has taught at the Vienna Academy of Music. (R)

Dernesch, Helga (*b* Vienna, 3 Feb. 1939). Austrian soprano. Studied Vienna. Début Berne, 1961, Marina in *Boris*. Wiesbaden, 1963-5; Cologne, 1965-8; Bayreuth 1965-7 in small roles, 1968 Eva; Scottish Opera since 1969, Gutrune, Leonore, Brünnhilde, Marschallin, Cassandra, Isolde. Salzburg Easter Festival 1969-74 as Brünnhilde and Isolde; London, C.G., since 1970 as Sieglinde, Chrysothemis, Leonore, Marschallin, Dyer's Wife. Created Elisabeth I in Fortner's *Elisabeth Tudor* (Berlin, 1972). Essentially a lyric soprano, she nonetheless embarked on the Wagnerian dramatic repertory with some success. Her personal beauty and warm personality make her a compelling performer on stage. (R)

Der Vogelfänger bin ich ja. Papageno's (bar.) aria introducing himself as the birdcatcher in Act 1, scene 1, of Mozart's *Der Zauberflöte.*

De Sabata, Victor (*b* Trieste, 11 Apr. 1892; *d* S. Margherita, 11 Dec. 1967). Italian conductor and composer. Studied Milan with Saladino and Orefice. After conducting in the concert hall he turned to opera, first at Monte Carlo, where he was assistant conductor from 1919; first opera there *La traviata*, 1918. Conducted the world première of *L'Enfant et les Sortilèges* (1925) and the first local performances of *Sadko, Rosenkavalier, Il trittico*, and *Turandot*; then from 1929 to 1953 was at Sc. first as conductor and then as musical and artistic director. Conducted *Tristan* at Bayreuth 1939, and appeared with the Sc. Company at C.G. 1950, conducting an unforgettable *Otello* and *Falstaff*. His incandescent and exciting readings of Verdi and Wagner reminded many listeners of Toscanini's. His opera *Il Macigno* was produced at Sc. in 1917. (R)

Deschamps-Jehin, (Marie-) **Blanche** (*b* Lyons, 18 Sept. 1857; *d* Paris, June 1923). French contralto. Studied Lyons and Paris. Début Brussels, Alhambra, 1874, in *Giroflé-Girofla*. Brussels, La M., 1879-85, where she created title-role in Massenet's *Hérodiade* (1881) and Uta in Reyer's *Sigurd* (1884). Paris, O.C., 1885-91, where she created Margaret in Lalo's *Roi d'Ys* (1888); returned there to create the Mother in *Louise* (1900). Paris, O., 1891-1902, making her début there in Nov. 1891 as Fidès and Catherine de Medici in Act 4 of *Les Huguenots* (a role specially restored for that occasion). First Dalila at the O., 1892, and Fricka (*Walküre*) (1893); London, C.G., autumn 1891 as Carmen, highly praised by all critics, and in Bruneau's *Le Rêve*; 1892 in Bemberg's *Elaine* and Fidès. 1902-9 sang mostly in concerts with some appearances Monte Carlo opera. Considered one of the great French contraltos. Married to the conductor Léon Jehin (1853-1928). (R)

Desdemona. Otello's wife (sop.) in Verdi's and Rossini's *Otello.*

Des Grieux. The hero (ten.) of Massenet's *Manon* and Puccini's *Manon Lescaut.*

Desormière, Roger (*b* Vichy, 13 Sept. 1898; *d* Paris, 25 Oct. 1963). French conductor. Studied Paris Conservatoire. Conducted with Diaghilev Ballet 1925-30; joined O.C. 1937. In 1938 conducted first performance there of Chabrier's *Une Éducation manquée, L'Étoile*, and *Ariadne auf Naxos*, and important revivals of *L'Heure espagnole, Le Médecin malgré lui*, and *Pelléas*, which he conducted at C.G. in 1949. Music Director, O.C., 1944-6. Forced by ill health to retire 1950. (R)

Despina. Fiordiligi's and Dorabella's maid (sop.) in Mozart's *Così fan tutte.*

Dessau. Town in Anhalt, Germany. Operatic acitivity began at the end of the 18th cent. In 1798 Prince Leopold Friedrich Franz built the Hoftheater (cap. 1,000), which was the largest in Germany after Berlin and Bayreuth. A strong Wagner tradition was established there in the second half of the 19th cent. *Die Meistersinger* was performed there in 1869 soon after its Munich première, and Bayreuth artists frequently appeared there, under Knappertsbusch, Schmitz, Rother, and others. The Opera House (cap. 1,245), opened in 1885, was rebuilt in 1938 and again in 1949.

Dessau, Paul (*b* Hamburg, 19 Dec. 1894). German composer and conductor. Studied Berlin. Worked in the Hamburg Stadttheater, 1912, later in Cologne and Mainz, then Berlin Stä. O. 1925-33; left Germany 1933. Returned to Berlin 1948. His operas are *Giuditta* (1912), the very successful *Die Verurteilung des Lukullus,* to a text by Brecht (1951, several revisions), *Puntila* (1966), *Lanzelot* (1969), *Einstein* (1974).

Destinn (Destinnová, orig. Kittlová), **Emmy** (orig. Emilie Pavlína, then Ema) (*b* Prague, 26 Feb. 1878; *d* České Budějovice, 28 Jan. 1930). Czech soprano. Studied Prague with Marie Lowe-Destinn, whose name she adopted for professional purposes. Début Dresden, 1897, Santuzza; London, C.G., 1904-14, 1919; N.Y., Met., 1908-16 and 1919-21. Chosen to sing Senta in first Bayreuth *Fliegende Holländer* (1901). The first Berlin Salome (1906); at C.G., the first Butterfly (1905), Tatyana (1906), Tess (1908), and Minnie (1911), which she had created at the world première of *La fanciulla del West* in N.Y. (1910). Under the name of Ema Destinnová returned to London 1919 as Aida. Retired from stage in 1927. Her voice, of a highly individual timbre, was even in range and impeccably produced, added to which she was a remarkably fine actress, especially in tragic roles. (R)

Destouches, André (*b* Paris, bapt. 6 Apr. 1672; *d* Paris, 7 Feb. 1749). French composer. Studied n Paris, then served as a soldier in Siam, returning to study further in Paris with Campra. His first opera *Issé* (1697) was a great success, and was followed by *Amadis de Grèce* (1699), *Marthésie* (1699), *Omphale* (1700), *Le Carnaval et la folie* (1703), and *Callirhoé* (1712). In 1713 he became Inspector General of the Opéra. Further operas were *Télémaque* (1714), *Sémiramis* (1718), *Les Éléments* (1721), and *Les Stratagèmes de l'amour* (1726). He was director of the O., 1728-31. Louis XIV was a great admirer of Destouches, who has a place in French operatic history not only as an important successor of Lully but as an influence on Rameau; his music is remarkable for its melodic elegance.

Destouches, Franz Seraph von (*b* Munich, 21 Jan. 1772; *d* Munich, 9 Dec. 1844). German composer. Studied Vienna with Haydn. His first opera was *Die Thomasnacht* (1792). He was music director in Erlangen in 1797, moving to Weimar in 1799 as a leader of the theatre orchestra. Other operas were *Das Missverstandnis* (1805), *Die blühende Aloë* (*c*1805), and *Der Teufel und der Schneider* (1843, prod. 1851).

Detmold. Town in Northern Westphalia, Germany. Singspiels were given in the 1770s, and in 1778 a Komödienhaus was opened. The Hoftheater was opened in 1825 under A. Pichler, and Lortzing and his wife worked in the company 1826-33; the theatre closed in 1848. Reopened 1852, it was burnt down in 1912, and reopened as the Landestheater in 1919 (cap. 730) with Lortzing's *Undine*.

Detroit. Town in Michigan, U.S.A. Opera in Detroit dates back to the middle of the last century when seasons were given by the De Vries and Pyne-Harrison Companies, and by an Italian ensemble under Arditi. Then came visits from the Damrosch, Met., and other Companies. In 1928 the Detroit Civic Opera Company was formed by Thaddeus Wroński; in 1934 it became associated with the Detroit Symphony Orchestra and between then and the war gave performances of several works including *Tristan*, *La Rondine*, *Peter Ibbetson*, and *Il Dibuk* (Rocca). In 1920 the Overture to Opera Company was formed, renamed the Michigan Opera T. in 1973. The performances are given in English.

Deus ex machina (*Lat* the god from the machine). The theatrical device, originating in Greek drama, whereby a god is lowered on a cloud or in a triumphal car in order to resolve the complexities of the plot. A classic instance occurs at the end of Monteverdi's *Orfeo*, when Apollo descends to remove his son Orpheus to Heaven. By extension, the term is used of any arbitrary last-minute solution to cut the tangled threads of a plot and bring about a happy ending.

Deutekom, Christina (orig. Stientje Engel) (*b* Amsterdam, 28 Aug. 1932). Dutch soprano. Studied Netherlands Opera Studio. Début Netherlands Opera, 1963, Queen of Night. N.Y., Met., 1967; London, C.G., 1968, in same role. Since then has established herself as a leading coloratura soprano in Italy in such roles as Lucia, Norma, and Rossini's Armide; also sings more dramatic roles including Abigaille, Odabella, Giselda, Leonora in *Trovatore*, and Donna Anna. Has an outstanding coloratura technique. (R)

Deutsche Oper am Rhein. See *Düsseldorf-Duisburg*.

Deux Aveugles de Tolède, Les (The Two Blind Men of Toledo). Opera in 1 act by Méhul; text by Benoît Marsollier. Prod. Paris, O.C., 28 Jan. 1806. Also operas *Les Deux Aveugles de Franconville* (Ligon, *c*1780), *Les Deux Aveugles de Bagdad* (Fournier, 1782), *Les Deux Petits Aveugles* (A.-E. Trial, 1792), *Les Deux Aveugles* (Offenbach, 1855).

Deux Journées, Les (The Two Days). Opera in 3 acts by Cherubini; text by Jean Nicolas Bouilly. Prod. Paris, T. Feydeau, 16 Jan. 1800; London, C.G., 14 Oct. 1801; New Orleans 12 Mar. 1811. One of Cherubini's most important works, also formerly known as *The Water Carrier* in England. Another opera on the subject is by Mayr (*Le due giornate*, 1801; text by Foppa, after Bouilly). Armand (ten.) falls into disfavour with Mazarin and arranges with the water-carrier Mikéli (bass) to escape from Paris in a barrel. He and his wife are caught, but Mikéli brings news of their pardon. Sequel *Michelli und sein Sohn* by Clasing (1806).

Devil and Daniel Webster, The. Opera in 1 act by Douglas Moore; text by composer, after Stephen Vincent Benét's story (1937). Prod. N.Y., Martin Beck T., 18 May 1939. Jabez Stone is rescued from a pact selling his soul to the devil by Daniel Webster's brilliant defence before a jury of famous villains of history.

Devil and Kate, The (Cz. *Čert a Káča*). Opera in 3 acts by Dvořák; text by Adolf Wenig, after the folk-take included in Božena Němcová's *Fairy Tales* (1845). Prod. Prague, N., 23 Nov. 1899; Oxford 22 Nov. 1932, with Turner, Ward, Manning, Wild, Beard, cond. Jacques.

Kate (con.), a stout elderly maid, fails to secure a dancing partner at a country fair, so says she would dance with the devil himself, Marbuel (bar.), who now carries her off. Her garrulity oppresses even Hell, which gladly relinquishes her to a rescuer. Marbuel returns to earth to capture the domineering lady of the manor, but vanishes at the sight of Kate.

Devils of Loudun, The. Opera in 3 acts by Krzysztof Penderecki; text by composer, after John Whiting's drama *The Devils* (1961) based on Aldous Huxley's historical study *The Devils of Loudun* (1952) examining a celebrated 17th-cent. case. Prod. Hamburg, S.O., 20 June 1969, with Troyanos, Hiölski, cond. Czyz; Santa Fe 14 Aug. 1969, with Davidson, Reardon, cond. Skrowaczewski; London, Col., 1 Nov. 1973, with Barstow, Chard, cond. N. Braithwaite. The plot describes how the priest Urbain Grandier (bar.) engenders a diabolic obsession in a convent of Ursuline nuns, above all in the prioress Jeanne (sop.). He is eventually tortured and burnt at the stake.

Devil's Wall, The (Cz. *Čertova stěna*). Opera in 3 acts by Smetana; text by E. Krásnohorská. Prod. Prague, Cz., 29 Oct. 1882, with Fibichová, Reichová, Sittová, Vávra, Lev, Krössing, Hynek, Chlumský, cond. A. Čech. An extremely complicated dynastic love story, involving much confusion between the Devil (bass) and his double, the hermit Beneš (bass).

Devin du Village, Le (The Village Soothsayer). *Intermède* in 1 act by Jean-Jacques Rousseau; text by composer. Prod. Fontainebleau 18 Oct. 1752; public prod. Paris, O., 1 Mar. 1753 with Laporte, Leroy, Troy; London, D.L., 21 Nov. 1766; N.Y. 21 Oct. 1790. One of the most successful and influential works of its age, and Rousseau's most famous composition. Of its innumerable parodies, imitations, and adaptations, the most famous is Mozart's **Bastien und Bastienne*. Colette (sop.) learns that her beloved *Colin (ten.) has been unfaithful to her and seeks the aid of a Soothsayer (bar.) who advises her to display utter indifference to Colin's advances. At the same time, the Soothsayer tells Colin that Colette has fallen in love with someone else. The trick works and the lovers are reunited.

Devriès. Dutch family of singers.
(1) **Rosa van Os de Vries** (*b* Deventer, 1828; *d* Rome, 1889). Soprano. Début The Hague 1846, Rachel; then New Orleans 1849-51; London, Ly., 1856; Milan, Sc., and Naples, S.C., 1855-65. Her 4 children Gallicized their name to Devriès:
(2) **Jeanne** (*b* New Orleans 1850; *d*?). Soprano. Studied with Duprez. Début Paris, T.L., 1867 as Amina, and same year created Catherine in *La Jolie fille de Perth* there. In 1875 she married the tenor Étienne Dereims (1845-1904).
(3) **Fidès** (*b* New Orleans 22 Apr. 1851; *d* ?, 1941). Soprano. Also studied with Duprez. Paris, O., 1869-71, created Chimène in *Le Cid* (1885); repertory included Ophelia, Agathe, Marguerite.

(4) **Maurice** (*b* New York, 1854; *d* Chicago, 1919). Baritone. Début Liège, 1874; Brussels, La M., 1882-4; created Gunther in Reyer's *Sigurd*. N.Y., Met., 1895-7, début as Mercutio; Bustamento in 1st U.S. prod. of *La Navarraise* (1895). Later taught in Chicago.
(5) **Hermann** (*b* New York, 25 Dec. 1858; *d* Chicago, 24 Aug. 1949). Bass. Studied Paris with Faure. Début Paris, O., 1878, Méru (*Les Huguenots*); O.C., 1880-5; Brussels, La M., 1800; London, C.G., 1899; Chicago, N.Y., Met., 1898-1900. Toured with the Savage Grand Opera Company. Left the stage 1910; taught, then became music critic of the *Chicago American Herald*, 1915-44.
(6) **David** (*b* Bagnères-de-Luchon, 1881; *d* Neuilly, 1934). Studied Paris with Lhérie and Duvernoy. Tenor. Grandson of Rosa and nephew of above. Début Paris, O.C., 1904, Gérald (*Lakmé*); sang regularly at Paris, O. and O.C., creating a number of roles including Philodème in D'Erlanger's *Aphrodite* (1906); New York, Manhattan Opera, 1909-10; London, C.G., 1910 as Pelléas; Brussels, LaM., 1920-21. One of the finest lyric tenors of his generation in the French repertory. (R)

Dexter, John (*b* Derby, 2 Aug. 1925). British producer. After directing films and straight theatre turned to opera with *Benvenuto Cellini*, London, C.G., 1966. Hamburg State Opera from 1969, where his productions included *Vêpres siciliennes, From the House of the Dead, Billy Budd,* and *Boris Godunov*. Staged first British performance of Penderecki's *The Devils of Loudun* for the E.N.O., 1973. Director of productions, N.Y., Met., 1974. A highly gifted and stimulating producer.

Diaghilev, Sergey (Pavlovich) (*b* Novgorod, 19 Mar. 1872; *d* Venice, 19 Aug. 1929). Russian impresario. Although renowned as founder of the Russian Ballet Company that bore his name, he was also an important figure in opera, in Paris (1907-9), Paris and London (1913-14), and Paris and Monte Carlo (1922-4). In 1907 he presented scenes from *Sadko, Tsar Saltan, Boris,* and *Ruslan and Lyudmila* in concert form at the Paris O. and in 1908 the first full stage performance outside Russia of *Boris,* with Shalyapin. In 1909 he gave *Ivan the Terrible* in Paris; in 1913, at the T. des Champs-Élysées, the first performance outside Russia of *Khovanshchina;* and in June and July that year, the first Russian season at Drury Lane. In 1914, in association with Beecham, he gave seven Russian operas (*Boris, Ivan, Prince Igor, Golden Cockerel, Nightingale, May Night,* and *Khovanshchina*). In Paris was responsible for the first performance of Stravinsky's *Mavra* (1923) and *Oedipus Rex* (1927), and in Monte Carlo in 1923 prod. Gounod's *Le Médecin malgré lui* (with recitatives by Satie), *La Colombe* (with recitatives by Poulenc), *Philémon* *et Baucis,* and Chabrier's *Une Éducation manquée* (recitatives by Milhaud).

Bibl: A. Haskell: *Diaghilev* (1935).

Dialect in opera. A number of attempts have been made since the 18th cent. to write operas in a local dialect, and with the reawakening of interest in local cultures and languages there is no reason to suppose the genre extinct. Many more operas make occasional use of dialect words, phrases, even long passages, generally in the mouths of the lower orders. The most famous is Strauss's *Der Rosenkavalier,* in which use of the Viennese dialect which everyone privately knew was spoken at court gave considerable offence. Some operas entirely in dialect are as follows:

Bavarian: Orff's *Die Bernauerin* (Stuttgart, 1947).

Neapolitan: Vinci's *Lo cecato fauzo* (1719); Miceli's *La sonnambula* (1870); D'Arrienzo's *Monzù Gnazio* (1866), *I due mariti* (1872).

Piedmontese: a version of Donizetti's *Lucia di Lammermoor* (Turin, 1859).

Plattdeutsch: Schoeck's *Vom Fischer un syner Fru* (Dresden, 1930).

Provençal (Occitan): Mondonville's 'pastouralo Toulouzeno' *Daphnis et Alcimadaure* (Fontainebleau, 1754; also given a concert perf. at Montpellier in the town's *patois,* 1758); a version of Duni's *Les Deux Chasseurs et la laitière* as *La Laytayro dé Naubernad* (pubd Toulouse, 1783).

Walloons: Jean-Noël Hamal's *Li Voyèdge di Thaufontaine* (Liège, 1757), *Li Lidjwès ègadji* (Liège, 1757), *Li Fiesse di Hoûte-si-Ploû* (Liège, 1758), *Les Ypocontes*; Ysaye's only opera, *Piér li houïeu* (Peter the Miner, Liège, 1931).

Dialogues des Carmélites (The Carmelites). Opera in 3 acts by Poulenc; text by Ernest Lavery, after the drama by Georges Bernanos, adapted from Gertrude von Le Fort's novel *Die letzte am Schafott* (1931) and a film scenario by Fr Brückberger and Philippe Agostini, in turn on the recollections of one of the original nuns of Compiègne, Sister Marie of the Incarnation. Prod. Milan. Sc., 26 Jan. 1957, with Zeani, Gencer, cond. Sanzogno; San Francisco 20 Sept. 1957, with Price, Turner, cond. Leinsdorf; London, C.G., 16 Jan. 1958, with Morison, Sutherland, Watson, cond. Kubelík. The opera tells of the martyrdom of Carmelite nuns during the French revolution.

Diamand, Peter (*b* Berlin, 8 June 1913). Austrian, naturalized Dutch, administrator. Studied Berlin. Secretary to Schnabel 1934-8. Assistant to director of Netherlands Opera 1946-8; secretary and artistic director Holland Festival 1947-65 and artistic adviser Netherlands Opera over same period, basing the Holland Festival productions on that organization; succeeded in persuading Giulini to conduct opera at eight Holland Festivals. Edinburgh Festival Director 1965-78.

Diamants de la Couronne, Les (The Crown Diamonds). Opera in 3 acts by Auber; text by Scribe and Vernoy de St Georges. Prod. Paris, O.C., 6 Mar. 1841; New York 12 July 1843, with Calvé, Cossas, Bailly; London, Princess's T., 2 May 1844. Also subject of operetta *Jadwiga* by Dellinger (1901).

Dibdin, Charles (*b* Southampton, bapt. 4 Mar. 1745; *d* London, 25 July 1814). English composer, singer, and musical factotum. After some successes in pieces of his own authorship and composition at C.G., became famous for his long series of musical pieces and his sea songs. His illegitimate son, Charles, followed in these footsteps, no less vigorously if without equal success.

Dich, teure Halle. Aria opening Act 2 of Wagner's *Tannhäuser* in which Elisabeth (sop.) greets the Hall of Song in the Wartburg where the song contest is to take place.

Dickens, Charles (*b* Landport, 7 Feb. 1812; *d* Gadshill, 9 Jan. 1870). English writer. His solitary excursion as a librettist, made just before the first instalment of *The Pickwick Papers,* was for Hullah's *The Village Coquettes* (1836). Operas on his works are as follows:

The Pickwick Papers (monthly, 1836-7): C. Wood (1922); Coates (1936); E. Solomon (1889); N. Burnand (1956).

Barnaby Rudge (1841): J. Edwards (*Dolly Varden,* 1902).

A Christmas Carol (1843): Herrmann (1954); Cikker (*Mr Scrooge,* comp. 1958, prod. 1963); D. Gray (1960); Kalmanov (*Mister Scrooge,* 1966); J. Cohen (1970).

The Cricket on the Hearth (1846): Gallignani (1873); Goldmark (1896); Zandonai (1908); Mackenzie (1914).

A Tale of Two Cities (1889): Benjamin (1949-50, prod. 1957).

Dickie, Murray (*b* Bishopton, 2 Apr. 1924). Scottish tenor. Studied Vienna with Pollmann, London with Dino Borgioli, and Milan with Guido Farinelli. Début London, Cambridge T., with New London Opera Company, 1947, Almaviva. C.G. 1948-52 when he created the Curé in *The Olympians* (1949); Gly. from 1950; Vienna since 1952, where he has enjoyed considerable success as David, Pedrillo, Jacquino, and in other light tenor roles. From 1975 began to produce opera; his English version of *Eine Nacht in Venedig* was staged by E.N.O. at Coliseum 1976. (R)

Dick Johnson. The cowboy hero (ten.) of Puccini's *La fanciulla del West.*

Dido and Aeneas. Opera in a prologue and 3 acts by Purcell; text by Nahum Tate, after Book

4 of Virgil's *Aeneid* (unfin., 19 B.C.). Prod. Josias Priest's School for Young Gentlewomen, Dec. ?1689 or poss. summer 1690; public prod. *c* Feb. 1700 and 9 Feb. 1704, then not revived on stage until 20 Nov. 1895, by R.C.M. at Ly. for bicentenary of Purcell's death; N.Y., Hotel Plaza, 10 Feb. 1923.

Various versions of the opera survive, the one most generally accepted by scholars being the MS now in the Library of St Michael's College, Tenbury. The libretto includes the text of an elaborate mythological Prologue, not in the Tenbury score: this was included in the original production, when an Epilogue by D'Urfey was spoken. It is not known whether Purcell set the Prologue: we know the opera only as an adaptation, 'A Mask in Four Musical Entertainments', made at the beginning of the 18th cent. The libretto has a different arrangement of the acts.

Dido (sop.) cannot bring herself to declare her love for Aeneas (ten.). Belinda (sop.) and the court succeed in making her yield, and a chorus celebrates the triumph of love and beauty.

The Witches assemble in their cave to plot the downfall of Dido and of Carthage. They agree to conjure up a storm so as to force the royal lovers, out hunting, to take shelter in the cave; here one of the Witches, disguised as Mercury, will remind Aeneas of his duty to go on to Italy. Dido and Aeneas are entertained with a masque of Diana and Actaeon: the storm drives Aeneas alone to the cave, where he is deceived by the false Mercury.

At the harbour, Aeneas plans to leave, while the Witches exult in their success: they plan to sink his fleet and fire Carthage. When Dido appears she silences Aeneas's explanations, and in the famous lament 'When I am laid in earth' she takes her leave of life; Cupids mourn above her tomb.

Dido's betrayal has been treated operatically some 90 times, including almost 40 settings of Metastasio's *Didone abbandonata*.

Didur, Adam (*b* Wola Sękowa, 24 Dec. 1874; *d* Katowice, 7 Jan. 1946). Polish bass. Studied Lwów with Wysocki and Milan with Emmerich. After concert début in Milan, 1894, stage début Rio, Méphistophélès. Warsaw Opera 1899-1903; Milan, Sc., 1903-6; London, C.G., 1905 Colline, Leporello, Mefistofele; first London Archibaldo 1914; Buenos Aires, 1905-8; N.Y., Manhattan Opera, 1907-8, Met., 1908-32 where he created Ashby in *La fanciulla del West* and Woodcutter in *Königskinder*, and was the first U.S. Boris (1913). Sang at Gatti-Casazza's farewell in Feb. 1933 as Pistol. Returned to Poland and was appointed director of the Warsaw Opera in 1939, but was prevented from carrying out his plans by the outbreak of war and bombing of Warsaw. Moved

to Katowice where he taught and formed an opera company which opened on 14 March 1945 with *Halka*. He was then appointed director of Katowice Conservatory. His pupils included Marian Nowakowski and Eugenia Zareska. (R)

Die Frist ist um. The Flying Dutchman's (bar.) soliloquy in Act 1 of Wagner's *Der fliegende Holländer,* in which he reflects that once again the term of seven years' wandering, to which he is sentenced by the curse upon him, has expired and he may land to seek salvation in the redeeming love of a woman who will sacrifice herself for him.

Dies Bildnis ist bezaubernd schön. Tamino's (ten.) aria in Act 1 of Mozart's *Die Zauberflöte,* declaring his love for Pamina at first sight of her portrait.

Dietsch, (Pierre-) **Louis** (-Philippe) (*b* Dijon, 17 Mar. 1808; *d* Paris, 20 Feb. 1865). French conductor and composer. Studied Dijon Cathedral and Paris, latterly at Conservatoire with Rejcha. Having won a *premier prix* for double bass, he played at the T.I. and O., becoming chorus master of the O. at Rossini's recommendation in 1840. Conductor, O., 1860-3; left after an argument with Verdi. He is perhaps best known for his unfortunate contacts with Wagner. His *Le Vaisseau fantôme* (1842) was not, as Wagner asserted, based on a translation of *Der fliegende Holländer*. In 1861 he conducted the notorious Paris performance of *Tannhäuser,* against Wagner's wishes and evidently incompetently.

Di Luna, Conte. The villainous young noble of Aragon (bar.), in love with Leonora, in Verdi's *Il trovatore*.

Dimitrescu, Giovanni (orig. Ion Dumitrescu) (*b* Iaşi, 30 Dec. 1860; *d* London, March 1913). Romanian tenor. Studied Iaşi and Bucharest with Giuseppe Cima. Début Bucharest 1885, Ernani. After a further period of study in Milan with various teachers including Lamperti, sang Duke of Mantua and Manrico at T. Filodrammatici, Milan. Toured Australia with Italian company 1889; London, C.G., 1890 and 1892 as Enzo, Radamès, Don José, Don Ottavio, etc. C.R., 1890-2; Warsaw, St Petersburg, Moscow, Kiev, where he was admired in both lyric and dramatic roles, and regarded the greatest Raoul and Vasco ever heard there, being compared to Tamberlik. Also sang extensively in Italy and S. America.

Di Murska, Ilma (*b* Zagreb, 4 Jan. 1836; *d* Munich, 14 Jan. 1889). Croatian soprano. Studied Vienna, and Paris with Mathilde Marchesi. Début Florence 1862; London, H.M.'s 1865, Lucia; N.Y. 1873, Amina. First London Senta 1870, which she sang in Italian. Her voice had a compass of nearly 3 octaves, and she excelled as Constanze and the Queen of Night, as well as in more dramatic parts. Toured U.S.A. and Australia 1873-6. Taught U.S.A. 1880.

D'Indy, Vincent (b Paris, 27 Mar. 1851; d 2 Dec. 1931). French composer. Apart from a number of projects and the unimportant 1-act opéra comique, Attendez-moi sous l'orme (1882), D'Indy's first opera was Le Chant de la cloche (concert perf. Paris, 1886; prod. Brussels, 1912); this is a so-called légende dramatique based on Schiller and heavily indebted to Parsifal. He further expressed his love of Wagner, his ancestral feeling for the Cévennes, and his discipleship of Franck in his next and most important stage work, the action musicale, Fervaal (1897). L'Étranger (1903) continues in the same line while discovering a greater refinement of texture. Nevertheless, this work came to stand for values opposite to those that had recently been expressed in Pelléas et Mélisande (1902). La Légende de St Christophe (1920), a drame sacré, continued to oppose the new values in an extraordinary, ambitious mélange of Wagner and medieval mysteries. His last stage work, Le Rêve de Cinyras (1927), is an unambitious operetta.
Bibl: N. Demuth: Vincent d'Indy (1951).

Dinner Engagement, A. Comic opera in 1 act by Lennox Berkeley; text by Paul Dehn. Prod. Aldeburgh 17 June 1954, with Sharp, Hooke, Cantelo, Nielsen, Young, cond. Tausky; Washington, University of Washington, 1958. The modern buffo plot concerns the attempts of a nouveau-pauvre couple to marry their daughter to a Prince – with ultimate success, though not through their schemes.

Dinorah, ou Le Pardon de Ploërmel. Opera in 3 acts by Meyerbeer; text by Barbier and Carré. Prod. Paris, O.C., 4 Apr. 1859, with Cabel and Faure; London, C.G., 26 July 1859, with Miolan-Carvalho; New Orleans, 4 Mar. 1861, with Patti, Melchissédec, Carrier, cond. Prévost. A slight pastoral opera about the peasant girl Dinorah (sop.), a goat-herd Hoël (bar.), and a hidden treasure.

Dio, mi potevi scagliar. Otello's (ten.) monologue in Act 3 of Verdi's Otello, the equivalent of 'Had it pleased heaven to try me with affliction' in Act 4, scene 2, of Shakespeare's Othello.

Dionysos. In Greek mythology, the god of wine; known to the Romans as Bacchus. The son of Zeus and Semele, he was taken to Naxos, and later led expeditions at the head of a group of Bacchae or Bassarids, inspired by his divine frenzy, and holding orgiastic feasts (Bacchanalia or Dionysia). Those who submitted to his conquests were introduced to the use of the vine and other benefits, but those

who, like Pentheus, resisted him, were savagely destroyed. He later married *Ariadne after she had been abandoned by Theseus on Naxos: in this role he appears as the god Bacchus (ten.) in Strauss's Ariadne auf Naxos. He also appears in Bliss's The Olympians. In late 19th-cent. German aesthetics, under the influence of Nietzsche's The Birth of Tragedy (1872), the Dionysian principle in art stands for the instinctive, physical, and elemental, however destructive, in opposition to the Apollonian principle of order, reason, and discipline: it is this antithesis which is at the centre of Britten's *Death in Venice, and is dramatized in Szymanowski's *King Roger and Henze's The *Bassarids.

Dippel, Andreas (b Kassel, 30 Nov. 1866; d Hollywood, 12 May 1932). German tenor and impresario. Studied Kassel, Berlin, Milan, and Vienna. Début Bremen 1887, Lionel in Martha; Bayreuth 1889 in small roles; N.Y., Met., 1890; London, C.G., 1897-1900. Joint manager of Met. with Gatti-Casazza 1908-10, and of Chicago Opera 1910-13. Spent last years as coach and musical adviser in Hollywood. Had an enormous repertory of some 150 roles, and was always ready to step in for an indisposed colleague. In London and New York substituted for Jean de Reszke in Wagner roles on several occasions. (R)

Di Provenza. The elder Germont's (bar.) aria in Act 2 of Verdi's La traviata, in which he tries to persuade his son Alfredo to return to the parental home in Provence away from his life with Violetta.

Di quella pira. Manrico's (ten.) aria in Act 3 of Verdi's Il trovatore, a rousing call to his followers to join him in saving his mother Azucena from being burnt alive. The famous high C which most tenors interpolate in the line 'O teco almeno, corrir a morir' is not in Verdi's score.

Di Stefano, Giuseppe (b Motta, 24 July 1921). Italian tenor. Studied Milan, with Montesanto; début 1946, Reggio Emilia, Des Grieux (Massenet). N.Y., Met., 1948, Duke of Mantua; London, C.G., 1961, Cavaradossi. In the early stages of his career, when he confined himself to lighter roles including Wilhelm Meister, Elvino, Fritz, and Nadir, his singing was notable for its unfailingly beautiful tone and the use of an exquisite pianissimo, the voice possessing a rich velvety sound. After 1953-4 he assumed heavier roles, adding Don José, Canio, Turiddu, Radamès, Alvaro, and Osaka in Mascagni's Iris to his repertory. (R)

Di tanti palpiti. Tancredi's (con.) love song in Act 1 of Rossini's Tancredi. It was possibly the most popular aria of its day, and was sung and whistled in the streets all over Europe. In Venice it was known as the aria dei risi (Rice

Aria) as Rossini was alleged to have composed it in four minutes while waiting for the rice to cook–an impossible time for either event.

Dite alla giovine. Part of the duet between Violetta (sop.) and the elder Germont (bar.) in Act 2 of Verdi's *La traviata,* in which she begs him to make her sacrifice known to his daughter.

Dittersdorf, Karl Ditters von (*b* Vienna, 2 Nov. 1739; *d* Neuhof, 24 Oct. 1799). Austrian composer. Of his 40-odd operas, many of them very popular in their day for their bright, tuneful but shallow invention, almost the only one to be revived from time to time is *Doktor und Apotheker* (1786). The work's liveliness and humour set an example for German comic opera.

Divinités du Styx. Alceste's (sop.) aria in Act 1 of Gluck's *Alceste,* offering to die in place of her husband.

Djamileh. Opera in 1 act by Bizet; text by Louis Gallet, after Alfred de Musset's poem *Namouna* (1832). Prod. Paris, O.C., 22 May 1872, with Prelly (described by Gauthier-Villars as 'the voiceless Venus'), Duchesne, Pontel, cond. Deloffre; Manchester, 22 Sept. 1892; Boston, Opera House, 24 Feb. 1913, with Marcel, Laffitte, Giacone, cond. Weingartner. Haroun pensions off his old mistress once a month and is bought a new one in the market by his servant Splendiano. Djamileh, the current mistress, falls in love with Haroun, and bargains with Splendiano to be readmitted disguised: this ruse wins Haroun's heart.

Dmitry. The Pretender (ten.) in Mussorgsky's *Boris Godunov* and in Dvořák's *Dmitrij.*

Dobrowen (or Dobrovein, orig. Barabeychik), **Issay** (Alexandrovich) (orig. Ishok Israelevich) (*b* Nizhny-Novgorod, now Gorky, 27 Feb. 1891; *d* Oslo, 9 Dec. 1953). Russian conductor, pianist, and producer. Studied Moscow, with Taneyev and others, and Vienna with Godowsky. Début Moscow, Kommisarzhevsky T., 1919 Hoffmann; Moscow, B., 1921-2. Engaged by Fritz Busch to produce the first German *Boris,* Dresden 1923; conducted *Onegin* and other operas there. Berlin, Volksoper, 1924-5. Sofia 1927-8, where he conducted the local première of *Tiefland* as well as doing much for the Opera there. Berlin, Stä. O., 1928-9 as producer. Between then and 1936 rarely conducted opera, but was a frequent visitor to Budapest Opera 1936-9. Stockholm, Royal Opera, as conductor and producer 1941-5. Was responsible for several Russian operas at Milan, Sc., 1948-53. Conducted *Boris* at C.G. 1952. (R)

Docteur Miracle, Le. (1) Operetta in 1 act by Bizet; text by Battu and Halévy. Prod. Paris, B.P., 9 Apr. 1857; London, Park Lane Group, 8 Dec. 1957.

(2) Operetta in 1 act by Lecocq; text by Battu and Halévy. Prod. Paris, B.P., 8 Apr. 1857. Both works were entries in a competition arranged by Offenbach (who offered 1,200 francs and a gold medal), being awarded the joint first prize among 78 entrants by a jury headed by Auber, Halévy, Scribe, and Gounod.

Doctor Miracle. The evil doctor (bass) in the Antonia episode of Offenbach's *Les Contes d'Hoffmann.*

Dodon. The King (bass) in Rimsky-Korsakov's *The Golden Cockerel.*

Dohnányi, Christoph von (*b* Berlin 8 Sept. 1929). German conductor. Studied Berlin, Munich, Tanglewood under Bernstein, and Tallahassee, Florida, with his grandfather Ernő von Dohnányi. Début Frankfurt 1965 *Die Entführung aus dem Serail*; Lübeck, music director, 1957-62; Kassel, 1962-4; Generalmusikdirektor, Frankfurt, 1968-76; Hamburg from 1976. Guest appearances Munich, Berlin, Salzburg. Conducted premières of Henze's *Der junge Lord* (1965) and *The Bassarids* (1966). Chicago, 1969 *Fliegende Holländer,* 1970 *Rosenkavalier;* N.Y., Met. 1972. (R)

Doktor Faust. Opera in 2 prologues, an interlude, and 3 scenes by Busoni (completed by Jarnach); text by composer after the Faust legend and Marlowe's treatment of it in *Dr Faustus* (1589), also the 18th-cent. German puppet play. Prod. Dresden 21 May 1925, with Seinemeyer, Strack, Burg, cond. Busch; broadcast concert perf. London, Q.H., 17 Mar. 1937, with Blyth, Joses, Noble, cond. Boult; N.Y., Carnegie Hall, 1 Dec. 1964, with Bjoner, Shirley, Fischer-Dieskau, cond. Horenstein (concert); prod. Reno, Nevada, 25 Jan. 1974. Faust (bar.) invokes the help of Mephistopheles (ten.) to help him regain his lost youth. Faust elopes with the Duchess of Parma (sop.) shortly after her marriage to the Duke (ten.). At an inn in Wittenberg, Faust hears of the Duchess's death, and he too longs to die. He meets a beggar woman, who turns out to be the Duchess, clasping the corpse of a child. Faust offers his own life if the child can be revived. As Faust dies, a young man rises from the body of the dead child.

Also opera by H. Reutter (*Dr Johannes Faust,* 1936). See also *Faust.*

Doktor und Apotheker. Singspiel in 2 acts by Dittersdorf; text by G. Stéphanie, after a French drama *L'Apothicaire de Murcie* by 'le Comte N. . .'. Prod. Vienna, B., 11 July. 1786. Adaptation by S. Storace, London, D.L., 25 Oct. 1788; this version also Charleston, City T., 26 Apr. 1796. Orig. version, N.Y., Terrace Garden, 30 June. 1875. Dittersdorf's most successful opera, often revived.

Domanínská (orig. Klobásková), **Libuše** (*b* Brno-Král, 4 July 1924). Czech soprano. Studied at Brno. Début Brno 1945, Blaženka (*The Secret*). Brno Opera 1945-55; Prague, N., since 1955. Vienna V. O., 1958, Abigaille, and guest appearances with the Prague Company; Moscow, Brussels, Holland, and Edinburgh Festivals as Jenůfa, Jitka in *Dalibor*. (R)

Domgraf-Fassbaender, Willi (*b* Aachen, 19 Feb. 1897; *d* Nuremberg, 13 Feb. 1978). German baritone. Studied Aachen, where his family had sent him to study church music; was heard by Erich Orthmann, conductor of the Aachen Opera, singing a solo part in a concert of church music and was immediately engaged for the local opera house, where he made his début in 1922. Further study Milan with Borgatti and Munich with Jacques Stückgold. After engagement in Berlin, Düsseldorf, and Stuttgart, became first lyric baritone at Berlin S. O. in 1928, where he remained until the end of the war. English début Gly., opening night of the first season, 1934, as Figaro; reappeared there in 1935 and 1937 as Figaro, Guglielmo, and Papageno. After the war sang in Hanover, Vienna, Munich, and Nuremberg, where he was *Oberspielleiter* 1953-62. From 1954 he taught at the Nuremberg Conservatory. Father of Brigitte *Fassbaender. (R)

Domingo, Placido (*b* Madrid, 21 Jan. 1941). Spanish tenor. Studied piano, conducting with Markevitch, and finally singing in Mexico. Début 1957 as baritone in Caballero's *zarzuela Gigantes y cabezudos*. First major role as tenor, Alfredo 1960. Israel National Opera 1962-5, singing more than 300 performances of 12 operas, most of them in Hebrew. N.Y. City Opera, 1966 in U.S. première of Ginastera's *Don Rodrigo*. N.Y., Met., since 1968; C.G. since 1971 Cavaradossi; 1973 Don José; 1974 Rodolfo, Dick Johnson, and Radamès. S.F., Vasco da Gama in *L'Africaine*, 1972; Paris, O., Arrigo in *Vêpres siciliennes*, 1974. Hamburg 1975, Otello. Conducted *Attila*, Barcelona 1973. The leading lyric-dramatic tenor since the death of Björling. (R)

Domino Noir, Le (The Black Domino). Opera in 3 acts by Auber; text by Scribe. Prod. Paris, O.C., 2 Dec. 1837, with Cinthie-Damoreau; London, C.G., 16 Feb. 1838; New Orleans Nov. 1839. Also opera by L. Rossi (1849).

Donalda (orig. Lightstone), **Pauline** (*b* Montreal, 5 Mar. 1882; *d* Montreal, 22 Oct. 1970). Canadian soprano. Studied Montreal and Paris with Duvernoy. Took the stage name from the 'Donaldas', the first women students allowed on the McGill Campus, named after Sir Donald Smith. Début Nice 1904, Manon. London, C.G., 1905, where she was sponsored by Melba, and thus sang there for several seasons, as Micaela, Zerlina, Gilda, Violetta, etc; created

Ah-Joe in Leoni's *L'Oracolo* (1905) and was the first London Concepción in *L'Heure espagnole*, (1919), delaying her retirement at Ravel's request for the purpose. Also sang N.Y., Manhattan Opera, 1906, and Paris. Married baritone Paul Seveilhac, and after his death the tenor Mischa Léon. After her retirement taught singing first in Paris 1922-37, and then in Montreal where she founded the Opera Guild of Montreal in 1942. Her pupils included the bass Joseph Rouleau. (R)
Bibl: C. Brotman: *Pauline Donalda* (1975).

Don Alfonso. The philosopher (bar.) who engineers the plot of Mozart's *Così fan tutte*.

Donauweibchen, Das (The Danube Sprite). Opera in 3 acts by Ferdinand Kauer; text (*Ein romantisches komisches Volksmärchen mit Gesang nach einer Sage der Vorzeit*) by K.F. Hensler. Prod. Vienna, L., 11 Jan. 1798. Kauer's most popular work, and one of the most popular of all operas in the first half of the 19th cent. all over Central and Eastern Europe. A second part followed, Vienna, L., 13 Feb. 1798, and a third, *Die Nymphe der Donau*, text by Berling; music by Bierey, Altona 25 July. 1801. Also a *Seitenstück, Das Waldweibchen*, by Kauer and Hensler, Vienna, L., 1 Apr. 1800.

Don Bartolo. The old doctor (bass) in Mozart's *Le nozze di Figaro* and, as Rosina's guardian, in Rossini's and Paisiello's *Il barbiere di Siviglia*.

Don Basilio. The priest and music-master (ten.) in Mozart's *Le nozze di Figaro* and (bass) in Paisiello's and Rossini's *Il barbiere di Siviglia*.

Don Carlos. Opera in 5 acts by Verdi; text by Méry and Du Locle after Schiller's drama (1787). Prod. Paris, O., 11 Mar. 1867, with Sass, Gueymard, Morère, Faure, Obin, cond. Hainl; London, C.G., 4 June 1867, with Lucca, Fricci, Naudin, Graziani, Petit, cond. Costa; N.Y., Ac. of M., 12 Apr. 1877, with Palmieri, Rastelli, Celada, Bertolasi, Dal Negro, cond. Maretzek. The 5-act version composed for Paris was revised by Verdi and Ghislanzoni for La Scala in 1884 (with Bruschi-Chiatti, Pasqua, Tamagno, Lhérie, Silvestri, cond. Faccio), dispensing with the Fontainebleau scene; this was restored in the 1887 version. Many other revisions and alterations have since been in currency.

Don Carlos (ten.), Infante of Spain, is betrothed to the beautiful Elisabeth de Valois (sop.). But to assure peace between France and Spain, she has to marry his father, King Philip (bass) instead. Carlos confides in his friend, Rodrigo, Marquis of Posa (bar.), who urges him to leave Spain and help bring peace to the Netherlands. Princess Eboli (mezzo), former mistress of the King and herself in love with Carlos, intrigues against him. The King, torn

137

between his human feelings and his duty to the Church as personified in the Grand Inquisitor (bass), orders Carlos's arrest as he meets Elisabeth for the last time. Carlos is saved from the Inquisition by the appearance of his Grandfather, Emperor Charles V (bass), who comes to lead Carlos to safety. Other operas on the subject are by Duplessis (1780), Deshayes (1799), Costa (1844), Bona (1847), Buzzolla (1850), De Ferrari (1854), Barthe (c 1860), and Moscuzza (1862).

Don Carlos di Vargas. Leonora's brother (bar.) in Verdi's *La forza del destino.*

Don Giovanni (orig. *Il dissoluto punito, ossia Il Don Giovanni*). *Dramma giocoso* in 2 acts by Mozart; text by Da Ponte, after the Don Juan legend and particularly after Bertati's libretto for Gazzaniga (1787). Prod. Prague, Nostic T., 29 Oct. 1787, with Saporiti, Micelli, Bondini, Baglioni, Bassi, Ponziani, cond. Mozart; London, Hm., 12 Apr. 1817, with Camporese, Hughes, Fodor, Naldi, Ambrogetti, Crivelli, cond. Weichsel; N.Y., Park T., 23 May 1826, in Da Ponte's presence, with four members of the Garcia family, Manuel sen. (Giovanni) and jun. (Leporello), Joaquina (Elvira), and Maria (Zerlina), cond. Étienne.

Leporello (bar.) is waiting by night outside the house of Donna Anna (sop.) whence his master Don Giovanni (bar.) emerges: Donna Anna tries to unmask her would-be seducer, and when her father the Commendatore (bass) draws a sword, Giovanni mortally wounds him before escaping. Anna and her lover Don Ottavio (ten.) swear vengeance on the unknown murderer. A former mistress of Giovanni's, Donna Elvira (sop.), interrupts a conversation between Giovanni and Leporello, but while he retails to her the list of his master's conquests, Giovanni again escapes. At the wedding of the peasants Masetto (bar.) and Zerlina (sop.), Giovanni's near-successful seduction of the bride is interrupted by Elvira; but Anna has recognized him as her attacker. She, Ottavio, and Elvira attend a party in Giovanni's palace, but when they unmask and accuse him, once more he eludes them. Giovanni now serenades Elvira's maid, having made Leporello lure Elvira away, and disguises himself as Leporello to evade a beating at the hands of the peasants. In the cemetery, Giovanni bids Leporello invite the statue of the Commendatore to supper: it accepts, and arrives to drag him down to Hell.
See also *Don Juan.*

Donizetti, Gaetano (*b* Bergamo, 29 Nov. 1797; *d* Bergamo, 8 Apr. 1848). Italian composer. Studied Bergamo with Salari, Gonzales, and J.S. Mayr, and Bologna with Pilotti and Padre Mattei. His student works include three unproduced operas. His parents opposed a musical

career, so he enlisted in the Austrian army; but he still found time for composition. His first success was *Enrico di Borgogna* (1818), with a text by his friend Merelli, which was produced at Venice, T.S.L. *Zoraide di Granata* (1822) was so successful that it procured him exemption from further military service. His early successful comedies, which include *L'aio nell'imbarazzo* (1824), *Oliva e Pasquale* (1827), and *Il giovedì grasso* (1828), belong to a world of Italian opera dominated by Rossini. With the next works, the influence of Rossini's French style is felt, but also that of Bellini: works of this period include *L'esule di Roma* (1828), *Alina, Regina di Golconda* (1828), *Il Paria* (1829), and *Elisabetta o Il castello di Kenilworth* (1829). Despite the growing influence of Verdi on his style, Donizetti found his mature voice with *Anna Bolena* (1830). *L'elisir d'amore* (1832) remains a classic of sentimental comedy, while *Torquato Tasso* (1833) and *Lucrezia Borgia* (1833) broke new ground as Romantic melodramas. *Lucia di Lammermoor* (1835), for all its familiarity as an example of Donizetti's style, is in fact uneven, including both original Romantic elements, and pages (some of them the most famous) of routine post-Rossini vocalization. Donizetti was always happy to write so as to give the best expression to the leading vocal talents of the day; hence the virtuosity of Fanny Tacchinardi-Persiani is reflected in parts of *Lucia,* while the dramatic gift of Pasta marks *Anna Bolena* and that of Ronzi di Begnis *Roberto Devereux,* the directness of Rosine Stoltz *La Favorite,* and the noble example of Ronconi, the writing for baritone in *Maria di Rohan* and *Maria Padilla.*

By the mid-1830s Donizetti was in full command of his dramatic gift, and though always willing to amend the content of his works to suit conditions, or to write to accommodate singers, he had begun to subordinate mere display to the needs of the drama. An example of this period is *Roberto Devereux* (1836). Commissions from Vienna and Paris encouraged him to develop his style to the needs of these new audiences. When in 1839 his *Poliuto* was forbidden by the Neapolitan censor, he went to Paris to produce the opera as *Les Martyrs* (1840): the work, characteristically, takes advantage of the resources of the O. without substantially altering its Italian nature. In the same year *Lucrezia Borgia* was withdrawn on the orders of Victor Hugo, who objected to Romani's adaptation of his tragedy. *La Fille du régiment* (1840) is another example of a work, Italian in essence, only lightly coloured with Gallicisms; *La Favorite* (1840), however, is a French Grand Opera, as is *Dom Sébastien* (1843). *Linda di Chamounix* (1842) manages by contrast to reconcile the Italian *semi-seria* genre with that of French *opéra comique.* With *Don Pasquale* (1843), the wit and subtlety which Donizetti had added to his idiom are returned to Italian opera with the greatest charm. Other works of his last years suggest further developments: *Maria Padilla* (1841) is much more freely composed, like the more strict and compact *Maria di Rohan* (1843) varying formal aria and recitative in a manner that virtually achieves continuous compositions.

A versatile and practical musician, Donizetti ranged widely in his subjects. Typical early works are comedies, his most typical later ones Romantic tragedies; and it was the latter genre that he regarded as his most important. Here, though always prone to relapse into triviality, he developed a gift for characterization and for dramatic momentum that can still be remarkably effective in the theatre. This was partly achieved by loosening the old firm divisions of recitative and aria, and interspersing arioso sections, perhaps varied with choral comments, that allow a much freer expressive range; yet even his most original moments could be followed by a trivial piece of uninspired soprano fireworks. Aware of the problem, he evolved the slow cabaletta, which allowed the singer more effective dramatic expression, with coloratura that was satisfying to the singer's vanity but more respectful of the audience's intelligence. Towards the latter part of his career, he also found ways of enriching his accompaniments (which can be negligible), and of chromatically inflecting his vocal lines subtly for expressive purposes without loss of tunefulness or singability. At the same time, he explored a richer vein of orchestration, and experimented with novel combinations of voices to vary the conventional ensemble patterns. In these matters, as in a good deal else, Donizetti is the most important direct forerunner of Verdi. The tunefulness of his 70 stage works, not to mention their superiority even at their most erratic over most contemporary operas, long ensured the survival of some; and since the 1950s, their championship by singers including Maria Callas, Leyla Gencer, Joan Sutherland, and Montserrat Caballé has helped to rediscover much excellent and long-forgotten music.
Bibl: W. Ashbrook: *Donizetti* (1965).

Don José. The hero (ten.) of Bizet's *Carmen*.

Don Juan. The legendary seducer and blasphemer, the essence of whose crime lies in his flouting of the conventions of man, by taking any woman for his pleasure, and of God, by mocking a dead man with the invitation of his statue to dinner. The tale was first set down in full dramatic form by Tirso de Molina (*El burlador de Sevilla y convidado de piedra*, 1630). Later developments of the legend assert not so much the punishment of a villain as the grandeur of a hero above the pettiness of society.

Operas on the legend are as follows. Melani (*L'empio punito,* 1669); Righini (1777); Calegari (1777); Tritto (1783); Albertini (1783); Gazzaniga (1787); Gardi (*Il nuovo convitato di pietra,* in hurried imitation of Gazzaniga, 1787); Fabrizi (1787); Reeve (1787); Mozart (1787); Paisiello (1790); Federici (1794, concocted by Da Ponte, music also by Gazzaniga, Sarti, and Guglielmi); Dibdin (music by many other hands also, 1817); Raimondi (1818); Carnicer (1822); Pacini (1832); D'Orgeval (*Don Juan de village,* 1863); Dargomyzhsky (1872); Manent (1875); Polignac (*Don Juan et Haidée,* 1877); Delibes (*Le Don Juan suisse,* 1880); Palmieri (1881); Vietinghoff-Scheel (1888); Linan and Videgain (1900); Helm (1911); Graener (*Don Juans letzte Abenteuer,* 1914); Benatzky (*Fräulein Don Juan,* 1915); Simon (1922); Lattuada (1929); Haug (1930); Casavola (1932); ColJet (*Le Fils de Don Juan,* 20th cent.); Malipiero (1963); Palester (1965); Taranu (1970); Slater (1972). A variant of the legend, *Don Juan de Mañara,* showing ultimate repentance, is derived from Prosper Merimée's story *Les Âmes du Purgatoire* (1834), based on the notorious Miguel de Mañara, who died in 1697; operas by Alfano (1914), Enna (1925), Goossens (1937), Tomasi (1956).

Don Magnifico. Cenerentola's father (bass) in Rossini's *Cenerentola.*

Donna Anna. The daughter (sop.) of the Commendatore and Don Ottavio's lover in Mozart's *Don Giovanni.*

Donna del lago, La (The Lady of the Lake). Opera in 2 acts by Rossini; text by Tottola, after Walter Scott's poem (1810). Prod. Naples, S.C., 24 Sept. 1819, with Pisaroni, Colbran, Davide; London, Hm., 18 Feb. 1823, with De Begnis, De Vestris, Curioni; N.Y. 26 Aug. 1829, with C. and R. Fanti, Ravaglia, Bordogni, Fabj, de Rosa. Revived Florence 1958. James V of Scotland – Giacomo in the opera (ten.) – loses his way and seeks shelter in the house of his enemy Douglas (bass), whose daughter Elena (sop.) has been forced to marry Roderick Dhu (ten.). In an uprising against the King, Roderick is killed, and Elena pleads with the King for her father's life and obtains his permission to marry her lover Malcolm (mezzo).

Donna Diana. Opera in 3 acts by Rezniček; text by composer, after Moreto's comedy *El Lindo Don Diego* (1654). Prod. Prague, 16 Dec. 1894.

Donna Elvira. A lady (sop.) of Burgos deserted by Don Giovanni in Mozart's opera.

Donna non vidi mai. Des Grieux's (ten.) aria in Act 1 of *Manon Lescaut,* in which he gives voice to his feelings as he sets eyes on Manon for the first time.

Donne Curiose, Le (The Inquisitive Women). Opera in 3 acts by Wolf-Ferrari; text by Luigi

Sugona after Goldoni's play of the same name. Prod. Munich, N. 27 Nov. 1903 in a German translation by H. Teibler as *Die neugierigen Frauen*, with Bosetti, Tordek, Breuer, Huhn, Koppe, Brodersen, Sieglitz, Bender, cond. Reichenberger; N.Y. Met., (first perf. in Italian) 3 Jan. 1912 with Alten, Farrar, Fornia, Mauborg, Jadlowker, de Segurola, Pini-Corsi, Didur, cond. Toscanini; first perf. in Italy Milan, Sc., 16 Jan. 1913 with Ferraris, Villani, Lollini, Solari, Navia, Govoni, Vannuccini, cond. Serafin. Set in 18th-century Venice, it tells of the suspicions of two married women and their friend, who believe that their husbands and lover are indulging in regular orgies at their men's club; they manage to gain admission to the club and discover that all their menfolk are doing is indulging in gourmet meals.

Don Ottavio. Donna Anna's lover (ten.) in Mozart's *Don Giovanni*.

Don Pasquale. *Opera buffa* in 3 acts by Donizetti; text by Ruffini and the composer after Anelli's libretto for Pavesi's *Ser Marc' Antonio* (1810). Prod. Paris, T.I., 3 Jan. 1843 with Grisi, Mario, Tamburini, Lablache; London, H.M.'s, 29 June 1843 with same cast but Fornasari replacing Tamburini; New Orleans, 7 Jan. 1845.

Don Pasquale (bass), a rich and crusty old bachelor, has decided to marry so that his nephew Ernesto (ten.) will not inherit his fortune as he disapproves of his choice of a bride, the attractive young widow Norina (sop.). The young couple, helped by Doctor Malatesta (bar.), a friend of them both as well as of Pasquale, arrange for the old man to go through a mock marriage with 'Sofronia', Norina in disguise, who is presented as Malatesta's sister, fresh from a convent. No sooner is the wedding ceremony over, than Sofronia reveals herself in her true colours and makes the old man's life a misery. Malatesta suggests that the marriage be annulled; Pasquale agrees and, admitting he has been fooled, forgives them all.

Don Quixote. See *Cervantes*.

Don Rodrigo. Opera in 3 acts by Ginastera; text by Alejandro Casona. Commissioned and prod. Buenos Aires, T. Colón, 24 July 1964 with Bandin, Cossutta, Mattiello, De Nanké, cond. Bartoletti; N.Y. State T. 22 Feb. 1966 to mark opening of City Opera's new home at the State T., Lincoln Centre, with Crader, Domingo, Clatworthy, Malas, cond. Rudel. The opera tells of the brief reign of Don Rodrigo, the last Visigoth King of Spain, whose defeat at the battle of Guadalete led to the fall of Spain to the Saracens.

Donzelli, Domenico (*b* Bergamo, 2 Feb. 1790; *d* Bologna, 31 Mar. 1873). Italian tenor. Studied Bergamo. Début there 1808 as comprimario in

Mayr's *Elisa*; further study Naples with Viga noni and Crivelli, where he sang with succes in Paisiello's *Nina pazza per amore* in 180! Rome from 1816. London, Hm., 1829. Cor tinued to sing in Italy and Vienna until 184 Rossini wrote a role for him in *Torvaldo e Do liska* (1815), and Mercadante in *Elisa e Claudi* Created Pollione at Sc. 1831, and was its firs interpreter in London. His voice was said t have been of baritone-like quality and som what limited in range; but he was praised fo his dramatic gifts.

Dorabella. Fiordiligi's sister (sop.) in Mozart' *Così fan tutte*.

Dorfbarbier, Der (The Village Barber). Opera i 1 act by Schenk; text by J. and P. Weidman produced as comedy 1785. Prod. Vienna, B., 3 Oct. 1796; N.Y. 15 Dec. 1847. Schenk's mos popular work, seen on virtually every Germa stage; 203 performances in 1816.

Dorn, Heinrich (*b* Königsberg, 14 Nov. 1804; Berlin, 10 Jan. 1892). German conductor an composer. A friend of many eminent mus cians in his day, he was an enemy of Wagne whom he anticipated by composing an oper *Die Nibelungen* in 1854 (to a text rejected b Mendelssohn). He was much admired as a cor ductor and teacher, especially in Königsber (1828), Leipzig (1829-32), Riga (1832-43), an Berlin (1849-69).

Dorset Garden Theatre. One of London's ea liest homes for music and drama. Erected b the widow of Sir William Davenant on plans b Wren and opened 1671, also known as th Duke's, later the Queen's. Demolished 170! Several of Purcell's works had first perfo mances there, including *King Arthur* (1691 *The Fairy Queen* (1692), and *The Indian Quee* (1695).

Dortmund. Town in N. Westphalia, German First theatre opened in 1837. Stadttheater (ca 1,200) opened in 1904 with *Tannhäuse* destroyed in 1943. During the inter-war yea the company included Teschemacher an Schmidt-Walter; Georg Hartmann wa administrator 1933-7. A new theatre (ca 1,130) opened in 1966 with *Der Rosenkavalie* Wilhelm Scheuchter was music director 196: 75; Marek Janowski 1975-9. Première have included Gurlitt's *Nana* (1958), Steffen *Eli* (1957), and the first German performance o Pizzetti's *Ifigenia* (1952). The company visite Leeds 1978.

Dorus-Gras, Julie (Aimée-Josèphe van Stee kiste) (*b* Valenciennes, 9 Sept. 1805; *d* Paris Feb. 1896). Belgian soprano. Studied Par Conservatoire with Henri and Blangini, an subsequently Paer and Bordogni. Début Bru sels 1826; Paris 1830 (début Adèle in *Le Com Ory*) where she succeeded Cinthie-Damorea prima donna in 1835. London 1839 (concerts), 1847, D.L., Lucia, which she sang in English, although not knowing the language; 1849, C.G., when she sang two of the roles she had created, Alice (*Robert le Diable*) and Marguerite de Valois. Also a famous Elvira (*Muette de Portici*), and sang that role in the performance of the opera in Brussels, Sept. 1830, which touched off the revolt of the Low Countries.

Osifey (Dositheus). The leader (bass) of the Old Believers in Mussorgsky's *Khovanshchina*.

Ostoyevsky, Fyodor (*b* Moscow, 30 Oct. 1821; St Petersburg, 28 Jan. 1881). Russian writer. Operas on his works are as follows:

Christ, the Boy, and the Christmas Tree (1848): Rebikov (*Yolka*, 1903).
White Nights (1848): Tsvetayev (1933); Cortese (1970); J. Buzko (1973).
From the House of the Dead (1862): Janáček (1930).
The Gambler (1866): Prokofiev (1929).
Crime and Punishment (1866): Pedrollo (1926); Sutermeister (*Raskolnikoff*, 1948); Mortimer (1967); Petrovics (1969).
The Idiot (1869): Bogdanov-Berezovsky (*Nastasya Filipovna*, 1968); L. Chailly (1970); J. Eaton (*Myshkin*, 1973).
The Brothers Karamazov (1880): Jeremiáš (1928); Ruyneman (1928); Blacher (*Der Grossinquisitor*, 1948).
Uncle's Dream (1859): H. Krasa (*Verlobung im Traum*, 1933).
The Crocodile: T. Wagner (1963).

Dotazione (*It* endowment). The term formerly used for the repertory of sets maintained by small theatres unable to afford new, specially designed sets for each production. Economic necessity has latterly brought about the practice of sharing sets even between major opera houses.

Dove sono. The Countess's (sop.) aria in Act 3 of Mozart's *Le nozze di Figaro*, mourning the loss of her husband's love.

Downes, Edward (Thomas) (*b* Birmingham, 17 June 1926). British conductor. Studied Birmingham, London, R.A.M., and privately with Hermann Scherchen. Originally a horn-player. Joined C.R. as a répétiteur 1951, and in the same position joined C.G. 1952, working with Kleiber, Kubelík, Kempe. Conducted C.G. company in Bulawayo 1953, and new productions of *Der Freischütz* and *Hoffmann* in 1953 and 1954. Conducted first British *Katerina Izmaylova* (1963), *Hamlet* (Searle, 1969), *The Bassarids* (B.B.C.), and premières of Bennett's *Victory* (1970) and Maxwell Davies's *Taverner* (1972). Music director Australian Opera 1972-6. Translated *Jenůfa, Katerina Izmaylova, Khovanshchina*, and *War and Peace*. As much

at home in Wagner as in Verdi and the Russian repertory. Has a fine knowledge of the voice and is uncompromising in his artistic attitudes. (R)

Down in the Valley. Folk opera by Kurt Weill; text by Arnold Sundgaard. Prod. Bloomington, 15 July 1948, with Bell, Aiken, Welsh, Campbell, Carpenter, Jones; Bristol, 23 Oct. 1957. In a series of flashbacks, the opera tells the story of a young couple, Brack Weaver and Jennie Parsons. Brack is awaiting execution for the killing, in self-defence, of Thomas Bouche, an unpleasant rival for Jennie's affections.

D'Oyly Carte, Richard. See *Carte*.

Dramaturg. The member of the staff of a German opera house who combines the duties of adapter of librettos, editor of programmes, and press officer, sometimes also producer and even actor.

Drame forain (*Fr* fair drama). The comedies staged at the Paris fairs in the 18th cent., known as *drames forains*, are an ancestor of **opéra comique*. Various companies played at the Foire Saint-Germain (Feb.-Apr.) and the Foire Saint-Laurent (Aug.-Sept.), giving light, irreverent, satirical comedies, often mocking the Opéra and Opéra-Comique, and nimbly evading all attempts at banning them. They used music and songs, though only incidentally, and the singing was by the actors rather than by professional singers; but the success of these highly popular pieces was such as to attract some very skilled writers. One of these was René Lesage (1668-1747), author among much else of the novel *Gil Blas*, who gave the form of these musical comedies a new control. Charles-Simon **Favart began his career writing for the fairs. From the *drame forain* he developed the **comédie mêlée d'ariettes*, and so advanced the development of *opéra-comique*.

Drame lyrique. A contemporary French term for a serious opera.

Dramma giocoso. An Italian term, current chiefly in the late 18th cent., for a comic opera which could include serious episodes: the most famous instance is Mozart's *Don Giovanni*.

Dramma per musica. An Italian term, current in the 17th and 18th cent., for a libretto destined for music, hence also the resulting opera, always serious.

Dreigroschenoper, Die (The Threepenny Opera). Opera in a prologue and 8 scenes by Weill; text a modern interpretation of *The *Beggar's Opera*, based on a translation by Hauptmann, with lyrics, drawn also from Kipling and Villon, by Brecht. Prod. Berlin, T. am Schiffbauerdamm, 28 Aug. 1928, with

Bahn, Lenja, Pausen, Gerron, Valetti, Ponto, Busch; N.Y., Empire T., 13 Apr. 1933; London, Royal Court T., 9 Feb. 1956, with D. Anderson, cond. Goldschmidt. The outline of the plot is very close to that of the work's original; it is set in Soho at the beginning of the 20th cent. and Macheath becomes Mack the Knife.

Drei Pintos, Die (The Three Pintos). Opera begun by Weber, but abandoned in 1821 in favour of *Euryanthe*; text by Theodor Hell, after Seidel's story *Der Brautkampf* (1819). Completed and scored by Mahler, with additions, using other music by Weber and with an interlude composed on themes in the opera by Mahler. Prod. Leipzig, 20 Jan. 1888, with Banmann, Artner, Rothhauser, Hedmont, Hübner, Grengg, Schelper, Köhler, Proft, cond. Mahler; London, John Lewis T., 10 Apr. 1962, with Tinsley, Brandt, Maurel. cond. Lloyd-Jones.

Don Pinto (bass) is intercepted by Don Gaston (ten.) on his way to Seville to marry Clarissa (sop.). Gaston, with the help of his servant Ambrosio (bar.), first tries to teach the inane Pinto the art of wooing and then makes him drunk. Taking his papers off him, thus becoming Pinto No. 2, Gaston sets off for Seville; but when he finds that Clarissa is secretly in love with Gomez (ten.), but cannot marry him, he passes on the Pinto papers: Gomez thus becomes the third Pinto. Eventually the real Don Pinto turns up and discloses himself to Clarissa's furious father Don Pantaleone (bar.); but all ends happily. The original scenario ordered events rather differently, and was arranged in its present form by Mahler and Carl von Weber, the composer's grandson.

Dresden. Town in Saxony, Germany. In 1617 Schütz reorganized the Kapelle on Italian models, and his *Dafne,* the earliest German opera, was produced for a Royal wedding nearby at Torgau in 1627 (with Rinuccini's text translated by Opitz; music lost). After the Thirty Years' War he was replaced by Bontempi and Albrici, and the line of opera that began with the opening of the Kurfürstliche Opernhaus in 1667 with Moniglia's *Teseo* was Italian. In 1707 this theatre was converted by Friedrich August into the Hofkirche, and performances were given in the Riesensaal of the Castle; he opened an enlarged Grosses Opernhaus in 1719. Under Friedrich August II, Hasse and his wife Faustina Bordoni worked there, under difficulties due to rivalry from the Italians. The opera house was altered by Galli-Bibiena in 1750. In 1755 Pietro Mingotti completed the Komödienhaus (Kleine Hoftheater), which lasted until 1841, and Angelo Mingotti opened a small wooden theatre in the court of the Zwinger for more popular types of opera (burnt down, 1748). Three Dresdeners, Naumann, Schuster, and Seidelmann, visited Italy on a grant in 1765, and Naumann in particular did

much on his return to influence taste in German direction. But the most popular an established form with the Court and nobili was Italian, and companies under Locatell Moretti, and Bustelli made successful visits. A an economy measure, Friedrich August wa obliged to open his opera house to the publi and this set a wider fashion for Italian oper though Singspiel remained popular: from 177 works by Hiller, Benda, Schweitzer, and othe were given by J.C. Wäser. Joseph Second opened his theatre on the Linckesche Bad i 1790, and E.T.A. Hoffmann was director of th company run by the Seconda brothers i Leipzig and Dresden in 1813-14.

In 1817 Weber was appointed as Roya German Kapellmeister; Francesco Morlacc was in charge of the Italian opera 1810-4 Weber instituted searching reforms in the sty of opera presentation, marking a crucial shi towards the concept of music drama. He wa succeeded by Reissiger in 1827. The ne Semper Opernhaus was opened in 1841. Aft the triumph of *Rienzi* in Dresden in 184 Wagner succeeded Morlacchi as Hofkapel meister; here his *Fliegende Holländer* (184: and *Tannhäuser* (1845) were produce Wagner had to leave after his part in the 184 revolution. In 1869 the opera house bur down; rebuilt on Semper's plans, it re-opene in 1878. Ernst von Schuch was conductor fro 1882, artistic director 1889-1914. During h time the company included Malten, Schuc Proska, Sembrich, Schumann-Heink, Buria Scheidemantel, later Siems, Von der Oste Perron, and Plaschke; premières include Strauss's *Feuersnot* (1901), *Salome* (1905 *Elektra* (1909), and *Rosenkavalier* (1911 Schuch was succeeded by Fritz Reiner. In 191 the theatre became the Staatsoper. Fritz Busc was appointed in 1922: his régime saw th performance of further Strauss operas, an Hindemith's *Cardillac* (1926), and the begi ning of the German Verdi revival with *Macbe* and *La forza del destino.* In 1933 Busch left an was succeeded by Karl Böhm 1934-43, and Ka Elmendorff 1943-5: further Strauss works ar Sutermeister's *Romeo und Julia* were pr mièred. Between the wars the compar included Seinemeyer, Cebotari, Rethber Höngen, Goltz, Ralf, Tauber, Pattiera Loren Schoeffler, Boehme, and Frick.

On 13 Feb. 1945, the theatre was gutte during the bombing of Dresden. The compar was housed in the town hall, 1945-8, under th direction of Joseph Keilberth. In 1948 it mov to the rebuilt Schauspielhaus (cap. 1,13 Rudolf Kempe was music director 1950 Franz Konwitschny 1953-5, Lovro von Matač 1956-8, Otmar Suitner 1960-4. Fred Larondel is Generalintendant, Horst Seeger Director Opera, Harry Kupfer Chief Producer. In Ju 1976 plans were announced for a new ope ouse to be built 1977-82, a complete reconstruction of the Semper theatre. It is intended to include a large number of technical sophistications, and to seat 1,310.

Bibl: H. Schnoor: *400 Jahre Deutsche Musik-kultur: Geschichte der Dresdener Hofkapelle* (1948).

Drottningholm Castle Theatre, Sweden. Built in 1764-6 by Carl Frederick Adelcrantz, it succeeded the first theatre built by Queen Louisa Ulrica, sister of Frederick the Great, in 1754 and destroyed by fire in 1762. The theatre saw much activity between 1777 and 1792 under Gustavus Adolphus III. It was rarely used from 1800 till 1922, when it was restored at the instigation of Agne Beiger, who worked in the Royal Library and accidentally discovered the original 18th-century scenery and stage machinery. Occasional performances were given by the Stockholm Opera. Since 1948 regular summer seasons of opera with works by Cimarosa, Handel, Gluck, Mozart, Haydn, Paisiello, etc. are given in the manner of the 18th century, with the orchestra in powdered wigs and satin coats. The English Opera Group was performed there in 1970 and 1971; and the Drottningholm productions of *Orfeo* and *Così in tutte* were seen at the 1972 Brighton Festival. Charles Farncombe has been music director since 1969.

Drury Lane, Theatre Royal. There have been our Drury Lane theatres on the same site. Although they have primarily been the home of drama and more recently of musicals, Drury Lane has been the scene of several important operatic seasons. The second theatre, opened in 1674, was designed by Wren; it saw the premières of several of Dryden's plays and masques for which Purcell wrote the music, and also the production of many ballad operas; Arne, Dibdin, Linley, and Storace were all connected with this theatre at various periods. The third D.L. (1794-1809) had Bishop as its music director (1806-9). The fourth and present theatre opened in Oct. 1812. Tom Cooke was the principal tenor from 1813 to 1835 and became music director in 1821. Alfred Bunn took over in 1831 and presented Malibran in *Fidelio, Sonnambula,* and other operas, which she sang in English. From 1835 to 1847 Bunn tried to establish English Opera on a permanent basis, and works by Balfe, Benedict, and Wallace were produced in rapid succession. In the mid-1850s seasons of English and Italian opera were given under the auspices of E.T. Smith, including the first performances in England of *Vêpres siciliennes* (in Italian). From 1867-77 the theatre became the home of Mapleson's Her Majesty's Opera, and it was here that the first performance in England of a Wagner opera was given, *Der fliegende Holländer* (or *L'Olandese dannato*), in July 1870.

In 1882 Richter and a German company gave a series of performances including the first in London of *Tristan* and *Meistersinger,* and from 1883 for a number of years Drury Lane was the scene of the London seasons of the Carl Rosa. In 1887 Augustus Harris started his Italian opera revival there, transferring the following year to Covent Garden; and in 1892 and 1893 he used Drury Lane for extra performances of German opera. From 1894 to 1913 there were some English seasons. In 1913 and 1914 Sir Joseph Beecham's Russian seasons had their home there (see Diaghilev). These included first performances in England of *Boris Godunov, Khovanshchina, Prince Igor, Ivan the Terrible, May Night, The Golden Cockerel,* and *The Nightingale.* During the First World War Beecham's English Company gave some of their London seasons there; but it was not until 1958 that opera was heard there again, when S.A. Gorlinsky gave a two months' season of Italian opera, including *William Tell,* which had had its first English performance there in 1830.

Dublin. Capital of Eire. Opera was first heard there in 1705-6 at the Smock Alley T. when D. Purcell's *The Island Princess* was produced. The oft-repeated accounts of Niccolini's appearances in *Rinaldo* in 1711 have been disproved in T.J. Walsh's *Opera in Dublin, 1705-1797* (1973). Italian opera was first given in 1761 by a company under the direction of Antonio Minelli that included the *De Amicis family and Zingoni: the first work given was Scolari's *La cascina* (19 Dec. 1761). After seven years of English Opera (1770-7), Italian opera returned to Dublin in the Fishamble Street T., and again on Smock Alley, where works by Paisiello, Anfossi etc. were performed. In 1784 Gluck's *Orfeo* (in English) had its first Dublin performance, with Mrs Billington as Eurydice; she was to appear there regularly for the next 13 years. Many of the performances were described by Michael *Kelly who, with Mrs Crouch, appeared in many operas in 1780s. In the 19th cent. the T. Royal was the scene of several outstanding seasons with artists who were heard regularly at the Italian Opera houses in London including Persiani, Grisi, Rubini, Mario, and Pauline Viardot, who sang Lady Macbeth in Verdi's opera in its only production in the British Isles before 1938. In 1871 the Gaiety T. was opened, and was the home of the Dublin seasons given by the Blanche Cole, Carl Rosa, Mapleson, Augustus Harris, O'Mara, and other touring companies, and from 1928 to 1938 the Irish Opera Society presented opera at the Gaiety T. In 1941 the Dublin Grand Opera Society was formed, and has given two seasons each year. The orchestra is that of Radio Eireann, and the chorus is made up of locals; but soloists from England and the Continent are regularly engaged; and occasionally whole foreign ensembles from Paris, Hamburg, Munich, and many artists from Eastern Europe. In addition to the more popular works in the repertory, Dublin has heard in recent years *La Favorite*, *Don Carlos, Simone Boccanegra, La Gioconda, The Queen of Spades, Pelléas et Mélisande, Cecilia* (Refice), and *Adriana Lecouvreur*.

Bibl: T. Walsh: *Opera in Dublin, 1705-1797* (1973); T. Walsh: *Opera in Old Dublin, 1819-1838* (1952).

Dubrovnik (It. Ragusa). Town in Dalmatia, Yugoslavia. Since the Second World War it has staged spectacular operatic performances in the open air as part of the annual summer festival.

Duca d'Alba II (The Duke of Alba). Opera in 4 acts by Donizetti; text by Scribe. Originally written for Paris, O., in 1840 but not produced; the libretto was later altered by Scribe and became the text of *Les Vêpres siciliennes*. Donizetti's score was recovered at Bergamo in 1875 and completed by Matteo Salvi, prod. Rome, T. Apollo, 22 Mar. 1882 with Bruschi-Chiatti, Gayarré, Paroli, L. Giraldoni, Silvestri, cond. M. Mancinelli: revived Spoleto 1959, in a production by Visconti when the original scenery was reproduced, with Tosini, Cioni, Quilico, Ganzarolli, cond. Schippers; N.Y., Town Hall, 20 Oct. 1959.

In this complicated story about the oppressed Flemings suffering under Spanish tyranny, Amelia (sop.), daughter of Egmont, is in love with Marcello (ten.), who is revealed to be the missing son of the Duke of Alba (bar.). Amelia, in an attempt to murder the Duke, instead kills Marcello, who has intervened to save his father's life. As he dies he begs the Duke to forgive Amelia.

Also opera by Pacini (1842).

Due Foscari, I (The Two Foscari). Opera in 3 acts by Verdi; text by Piave, after Byron's drama, *The Two Foscari* (1821). Prod. Rome, Arg., 3 Nov. 1844, with Barbieri-Nini, Ricci, Roppa, Bassini, Pozzolini, Mirri; London, H.M.'s, 10 Apr. 1847, with Montenegro, Fraschini, and Coletti; Boston 10 May 1847, with Rainieri, Perelli, Vila, Battaglini.

Jacopo Foscari (ten.), son of the Doge of Venice (bar.), is unjustly condemned to exile in Crete. Although the Doge knows him to be innocent and despite pleas from Jacopo's wife, Lucrezia (sop.), the Doge upholds the verdict of the Council of Ten. Jacopo dies of a broken heart and the Doge resigns his office. Also opera *I Foscari* by Zenger (1863).

Due litiganti, I (The Two Litigants). Correctly, *Fra due litiganti il terzo gode.* Opera in 3 acts by Sarti; text an altered version of Goldoni's *Le nozze.* Prod. Milan, Sc., 14 Sept. 1782; London, King's T., 6 Jan. 1784 (as *I rivali delusi*). In its

day immensely popular; Mozart not only used the aria 'Come un agnello' for a set of piano variations (K460), but quoted it, with certainty of recognition, in Don Giovanni's supper scene as the wind band's second piece – whereupon Leporello exclaims, 'Evvivano *I litiganti!*' Also opera by Pescetti (1749), Astaritta (1766).

Duenna, The; or The Double Elopement. (1) Opera in 3 acts composed and compiled by Thomas Linley, sen. and jun.; text by Sheridan Prod. London, C.G., 21 Nov. 1775; N.Y. 10 July 1786. One of the most successful English comic operas of the 18th cent., surpassing even *The Beggar's Opera* on its first run (75 performances as against 63).

(2) Opera in 4 acts by Prokofiev (sometimes known, from the translation of Prokofiev's Russian title, as *Betrothal in a Monastery*); text by Prokofiev with verses by Mira Mendelssohn after Sheridan. Prod. Leningrad, K., 3 Nov. 1946, with Ulyanov, Solomyak, Khalileyeva, Velter, Bugayev, Grudina, Freidkof, Orlov cond. Khaykin; N.Y., Greenwich Mews Playhouse, 1 June 1948 (pf duet acc. only) London, B.B.C. (Russian perf.), 1963.

(3) Opera in 3 acts by Roberto Gerhard; text by composer, after Sheridan. Wiesbaden (concert), 27 June. 1951.

Duet. A composition for two performers, with or without accompaniment, in which the interest is equally shared. The *duetto da camera* (chamber duet) for two voices was a popular form from about the late 17th cent. and from about the mid 18th cent. it became an important ingredient of opera, the love duet being its most familiar manifestation.

Dufranne, Hector (Robert) (*b* Mons, 25 Oct 1870; *d* Paris, 4 May 1951). Belgian bass baritone. Studied Brussels. Début Brussels, L. M., 1896, Valentine. Paris, O.C., 1899-1909 where he created Marquis de Saluces in Massenet's *Grisélidis* (1901), Golaud in *Pelléas* (1902), Amaury-Ganelon in Rabaud's *La Fille de Roland* (1904), title-role in Leroux' *Chemineau* (1907). Paris, O., from 1909 when he sang Jochanaan in the first Paris *Salome* (1910). N.Y., Manhattan Opera, 1908-10 first U.S. Golaud, Prior in *Le Jongleur de Notre Dame*, Coudal in *Sapho* (1910), Marquis in *Grisélidis* (1910); Chicago, 1910-22, where he created the Magician in *The Love of the Three Oranges* (1922). Sang title-role in Falla's *El retablo de Maese Pedro* in Princess de Polignac' private theatre in Paris, 1923. London, C.G. 1914, Golaud. Continued to sing until 1939. (R)

Dugazon (orig. Lefèvre), **Louise** (Rosalie) (*b* Berlin, 18 June 1755; *d* Paris, 22 Sept. 1821) French mezzo-soprano. Her father was dancer at the Opéra and she and her sister began their professional careers as dancers Persuaded by Grétry to study singing, she was accepted as a pupil by Favart. Grétry composed an air for her to sing in his *Lucille* (1769), but her adult début was as Pauline in Grétry's *Sylvain* (1774). In 1776 she married the actor and writer Jean Baptiste Henri Gourgault, known as Dugazon; and as Mme Dugazon she continued to sing until 1804, creating more than 60 roles at the Comédie Italienne, and later the Opéra-Comique, especially in operas by Grétry, Dalayrac, Isouard, and Boieldieu. After a voluntary exile during the Revolution, she returned to the stage in 1795. She made her farewell in 1804, when she sang Zemaide in *Le Calife de Bagdad* in the presence of Napoleon and Josephine. Her most famous role was as Dalayrac's Nina. She inspired a volume of laudatory odes as well as a host of paintings, and caused the genres in which she excelled to be known as 'jeunes Dugazons', and 'mères Dugazons'.

Her son **Gustave** (1782-1826) composed 5 opéras-comiques, 3 ballets, and an anthology of arias by Rossini.

Bibl: A. Pougin: *Figures d'Opéra-Comique* 1875); H. & A. Leroux: *La Dugazon* (1926); J. J. Olivier: *Mme Dugazon de la Comédie-Italienne, 1755-1821* (1917).

Dukas, Paul (*b* Paris, 1 Oct. 1865; *d* Paris, 17 May 1935). French composer. Dukas's only opera, *Ariane et Barbe-Bleue* (1907), is also his most ambitious and remarkable work. The first major opera to be influenced by *Pelléas et Mélisande*, it differs in its broader structural scheme, its scope for more elaborate musical development, its more brilliant scoring, and its simpler emotional appeal; some qualities of *Pelléas* are thus present but dispersed into a more conventional kind of opera. It was one of the first works to find more than Grand Guignol in the legend, and suggests, through Maeterlinck's text, that women prefer even the harshest marriage to lack of security. Dukas also helped Saint-Saëns to complete Guiraud's *Frédégonde*, and edited several of Rameau's operas.

Bibl: G. Favre: *Paul Dukas* (1948).

Duke Bluebeard's Castle (Hung., *A kékszakállú herceg vára*). Opera in 1 act by Bartók; text by Béla Balázs. Prod. Budapest, 24 May 1918, with Haselbeck, Kalman, cond. Tango; N.Y., C.C., 2 Oct. 1952, with Ayars, Pease, cond. Rosenstock; London, Rudolf Steiner T., 16 Jan. 1957, by Cape Town University Opera Club, with Desirée Talbot, Gregorio Fiasconaro, cond. Chisholm.

Bluebeard (bass) is not the Gilles de Rais monster of the *Ma Mère l'Oye* fairy-tale, but a sorrowing, idealistic man who takes Judith (sop.), his newest bride, home to his murky castle. She makes him unlock his secret doors one by one and when she has penetrated his innermost secret she takes her place, another

failure, among the other wives behind the last door, leaving Bluebeard in his loneliness.

Duke of Mantua, The. The licentious duke (ten.) who pursues Gilda in Verdi's *Rigoletto*.

Dulcamara. The quack (bass) in Donizetti's *L'elisir d'amore*.

Du Locle, Camille (*b* Orange, 16 July 1832; *d* Capri, 9 Oct. 1903). French librettist. His first libretto was for Duprato's *M'sieu Landry* (1856). In 1869 he was joint director of the Paris O. 1870-4 of the O.C., with Leuven, 1874-6 sole director. He is particularly notable for his work for Verdi. He continued the text of *Don Carlos* after Méry's death, and made a preliminary draft of *Aida* with Verdi before it was passed to Ghislanzoni; he also translated *Simon Boccanegra*, *La forza del destino* (with Nuittier), and the first two acts of *Otello*. His other librettos include that for Reyer's *Sigurd*, and *Salammbô*. Though a keen innovator, who encouraged Bizet in many ways, he was not a man of great dramatic gifts.

Dumas, Alexandre (1) (père) (*b* Villers-Cotterets, 24 July 1802; *d* Dieppe, 5 Dec. 1870). French writer. Operas on his works are as follows:
Henri III (1829): Flotow (*Le Comte de St Mégrin*, 1838, rev. as *La Duchesse de Guise*, 1840); Josse (*La Lega*, 1876); Hillemacher (1886).
Charles VII chez ses grands vassaux (1831): Donizetti (*Gemma di Vergy*, 1834); Cui (*The Saracen*, 1899).
Don Juan de Marana (1836): Enna (1925).
Kean (1836): Sangiorgi (1855).
Mademoiselle de Belle-Isle (1839): Samara (1905).
Othon l'Archer (1840): Reiss (1856); Minchejmer (*Otton Łucznik*, 1864).
Pasqual Bruno (1840): Hatton (1844).
Ascanio (1843): Saint-Saëns (1890).
Les Demoiselles de St Cyr (1843): Dellinger (1891); Humperdinck (*Heirat wider Willen*, 1905).
Les Trois mousquetaires (1844): Visetti (1871); Xyndas (1885); Dionesi (1888); Somerville (1899); De Lara (1921); Benatzky (1931).
Le Comte de Monte Cristo (1844): Dell'Aquila (1876); Caryll and others (1886).
Les Frères corses (1845): Fox (1888).
La Dame de Monsoreau (1846): Salvayre (1888).
Joseph Balsamo (1848): Litolff (*La Mandragore*, 1876).
Le Tulipe noir (1850): Flotow (*Il fiore di Harlem*, 1876).
Le Chevalier d'Harmental (1853): Messager (1896).
Also *Gloria Arsena* (Enna, 1917).
Also wrote *Piquillo*, opéra-comique, with Gérard de Nerval, music by Mompou, prod. O.C., 1837.

Dumas, Alexandre (2) (fils) (*b* Paris, 28 July 1824; *d* Paris, 27 Nov. 1895). French writer, son of above. Operas on his works are as follows: *La Dame aux Camélias* (1848): Verdi (*La traviata*, 1853); H. Forrest (*Camille*, 1930). *La Femme de Claude* (1873): Cahen (1896).

Duni, Egidio Romualdo (*b* Matera, 9 Feb. 1709; *d* Paris, 11 June 1775). Italian composer. After some travels, success in Italy with a French opera *Ninette à la cour* (1755) brought him to Paris, where he rapidly became one of the principal *opéra comique* composers of his day. In 1756 he wrote two Goldoni operas, *La Caseina* for Venice, and *La buona figliuola* for Parma. In Paris he had further success with *Le Peintre amoureux* (1757), and with a succession of 18 other works he established himself as one of the most popular composers of the day and a founder of *opéra comique*. His greatest successes include *La Fille mal gardée* (1758), *Nina et Lindor* (1758), *L'Isle des foux* (1760), *Les Deux chasseurs* (1763), *La Fée Urgèle* (1765), *La Clochette* (1766), *Les Moissonneurs* (1768), and *Les Sabots* (1768). He brought an Italian liveliness to the genre; and beginning with *La Fille mal gardée*, he gave French light opera a substance it hardly possessed in the days of the *drame forain*, using entirely original music, with trios and quartets as well as arias. In certain works the characters have a pathos and eloquence that greatly contributed to elevating the genre above the merely frivolous.

Dunn, Geoffrey (*b* London, 13 Dec. 1903). English tenor and producer. After early successes, especially as a character singer, he devoted himself to translating many foreign operas, among them Monteverdi's *L'incoronazione di Poppaea*, Handel's *Serse*, Wolf's *Der Corregidor*, Rimsky-Korsakov's *Mozart and Salieri*, Offenbach's *La Vie parisienne*, and Pizzetti's *Assassinio nella cattedrale*.

Dunque io son. The duet between Rosina (mezzo) and Figaro (bar.) in Act 1, scene 2, of Rossini's *Il barbiere di Siviglia*, in which he spins a story about his cousin, a poor student, who is in love with a certain girl – and eventually is given an already written letter for the disguised Count Almaviva.

Duodrama. The name given, by Mozart among others, to works for two actors with musical accompaniment. Mozart refers with enthusiasm to the best-known works of the genre, by Jiří Benda, and himself contemplated writing one, *Semiramis*.

Duparc, Elisabeth (*b* ?; *d* ?). French soprano. Known as 'La Francesina'. Sang in London 1738-45, creating Clotilda in Handel's *Faramondo* and the title role of his *Deidamia* as well as taking part in several of his dramatic oratorios. Burney called her style of singing 'lark-like'.

Duprez, Gilbert (Louis) (*b* Paris, 6 Dec. 1806; *d* Passy, 23 Sept. 1896). French tenor. Studied Paris Conservatoire, with Choron. Début Odéon 1825, Almaviva, with little success. Then went to Italy for further study and sang there 1829-35, in which year he was chosen by Donizetti to create Edgardo (*Lucia*) at Naples. Returned to Paris as tenor at the O. 1837-49, where he created the title role in *Benvenuto Cellini*, Fernando (*La Favorite*), Polyeucte (*Les Martyrs*), and several other parts, as well as taking over several of Nourrit's roles in Meyerbeer and Halévy works. From 1842 to 1850 professor of singing, Conservatoire; in 1853 founded his own school. His pupils included Battu, Miolan-Carvalho, Nantier-Didiée, and Albani. He composed eight operas and a quantity of other music, and wrote two books on singing. His wife, **Alexandrine Duperron** (1808-72) sang in Paris 1827-37; and their daughter **Caroline** (1832-75) was a soprano leggiero who, like her mother, appeared together with Duprez.
Bibl: G. Duprez: *Souvenirs d'un chanteur* (1880); *Récréations de mon grand âge* (1888).

Durastanti, Margherita (*b c*1685; *d* ?). Italian soprano and mezzo-soprano. After appearances in Italy 1709-16 in works by Handel, Scarlatti and others, was engaged for Dresden in 1719; London, King's T., 1719-24, creating leading roles in Handel's *Ottone, Flavio, Giulio Cesare*, and appearing in works by Scarlatti Ariosti, Bononcini, etc. The arrival in London of Cuzzoni and her increasing popularity probably contributed to Durastanti's withdrawal from the stage. However, she returned in 1733 with a company that included Carestini and the Negri sisters, to help Handel in his struggle against Porpora, and sang in Handel's *Arianna in Creta* in 1734, after which she retired finally.

Durch die Wälder. Max's (ten.) aria in Act 1 of Weber's *Der Freischütz*, in which he tells how once he wandered happily through the countryside, before misfortune befell him.

Durchkomponiert (*Ger* continuously composed). The term used for an opera in which there is no spoken dialogue or recitative, but continuous music into which separate numbers merge to a greater or lesser degree.

Dussek, Sophia. See *Corri*.

Düsseldorf-Duisburg. Two German industrial cities in North Rhine-Westphalia, Germany, which since 1956 have together housed the *Deutsche Oper am Rhein*, one of the strongest German operatic ensembles. Alberto Erede was Generalmusikdirektor 1958-62, Hermann Juch Intendant 1955-63; they were succeeded by Günter Wich and Grischa Barfuss in 1964. It has been the scene of the premières of Klebe's *Die Räuber* (1957) and the new version of Křenek's *Karl V* (1958); the company has specialized in 20th-cent. opera, revivals of Monteverdi, and complete cycles of works by Mozart, Janáček, and Strauss. Before the formation of the Deutsche Oper am Rhein, the Düsseldorf Company was under the direction of Hollreiser and then Szenkar. The Düsseldorf Opera House (cap. 1,041) was built in 1875 and rebuilt in 1956; the Duisburg Stadttheater (cap. 1,118) was built in 1912 and rebuilt in 1950.

Duval, Denise (*b* Paris, 23 Oct. 1921). French soprano. Début Bordeaux Oct. 1941 as Lola. Paris at Folies-Bergères 1944, where she was the first serious singer to appear since Lina *Cavalieri. Leading soprano O. and O.C. 1947-65. Created Thérèse (*Mamelles de Tirésias*), Blanche (*Carmélites*), Elle (*La Voix humaine*). Also noted as Concepción in *L'Heure espagnole*, and Princesse in *Mârouf*. Has sung with success in Italy, U.S.A., and elsewhere. Edinburgh Festival 1960 in British première of *La Voix humaine*; Gly. 1962, Mélisande. Retired 1965 and taught. (R)

Dux, Claire (*b* Witkowicz, 2 Aug. 1885; *d* Chicago, 8 Oct. 1967). German soprano. Studied Berlin and Milan with Teresa Arkel. Début Cologne 1906, Pamina. Berlin 1911-18; London, C.G., 1913, as first English Sophie (also sang Eva). The following year she sang Pamina under Beecham at D.L. Chicago 1921-4. Marrying a wealthy American, she retired from the stage at the height of her powers. (R)

Dvořák, Antonín (*b* Nelahozeves, 8 Sept. 1841; *d* Prague, 1 May 1804). Czech composer. Though some of his operas are popular in Czechoslovakia, they have not been accepted into foreign repertories. Even in their own country, *Alfred* (1870, prod. 1938), *Král a uhlíř* (King and Collier, 1874), the historical *Vanda* (1876), and the Romantic *Armida* (1904) have languished. But the sentimental humour of *Jakobín* (The Jacobin, 1889) is appreciated, as are the folk charms of *Tvrdé palice* (The Pigheaded Peasants, 1874, prod. 1881) and *Šelma Sedlák* (The Peasant a Rogue, 1878). *Čert a Káča* (The Devil and Kate, 1899) has had some success abroad, and *Dimitrij* (1882), whose plot begins where *Boris Godunov* ends, has had a few performances. Dvořák's greatest success has always been *Rusalka* (1901), a work of much charm which is as popular with Czech children as *Hänsel und Gretel* is with Germans. It is for his occasional delights rather than for his sense of musical drama that he is remembered as an opera composer.
Bibl: J. Clapham: *Antonín Dvořák* (1966).

Dvořáková, Ludmila (*b* Kolín, 11 July 1923). Czech soprano. Studied in Prague with Jarmila

Vavrdová. Début Ostrava 1949, Káta Kabanová. After appearances in Bratislava and Prague, and guest appearances in 1956 in Vienna as Leonore, was engaged for the Berlin S.O., 1960, making her début there as Oktavian. Bayreuth 1965-71 as Gutrune, Brünnhilde, Venus, Kundry; N.Y., Met., 1966-8; London, C.G., 1966-71 as Brünnhilde, Isolde, Leonore. Repertory also includes Dyer's Wife in *Frau ohne Schatten,* Ariadne, Marschallin, and Verdi roles. Possesses a warm, generous personality, if less than complete vocal technique. Married to the conductor Rudolf Vašata. (R)

Dybbuk, The. (1) Opera in prologue and 3 acts by Lodovico Rocca (*Il Dibuk*); text by R. Simoni, after Shelomoh An-Ski's drama (1916). Prod. Milan, Sc., 24 Mar. 1934, with Oltrabella, Palombini, Lo Giudice, Paci, Bettoni, Baronti, cond. Ghione. Chanon (ten.) is fascinated by the mysteries of the Kabala and tries to discover the means of winning riches so that he can marry Leah (sop.). He dies, but his spirit enters Leah's body.
(2) Opera in 3 acts by David Tamkin; text by Alex Tamkin. Comp. *c*1931, prod. N.Y., C.C., 4 Oct. 1951, with Neway, Russell, Bible, Rounseville, cond. Rosenstock. Also projected, partly sketched, opera by Gershwin, abandoned when he learnt that the rights belonged to Rocca. Other operas on the subject are by Füssel (1970) and Di Giacomo (1978).

Dyck, Ernest Van (Marie Hubert) (*b* Antwerp, 2 Apr. 1861; *d* Berlaer-lès-Lierre, 31 Aug. 1923). Belgian tenor. Studied with Saint-Yves Bax. Début Paris, T. Eden, 1887, in French première of *Lohengrin*. The following year, after a period of study with Mottl, sang Parsifal at Bayreuth, and continued to appear there in that role and as Lohengrin until 1912. Vienna, H., 1888-98, where he created title-role in *Werther* (1892). London, C.G., from 1891, including the 1907 winter season when he acted as manager and artistic director of a German company; N.Y., Met., 1898-1902. Famous in Wagner's Heldentenor roles. Much admired by Bernard Shaw. From 1906 taught singing in Brussels and Antwerp. (R)
Bibl: H. de Curzon: *Ernest van Dijck* (1933).

Dyer's Wife, The. The (anonymous) wife (sop.) of Barak the Dyer in R. Strauss's *Die Frau ohne Schatten.*

Dzerzhinsky, Ivan (Ivanovich) (*b* Tambov, 9 Apr. 1909; *d* Leningrad, 1978). Russian composer. Studied Moscow and Leningrad. When still a student, he entered his opera *The Quiet Don* (based on Sholokhov's then still unfinished novel) in a competition organised by the Bolshoy T. and the journal *Komsomolskaya Pravda*, without success. But revised, with help from Shostakovich and others, it was produced in Leningrad, Maly T., in 1935, conducted by another of the work's encouragers, Samuil Samosud. The opera was highly praised by Stalin and Molotov, and hence immediately became the prototype of Socialist Realist opera in its simple construction and direct language. His next work, *Virgin Soil Upturned* (1937), and his subsequent operas, failed to sustain this success.

E

Eames, Emma (*b* Shanghai, 13 Aug. 1865; *d* New York, 13 June 1952). American soprano. Studied Boston with Clara Munger, Paris with Marchesi. Début Paris, O., 1889, Juliette (chosen by Gounod), and during next two years created Colombe in Saint-Saëns's *Ascanio* and title role in De la Nux's *Zaïre*. Forced to leave Paris because of intrigues. C.G. début 1891, Marguerite, sang there until 1901 (not every season) where her success aroused Melba's jealousy. N.Y., Met., 1891-1909; Boston 1911-12. Retired when in her prime. Greatly admired as Aida, Desdemona, and Tosca, she also sang Elsa, Sieglinde, and Pamina. (R)
Bibl: E. Eames: *Some Memories and Reflections* (1927).

Easton, Florence (Gertrude) (*b* Middlesbrough, 25 Oct. 1884; *d* New York, 13 Aug. 1955). English soprano. Studied R.C.M. London, Paris with Elliot Haslam. Début Newcastle-on-Tyne, Moody-Manners Company, 1903, Shepherd (*Tannhäuser*). Joined Henry Savage Company, 1905; Berlin, Royal Opera, 1907-13; Hamburg 1914-16; N.Y., Met., 1917-29, 1935-6, during which time she created Lauretta (*Schicchi*) and Aelfrida in Deems Taylor's *The King's Henchman*. Sang Turandot at C.G. 1927, Brünnhilde and Isolde in 1932, and Tosca at S.W. 1934. One of the most versatile sopranos of the inter-war years, having a repertory of 88 roles in four languages, ranging from Brünnhilde to Carmen. She could learn a new score in 12 hours, and was always ready to step into any of her roles when a colleague fell ill. (R)

Ebers, John (*b* London, 1785; *d* London, *c*1830). English impresario. Originally a bookseller, manager of the King's T. 1820-7. His first season, which included first London perfs. of *La gazza ladra* and *Il turco in Italia,* ended in ruin because of the exorbitant demands of the singers. In 1822 he took a 4-year lease on the theatre, but was again ruined because the stage-manager, to whom he had sublet, absconded. In 1826 he lost a lawsuit over chorus payment. His company included De Begnis, Colbran, Camporese, Pasta, Vellutti, and Vestris. Among the operas he introduced to London were *La donna del lago, Il crociato in Egitto,* and *La vestale.*
Bibl: J. Ebers: *Seven years of the King's Theatre* (1828).

Ebert, Carl (*b* Berlin, 20 Feb. 1887). German producer and opera manager. Trained as an actor by Reinhardt and after engagements in Berlin and Frankfurt became general director of the State T. at Darmstadt 1927. In 1931 was appointed general director and producer of the Berlin Stä. O., where his productions came as a revelation to critics and public. Refused to collaborate with the Nazis and left Germany in 1933; besides producing opera in Florence and Buenos Aires, founded, with Fritz Busch, the *Glyndebourne Festival. Organized Turkish National T. and O. 1936-47; Director of opera department at University of Southern California 1948-56. Returned to Gly. 1947-59, and to his former position in Berlin 1956-61. N.Y., Met., 1959-62. His productions of Verdi and Mozart set a particularly high standard: his intensive rehearsals resulted in performances notable for their detail and fine ensemble. Staged première of *The Rake's Progress,* Venice 1951. His son **Peter** (*b* Frankfurt, 6 Apr. 1918) has worked at Gly.; was director of productions for Scottish Opera 1963-75. Augsburg 1968-73. Wiesbaden 1975-7. General administrator Scottish Opera from 1977.

Eboli. Ex-mistress (mezzo, originally soprano) of King Philip and lady-in-waiting to Elisabeth, in Verdi's *Don Carlos.*

Ecuador. Opera is of comparatively recent development; it began with the efforts of a musician of Italian origin, Pedro Pablo Traversari (*b* 1874; d. ?). Annual seasons are given by visiting European and South American companies at the T. Sucre in Quito.

Edelmann, Otto (Karl) (*b* Vienna 5 Feb. 1917). Austrian bass-baritone. Studied Vienna Academy with Lierhammer and Graarud. Début Gera 1938, Figaro. Resumed his career, which was interrupted by the war, in 1947 by joining the Vienna Opera. Bayreuth 1951-2, Hans Sachs; Salzburg 1953-4 Leporello, 1958, 1960 Ochs in opening of new Festspielhaus. San Francisco 1955, 1957, 1964; N.Y. Met., 1954-70, where his Baron Ochs was much admired. (R)

Edgar. Opera in 4 acts by Puccini; text by Ferdinando Fontana, after Alfred de Musset's verse drama *La Coupe et les lèvres* (1832). Prod. Milan, Sc., 21 Apr. 1889, with Pantaleoni, Cataneo, Gabrielesco, Magini-Coletti, cond. Faccio; London, Hammersmith Town Hall, 6 Apr. 1967, with Rubini, Doyle, Byles, Rippon, cond. Vandernoot N.Y., Carnegie Hall (concert), 13 Apr. 1977. Edgar (ten.) is torn between his love of Fidelia (sop.) and his passion for Tigrana (mezzo). He yields to the latter, but tiring of it returns to Fidelia, who is stabbed by the jealous Tigrana.

Edgardo. Edgar of Ravenswood (ten.), lover of Lucy, in Donizetti's *Lucia di Lammermoor.*

Edinburgh. Capital of Scotland. Apart from visits by touring companies, Edinburgh had little or no opera before the Second World War:

it was, however, the birthplace of the *Denhof Opera Company. Since 1947 it has been the home of the annual *Edinburgh Festival. From 1963 *Scottish Opera have given annual spring seasons at the King's T. and 1969-74 short winter seasons at either the King's or Lyceum Ts. S.W. Opera, and its successor the E.N.O., also pay regular visits to Edinburgh.

Edinburgh Festival. An annual summer festival founded in 1947 by the Glyndebourne Society Ltd at the instigation of Audrey *Christie and Rudolf *Bing, who was the festival's first artistic director, 1947-50. He was succeeded by Ian Hunter 1950-5. Between 1947 and 1955 Glyndebourne Festival Opera provided the opera, except in 1952 when the Hamburg State Opera paid its first visit to Great Britain. Robert Ponsonby succeeded Hunter and between 1956 and 1960 brought the Hamburg State Opera back for a second visit (1956), and also the Piccola Scala, Milan (1957), the Stuttgart Opera (1958), and the Stockholm Opera (1959). Lord *Harewood's régime (1961-5) saw visits by C.G. Opera (1961), Belgrade Opera (1962), S.C., Naples (1963), Prague National T. (1964), Bavarian State Opera, and Holland Festival Opera (1965). Peter Diamand succeeded Harewood, and since 1966 opera has been given by the Stuttgart Opera, 1966; Scottish Opera, 1967, 1968, 1970, 1972, 1974, 1975-7; Hamburg State Opera, 1968; Florence Opera, 1969; Frankfurt Opera and Prague Opera, 1970; Deutsche Oper, W. Berlin, 1971 and 1975; T. Massimo, Palermo, Deutsche Oper am Rhein, 1972; Hungarian State Opera 1973; Stockholm Opera, 1974; in addition, the Festival itself has mounted productions of Rossini and Mozart operas, and a successful *Carmen* 1977. John Drummond was appointed to succeed Diamand in 1979.

First performances in Great Britain since 1947 have included: *Mathis der Maler* (1952), *The Rake's Progress* (1953), *Oedipus Rex* and *Mavra* (1956), *La vida breve* (1958), *Aniara* (1959), *La Voix humaine* (1960), *Love of Three Oranges* and *The Gambler* (1962), *Dalibor*, *Resurrection* (Cikker), *From the House of the Dead* (1964), *Le pescatrici* (Haydn), *Intermezzo* (1965), *Lulu* (1966), *Orfeo ed Euridice* (Haydn, 1967), *Sette canzoni* (Malipiero, 1969), *Melusine* (Reimann, 1971), *Die Soldaten* (Zimmermann, 1972), *Blood Wedding* (Szokolay, 1973), *The Vision of Thérèse* (Werle, 1974), *Hermiston* (Orr, 1975), *Mary, Queen of Scots* (Musgrave, 1977). Mention should also be made of *Ariadne auf Naxos* (1st version), cond. Beecham (1950), *Le Comte Ory* (1954), Callas in *La sonnambula* (1957), *Adriana Lecouvreur* with Magda Olivero (1963), *The Trojans* with Janet Baker (1973), *Alceste* (1974), *Moses und Aron* (1976), and the Monteverdi cycle by the Zurich Opera in 1978.

Éducation manquée, Une. Operetta in 1 act by Chabrier; text by Leterrier and Vanloo. Prod. Paris, Cercle de la Presse, 1 May 1879, with Harding, Réval, Morlet; Tanglewood 3 Aug. 1953; London, Fortune T., 22 May 1955, with Zeri, Dickerson, Turgeon, cond. Jacob.

Edvina, Louise (orig. Marie-Louise Lucienne Martin) (*b* Montreal, *c*1880; *d* London, 13 Nov. 1948). French-Canadian soprano. Studied Paris with Jean de Reszke; début London, C.G., 1908 as Marguerite, singing there regularly until 1914, and again in 1919, 1920, and 1924. She was the first London Louise, Thaïs, Maliella (*Gioielli della Madonna*), Fiora, Francesca da Rimini. Also appeared in Boston, Chicago, and N.Y. An elegant singer, especially of French roles. (R)

Edwards, (Henry) **Sutherland** (*b* Hendon, 5 Sept. 1829; *d* London 21 Jan 1906). English critic. For many years critic of the St James Gazette. Writings include *History of Opera, from Monteverdi to Donizetti* (1862); *Life of Rossini* (1869); *The Lyric Drama* (1881); *Famous First Representations* (1886); *The Prima Donna* (1888).

Edwin and Angelina, or The Banditti. Opera in 3 acts by Victor Pelissier; text by E. H. Smith, after Goldsmith's ballad (1764). Prod. N.Y., John St T., 19 Dec. 1796. The second American opera (preceded only by *The *Archers*), performed only once.

Egk, Werner (*b* Auchsesheim, 17 May 1901). German composer. His first opera for the theatre was *Die Zaubergeige* (1935), successfully using numbers based on popular tunes. This was followed by *Peer Gynt* (1938), which became popular on receiving Hitler's approval. Next came *Columbus* (1942), a revision of the radio opera of 1933, *Circe* (1948), *Irische Legende* (1954), *Der Revisor* (1957), *Verlobung in San Domingo* (1963), and *17 Tage und 4 Minuten* (1966). Egk's dramatic flair and his capacity for drawing on the most readily acceptable aspects of his predecessors, notably Stravinsky, have made him a popular composer in Germany.

È il sol dell' anima. The Duke's (ten.) aria declaring his love to Gilda in Act 1, scene 2, of Verdi's *Rigoletto*, leading to the love duet.

Einem, Gottfried von (*b* Berne, 24 Jan. 1918). Austrian composer. His first operatic successes came with *Dantons Tod* (1947, after Büchner) and *Der Prozess* (1953, after Kafka). These were followed by *Der Zerrissene* (1964, text by Boris Blacher, after Nestroy) and *Kabale und Liebe* (1976). Another successful work, which has been widely performed, is *Der Besuch der alten Dame* (after Dürrenmatt, 1971). His work is direct and theatrically effective rather than dramatically profound, and is very eclectic.

EIN MÄDCHEN ODER WEIBCHEN

Ein Mädchen oder Weibchen. Papageno's (bar.) aria in Act 2, scene 5 of Mozart's *Die Zauberflöte*, in which he sings of his longing for a wife.

Einsam in trüben Tagen. Elsa's (sop.) aria, known as 'Elsa's Dream', in Act 1 of Wagner's *Lohengrin*, in which she recounts her dream of a rescuing hero.

Ein Schwert verhiess mir der Vater. Siegmund's (ten.) narration in Act 1 of Wagner's *Die Walküre.*

Eire. The first opera in Erse was O'Dwyer's *Eithne* (1910). Palmer's *Sruth na maoile* (The Sea of Moyle, 1923), on the Irish saga *The Children of Lir*, was given in Dublin. Other attempts at a national opera have been made; but Ireland's operatic tradition has mostly been maintained in expatriate composers, in a number of settings of Irish legends and the works of Irish playwrights by English composers, and in a long history of operatic performances that goes back to 1761.
See also *Dublin, Wexford.*

Eisenstein. A wealthy Viennese (ten.), husband of Rosalinde, in Johann Strauss's *Die Fledermaus.*

Eléazar. The Jewish goldsmith (ten.) in Halévy's *La Juive.*

Elegy for Young Lovers. Opera in 3 acts by Henze; text by W. H. Auden and Chester Kallman. Prod. Schwetzingen, 20 May 1961, by Bavarian State Opera, with Bremet, Benningsen, Rogner, Lear, Fischer-Dieskau, Kohn, cond. Bender; Gly., 19 July 1961, with Söderström, Dorow, Meyer, Turp, Alexander, Hemsley, cond. Pritchard; N.Y., Juilliard, 29 Apr. 1965, with Haywood, Shane, Wagner, Jones, Davison, Evans. Gregor Mittenhofer (bar.), the self-centred and egoistic poet, goes every year to the 'Schwarzer Adler' in the Austrian Alps, to seek inspiration for his work from the hallucinations of Hilda Mack (sop.). She is forever awaiting the return of her husband, who disappeared forty years earlier on their honeymoon. When his body is recovered from the glacier, the poet has to look elsewhere for inspiration and turns to the young lovers, Toni, his stepson (ten.) and Elisabeth (sop.). He sends them to the Hammerhorn to gather edelweiss, and there lets them die. Their death inspires his greatest poem 'Elegy for Young Lovers', which he reads silently before the audience in the closing scene of the opera.

Elektra. Opera in 1 act by Richard Strauss; text by Hugo von Hofmannsthal, after his drama (1903), in turn after Sophocles's tragedy (411 or 410 B.C.). Prod. Dresden, Hofoper, 25 Jan. 1909, with Krull, Siems, Schumann-Heink, Perron, cond. Schuch; N.Y., Manhattan Opera,

ELISABETTA, REGINA D'INGHILTERRA

1 Feb. 1910 (in French), with Mazarin, Baron, Gerville-Réache, Huberdeau, cond. De la Fuente; London, C.G., 19 Feb. 1910, with Walker, Rose, Bahr-Mildenburg, Weidemann, D'Oisly, cond. Beecham.
Elektra (sop.) mourns the death of her father Agamemnon; she tries to persuade her sister Chrysothemis (sop.) to help her avenge it. Her mother Klytemnestra (mezzo), Agamemnon's murderer, is plagued by nightmares and fears, but finds some comfort in news of the death of Elektra's absent brother Orest. Alone, Elektra begins to dig up the axe that had slain Agamemnon, but is interrupted by a stranger in the courtyard: it is Orest (bassbar.), not dead but secretly returned. He enters the palace and kills Klytemnestra; when Klytemnestra's lover Aegisth (ten.) appears, Elektra lights his way into the palace and to his own murder. She dances in triumph, and collapses dead.
Other operas on the subject are by Lemoyne (1782), Häffner (1785), and Gnecchi (*Cassandra*, 1905). The similarity between certain motives in the latter work and in Strauss's caused some stir at the time, and there were suggestions of both telepathy and plagiarism. See also *Idomeneo.*

Elenco artistico (*It* catalogue of artists). Properly, the names of the performers in a company or special production or season, published on a poster. More recently, the complete list of artists, including producers, designers, conductors, etc., engaged by an Italian opera house. In Germany the information is contained in the season's *Spielplan.

Eletsky. A Russian prince (bar.), in love with Lisa and Hermann's rival, in Tchaikovsky's *The Queen of Spades.*

Elisabeth. The daughter (sop.) of the Landgrave in Wagner's *Tannhäuser.*

Elisabeth de Valois. The wife (sop.) of King Philip in Verdi's *Don Carlos.*

Elisabetta, Regina d'Inghilterra (Elizabeth, Queen of England). Opera in 2 acts by Rossini; text by Giovanni Schmidt, after Carlo Federici's drama (1814). Prod. Naples, S.C., 4 Oct., 1815, with Colbran, Dardanelli, Manzi, Nozzari, Manuel Garcia, Chizzola; London, King's T. 30 Apr. 1818, with Fodor, Corri, Crivelli, Garcia. The overture and finale were taken from *Aureliano in Palmira*, and the former now replaces the lost overture to *Il barbiere di Siviglia*. A special performance was recorded by Italian Radio for the coronation of Queen Elizabeth II in 1953.
Queen Elizabeth I (sop.) learns from the Duke of Norfolk (ten.) that her favourite, Leicester (ten.), has secretly married Mathilde (sop.). Unable to persuade Leicester to give up

Mathilde, she has him imprisoned; when Norfolk's intrigues eventually lead to his arrest, the Queen shows her magnanimity by pardoning Leicester and Mathilde.

Other operas on Elizabeth I are by Pavesi (1810), Carafa (1818) Donizetti (*Roberto Devereux*, 1837), Giacometti (1853), Klenau (1939), Walter (1939), and Britten (*Gloriana*, 1953).

Elisir d'amore, L' (The Love Potion). Opera in 2 acts by Donizetti; text by Romani, after Scribe's libretto for Auber's *Le Philtre* (1831). Prod. Milan, T. della Canobbiana, 12 May 1832, with Sabine Heinefetter, Dabadie, Genero, Frezzolini; London, Ly., 10 Dec. 1836; N.Y., Park T., 18 June 1838., with Caradori-Allan, Jones, Morley, Placide. Nemorino (ten.) acquires courage to approach Adina (sop.) through faith in an elixir provided, in exchange for his last coin, by the quack Dulcamara (bass). His confident behaviour so annoys her that she decides to marry his rival, the recruiting sergeant Belcore (bar.), without delay. In Act 2 Nemorino complains to Dulcamara, who recommends another bottle; Nemorino pays for this by signing on with Sgt Belcore. News of the death of Nemorino's rich uncle makes him suddenly desirable to the village girls; Adina is now sad, but is quickly consoled by Nemorino. Dulcamara points triumphantly to the potency of his wares. Also opera by Kate Loder (*c* 1840s).

Elizza, Elise (Elisabeth Letzergroschen) (*b* Vienna, 6 Jan. 1870; *d* Vienna, 3 June 1926). Austrian soprano. Studied Vienna with Adolf Limley. Début in operetta, Carl T. 1892, Margit in Weinberger's *Lachenden Erben*. Olomouc, 1894. Further study with Materna. Vienna, O., 1895-1919, after which she taught in Vienna. Considered to have had one of the most beautiful voices of her day; repertory included Wagner and also coloratura soprano roles. (R)

Elle a fui, la tourterelle. Antonia's (sop.) aria at the piano, in the 'Antonia' act of Offenbach's *Les Contes d'Hoffmann.*

Ellen Orford. The schoolmistress (sop.) who befriends Peter in Britten's *Peter Grimes.*

Elleviou, Jean (orig. Pierre-Jean-Baptiste-François) (*b* Rennes, 14 June 1769; *d* Paris, 5 May 1842). French tenor. Début Paris, Comédie Italienne, 1790, in Monsigny's *Le Déserteur*, as *basse-taille*, changing to tenor and making new début, 1791, in première of Dalayrac's *Philippe et Georgette*. After difficulties with the authorities in the French Revolution, he was forced to interrupt his career, and only rejoined the Comédie Italienne in 1797, singing there until 1801 in a wide variety of roles. His versatility was remarkable: when he moved to the O.C. in 1801 he sang leading roles in new works by Grétry (with whom he had a particular

affinity), Dalayrac, Boieldieu, Monsigny, Méhul, and other composers, singing 40 new parts, among them title roles of Méhul's *Joseph* and Boieldieu's *Jean de Paris*. A contemporary account describes his voice as not strong, but flexible and used with art and charm. He wrote the libretto for Berton's *Délia et Verdikan,* and perhaps others.
Bibl: E.H.P. de Curzon: *Jean Elleviou* (1930).

Elmendorff, Karl (*b* Düsseldorf, 25 Jan. 1891; *d* Taunus, 21 Oct. 1962). German conductor. Studied Cologne, Hochschule für Musik, with Steinbach and Abendroth. Düsseldorf, Hagen, Wiesbaden (1932-6); Munich, Mannheim (1936-42), Dresden (1942-5), Cassel (1948-51), and Wiesbaden again (1952-6). A distinguished Wagnerian: he conducted at Bayreuth 1927-42, also Wagner performances at the Florence Festival and elsewhere in Italy. (R)

Elmo, Cloe (*b* Lecce, 9 Apr. 1910; *d* Ankara, 24 May 1962). Italian mezzo. Studied Rome with Ghibaudo, Rinolfi, and Pedrini. Début Cagliari 1934, Santuzza. Soon reached Milan Sc., where she sang regularly 1936-43, and after the Second World War. N.Y., Met., 1947-9. Chosen by Toscanini for Mistress Quickly in his *Falstaff* recording. Created leading mezzo roles in operas by Rocca, Frazzi, Pedrollo, and Malipiero. From 1954 until her death taught at the Ankara Conservatory. (R)

Elsa. Daughter (sop.) of the Duke of Brabant, heroine of Wagner's *Lohengrin.*

Elsner, Józef Ksawery (*b* Grotków, 1 June 1769; *d* Elsnerówka, 18 Apr. 1854). Polish composer, conductor, teacher, and writer. Studied Wrocław and Vienna. Conducted Lwów 1792 and Warsaw 1799, where he remained until his death. Principal, Warsaw Conservatory, 1821: his most famous pupil was Chopin. His stage works include 32 operatic pieces, ranging from full-scale operas to vaudevilles and opera-ballets. Among the more important are *Andromeda* (1807: composed in honour of Napoleon, who attended the second perf.), *Leszek Biały* (Leszek the White, 1809), and *Król Łokiełek* (King Łokietek, 1818). His operatic activity gave considerable encouragement to Polish opera, though the works themselves were soon forgotten and contained little relevant to the development of Polish national opera as an art.

Elvino. A well-to-do young Swiss farmer (ten.), hero of Bellini's *La sonnambula.*

Elvira. (1) A lady (sop.), of Burgos, deserted by Don Giovanni in Mozart's opera.
(2) The Bey's about-to-be-discarded wife (sop.) in Rossini's *L'Italiana in Algeri.*
(3) Daughter of Gualtiero Valton, heroine (sop.) of Bellini's *I Puritani.*
(4) A Spanish noblewoman (sop.), heroine of Verdi's *Ernani.*

Emperor Jones, The. Opera in 2 acts by Louis Gruenberg; text by Kathleen de Jaffa, after Eugene O'Neill's drama (1921). Prod. N.Y., Met., 7 Jan. 1933, with Tibbett, cond. Serafin; also Amsterdam (1934) and Rome (1952, with Rossi-Lemeni, cond. Gavazzeni). Brutus Jones (bar.), an ex-Pullman porter and escaped convict, rules his island in the Caribbean, with all the outward trappings of royalty. He has systematically fleeced his people and is making preparations to flee, warned by Henry Smithers (ten.), that the tribesmen are about to revolt. Jones flees into the jungle and is confronted (in hallucinations) by his past victims. He begs God for forgiveness; but discovered by the witch doctor who has summoned the tribesmen, he kills himself with his last bullet, a silver one he has saved for this purpose.

Encore (*Fr* again). The word shouted by members of a British audience to demand the repeat of a number, hence the word applied to the actual repeat. On the Continent, the word *bis* (*Fr* and *It*, from *Lat*, twice, again) is used, and can similarly be formed into a noun (*It: chiedere un bis*, to call for an encore) or a verb (*Fr: il fut bissé*, he was encored). Though known in the ancient theatre, the practice originally began in opera with the rise of virtuoso singers in the 17th cent., and has been very controversial; audiences have come into conflict with artists (almost invariably conductors) who insist on artistic continuity. Toscanini was a leading example of a conductor who quarrelled with audiences over his refusal to allow encores. The practice became at one time virtually automatic in the D'Oyly Carte Opera Company, with the encore point printed into the orchestral parts and singers ready with new 'business' for each comic repeat. Caruso was obliged to repeat 'La donna è mobile' five times at Rio de Janeiro in 1903; a whole scene of *Otello* was encored at Florence in 1951; however, the longest encore on record was that of an entire opera, *Il *matrimonio segreto* at its première in 1792.

Enfant et les sortilèges, L' (The Child and the Enchantments). *Fantaisie lyrique* in 2 parts by Ravel; text by Colette. Prod. Monte Carlo, 21 Mar. 1925, with Gauley, Orsone, Lafont, Warnery, cond. De Sabata; San Francisco 19 Sept. 1930, with O. Mario, Gruninger, Farncroft, Picco, cond. Merola; Oxford, Town Hall, 3 Dec. 1958, by Oxford University Opera Club, with C. Hunter, cond. Westrup. Toys, books, and furniture rebel against a bad child who has ill-used them; fleeing to the garden he finds the trees and animals equally hostile. They relent when he bandages the paw of a baby squirrel hurt in the rumpus. The child runs back to the comforting figure of his mother.

English National Opera. See *Sadler's Wells*.

English Opera Group, The. A company founded by Britten, John Piper, and Eric Crozier in 1946 after the first performance at Glyndebourne of Britten's *The Rape of Lucretia,* 'to be devoted to the creation and performance of new operas . . . and to encourage poets and playwrights to tackle the writing of librettos in collaboration with composers'. Since its foundation the Group has been responsible for the foundation and artistic direction of the *Aldeburgh Festival, the formation of the Opera Studio, subsequently the Opera School and then the National School of Opera, under Joan Cross and Anne Wood, and the commissioning and/or production of new works by Britten (*Albert Herring, Beggar's Opera, Turn of the Screw, Noyes Fludde,* the three Church Parables, *Owen Wingrave* (for T.V.), and *Death in Venice),* Berkeley (*Ruth, A Dinner Engagement,* and *Castaway),* Birtwistle (*Punch and Judy),* Williamson (*English Eccentrics),* Walton (*The Bear),* and Crosse (*Purgatory, The Grace of Todd),* as well as the revival of works by Purcell, Bickerstaffe, and Holst. Besides performing in England the Group has visited Holland, France, Germany, Italy, Scandinavia, and Canada. The management and financial responsibility of the Group were assumed by Covent Garden in 1961. In 1964 the Group was the first British opera company to visit the U.S.S.R.; in 1967 the Group appeared in Montreal for EXPO; and in 1971 performed *A Midsummer Night's Dream* in San Francisco. Colin Graham is director of productions, and Steuart Bedford chief of music staff. In 1975 it was reorganized as the English Music T., on a more regular basis, though in 1977 its activities were reduced as a result of a cut in the Arts Council grant.

Enna, August (*b* Nakskov, 13 May 1859; *d* Copenhagen, 3 Aug. 1939). Danish composer of Italian origin. Self-taught. After holding various conducting appointments, and writing several unsuccessful operas, he won a following with *Heksen* (The Witch, 1892). Though none of his subsequent operas equalled this in success, he wrote a number of works in late-Romantic vein which were popular in Denmark and to some extent in Germany; these include some Hans Andersen operas, e.g. *Prinsessen paa Aerten* (The Princess and the Pea, 1900, inaugurating the Århus theatre), and a Hugo opera, *Komediante* (The Actors, 1920, after *L'Homme qui rit*).

Enrico. Henry Ashton (bar.), brother of Lucy, in Donizetti's *Lucia di Lammermoor.*

Ensemble (*Fr* together). As a noun, used in English as well as French and German either for a group of performers or for their musical unanimity.

Ente autonomo (*It.* autonomous being,

independent organization). The name given to the independent, self-governing corporations which control leading Italian opera houses (e.g. Milan, Sc., and Naples, S.C.), as opposed to the commercial impresario who is given a concession to manage short seasons in smaller provincial theatres. The Ente Autonomo idea was formulated during Toscanini's 1922-9 régime at Sc., and soon adopted by the major Italian theatres.

Entführung aus dem Serail, Die (The Abduction from the Seraglio). Opera in 3 acts by Mozart; text by Gottlob Stephanie, altered from Christoph Friedrich Bretzner's libretto for André's *Belmont und Constanze* (1781), in turn adapted from one of various English and Italian plays and comic operas on the subject. Prod. Vienna, B., 16 July 1782, with Cavalieri, Teyber, Adamberger, Fischer, cond. Mozart; London, C.G., 24 Nov. 1827, in a version with extra characters by Kramer, with Hughes, Vestris, Sapio, Wrench, Benson, cond. Smart; N.Y., Brooklyn Athenaeum, 16 Feb. 1860, with Johansson, Rotter, Lotti, Quint, Weinlich.

Belmonte (ten.) arrives at the Pasha's palace in Turkey seeking Constance (sop.), who has been captured with her English maid Blonde (sop.) and with his servant Pedrillo (ten.). Despite the suspicions of the Pasha's steward Osmin (bass), who is in love with Blonde, Pedrillo gains admittance to the service of the Pasha (speaking part), who has been rejected by Constance. Blonde repels Osmin and, with the great aria 'Martern aller Arten', Constance declares that not even torture will make her accept the Pasha. Pedrillo makes Osmin drunk in order to facilitate the captives' escape. They are caught, but the Pasha magnanimously pardons and frees them.

Other operas on the subject are by Dieter (*Belmonte und Konstanze*, text Bretzner, 1784) and Knecht (1787).

Entr'acte (*Fr* between acts). In opera, a piece of orchestral music played between the acts or scenes.

Entrée (*Fr* entry). In opera, (1) a march-like piece played for the entrance of an important person or a group of dancers, in the operas of Lully and his contemporaries, (2) a term for an 'act', when each *entrée* has its own separate plot, as in Rameau's *Les Indes galantes*.

Enzo. A Genoese noble (ten.), La Gioconda's lover in Ponchielli's *La Gioconda*.

Épine, Francesca Margherita de l' (*b* ?; *d* London, 9 Aug. 1746). Italian soprano who appeared at D.L. between 1704 and 1718. Said to have been the first Italian to sing publicly in England. In 1710 sang in *Alamahide*, the first opera to be sung wholly in Italian in England, and subsequently in Handel's *Rinaldo* and *Il*

pastor fido. Married Pepusch in 1718, when she retired from the stage; said to have brought Pepusch a fortune of £10,000. Because of her ugly appearance, Pepusch called her 'Hecate', and no portrait of her was ever made.

Era la notte. Iago's (bar.) aria in Act 2 of Verdi's *Otello*, in which he pretends to substantiate his accusations against Desdemona by alleging that he once heard Cassio talking in his sleep about Desdemona and their love for one another.

Erb, Karl (*b* Ravensburg, 13 July 1877; *d* Ravensburg, 13 July 1958). German tenor. Joined Stuttgart Opera chorus 1907, and five months later sang solo role in *Der Evangelimann*. After engagements in Lübeck and Stuttgart, joined Munich Opera in 1913, remaining there until 1925, and creating title role in *Palestrina*, 1917. London, C.G., 1927, Belmonte. A fine Mozart singer. Husband of Maria *Ivogün. (R)

Erda. The Earth Goddess (con.) and mother, by Wotan, of the Valkyries in Wagner's *Ring*.

Erede, Alberto (*b* Genoa, 8 Nov. 1909). Italian conductor. Studied Genoa, Milan, and Basle; then with Weingartner 1929-31, and Busch in Dresden. Début Turin 1935, *Ring*. Brought by Busch to Gly., where he conducted several performances before the war. He returned to England in 1946 to become music director of the New London Opera Company U.S. with Salzburg Opera Guild, 1937-8. N.Y., Met., 1950-4. Deutsche Oper am Rhein from 1956, Generalmusikdirektor 1958-62. Bayreuth (*Lohengrin*) 1968. A fine trainer of young singers and a great believer in team work and ensemble. (R)
Bibl: L. Rognoni: *Alberto Erede* (1954).

Erhardt, Otto (orig. Martin Ehrenhaus) (*b* Breslau, 18 Nov. 1888; *d* San Carlos de Bariloche, 18 Jan. 1971). German producer. Studied music and history of art and began career as a violinist. He staged the first German production of Monteverdi's *Orfeo* (Breslau, 1913). Düsseldorf 1918-20. Stuttgart 1920-7, where his *Boris Godunov* (1921) was one of the first Expressionist productions; he also produced Busoni's *Doktor Faust* (1927) incorporating film sequences. Dresden 1927-31, where he produced the first performance of Strauss's *Die aegyptische Helena* (1928). Chicago 1930-2. C.G. 1933-5, producing English premières of Strauss's *Arabella*, and Weinberger's *Shvanda* (1934). Vienna 1934-7. Buenos Aires, Colón, 1939-56. N.Y., City Opera, 1954-6, 1967.

Erismena, L'. Opera in a prologue and 3 acts by Cavalli; text by Aurelio Aureli. Prod. Venice S. Apollinare 26 Dec. 1655; revised in 1670. Revived in version made by Lionel Salter,

London, B.B.C., 13 May 1967, with Robinson, Neville, Sinclair, Esswood, Herincx, cond. Salter; first English stage perf. London, King's College, 1 Apr. 1974, cond. Bedford. Version by Alan Curtis prod. Hague, Kon. Schouwburg, 26 June 1974, cond. Curtis.

Eri tu. Anckarstroem's (Renato's) (bar.) aria in Act 3, scene 1, of Verdi's *Un ballo in maschera*, resolving to punish not his supposedly unfaithful wife but his friend and king, Gustavus (Renato).

Erkel, Ferenc (*b* Gyula, 7 Nov. 1810; *d* Budapest, 15 June 1893). Hungarian composer, conductor, and pianist. Studied Poszony, with Klein. Moved to Koloszvár (now Cluj), where he first heard early attempts at Hungarian opera; later settled in Buda as opera conductor of the Hungarian T. Company (*c*1835). Gave up a developing career as a pianist on hearing Liszt, and turned increasingly to composition, achieving early success with his first opera, *Bátori Mária* (1840). He followed this up with *Hunyadi László* (1844), the most successful of his operas in Hungary. Though drawing on Viennese and Italian elements, it achieves a genuinely Hungarian character by its use of Hungarian-inflected recitative and by the incorporation of national dances, especially the *verbunkos*. Erkel also tried to develop a Hungarian equivalent of the English ballad operas known as *népszínmű*, in which were incorporated both ballads and original songs: these included *Két pisztoly* (Two Pistols, 1844), and became very popular. Other commitments and the need to earn a living prevented him from returning to opera for some years; but in 1861 he produced *Bánk bán*, based on a previously censored play and written in collaboration with his two sons Gyula and Sándor. Here the experiments of *Hunyadi László* are taken a stage further, with Hungarian elements more fully incorporated into fluent and original structures, and with more vivid and penetrating characterization. This was also the first composed work to make use of the cimbalom.

None of Erkel's subsequent operas achieved a comparable success. He attempted comic opera on the one hand, with *Sarolta* (1862) and *Névtelen hősök* (Unknown Heros, 1880), in which there is copious use of popular tunes and rustic scenes; and national music drama on the other, with *Dósza György* (1867) and *Brankovics György* (1874), in which Hungarian musical characteristics are absorbed into a continuous musical flow, with the orchestra taking a prominent role. Though there are in them anticipations of Liszt and even of Bartók, the shadow of Wagner falls more heavily across them, and deepens with Erkel's last opera, *István király* (King Stephen, 1885, mostly by Gyula Erkel). He left the National T. in

1874, being succeeded by Richter, though he continued to conduct his own works and to play in public. *Hunyadi László* and *Bánk bán* have remained in Hungarian repertories, and have occasionally been performed abroad; with them, Hungarian national opera was founded.

Bibl: A. Németh: *Erkel Ferenc* (1967).

Ermolenko-Yuzhina (orig. Plugovskaya), **Nataliya** (Stepanovna) (*b* Kiev, 1881). Russian soprano. Studied Kiev with Zotovoy, Paris with Vidal. First sang in Tsereteli's private opera company. Début Kiev 1900, Lisa in *Queen of Spades*. St Petersburg, M., 1901-4, 1910, 1916-18; Moscow, B., 1904-16; Moscow, Z., 1908-10. Paris, Diaghilev season, 1908, Marina Paris O., from 924. Her roles included Wagner's Elsa, Brünnhilde, Sieglinde, and Gutrune (she sang the latter in the famous 1905 Maryinsky *Götterdämmerung*), the Russian repertory, including Yaroslavna (which she sang to Pavel Andreyev's Igor and Shalyapin's Galitzky in 1915), Marfa, and Tatyana, also Aida, Agathe, Carmen, and Violetta. Married the tenor David Yuzhin (Jushin). (R)

Ernani. Opera in 4 acts by Verdi; text by Piave, after Victor Hugo's tragedy *Hernani* (1830). Prod. Venice, F., 9 Mar. 1844, with Loewe, Guasco, Superchi, Selva; London, H.M.'s, 8 Mar. 1845, with Rita-Borio, Moriani, Botelli, Fornisari, cond. Costa; N.Y., Park T., 13 Apr. 1847, with Tedesco, Perelli, Vita, Novelli, cond. Arditi. Elvira (sop.), who is about to marry her elderly kinsman Don Ruy Gomez (bass), is in love with Ernani (ten.), in reality Don Juan de Aragon, outlawed by the King of Castile. She is also loved by Don Carlo, King of Castile (bar.), recently elected Holy Roman Emperor, who removes her from her father's castle. Ernani and Silva (bass) join together to rescue Elvira and plot against the king's life. Ernani gives Silva a silver hunting-horn, promising that when it is sounded, he will take his own life. Carlo pardons his enemies and agrees to the marriage between Elvira and Ernani; as the couple prepare for the wedding, Silva sounds the hunting-horn and Ernani, in fulfilment of his promise, stabs himself and dies in Elvira's arms.

Other operas on the subject are by Gabussi (1834), Mazzucato (1844), Laudamo (1849), and Hirschmann (1909).

Ernani, involami. Elvira's (sop.) aria in Act 1 of *Ernani*, in which she sings of Ernani and hopes that he will flee with her.

Ernesto. Norina's lover (ten.) in Donizetti's *Don Pasquale*.

Ernster, Deszö (*b* Pécs, 23 Nov. 1898). Hungarian bass. Début Düsseldorf 1925. Bayreuth 1931; Graz, 1935-7. America with Salzburg

Opera Guild 1937; interned in concentration camp during war, but returned to America in 1946 and became leading bass at N.Y., Met., in German repertory. Sang Hagen at C.G., 1949 and 1954, and Banquo and Alfonso at Gly. in 1952. Deutsche Oper am Rhein 1950-67. (R)

Ero the Joker (Serb. *Ero s onoga svijeta*: Ero from the other world). Opera in 3 acts by Jakov Gotovac; text by Milan Begović, after a Dalmatian folk tale. Prod. Zagreb 2 Nov. 1935; London, Stoll, by Zagreb Company, 28 Jan. 1955, with Tončić, Radev, Gostič, Krisžaj, Kučić, cond. Gotovac. One of the most popular of all Yugoslav operas.

Ershov, Ivan (Vasilyevich) (*b* Novocherkassk, 20 Nov. 1867; *d* Leningrad, 21 Nov. 1943). Russian tenor. Studied Moscow 1888 with Alexandrova-Kochetova, then St Petersburg 1888-93 with Gabel and Paleček. Début St Petersburg, M., 1893, Faust. Appeared in Italy 1894 (Don José, Canio); then Kharkhov 1894-5 (Romeo, Faust, Raoul, Ernani). St Petersburg, M., 1895-1929. He covered a wide stylistic range, including in his repertory (of 58 roles), Florestan, Wagner roles (Siegfried, Siegmund, Tristan, Lohengrin, Tannhäuser), and many Russian roles, among them Glinka's Sobinin and the Finn, Rimsky-Korsakov's Tsar Berendey, Sadko, and (the first) Grishka Kuterma, and Mussorgsky's Golitsyn. He also sang in some modern operas, including Prokofiev's *Love of the Three Oranges* (Truffaldino). His voice was praised for its strength, resonance, and clarity, and he was admired as an actor, by many Russians above Shalyapin. Taught Petrograd (Leningrad) Conservatory, 1916-41, also producing opera there. (R)
Bibl: V. Bogdanov-Berezovsky: *Ivan Ershov* (1951).

Erwartung (Expectation). *Mimodrama* in 1 act by Schoenberg; text by Marie Pappenheim. Prod. Prague, Neues Deutsches T., 6 June 1924, with Gutheil-Schoder, cond. Zemlinsky; London, S.W., 4 Apr. 1960, by New Opera Company, with Harper, cond. Lovett; Washington 28 Dec. 1960, with Pilarczyk, cond. Craft.

Escamillo. The toreador (bar.) in Bizet's *Carmen*.

È scherzo od è follia. Quintet sung by Oscar (sop.), Mam'zelle Arvidson (Ulrica) (mezzo), Gustavus (Riccardo) (ten.), Ribbing (Sam) (bass), and Horn (Tom) (bass) in Act 1, scene 2 of Verdi's *Un ballo in maschera*, in which the characters react variously to the prophecy that Gustavus will die by the hand of a friend.

Essen. Town in North Rhine Westphalia, Germany. Opera is given in the Städtische Bühnen (cap. 800), built in 1892, and rebuilt after the war in 1950. Premières of works by Fortner, Klebe, and Reutter have been staged there, as

well as the first performances in Germany of *Karl V* (1950), *Lulu* (1953), *Il prigioniero* (1954), *The Fairy Queen* (1959), and Martinů's *Mirandolina* (1960).

Esterház. Castle near Süttör, Hungary. The summer residence of the Princes Esterházy, built in 1766; it included a theatre (cap. 400). Opera was originally given twice a week under *Haydn, with a repertory that concentrated on his own works but also included works by Piccinni, Sacchini, Salieri, Anfossi, Cimarosa, Dittersdorf, and others. There was also a marionette theatre on the other side of the park, at which Haydn's *Philemon und Baucis* was prod. 1773. Burned down in 1779, the castle was rebuilt with an enlarged theatre that was reopened with Haydn's *La fedeltà premiata* in 1781.
Bibl: M. Harányi: *The Magnificence of Eszterház* (1954, trans. 1962).

Estonia. During the period of German hegemony, a few operas were given by the musical society Wanemuine in Tallinn, and a tradition of operetta developed. With independence in 1918, new impetus was given to theatrical life, and an opera and ballet company was formed in 1923. Though earlier operas had been written by Estonian composers, notably *Sabina* (1906) by Artur Lemba (1885-1963), the first true Estonian opera was *Vikerlased* (The Vikings, 1928) by Evald Aav (1900-39). This was followed by *Kaupo* (1932), by Adolf Vedro (*b* 1890). Lemba's later works included *Armastus ja Surm* (Love and Death, 1931) and *Elga* (1934). Under Soviet rule, from 1944, operatic life has further developed. New Estonian operas have included *Tasuleegid* (1945) by Eugen Kapp (*b* 1908), also composer of a children's opera, *Talvemuinasjutt* (Winter Story, 1959); *Lembitu* (1961) by his cousin Wilhelm Kapp (1913-64); *Pühajärv* (The Holy Lake, 1947), *Iormide Rand* (The Shore of Storms, 1950), *Käsi Käes* (Hand in Hand, 1955) and *Vigased Pruudid* (Fallible Wives, 1959) by Gustav Ernesaks (*b* 1908); the satirical opera *Korolyu Kholodno* (The King is Cold, 1967) by the jazz and popular composer Valter Ojakäär (*b* 1923); and works by Leo Normet (*b* 1922), Eino Tambert (*b* 1930), and Velyo Tormis (*b* 1930). Opera is given in a theatre built in 1913 (cap. 800).

Esultate! Otello's (ten.) opening lines in Act 1 of Verdi's opera, announcing victory over the Turks.

Etcheverry, Henri-Bertrand (*b* Bordeaux, 29 Mar. 1900; *d* Paris, 14 Nov. 1960). French bassbar. Studied Paris. Début Paris, O., 1932, Ceprano (*Rigoletto*); O.C. from 1937 where he was considered the best Golaud of his generation. London, C.G., 1937 Barbe-Bleue, 1949 Golaud. Created roles in a number of contemporary works including Hahn's *Le Marchand de* *enise*. His most popular roles, apart from Bolaud, were Boris, Méphistophélès, and St ris. (R)

toile du Nord, L' (The Star of the North). Opera n 3 acts by Meyerbeer; text by Scribe, after ellstab's text for *Ein Feldlager in Schlesien*, ased in turn on an episode in the life of Fredrick the Great. Prod. Paris, O.C., 16 Feb. 1854, s *L'Étoile du nord* with Duprez, Battaile, ourdan, Lefèbvre – 100th perf. on 1st anniversary; London, C.G., 19 July 1855, with Bosio, Marai, Gardoni, Formes, Lablache, Zelger, ond. Costa; New Orleans 5 Mar. 1855, with retti, Martial, Holtzem, Génibrel, Laget, Beccers. Originally composed as *Ein Feldlager in chlesien* to open the new Berlin Opera, 7 Dec. 844, with Tuczek: eight days after the première, she was replaced by Jenny Lind, who ang the work widely, in the revised version for ienna (1847) under the new title *Vielka*. Tsar eter (bass) loves the village girl Katherine sop). She substitutes herself for her brother en.) in the Russian Army, and informs the sar of a conspiracy. Disguised as a carpenter, e Tsar woos Katherine and makes her his sarina.

ugene Onegin. Opera in 3 acts by chaikovsky; text by composer and Konstantin hilovsky, after Pushkin's poem (1831). Prod. oscow, Conservatory, Maly T., 29 Mar. 1879, ith Klimentova, Levitskaya, Reiner, Konshina, ilev, Medvedev, Makhalov, Tarkhov, cond. N. ubinstein; professional première, Moscow, ., 23 Jan. 1881, with Verny, Krutikova, unevich, Khokhlov, Usatov, Bartsal, bramov, cond. Bevignani; London, Olympic ., 17 Oct. 1892, with Fanny Moody, Oudin, lcKay, Manners, cond. Henry Wood; N.Y., let., 24 Mar. 1920, with Muzio, Perini, Marnelli, De Luca, Didur, cond. Bodanzky.

The opera takes place in St Petersburg in the arly 19th century. Tatyana (sop.), the young nd impressionable daughter of Madame arina (mezzo), falls in love with the Byronic negin (bar.), a friend of her sister Olga's betothed, Lensky. Tatyana stays up all night vriting an impassioned letter to Onegin telling im of her feelings. The following day he meets er in the garden and, lecturing her on aidenly reticence, urges her to forget him.

Tatyana's birthday is being celebrated by a all. Some of the elderly women gossip about atyana and Onegin, who have been dancing ogether. Onegin, annoyed, dances with Olga mezzo), who had promised the dance to ensky (ten.). The latter remonstrates with his ancée, who is so piqued that she offers a urther dance to Onegin. Monsieur Triquet en.), the French tutor, sings a song in praise of atyana. When the dancing is resumed, Lensky uarrels with Onegin and challenges him to a uel. Early next morning the two men meet

beside an old mill near a stream. Lensky is killed.

Six years have passed and Onegin, who has been abroad, returns to St Petersburg. A ball is in progress at the palace of Prince Gremin (bass) who has married Tatyana. Onegin is one of the guests, and when he meets Tatyana again he realizes that he loves her. He writes asking her to see him again. She agrees and he comes to her boudoir. He tells her he loves her and urges her to flee with him. At first Tatyana wavers, and then responds ardently; but after a few moments she reminds Onegin of her duty to her husband, and sends him away for ever.

Euridice. (1) Opera in prologue and 6 scenes by Peri; text by Ottavio Rinuccini. Prod. Florence, Pitti Palace, 6 Oct. 1600, as part of the wedding celebrations for Henri IV of France and Maria de' Medici; Saratoga Springs, 9 Apr. 1941. The first opera of which the music is extant.

(2) Opera in prologue and 6 scenes by Caccini; text by Ottavio Rinuccini. Prod. Florence, Pitti Palace, 5 Dec. 1602.

In this version of the popular Orpheus legend, Euridice dances with her companions, and Orpheus is apostrophizing the beauties of nature when Daphne arrives to announce Eurydice's death. Venus allows him to descend to Hades to beg Pluto for the return of his bride. The plot omits the famous condition whereby Orpheus must not look back as he leads her back to the world, and the opera ends happily.

Euryanthe. Opera in 3 acts by Weber; text by Helmina von Chezy, after a medieval French romance. Prod. Vienna, Kä., 25 Oct. 1823, with Sontag, Haitzinger, Grünbaum, Forti, Seipelt, Teimer, Rauscher, cond. Weber; London, C.G., 29 June 1833, with Schröder-Devrient; N.Y., Met., 23 Dec. 1887, with Lilli Lehmann, Brandt, Alvary, Fischer, Elmblad, cond. Seidl. Lysiart (bar.), angered by Adolar's (ten.) protestations of love for Euryanthe (sop.), wagers that he can seduce her. She has meanwhile given away a family secret about a suicide to the evil Eglantine (mezzo), who has won her confidence. When Lysiart accuses her of infidelity before the Court, she fails to deny it, and the miserable Adolar leads her into the desert to kill her. But when she saves his life, he abandons her instead, to be found by the King and a hunting party. Lysiart, who has won Adolar's possessions and estate in the wager, is about to marry Eglantine when Adolar arrives; the plot is disclosed, and he is reunited with Euryanthe. Also opera on the subject by Carafa (1828).

Eva. Pogner's daughter (sop.), heroine of Wagner's *Die Meistersinger von Nürnberg*.

Eva. Opera in 3 acts by J. B. Foerster; text by composer, after Gabriela Preisová's drama *Gazdina roba* (The Innkeeper's Daughter). Prod. Prague, N., 1 Jan. 1899.

Evangelimann, Der (The Evangelist). Opera in 2 acts by Kienzl; text by composer, after L. F. Meissner's story (1894). Prod. Berlin, O., 4 May 1895, with Pierson, Goetz, Sylva, Bulss, Mödlinger, cond Muck; London, C.G., 2 July 1897, with Engle, Schumann-Heink, Van Dyck, Bispham, Pringle, cond. Flon; Chicago, Gt Northern T., 3 Nov. 1923, with Mörike, Metzger, Ritter, Zador.

Evans, (Sir) **Geraint** (*b* Pontypridd, S. Wales, 16 Feb. 1922). Welsh baritone. Studied Hamburg with Theo Hermann and Geneva with Fernando Carpi. Début London, C.G., 1948, Nightwatchman (*Meistersinger*), since when he has established himself as one of the leading British baritones of the day, singing Figaro, Papageno, Beckmesser, etc. Sang regularly at Glyndebourne 1949-61, Guglielmo (*Cosi*), Masetto, Leporello, Abbate (*Arlecchino*), and Falstaff. San Francisco since 1959; Milan, Sc., 1960; Vienna 1961; Salzburg since 1962. His voice is a warm lyric baritone of considerable range; his diction is admirable and his characterization lively and humane. Among the roles he has created in London are Mr Flint (*Billy Budd*), Mountjoy (*Gloriana*), and Antenor (*Troilus and Cressida*). Celebrated his 25th anniversary at Covent Garden singing title-role in new production of *Don Pasquale*. Has also produced for W.N.O.C. and in Chicago and San Francisco. Awarded C.B.E. 1959; knighted 1969. (R)

Everding, August (*b* Bottrop, 31 Oct. 1928). German producer and administrator. Studied Bonn and Munich. After engagements in the straight theatre, including Munich, where he was general administrator of the Munich Kammerspiele 1963-73, succeeded Liebermann at Hamburg S.O. 1972; Munich from 1976. Guest producer Vienna, San Francisco, London. Bayreuth, 1969 *Fliegende Holländer,*

1974 *Tristan und Isolde.* Hamburg from 1973

Evirato. See **Castrato.**

Excursions of Mr Brouček, The (Cz., *Výlety pana Broučka*). Opera in 2 parts by Janáček text by composer, with suggestions, contributions, and amendments by F. Gellner, V. Dyke and F. S. Procházka, after Svatopluk Čech's novels (1888, 1889). Part 1, *Výlet pana Broučka do měsíce* (Mr Brouček's Excursion to the Moon); Part 2, *Výlet pana Broučka do XV sto* (Mr Brouček's Excursion to the 15th cent). Prod. Prague, Cz., 23 Apr. 1920, with Štork Miřiovská, Jeník, Zítek, Novák, Crhová, Pivoňková, Soběský, Hruška, Lebeda, Novotný cond. Ostřil; Edinburgh, King's T., 3 Sept. 1970 by Prague Nat. T., with Blachut, Tattermusch ová, Židek, D. Jedlička, Berman, Lermariová Prochazková, R. Jedlička, Karpišek, Vonásek cond. Krombholc. In the first of Mr Brouček's magic excursions, to the Moon, he encounters a fantastic aesthetic world: though the work's ostensible purpose is to lampoon his bourgeois complacency and Philistinism, he actually emerges in a more sympathetic light than the posturing Moon dwellers. His second excursion to the 15th cent., where he behaves in a cowardly fashion before being restored to the present.

Exit Aria. See *Aria.*

Ezio. Opera in 3 acts by Handel; text by Metastasio. Prod. London, King's T., 26 Jan. 1732 with Strada, Senesino, Bertolli, Bagnolessi N.Y, Gate T., 11 May 1959, with Caplan, Cornell Edgar, Smith, Warwick, cond. Saffir. Among some two dozen other settings are those by Auletta (1728), Porpora (1728), Lampugnan (1736), Jommelli (1741), G. Scarlatti (1744) Hasse (1755), Traetta (1757), Gluck (1763), J. C Bach (1764), Gazzaniga (1772), and Mercadante (1827).

F

Fabbri, Guerrina (b Ferrara, 1868; d Turin, 21 Feb. 1946). Italian contralto. A coloratura of the Supervia type renowned for her *Cenerentola* and *L'Italiana in Algeri*. Début Viadana 1885, La Cieca; London, D.L., Amneris on opening night of Augustus Harris's famous 1887 season. Heard again in London 1891 as Orfeo, Fidalma, and Cenerentola. N.Y., Met., 1891-2, 1909-10. Last performance Genoa, 1925 in *Quatro rusteghi*. (R) Her sister **Vittorina** sang as a mezzo-soprano 1889-95.

Fabri, Annibale Pio (b Bologna, 1697; d Lisbon, 12 August 1760). Italian tenor, known as 'Il Balino' or 'Il Bolognese'. Studied with Pistocchi, début ?1716 Bologna in Bassani's *Alarico Re de' Goti*. After appearances in Venice in operas by Vivaldi, Lotti, Porpora, etc. he was engaged by Handel in 1729 for London, where he made his début in *Tolomeo* and sang in the premières of *Lotario* (1729), *Partenope* (1730), and *Poro* (1731). Principal of Academia Filarmonica, Bologna; cantor of the Royal Chapel Lisbon, 1750. Composed two oratorios and some voice exercises. His wife **Anna Maria Fabri** (b Bologna) sang with her husband, 1711-16 in various Italian theatres.

Faccio, Franco (Francesco Antonio) (b Verona, 8 Mar. 1840; d Monza, 21 July 1891). Italian conductor and composer. Studied Milan. Until the 1870s was primarily known as a composer and teacher. His *I profughi fiamminghi* was performed at Milan, Sc., 1863. His greatest success was with *Amleto* (1865, rev. 1871): the work benefits greatly from Boito's libretto, but despite his vivid sense of theatre, Faccio was unable to rise to the formidable demands of the subject. He conducted in Germany and Scandinavia, Lorini's Company, 1867. Conductor Milan, Sc., 1871-90: conducted premières of *Otello*, *La Gioconda*, *Dejanice*, *Edgar*, also first Milan Wagner opera (*Lohengrin*, 1873). Conducted first London *Otello*, 1889. Verdi admired Faccio's talent as a composer, but an ode to Faccio written by Boito after the première of *I profughi fiamminghi* gave Verdi offence and it was some time before the breach was healed. Faccio's sister **Chiarina** (1846-1923) was a soprano.
Bibl: R. de Rensis: *Franco Faccio e Verdi* (1934).

Fafner. With Fasolt, one of the two giants (bass) in Wagner's *Das Rheingold*. He has turned into a dragon in *Siegfried*.

Failoni, Sergio (b Verona, 18 Dec. 1890; d Sopron, 25 July 1948). Italian conductor. Studied Verona and Milan. Début Como 1921,

conducting Rameau's *Platée*. Held appointments at various Italian theatres, including Sc. 1932-4, 1940-1, 1946-7 and was a well-known figure at the Verona Arena. His most important work was at the Budapest State Opera, where he was music director, 1928-47. (R)

Fair Maid of Perth. See *La Jolie Fille de Perth*.

Fairy Queen, The. 'Opera' in a prologue and 5 acts by Purcell; text an anonymous adaptation (by Elkanah Settle?) of Shakespeare's comedy *A Midsummer Night's Dream* (1595-6). Prod. London, Dorset Gardens, Apr. 1692; next stage prod., Cambridge 10 Feb. 1920; San Francisco 30 Apr. 1932. The score was lost by Oct. 1701, when an advertisement offered 20 gns. for its recovery; it was found in 1901 by J. S. Shedlock (not quite complete) in the library of the R.A.M. The first work staged by C.G. Opera on its formation in 1946. Not really an opera, but a succession of masques.

Falcon, Marie Cornélie (b Paris, 28 Jan. 1812; d Paris 25 Feb. 1897). French soprano. Studied Paris Conservatory with Henri and Pelegrini, later with Bordogni and Nourrit. Début Paris, O., 1832 Alice (*Robert le Diable*). Her career lasted only until 1838, when she lost her voice and had to retire; an attempted come-back at the Opéra in March 1840 ended in disaster. Created Mme Ankerstroem (*Gustavus III*), Rachel (*La Juive*), Valentine (*Huguenots*), and was a famous Donna Anna and Giulia (*Vestale*). Donizetti, who had hoped that she would create Pauline in *Les Martyrs*, noted in a letter that 'after she has sung for a short time, her voice seems veiled'. Her name became synonymous with the dramatic soprano roles in which she was unapproachable, and the term *falcon* still survives to describe this type of voice.
Bibl: C. Bouvet: *Cornélie Falcon* (1927).

Fall, Leo (b Olomouc, 2 Feb. 1873; d Vienna, 16 Sept. 1925). Austrian composer. Studied Vienna, with R. and J. N. Fuchs. Conducted in Berlin, Hamburg, and Cologne; settled in Vienna 1906. With Lehár and Kalmán, he was one of the most popular Viennese operetta composers of his time. His early operas were unsuccessful, but he found his métier in operetta with his light melodic grace and his neatness of invention: they include *Der Rebell* (1905, later reworked as *Der liebe Augustin*, 1912), *Der fidele Bauer* (1907), *Die Dollarprinzessin* (1907), *Eternal Waltz* (1911), *Die Rose von Stamboul* (1916), *Madame Pompadour* (1923), and *Jugend im Mai* (1926). Some of his operettas were very popular in London.

Falla, Manuel de (b Cádiz, 23 Nov. 1876; d Alta Gracia, 14 Nov. 1946). Spanish composer. *La vida breve* (1905) is an early work, with a weak plot; but already Falla's authentic voice is to be heard behind the different manners he adopts. Despite unevenness, it is a work of genuine dramatic power. *El retablo de Maese Pedro* (1923) handles an incident in *Don Quixote*. The forces are miniature, and there is a disciplined refinement and intensity in Falla's mature style that is more essentially Spanish than the surface colour of the earlier work. His *Atlantida* (completed by Halffter) is a work of vast ambition and intermittent power (concert perf., Barcelona 24 Oct. 1961; prod. Milan, Sc., 18 June 1962). (R)

Bibl: J. Pahissa: *Vida y obra de Manuel de Falla* (1947; trans., *Manuel de Falla*, 1954).

Falsetto (*It* lit. dim. of *falso*: false, altered; or poss. from *Lat fauces*: throat). The artificial method of voice production employed by male singers, using only a partial vibration of the vocal cords. Weak in timbre, and capable of only the smallest expressive variety, it is normally used in opera only for special effects, whether for extreme refinement and softness of tone, as perhaps at the end of the Romance in *Les Pêcheurs de perles,* or satirically, as usually by Falstaffs imitating Mistress Ford allegedly sighing, 'Io son di Sir John Falstaff'. There is a long passage of falsetto in Weber's *Die drei Pintos*. In the 19th cent. a singer who specialized in a version of falsetto singing was sometimes known in Italy as *falsettone*, or *falsetto rinforzato*.

Falstaff. Opera in 3 acts by Verdi; text by Boito, after Shakespeare's comedy *The Merry Wives of Windsor* (1600-1) and *Henry IV* (Pt. 1, 1597; Pt. 2, 1598). Prod. Milan, Sc., 9 Feb. 1893, with Zilli, Stehle, Guerrini, Pasqua, Garbin, Maurel, Pini-Corsi, Paroli, Pellagalli-Rossetti, Arimondi cond. Mascheroni; London, C.G., 19 May 1894, with Zilli, Olghina, Ravogli, Kitzu, Beduschi, Pessina, Pini-Corsi, cond. Mancinelli; N.Y., Met., 4 Feb. 1895, with Eames, De Lussan, Scalchi, De Vigne, Russitano, Maurel, Campanari, cond. Mancinelli.

Sir John Falstaff (bar.) sends identical love-letters to Alice Ford (sop.) and Meg Page (mezzo). The two women dispatch Mistress Quickly (mezzo) to the Garter Inn to tell Falstaff that Ford (bar.), Alice's husband, is out of the house between two and three o'clock. Ford has been plotting to marry off his daughter Nannetta (sop.), in love with the young Fenton (ten.), to Dr Caius (ten.); he suspects his wife and, disguising himself as Master Brook, goes to see Falstaff and asks his help to procure Alice for himself. The rest of the opera shows how the Merry Wives get their revenge on Falstaff and at the same time thwart Ford's plans for Nannetta.

Other operas on the subject are by Dittersdorf (1796), Salieri (1798), Balfe (1838), Nicolai (1849), and Adam (1856).

Fancelli, Giuseppe (*b* Florence, 24 Nov. 1833; *d* Florence 23 Dec. 1887). Italian tenor. Début Milan, Sc., 1860 probably as Fisherman in *Guillaume Tell*; London C.G., 1866-8, 1870-2, Alfredo, Edgardo, Elvino, Pollione, Raoul, etc., also at D.L. First Sc. Radamès 1872. Had a vibrant and telling voice and, according to Klein, held a high C with an ease unsurpassed even by Tamagno and Caruso. He could not read music, and his dramatic gifts were very limited.

Fanciulla del West, La (The Girl of the [Golden] West). Opera in 3 acts by Puccini; text by Civinini and Zangarini, after Belasco's drama *The Girl of the Golden West* (1905). Prod. N.Y., Met., 10 Dec. 1910, with Destinn, Caruso, Amato, cond. Toscanini; London, C.G., 29 May 1911, with Destinn, Bassi, Ghilly, cond. Campanini; Rome, C., 12 June 1911, with Burzio, Bassi, Amato, cond. Toscanini.

The opera, set in California in the days of the Gold Rush, tells of the love of Minnie (sop.), owner of the Polka saloon, for Dick Johnson (ten.), who in reality is Ramerrez, a notorious bandit. The Sheriff, Jack Rance (bar.), is also in love with Minnie, and when he reveals to her that Johnson is a bandit, she sends the latter away. But when he is wounded, Minnie, who has relented, hides him in the loft of her cabin. Drops of blood from the ceiling reveal to Rance that Johnson is there. Rance and Minnie play poker: if she should win Rance must let Johnson go free; if she loses, she will marry Rance. By cheating, she wins the game. But Johnson is captured and is condemned to be hanged. Minnie rides up on horseback and successfully pleads for Johnson's life. Together they set off to start a new life together.

Fanget an! Walther's (ten.) trial song in Act 1 of Wagner's *Die Meistersinger*.

Faninal. A wealthy, newly ennobled merchant (bar.), Sophie's father, in Strauss's *Der Rosenkavalier*.

Faramondo. Opera in 3 acts by Handel; text by Zeno, altered. Prod. London, Hm., 18 Jan. 1738, with Francescina, Lucchesi, Caffarelli, Montagna, Lottini, Merighi. Unsuccessful: ran 8 nights. Zeno's text was first set by Pollarolo (1699), later by Porpora (1719).

Farewell. The name commonly given to the last performance in public of a favourite artist. Some singers, especially sopranos, have announced their farewell seasons years before they took their actual leave of the stage – Grisi is a notable example. Melba's Farewell, including her speech, at C.G. in 1926, was recorded by H.M.V. German provincial houses give 'Abschied' performances for a favourite singer when he or she leaves to take up an engagement in another theatre.

Farinelli (orig. Carlo Broschi) (*b* Andria, 24 Jan. 1705; *d* Bologna, 15 July 1782). Italian male soprano. Studied with Porpora; début 1722 in his teacher's *Eumene*. In 1727 he was defeated in a public exhibition of vocal skill by Bernacchi, who then consented to teach him further. He sang in Vienna and London, where he became a great favourite, women fainting from excitement at his performances. Became the star performer in Porpora's rival company to Handel's at Lincoln's Inn Fields. Sang in Madrid in 1737; his voice so cheered the melancholia of Philip V that he was offered 50,000 francs a year to remain in Madrid. This he did for 25 years, singing him the same four songs every night. He persuaded Philip's successor, Ferdinand VI, to establish an Italian opera in Madrid, and in 1750 received the Cross of Calatrava. On Charles III's accession he had to leave Spain for political reasons. When he was visited by Burney in Bologna in 1771 he no longer sang, but played the harpsichord and viola d'amore; he had a fine collection of pictures by Murillo and Ximenes.

Operas on him are by Barnett (1839), Espín y Guillén (1854), Zumpe (1886), and Bretón (1901).

Bibl: J. Desastre: *Carlo Broschi* (1903).

Farinelli, Giuseppe (orig. Francesco Finco) (*b* Este, 7 May 1769; *d* Trieste, 12 Dec. 1836). Italian composer. Studied Este, Venice with Martinelli, later Naples. A follower of Cimarosa in style, he composed 20 *opere serie* and 38 comic operas, many of which were popular on Italian stages until the coming of Rossini. The most successful include *Teresa e Claudio* (1801), *Chi la dura la vince* (1803), and *I riti d'Efeso* (1803).

Farrar, Geraldine (*b* Melrose, Mass., 28 Feb. 1882; *d* Ridgefield, 11 Mar. 1967). American soprano. At the age of 10 appeared in a pageant, as Jenny Lind, when her voice attracted attention. Studied in Boston, N.Y., and Paris, then (on Nordica's advice) in Berlin with Graziani. Début there, Hofoper, 1901, Marguerite. Heard by Lilli Lehmann, whose pupil she then became. N.Y. début 1906, Juliette; remained a member of the Met. until her retirement in 1922, singing nearly 500 times in 29 roles. Created Amica (Mascagni) (Monte Carlo, 1905), the Goosegirl in *Königskinder* (1910), Madame Sans-Gêne (1915), and Suor Angelica (1918). An outstanding Butterfly, Manon, and Zazà. She enjoyed great popularity, especially among young female opera-goers, who were nicknamed 'Gerryflappers'. She made more than a dozen films. (R)

Bibl: G. Farrar: *The Story of an American Singer* (1916), rev. as *Such Sweet Compulsion* (1938).

Fasano, Renato (*b* Naples, 21 Aug. 1902). Italian composer and conductor. Studied Naples. Founded the Collegium Musicum Italicum in Rome (1941) and subsequently the Virtuosi di Roma; and in 1957 the Piccolo T. Musicale Italiano, which has appeared throughout Europe and the U.S.A. giving performances of operas by Galuppi, Cimarosa, Paisiello, Pergolesi, Rossini, etc. (R)

Fasolt. With Fafner, one of the giants (bass) in Wagner's *Das Rheingold*.

Fassbaender, Brigitte (*b* Berlin, 3 July 1939). German mezzo-soprano. Daughter of baritone Willi *Domgraf-Fassbaender. Studied with her father and at Nuremberg Conservatory. Début Munich, P., 1961, Nicklausse. Member of Bavarian State Opera since 1961; London, C.G., 1971, Oktavian; San Francisco, 1971, Carmen; Salzburg, 1973, Fricka. Especially successful in *travesti* roles, but also as Dorabella, Marina, and Charlotte. Possesses a large and attractive voice and vivid stage personality. (R)

Fassbender, Zdenka (*b* Děčín, 12 Dec. 1879; *d* Munich, 14 Mar. 1954). Bohemian soprano. Studied Prague with Sophie Lowe-Destinn; début Karlsruhe 1899. Leading dramatic soprano Munich 1906-19; specially noted for her Strauss and Wagner. Sang Elektra and Isolde in London under Beecham, 1910 and 1913. Married Felix *Mottl.

Fauré, Gabriel (*b* Pamiers, 12 May 1845; *d* Paris, 4 Nov. 1924). French composer. *Prométhée* (1900) shows the influence of Wagner, though the treatment is essentially classical, portraying and suggesting, rather than conveying, emotion. Wagner's shadow still falls across *Pénélope* (1913), together with the heavier one of Romantic convention – an opening spinning chorus, a final 'Gloire à Zeus'. But it is in this work that Fauré comes closest to exemplifying the true connection between the French and the Greek genius – a spare, brilliant quality of thought rather than the Hellenistic languor on which the comparison generally rests.

Bibl: C. Koechlin: *Fauré* (1927; trans., 1945); N. Suckling: *Fauré* (1946).

Faure, Jean-Baptiste (*b* Moulins, 15 Jan. 1830; *d* Paris, 9 Nov. 1914). French baritone. Studied Paris Conservatoire. Début Paris, O.C., 1852 in *Galathée* (Massé). O. 1861-9, 1872-6, and 1878, creating Nelusko (*L'Africaine*), Posa (*Don Carlos*), Hamlet, etc. Début C.G. 1860, Hoël (*Dinorah*), and sang there and at D.L. and H.M.'s frequently until 1877; last appearances Marseilles and Vichy, 1886. Was an admired Don Giovanni and William Tell. From 1857 to 1860 taught singing at the Conservatoire. He wrote two books on singing, and was the subject of two portraits by Manet. His wife, **Con-**

stance Caroline Lefèbvre (1828-1905) sang at the O.C., 1849-59.

Faust. A wandering conjuror who lived in Germany c1488-1541. The legend that he had sold his soul to the Devil, in exchange for a fixed period of renewed youth and other favours, was first set down and published in the *Historia von D. Johann Fausten* (compiled by Johann Spies, 1587); it inspired various writers, especially Marlowe in his *Tragicall History of Dr Faustus* (1588-93) and Goethe in his *Faust* (Pt. 1, 1808; Pt. 2, 1832).

Operas deriving from Goethe's treatment of the legend are by Lutz (*Faust et Marguerite*, 1855), Gounod (1859), Barbier (a *saynète bouffe, Faust et Marguerite*, 1869), Brüggemann (Faust tetralogy: *Doktor Faust*, 1910; *Gretchen*, 1910; *Faust und Helena*; *König Faust*, unfin.), and N.V. Bentzon (*Faust*, 1964, after Goethe, Kafka, and Joyce).

Operas deriving from other sources are by Hanke (*La Ceinture du Docteur Faust*, c1796), I. Walter (*Dr Faust*, 1797), Spohr (1816), W. Müller (*Dr Fausts Mantel*, 1817), Saint-Lubin (*Le Cousin du Docteur Faust*, 1829), Busoni (*Doktor Faust*, 1925), Reutter (*Dr Johannes Faust*, 1936, rev. 1955), Engelmann (*Dr Fausts Höllenfahrt*, 1951), J. Berg (*Dr Johannes Faust*, 1967).

Berlioz's *La Damnation de Faust* (1846), though not an opera, has repeatedly been staged.

Faust. Opera in 5 acts by Gounod; text by Barbier and Carré, after Goethe's poem (Pt. 1, 1808; Pt. 2, 1832). Prod. Paris, T.L., 19 Mar. 1859, with M. Carvalho, Faivre, Barbot, Reynald, Balanque, cond. Deloffre; 500 perfs. by 1887, 1,000 by 1894, 2,000 by 1934; London, H.M.'s, 11 June 1863, with Tietjens, Trebelli, Giuglini, Santley, Gassier – and in every C.G. season 1863-1911; Philadelphia 18 Nov. 1863, with Frederici, Gross, Himmer, Steinecke, Graffi. Inaugural opera at Met. 22 Oct. 1893, with Nilsson, Scalchi, Campanini, Del Puente, Novara, cond. Vianesi. One of the most successful operas ever written, with translations into at least 25 languages. The opera inspired a poem *Fausto* by Estanislao del Campo.

Faust (ten.) makes a bargain with Méphistophélès (bass): in return for eternal youth and the beautiful Marguerite (sop.), he promises Méphistophélès his soul. Valentine (bar.), Marguerite's brother, entrusts the care of his sister to the faithful Siebel (mezzo) while he goes off to the wars. On his return he finds Marguerite has been betrayed by Faust, and challenging him to a duel is killed. Marguerite, in prison for killing her baby, refuses to go with Faust and Méphistophélès; as she ascends to Heaven, Faust is dragged down to Hell by Méphistophélès.

Favart, Charles-Simon (*b* Paris, 13 Nov. 1710; *d* Belleville, 12 Mar. 1792). French librettist and impresario. Stage manager, O.C., then summoned to Brussels by the Maréchal de Saxe to organize a theatre for the troops in Flanders. Succeeded Monnet as director of the *Opéra-Comique 1758, holding the position until his retirement in 1769. In 1781 the O.C. assumed his name. He provided more than 150 librettos for different composers, among them Grétry, Philidor, and Gluck.

The first important French comic librettist, Favart began his career writing *vaudevilles, *drames forains*, and other pieces, developing in the 1750s the librettos with a continuous story, invented or at least developed from an original by himself, into which songs were fitted: this was the *comédie mêlée d'ariettes*. His parodies were witty and on the whole good-natured, even constructive: his *Arlequin-Dardanus* (1739), parodying Rameau's *Dardanus* (1739), so impressed the librettist, La Bruère, that the text was revised for the next production. His shafts pierced not only fellow librettists, but composers, singers, and the stage management of the Opéra. In the 1760s he turned to adaptations, in an attempt to fashion an indigenous French comic opera in the wake of the *Guerre des Bouffons. He gave the lighthearted plots a tinge of sentimentality, especially in the female lead (the *ingénue). These librettos were characterized by their nimble pace, and their ingenious tangle of intrigue to which *couplets add a point of brief repose.

Favart's pastoral comedies include *Le Caprice amoureux, ou Ninette à la cour,* set by Duni (1755), a piece which typifies his ability to turn a parody (of Goldoni) into a work that develops the comic genre: there are in it anticipations of many subsequent *ingénues* in Ninette (e.g. Zerlina) and even of whole situations, and other of Favart's librettos contain suggestions of characters that were to become famous through later comic operas. *Soliman second, ou Les Trois Sultanes* (set by Gilbert, 1761) is an early example of the 'Turkish' plots of Mozart's *Entführung* and other works. Favart was also largely responsible for a new naturalistic treatment of peasants and rustic life, often sentimental but more accurately observed and more respectful of simple people. He helped substantially to make possible the realism of later *opéra-comique*.

After the death of his wife (see below) in 1772, Favart gave up writing for the theatre and withdrew to his country house at Belleville. *Bibl:* C. S. Favart: *Mémoires et correspondance littéraire* (ed. A. P. Favart and H.F. Dumolard, 3 vols., 1808); A. Font: *Essai sur Favart et les origines de la comédie mêlée de chant* (1894).

Favart, Marie (orig. Marie-Justine-Benoîte Duronceray) (*b* Avignon 15 June 1727; *d* Paris, 21 Apr. 1772). French soprano. Wife of above, daughter of André-René Duronceray, musician of the Chapel Royal of Louis XV. Début 1744 under name of Mlle de Chantilly in *Les Fêtes publiques*. Married Favart 1745. Under the protection of the Maréchal de Saxe and accompanied by her husband, she took part in performances in Flanders. She was the leading soubrette at in Paris, T.I., from 1751, scoring a great success in *La serva padrona*, and in several works for which her husband had written the libretto, including *Les Amours de Bastien et Bastienne*. Her successes aroused much hostility and jealousy. She intrigued to close her husband's theatre, the O.C., by performing works at the Italien created for the Comique. Louis XV decreed the amalgamation of the two theatres in February 1762. She fell ill in June 1771 and died the following spring. Her son, **Charles-Nicolas-Justin Favart** (1749-1806) sang at the O.C. and T.I.; a second son **Antoine Pierre Charles** (1784-*c*1867) was co-author of a vaudeville, *La Jeunesse de Favart*. Operetta on her life, *Mme. Favart*, by Offenbach (1878).
Bibl: A. Pougin: *Madame Favart* (1912).

Favero, Mafalda (*b* Ferrara, 6 Jan. 1905). Italian soprano. Studied Bologna with Alessandro Vezzani. Début Cremona, T. Ponchielli, under pseudonym Maria Bianchi, as Lola. Parma 1927, Liù. Engaged by Toscanini for Milan Sc. 1929, and sang there regularly until 1942 and again 1945-50, creating Gasparina (*Il campiello*) and *La dama boba*. London, C.G., 1937 and 1939; San Francisco, N.Y., Met., 1938. A fine Mimì, Manon, Thaïs, Adriana Lecouvreur, and Zazà. (R)
Bibl: I. Buscaglia: *Mafalda Favero nella vita e nell' arte* (1946).

Favola d'Orfeo, La (The Legend of Orpheus). *Favola in musica* in a prologue and 5 acts by Monteverdi; text by Alessandro Striggio. Prod. (privately) Mantua, Accademia degl'Invaghiti, Feb. 1607, and 24 Feb. 1607, Mantua, Court T., with Gualberto. Revived Paris 25 Feb. 1904, concert version by Schola Cantorum (arr. D'Indy); first modern stage perf. there, T. Réjane 1911. N.Y., Met., concert perf., 14 Apr. 1912, with Fornia, Weil, Witherspoon; first U.S. prod. Northampton, Smith College, in Malipiero version, 14 May 1929, with Kullman. First English perf., concert, London, Institut Français, in D'Indy version, 1924; first English prod., Oxford, 7 Dec. 1925, opening prod. of Oxford University Opera Club, cond. Westrup. Of many editions, the most famous (in some cases notorious) are those by Eitner (1881), D'Indy (?1903), Orefice (1909), Malipiero (1923), Orff (1923), Westrup (1925), Benvenuti (1934), Respighi (1935), Hindemith (1954), Wenzinger (1957), Maderna (1967), Stevens (1967), and Leppard (1967).

After a prologue, nymphs and shepherds are discovered rejoicing at the coming marriage of Orpheus (ten. or bar.) and Eurydice (sop.). In a wood, Orpheus sings to nature, but is interrupted by the Messenger (con.) bringing the news of Eurydice's death. He descends to Hades to find her, and is comforted by Hope; lulling Charon (bass) with his song, he crosses the Styx and wins the agreement of Pluto (bass) and Proserpina (sop.) that he may take her back to earth if he will not turn round to look at her on their journey. Unable to resist assuring himself that she is indeed there, he turns just as they reach the light, and she is snatched back to Hades. Orpheus laments his lot, but is consoled by Apollo (bass) with the promise of immortality with Eurydice.

Favola per musica, or **Favola in musica.** A 17th-cent. term for an opera libretto of legendary or mythological nature.

Favorite, La (The Favourite). Opera in 4 acts by Donizetti; text by Royer and Vaëz, after Baculard d'Arnaud's drama *Le Comte de Comminges* (1764) and other material. Prod. Paris, O., 2 Dec. 1840 with Stolz, Elian, Duprez, Barroilhet, Levasseur, Wartel, cond. Habeneck; New Orleans 9 Feb. 1843 with Lagier, Allard, Victor, Blès cond. Prévost; London, D.L., 18 Oct. 1843. Originally to be entitled *L'Ange de Nisida*, it has been given also as *Dalila, Leonora di Guzman*, and *Riccardo e Matilda*.

The action takes place in Spain in 1340 and tells of the unhappy love of Fernando (ten.), a novice in the Monastery of St James, for Leonora de Gusman (mezzo), mistress of Alfonso XI (bar.), King of Castile.

Federici, Vincenzo (*b* Pesaro, 1764; *d* Milan, 26 Sept. 1826). Italian composer. He wrote 14 *opere serie* and one comic opera (*La locandiera scaltra*, 1812). Conducted Bianchi's *La villanella rapita* in London in 1790, then his own *L'usurpatore innocente*. Connected with King's T. for 10 years. Returned to Italy 1802, settling in Milan, where he taught at the Conservatory. Though not of great originality, his operas are well fashioned and were very successful in their day; in style they are close to Fioravanti and Paisiello.

Fedora. Opera in 3 acts by Giordano; text by Colautti, after Sardou's drama (1882). Prod. Milan, T.L., 17 Nov. 1898, with Bellincioni, Caruso, cond. Giordano; London, C.G., 5 Nov. 1906, with Giachetti, Zenatello, cond. Mugnone; N.Y., Met., 5 Dec. 1906, with Cavalieri, Caruso, cond. Vigna.

The story of the tragic love of Count Loris Ipanov (ten.), a Russian nihilist, for the Princess Fedora Romanov (mezzo or sop.).

Fedra. (1) Opera in 3 acts by Pizzetti; text by D'Annunzio. Prod. Milan, Sc., 20 Mar. 1915, with Kruscneniski, Anitua, Di Giovanni, Grandini, cond. Marinuzzi.

The opera, based on Euripides's *Hippolytus*, tells how Phaedra (sop.) the wife of Theseus (bar.), falls in love with her stepson, Hippolytus (ten.) and when rejected by him hangs herself, leaving behind a letter falsely accusing Hippolytus of dishonouring her.

(2) Opera in 1 act by Romano Romani; text by Alfredo Lenozoni. Prod. Rome 3 Apr. 1915, with Raisa; London, C.G., 18 June 1931, with Ponselle. Other operas on the subject by Lemoyne (1786), Paisiello (1788), ?Niccolini (1803), Orlandi (1820), Mayr (1821), Lord Burghersh (1824).

Feen, Die (The Fairies). Opera in 3 acts by Wagner; text by composer after Gozzi's comedy *La donna serpente* (1762), first used in Himmel's *Die Sylphen* (1806; the first German Gozzi setting). Prod. Munich 29 June 1888, cond. Fischer; Birmingham, by Midland Music Makers, 17 May 1969, cond. Lee. Wagner's first completed opera, comp. 1833-4. The first production was rehearsed by Richard Strauss, who was to have conducted it; but Perfall, the Intendant, decided that 'so important a novelty cannot be left to the third conductor'. The incident precipitated Strauss's departure from Munich in the following year.

Pursuing a doe, Prince Arindal (ten.) plunges into a river and awakes in the castle of the fairy Ada (sop.). They fall in love, and marry on condition that for eight years he shall not ask her origin. At the end of this time he does ask the question, and she and her castle and her children vanish; Arindal is cast back into the world of humans. Meanwhile his father has died and the city is threatened with invasion. Arindal does not know that Ada is subject to the fairies' insistence that she must remain one of them, and may only shed her immortality for Arindal by surviving a set of ordeals; she must lay dreadful tests upon him, and he must endure them without cursing her. Arindal is driven beyond his endurance and does curse her; and when the truth is revealed he goes mad when she turns to stone. But with the help of the magician Groma, Arindal pursues her into the underworld and overcomes the spirits who defend her; with his lyre, he melts the cold stone and wins back his bride. She must remain a fairy, but he can now join her in her realm.

Casella used the same text for his *La donna serpente* (1932).

Feinhals, Fritz (*b* Cologne, 14 Dec. 1869; *d* Munich, 30 Aug. 1940). German baritone. Studied Milan with Giovannini and Selva. Début Essen 1895, Silvio. Leading baritone Munich Opera 1898-1927; London, C.G., 1898 and 1907; N.Y., Met., 1908. A famous Sachs, Wotan, Telramund, Amfortas, and Kurwenal;

but also heard often in Mozart and Verdi. (R)

Fel, Marie (*b* Bordeaux, 24 Oct. 1713; *d* Chaillot (Paris) 5 Feb. 1794). French soprano. Début Paris, O., 1734, where she remained until 1758. Created L'Amour in *Castor et Pollux*, and roles in operas by Lully, Leclair, Mondonville, Rousseau, Brassac, and Dauvergne. Famous for her performance of Jélyotte in *Le Devin du village*. Her brother, **Antoine** (1694-1771), sang at the O. and also was a composer.

Feldlager in Schlesien, Ein. See *Étoile du Nord*.

Felsenstein, Walter (*b* Vienna, 30 May 1901; *d* Berlin, 8 Oct. 1975). Austrian producer. Studied Graz and Vienna. Originally an actor in Lübeck, Mannheim, etc. Subsequently opera producer in Cologne, Frankfurt, Munich, and Zürich. Producer and Intendant of Berlin K.O. 1947-75, where his productions of *The Cunning Little Vixen*, *Figaro*, *Contes d'Hoffmann*, *Zauberflöte*, *Carmen*, and *Otello* won international acclaim. Helped to train Götz *Friedrich and Joachim *Herz.
Bibl: G. Friedrich: *Walter Felsenstein* (1967); S. Stomper and I. Kobán (ed.): *Walter Felsenstein Schriften zum Musiktheater* (1976).

Fenice, Teatro La. See *Venice*.

Fenton. Anne's (Nannetta's) lover (ten.) in Nicolai's *Die lustigen Weiber von Windsor* and Verdi's *Falstaff*.

Fenton (orig. Beswick), **Lavinia** (*b* London, 1708; *d* Greewich, 24 Jan. 1760). English soprano. Originally an actress, she sang Polly Peachum at the first performance of *The Beggar's Opera* (1728). After singing the role more than 60 times she left the stage and became the mistress of the Duke of Bolton, whom she married in 1751.

Feo, Francesco (*b*? Naples, ? 1685; *d* Naples, 1761). Italian composer. Studied Rome, later taught in Naples, including among his pupils Jommelli and Pergolesi. An important composer of Neapolitan opera, he wrote a large number of works that were successful in their day; of them, *Siface* (1723) and *Ipermestra* (1724) are the best known.

Ferencsik, János. (*b* Budapest, 18 Jan. 1907). Hungarian conductor. Studied Budapest. Répétiteur at the State Opera 1927-30; conductor from 1930; music director since 1950. Many guest appearances incl. Vienna 1948-50 and subsequently; San Francisco 1962-3; Edinburgh Festival with Budapest Company 1963, 1973. (R)

Fermata (*It* stop, pause). The term used for a pause on a held note or chord; the Italians use the word *corona*.

Fernand Cortez. Opera in 3 acts by Spontini; text by Esménard and De Jouy, after Alexis

Piron's tragedy (1744). Prod. Paris, O., 28 Nov. 1809 with Branchu, Lainez, Laïs, Laforet, Dérivis, Bertin – c250 perfs. by 1840; N.Y., Met., 6 Jan. 1888, with Meisslinger, Alvary, Nieman, Fischer, Elmblad, cond. Seidl; never in London, initially through Bishop's (unsuccessful) opera on same subject, text by Planché, C.G., 1823. Cortez (ten.), conqueror of Mexico, has fallen in love with Amazily (sop.), daughter of king Montezuma (bass). With her help he puts down a mutiny by his own men and rescues his brother from being sacrificed to the Aztec gods. Also opera by Ricci (1830).

Fernández Caballero, Manuel (b Murcia, 14 Mar. 1835; d Madrid, 26 Feb. 1906). Spanish composer. One of the most popular of all zarzuela composers; his 220-odd pieces include El salto del pasiego, Los Hijos del Capitán Grant, La Viejecita, and El Señor Joaquín.

Ferne Klang, Der (The Distant Sound). Opera in 3 acts by Schreker; text by composer. Prod. Frankfurt 18 Aug. 1912. Schreker's first and best-known opera.

Ferni. Italian musical family.
(1) **Carolina** (b Como, 20 Aug. 1839; d Milan, 4 June 1926). Italian soprano and violinist. Studied violin Paris and Brussels, and voice with Pasta. Début Turin, 1862, Leonora in Favorite. Milan, Sc., 1866-8. Repertory included Norma, Selika, Saffo, and Mercuri's Violino del Diavolo in which she both sang and played the violin. Retired from stage 1883 and opened a school for singing in Milan and later in St Petersburg. Her pupils included Caruso and Burzio. She married the baritone Leone *Giraldoni; their son, **Eugenio**, who created Scarpia, was also one of her pupils.
(2) **Vincenzina** (b Como, 1873; d Turin, June, 1926). Italian soprano and violinist. Sister of (1). After a short career married the Spanish baritone Manuel Carbonell Villar (1856-1928) and retired from stage.
(3) **Virginia** (b Turin, 1849; d Turin, 4 Feb. 1934). Italian soprano. Cousin of (1) and (2). She was a child prodigy; appeared when 7 years old singing Spanish songs and accompanying herself on the violin. Stage début shortly after as Siebel. Successful career in Europe and America, retired 1896. Repertory included Carmen, Mignon, Loreley, and Margherita and Elena (Mefistofele). Married the violinist Germano.

Ferrando. An officer (ten.), Dorabella's lover, in Mozart's Così fan tutte.

Ferrani (orig. Zanazzio), **Cesira** (b Turin, 8 May 1863; d nr Biella, 4 May 1943). Italian soprano. Studied with Antonietta Fricci. Début Turin 1887, Micaëla. Created Manon Lescaut (1893), Mimì (1896). Celebrated for her interpretations of Eva and Elsa, and chosen by Toscanini as

first Mélisande in Italy (Milan. Sc., 1908). In Rome in 1909 Pelléas was hissed off the stage and Ferrani retired to Turin, where she founded a salon which became the centre of intellectual life there for many years. (R)

Ferrara. Town in Emilia, Italy. The first theatre was built in 1610 by the Accademia degli Intrepidi. It was taken over by the Marchese Pio Enea degli Obizzi, 1640, and burned down in 1679. The T. Comunale opened in 1789 and was the scene of the première of Rossini's Ciro in Babilonia (1812). The Arena Tosi-Borghi, built in 1856, was turned into the T. Verdi in 1913 and is the scene of short opera seasons every spring and autumn. Gatti-Casazza was manager at the Comunale 1894-7, and Serafin made his début there in 1902.

Ferrarese, La. See Gabrieli, Adriana.

Ferrari, Benedetto (b Reggio, 1595; d Modena, 22 Oct. 1681). Italian composer and librettist. Studied Rome. In 1637 he wrote the libretto of the first publicly performed opera, Manelli's Andromeda for the T. Tron di S. Cassiano in Venice. He was one of the first to set his own librettos to music.

Ferrari, Giacomo (Gotifredo) (b Rovereto, bapt. 2 Apr. 1763; d London, Dec. 1842). Italian composer. Studied Verona, Rovereto, and in Switzerland. Worked in Paris at the T. de Monsieur, 1787, also writing extra music for Bianchi's La villanella rapita and other operas. In London from 1792: his first opera here was I due Svizzeri (1799), and this was followed by several others, including L'eroina di Raab (1813) for Catalani. He published A Concise Treatise on Italian Singing (2 vols, trans. Shield, 1818 and 1825). His son **Adolfo Ferrari** (1807-70) was a singer, as were Adolfo's wife Johanna Thompson and their daughter Sophia Ferrari.

Ferrari-Fontana, Edoarda (b Rome, 8 July 1878; d Toronto, 4 July 1936). Italian tenor. After completing his medical studies, he decided to enter diplomatic service and worked as secretary to the Italian consul in Montevideo 1902-8. Began to study singing and took part in operetta and light opera performances in Argentina and Milan. Persuaded by Serafin to study singing seriously 1907-9. Début Turin 1910, Tristan, replacing at short notice the indisposed Borgatti. Milan, Sc., 1912-14, where he created Avito (L'amore dei tre re). N.Y., Met., 1913-15; Chicago, Boston. Especially successful in Buenos Aires 1911-12 and 1920 as Tristan, Siegmund, Siegfried, and Tannhäuser. After leaving stage taught in Toronto 1926-36. Married to Marguerite *Matzenauer. His records show him to have had a rich, clear voice, a solid technique, and excellent enunciation. (R)

Ferretti, Jacopo (*b* Rome, 16 July 1784; *d* Rome, 7 Mar. 1852). Italian librettist. After an early failure with his libretto for Fioravanti's *Didone abbandonata* (1810), a reworking of the Metastasio, he made the brilliant version of the old Cinderella story, *Cenerentola* (1817), for Rossini. He also wrote *Matilde di Shabran* for Rossini, and *Torquato Tasso* for Donizetti, as well as librettos for Zingarelli, Mayr, P. C. Guglielmi, Coccia, Mercadante, Pacini, L. Ricci, Coppola, and many others. His verses, especially for *opera buffa*, are distinguished by their verbal elegance and sharp social comment, and he was always willing to modify his own or other men's work to ensure a greater acceptance for the opera.

Ferri, Baldassare (*b* Perugia, 9 Dec. 1610; *d* Perugia, 18 Sept. 1680). Italian male soprano. Studied in Rome, probably with V. Ugolini. Heard by Ladislas VII in 1625, who took him to Poland, where he remained until 1655. Although Poland and Sweden were at war, Queen Christina begged Sigismund III to allow Ferri to go to Stockholm to sing. The request was granted, and Ferri sang with great success in the Swedish capital; a medal was struck in his honour. From 1655 to 1675 he sang in Vienna, becoming enormously rich: when he died he left 600,000 scudi for a charitable institution to be built in Perugia. In Vienna the Emperor Leopold I hung Ferri's portrait in his bedroom, with the inscription 'Baldassare Ferri, Re dei Musici'. One of the first of the great star castrati.

Ferrier, Kathleen (*b* Higher Walton, 22 Apr. 1912; *d* London, 8 Oct. 1953). English contralto. Studied with J. E. Hutchinson and Roy Henderson. Was established as a concert singer before her opera début in 1946 in Britten's *The Rape of Lucretia* in its world première at Gly. Sang Orfeo at Gly., 1947, and in Holland, and at C.G. under Barbirolli in 1953. Her beautiful voice, warm stage presence, and deep sincerity made her one of the best loved singers of her day. (R)
Bibl: W. Ferrier: *The Life of Kathleen Ferrier* (1955; reissued, with *Kathleen Ferrier, a Memoir* (ed. Cardus, 1954) 1971).

Fervaal. *Action dramatique* in a prologue and 3 acts by D'Indy; text by composer. Prod. Brussels, M., 12 Mar. 1897, with Raunay, De la Tour, Seguin, cond. Flon.

The action, which takes place in the Midi of France at the time of the Saracen invasions, tells how Fervaal (ten.) a Celtic chief, wounded in battle, is nursed back to health by Guilhen (sop.), a Saracen sorceress. Arfagard (bar.), a Druid, forces Fervaal to leave Guilhen, who, thinking herself betrayed, lures the Celts to their deaths.

Festa (Maffei), **Francesca** (*b* Naples, 1778; *d* St Petersburg, 21 Nov. 1835). Italian soprano. Sister of the conductor and violinist, Giuseppe Festa. Studied Naples with Aprile, Milan with Pacchiarotti. Début Naples, T.N., 1799; Milan, Sc., 1805, 1814, 1816-17, 1819, 1824. She created Fiorilla (*Turco in Italia*) and roles in operas by Mosca, Pavesi, Paer, etc., also first Scala Donna Anna and Cenerentola. Paris, Odéon, 1809-11, Munich 1821, St Petersburg 1829. Said to have had a voice of sensuous appeal.

Festivals. The term derives from the Latin *festivitas* (merriment), and was used at the time of the Renaissance to describe the celebrations with music that took place in the Royal courts to mark special occasions, as, for example, the meeting at Bologna in 1515 between Francis I and Pope Leo X. In more modern times the word came to be applied to a grand musical occasion, in the first place dedicated to one composer, as, for example, the Handel Festival in England in 1862, the Haydn Festivals in Austria in 1808-11, and the Beethoven celebrations in Germany in 1845.

Summer festivals are very much a product of the post-1945 period, and are often highly commercialized affairs, arranged to attract the tourist from abroad. There are of course honourable exceptions, especially the now annual Bayreuth Festival (July–Aug.) which is the oldest of the European opera festivals, having started in 1876. Wiesbaden (May) began in 1900. The Munich Opera Festival (mid-Aug.– early Sept.) was begun in 1901; Salzburg (July–Aug.) was established in 1920; Zurich (June) in 1932; Florence (May–June) in 1933; Glyndebourne (May–Aug.) in 1934; Edinburgh (Aug.–Sept.) in 1947; Aldeburgh (June) in 1948; Aix-en-Provence (July) in 1948; Holland (June–July) in 1949; Wexford (Oct.–Nov.) in 1951; Spoleto (June–July) in 1958. The Salzburg Easter Festival was established in 1967 by Karajan. Other summer festivals include those at Bregenz, Orange, Schwetzingen, and Drottningholm. In the U.S.A. the most important opera festival takes place at Santa Fe in New Mexico. See also separate entries for above-named places.

Feuersnot (Fire-famine). *Singgedicht* in 1 act by Richard Strauss; text by Ernst von Wolzogen, after a Flemish legend, *The Quenched Fires of Audenaarde,* in J.W. Wolf's *Sagas of the Netherlands* (1843). Prod. Dresden 21 Nov. 1901, with Krull, Petter, Scheidemantel, cond. Schuch; London, H.M.'s, 9 July 1910, with Fay, Oster, Radford, cond. Beecham; Philadelphia 1 Dec. 1927, with Stanley, Salzinger, Rasely, Albert Mahler, Nelson Eddy, cond. Smallens.

Kunrad (bar.) is so enraged at his public humiliation by Diemut (sop.) that he conjures the extinction of all fire; this is restored at the moment of his acceptance by the repentant

Diemut. The opera pokes fun at the Munichers who rejected Richard I (Wagner), and then his disciple, Richard Strauss.

Février, Henri (b Paris, 2 Oct. 1875; d Paris, 8 July 1957). French composer. Studied Paris with Fauré, Leroux, Messager, Pugno, and Massenet. His first opera was *Le Roi aveugle* (Paris 1906) which achieved only a moderate success; this was followed in 1909 by *Monna Vanna*, his most successful work, which was produced in several countries and has had several revivals in Paris. He wrote several more works for the stage which were in the tradition of Massenet, but also show the influence of Debussy and the Italian *verismo* school. He wrote *André Messager: mon maître, mon ami* (1948).

Fiamma, La (The Flame). Opera in 3 acts by Respighi; text by Guastalla after Hans Werner Jensen. Prod. Rome, T.R., 23 Jan. 1934, with Cobelli, Minghetti, Tagliabue, cond. Respighi; Chicago 2 Dec. 1935, with Raisa, Barova, Bentonelli, Morelli, cond. Hageman.

Silvana (sop.), daughter of a witch, Agnes de Cervia, is married to Basilio (bar.), ruler of Ravenna. She is unable to stop her mother being hanged. Agnes curses Basilio's family, including her daughter, who then falls in love with Agnes's stepson Donello (ten.). When Silvana confesses her adultery, Basilio falls dead, and Silvana, accused of witchcraft herself, is condemned to death.

Fibich, Zdeněk (b Všebořice, 21 Dec. 1850; d Prague, 15 Oct. 1900). Czech composer. It is for his seven operas that Fibich is chiefly remembered. *Bukovín* (1874) and *Blaník* (1881) are both early and uneven, but with *Nevěsta mesinská* (The Bride of Messina, 1884), Fibich's skill and imagination as an opera composer became fully apparent. *Bouře* (The Tempest, 1895) is said to be effective. Fibich's last three operas were written with Anežka Schulzová, the poet for whom he abandoned his family. *Hedy* (1896) contains fine music, but his masterpiece is *Šárka* (1897), a powerful and musically gripping treatment of the popular Czech legend. *Pád Arkuna* (The Fall of Arkun, 1900) turns away from popular taste. Though less gifted melodically than either Smetana or Dvořák, Fibich had a considerable gift for symphonic thought in opera. He makes much use of Leitmotiv in his trilogy of melodramas *Hippodamie*, consisting of *Námluvy Pelopovy* (The Wooing of Pelops, 1889), *Smír Tantalův* (The Atonement of Tantalus, 1890), and *Smrt Hippodamie* (The Death of Hippodamia, 1891). *Bibl:* K. Jirák: *Zdeněk Fibich* (1947).

Fidelio, oder Die eheliche Liebe. Opera in 3 acts by Beethoven; text by Josef Sonnleithner, a German version of Bouilly's *Léonore, ou L'Amour conjugal*, music by Gaveaux (1798)

and then set, in an Italian version, by Paer (1804) and Mayr (1805). Altered and reduced to 2 acts by Stefan von Breuning in 1806; given final form by Georg Friedrich Treitschke in 1814. First version prod. Vienna, W., 20 Nov. 1805, with Milder, Demmer, Meier, Rothe, Weinkopf, Caché, cond. Seyfried; 2nd version, W., 29 Mar. 1806; 3rd version, Kä., 23 May 1814. London, H.M.'s, 18 May 1832, with Schröder-Devrient, Haitzinger, cond. Chelard; N.Y., Park T., 9 Sept. 1839, with Inverarity, Manvers, Giubilei, Martyn.

The overture now usually played is entitled *Fidelio*. Three other overtures exist, *Leonore No. 1* (composed for a projected performance in Prague), *Leonore No. 2* (actually the first, played at the première), and *Leonore No. 3*. There is a long-standing tradition of using the last as an interlude between the final scenes; but it fits neither harmonically, instrumentally, nor dramatically, intruding an orchestral summary of parts of the drama. At the Vienna Kä. on 28 Sept. 1841 Nicolai placed it between the two acts. Carl Anschütz set it before the final scene in Amsterdam, late April 1849, and at London, D.L., 19 May 1849. Balfe followed suit at H.M.'s in 1851, as did Augusto Vianesi in Paris (T.I.) in Jan. 1852 (reported by Berlioz). Levi played it after the opera in Rotterdam in 1863. Anschütz played three overtures (not known which) in Philadelphia, 9 Nov. 1863, one before each act; others in U.S. gave *Leonore No. 3* before the final scene, incl. Seidl (Met., 1890-1). Mahler did so, Vienna 1904 (and has often been credited with introducing the idea). Other conductors who have done it include Busch, Reiner, Szell, Beecham, Walter, Kleiber, Furtwängler, Toscanini, Strauss (after initial doubts), and Klemperer (later giving it up).

Florestan (ten.), a Spanish nobleman, has been thrown into prison. His wife Leonore (sop.) has followed him disguised as a boy, Fidelio, in the hope of rescue. The kindly jailer Rocco (bass) employs 'Fidelio', with whom his daughter Marzelline (sop.) falls in love, to the annoyance of her lover Jacquino (ten.). The famous quartet expresses their reactions. The tyrannical governor Pizarro (bass-bar.) decides to kill Florestan to prevent his discovery at an impending inspection. Leonore persuades Rocco to allow the prisoners out for a while; they emerge groping towards the sunlight. But Florestan is not among them.

Florestan is chained in his dungeon, whither Rocco comes with Leonore to dig the prisoner's grave. Pizarro tries to kill Florestan, but is prevented by Leonore with a pistol. Far-off trumpets announce the arrival of the inspecting minister. The prisoners are all released; Pizarro is arrested, and Leonore herself unshackles Florestan.

Fidès. John of Leyden's mother (mezzo) in

167

Meyerbeer's *Le Prophète*.

Fiery Angel, The. Opera in 5 acts by Prokofiev; text by composer, after Valeriy Bryusov's historical novel, first published in the magazine *The Scales*, 1907-8. Concert perf., Paris, 25 Nov. 1954, with Marée, Depraz, cond. Bruck. Prod. Venice, F., 14 Sept. 1955, with Dow, Panerai, cond. Sanzogno; London, S.W., 27 July 1965, by New Opera Company with Collier, Shaw, cond. Lovett.; N.Y., C.C., 22 Sept. 1965, with Schauler, Milnes, cond. Rudel.

At an inn, Rupprecht (bass) meets Renata (sop.) in a state of possession in which she mistakes him for Heinrich, a former lover whom she associated with her guardian angel. He agrees to take her to Cologne to look for Heinrich (bar.), having fallen in love with her himself. The couple try by magic to find Heinrich; Rupprecht is equally disappointed by a visit to the magus Agrippa of Nettesheim. Renata has met and been repulsed by Heinrich; she urges Rupprecht to fight him. Rupprecht loses, but wins Renata. Renata threatens to leave Rupprecht, whose obsessive physical passion for her contrasts with memories of her 'guardian angel'. In a garden by the Rhine, Renata hurls a knife at Rupprecht, accusing him of being possessed by the Devil, as Faust and Mephistopheles enter. Rupprecht watches Mephistopheles angrily devour a slow-moving serving-boy and then resurrect him from a nearby rubbish dump. He joins the party. Rupprecht is in the suite of the Inquisitor, who is investigating a story of diabolical possession in a convent. The source of the trouble is a new nun – Renata. Signs of possession appear; as the exorcism rite begins, hysteria seizes the community and the opera ends with the Inquisitor sentencing Renata to be burnt alive for having dealings with evil spirits.

Fiesco. A Genoese nobleman (bass) in Verdi's *Simone Boccanegra*.

Figaro. The Barber of Seville (bar.) in Rossini's and Paisiello's operas of that name, subsequently Count Almaviva's valet (bar.) in Mozart's *Le nozze di Figaro*. Another opera on the character by C. Rossi (*La figlia di Figaro*, 1846). See also *Beaumarchais*.

Figlia del Reggimento, La. See *Fille du Régiment, La*.

Figlia di Jorio, La (The Daughter of Jorio). Opera in 3 acts by Pizzetti; text, word - for - word setting of D'Annunzio's tragedy (1903). Prod. Naples, S.C., 4 Dec. 1954 with Petrella, Nicolai, Picchi, Guelfi, cond. Gavazzeni. One of Pizzetti's most successful operas An earlier version by Franchetti was prod. Milan, Sc. 1906 with Pandolfini, De Cisneros, Zenatello, Giraldoni, Didur, cond. Mugnone.

The action takes place in the Abruzzi area of Italy. Mila (sop.), fleeing from the peasants who think she is a witch, is saved by Aligi (ten.), who falls in love with her. His father, Lazaro (bar.), tries to prevent their liaison and has Aligi beaten and imprisoned. He escapes, and kills his father whom he discovers about to rape Mila; but she says she is the guilty one and is burned as a witch.

Figner (Mei-Figner), **Medea** (orig. Amedea Mei Zoraide) (*b* Florence, 4 Mar. 1859; *d* Paris, 8 July 1952). Italian, later Russian, mezzo-soprano, later soprano. Studied Florence with Bianchi, Carlotta Carozzi-Zucchi, and Heinrich Panofka. Début Florence 1874 in Verdi Requiem; stage début same year Sinaluga, Azucena. After successes in Madrid, Barcelona, Bucharest in the mezzo repertory, including Carmen, Leonora in *Favorite*, she met Nikolay *Figner, who was just embarking on his successful career; she followed him to South America, 1886, where they both appeared with Claudio Rossi's company in Rio and elsewhere. They married in Feb. 1889, were divorced in 1903. She sang in St Petersburg, 1887, with Figner, and made a triumphant first appearance as Valentine in *Huguenots*. London, C.G., 1887. Regularly at St Petersburg until 1912, where she created Lisa in *Queen of Spades*, Yolanta, and roles in Nápravník's *Dubrovsky* and *Francesca da Rimini*. Although her official farewell was as Carmen in 1912, she made occasional appearances until 1916 as Carmen and Valentine. She left Russia in 1919 and settled in Paris, though she returned to Russia for visits and recordings until 1930. She continued to make records until 1930, and in 1949 recorded an interview with the Danish critic Knud Lindencrone (released 1975), in which she recalled working with Tchaikovsky, and even sang extracts from *Queen of Spades*, *Dubrovsky*, and other works. Her recordings reveal a beautiful voice, impeccable technique, and dramatic temperament. (R) Her daughter, **Lydia Nikolayevna Figner–Gérard**, studied with her mother and sang with the Russian Opera in Paris and the French provinces, after which she taught singing in Paris.
Bibl: M. Figner: *Moi vospominaniya* [My memoirs] (1912).

Figner, Nikolay (Nikolayevich) (*b* Kazan, 21 Feb. 1857; *d* Kiev, 13 Dec. 1918). Russian tenor. He abandoned a career in the Navy in 1881 to study singing in St Petersburg with Pryanishnikov and Everardi; he later also studied in Naples with De Roxas. Very successful début Naples, T. Sannazaro, 1882, in *Philémon et Baucis*. After engagements in Parma, Bologna, and other Italian cities, he joined Claudio Rossi's company touring Brazil, where he took part in the performances at which Toscanini began his career. He was instrumental in securing the young conductor's engagement in the first Turin performance of *Edmea*, in which Figner himself sang. London, C.G., 1867, Elvino, Ernani, Duke of Mantua. St Petersburg, M., 1887-1907; in private Russian theatres 1907-10. Director, St Petersburg, Narodny Dom, 1910-15. Deeply admired by Tchaikovsky, who wrote Hermann (*Queen of Spades*) for him and Lisa for his wife; also Vaudémont in *Yolanta*. Created Vladimir in Nápravník's *Dubrovsky*, and sang other Russian roles; famous as Raoul, Otello, Radamès, Lensky, Canio, and Don José. Records made late in his career reveal fine musicianship, phrasing, and technique, if not an outstanding voice. He married, in 1889, Medea Mei, thenceforth known as Medea Mei-*Figner. (R)

Filar il tuono (or **Filar la voce**, or **un filo di voce**) and **Filer la voix** (or **Filer le son**) (*It* and *Fr* to spin the voice, or tone). A term, mentioned by G.B. Mancini in his *Pensieri e reflessioni pratiche sopra il canto figurato* (1774), and in common operatic usage with various interpretations. It is usually taken to mean an instruction to hold a long, soft note without crescendo or diminuendo. Verdi marks *un filo di voce* for the final A of Violetta's 'Addio del passato' in *La traviata*. According to other authorities, it may also require a diminuendo from piano to pianissimo, or even a swelling of tone, synonymously with *messa di voce. To be skilled in the technique, however interpreted, is in Italian *avere dei bei filati*.

Fille de Madame Angot, La (Madame Angot's Daughter). Operetta in 3 acts by Lecocq; text by Clairvaille, Siraudin, and Koning, after A. F. Eve Maillot's *vaudeville, Madame Angot ou La Poissarde parvenue* (1796). Prod. Brussels, Alcazar, 4 Dec. 1872 with Desclauzas; London, St J.'s, 17 May 1873, with Aimée; N.Y. 25 Aug. 1873. Lecocq's most popular work, and one of the most successful post-Offenbach operettas.

Fille du régiment, La (The Daughter of the Regiment). Opera in 2 acts by Donizetti; text by Vernoy de St-Georges and Bayard. Prod. Paris, O.C., 11 Feb. 1840, with Bourgeois, Boulanger, Blanchard, Marié de l'Isle, Henry, cond. Donizetti; Italian version, trans. and adapted by C. Bassi with recitatives by Donizetti replacing dialogue, Milan, Sc., 3 Oct. 1840, with Abbadia, Salvi, Scalese, cond. Donizetti; New Orleans 2 Mar. 1843 with Place, Blès; London, H.M.'s, 27 May 1847, with Lind, Lablache. Donizetti's first French opera, and one of his most successful works: 44 perfs. in 1840. Marie Julie Boulanger, who sang the Marquise de Berkenfeld) was the grandmother of Nadia Boulanger.

Marie (sop.), brought up in a regiment by the kindly Sulpice (bass), loves Tonio (ten.), but when it is announced that she is a Marquise's niece she has to leave. The Marquise (mezzo) teaches Marie noble ways; French soldiers,

Tonio among them, storm the castle, and Marie succeeds, with the soldier's help, in getting her way and returning to Tonio.

Film opera. Even in the days of the silent film, several films of operas were made: in 1903 Pathé produced a film of *Faust*, and in 1909 there were three different versions of *Rigoletto*, one made in France using Hugo's original book and Verdi's music, and one in the U.S.A. entitled *The Fool's Revenge*. In 1910 a gramophone record of a bass of the Paris Opéra singing 'Vous qui faites' from *Faust* was played behind a cinema screen showing the singer in action. In the same year there were two *Carmen* films, one of which was called *The Cigarette Maker of Seville*, and also *Manon* and *Il trovatore* in France. In 1911 there was an *Aida* and a Russian film of *A Life for the Tsar*. Between 1912 and 1915 Italy produced films of *Parsifal*, *Figaro*, and *Manon* with Lina Cavalieri and Lucien Muratore. In 1915 Cecil B. De Mille produced *Carmen* with Geraldine Farrar: subsequent *Carmen* films included *Gypsy Blood* with Pola Negri, directed by Ernst Lubitsch (Germany 1919), and *The Loves of Carmen* with Dolores Del Rio (Hollywood 1927). In 1917 Samuel Goldwyn persuaded Mary Garden to make a film of *Thaïs*. Other opera films of this time included Mary Pickford in *Madam Butterfly*, Farrar in *Tosca*, Lillian Gish and John Gilbert in *La Bohème* (produced by Irving G. Thalberg), and *Faust* with Emil Jannings and Yvette Guilbert. In 1918 Caruso was persuaded to star in a silent film called *My Cousin*. In 1926 Strauss made a special version of his *Rosenkavalier* score for a film first shown in London with Strauss himself conducting an enlarged orchestra in the pit of the Tivoli cinema.

In 1926 Martinelli, Marion Talley, and Anna Case made the first Vitaphone sound films of opera arias, and later Fortuno Gallo produced a film, *Pagliacci*, in sound with his San Carlo Touring Opera. By 1932 an organization known as Educational Films released a series of 18-minute 'operalogues' of *Martha*, *Carmen*, *Cavalleria rusticana*, etc., and MGM were starring Grace Moore, Lawrence Tibbett, Lily Pons, and Jan Kiepura in feature films which included operatic sequences. During the 1930s opera films made in Europe included a *Bartered Bride* with Jarmila Novotná, *Louise* with Grace Moore, under the supervision of Charpentier, *Madama Butterfly* with Maria Cebotari, *Pagliacci* with Tauber, and *The Last Rose* (a film based on *Martha*) with Helge Roswaenge. Mention should also be made of a film of *Don Quixote* with Shalyapin, with music by Ibert, produced by Pabst. Other singers who appeared in films at that time included Kirsten Flagstad, who sang Brünnhilde's Battle Cry in *The Big Broadcast of 1938*, Lucrezia Bori,

Gladys Swarthout, Risë Stevens, Gigli, and Charles Kullman.

Despite all this activity, it was many years before opera received serious consideration as film entertainment, and great difficulty has been experienced in overcoming the essential contradiction of the medium, namely the remoteness and formalization of the stage, with voice and personality projected to meet the audience. In addition, the cinema destroys the barrier of the footlights, and needs to vary its distances, from vast panorama to intimate close-up. Some operas have been shot as if on stage, e.g. the Italian *Barber of Seville*; this merely stresses at one remove the artificiality that is acceptable in the theatre. Some have attempted to compromise by using the cinema's greater mobility of viewpoint without taking the action beyond the natural limits of the stage, e.g. Paul Czinner's productions of the Salzburg *Don Giovanni* and *Der Rosenkavalier*, and the Zeffirelli-Karajan *La Bohème*. Some have removed the opera from the theatre altogether, and made free use of distant landscape shots, panning shots, and close-ups, e.g. Stroyeva's Bolshoy *Boris Godunov* – one of the most successful film operas to date. The voices are usually added after the action has been photographed: this helps to overcome the disadvantage that a singer rarely looks attractive in close-up. There have been several more Russian and Italian filmed operas including *Katerina Izmaylova*, *Aida*, and *La traviata*. Felsenstein directed films of *Otello* and *Contes d'Hoffmann* in productions based on his work at the Komische Oper, in East Berlin; the Hamburg State Opera productions of *Meistersinger*, *Figaro*, *Freischütz*, *Wozzeck*, *Zar und Zimmermann*, and *Elektra* have also been committed to film, as have several of Karajan's spectacular Salzburg productions. Seasons of film opera at London's Royal Festival Hall have become regular attractions during the summer months.

Filosofo di campagna, Il (The Country Philosopher). Opera in 3 acts by Galuppi; text by Goldoni. Prod. Venice, S. Sam., 26 Oct. 1754; London, King's T., 6 Jan. 1761 with three of the Baglioni family in principal roles; Boston, Conservatory, 26 Feb. 1960. Don Tritemio (bar.) lives in the country with his daughter Eugenia (sop.) and her companion Lesbina (sop.), to whose charms he has succumbed. Nardo (bar.), a rich farmer, has been chosen by Tritemio as the husband of Eugenia, but she is in love with Rinaldo (ten.). With the help of Lesbina, who disguises herself as Eugenia, she successfully arouses Rinaldo's jealousy. He then beats Nardo, but falls in love with Lesbina. The two couples marry.

Finale (*It* end). The last movement of a piece of music, in opera of an act. It was important in the

days of set arias and recitative as the strong climax to an act, and was first developed by Alessandro Scarlatti. Piccinni, following examples in Galuppi, introduced a sectional construction, using passages in different tempos and keys. But very early on, the finale tended towards a continuous design, absorbing aria, ensemble, and freer passages of near-recitative or recitative proper. Outstanding examples are the finales to Acts 2 and 4 of Mozart's *Figaro*.

Finch'han dal vino. Don Giovanni's aria in Act 1 of Mozart's *Don Giovanni*, in which he bids Leporello prepare for the party. Often known as the Champagne Aria, from a tradition of the performer singing it with a glass of champagne in his hand.

Finland. The first operatic performances were given in Helsinki by amateurs, in Swedish. This long remained the official language; Fredrik Pacius's (1809-91) *Kung Carls jakt* (King Charles's Hunt, 1852) is often regarded as the first Finnish opera, but the composer was of German origin and the work was in Swedish. His *Prinsessan av Cypern* (The Princess of Cyprus, 1860) inaugurated the first permanent theatre in Helsinki, and led to some attempts at Finnish-language opera. But Pacius's last opera, *Lorelei* (1887), was given in German; even Sibelius's only opera, *Jungfruburen* (The Maiden's Bower, 1896) was given in Swedish. The first opera to a Finnish text was Oskar Merikanto's (1868-1924) *Pohjan Neiti* (The Maid of Bothnia, comp. 1819, prod. Viipuri, open-air, 1908). The most successful Finnish opera has been Leevi Madetoja's (1887-1947) *Pohjalaisa* (The East Bothnians, 1924), which draws on folk melodies.
See also *Helsinki*.

Finta giardiniera, La (The Feigned Garden-Girl). *Opera buffa* in 3 acts by Mozart; text, possibly by Calzabigi, for Anfossi's opera (1774), altered by Coltellini. Prod. Munich 13 Jan. 1775, with Rosa and Teresina Manservisi, ?Rossi, Consoli; N.Y., Mayfair, 18 Jan. 1927, with Chamberlin, Millay, Sheridan, Echolls, Rogers, Hale, Campbell, cond. Marrow; London, Scala, 7 Jan. 1930, with Eadie, M. Parry, Lemon, Leer, Wendon, Michael, Comstock, cond. Heward.

The Countess Violante Onesti (sop.) is believed to have died from a wound at the hands of her lover Count Belfiore (ten.) during a quarrel. He has fled, but she is seeking him forgivingly, and takes a post as a gardener under the name of Sandrina. Her employer, the Podestà Don Anchise (ten.), has fallen in love with her, to the annoyance of his maid Serpetta (sop.), who has designs on him herself. When Sandrina finds Belfiore paying court to the Podestà's niece Arminda (sop.), she is determined to punish him. But when his arrest for the murder of Countess Onesti is announced, she reveals her disguise; she then pretends to Belfiore that she is not Violante Onesti after all. After many fantastic confusions, all is resolved. Another opera on the subject is by Piccinni (1770).

Finta semplice, La (The Feigned Simpleton). *Opera buffa* in 3 acts by Mozart; text by Coltellini, after a libretto by Goldini first set by Perillo (1764). Prod. Salzburg, 1 Court, 1 May 1769, with M. Haydn, Fesemayer, Meissner, Spitzeder, Braunhofer, Hornung, Winter; London, Palace T., 12 Mar. 1956, with Siebert, Oravez, Küster, Maran, Jaresch, Raninger, Pernerstorfer, cond. Maedel; Boston 27 Jan. 1961 with Dalapas.

Finto Stanislao, Il (The False Stanislas). Opera in 2 acts by Jírovec (Gyrowetz); text by Romani. Prod. Milan 5 July. 1818. Text set by Verdi in 1840 for *Un*giorno di regno*. Another opera on the subject is by Mosca (1811).

Fioravanti, Valentino (*b* Rome, 11 Sept. 1764; *d* Capua, 16 June 1837). Italian composer. He wrote some 77 operas: nevertheless, the last of them was called *Ogni eccesso è vizioso* (1824). Fresh and easily written, they were popular in their day, though only *Le cantatrici villane* (1803) has been at all frequently revived, especially in Germany as *Die Dorfsängerinnen*. He was essentially a buffo composer, with a lively feeling for the manner of which Cimarosa was the master. His son **Vincenzo** (*b* Rome, 5 Apr. 1799; *d* Naples, 28 Mar. 1877) was obliged to study music in secret, and experienced many difficulties in his career as a composer; but his operas, like those of his father most successful when in buffo vein, were popular in Naples. *Il ritorno di Pulcinella dagli studi di Padova* (1837) had a wider success and was even performed in London and America, due to adaptation by the singer Carlo Cambiaggio.

A second son of Valentino, **Giuseppe** (? – ?), was one of the best buffo basses of his day: he took part in a number of premières including those of Rossini's *Bianca e Faliero* and *Matilde di Shabran*, and Donizetti's *La zingara, Alfredo il Grande, L'ajo dell'imbarazzo*, and *Betly*. Giuseppe's two sons **Valentino** (1827-79) and **Luigi** (1829-1887) were also buffo basses, specializing in the same roles as their father.

Fiordiligi. Dorabella's sister (sop.) in Mozart's *Così fan tutte*.

Fioritura (*It* flourish). An ornamental figure, written or improvized, decorating the main line of the melody. Also known, less correctly, as *coloratura.

Fischer, Anton (*b* Ried, bapt. 13 Jan. 1778; *d* Vienna, 1 Dec. 1808). German composer and tenor. Studied with his brother, the composer Matthäus Fischer; then joined chorus of Josef-stadt T. and moved to the Vienna W. under Schikaneder in 1800. Here he sang small tenor roles, became assistant Kapellmeister in 1806 (when the theatre had moved to the Wien), and wrote many popular stage works in light and easily enjoyable vein. Among his Singspiels his great triumph was *Das Hausgesinde* (1808, 115 performances).

Fischer, Emil (*b* Brunswick, 13 June 1838; *d* Hamburg, 11 Aug. 1914). German bass-baritone. Studied with his parents, both of whom were opera singers. Début Graz 1857 as the Seneschal in *Jean de Paris* (Boieldieu). Engaged Pressburg, Stettin, Brunswick, Danzig, and Dresden. C.G. 1884 as Sachs. Broke his contract with Dresden the following year to join the Met., where he remained until 1891. The first American Sachs, Steffano (*Rienzi*), King Mark, Wotan (*Rheingold*), Wanderer, Lysiart, Hagen. He settled in New York and became a teacher, but sang many performances with the Damrosch Company, 1894-8. In Mar. 1907 a Testimonial Performance which realized $10,000 was given in his honour at the Met., in which he sang Sachs in Act 3, scene 1, of *Meistersinger*.

Fischer, Ludwig (*b* Mainz, 18 Aug. 1745; *d* Berlin, 10 July 1825). German bass. Contemporary and great friend of Mozart. Studied with Raaff. Début Mannheim 1772 in Salieri's *Fiera di Venezia*. The original Osmin; sang with success in Munich, Vienna, Berlin, and Paris. Possessed a compass of two-and-a-half octaves, and was regarded as the greatest German bass of his day. Appeared in London as the Count in the first performance in England of *Figaro* in 1812, but his German method of singing was not liked, though the critic of the *Examiner* wrote: 'He however breathes in tune, and that is praise due to no other male performer at the theatre.' His wife **Barbara Strässer** (*b* 1758) sang at Mannheim 1772-89; their four children, **Joseph** (1780-1862), **Josepha** (*b* 1782), **Thérèse Wilhelmina** (*b* 1785), and **Louise** were all singers.

Fischer, Res (*b* Berlin, 8 Nov. 1896; *d* Stuttgart, 4 Oct. 1974). German contralto. Studied Stuttgart. Début Basle 1927. Engagements followed at Frankfurt, 1925-41, and Stuttgart, where she was leading contralto from 1941. Created the title role in Orff's *Antigonae* at Salzburg in 1949, and has appeared as a guest artist all over Europe, including London (Klytemnestra with Stuttgart Opera, 1955). (R)

Fischer-Dieskau, Dietrich (*b* Berlin, 28 May 1925). German baritone. Studied Berlin with Georg Walter and Weissenborn. Prisoner of war in Italy, but was able to begin his career in 1947. Stage début Berlin Stä. O. 1948, Posa; here he has been leading baritone ever since. Munich and Vienna since 1949; Bayreuth 1954-

171

6, Wolfram, Herald (*Lohengrin*), Kothner, Amfortas; Salzburg since 1957. London, C. G., 1965, Mandryka; 1967, Falstaff. Roles include Dr. Faust (Busoni), the Count, Falstaff, Jochanaan, Mandryka (*Arabella*), Mathis der Maler, Wozzeck, Onegin, Don Giovanni, Renato (*Ballo in Maschera*), Sachs. Created Mittenhofer (*Elegy for Young Lovers*). One of the great singers of this century, and an equally thoughtful interpreter of Lieder and opera. Has also conducted, including opera recordings. (R)
Bibl: F. Horzfeld: *Dietrich Fischer-Dieskau* (1958).

Fischietti (or Fischetti), **Domenico** (*b* Naples, *c*1725; *d* Salzburg, *c*1810). Italian composer. He was active as an opera composer in Naples, Palermo, Venice, Prague, and Dresden, and became Hofkapellmeister (1772-9) in Salzburg, in preference to Leopold Mozart, though he continued to visit Italy for productions of new operas. Mozart thought highly of him.

Fisher, Sylvia (*b* Melbourne, 18 Apr. 1910). Australian soprano. Studied Melbourne Conservatory with Adolf Spivakovsky. Début Melbourne 1932, Hermione in Lully's *Cadmus and Hermione*, while still a student. Stage début London, C.G., 1949, Leonore (*Fidelio*). The company's leading dramatic soprano until 1958, being especially successful as the Marschallin, Sieglinde, and the Kostelnička. Made guest appearances in Italy, 1952 and Chicago, 1959. E.O.G. 1963-71 as Mrs Grose in *Turn of the Screw*, and Female Chorus in *Rape of Lucretia*. Created Miss Wingrave in *Owen Wingrave*, B.B.C./T.V. 1971, C.G. 1973. S.W., as Queen Elizabeth in *Gloriana*, and Kostelnička in *Jenůfa*.(R)

Flagstad, Kirsten (Malfrid) (*b* Hamar, Norway, 12 July 1895; *d* Oslo, 7 Dec. 1962). Norwegian soprano. Studied with her mother and Ellen Schytte-Jacobsen. Début Oslo 1913, Nuri (*Tiefland*). Until 1933 she appeared only in Scandinavia, in a vast repertory of opera and
• operetta, and was on the verge of retiring in 1933 when she was engaged to sing small roles at Bayreuth. In 1934 she sang Sieglinde there and an engagement for the N.Y., Met. followed where she made her début in 1935 in the same role. During her initial N.Y. season sang Brünnhilde and Kundry for the first time in her life, immediately establishing herself as the greatest Wagner soprano of the day. Appeared at C.G. in 1936 and 1937, and after the war did much to restore the Wagner repertory there, not only singing Isolde, Kundry, Sieglinde, and Brünnhilde in German, but learning the *Walküre* Brünnhilde in English. Sang Dido in English at the *Mermaid T. in London. Retired in 1954, but continued to record. Director of the Norwegian National Opera 1959-60. Her voice

was not sensuous in quality, but was of great power and radiance, and superbly projected. (R)
Bibl: K. Flagstad (with L. Biancolli): *The Flagstad Manuscript* (1952); E. McArthur: *Flagstad: A Personal Memoir* (1965).

Flavio. Opera in 3 acts by Handel; text by Haym, partly based on Corneille's tragedy *Le Cid* (1637) and altered from a libretto *Flavio Pertarido* by Ghigi composed by Pollarolo (1706). Prod. London, Hm., 25 May 1723, with Cuzzoni, Durastini, Robinson, Senesino, Boschi, Berenstadt. Revived Abingdon 1969.

Fledermaus, Die (The Bat). Operetta in 3 acts by Johann Strauss; text by Haffner and Genée, after a French *spirituel vaudeville*, *Le Reveillon* (1872), by Meilhac and Halévy, based in turn on Roderich Bendix's comedy *Das Gefängnis* (1851). Prod. Vienna, W., 5 Apr. 1874, with Charles-Hirsch, Geistinger, Szika, and Lebrecht cond. Strauss; N.Y., Stadt T., 21 Nov. 1874, with Cotrelly, Fiebach, Schnelle, Fritze, cond. Bial; London, Alhambra, 18 Dec. 1876, with Cabella, Chambers, Loredan, Rosenthal, cond. Jacobi.

Rosalinde (sop.) is being serenaded by her former admirer Alfred (ten.), an opera singer; her husband, Eisenstein (ten.), is about to go to prison for having insulted the tax collector. His friend Dr Falke (bar.) comes supposedly to conduct him to prison, but suggests that they both should go to the party being given by Prince Orlofsky (mezzo, now often ten.), and that Eisenstein should present himself at the prison the following morning. When the two men have gone off, Alfred returns; his tête-à-tête with Rosalinde is disturbed by the arrival of Frank (bar.), the prison governor who has come to conduct Eisenstein to jail. He mistakes Alfred for Eisenstein and takes him off to prison. Rosalinde, also invited to Orlofsky's party, arrives there masked, pretending to be a Hungarian countess; Eisenstein flirts outrageously with her. The plot is further complicated by the fact that Eisenstein's maid, Adele (sop.), wearing one of her mistress's dresses, is also at the party. All misunderstandings are cleared up the following morning in the prison.

Fleischer-Endel, Katherina (*b* Mühlheim, 27 Sept. 1873; *d* Dresden, 18 July 1908). German soprano. Studied Dresden with August Iffert. Début Dresden in concert 1893, in opera 1894 as Bridesmaid (*Freischütz*). Dresden, H., 1894-7; Hamburg, 1897-1917. London, C.G., 1905, 1907, Sieglinde, Eva, Elisabeth. N.Y., Met., 1906-7. Bayreuth 1904-8 Elisabeth, Elsa, Sieglinde, 3rd Norn, Brangaene. Guest appearances Berlin and other German houses. After leaving stage taught singing in Dresden. (R)

Flensburg. City in Schleswig-Holstein. The Städtische T. (cap. 610) opened in 1894.

leta, Miguel (*b* Albalate, 28 Dec. 1897; *d* La Coruña, 30 May 1938). Spanish tenor. Studied Barcelona Conservatory. Début Trieste 1919, Paolo (*Francesca da Rimini*); N.Y., Met., 1923-; Milan, Sc., 1923-6 where he created Calaf. Also the first Romeo in Zandonai's *Giulietta e Romeo* (Rome 1922). (R) His son **Pierre Fleta** (*b* 1925) has appeared at Brussels, La M., and in France. (R)

liegende Holländer, Der (The Flying Dutchman). Opera in 1 act, later 3 acts, by Wagner; text by composer, after the legend as told in Ch. 7 of Heine's *Aus den Memoiren des Herren von Schnabelewopski* (1831). First used as scenario for *Dietsch's *Le Vaisseau fantôme* (1842). Prod. Dresden, Hofoper, 2 Jan. 1843, with Schröder-Devrient, Wächter, Reinhold, Risse, Bielezizky, cond. Wagner; London, D.L. 23 July 1870, with Di Murska, Corsi, Perotti, Rinaldini, Foli, Santley, cond. Arditi (in Italian: first Wagner opera in London); Philadelphia, Ac. of M., 8 Nov. 1876 with Pappenheim, Maccei, Preusser, Sullivan, cond. Carlberg (in Italian).

The Dutchman (bar.) has been condemned, for his blasphemy, to sail his ship until redeemed by a faithful woman. This salvation he is allowed to attempt once every seven years. In one of these periods he is driven by storms to a Norwegian harbour. He moors beside the ship of Daland (bass), who, impressed by the Dutchman's wealth, offers him shelter. Daland's daughter Senta (sop.) sings to her friends, as they spin, the Ballad of the flying Dutchman. Her lover Erik (ten.) pleads his own cause, unsuccessfully. But when the Dutchman enters, she is confused by his declaration of love. The Dutchman overhears Erik being rejected again, and concludes that he too may be deserted by Senta. He sets sail; but Senta leaps to him from a cliff-top. Her faith redeems him, and together they are seen rising heavenwards.

Another opera on the subject by Rodwell (1827).

lorence (It. Firenze). Town in Tuscany, Italy. Birthplace of opera when Peri's *Dafne* was performed there in 1597 as a result of the establishment of the *Camerata. In 1656 the T. della Pergola was built at No. 1 Via della Pergola; it was considerably altered by Antonio Galli-Bibiena in 1738, and again in 1857 (cap. 1500). Lanari managed the theatre in the 1830s and 1840s, and it was there that the first performances in Italy of *Figaro* (1788), probably *Don Giovanni* (1792), and *Die Entführung aus dem Serail* (1935) took place, also the premières of Donizetti's *Parisina*, Verdi's *Macbeth* and Mascagni's *I Rantzau*. It was there too, that the first Italian performance of *Les Huguenots* was given under the title of *Gli anglicani*, as well as *Le Prophète*, *Robert le Diable*, and *Dinorah*.

The T. Comunale was built, without a roof, in 1864, and covered over in 1883. Originally called the T. Politeama Fiorentino Vittorio Emmanuele, it was renamed the Comunale in 1932 when it was taken over by the Florentine authorities. From 1919 to 1928 regular winter seasons were given, and in 1928 plans were set on foot to make it the centre of the Florence *Maggio Musicale, and permanent home of Gui's Stabile Orchestrale Fiorentina. In addition to performances during the Florence Festival, the Comunale gives regular winter and summer seasons. It was rebuilt and modernized 1959-60; reopened 1961 (cap. 2,500).
Bibl: L. Pinzauti: *Il Maggio Musicale Fiorentino* (1967); A. Nagler: *Theatrical Festivals of the Medici* (1964).

Florestan. A Spanish nobleman (ten.), Leonore's husband, in Beethoven's *Fidelio*. The name was popular for characters in pastoral opera, and is also that of the governor of the prison in Grétry's *Richard Cœur de Lion*.

Floridante. Opera in 3 acts by Handel; text by Rolli. Prod. London, Hm., 20 Dec. 1721, with Robinson, Salvai, Senesino, Boschi.

Flotow, Friedrich von (*b* Teutendorf, 27 Apr. 1812; *d* Darmstadt, 24 Jan. 1883). German composer. Studied Paris with Rejcha. Though he wrote part of Grisar's *Lady Melvil* (1838; reworked by Grisar as *Le Joaillier de St James*, 1862) and *L'Eau merveilleuse* (1839), his first public success was with *Le Naufrage de la Méduse* (1839, with Pilati; reworked as *Die Matrosen*, 1845). He wrote several other operas for Paris, including *La Duchesse de Guise* (1840), *L'Esclave de Camoëns* (1843), and *L'Ame en peine* (1846). He achieved further success by rewriting, as a full opera, his *Alessandro Stradella* (1844), originally a *pièce lyrique* of 1837. This was followed by his most enduring success, after its triumphant première in Vienna, *Martha* (1847): the work was also refashioned from earlier material, a ballet *Lady Harriette* (1844) to which Flotow had contributed an act. Few of his later operas approached this in popularity, though he had some success with *La Veuve Grapin* (1859), *Zilda* (1866), and *L'Ombre* (1870). He was Intendant at Schwerin, 1855-63.

Flotow's music is light, damagingly so when he tackles large subjects, but at its best has a grace, fluency, and charm that have continued to please audiences. In his light romantic comedies, situation is more important than characterization, and reality does not intrude very far. Despite his German origins, and his German and Viennese successes, his real arena was Paris, where he made a successful career by ingeniously and with sound instinct modifying some of the more sentimental features of German Romantic opera to appeal to French taste.

Flower Duet. The name often given to the duet 'Scuoti quella fronda di ciliego', sung by Butterfly (sop.) and Suzuki (mezzo) in Act 2 of Puccini's *Madama Butterfly* as they strew the house with flowers against Pinkerton's expected return.

Flower Song. The name usually given to José's (ten.) aria 'La fleur que tu m'avais jetée', in Act 2 of Bizet's *Carmen*, telling Carmen how he has treasured the flower she threw him, and with it the hope of her love.

Floyd, Carlisle (*b* Latta, 11 June 1926). American composer. Studied Syracuse University, and privately with Firkušný. Came to the fore with his opera *Susannah* (1955), which revealed a distinct talent for the stage. This was followed by *Wuthering Heights* (1958), *The Passion of Jonathan Wade* (1962), *Markheim* (1966), *Of Mice and Men* (1970), and *Bilby's Doll* (1976).

Flying Dutchman, The. See *Fliegende Holländer, Der*.

Fodor-Mainvielle, Joséphine (*b* Paris, 13 Oct. 1789; *d* Saint-Genis, nr Lyons, 14 Aug. 1870). French soprano. Daughter of the violinist Joseph Fodor, and wife of the actor Mainvielle (whom she married in 1812). Début St Petersburg 1808 in Fioravanti's *Le cantatrici villane*. London, King's T. 1816-18, where she sang with great success in Mozart (Fiordiligi, Vitellia, Countess, Zerlina); the first London Rosina and Elisabetta in Rossini's *Elisabetta, Regina d'Inghilterra*. Appeared with success in Paris, Naples, and Vienna, where she sang 60 performances of Semiramide in the 1824-5 season. On 9 Dec. 1825, when she was singing this role for the first time in Paris, before an audience that included Rossini and Cherubini, she lost her voice at the beginning of the second scene; after a long delay she agreed to finish the opera, but collapsed at the end of the evening, her voice quite gone. She retired to Naples, attempting two come-backs at the S.C. in 1828 and 1831, and then retired to Fontainebleau. Her daughter **Enrichetta** sang in Berlin 1846-9. *Bibl:* J. Fodor-Mainvielle: *Conseils et réflexions sur l'art de chant* (1857).

Foerster, Josef Bohuslav (*b* Prague, 30 Dec. 1859; *d* Nový Vestec, 29 May 1951). Czech composer. His six operas show an increasing metaphysical interest. *Debora* (1893) and *Eva* (1899) reflect real life. *Jessika* (1905) is based on *The Merchant of Venice*, which title it later took (*Kupec benátský*). With *Nepřemožení* (The Invincibles, 1919), *Srdce* (The Heart, 1923), and *Bloud* (The Simpleton, 1936), the characters are increasingly identified with moral states; the expression is inward, personal and symbolic, the drama spiritual. His wife Berta *Foerstrová-Lautererová was a dramatic soprano. *Bibl:* Z. Nejedlý: *J.B. Foerster* (1910).

Foerstrová-Lautererová, Berta (*b* Prague, 11 Jan. 1869; *d* Prague, 9 Apr. 1936). Czech soprano; wife of above. Studied Prague with Antonia Poldková and Tauwitz. Début Prague N., 1887, Agathe. Here she created Julia in Dvořák's *Jakobín* and Xenia in his *Dimitrij*; also first Prague Desdemona and Tatyana, which she sang in presence of Tchaikovsky. Hamburg, 1893-1901, where she became one of Mahler's favourite singers. He summoned her to Vienna, where, as Foerster-Lauterer, she remained until 1913. Vienna roles included Adalgisa, Euryanthe, Lisa, Nedda, and Frasquita in *Corregidor*, which she created. Admired by Cosima Wagner, who invited her to sing Elsa at Bayreuth: this she was unable to do. Married Josef Bohuslav Foerster in 1892. Retired from stage 1914. (R)

Foignet, Charles Gabriel (or Jacques) (*b* Lyons, 1750; *d* Paris, 1823). French singer and composer. From 1791 he wrote *opéras-comiques* and *vaudevilles*, initially with Louis Simon, for the newly opened Paris public theatres; of one of these, the T. Montansier, he and Simon became two of the joint administrators, and he also founded the T. des Victoires-Nationales, and directed the T. des Jeunes-Artistes. His son **François Foignet** (*b* Paris, 17 Feb. 1782; *d* Strasbourg, 22 July. 1845) was a singer and composer who made his name at the Jeunes-Artistes, especially in his own *opéra-comique La Naissance d'Arlequin* (1803). On Napoleon's closure of the small Paris theatres in 1807, he worked in Liège, Bruges, Marseilles, Nantes, Angulème, and elsewhere.

Foli (Foley), **A**(llan) **J**(ames) (*b* Cahir, Tipperary 7 Aug. 1835; *d* Southport, 20 Oct. 1899). Irish bass. Studied Naples. Début Catania 1862 Elmiro in Rossini's *Otello*. After appearances in other Italian cities, London début H.M.'s 1865 Saint-Bris. Sang more than 60 operas at C.G. H.M.'s and D.L. Appeared in America with Mapleson's company 1878-9 and in Russia and Austria. The Daland of the first Wagner performance in London, 1870. Possessed a powerful voice, ranging from E to f'.

Fomin, Evstigney (Ipatyevich) (*b* St Petersburg 16 Aug. 1761; *d* St Petersburg, end Apr./beginning May 1800). Russian composer. Studied St Petersburg with Sartori and Raupach, Bologna with Padre Martini. From 1797 he worked as répétiteur in the St Petersburg Opera. On his return from Italy, he wrote a ballet-opera *Novgorodsky Bogatyr Boyeslavovich* (Boyeslavovich, the Novgorod Hero) in which he makes some use of folktunes; this was to a text by Catherine the Great. His other operas include *Yamshchiki na Podstave* (The Post Drivers, 1787), *Amerikantsy* (The Americans, 1788), and *Zolotoye Yabloko* (The Golden Apple, prod. 1803): the first is remarkable for its use of Russian folk music, including folk polyphony, and for its vivid depiction of the life of the coach drivers, and is thus an important example for the future development of national Russian opera. However, Fomin's most outstanding opera is the melodrama *Orpheus and Eurydice* (1788), an enterprising work that includes a number of technical and instrumental experiments. The most talented Russian opera composer of the end of the 18th cent., though he did not live to develop his gifts fully.

Fontana, Ferdinando (*b* Milan, 30 Jan. 1850; *d* Lugano, 12 May 1919). Italian playwright and librettist. Wrote *Aldo e Clarenza* for Massa (1878), but best known as the author of two of Puccini's earliest opera texts, *Le Villi* (1884) and *Edgar* (1889), a collaboration arranged (with some haggling about fees) by Ponchielli. Also librettist of Franchetti's *Asrael* (1888), and made the Italian translations of *Tiefland* and *Die lustige Witwe*.

Foppa, Giuseppe (Maria) (*b* Venice, 12 July 1760; *d* Venice, 1845). Italian librettist. Apart from a brief period in Lisbon (1797-8), lived largely in Venice, where he wrote over 80 works for composers including Andreozzi, Bertoni, Bianchi, Coccia, Farinelli, Fioravanti, Generali, Mayr, Nasolini, Paer, Pavesi, Rossini (*L'inganno felice, Il signor Bruschino*, and *Sigismondo*), Spontini (*Le metamorphose di Pasquale*), and Zingarelli. His talent was for comedy, and his texts draw on the stock characters and situations of the 18th cent. and especially of the *commedia dell'arte*, somewhat under the influence of Goldoni. From the *commedia dell'arte* he selected and gave prominence to a number of scenes, including the Mad Scene with flute obbligato, which thereupon entered operatic currency. In his serious operas he showed more Romantic inclinations; he was one of the first librettists to introduce Shakespearean subjects into opera (though in the Ducis versions), e.g. *Giulietta e Romeo* for Zingarelli.

Ford. A citizen of Windsor (bar.), Alice's husband, in Verdi's *Falstaff*. In Nicolai's *Die lustigen Weiber von Windsor* he is Herr Fluth (bar.).

Formes, Karl (*b* Mülheim, 7 Aug. 1815; *d* San Francisco, 15 Dec. 1889). German bass. Son of a sexton; first sang in a Benefit concert to raise funds for Cologne Cathedral. Stage début Cologne 1841, Sarastro. Mannheim, Vienna from 1845, where he created Plunkett in *Martha* 1847); London, D.L., 1849; N.Y. 1857. Married the American soprano Pauline Gravewood,

with whom he established a singing school in San Francisco. His brother **Theodor** (1826-74), who sang in Europe (first Berlin Tannhäuser and Lohengrin) and U.S.A., died insane.

Formichi, Cesare (*b* Rome 15 Apr. 1883; *d* Rome, 21 July 1949). Italian baritone. Studied Rome with Lombardo. Début Milan, T.L., 1911. London, C.G., 1924; Chicago 1922-32. Admired for his Scarpia, Rigoletto, etc., and in Italy for his Wagner interpretations. In 1937 was responsible for the badly organized Italian performances during the Coronation season at C.G.; also acted as artistic director of the Vichy Casino. (R)

Forsell, John (orig. Carl Johan Jacob) (*b* Stockholm, 6 Nov. 1868; *d* Stockholm, 30 May 1941). Swedish baritone. Début Stockholm 1896, Figaro; sang there regularly until 1909 when he went to the N.Y. Met for one season. Also appeared in London, Berlin, Vienna. One of the finest Don Giovannis of his generation; he sang this role at Salzburg under Schalk in 1930. Intendant of the Stockholm Opera 1923-39. Professor of singing at Stockholm Conservatory: his pupils included Jussi Björling and Svanholm. (R)

Forti, Anton (*b* Vienna, 8 June 1790; *d* Vienna, 16 June 1859). Austrian baritone and tenor. Esterház 1807-11; Vienna, W., 1811-13 and Court T., from 1813. He sang some tenor roles, e.g. Rossini's Otello (1819), Max (1821), and Titus (1823), while also singing Pizzaro and other baritone roles. He made guest appearances in Prague, Hamburg, and Berlin. In 1823 he created Lysiart. He was also famous as Don Giovanni and Figaro, as well as for his Pizzaro (which he had sung in the 1814 version). He retired in about 1833, having won first prize in a State lottery, but returned occasionally to the stage from 1834: he was still singing in Vienna in 1841 (e.g. in Hérold's *Le Pré aux clercs* and Thomas's *Le Panier fleuri*). His wife **Henriette Forti** (orig. Theimer) was a soprano who sang light roles in Prague in the 1820s, at Frankfurt in 1826, and at Munich and Berlin in 1830: a successful Zerlina and Cherubino, and a brilliant page in Boieldieu's *Jean de Paris*.

Fortner, Wolfgang (*b* Leipzig, 12 Oct. 1907). German composer. Interest in amateur music-making led to his first stage work, the school opera *Cress ertrinkt* (1930). *Die Witwe von Ephesus* (1952) is a pantomime in 1 act with small orchestra. His two Lorca operas, *Bluthochzeit* (1957) and *In seinem Garten liebt Don Perlimpin Belisa* (1962) reconcile serial and diatonic musical idioms. Has also written a T.V. opera, *Der Wald*, an *opera buffa, Corinna* (1958), and *Elisabeth Tudor* (1972).

Fort Worth. Town in Texas, U.S.A. The Fort Worth Opera Association, founded in May

LA FORZA DEL DESTINO

1946 (first production *La traviata,* November 1946), gives an annual opera season with principal roles sung by guest artists. In October 1963 it received a Ford Foundation Grant to enable it to increase its activities from three to four productions a season. Most works are sung in English.

Forza del destino, La (The Force of Destiny, or The Power of Fate). Opera in 4 acts by Verdi; text by Piave, after the drama *Don Alvaro, ó La Fuerza del Sino* (1835), by Angel de Saavedra Ramírez de Banquedano, Duke of Rivas, and on a scene from Schiller's drama *Wallensteins Lager* (1799). Prod. St Petersburg, Imperial T., 10 Nov. (OS; 22 Nov. NS) 1862, with Barbot, Nantier-Didiée, Tamberlik, Graziani, Bassini, Angelini; N.Y., Ac. of M., 24 Feb. 1865, with Carozzi-Zucchi, Morensi, Massimiliani, Bellini cond. Bergmann; London, H.M.'s, 22 June. 1867, with Tietjens, Trebelli. Mongini, Santley Gassier, cond. Arditi.

Don Alvaro (ten.) has accidentally killed the Marquis of Calatrava (bass), father of his beloved Leonora (sop.). Cursed by her dying father, she takes refuge in a monastery, while her brother Don Carlo (bar.) pursues Alvaro in search of vengeance. Leonora and her brother die, but Alvaro lives on, a victim of destiny.

Another opera on the subject is by Del Campo (*El Final de Don Alvaro,* 1910).

Forzano, Giovacchino (*b* Borgo S. Lorenzo, 19 Nov. 1883; *d* Rome, 18 Oct. 1970). Italian librettist and producer. Studied to become a singer, and actually appeared in baritone roles in the Italian provinces. Provided librettos for *Lodoletta, Il piccolo Marat, Gianni Schicchi, Suor Angelica, Sly, Il Re, Oedipus Rex* (Leoncavallo), *Palla di Mozzi* (Marinuzzi). Began producing operas in 1904 and was responsible for the staging of the world premières of *Turandot, Nerone* (Boito), *La cena delle beffe* (Giordano), and *I cavalieri di Ekebù* (Zandonai). Worked at C.G., Vienna S.O., Verona Arena, Rome, and Naples.

Foss (orig. Fuchs), **Lukas** (*b* Berlin, 15 Aug. 1922). American composer of German origin. His first opera, *The Jumping Frog of Calaveras County* (1950), gave evidence of a fertile and brilliant talent. His second opera, *Griffelkin,* was produced on T.V. in 1955.

Four Saints in Three Acts. 'An opera to be sung' in 4 (*sic*) acts by Virgil Thomson; text by Gertrude Stein. Concert perf. Ann Arbor 20 May 1933; prod. Hartford, by Society of Friends and Enemies of Modern Music, Avery Memorial T., 8 Feb. 1934; Paris, 1952. The action takes place in Spain and takes the form of an allegory in which Saint Theresa, surrounded by men, and Saint Ignatius, surrounded by women, work together and help one another to become

saints. Originally performed by an all-negro cast.

Fox, Carol (*b* Chicago, 15 June 1926). American manager. Studied singing Chicago, New York, and in Italy. Founder with Nicola Rescigno and Lawrence Kelly of the Lyric Opera of Chicago in 1952; General Manager since 1956. Has raised the standard of opera in Chicago to European levels, engaging outstanding singers, conductors, producers, and designers, and enlarging the repertory.

Fra Diavolo. *Opéra-comique* in 3 acts by Auber; text by Scribe. Prod. Paris, O.C., 28 Jan. 1830 with Boulanger, Prévost, Chollet, Féréol; London, D.L., 1 Feb. 1831; N.Y. 17 Oct. 1831, with Saint-Clair, Milon, Saint-Aubin, Privat.

Fra Diavolo (ten.), a notorious bandit, passing himself off as the Marquis of San Marco, compromises Zerlina (sop.), the daughter of an innkeeper, while engaged in an elaborate plot to steal the jewels of Lady Pamela (mezzo), wife of Lord Cockburn (bass). Betrayed by his associates, Fra Diavolo is shot, having cleared Zerlina of any involvement and reunited her with her lover, Lorenzo (ten.) An alternative ending has Fra Diavolo taken prisoner.

Also parody by Drechsler (1830).

Fra Gherardo. Opera in 3 acts by Pizzetti; text by composer after the Chronicles of Salimbene da Parma (13th cent.). Prod. Milan, Sc., 16 May 1928, with Cristoforeanu, Stignani, Trantoul, Baccaloni, cond. Toscanini; N.Y., Met., 21 Mar. 1929, with Müller, Claussen, Johnson, Pinza, cond. Serafin. Gherardo (ten.), a weaver, joins the order of the White Friars following a love affair with Mariola (sop.). He leads a revolt of the oppressed people of Parma against the nobles and dies at the stake; Mariola is killed by a madwoman.

Françaix, Jean (*b* Le Mans, 23 May 1912). French composer. His first opera was a chamber opéra-comique, *Le Diable boîteux* (1937). This was followed by the musical comedy *L'Apostrophe* (1942), the 4-act *La Main de gloire* (1950), *Paris à nous deux* (1954), and *La Princesse de Clèves* (1965).

France. During Louis XIV's minority, an attempt was made by Mazarin to establish Italian opera in Paris. Among the works heard were those of Cavalli, who visited Paris in 1660. The first attempts at a national genre based on the Italian example came with the foundation of the *Académie de Musique (the beginnings of the *Opéra) by Perrin and Cambert in 1669 They were succeeded by *Lully, who had provided dances and music for Molière and in 1672 composed what is often considered the first French opera, *Les Fêtes de l'amour et de Bacchus.* Lully set a standard of French recitative gave dance (after the example of the *ballet de*

LA FORZA DEL DESTINO — FRANCE

176

cour) the central place it long retained in French opera, and established the tradition of spectacle and formal manners in opera, reflecting the lustre of the roi soleil. The rigidity of the style, vigorously mocked in the *drame forain, made it difficult for a less imposing musician than Lully to develop French opera significantly, despite the work of *Campra and *Destouches, until *Rameau. The contrasting pomposity but grandeur of the *tragédie lyrique on the one hand, on the other the flimsiness but gaiety of the works that led to the new term *opéra comique in 1715, was to be a familiar polarization throughout French operatic history.

The essentially French nature of this contrast, and of the love of forming factions, was shown when a troupe of Neapolitan opera buffa singers visited Paris in 1746 and 1752. There ensued the *Guerre des Bouffons. On the Italian side, Rousseau wrote Le Devin du village (1752). Though the liveliness of the Italians carried most Parisians with them, Paris naturalized their style of comic opera and made it French. Having written Orfeo (1762) with Calzabigi under some influence of Rameau, Gluck came to Paris in 1774 for Iphigénie en Aulide and French versions of Orfeo and Alceste. Gluck's success rekindled controversy, and Piccinni, composer of a number of popular Neapolitan comedies, was (against his will, and despite his admiration for Gluck) made the subject of a rival faction. French light opera continued as plays in which music played a subsidiary if essential role, though *Duni (e.g. Les Moissonneurs, 1768) and *Philidor (e.g. Tom Jones, 1765) gave naturalism and freshness greater expressive weight in a pre-Romantic manner. A third important figure of the period was *Monsigny (e.g. Le Déserteur, 1769), who without loss of immediacy in treatment gave opéra comique still more substance.

With the Revolution, opéra comique developed into a major vehicle for social comment (and was to be the most important single ancestor of Romantic opera). *Grétry, *Dalayrac, *Catel, and others brought into opera many new ideas, from different ages and exotic countries, from different social milieus, and from fairytale and the supernatural as well as Nature and a Rousseau-inspired respect for Natural Man. The most gifted and original of this important group was *Méhul (e.g. Joseph, 1807), who wrote some light works but whose real gift was for the passionate and tragic. An important consequence, especially given the French attention to clarity of verbal expression, was the growth of interest in carrying on the action during a musical number. Once again it was an Italian, *Cherubini, who, together with Méhul, gave an important lead to opéra comique, e.g. with Lodoiska (1791). Another impor-

tant composer of dawning Romanticism was Le Sueur (La Caverne, 1793). A significant genre to emerge from the political upheavals of the period was *Rescue opera, initially with Berton's Les Rigueurs du cloître (1790).

The age of Napoleon gave France a renewed taste for grandeur, expressed now not to glorify aristocratic order but, among other features, to celebrate the Hero, conquest, and historical movements; the audience, especially after the fall of Napoleon, was increasingly a prosperous bourgeoisie, uneducated in taste but impressed by pomp and expensive spectacle. The style was, once again, set by an Italian, *Spontini, with La Vestale (1809); this initiated a genre of large, loud, long operas, usually on historical subjects, demanding elaborate pageantry in their staging. Characteristic works which, in the wake of Spontini (Napoleon's preferred composer), formed the new style of *Grand opera in the 1820s included *Auber's La Muette de Portici (1828) and Rossini's Guillaume Tell (1829). This manner was brought to its highest point by *Meyerbeer, initially with Robert le Diable (1831) and most successfully with Les Huguenots (1836). It was matched by *Halévy in La Juive (1836).

For the first half of the 19th cent. the supremacy of Paris as an operatic centre was unquestioned, and the style of the Opéra influenced composers from Verdi and Tchaikovsky to Wagner. Not all French composers were able to match its demands: Benvenuto Cellini failed to obtain a footing at the Opéra in 1838, and Berlioz wrote Les Troyens without hope of production, and saw it first staged in Germany. Once again in French operatic history, the grandeur and strength that impressed so many musicians brought with it an inflexibility that excluded too much, and too many composers. Not surprisingly, the vivacity that remained another vital strain in French artistic life found expression in comic opera. *Boieldieu and *Hérold had written lively and popular works that were significant in the history of Romantic opera; Auber had (to Wagner's dismay) moved from the nobility of La Muette to a series of lighter and thinner works, most successfully with Fra Diavolo (1830). *Adam had a great success with Le Postillon de Longjumeau (1836). A reconciliation between the two strains of grand opera and opéra-comique was one of the reasons for the outstanding popularity of *Gounod's Faust (1859). A more significant step came with *Bizet's Carmen (1875), whose brilliant invention and passionate naturalism captivated musicians all over Europe, and was an important example for *verismo. The sentimental strain in French opera exploited by Gounod was given a distinctive new colouring by *Massenet, especially in the combination of sex and religion in

Hérodiade (1881) and *Thaïs* (1894) and in the romantic tragedies *Manon* (1884) and *Werther* (1886). The realistic strain found new life in the work of Bruneau, who had Zola as his librettist, and of Charpentier in the very popular *Louise* (1900). Meanwhile, the love of farce had been indulged with a brilliant tradition of operetta that reached its most characteristic form in the irreverent, irresistible works of *Offenbach: also popular were Audran, Planquette, Lecocq, and others.

The effect of Wagner went more deeply in France than in any country outside Germany, and a number of works were written either accepting or constructively rejecting the influence. *Debussy's *Pelléas et Mélisande* (1902) both rejects Wagner and is tinged by him; it is deeply French in its delicacy, its literary awareness, its care for good declamation, its subtle use of the orchestra. Wagnerisms had crept into the work of D'Indy, Chabrier, Lalo, Dukas, and Franck, too much so for their regular acceptance into the mainstream of French opera, despite many fine inventions. However, Chabrier also showed his light touch, as in his turn did Ravel with two delightful one-act comedies. Roussel, in *Padmâvatî*, attempted a recreation of opera-ballet. In modern times, the grand opera tradition has proved less adaptable to new ideas, despite the example of a few works such as Milhaud's *Christophe Colombe* (1930), than that of light opera. Poulenc's talent was to prove more characteristically employed in *Les Mamelles de Tirésias* (1947) than in his deeply felt attempt at a serious opera, *Les Dialogues des Carmélites* (1957). The youngest generation of composers has shown an interest in experimenting with new dramatic forms in almost all kinds and traditions.

See also *Aix-en-Provence, Bordeaux, Colmar, Lille, Lyons, Marseilles, Monaco, Mulhouse, Nancy, Nantes, Nice, Opéra du Rhin, Orange, Paris, Rouen, Strasbourg, Toulon, Toulouse.*

Francesca da Rimini. Opera in 4 acts by Zandonai; text by Tito Ricordi, after D'Annunzio's tragedy (1902). Prod. Turin, T.R., 19 Feb. 1914, with Cannetti, Crimi, Cigada, Nessi, cond. Panizza; London, C.G., 16 July 1914, with Edvina, Martinelli, Cigada, Paltrinieri, cond. Panizza; N.Y., Met., 22 Dec. 1916, with Alda, Martinelli, Amato, Bada, cond. Polacco.

The story, based on Canto V of Dante's *Inferno,* tells how Francesca (sop.) falls in love with Paolo (ten.), thinking him to be his brother, Gianciotto (bar.), whom she is to marry, and who has in fact sent Paolo to bring her to him. Malatestino (ten.), another brother, who has made unsuccessful advances to Francesca, betrays the lovers. They are discovered in one another's arms by Gianciotto, who kills Paolo. There are some 30 operas on the subject. See *Dante.*

Franchetti, Alberto (*b* Turin, 18 Sept. 1860; *d* Viareggio, 4 Aug. 1942). Italian composer. His private means allowed him prolonged and carefully selected training in Italy and Germany (with Rheinberger in Munich, Draeseke in Dresden), and later helped to stage his nine operas under the best conditions. His first opera was *Asrael* (1888), followed by *Cristoforo Colombo* (1892). *Germania* (1902) was prod. in England, though *La figlia di Jorio* (1906) has been the most successful. His wealth and his fondness for spectacular tableaux led him to be compared to Meyerbeer in Italy.

Franci, Benvenuto (*b* Pienza, nr Siena, 1 July 1891). Italian baritone. Studied Rome with Cotogni and Rosati. Début Rome, 1918, Giannetto in *Lodoletta.* Leading baritone Rome Opera 1928-49 and at Sc. from 1923 where he created Manuel in Boito's *Nerone,* Neri in *La cena delle Beffe,* and Cristana in *I Cavalieri di Ekebù.* London, C.G., 1925, 1931, and 1946, where his Scarpia (opposite Jeritza), Rigoletto, and Gérard were greatly admired. Also famous for his William Tell, Macbeth, Barnaba, and Telramund. (R) His daughter **Marcella** had a short career as a soprano after the Second World War; his son **Carlo** (*b* Buenos Aires, 18 July 1927) is a conductor and composer. (R)

Franck, César (*b* Liège, 10 Dec. 1822; *d* Paris, 8 Nov. 1890). French composer of Belgian origin. Even D'Indy allowed that Franck's operas were insignificant, less operatic than some of the sacred music. The early comic opera *Le Valet de ferme* (1851-2) was never produced. *Hulda* (1882-5) was produced at Monte Carlo, 1894. *Ghisèle* (1888-90) was finished by Bréville, Chausson, D'Indy, Coquard, and Rousseau, and produced at Monte Carlo, 1896.

Franck, Johann Wolfgang (*b* ? Nuremberg, ? 1641; *d* ? London, ? after 1696). German composer. After writing some operas for the Court of Ansbach, he was compelled to flee to Hamburg following his murder of one of his musicians, and wounding of his wife. In Hamburg, he won a high reputation as an opera composer, writing 14 in the years 1679-86. He moved to London in 1690. *Die drey Töchter Cecrops* (1679) is the earliest extant German opera in full score. He is an important early composer of German opera, remarkable especially for his successful reconciliation of the characteristics of Venetian opera (in particular Cavalli) with German opera, and for the fluency of melodic declamation he thereby achieved.

Franckenstein, Clemens von (*b* Wiesentheid, 14 July 1875; *d* Hechendorf, Pilsensee, Bavaria, 19 Aug. 1942). German composer, conductor, and Intendant. Studied Vienna with Bruckner; also Munich and Frankfurt. Conducted Moody-Manners Company 1902-7; then held posts in

Wiesbaden, Berlin, and Munich. Director Munich Opera 1912-18, and then 1924-34, when it enjoyed great prestige. Composed four operas. His brother was for many years Austrian Ambassador to Great Britain. His wife, **Maria Nezadal** (*b* Pardubice, 21 Feb. 1897), a Czech soprano, sang in Munich, Vienna, and London. (R)

Frankfurt am Main. Town in Hesse, Germany. The first opera performance was of Theile's *Adam und Eva*, given by Johann Velten's company in the Haus zum Krachbein on 4 June 1698. Throughout the 18th cent. the city was dependent upon similar travelling companies. Not possessing a Court Opera, Frankfurt had no tradition of *opera seria*, and was more readily drawn to opera buffa, Singspiel, and opéra comique. Between 1770 and 1777 Theobald Marchand was the first to give opéra comique in German. The popularity of Singspiel extended to the young Goethe, whose first Singspiel text, *Erwin und Elmire*, was set by André in 1777. Other companies to work in the city included those of Abel Seyler (with Neefe as composer), Böhm, and Grossmann (with Stegmann as composer).

In 1782 the Städtisches Comödienhaus opened in the Paradeplatz (later Theaterplatz) with a repertory that centred on Mozart. Many of his operas were given in the remaining years of the century, as part of a repertory that also included other standard works of German opera of these years such as Winter's *Unterbrochene Opferfest*, Weigl's *Corsar*, Salieri's *Axur*, and Paer's *Camilla*. Fränzl was music director 1792-5, being succeeded by Kunzen and then in 1796 by Carl Cannabich. Though there was difficulty in providing a chorus, Cannabich benefited from the presence of a large orchestra from the dissolved Kapelles of various Rhineland cities. The repertory of these years continued to be based on Mozart and Singspiel, with the gradual addition of more French opéra comique. The orchestra continued to improve, and in 1804 was awarded a Benefit: they chose the most popular work in Frankfurt, *Camilla*, and gave the proceeds to a deceased colleague's widow. Another prominent feature of these early years of the 19th cent. was an emphasis on sumptuous décor, with the use of perspective in the splendid sets of Giorgio Fuentes (in Frankfurt 1796-1805) anticipating the architectural solidity of *Cicéri at the Paris O. His most famous designs, for Mozart's *Titus*, Weigl's *Corsar*, and Salieri's *Palmira*, impressed Goethe, who tried to win him for Weimar.

Frankfurt was the scene of the première of Weber's *Silvana* in 1810, and followed this with other of his works, Spohr was briefly director 1818-19, producing his *Zemire und Azor* there in 1819. Later the repertory was extended to

include Auber, Halévy, and Meyerbeer, also Wagner and Verdi; the most important singers of these decades included Henriette Sontag, Wilhelmine Schröder-Devrient, Jenny Lind, Josef Tichatschek, and Johanna Wagner. In 1842 the theatre passed into private hands, and was enlarged in 1855. Wagner directed an important season in 1862, including a new production of *Lohengrin*.

In 1880 a new theatre, exclusively for opera, was opened in the presence of Kaiser Wilhelm I. Otto Dessoff was music director; then Ludwig Rottenberg took over, and between 1889 and 1923 gave a number of German premières including that of *Pelléas and Louise*, and the world première of Schreker's *Der ferne Klang*. His ensemble included Selma Kurz, his music staff Pollak, Brecher, and Szenkar. Clemens Krauss was music director 1924-9, with Wallerstein as producer and Siewerth as designer; the company included Kern, Ursuleac, Voelker, and Siegler, and though high standards were achieved, there was less interest shown in contemporary music. Krauss and Wallerstein were followed by Steinberg and Graf, who staged the première of Schoenberg's *Von Heute auf Morgen* (1930). During the Nazi régime Bertil Wetzelberger and Konwitschny were music directors, and the ensemble included Clara Ebers, Res Fischer, Theo Herrman, and Paul Kötter. Premières included Egk's *Die Zaubergeige* (1935), Reutter's *Dr Johannes Faust* (1937), and Orff's *Carmina Burana* (1937) and *Die Kluge* (1943). The opera house was bombed in 1943. From 1945 to 1951 opera was given on a temporary stage in the Stock Exchange, under Bruno Vodenhoff. In 1951 the company moved to the rebuilt Schauspielhaus, with Harry Buckwitz as Intendant and Georg Solti as music director 1952-61. Solti was succeeded by Matačić (1961-5), Christoph von Dohnányi (1968-77), and Michael Gielen (from 1977). Since 1951 the company has included Ileana Cotrubas, Christa Ludwig, Hanny Steffek, Anja Silja, Theo Adam, Ernst Kozub, Sandor Konya, and Alberto Remedios.

Franklin, David (*b* London, 17 May 1908; *d* Worcester, 22 Oct. 1973). English bass. Sang first as an amateur; heard by John Christie in 1934, then by Fritz Busch, who sent him to Vienna to study with Jani Strasser. Début Gly. 1936, Commendatore; regularly there until 1939. Leading bass at C.G. 1947-50; sang Mars in the première of Bliss's *Olympians*. Left the stage in 1951, following a throat operation, to teach, lecture, and write: librettist of Phyllis Tate's *The Lodger*. He brought to all his roles great intelligence, humour, and a fine sense of the theatre. (R)
Bibl: D. Franklin: *Basso Cantante* (1969).

Frantz, Ferdinand (*b* Kassel, 8 Feb. 1906;

d Munich, 25 May 1959). German bass-baritone. Début Kassel 1927, Ortel (*Meistersinger*). Hamburg (1937-43); Munich 1943-59; N.Y., Met., 1949-51, 1953-4; London, C.G., 1953-4. Although originally a bass, singing Pogner, Gurnemanz, Landgrave, King Mark, etc., he could also sing baritone roles and became a distinguished Hans Sachs, Wotan, Kurwenal, and Pizarro. Married to the soprano Helena Braun (*b* Düsseldorf, 1903). (R)

Franz, Paul (orig. François Gautier) (*b* Paris 30 Nov. 1876; *d* Paris, 20 Apr. 1950). French tenor. Studied with Louis Delaquerrière. Début O. 1909, Lohengrin. Remained leading tenor there until 1938, singing in the first Paris *Parsifal* (1914) and in many other premières both in Paris and at Monte Carlo, as well as Aeneas in the 1922 revival of *Les Troyens* at the O. London, C.G., 1910-14. Professor of singing at the Conservatoire from 1938. (R)

Fraschini, Gaetano (*b* Pavia, 16 Feb. 1816; *d* Naples, 23 May 1887). Italian tenor. Studied with F. Moretti. Debut 1837 Pavia in *Gemma di Vergy* replacing an indisposed leading tenor. Milan, Sc., 1840. Greatly admired by Verdi; he created the leading tenor roles in *Attila*, *Il corsaro*, *La battaglia di Legnano*, *Un ballo in maschera*, *Alzira*, and *Stiffelio*; also created Genaro in Donizetti's *Caterina Cornaro*. London. H.M.'s, 1847; D.L., 1868. The opera house in Pavia is named after him.

Frau ohne Schatten, Die (The Woman without a Shadow). Opera in 3 acts by Strauss; text by Hugo von Hofmannsthal, after his own story (1919). Prod. Vienna, O., 10 Oct. 1919, with Lehmann, Jeritza, Weidt, Oestvig, Mayr, cond. Schalk; San Francisco, 18 Sept. 1959 with Schech, Lang, Dalis, Feiersinger, Yahia, cond. Ludwig; London, S.W., by Hamburg Opera, 2 May 1966, with Tarrés, Kuchta, Dalis, Kozub, Crass, cond. Ludwig.

The Princess (sop.), who has married an Eastern Emperor (ten.), is neither human nor fairy and therefore cannot have a child; unless she can find this shadow, or power to bear children, the Emperor will be turned into stone. The Nurse (mezzo) takes her to the house of Barak (bar.), whose wife (sop.) is ready to sell her shadow in exchange for treasure, but her husband tells her of the folly of such an action. The Empress learns that she can obtain the shadow of Barak's wife by drinking the water of a nearby fountain; but she refuses to do this and thus bring tragedy into Barak's life. She is rewarded for this unselfish act by the spirit world, who give her the long-desired shadow.

Frazzi, Vito (*b* San Secondo Parmense, 1 Aug. 1888; *d* Florence, 8 July 1975). Italian composer. He composed two ambitious operas *Re Lear* (1939) and *Don Chisciotte* (1951), and edited early Italian operas.

Freia. The goddess of youth (sop.) in Wagner's *Das Rheingold*.

Freiburg im Breisgau. Town in Baden-Württemberg, Germany. A theatre opened in 1785, and opera was given regularly from 1790, the repertory being based on Mozart, Schenk, Müller, Paisiello, Dittersdorf, and Wranitzky. The Grosses Haus was opened in 1910; destroyed in 1944, it reopened in 1949 (cap. 1,133). Dallapiccola's *Volo di Notte* had its German première there, 1952.

Freischütz, Der (The Freeshooter, i.e. the marksman with magic bullets). Opera in 3 acts by Weber; text by Friedrich Kind, after a tale in the *Gespensterbuch* (1811) of Johann Apel and Friedrich Laun. Prod. Berlin, Sch., 18 June 1821, with Seidler, Eunicke, Stümer, Blume, Wauer, Rebenstein, Wiedemann, Hillebrand, Gern, Reinwald, cond. Weber – 500 perfs. there by 1884; London, Ly., 22 July 1824, with Paton, Stephens, Braham; N.Y., 2 Mar. 1825 with Kelly, De Luce, Keene, Clarke, Richings.

Max (ten.) is in love with Agathe (sop.), daughter of the head ranger Cuno (bass). He is eager to win a shooting competition to decide the next head ranger and thereby become eligible to marry Agathe, but loses in a trial. Kaspar (bass) has sold his soul to the evil spirit Samiel (speaker), and must bring another victim; Max agrees to get magic bullets from Samiel.

Agathe, apprehensive though soothed by Aennchen (sop.), is interrupted by Max, who pretends he must fetch a stag he has shot in the haunted Wolf's Glen. Amid weird sights and sounds in the Glen, Kaspar forges seven bullets for Max – the last to go where Samiel wills, though Max does not know this.

Preparing to marry Max, Agathe prays for protection; she has had bad dreams, but Aennchen again comforts her. Max amazes everyone at the shooting contest with his remarkable shots. The Prince orders Max to shoot a passing dove with the seventh; Agathe's voice is heard begging him not to. Max fires. Agathe falls, but it is Kaspar who now has to die instead. Max confesses his pact with Samiel, but eventually on the intercession of the Hermit (bass) is promised forgiveness.

Other operas on the subject are by Neuner (1812), Rosenau (1816), and Roser (1816).

Fremstad, Olive (orig. Olivia Rundquist) (*b* Stockholm, 14 Mar. 1871; *d* Irvington, N.Y., 21 Apr. 1951). Swedish, later American, soprano. Début Boston 1890 as Lady Saphir (Sullivan's *Patience*). Studied Berlin with Lilli Lehmann 1893; début Cologne 1895, Azucena. Engagements followed in Munich, Vienna, and Bayreuth; C.G. début 1903, and same year N.Y., Met., as Sieglinde. Leading soprano there until 1914. One of the great Isoldes and Brünnhildes of the century; at her farewell appearance in N.Y. 1914 was given 19 curtain calls and 21 minutes of applause. Made her last operatic appearance in Milwaukee in 1918 as Tosca, and continued to appear in concerts until 1920. (R)

Freni, Mirella (*b* Modena, 27 Feb. 1935). Italian soprano. Studied with Campogalliani. Début Modena 1955, Micaëla. After appearances in the Italian provinces and a season with the Netherlands Opera (1959-60) was engaged for Gly. 1960, Zerlina; 1962, Susanna and Adina. London, C.G., since 1961, Nannetta, Zerlina, Violetta, Marguerite, and Susanna; Milan, Sc., 1963, Mimì in the Karajan-Zeffirelli *Bohème*. Chicago, 1963, Marguerite. Repertory also includes Liù, Elvira in *Puritani*. Since 1970 her voice has darkened, and she has been singing heavier roles, including Desdemona, Elisabeth de Valois, Amelia in *Boccanegra*. One of the most musical Italian sopranos of recent years, with a charming personality. (R)

Frère Laurent. The holy man (bass) and friend of Romeo and Juliet in the operas by Gounod and Sutermeister.

Fretwell, Elizabeth (*b* Melbourne, 1922). Australian soprano. Début Australian National Opera 1947, Senta. Came to Britain 1954; after singing Aida and Musetta with the Dublin Grand Opera, engaged as leading soprano at S.W. 1955, where her Violetta earned high praise. Created the part of Blanche in *The Moon and Sixpence* (Gardner); the first British Ariadne. (R)

Frezzolini, Erminia (*b* Orvieto, 27 Mar. 1818; *d* Paris, 5 Nov. 1884). Italian soprano. Studied with her father, Giuseppe Frezzolini, a well-known buffo and first Dulcamara, and later with Nencini, Ronconi, Manuel Garcia, and Tacchinardi. Début Florence 1838, Beatrice di Tenda. London 1842 and 1850. Created Viclinda (*Lombardi*) and the title role in Verdi's unsuccessful *Giovanna d'Arco* (1845); the first N.Y. Gilda. Retired in 1860, but returned to the stage in 1863, singing again until 1868.

Fricci (orig. Frietsche), **Antonietta** (*b* Vienna, 8 Jan. 1840; *d* Turin, 7 Sept. 1912). Austrian soprano. Studied Vienna with Marchesi and in Italy. Début Pisa 1858, Violetta; London, C.G., 1862, where she was the first London Eboli (1867); Milan, Sc., 1865-73; first Italian Selika and Eboli, and elsewhere in Italy. Famous for her Norma, Lady Macbeth, and Lucrezia Borgia. Retired 1878 and taught in Florence and Turin; her pupils included Cesira Ferrani. Married the tenor Pietro Neri-Baraldi (1828-1902).

Frick, Gottlob (*b* Olbronn, 28 July 1906). German bass. Studied Stuttgart Conservatory with Neudörfer-Opitz. Joined chorus Stuttgart Opera 1927, remaining there until 1931. Début as soloist, Coburg 1934, Daland. After engage-

ments in Königsberg and Freiburg, joined Dresden State Opera 1940, remaining there until 1950, creating Caliban in Sutermeister's *Die Zauberinsel* and The Carpenter in Haas's *Die Hochzeit des Jobs*. Berlin, Stä. O., 1950-3; Munich and Vienna since 1953. London, C.G., 1951 and 1957-67, 1971 as Hunding, Hagen, Gurnemanz, Daland, Rocco. N.Y., Met., 1962. Bayreuth, 1957-64 Pogner, Hagen, Hunding, Fasolt. Repertory also includes Sarastro, Caspar, Philip, Padre Guardiano. Officially retired 1970, but in 1976 was still making occasional appearances in Munich, Stuttgart, and Vienna. One of the few large-voiced 'black' German basses of the post-Second World War period. His Gurnemanz was considered the equal of Ludwig Weber's. (R)

Fricka. Wotan's wife (sop.) in Wagner's *Ring*.

Fricsay, Ferenc (*b* Budapest, 9 Aug. 1914; *d* Basle, 20 Feb. 1963). Hungarian conductor. Studied with Kodály and Bartók. When 19 appointed conductor at Szeged. First conductor Budapest Opera 1939-45, and was in Budapest from 1945 when he took over the première of Einem's *Dantons Tod* at Salzburg from Klemperer, who was indisposed. Director Berlin Stä. O. 1951-2 (resigning after differences with the management); Munich State Opera 1956-8; returned to Berlin to conduct at the rebuilt Deutsches Opernhaus 1961. Recorded several operas with R.I.A.S. Orchestra of Berlin, which he trained into a fine instrument. Conducted premières of *Le Vin Herbé* and *Antigonae* at Salzburg. (R)

Friedenstag (Peace Day). Opera in 1 act by Richard Strauss; text by Gregor, after Calderón's drama *La Rendención de Breda* (1625). Prod. Munich, 24 July 1938, with Ursuleac, Patzak, Hotter, cond. Krauss; Los Angeles, University of S. California, 2 Apr. 1957, cond. Ducloux.

On the day that the Peace of Westphalia is signed in October 1648, the Commandant (bar.) of Breda refuses to surrender to the Commander of the besieging army (bass), despite the latter's kind words and proferred peace. Only when the Commandant's wife Maria (sop.) begs her husband to acknowledge that peace has really come and that brotherhood has replaced hatred, does he throw away his sword and embrace his former enemy. The opera ends with a paean to peace.

Friedrich, Götz (*b* Naumburg-Saale, 4 Aug. 1930). German producer. Studied Weimar. Berlin, K. O., 1953-62, first as assistant to Felsenstein, then chief producer. First production *Così fan tutte*, Weimar, 1958. Guest appearances Bremen, Kassel, and other West German cities. Holland Festival, *Falstaff* (1972); *Aida* (1973); Bayreuth, *Tannhäuser* (1972);

Freischütz (1977); London, C.G., *Ring* (1974-6); *Idomeneo* (1978). His productions, tinged with left-wing political motivation, are both controversial and stimulating. Appointed principal producer C.G., 1976.

Froh. The God of Spring (ten.) in Wagner's *Das Rheingold.*

From the House of the Dead. See *House of the Dead, From the.*

Fuchs, Marta (*b* Stuttgart, 1 Jan. 1898; *d* Stuttgart, 22 Sept. 1974). German soprano, originally mezzo. Début Aachen 1928. Dresden Opera 1930-6; Berlin S.O. 1936-42; Stuttgart 1949-51. London, C.G., with Dresden Opera, 1936, Marschallin, Ariadne, Donna Anna. One of the best German dramatic sopranos of her day; was a distinguished Isolde, Brünnhilde, and Kundry, all of which she sang at Bayreuth. (R)

Fugère, Lucien (*b* Paris, 22 July 1848; *d* Paris, 15 Jan. 1935). French baritone. Début 1870 at the Café-Concert, Ba-ta-can, Paris. Engaged for the B.P. in 1874, and in 1877 reached the O.C., where he remained until 1910, singing more than 100 roles, of which more than 30 were world premières including Le Père in *Louise.* He was also the first Paris Schaunard and Boniface (*Le Jongleur de Notre-Dame*) and a famous Papageno, Figaro, and Leporello. He sang the latter role at C.G., in 1897. Paris, Gaîté-Lyrique, 1910-19; returned to O.C. 1919, jubilee 5 Mar. 1920. Awarded Légion d'honneur 1928. He continued to sing until he was 80 when he celebrated his birthday in a performance of *La Basoche* at Le Touquet. (R)
Bibl: R. Duhamel: *Lucien Fugère* (1929).

Fürsch-Madi(er), Emma (*b* Bayonne, 1847; *d* Warrenville, New Jersey, 20 Sept. 1894). French soprano. Studied Paris Conservatoire.

Début Paris 1868; London, C.G., 1881, Valentine (*Huguenots*); New Orleans, with French Company, 1873-4; N.Y., Met., 1883-4 and 1893-4. A regular visitor to London until 1890; an excellent Donna Anna, Aida, and Lucrezia Borgia.

Furtwängler, Wilhelm (*b* Berlin, 25 Jan. 1886; *d* Baden-Baden, 30 Nov. 1954). German conductor. Studied Munich with Rheinberger and Schillings. After early engagements in Zurich, Strasbourg, and Lübeck, appointed to Mannheim in 1915, where he remained until 1920. There then followed a period devoted mostly to the concert hall, but from 1924 his Wagner performances in Berlin and Paris attracted great attention. He conducted at Bayreuth in 1931, 1936, 1937, 1943, and 1944; and the opening concert there after the war (1951) devoted to the Choral Symphony. C.G. début 1935, *Tristan*; returned in 1937 and 1938 to conduct the *Ring*. A regular visitor to Salzburg and Vienna; and his Wagner performances at La Scala and for the Italian Radio set a high standard. His position during the Nazi régime has been the subject of much controversy and he was refused permission to conduct in America.(R)
Bibl: B. Gavoty and R. Hauert: *Wilhelm Furtwängler* (1954).

Fux, Johann Joseph (*b* Hirtenfeld, 1660; *d* Vienna, 13 Feb. 1741). Austrian composer. Though best known for his *Gradus ad Parnassum*, formulating rules of counterpoint, and for his sacred music, he wrote 19 operas, among them *Costanza e fortezza* (1723) for the coronation of Charles VI in Prague. In them, he infused Viennese opera with some of the spirit of Neapolitan opera, making use of *da capo* arias and giving them a novel depth of feeling.
Bibl: L. von Köchel: *J.J. Fux* (1872).

G

Gabrieli, Adriana (*b* Ferrara, *c*1755; *d* Venice, 1799 or later). Italian soprano. Known as La Ferrarese, and Ferraresi Del Bene after her marriage with Luigi Del Bene, with whom she eloped in 1783. Studied Venice, probably with Sacchini; heard there in 1770 by Burney, who wrote that she had a 'fair natural voice of extraordinary compass'. London, H.M.'s, 1785 in Cherubini's *Demetrio*, and in 1786 created Epponina in his *Giulio Sabbino*. Milan, Sc., 1787; Trieste 1788; Vienna 1788-92, where she created Fiordiligi (1790) – indeed one of the 'dame ferraresi', as Da Ponte (whose mistress she became) calls the two sisters in the libretto. In 1789 Mozart composed for her the aria 'Al desio di chi t'adora' which she sang instead of Susanna's 'Deh vieni' in Act 4 of *Figaro*; but he did not have a very high opinion of her, for he wrote of Allegrandi in 1789, 'She is far better than Ferrarese, but that is not saying much'. In 1792, after quarrels with singers and other scandals, she was dismissed from the Court.

Gabrielli, Caterina (*b* Rome, 12 Nov. 1730; *d* Rome, 16 Feb. 1796). Italian soprano. Daughter of Prince Gabrielli's cook, and known as La Coghetta. Studied Rome with Francesco Garcia, and Naples with Porpora. Début probably Venice 1754 as Ermione in Galuppi's *Antigona* (appearances in Lucca and Naples in 1747 and 1750 have not been confirmed). Created a number of roles in Gluck's Italian operas 1755-60. London début 1775. According to Burney she possessed a remarkably flexible voice of a thrilling quality. Her personal beauty and capriciousness involved her in many intrigues with royalty and nobility all over Europe. Her sister **Francesca** or **Checca**, often confused with Adriana Gabrieli (above), was a poor singer, who accompanied Caterina as a *seconda donna* in many operas. Their brother **Antonio** sang in Moscow and Venice and was a violinist at the T. di Lucca, 1778.

Gadski, Johanna (Emilia Agnes) (*b* Anclam, 15 June 1872; *d* Berlin, 22 Feb. 1932). German soprano. Studied Stettin with Schroeder-Chaloupka. Début Berlin, Kroll Opera, 1889, Undine; N.Y., with Damrosch Company, 1895, Elsa; London, C.G., 1899, Elisabeth. Member of N.Y., Met., 1898-1904 and 1907-17; specially noted for her Wagner interpretations. Left America when her husband was deported as an enemy alien, 1917; when she returned with a Wagnerian touring company 1929-31 she was past her prime. Also appeared at Bayreuth (1899) and Munich Festivals (1905-6). (R)

Gafforini, Elisabetta (*b* Milan, ?1775; *d* ?). Italian mezzo-soprano. Sang Venice, F., as prima donna in operas by Bianchi and Andreozzi; Milan, Sc., 1801-2, 1808, 1810. Created roles in operas by Fioravanti, Mosca, Orlandi, Pavesi, etc. Greatly admired by Stendhal.

Gagliano, Marco da (*b* Gagliano, May 1582; *d* Florence, 25 Feb. 1643). Italian composer. One of the fathers of opera. According to Peri, his *Dafne* (1608) was the finest of the early settings of the subject. The important preface to this work, written a century and a half before the preface to Gluck's *Alceste*, shows the same determination to banish singers' abuses in favour of dramatic naturalness, and gives practical advice on performance. He collaborated with Peri on *Il Medoro* (1616), but the music of this and of two other opera-oratorios is lost. His last opera, *La Flora* (1628, with Peri) survives. A severe self-critic, he printed only music he considered worthy of survival.

Gailhard, Pierre (*b* Toulouse, 1 Aug. 1848; *d* Paris, 12 Oct. 1918). French bass and manager. Studied Toulouse and Paris Conservatoires. Début Paris, O.C., 1867, Falstaff in Thomas's *Le Songe d'une nuit d'été*; London, C.G., 1879 where his Méphistophélès was considered the best since Faure. Manager of the Paris O., with Ritt 1884-91, with Bertrand 1893-9, with Capoul 1900-5, and by himself 1905-8. Sang in the premières of several works by Offenbach, Auber, Thomas, etc., and was responsible for the French premières of most of Wagner's major works and the engagements in Paris of the De Reszkes, Renaud, Melba, etc. (R) His son **André** (1885-1966) was a composer, and a number of his works were produced in France.

Galeffi, Carlo (*b* Malamocco, nr Venice, 4 June 1884; *d* Rome, 22 Sept. 1961). Italian baritone. Studied with Di Como and Sbriscia. Début Rome T. Quirino, 1903, Enrico. N.Y., Met., 1910; Chicago 1919-21. Sang in leading opera houses of Europe, and was a great favourite in South America. Created Fanuel in Boito's *Nerone*, Manfredo in Montemezzi's *L'amore dei tre Re*, and the leading baritone roles in two Mascagni operas – *Parisina* and *Isabeau*. He was also the first Italian Amfortas and European Schicchi and Michele. Famed for his interpretations of Rigoletto, Nabucco, Boccanegra, and Tell. Last appearance, April 1954. (R)

Bibl: A. Marchetti: *Carlo Galeffi* (1973).

Galilei, Vincenzo (*b* Santa Maria a Monte, *c*1520; *d* Florence, buried 2 July 1591). Italian composer. The father of the astronomer, he was prominent among the group of musicians who met at the palace of Giovanni Bardi in Florence towards the end of the 16th cent., and out of whose discussions opera was born. According to G. B. Doni, Galilei was the first of the group to compose melodies for a single voice; and he was a pioneer of the *stile rappresentativo*. See *Camerata*.

Galitsky, Prince. Igor's brother-in-law (bass), in Borodin's *Prince Igor*.

Gall (orig. Galle), **Yvonne** (*b* Paris, 6 Mar. 1885; *d* Paris, 21 Aug. 1972). French soprano. Studied Paris Conservatoire. Début Paris, O., 1908, Mathilde; sang regularly at the O., 1908-35 and O.C., 1921-34. Chicago 1918-21 in French and Italian repertory, including Isaura in Marinuzzi's *Jacquerie*, Juliette, and Concepcion; London C.G., 1924, Tosca; San Francisco, 1931; Milan, Sc., and other Italian houses. Sang Phébé in Rameau's *Castor and Pollux* at 1935 Florence Festival. Created roles in works by Busser, Magnard, etc. and was the first Tatyana and Woglinde at the O. (R)

Galli, Caterina (*b* ?, *c*1727; *d* London, 1804). Italian mezzo-soprano. Début London, 1743 in Galuppi's *Enrico*. A great favourite in London, performing leading roles in Handel's *Theodora*, *Jephtha*, and *Joshua*. Reappeared in the 1770s at the King's T. Became companion of Martha Ray, the mistress of the Earl of Sandwich, and was with her when she was murdered outside C.G., in 1779. She became extremely poor, and when 70 was induced to reappear in oratorio at C.G.

Galli, Filippo (*b* Rome, 1783; *d* Paris, 3 June 1853). Italian tenor, later bass. Début Naples 1801, and for 10 years one of the leading Italian tenors. A serious illness changed his voice to bass, and, encouraged by Paisiello, he became one of the greatest basses of the day. His first appearance as such was at Venice, 1812, in the première of *L'inganno felice* by Rossini, who also wrote Fernando in *La gazza ladra,* the title role in *Maometto II*, Mustafà, and other roles for him; also created Henry VIII in Donizetti's *Anna Bolena*. London, King's, from 1827. After 1840 his vocal powers declined and he became chorus master at Lisbon and Madrid; he taught at the Paris Conservatoire 1842-8; and from then until his death he lived in poverty. His brother **Vincenzo** (1798-1858) was a buffo bass. Début Milan, Sc., 1824, where he sang regularly until 1840; also appeared in London, New York, and Vienna.

Galli-Curci, Amelita (*b* Milan, 18 Nov. 1882; *d* La Jolla, 26 Nov. 1963). Italian soprano. Studied Milan with Garignani and Sara Dufes, but mostly self-taught. Début Trani 1906, Gilda; Chicago 1916; N.Y., Met., 1921-30. Renowned for her Gilda, Violetta, Elvira (*Puritani*), Dinorah, etc. She possessed a pure limpid voice of amazing agility, but never quite overcame a tendency to sing slightly sharp. A throat illness forced her to retire; after an operation in 1935 she attempted a come-back, singing Mimì in Chicago 1936, but with little success. She then finally retired. She never appeared in opera in England. (R)
Bibl: E. C. La Massena: *Galli-Curci's Life of Song* (1945).

Galli-Marié, Célestine (orig. Marié de l'Isle) (*b* Paris, Nov. 1840; *d* Vence, nr Nice, 22 Sept. 1905). French mezzo. Studied with her father, Félix Mécène Marié de l'Isle. Début Strasbourg 1859. Engagements followed in France, Belgium, and Italy. Paris, O.C., 1862-85, where she created Mignon (1866) and Carmen (1875). Sang in London, H.M.'s, 1886 with a French company. In 1890 participated in a performance of *Carmen* at the O.C. with Melba, Jean de Reszke, and Lassalle to raise funds for a Bizet memorial. Modest Tchaikovsky praised the manner in which she 'managed to combine with the display of unbridled passion an element of mystical fatalism'. Also created parts in operas by Gevaert, Guiraud, Maillart, Massé, and Massenet (*Don César de Bazan*).

Gallo, Fortune (*b* Torremaggiore, 9 May 1878; *d* New York, 28 Mar. 1970). Italian impresario. Established himself in America after 1895 as manager of several touring companies. In 1909 founded the *San Carlo Touring Company and was a pioneer of the production of opera sound films.
Bibl: F. Gallo: *Lucky Rooster* (1968).

Galuppi, Baldassare (*b* Burano, 18 Oct. 1706; *d* Venice, 3 Jan. 1785). Italian composer. He wrote 91 operas, beginning (unsuccessfully) with one at the age of 16. Studied with Lotti. He later had some success in Venice, London, and St Petersburg (1765-8). In Burney's view, he had more influence on English music than any other Italian. His fame rests mainly on his *opere buffe*, especially those written during his 15-year collaboration with Goldoni: these include *Il mondo della luna* (1750), *Il mondo alla roversa* (1750), *Le virtuose ridicole* (1752), and *Il filosofo di campagna* (1754). Dent declared that, while his melody was attractive but not strikingly original, 'he had a firmer grasp of harmony, rhythm, and orchestration than most of his Italian contemporaries' (*Grove's Dictionary*, 5th ed.). He is also important in the history of opera as a pioneer of the *finale, joining several separate movements into a concerted whole in which the dramatic action reaches a crucial situation that is then developed.
Bibl: A. della Corte: *Baldassare Galuppi* (1948).

Galvani, Giacomo (*b* Bologna, 1 Nov. 1825; *d* Venice, 7 May 1889). Italian tenor. Studied Bologna with Gamberini and Zamboni. Début Spoleto, 1849, *Masnadieri*. Appearances all over Europe until 1889, when he abandoned singing to manage in collaboration with Ciampi a company which toured Russia. Taught singing in Moscow and from 1887 in Venice. Said to have sung in the style of Rubini,

nd was considered on ideal interpreter of the
ossini and Donizetti repertory.

iambler, The. Opera in 4 acts by Prokofiev;
ext by composer, after Dostoyevsky's story
1866). Prod. Brussels, La M., 29 Apr. 1929, with
eblanc, Andry, Ballard, Lense, Rambaud,
'ovanovitch, cond. De Thoran, in French trans.
y Paul Spaak; N.Y., 85th St Playhouse, 4 Apr.
957, with Beauvais, Bering, Lane, Falk, cond.
2 pianos) Georgette Palmer; Edinburgh, by
ielgrade Opera Company, 28 Aug. 1962, with
leybalova, Miladinović, Cakarević, Starc,
ındrašević, Cvejić, cond. Danon. Orig. pro-
ected prod., Petrograd 1917, cancelled due to
evolution; second projected Leningrad prod.,
927, postponed.
Alexey is in the service of a General in the
ierman spa of Roulettenburg. In love with the
oquettish Mlle Blanche and, having gambled
way most of his money, in debt to a French
Marquis, the General anxiously awaits the
leath of his rich grandmother. But she turns
ıp, and proceeds to lose her fortune at the
ables. The General's daughter Pauline, whom
Alexey loves, is now faced with marrying the
Marquis; to prevent this, Alexey tries to win
ome money and succeeds in breaking the
ıank. But when he presents her with the
noney, she hysterically flings it in his face.

iarbin, Edoardo (b Padua, 12 Mar. 1865; d
3rescia, 12 Apr. 1943). Italian tenor. Studied
Milan with Selva and Orefice. Début Vicenza,
891, Alvaro. Milan, Sc., 1893 where he created
'enton; T. Lirico, Milio in Zazà (1900). London,
C.G., 1908, and guest appearances in South
America, France, Poland, and Russia. Although
ı lyric tenor, he was especially effective in ver-
smo roles and was a gifted actor. Married the
oprano Adelina *Stehle. (R)

iarcia. Family of singers and teachers of
inging, of Spanish origin.
(1) **Manuel** (del Popolo Vicente) (b Seville, 22
ian. 1775; d Paris, 9 June 1832). Spanish tenor,
omposer, and teacher. Father of (3), (4), (5);
ıusband of (2). Studied Seville with Antonio
Ripa; début Cadiz, 1798, in a tonadilla. Paris,
C.I., 1808 in Paer's Griselda. Created Norfolk in
Rossini's Elisabetta, Regina d'Inghilterra
Naples, S.C., 1815), Almaviva in Barbiere di
iiviglia (Rome, A., 1816); London Hm., 1818;
irst London Almaviva, Norfolk, Lindoro
Italiana in Algeri); also heard as Sesto
Clemenza di Tito), Ferrando, and Tamino;
eturned London, 1819, 1823-5, when he sang
ıtle-role in Rossini's Otello and the baritone
oles of Guglielmo in Così and Don Giovanni.
N.Y., 1825-6, where he founded an Italian
ıpera, with a company that included Crivelli,
Angrisani, De Rosich, his daughter Maria
Malibran), his son Manuel, and his second
vife, Joaquina. On 26 May 1826 he gave the

first performance in America of Don Giovanni
with himself, wife, son, and daughter in the
cast, and with Da Ponte in the audience. He
later took the company to Mexico, where he
was robbed by bandits of some £6,000 in gold.
He wrote many operas including 17 in Spanish,
18 in Italian, and 8 in French. In 1827 he settled
in Paris as a teacher. His pupils included his two
daughters Maria (Malibran) and Pauline (Viardot), his son Manuel, Méric-Lalande, Nourrit,
and Favelli.
(2) **Joaquina** (b Sithces, 28 July 1780; d Brussels, 10 May 1854). Spanish singer. Second
wife of (1), mother of (3).
(3) **Manuel** (b Madrid, 17 Mar. 1805; d
London, 1 July 1906). Spanish baritone and
teacher. Son of (1) and (2); brother of (4) and
(5); husband of (6); father of (7). Studied with
his father. Début N.Y., 1825, Figaro. Paris 1829,
but vocal difficulties forced him to abandon the
stage and devote himself to teaching, first in
Paris, and from 1848 in London. First to undertake the scientific study of voice production;
invented the laryngoscope. Professor, R.A.M.,
London, 1848-95. His many pupils included
Lind, Frezzolini, Mathilde Marchesi, and
Santley: Henry Wood, who accompanied for
his classes, called him the finest teacher of his
day. Writings include Mémoires sur la voix
humaine (1840); Traîté complet de l'art du
chant (1847); Hints on Singing (1894).
(4) **Maria-Felicita** (b Paris, 24 Mar. 1808; d
Manchester 23 Sept. 1836). Spanish mezzo-
contralto. Daughter of (1); sister of (5) and (7);
half-sister of (3). Married E. Malibran, and then
C. de Beriot. See Malibran.
(5) **Pauline** (b Paris, 8 July 1821; d Paris, 18
May, 1910). Spanish-French mezzo-soprano.
Daughter of (1); sister of (5) and (6); half-sister
of (3). Married Louis Viardot. See Viardot.
(6) **Eugenia** (b Paris, 1815; d Paris, 12 Aug.
1880). French soprano and teacher. First wife of
(3), mother of (7). Studied with her husband.
Sang in Italy including Milan, Sc., as Abigaille,
1846, Paris and London.
(7) **Gustave** (b Milan, 1 Feb. 1837; d Paris, 12
June 1925). Italian baritone and teacher. Son of
(3) and (6); father of (8). Studied with his
father. Début, London, H.M.'s Don Giovanni.
Italy, including Sc., 1862-80. Later a teacher in
London.
(8) **Alberto** (b London, 6 Jan. 1875; d
London, 10 Aug. 1946). English baritone and
teacher. Son of (9) by his second wife. Taught
London, R.C.M. and G.S.M.
Bibl: J. M. Levien: The Garcia Family (1932),
rev. as Six Sovereigns of Song (1948).

Gardelli, Lamberto (b Venice, 18 Nov. 1915).
Italian conductor and composer. Studied
Pesaro and Rome. Répétiteur, T. dell'Opera,
Rome, under Serafin. Début Rome 1945,
Rigoletto; Stockholm Opera 1946-55;

Budapest Opera, 1961-5; Gly. 1964-5, 1968, *Macbeth, Anna Bolena;* N.Y., Met., 1966-8; London, C.G., 1968-9, 1970-1, 1975-6. Has composed four operas, including *Alba Novella* (1937), *Il sogno* (1942). (R)

Garden, Mary (*b* Aberdeen, 20 Feb. 1874; *d* Aberdeen, 3 Jan. 1967). Scottish soprano. Went to America as a child, studied singing in Chicago. In 1896 sent by wealthy patroness to Paris where her teachers included Sbriglia (for a week), Bouhy, Marchesi, and Fugère. Befriended by Sybil *Sanderson, who recommended her to Carré at the O.C., in 1900. Caused a sensation by taking over the role of Louise from Rioton, its creator, half-way through a performance in April that year. Created Mélisande (1902), Leroux's *La Reine Fiammette,* Saint-Saëns's Hélène, Massenet's Chérubin and Sapho, and Erlanger's Aphrodite. N.Y., Manhattan Opera, 1907. Thaïs. Joined Chicago Opera 1910 and became its director 1919-20, running up an enormous deficit; continued to sing with the company until 1931. Her last U.S. operatic appearance was an outdoor Carmen at Cincinnati; her last appearance was as Katiusha (*Risurrezione*) at the Paris O.C., 1934. (R)
Bibl: M. Garden: *The Mary Garden Story* (1951).

Gardner, John (Linton) (*b* Manchester, 2 Mar. 1917). English composer. Coached and conducted at C.G. (1946-53) and played the broken-down piano on stage in *Wozzeck.* His first opera, *The Moon and Sixpence,* was prod. S.W., 1957, his second, *The Visitors,* Aldeburgh 1972.

Gardoni, Italo (*b* Parma, 12 Mar. 1821; *d* Paris, 26 Mar. 1882). Italian tenor. Studied with De Cesari. Début Viadana 1840, Roberto Devereux. After engagements in France, Italy, and Germany, came to London in 1847 and created the tenor role in Verdi's *I masnadieri.* Returned to London regularly until 1874.

Gasparini, Francesco (*b* Camaiore, 5 Mar. 1668; *d* Rome, 22 Mar. 1727). Italian composer. Studied with Corelli and Pasquini. Wrote 61 operas, most of them for Venice. One of the most successful was *Ambleto* (1705), the first Hamlet opera, though not based on Shakespeare and using a different plot. He was one of the first Italian composers to have operas performed in London. Heroic, tragic-comic, and comic, they are based on a strict recitative – *da capo* aria scheme.

Gassier, Edouard (*b* Draguignan, 30 Aug. 1820; *d* Havana, 18 Dec. 1872). French bass-bar. Studied Paris Conservatoire. Début Paris, O.C., 1845. After appearances in Italy engaged for the T.I., Paris, 1854, and the following year London, D.L. Sang regularly in London until

1870. The first London Méphistophélès, Page (*Merry Wives*), Melitone, Thoas (*Iphigénie en Tauride*). His wife **Josefa Gassier** (1821-1866) (*née* Fernández) was a Spanish soprano who first sang in London 1846 under her maiden name; created Annetta (*Crispino e la Comare*), Venice 1850.

Gassmann, Florian (Leopold) (*b* Most (Brüx), 3 May 1729; *d* Vienna, 20 Jan. 1774). German composer. He wrote 25 operas, which won respect from Burney, among others. He was most successful in comic opera (e.g. the *dramma giocoso, La contessina,* 1770), which gave rein to his gift for characterization and, in this particular instance, to his ability to contrast noble and peasant with a sharpness of observation that has been said to anticipate *Figaro.* He also wrote *opera seria,* and in his last such work, *Ezio* (1770), reflected some of Gluck's reforms. That his heart may have been in comedy, however, is suggested by his satirical *commedia per musica* setting of Calzabigi's *L'opera seria* (1769). His daughters, **Maria Anna Gassmann** (*b* Vienna, 1771; *d* Vienna, 27 Aug. 1852) and **Theresa Maria Gassmann** (*b* Vienna, 1 Apr. 1774; *d* Vienna, 8 Sept. 1837), were singers, the latter having the more successful career in Vienna.

Gatti-Casazza, Giulio (*b* Udine, 3 Feb. 1869; *d* Ferrara, 2 Sept. 1940). Italian impresario. After training as an engineer, took his father's place as director of the T. Municipale, Ferrara, 1893. His success led to his appointment as director of La Scala in 1898, where with Toscanini he did much for the theatre's prestige, giving the first performances in Italy of *Boris Godunov* and *Pelléas et Mélisande,* and popularizing Wagner. Director of N.Y., Met., 1908-35, during which period he presented more than 5,000 performances of 177 works. He made the Met., internationally famous by the standard of the productions and the galaxy of stars he assembled. Married first the soprano Frances *Alda and then the dancer Rosina Galli.
Bibl: G. Gatti-Casazza: *Memories of Opera* (1941).

Gaubert, Philippe (*b* Cahors, 3 July 1879; *d* Paris, 8 July 1941). French conductor and composer. Studied Paris Conservatoire. After various orchestral appointments, became principal conductor at the Paris O., in 1920, a position he held until his death. Conducted *Alceste* and *Ariane et Barbe-Bleue* in London in 1937. His opera *Naïla* was produced in Paris in 1927. (R)

Gavazzeni, Gianandrea (*b* Bergamo, 25 July 1909). Italian conductor, critic, and composer. Studied Milan Conservatory. Until 1940 he was mostly engaged in composition, occasionally conducting performances of his own works.

Since 1948 he has conducted regularly at Milan Sc.; Gly. 1965, N.Y., Met., 1976. He has published books on Donizetti, Pizzetti, Wagner, and Mussorgsky. (R)

Gay, John (*b* Barnstaple, 16 Sept. 1685; *d* London, 4 Dec. 1732). English poet, playwright, and theatre manager. He provided librettos for Handel's *Acis and Galatea* and Pepusch's *The Beggar's Opera* and *Polly*. He also obtained Davenant's letters patent, which enabled him to build the first *Covent Garden Theatre in 1732.

Gay, Maria (*b* Barcelona, 13 June 1879; *d* New York, 29 July 1943). Spanish mezzo-contralto. Voice discovered while in prison after being arrested for singing a revolutionary song. Originally self-taught, then studied with Adiny in Paris. Début Brussels, La M., 1902, Carmen; London, C.G., 1906, same role; N.Y., Met., 1908; Chicago 1913-27. Married *Zenatello in 1913, with whom she set up a singing school in 1927. Her pupils included Nino Martini and Hilde Reggiani. She and her husband were responsible for the discovery of Lily Pons and for the engagement of Callas at the Verona Arena, 1947. (R)

Gayarre, Julián (orig. Gayarre Sebástian) (*b* Valle de Roncal, 9 Jan. 1844; *d* Madrid, 2 Jan. 1890). Spanish tenor. Studied Madrid. Début Varese, 1867, Nemorino. London, C.G., 1877, where he created a furore by his singing of Fernando (*Favorite*). Sang in London regularly until 1881, and again 1886-7; his greatest years were 1876-86. Sobinin in first London *Life for the Tsar*; created Enzo in *La gioconda*, title role in *Duca d'Alba*. Regarded by many who heard him as the supreme tenor of his time, with unique powers of expressive singing; Gounod, after listening to him sing a *Faust* aria privately, exclaimed enthusiastically, 'I have never heard my music sung like that'. Latterly his voice began to deteriorate: at a performance of *Les Pêcheurs de perles* in Madrid on 8 Dec. 1889, he failed in Nadir's aria, and again on being recalled by the sympathetic public; and murmuring 'Esto se acabó' ('It's all over'), he withdrew. He died 25 days later.
Bibl: F. Hernandel Girbal: *Julián Gayarre, el tenor de la voz de angel* (1955).

Gayer, Catherine (*b* Los Angeles, 11 Feb. 1937). American soprano. Studied Los Angeles and Berlin. Début Venice, F., 1961 The Companion in *Intolleranza* (Nono). Berlin, D., since 1961; guest appearances Milan, Sc., Vienna, Salzburg, Edinburgh. Created Nausikaa in Dallapiccola's *Ulisse* (1968), title role in Reimann's *Melusine* (1971), Christina in Orr's *Hermiston* (1975). Repertory also includes Constanze, Queen of Night, Queen of Shemakha, Sophie, Zerbinetta, Jenifer (*Midsummer Marriage*), Mélisande, and Lulu. A highly-gifted artist whose performances, especially of 20th-century music, are outstanding. (R)

Gaztambide (y Garbayo), **Joaquín** (Romualdo) (*b* Tudela, 7 Feb. 1892; *d* Madrid, 18 Mar. 1870). Spanish composer. Studied Pamplona and Madrid, with P. Albéniz and Carnicer. From 1848 he was director of the T. Español, where the first of his *zarzuelas*, *La Mensajera*, was given in 1849. A pioneer on behalf of new and foreign music, he introduced Wagner to Spain. In 1869 he toured South America with his own *zarzuela* company, but fell ill while travelling and died on his return home. Of his 44 *zarzuelas*, the best known is *La catalina* (1854).

Gazza ladra, La (The Thieving Magpie). *Opera semi-seria* in 2 acts by Rossini; text by Gherardini, after the comedy *La Pie voleuse* (1815) by Baudouin d'Aubigny and Caigniez. Prod. Milan, Sc., 31 May 1817, with Giorgi-Belloc, Gallianis, Castiglioni, Monelli, Botticelli, Galli, Ambrosi, Biscottini, Rossignoli, De Angeli; London, Hm., 10 Mar. 1821, with Camporese; Philadelphia, Oct. 1827.

Ninetta (sop.), a servant girl, is engaged to Giannetto (ten.), the son of the farmer in whose house she works. She is accused of stealing a silver spoon, and the Podestà (bass), whose advances Ninetta has repulsed, brings her to trial and she is condemned to death. Only when she is on the way to execution is it discovered that the real thief was a magpie who flew into the farmhouse window.

Gazzaniga, Giuseppe (*b* Verona, 5 Oct. 1743; *d* Crema, 1 Feb. 1818). Italian composer. Studied Naples, with Porpora and Piccinni. He was most successful in *opera buffa*, in which form his racy, conventional manner proved effective in his own day, and earns him a place in history as one of the minor forerunners of Rossini. However, he is best known for his 1-act *Don Giovanni Tenorio* (1786), one of his most successful works. Both libretto (by Bertati) and music were known to Da Ponte and Mozart before they wrote their *Don Giovanni*, and their work was certainly influenced not only by such conventions as the *catalogue aria, but more specifically in other places, e.g. in the aria 'Notte e giorno faticar', and perhaps in the construction of the work as a *dramma giocoso*, deriving from Gazzaniga's interlarding of serious scenes with farcical ones and his buffo finale as Giovanni is damned.

Gazzaniga (Malaspina Albites), **Marietta** (*b* Voghera, 1824; *d* Milan, 2 Jan. 1884). Italian soprano. Studied with Cetta and Mazzucato. Début Venice 1842. Created title-role in *Luisa Miller* (1849), Lina in *Stiffelio* (1850), and title-roles in operas by Pacini, Coppola, and Mazzucato. Milan, Sc., 1851-3, 1862.

Gdańsk (Ger. Danzig). Town in Poland, from

1918-39 a Free City. Some performances were given in the early 17th cent in the Budynek do Szermierki (Fencing School), and one work staged was *Tragedia o Bogaczu i Łazarzu* (The Tragedy of the Rich Man and Lazarus, 1643), with music by Marcin Grȩboszewski. Johann Meder (1649-1719) tried to introduce opera with his *Nero* (1695), but *Die widerverehelichte Coelia* (1698) had, owing to opposition from the town council, to be given at Schottland. A new theatre, the Schauspielhaus, opened in 1801; here a German company gave opera around 1810. Open-air opera was given at nearby Sopot 1929-39, including works by Wagner in some famous festivals, 1924-42. The theatres were destroyed in the war, but in 1949 the T. Wybrzeże began staging opera, performed by the Studio Operowe. In 1953 this joined with the symphony orchestra to form the State Baltic Opera and Philharmonic company.

Gebet. See *Preghiera*.

Gedda (orig. Ustinov), **Nicolai** (*b* Stockholm, 11 July 1925). Swedish tenor, of Russian origin. Studied Stockholm, with Carl Martin Oehmann and N.Y., with Paola Novikovna. Début Stockholm, 1952, in *Le Postillon de Longjumeau*. His success was immediate and led to engagements in Milan, Sc., 1953, where he sang Don Ottavio and created the Husband in Orff's *Trionfo d'Afrodite*. London, C.G., 1954, Duke of Mantua; Paris O., 1954, Huon. N.Y., Met., since 1957, where he has sung many roles in French and Italian repertory, and created Anatol in Barber's *Vanessa*. This he also sang in Salzburg, where he had appeared in 1957 in Liebermann's *School for Wives*. Returned C.G., 1968, as Benvenuto Cellini. A musicianly and aristocratic artist, generally considered the best tenor exponent of French opera of the 1960s and 1970s. (R)

Geliot, Michael (*b* London, 27 Sept. 1933). English producer. Studied Cambridge, where he staged the first production in England of Liebermann's *School for Wives*, 1958. Stage manager, S.W., 1960-1; produced Burt's *Volpone* there for New Opera Company, 1961; *Mahagonny*, 1963. Produced for Scottish Opera, Wexford, W.N.O., resident producer there 1965-78, and Director of Productions 1969-78. London, C.G., *Taverner*, 1972, *Carmen*, 1973. Netherlands Opera, *Wozzeck*, 1973; Munich Festival, *Fidelio*, 1974. Although he has produced Mozart, Verdi, and Berlioz, his greatest successes have been in contemporary opera. He works closely with the designer Ralph *Koltai, with whom he shares an approach to opera by way of modern methods of music theatre.

Gelsenkirchen. Town in North Rhine Westphalia, Germany. Until the mid-1930s, Opera

was generally given by visiting ensembles from Düsseldorf and Duisburg. The City T. opened 1935, and was destroyed by bombs in 1944. The new theatre opened 1959 (cap. 1,050) and with neighbouring Bochum formed the Musiktheater im Revier (with Ljubomir Romansky as music director).

Gencer, Leyla (*b* Istanbul, 10 Oct. 1924). Turkish soprano. Studied Istanbul with Arangi-Lombardi. Début Ankara 1950, Santuzza. Further study Italy with Apollo Granforte. Italian career began Naples, S.C., 1953; Milan, Sc., since 1956, where she created Mme Lidoine (*Carmélites*) 1957, and First Woman of Canterbury (*Murder in the Cathedral*) 1959. San Francisco 1956-8; Salzburg 1961; London, C.G., 1962, Elisabeth de Valois and Donna Anna; Gly. 1962, Countess Almaviva, and 1955, Anna Bolena; Edinburgh Festival 1969, Maria Stuarda, and 1972, Elisabeth in Rossini's *Elisabetta, Regina d'Inghilterra*. Also sings Renata (*Fiery Angel*), Lida (*La battaglia di Legnano*), Lucrezia (*I due Foscari*), and Norma. A highly dramatic singer and actress. (R)

Genée, (Franz Friedrich) **Richard** (*b* Danzig, 7 Feb. 1823; *d* Baden, nr Vienna, 15 June 1895). German conductor, librettist, and composer. After conducting at theatres in Reval, Riga, Cologne, Düsseldorf, Mainz, Schwerin, and Prague, he was at the W., Vienna, 1868-78. Of his operettas, only *Der Seekadett* (1876) and *Nanon* (1877) had any great success, but he is well known for his brilliant and witty librettos, especially for Johann Strauss (e.g. *Die Fledermaus*, with Haffner), Suppé, and Millöcker, often in collaboration with F. Zell (Camillo Walzel). He also translated works by Lecocq, Offenbach, and Sullivan.

Generali (orig. Mercandetti), **Pietro** (*b* Masserano, 23 Oct. 1773; *d* Novara, 3 Nov. 1832). Italian composer. Studied Rome and Naples, making his operatic début at 17 with *Gli amanti ridicoli* (1800); after the success of *Pamela nubile* (1804), a version of Goldoni's *La buona figliuola*, he was in great demand, both in Italy and in Vienna. Director of Santa Cruz T., Barcelona, 1817-21. Back in Italy, he settled first in Naples, then (1827) Novara. His music has an easy brilliance which at first won him much popularity, but it lacks the individuality of Rossini, whose orchestral effects he partly anticipates and whose operas were largely responsible for his eclipse.

Generalintendant (or **Intendant**) (*Ger* superintendent). The name given to the administrator of a German opera house – often but not necessarily the artistic or musical director.

Generalmusikdirektor (*Ger* chief music director). The title given to the senior musician in a German opera house; his responsibilities include all decisions of musical policy, staffing, repertory, etc., and he also acts as chief conductor.

Generalprobe (*Ger* principal rehearsal). The final, dress rehearsal in a German opera house. Usually opened to critics, professional colleagues, possibly opera clubs or school parties and other invited individuals or groups, it virtually constitutes the first performance of a new opera or production, and is rarely interrupted for further work. The final rehearsal at which matters may still be adjusted is the preceding *Hauptprobe. See also *Probe.

Geneva. Capital of Switzerland. The first opera performed there was Grétry's *Isabelle et Gertrude* (1777). A new theatre (cap. 1,200) opened in 1783; this was the home of opera in Geneva

opened with *Guillaume Tell*. Premières of works by Lacombe, Jaques-Dalcroze, and Aubert were given; the theatre burned down in May 1951. The present theatre (cap. 1,500) opened on Dec. 1962 with a performance of *Don Carlos* in the original French produced by Marcel Lamy; he was the theatre's director until 1965 when he was succeeded by Herbert Graf, whose régime opened with *Die Zauberflöte* in the Kokoschka settings, cond. Ansermet. The theatre is run on the *stagione* system, and as well as popular works, the Graf régime included Milhaud's *La Mère coupable,* Bloch's *Macbeth,* Rameau's *Platée,* Massenet's *Don Quichotte,* Chabrier's *L'Étoile,* and Honegger's *Antigone.* There have also been visits by companies from abroad, including the Brno Opera and the English Opera Group. Graf announced his retirement in 1972, but died during his last year in office. He was succeeded by Jean-Claude Riber.

Gennaro. (1) A young soldier (ten.), actually Lucrezia Borgia's son, hero of Donizetti's *Lucrezia Borgia.* (2) The blacksmith (ten.) in Wolf-Ferrari's *I gioielli della Madonna.*

Genoa (It. Genova). Town in Liguria, Italy. The first opera performed there was Ferrari's *Il pastor regio,* during the 1640s. Genoa did not possess an opera house worthy of so prosperous a town until King Charles Felix (Carlo Felice) urged the building of an opera house there in 1821. The architect was Carlo Barabino, and the beautiful T. Carlo Felice (cap. 2,500) was opened on 7 Apr. 1828 with Bellini's *Bianca e Fernando.* Mariani was music director 1852-73; he was succeeded by Giovanni Rossi, who remained until 1879, and conducted the première of Gomez's *Salvator Rosa* (1874). Between 1891 and 1894 the theatre was the scene of the young Toscanini's early triumphs. In 1892, as part of the celebrations for the 400th anniversary of Columbus's discovery of America, the theatre was redecorated and the

management commissioned Franchetti to compose an opera on the famous explorer, which Mancinelli conducted (*Cristoforo Colombo,* Oct. 1892). Wagner's operas have always enjoyed a great popularity there, and Strauss's works have also been given frequently. The theatre was destroyed during the Second World War, but has been partially rebuilt (cap. 1,500) and seasons are given there and at the T. Margherita. Celestina Lanfranco, Italy's first woman intendant since Emma Carelli in Rome, directed the theatre from 1945 to 1970; she gave the first performances in Italy of *Capriccio* (1953), *Le Mystère de la Nativité* (Martinů, 1963), and the first Genoa performances of *Wozzeck* and *Katerina Izmaylova.*

Genoveva. Opera in 4 acts by Schumann; text by Robert Reinick, altered by composer, after Tieck's tragedy *Das Leben und Tod der heiligen Genoveva* (1799) and Hebbel's tragedy *Genoveva* (1843). Prod. Leipzig 25 June 1850, with Mayer, Günther-Baumann, Wiedemann, Brussin, cond. Reitz; London, D.L., by R.C.M., 6 Dec. 1893. Schumann's only opera. Hebbel's tragedy was also set by Natanael Berg (1947) and Eidens (20th cent.). Also opera *Golo und Genoveva* (1838) by Huth.

Gentele, Göran (*b* Stockholm, 20 Sept. 1917; *d* Sardinia, 18 July 1972). Swedish producer and administrator. After twelve years at the National T., Stockholm, 1941-52, joined the Royal Opera, Stockholm, as producer, 1952-63, and succeeded Svanholm as director, 1963-71. Produced more than 24 operas in Stockholm, including the controversial *Ballo in maschera,* and Blomdahl's *Aniara;* London, C.G., 1961, *Iphigénie en Tauride.* Appointed general manager N.Y. Met., 1970, to succeed Bing in Sept. 1972, but was killed in car crash a few weeks before he was due to take up his appointment.

Gentili, Serafino (*b* Venice, *c*1775; *d* Milan, 13 May 1835). Italian tenor. Début Ascoli Piceno 1796. Naples, 1800-3; Paris, 1809; Milan, Sc., 1812-28; Dresden 1822-4. Created Lindoro in *L' italiana in Algeri* (Venice, 1813). During last years of career sang as Gentili Donati so as not to be confused with Pietro Gentili, another tenor. His daughter, Guistina Bonora, sang with him 1820-8.

Gentle Shepherd, The. A Scots ballad opera in 5 acts; text by Allan Ramsay. Prod. Edinburgh, Taylor's Hall, 29 Jan. 1729; London, D.L., Anglicized as *Patie and Peggie* by Theophilus Cibber, 20 Apr. 1729. Many other versions: that by Richard Tickell prod. D.L. 29 Oct. 1781; N.Y. 7 Jan. 1786. Originally a comedy without songs (1725), it was changed into a ballad opera after the success of *The Beggar's Opera* at Haddington in 1738, and quickly reached a similar standing in Scotland.

Georgia. The first Georgian opera house (now

Paliashvili T.) opened in Tiflis in 1851, when performances were given by visiting Italian companies. Later, Russian opera was also given. In 1898 a concert performance was given in St Petersburg of part of *Daredzan Tsviery*, by Meliton Balanchivadze (1863-1937) (prod. Tiflis 1926 as *Tamara Kovarnaya* (The False Tamara)). Other works that followed included *Skazanye o Shota Rustaveli* (The Tale of S.R., 1919) by Dmitry Arakishvili (1873-1953); *Abesalom i Eteri* (1919) and *Daysy* (Twilight, 1923) by Zachary Paliashvili (1871-1933); and *Keto i Kote* (1919) by Victor Dolidze (1890-1933). With the Revolution, a new impetus was given to national opera: new works followed from these composers, and among many other operas have been *Deputat* (1939) by Shalva Taktakishvili (1900-65); *Rodina* (Fatherland, 1939) by Iona Tuskiya (1901-63); *Bakhtrioni* (1936) and *Lado Ketskhoveli* (1941) by Grigory Kiladze (1902-62); *Mziya* (1950) by Andrey Balanchivadze (*b* 1906, son of Meliton and brother of the choreographer George Balanchine); *Skazanye o Tariele* (The Tale of Tariel, 1946) by Shalva Mshevelidze (*b* 1904); *Neproshenye Gosti* (The Uninvited Guests, 1950) by Alexander Bukiya (*b* 1905); and *Mindiya* (1961) and the triptych *Tri Novelly* (Three Stories, 1967) by Otar Taktakishvili (*b* 1924). The main operatic centre is the T. Opery i Balety Paliashvili in Tiflis.

Gérard. A Revolutionary leader (bar.) in Giordano's *Andrea Chénier*.

Gerhard, Roberto (*b* Valls, 25 Sept. 1896; *d* Cambridge, 5 Jan. 1970). Spanish composer. His only opera, based on Sheridan's *The Duenna*, is a brilliant, intelligent setting which suggests that in more favourable circumstances he might have developed this side of his talent more fully. Written in 1947, it has been broadcast, and given concert perf., Wiesbaden 1951.

Gerl, Franz Xaver (*b* Andorf, 30 Nov. 1764; *d* Mannheim, 9 Mar. 1827). German bass and composer. Sang in the Salzburg Choir under Leopold Mozart. Joined Schikaneder's company in 1788 and was first bass at the T. auf der Wieden, 1789-93. Mozart wrote the aria 'Per questa bella mano' (K. 612) for him. The first Sarastro (1791); his wife Barbara Reisinger (1770-1806) was the first Papagena. He collaborated with *Schack in providing music for a number of operas performed in Vienna. His brother **Judas Thaddäus Gerl** (1774-1844) was also a bass.

German (Jones), (Sir) **Edward** (*b* Whitchurch, 17 Feb. 1862; *d* London, 11 Nov. 1936). English composer. Hopes that he might prove Sullivan's successor in the field of light opera were encouraged by the success of *Merrie England* (1902), but his gift was much more slender.

Tom Jones (1907), loosely after Fielding, and *Fallen Fairies* (1909), with text by Gilbert, were popular in their day. His music has a simple melodiousness, reflecting dramatic situations; it can be pretty, even dainty, or robust and jingoistic, and is admirably written for the voice. Most of the numbers in his operettas are lyrical and decorative, and have no rhythmic or harmonic complication, though the finale of Act 1 of *Merrie England* suggests that he had in him a vein of dramatic music that never found an effective outlet. He completed Sullivan's *The Emerald Isle* (1901).

Bibl: W. H. Scott: *Sir Edward German* (1932).

Germany. For many years the history of German opera was that of Italian composers established at German Courts, e.g. Pallavicini at Dresden, Draghi at Vienna. The first German opera was Heinrich Schütz's *Daphne*, given at Torgau, near Dresden, in 1627; the libretto was a translation of Rinuccini, and the music is lost. The first extant German opera is *Seelewig*, by Sigismund Staden, privately performed at Nuremberg in 1644. German opera was long primitive, often on religious subjects, and consisting of musical numbers interpolated into a play. With a permanent opera house established at Hamburg from 1678, a chance was given to Reinhold *Keiser, then to *Handel. Meanwhile, beside these attempts, and the ever-present Italian opera, *Singspiel developed, as exemplified in the works of Johann Adam *Hiller. An indication of the condition of German opera in the 18th cent. may be had from *Mozart's reluctance as a boy to compose one. His *Entführung aus dem Serail* (1782) is based on Singspiel methods, differing only in musical quality; the genre is raised to the level of greatness with *Die Zauberflöte*. This was also the basis, with the example of French *rescue opera, for *Beethoven's *Fidelio* (1805, rev. 1806 and 1814).

However, the works of isolated geniuses did not constitute a tradition, and many German composers in the early 19th cent. attempted to form one. One of the most popular of all German operas written before the end of 18th cent. was *Winter's *Das unterbrochene Opferfest* (1796); other composers aiming to develop an independent German opera included *Spohr, *Schubert, *Poissl, and E.T.A. *Hoffmann. However, it was *Weber who grasped that the real example for German Romantic opera lay not with Singspiel but with French Revolutionary *opéra comique*, since it was here that a more advanced technique had developed for the handling of popular subjects, free from the formalities of Italian *opera seria*. The performance of *Der Freischütz* in Berlin in 1821 was a turning-point in the history of German opera. Weber took his reforms further with *Euryanthe* (1823), the most artistically successful continuous opera of its day; his death in 1826 left the field to a number of minor figures, including *Marschner, *Lortzing, *Nicolai, and *Lindpaintner, who took up a number of the themes Weber had identified in his operas as distinctively German. These included the supernatural, Nature, medieval subjects, popular settings, melodies based on folk song, or stories based on folk legend. There was, musically, an increased tendency towards continuity, and to structures based on motive rather than separate numbers; the characters grew in psychological subtlety with the development of new expressive means, especially *Leitmotiv.

These elements, and much else, in Romantic opera were the basis of the growth and the reforms of *Wagner, whose life work culminated in the first Bayreuth Festival in 1876. By now a German tradition was flourishing, with theatres in all important towns and numerous composers working both in them and independently. Many composers associated themselves with Wagner and attempted to write operas in his manner and according to his methods; others reacted sharply against him. The most successful of his followers were all minor figures, however, such as *Cornelius. The inspiration of Wagner and the New German School fired Richard *Strauss to his first operas; but though he produced his first opera, Guntram, in 1894 and his last, Capriccio, in 1942, his work is rooted in the 19th cent. and grows little beyond it except onto the fringes of Expressionism with Salome and Elektra. There was strong reaction against Wagner in the 1920s, especially from *Hindemith and *Weill.

In modern times, especially with the resumption of normal operatic life after the censorships and the anti-Semitic policies of the Nazis and then the hardships of war, operatic activity in Germany has been as rich as anywhere in the world, both in terms of new works written and opera houses performing wide repertories. A German opera house remains an important training ground for singers and music staff alike, providing unrivalled experience of opera for beginners and serving audiences with a wide repertory.

See also Aachen, Augsburg, Baden-Baden, Bayreuth, Berlin, Bielefeld, Bonn, Bremen, Breslau (under Wrocław), Brunswick, Chemnitz, Coburg, Cologne, Darmstadt, Dessau, Detmold, Dortmund, Dresden, Düsseldorf, Essen, Flensburg, Frankfurt am Main, Freiburg im Breisgau, Gelsenkirchen, Göttingen, Hagen, Halle, Hamburg, Hanover, Herrenhausen, Kaiserslautern, Karlsruhe, Kassel, Kiel, Königsberg (under Kaliningrad), Krefeld, Leipzig, Lübeck, Magdeburg, Mainz, Mannheim, Munich, Münster, Nuremberg, Oldenburg, Osnabrück, Pforzheim, Regensburg, Riga (under Latvia), Rostock, Saarbrücken, Schwerin, Stuttgart, Trier, Weimar, Wiesbaden, Würzburg, Wuppertal.

Germont. Alfredo's father Giorgio (bar.) in Verdi's La traviata. Often referred to as Germont père.

Gershwin, George (b New York, 26 Sept. 1898; d Hollywood, 11 July 1937). American composer. His first opera, Blue Monday (1923), later renamed 135th Street, was a 1-act piece using jazz-type recitative to connect popular songs. It was unsuccessful. Porgy and Bess (1935) mixes, without reconciling, jazz and 'serious' music, but triumphs by its melodic charm and exuberance, its brilliant colour, humour, and dramatic vitality, and by its power of touching characterization. On 26 Dec. 1955, in Leningrad, a travelling Porgy company became the first American theatrical group to perform in the Soviet Union.

Bibl: D. Ewen: A Journey to Greatness (1956).

Gerster, Etelka (b Kassa, now Košice, 25 June 1855; d Pontecchio, 20 Aug. 1920). Hungarian soprano. Studied Vienna with Marchesi. Heard by Verdi who recommended her to the Fenice, Venice, where she made her début as Gilda in 1877. Appearances followed in France, Germany, and Italy. London, H.M.'s, 1877 as Amina, singing there for the next three years, and C.G. 1890, when she was past her prime. She appeared in America 1879-87 where she almost rivalled Patti in popularity: a bitter dislike arose between the two singers. In 1896 she opened a school for singing in Berlin, which functioned until 1917. Her roles included Queen of Night, Rosina, Lucia, and Violetta. She published a treatise on singing, Stimmführer (1906).

Gerster, Ottmar (b Braunfels, 29 June 1897; d Leipzig, 31 Aug. 1969). German composer. His Enoch Arden (1936), after Tennyson, used popular tunes in separate numbers as well as Leitmotiv; together with Die Hexe von Passau (1941), this has been by far his most successful opera.

Gerusalemme. See I Lombardi.

Gerville-Réache, Jeanne (b Orthez, 26 Mar. 1882; d New York, 5 Jan. 1915). French contralto. Studied Paris with Rosine Laborde and Pauline Viardot. Début Paris, O.C., 1899, Orpheus; O.C., 1899-1903, creating Catherine in Le Juif polonais and Geneviève in Pelléas et Mélisande; Brussels, La M., 1903-4; London, C.G., 1905, Orpheus; N.Y., Manhattan Opera, 1907-10, in variety of roles including Anita in La Navarraise, Delilah, Hérodiade, Klytemnestra in first U.S. Elektra, and Geneviève; 1910-15 appearances with Chicago Opera, Boston, National Opera Company, of Canada. Possessed a true contralto voice and great dramatic power. (R)

Gesamtkunstwerk (*Ger* unified work of art). A term, associated with Wagner and discussed by him in *Das Kunstwerk der Zukunft* (The Art Work of the Future, 1849) and in other places, to describe a dramatic form in which all the arts – poetry, drama, the visual arts, music, song – should be united so as to form a new and complete work of art.

Ghedini, Giorgio (Federico) (*b* Cuneo, 11 July 1892; *d* Nervi, 25 Mar. 1965). Italian composer. The most popular of his operas have been *Re Hassan* (1939) and *Billy Budd* (1949); he has also written *Le Baccanti* (1948, after Euripides), and *L'ipocrita felice* (1956, after Max Beerbohm; orig. radio opera *Lord Inferno*, 1952).

Ghent (Fr. Gand, Flem. Gent). Town in E. Flanders, Belgium. The first opera performances were in 1698, when Lully's *Thesée* was given by a company of 40, who were allowed free accommodation. Opera is now given regularly at the Royal Opera, opened Aug. 1840 as the T. Lyrique, renamed Royal Opera, 1921. Until 1940 all performances were sung in French. During the German occupation, 1940-4, performances were sung in Flemish. After 1947 the French and Italian repertory were sung in French and German, and other works in Flemish; more recently, Italian opera has been given in the original language. A very large repertory and appearances by outstanding international artists have been two of the prominent features of the post-war period; first under Vina *Bovy 1947-55; then under Constant Meillander (1955-61). Meillander was succeeded by Karel Locufier, who died in 1972. The present director is Bart Lotigiers.
Bibl: G. Verriest: *Het lyrisch toneel Te Gent* (1964).

Ghiaurov, Nikolay (Georgyev) (*b* Lydjene, nr Velingrad, 13 Sept. 1929). Bulgarian bass. Studied Sofia, with Brambarov, 1949, Leningrad 1950-1, Moscow. Début Moscow, opera studio, 1955, Don Basilio, then on public stage, Sofia 1956. International appearances since 1957, incl. Paris, O., Méphistophélès, Ramfis etc; Milan, Sc., 1959, Boris, Philip II; London, C.G., 1962, Padre Guardiano; Vienna since 1962; Chicago since 1964; Salzburg since 1965. Other roles include Don Giovanni, Pimen, Creon (*Medea*). One of the finest basses of his kind since Pinza, especially good as Méphistophélès and in Verdi. (R)

Ghiringhelli, Antonio (*b* Brunello, 5 Mar. 1903). Italian administrator. Studied law at Genoa. After Italian liberation in 1945, invited by Mayor of Milan, Antonio Greppi, to supervise the rebuilding of Sc. and eventually to become its general administrator, a position he held successfully until 1972. He was instrumental in the building of a second auditorium (La Piccola Scala), and of taking the Sc. company on successful overseas visits, notably to London, Vienna, and Moscow. He established the Sc. schools for young singers and stage designers, and developed the theatre's ballet school.

Ghislanzoni, Antonio (*b* Lecco, 25 Nov. 1824; *d* Caprino Bergamasco, 16 July 1893). Italian librettist and baritone. As a singer, he made his début in Sanelli's *Luisa Strozzi* in 1846, and sang in various Italian towns before being arrested for revolutionary activities and deported to Corsica; resuming his career on his release, he sang Don Carlo in *Ernani*, Paris 1851. At this time he also formed a company and began writing librettos. The loss of his singing voice compelled him to turn to writing novels and criticism as well as further librettos, and to editing periodicals. His 85-odd librettos include those for Kashperov's *Maria Tudor* and Petrella's *I promessi sposi*, and for works by Ponchielli, Gomes, Cagnoni, Braga, and Catalani. He is most famous for his work on *Aida*, with which Verdi was very pleased.
Bibl: A. Ghislanzoni: *Reminiscenze artistichi* (n.d.).

Giacosa, Giuseppe (*b* Colleretto Parella, 21 Oct. 1847; *d* Colleretto Parella, 2 Sept. 1906). Italian playwright and librettist. After practising law, he turned to writing, also holding various teaching posts including that of professor of drama at the Verdi Conservatory. As a dramatist, he is regarded in Italy as one of the most important representatives of *verismo*; he is also remembered as the part-author with Luigi *Illica, for whose dramatic structures he provided the versification of three operas for Puccini, *La Bohème, Tosca,* and *Madama Butterfly.*

Gianni Schicchi. Opera in 1 act by Puccini; text by Forzano, after an episode (perhaps based on fact) mentioned in Canto XXX, l. 32, of Dante's *Inferno* (*c*1307-21). The third part of Puccini's *Trittico*: prod. N.Y., Met., 14 Dec. 1918, with Easton, Crimi, De Luca, cond. Moranzoni; Rome, C., 11 Jan. 1919, with Dalla Rizza, E. Johnson, Galeffi, cond. Marinuzzi; London, C.G., 18 June 1920, with Dalla Rizza, Burke, Badini, cond. Bavagnoli.

The relatives of the recently dead Buoso Donati try to alter in their own favour his will leaving his fortune to a monastery. Schicchi (bar.) is called in, and yields to pleas for help from his daughter Lauretta (sop.), in love with Buoso's nephew Rinuccio (ten.). He offers to impersonate the dead man, whose death is not yet public, and dictate a new will leaving money to the relatives; first he warns them of the serious penalties involved in the event of discovery. In bed, disguised as Buoso, he then leaves the most valuable properties to himself, later giving the house to the lovers.

Giannini. Italian family of singers and composers.

(1) **Ferruccio** (*b* Ponte d'Arnia, 15 Nov. 1868; *d* Philadelphia, 17 Sept. 1948). Italian tenor. Emigrated to U.S.A. in 1885; studied Detroit with Eleodoro De Campi (a Lamperti pupil). Début Boston, 1891. Made the first operatic records for Emile Berliner, 1896. Married the violinist Antonietta Briglia and settled in Philadelphia, where they opened a small theatre in which operas, plays, and concerts were given. They had six children, including:

(2) **Euphemia** (*b* Philadelphia, 8 Nov. 1895). Studied Milan with Adele Gigola. Début, Turin, Mimì. Returned to U.S.A., 1917, and after a short career in concert and opera taught singing at the Curtis Institute, Philadelphia, where her pupils included Frank Guarrera, Anna Moffo, David Lloyd, and Ellen Faull.

(3) **Dusolina** (*b* Philadelphia, 19 Dec. 1902). Soprano. Studied New York with Sembrich. Début in concert, N.Y., 1923 (though she had sung La Cieca in *La Gioconda* and Azucena when still a child at her father's theatre). Hamburg, 1925, Aida and Santuzza, followed by appearances in Berlin, Vienna, London (C.G. 1928, Aida). Salzburg, 1934-6, Donna Anna and Alice; N.Y., Met., 1935-42; City Opera, 1944, Carmen, Santuzza, Tosca; San Francisco, Chicago, and other American cities. Reappeared in Europe 1947-50. Created Hester in her brother's opera, *The Scarlet Letter* (Hamburg 1938). After retiring taught master classes in Zurich and elsewhere. Considered one of the most exciting singers of her day. Had a range from a to E'''. A prolific recording artist. (R)

(4) **Vittorio** (*b* Philadelphia, 19 Oct. 1903; *d* New York, 28 Nov. 1966). American composer. Studied Milan and Juilliard School. Operas include *Lucidia* (Munich 1934), *The Scarlet Letter* (Hamburg 1938), *The Taming of the Shrew* (Cincinnati 1953), and *The Harvest* (Chicago 1961).

Giannini, Francesco. Italian tenor. Not related to above family. Sang with the Strakosch, Angelo, Giulia Valda, and Mapleson companies in the U.S.A., sometimes under the name of Isaaco Giannini, and in London, C.G., between 1885 and 1892. His brother **Enrico Giannini** (Grifoni) sang at the N.Y., Met., 1891-2. Other Giannini family singers included Giuseppe, Felice, Ernesto, and Filippo.

Gibson, (Sir) **Alexander** (*b* Motherwell, 11 Feb. 1926). Scottish conductor. Studied Glasgow, Royal Scottish Academy of Music; London, R.C.M.; later with Markevitch at Salzburg and Paul van Kempen at Siena. Répétiteur, S.W., 1951-2, conductor 1954-7. Music director 1957-9, during which period he conducted première of Gardner's *Moon and Sixpence*. Founded *Scottish Opera 1962 and as music director has conducted most of its Wagner, Strauss, and Mozart performances as well as *The Trojans, Pelléas et Mélisande,* and British première of

Volo di notte. Washington Opera 1972. A versatile, energetic, and sensitive musician, and very much a 'singers' conductor'. Knighted 1977. (R)

Gielen, Michael (Andreas). (*b* Dresden, 20 July 1927). German, later naturalized Argentinian, conductor. Son of the producer Josef Gielen, he was brought up in Buenos Aires where he studied with E. Leuchter and later in Vienna with J. Polnauer. Début Vienna, 1954 *Jeanne au Bûcher*; Buenos Aires, C. 1947-50; Vienna, S. 1950-60; Stockholm, Royal Opera, as chief conductor 1960-5; Netherlands Opera 1972-7; Frankfurt Opera as musical director since 1977. Has specialized in contemporary scores and conducted world première of Zimmerman's *Die Soldaten,* Cologne 1965. (R)

Giesecke (or Gieseke), **Karl Ludwig** (orig. Johann Georg Metzler) (*b* Augsburg, 6 Apr. 1761; *d* Dublin, 5 Mar. 1833). German dramatist. He worked in Vienna for Schikaneder, writing opera texts among other pieces and translating librettos, including Mozart's *Figaro* and *Così.* His claim to the part-authorship of Mozart's *Zauberflöte* is doubtful.

Gigli, Beniamino (*b* Recanati, 20 Mar. 1890; *d* Rome, 30 Nov. 1957). Italian tenor. Studied Rome, Santa Cecilia, with Enrico Rosati. Won first prize in international contest at Parma, 1914 ('We have found the tenor', wrote Bonci in his report). Début Rovigo 1914, Enzo (*Gioconda*). Milan, Sc., 1918, Faust in Boito celebrations under Toscanini. N.Y., Met., 1920-32 and 1938-9, where he was regarded as Caruso's successor. London, C.G., 1930-1, 1938-9, and 1946, in the latter year singing with his daughter Rina in *Bohème* and *Pagliacci* and appearing on the same evening as both Turiddu and Canio. Left America for Italy in 1932 in protest against salary cuts at the Met., and was outspoken in his criticism of the United States. Returned to U.S.A., 1938-9.

His voice was one of the most beautiful of this century, and his technique was as secure at 60 as it had been when he was a young man. He did not always display good taste, and his acting was generally rudimentary. Nemorino, the Duke of Mantua, Des Grieux, Cavaradossi, Lionel and Chénier were among his best roles. (R)

Bibl: R. de Rensis: *Il cantore del popolo* (1934); B. Gigli: *Memorie* (1957, trans. as *The Memoirs of Beniamino Gigli,* 1957).

Gilbert, W. S. ((Sir) William Schwenk) (*b* London, 18 Nov. 1836; *d* Harrow Weald, 29 May 1911). English poet, playwright, and librettist. His earliest dramatic work was a burlesque of Donizetti's *L'elisir d'amore* entitled *Dulcamara, or The Little Duck and the Great Quack* (1866). His long collaboration with *Sullivan on the so-called *Savoy Operas provided English opera with a vein of comedy which has never been consistently excelled. Idiosyncratic and ingenious, he was a versifier of matchless brilliance, with a mastery of the *patter song that is the equal of anything in the whole of *opera buffa*. His satire of various British institutions – the Navy, the House of Lords, the Police – is as apt as that of more exotic manifestations such as the Japanese Exhibition (in *The Mikado*) and the aesthetic movement (in *Patience*), and ultimately as inoffensive. Of a number of personal quirks, the one that has caused posterity most difficulty is his obsession with the middle-aged, plain, but love-lorn spinster, e.g. Katisha in *The Mikado*. His extraordinary technical proficiency was always musically stimulating to Sullivan.

Gilda. Rigoletto's daughter (sop.) in Verdi's *Rigoletto*.

Gilibert, Charles (*b* Paris, 29 Nov. 1866; *d* New York, 11 Oct. 1910). French bass–baritone. Studied Paris Conservatoire. Début Paris, O.C., 1889; London, C.G., 1894-1909; N.Y., Met., 1900-3, and Manhattan Opera 1906-10. First London Le Père (*Louise*) and Boniface (*Le Jongleur de Notre-Dame*). (R)

Gilly, Dinh (*b* Algiers, 19 July 1877; *d* London, 19 May 1940). French baritone. Studied Paris Conservatoire and with Cotogni. Début Paris, O., 1899. Priest in *Sigurd*; N.Y., Met., 1909-14, where he was heard by Kirkby Lunn, who recommended him to C.G. Début there 1911, Amonasro; remained until 1914, reappeared 1919-24. First London Jack Rance and Athanael. Did not possess a great voice, but was an intelligent and musical singer. Settled in England and appeared at C.G., with the Beecham, Carl Rosa, and B.N.O., companies. Married the contralto Edith Furmedge and opened a singing school in London. Pupils included Brownlee and Noble. (R) **Renée Gilly,** his daughter, studied with him and made her début Paris, O.C., 1933 as Charlotte. Sang Carmen at C.G., 1937. (R)

Giménez (or Jiménez) (y Bellido), **Jeronimo** (*b* Seville, 10 Oct. 1854; *d* Madrid, 19 Feb. 1923). Spanish composer and conductor. Studied Seville, becoming director of the Seville Opera at the age of 17. He then studied in Paris with Alard, Savart, and Thomas. After travels in Italy, he became director of the T. Apolo in Madrid (1885), then of the T. de la Zarzuela, where he conducted the first Spanish *Carmen*. He wrote many zarzuelas, especially in the 1-act form known as the *género chico*, making much use of Spanish song and dance. They include *Tannhauser el estanquero* (1890), *Tannhauser cesante* (1890), *Trafalgar* (1890), *El barbero de Sevilla* (1901), *Los viajes de Gulliver* (1911), and *Tras Tristan* (1918).

Ginastera, Alberto (Evaristo) (*b* Buenos Aires, 11 Apr. 1916). Argentinian composer. Studied Buenos Aires Conservatory. His long list of works includes the operas *Aeroporto* (1961), *Don Rodrigo* (1964), *Bomarzo* (1967 – his greatest success), and *Beatrix Cenci* (1971).

Gioconda, La (The Joyful Girl). Opera in 4 acts by Ponchielli; text by 'Tobia Gorrio' (Arrigo Boito), after Hugo's drama *Angelo, tyran de Padoue* (1835). Prod. Milan, Sc., 8 Apr. 1876 (two months after Cui's setting of the subject was prod. in St Petersburg), with Mariani Masi, Biancolini, Gayarre, Aldighieri, cond. Faccio; London, C.G., 31 May 1883, with Marie Durand, Stahl, Marconi, Cotogni, cond. Bevignani; N.Y., Met., 20 Dec. 1883, with Nilsson, Fursch-Madi, Stagno, Del Puente, cond. Vianesi.

La Gioconda (sop.), a street singer, is in love with Enzo Grimaldo (ten.), who does not return her love, as he is in love with Laura (mezzo), wife of the nobleman Alvise (bass). La Gioconda refuses the advances of Barnaba (bar.), a spy of the Inquisition; in revenge he orders the arrest of La Cieca (alto), Gioconda's mother, accusing her of witchcraft. Laura successfully pleads with her husband and saves the old woman's life; in return for this, La Gioconda helps Laura and Enzo escape Alvise's vengeance (Barnaba having informed against them) by promising herself to Barnaba. When he comes to claim her, she kills herself.

Gioielli della Madonna, I (The Madonna's Jewels). Opera in 3 acts by Wolf-Ferrari; text by Golisciani and Zangarini, German version *Der Schmuck der Madonna* by Hans Liebstöckl. Prod. Berlin, Kurfürstenoper, 23 Dec. 1911, with Ida Salden, Marak, Wiedemann; Chicago, Auditorium, 16 Jan. 1912, with Carolina White, Bassi, Sammarco; London, C.G., 30 May 1912, with Edvina, Martinelli, Sammarco. Prod. Genoa, 6 Feb. 1913, with Boccolini, Calleja, V. Borghese; then not in Italy again, because of the allegedly profane subject, until Rome, 26 Dec. 1953.

Raffaele (bar.) is willing even to steal the Madonna's jewels to prove his love for Maliella (sop.); but Gennaro (ten.) wins her by this very deed. Remorsefully she confesses to the enraged Raffaele and rushes away to drown herself, while Gennaro returns the jewels to an image of the Madonna, and then stabs himself.

Giordani, Tommaso (*b* Naples, *c*1730; *d* Dublin, 23 or 24 Feb. 1806). Italian composer. As member of a family strolling opera company, he came to England, then to Ireland. He wrote over 20 operas for London and Dublin and played an active part in the musical life of both cities.

Giordano, Umberto (*b* Foggia, 28 Aug. 1867; *d* Milan, 12 Nov. 1948). Italian composer. His ten operas matched the current taste for violent *verismo* in post-Mascagni vein; but even in the most successful of them, *Andrea Chénier* 1896) and *Fedora* (1898), the final impression s of clever exploitation of the proven devices 'or theatrical and vocal effect rather than genuinely creative composition. He composed nothing for the stage after *Il Re* (1929). *Bibl:* D. Cellamare: *Umberto Giordano* (1949).

Giorgetta. Michele's wife (sop.) in Puccini's *Il tabarro.*

Giorgi, Teresa. See *Belloc.*

Giorgi-Banti, Brigida. See *Banti.*

Giorgi-Righetti, Geltrude. See *Righetti, Geltrude Giorgi.*

Giorno di Regno, Un (King for a Day) (later known as *Il finto Stanislao* (The False Stanislas)). *Melodramma giocoso* in 2 acts by Verdi; text by Romani, after A.V. Pineu-Duval's comedy *Le Faux Stanislas* (1808). Prod. Milan, Sc., 5 Sept. 1840, with Rainieri-Marini, Abbadia, Salvi, Ferlotti, Scalese, Rovere, Vaschetti, Marconi; N.Y., Town Hall, 18 June 1960; London, St Pancras Town Hall, 21 Mar. 1961, with Jolly, Jonic, Hallett, Hauxvell, Garrett, cond. Ucko. Verdi's second opera, and his only comedy apart from *Falstaff.* The text was first set by Gyrowetz *(Il finto Stanislao,* 1818).

The Cavalier di Belfiore (bar.), a French officer, impersonating Stanislas, the King of Poland, successfully persuades the parents of Giulietta (mezzo-sop.) to allow their daughter to marry Edoardo (ten.). At the same time, he becomes reconciled to the Marchesa del Poggia (sop.), a young widow, who thinks she has been deserted by him.

Giovanna d'Arco (Joan of Arc). Opera in a prologue and 3 acts by Verdi; text by Solera, after Schiller's tragedy *Die Jungfrau von Orleans* (1801). Prod. Milan, Sc., 15 Feb. 1845, with Frezzolini-Poggi, Poggi, Colini, Marconi, Lodetti; N.Y., Carnegie Hall, 1 Mar. 1966, with Stratas, Mori, Milnes, cond. Cillario; London, R.A.M., 20 May 1966, with Carr, West, Charles, cond. Treacher.

Joan (sop.) is loved by Charles, the Dauphin (ten.), but she refuses to yield to his advances as she has heard heavenly voices telling her not to give in to worldly temptations. Joan's father, Giacomo (bar.), denounces his daughter at Charles's coronation, but she is freed from prison to lead the French army against the English, and dies from wounds received in battle.
See also *Joan of Arc.*

Giovanna de Guzman. See *Vêpres siciliennes, Les.*

Giraldoni, Eugenio (*b* Marseilles, 20 May 1871; *d* Helsinki, 23 Oct. 1924). Italian baritone. Son of the baritone Leone Giraldoni and the soprano

Carolina Ferni, herself a pupil of Pasta and a famous dramatic soprano. Studied with his mother. Début Barcelona 1891, Escamillo. N.Y., Met., 1904–5. Created Scarpia, Rome, 1900; a famous Gérard and Boris. (R)

Giraldoni, Leone (*b* Paris, 1824; *d* Moscow, 1 Oct. 1897). Italian baritone, father of above. Studied Florence with Ronzi. Début Lodi 1847. Created Donizetti's Duca d'Alba, Verdi's Boccanegra and Renato. Retired 1885 and taught in Italy and from 1891 in Moscow. Married the soprano Carolina *Ferni (1839-1926).

Giraud, Fiorello (*b* Parma, 22 Oct. 1870; *d* Parma, 28 Mar. 1928). Italian tenor, son of the tenor Lodovico Giraud (1846–82). Studied Parma with Babacini; début Vercelli, 1891, Lohengrin. Leading Italian Wagnerian (Siegfried, Tristan). Created Canio (*Pagliacci*) 1892, and first Italian Pelléas, Milan (1908); also admired in Puccini roles. (R)

Girl of the Golden West, The. See *Fanciulla del West, La.*

Giuditta. Opera in 3 acts by Lehár; text by Paul Knepler and Fritz Löhner. Prod. Vienna, S.O., 20 Jan. 1934, with Novotná and Tauber. Lehár's only full-scale opera. Mussolini rejected the proposed dedication on the grounds that the work's depiction of an Italian officer leaving the colours for a woman was unthinkable in Fascist Italy.

Giuditta (sop.) leaves her husband to accompany Octavio (ten.), an army officer who has seduced her, to Africa. When he departs with his regiment, Giuditta becomes a dancer. Octavio deserts from the army and becomes a pianist in a restaurant. The two meet again in the restaurant, where Giuditta is supping with her new admirer; as they leave, Octavio remains playing the piano as a waiter turns out the lights.

Giuglini, Antonio (*b* Fano, 1827; *d* Pesaro, 12 Oct. 1865). Italian tenor. Studied with Cellini. Début Fermo. London, H.M.'s 1857, Fernando (*La Favorita*). Appeared there, D.L., and Ly., for the next seven years with great success. The first London Riccardo (*Ballo*), Rodolfo (*Luisa Miller*), and Arrigo (*Les Vêpres siciliennes*). Showed signs of insanity in 1865 in St Petersburg and when he returned to London in the spring of that year had to be confined to an asylum. Was taken back to Italy in the autumn and died shortly afterwards.

Giulietta. The courtesan (sop. or mezzo), one of Hoffmann's loves in Offenbach's *Les Contes d'Hoffmann.*

Giulietta e Romeo. See *Romeo and Juliet.*

Giulini, Carlo Maria (*b* Barletta, 9 May 1914). Italian conductor. Studied Rome, Santa Cecilia. Music director of Radio Italiana 1946-51; Milan,

Sc., 1951-6; London, C.G., 1958-67, where his direction of Don Carlos earned him the highest praise. Has conducted at the leading European Festivals including Edinburgh, Aix, Holland, and Florence. Successfully collaborated with the producer *Visconti and Callas in a number of productions at La Scala, including Alceste and Traviata. One of the most outstanding post-war Italian conductors. (R)

Giulio Cesare (Julius Caesar). Opera in 3 acts by Handel; text by Nicola Francesco Haym. Prod. London, Hm., 20 Feb. 1724, with Cuzzoni, Durastanti, Robinson, Bernardi; Northampton (Mass.), Smith Coll., 14 May 1927. Other operas on Caesar are by Cavalli (1646), Sartorio (1677), Freschi (1682), Strungk (1694), Novi (1703), Keiser (1710), Perez (1762), Bianchi (1788), Andreozzi (1789), Robuschi (1790), Zingarelli (1790), Curci (1796), Seyfried (1811), Nicolini (1816), Garcia Robles (19th cent.), Malipiero (1936), Klebe (1959). See also Shakespeare.

Giustino. Opera in 3 acts by Handel; text an altered version of Beregani's libretto, first composed by Legrenzi (1683). Prod. London, C.G., 27 Feb. 1737, with Strada, Bertolli, Annibali, Conti, Beard, Negri. Revived Abingdon, 1967.

Gizziello (orig. Gioacchino Conti) (b Arpino, 28 Feb. 1714; d Rome, 25 Oct. 1761). Italian male soprano. Studied with Gizzi, from whom he took his stage name. Début Rome 1730. London 1736 in Handel's Ariodante; subsequently created leading roles in same composer's Atalanta, Arminio, Giustino, and Berenice. From 1743 to 1753 he was mostly in Lisbon, but managed to visit Naples in 1747 to take part in a celebrated performance of Achille in Sciro with Caffarelli. Retired 1753.

Gläser, Franz (Joseph) (b Obergeorgenthal (Horní Jiřetín), 19 Apr. 1798; d Copenhagen, 29 Aug. 1861). Bohemian composer.. Studied Prague, with Pixis. Conducted in Vienna, 1817–30, then in Berlin. Moved to Copenhagen as music director, 1842. Of his many works (over 50 for the stage), the most popular was Des Adlers Horst (1832), once in most German repertories and known to Wagner; it includes 'pre-Wagnerian' features such as an apostrophe to the sun and the use of insistently repeated short figures for creating dramatic tension. In Copenhagen, he wrote two operas to texts by Hans Andersen, Bryllupet vet Como-Søen (The Wedding on Lake Como, 1849) and Nøkken (The Water-Sprites, 1853).

Glasgow. Town in Scotland. Apart from the usual visits by touring opera companies, there have been seasons by the Glasgow Grand Opera Society, formed in 1905, which has given Goldmark's The Queen of Sheba (1921), Ponchielli's I promessi sposi (1932), Idomeneo (1933), Les Troyens (1935), and Béatrice et

Bénédict (1936). These last three were all British premières and were given under the direction of Erik Chisholm. Since 1945 the Society's productions have included Mefistofele, Le Roi d'Ys, Nabucco, and MacCunn's Jeannie Deans. The first season of *Scottish Opera was given there in 1962 (Madama Butterfly and Pelléas et Mélisande). Opera was given regularly in the King's T. until the restored Empire T. was opened as the home of Scottish Opera, 1976.

Glastonbury. See Boughton.

Glinka, Mikhail (Ivanovich) (b Novospasskoye, 1 June 1804; d Berlin, 15 Feb. 1857). Russian composer. Though he made sketches for operas on Scott's Rokeby, Zhukovsky's Marina Grove (later incorporated into A Life for the Tsar), and Shakhovskoy's The Bigamist (lost), Glinka completed only two operas, A Life for the Tsar (1836; first entitled, and now known in Russia as, Ivan Susanin) and Ruslan and Lyudmila (1842), on which his position as the father of Russian opera rests.

Despite its debt to Italian music in its writing for the voice, and to French music in its spacious choral scenes and its ballet, A Life for the Tsar is intrinsically Russian. Even these two influences are characteristic of what were to be constant stimuli in later Russian opera; Glinka also showed the way in his ability to bring national music into the framework of what his 'initial plan' for the work described as a 'national heroic-tragic opera'. Though he quotes little, he has assimilated essential Russian musical characteristics – such as the podgolosok or folk polyphony, the sound of the balalaika, and certain distinctive melodic traits – and made them the basis of his own invention. Previous Russian composers had drawn upon these and similar sources: it is the action of a major musical mind upon them, using them not as quotation but as the basis for a personal language, that gives A Life for the Tsar its position as the first work of Russian opera's maturity.

Ruslan and Lyudmila is by contrast a brilliant fairy-tale, a riot of colourful episodes that gave Glinka rich opportunity to indulge his talent in this direction without taxing too severely his limited structural ability. Even the most effective and attractive parts of the score show a mixture of manners, in each of which Glinka distinguishes himself without unifying them into a stylistic dramatic whole. Yet the importance of Ruslan to the history of Russian opera is incalculable, for it marked the first appearance of the 'orientalism' and the love of magic, together with the sense of a legendary hero, that was to fascinate Borodin, Mussorgsky, and Rimsky-Korsakov, and was to leave its mark even upon Tchaikovsky's operas.

Bibl: D. Brown: Mikhail Glinka (1974).

Gloriana. Opera in 3 acts by Britten; text by William Plomer, after Lytton Strachey's study *Elizabeth and Essex* (1928). Commissioned by C.G. for the Coronation of Queen Elizabeth II, and prod. at a Gala Performance in her presence, 8 June 1953, with Cross, Vyvyan, Sinclair, Pears, G. Evans, Matters, Dalberg, cond. Pritchard; Cincinnati 8 May 1956, with Borkh, Danco, Rankin, Alexander, Uppman, cond. Krips. The plot describes the events of the later years of Queen Elizabeth I's (sop.) reign, and in particular her relationship with the Earl of Essex (ten.).

Glossop, Peter (*b* Sheffield, 6 July 1928). English baritone. Studied Sheffield with Leonard Mosley and Eva Rich. Début Sheffield Operatic Society, 1949, Dr Coppelius and Dr Miracle. London, S.W., 1952 (in chorus), 1953–62 principal; roles included Rigoletto, Di Luna, Scarpia, Onegin, and Zurga; C.G. since 1966, mostly in the Italian repertory, but also as Demetrius in *A Midsummer Night's Dream,* Billy Budd, Herald in *Lohengrin,* Donner, and Jochanaan. Milan, Sc., 1966 and subsequently. Also appearances in Mexico, San Francisco, N.Y., Met. Has a true Verdi baritone voice, and is an extrovert performer. (R)

Gluck, Alma (orig. Reba Fiersohn) (*b* Bucharest, 11 May 1884; *d* New York, 27 Oct. 1938). American soprano of Romanian birth. Studied N.Y. Début N.Y., Met., 1909, Sophie (*Werther*). After three seasons at the Met., and a further period of study with Sembrich, she devoted herself to the concert platform. (R) Her daughter Marcia Davenport has written a *Life of Mozart,* a biography of Toscanini, and an operatic novel *Of Lena Geyer* based on incidents in her mother's life.

Gluck, Christoph Willibald von (*b* Erasbach, 2 July 1714; *d* Vienna, 15 Nov. 1787). German composer, (?) of Bohemian stock. Gluck is opera's second founder. His first opera, *Artaserse* (1741), had a Metastasio libretto, and to begin with he accepted the Metastasian conventions of the day – *da capo* arias, profusely ornamented, sung perhaps by castratos and linked in *recitativo secco.* Established in Vienna after a London visit, he gradually became dissatisfied with the tyranny of singer over composer which these artifices represented. The librettist Durazzo encouraged his restlessness, though their *L'innocenza giustificata* (1755) is as blameless as its title. In 1758 a Viennese vogue gave him the chance to set a number of French *opéras comiques*; if their strings of numbers linked by speech represented no formal advance, Gluck was now writing music for characters more vividly alive than the two-dimensional Metastasian gods and kings. In 1761 he set Gaspar Angiolini's *Don Juan,* a dramatic *ballet d'action* in place of the conventional *divertissement en danse.*

Then in 1762 came *Orfeo ed Euridice,* in which Gluck, stimulated now by his librettist Calzabigi, stood forward as reformer: *recitativo accompagnato* made the music more fully continuous, and the singers' claims were set below the aim of a purer, more genuinely classical approach to drama in music. A few conventional operas followed; then in *Alceste* (1767) opera finally became music drama, and in the famous preface Gluck declared his aims: to purge singers' abuses, to 'restrict music to its true office by means of expression and by following the situations of the story', and to strive always for complete clarity and simplicity. *Alceste* triumphed. *Paride ed Elena* followed in 1770, and then Gluck turned to French opera. *Iphigénie en Aulide* (1773) was reluctantly accepted by the Paris Opéra, and its production in 1774, followed by new versions of earlier operas, touched off an artistic rivalry with Piccinni, to the city's delight. In *Armide* (1777) Gluck set out to be 'more of the poet and painter than the musician', and claimed to have discovered how to identify characters musically. *Iphigénie en Tauride* (1779) was an instant success, but *Écho et Narcisse* (1779) failed. Gluck returned to Vienna, where he composed little more.

It is the simplicity he sought that remains Gluck's greatest quality – a simplicity that can be barren but frequently reaches the sublime. His greatness was achieved with a bewildering lack of technical resources, but such is his mastery that this is almost always turned to positive, expressive account. Said Berlioz, 'La nudité ne convient qu'aux désses.'
Bibl: E. Newman: *Gluck and the Opera* (1895, R/1964); P. Howard: *Gluck and the Birth of Modern Opera* (1963).

Glückliche Hand, Die (The Favoured Hand). *Drama mit Musik* in 1 act by Schoenberg; text by composer. Prod. Vienna, V.O., 14 Oct. 1924, with Jerger, Pfundmayr, Hunstiger, cond. Stiedry; Philadelphia, Ac. of M., 11 Apr. 1930. The subject is the artist's quest for happiness; this is undertaken by a man (bar.), who is the protagonist, though there are mimed parts for another man and a woman, and a chorus which comments at the start and finish.

Glyndebourne. The name of the house and estate of John Christie near Lewes, Sussex, in the grounds of which a festival opera house was built in 1934 for the purpose of giving model performances of opera in ideal surroundings. The inspiration behind the venture came from Christie's wife, the soprano Audrey *Mildmay. The first Glyndebourne Festival opened on 28 May 1934 with *Figaro,* followed the next evening by *Così fan tutte.* The conductor was Fritz Busch and the producer Carl Ebert, who between them set a standard in musical ensemble and production which far exceeded anything seen or heard in English opera at that time.

By 1939 the theatre had been enlarged, and the seating capacity was increased from 300 to 600; the present capacity is 800. The repertory then included *Figaro, Così, Entführung, Zauberflöte, Don Giovanni, Don Pasquale,* and Verdi's *Macbeth* (first perf. in England). Audrey Mildmay, Ina Souez, Luise Helletsgrüber, Irene Eisinger, Margherita Grandi, John Brownlee, Dino Borgioli, Willi Domgraf-Fassbänder, David Franklin, Heddle Nash, Roy Henderson, Mariano Stabile, and Francesco Valentino were among the regular artists. During the war years Glyndebourne became the home of evacuees. It reopened in 1946, when the English Opera Goup produced *The Rape of Lucretia;* in 1947 the same organization gave *Albert Herring,* and Ebert returned to produce *Orfeo* with Ferrier. In 1948 and 1949 there were no opera performances, though Glyndebourne, under the general management of Rudolf *Bing, was responsible for the opera at the first five Edinburgh Festivals. Glyndebourne resumed its own annual summer festivals in 1950, when Busch returned to collaborate again with Ebert. Busch died in 1951, and his place as chief conductor was taken by Vittorio Gui, who was responsible for the inclusion of several of Rossini's operas in the repertory. Ebert retired at the end of the 1959 Festival and was succeeded by Rennert, who with Gui became Artistic Counsellor – Gui as Head of Music, Rennert Head of Production. In 1963 John Pritchard was given the title of Music Counsellor when Gui resigned from his official position, though he continued to conduct until 1965. In 1968 Rennert resigned, following his appointment to Munich, and Moran Caplat, who had been connected with Glyndebourne since 1945, first as assistant manager and then as general manager, was appointed general administrator; the following year Pritchard became music director. In 1971 John Cox was appointed director of production. Although Raymond Leppard has held no official position at Glyndebourne, his close connection with the house since 1962 has resulted in the expansion of the repertory to include works by Monteverdi and Cavalli. Pritchard was succeeded by Bernard Haitink in 1977.

Additions to the repertory in the post-war period have included *La Cenerentola, L'italiana in Algeri, Il barbiere di Siviglia, Le Comte Ory, La pietra del paragone, Falstaff, Arlecchino, Il segreto di Susanna, Ariadne auf Naxos, Idomeneo, Alceste, The Rake's Progress, Der Schauspieldirektor, Rosenkavalier, Fidelio, I Puritani, L'elisir d'amore, Elegy for Young Lovers* (Henze), *L'incoronazione di Poppea, Pelléas et Mélisande, Capriccio, Anna Bolena,* *Werther, L'Ormindo, La Calisto, Eugen Onegin, Il Turco in Italia, The Rising of th Moon, The Queen of Spades, Il ritorno d'Uliss in patria, The Visit of the Old Lady, The Cunnin Little Vixen, Intermezzo,* and *Die schweigsam Frau;* and at Edinburgh, *La forza del Destin* and *Un ballo in maschera.* The post-wa generation of Glyndebourne artists ha included Janet Baker, Jane Berbié, Ileana Cot rubas, Denise Duval, Anne Howells, Sen Jurinac, Ilva Ligabue, Kerstin Meyer, Margare Price, Graziella Sciutti, Elisabeth Söderströr Josephine Veasey, Sesto Bruscantini, Gerain Evans, Hugues Cuénod, Paolo Montarsol Marius Rintzler, Michel Roux, George Shirley Richard Van Allan, John Wakefield; th conductors Vittorio Giu, John Pritchard Andrew Davis, Carlo Felice Cillario, Lambert Gardelli, Bernard Haitink, Raymond Leppard Paul Sacher, and Silvio Varviso; the producer Ebert, Rennert, John Cox, Peter Ebert, Gian franco Enriquez, Mikhail Hadjimishchev, Pete Hall, Michael Redgrave, Franco Zeffirelli; an the designers Osbert Lancaster, Oliver Messe Lorenzo Ghiglia, Henry Bardon, Peter Rice Emmanuele Luzzati, Ita Maximovna, Joh Bury, and Michael Annals.

Bibl: S. Hughes: *Glyndebourne* (1965).

Glyndebourne Touring Opera. A company o young singers from Glyndebourne establishe with support from the Arts Council and th Gulbenkian Trust to take Glyndebourn productions to major cities outside Londor Brian Dickie is the company's administrator Myer Fredman was musical director until 1975 Kenneth Montgomery 1957–7; Nichola Braithwaite from 1977. Works taken on tou have included *L'Ormindo, Macbeth, Eugen Onegin, Werther, Il Turco in Italia, Ariadne au Naxos, L'elisir d'amore* as well as the mor familiar Mozart repertory. Most operas ar given in their original language.

Glynne, Howell (*b* Swansea, 24 Jan. 1906; Toronto, 24 Nov. 1969). Welsh bass. Studie with Ben Davies and Reinhold von Warlich Joined C. R. chorus, occasionally taking sma roles, and in Sept. 1931 sang Sparafucile Leading bass at S.W. 1946-51 and again 1956 64; C.G. 1951-6. Fiesco in the English premièr of *Simone Boccanegra,* and Mr Crusty in Th *School for Fathers* at S.W.; created Lavatte i Bliss's *The Olympians* at C.G. Possessed a ric voice and a flair for buffo roles. Taught Toront Conservatory 1964-9. (R)

Goat's trill. See *Bleat.*

Gobatti, Stefano (*b* Bergantino, 5 July 1852; Bologna, 17 Dec. 1913). Italian composer. Th astounding success of his first opera, *I Go* (1873), which had 52 curtain calls, won him th honorary citizenship of Bologna and the clain by his admirers that here was the new Verdi

The enthusiasm quickly faded, and Verdi himself called *I Goti* 'the most monstrous musical abortion ever composed'. The failure of his other operas, *Luce* (1875) and *Cordelia* (1881), *Masias* (comp. 1900) was never staged), coupled with misfortune, debt, and slander (he was accused of possessing the evil eye), caused him to to devlop persecution mania, and he died in an institution.

Gobbi, Tito (*b* Bassano del Grappa, 24 Oct. 913). Italian baritone. Originally studied law, then turned to singing. Studied Rome with Crimi; début Gubbio, 1935, Rodolfo (*Sonnambula*); London, C.G., since 1950; San Francisco 948; Chicago since 1954. Has sung at all the leading Italian opera houses, and appeared regularly in Vienna. Intelligence, musicianship, and acting ability, allied to a good if not very large voice, have made Gobbi one of the finest singing actors of his generation. A distinguished Verdi and Puccini interpreter (Rigoletto, Macbeth, Boccanegra, Posa, Iago, Falstaff, Scarpia, Rance, Michele); also a celebrated Wozzeck and Figaro. Has a repertory of nearly 00 operas, and has made 26 films. Début as producer, Chicago and C.G., 1965, *Simon Boccanegra*. (R)

Godard, Benjamin (Louis Paul) (*b* Paris, 18 Aug. 849; *d* Cannes, 10 Jan. 1895). French composer. Studied Paris, with Reber and Vieuxtemps. The most successful of his six operas was *La Vivandière* (1895); the others were *Les Bijoux de Jeanette* (1878), *Pedro de Zalaméa* 1884), *Jocelyn* (1888; from this comes the famous *Berceuse*), *Dante et Béatrice* (1890), and *Les Guelfes* (1902).

Goehr, Walter (*b* Berlin, 28 May 1903; *d* Sheffield, 4 Dec. 1960). English conductor and composer, of German birth. Studied Berlin, with Schoenberg. He wrote the first radio opera, *Malpopita* (1930). Moved to England and became an influential conductor and teacher, by way of his position with Columbia Records, the B.B.C., and Morley College. He won a Grand Prix du Disque for his edition and performance of Monteverdi's *Poppea* (1954), and was one of the first conductors in England to arouse wider interest in baroque music, especially Purcell and Monteverdi. (R) His son **Alexander** (*b* Berlin, 10 Aug. 1932) is a composer and teacher. Studied Paris, with Messiaen. He has held American professorships, Professor of Music at Leeds 1971–6, now Professor of Music at Cambridge. His first opera, *Arden Must Die* (1967), had its première at Hamburg: it revealed a vivid dramatic talent, which Goehr put to very different but effective use in the dramatic madrigal' *Naboth's Vineyard* (1968) and *Shadow Play* (1970). The former, in some ways a re-creation of the dramatic entertainments that immediately preceded opera and specifically of the style of Monteverdi's *Il*

combattimento di Tancredi e Clorinda, uses two mimes, singers, and instruments; the latter (based on the episode of the Cave in Plato's *Republic*) uses speaker, tenor, and instruments. They are among the most imaginative attempts to develop a tradition of *Music Theatre in England.

Goethe, Johann Wolfgang von (*b* Frankfurt, 28 Aug. 1794; *d* Weimar, 22 Mar. 1832). German poet and dramatist. Goethe's deep interest and involvement in music included early experience singing bass in a choir, learning some instruments, and attending with admiration operas and Singspiels, especially those by Hiller. He was also much impressed by the visit of Marchand's company to Frankfurt, 1771-7, and came to know the composer Johann André. His own Singspiel texts were *Erwin und Elmire, Claudine von Villa Bella, Lila, Die Fischerin, Jery und Bätely*, and *Scherz, List und Rache;* he also wrote a second part to *Die Zauberflöte*. When he was director of the Weimar theatre, 1791–1817, his repertory included operas: his preferred composer was Mozart (280 perfs.) followed by Dittersdorf (139 perfs.), then French composers. Among the adaptations he made was one of Mozart's *Der Schauspieldirektor*. Operas on his works are as follows.

Die Laune des Verliebten (1765): Gürrlich (1812).
Die Mitschuldigen (1769): Riethmüller (1957).
Götz von Berlichingen (1773): Goldmark (1902).
Satyros (1773): Baussnern (1922); Bořkovec (1942).
Der Jahrmarktfest zu Plundersweilern (1773): Anna Amalia (1775); A. B. Eberwein (1818).
Erwin und Elmire (1774): André (1775); Duchess Anna Amalia of Sachsen-Weimar (1776); Wolf (1780); Schweitzer (1780); E. W. Wolf (1780); Vogler (1781); Agthe (1785); Stegmann (1786); Rupprecht (1790); Reichardt (1791); Bergt (c1805); Schoeck (1916).
Clavigo (1774): Ettinger (1926).
Die Leiden des jungen Werthers (1774): R. Kreutzer (1792); Pucitta (1802); Benvenuti (1811); Coccia (1814); Aspa (1849); Gentili (1862); Massenet (1882); Parody by W. Müller (1830).
Claudine von Villa Bella (1774; rev. 1779 as Singspiel): André (1779); Beecke (1780); G. Weber (1783); Reichardt (1789); Kerpen (late 18th cent.); Schneider (1807); Blum (1810); Kienlen (1810); Eisrich (1813); Schubert (part comp.), 1815); Eberwein (1815); Kienlen (1817); Coccia (1817); Gläser (1826); Stolze (1831); Drechsler (after 1836); Müller (*c* 1850); J. H. Franz (Hochberg) (1864); Seidel (1871); Knappe (1882); Irmler (1932).

Stella (1776): Deshayes (*Zélia*, 1791; *La Suite de Zélia*, 1792).

Lila (1776): Seckendorf (1776); Reichardt (1790); Seidel (1818).

Die Geschwister (1776); Rottenberg (1916); Veidl (1916); Meyerolbersleben (1932).

Proserpina (1777); Seckendorf (1777).

Jery und Bätely (1780): Seckendorf (1779); Reichardt (1789); Winter (1790); Schaum (1795); Bierey (1803); K. Kreutzer (1810); Frey (1815); Seidel (comp. 1815); Marx (1825); Bergt (early 19th cent.); Hartmann (1833); Adam (1834); Rietz (1840); H. Schmidt (before 1846); Stiehl (1868); Bronsart (1873); Bolck (1875); Pfaff (1910); Dressel (1932); Kniese (1937). Scribe and Mélesville's text for Adam's *Le Chalet* (1834), re-worked for Donizetti's *Betly* (1836) is derived from it.

Die Fischerin (1782): Corona Schröter (1782: she also sang Dortchen in it, thus becoming the first composer and first singer of *Erlkönig*); Eberwein (1818).

Scherz, List und Rache (1784): P.C. Kayser (1786); Winter (1790); E.T.A. Hoffmann (1801); Kienlen (1805); Bruch (1858); Wellesz (1928); Irmler (*c* 1930).

Egmont (1787): Dell'Orefice (1878); Salvayre (1886); Meulemans (1960).

Märchen (1794): Klebe (1969).

Wilhelm Meisters Lehrjahre (1796): Thomas (*Mignon*, 1866).

Der Zauberlehrling (1797): Döbber (1907); Braunfels (1954, TV).

Die Braut von Korinth (1797); Devasini (1846); Duprato (1867).

Der Gott und die Bajadere (1797); Auber (1830).

Hermann und Dorothea (1798): Missa (1911).

Faust (Pt. 1, 1808; Pt. 2, 1832): Joseph Strauss (*c* 1814); Lickl (1815); Seyfried (1816); I. Walter (1819); Horn (1825); Béancourt (1827); Berlioz (non-operatic, but sometimes staged: *La Damnation de Faust*, 1846, incorporating and revising *Huit Scènes de Faust*, 1829); Lindpaintner (1831); Bertin (1831); Pellaert (1834); Rietz (1836); Gregoir (1847); Hennebert (1853); Lutz (1855); Gounod (1859); Boito (*Mefistofele*, 1868); Lassen (1876); Zöllner (1887); Souchay (1940).

Pandora (1808): Lassen (1886); Gerster (1949).

R. Wagner-Régeny's *Prometheus* (1959) includes a setting of Goethe's poem. Lehár's *Friederike* (1928) is an operetta on the Friederike Brion episode in Goethe's life.

Goetz. See *Götz*.

Gogol, Nikolay (Vasilyevich) (*b* Sorochintsy, 31 Mar. 1809; *d* Moscow 4 Mar. 1852). Russian writer. Most Gogol operas are on the stories in *Evenings on a Farm near Dikanka* (1831–2): *Christmas Eve:* Tchaikovsky (*Vakula the Smith*, 1874; rev. as *Cherevichki* (The Slippers)

1885); N. Afanasev (19th. cent.); Solovyov (1875, prod. 1886); Lysenko (operetta, 1874; opera, 1883); Rimsky-Korsakov (1895); Bogoslovsky (1929); Peysin (1929); Gertman (?); Shtzurovsky (?).

May Night: Sokalsky (1876); Rimsky-Korsakov (1879); Lysenko (1884); Ryabov (1937); Baumilas (*c* 1956).

The Lost Charter: Yaroslavenko (1922).

St John's Eve: Tikots (?1912).

The Terrible Revenge: N. Kochetov (1903).

Sorochintsy Fair: Mussorgsky (unfin. 1880); Yanovsky (1899); Ryabov (1936); V. Alexandrov (?).

The Portrait (1835, rev. 1842): Rosenberg (1956).

The Wedding (1834, 1 act only): Mussorgsky (1868, unfin.: prod., piano acc., 1909); A. Jiránek (early 20th cent.); Martinů (1953); Grechaninov (1946, prod. 1950).

The Coach: Kholminov (20th cent.).

The Nose (1835): Shostakovich (1930); W. Kaufmann (1953).

The Diary of a Madman (1835); Searle (1958); Ancelin (*Journal d'un fou*, 1975).

Viy (1835): Kropivnitsky (late 19th cent.); Goryelov (1897); K. Moor (1903); Dobronić (1 act of *Vječnaja Pamjat*, 1947); Verikovsky (1946); Staritsky (?).

Taras Bulba (1835): Vilboa (19th cent., unprod.); Afanasyev (19th cent., unprod.); Sokalsky (1878, rev. 1905 as *The Siege of Dubno*); V. Kühner (1880); Elling (*Kosakkerne*, 1896); Lysenko (1890, prod. 1924); Kashperov (1887); Berutti (1895); Trailin (*c*1885, prod. 1914); M.S. Rousseau (1919).

The Inspector General (1836): K. Weis (1907); Shvedov (comp. 1934); Zádor (1935); Zanella (1940); Egk (1957). Also, based on Gogol's idea, Chukhadjyan (*Arifin Khilesi*, 1872).

The Greatcoat (1842): W. Kaufmann (*Bashmashkin*, 1952); Marttinen (1965); Kholminov (20th cent.).

Golaud. Mélisande's husband (bass-bar.), half-brother of Pelléas, in Debussy's *Pelléas et Mélisande*.

Golden Cockerel, The. Opera in 3 acts by Rimsky-Korsakov; text by Belsky, after Pushkin's poem (1834). Prod. Moscow, Z., 7 Oct. 1909, with Dobrovolskaya, Speransky, Pikok, Rostovtseva, Zaporozhets, Ernts, Dikov, Klopotovskaya, cond. Cooper; London, D.L., 15 June 1914, with Dobrovolskaya, Petrenko, Petrov, Altechevsky, cond. Cooper; N.Y., Met., 6 Mar. 1918, with Barrientos, Didur, Diaz, cond. Monteux.

The 14th and last of Rimsky-Korsakov's operas. The censor refused to sanction performance during the composer's lifetime owing to the alleged reference in King Dodon's Court to that of Tsar Nicholas II, and the implied critim of the inefficient conduct of the Russo-panese War. The composer wanted his ngers also to dance, but this was found too hausting, and so for the Petrograd produc-n Fokine devised the idea of having the ngers seated in the theatre boxes, with e action mimed by dancers. Despite pro-sts from the composer's family, this version roduced the work to Western Europe; t later productions in New York and London verted to the original.

The opera tells of the miraculous golden coc-rel, given to the old King Dodon (bass) by the strologer, (ten.) which crows at the sign of minent danger. Dodon brings back the autiful Queen of Shemakha (sop.) to his cap-; when the Astrologer demands payment the cockerel he is killed by Dodon, and the ckerel kills the King.

Idmark, Karl (orig. Károly) (b Kesthely, 18 ay 1830; d Vienna, 2 Jan. 1915). Austro-ngarian composer. His first opera, *Die nigin von Saba* (1875) was also his most ccessful: colourful and tuneful, it was taken all over Germany and also in England and nerica. Goldmark's later operas were *Merlin* 386), *Das Heimchen am Herd* (1896), *Die iegsgefangene* (1899), *Götz von Ber-hingen* (1902), and *Ein Wintermärchen* 02). His eclectic style, drawing on influences disparate as Mendelssohn and Hungarian k music, was also influenced by Wagner, and was less successful when attempting monu-ental opera in a manner somewhere bet-en Meyerbeer and Wagner than when lulging his agreeable melodic vein in less abitious and lighter pieces.

l: K. Goldmark: *Erinnerungen aus meinem ben* (1922, 2/1929).

doni, Carlo (b Venice, 25 Feb. 1707; d Paris, eb. 1793). Italian dramatist. His brilliant com-ies were the basis for numerous librettos, pecially for Galuppi, Vivaldi, G. Scarlatti, chietti, Gassmann, Piccinni, and Haydn, and modern times have been used especially by lf-Ferrari.

Idovsky, Boris (b Moscow, 7 June 1908). ssian, now naturalized American, opera pro-cer and conductor. Studied Moscow, Berlin, d Budapest, and at the Curtis Institute, N.Y., h Reiner. Has held appointments in the era departments of the Cleveland Institute of sic, the New England Conservatory, and the erkshire Music Center, where he was the anizer of the productions of *Peter Grimes,* ert Herring, La clemenza di Tito,* etc.

dschmidt, Berthold (b Hamburg, 18 Jan. 3). British composer and conductor of rman birth. In 1926–7, asst. cond. Berlin S. 1927–9, cond. Darmstadt Opera; 1931–3, stic adviser Berlin Stä. O.; 1947, cond. Glyn-bourne Opera at Edinburgh. His operas are

Der gewaltige Hanrei (1932) and *Beatrice Cenci* (1951), a prize-winner in the Arts Council competition for the Festival of Britain, but not produced.

Goldschmied von Toledo, Der (The Goldsmith of Toledo). Pasticcio, compiled from music by Offenbach, by Stern and Zamara; text by Zwerenz, after Hoffmann's story *Das Fräulein von Scuderi* (1818). Prod. Mannheim 7 Feb. 1919; Edinburgh 16 Mar. 1922 by B.N.O.C., subsequently at C.G. See also *Cardillac.*

Goltz, Christel (b Dortmund, 8 July 1912). German soprano. Studied with Ornelli-Leeb in Munich. Joined chorus of Furth Opera 1935; début there as Agathe. Dresden State Opera 1936–50; London, C.G., 1951; N.Y., Met., 1954. Sang regularly in Munich, Vienna, and Berlin until 1970. Created Orff's *Antigonae,* Dresden 1949, and Liebermann's *Penelope,* Salzburg 1954. Possessed a clear and brilliant voice, three octaves in range, and sang and enacted her roles with great intensity. A renowned Salome, Elektra, and Marie (*Wozzeck*). (R)

Gomes, (Antonio) **Carlos** (b Campinas, 11 July 1836; d Pará, 16 Sept. 1896). Brazilian com-poser of Portuguese origin. His first opera was *Noite de Castello* (1861); this was followed by *Joanna de Flandres* (1863), for which he won a scholarship to Italy. Here he studied with L. Rossi, and wrote several operas that were more Italian in style before a triumphant return to Brazil. *O Guarani* (1870) has been given with success in Italy and England; other successful operas include *Salvator Rosa* (1874), *Maria Tudor* (1879), and *O Escravo* (1889). *Bibl:* J. Britto: *Carlos Gomes* (1956).

Gomez, Jill (b New Amsterdam, British Guiana, 21 Sept. 1942). British soprano. Studied London, R.A.M. and G.S.M. Début in Cambridge University Opera 1967, Mermaid in *Oberon*; Gly. Touring Company 1968 Adina; Gly. Festival 1969, Mélisande, and subse-quently C.G., 1970 creating Flora in Tippett's *The Knot Garden* and subsequently as Tytania and Lauretta. E.O.G., creating the Countess in Musgrave's *Voice of Ariadne,* Aldeburgh 1974. Appearances with Scottish Opera, W.N.O. Repertory includes Pamina, Elizabeth Zimmer in *Elegy for Young Lovers,* Anne Trulove, and Jenifer in Tippett's *Midsummer Marriage.* Pos-sesses a pure lyric soprano and an engaging stage presence. (R)

Gonzaga, Pietro (b Longarone, 25 Mar. 1751; d St Petersburg, 6 Aug. 1831). Italian designer. He joined Milan Sc. as a scene-painter, 1779, then worked in other Italian cities and visited Russia in order to build a private theatre for Prince Yusupov (1789), but returned to contri-bute to the inauguration of Venice, F. Back in Russia, he worked in various theatres, where he developed his interest in architectural scenery and perspective in sets that foreshadow much of Romantic practice.

Good Friday Music (Karfreitagzauber). The music in Act 3, scene 1, of Wagner's *Parsifal*, as Parsifal, returning after his wanderings, is annointed in preparation for his entry into the Castle of the Grail.

Goodall, Reginald (*b* Lincoln, 13 July 1905). Studied London, R.C.M., Munich, and Vienna. London, C.G., répétiteur with Coates-Rosing Company, 1936. S.W. 1944–6, cond. première of *Peter Grimes* there 1945 and *The Rape of Lucretia* at Gly., sharing it with Ansermet 1966. C.G., since 1946, conducting *Manon, Meistersinger, Fidelio* and much of the Italian repertory during the Rankl period, then, only rarely, works including *Walküre, Tristan, Parsifal, Salome*. Invited to conduct English *Mastersingers* at S.W. in 1968, the success of which led to his preparing and conducting Sadler's Wells Opera's *Ring* in English at the London Coliseum with great success. Late in his career he was recognized as a great Wagner conductor in the Furtwängler-Knappertsbusch tradition, with an exceptional understanding of the works' architecture and inner drama, expressed in slow tempos and great beauty of line and tone. (R)

Goossens, Eugène I (*b* Bruges, 25 Feb. 1845; *d* Liverpool, 30 Dec. 1906). English conductor of Belgian origin. Came to England in 1873; in 1882 joined Carl Rosa, with whom cond. first performance in English of *Tannhäuser* (1882). In 1892 cond. command performance *La Fille du régiment* before Queen Victoria. His son **Eugène II** (*b* Bordeaux, 28 Jan. 1867; *d* London, 31 July 1958) worked under him in the C.R.; then principal cond. in succession of Burns-Crotty, Arthur Rouseby, and Moody-Manners companies. Principal cond. C.R., 1899–1915, maintaining high standards set by his father, and making many additions to the repertory. Joined Beecham's company at Birmingham 1917, and cond. in Beecham season at H.M.'s. Opened 1918 Beecham season at D.L., with *Ivan the Terrible*. Married **Annie Cook**, former contralto of Carl Rosa and daughter of basso buffo T. Aynsley Cook; their five children included **Eugène III** (*b* London, 26 May 1893; *d* London, 13 June 1962), composer and conductor. Eugène III began conducting career assisting Beecham and his father. Cond. some performances of B.N.O.C. and C.R. Latterly he conducted little opera, though he directed his own *Judith* (1929) and *Don Juan de Mañara* (1937) at C.G., and performances in Philadelphia and Cincinnati in the 1930s. Both operas have librettos by Arnold Bennett. In them his operatic experience is evident in the dramatic presentation of librettos whose merits are primarily literary, though his own highly chromatic yet chaste style is itself not essentially operatic. Director N.S.W. Conservatory of Music 1947-56, helping many Australian singers at the start of their careers. (R) *Bibl:* E. Goossens [III]: *Overture and Beginners* (1951).

Gorgheggio (*It* warbling). A rapid decorative vocalization consisting of numerous rising and falling notes. It was already unpopular with composers in the 17th cent., and became in the 18th cent. and 19th cent. one of many devices whereby singers would introduce evidence of their own virtuosity, especially in the *aria d' bravura*, without regard to musical or dramatic sense.

Gorr, Rita (orig. Marguerite Geirnaert) (*b* Ghent, 18 Feb. 1926). Belgian mezzo-soprano. Début Antwerp 1949, Fricka; Strasbourg 1949–52. Won first prize at International Contest at Lausanne 1952, after which she was engaged at the Paris O. London, C.G., since 1959; N.Y., Met., 1962. Has sung in Lisbon Naples, Rome with success, and in 1958 sang Fricka at Bayreuth. Repertory includes Kundry Dalila, Hérodiade, Charlotte, Oktavian, and Orphée. (R)

Gorrio, Tobia. See *Boito, Arrigo*.

Gossec (orig. Gossé), **François** (Joseph) (*b* Vergnies, 17 Jan. 1734; *d* Passy, 16 Feb. 1829). French composer of Belgian descent. Studied Antwerp, then Paris with Rameau. Assistant director, Paris, O., 1780-2, then on the board until 1784. His greatest popular successes were with his comedies, especially *Les Pêcheurs* (1766) and *Toinon et Toinette* (1767); even here, his attempt to give greater interest to the orchestra led to the reproach that he was 'learned'. Later he attempted a large-scale national French opera in the 5-act (later 4-act) *tragédie lyrique, Sabinus* (1773), which treats a story of the Gauls resisting the Romans in a manner that anticipates Spontini. He was a great admirer of Gluck, as is revealed particularly in his *Thésée* (1782). *Bibl:* J.-G. Prod'homme: *François-Joseph Gossec* (1949).

Göteborg (Gothenburg). Town in Sweden Early opera performances were given by German companies in the 1830s. In Sept. 1859 the New T. (cap. 650) was opened, and performances were again given by visiting companies, including the first performances in Sweden of *Nabucco* in 1865. In October 1889 the theatre was renamed the Stora T. and was bought by Albert Ranft, who was the administrator until 1920, when he sold it to a joint stock company and it became the Lyric T. of Göteborg. In 1965 it was taken over by the government. Chief conductors have included Tullio Voghera, Gunnat Stern, and Sixten

Ehrling. It was at Göteborg that Flagstad sang her first Agathe in 1928, and *Les Vêpres Siciliennes* had its first and only Swedish production. In September 1971 performances were given in the new Scandinavium Arena, which was inaugurated with *Aida* with Nilsson; in three days more than 30,000 people heard the opera. The present administrator is Lars Johan Werle.

Gotovac, Jakov (*b* Split, 11 Oct. 1895). Yugoslav conductor and composer. Studied Split, then Vienna with Marx. His best-known opera is *Ero s onoga svijeta* (Ero from the Other World; usually known in English as *Ero the Joker, 1935). This is a consciously folk-influenced, eclectic piece transferring tried Italian methods to a local setting with some success. His other operas are *Morana* (1930), *Kamenik* (1946), *Mila Gojsalića* (1952), *Stanac* (1959), *Dalmaro* (1958), a Singspiel, *Derdan* (1955), and the opera-oratorio *Petar Svačić* (1969). Cond. Zagreb opera, 1923–57.

Götterdämmerung. See *Ring des Nibelungen.*

Göttingen. Town in Lower Saxony, Germany. The City T. (cap. 740) opened in 1890. In 1920 the Handel Renaissance began there with a performance of *Rodelinda* under the direction of Oskar Hagen, who was the moving figure in establishing the Handel Festival there, and who was responsible for the new version of this and other Handel works. Operas performed there 1921–39 were *Ottone, Theophano, Giulio Cesare, Serse, Ezio, Radamisto, Apollo e Daphne, Acis and Galatea, Partenope, Scipio,* and *Tolomeo.* The festivals were resumed in 1946 with the first performance in Germany of *Arianna.* Since 1967 the operas have included *Teseo, Il Pastor Fido, Ariodante, Flavio, Riccardo Primo,* and *Semele.* In 1949 Purcell's *Fairy Queen* was produced.

Götz, Hermann (Gustav) (*b* Königsberg, 7 Dec. 1840; *d* Hottingen, 3 Dec. 1876). German composer. Studied Königsberg, then Berlin (Stern Conservatory), with Stern and Bülow. His *Der widerspenstigen Zähmung* (1874, after *The Taming of the Shrew)* became a European success, and was much admired by Shaw on its London production. The music is tender, elegant, and well constructed, especially in the finales, with which Götz hoped to create a modern equivalent of his beloved Mozart. His characterization is deft, his humour neat; his Romanticism lies in details of treatment rather than in a more fundamental attitude. Nevertheless, the work is one of the best German comedies of the 19th cent. *Francesca da Rimini,* completed by Ernst Frank and prod. 1877, was unsuccessful.
Bibl: E. Kreuzhage: *Hermann Götz* (1916).

Gounod, Charles (*b* Paris, 17 June 1818; *d* Saint-Cloud, 18 Oct. 1893). French composer.

He declared that 'the composer who would achieve a successful career must create it through writing operas'. His first, *Sapho* (1851), indicates his gifts in this direction; Adam suggested Gluck as the main influence. *La Nonne sanglante* (1854) attempted the melodramatic, but Gounod recovered himself in the witty *Le Médecin malgré lui* (1858) and in *Philémon et Baucis* (1860); both have charm and certainty of touch. Meanwhile he had been at work on *Faust* (1859), his masterpiece. With it Gounod became the foremost French composer of his day, though it held the seeds of his decline: the grand manner so enraptured him that he never really escaped back to the style of which he was potentially a great master. The finest moments of *Faust* are not those of high drama, but the humbler delights in which the score abounds. *La Colombe* (1860) was a 2-act piece, prod. at Baden-Baden; Gounod's conquest of the Opéra was unhappily not clinched with *La Reine de Saba* (1862) or *Roméo et Juliette* (1867), which suffer from adherence to the musical conventions of the day, though it is in *Roméo* that some of his most beautiful and dramtically apt music is to be found. *Mireille* (1864) has a much simpler charm. Religious music claimed him almost completely until 1876, when he returned without conspicuous success to opera. *Cinq-Mars* (1877), *Polyeucte* (1878), and *Le Tribut de Zamora* (1881) represent a more sanctimonious, grandiose side of his nature that stifled what were undoubtedly original and appealing expressive gifts. *Mireille* and *Roméo* remain in the French repertory; the once ubiquitous *Faust* seems to have lost some of its former popularity.
Bibl: J.-G. Prod'homme and A. Dandelot: *Gounod* (2 vols., 1911).

Goyescas. Opera in 3 scenes by Granados, amplified and scored from piano pieces after Goya's paintings; text added by Fernando Periquet. Prod. N.Y., Met., 28 Jan. 1916—first Spanish opera in N.Y., with Fitziu, Perini, Martinelli, De Luca, cond. Bavagnoli; London, R.C.M., 11 July 1951. The song 'The Lover and the Nightingale' occurs in scene 2.

When he hears that Rosario (sop.) has been invited to a ball by his rival, the toreador Paquiro (bass.), Fernando (ten.) decides to go too. He is fatally wounded by Paquiro in a duel, and dies in Rosario's arms.

Gozzi, Carlo (*b* Venice, 13 Dec. 1720; *d* Venice, 14 Apr. 1806). Italian playwright, whose comic *fiabe drammatiche,* many of them written in opposition to Goldoni, were a popular source for operas, especially in Germany since the beginning of the Romantic movement; some were translated by Schiller. Operas on his works include the following:
L'amore delle tre melarance (1761): Prokofiev (1919).

Il corvo (1761): A. J. Romberg (1794); J. P. E. Hartmann (1832).

Il Re cervo (1762): Henze (1956).

La donna serpente (1762): Himmel (*Die Sylphen,* 1806); Wagner (*Die Feen,* 1888); Casella (1931).

Turandot (1762): Blumenroeder (1810); Reissiger (1835); Hoven (1839); Lövenskiold (1854); Bazzini (1867); Busoni (1917); Puccini (1924, unfin.); Zabel (1928).

I pitocchi fortunati (1764); Benda (*Das tartarische Gesetz,* 1780); Zumsteeg (do., 1780). Also Calandro (*I tre matrimoni,* 1756, text attrib. Gozzi).

Graf, Herbert (*b* Vienna 10 Apr. 1904; *d* Geneva, 5 Apr. 1973). Austrian, later American, producer. Son of famous Viennese critic Max Graf. Studied Vienna and held appointments in Münster, Breslau, and Frankfurt. Left Germany during Hitler régime and went to America, where he staged opera in Philadelphia, and was at the N.Y. Met. 1936-60. Director Zurich Opera 1960-3; Geneva, Grand T., 1965-73. Produced regularly at Salzburg, Milan, Sc., Verona, Holland Festival. Responsible for Handel's *Samson, Boris,* and *Parsifal* at C.G., 1958-9. A traditional producer in the best sense; remembered for his discovery and encouragement of young talent. Wrote *Opera for the People* (1951) and *Producing Opera for America* (1961).

Graham, Colin (*b* London, 22 Sept. 1931). British producer and administrator. Studied London, R.A.D.A. Began producing opera in 1954. E.O.G., 1958, director of productions 1963-75. Staged first performance of Britten's *Noyes Fludde, Curlew River, The Burning Fiery Furnace, The Prodigal Son, Owen Wingrave,* and *Death in Venice.* London, New Opera Company, and Handel Opera since 1958. S.W., since 1961. Produced first stage perfs. in England of *Cunning Little Vixen, From the House of the Dead, War and Peace,* and premières of *Mines of Sulphur,* and *Penny for a Song,* for which he also wrote the libretto. C.G., *Orfeo* (1961), *Hoffmann* (1962) *Owen Wingrave* (1973), *Death in Venice* (1973). One of the most gifted and musical of British producers, especially successful in the handling of the chorus in large crowd scenes, as in *War and Peace* and *Forza del destino,* and in his perceptive character realization. Notable for his close collaboration with Britten on the three Church Parables in formulating their dramatic convention. Director, English Music Theatre Company from 1975-8; appointed director of productions, E.N.O., 1978.

Gramophone. Opera and opera singers have played an important part in the history of the gramophone; indeed, it has been said with some truth that 'Caruso made the gramophone

and the gramophone Caruso'. In the mid-1890s Gianni Bettini began to record the voices of singers in New York on cylinders, and he offered for sale items by Ancona, Saléza, Plançon, Van Dyck, and Van Rooy; it is also known that he possessed cylinders made by Arnoldson, Calvé, Melba, Nordica, Sembrich, Nicolini, Campanini, Tamagno, the De Reszkes, Lassalle, and Maurel. Meanwhile Emil Berliner had perfected his machine, which played a disc. In Europe, the Gramophone Company was established in 1898, and by 1902 its artists included Caruso, Shalyapin, Calvé, and Battistini. Various other companies quickly established themselves, and virtually every singer of note began to record. The first 'complete' opera recording (with many cuts) was *Il trovatore,* made sporadically between 1903 and 1906 and sung by sixteen different singers. There was also a virtually complete *Pagliacci* conducted by the composer. In Germany there was a *Fledermaus* in 1907, *Faust* (Destinn, Jörn, Knüpfer) in 1908, *Carmen* (Destinn, Jörn), *Cavalleria* (Hempel), and *Pagliacci.* In France nine complete operas were recorded by the Pathé Company before 1914, including *Roméo et Juliette* (Gall, Affre, Journet), *Faust,* and *Carmen.*

Electrical recording replaced the acoustic techniques in the 1920s. Sizeable extracts from *Parsifal, The Ring,* and *Tristan* were recorded at Bayreuth in 1927, and excerpts from a live performance in Berlin of *Meistersinger* (Schorr, List, Schützendorf, Hutt, Blech) in 1928. In the same year complete recordings of operas by the company of La Scala, Milan, began in Europe with *Rigoletto*; the popular Verdi-Puccini repertory was nearly all recorded twice, once by H.M.V. and once by Columbia; in Paris, performances of *Carmen, Pelléas, Faust,* and *Manon* were quickly recorded. In the 1930s and even during the war years the Italian studios were able to record Gigli in complete performances of *Pagliacci, Cavalleria, Tosca, Bohème, Madama Butterfly, Andrea Chénier, Ballo in maschera,* and *Aida*; and during the occupation of France there were complete recordings made of *Pelléas* and *La Damnation de Faust.* In America in 1947 Columbia signed a contract with the Met., and its first complete opera was *Hänsel und Gretel.*

The advent of long-playing recording opened up a whole new horizon, and since 1950 the operatic gramophone repertory has been widened to include complete recordings of many works that even ten years ago were only names in reference books. Not only have the popular works been recorded and re-recorded, but the old favourites of the last century by Rossini, Bellini, Donizetti, and unfamiliar Verdi works have all appeared; the Slavonic repertory (Czech and Russian) and many important modern works can now be heard in one's own home. If no composers have yet written specially for the gramophone, as they have for radio and television, contemporary operas by Britten, Menotti, Stravinsky, and others are also available. The coming of stereophonic sound meant another bout of re-recording the standard repertory, as well as first recordings of *Der Ring des Nibelungen* and Britten's operas by the Decca team under John Culshaw, which evolved new and brilliantly successful 'production' techniques to create a realistic, non-theatrical image of the opera in the mind's eye and ear. Philips Records have recorded several operas during the post-war Bayreuth Festivals and the Berlioz and Mozart operatic repertory under Colin Davis with the Covent Garden orchestra and chorus. Similarly, Deutsche Grammophon has recorded most operas produced and conducted by Karajan at the Salzburg Easter Festival and some Verdi operas at Milan, Sc., under Abbado.

Along with all the benefits and pleasures of the gramophone there remains the danger that recorded opera may become so artificial, so contrived, that the theatrical impulse vanishes from the finished product; one must also recognize that gramophone records of great singers make for a celebrity-minded operatic public which has little time for performances by an ensemble without 'stars', and which expects its stars to shine as brightly in the opera house as they do on records.

Granados (y Campina), **Enrique** (*b* Lérida, 27 July 1867; *d* English Channel, 24 Mar. 1916). Spanish composer. *María del Carmen* (1898) was an immediate success on its Madrid production; this was followed by five works to texts by Apeles Mestre – *Petrarca* (unprod.), *Picarol* (1901), *Follet* (1903), *Gaziel* (1906), and *Liliana* (1911) – before he revised some of his piano pieces based on Goya to make his masterpiece, *Goyescas* (1916). Though influenced by late 19th-cent. Central European Romantic traditions, Granados's music is Spanish not merely in its contours but in its essential techniques. His son **Edoardo** (*b* Barcelona, 28 July 1894; *d* Madrid, 2 Oct. 1928) composed 13 *zarzuelas*; the best known were *Bufón y hostelero* and *La Ciudad eterna*.
Bibl: J. Subirá: *Enrique Granados* (1926).

Grand opera. In common English usage, serious opera without spoken dialogue. In French, more precisely, *grand opéra* as opposed to *opéra comique* means a serious epic or historical work, in four or five acts, which uses the chorus actively and includes a ballet. It was the characteristic operatic form of the Paris Opéra, especially in the first four decades of the 19th cent., in the wake of the Revolution and with the emergence of a wealthy middle class devoted to spectacle.

Great importance was therefore attached to magnificence of effect, both on the stage with the reforms of *Cicéri, and among singers with the disappearance of the castrati and the emergence of a new type of heroic dramatic singer. The composer who first answered these demands and set new standards was Spontini, with *La Vestale* (1807), *Fernand Cortez* (1809), and *Olimpie* (1819); and among the most important grand operas of the years that followed at the Opéra were Auber's *La Muette de Portici* (1828), Rossini's *Guillaume Tell* (1829), Meyerbeer's *Robert le Diable* (1831) and *Les Huguenots* (1836), and Halévy's *La Juive* (1835). The style left its mark upon Wagner's early operas, especially *Rienzi* and *Tannhäuser* (rewritten for Paris), and long survived as an influence on the music demanded by the Paris Opéra.

Grandi, Margherita (orig. Marguerite Garde) (*b* Hobart, 10 Dec. 1895). Tasmanian soprano. Studied London, R.C.M., Paris with Calvé, and later Milan with Russ. Début, Paris, O.C., in *Werther* under name of Djema Vécla (anagram of Calvé); used this name until she married the Italian scene–designer Giovanni Grandi. Created title-role in Massenet's *Amadis*, Monte Carlo, 1922. Went to Italy, second début 1932, Milan, T. Carcano, Aida. Sang Maria in first Italian performance of Strauss's *Friedenstag* (1940). Gly., 1939, Lady Macbeth; London, Cambridge T., 1947, Tosca and Donna Anna; C.G., 1949-50, created Diana in Bliss's *Olympians*, also sang Leonora (*Trovatore*) and Tosca. One of the few singers of her day who possessed the 'grand style'; her Tosca and Lady Macbeth were sung and acted with a sweep and conviction rare on the opera stage. (R)

Grane. Brünnhilde's horse in the *Ring*. Seldom seen on the stage since the war, but formerly ridden with effect into the flames by singers including Leider and Lawrence.

Grassi, Cecilia (*b* Naples, *c*1740; *d* ?). Italian soprano. Début Venice 1760. Created Larissa in Gluck's *Trionfo di Clelia* (1763); London, Hm., 1761-7, 1770-1, where she was first London Eurydice. Married J. C. Bach in London 1774 and left the stage. According to Burney, she had a voice of rare sweetness and expression, but few artistic gifts.

Grassini, Josephina (orig. Giuseppina) (Maria Camilla) (*b* Varese, 8 (?18) Apr. 1773; *d* Milan, 3 Jan. 1850.) Italian contralto. Studied Varese with Zucchinetti. Heard by General Alberico Belgioioso, who took her to Milan to study with Secchi and the castrato Crescentini. Début Parma, 1789, in Guglielmi's *Pastorella nobile* and immediately afterwards in Cimarosa's *La ballerina amante*; Milan, Sc., 1790-1800 in operas by Guglielmi, Paisiello, Salieri, Zingarelli, Portogallo, etc. In 1800, after Marengo, a gala performance was given at La Scala for Napoleon's return to Milan; he was struck by her 'beauté théâtrale et par les sublimes accents de sa voix' and took her to Paris. In London, 1804, she became Billington's rival. Not everyone admired her voice: according to Mount–Edgcumbe, 'No doubt the deaf would have been charmed by Grassini, and the blind must have been delighted with Mrs Billington'. Sang in English première of Cimarosa's *Gli Orazi e Curiazi*.

Returned to Paris in 1806, where she became Napoleon's favourite, and received an income of 36,000 francs plus a payment of 15,000 francs. Especially successful in Nasolini's *Morte di Cleopatra*, Paër's *Didone abbandonata*, and particularly Cherubini's *Pimmalione*. After Napoleon's fall in 1815 she had to leave Paris, and returned to Milan in 1817, where she had little success. Continued to sing in public until 1829, and then turned to teaching; her pupils included Pasta and Giuditta and Giulia Grisi.

Bibl: A. Gavoty: *La Grassini* (1947).

Grau, Maurice (*b* Brno, 1849; *d* Paris, 14 Mar. 1907). Czech impresario. Went to America when a child. Began management in 1872, organizing tours of Bernhardt, Offenbach, and the Kellogg Opera Company. Joined Abbey 1890 to give season at N.Y., Met., and from 1891 to 1897 directed Met., with Abbey and John B. Schoeffel; became sole manager of theatre 1897-1903. On death of Augustus Harris appointed managing director of C.G., London, a position he held until the end of the 1900 season.

Graun, Carl Heinrich (*b* Wahrenbrück, 1703 or 1704; *d* Berlin, 8 Aug. 1759). German composer and tenor. Studied Dresden; début Brunswick, where he produced several of his own Italian works and met the Crown Prince of Prussia, later Frederick the Great, who invited him to become Court Kapellmeister in Berlin in 1740. Here he produced the bulk of his work. After Hasse, he was the most important representative of Italian opera in Germany, upholding a strict form – with arias in which singers' coloratura was encouraged – that did a certain amount to weaken Gluck's reforms. However, he himself moved in the direction of reform with *Silla* (1753); text by Frederick the Great), *Semiramide* (1754), and *Montezuma* (1755; text by Frederick the Great).

Graupner, (Johann) **Christoph** (*b* Kirchberg, 13 Jan. 1683; *d* Darmstadt, 10 May 1760). German composer. Studied Leipzig, with Schelle and Kuhnau. Accompanist at Hamburg under Keiser, 1707; Kapellmeister Darmstadt, 1712; later renounced the stage. He wrote 5 operas

for Hamburg, beginning with *Dido* (1707), which follow Keiser's style.

Gravenhage, 's. See *The Hague.*

Graz. Town in Styria, Austria. The first opera house was a modest affair built during the seasons of the Mingotti company, 1736-46. A taste for Italian opera grew, and the Nationaltheater was opened in 1776 with Sacchini's *La contadina in corte*. From 1791 more German opera was given, and in the new century still more German Singspiels and some works by Grétry. Under the director Franz Hysel, Mozart's operas were regularly given. The first Graz *Fidelio* was given in 1816, the first *Freischütz* in 1822. A fire destroyed the theatre in 1823, and the New Landestheater opened in 1825; the company included Nestroy as singer and actor. Later singers included Tichatschek. When the censorship was abolished in 1848, many new plays were introduced as well as operas by Rossini, Bellini, Donizetti, and increasingly Verdi. In 1854, three years before Vienna, Graz heard *Tannhäuser*. The first complete Graz *Meistersinger* was given under Karl Muck 1885. Muck also conducted *Lohengrin* 1899 to open the new Opernhaus (cap. 1400). In 1906 the first Austrian *Salome* was given. The present Intendant is Carl Nemeth. Singers who worked in Graz early in their career include Welitsch, Manowarda, Schorr, and Töpper; also the conductors Franz Schalk and Karl Rankl.

Graziani, Francesco (*b* Fermo, 26 Apr. 1828; *d* Fermo, 30 June 1901). Italian baritone. Studied with Cellini. Début Ascoli Piceno 1851 in *Gemma di Vergy.* London, C.G., 1855-80 (début as Carlos in *Ernani*). The first London Luna, Nelusko, Posa, and Amonasro. Paris 1853-61. Created Don Carlo (*Forza del destino*), St Petersburg 1862. U.S.A. 1854. He possessed one of the most beautiful and mellow voices of the last century, but apparently little artistry, for he was constantly criticized for his unmusical and poor phrasing and his unpurposeful acting. A friend of Mazzini, he worked strenuously in the cause of Italian independence.

Graziani, Lodovico (*b* Fermo, 14 Nov. 1820; *d* Fermo, 15 May 1885). Italian tenor. Brother of above. Studied with Cellini. Début Bologna 1845 in Cambiaggio's *Don Procopio.* Created Alfredo in *La traviata* (Venice 1853); Milan, especially successful in Verdi repertory. A third brother, **Vincenzo** (*b* Fermo, 16 Feb. 1836; *d* Fermo, 2 Nov. 1906), was a baritone. Début 1861, Belcore; had to abandon career because of deafness.

Great Britain. For most of the 17th cent. the popular form of dramatic musical entertainment in England was the masque, which was much influenced by the French *ballet de cour* and little by Italian opera. However, in 1656 the first work that can be called an opera, *The Siege of Rhodes*, was given at Rutland House with music (now lost) by various composers including Locke. This work was notable for the first appearance of a woman upon the stage in England. In 1674 several attempts at opera followed: these included *Ariane* by Cambert and Grabu and *Psyche* by Locke; but the next real opera was *Blow's *Venus and Adonis* (*c*1680).

This served as the model for English opera's first (and for many years only) masterpiece, *Purcell's *Dido and Aeneas* (*c*1689). Purcell's collaboration with Dryden, e.g. on *The Tempest*, produced some superb stage music, but the conventions of the time were against the flowering of the genre into a true operatic tradition: *King Arthur* (1691) stands on the brink of authentic English opera. With Purcell's death in 1695, the way was open for Italian fashions to conquer England: the first complete Italian opera to be sung in English was Bononcini's *Camilla* (1706), the first in Italian the anonymous *Almahide* (1710). In 1710 *Handel arrived in England, and for 30 Years from 1711 he produced a series of Italian operas for London.

The first effective counter to the Italian domination of operatic life was *The Beggar's Opera* (1728); its immense popularity triggered off a whole series of *ballad operas which in turn played an important part in the ancestry and growth of German *Singspiel. In 1762 *Arne made a new attempt at English opera with *Artaxerxes*. It was not taken up, and for years to come English opera was synonymous with *pasticcio. One of the most successful composers of the day was *Bishop, who wrote dramatic works in every vein, adapting many popular European works and adding numbers of his own in varying degrees. The plot, the dialogue, the scenery (including the stage machinery and transformations between scenes) were all accorded priority over the music.

These conditions dismayed Weber when he accepted the commission for *Oberon* (1826), but the work's success greatly helped to pave the way for English Romantic opera. The first significant work in the genre was John *Barnett's *The Mountain Sylph* (1834). This was followed by Michael *Balfe's *The Siege of Rochelle* (1835): of his thirty operas, by far the most successful was *The Bohemian Girl* (1843). A classic of the period was William *Wallace's *Maritana* (1845). Another important figure was Edward *Loder, whose *Raymond and Agnes* (1855) shows greater ability than its predecessors to build up continuous forms. However, most of these works, for all their qualities, show English opera still very much under foreign influence, especially now German and

French. The *Carl Rosa Opera Company loyally staged works by English composers, including *Cowen, *Mackenzie, and *Stanford: the latter's *Shamus O'Brien* (1896) won a following. But the most popular figure of the latter years of the century was *Sullivan, who drew upon the whole of recent operatic history to fertilize his clever, Romantic idiom in the famous series of Savoy Operas. A serious attempt to transfer the tried methods of German opera to the English stage was made by Ethel *Smyth with *The Wreckers* (1909); this was championed by Beecham, who also devoted an important part of his life's work to propagating the music of *Delius, including his operas.

Meanwhile, a new attempt was being made to discover a more authentic English idiom by way of folk song. The collection of folk songs was inaugurated by Cecil Sharp and also undertaken by *Holst and *Vaughan Williams. Holst began his operatic career in Germanic vein, but discovered a new originality, partly through his invention of a more authentic English musical declamation, with *Savitri* (1908, prod. 1916). Vaughan Williams wrote an English counterpart to Smetana's *The Bartered Bride* in *Hugh the Drover* (comp. 1911-14, prod. 1924). Attempts at English Wagnerian opera were made by Rutland *Boughton and Josef *Holbrooke, but Vaughan Williams discovered a more authentic national manner; and if his operas, and Holst's, reflect the belated state of English opera's growth in European terms, they served to open up new vistas. Attempts at opera were made during the 1920s and 1930s; but it was with *Britten's *Peter Grimes* (1945) that England at last found operatic maturity. The success of this work, coupled with the new audience that had developed for opera, encouraged Britten and a whole generation of composers, many of whom had been reluctant to write opera in economic conditions discouraging for its presentation. Since the Second World War, every British composer of importance has attempted opera, and a vigorous operatic life, based on new works as well as the standard repertory, has developed with the growth of national companies in Scotland and Wales. Belatedly, England has become a major operatic nation.

Se also *Abingdon, Aldeburgh Festival, Arts Council, Beecham Opera Company, Birmingham, British Broadcasting Corporation, British National Opera Company, Cambridge, Carl Rosa Opera Company, Chelsea Opera Group, Covent Garden, Denhof Opera Company, Edinburgh, Edinburgh Festival, English National Opera, English Opera Group, Glasgow, Glyndebourne Touring Company, Handel Opera Society, Intimate Opera Company, Liverpool, London, Manchester, Opera for All, Oxford, Scottish Opera, Welsh National Opera Company.*

Greece. The Ionian Islands, subject to Venice 1386-1797 and to Britain 1815-64, acquired their first knowledge of opera when visiting Italian companies gave seasons at the T. San Giacomo in Corfu during the 18th cent. Seasons were also given in the other islands, and local composers went to study in Italy. The first was the Corfiote, Spiridon *Xyndas (1814-96), composer of various operas in Italian and of the first opera in Greek, *O Ypopsyphios Vouleftis* (The Parliamentary Candidate, comp. 1857, prod. Corfu 1867); his popularity was enormous. His successors include the Zakynthian, Pavlos Karrer (1829-96), composer of two operas on Greek plots, *Markos Botsaris* (1857) and *Kyra Phrosyni* (1869); Spiros Samaras (1863-1917), whose most successful opera was *Rhea* (1908); and Eduardos Lambelet (1820-1903).

The mainland, occupied by the Turks from the 14th cent. until 1821, had no experience of opera until the visits of Italian companies in 1840. These proved immensely popular, and seasons were given in Athens, Piraeus, and Patras. Greek national opera began to evolve through the introduction into Italian forms of Greek folk songs and folk subjects and Byzantine chant. A successful pioneering work was *O Protomastoras* (The Master Builder, libretto by Nikos Kazantzakis, 1916) by Manolis *Kalomiris (1883-1962), whose later operas include *To Daktilidi tis Manas* (The Mother's Ring, 1919), *Xotika Nera* (The Shadowy Waters, to W. B. Yeats's drama, 1950), and *Constantine Palaeologus* (1962). Other significant Greek composers have included Dionysios *Lavrangas (1864-1941; *Dido*, 1909); Marios Varvoglis (*b* 1895; *To Apoghevma tis Agapis* (The Afternoon of Love), 1944); Gheorghios Sklavos (*b* 1888; *Lestenitsa*, comp. 1923, prod. 1947; *Amphitryon,* comp. 1942, prod. 1955); Petros Petridis (*b* 1892; *Zemphira*, 1957); Menelaos Pallandios (*b* 1914; *Antigone*, 1942); and Solon Michailidis (*b* 1905; *Odysseus*, 1955). See also *Athens, Corfu.*

Gregor, Joseph (*b* Czernowitz, 26 Oct. 1888; *d* Vienna, 12 Oct. 1960). Austrian librettist and writer. He wrote the librettos for Strauss's *Friedenstag, Daphne,* and *Die Liebe der Danae.* For many years he was stage archivist of the Austrian National Library. Among his writings, especially on the Viennese theatre, are *Kulturgeschichte der Oper* (1941, 3/1950), also *Richard Strauss* (1939, 3/1952).
Bibl: R. Strauss and J. Gregor (ed. R. Tenschert): *Briefwechsel* (1955).

Greindl, Josef (*b* Munich, 23 Dec. 1912). German bass. Studied Munich with Bender and Bahr-Mildenburg. Début Munich in a semi-professional performance of *Freischütz*, 1935, then Krefeld as Hunding, 1936. Berlin since 1942, first S.O., then Sta. O. Bayreuth 1943, and leading bass there 1951-70. Moses in the first German stage performance of *Moses und Aron* (1959). Has also appeared in England, Italy, and North and S. America. Professor of singing at Saarbrücken since 1961. (R)

Gresse, André (*b* Lyons, 23 Mar. 1868; *d* Paris, 1937). French bass. Son of the bass Léon Gresse, the first Paris Lodovico, Pogner, and Hunding. Studied with Taskin, Melchissedec, and Duvernoy. Début Paris, O.C., 1896, Commendatore; Paris O., from 1901. First Fasolt, Titurel, King Mark, at the Opéra. Created Sancho Panza (Massenet's *Don Quichotte*). (R)

Gretel. Hänsel's sister (sop.) in Humperdinck's opera.

Grétry, André (Ernest Modeste) (*b* Liège, 11 Feb. 1741; *d* Montmorency, 24 Sept. 1813). French composer, of Walloon descent. While studying in Rome, he had a success with his intermezzo *La Vendemmiatrice* (1765), but his aim was Paris and *opéra comique.* Encouraged by Voltaire, whom he had met in Geneva, he arrived in Paris in 1767; and here his works (especially *Le Tableau parlant,* 1769) quickly found favour. Some 50 operas followed in 35 years; as well as comedies and fairy stories – of which *Zémire et Azor* (1771) is the best known – he attempted serious opera. His most ambitious work is *Richard Coeur de Lion* (1784), which anticipates *rescue opera and looks even further ahead in the direction of Leitmotiv with its nine-fold varied repetition of Blondel's song.

The neatness with which Grétry as a theorist labelled the constituents of music was at once his strength and weakness as a composer. That the theorist saw the composer's shortcomings is revealed in several comments: he knew himself to be a good melodist but to lack harmonic or contrapuntal art. He tried to relegate harmony to the position of 'the base of the statue'. His works are graceful, untroublesome, always effective, and in certain instances unexpectedly imaginative in handling; but in most of his *opéras comiques* the harmonic poverty and the enervating tidiness of the conception tend to dominate.
Bibl: E. Closson: *Grétry* (1920).

Grieg, Edvard (Hagerup) (*b* Bergen, 15 June 1843; *d* Bergen, 4 Sept. 1907). Norwegian composer. Only 3 scenes of his sole attempt at opera, *Olav Trygvason* (1873), were completed; they survive as a cantata.

Grimaldi. See *Nicolini.*

Grisar, Albert (*b* Antwerp, 26 Dec. 1808; *d* Asnières, 15 June 1869). French composer. Studied Paris, with Rejcha. His first opera, *Le Mariage impossible* (1833), won him a subvention for further study in Paris. He produced a number of works in Paris, some in collaboration with Flotow (*Lady Melvil,* 1838, and *L'Eau merveilleuse,* 1839) and with Boieldieu (*L'Opéra à la cour,* 1840). After further study in Naples with Mercadante, he returned to Paris, where he produced 11 more operas. These are lively and with a quick ear for comedy, anticipating some of the features of Hervé, Lecocq, and even Offenbach.

Grisélidis. Opera in a prologue and 2 acts by Massenet; text by Silvestre and Morand. Prod. Paris, O.C., 20 Nov. 1901, with Bréval, Tiphaine, Maréchal, Fugère, Dufranne, cond. Messager; N.Y., Manhattan Opera, 19 Jan. 1910, with Garden, Dalmorès, Dufranne, Huberdeau, cond. De la Fuente.

Alain loves Grisélidis, wife of the Marquis. The Devil tries to persuade her of her husband's infidelity and to accept Alain. She resists, and he takes her child, which is eventually retrieved by the Marquis. Also opera by Franckenstein (1898).

Grisi, Giuditta (*b* Milan, 28 July 1805; *d* Robecco, 1 May 1840). Italian mezzo-soprano. Niece of Grassini and cousin of Carlotta Grisi, the dancer. Studied Milan; début Vienna 1825, Faliero in Rossini's *Bianca e Faliero.* Bellini wrote Romeo for her in *I Capuleti e i Montecchi* (1830). Appeared in London and Paris but was overshadowed by her sister Giulia. Taught the *Grassini sisters.

Grisi, Giulia (*b* Milan, 22 May 1811; *d* Berlin, 29 Nov. 1869). Italian soprano. Sister of above, who was her first teacher; also studied Milan with Filippo Gugliena. Début as mezzo-soprano 1828, Milan, in Rossini's *Zelmira.* Created Adalgisa in *Norma,* Sc. Dissatisfied with conditions in Milan and unable to obtain a release from Sc., she fled Italy and went to Paris, where her aunt Grassini, her sister, and Rossini were at the T. I.; here she obtained an engagement. Sang regularly in Paris 1832-48 and 1856-8, where she created Elvira in *Puritani* and Norina in *Don Pasquale,* the former with Rubini, the latter with Mario, whom she married. London début 1834. Except in 1842, sang in London every season until 1861, first at King's T. (later Her Majesty's Opera), then C.G. An attempted reappearance in 1866 at H.M.'s as Lucrezia Borgia was disastrous. Appeared in America 1854-5. Her voice was rich, beautiful, and flexible, and suitable for lyric and dramatic roles.

Grist, Reri (*b* New York, 1932). American soprano. Studied New York, Queen's College. Début Cindy Lou (Micaela) in *Carmen Jones* 1957. Opera début, Santa Fe, 1959, Blonde. Engaged by Graf for Zurich 1961-4. Gly., 1962, Zerbinetta; London, C.G., 1962 Queen of Shemakha, 1964 Olympia, 1967 Gilda, 1971 Susanna, 1975 Oscar; N.Y., Met., since 1966; Salzburg since 1964. Repertory also includes

Adina, Adele, Sophie, Aminta. A lively artist with a girlish and sweet voice. (R)

Griswold, Putnam (*b* Minneapolis, 23 Dec. 1875; *d* New York, 26 Feb. 1914). American bass-baritone. Studied London, R.C.M., and with Randegger. Début London, C.G., 1901 as Renato in première of Stanford's *Much Ado about Nothing;* then followed further study with Bouhy in Paris and Emmerich in Berlin. After appearances in Germany he toured America with Savage Company as Gurnemanz. N.Y., Met., 1911-14. A famous Daland, Pogner, and King Mark.

Grob-Prandl, Gertrud (*b* Vienna, 11 Nov. 1917). Austrian soprano. Studied Vienna with Burrian. Début Vienna, V.O., 1938, Santuzza; Zurich 1946-7. Vienna, S.O., 1947-64. London, C.G., 1951, Turandot. Appearances at all leading theatres in Europe and S. America. Noted for her Brünnhilde, Isolde, and Ortrud. (R)

Grossi, Giovanni. See *Siface.*

Grossmächtige Prinzessin. Zerbinetta's (sop.) recitative and aria in Strauss's *Ariadne auf Naxos,* in which she tries to convert Ariadne to her fickle view of love. One of the most difficult coloratura arias in opera.

Groves, (Sir) Charles (Bernard) (*b* London, 10 Mar. 1915). English conductor. Studied R.C.M. Chorus Master B.B.C. Opera Unit 1937-9; conductor B.B.C. Northern Orchestra 1945-51, during which time he conducted several studio perfs. of opera including Holst's *The Perfect Fool,* Dohnányi's *The Tenor,* and *Hänsel und Gretel.* Musical director W.N.O. 1961-3 where he conducted first perf. in Great Britain of *La battaglia di Legnano* and productions of *I Lombardi* and *Vespri siciliani.* S.W./E.N.O. as guest from 1971, music director since 1978: conducted world première of Crosse's *Story of Vasco* (1974), then *Euryanthe* (1977), and *Due Foscari* (1978). (R)

Grozăvescu, Trajan (*b* Cluj, 1894; *d* Vienna, 15 Feb. 1927). Romanian tenor. Studied Bucharest and Milan. Début Bucharest; Vienna, V., 1924, S., 1925-7, first Chénier at S.O.; guest appearances Berlin, S. Especially successful in Verdi repertory. Promising career ended tragically when his jealous wife shot him in Vienna, before a scheduled guest appearance in Berlin. (R)

Bibl: M. Demeter-Grozăvescu and I. Voledi: *Trajan Grozăvescu* (1965).

Gruhn, Nora. See *Grünebaum.*

Grümmer, Elisabeth (*b* Niederjeutz, 31 Mar. 1911). German soprano. After three years as an actress at Aachen was urged by Karajan to become a professional singer; début Aachen, 1940 as First Flower Maiden in *Parsifal.* After an engagement in Duisburg and guest appearances elsewhere, engaged as leading lyric soprano, Berlin, Stä. O., 1946; London, C.G., 1951, Eva; Bayreuth, 1957-61, Eva, Elsa, Freia, Gutrune; N.Y., City O., 1967; Gly., 1956 Countess and Ilia. Guest appearances Vienna, Munich, Hamburg. A distinguished Agathe, Oktavian, Marschallin. Her beautiful voice and aristocratic style particularly suited her to Mozart and Strauss. Teaches voice at Berlin Hochschule. (R)

Grünbaum (orig. Müller), **Therese** (*b* Vienna, 24 Aug. 1791; *d* Berlin, 30 Jan. 1876). Austrian soprano. Daughter of Wenzel *Müller. Studied with her father and appeared as a child in various works. Moved to Prague in 1807, where she sang in the first German *Don Giovanni* (Zerlina: later a famous Donna Anna). In 1816 she went to the Kä, in Vienna, where for ten years she was the leading soprano, singing Rossini's Desdemona among many other roles, and creating Eglantine (*Euryanthe*). Berlin 1828-30; here she opened a singing school. Her husband **Johann Christoff** (*b* Haslau, 28 Oct. 1785; *d* Berlin, 10 Oct. 1870) was a tenor who made his début in Regensburg in 1804. Prague 1808-18, then Vienna and Berlin. Translated many librettos into German. Their daughter **Caroline** (*b* Prague, 18 Mar. 1814; *d* Brunswick, 26 May 1868) was a soprano who made her début as Emmeline (*Schweizerfamilie*) in 1828. Berlin 1832, where she created Anna (*Hans Heiling*). Retired 1844.

Gründgens, Gustav (*b* Düsseldorf, 22 Dec. 1899; *d* Manila, 7 Oct. 1963). German actor, producer, and administrator. Studied Düsseldorf. Engaged by Klemperer to produce *Figaro* and *Così fan tutte* at Berlin, Kroll Opera, 1931. *Zauberflöte*, Berlin, S.O., under Karajan, 1938. Intendant Düsseldorf, 1947-55. Produced operas at Florence, Salzburg Festivals, and in Germany.

Grunebaum, Hermann (*b* Giessen, 8 Jan. 1872; *d* Chipstead. 5 Apr. 1954). German, later English, conductor and coach. Studied Frankfurt with Humperdinck, and Berlin. Début 1893 Coblenz. Chorus-master London, C.G., 1907-33; assisted Richter in preparing the English *Ring* at C.G., 1908-9. In collaboration with T. C. Fairbairn founded London School of Opera, where he conducted the première of Holst's *Savitri* in 1916. Director of opera class at R.C.M., 1924-46, where his achievements included complete performances of *Parsifal* by students in 1926, in which he shared the conducting with Boult. His daughter **Nora Gruhn** (*b* 6 Mar. 1905) studied Munich; début Kaiserslautern 1928; sang at C.G., 1929-32, and S.W., 1932-6 and 1945-8. Lady Felicia in first English performance of *School for Fathers*: also appeared at Cologne 1930-1. (R)

Gruppetto (*It* little group). Its most common form is the alternation of a main note with two subsidiaries, immediately above and below. Beginning as one of the myriad ornaments of baroque composition, it survived with particularly beautiful effect in Wagner.

Guadagni, Gaetano (*b* Lodi, *c*1725; *d* Padua, Nov. 1792). Italian male contralto, later soprano. Début Parma 1747. Went to London in 1748 as member of a burletta company. Heard by Handel who engaged him to sing in *Samson* and *Messiah*; studied acting with Garrick. Dublin 1751-2; Paris and Versailles, 1754; Lisbon, where he studied with Gizziello. Created title role in Gluck's *Orfeo* (1762) and *Telemaco* (1765). Returned to London 1769: thought by Burney to have no equal on the operatic stage as an actor. Returned to Italy 1774; retired from stage 1776 and settled in Padua, where he continued to sing for several years at the Basilica di San Antonio. In his retirement, produced operas on a domestic puppet stage. His sister **Lavinia Maria** (*b* Lodi, 21 Nov. 1735; *d* Padua, *c*1790) appeared in comic opera 1756-74.

Guarducci, Tommaso (*b* Montefiascone, *c*1720; *d* ?). Italian male soprano. Studied Bologna, with Bernacchi. Naples, S.C., 1758-9, 1762; London, H.M.'s, 1767, creating leading roles in J. C. Bach's *Carattaco* and Vento's *Conquista del Messico*. According to Burney he was 'tall and awkward in figure, inanimate as an actor, and in countenance ill-favoured and morbid; but a man of great probity and worth in his private character, and one of the most correct singers. His voice was clear, sweet, and flexible. His shake and intonations were perfect, and by long study and practice he had vanquished all the difficulties of his art, and possessed himself of every refinement.'

Guarnieri, Antonio (*b* Venice, 1 Feb. 1880; *d* Milan, 25 Nov. 1952). Italian conductor. Played the cello in the Martucci Quartet; turned to conducting at Siena 1904, and rapidly became successful. Engaged on a 7-year contract for Vienna 1912, but quarrelled because of the conditions of work and soon resigned. Milan, Sc., 1922-3, and followed Toscanini there 1929, conducting there regularly until shortly before his death. Conducted the first performances in Italy of Bloch's *Macbeth* and Respighi's *Belfagor*. Highly regarded as a musician and technician by his colleagues and singers. (R) His sons **Arrigo** (*b* Lugo di Romagna, 22 May 1910; *d* Rome, 22 Nov. 1975) and **Ferdinando** (*b* Milan, 19 Nov. 1936) were both conductors.

Guatemala. The first opera given was Dalayrac's *Adolphe et Clara* at the T. Fedriani (1830). Some Italian works were staged at the T. de Oriente in 1845, and a few seasons followed, some of them by amateurs. In 1850 another season was presented including, as well as Italian works, *La Mora generosa* by the Guatemalan José Escolástico Andrino. The success of Rossini's *Barbiere* in various seasons encouraged the government to arrange for regular visits of Italian and French companies. The first experience of *zarzuela* in 1873 in turn led to regular visits by companies from other countries. Guatemalan opera has been slow to develop, but a few composers have written characteristic works based on folk or Maya music, including Jésus Castillo (*Quiché-Vinak*).

Gudehus, Heinrich (*b* Altenhagen, nr Celle, 30 Mar. 1845; *d* Dresden, 9 Oct. 1909). German tenor. Studied Brunswick with Malwina Schnorr von Carolsfeld and Berlin with Gustav Engel. Début Berlin 1871, Nadori in Spohr's *Jessonda*. After engagements in Lübeck, Freiburg, and Bremen, was leading tenor at Dresden 1880-90; Bayreuth 1882-9, where he sang Parsifal (in the work's second performance), Tristan, and Walther. First C.G. Tristan and Walther. First London Parsifal (concert version, R.A.H., 1884). N.Y., Met., 1890-1.

Gueden, Hilde (*b* Vienna, 15 Sept. 1917). Austrian soprano. Studied Vienna with Wetzelsberger. Début 1934 in operetta; opera début Zurich 1939, Cherubino; Munich 1941-2, Despina, Sophie, Zerlina. Vienna, S.O., 1946-73; London, C.G., with Vienna Company 1947; N.Y., Met., 1951-60. A versatile artist equally at home in Mozart and Lehár, Johann and Richard Strauss. Also sang in a number of modern works including *Mahagonny*, *Rape of Lucretia*, Blacher's *Romeo und Julia*, and *The Rake's Progress*. (R)

Guelfi, Giangiacomo (*b* Rome, 21 Dec. 1924). Italian baritone. After studying at Florence for the law, turned to singing. Studied with Ruffo. Début Spoleto, 1950, Rigoletto. Milan, Sc., since 1952, Chicago 1954 and subsequently; N.Y., Met., 1970 Scarpia, Jack Rance; London, C.G., 1957, Scarpia; D.L., 1958, Gérard. Created Lazaro in Pizzetti's *La figlia di Jorio* (Naples, 1954). A powerful, vigorous singer, with an exciting voice. (R)

Guerre des Bouffons (*Fr* war of the comic actors; also *querelle des bouffons*). The controversy that from 1752 to 1754 divided Paris into two parties, those upholding French serious opera (Lully, Rameau, Destouches, etc.) and those upholding the Italian *opera buffa* (Pergolesi, etc.). Though Pergolesi's *La serva padrona* had been given in Paris in 1746 without arousing controversy, the performance in 1752 given by a visiting company of actors (*buffi*) precipitated the quarrel. The opponents were the King, Mme. de Pom-

padour, the Court, and the aristocracy, defending traditional French opera, and intellectuals and connoisseurs defending the Italians: the latter included Rousseau, Diderot, D'Alembert, and the Queen, their argument being that Italian opera had refreshed a moribund tradition with greater expression and above all greater simplicity and naturalness and less reliance on elaborate contrapuntal techniques. Rousseau's contribution was his famous *Lettre sur la musique française* (1753). French musicians who sided with the *buffi* evolved, in answer to the Italians, the *comédie mêlée d'ariettes*. The quarrel was also known as the *guerre des coins* (war of the corners), from the habit of the supporters of the French of gathering by the King's box, while their opponents gathered by the Queen's.

Guéymard, Louis (*b* Chapponay, 17 Aug. 1822; *d* Paris, July 1880). French tenor. Début Lyons, 1845; Paris O., 1848 in *Robert le Diable*. Leading tenor at O., until 1868; created Arrigo (*Vêpres siciliennes*) Jonas (*Prophète*), Assad (*La Reine de Saba*). New Orleans 1873-4. London C.G., 1852. His wife, **Pauline Lauters-Guéymard** (*b* Brussels, 1 Dec. 1834; *d* ?), Belgian soprano, made her début Paris, T.L., 1854; O., 1857-76; created Eboli, Queen (*Hamlet*), Reine de Saba (Gounod).

Guglielmi, Pietro Alessandro (*b* Massa di Carrara, 9 Dec. 1728; *d* Rome, 18 Nov. 1804). Italian composer. Studied with his father, and with others including Durante. He began his career in Naples, probably with *Lo solachianello 'mbroglione* (1757), following this with an opera seria for Rome, *Tito Manlio* (1763). He was in London as composer to the King's T., 1767-72, when he also introduced a version of Gluck's *Orfeo* to London; his own works had difficulty in competing with Piccinni's lighter works. Back in Italy, he found comparable difficulty in regaining his former popularity in the face of competition from Cimarosa and Paisiello. He wrote 103 operas, which Burney credited with 'some Neapolitan fire' marred by haste and lack of self-criticism. His *opere serie* have a certain originality, especially in their development of the use of chorus and orchestra, and their expansion of the finales. He was, none the less, more at home with opera buffa, in which he showed a natural, lively feeling for the absurd, and was able to introduce some ingenious effects, such as contrasting melodies for singers and orchestra which were developed in the finales. He was admired by Rossini. His eldest son, **Pietro Carlo** (*b* ? Naples, *c*1763; *d* Naples, 28 Feb. 1817), was a composer who visited Spain and Portugal, was back in Italy by 1795, and in the following decade wrote many operas for Italian cities in a style described as light and fluent. He went abroad again in 1807, visiting London, and returned by 1810 or 1811. He wrote three operas for La Scala in 1813. His best work was *Paolo e Virginia*, for Naples (1816). A follower of his father, whose inventiveness he lacked. His brother **Giacomo** (*b* Massa, 16 Aug. 1782; *d ?*, 1846), Pietro Alessandro's 8th son, was a tenor who created Don Ramiro in Rossini's *Cenerentola*. His pupils included Grisi and Tamberlik.

Guglielmo. A young officer (bar.), Fiordiligi's lover, in Mozart's *Così fan tutte*.

Guglielmo Ratcliff. Opera in 4 acts by Mascagni; text by Andrea Maffei, a literal translation of Heine's tragedy (1822). Prod. Milan, 16 Feb. 1895, with Stehle, De Negri, Pacini, cond. Mascagni.

William Ratcliff (ten.) is haunted by the visions of a man and a woman; in Maria (sop.), daughter of MacGregor (bass), he finds the realization of the woman, and swears to kill anyone who tries to marry her; Count Douglas (bar.) does so, and William challenges him to a duel, but Douglas spares his life. Maria prepares for her marriage with Douglas and learns from her nurse, Margherita (mezzo), that her mother and William's father had once been in love but were prevented from marrying; she had, instead, married MacGregor, who had then killed William's father. William, himself wounded, bursts into Maria's room, kills her and then dies. When Douglas sees the two bodies he kills himself.

See also *William Ratcliff*.

Gui, Vittorio (*b* Rome, 14 Sept. 1885; *d* Florence, 16 Oct. 1975). Italian conductor and composer. Studied Rome, Santa Cecilia, under Falchi. Début Rome, T. Adriano, 1907, *La Gioconda*. Milan, with Toscanini, 1923-5 and 1932-4; London, C.G., 1938-9 and 1952; Gly. 1952-65. Founded T. di Torino 1925, where cond. first Italian *Ariadne auf Naxos* and *L'Heure espagnole*. Established the Florence Orchestra 1928, from which emerged the Florence Maggio Musicale in 1933. One of the finest Italian conductors of Gluck, Mozart, and Rossini, and responsible for revivals of several neglected operas in Italy, including *Comte Ory*, *Alceste*, and *Così fan tutte*. His own works include *Fata Malerba* (Turin 1927). (R)

Guillaume Tell (William Tell). Opera in 4 acts by Rossini; text by Étienne de Jouy, Florent Bis, and Armand Marast, after Schiller's dramatic version (1804) of the legend first set down in a ballad (before 1474). Prod. Paris, O., 3 Aug. 1829, with Cinti-Damoreau, L. Dabadie, Mori, H. Dabadie, Nourrit, Levasseur, Bonel, Prévost, dancers incl. Taglioni; London, H.M.'s, 11 July 1839 (orig. version), with Persiani, Rubini, Tamburini, Lablache, cond. Costa; N.Y., 19 Sept. 1831, with Saint-Clair, Privat, Saint-Aubin.

The opera tells the familiar story of William Tell (bar.), who rallies the Swiss against the Austrians; a sub-plot tells of the love of the Swiss patriot Arnold (ten.) for the Austrian Mathilde (sop.). Other operas on the subject are by Grétry (1791), B. A. Weber (1795), Carr (1796), and Baillou (1797).

Guiraud, Ernest (*b* New Orleans, 23 June 1837; *d* Paris, 6 May 1892). French composer. The son of the composer Jean-Baptiste Guiraud (*b* Bordeaux, 1803; *d* New Orleans, *c*1864) who had left France when he failed to win a hearing for his operas, Ernest Guiraud is best known for his recitatives for Bizet's *Carmen* and his completion of the orchestration of Offenbach's *Les Contes d'Hoffmann*. His own operas include *Le Kobold* (1870), *Madame Turlupin* (1872), *Piccolino* (1876), and *Frédégonde*, which was unfinished at his death and was completed by Saint-Saëns and Dukas and staged in 1895. A well-loved teacher; his pupils included Debussy. His *Traité d'instrumentation* (1895) was the first French work of its kind to evaluate the scores of Wagner.

Gulbranson (orig. Norgren), **Ellen** (*b* Stockholm, 4 Mar. 1863; *d* Oslo, 2 Jan. 1947). Swedish soprano. Studied Stockholm and Paris with Marchesi. Début Stockholm 1886 (concert), 1889 (stage), Amneris. Bayreuth's only Brünnhilde 1897-1914, also sang Kundry 1899-1906. London, C.G., 1900 and 1907-8. Greatly admired by Melba, who begged her to come and sing some of her Wagner repertory to her in private. (R)

Gunsbourg, Raoul (*b* Bucharest, 25 Dec. 1859; *d* Monte Carlo, 31 May 1955). Romanian composer and impresario. After managing opera in Russia and Nice, became director of the Monte Carlo Opera in 1890, a position he held until 1950. Under his régime Monte Carlo saw the premières of many important works, including the stage version of *La Damnation de Faust* (1893) (his own adaptation), *Le Jongleur de Notre-Dame* (1902), *Don Quichotte* (1910), *Pénélope* (Fauré) (1913), *La Rondine* (1917), *L'Enfant et les Sortilèges* (1925), *Judith* (Honegger) (1926), and *L'Aiglon* (Honegger-Ibert) (1937). His own operas included *Le Vieil aigle* (Monte Carlo 1909, Chicago 1916) and *Ivan le terrible* (Brussels 1910).

Bibl: R. Gunsbourg: *Cent cens de souvenirs ... ou presque* (1959).

Gunther. Hagen's half-brother (bar.), King of the Gibichungs, in Wagner's *Götterdämmerung*.

Günther von Schwarzburg. Singspiel in 3 acts by Holzbauer; text by Anton Klein. Prod. Mannheim, 5 Jan. 1777. Though described as a Singspiel, the work (Holzbauer's only German opera) was an attempt to create a German national opera on a substantial scale, using recitatives to replace spoken dialogue. The first German opera published in full score.

Guntram. Opera in 3 acts by Richard Strauss; text by composer. Prod. Weimar, 10 May 1894, with Pauline de Ahna, Zeller, cond. Strauss. Set in 13th-cent. Germany, it tells of Guntram (ten.) and Friehold (bass), members of the Holy Society of Peace, to which they have vowed fidelity and obedience; and of Guntram's love for Freihild (sop.), daughter of Duke Robert (bar.).

Gura, Eugen (*b* nr Žatec, 8 Nov. 1842; *d* Aufkirchen, 26 Aug. 1906). German bass-baritone. Studied Vienna and Munich. Début Munich 1865 in *Der Waffenschmied* (Lortzing). Appeared in Breslau, Leipzig, and Hamburg 1876-83 and again in Munich 1883-96. Created Donner and Gunther, Bayreuth 1876; also heard there as Mark and Sachs. First London Mark and Sachs, D.L., 1882, when he also sang Lysiart in revival of *Euryanthe*.
Bibl: E. Gura: *Erinnerungen aus meinem Leben* (1905).

Gura, Hermann (*b* Breslau, 5 Apr. 1870; *d* Bad Wiessee, 13 Sept. 1944). German baritone, son of above. Studied Munich. Début Weimar 1890, Dutchman. Later became a producer; director of the Berlin K. O., from 1911; was responsible for the first London production of *Rosenkavalier* and other works in the 1913 Beecham season at C.G., when he also sang Beckmesser. Director Helsinki Opera, 1920-7. (R) His wife **Annie Gura-Hummel** (*b* 1884), soprano, sang the Goose-girl in the first London production of *Königskinder* (1911). (R) Their daughter, **Anita Gura** (*b* 1911), was also a soprano.

Gurlitt, Manfred (*b* Berlin, 6 Sept. 1890; *d* Tokyo, 29 Apr. 1972). German composer and conductor. Studied with Humperdinck and Karl Muck. After various appointments, music director Bremen 1914-27. His works were banned by the Nazis, and he settled in Japan, where he organized opera performances. His nine operas include a setting of *Wozzeck* made at about the same time as Berg's, and independently successful on its production in 1926, and another based on Zola's *Nana* (1958). He returned to Germany in 1953 to direct some of his works. (R)

Gurnemanz. The veteran Knight of the Grail (bass) in Wagner's *Parsifal*.

Gustave III, ou Le Bal masqué. Opera in 5 acts by Auber; text by Scribe, based on fact. Prod. Paris, O., 27 Feb. 1833; London, C.G., 13 Nov. 1833, trans. Planché; N.Y., 21 July 1834. See also *Ballo in maschera, Un*.

Gutheil-Schoder, Marie (*b* Weimar, 10 Feb. 1874; *d* Bad Ilmenau, 8 Oct. 1935). German soprano. Studied Weimar with Von Milde and also coached roles with Strauss. Début Weimar, 1891, as First Lady in *Magic Flute*. Engaged by Mahler for Vienna 1900, remaining there until 1926. At first she was attacked by the Viennese critics as 'the singer without a voice', but later became a firm favourite as Carmen, Pamina, Elvira, Elektra, and Octavian. Only London appearance, C.G., 1913, as Octavian. Taught, also worked as producer Vienna, S.O., and Salzburg. (R)

Guthrie, (Sir) **Tyrone** (*b* Tunbridge Wells, 2 July 1900; *d* Newbliss, 15 May 1971). British producer. Connected with Old Vic since 1933, became director of the S.W. Opera in 1941, and produced *Figaro*. When Joan Cross became Director of Opera, Guthrie remained director of the Vic-Wells organization, and continued his operatic work with productions of *Bohème* and *Traviata*. Other operas he produced for S.W. included a highly controversial *Carmen*, and *The Barber of Seville*. At C.G., he was responsible for *Peter Grimes* (1946) and *Traviata* (1948), and at the N.Y. Met. for *Carmen* (1952) and *Traviata* (1957). Guthrie eschewed tradition and aimed at great naturalness in his productions; he handled crowd scenes with much success, but his approach to opera was not always dictated by the music.

Gutrune. Gunther's sister (sop.) in Wagner's *Götterdämmerung*.

Gwendoline. Opera in 2 acts by Chabrier; text by Catulle Mendès. Prod. Brussels, La M., 10 Apr. 1886, with Thuringer, Engel, cond. Dupont. The Viking King Harald loves Gwendoline, daughter of his prisoner, the Saxon Armel, who pretends to consent to their marriage but arranges for her to kill Harald. She refuses, and commits suicide when Armel kills Harald.

Gye, Frederick (*b* London, 1809; *d* Dytchley, 4 Dec. 1878). English impresario. Manager of C.G., 1849-77. Joined by Mapleson for two seasons at C.G., 1869-70. During his régime he introduced many operas to the London public, including *Don Pasquale, Rigoletto, Il trovatore, Don Carlos, Aida, Lohengrin*, and *Tannhäuser*, and singers including Patti, Albani, Lucca, Tamberlik, Faure, Maurel. Statue stands today in the foyer, C.G. His son Ernest succeeded him, and married Albani.

Gyrowetz, Adalbert (Mathias) (orig. Vojtěch Matyás Jírovec) (*b* Budějovice, 20 Feb. 1763; *d* Vienna, 19 Mar. 1850). Bohemian composer. After successes in Vienna, Naples, and Paris, he went to London. *Semiramide* was commissioned for the Pantheon, but the score was destroyed when the theatre burnt down in 1792. Back in Vienna, he wrote more operas, among them the successful *Der Augenarzt* (1811) and *Hans Sachs im vorgerückten Alter*

(1834). The latter was on the subject later used by Wagner in *Die Meistersinger*; his *Il finto Stanislao* (1818) was to the Romani libretto later used by Verdi. In all he wrote some 30 operas, Singspiels, and melodramas, of which *Agnes Sorel* (1806) was an outstanding success. He was liked and admired by Mozart and Beethoven, and especially by Haydn, whose music he deeply admired and whose style he cultivated in his own works.

H

Hába, Alois (*b* Vizovice, 21 June 1893; *d* Prague, 26 Nov. 1973). Czech composer. Studied Prague with Novák (1914-15), Vienna and Berlin with Schreker (1918-22). The principal advocate of microtonal music, he wrote works for specially constructed instruments, including operas. *Matka* (The Mother, 1931), in the quarter-tone scale, was prod. Munich, and revived in Czech, Prague 1947. *Nová země* (New Earth, comp. 1935-6) is in the normal semitonal system. *Přijd' království Tvé* (Thy Kingdom Come, 1934) requires the singers to master sixth-tones. Though it aroused much interest on its first performance and revival, *Matka* has not been taken up by other theatres (apart from Florence, 1964), largely because of the obvious difficulty for most singers of pitching the quarter-tone intervals accurately. After 1948, Hába's microtonal composition class at the Prague Conservatory was dissolved, though he continued composing and teaching, his pupils including Karel Ančerl. His brother **Karel** (*b* Vizovice, 21 May 1898) studied Prague with Novák, then with Alois Hába. His operas are *Jánošík* (1934), *Stará historie* (Ancient History, 1940), and a children's opera, *Smolíček* (1950).

Habanera. A song and dance of primitive origin, deriving from the dancing of the *ñañigos*, a coloured people of a district of Havana (whence its name); it spread through S. America, where it became the ancestor of the dance-hall tango, and reached Spain. The most familiar operatic example is Carmen's 'L'amour est un oiseau rebelle', in Act 1 of Bizet's opera, which reflects its characteristic rhythm and its erotic nature. Bizet first wrote another melody (in 6/8), replacing it with the familiar version based on Sebastián Yradier's song 'El Arregilito'. Also the title of an opera by Laparra (1908).

Habich, Eduard (*b* Kassel, 3 Sept. 1880; *d* Berlin, 15 Mar. 1960). German baritone. Studied Frankfurt, with Max Fleisch. Début Coblenz 1904. Berlin, S.O., 1910-30; London. C.G., 1924-36; N.Y., Met., 1935-7; Bayreuth (Alberich, Klingsor 1911-31). Also a famous Beckmesser and Faninal. After leaving the stage, taught in Berlin. (R)

Hadjibeyov. Azerbaijani family of musicians.
(1) **Zulfugar Abdul Hussein-ogly** (*b* Shusha, 17 Apr. 1884; *d* Baku, 30 Sept 1950). Composer. Self-taught. His works include the opera *Ashug-Garib* (1916) and musical comedies.
(2) **Uzeir Abdul Hussein-ogly** (*b* Agjabedi, nr

Shusha, 17 Sept. 1885; *d* Baku, 23 Nov. 1948). Composer and conductor. Studied Gori, Moscow with Ladukhin, St Petersburg with Kalafaty. Founded first Azerbaijani music school 1922. Produced his opera *Leila and Medjnun*, Baku 1908. His other operas are *Sheikh Senan* (1909), *Rustum and Sohrab* (1910), *Asli and Kerem* (1912), *Shah Abbas and Hurshidbanu* (1912), *Harun and Leila* and – his most famous work – *Kyor-ogly* (1937). He also wrote many successful musical comedies.
(3) **Hussein Aga Sultan-ogly** (*b* Shemakha, 19 May 1898; *d* Baku, 10 Nov. 1972). Tenor. Studied with Speransky. Appeared singing female roles, 1916. Azerbaijan O., 1920, especially in works by Zulfugar Hadjibeyov, and as Lensky and Almaviva.
(4) **Sultan Ismail-ogly** (*b* Shusha, 8 May 1919). Composer and conductor. Studied with his uncle. Conducted Baku musical comedy company 1938-40. Composer of many musical comedies.

Hadley, Henry (Kimball) (*b* Somerville, 20 Dec. 1871; *d* New York, 6 Sept. 1937). American composer. Studied Boston, with Emery and Chadwick, Vienna with Mandyczewski. His operas are *Safié* (1909), *Azora* (1917), *Bianca* (1918), *Cleopatra's Night* (1920), a radio opera *A Night in Old Paris* (1933), *Nancy Brown*.

Hafgren, Lily (Johana Maria) (*b* Stockholm, 7 Oct. 1884; *d* Berlin, 27 Feb. 1965). Swedish soprano. Daughter of Johan Erik Hafgren, theatre manager, and Maria Malmgren, concert soprano. Studied Frankfurt, and began career as concert pianist; heard singing by Siegfried Wagner, who advised her to become a singer. Studied Stuttgart with Max Fleisch. Début Bayreuth, 1908, Freia; returned 1911, 1912, 1924 as Eva; Mannheim 1908-12, Berlin, H., 1912-21. Guest appearances in Milan, Paris, Rome, etc. Last appearances Dresden, 1933-4. First Berlin Empress in *Frau ohne Schatten* and a famous Isolde and Brünnhilde. Especially praised as an actress. Married the Intendant Waag and later the industrialist Georg Dinkela; appeared as Hafgren-Waag and later as Hafgren-Dinkela. (R)

Häfliger, Ernst (*b* Davos, 6 July 1919). Swiss tenor. Studied Zurich, Vienna under Patzak, and Geneva under Carpi. Début Zurich, 1943, Tiresias in Orff's *Antigone*. Berlin, Stä. O., 1953-74; Gly., 1956. Excels in Mozart and in modern music. (R)

Hagen. Alberich's son (bass) and Gunther's half-brother in Wagner's *Götterdämmerung*.

Hagen. Town in N. Rhine Westphalia, Germany. The theatre was opened in 1911 (cap. 830) and destroyed in the Second World War; rebuilt (cap. 940), opened in 1949 with *Der Rosenkavalier*.

Hague, The. See *The Hague*.

Hahn, Reynaldo (*b* Caracas, 9 Aug. 1875; *d* Paris, 28 Jan. 1947). French composer. Studied Paris with Dubois, Lavignac, and Massenet. From 1934 he was music critic of *Figaro*, also working as a conductor; director Paris O., 1945-6. Of his numerous stage works, including operas and operettas, the most successful were the operettas *Ciboulette* (1923) and *Mozart* (1925).

Haitink, Bernard (*b* Amsterdam, 4 Mar. 1923). Dutch conductor. Studied Amsterdam. Opera début 1963 Holland Festival, *Fliegende Holländer*; 1966 *Don Carlos,* after which he did not conduct opera again until Gly. 1976 *Rake's Progress*; succeeded Pritchard there as music director 1978; London, C.G., 1976 *Don Giovanni,* 1977 *Lohengrin*. (R)

Haizinger (Haitzinger), **Anton** (*b* Wilfersdorf, 14 Mar. 1796; *d* Vienna, 31 Dec. 1869). Austrian tenor. Studied Vienna with Wölkert, Mozzati, and Salieri. Début Vienna, W., 1821, Gianetto (*La gazza ladra*). Created Adolar (*Euryanthe*) which he sang in London, C.G., 1833, when he was also heard as Florestan, Tamino, and Max, all opposite Schröder-Devrient. Later established a singing school at Karlsruhe, and published a handbook on singing. He was much praised for the intelligence and musicianship of his singing: P.A. Wolff admired 'his sympathetic voice, his moving delivery, his excellent technique'.

Halász, László (*b* Debrecen, 6 June 1905). Hungarian, later naturalized American, conductor and manager. Studied Budapest; began professional career as pianist. Held conducting appointments in Budapest (1929-30), Prague (1930-2), Vienna (1933-6), and Salzburg (1929-36). American début St Louis 1936, *Tristan und Isolde*. Director St Louis Grand Opera Association 1939-42; N.Y., C.C., 1943-51, when he was dismissed after differences with the Board of directors. Subsequently conducted in Europe.

Halévy, (Jacques François) **Fromental** (Elie) (orig. Elias Lévy) (*b* Paris, 27 May 1799; *d* Nice, 17 Mar. 1862). French-Jewish composer. Studied Paris with Berton and Cherubini, and won Prix de Rome 1819. He had his first success with *Clari* (1829), in which Malibran sang the title role at the Paris T.I. But his real fame dated from 1835, when his masterpiece *La Juive* was produced: this is one of the most important works of French *Grand Opera, and though cast in the mould of Meyerbeer it achieves a certain individual grandeur and effectiveness. Wagner admired in it 'the pathos of high lyric tragedy' and Halévy's capacity in it for reconstructing the atmosphere of antiquity without reference to many circumstantial details. Wagner further regarded *La Juive* and

La Reine de Chypre (1841) as 'two monuments in the history of the art of music'; the latter work contains suggestions of his own Tarnhelm and of the *Tristan* love potion, but is also pre-Wagnerian in its chromatic harmony, and in its freedom of movement between numbers (though many of these are conventional in manner). Of Halévy's other operas, another success was the comedy *L'Éclair* (1835). He taught at the Conservatoire from 1827, his pupils including Gounod, Massé, and Bizet (who married his daughter). His brother **Léon Halévy** was an author and dramatist, whose son **Ludovic Halévy** (*b* Paris, 31 Dec. 1833; *d* Paris, 7 May 1908) collaborated with Meilhac in writing librettos for Offenbach, Bizet, and Delibes, sometimes as 'Jules Servières' and 'Paul D'Arcy'.

Halka (Helen). Opera in 2 (later 4) acts by Moniuszko; text by Włodzimierz Wolski, after K.W. Wójcicki's story *Góralka*. 2-act version concert perf. Wilno 1 Jan. 1848, prod. Wilno 28 Feb. 1854; 4-act version prod. Warsaw 1 Jan. 1858; N.Y., People's T., June 1903; London, University College, 8 Feb. 1961. Halka loves Janusz who loves Sophie. Janusz seduces Halka, but forsakes her; she kills herself while Janusz and Sophie are being married.

Sequel *Pomsta Jontkowa* (Jontek's Revenge, 1926) by Wallek-Walewski.

Hall, Peter (*b* Bury St Edmunds, 22 Nov. 1931). British producer and administrator. Studied Cambridge, where he became director of Arts T., 1955. Managing Director Royal Shakespeare T., 1960-9. Prod. *Moses and Aaron*, London, C.G., 1965, followed by *The Magic Flute* (1966), *The Knot Garden* (1970), *Eugene Onegin* (1971), and *Tristan and Isolde* (1971). Appointed co-director of Royal Opera with Colin Davis in 1969 (effective from Sept. 1971), but resigned before taking up the post on the grounds that the period of 26 weeks a year stipulated in his contract was too short a time to do his job properly – though more fundamental reasons have been suggested, including his unwillingness to accept the star system. Gly. since 1970, producing *Calisto, Il ritorno d'Ulisse in patria, Le nozze di Figaro, Don Giovanni,* and *Così fan tutte*. Hall regards opera as total musical theatre and his productions are notable for their powerful sense of drama and for their original approach; at his finest with a major dramatic singer, as with Janet Baker at Gly., he also possesses the ability to draw exceptional performances from an entire cast.

Halle. Town in Saxony, Germany. Birthplace of Handel. The first stage performances date from 1616. Duke August built the first Court Opera in 1654, opened with *Die Hochzeit des Thetis* by the music director, Philipp Stolle, thus making the city one of the earliest operatic centres in Germany. For long, Singspiel-style works were the staple fare, and in the early 19th cent. the city remained chiefly dependent on travelling companies for its introduction to Romantic opera. The T., des Friedens was opened in 1886; destroyed in 1945, it reopened in 1951 (cap. 1,035). Since the war, there has been an annual Handel Festival, and revivals have included *Deidamia* (1953), *Ezio* (1954), *Radamisto* (1955), *Poro* (1956), *Admeto* and *Tamerlano* (1958); *Imeneo* (1960), *Orlando* (1961), *Siroe* (1962), *Amadigi* (1963), *Tolomeo* (1964), *Scipio* (1965), *Alcina* (1966), *Agrippina* (1967), *Rodelinda* (1969), *Ariodante* (1971), *Serse* (1973), *Faramondo* (1976), and *Teseo* (1977).

Hallé, (Sir) **Charles** (orig. Carl Halle) (*b* Hagen, 11 Apr. 1819; *d* Manchester, 25 Oct. 1895). English pianist and conductor of German birth. Though most famous for the foundation of the orchestra which bears his name, his work for opera included seasons conducting in Manchester 1854-5 and at H.M.'s 1860-1. He was also responsible for the first English concert performance of Berlioz's *Damnation de Faust*.

Hallström, Ivar (*b* Stockholm, 5 June 1826; *d* Stockholm, 11 Apr. 1901). Swedish composer. He is best known for his operas, of which the most popular was *Den bergtagna* (The Girl Bewitched by the Mountain Spirit, 1874); this was widely performed, and its light, easy use of folk melodies won the composer a following abroad as in Sweden. Of his other works, one of the most successful was the operetta *Den förtrollade Katten* (The Enchanted Cat, 1869).

Hamburg. City-state in N. Germany. The first independent public opera house in Germany was the T. auf dem Gänsemarkt, opened in 1678 with Theile's *Adam und Eva*. J. W. Franck was Kapellmeister 1679-86. Under R. *Keiser, who wrote at least 116 operas for Hamburg, the city developed a vigorous operatic life, and in 1705 saw the premières of Handel's first operas, *Almira* and *Nero*. J. Mattheson, who was conductor and singer (1697-1705), produced his *Boris* (1710) and *Heinrich IV* (1711). For a period the city was then dependent on visiting companies. The first Mozart operas were heard from 1787. In 1809 the theatre became the Stadttheater; the new building designed by Schinkel was inaugurated operatically in 1827 with *Jessonda*. A strong operatic life developed, with Italian as well as German and French works featuring in the repertory. In 1851 the opera became the Grosse Oper, directed by Lachner; singers included Kindermann, Tichatschek, and Tietjens. B. Pollini, who was director from 1873, brought many famous singers to the city, including Klafsky, Schumann - Heink, and Niemann. The theatre

also gave an early welcome to Wagner's works, and was the scene of the first German *Otello* (1888) and *Eugene Onegin* (1892, under Mahler, in Tchaikovsky's approving presence). The Stadttheater was built in 1874. Bülow was music director 1888-91, Mahler 1891-7, Weingartner 1912-14, Pollak 1917-31, Böhm 1931-3, Jochum 1933-44, Grüber 1946-51, Ludwig 1951-71, Stein 1971-7, Dohnányi (also Intendant) from 1977. The Staatsoper, inaugurated in 1933, was bombed in 1943, but in 1945 the stage part of the old opera house was refitted to accommodate stage, orchestra, and auditorium. In 1949 the auditorium was enlarged; and in 1955 the new opera house, (cap. 1,649) was opened. Rennert was Intendant 1946-56, Heinz Tietjen 1956-9, Rolf Liebermann 1959-72, August Everding 1972-7. Since 1946 Hamburg has staged more than 40 contemporary operas, and in 1961 Liebermann was able to give a week of contemporary works. Premières have included Henze's *Der Prinz von Homburg*, Goehr's *Arden Must Die*, Searle's *Hamlet*, and Penderecki's *The Devils of Loudun*.
Bibl: [various]: *300 Jahre Oper in Hamburg* (1977).

Hamlet. Opera in 5 acts by Thomas; text by Barbier and Carré, after Shakespeare's tragedy (1600-1). Prod. Paris, O., 9 Mar. 1868, with Nilsson, Guéymard, Collin, Faure, Belval, Castelmary, cond. Hainl; London, C.G., 19 June 1869, with Nilsson, Sinico, Corsi, Santley, Bagagiolo, cond. Arditi; N.Y., Ac. of M., 22 Mar. 1872, with C. Nilsson, Cary, Brignoli, Barre, James, Coletti. Also opera by Searle, prod. Hamburg, 5 Mar. 1968, with Anderson, Meyer, Dowd, Krause, cond. Kuntzsch; London, C.G., 18 Apr. 1969, with Howells, Johnson, Dowd, Braun, cond. Downes. For other operas on subject, see *Shakespeare*.

Hammerstein, Oscar (*b* Stettin, 8 May 1846; *d* 1 Aug. 1919). German, later naturalized American, impresario. Went to America as an immigrant and made a fortune from inventing a cigar-making machine. Wrote plays and built a number of theatres. Turned to opera in 1906 when he built the *Manhattan Opera House, where he established a brilliant company and an interesting repertory which threatened to rival the Met. In 1908 he built the Philadelphia O. H., which he ran in association with his N.Y. Company. In 1910 the Met. purchased his interests and stipulated that he should not produce opera in the U.S. for ten years. He went to London and built the London O.H. (Stoll Theatre) in 1911, which could not stand up to the opposition of C.G. and collapsed after two seasons. In 1913 he built the Lexington Opera House in N.Y. and attempted to produce opera there, but was restrained legally by the Met. His grandson, **Oscar Hammerstein II** (*b* 12 July

1895), is known for his work in American musicals.

Bibl: J. Cone: *Oscar Hammerstein's Manhattan Opera Company* (1966).

Hammond, (Dame) **Joan** (*b* Christchurch, New Zealand, 24 May 1912). New Zealand soprano. Studied Sydney Conservatory, Vienna, and London with Dino Borgioli. Début as singer 1931; stage début Sydney, 1932, in small roles with visiting Italian opera company. Vienna 1939. C. R., 1942-5 and guest appearances C.G., 1948-51; S.W., 1951 and 1959, when she sang the title role in the first British stage performance of *Rusalka.* Has made guest appearances in opera in N.Y., Russia, and Spain. Retired 1965. (R)

Bibl: J. Hammond: *A Voice, a Life* (1970).

Hammond-Stroud, Derek (*b* London, 10 Jan. 1929). English baritone. Studied London with Elena Gerhardt, Munich with Hüsch. Début London, St Pancras Town Hall 1955, Creon in Haydn's *Orfeo.* S.W. since 1962; especially successful in the buffo repertory, including Bartolo, Melitone, Don Magnifico; also Alberich, and an outstanding Beckmesser. C.G., since 1971 as Faninal, Yamadori, and Sacristan. Gly., 1973. N.Y., Met., 1977. An outstanding character actor, with a sharp eye for detail and excellent clarity of diction. (R)

Handel, George Frideric (orig. Georg Friedrich Händel) (*b* Halle, 23 Feb. 1685; *d* London, 14 Apr. 1759). German, later English, composer. Studied with Zachau, the Halle organist, becoming assistant organist himself in 1697. Leaving for Hamburg in 1703, he joined the opera house under Reinhard *Keiser; here his first operas, *Almira* and *Nero* (lost), were produced in 1705. Two more, *Florinda* and *Dafne,* were written before he left for Italy in 1706. These are modelled on Keiser's operas, not least in their mixture of styles. In Florence he wrote *Rodrigo* (*c*1707 or 1708, partly lost) and in Venice *Agrippina* (1709), which shows him struggling to assert his personality against the influence of Alessandro Scarlatti: the Italian style he absorbed on this journey coloured much of his later work. He returned to Germany in 1710 before journeying on to London.

Here he found Italian *opera seria, with all its stultifying conventions, the ruling social passion and the dominant force on music. *Rinaldo* (1711, at the Queen's, later King's, Theatre) typifies this pattern. *Rinaldo* was a success and swiftly led to *Il pastor fido* (1712), which drew on previous works; *Teseo* (1713), Handel's only 5-act opera; and *Silla* (1713). *Amadigi* (1715) is a more mature piece, developing the bolder orchestral effects achieved by great variety of instrumental means, which increase in number as time goes by.

Five years elapsed, during which Handel became a director with Bononcini and Ariosti of the Royal Academy of Music (an operatic business venture that functioned 1720-8) and went to scour Italy for singers, before *Radamisto* (1720), in which his style is fully mature. The orchestration is richer, the invention more personal and confident, the forms treated with greater originality wherever convention permitted. It is a more striking opera than the three which followed: *Muzio Scevola* (1721), of which Handel wrote only Act 3; *Floridante* (1721), in which the music has to survive an unusually stilted libretto; and *Ottone* (1723), a still more conventional piece with a few striking numbers. *Flavio* (1725) also suffers from a stilted libretto. But by now Handel's ascendancy over his great London rival Bononcini was established, and he could command the services, if not predict the behaviour, of all the great singers of the day.

With *Giulio Cesare* (1724) the range of effects is widened and the conventions begin to be more richly vitalized. It has many thrilling orchestral effects, including a stage orchestra. But in total achievement it is perhaps excelled by *Tamerlano* (1724), which contains much great music, including a wealth of accompanied recitatives, that culminates in an elaborate death scene, linking seven movements of aria and recitative, that is one of the most powerful scenes in all Handel. *Rodelinda* (1725) maintains this level of invention. Both are remarkable for that rarity with Handel, an important tenor part.

The 1725-6 season was the one in which the engagement of Faustina Bordoni precipitated the notorious rivalry with Cuzzoni: partisanship led to rowdy scenes at the opera house, lampoons were published, and Handel's rivalry with Bononcini was played up. In Feb. 1726 Handel became an English citizen. *Scipione,* which dates from this year, is comparatively dull; it was quickly followed by *Alessandro,* in which Bordoni made her début with Cuzzoni. *Admeto* (1727) sets a thoroughly conventional classical plot of the day, but the arias are extremely fine; much the same is true of *Riccardo Primo* (1727) (which anticipates Verdi's *Otello* by opening with a storm off the coast of Cyprus). Only *Siroe* (1728) and *Tolomeo* (1728) followed before the Academy collapsed.

Having set himself up again at the King's Theatre with Heidegger, Handel made a fresh recruiting trip to Italy and returned for *Lotario* (1729), which failed: it is distinguished chiefly for its impressive Handelian matriarch figure. *Partenope* (1730), to an excellent comic libretto, strikes out in a new direction, though it contains a fine, typically Handelian battle scene whose noisy orchestral symphony caused much audience uneasiness. *Poro* (1731) is a striking work, but *Ezio* (1732), which is all solo *da capo* arias except for a chorus at the end, is more conventional. *Sosarme* (1732) contains another fine matriarch, as well as an excellent long finale and some good bass arias, but is musically uneven. *Orlando* (1733) is on an altogether higher level of invention – it is also notable for its striking scenic and structural effects: the hero's madness is portrayed in a scene of linked movements and symbolized by the first use in history of 5/8 time.

In the next year Handel and Heidegger gave up their partnership under pressure from the rival 'Opera of the Nobility' at Lincoln's Inn Fields, which had lured away the best singers; they vacated the King's Theatre to their rivals, and Handel moved to Lincoln's Inn Fields, having produced *Arianna* (1734), a decline from *Orlando's* richness. But in 1735 the new season opened, this time at Covent Garden, with *Ariodante*, a spectacular if uneven opera that included a ballet (Handel had secured the services of the French dancer Marie Sallé). From about this time, too, simple use is made of a separate chorus; previously the final *coro* implied an ensemble of soloists. *Ariodante's* immediate successor was *Alcina* (1735), a piece rich in scenic effects and distinguished by some of Handel's most passionate and touching arias. *Atalanta* (1736) is a lighter work (it ends with a display of fireworks), though a finely imagined one. Handel's serious decline in health is reflected in the poverty of *Arminio* (1737) and *Giustino* (1737) (which includes a consort of recorders). *Berenice* (1737) is basically dull, apart from the overture (with its famous minuet) and one or two numbers. It successor, *Faramondo* (1738), is a little broader in range. *Serse* (1738) has become celebrated through the *Larghetto* 'Ombra mai fù', now inescapably known as 'Handel's Largo'; it is a light and entertaining opera, with a buffo servant who antedates Leporello. *Imeneo* (1740), called by Handel an operetta, is a little like his last opera *Deidamia* (1741), an ironic, almost anti-heroic comedy with touches of sentiment.

The revival of Handel's operas dates from Germany in the 1920s, and has gathered force in recent years, especially in England. The artificiality of *opera seria* has proved less of a stumbling-block than expected: perhaps its very formality and neatness offers something to a society lacking these qualities and failing to find them in the music of its own time. The dramatic force which the genre still holds is impressive, and producers who attempt 'special' presentation of works written by a composer with shrewd stage sense quickly discover their error. Difficulties remain, for few singers possess the elaborate technique of Handel's day, and the castrato parts must either be transposed or given to a woman or a countertenor.

However magnificently Handel filled *opera seria* form and however boldly he tried to trans-cend its cramping conventions, the attempt to establish it as a living art form was bound to fail; accordingly he turned his attention to oratorio. But inevitably most of his oratorios are intensely dramatic in conception: the scores contain stage directions, and though after 1732 he had no stage performances in view, there is evidence that he 'visualized' his heroes and their actions while composing their music. It is not surprising, then, that when writing in a dramatic form liberated from *opera seria* conventions, he should have achieved greater dramatic range. Many problems attend the staging of these dramatic oratorios, not least the question of how to place the chorus, which now played a large part. Another major effect on Handel was his release from the domination of the *da capo* aria and the elimination of castratos and star singers. Thus the oratorio arias have richer accompaniments. Indeed, the whole dramatic structure becomes more organic. Religious scruples and mistrust of the theatre as a den of vice long kept these dramatic oratorios out of the theatre, and it was not until the German revival of interest in Handel's operas after the First World War that the dramatic oratorios began appearing on the stage. Almost all have now done so in England, some repeatedly, staged by both professionals and enthusiastic amateurs.

Bibl: G Abraham (ed.): *Handel: a Symposium* (1954), incl. chapter on the operas by E. J. Dent; W. Dean: *Handel and the Opera Seria* (1970).

Handel Opera Society, England. Founded in 1955 at the instigation of Prof. E.J. Dent, with aim of 'reviving public interest in professional stage performances [in Great Britain] of Handel's dramatic works'. It began its activities with a production of *Deidamia* in Dent's translation at the St Pancras Town Hall., London, conducted by Charles Farncombe, who has been the company's music director ever since. Between 1955 and 1977 the Society has staged a further 21 Handel works: *Hercules* (1956), *Alcina* with Sutherland (1957), *Theodora* (1958), *Semele* and *Rodelinda* with Sutherland and Baker (1959 – the first year in which the Society's annual season was given at S.W.), *Radamisto* (1960), *Rinaldo* (1961), *Jephtha* (1962), *Serse* and *Giulio Cesare* with Sutherland (1963), *Riccardo Primo* (1964), *Saul* (1965), *Orlando* with Baker (1966), *Scipione* (1967), *Susanna* (1969), *Samson* (1970), *Ottone* (1971), *Atalanta* (1973). *Ariodante* (1974), *Belshazzar* (1976), and *Ezio* (1977). The Society's productions have also been seen in Liège, Göttingen, Herrenhausen, Halle, and Drottningholm.

Hann, George (*b* Vienna, 30 Jan. 1897; *d* Munich, 9 Dec. 1950). Austrian bass-baritone. Studied Vienna with Lierhammer. Munich State Opera 1927-50. Also appeared Salzburg,

Vienna. One of the best buffo artists in Germany, and especially remembered for his Kecal, Falstaff, Ochs, La Roche (which he created), and Leporello; he also sang dramatic roles incl. Gunther, Amfortas, Pizarro, and Sarastro. London, C.G., while still a student in 1924, Cappadocian in *Salome*; 1947 with Vienna Company as Pizarro, Leporello, and Nazarene. (R)

Hanover (Ger., Hannover). Town in Lower Saxony, Germany. Musical performances were given in the Residenz in the early 17th cent; the first opera given there was probably Cesti's *Orontia* in 1649. The first opera house (cap. 1,200) was inaugurated in 1689 with Steffani's *Enrico Leone*; Steffani composed a further nine operas for Hanover, and was music director until 1698. After his departure guest companies performed until Marschner was appointed music director in 1831. The Royal Opera House (cap. 1,300) was opened in Sept. 1852 with Marschner's *Natur in Kunst*. Successive music directors included Ludwig Fischer, Bülow, Arno Grau, and Rudolf Krasselt; singers have included Gertrud Kappel, Tiana Lemnitz, Albert Niemann, and Theodor Wachtel. Operas premièred in Hanover up to 1943, when the theatre was badly damaged by bombs, include Stanford's *The Veiled Prophet*, Wellesz's *Prinzessin Girnara*, and Wolf-Ferrari's *Der Kuckuck in Theben* (Gli Dei a Tebe), as well as the first German *A Life for the Tsar*.

After the Second World War, Franz Konwitschny was music director 1945-9, Johannes Schüler, who had been 1st conductor under Krasselt, 1949-60, Günther Wich 1961-5, Georg Alexander Albrecht since 1965. The rebuilt opera house (cap. 1,554) was opened in 1950 and premières have included Henze's *Boulevard Solitude* (1952) and Meyerowitz's *Die Doppelgängerin* (1967), the first German *Albert Herring*, and important revivals of Verdi's *I masnadieri* (1964), Busoni's *Dr Faust* (1967), and Smetana's *The Secret* (1969). See also *Herrenhausen*.

Hans Heiling. Opera in prologue and 3 acts by Marschner; text by Devrient, after an old folk tale. Prod. Berlin, H., 24 May 1833, with Grünbaum, Valentini, Devrient, Bader, cond. Marschner; Oxford, 2 Dec. 1953, with Blacker, Rawson, Wasserman, Townend, cond. Westrup. Another opera on the subject is by Volkert (1847).

Hans Sachs. See Sachs, Hans.

Hänsel und Gretel. Opera in 3 acts by Humperdinck; text by Adelheid Wette (composer's sister), after the story in the Grimm brothers' *Kinder- und Hausmärchen* (1812-14). Prod. Weimar, 23 Dec. 1893, with Kayser, Schubert, Tibelti, Finck, Wiedey, cond. R. Strauss;

London, Daly's 26 Dec. 1894, with Douste, Elba, Miller, Lennox, Copland, cond. Arditi; N.Y., Daly's, by A. Harris's Company, 8 Oct. 1895, with Douste, Elba, Meisslinger, Gordon, Brani, Johnston, Bars, cond. Seidl. Another opera on the tale is by Reichardt (1773).

Hanslick, Eduard (*b* Prague, 11 Sept. 1825; *d* Baden, nr Vienna, 6 Aug. 1904). German music critic. His first work on aesthetics, *Vom Musikalisch-Schönen* (1854), remains his most important book, and sets out to establish and argue a case for non-representational music, and for form expressed in sound as being the only content of music. This placed him in opposition to Liszt, and especially to Wagner, whose early works he admired but whose later course he both feared and deplored in direct proportion to his deep admiration for Wagner's talent. This led to his being pilloried by Wagner in the guise of Beckmesser (originally named Hans Lich). They were never reconciled, but Hanslick's final tribute to Wagner after the latter's death is generous and moving. He has passed into history as the epitome of the rigid, ultra-conservative critic attempting to halt progress; but his conservatism was based on deeply felt, thoroughly argued artistic criteria, and it was these that gave his writings, during his long years as a Viennese music critic, so much weight, and which make his essays still well worth reading.
Bibl: E. Hanslick (trans. H. Pleasants): *Vienna's Golden Years of Music, 1890-1900* (1951).

Hardy Thomas (*b* Upper Bockhampton, 2 June 1840; *d* Dorchester, 11 Jan. 1928). English poet and novelist. Operas on his works are as follows:
Far From the Madding Crowd (1873): E. Harper (*Fanny Robin*, 1976).
The Mayor of Casterbridge (1886): Tranchell (1951).
Three Strangers (1888): Bath (20th cent); Gardiner (1936).
Tess of the D'Urbervilles (1891): D'Erlanger (1906).
The Queen of Cornwall (1923): Boughton (1924).

Harewood, Earl of (George Henry Hubert Lascelles) (*b* London, 7 Feb. 1923). English critic and administrator. Son of H.R.H. the Princess Royal, and first cousin of H.M. Queen Elizabeth II, Lord Harewood has inherited his great-great-grandparents' (Queen Victoria and Prince Albert) love for music, in particular for opera. He founded the magazine *Opera* in 1950; served on the Board of Directors at C.G. 1951-3 and 1969-72; and was controller of opera planning there 1953-60. Artistic director of Leeds Festival 1958-74; Director of Edinburgh Festival 1961-5. Managing Director, S.W., later E.N.O., from 1972. Compiled rev. editions of

Kobbé's *Complete Opera Book*, 1953 and 1976. He has championed the E.O.G., the Opera School, and other native operatic enterprises.

Harmonie der Welt, Die (The Harmony of the World). Opera in 5 scenes by Hindemith; text by composer. Prod. Munich, P., 11 Aug. 1957 with Fölser, Töpper, Holm, Josef Metternich, cond. Hindemith. Based on the life of the astronomer Kepler and his musical theories of planetary motion, the work is, like *Mathis der Maler*, a study of the artist's or philosopher's relationship to the political and social movements of his times.

Harper, Heather (Mary) (*b* Belfast, 8 May 1930). Irish soprano. Studied London, T.C.M., and with Helene Isepp and Frederic Husler. Début Oxford University Opera Society 1954, Lady Macbeth. Gly. Chorus 1955, 1959 First Lady, 1963 Anne Trulove. E.O.G., 1956-75; London, New Opera Company, 1960, *Erwartung*. C.G., since 1962; Helena in *Midsummer Night's Dream*, Gutrune, Eva, Antonia, Ellen Orford, Hecuba, Arabella; created Mrs Coyle, Nadia (*The Ice Break*). Bayreuth, 1967, Elsa; Buenos Aires, C., since 1969 as Vitellia (*La clemenza di Tito*), Marguerite, Arabella; San Francisco and N.Y., Met. (R)

Harris, (Sir) **Augustus** (*b* Paris, 1852; *d* Folkestone, 22 June 1896). English impresario. Son of stage-manager of C.G. Was Mapleson's assistant manager, and then in 1879 became lessee of D.L. Brought C.R. to London 1883 and managed their seasons until 1887, when he gave a trial season of Italian opera at D.L. with great success. He took C.G. for the following year, and in 1888-96 achieved great artistic and financial success with the help of a brilliant company that included Melba and the De Reszkes. He introduced opera in the original language to C.G., and did much to popularize Wagner.

Harrison, Julius (*b* Stourport, 26 Mar. 1885; *d* Harpenden, 5 Apr. 1963). English conductor. Studied Birmingham under Bantock. C.G., 1913 with Raymond Roze's Company. Sent by Grand Opera Syndicate to Paris the following year to help Nikisch and Weingartner prepare performances of *Parsifal, Tristan,* and *Meistersinger*. Conductor Beecham Company and B.N.O.C. 1922-7 (R)

Harrison, William (*b* London, 15 June 1813; *d* London, 9 Nov. 1868). English tenor and impresario. Studied R.A.M. Début C.G. 1839 in *Rooke's Henrique*. After seasons at D.L., where he created leading tenor roles in *The Bohemian Girl, Maritana,* and other works, he established, in 1856, an English opera company in conjunction with the soprano Louisa Pyne. The company performed every autumn and winter at C.G. 1858-64, and gave the first performances

of works by Balfe, Wallace, Benedict, and others.

Harshaw, Margaret (*b* Narbeth, Penn., 12 May 1912). American soprano, orig. mezzo. Studied Philadelphia, Juilliard School, N.Y. Début N.Y., 1935. Won Met. Auditions of Air 1942. N.Y., Met., 1942-64, first as mezzo. In 1950 discovered her voice was changing and after singing Senta in 1951 and the *Götterdämmerung* Brünnhilde in 1952 established herself as one of the leading Wagner sopranos of the day. London, C.G., 1953-6 and 1960, Brünnhilde; Gly., 1955, Donna Anna. Retired 1964; teaches at Bloomington, where she sang a *Walküre* Brünnhilde, 1970. (R)

Hart, Fritz (Bennicke) (*b* London, 11 Feb. 1874; *d* Honolulu, 9 July 1949). English conductor and composer. Studied London, R.C.M., with Stanford. In 1915 became director of the Melbourne Conservatory, where Melba taught and where many of his 22 operas were produced. A gifted writer, he provided most of his own librettos, favouring Celtic Twilight subjects; and his intense practical sense (he had appeared as an actor) helped to make his works theatrically effective.

Hartford. Town in Connecticut, U.S.A. Until 1941 opera was given by visiting companies, including the Metropolitan from New York and the Naples S.C. In 1941 Frank Pandolfi, a lawyer and singing teacher, launched the Connecticut Opera Association with a performance of *Carmen*. Since then 5 or 6 operas a season, with star casts and minimal production, are given to large audiences, many of whom travel from Boston and New York to hear artists in roles they have not sung in New York, e.g. Stignani as Azucena, Sutherland as Mary Stuart, and Magda Olivero as Adriana Lecouvreur. The Hartt Opera T., attached to the University of Hartford, performs rarely-heard works in modern and often controversial productions.

Hartman, Georg (*b* Nuremberg, 19 Feb. 1891; *d* Munich, 9 Jan. 1972). German producer and administrator. After several years in the straight theatre (1912-19), he began to produce opera, first at Erfurt, then Hanover (1919-20) and Dresden (1920-23). Generalintendant Lübeck (1923-5), Dessau (1925-33, 1946), Dortmund (1934-7), Duisburg (1938-44). Appointed Intendant of Bavarian State Opera, Munich, 1947-52, and produced a number of important works during the Solti regime there, including *Mathis der Mahler, Raskolnikoff,* and operas by Wagner, Verdi, and Strauss.

Hartmann, Karl Amadeus (*b* Munich, 2 Aug. 1905; *d* Munich, 5 Dec. 1963). German composer. His chamber opera *Der Simplicius Simplicissimus Legend* (comp. 1934, prod. Cologne 1949, rev. 1955) has been popular in Germany.

Hartmann, Rudolf (*b* Ingolstadt, 11 Oct. 1900). German producer and manager. Studied stage design Munich, and in Bamberg under Berg-Ehlert. Engaged as *Oberspielleiter* Altenberg 1924; Nuremberg 1928-34 and 1946-52; Berlin State Opera 1934-8, where he began his collaboration with Clemens Krauss and produced the première of *Die Zaubergeige*; Munich 1938-44, and 1953-67 Staatsintendant there. Staged premières of *Friedenstag* and *Capriccio* there and revivals of most of Strauss's major works as well as première of *Liebe der Danae*, Salzburg, 1952. London, C.G., *Elektra* 1953, *Arabella* 1965, *Frau ohne Schatten* 1967; new *Ring* production 1954. Hartmann has no special theories on production but inclines towards tradition.
Bibl: R. Hartmann: *Oper-Regie und Bühnenbild Heuto* (1977).

Harwood, Elizabeth (*b* Kettering, 27 May 1938). English soprano. Studied Manchester, R.C.M. Début Gly., 1960, Second Boy (*Zauberflöte*); London, S.W., 1961-5 and since 1965 as guest artist; especially successful in Mozart repertory, and as Countess Adèle (*Comte Ory*), Zerbinetta, Gilda, Manon; C.G., since 1967, Fiakermilli in *Arabella*; Bella (*Midsummer Marriage*); Gilda, Oscar, Marzelline, Norina; Scottish Opera since 1961, Fiordiligi, Sophie, Lucia. Toured Australia with Sutherland 1965; Aix-en-Provence 1967-9; Salzburg since 1970 as Constanze, Fiordiligi, Donna Elvira, and Countess. Her beautiful voice and appearance are allied to a warm stage personality. (R)

Háry János (John Háry). Opera in prologue, 5 parts, and epilogue by Kodály; text by B. Paulini and Z. Harsányi, after János Garay's poem. Prod. Budapest 16 Oct. 1926, with Nagy, Palló, cond. Rékai; N.Y., Juilliard School, 18 Mar. 1960, with Anker, Whitesides, cond. Waldman; London, Camden Town Hall, 28 Nov. 1967, with Temperley, Olegario, cond. Wales.

Häser, Charlotte (Henriette) (*b* Leipzig, 24 Jun. 1784; *d* Rome, 1 May 1871). German soprano, daughter of the composer Johann Georg Häser (1729-1809) and sister of the composer and singing teacher August Ferdinand Häser (1779-1844). Studied with her father. Appeared with success in Dresden, leaving in 1806 for Italy. Here she triumphed, becoming one of the first German singers to make an international reputation and being hailed as 'la divina Tedesca'. After further successes in Germany, where she was much admired by Spohr, she married and retired to Rome. She was one of the first women to sing men's roles (e.g. Tamino). A contempory account praises the simplicity and musicianship of her singing, and its absence of intrusive flourishes, finding her tone full and affecting if rather cutting in the high register.

Hasse, Johann (Adolf) (*b* Bergedorf, bapt. 25 Mar. 1699; *d* Venice, 16 Dec. 1783). German composer. Sang as tenor in Hamburg (1718) and Brunswick (1719). After his first opera *Antioco* was produced in Brunswick in 1721, he went to Italy to study with Porpora and A. Scarlatti. Here he established his reputation firmly with *Sesostrate* (1726), becoming so popular as to win the name 'il caro Sassone' (though not in fact a Saxon). In 1730 he married Faustina *Bordoni, then at the height of her fame, and wrote a number of his operas for her. Directed the Dresden Opera from 1731, and though his position was initially made difficult by rivalries and jealousies, he was appointed Oberkapellmeister 1750. Visited London in 1734, producing his *Artaserse* as a counterattraction to Handel. His 30-year reign in Dresden firmly established Italian opera there as the art of the Court and aristocracy. After the siege of Dresden in 1760, during which he lost most of his MSS, he moved to Vienna (1763), finally settling in Venice (1773).

Conservative in style, and already outdated by Gluck's reforms during his Vienna period, Hasse's music typifies *opera seria* as it was established in Germany during the mid-18th cent. He set almost all the texts by his contemporary Metastasio, including 56 operas and 13 intermezzi; their form consists of the traditional pattern of *opera seria*, with *da capo* arias in which the main burden of the dramatic expression is contained in melody that at its finest reaches great elegance and richness.
Bibl: R. Gerber: *Der Operntypus J.A. Hasses* (1925).

Hasselmans, Louis (*b* Paris, 25 July 1878; *d* San Juan 27 Dec. 1957), French conductor. Studied Paris Conservatoire. Début with Lamoureux Orchestra; Paris, O.C., 1909-11; Montreal Opera 1911-13; Chicago 1918-20; N.Y., Met., 1921-36, where he conducted N.Y. premières of *L'Heure Espagnole* and *Habanera*.

Hastreiter, Helene (*b* Louisville, Kentucky, 14 Nov. 1858; *d* Varese, 6 Aug. 1922). American mezzo. Studied Madison, Wisc. Début (aged 16) Chicago, in *Masaniello*. Went to Europe 1880 and studied Milan with the Lampertis; début Trieste. Engaged by Mapleson 1886-7 and by Theodore Thomas for the American Opera Company 1885-6. London, H.M.'s and C.G., 1887-8. Repertory included Orfeo, Ortrud, Senta.

Hatto, Jeanne (Marguerite Jeanne Frère) (*b* St Armour, 30 Jan. 1879; *d* Paris, Mar. 1958). French soprano. Studied Lyons and Paris, début Paris, O., 1899, Brünnhilde in *Sigurd*. Sang regularly at the O. until 1922, creating Iole (*Astarte*), Geneviève in Chausson's *Le Roi Arthus*, and Floria in Saint-Saëns's *Les Barbares*. Repertory also included Elisabeth, Sieglinde, Marguerite, Tenaire (*Castor et Pollux*), Diane (*Hippolyte et Aricie*), Monna Vanna, Donna Elvira, and Salammbô. (R)

Hauer, Josef (Matthias) (*b* Wiener-Neustadt, 19 Mar. 1883; Vienna, 22 Sept. 1959). Austrian composer. His theories of atonal music, which preceded and were respected by Schoenberg, found expression in two operas, *Salambo* (excerpts broadcast 1930) and *Die schwarze Spinne* (not prod.).

Hauk, Minnie (orig. Mignon Hauck) (*b* N.Y., 16 Nov. 1851; *d* Triebschen, 6 Feb. 1929). American soprano. Studied New Orleans and New York. Début Brooklyn 1866, Amina; London, C.G., 1868. Appeared with success in Paris, Brussels, Moscow, Berlin. The first American Juliette (which she sang the day before her 16th birthday), Carmen, and Manon; first London Carmen. Appeared for one season at N.Y., Met., 1890-1 and then organized her own opera company, but after season's tour suddenly retired from the stage at the height of her powers and went to live with her husband in Wagner's villa at Triebschen. She lost her fortune during the First World War and was supported by funds raised by American opera-lovers.
Bibl: M. Hauk: *Memories of a Singer* (1925).

Hauptprobe (*Ger* Chief rehearsal). In German opera houses, the final rehearsal before the Dress Rehearsal, or *Generalprobe.

Hauptstimme. *Ger* Principal voice or role.

Häusliche Krieg, Der. See *Verschworenen, Die*.

Haute-Contre (*Fr* High counter [tenor]). A high tenor, but not (as often stated) falsetto; the voice of most leading male roles in French opera from Lully to Rameau. Its range was normally about d – b[1].

Havana. Capital of Cuba. The first theatre opened with an operatic setting of Metastasio's *Didone abbandonata* in 1776. The T. Coliseo, which this inaugurated, was renamed the T. Principal in 1803; it was severely damaged by cyclones in 1844 and 1846. Meanwhile there had been opened the T. Tacon, modelled on the T. Real of Madrid and the T. Liceo of Barcelona, and in its day said to be the largest opera house in the world. It was for long the home of visiting European companies. In 1915 it was reinaugurated as the T. Nacional with *Aida*, under Serafin. A number of other theatres have housed zarzuelas and operettas.
    A Havana Italian Opera Company, organized by Francesco Marty under the direction of Arditi and with leading French and Italian singers, appeared in New Orleans 1837, New York 1847-50.

Hawes, William (*b* London, 21 June 1785; *d* London, 18 Feb. 1846). English composer.

From 1824 he directed at the Ly., where he introduced Weber's *Der Freischütz*, with some airs of his own (1824). Apart from his own operettas, he was responsible for adapting many operas for the English stage, among them *Così fan tutte, Don Giovanni,* and *Der Vampyr*.

Haydn, (Franz) **Joseph** (*b* Rohrau, 31 Mar 1732; *d* Vienna, 31 May 1809). Austrian composer. Haydn's first five operas are lost, but 15 survive, largely neglected. There were also five puppet operas, of which only *Philemon und Baucis* (1773) is extant. Yet Haydn rated opera high in his interests, and used to say that if he had gone to Italy he might have become a first-rate opera composer. Weak librettos are partly to blame for dragging some fine music into obscurity. Though bound to convention, in his case a mixed one of *opera seria* and *opera buffa*, Haydn's operas give a steadily larger role to the music: their mixture of comic and serious elements was one developed with genius by Mozart. The beginnings are already discernible in *Lo speziale* (1768). The later operas discard, or develop out of recognition, the *aria da capo*, and greater importance is allotted to ensembles. *Il mondo della luna* (1777) (frequently revived in a new edition by Robbins Landon (1959)) has some subtle orchestral commentaries; and in *La vera costanza* (1779), still more in *L'isola disabitata* (1770), the music has a deliberately Gluckian indissolubility from the drama. With *La fedeltà premiata* (1780) Haydn began to lose interest in opera of a mixed nature; *Armide* (1784) is a wholly serious work. *L'anima del filosofo* (1791) was the only opera not limited by the needs of the Esterház company. In it Haydn tried to develop *opera seria* along Gluck's lines: greater dramatic use is made of the chorus, for instance. But it shows, in Geiringer's words, 'that Haydn did not feel himself sufficiently at home in opera composition to free himself completely from the bondage of the prevailing taste and to create musical drama'.
    Operas on his life are by Hetzel (*La Jeunesse de Haydn*) and Suppé (*Joseph Haydn*, 1887).
Bibl: K. Geiringer: *Haydn* (1947).

Hayes, Catherine (*b* Limerick, 25 Oct. 1825; *d* London, 11 Aug. 1861). Irish soprano. Studied Dublin with Sapio, Paris with Garcia, Milan with Felice Ronconi. Début Marseilles 1845, Elvira (*Puritani*). After successful appearances in Italy and Austria, appeared at C.G. 1849 as Linda, Lucia, and other roles. Thackeray pays her tribute in his *Irish Sketch-Book*.

Head voice. A method of tone production in the upper register, so called from the sensation experienced by the singer of the voice functioning at the top of the head. The tone is weak but light and clear.

223

Hedmont, Charles (orig. Emmanuel Christian Hedmont) (*b* Ontario, 24 Oct. 1857; *d* London, 25 Apr. 1940). Canadian tenor. Studied Montreal and Leipzig. Début Berlin under name of Emanuel Hedmont. Leipzig, 1882-7, sharing leading tenor roles with Lederer; especially successful as Max, Ottavio, Belmonte, Tamino, and Idomeneo. Bayreuth, 1886, David. Principal tenor, C.R., 1891-1909. Presented a season of opera in English at C.G., autumn 1895, which included first performance in English of *Walküre* in which he sang Siegmund. Sang Loge in the English *Ring* under Richter at C.G., 1908, and also acted as stage manager. Also appeared in U.S.A.

Heger, Robert (*b* Strasbourg, 19 Aug. 1886; *d* Munich, 14 Jan. 1978). German conductor and composer. Studied Strasbourg, Zurich, and Munich. Début, Ulm, 1909; held appointments in Barmen, Vienna, Nuremberg, Munich, Berlin S.O. 1933-44, Stä.O., 1944-50; Kassel, music director of rebuilt S.O. 1935-41, where he conducted several premières, including *Tobia Wunderlich* (Haas) and *Elisabeth von England* (Klenan). Returned to Munich 1950. London, C.G., 1925–35 and with Munich company 1953, when he directed first London performance of *Capriccio*. Has composed 4 operas. (R)

Heidegger, John (orig. Johann Jakob) (*b* c1659; *d* London, 4 Sept. 1749). English impresario of Swiss birth. Manager King's Theatre, Haymarket, 1708-34; in partnership with Handel 1729-34. Wrote libretto for Handel's *Amadigi.*

Heilbron (Heilbronn), **Marie** (*b* Antwerp, 1851; *d* Nice 31 Mar. 1886). Belgian soprano. Studied Paris. Début Paris, O.C., 1867 in Massenet's first opera, *La Grand' Tante*. Paris, O., 1879-80 as Marguerite, Zerlina, and Ophelia. Created Manon at O.C., 1884. Milan, Sc., 1879; London, C.G., 1874, 1879.

Heine, Heinrich (orig. Harry) (*b* Düsseldorf, 13 Dec. 1797; *d* Paris, 17 Feb. 1856). German poet, playwright, and novelist. A close friend of Meyerbeer, and critic of the Augsburg *Allgemeine Zeitung*: he wrote valuable reports on Paris musical life. His *Almansor* (1823) was the basis of an opera partly composed and later destroyed by Debussy. Operas on his works are as follows:

Almansor (1823): Behrend (1931).
William Ratcliff: Cui (1869); Bavrinecz (1885); Pizzi (1889); Mascagni (1895); Leroux (1906); Dopper (1909); Andreae (1914).
Der Schelm von Bergen (1846): Olschlegel (1888); Obar (1892); Char (1895); Sahlender (1895); Behm (1899); Niehr (1900); Gerlach (1903); Atterberg (1934).
Memoiren des Herrn von Schnabelewopski (1831): Wagner (*Der fliegende Holländer*, 1843).

Heinefetter, Maria (*b* Mainz, 16 Feb. 1816; *d* Vienna, 23 Feb. 1857). German soprano. Sang with success in Vienna as Mme Stöckl Heinefetter. London, C.G., with German company 1842, the first London Valentine in *Huguenots*. Died insane. She had four sisters. **Sabine** (*b* Mainz, 19 Aug. 1809; *d* Illemau, 18 Nov. 1872), soprano, was originally a harpist and was encouraged to take up singing by Spohr. Studied Paris with Tadolini, and sang at Théâtre des Italiens until 1842; then in Italy, Vienna and Dresden. Retired 1844. Like Maria she died insane. **Kathinka** (1820-58) sang in Paris and Brussels from 1840 onwards; and **Eva** and **Clara** were also opera singers.

Heinrich. The King of Saxony (bass) in Wagner's *Lohengrin;* also known as Heinrich der Vogler (Henry the Fowler).

Heinrich, Rudolf (*b* Halle, 10 Feb. 1926; *d* London, 1 Dec. 1975). German scene designer. Studied Burg Giebichenstein. Leipzig 1948-50; Halle, 1950-4; Berlin, K.O., 1954-61, where he was Felsenstein's chief designer (*Carmen, Cunning Little Vixen, Hoffmann, Otello, Traviata, Midsummer Night's Dream*). Free lance after 1961, designing productions for N.Y. Met. (*Salome, Elektra, Tosca*), Boston (*Boris Godunov*), Munich, and Milan. At Santa Fe he designed and produced *Lulu*. Married the American soprano Joan Carroll. His approach to opera is coloured by Brecht's theories.

Heldenbariton (*Ger* Heroic baritone). See *Baritone.*

Heldentenor (*Ger.* Heroic tenor). See *Tenor.*

Heldy, Fanny (orig. Marguerite-Virginia Emma Clementine Deceuninck) (*b* Ath, 29 Feb. 1888; *d* Paris, 13 Dec. 1973). Belgian soprano. Studied Liège and Brussels. Début Brussels, La M., 1910, Elena in Gunsbourg's *Ivan le Terrible*. Sang at La M. until 1917, returning regularly as guest. Paris, O.C., 1917-20; O., 1920-39; London, C.G., 1926, 1928. Chosen by Toscanini to sing Louise and Mélisande at Milan Sc. Created L'Aiglon, Monaco 1937. Admired in these roles and as Manon, Thaïs, and Concepción. (R)

Helm, Anny (*b* Vienna 20 July 1903). Austrian soprano. Studied Vienna with Gutheil-Schoder and Gertrude Förstel, and Berlin with Ernst Grenzebach. Début Magdeburg 1924. Berlin, S.O., 1926-33; Bayreuth 1927-31, Brangaene, Venus; London, C.G., 1939, Venus. From 1935 lived in Italy and sang as Anny Helm-Sbisa (her husband, Giuseppe Sbisa, was for many years director of the T. Giuseppe Verdi, Trieste). Repertory also included Donna Anna, Alceste, Brünnhilde, Isolde, Elektra, Lady Macbeth (Bloch), and Turandot. (R)

Helsinki (Swed., Helsingfors). Capital of Finland. Opera was given by touring German companies in the early 19th cent. The Russky T., built in 1879, was used, after Finland's achievement of independence, for opera; a miniature version of the Kirov T. (cap.669), it is now used by the Suomen Kansallisooppera. The first permanent Finnish company was founded in 1873, but regular opera had a chequered career until 1911, when Edward Fazer and Aíno Ackté started a company as a private enterprise; in 1914 this became the Suomalainen Ooppera. Frazer was director 1911-38 (with Armas Järnefelt as artistic director 1932-6 and Ackté 1938-9), to be succeeded by Oiva Soini 1939-52. Jussi Jalas was music director until 1973, Leif Segerstam from 1973. An annual festival takes place in May.

Heming, Percy (*b* Bristol, 6 Sept. 1883; *d* London, 11 Jan. 1956). English baritone. Studied London, R.A.M., with Frederick King, Dresden with Henschel. Début Beecham Co. 1915, Mercutio. Sang Marcello on the opening night of the B.N.O.C.'s first C.G. season and became one of its leading baritones; then joined the C.G. English Touring Company. S.W., 1933-5. Assistant artistic director C.G., 1937; artistic director C.G. English Company 1937-9; artistic adviser C.G., 1946-8. Sang a great variety of roles ranging from Bartolo to Amfortas, Kecal to Scarpia. Toured U.S.A. as Macbeth. (R)

Hempel, Frieda (*b* Leipzig, 26 June 1885; *d* Berlin, 7 Oct. 1955). German soprano. Studied Berlin with Nicklass-Kempner. Début Schwerin: her success resulted in the Kaiser asking the Schwerin authorities to release her to sing in Berlin, where she made her début as Frau Fluth (*Lustigen Weiber*) in 1905. London, C.G., 1907, Bastienne. N.Y., Met., 1912, Marguerite de Valois and regularly until 1919. Chicago Opera, 1914 and 1920-21. The first Berlin and N.Y. Marschallin, a role she sang in London in 1913. Such was her amazing versatility that she could sing Eva and Euryanthe as well as Queen of Night, Rosina, and Oscar. After 1921 she devoted her time to the concert hall and was famed for her Jenny Lind recitals in costume. (R)
Bibl: F. Hempel: *Mein Leben dem Gesang* (1955).

Hemsley, Thomas (Jeffery) (*b* Coalville, 12 Apr. 1927). English baritone. Studied with Lucie Manén. Début London, Mermaid T. 1951, Aeneas (Purcell) to Flagstad's Dido. Gly. from 1953, including Dr. Reischmann in English language première of Henze's *Elegy for Young Lovers* (1961). E.O.G. from 1955, creating Demetrius in *A Midsummer Night's Dream*. Aachen O. 1953-6, Düsseldorf, Deutsche Oper am Rhein 1953-63. Bayreuth, Beckmesser 1968-70. (R)

Henderson, Roy (*b* Edinburgh, 4 July 1899).

British baritone and teacher. Studied London, R.A.M. Début London, C.G., 1929, Donner. Gly., 1934-9 as Count Almaviva, Guglielmo, Masetto, and Papageno. Teacher of Ferrier and many other singers. (R)

Henry VIII. Opera in 4 acts by Saint-Saëns; text by Détroyat and Silvestre. Prod. Paris, O., 5 Mar. 1883, with Krauss, Richard, Renaud, Lassalle, cond. E. Altes; London, C.G., 14 July 1898, with Pacary, Heglon, Renaud, cond. Mancinelli.

Concerns the love of the King (bar.) for Anne Boleyn (sop), whom he marries despite her love for Gomez (ten.), the Spanish Ambassador, and in the face of the Pope's disapproval. Operas on Henry VIII's wives include Donizetti's *Anna Bolena* (1830) and Lillo's *Caterina Howard* (1849).

Hensel, Heinrich (*b* Neustadt, 29 Oct. 1874; *d* Hamburg, 23 Feb. 1935). German tenor. Studied Vienna and Milan. Début Freiburg, 1897; London, C.G., 1911, Loge and 1912-14; N.Y., Met., 1911, Lohengrin. Hamburg, 1912-29. First London Parsifal, a role he also sang at Bayreuth. Married the soprano **Elsa Schweitzer** (1878-1937), who sang at Dessau and Frankfurt.

Henze, Hans Werner (*b* Gütersloh, 1 July 1926). German composer. His first opera was *Das Wundertheater* (1948, 1 act) after Cervantes; then followed the radio opera *Ein Landarzt* (1951) and *Boulevard Solitude* (1950-1, prod.1952). The latter, a version of the Manon Lescaut story, was an instant success at its première; it makes much use of ballet, in which Henze has shown great interest, and is constructed in separate numbers, as is the radio opera which came next, *Das Ende einer Welt* (1953). This first reveals, in the form of a puncturing satire on snobbish arty society, Henze's consistent interest in the problem of the artist as man and his relationship and duty to his fellows.

König Hirsch (1952-5, prod, 1956) is a very large-scale treatment of a Gozzi fable, concerning the conflicting claims on a king's duty, and aroused violent enthusiasm and antagonism. Henze's special gift for a somewhat fantastic vein of lyricism was first fully revealed here, and this was perhaps brought to flower by his growing love of Italy, where he has latterly lived. In emphasizing the poetic timelessness of the hero's predicament in his next opera, *Der Prinz von Homburg* (1960), he further showed his distaste for German military values; these are subdued in his operatic treatment of Kleist's ambivalent soldier-dreamer. The score reveals a new power in absorbing the various influences and manners to which Henze has been dangerously subject by virtue of his sheer skill at all forms of musical language, while the vein of fantasy is undiminished. *Elegy for Young Lovers* (1961) concerns a great poet who feeds his art with the lives of all those around him, callously destroying them in the process if need be; a further treatment of Henze's ideas about the relationship between the artist and society, here portrayed as predator and prey, it is more disciplined in manner without excluding an affecting lyricism. *Der junge Lord* (1965) is a tart little satire on the *petit bourgeois* element in German life which Henze despises.

The *Bassarids* (1966), like *Elegy* to a text by W. H. Auden and Chester Kallman, is a more richly composed work, setting a new treatment of *The Bacchae*. Instructed by Auden to 'make his peace with Wagner' before beginning work on it, the opera shows a stronger, less wary acknowledgement of the German tradition than previously, and includes some fine large-scale music. A number of music theatre works followed, incl. *El Cimarrón* (1970) and *La cubana* (1974). *We Come to the River* (1976) marked Henze's return to opera, after a 10-year absence, with a work on a left-wing political subject using his familiar Romantic language. (R)

Herbert, Victor (*b* Dublin, 1 Feb. 1859; *d* New York, 26 May 1924). Irish-American composer. Went to N.Y. in 1886, where his wife, Therese Herbert-Förster (1861-1927), sang in the German Opera at the Met. while he was a cellist in the orchestra. Remembered chiefly as the composer of a large number of tuneful and highly successful operettas, Herbert also wrote two operas, *Natoma* (1911) and the 1-act *Madeleine* (1914).

Herincx, Raimund (*b* London, ?). English bass-baritone of Belgian parentage. Studied Belgium with Van Dyck and Italy with Valli. Début 1950, W.N.O., Figaro, 1956 title role in *Mefistofele*; S.W./E.N.O. from 1957, singing over 40 roles; C.G., 1968 King Fisher (*Midsummer Marriage*), returning to create Faber in *The Knot Garden* (1970) and the White Abbot in *Taverner* (1972), as well as singing Escamillo and Alfio; also created Segura in *Our Man in Havana* (Williamson). Boston 1967; Seattle 1977. Repertory also includes Wotan, Nick Shadow, Macbeth, Mephistopheles (Berlioz), and Creon and the Messenger (*Oedipus Rex*). (R)

Her Majesty's Theatre, Haymarket (for history before 1837, see *King's Theatre*). The King's T. was renamed Her Majesty's on the accession of Queen Victoria in 1837, during the management of *Laporte. Two years later, following Laporte's refusal to re-engage Tamburini as a protest against the clique of singers known as *La Vieille Garde*, he was succeeded by *Lumley, whose management lasted until 1859; and Lumley by *Mapleson 1862-7 and 1877-87. From 1847, the year C.G. opened, both

Lumley and Mapleson had to face the rivalry of a second Royal Italian Opera in London. Although the theatre was burnt down in 1867 and rebuilt two years later, it did not become an opera house again until 1877, which was the last year in which Tietjens sang. During the Lumley and Mapleson managements the first performances in England of many operas were given. These included the later Donizetti works, most of the early and middle Verdi works, *Les Pêcheurs de perles, Faust, Carmen,* and *Mefistofele*. The C.R. Company's London seasons of 1879, 1880, and 1882 were given there, and in the latter year a German company under Seidl gave the first London performance of the *Ring*. In 1886 there took place a French season in which Galli-Marié sang her original role of Carmen, and the following year Patti made her only appearance in that house. The theatre was pulled down in 1891 and the present building opened in 1897 under the management of Beerbohm Tree. There in the early 1900s occasional performances were given by the R.C.M. student class. *The Wreckers* received its English première there under Beecham in 1909; in the following year Beecham gave his season of *opéra comique* and in 1913 the London première of *Ariadne auf Naxos*. After the B.N.O.C. left C.G. in 1924, their London West End seasons were given there. The theatre has not housed opera for the last 50 years, except for Bernstein's opera-ballet *West Side Story* and the 1962 Tyrone Guthrie productions of Gilbert and Sullivan.

Hermann. A young officer (ten.), hero of Tchaikovsky's *The Queen of Spades*.

Hérodiade. Opera in 4 acts by Massenet; text by Paul Milliet and 'H. Grémont' (Georges Hartmann), after Flaubert's story (1877). Prod. Brussels, La M., 19 Dec. 1881, with Duvivier (as Salome), Deschamps, Vergnet, Manoury, cond. Dupont; New Orleans 13 Feb. 1892, with Cagniant, Duvivier (as Hérodiade), Verhees, Guillemot, Rey, Dulin, Rossi; London, C.G., 6 July 1904 (as *Salome*) with Calvé, Lunn, Dalmorès, Renaud, Plançon, cond. Lohse. The story is that of Salome, though it differs from Strauss's treatment in that John the Baptist (ten.) admits his love for Salome (sop.), who stabs herself after the jealous Herod (bar.) has had him killed.

Hérold, (Louis-Joseph-) Ferdinand (*b* Paris, 28 Jan. 1791; *d* Paris, 19 Jan. 1833). French composer. Studied Paris with his father, the composer Joseph Hérold, with Adam, Catel, and Méhul. Winning the Prix de Rome, he went to Italy and had his first opera *La gioventù di Enrico Quinto* successfully produced in Naples, 1815. Back in Paris, he collaborated with Boieldieu on *Charles de France* (1816), but had his first great success with *Les Rosières* (1817), following this up with another, *La Clochette* (1817). There followed other short, light works written while he was working as accompanist at the T.I., 1820-7; in 1827 he moved to the O. as répétiteur. He had renewed success with *Marie* (1826), a work combining elements of Italian vocal writing and Singspiel within an essentially French framework. Ambitious and hardworking, he continued trying to develop and improve his art, which reached its high point shortly before his early death with *Zampa* (1831) and *Le Pré aux clercs* (1832).

With the latter two works alone, Hérold earns a place as an important minor figure in the history of French opera. Though there are suggestions in his music of Rossini and (especially in *Zampa*) of Weber, not least in the increased importance given to the orchestra, he is essentially a follower of Boieldieu, with an individual vein of melody that attempts greater depths of Romantic feeling without forfeiting lightness of manner. His early death was a disaster for French opera: as he himself remarked in his last illness, 'I was just beginning to understand the stage.'

Herold, Vilhelm (Kristoffer) (*b* Hasle, 19 Mar. 1865; *d* Copenhagen, 15 Dec. 1937). Danish tenor. Studied Copenhagen; début Copenhagen 1893; Faust; Chicago 1893; London, C.G., 1904, Lohengrin, when his voice was compared to J. de Reszke's. Member of Stockholm Opera 1901-3, 1907-9. Opera director at Royal T. Copenhagen, 1922-4. Sang Pedro in *Tiefland* at Oslo in 1913 in the performance in which Flagstad made her début as Nuri. (R)

Herrenhausen. Suburb of *Hanover where festival performances are given in the baroque Heckentheater, built 1689-93 by Duke Johann Friedrich. In 1945, after the Hanover Opera was destroyed, a temporary theatre was established at Herrenhausen, and in 1945 the first post-war opera performances in all Germany were given there. Since 1954, when an annual summer festival was established, performances have been given both in the theatre and in the open-air, of operas by Monteverdi (*Orfeo*, *L'incoronazione di Poppea*), Handel (*Deidamia*, *Acis and Galatea*, *Ariodante*, *Giulio Cesare*, *Susanna*, *Serse*, *Scipione*), Mozart (*La clemenza di Tito*), and Scarlatti (*Il trionfo dell'-onore*).

Hertz, Alfred (*b* Frankfurt, 15 July 1872; *d* San Francisco, 17 Apr. 1942). German, later naturalized American, conductor. Studied Frankfurt; début Halle 1891. After appointments in Germany, went to N.Y., Met., in 1902 where he was conductor of German opera until 1915. He conducted the first American performances of *Parsifal* in 1903, which so enraged Cosima Wagner that the doors of all German opera houses were henceforth closed to him. He conducted the world premières of *Königskinder*, *Cyrano de Bergerac* (Damrosch), and the American premières of *Rosenkavalier* and *Salome*. He appeared in London, C.G., in 1910.

Herz, Joachim (*b* Dresden, 14 June 1924). German producer and administrator. Studied Dresden with Ernst Hintze (conducting), Heinz Arnold (producing); while studying, was répétiteur at Dresden Opera School. Further musical studies Berlin 1949-51. Producer Dresden-Radebeul touring opera, 1951-3; Berlin, K.O., as assistant to Felsenstein 1953-6; Cologne, 1956-7. Chief producer Leipzig Opera 1957, director of opera company 1959-76. Guest engagements Moscow, Buenos Aires, Hamburg, Frankfurt, Vienna, etc. London, E.N.O., *Salome*, 1975. A disciple of Felsenstein and believer in the concept of music theatre. Has also directed *Fliegende Holländer* on film (1963) and *Serse* for Danish TV (1973). Appointed director of Berlin K.O. after Felsenstein's death in 1976.
Bibl: H.-J. Irmer and W. Stein: *Joachim Herz* (1977).

Herzeleide. Kundry's (sop.) narration in Act 2 of *Parsifal*, in which she tells Parsifal of his mother.

Hesch, Wilhelm (orig. Vilém Heš) (*b* Týnec nad Labem, 3 July 1860; *d* Vienna, 3 Jan. 1908). Bohemian bass. Début Brno 1880, Kecal. Hamburg, 1893; Vienna 1894-1908 – leading bass during Mahler regime. Distinguished in Mozart repertory (Leporello, Osmin, Figaro, Sarastro, Alfonso) and as Rocco, Caspar, and Kecal, and in Wagner. (R)

Heuberger, Richard (Franz Joseph) (*b* Graz, 18 June 1850; *d* Vienna, 28 Oct. 1914). Austrian composer and critic. Wrote criticism for Viennese and Munich newspapers, succeeding Hanslick on the *Neue Freie Presse* in 1896; but best known for his series of operettas. The most successful was *Der Opernball* (1898); others are *Abenteuer eines Neujahrsnacht* (1886), *Manuel Venegas* (1889), *Mirjam* (1894), and *Barfüssele* (1905).

Heure Espagnole, L' (The Spanish Hour). Opera in 1 act by Ravel; text by Franc-Nohain, after his own comedy. Prod. Paris, O.C., 19 May 1911 with Vix, Périer cond. Ruhlmann; London, C.G., 24 July 1919 with Donalda, Maguénat, cond. Pitt; Chicago 5 Jan. 1920, with Gall, Maguénat cond. Hasselmans.

The clockmaker Torquemada (ten.) goes off to attend to the town clocks, leaving a customer, the muleteer Ramiro (bar.), in the shop to await his return. Concepción, (sop.), who is accustomed to receive her lovers in her husband's absence, sets him carrying clocks about. Gonzalve (ten.) a poet, enters and serenades her protractedly. On the arrival of a second lover, Don Inigo Gomez (bass), Ramiro is made to carry Gonzalve, hidden in a clock, up to the bedroom. The same happens to Don Inigo, while the first clock is brought down. Annoyed by their ineffectiveness, Concepción eventually admiringly orders Ramiro upstairs again – without a clock. Torquemada returns, finds the two lovers inside clocks 'examining' them, and effects a quick sale.

Hidalgo, Elvira de (*b* Aragón, 27 Dec. 1892). Spanish soprano. Studied Barcelona and Milan, with Bordalba and Vidal. Début Naples, 1908, Rosina. Sang all over the world. The last of the Spanish *soprani d'agilità*, who included Pacini, Galvany, Barrientos, and Pareto. Her repertory included Linda, Elvira, and Gilda. She taught in Athens, where she was the only teacher of Maria Callas; then in Ankara 1949-59, and since 1959 in Milan. (R)

Hilgermann, Laura (*b* Vienna, 13 Oct. 1867; *d* Vienna, 1937). Austrian mezzo. Studied Vienna with Karl Maria Wolf and S. Rosenberg. Début Prague, 1885, Azucena. Prague 1885-9; Budapest 1890-1900. Engaged by Mahler for Vienna 1900, remaining member of company until 1920; after leaving stage taught in Vienna. Roles included Dorabella. (R)

Hill, Karl (*b* Idstein, 9 May 1831; *d* Sachsenberg, 12 Jan. 1893). German baritone. Frankfurt 1858-9, Schwerin 1868-90, first Bayreuth Alberich (1876) and Klingsor (1882). Died insane.

Hiller (orig. Hüller), **Johann Adam** (*b* Wendisch-Ossig, 25 Dec. 1728; *d* Leipzig, 16 June 1804). German composer. Studied in Dresden, where he also sang as a boy and played the flute. Among his posts was that of Kapellmeister in Leipzig. More than any other single composer, he is the founder of *Singspiel, introducing into the pieces played by the Leipzig theatre company (who were not trained singers) separate Lieder which in his hands bore an added dramatic and characteristic force. He even included ensembles and something near the beginnings of the dramatic scena. The best known of his many Singspiels are *Der Teufel ist los* (1766) and *Die Jagd* (1770). His songs from these works became very popular throughout Germany, and it was Hiller's example that led to Goethe's interest in Singspiel.

Hin und Zurück (There and Back). *Sketch mit Musik* in 1 act by Hindemith; text by Marcellus Schiffer, after an English revue sketch. Prod. (with works by Milhaud, Toch, and Weill) Baden-Baden 17 July 1927, with J. Klemperer, Mergler, Lothar, Giebel, Pechner, cond. Mehlich; Philadelphia, 22 Apr. 1928; London,

S.W., 14 July 1958, by Opera da Camera of Buenos Aires, with Chevaline, Valori, Feller, cond. Sivieri.

After the murder of his unfaithful wife by a husband, supernatural intervention reverses the plot: the wife comes back to life, the lover retreats, the husband puts away his revolver, and all ends as it began.

Hindemith, Paul (*b* Hanau, 16 Nov. 1895; *d* Frankfurt, 28 Dec. 1963). German composer. His first three (1-act) operas are now forgotten –they are *Mörder, Hoffnung der Frauen* (text by Kokoschka) (1921), a Burmese marionette play *Das Nusch-Nuschi* (1921), and *Sancta Susanna* (1922). *Cardillac* (1926, rev. 1952) treated a tragic subject with emotional intensity, while *Neues vom Tage* (1929) is a sharp satire on the Press. Determinedly modern, the latter work includes an aria sung by the heroine in her bath praising the merits of electric heating over gas: this brought an injunction from the local gas company. *Mathis der Maler* (1938) is based on the life of the painter Matthias Grünewald, and aroused violent Nazi antagonism for its portrayal of peasants rebelling against authority, with the artist first siding with them and then withdrawing into his work. Even Furtwängler's vigorous advocacy could not prevent a ban on the scheduled Berlin première in 1934. *Die Harmonie der Welt* (1957) is based on the life of the astronomer Kepler, whose laws of planetary motion have a musical basis. Here Hindemith's thoughtfully evolved harmonic theories, which are founded on the harmonic series and its resulting tensions and relationships, are defended dramatically as being founded on natural laws rather than on the arbitrary rules which he saw as the weakness of dodecaphony. But the central dramatic theme, as in *Mathis*, is the relationship of the artist or scientist to the social or political movements of his time, and of his private life to his work. Hindemith's last opera, after Thornton Wilder, was a drama of different generations appearing simultaneously, *Der lange Weihnachtsmahl* (1961).
Bibl: G. Skelton: *Paul Hindemith* (1975).

Hines (orig. Heinz), **Jerome** (*b* Hollywood, 8 Nov. 1921). American bass. Studied Los Angeles. Début San Francisco, 1941, Biterolf. After appearances with various small U.S. companies, auditioned and engaged for N.Y. Met., 1947. Milan, Sc., 1958-9, Hercules (Handel); Edinburgh Festival, 1953, Nick Shadow. A fine Boris, Grand Inquisitor, and Gurnemanz, which he sang at Bayreuth 1958; returned 1959-60, King Mark and Wotan. (R)

Hislop, Joseph (*b* Edinburgh, 5 Apr. 1884; *d* Lundin Links, 3 May 1977). Scottish tenor and teacher. Studied Stockholm with Gillis Brett, and Italy. Début Stockholm, 1914, Faust.

London, C.G., 1920-8; Chicago 1920; toured U.S.A. with Scotti Company, 1921. A fine Puccini and Verdi singer who also specialized in the French repertory (Faust, Roméo, Des Grieux); last appearance Stockholm 1937. Taught in Stockholm 1936-49 where one of his pupils was Birgit Nilson. Later adviser on singing at C.G. and S.W. (R)

Hoengen, Elisabeth (b Gevelsberg, Westphalia, 7 Dec. 1906). German mezzo-soprano. Studied Berlin with Hermann Weissenborn. Début Wuppertal 1933. After engagements at Düsseldorf (1935-40) and Dresden (1940-3), became leading singer at Vienna, S.O. London, C.G., 1947, with Vienna Company, and 1959-60; N.Y., Met., 1951-2. An impressive singing actress, particularly noted for her Lady Macbeth, Klytemnestra, Herodias, and Ortrud. From 1957 taught in Vienna. (R)

Hoesslin, Franz von (b Munich, 31 Dec. 1885; d nr Sète, 28 Sept. 1946). German conductor. Studied Munich with Reger and Mottl. Début St Gall, 1908. Held appointments at Riga, Lübeck, Mannheim, Berlin, Dessau, Barmen-Elberfeld, and Breslau. Bayreuth 1927-8, 1934, 1928-40. Then followed his Jewish wife into exile in Switzerland. Killed in air-crash. (R)

Hoffman, Grace (Goldie) (b Cleveland, 14 Jan. 1925). American mezzo. Studied New York with Friedrich Schorr and Milan with Mario Basiola. Début 1951, Lola in U.S. touring company. Florence 1951, Priestess in Aïda. Zurich 1953-5; Stuttgart since 1955. London, with Stuttgart Company 1955, C.G., 1959-60, 1961, 1964-6, 1970-1; N.Y., Met., 1958. Bayreuth since 1957, and guest appearances elsewhere in Europe. Equally at home in Verdi and Wagner; has sung successfully as Eboli, Brangaene, and Kundry. (R)

Hoffmann, E.T.A. (Ernst Theodor Amadeus, orig. Wilhelm) (b Königsberg, 24 Jan. 1776; d Berlin, 25 June 1822). German novelist, critic, conductor, and composer. One of the most famous and influential figures of the Romantic movement in literature. Directed the Bamberg T. Company 1808, and the Seconda Company in Leipzig and Dresden 1813-14. After a Singspiel Die Maske (1799), he wrote Scherz, List und Rache for Posen (1801); two Singspiels (not prod.) followed, Der Renegat (1804) and Faustina (1804), then Die lustigen Musikanten (1804), Der Canonicus von Mailand (1805), Liebe und Eifersucht (1808), Der Trank der Unsterblichkeit (1808), Dirna (1809), Aurora (1812), Saul (1811), and – his most famous opera – Undine (1816). All are number operas with dialogue, though Aurora and Undine have important freely composed finales.

Undine anticipates much in later Romantic opera. It was greatly admired by Weber, whose review is famous for its statement of Romantic

ideals, as an example of, 'the opera Germans want, a self-contained work of art in which all elements, contributed by the related arts in collaboration, merge into one another and are absorbed in various ways so as to create a new world'. Undine also contains another curious anticipation of Wagner in its final destruction of the lovers in what is referred to as a Liebestod (though the music at this point is quite un-Wagnerian). As a critic Hoffmann took an equivocal position about Romanticism: he had a wary friendship with Weber, whose Freischütz was attacked in some notorious anonymous articles possibly by him; in Berlin in 1821 he translated the rival opera Olympie for Spontini. But his writings, especially his short stories such as the sensitive and imaginative tale Don Juan (reflecting his love for Mozart, whose middle name he took in homage), influenced more than a generation of Romantic writers and composers.

Hoffmann himself appears in operas by Laccetti (Hoffman, 1912), Kosa (Anselmus diák, 1944), and Besch (1945), and in Offenbach's setting of three of his stories, Les *Contes d'Hoffmann (1881): these are Der Sandmann, Geschichte vom verlorenen Spiegelbilde, and Rath Krespel. Operas on his works are as follows:
Fantasiestücke in Callots Manier (1814): Malipiero (I Capricci di Callot, 1942).
Der goldene Topf (1815): Braunfels (unfin.): Petersen (1941); Kosa (1945).
Die Elixiere des Teufels (1816): Rodwell (1829).
Nussknacker und Mausekönig (1816): Szeligowski (Kratatuk, 1955).
Der Sandmann (1817): Adam (La poupée de Nuremberg, 1852); Audran (La Poupée, 1896).
Das Majorat (1817): Weigl (Die eisene Pforte, 1823).
Klein Zaches (1819): Hausegger (Zinnober, 1898).
Meister Martin der Küfer und seine Gesellen (1819): Weissheimer (1879); Blockx (Maître Martin, 1892); Lacombe (1897).
Die Bergwerke von Falun (1819): libretto by Wagner for Dessauer (unused, 1842); Holstein (Der Haideschacht, 1868).
Rath Krespel (1819): Cadaux (Le Violon de Crémone, n.d.).
Die Brautwahl (1820): Busoni (1912).
Signor Formica (1820): Rastrelli (1832); Schütt (1892).
Das Fräulein von Scuderi (1819): Stern and Zamarra (Der Goldschmied von Toledo, 1919); Hindemith (Cardillac, 1926, rev. 1952).
Die Königsbraut (1821): Offenbach (Le Roi Carotte, 1872).
Prinzessin Brambilla (1821): Braunfels (1909).
Also: Elsner (Stary trzpiot i młody medrzec, 1805); Harsányi (Illusion, 1949).

Bibl: E. Istel (ed.): *E.T.A. Hoffmanns musikalische Schriften* (1907).

Hofmann, Ludwig (*b* Frankfurt, 14 Jan. 1895; *d* Frankfurt, 28 Dec. 1963). German bass-baritone. Studied Frankfurt and Milan. Début Bamberg 1918. London, C.G., 1932, 1939, and 1955; N.Y., Met., 1932-8. Berlin, Stä. O., 1918-32; S.O., 1932-5. Vienna 1935-55. Appeared regularly Bayreuth and Vienna in both Wagner bass and baritone roles and the Italian and French repertory. (R)

Hofmannsthal, Hugo von (*b* Vienna, 1 Feb.1874; *d* Rodaun, 15 July 1929). Austrian poet and dramatist. Operas of Strauss for which he wrote librettos are *Elektra* (1906-8), *Der Rosenkavalier* (1909-10), *Ariadne auf Naxos* (1st version, 1911-12; 2nd version,.1915-16), *Die Frau ohne Schatten* (1914-17), *Die ägyptische Helene* (1924-7; rev. 1933), and *Arabella* (1930-2). The collaboration is recorded in detail in their published correspondence. He also wrote the libretto for Wellesz's *Alkestis* (1924); his play *Die Hochzeit der Sobeide* was the source of Cherepnin's opera (1933); and his *Das Berwerk zu Falun* of Wagner-Regény's opera (1961).
Bibl: F. and A. Strauss (ed.): *Briefwechsel Richard Strauss und Hugo von Hofmannsthal* (1926, 2/1955; Eng. trans. 1961).

Hofoper (*Ger* Court Opera). The name given in pre-1918 days to the Court or Royal Opera houses in a number of German and Austrian cities, including Munich and Vienna.

Ho-jo-to-ho! Brünnhilde's war-cry in Act 2 of Wagner's *Die Walküre.*

Holbrooke, Josef (*b* Croydon, 5 July 1878; *d* London, 5 Aug. 1958). English composer. Studied London, R.A.M., with Corder. His first opera was *Pierrot and Pierrette* (1909). He then devoted himself to a massive quasi-Wagnerian trilogy on Celtic legends, *The Cauldron of Annwyn,* whose constituent parts were *The Children of Don* (1912), *Dylan, Son of the Wave* (1914), and *Bronwen* (1929). He also wrote three slighter works, *The Enchanter* (1915), *The Stranger* (1924), and *The Snob.* Holbrooke's music has considerable imaginative power. The Celtic trilogy suffered from the turn away from Wagner at about the time it was being composed, but is also damaged, despite some pages which suggest a feeling for mythical opera, by a lack of self-criticism.

Holland. Hacquart's *De triomfeerende Min* (The Triumph of Love), written in 1679 to celebrate the Peace of Nijmegen, was rather more than incidental music to a play though hardly yet an opera. Slow to develop an independent tradition, Holland was for long dependent on visiting Italian, French, and German companies. The many short-lived Dutch national opera companies were shared between Amsterdam and The Hague. An early attempt at Dutch opera was by J.B. van Bree (1801-57) with *Sapho* (1834). However, despite encouragement to opera, little developed, though an enlightened welcome was given to much foreign opera that was staged in Holland. The Wagner Vereeniging (1883) had great success in stimulating interest in its subject. A new impulse came in modern times, especially with the example of Willem Pijper (1894-1947) and his *Halewijn* (1933). Henk Badings (*b* 1907) had some success with *De Nachtwacht* (The Night Watch, 1942).

The Holland Festival, founded 1947 by H.J. Reinink, with Peter Diamand as secretary and later artistic guiding light, is unique in being a nation-wide festival, centred on Amsterdam and The Hague. It embraces music, drama, and the visual arts as well as other entertainments. Opera has always played an important part, and the programmes have shown a high regard for quality as well as great enterprise. Operas have included *Oberon* (1950), *Lulu* (1953), *From the House of the Dead* (1954), *Von Heute auf Morgen* and *Erwartung* (1958), *Benvenuto Cellini* (1961), and Haydn's *Orfeo.*
See also *Amsterdam, The Hague, Maastricht.*

Holm, Richard (*b* Stuttgart, 3 Aug. 1912). German tenor. Studied Stuttgart with Rudolf Ritter. After concert and radio appearances in Stuttgart 1936-7, engaged by Kiel Opera in 1937. After engagements in Nuremberg and Hamburg, joined Bavarian State Opera, Munich, in 1948. London, C.G., 1953, David; 1958-60, 1964-6 Loge; also Flamand in first London *Capriccio* with Munich Opera; Gly. 1950, Belmonte; N.Y., Met., 1952-3 David; appearances at Bayreuth, Salzburg, Vienna, etc. Repertory also includes Xerxes, Titus, Tamino, which he sang in Felsenstein's production of *Zauberflöte* at Berlin K.O. Novagerio in *Palestrina,* Robespierre in *Dantons Tod,* and Aschenbach in *Death in Venice.* A well-schooled and sensitive performer with pleasing if not very large voice. Professor of singing at the Munich Hochschule für Musik since 1967. (R)

Holst, Gustav (Theodore) (*b* Cheltenham, 21 Sept. 1874; *d* London, 25 May 1934). English composer of Swedish origin. His first five operatic works are now forgotten: the first four are said to be pale Sullivan; and Holst afterwards dismissed the fifth, *Sita* (1899-1906, unprod.) as 'good old Wagnerian bawling'. Wagner's influence is superficial (there is a poor attempt to match his *Stabreim* in English); it is abandoned in the next opera, also on a Sanskrit subject, *Savitri* (comp. 1909, prod. 1916). This 1-act opera, the first important English chamber opera since *Dido and Aeneas,* is a pioneer work: it points forward to the modern chamber opera taken up especially by Britten, it dispenses with the proscenium arch (and can well be performed in the open air), and it shows an understanding of Eastern ideas far in advance of its time. Using only three voices (and a wordless chorus) and 12 instruments, it achieves a very strong and individual atmosphere with great economy of means, not least through a characteristic and imaginative dramatic use of bitonality.

The Perfect Fool (1923) displays an essential Holstian dichotomy: an earthy, conversational manner is set against one more ethereal and remote. At The Boar's Head (1925) collects all the Falstaff episodes from Shakespeare's Henry plays, and though lively and energetic is almost self-defeatingly ingenious. The Tale of the Wandering Scholar (1934, later retitled The Wandering Scholar; rev. Britten 1951; ed. Britten and I. Holst, 1968) is a 1-act chamber opera which returns with success to the comic style he originally sought. Laconic and deft, it has a certain dryness, but at its best the dryness of good wit.

Bibl: I. Holst: The Music of Gustav Holst (1951, 2/1968).

Holzbauer, Ignaz (Jakob) (b Vienna, 17 Sept. 1711; d Mannheim, 7 Apr. 1783). Austrian composer. Studied in Venice. He held various posts as Kapellmeister, including in Vienna (1744-6), Stuttgart (1750), and Mannheim (1753). The most famous of his operas was Günther von Schwarzburg (1776); which was much admired by Mozart; this is significant as the first effort at using a German subject in a full-length German opera, with recitative replacing the dialogue of Singspiel and with the individual numbers showing some attempt at a loosening of form.

Home, Sweet Home. Originally an aria in Bishop's Clari, or The Maid of Milan (called by the composer a 'Sicilian Air'); also occurs in altered form in Donizetti's Anna Bolena, which resulted in Bishop's bringing an action for 'piracy and breach of copyright'. It used to be sung by Patti, Melba, and other prima donnas in the Lesson scene in The Barber; they often accompanied themselves on a piano wheeled on to the stage for the purpose.

Homer, Louise (orig. Louise Dilworth Beatty) (b Pittsburgh, 28 Apr. 1871; d Winter Park, Florida, 6 May 1947). American contralto. Studied Philadelphia and Boston, where she met the composer Sidney Homer and married him. He took her to Paris, where she studied with Fidèle König and Lhérie. Début Vichy 1898 Leonora (La favorite). London, C.G., 1899, Lola; San Francisco 1900, Amneris. Leading contralto N.Y., Met., 1900-19. Sang Orfeo and Hate (Armide) in the famous Toscanini performances at the Met. Created the Witch in Königskinder (1910), and leading roles in Manrù

(Paderewski), Mona (Parker), and The Pipe of Desire (Converse). Returned to Met., 1927-9. Much admired in Wagner. (R)

Bibl: A. Homer: Louise Homer and the Golden Age of Opera (1974).

Honegger, Arthur (b Le Havre, 10 Mar. 1892; d Paris, 27 Nov. 1955). French-born composer of Swiss parentage. His first dramatic work, Le Roi David (1921), established him as a composer of importance; already in it is present the extremely characteristic opposition of a delicate, simply framed style, often expressed almost archaically, to an aggressive, barbaric modernity associated with thick harmony and severe rhythms. This was followed by the opera Antigone (1927), the Biblical opera Judith (1926), the melodrama Amphion (1931), the operetta Les Aventures du Roi Pausole (1930), and the stage oratorio Cris du Monde (1930-1) before his best-known work, the stage oratorio Jeanne d'Arc au bûcher (1936). This is marked by the same unerringly apt use of means, sometimes very slender means, within a large framework as in David. Part melodrama (the main role is spoken), part oratorio, part opera, it is the most successful realization of Honegger's essential dualism. The attempts to fuse his opposing elements continue (as before, the special titles perhaps reflect what he felt as a special problem) in the opera L'Aiglon (1937, with Ibert), the 'spectacle' Les Mille et Une Nuits (1937), the operetta Les Petites Cardinal (1937), the dramatic legend Nicolas de Flue (1941), and the opera Charles le Téméraire (1944).

Hook, James (b Norwich, 3 June 1746; d Boulogne, 1827). English composer. He wrote some 30 operas and operettas for London theatres; very popular in their day, these were essentially plays with interpolated numbers, often based on popular or folk tunes.

Hopf, Hans (b Nuremberg, 2 Aug. 1916). German tenor. Studied Munich with Paul Bender. Début 1936 with Bayerische Landesbühnen. After engagements at Augsburg, Oslo, Dresden, and Berlin, joined Munich Opera 1949. London, C.G., 1951-3, 1963; N.Y., Met., 1952-5. Has participated in Bayreuth, Salzburg, and Munich Festivals; among his best roles are Max (Freischütz), the Kaiser (Frau ohne Schatten), and Otello. Repertory also includes Siegfried and Tristan. (R)

Horn, Charles Edward (b London, 21 June 1786; d Boston, 21 Oct. 1849). English singer and composer. Studied with his father Karl Friedrich Horn, and Bath with Rauzzini. Début London, Ly., 1809. He took part in many English operatic ventures as singer and conductor, and was responsible for bringing Balfe to London in 1823. As well as his own works, he sang Caspar in Der Freischütz at D.L., 1824. His voice was said to be poor but of extensive range, so that he could sing tenor as well as baritone parts.

Horn's operas are for the most part plays with inserted songs, sometimes the work of others. *Paul Pry* (1826) includes 'Cherry Ripe'. His only full-scale opera was *Ahmed el Ramel* (1840, lost); however, he was possibly the first composer to write an all-sung English opera, *Dirce* (1823); though lost apart from a single duet, this seems to have been a Metastasian opera using recitative. He also produced some operas in America, including five in N.Y., and adapted others.

Horne, Marilyn (*b* Bradford, Penn., 16 Jan. 1929). American mezzo-soprano. Studied University of Southern California with William Vennard and attended Lotte Lehmann's master-classes. In 1954 she dubbed the singing voice for Dorothy Dandridge in film *Carmen Jones.* Début Gelsenkirchen, 1957, Giulietta; remained there until 1960, singing variety of roles including Marie (*Wozzeck*), Minnie, Fulvia (*Ezio*). San Francisco, 1960; N.Y., American Opera Society, 1962, Agnese in *Beatrice di Tenda* with Sutherland, which began a collaboration between the two artists that continued in the Bellini and Rossini repertory. London, C.G., 1965 Marie, 1967 Adalgisa; Milan, Sc., 1969, Neocle (*L'assedio di Corinto*); N.Y., Met., since 1970. Repertory also includes Arsace, Adalgisa, Isabella, Rosina, Carmen. Possesses a large rich voice of enormous compass (she has also sung some Wagner) and an outstanding vocal technique. (R)

Hosenrolle. See *Travesti.*

Hotter, Hans·(*b* Offenbach-am-Main, 19 Jan. 1909). German bass-baritone. After a period as organist, choirmaster, and student of church music, he turned to opera. Studied with Matthaeus Roemer, a De Reszke pupil. Début Opava 1929, Speaker (*Zauberflöte*). After engagements in Prague, Breslau, and Hamburg (1934-8) he became a member of the Munich and Vienna Operas, dividing his time between these two houses. London, C.G., 1947 with Vienna Company and regularly until 1967, especially in Wagner; N.Y., Met., 1950-4. Created the Commandant (*Friedenstag*) and Olivier (*Capriccio*). He established himself as the leading exponent of Wotan at postwar Bayreuth; he is also a distinguished Dutchman, Borromeo (*Palestrina*), and Grand Inquisitor. An intellectual singer in the best sense of the word, and highly endowed as an actor and musician. Responsible for the new production of *The Ring* at C.G., 1961-4. He sang his last Wotan in Paris, June 1972. (R)

House of the Dead, From the (Cz., *Z mrtvého domu*). Opera in 3 acts by Janáček; text by composer, after Dostoyevsky's novel based on his prison reminiscenses (1862). Prod. Brno, 12

Apr. 1930, with Šíma, Žlábková, Fischer Olšovský, Pelc, Šindler, Pribytkov, cond Bakala; Edinburgh, by Prague Nat. T., 28 Aug 1964, with Jedlička, Tattermuschová, Blachu Kocí, Zídek, Karpísek, Švorc, cond. Grego N.Y., Net T.V., 3 Dec. 1969, with Rounsevill Lloyd, Jagel, Reardon, cond. Hermann Adler

Though virtually without plot, the opera' handling of scenes from Siberian prison life i framed by the arrival and eventual departure c a political prisoner, Alexander Goryanchiko (bass) (in the book, Dostoyevsky himself). It i also lent continuity by being constructe around a series of long narratives by sever prisoners. Janáček's original ending was wit the remaining prisoners being herded bac into the House of the Dead, their prison, by guard; a revised version by Bakala an Chlubna maintains the optimism of the fin chorus to the end.

Houston. Town in Texas, U.S.A. The Housto Grand Opera Association was founded in 195 and until 1966 a limited annual season of thre to four operas a year was given in the Housto Music Hall (cap 3,000), under the music directo Walter Herbert. In Oct. 1966 the Jesse H. Jone Hall for the Performing Arts (cap 3,000) wa opened, and became the home of the compan and the number of annual productions wa increased to five (six in 1970). In 1973 Davi Gockley, associate director, was appointe general director in succession to Hubert an increased the number of performances pe season from 27 to 45, performing each opera i English and the original language and givin chances to young American artists. The pre mière of Pastieri's *The Seagull* was given i Mar. 1974.

Hugh the Drover. Opera in 2 acts by Vaugha Williams; text by Harold Child. Prod. Londor R.C.M., 7 July 1924 (dress rehearsal, with D Foras, Benson, Trefor Jones, Leyland White cond. Waddington); first public performance H.M.'s 14 July 1924, by B.N.O.C., with Mar Lewis, Willis, Tudor Davies, Frederic Collie cond. Sargent; revived with added Act 2 sc. ' R.C.M. 15 June 1933, cond. Beecham Washington, 21 Feb. 1928, with Montan Tudor Davies, cond. Goossens.

Mary (sop.) is engaged to John the Butche (bass-bar.), whom Hugh (ten.) defeats in boxing match for her hand. He is then accuse of being a Napoleonic spy, but the arrestin sergeant recognizes him and removes Joh instead. Hugh leaves with Mary.

Hughes, Arwel (*b* Rhosllanerchrugog, 25 Au 1909). Welsh composer. His *Menna* (1953) wa an early Welsh opera on a national theme.

Hugo, Victor (*b* Besançon, 26 Feb. 1802; Paris, 22 May 1885). French poet, novelist, an playwright. His only attempt at a libretto wa

is adaptation of *Notre-Dame de Paris* as *smeralda* for Bertin (1836); but his vigorous iomantic polemics, both by precept and by xample, exercised a great influence on libret-ists and hence upon Romantic opera. Operas ›n his works are as follows:
Marian Delorme (1829): Bottesini (1862); Pedrotti (1865); Ponchielli (1885).
es Orientales (1829): J. Cohen (*Les Bluets*, 1867).
Hernani (1830): Bellini (unfin., sketched 1830); Gabussi (1834); Mazzucato (1843); Verdi (1844); Laudamo (1849); Hirschmann (1908).
Notre-Dame de Paris (1831): L. Bertin (1836); Birch-Pfeiffer (1836); Rodwell (*Quasimodo*, 1836); Prévost (*c*1840); Mazzucato (1838); Dargomzyhsky (1847); Poniatowski (1847); Battista (censored title *Ermelinda*, 1851; rev. as *Esmeralda*, 1857); Lebeau (1857); W. Fry (1864); Wetterham (1866); Campana (1869); Pedrell (*Quasimodo*, 1875); G. Thomas (*Esmeralda*, 1883); Giro (1897); F. Schmidt (1914); Bosch y Humet (*Febo*, early 20th cent).
e Roi s'amuse (1832): Verdi (*Rigoletto*, 1851).
ucrèce Borgia (1833): Donizetti (1833).
Marie Tudor (1833): Balfe (*The Armourer of Nantes*, 1836); Schoberlechner (*Rossana*, 1839); Ferrari (*Maria d'Inghilterra*, 1840); Pacini (1843); Bognar (1856); Kashperov (1860); Chiaromonte (1862); Blaramberg (*Maria Burgundskaya*, 1878); Gomes (1879); Wagner-Régeny (*Der Günstling*, 1935).
Angelo (1835): Mercadante (*Il giuramento*, 1837); Ponchielli (*La gioconda*, 1876); Cui (1876); Villate (1880); Bruneau (1928).
Ruy Blas (1838): Poniatowski (1843); Besanzoni (1843); G. Rota (1858); W. Glover (1861); Zenger (1868); Marchetti (1869); G. Braga (comp. 1868); F. Franchetti (1868); Pietri (1916).
es Burgraves (1843): Salvi (1845); Dobrzyński (1860); Orsini (1881); Podesta (1881); L. Nielsen (1917); Sachs (1926).
es Misérables (1862): Duniecki (1864); Bonsignore (1925); Michetti (*Vagabonda*, 1933); after Pt 1: Ratbert (*L'Italie*); Pt 2, les Pauvres gens: Gilson (*Zeewik*, 1904).
'Homme qui rit (1869): Ronzi (1894); Enna (*Komedianter*, 1920); Pedrollo (1920).
Torquemada (1882): Rota (1943).
a Légende des siècles (1859-85): Mancinelli (*Isora di Provenza*, 1884).
a Grand-mère: Silver (1930).

Huguenots, Les. Opera in 5 acts by Meyerbeer; ext by Scribe and Deschamps. Prod. Paris, O., 29 Feb. 1836, with Falcon, Dorus-Gras, Nourrit, .evasseur; New Orleans 29 Apr. 1839, with Julia Calvé, Banberger, Huymann, Bailly; .ondon, C.G., 20 June 1842, with Stöckl-Heinefetter, Lutzer, Wettlaufer, Breiting, Mel-

linger, Schwener, Staudigl, cond. Lachner. At the Met., in the 1890s the performances were known as the *nuits des sept étoiles*, when the cast included Nordica, Melba, Scalchi, Jean and Édouard de Reszke, Maurel, and Plançon. It was the work chosen to open the present C.G. building in 1858.

Hullah, John (Pyke) (*b* Worcester, 27 June 1812; *d* London, 21 Feb. 1884). English composer and manager. Studied London with Horsley and Crivelli. Wrote the music to Charles Dickens's *The Village Coquettes* (1836). His *The Barbers of Bassora* and *The Outpost* were produced at C.G., in 1837 and 1838. He subsequently turned to teaching and the training of teachers.

Hummel, Johan Nepomuk (b Poszony, 14 Nov. 1778; *d* Weimar, 17 Oct. 1837). Austro-Hungarian composer and pianist. Opera played a small part in his output, and the best known of his dramatic works is *Mathilde von Guise* (1810): this attempts to adapt Mozartian methods to Romantic manners. He also wrote a new finale to Auber's *Gustave III* in 1836.

Humming Chorus. The name usually given to the hidden chorus which ends the first scene of Act 2 of Puccini's *Madama Butterfly* as Butterfly, Suzuki, and the baby take up their stance at the *shosi* awaiting Pinkerton.

Humperdinck, Engelbert (*b* Siegburg, 1 Sept. 1854; *d* Neustrelitz, 27 Sept. 1921). German composer. He assisted Wagner in the preparation of *Parsifal* at Bayreuth in 1880-1, even composing a few bars of it (later discarded) to cover a transformation. His own first opera, *Hänsel und Gretel* (1893), has remained his most successful. Its simple nursery tunes are used in a superficially Wagnerian manner, though there is no systematic attempt to develop an association between persons or ideas and a musical motive. A work of unique charm, it has been an enduring success with German children, perhaps still more with nostalgic German parents. His next work, *Die sieben Geislein* (1895), was also based on a story from the Grimms; and this was followed by what was later to be his most popular work after *Hänsel*, *Königskinder* (1897), which made constructive use of melodrama. *Dornröschen* (1902) was a third attempt to write a fairy-tale opera, but proved less successful than *Hänsel*. *Die Heirat wider Willen* (1905), after Dumas, was first conducted in Berlin by Richard Strauss; here Humperdinck seems to look back to an earlier tradition in German Romantic opera before Wagner. The better known version of *Königskinder*, given in N.Y. in 1910, was a recomposition of the melodrama of 1897. Later works were two Spielopern, *Die Marketenderin* (1914) and *Gaudeamus* (1919); these are said to suffer from weak librettos. His son

Wolfram Humperdinck (*b* Frankfurt, 29 Apr. 1893) worked as a producer in Detmold, Leipzig 1933-41, then was Intendant at Kiel 1941-5.

Hunding. A Neiding (bass), husband of Sieglinde, in Wagner's *Die Walküre*.

Hungary. The Turkish occupation from 1541 to 1686 inhibited the development of national music, and Hungary's first opera performances were given in Poszony by visiting Italian companies (*Mingotti, 1740; Bon, 1760; Zamperini, 1764). From 1762 Haydn directed his operas at Kismarton (Eisenstadt); and in 1768 his *Lo speziale* opened Prince Esterházy's theatre at Esterház, where many of his operas were performed. Other nobles' theatres included that of Count Erdődy at Poszony, where the first Mozart opera in Hungary was given (*Entführung*, 1785), and that of Bishop Patachich at Nagyvárad, where Dittersdorf worked (1764-9). In Buda and Pest performance were given in German (from 1787) and in Hungarian (1793-6, 1807-15). From 1790 a Piarist School in Pest had begun working towards national opera by staging Singspiels and opere buffe; but the first Singspiel in Hungarian was *Pikkó Herceg* (Prince Pikkó, 1793) by Jószef Chudy (1751 or 1753–1813) (music lost, but evidently Hungarian songs interpolated in a Viennese-style *Zauberposse*).

In the early years of the 19th cent., the German company included works, especially by Mozart, Beethoven, and Weber, which keenly interested Hungarian musicians; the inclusion of many Italian and French works (Rossini, Bellini, Donizetti, Verdi, Auber, Meyerbeer) soon after their premières gave an example to the tentatively emerging Hungarian national opera. Some composers, including János Lavotta (1764-1820), Antal Csermák (1774-1822), and János Bihari (1764-1827), began using Hungarian elements in their operas; others incorporated sections of foreign works into their operas. The first true Hungarian opera (though in fact it includes German and Italian elements) was *Béla Király Futása* (King Béla's Flight, 1822) by Jószef Ruzitska (1758-1823), which made use of the national *verbunkos* music, and became very popular. Other operas followed, notably Ruzitska's *Kemény Simon* (1822), *Csel* (The Trick, 1839) by András Bartay (1799-1854), *Visegrádi Kincskeresők* (The Treasure-Seekers of Visegrad, 1839) by Mark Rózsavölgyi (1789-1848) and *Benyovszky* (1847) by Ferenc Doppler (1821-83). These combine large dramatic scenes based on Italian and Viennese models with lyrical and heroic episodes deriving their style from the *verbunkos*.

The true founder of Hungarian opera was Ferenc *Erkel, the first composer gifted enough to fuse the above elements into a vivid and personal musical language. From 1838 he directed the Nemzeti Szinház (National T.) which had opened in Pest on 22 Aug. 1837. Hitherto Hungarian opera companies had worked in provincial towns, from 1799 in Koloszvár (*Cluj) and Debrecen, from 1818 in Székesfehérvár, from 1828 in Kassa (*Košice). Erkel's most important fellow-composer was Mihály *Mosonyi; others included Karoly Thern (1817 86), Ferenc Doppler (1821-83), Károly Doppler (1825-1900), György Császár (1813-50), Ignác Bognár (1811-83), and Károly Huber (1828-85) but for all their useful experimental work they could not match Erkel's example. A parallel development, to which Erkel contributed, was the *népszinmű*, or popular play, which had musical insertions similar to ballad opera.

In 1884 Erkel moved to the newly opened Operaház (Opera House), where he directed a large repertory. His death in 1893 opened the theatre to Wagner, whom he had tried to resist, and of a Wagnerian generation which followed in the period of Hans *Richter's direction, the most outstanding was Ödön Mihalovich (1842-1929), composer of Wagnerian operas including *Toldi szerelme* (The Love of Toldi, 1893) and a founder of the Budapest Wagner Society. A number of composers found international careers, especially in other Habsburg lands: those who continued to work for national opera at home included Ferenc Sáros (1855-1913), Jenő Sztojanovics (1846-1919) and Emil *Abrányi. Their work helped to pave the way for the major talents of Béla *Bartók and Zoltán *Kodály. Other successful opera composers of the inter-war years included Ferenc Farkas (*b* 1905), Leó Weiner (1885-1960), Albert Siklós (1878-1942), Jenő Kenessy (*b* 1906), Jenő Adam (*b* 1896) and Pál Kadosa (*b* 1903). Since 1945 opera has continued to spread and develop, and new companies have been formed in many provincial and industrial centres. Emil Petrovice's (*b* 1930) operas include *C'est la guerre* (1962), *Lysistrata* (1971), and *Crime and Punishment* (1970). Sandor Szokolay (*b* 1931) has established himself with *Blood Wedding* (1964), *Hamlet* (1968), and *Samson* (1973).

See also *Budapest, Debrecen, Eszterháza, Pécs, Szeged*.

Hüni-Mihacsek, Felice (*b* Pécs, 3 Apr. 1891; *d* Munich, 26 Mar 1976). Hungarian soprano Studied Vienna with Rose Papier. Début Vienna 1919; Munich State Opera 1926-45. One of the best Mozart singers of the inter-war years (Fiordiligi, Constanze, Queen of Night, Donna Anna), and also a distinguished Marschallin and Eva. Last stage appearances Munich 1953, Marschallin. (R)

Hunter, Rita (Nellie) (*b* Wallasey, 15 Aug. 1933) English soprano. Studied with Edwin Francis, Eva Turner, and Redvers Llewellyn. After appearing in the choruses of musical comedies, joined S.W. Chorus in 1954, remaining there for two years, occasionally singing small roles (eg. First Bridesmaid in *Figaro*). C.R. 1956-8 as Inez, Frasquita, etc. S.W. as soloist from 1959; her roles included Marcellina in *Figaro*, Senta, Odabella; from 1968, Leonora (*Trovatore*), Donna Anna, Brünnhilde in the E.N.O. *Ring*, Amelia, and Elisabeth de Valois. London, C.G., as Third Norn 1963; N.Y., Met., from 1972, Brünnhilde, Santuzza, Aida; San Francisco, 1975, Norma. A strong, brilliant, and very pure voice and an appealing personality distinguish her stage presence, despite her substantial physique. (R)

Hunyadi László. Opera in 4 acts by Erkel; text by Béni Egressy, after the drama by Lőrinc Tóth. Prod. Budapest 27 Jan. 1844.

Huon of Bordeaux. A knight (ten.), Duke of Guienne, hero of Weber's *Oberon*.

Hüsch, Gerhard (*b* Hanover, 2 Feb. 1901). German baritone. Studied with Hans Emge. Début Osnabrück 1923 as Liebernau (*Waffenschmied*). Engagements in Cologne (1927-30) and Berlin (1930-42), first at the Stä. O., then at the S.O. London, C.G., 1930, Falke in Walter's famous *Fledermaus* production; subsequently heard as Papageno. Bayreuth 1930-1 when he sang an outstanding Wolfram in *Tannhäuser*. After a few post-war appearances, devoted himself to teaching; pupils include Hammond-Stroud.(R)

Hyde, Walter (*b* Birmingham, 6 Feb. 1875; *d* London, 11 Nov. 1951). English tenor. Studied R.C.M. with Garcia and as a student appeared in *Euryanthe* and Stanford's *Much Ado About Nothing*. After singing in light musical plays was engaged by Pitt to sing Siegmund in the English *Ring* at C.G. under Richter. Appeared regularly at C.G. from 1908 to 1923, and was member of the Beecham Company and subsequently the B.N.O.C., of which he became a director. N.Y., Met., Siegmund; U.S. tour 1912 in *Robin Hood*. The first London Sali (*A Village Romeo and Juliet*) and a notable English Parsifal. (R)

Hymn to the Sun. Aria sung by the Queen of Shemakha (sop.) in Act 2 of Rimsky-Korsakov's *The Golden Cockerel*.

I

Iago. A Venetian soldier, ensign to Otello, (bar.) in Verdi's and (ten.) in Rossini's *Otello*.

Iaşi (Jassy). Town in Romania, capital of Moldavia. Opera was given in the T. Naţional under the composer Alexander Flechtenmacher in 1844-7, and by visiting companies. The present company was formed in 1956; in 1958 the T. Naţional was modernised, and the company began touring towns and villages of Moldavia.

Ibert, Jacques (*b* Paris, 15 Aug. 1890; *d* Paris, 5 Feb. 1962). French composer. Studied Paris with Gédalge, Ducasse, Fauré, and Vidal. His nine operas include the successful *Angélique* (1927), *Le Roi d'Yvetot* (1930), *Gonzague* (1933), and (with Honegger) *L'Aiglon* (1937). Director, Union des Théâtres Lyriques, Paris, 1955-7.

Ibsen, Henrik (*b* Skien, 20 Mar. 1828; *d* Oslo, 23 May 1906). Norwegian playwright. Operas on his works are as follows:
The Feast at Solhaug (1856): Stenhammar (1899).
Olav Liljekrans (1856): A. Eggen (1940).
The Warriors at Helgeland (1858): Rerny (*Hjördis*, 1900); K. Moor (*Hjördis*, 1905); Sandby (1920).
Peer Gynt (1867): Ullmann (20th cent.); Heward (unfin., from 1922).
The Doll's House (1879): Mack (1967).
Kongsemnerne (1863): Bucht (1966).
Terje Vigen: Lie (1904).

Ice Break, The. Opera in 3 acts by Tippett; text by composer. Prod. London, C.G., 7 July 1977, with Harper, McDonnell, Barstow, Vaughn, C. Walker, Shirley-Quirk, R. Kennedy, J. Dobson, also Anne Wilkins and James Bowman representing a single character, cond. C. Davis. The subject of the opera is stereotypes – their imprisoning characteristics and the need for rebirth. After 20 years in prison camps, Lev (bass) arrives in a new world to join his wife Nadia (lyric sop.), who has emigrated with their baby son Yuri. Also at the airport are Yuri's girl friend Gayle (dramatic sop.) and her black friend Hannah (rich mezzo), there to meet the black 'champion' Olympion (ten.) together with his fan club. Out of a series of violent tensions, individual and collective, there develops a riot in which Olympion and Gayle are killed and Yuri (bar.) is near-fatally injured. Nadia dies peacefully. During an interlude in which a group attempts a psychedelic 'trip', the messenger Astron (lyric mezzo and high ten. or counter-ten.) is mistaken for God, though he disclaims his divinity. Yuri is operated on by

ILIA

Luke (ten.), a young doctor, and, released from the cracking plaster, he finds reconciliation with his father.

Ich baue ganz auf deine Stärke. Belmonte's (ten.) aria in Act 3 of Mozart's *Die Entführung aus dem Serail*, which he is instructed by Pedrillo to sing to conceal the placing of the ladders to the Seraglio windows. Often omitted.

Idomeneo, Re di Creta. Opera in 3 acts by Mozart; text by G. B. Varesco, after Danchet's libretto for Campra's *Idomenée* (1712) and the ancient legend. Prod. Munich, 29 Jan. 1781, with D. Wendling, E. Wendling, Raaf, Del Prato, Panzacchi; Glasgow, 12 Mar. 1934; Tanglewood, 4 Aug 1947, with Bollinger, Trickey, Lenchner, Laderoute, Guarrera, cond. Goldovsky. Idomeneo, King of Crete (ten.) has sent home from Troy captives including Ilia (sop.), daughter of Priam. She and Idomeneo's son Idamante (sop. or ten.) are in love, though he has not declared himself: Elettra (sop.) also loves him. The impending return of Idomeneo is the sign for an amnesty of prisoners. But a sudden storm causes the King to vow to the sea god a sacrifice of the first living thing he meets on shore. This is his son. Horrified, he hurries away without speaking; a joyful chorus welcomes the warriors.

The King tries to evade his vow by sending Idamante to escort Elettra home to Argos, much to the distress of Ilia. But a storm arises, followed by a monster who ravages the island. The people hold that some unknown sinner has offended the gods, and Idomeneo admits his guilt and is ready to die.

Idamante and Ilia declare their love before he sets out to attack the monster. Elettra, mad with jealousy, interrupts, followed by the King, who is torn between anxiety for his son and guilt. He is forced, by the people's demand for a victim, to reveal the truth. The High Priest hesitates to make the sacrifice on hearing that the monster has been killed by Idamante, who nevertheless offers himself as a victim so as not to break his father's vow. But the voice of the god spares him, announcing that Idomeneo must abdicate. Idamante ascends the throne with Ilia at his side.

Other operas on the subject are Campra (1712), Galuppi (1756), Gazzaniga (1790), Paisiello (1792), Paer (1794), Federici (1806), and Farinelli (1812).

I have attained the highest power. Boris's (bass) monologue in Act 2, scene 2 of Mussorgsky's *Boris Godunov*.

Il balen. Di Luna's (bar.) aria in Act 2, scene 2 of Verdi's *Il trovatore*, in which he sings of the tempest raging within his heart.

Ilia. A Trojan princess (sop.), daughter of King Priam, in Mozart's *Idomeneo*.

lacerato spirito. Fiesco's (bass) aria in the prologue to Verdi's *Simon Boccanegra*, in which he sings of his tortured soul.

lica, Luigi (*b* Piacenza, 9 May 1857; *d* Piacenza, 6 Dec. 1919). Italian playwright and librettist. He wrote or collaborated on some 80 librettos or some of the leading composers of his day, beginning with Smareglia's *Il vassallo di Szigeth* (1889). Others include Catalani's *La Vally* (1892), Giordano's *Andrea Chénier* (1896), Mascagni's *Iris* (1898) and *Le maschere* (1901), and D'Erlanger's *Tess* (1906); but he is most famous for his collaboration on Puccini's *Manon Lescaut* (1893) and, with Giuseppe Giacosa, *La Bohème* (1896), *Tosca* (1900), and *Madama Butterfly* (1904). A man of exuberant and violent passions, also a quick and inventive worker, he was at his best at inventing strong characters and situations. He lacked Giacosa's sensibility, but complemented him well, and in Puccini's words 'he had plenty of imagination'. He reflected a French influence in his work, in the conflict of a powerful love element with social or political tensions, portrayed in plots of some accuracy in historical atmosphere and detail, and supported by adding thorough stage directions (a French practice which he introduced into Italian opera).

mio tesoro. Don Ottavio's (ten.) love song to Donna Anna in Act 2, scene 2 of Mozart's *Don Giovanni*.

mbroglio (*It* entanglement, intrigue, orig. from the *Broglio*, the arcade of the Doge's Palace in Venice in which such intrigues were conducted). A scene in which confusion is suggested by great diversity, both melodic and rhythmic, of the parts given to the singers or groups of singers. Though originating in 18th cent. Italian opera, the imbroglio at its most advanced and intricate can be seen in the end of Act 2 of Wagner's *Die Meistersinger*.

neneo. Opera in 3 acts by Handel; text anon. Prod. London, Lincoln's Inn Fields, 22 Nov. 740, with Francesina, Edwards. A failure, not revived between 1742 and 1960.

nmolation. The name generally given to the scene of Brünnhilde's death in Act 3 of Wagner's *Götterdämmerung* as she rides (or in most modern productions, walks) into the flames of Siegfried's funeral pyre.

nmortal Hour, The. Opera in 2 acts by Boughton; text by 'Fiona Macleod' (William Sharp). Prod. Glastonbury, Assembly Rooms, 26 Aug. 1914, with Lemon, Jordan, Austin, Boughton (replacing an unwell singer as alua), cond. Kennedy Scott; N.Y., Grove St. ., 6 Apr. 1926, with Borden, Kuschke, Mordurst, Vining, Cox, Rothwell, Gurney, cond. imboni. The opera had an outstandingly successful season of 216 nights at the Regent

T., London, from 13 Oct. 1922 to the following April; this was followed by another run of some 160 performances from 17 Nov. 1923, and by others, with the work reaching over 500 London performances by 1932. A revival at S.W. in 1953 was unsuccessful.

The fairy Etain (sop.) and the king Eochaidh (bar.) are to be married. The fairy prince Midir (ten.) enchants Etain, and she follows him to the Land of Heart's Desire. Dalua (bar.), the Shadow God, touches Eochaidh and he falls dead.

Impresario (from It. *impresa*, undertaking). Organizer and/or manager of an opera company. The Italian equivalent of Ger. *Schauspieldirektor*, both in general use and as title for Mozart's opera.

In alt. The term used to describe the notes in the octave immediately above the top line of the treble stave, running from g'' to f'''. The next octave, from g''' to f'''', is **in altissimo**.

Incledon, Charles (*b* St Keverne, Cornwall, 5 Feb. 1763; *d* London, 18 Feb. 1826). English tenor. As choirboy at Exeter Cathedral studied under Langdon and Jackson. Went to sea, where his fine tenor voice impressed Admiral Pigot. Engaged Southampton 1784, Bath 1785, where he was heard by Rauzzini, who gave him lessons. London, C.G., from 1790. Appeared in operas by Shield and Arnold. His son, **Charles,** (1791-1865) appeared briefly in London in the 1820s at Drury Lane as Meadows in *Love in a village* and in *The Waterman*, and then taught in Vienna.

Incoronazione di Poppea, L' (The Coronation of Poppaea). Opera in a prologue and 3 acts by Monteverdi; text by G. F. Busenello, after Tacitus, *Annals* xiii-xv (*c* AD 117). Prod. Venice, S.G.P., autumn 1642; Northampton. Mass., Smith Coll., 27 Apr. 1927 with Fatman, Miliette, Donovan, Lyman, Pitts, Sinclair, McNamara, cond. Josten; Oxford, Univ. Opera Club, 6 Dec. 1927, ed. and cond. Westrup; Glyndebourne (Leppard version) 29 June 1962, with Laszlo, Bible, Dominguez, Lewis, Cava, Marimpietri, Alberti, cond. Pritchard. Monteverdi's last opera; the first on an historical (other than Biblical) subject.

The Emperor Nero (Nerone) (ten.) has fallen in love with Poppea (sop.) and wants to divorce Ottavia (mezzo). Poppea suspects the old philosopher Seneca (bass) of being involved in a plot against her, and Nero compels him to take his own life. Ottavia persuades Ottone (bar.) to murder his former mistress Poppea, but he is caught, and only saved by his lover Drusilla (sop.), who confesses her own intention to murder Poppea, also revealing Ottavia's plot. Ottone and Drusilla are banished; Ottavia is divorced; and Nero and Poppea celebrate their marriage and Poppea's coronation.

Indes Galantes, Les. Opera-ballet in a prologue and 4 *entrées* by Rameau; text by Louis Fuzelier. Prod. Paris, O., 23 Aug. 1735 with prologue and 2 *entrées* – third added at third performance, fourth added 10 Mar. 1736, with Eremans, Petipas, Pelissier, Antier, Cuignier, Jelyotte, Dun, De Clusse, cond. Cheron; N.Y., T.H., 1 Mar. 1961, with Raskin, Ferriero, Bressler, Shirley, Trehy, cond. Dunn. In its final form the work tells four tales of love in different parts of the world: the *entrées* are *Le Turc généreux, Les Incas du Pérou, Les Fleurs,* and *Les Sauvages.* Rameau's third opera and greatest success. Revived Paris, O., 1952, and perf. 246 times in the following ten years.

India. Indian musical theatre is a mixed genre that does not match the normal Western idea of opera. The fusion of epic poetry with the music and dancing of the temple led to Sanskrit musical drama (*geya nataka*), of which classics included the *c.* 4th cent. Kalidasa's *The Recognition of Shakuntala* (a story well known in Europe and the subject of several operas, including one by Schubert). The situations were formal, revolving round the stereotypes of hero, heroine, villain, and clown. The accompaniment was by instruments from eight to 60 in number, and was designed to frame a mood shared between performers and audience rather than to set words or illustrate actions; the songs were sung by members of the orchestra. There was a minimum of scenery or props.

With the Moslem raids of the 12th cent. and the rise of the Mogul Empire, Sanskrit music drama loosened its ritual forms; more realistic acting was demanded, with singing as well as dancing by the actors. Culturally, North and South India were divided. In the North, the emphasis was on pageantry and formal drama which made great demands on performers and audience alike: one drama, the *Ramalila,* takes a fortnight to perform, the *Krishnalila* a month, and both are still performed on the sites of their legendary events. In the South, musical drama is dependent more on the village storyteller's art, and tends to consist of a narration illustrated with song, dance and mime, though the subjects are also mythological. A later development, *charitram,* is closer to Western opera, with less improvisation and a more disciplined balance between drama and music. In each, vocal standards are regarded as being as irrelevant to the detail of the execution as handwriting is to a composer, though this has not prevented the recent emergence of popular singers. In the North, the wealthy 19th cent. amateur Wajid Ali Shah developed a genre of musical drama illustrating medieval paintings that depicted ragas by means of tableaux, with miming actors and an instrumental ensemble. Around 1900 the Parsis toured a kind of musical

theatre which won popularity by virtue of its large numbers of performers and its accent on spectacle. Bengali theatre, inclined to similar ideas, was restrained by the example of Rabindranath Tagore (1861-1941), who attached the highest importance to his music and insisted on simplicity of form and seriousness of theme. Familiar with Western music, he was not afraid to use European folk song and traditional Indian music in a dramatic form he called Rabindra-Sangeet: one of his works, *Shyama* (1939), is a simple ballad opera on a tragic story. He is the first Indian to achieve a successful cross-fertilization of East and West in drama.

Performances of Western opera were sometimes staged during the British Raj. Scenes from *Don Giovanni* were given in 1833 and *Cenerentola* was given in 1834 in Calcutta, for instance; *Cavalleria rusticana* was given at Simla in 1901, Linley's *The Duenna* in Calcutta in 1915 and in Bombay in 1925. The so-called Opera House in Calcutta was really intended for drama and variety, though Pollard's Lilliputian Opera Company (probably a concert party group) performed there in 1896-7.

New Indian operas produced within the first decade of independence include *Meena Gurjari,* by Nat Mandal; this makes use of Punjabi folk songs, treated in Leitmotiv manner and demanding part-singing, even a vocal trio.

Indiana. See *Bloomington.*

In diesen heil'gen Hallen. Sarastro's (bass) aria in Act 2 of *Die Zauberflöte,* in which he tells Pamina that no thought of violence is entertained within the sacred walls of the temple of Isis and Osiris.

Indy, d'. See *D'Indy.*

In fernem Land. Lohengrin's (ten.) narration in the last scene of Wagner's *Lohengrin,* in which he discloses his identity and tells of the Holy Grail. In German known as the *Gralserzählung.*

Ingénu(e) (*Fr* artless, innocent). The *ingénue* of 18th cent. French opera, a development by Favart of the **damigella* of 17th cent. Italian opera, was as a type a girl of 15 or 16 whose innocence and light approach to love had a pronounced sentimentality but was also marked by a latent sensuousness; her tendency to tears was part of her charm, and this characteristic helped to develop the *comédie larmoyante,* or sentimental comedy, which was a part of French comic opera in the later 18th cent. The *ingénu,* a less common or typical character, was usually little more than a village simpleton.

Inghelbrecht, Désiré-Émile (*b* Paris, 17 Sept. 1880; *d* Paris, 14 Feb. 1965). French conductor and composer. Paris, Ch. E., 1913; O.C., 1924-5, 1932-3; O., 1927-8, 1949-50. (R)

Bibl: D.-E. Ingelbrecht: *Mouvement contraire* (1947).

Inghilleri, Giovanni (*b* Porto Empedocle, 9 Mar. 1894; *d* Milan, 10 Dec. 1959). Italian baritone and composer. Début Milan, Teatro Carcano, 1919, Valentine. Sang regularly in Rome and other Italian centres. London, C.G., 1928-30, 1935; Chicago 1929-30. His roles included Gérard (which he sang on the 50th anniversary of the première of *Chénier* under the composer's direction at Sc.), Scarpia, Amfortas, and Shaklovity in *Khovanshchina,* which he continued to sing until 1953. Created leading roles in Casella's *La donna serpente,* Malipiero's *Giulio Cesare,* and Cattozzo's *I misteri dolorosi.* After leaving the stage, taught in Pesaro and Milan. His compositions include the opera *La burla,* a ballet and several songs. (R)

Innsbruck. Town in the Tyrol, Austria. The Comedi-Haus, built 1629-31 by the Archduke Leopold, was the first real German-speaking theatre in Europe. It had a small orchestra and forty-one singers who performed operas, mostly for the court. Leopold's son, the Archduke Ferdinand Karl, commissioned the court architect Christoph Gumpp to build a new and larger theatre opposite the Imperial Palace on the site of the present opera house. He engaged mostly Italian artists on a permanent basis, including the composer Cesti, who remained as court composer for eight years, and whose *Cleopatra* was the opening opera of the new house, in 1653. In 1655 Queen Christina stayed at Innsbruck on her way to Rome, and the première of Cesti's *L'Argia* (which lasted five-and-a-half hours and had three ballets) was produced in her honour. A third Cesti work, *Veneri cacciatrice,* had its première in Innsbruck in 1659. This was the year in which the first permanent theatre and opera companies were formed in the city. Ferdinand's successor, Sigmund Franz, discovering that his brother had died virtually bankrupt, dismissed the ensemble, including Cesti who then went to Vienna. During the governorship of Karl Lothringen, amateur performances were given, including Cesti's *La magnanimità d'Alessandro* with a cast that included six Counts, eight Countesses, one Marchese, and one Baron. His successor, Karl Philipp von Pfalz-Neuburg, brought his own private orchestra to Innsbruck under Johann Jakob Greber, who was also a composer.

Greber went to Mannheim in 1717; then followed the reign of Maria Theresia, who banned all religious plays, dismissed the court orchestra and converted the southern part of the main theatre into a public library. In 1775-6 Schikaneder was engaged as producer/actor and librettist.

In the first half of the 19th cent. there were

700 opera productions in Innsbruck, of which 200 were first local productions. A further expansion of the repertory followed with works by Verdi and Wagner. Since 1886 the theatre has belonged to and been run by the municipality. In 1827 the house was modernized and in 1938, with the German annexation of Austria, it became a Landestheater: a permanent opera company was engaged, and in 1940 Strauss attended a performance of *Salome.* After the war the theatre was renamed the Tirolese Landestheater, and Siegfried Nessler, brother of the composer, was appointed music director; Robert Nessler was Kapellmeister and operetta conductor. He engaged the young Leonie Rysanek, who made her début in 1949, and gave two premières, Robert Nessler's *Die Brautnacht* (1956) and Respighi's *Cesare Borgia* (1957). The house was closed and completely rebuilt in 1961-7 (cap. 793); reopened in December 1967 with *Die Meistersinger.* First performances in Austria have included Egk's *Die Verlobung in San Domingo* and Henze's *Boulevard solitude.*

In quelle trine morbide. Manon Lescaut's (sop.) aria in Act 2 of Puccini's opera, in which she sings of the chill in the splendour among which she lives, and wishes she were back in the humble dwelling where she and Des Grieux were so happy.

In questa reggia. Turandot's (sop.) narration in Act 2, scene 2 of Puccini's opera, in which she recounts how the rape of her ancestress Princess Lo-u-Ling made her resolve to be revenged upon all men through her vow to set riddles to those who seek her love, with death as the price of failure.

Inszenierung (*Ger* production). Hence *Neuinszenierung,* for the new production of an opera.

Intendant (*Ger* superintendent). The administrator of a German opera house; not necessarily the artistic or music director.

Intermezzo (*It* interlude). (1) Originally a short musical entertainment appearing in the course of a dramatic entertainment. The *intermedi* of plays were part of the process that led to the development of opera; these first appeared as early as the end of 15th cent., and were common in the 16th cent. As early as 1623 an opera, *L'amorosa innocenza,* was performed in Bologna with intermezzi that, though separately inserted, formed a continuous opera of their own, *Il coronazione di Apollo.* This joining together of a serious and a comic entertainment became very popular throughout the 17th cent., and by early 18th cent. Neapolitan opera the appeal of the more realistic, popular genre in contrast to the gods and kings and heroes of *opera seria* had become too strong to be contained: a separate form was developing.

239

The most famous intermezzo was Pergolesi's *La serva padrona*, originally part of his *opera seria*, *Il prigionier superbo* (1733), but still surviving independently of its long-forgotten 'host' opera. If *opera seria* stood for the establishment of order and the importance of conformity to social and moral standards, the intermezzo satisfied the complementary human wish not to conform, and so came to make the larger entertainment seem artificial and stilted. It is thus the beginning of *opera buffa*.

(2) The word is also used in the sense of an interlude, a short piece of music or even a short scene interpolated in the course of an opera. An orchestral intermezzo may be virtually a miniature tone-poem, perhaps denoting the passing of time (as between scenes 1 and 2 of Mascagni's *Cavalleria rusticana*) or describing or summarizing events between scenes (as between Acts 3 and 4 of Puccini's *Manon Lescaut*). A dramatic intermezzo, or interlude, may take the form of a scene to some degree outside the main plot (as with the choral interlude between Acts 1 and 2 of Schoenberg's *Moses und Aron*). Henze's 'opera seria', *The Bassarids* (1966), includes a dramatic intermezzo, *The Judgement of Calliope*, which though relevant to the main plot is a conscious reversion to the earlier practice described under (1) above.

Intermezzo. Opera in 2 acts by Strauss; text by composer. Prod. Dresden, 4 Nov. 1924, with Lehmann, Correck, cond. Busch; N.Y., Lincoln Center, 11 Dec. 1963, with Curtin, Bell, cond. Scherman; Edinburgh, King's T., 2 Sept. 1965 with Steffek, Prey, cond. Zallinger. Based on incidents in Strauss's own life when his happy marriage was threatened by his having received, by mistake, a passionate love-letter from an unknown female admirer. Strauss becomes Robert Storch (bar.), his wife Pauline is renamed Christine (sop.). Also opera by G. F. Maio (1752).

Intimate Opera Company. Founded by the baritone Frederick Woodhouse in 1930, with Geoffrey Dunn and Margaret Ritchie, the company toured Great Britain with a repertory that included *La serva padrona*, *Bastien und Bastienne*, Arne's *Thomas and Sally*, Dibdin's *The Grenadier*, and Carey's *True Blue*. In 1936 Ritchie was succeeded as the company's soprano by Winifred Radford, who brought works by Offenbach into the repertory. In 1938 the company visited the U.S.A. and had a successful season at the Little T. on Broadway. After the war the Arts Council began to help the company. In 1952 Antony Hopkins was music director; he was succeeded by Winifred Radford, with Joseph Horovitz as music director. In 1973 William Dickie assumed the general management of the company. In addition to works by Purcell, Storace, Mozart, etc. the group has produced works by Hopkins, Horovitz, Geoffrey Bush, and Gerald Cockshott. Singers who have appeared with the company include Patricia Hughes, Ann Dowdall, Elizabeth Gale, Winifred Radford, Eric Shilling, Stephen Manton, Duncan Robertson, Leyland White, Donald Francke, and Robert Bateman. Recent productions have been staged by Dennis Arundell and Anthony Besch.

Intonation. The quality of singing or playing in tune.

Intrusive H. A common singer's fault found chiefly in long runs on one syllable: each new note is started with an unvocalized breath so that the effect is not 'a-a-a-' but 'ha-ha-ha-'. An accusation of this fault levelled against Steuart Wilson by a schoolmaster in a letter to the *Radio Times* in 1933 led to a libel action. Wilson won his case, in which a large number of musicians were called as witnesses, and was awarded £2,100 damages against the B.B.C. and the schoolmaster. He spent it on a production of Boughton's *The Lily Maid*.

Invano, Alvaro. The duet between Carlo (bar.) and Alvaro (ten.) in Act 4, scene 1 of Verdi's *La forza del destino*, in which Alvaro, now Padre Raffaello, tries to dissuade Carlo from challenging him to a duel.

Invisible City of Kitezh, The (Full title: *The Legend of the Invisible City of Kitezh and the Maiden Fevronia*). Opera in 4 acts by Rimsky-Korsakov; text by V. I. Belsky, after the legend. Prod. St Petersburg, M., 20 Feb. 1907, with Filippov, Labinsky, Kuznetsova-Benois, Ershov, Sharonov, Markovich, Zabela, cond. Blumenfeld; London, C.G. (concert), 30 Mar. 1926, with Smirnova, Davidova, Pozenkovsky, Carewia, Kaidonov, cond. Coates; Ann Arbor (concert), 21 May 1932; Philadelphia, 4 Feb. 1936, with Palmer.

Iolanta. See Yolanta.

Iphigenia. In classical mythology, the daughter of Agamemnon and Clytemnestra. Agamemnon killed a hart in the sacred grove of Artemis, who then becalmed the Greek fleet waiting to sail from Aulis for Troy. Agamemnon decided to follow the priest Calchas's advice and sacrifice Iphigenia, but Artemis carried her off to Tauris to be a priestess. There she was discovered years later by her wandering brother Orestes, and brought home again to Mycenae.

The legend was given dramatic expression by Euripides in his *Iphigenia in Aulis* (?406 B.C., unfin.) and *Iphigenia in Tauris* (414-1 B.C.), and has been treated by numerous composers, the first (anon.) in 1632. Besides Gluck's two operas (see below), there are at least 30 settings of *Iphigenia in Aulis* between 1632 and 1819, and more than 15 of *Iphigenia in Tauris* between 1704 and 1817.

Iphigénie en Aulide. Opera in 3 acts by Gluck; text by Roullet, after Racine's tragedy (1674) based on Euripides' tragedy (?406-5 B.C., unfin.). Prod. Paris, O., 19 Apr. 1774, with Arnould, Duplant, Legros, Larrivée, cond. Gluck; Oxford, 20 Nov. 1933, with Green, Philips, Heseltine, Dance, Wade, Downing, Douglas, cond. Harvey; Philadelphia, 22 Feb. 1935, with Tentoni, Van Gordon, Bentonelli, Baklanov, cond. Smallens.

Iphigénie en Tauride. Opera in 4 acts by Gluck; text by Guillard, after Euripides' drama (414–12 BC). Prod. Paris, O., 18 May 1779, with Levasseur, Larrivée, Legros, cond. Francoeur; London, King's T., 7 Apr. 1796, with Giorgi-Banti, Roselli, Viganoni, Rodevino; N.Y., Met., 25 Nov. 1916, with Kurt, Sembach, Weill, cond. Bodanzky.

Ippolitov-Ivanov (orig. Ivanov), **Mikhail** (Mikhailovich) (*b* Gatchina, 19 Nov. 1859; *d* Moscow, 28 Jan. 1935). Russian composer. Studied St Petersburg with Rimsky-Korsakov. Between 1887 and 1934 wrote seven operas, including *Ruth* (1887), *Azra* (1890), *Asya* (1900), *Treachery* (1910), *Ole the Norseman* (1916), and *The Last Barricade* (1933). Lived at Tiflis 1882-93, conducting opera there from 1884. Conducted the Mamontov and Z. companies in Moscow 1899–1906, and at the B. from 1925. Greatly stimulated operatic activity in Georgia, and in Moscow introduced a number of new operas to the Russian repertory, including *Tsar Saltan* and *The Tsar's Bride*.
Bibl: S. Bugoslavsky: *M.M. Ippolitov-Ivanov* (1936).

Iris. Opera in 3 acts by Mascagni; text by Illica. Prod. Rome, C., 22 Nov. 1898 with Darclée, De Lucia, Caruso, cond. Mascagni; revised and given at Milan Sc., 19 Jan. 1899; Philadelphia 14 Oct. 1902, with Farneti, Schiavazzi, Bellati, cond. Mascagni; London, C.G., 8 July 1919, with Sheridan, Capuzzo, Couzinou, cond. Mugnone. The opera, set in 19th-century Japan, tells of the vain attempt by Osaka (ten.) to win the love of the pure young Iris (sop.). He arranges with Kyoto (bar.), the keeper of a brothel, to have her abducted, and her blind father, thinking she has gone there voluntarily, curses her and flings mud at her. Iris drowns herself in a sewer.

Irische Legende. Opera in 5 scenes by Egk; text by the composer after W. B. Yeats's drama *The Countess Cathleen* (1892). Prod. Salzburg, Festspielhaus, 17 Aug. 1955, with Borkh, Klose, Lorenz, Böhme, Frick, cond. Szell. In Ireland, some time in the future, the Devil has caused a famine and the people sell their souls to him in exchange for food. Countess Cathleen (sop.) offers to sell her soul not only for this reason, but because her lover, the poet Aleen (bass), has been abducted by demons. Like Mar-

guerite in *Faust*, she is saved and ascends to heaven.

Irmelin. Opera in 3 acts by Delius; text by composer. Prod. Oxford, New T., 4 May 1953, Graham, Copley, Round, Hancock, cond. Beecham. The Princess Irmelin (sop.) awaits her true love. Nils (ten.), a prince disguised as a swineherd, is searching for the ideal woman; he is told he will find her at the end of the silver stream, and there he finds Irmelin.

Isaac, Adèle (Lelong) (*b* Calais, 8 Jan. 1854; *d* Paris, *c* 22 Oct. 1915). French soprano. Studied Paris, with Duprez. Début Paris, T. Montmartre, 1870, *Noces de Jeannette*. Paris, O.C., 1873, 1878–83, 1883–8; created Olympia, Antonia, Giulietta (*Hoffmann*), Minka (*Roi malgré lui*); Paris, O., 1883–5; Rome, A., 1888. Retired 1894. Considered a fine interpreter of Mozart (Susanna, Zerlina, etc.) and of the operas of Hérold, Halévy, Thomas, and Gounod.

Isabeau. Opera in 3 acts by Mascagni; text by Illica. Prod. Buenos Aires, C., 2 June 1911, with Farnetti, Saludas, Galeffi, cond. Mascagni; Chicago 12 Nov. 1917, with Raisa, Crimi, Rimini, cond. Campanini. Unwilling to choose a husband, the Princess Isabeau (sop.) is made to ride naked through the streets in the middle of the day; anyone who dares look at her will be condemned to death. This edict is disobeyed by Folco (ten.), a young forester, and Isabeau falls in love with him; the crowd, however, lynch him, and Isabeau kills herself over his dying body.

Isabella. The heroine (mezzo) of Rossini's *L'italiana in Algeri*.

Isolde. The Irish princess (sop.) in Wagner's *Tristan und Isolde*.

Isolier. The Count's page (mezzo) in Rossini's *Le Comte Ory*.

Isouard, Nicolò (*b* Musta, Malta, 6 Dec. 1775; *d* Paris, 23 Mar. 1818). Maltese composer, often known simply as Nicolo. Studied Palermo, then Naples with Sala and P. Guglielmi. The first of his 40-odd operas, *L'avviso ai maritati* (1794), was unsuccessful. He was more fortunate with *Artaserse* (1794). He then wrote a number of operas for the theatre in Valetta. In 1799 he went to Paris, where he produced *Le Tonnelier* (1799) among a number of operas of which *Cendrillon* (1810) was the most successful; of many others that were popular, one of the most important and characteristic was *Jeannot et Colin* (1814). On Boieldieu's return from Russia, he lost some of his following. His comedies were generally escapist, a distraction from current events rather than a reflection or witty distortion.

Israel. In 1920 Mordecai Golinkin organised a Benefit in Petrograd with Shalyapin, and the proceeds enabled him, once he had emigrated to Palestine, to mount a performance of *La traviata* in a Tel Aviv cinema and launch the Palestine Opera Company. By 1927, when the company was obliged to disband, he had presented over 20 operas, all in Hebrew, including *Samson et Dalila*, *La Juive*, and Rubinstein's *The Maccabees*. He continued his activities, however, and was one of the founders of the Palestine Folk Opera in 1941: the repertory included M. Lavry's *Dan ha-Shomer* (Dan the Guard, 1945). He retired in 1953. In 1945 the soprano Edis de Philippe arrived in Palestine, and gained support for a national opera company to be formed to coincide with the foundation of the Jewish state. On 29 Nov. 1947, the date on which the U.N.O. voted the partition of Palestine, she mounted a gala performance of operatic excerpts by the new Hebrew Nat. O., soon followed by a production of *Thaïs* with herself in the title-role. In 1958 the company, now the Israel National Opera Company, moved into a permanent home, the former Knesset (Parliament) in Tel Aviv (cap. *c*900). By the 25th anniversary season there had been 43 productions. Most operas are performed in Hebrew, except for Russian works, and an international repertory includes operetta and musicals and finds a place for works with special associations (e.g. *Samson et Dalila*, *Nabucco*, Goldmark's *Die Königin von Saba*). Wagner and Strauss are still excluded on grounds of being associated with Nazism. In 1933 a Chamber Opera was formed, under Benno Frankel, and more recently concert performances have been given by a Chamber Opera Group under Gary Bertini. Placido Domingo, among others, began his career with the Israel Nat. O.C.

Operas by *sabras* (native-born Israelis) include *Alexandra* (1959) and *Independence Night Dream* (1973) by Menachem Avidom. Operas by composers settled in Israel include *Ashmedai* and *Masada* (1973) by Josef Tal (*b* 1910); and *The War of the Sons of Light* (1972) by Ami Maayani (*b* 1936). Performance are also given in Haifa and Jerusalem.

Istanbul. Town in Turkey, formerly Byzantium, then Constantinople, capital of the Ottoman Empire 1453–1924. The first theatre on Western models was the Naum T., opened by the Syrian Mihail Naum in 1844 with Donizetti's *Lucrezia Borgia*, followed by other Italian works. An Italian company played in the 1845–6 season. The theatre was burnt down, but reopened by Naum in 1848 with *Macbeth*. The 1849–50 season included six operas by Verdi, Bellini, and Donizetti, given by an Italian company of 36. The 1850–1 season opened with *Robert le Diable* and included Verdi's *Attila*. Naum went on to stage *Il trovatore* (1858) and *Barbiere* (1854), but despite the

242

grant of a monopoly he had to be supported with a subsidy. In 1864–5 another Italian company, which included Adelaide Ristori, opened with *I vespri siciliani*, and the following season saw further Verdi works. In the rebuilt theatre, *La muette de Portici* was given in 1869, but the theatre was burnt down in the following year. A private opera house (cap. 300) had been built by Sultan Abdul Mejid in his Dolmabahçe Palace, with Giuseppe Donizetti (brother of the composer) as director, in 1859; this was burnt down in 1863. Another theatre was built by Sultan Abdul Hamid in the Yildiz Palace in 1889; opera was given here until 1908. Despite other enterprises, opera was not established on a permanent basis until 1959, with the obtaining of municipal grants and the foundation of an opera house.

Italiana in Algeri, L' (The Italian Girl in Algiers). Opera in 2 acts by Rossini; text by Angelo Anelli, originally set by Luigi Mosca (1808). Prod. Venice, S.B., 22 May 1813, with Marcolini, Annibaldi, Berni Chelli, Gentili, Galli, Rosich; London, Hm., 26 Jan. 1819, with Giorgi-Belloc Ambrogetti, Garcia Placci; N.Y., 5 Nov. 1832, with Saccomano, Marozzi, Verducci, Manetti, Orlandi, Fornasari, Sapignoli, cond. Rapetti.

Isabella (mezzo), 'l'italiana' of the title, has been sailing the seas in search of her lover Lindoro (ten.), who is a slave of Mustaphà (bass), Bey of Algiers. A storm drives Isabella's ship to the shores of Algiers, and she arrives at the court accompanied by her elderly admirer Taddeo, whom she passes off as her uncle. The Bey falls in love with her, and after many complications Lindoro and Isabella plan to enrol Mustaphà in the order of the 'Pappatacci'. The most important rule of the order is to eat and be silent, and be a model husband. Isabella and Lindoro are able to sail away reunited, and the Bey returns to his neglected wife Elvira (sop.).

Italy. Though opera has its origins in earlier dramatic forms, its invention is generally accepted as dating from the discussions of the *Camerata in Florence around the year 1600. The first opera is *Peri's *Dafne* (1597); the first of which the music survives is his *Euridice* (1600). Opera was an Italian invention; and for many years Italy was the home of the art, and an inspiration to other countries.

One of opera's greatest geniuses was Claudio *Monteverdi (1587–1643). Not only is his music of the highest inspiration, but his vision of opera as a drama in music has remained valid through all its long history. The music of the early Florentine opera had consisted mostly of recitative over a thorough bass, pursuing the intention of the Camerata to imitate (as they thought) ancient Greek drama. Monteverdi greatly enriched the genre, both in form and in subtlety of characterization, giving the recitative expressive force, the orchestra colour, and the set numbers great power. His *Orfeo* (1607) also suggests in its opening toccata what was to become the overture, and his skilful use of ritornellos helps to strengthen the drama with a degree of musical unity.

By the 1630s other Italian cities, especially Rome, had begun to show an interest in opera, This school of opera began to differentiate more clearly between aria and recitative: in the operas of Stefano Landi (*c*1590–*c*1655) there is an increased emphasis on melody in the arias, while in his *Il Sant' Alessio* (1632) a sinfonia before Act 2 suggests the arrangement of the later Italian overture in its three-movement structure; these works also made increased use of ensemble.

With the opening to the public of the T. San Cassiano in Venice in 1637, opera was made available to a wider audience than the aristocracy. At the same time, the formality of the manner had begun to demand comic relief. Venetian opera of this period, as exemplified above all in the works of Monteverdi, *Cesti, and *Cavalli, developed greater variety and expressiveness, with more complicated plots, livelier characterization, comic episodes, and numbers which displayed some of the favourite singers who had begun to make careers in opera and to cultivate the art of *bel canto*. With the firmer separation between recitative and aria, the latter developed greater formality, including the *da capo* form. The orchestra's importance also increased, both for expressive purposes in accompaniment and to provide interludes, ritornelli etc. Opera continued to spread across Italy, back to Florence with Cesti, and to Naples with the work of Francesco Provenzale (?1627–1704). Among the first Italians to establish themselves in Germany was Agostino *Steffani.

By the beginning of the 18th-cent., Italian opera had achieved a standardization that, though rigid, provided an example for native and now also for foreign composers. The genre *opera seria* was particularly firmly established in Naples, whence its description as *Neapolitan opera. In organizing the free forms of 17th-cent. opera into a firm 3-act structure, Apostolo *Zeno and Pietro *Metastasio dispensed with much that threatened dramatic logic, but provided a confining strictness. The subject of *opera seria* was generally classical history and legend, with action and reflection scrupulously balanced in the course of recitative and aria: in general, the action took place in recitative, with the arias providing points of reflection and repose also of musical expression and the chance of personal display by the singer. To this pattern the other operatic ingredients were subject; and great attention devolved upon the *aria. This form not only gave opera a strict framework in which com-

posers could work; it encouraged the rise of a school of virtuoso singers, especially the *castrato. The major figure in 18th-cent Italian opera seria was Alessandro *Scarlatti; others were Nicola *Porpora, Leonardo *Leo, and Johann Adolf *Hasse. But the composer who produced the greatest work in the convention was *Handel. Subsequent composers of *opera seria* include Nicolò *Piccinni, Antonio *Sacchini, Antonio *Salieri, the young *Gluck, and the young *Mozart. It was the strictness and high seriousness of *opera seria* that led to the insertion of comic episodes, developing into to *Intermezzo and hence into comic opera.

Reaction against so strict a form was inevitable, and Niccolo *Jommelli and Tommaso *Traetta helped to pave the way for opera's second founder, *Gluck. By now, Italian opera had begun to spread across Europe and to establish itself firmly in most countries. Germany was dependent for long on the many travelling companies that crossed Europe, such as those of the brothers *Mingotti; Russia cultivated its national tradition in what became the classic method of first importing Italians to show the way, then sending native composers to study in Italy, and finally developing a national genre, based on folksong and folk legend grafted at first onto Italian models. By the early 19th cent., Germany and France were becoming independent of Italian example, and the Paris Opéra had formed a style that in turn influenced Italians, including *Cherubini, *Spontini, and even *Rossini and *Verdi.

However, Italian opera continued as a central tradition, and continued to produce numerous composers. Rossini revealed the comic possibilities to an unexcelled degree, while also showing mastery of Romantic opera and Grand opera; and the work of countless composers delighted their compatriots, visiting foreigners, and audiences abroad. Italian Romantic opera reaches its full stature in the work of *Bellini and *Donizetti; its greatest master was *Verdi. For all the advances which had been made, Italian opera remained grounded on its original principles – melody that was a stimulus to the finest vocal art, dramatic plots, clarity of presentation, and powerful emotions presented with a sense of drama.

Such was the strength of this tradition that little effective influence reached Italy, though there were composers who felt the force of Wagner. But partly in reaction to the drama that dealt with grand and heightened emotions, there developed the manner known as *verismo, the so-called *'squarcio di vita'*, or 'slice of life', referred to in an early classic of the genre, *Leoncavallo's *Pagliacci*. Other important *verismo* composers were *Mascagni, *Giordano and *Puccini, whose work proved immensely popular and stimulating to other countries' composers, especially the French. Puccini is the last composer most of whose works are still in the world-wide repertory.

Italian opera has remained vigorous, and continues to draw composers, from Puccini's successors such as *Zandonai, *Malipiero and many others, to the younger generation. Only in the most recent times has there been some falling away, as novel operatic methods in other countries challenge the traditional Italian qualities. See also *Bari, Bergamo, Bologna, Brescia, Cagliari, Catania, Como, Ferrara, Florence, Genoa, Mantua, Milan, Naples, Novara, Padua, Palermo, Parma, Pesaro, Piacenza, Ravenna, Reggio Emilia, Rome, Siena, Spoleto, Treviso, Trieste, Turin, Udine, Venice, Verona, Vicenza.*

Ivanhoe. Opera in 5 acts by Sullivan; text by Julian Sturgis, after Scott's novel (1819). Prod. for inauguration of short-lived Royal English Opera House (now Palace T.) in Cambridge Circus, London, 31 Jan. 1891, with Macintyre, Ben Davies, ffrangcon-Davies, cond. Sullivan. Sullivan's only grand opera, and perhaps the only grand opera ever to have a continuous run (160 perfs.). Other operas on the subject are by Rossini (1826), Pacini (1832), Savi (1863), and Ciardi (1888).

Ivan Susanin. See *Life for the Tsar, A.*

Ivan the Terrible. See *Maid of Pskov, The.* Ivan IV also appears in Rimsky-Korsakov's *The Tsar's Bride,* and plays a crucial part in the plot of Tchaikovsky's *The Oprichnik,* though the censor refused to allow him to be portrayed on stage.

Ivanov, Nikolay (Kuzmich) (*b* Voronezh, 22 Oct. 1810; *d* Bologna, 19 July 1880). Russian tenor.

Member of the Imperial Choir at St Petersburg. He received much encouragement from Glinka, at whose suggestion he went to Italy to study in Milan and Naples with Bianchi, A. Nozzari, and J. Fodor-Mainvielle. Début Naples, S.C., 1832, Percy (*Anna Bolena*). Paris, T.I., 1833–7; London, King's T., 1834, when Mount-Edgcumbe found his style 'chaste and simple, but with little execution'; Chorley, on the other hand, wrote, 'Nothing could be more delicious as to tone – more neat as to execution'. He returned to London, 1835 and 1837. He was a close friend of Rossini and one of the group who sang at Bellini's funeral. He retired in 1852.

Ivogün, Maria (orig. Maria Kempner) (*b* Budapest, 18 Nov. 1891). Daughter of a Hungarian officer and the singer Ida von Günther (not, as often stated, of Mizzi Günther, creator of Hanna Glawari in *The Merry Widow*). Studied Vienna with Amalie Schlemmer-Ambros. Engaged by Bruno Walter for Munich Opera;

created Ighino in *Palestrina*; N.Y., with German Opera, 1923; Berlin, Stä., 1925–34; London, C.G., 1924, 1927; Chicago 1922–3; Salzburg 1925, 1930. Last stage appearance as Zerbinetta, Berlin 1934, after which she devoted herself to teaching. Her pupils include Schwarzkopf and Rita Streich. One of the finest coloratura sopranos of the inter-war years; greatly admired as Constanze, Queen of Night, Zerbinetta, Gilda, Norina, Mistress Ford (Nicolai), and Oscar. In addition to Ighino, created leading roles in operas by Korngold and Braunfels. Married first to tenor Karl Erb and then the accompanist Michael Raucheisen. (R)

J

Jackson. Town in Mississippi, U.S.A. The home of the American all-black opera company, founded in 1971 by leading members of Jackson State University and Utica Junior College. It performs in Municipal Auditorium and began activities in May 1971 with *Aida*. Since then it has produced William Grant Still's *Highway 1 USA* and Bayou Legend and Lay's *The Juggler of Our Lady* and *Jubilee* (all world premières), as well as *Carmen, Otello, Der fliegende Holländer,* and *L'elisir d'amore,* the latter set in the steamboat era in Mississippi. Debria Brown and Faye Robinson are among its artists who have since made international careers. Walter Herbert was music director from 1971 until his death in 1975.

Jacobin, The (Cz., *Jakobín*). Opera in 3 acts by Dvořák; text by Marie Červinková-Riegrová. Prod. Prague, Cz., 12 Feb. 1889 with Foerstrová-Lautererová, Cavallarová, Veselý, Heš, Kroessing, cond. Čech. London, St George's Hall, 22 July 1947 by Workers' Music Assoc. with Vowles, Taplin, Lensky, Dargavel, Laurie, Davidson, R. Davies, cond. Corbett. The Jacobin returns from an exile caused by his political views and with the help of the musician Benda manages to regain his former position.

Jacovacci, Vincenzo (*b* Rome, 14 Nov. 1811; *d* 30 Mar. 1881). Italian impresario. After various theatrical enterprises and escapades (including being arrested for selling too many tickets for the première of Donizetti's *Adelia,* with Giuseppina Strepponi in the title role), he became one of the leading impresarios of mid-19th cent. Italy. He championed Verdi, giving the premières of *Il trovatore* (1853) and *Un ballo in maschera* (1859) and the Italian première of *La forza del destino* (1863) at the T. Apollo, Rome. However, his sharp business sense led him to engage inferior singers, to Verdi's annoyance. His productions were nevertheless based on spectacle and a sense of show that attracted the public.

Jacquino. Rocco's young assistant gaoler (ten.) in Beethoven's *Fidelio.*

Jadlowker, Hermann (*b* Riga, 5 July 1877; *d* Tel Aviv, 13 May 1953). Latvian tenor. Studied Vienna with Josef Gänsbacher. Début Cologne, 1897, Gomez in *Nachtlager von Granada.* Königsberg, Stettin, Rostock, Riga, Karlsruhe 1906–10; Berlin, Kroll, from 1907; Boston 1910–12; Berlin, Hofoper, 1911–12, 1922–3; N.Y., Met., 1910–13, where he created the King's son (*Königskinder*); also created Bac-

chus (*Ariadne*) Stuttgart 1912. In 1929 returned to Riga as chief cantor in the synagogue. Taught singing Riga Conservatory 1936–8, and from 1938 in Tel Aviv. His repertory included Raoul, Florestan, Don Carlos, Lohengrin, Parsifal. Made more than 200 records, which reveal a superb technique and a command of the florid style. (R)

Janáček, Leoš (*b* Hukvaldy, 3 July 1854; *d* Ostrava, 12 Aug. 1928). Czech composer. A passionate humanist, Janáček increasingly found opera to be the form in which he could best express his intense love of life and of people. His operas contain his greatest work, and it is chiefly upon them that his reputation rests. *Šárka* (1887; rev. 1888, 1918, prod. 1925) treats the Czech legend with skill and an occasional foretaste of his mature style, but in *Počátek románu* (The Beginning of a Romance, 1894) he reverted, in the attempt to compose a light folk comedy, to an unsuccessful version of opera based on folksongs and dances. Then came *Její Pastorkyňa* (Her Foster-Daughter, generally known as *Jenůfa,* 1894–1903). Though produced in Brno in 1904, it was not until a visitor who had overheard some of the music succeeded in obtaining a Prague performance (1916) that Janáček suddenly became famous. *Jenůfa* is his lyrical masterpiece, a wise and tender setting, in an idiom now fully mature, of a romantic plot marked with characteristic truthfulness of observation. For the first time Janáček's lifelong interest in speech-melodies is turned to expressive use; the short phrases of his own abrupt Lachian dialect are at the root of his musical idiom. In *Osud* (Fate, 1904, prod. 1958), some charming music is contained in an unsatisfactory libretto. *Výlety pana Broučka* (The Excursions of Mr Brouček, 1920) caused Janáček some difficulty: the first part, *Výlet pana Broučka do Měsíce* (Mr Brouček's Excursion to the Moon), needed much revision before he was satisfied; *Výlet pana Broučka do XV stol* (Mr Brouček's Excursion to the 15th century) followed. The former satirizes the bourgeois stolidity of Mr Brouček in a fictitious society run on artistic principles, though in fact the audience tends to sympathize with Mr Brouček's rugged common sense. The latter part is set in the Hussite Wars, and though both are intensely Czech in character, the work – not only for the beauty of some of the music – has proved more exportable than was originally believed likely.

Káťa Kabanová (1921), which followed soon after, is an expression of Janáček's lifelong attraction to Russian subjects: he contemplated an opera on *Anna Karenina,* with which the plot has a certain kinship, in 1907. It is a sombre work, more closely composed than *Jenůfa* but no less lyrical or sympathetic in its treatment of human predicaments. With *Příhody Lišky Bystroušky* (The Tales of Fox Sharpears, known in English as *The Cunning Little Vixen*, 1924), Janáček turns to nature for his subject. His animals have intensely vivid and very accurately observed natures, as do the village and rustic characters who live close by them and become involved with them (though there is no attempt to equate the two, as in the German version by Max Brod). Musically, the opera is still more laconic than earlier works, with the sounds of the woods made the substance of beautifully devised themes; and the final pages are the most rapturous affirmation of his love of Nature, as real, tough, and enduring, that Janáček ever made.

Věc Makropulos (The Makropoulos Case, or The Makropoulos Business, 1926) turns away from nature to an urban world of legal wrangles and theatrical life, and at the centre of it is the unnatural figure of the singer whose use of an elixir of life has condemned her to a miserable immortality; yet the theme is related in that Janáček is pointing to the justness of a natural life span, and insisting that it is the certainty of death that gives beauty and meaning to life. More drily scored than its predecessors, it is a brilliantly swift, subtle piece of work, his most intricate opera; the final pages are another rapturous affirmation of the natural order. In *Z mrtvého domu* (From the House of the Dead, 1930), a setting of Dostoyevsky's prison diaries, Janáček crystallized his idiom into its most concise, most intensely expressive form. Though the work has no plot and little incident, the strength of his musical portraits of the prisoners in their harsh life, and his genius for making these relate in a musically governed whole, give the opera a unique and profoundly moving character. His love, never sentimental in its declarations, is here extended to all men, especially when brought to their lowest. At the head of the score he set the words, 'In every human being there is a spark of God'.
Bibl: J. Vogel: *Leoš Janáček* (1958, trans. 1962).

Janků, Hana (Svobodá-) (*b* Brno, 25 Oct. 1940). Czech soprano. Studied Brno with Jaroslav Kvapil. Début Brno 1959; remained until 1960 and sang Leonora (*Trovatore*), Turandot, Libuše, Milada, Rusalka, and Turandot. Milan, Sc., 1967, Turandot; Deutsche Oper am Rhein and Berlin D. O. since 1970. London, C.G., 1973, Tosca. San Francisco, Mexico, etc. Repertory also includes Gioconda, Ariadne, and Kundry. Possesses a fine lyric-dramatic soprano voice of great power. (R)

Janowitz, Gundula (*b* Berlin 2 Aug. 1937). German soprano. Studied Graz. Début Vienna, S., 1960 Barbarina; Bayreuth 1960-62; Salzburg since 1963; Glyndebourne 1964, Salzburg

Easter Festival 1967–8 Sieglinde; N.Y. Met., 1967 Sieglinde; Berlin, D., since 1966. London, C.G. 1976 Donna Anna. Repertory also includes Agathe, Elisabeth, Fiordiligi, Empress in *Frau ohne Schatten*, Arabella. Possesses a rich, creamy, and beautiful voice, but is not a very vivid dramatic artist. (R)

Jansen (orig. Toupin), **Jacques** (*b* Paris, 22 Nov. 1913). French baritone. Studied with Panzéra. Début Paris, O.C., 1941, Pelléas; N.Y. Met., 1949 and London, C.G., 1949 in same role. Has appeared at Buenos Aires, C., and throughout Italy. His roles include Mârouf, Fragonard, and Valerien in Hahn's *Malvina*. (R)

Janssen, Herbert (*b* Cologne, 22 Sept. 1895; *d* New York, 3 June 1965). German, later naturalized American, baritone. Studied Cologne and Berlin with Daniel. Début Berlin 1924. London, C.G., 1926, and every season until 1939; N.Y., Met., 1939–51. Greatly admired as Amfortas, Wolfram, Gunther, and Kurwenal, all of which he sang in Bayreuth, London, and New York. During the war years, when there was a shortage of dramatic baritones in America, he unwisely undertook Wotan and Sachs, which were too heavy for him. His Kothner in *Meistersinger* has rarely been bettered. (R)

Japan. Japanese musical theatre is the most important form of Japanese drama, and is entitled the No Play ('accomplishment' or 'art' play). Several elements, including the narrative courtly dances of Bugaku and the importation of Gagaku from Korea in 612, combined to bring No to its flowering in the 14th cent.; nothing of importance has been written since 1600. The No Play is a fusion of song (*uta*) by a chorus (*ji*) of 8–10, recitation (*kotoba*), dance (*mai*), and instrumental music (*hayashi*), the latter provided by flute and three drums of variable, determinate pitch. An average evening of No consists of several plays, each lasting up to about three-quarters of an hour, first a warrior play, second a female-wig play in which a man impersonates a woman, often mad or in tragic circumstances, third a play of freer nature and subject, usually sensational, and a concluding dance play. The most famous author of No Plays was Zeami Motokiyo (1363–1443), who also composed, directed, acted, and danced; his son, Jūro Motomasa (1395–1431), was the author of *Sumida-gawa*, a celebrated female-wig play now also well known in the West as the source of *Britten's *Curlew River*. This 'operatic' treatment of No was anticipated by Yoshiro Irino's *The Silken Drum* (1962), a dodecaphonic T.V. opera which won the Second Salzburg Prize in 1962.

Western opera was first given in Japan on a regular basis by the Fujiwara O.C., founded in 1933 by the tenor Yoshie Fujiwara; this remains the most important Japanese company, and with Government subvention has continued a successful policy of staging a widely selective repertory of classics with Japanese, and occasionally Western, singers. The Nikikai troupe, a kind of singers' co-operative founded in 1952, has reflected the Japanese enthusiasm for Wagner with a production of *Parsifal* (1967) and initiated a Japanese *Ring* with *Walküre* in 1973. Other standard Western works, including *Figaro* and *Der fliegende Holländer,* have been given in the company's distinguished history. Opera is given in the Nissei T. (cap. 1,350), opened in Tokyo in 1964. Of many other groups, companies, occasional enterprises, and student ventures, the Tokyo Chamber Opera Group has been outstanding; founded in 1970, it gives five productions a year. In spite of poor conditions, it has given successful versions of works from *The Play of Daniel* to *Arlecchino,* as well as operas by Monteverdi, Britten, Haydn, Hindemith, and a new Japanese opera, *The Old Tale of the Enslaver Tarobe* (1973), by Yoshiya Mamiya. There have also been many visits by Western companies, e.g. from Italy, Paris (1962), Bayreuth (1964), and West Berlin (1970). The N.H.K. Radio and T.V. imports opera every second year. The Osaka Expo 1970 included in the Festival Hall performances of *Lohengrin* and *Moses und Aron* by the German Opera, Berlin, *Rheingold* by the Nikikai Opera Company, Paisiello's *Il barbiere di Siviglia* by the Piccolo T. Musicale of Rome, and Russian operas by the Bolshoy. Much other activity has assured Japan of a secure position on the international opera circuit.

In 1960 *Gracia Hokosawa,* by Vincenzo Cimatti, an Italian priest resident in Japan, was performed in Tokyo. Japanese operas include the 1-act *Kurai Kagami* (The Black Mirror, 1960) by Yasushi Akutagawa (*b* 1925) and *Arima Kohi* (1967) by Sadao Bekku (*b* 1922), a pupil of Milhaud and Messiaen; but the most important Japanese opera composer is Ikuma Dan (*b* 1924), who wrote the popular 1-act *Yuzuru* (The Silver Heron, 1951: to the same plot as Sven-Erik Bäck's *Crane Feathers*), *Kikimimi Zukin* (The Listening Cowl, 1955), *Yokihi* (1958), and *Hikarigoke* (The Shining Moss, 1972), a tale of cannibalism among an isolated naval party. Other works include Kan Ishii's *Kesa and Morito* (1969) and Saburo Takata's *The Dark Blue Wolf* (1973), on Genghis Khan.

Järnefelt, (Edvard) **Armas** (*b* Viipuri, 14 Aug. 1869; *d* Stockholm, 23 June 1958). Swedish conductor and composer of Finnish birth. Studied Helsinki with Wegelius and Busoni, Berlin with Becker, Paris with Massenet. Assistant conductor Magdeburg 1896, Düsseldorf 1897; cond. Wagner operas Helsinki 1904; Stockholm Opera 1905–6, 1907–32; Helsinki

Opera 1932–6. Married first **Maikka Pakarinen** (**Järnefelt**) (*b* Joensuu, 26 Aug. 1871; *d* Turku, 4 July 1929), a soprano who was a pupil of Marchesi, and sang as Maikka. They divorced in 1908 (she then married Selim Palmgren), and in 1910 he married **Liva Edström** (*b* Vänersborg, 18 Mar. 1876; *d* Stockholm, 24 June 1971), a soprano who sang at the Stockholm Opera 1898–1926.

Jean de Paris (John of Paris). Opera in 2 acts by Boieldieu; text by C. Godard d'Aucour de Saint-Just. Prod. Paris, O.C., 4 Apr. 1812; London, C.G., arr. Bishop with additions, with Stephens; New York, same version 25 Nov. 1816. Other operas on the subject are by Morlacchi (text by Romani, after Saint-Just, 1818) and Donizetti (text by Romani for Morlacchi, 1839).

The young widowed Princess of Navarre is destined to marry the Crown Prince of France, but intends first to spend some time travelling. At a Pyrenean inn, preparations for her arrival are interrupted by the arrival of the suite of 'Jean de Paris' (the Prince in disguise); they take possession of the inn. The Princess's Seneschal is outraged, but Jean declares that the Princess may be his guest. She recognizes him, but conceals this, telling him as they dance that she has already chosen her husband; all is disclosed, and the Prince and Princess are united.

Jeanne d'Arc au Bûcher (Joan of Arc at the Stake). Oratorio *dramatique* by Honegger; text by Claudel. Prod. Basle 12 May 1938, with Ida Rubinstein; San Francisco 15 Oct. 1954, with Dorothy Maguire; London, Stoll, 20 Oct. 1954, with Ingrid Bergman. See also *Joan of Arc.*

Je crois entendre encore. Nadir's (ten.) aria in Act 1 of *Les Pêcheurs de Perles,* in which he sings of his love for Leila.

Jehin, Léon (*b* Spa, 17 July 1853; *d* Monte Carlo, 14 Feb. 1928). Belgian conductor. Studied Liège and Brussels. Conductor Brussels, La M., 1882–8; Paris, O., 1889–93; London, C.G., 1891–2 where he directed first London performances of *Philémon et Baucis* and *Le Rêve.* Subsequently at Monte Carlo Opera. Married the mezzo-soprano Marie Blanche *Deschamps.

Jeník. A young villager (ten.), son of Tobias Micha by his first marriage, in Smetana's *The Bartered Bride.*

Jenůfa (Cz., *Její pastorkyňa*: Her Foster-Daughter). Opera in 3 acts by Janáček; text by composer, after Gabriela Preissová's drama (1890). Prod. Brno, 21 Jan. 1904, with Kabeláčová, Svobodová, Staněk-Doubravský, Procházka, cond. Hrazdira; N.Y., Met., 6 Dec. 1924, with Jeritza, Matzenauer, Oehmann, Laubenthal, cond. Bodanzky; London, C.G., 10 Dec.

1956, with Shuard, Fisher, Lanigan, E. Evans cond. Kubelík.

In the mill of Grandmother Buryjovka in the Moravian mountains lives the ne'er-do-well Števa Buryja (ten.); his stepbrother Laca Klemeň (ten.) is a farm-hand and their cousin Jenůfa (sop.) helps in the house. She is the stepdaughter of Grandmother Buryjovka's daughter-in-law, who, from her position as sexton, is known as the Kostelnička (sop.). Jenůfa is expecting Števa's child, and anxiously awaits the result of a conscription ballot to know whether he will return and marry her. He returns, unrecruited but also drunk, and the Kostelnička forbids him to marry Jenůfa until he has proved his worth by a year's total abstinence. When Števa, who is only physically attracted to Jenůfa, leaves, Laca offers her flowers and tries to kiss her; on being repelled, he slashes her face with a knife.

Jenůfa has secretly had a son. The Kostelnička, tormented by the disgrace, sends for Števa to marry Jenůfa; but he denies responsibility, and says that he is engaged to the mayor's daughter Karolka (mezzo). Laca appears, penitent and willing to marry Jenůfa though shocked by hearing of the birth of Števa's child. The Kostelnička, hoping to help the marriage on, tells Laca that the child had died; she takes it and drowns it in a brook. When Jenůfa awakes, she is also told that the child has died.

Jenůfa and Laca are about to be married, as are Števa and Karolka. As the ceremony begins, news comes that the body of a baby has been found under the ice. Jenůfa realizes the truth and reveals whose baby it is. To save her from being accused, the Kostelnička steps forward and confesses her guilt. Comforted by Jenůfa's forgiveness, she is led away. Jenůfa now turns to Laca and gives him his freedom; but he is faithful, and as the curtain falls they pledge their love.

Jeremiáš, Otakar (*b* Písek, 17 Oct. 1892; *d* Prague, 5 Mar. 1962). Czech composer. Son of Bohuslav Jeremiáš (1859–1918), founder of the South Bohemian Conservatory, and younger brother of the composer Jaroslav Jeremiáš (1889–1919). Studied with his father and in Prague with Novák. Among other activities, he was director of the National T. 1945–7. His own operas, post-Janáček in manner, include an ambitious and respected setting of *The Brothers Karamazov* (1928) and a Till Eulenspiegel one, *Enšpígl* (1949).

Jerger, Alfred (*b* Brno, 9 June 1889; *d* Vienna, 18 Nov. 1976). Austrian baritone. Studied Vienna. Passau 1913 as conductor; Zurich 1913–14 as Korrepetitor. Began singing in 1915 (*Die drei Pintos*); formal début Munich 1919. Vienna 1921, and leading baritone there until 1953; created The Man (*Glückliche Hand*).

Appeared regularly at Salzburg as Don Giovanni, Pizarro, Guglielmo, and Count Almaviva. Created Mandryka, Dresden 1933 and sang same role at C.G. 1934. From 1947 produced at the Vienna V.O. and taught at the Academy. (R)

Jeritza, Maria (orig. Mimi Jedlitzková) (*b* Brno, 6 Oct. 1887). Czech (Moravian) soprano. Studied Brno, Prague with Auspitz, and later in N.Y. with Sembrich. At Dortmund 1906–7. Official début Olomouc 1910, Elsa. Vienna, V.O. 1911; Blanchefleur in Kienzl's *Der Kuhreigen*. Vienna, S.O., 1911–32, 1949–52; created the Empress in *Frau ohne Schatten* and was the first Vienna Minnie in *La fanciulla del West*. Chosen by Strauss to create title role in *Ariadne auf Naxos*, Stuttgart 1912. N.Y., Met., 1921–32, 1951; London, C.G., 1925–6. Was the first American Jenůfa, Marietta, and Turandot, and was renowned for her Thaïs, Maliella, Tosca, Carmen, and Fedora. Her personal beauty, acting ability, and lovely voice combined to make her one of the most sought-after artists of the inter-war years. (R)
Bibl: M. Jeritza: *Sunlight and Song* (1924).

Jerum! Jerum! Hans Sachs's (bar.) cobbling song in Act 2 of Wagner's *Die Meistersinger von Nürnberg*.

Jérusalem. See *Lombardi, I*.

Jessonda. Opera in 3 acts by Spohr; text by E. H. Gehe, after Antoine Lemierre's tragedy, *La Veuve de Malabar*. Prod. Kassel, 28 July 1823, with Schröder-Devrient, Beltheim, Keller, Bergmann, Mayer, Tourny, cond. Spohr; London, Prince's, T., 18 June 1840; Philadelphia, 15 Feb. 1864.

The Rajah's widow Jessonda (sop.) must die, according to custom, on his funeral pyre. Nadori (ten.), a young priest of Brahma, must announce this to her; but he falls in love with her sister Amazili (sop.) and promises to help save Jessonda. Purifying herself for her ordeal, Jessonda is recognized by her former lover, the Portuguese general Tristan d'Acunha, besieging Goa. A truce forbids him to attack and rescue her; but when he finds that the priest Daudon has broken the truce, he feels free to enter the temple by a secret passage and rescue Jessonda.

Jewels of the Madonna, The. See *Gioielli della Madonna, I*.

Jírovec. See *Gyrowetz*.

Joan of Arc (*b* Domrémy, 6 Jan. 1412; *d* Rouen, 30 May 1431). The French martyr who led an army against the English besieging Orléans, and was burnt at the stake. Operas about her are by Andreozzi (1789), R. Kreutzer (1790), Carafa (1821), Vaccai (1827), Pacini (1830), Balfe (1837), Vesque von Püttlingen (1840),

Verdi (1845), Langert (1862), Duprez (1865), Mermet (1876), Bruneau (1878), Tchaikovsky (1879), Chausson (1880), Rezniček (1886), Widor (1890), Wambach (1900), Morera (1907), Roze (1911), Marsh (1923), Anderson (1934), Honegger (1938), Bastide (1949), Dello Joio (*The Triumph of St Joan*, 1950; *The Trial at Rouen*, 1956); Humphreys (1968). See also *Giovanna d'Arco.*

Jochanaan. John the Baptist (bar.) in Strauss's *Salome.*

Jochum, Eugen (*b* Babenhausen, 1 Nov. 1902). German conductor. Studied Augsburg and Munich. After working in Munich (1924–5), Mönchen-Gladbach (1925–6), Kiel (1926–9), and Mannheim (1929–30), was Generalmusik-direktor, Duisburg, 1930–2 and Hamburg, 1934–5. His Bayreuth appearances include 1953 (*Tristan*), 1954 (*Tannhäuser*), 1971–3 (*Parsifal*). His brother **Georg Jochum** (*b* Babenhausen, 10 Dec. 1909; *d* Mülheim, 1 Nov. 1970) was a conductor who worked in Münster and Frankfurt (1934–7), Plauen, and Linz (Generalmusikdirektor 1940–5).

John Lewis Partnership Music Society. An amateur society, sponsored by the public-spirited John Lewis shops in London, which with the help of professional conductors (generally James Robertson), producers, and designers has produced a number of operas since 1947 of a remarkably high artistic standard, including the first stage performances in England of Dvořák's *Rusalka* (1950) and *The Peasant a Rogue* (1963), Sutermeister's *The Black Spider* (1954), Floyd's *Susannah* (1968), and Chabrier's *L'Etoile* (1970), the première of Hugo Cole's *The Tunnel* (specially commissioned by the John Lewis Partnership) (1960), and such rarities as Wolf-Ferrari's *Le donne curiose*, Puccini's *Le villi*, Smetana's *The Kiss*, Boieldieu's *La Dame blanche*, Bizet's *Don Procopio*, Offenbach's *La Périchole*, and the Weber-Mahler *Die drei Pintos.*

Johnson, Edward (*b* Guelph, Ontario, 22 Aug. 1878; *d* Toronto, 20 Apr. 1959). Canadian tenor and manager. Studied N.Y. with Mme von Feilitsch and Florence with Vincenzo Lombardi. Début (as Eduardo di Giovanni) Padua 1912, Chénier. Engaged for Milan Sc. 1913–14 where he created Parsifal in Italy. Between 1914 and 1919 he created in either Milan or Rome leading tenor roles in Montemezzi's *La nave*, Pizzetti's *Fedra*, and Alfano's *L'ombra di Don Giovanni*; he was also the first Italian Rinuccio and Luigi, and an admirable Siegfried and Tannhäuser. Chicago Opera 1919–22; N.Y., Met., 1922–35; sole appearance London, C.G. (with B.N.O.C., 1923), as Faust. At Met. created leading tenor roles in *The King's Henchman, Peter Ibbetson*, and *The Merry Mount.* Was also a distinguished Pelléas. Manager of *Met-

ropolitan 1935–50, and after his retirement played an active part in the opera class in the Music Faculty at Toronto University. (R)
Bibl: R. Mercer: *The Tenor of his Time* (1976).

Johnston, James (*b* Belfast, *c* 1900). Irish tenor. Début Dublin 1940, Duke of Mantua; London, S.W., 1945–50 Duke of Mantua; London, S.W., 1945–50 and guest artist until 1957. C.G. 1950–8. Created Hector in Bliss's *Olympians* and was the first Gabriele Adorno in *Simone Boccanegra* at S.W. 1948. His lyric-dramatic voice admirably suited him for Canio, Radamès, Manrico, Calaf, and Don José. He sang Italian roles with a ringing tone and an intensity rare among British singers. (R)

Jolie fille de Perth, La (The Fair Maid of Peth). Opera in 4 acts by Bizet; text by St Georges and Adenis, loosely based on Scott's novel, *The Fair Maid of Perth* (1832). Prod. Paris, T.L., 26 Dec. 1867, with Devriès, Ducasse, Lutz, Barré; Manchester, 4 May 1917, with Nelis, Clegg, Hyde, Millar, cond. Beecham.

Henry Smith (ten.), an armourer, is lamenting the absence of his beloved Catherine Glover (sop.). He gives shelter to the gipsy Mab (sop. or mezzo); then he welcomes Catherine, her father Simon (bass) and Ralph (bass or bar.), who is jealous of Smith. The Duke of Rothsay (bar. or ten.) invites Catherine to his castle, to Smith's rage, and asks Mab, his former mistress, to help him abduct her: Mab pretends to agree, but after many complications brings about a happy ending.

Jommelli, Niccolò (*b* Aversa, 10 Sept. 1714; *d* Naples, 25 Aug. 1774). Italian composer. Studied Naples with Muzillo and Feo. His first operatic success was *L'errore amoroso* (1737), followed by *Odoardo* (1738). He had further successes in Rome (*Ricimero* and *Astianatte*, 1740) and in Bologna (*Ezio*, 1741), where he also studied with Padre Martini. The success of *Merope* in Venice (1741) won him an appointment at the Ospedale dei Incurabili (1741–7); *Semiramide* (1743) and *Sofonisba* (1746) followed. In Vienna from 1749, he wrote five operas; he also worked in Rome, and his operas include *Artaserse* (1749), which has an early use of *crescendo, and *Ifigenia in Aulide* (1751). Appointed at Stuttgart from 1753: his operas here, which include *La clemenza di Tito* (1753) and *Fetonte* (1753), show a subtler and fuller use of the orchestra, and especially an ability to move away from *da capo* aria, whose rigidities he resisted except for special dramatic purposes, and to give extra expressive weight to accompanied recitative. He also wrote opera buffa, including *La critica* (1766), though his gift really lay in opera seria. Returning to Naples in 1769, he found himself forgotten, his reforms unwelcome: his last operas, *Armida* (1770) and *Ifigenia in Tauride*

(1771), were failures. Of 82 known operas and divertissements, 53 survive.

Bibl: H. Abert: *Niccolò Jommelli als Opernkomponist* (1908, R/1969).

Jommellino. See *Andreozzi.*

Jones, Gwyneth (*b* Pontnewynydd, 7 Nov. 1936). Welsh soprano. Studied London, RCM, with Arnold Smith and Ruth Packer, Siena, and Geneva with Maria Carpi. Engaged as a mezzosoprano Zurich 1962, début as Orpheus (Gluck). London, C.G., since 1963 as soprano. Vienna since 1966; Bayreuth since 1966; Sieglinde, Senta, Kundry, Venus, Elisabeth, Brünnhilde; Vienna since 1966; Munich, Milan, San Francisco. Repertory also includes Medée, Leonore, Donna Anna, Salome, Octavian, Marschallin, Helena, and Verdi dramatic soprano roles. An uneven vocalist, at her best exciting, and dramatically vivid. (R)

Jones, Parry (*b* Blaina, Monmouthshire, 14 Feb. 1891; *d* London, 26 Dec. 1963). Welsh tenor. Studied London, R.C.M., Italy with Colli, Dresden with Scheidemantel, and England with John Coates. After touring America and surviving the torpedoing of the *Lusitania* in 1915, he sang with the Beecham and D'Oyly Carte Companies. Leading tenor C.R. 1919–22, and B.N.O.C. 1922–8; C.G., 1925–6, 1930–2, 1935, 1937 in small roles. Sang in the first English performances of *Wozzeck, Mathis der Maler, Doktor Faust* and other works in B.B.C. concert performances. C.G. 1949–53, especially as Shuisky and the Captain (*Wozzeck*). Taught at London, G.S.M. (R)

Jongleur de Notre-Dame, Le (Our Lady's Juggler). Opera in 3 acts by Massenet; text by Maurice Léna, after a story by Anatole France in *L'Etui de nacre* (1892). Prod. Monte Carlo, 18 Feb. 1902, with Maréchal, Renaud, Soulacroix, cond. Jéhin; London, C.G., 15 June 1906, with Laffitte, cond. Messager; N.Y. 27 Nov. 1908, with Mary Garden as Jean (orig. tenor role), cond. Campanini.

Jonny spielt auf (Johnny strikes up). Opera in 2 parts (11 scenes) by Křenek; text by composer. Prod. Leipzig, 10 Feb. 1927, with Cleve, Schulthess, Beinert, Horand, Spilcker, cond. Brecher; N.Y., Met., 19 Jane 1929, with Bohnen, Schorr, cond. Bodansky.

Jonny (bar.), a jazz-band leader, steals a violin from Daniello (bar.) and becomes so immensely successful that his performance from the North Pole sets the world dancing the Charleston.

Jonson, Ben (*b* London, *c* 11 June 1572; *d* London, 6 Aug. 1637). English poet and dramatist. Operas on his works are as follows: *Volpone* (1606): Gruenberg (1945); Demuth (1949); Antheil (1953); Coombs (1957); Zillig (1957); Zimmermann (1957); Burt (1960).

Epicoene (1609): Salieri (*Angiolina*, 1800); Lothar (*Lord Spleen*, 1930); Strauss (*Die schweigsame Frau*, 1935). *The Alchemist* (1610): Lang (1969). *Catiline* (1611): Hamilton (1974). *The Masque of Oberon* (1615): Arne (*The Fairy Prince*, 1771).

Joplin, Scott (*b* Texacarna, 24 Nov. 1868; *d* New York, 1 Apr. 1917). American composer. Best known for his popular piano rags, Joplin also wrote the first ragtime operas. *A Guest of Honour*, to his own libretto, was composed in the early years of the century; *Treemonisha* was published in 1911, and given a single performance in 1915 without scenery and with the composer at the piano; revived 1975. It has also been recorded.

Joseph. Opera in 3 acts by Méhul; text by Duval. Prod. Paris, O.C., 17 Feb. 1807, with Gavaudan, Elleviou, Solie; Philadelphia 15 Oct. 1828; London, D.L., concert, 7 Apr. 1841; London, C.G., 3 Feb. 1914, with Jonsson, Sembach, Van Hulst, Kiess, Plaschke, cond. Pitt.

Under the assumed name of Cleophas, Joseph (ten. or sop.) has saved Egypt from famine; his blind father, Jacob (bar.), and brothers arrive in Memphis to beg for food, but do not recognize him. When he reveals his identity, he forgives his brothers and begs his father to do likewise.

Journet, Marcel (*b* Grasse, 25 July 1867; *d* Vittel 7 Sept. 1933). French bass. Studied Paris Conservatoire with Obin and Seghettini. Début Montpellier 1891, *La favorite.* Brussels, La M., 1894–1900; London, C.G., 1897–1907, 1927–8; N.Y. Met., 1900–1908; Chicago 1915–19. Paris, O., 1908–31, where first Fafner, Klingsor, Phanuel (*Hérodiade*), Dosifey, and Sultan in *Mârouf.* Milan, Sc., 1917, 1922–7: created Simon Mago in Boito's *Nerone* and was much admired as the Father (*Louise*), Golaud, Méphistophélès, Escamillo, the Wanderer, and especially Hans Sachs. Repertory also included William Tell, Tonio, Athanael, and Gurnemanz. His recordings reveal a well-schooled and beautiful voice, which carried on the tradition of the best French basses as exemplified by Delmas and Plançon. (R)

Jouy, (Victor Joseph) **Étienne** (de) (*b* Jouy-en-Josas, 12 Sept. 1764; *d* St Germain-en-Laye, 4 Sept. 1846). French playwright, librettist, and journalist. As librettist at the Paris Opéra, he worked for some of the most successful composers of the day, including Méhul, Boieldieu, Catel, and Dalayrac; but his greatest and most characteristic collaborations were with Cherubini (*Les Abencérages*), Rossini (*Guillaume Tell* and the revision of *Moise*), and especially Spontini (*La vestale, Fernand Cortez,* and *Milton*). His vivid appreciation of the sensational could go to extremes – he introduced horses into *Cortez* on the plea that the surprise thus occasioned matched that of the original Aztecs on beholding horses; but at his finest, as in *La vestale,* he responded to the demands of the heroic and spectacular in French *grand opera with some imposing scenes and verses.

Juch, Emma (*b* Vienna, 4 July 1863; *d* New York, 6 Mar. 1939). American soprano. Her parents were both Austrian by birth, but had become naturalized Americans, and she was born while they were on a visit to Austria. Studied with her father and Murio-Celli. Début London, H.M.'s, 1881, Philine (*Mignon*); N.Y., Ac. of M., 1881, same role. Then joined the American Opera Company, subsequently the National Opera Company, which foundered in 1889 and was reorganized by her as the Juch Grand Opera Company, which toured the U.S., Canada, and Mexico until 1891, after which she withdrew from opera. A great champion of opera in English. Her pure diction was often quoted as a model. She possessed an enormous vocal range and sang the Queen of Night and Senta with equal success. (R)

Judith. A Jewish heroine who, in the book of the Apocrypha named after her, made her way into the tent of Nebuchadnezzar's general Holofernes and cut off his head, thus saving her native town of Bethulia. Operas on the subject (many after Hebbel's tragedy, 1839) by L. Koželuch (1799), Fuss (1814), Raimondi (1827), Levi (1844), Hebenstreit (1849, on Nestroy's parody of Hebbel), E. Naumann (1858), A. Peri (1860), Serov (1863), Doppler (1870), Silveri (1885), Falchi (1887), Ettinger (1921), Chishko (1923), Rezniček (1923), Honegger (1926), Goossens (1929), Gnecchi (1953).

Juilliard School, New York. One of America's leading musical academies, the Juilliard School has always favoured opera in English. The first opera it staged was *Hänsel and Gretel* in 1929, since when it has staged many works, including the American stage premières of Britten's *The Beggar's Opera* (1950) and Strauss's *Capriccio* (1954). Albert Stoessel was the school's music director 1929-43, and after his death he was succeeded by Wilfred Pelletier and Edgar Schenkman. In 1947 William Schuman, president of the school, appointed Frederic Cohen head of the opera department which became the Juilliard Opera T. Moved to a splendidly equipped new building in Lincoln Centre 1970; Peter Mennin is the director. Past students of the school include Frances Bible, Gloria Davy, Mack Harrell, Margaret Harshaw, Charles Kullman, Evelyn Lear, Risë Stevens, Leontyne Price, Thomas Stewart, and Shirley Verrett.

Juive, La (The Jewess). Opera in 5 acts by Halévy; text by Scribe. Prod. Paris, O., 23 Feb. 1835, with Falcon, Dorus-Gras, Nourrit, Levas-

seur; New Orleans 13 Feb. 1844, with Fleury-Joly, Lecourt, Grossett, Blès, cond. Prévost; London, D.L., 29 July 1846, with Julien, Charton, Laborde, Zelger, cond. Henssens. The opera, set in 15th cent. Constance, tells of the persecution of the Jews in that city led by Cardinal Brogni (bass), and how Rachel (sop.), the supposed daughter of Eleazar the goldsmith, refuses to betray her lover Leopold (ten.), prince of the Empire. She is condemned with her 'father' to death by being thrown into a cauldron of boiling water. As she goes to her death Eleazar reveals she is not his daughter but that of Cardinal Brogni.

Julien. Opera in a prologue and 4 acts by Charpentier; text by composer. Prod. Paris, O.C., 4 June 1913, with Carré, Rousselière, cond. Wolff; N.Y., Met., 26 Feb. 1914, with Farrar, Caruso, cond. Polacco. A sequel to *Louise*, but unsuccessful, receiving only 20 Paris performances; never revived. The dead Louise (sop.) appears to Julien (ten.) in a vision and attempts to rekindle his faith in art and beauty. Julien, however, is frustrated in the attempt to find his soul by this means, and dies.

Julietta. Lyrical opera in 3 acts by Martinů; text by composer, after Georges Neveux's drama *Juliette, ou La Clé des songes* (1930). Prod. Prague, N., 16 Mar. 1938, with Horáková, Podvalová, Gleich, Ludek, Mandaus, cond. Talich; London, Col., 5 Apr. 1978, with Roberts, Kale, Du Plessis, Wicks, cond. Mackerras.

Juliette. Roméo's lover (sop.) in Gounod's *Roméo et Juliette.*

Julius Caesar. See *Giulio Cesare.*

Jullien, Louis (*b* Sisteron, 23 Apr. 1812; *d* Paris, 14 May 1860). French conductor. Conducted in London from 1840, where his flamboyant personality attracted much attention to his concerts, directed opera, and composed an unsuccessful opera *Pietro il Grande* (C.G. 1852, with Tamberlik), which he financed himself. Originator of the unsuccessful speculation at D.L. in 1847 when English operas were to be given with Berlioz as conductor and with Bishop superintending rehearsals.

Junca, Marcel (*b* Bayonne, 1818; *d* Lormes, 4 Oct. 1878). French bass. Studied Toulon and Paris. Début Metz, 1839. Lyons 1840-1; Paris 1847-55. Appearances Milan, Sc., created Mefistofele (Boito); Buenos Aires, C., created Salvator Rosa (Gomez). Sang Padre Guardiano in revised *Forza* (Milan, 1869); repertory also included Silva, Philip, Alfonso (*Lucrezia Borgia*). Also created Mossoul (*Si jétais roi*). Retired from stage 1877.

Junge Lord, Der (The Young Lord). Comic Opera in 2 acts by Henze; text by Ingeborg Bachmann, after a parable in Hauff's *Der*

Scheik von Alexandria und seine Sklaven (1827). Prod. Berlin, D., 7 Apr. 1965, with Mathis, Otto, Johnson, Graf, McDaniel, Driscoll, Hesse, Grobe, cond. Dohnányi; San Diego 17 Feb. 1967, with Lynn, Curatillo, Turner, Toscano, Fredericks, Cole, Remo, cond. Herbert; London, S.W., by Cologne Opera, 14 Oct. 1969, with Fine, Ahlin, Harper, Mohler, Nicolai, cond. Janowski.

Sir Edgar (silent role) introduces his nephew, Lord Barratt (ten.), to the inhabitants of the small German provincial town of Grünwiesel. The young lord shocks the local snobbish establishment, but his behaviour is sycophantically condoned until it is revealed that he is a circus ape dressed in man's clothing.

Jürgens, Helmut (*b* Höxter an der Wese, 19 Jun. 1902; *d* Munich, 28 Aug. 1963). German designer. Technical director Düsseldorf 1930-8; Frankfurt 1938-45. Chief designer Bavarian State Opera, Munich 1948-63. Designed more than 100 productions for the Prinzregenten and Cuvilliés theatres; also *Meistersinger, Frau ohne Schatten, Fidelio,* and *Aida* for the rebuilt National T., 1963. Professor of scene design at Munich Academy of Visual Arts.

Jurinac, Sena (orig. Srebrenka) (*b* Travnik, 24 Oct. 1921). Yugoslav soprano. Studied Zagreb with Maria Kostrenčić. Début Zagreb 1942, First Flower Maiden, then Mimì. Member of Vienna S.O. since 1944; London, C.G., with Vienna Company 1947, Dorabella; 1959-63, 1965, 1973. Gly. Festivals 1949-56; San Francisco 1959. One of the finest Mozart singers of her day – a beautiful Cherubino, Fiordiligi, Ilia, Donna Elvira, and Pamina. As her voice grew in size she assumed heavier roles – Donna Anna, the Countess. Considered by many people to be the finest Octavian of the century and the best Composer (*Ariadne auf Naxos*) since Lotte Lehmann. Since 1957 she has sung Elisabeth de Valois, Desdemona, and Butterfly with equal success. Chosen by Klemperer as Leonore for his C.G. *Fidelio* (1961); later sang Marschallin and Iphigenia there. (R)
Bibl: U. Tamussino: *Sena Jurinac* (1971).

Jushina. See *Ermolenko-Yuzhina.*

K

Kabaivanska, Raina (Yakimova) (*b* Burgas, 15 Dec. 1934). Bulgarian soprano. Studied Sofia with Prokopova and Yosifov. Début Sofia, 957, Tatyana; further study in Milan with Zita Fumagalli-Riva, and in Vercelli with Giulia Tess. Italian début Fano, 1959, Nedda (as Raina Kabai); Milan, Sc., since 1961; London, C.G., 962, Desdemona, 1963 Liù; N.Y., Met., since 962. Repertory includes Verdi and Puccini as well as title-roles in *Francesca da Rimini, La Wally, Adriana Lecouvreur*. Sang Hélène in Callas's prod. of *Vespri Siciliani* which opened rebuilt Turin, T.R., 1973. A well-schooled singer with beautiful stage presence and dramatic temperament. (R)

Kabalevsky, Dmitry (Borisovich) (*b* St Petersburg, 30 Dec. 1904). Russian composer. Studied Moscow, with Myaskovsky. His fluent talent and easy tunefulness have found expression in five operas: *The Master of Clamecy* after Romain Rolland's *Colas Breugnon*, under which title the overture is known; 1938, rev. 1968, prod. 1970); *Under Fire* (or *Before Moscow*, 1943); *The Family of Taras* (1950); *Nikita Vershinin* (1955); and *The Sisters* (1969).

Kaiserslautern. Town in Rhineland-Palatinate, Germany. A resident company was established in 1787. The theatre (cap. 1,200) opened 1862 with *Preciosa*. It burned down 1867; a second theatre was opened 1897, and destroyed 1944. The new theatre (cap. 750) opened 1950. Music directors have included Rudolf Moralt, Hubert Albert, Erich Riede, and, since 1969, Wilfried Emmert.

Kaliningrad (Ger. Königsberg). Town in Russia, formerly Prussia. The German town of Königsberg, as it remained until 1945, first saw opera with Heinrich Albert's *Cleomedes* (1635). The first opera house was built in 1753, and Singspiels were given. After the Russian occupation of 1758-62, Austrian officers imprisoned in the city helped to foster a knowledge of Viennese music. Mozart was first given in 1793 (*Don Giovanni*) and predominated in the repertory in the early years of the 19th cent., together with French opera. After the theatre burnt down in 1798, a plain new one was erected and took over the ensemble of the Schuch sisters which had meanwhile been a regular visitor. With Hiller's son Friedrich Adam as music director, the company played in Königsberg in the winter, in Danzig in the summer, with visits to Elbling. Economic difficulties followed, and the new Schauspielhaus (1806) burnt down in 1808. The old theatre reopened, with rather an

ill-assorted company and a repertory of the standard French and German works. A new theatre opened 1810 (cap. *c*750) but organizational difficulties affected standards. Hiller died in 1812, and yet another economic crisis led to the dismissal of Minna Planer, Wagner's first wife, in 1837. A Wagner tradition developed during the second half of the century, with ten Wagner works receiving over 200 perfs. 1889-1900. The Ostpreussisches Landestheater (cap. 1425) was rebuilt 1910. Frida Leider was in the company 1918-19; subsequent company singers have included Gottlob Frick, Josef Herrmann, Paul Kuen, and Arno Schellenberg. Karl Rankl once worked there as conductor, Günther Rennert as producer.

Kalisch, Alfred (*b* London, 13 Mar. 1863; *d* London, 17 May 1933). English critic and librettist. Originally a barrister, he took up musical journalism in 1894, and was critic of *The Star, The World, Morning Leader* and from 1912 of *The Daily News*. Translated *Salome, Elektra, Rosenkavalier, Ariadne auf Naxos*, and other works into English. He was a great champion of Strauss's operas, writing many pamphlets and articles and delivering lectures on them. Apart from Beecham, he probably did more than anyone else for Strauss in England.

Kalisch, Paul (*b* Berlin, 6 Nov. 1855; *d* St Lorenz am Modensee, 27 Jan. 1946). German tenor. Originally an architect. His voice was discovered by Pollini, who sent him to Milan to study with Lamperti. Début (as Paolo Alberti), Rome, 1879, Edgardo. Milan, Sc., 1882 under same name. After five years in Italy and a period in Munich, he was engaged for the Berlin Opera 1884-7. London, H.M.'s 1887, 1888. N.Y., Met., 1888-92 where he sang Tannhäuser in the first American performance of the Paris version of the opera, Nureddin in the American première of *Der Barbier von Bagdad*, Pollione in the 1890 Benefit performance for Lilli Lehmann, whom he had married in 1888, and Manrico when Lehmann sang her first role in Italian in 1891.

Kálmán, Emmerich (orig. Imre) (*b* Siófok, 24 Oct. 1882; *d* Paris, 30 Oct. 1953). Hungarian composer. Studied Budapest with Koessler. From 1938 he lived in Vienna, where he won a following as a composer of lively and tuneful operettas. The most successful were *Czardasfürstin* (1915), *Gräfin Maritza* (1924), and *Die Zirkusprinzessin* (1926). He then lived in America and from 1945 in Paris, where he wrote his last operetta, *Arizona Lady* (completed by his son, 1954).
Bibl: J. Bistron: *Emmerich Kálmán* (1932).

Kalomiris, Manolis (*b* Smyrna, 14 Dec. 1883; *d* Athens, 3 Apr. 1962). Greek composer. Studied Vienna with Grädener. His operas are *O Protomastoras* (The Master Mason, after Kazantzakis, 1916), *To Dakhtilidi tis Manas* (The

Mother's Ring, 1917), *Anatoli* (Sunrise, 1945), and *Ta Xotika Nera* (The Shadowy Waters, after Yeats, 1951).

Kalter, Sabine (*b* Jaroslaw, 28 Mar. 1890; *d* London, 1 Sept. 1957). Hungarian mezzo-soprano. Début Vienna, V.O., 1911. Leading mezzo-soprano Hamburg 1915-35, where her Lady Macbeth and Wagner interpretations were greatly admired. Forced to leave Germany, she went to London where she sang at C.G. 1935-9 as Fricka, Ortrud, Brangaene, and Herodias. (R)

Kamionsky, Oscar (Isayevich) (*b* Kiev, 1869; *d* Yalta, 15 Aug. 1917). Russian baritone. Studied St Petersburg with Camille Everard, and in Naples with Rossi. Début Naples 1891; most of career from 1893 in Russia: Kharkov 1893-4, 1898-9; Kiev 1894-5, 1902-4; Rostov-on-Don 1895-6; Tiflis 1896-8, 1899-1901. Guest appearances Moscow, St Petersburg, Baku, Odessa, Kazan, etc. St Petersburg, Tseretoli company, 1904-5; Moscow, Z., 1905-8, 1913-14. Retired 1915. Repertory included Onegin, Mazeppa, Renato, and Figaro. Known as 'the Russian Battistini'. (R)

Kammersänger (Kammersängerin) (*Ger* Chamber singer). High honorary title given by the German and Austrian governments to distinguished singers. Originally the title was bestowed by the various courts.

Kanawa, Kiri Te. See *Te Kanawa, Kiri.*

Kansas City. The Kansas City Lyric T., founded by Russell Patterson and Morton Walker in 1958, opened in Sep. 1958 (*La bohème*) with a policy of giving opera in English with young American artists. In the first decade of its existence it gave 200 performances of 30 operas, including several American works, e.g. *Vanessa, The Crucible,* and *The Sweet Bye and Bye.*

Kapellmeister (*Ger* chapel master). Originally the choirmaster in a court chapel, and formerly generally used in Germany for a conductor.

Kapp, Julius (*b* Steinbach, 1 Oct. 1883; *d* Hinang bei Alstädten im Algau, 18 Mar. 1962). German musicologist. Connected with Berlin S.O. from 1921; first as editor of *Blätter der Staatsoper* and then as Dramaturg. He adapted many operas for the German stage, including *Les Huguenots, Les Troyens,* and *Guillaume Tell.* He wrote books on Wagner, Meyerbeer, Berlioz, Weber, and Schreker, and several historical works on the Berlin Opera.

Kappel, Gertrud (*b* Halle, 1 Sept. 1884; *d* Munich, 3 Apr. 1971). German soprano. Studied piano Leipzig with Nikisch. Début Hanover 1906, Leonora (*Trovatore*); leading soprano Munich 1927-31; London, C.G., 1912-14, 1924-6; N.Y., Met., 1928-36. A famous

Brünnhilde and Isolde, she also sang Elektra and the Marschallin with success. She was admired by many above Leider and Flagstad in Wagner. Retired 1937. (R)

Karajan, Herbert (orig. Heribert) **von** (*b* Salzburg, 5 Apr. 1908). Austrian conductor. Studied Salzburg Mozarteum with Schalk and Vienna Conservatory. Début Salzburg, Landestheater, 1927 (*Fidelio*). Ulm 1927-34; Aachen 1934-8; Berlin S.O. 1938-45; Vienna, S.O., as artistic director 1956-64. Milan, Sc., since 1948; Bayreuth 1951-2; artistic director Salzburg Festival 1958-60 and from 1964. Established his Salzburg Easter Festival in 1963, giving one opera of the *Ring* each year, but never a complete cycle; and then *Parsifal, Tristan, Meistersinger* and *Trovatore*; these performances with the Berlin Philharmonic were subsequently recorded and Karajan also hoped to have them made into films. Karajan possesses one of the most remarkable conducting talents of the day. His very personal, high-powered approach to classical composers has sharply divided opinion. His catholic taste is evident in his direction of such different works as *Lucia di Lammermoor* and *Il trovatore* on the one hand, and the German repertory from Mozart to Strauss on the other. As a producer he is more fascinated by lighting and stage techniques, and as a conductor by beauty of sound, especially orchestral, than by dramatic meaning. *Bibl:* P. Robinson: *Karajan* (1975).

Karfreitagzauber. See *Good Friday Music.*

Karlsruhe. Town in Baden-Württemberg, Germany. Opera was first given in the 17th cent. in the Residenz Durlach, and a number of performances and visits from travelling companies took place in the 18th cent. A new theatre was opened in 1810 with Paer's *Achilles*; this burned down in 1847. The Court T. opened in 1851, and was destroyed in 1944. Music directors in the first part of the 19th cent. included Franz Danzi, who staged many works by his friend Weber, and Joseph Strauss (1824-63), who was responsible for a major growth in operatic life and the foundation of a Wagner tradition. After the Second World War the former Staatstheater and Konzerthalle were used for opera; this was rebuilt in 1954 (cap. 1,055). Music directors have included Hermann Levi (1864-72), Felix Mottl (1880-1904), Joseph Krips (1926-33), Joseph Keilberth (1933-40), Alexander Krannhals (1955-62), Arthur Grüber (1962-77), and Christof Prick (from 1977). The most important event was the first performance of Berlioz's *Les Troyens*; also the first German *Yolanta* (1894), *King Priam* (1963), and *Midsummer Marriage* (1973). Artists who began their careers there include Schnorr von Carolsfeld, Jadlowker, Köth, Jess Thomas, and Barry McDaniel.

Karl-Marx-Stadt (until 1953, Chemnitz). Town in Saxony, Germany. Former Opera-House opened 1909, destroyed during Second World War. New theatre (cap. 1,073) opened 1950.

Kärntnertortheater. T. in Vienna dating from 1761. Originally home of drama, but from 1790 used for opera and operetta. *Barbaia was director 1821-8, and invited Rossini to give a season of opera there 1821. Premières of *Euryanthe*, *Linda di Chamounix*, *Maria di Rohan*, and *Martha*.

Kaschmann (orig. Kašman), **Giuseppe** (*b* Mali Losing, 14 July 1847; *d* Rome, 7 Feb. 1925). Italian baritone. Studied Udine with Giovanini. Début Zagreb, 1869, and sang at inauguration of Zagreb Opera 2 Oct. 1870 (title-role in Zajc's *Mislav*); Milan, Sc., 1878; N.Y., Met., 1883 for inaugural season, and sang the first Enrico *Lucia*) in that theatre; returned in 1896 to sing Telramund in *Lohengrin* in German. Bayreuth, 1892, 1894, Amfortas and Telramund. With advancing years he turned to buffo roles, and was singing Pasquale and Bartolo when he was nearly 70; in 1921 appeared in Cimarosa's *Astuzie femminili* in Rome. (R)

Kashperov, Vladimir (Nikitich) (*b* Chufarova, 6 Sept. 1826; *d* Romantsevo, 8 July 1894). Russian composer and singing teacher. Studied with Fotta and Henselt in St. Petersburg (where his *The Gypsies* was part prod. 1850), and on Glinka's recommendation Berlin with Dehn. In Italy he studied singing techniques. His Italian operas were *Maria Tudor* (text by Ghislanzoni, Milan 1859) and *Rienzi* (Florence, 1863). Back in Russia, he wrote *Consuelo* (1865), and on national subjects *The Storm* (1867) and *Taras Bulba* (1893). A respected professor of singing, Moscow Conservatory 1866-72.

Kašlík, Václav (*b* Poličná, 28 Sept. 1917). Czech producer, composer, and conductor. Studied Prague with Talich. Début Brno, 1941, conducting and producing *Orfeo*. Music director Brno, 1943-5; Prague, T. of 5 May, music director, 1945-8; National T. since 1948 as chief producer. Guest appearances all over Europe including Milan, Sc., where he produced *Cardillac* and *Samson et Dalila*, and Venice, F., where he produced the première of Nono's *Intolleranza*. Also staged premières of Martinů's *Mirandolina*, *Julietta*, and *Greek Passion*. London, C.G., 1969, *Pelléas*, 1972 *Nabucco*, 1973 *Tannhäuser*. Works in close collaboration with Josef *Svoboda developing the 'laterna magica' techniques for opera, which include projection, film, stereophonic sound, etc. He sums up his credo as trying with modern techniques 'to present contemporary feelings and problems amusingly, even in a form which is so often so stiff as opera'.

Kaspar. See *Caspar*.

Kassel. Town in Hesse, Germany. The Ottoneum, built in 1603-5, was the first permanent theatre in Germany. Ruggiero Fideli gave annual seasons of Singspiel there 1701-21. A new Italian opera house was opened in the Palace of Prince Maximilian in 1764 with Fiorillo's *Diana e Endimione*, and 1776-85 French opera was given at the Bauhaus. French opera prevailed under Blangini (1809-14), when the conductor, Legaye, was remarked upon for directing the orchestra 'in the French manner, with a baton.' A very large, predominantly French, repertory was given. In February 1814 the new Hoftheater opened with Winter's *Unterbrochene Opferfest*, beginning the tradition of German opera which continued under Spohr (1822-57) and Mahler (1883-5). Later directors have been Paul Bekker (1925-7 with Křenek as Dramaturg), Ernst Legal (1927-8), Heger (1935-43), Ellmendorf (1948-51), Paul Schmitz (1951-63), Christoph von Dohnányi (1963-6), Gerd Albrecht (1966-72), James Lockhart (since 1972). The former theatre was destroyed in 1943 and the new Staatstheater (cap. 1,010) opened in September 1959 with the première of Wagner-Régény's *Prometheus* (in the interim performances were given in the Stadthalle). Premières in Kassel have included Spohr's *Jessonda* (1823), Křenek's *Orpheus* (1926), Haas's *Tobias Wunderlich* (1937), Reuther's *Dr Johannes Faust* (1947), Klebe's *Die Raüber* (1962), Henze's *König Hirsch* – second version (1963). During the Second World War Kapp's Nazi version of Verdi's *Nabucco* was produced there in 1942. Singers who have been members of the Kassel company include Sabine Heinefetter, Fritz Windgassen, Heinrich Pflanzl, Gerda Lammers, and Willi Domgraf-Fassbänder.

Kastorsky, Vladimir (Ivanovich) (*b* Bolshiye Soly, 14 Mar. 1871; *d* Leningrad, 2 July 1948). Russian bass. Studied with Gabel and Cotogni. Début 1894 with Champagner's touring company; St Petersburg, M., from 1899; later member of Z. company. Repertory included Miller in *Rusalka*, Gremin, Pimen, Hagen, Wotan, King Mark. Sang in Diaghilev's Russian seasons in Western Europe 1907-8. A fine artist with a strong, dark voice. (R)

Káťa Kabanová. Opera in 3 acts by Janáček; text by composer, after Ostrovsky's tragedy *The Storm* (1859). Prod. Brno 23 Nov. 1921, with Veséla, Hladiková, Zavřel, Šindler, Pustinská, Jeral, cond. Neumann; London, S.W., 10 Apr. 1951, with Shuard, R. Jones, cond. Mackerras; Cleveland, Karamu House, 26 Nov. 1957, with piano, then Bear Mountain, Empire State Music Festival, 2 Aug. 1960, with Shuard, Doree, Petrak, Gari, Frankel, cond. Halasz.

Káťa (sop.) is married to Tichon (ten.), whose mother Kabanicha (con.) hates her. She loves Boris (ten.), in spite of attempts to remain loyal to her husband, and meets him secretly outside her garden while her friend Varvara (sop.) meets the teacher Kudrjaš (ten.). During the storm, Káťa confesses her guilt to her family and other sheltering passersby; she escapes from Tichon's arms, and saying good-bye to Boris, throws herself into the Volga.

Katerina Izmaylova. See *Lady Macbeth of the Mtsensk District, The.*

Kazakhstan. The Kazakh Opera and Ballet T., organized in Alma Ata (formerly Verny) in 1937, opened with the musical comedy *Ayman and Sholpan* (1934) by Auezov. There followed eight operas based on folk music by Evgeny Brusilovsky (*b* 1905), including the first Kazakh opera, the Romantic *Kiz-Zhibek* (1934), *Zhalbir* (1935), and *Dudaray* (1953), on a symbolic tale of love between the Russian heroine and a Kazakh *dzhigit* (horseman). The first two were given in Moscow in a Kazakh festival in 1936. Other operas have included, notably, *Birzhan i Sara* j)1946), on the 18th cent. Kazakh poet Birzhan Kozhagulov, by Mukan Tulebayev (1913-60). The repertory at Alma Ata is based on Russian classics, with a number of French and Italian works. Opera is given in the Kazakh National T. 'Abay', so named in 1945 after the composer and poet Abay Kunanbayev (1845-1904). An opera on his life, *Abay* (1944), was written by Achmet Zhubanov (*b* 1906) in collaboration with Latif Khamidy (*b* 1906), also composer of *Dzhambul i Aykumis* (1946).

Kecal. The marriage-broker (bass) in Smetana's *The Bartered Bride.*

Keil, Alfredo (*b* Lisbon, 3 July 1850; *d* Hamburg, 4 Oct. 1907). Portuguese composer, of German and Alsatian descent. Studied in Lisbon and Nuremberg, returning to Lisbon in 1870 and exhibiting as a painter. A man of wide culture, he began publishing light music and in 1883 produced a 1-act comedy, *Susana*; this was followed by a successful 4-part opera, *Donna bianca* (1883), then by *Irene* (1893) and *Serrana* (1899). The operas are in Portuguese (though its première was in an Italian translation). In *Susana*, Keil created a Portuguese operatic idiom, and is usually considered to have written the first Portuguese opera and founded with it a national genre.

Keilberth, Joseph (*b* Karlsruhe, 19 Apr. 1908; *d* Munich, 20 July 1968). German conductor. Studied Karlsruhe; joined local opera company as Korrepetitor 1925. Generalmusikdirektor 1935. Conductor Dresden 1945-50; Munich 1951, Generalmusikdirektor 1959-68. Conducted *The Ring* and other works at Bayreuth 1952-6, and appeared as guest conductor at other European festivals, including Edinburgh. His readings of Strauss were particularly admired. Died while conducting a festival performance of *Tristan*. (R)

Keiser, Reinhard (*b* Teuchern, bapt. 12 Jan 1674; *d* Hamburg, 12 Sept. 1739). German composer. Studied Leipzig. His first opera *Basilius,* was produced in 1693, where he studied with Kusser; in 1695 he followed Kusser to Hamburg, where he wrote over 7 operas. In 1703 he took over the direction of its opera, at first with Drüsicke and from 1707 alone; and after various visits (notably to Copenhagen and Ludwigsburg) settled there again in 1724. His importance to German opera, both through his compositions and by his work in creating the highest standards at Hamburg, is enormous. Mattheson called him the first dramatic composer in the world, and for a time he assured the position of German opera. Influenced by Lully and Scarlatti in his vocal writing, he was a pioneer in the characteristic German art of enriching orchestral accompaniments and in writing virtuoso part for instruments. Among his violinists (later harpsichordist) was Handel, whose first opera *Almira* was to some extent modelled on Keiser and who inherited from him a taste for picturesque accompaniments. Handel borrowed from Keiser's works several times at later stages in his career. Keiser's many operas, of which *Störtebecker und Goedje Michel* (1701) was one of the most popular, had a great success in their day; but their range of manner and influences, which won them quick popularity in an international and polyglot trading city, could not assure them more permanent value. Keiser's allegedly dissolute character was the subject of an opera to his own melodies arranged by Benno Bardi, *Der tolle Kapellmeister* (Danzig, 1931).

Kelemen, Zoltan (*b* Budapest, 1933). Hungarian bass. Studied Budapest and Rome with Maria Teresa Pediconi. Début Augsburg, 1962. Sings regularly in Cologne, Düsseldorf, Hamburg, Munich. Bayreuth, 1962, in small roles since 1964 as Alberich; Salzburg, since 1966 Rangoni, Bartolo, Alberich; London with Cologne Opera at S.W., 1969, Lord Mayor in *Junge Lord*; C.G., since 1970, Alberich. N.Y. Met Roles also include Osmin, Dulcamara, Leporello, Falstaff, and Schicchi. (R)

Kellogg, Clara Louise (*b* Sumterville, 12 July 1842; *d* New Haven, 13 May 1916). American soprano and impresario. Début N.Y., Ac. of M. 1861, Gilda. First N.Y. Marguerite. Sang in London 1867 and 1872, when she joined Pauline Lucca in management of Lucca Kellogg Company. Organized English company in America 1873-89.
Bibl: S. L. Kellogg: *Memoirs of an American Prima Donna* (1913).

Kelly, Michael (*b* Dublin, 25 Dec. 1762; *d* Margate, 9 Oct. 1826). Irish tenor and composer. Studied with Morland and Arne, and later with

Rauzzini. Début Dublin 1779, Count in Piccinni's *La buona figliuola*. Went to Naples where he studied for a further period. After appearances throughout Italy went to Vienna where he was engaged at the Court T. and created Basilio and Curzio in Mozart's *Figaro* (1786). Appeared London, D.L., 1787; King's T. 1793, where besides being leading tenor was acting manager. Farewell appearance Dublin Oct. 1811, in *The Bard of Erin,* one of his many compositions. His two volumes of *Reminiscences* published in 1826 give an amusing and valuable picture of the opera stage of his day. Known in Italy as Signor Occhelli.
Bibl: S. Ellis: *The Life of Michael Kelly* (1930). M. Kelly: *Reminiscences* (1826; ed. Van Thal as *Solo Recital,* 1972).

Kemble, Adelaide (*b* London, 1814; *d* Warsash House, Hants, 4 Aug. 1879). English soprano. Younger daughter of the actor Charles Kemble. After a short career as a concert singer, went to Italy where she studied with Pasta and made début at Venice as Norma 1838. After appearances throughout Italy she returned to England where she sang Norma in English at C.G. 1841. Leading member of the English Company at C.G. 1841-2, appearing with great success in *Figaro, Sonnambula, Semiramide,* and *Norma.* Retired 1843 upon her marriage to Edward John Sartoris. Accounts of her career are included in her sister's (Fanny Kemble's) *Record of a Girlhood.*

Kemp, Barbara (*b* Cochem, 12 Dec. 1881; *d.* Berlin, 17 Apr. 1959). German soprano. Studied Strasbourg; début there 1903. After engagements at Rostock and Breslau, became leading soprano at Berlin 1913-32. N.Y., Met., 1922-4; Bayreuth (Senta and Kundry) 1914-27. Stage director in Berlin in the 1930s where she produced her husband's *Ingwelde* in 1938. (R)

Kempe, Rudolf (*b* Niederpoyritz, 14 June 1910; *d* Zurich, 11 May 1976). German conductor. Studied Dresden with Fritz Busch. First oboe Leipzig Gewandhaus Orchestra 1929-36. Répétiteur and junior conductor Leipzig Opera 1925-9, where he made his conducting début, 1935, *Wildschütz.* Chemnitz 1942-8, Weimar 1948-9; Generalmusikdirektor Dresden 1949-52; Munich 1952-4. London début, C.G., with Munich Company 1953, and appeared there regularly until 1974; N.Y., Met., 1954-6; Bayreuth 1960, conducting new prod. of the *Ring; Lohengrin* 1967. Although Kempe first made a name for himself in Strauss and Wagner, he was one of the few German opera conductors whose readings of Puccini and Verdi commanded respect. He was a first-rate orchestral trainer, and procured the most beautiful playing from his instrumentalists; indeed his 'chamber-music' approach to the *Ring* and other works was adversely criticized. (R)

Bibl: C. Kempe-Oettinger: *Rudolf Kempe* (1977).

Kern, Adele (*b* Munich, 25 Nov. 1901). German soprano. Début Munich 1924, Olympia; Vienna 1929-30; Munich 1937-46. London, C.G. 1931 and 1933. Appeared regularly at Salzburg 1927-35; at Berlin and in S. America. One of the brilliant company of singers in the Clemens Krauss régimes in Vienna and Munich. Especially famous for her Sophie, Zerbinetta, and Mozart soubrette parts. (R)

Kern, Patricia (*b* Swansea, 4 July 1927). Welsh mezzo-soprano. Studied London, G.S.M. with Parry Jones. Début 1952 in Opera for All's *Cenerentola.* After appearances with W.N.O. and in Dublin, joined S.W. 1959; especially successful as Cherubino, Dorabella, Cinderella, Rosina, Pippo (*La gazza ladra*), and Messenger in Monteverdi's *Orfeo;* created Josephine in *Violins of Saint-Jacques.* London, C.G., 1967-72 as Zerlina, Suzuki, and Cherubino. Also appeared Spoleto, Dallas, Washington, N.Y. City Opera, and in Canada. (R)

Kerns, Robert (*b* Michigan, 1933). American baritone. Studied Detroit. Début Ohio, 1955, Sharpless. N.Y., City O., 1959. Spoleto 1960; Vienna, S.O. since 1962; London, C.G. since 1964 as Billy Budd, Guglielmo, Count Almaviva, Figaro (Rossini), and Choroebus; Salzburg since 1967. Repertory also includes roles in Verdi, Wagner, and Strauss. (R)

Kertész, István (*b* Budapest, 28 Aug. 1929; *d* nr Tel-Aviv, 16 Apr. 1973). Hungarian conductor. Studied Budapest, and Rome with Previtali. Début Budapest 1954, *Entführung;* Augsburg 1958-63; Cologne 1964-73. London, C.G. 1966-8. Mozart specialist; also gave notable performances of *The Fiery Angel, Billy Budd, Carmélites.* (R)

Bibl: K. Richter: *István Kertész* (1974).

Khaikin, Boris (Emmanuilovich)**,** (*b* Minsk, 26 Oct. 1904). Russian conductor. Studied Moscow Conservatory. Moscow, Stanislavsky T., 1928-35; Leningrad, M. 1936-45; Leningrad, Kirov, 1943-54; Moscow, B. since 1954. Conducted many world premières, including Prokofiev's *The Duenna* and *The Story of a Real Man.* Guest apperances Florence, 1953 *Knovanshchina,* and Leipzig 1964 *Queen of Spades.* (R)

Khokhlov, Pavel (Akinfiyevich) (*b* Spassky, 2 Aug. 1854; *d* Moscow, 20 Sept. 1919). Russian baritone. Studied in Moscow with Yury Arnold (who upset his voice by making him study bass parts) and Alexandrova-Kochetova. Début Moscow, B., 1879, Valentine. He remained with the company until his retirement in 1900. St Petersburg, M., 1881, 1887-8. His warm voice and personality were very popular, and he was especially famous as Eugene Onegin (which he sang at the first public performance, 1881, and thereafter 138 times in Moscow). His other most famous role was the Demon; further roles included Don Giovanni, Di Luna, Germont père, Wolfram, Telramund, Ottokar, Boris, and Prince Igor. A conscientious artist, who continually re-studied his roles, he nevertheless suffered an early vocal decline, as even his friend and admirer Tchaikovsky admitted, by 1886.

Bibl: V. Yakovlev: *P. A. Khokhlov* (1950).

Khovanshchina (Russ., The Khovansky Affair). Opera in 5 acts by Mussorgsky; text by composer and Stasov. Left unfinished; completed and orch. by Rimsky-Korsakov. Prod. St Petersburg, Kononov T., 21 Feb. 1866, by amateurs, cond. Goldstein; St Petersburg, 8 Nov. 1893 by artists of the Russian Opera Society; Moscow 1897, by Russian private opera company, with Bedlevich, Selyuk, Shalyapin, Karklin, Sokolov, Inozemtsev, Antonova, cond. Esposito; Moscow, Z., 1910 with Zaporozhets, Sekar-Rozhansky, Petrova-Zvantseva, Petrov, Shevelyov, cond. Palitsyn; first major production, St Petersburg, M., 7 Nov. 1911, with Zbruyeva, Ershov, Labinsky, P. Andreyev, Sharonov, Shalyapin, cond. Coates; London, D.L., 1 July 1913, with Petrenko, Andreyev, Zaporozhets, Shalyapin, cond. Cooper; Philadelphia 18 Apr. 1928, with Fedotova, Crima, Windheim, Shvetz, Figaniak, cond. Grigaitis. Other versions by Stravinsky and Ravel (Paris 1913) and Shostakovich (Leningrad 1960).

The opera, based on the complicated political events of the time of the accession of Peter the Great in 1682, concerns the strife between various factions. The Streltsy, or Guards, are led by Prince Ivan Khovansky (bass), whose son Andrey (ten.) in a sub-plot tries to rape a German girl Emma (sop.), but is prevented by his former mistress Marfa (sop.). The rival faction is led by Prince Golitsyn (ten.). An important part is also played by the Old Believers, the ultra-orthodox group in the Church who had refused to accept the reforms of the 1650s: they are led by Dosifey (bass), and are eventually killed, together with the reconciled Marfa and Andrey.

Khrennikov, Tikhon (Nikolayevich) (*b* Elets, 10 June 1913). Russian composer. His operas are *In the Storm* (1939), *Frol Skobeyev* (1950), and *The Mother* (1957).

Kiel. German town, capital of Schleswig-Holstein. Opera has been given there since 1764. The first city theatre was built 1841, rebuilt 1907 (cap. 960), destroyed 1944. The new theatre (cap. 918) opened 1953. Georg Hartmann was Intendant 1924-32, Sellner 1950-5, and since 1976 Claus Henneberg. Music directors have included Georg Winkler

1950-59, Peter Ronnefeld 1963-5, and Hans Zender 1969-76. The first German performances of *The Medium* and Milhaud's *La Mère coupable* were given there.

Kienzl, Wilhelm (*b* Waizenkirchen, 17 Jan. 1857; *d* Vienna, 3 Oct. 1941). Austrian composer. Studied in Graz, Prague, Leipzig, and Vienna. A confirmed Wagnerian, he showed in his operas that Wagner's principles could apply to music below that of the loftiest music drama. *Urvasi* (1886) attracted some attention; *Heilmar der Narr* was not produced until 1892 through staging difficulties; and then with *Der Evangelimann* (1895) Kienzl produced his greatest success. Seven less popular operas followed. He also edited Mozart's *La clemenza di Tito* and published a study of Wagner, with whose family he had once lived in Bayreuth.

Bibl: W. Kienzel: *Meine Lebenswanderung* (1926).

Kiepura, Jan (*b* Sosnowiec, 16 May 1902; *d* New York, 15 Aug. 1966). Polish tenor. Studied Warsaw with Brzeziński, Milan with Leliva. Début Lwów, 1924, Faust. Guest appearances 1926-39 Vienna, Berlin, Milan, Paris, and Budapest. N.Y., Met., 1938-41; Chicago 1931-2, 1939-42 and appearances elsewhere in the U.S.A. Famous interpreter of Don José, Des Grieux, Calaf, Cavaradossi, and Rodolfo. Strikingly handsome, and had considerable success in several films, into which he introduced operatic arias. Married the Hungarian soprano Martha Eggerth (*b* 1912) with whom he sang both in America and Europe in performances of *The Merry Widow*. (R) His brother **Władisław Kiepura** (*b* 30 Mar. 1904) sang as Ladis Kiepura.

Kindermann, August (*b* Potsdam, 6 Feb. 1817; *d* Munich, 6 Mar. 1891). German bass-baritone. Began career in chorus of Berlin Opera 1836. Sang bass and baritone roles Leipzig 1839-46. Munich Opera 1846-91, where he celebrated his 25th anniversary in 1871 singing Figaro, and his 40th in 1886 as Stadinger in *Waffenschmied*. Titurel in the first performance of *Parsifal* at Bayreuth 1876. His elder daughter **Marie** enjoyed a career at Kassel; a younger daughter was **Hedwig *Reicher-Kindermann,** another daughter **Franziska** sang in Munich; and a son, **August**, sang in Weimar and Hamburg.

King, James (*b* Dodge City, 22 May 1925). American tenor. Studied with Martial Singher. Début as baritone 1961; after further study, début as tenor, San Francisco 1961, José. Berlin, D., since 1962; Bayreuth since 1965 as Siegmund, Lohengrin, Parsifal; N.Y., Met., since 1966; London, C.G., since 1966 as Kaiser, Siegmund, Manrico, Calaf, Florestan. (R)

King Arthur, or The British Worthy. 'A dramatick opera' in prologue, 5 acts, and epilogue by Purcell; text by Dryden. Prod. London, Dorset Gardens, prob. early June 1691, with Betterton, Williams, Hodgson, Kynaston, Sandford, Alexander, Bowen, Harris, Bracegirdle, Richardson, Butler, Bowman; N.Y., 28 Apr. 1800.

There are some 30 operas on Arthurian legends.

King Mark. The King of Cornwall (bass) in Wagner's *Tristan und Isolde.*

King Priam. Opera in 3 acts by Tippett; text by composer, after Homer's *Iliad.* Prod. Coventry T., 29 May 1962, with Collier, Veasey, Elkins, Lewis, Robinson, Godfrey, Dobson, Lanigan, cond. Pritchard; Karlsruhe, 26 Jan. 1963, with Moussa-Felderer, Wolf-Ramponi, Graf, Reynolds, Harper, Vandenburg, cond. Grüber.

Priam (bass-bar.), supported by Hecuba (sop.), chooses the death of his baby son Paris, who (it is prophesied by the Old Man (bass)) will cause his father's death. But he is relieved to find, in the next scene, when out hunting, that the boy (sop.) has been spared; he and Hector (bar.) take him to Troy. Here Paris (ten.) and Hector quarrel; Paris fetches Helen (mezzo) from Sparta. In the last scene of the act, Hermes (ten.) arranges the Judgement of Paris; Aphrodite (i.e. Helen) is chosen.

In the war that ensues, Achilles (ten.) is sulking in his tent; the Trojans drive the Greeks back and fire their ships, but are weakened by Hector and Paris quarrelling. Patroclus (bar.) puts on Achilles's armour but is killed by Hector. The Trojans' rejoicing is interrupted by Achilles's war-cry.

The women reflect upon their role in the war. News of Hector's death at the hands of Achilles is brought to Priam. He goes to beg his son's body, and rouses Achilles's pity. He then withdraws into himself, and is killed before the altar by Achilles's son.

King Roger (Pol., *Król Roger*). Opera in 3 acts by Szymanowski; text by Jarosław Iwaszkiewicz and composer. Prod. Warsaw 19 June 1926, with Mossakowski, Korwin-Szymanowska, Dobosz, Wraga, cond. Młynarski; London, S.W., by New O.C., 14 May 1975, with Knapp, cond. Mackerras.

Queen Roxane (sop.) falls in love with a shepherd-prophet (ten.) from India, denounced as a heretic. King Roger (bar.) is finally converted, and the work closes with a bacchanal in a Greek temple.

Also opera on the subject by H. Berton (1817).

King's Henchman, The. Opera in 3 acts by Deems Taylor; text by Edna St. Vincent Millay. Prod. N.Y., Met., 17 Feb. 1927, with Easton, Johnson, Tibbett, cond. Serafin.

Eadgar (bar.), King of England, sends Æthelwold (ten.) to win the Princess Ælfrida (sop.) for him; Æthelwold marries her, sending word

that she is ugly, but when Eadgar comes to visit them and finds how beautiful she is, Æthelwold kills himself in remorse.

King's Theatre, Haymarket. Built by Vanbrugh to house the Lincoln's Inn Fields T. Company and opened on 9 Apr. 1705 as the Queen's Theatre with Greber's *Gli amori d'Ergasto,* the first Italian opera to be heard in London. Opera alternated with the drama until the end of 1707, when the theatre became wholly devoted to opera. At first some works were sung in English, others in Italian, and some in a mixture of both tongues; but from 1710 onwards the theatre in the Haymarket was the exclusive home in London of Italian opera. The Queen's T. was renamed the King's in 1714 on the accession of George I, and became Her Majesty's in 1837 on the accession of Queen Victoria. *Heidegger was the theatre's manager 1710-34 and in the years 1729-34 shared the management of the theatre with Handel. During the whole of this period more than 24 of Handel's operas, 7 of his pasticcios, and one or two of his secular choral works and oratorios all received their first performances there. From the time of Handel until the fire of 1789 the English premières of many long-forgotten operas by Bononcini, Tarchi, Cimarosa, and other Italians were given. The new King's T., then the largest in England (cap. 3,300), was designed by a Polish architect, Michael Nowosielski, and opened on 16 Jan. 1793 with Paisiello's *Il barbiere di Siviglia.* The company was under the management of Storace and Kelly. During the years 1793-1820 *Iphigénie en Tauride, La clemenza di Tito, Così fan tutte, Die Zauberflöte, Figaro, Don Giovanni, Il barbiere di Siviglia, L'italiana in Algeri, La Cenerentola,* and *Tancredi* all received their first English performances there. The singers included Giorgi–Banti, Teresa Bellochi, Mrs. Billington, Catalani, Joséphine Fodor-Mainvielle, Grassini, Mara; Ambrogetti, Graham, Garcia, Kelly, Levasseur, and Naldi. During the régime of Ebers (1821-7) more Rossini works, including *La gazza ladra, La donna del lago, Otello, Il turco in Italia, L'italiana in Algeri,* and Spontini's *La vestale,* were produced, as well as the first Meyerbeer opera to be heard in England, *Il crociato in Egitto.* New singers included Brambilla, Camporose, Colbran, Caradori, De Begnis, Pasta, and Velluti. Ebers was succeeded as manager by *Laporte (1821-31 and 1833-41), during whose régime the theatre became Her Majesty's Royal Italian Opera House. (For the continuation of this history, see *Her Majesty's.*)

Bibl: D. Nalbach: *The King's Theatre, 1704-1867* (1972).

Kipnis, Alexander (*b* Zhitomir, 13 Feb. 1891; *d* Westport, Conn., 14 May 1978). Russian bass. Studied Warsaw, where he graduated as a conductor; then Berlin with Grenzebach. Although an enemy alien during the First World War, was allowed to continue his studies in Germany and made his début at Hamburg 1915; Wiesbaden 1916-21; Berlin, Stä. O., 1921-9, S.O. 1930-5; Chicago Opera 1923-32 and after 1938; N.Y., Met., 1939-46. Buenos Aires 1926-36. London, C.G., 1927, début as Marcel in the ill-fated revival of *Les Huguenots*; returned 1929-35, and was especially admired as Gurnemanz, Hagen, Mark, and Rocco. Bayreuth 1927-33; he also sang Sarastro at Gly. and Salzburg. Forced by Hitler to leave Germany, he settled in America, and eventually became an American citizen. Considered one of the finest singers in German opera of his day, but also a distinguished Boris and Arkel; had a beautiful voice of great flexibility and colour. (R)

Kirchhof, Walter (*b* Berlin, 17 Mar. 1879; *d* Wiesbaden, 26 Mar. 1951). German tenor. Studied with Lilli Lehmann and in Milan. Début Berlin 1906, Faust; here he was leading tenor until 1920 and also appeared 1923-4, 1928-9, 1932. London, C.G., 1913 and 1924; N.Y., Met., 1926-31. Renowned mostly as a Heldentenor, though he also sang Max in *Jonny spielt auf* and Pietro in *Boccaccio* in N.Y. (R)

Kirghizistan. The first musical theatre in Kirghizistan was formed in Frunze (formerly Pishpek) in 1936. The operettas *Altin kiz* (The Golden Girl, 1937) and *Adzhal orduna* (Life, not Death, 1938) and the opera *Aychuzek* (1939) were written for it, all in collaboration by three composers, Vladimir Vlasov (*b* 1903), Abdilas Maldibayev (*b* 1906), and Vladimir Fere (*b* 1902). Broadly, Maldibayev was responsible for the melodic material, the others for constructing the works. Vlasov and Fere also collaborated on *Za schaste naroda* (For the People's Happiness, 1941), all three again on *Patrioty* (1941). Mikhail Rauchberger (*b* 1901) wrote *Kokul* (The Golden Forelock, 1943). In 1942 the Frunze theatre was renamed the Kirghiz Opera and Ballet T. Manas, by the same three composers, was produced there but withdrawn after accusations of formalism; they then wrote *Kel Boyunda* (1951). Other Kirghiz operas include *Aysha i Aydar* (1952) by Sergey Germanov (*b* 1988) and Achmet Amanbayev (*b* 1920), and *Molodye Serdtse* (Young Hearts, 1953) by Mukash Abdrayev (*b* 1920). The celebrated folk singer and musician Toktogul Satilganov (*c*1864-1933) left a large number of songs and melodies which were taken up by Kirghiz composers, and which are used in the three operas on his life bearing his name, in 1940 by Alexander Veprik (1899-1958), in 1956 by Abdrayev and Maldibayev, and in 1958 by Vlasov, Maldibayev, and Fere.

Kirkby Lunn, Louise. See *Lunn*.

Kirov Theatre. See *Leningrad*.

Kirsten, Dorothy (*b* Montclair, N.J., 6 July 1917). American soprano. Studied N.Y., Juilliard School. Protégée of Grace Moore, who arranged for her début at the Chicago Opera in 1940 as Pousette in *Manon*. N.Y. City Opera; Met., 1945-57, 1959-75; her roles have included Louise, which she studied with Charpentier, Fiora, Cio-Cio-San, Marguerite, Minnie, and Manon Lescaut. Has appeared in a number of films including *The Great Caruso*. Toured U.S.S.R. 1962. (R)

Kiss, The (Cz. *Hubička*). Opera in 3 acts by Smetana; text by Eliška Krásnohorská, after the story (1871) by 'Karolina Světlá' (Joanna Mužáková). Prod. Prague, P., 7 Nov. 1876, with Sittová, Cachová, Lauşmannová, Vávra, Čech, Lev, Mareš, Šára, cond. Čech; Chicago, Blackstone T., 17 Apr. 1921; Liverpool, 8 Dec. 1938 (amateur); London, King's T., Hammersmith by C.R., 15 Oct. 1948, cond. Tausky.

The widower Lukaš is anxious to exchange a betrothal kiss with Vendulka, but she refuses to kiss him before they are married; such an act is said to rouse the ghostly wrath of a dead wife. After many complications, Lukaš succeeds.

Kitezh. See *Invisible City of Kitezh, The.*

Kittel, Hermine (*b* Vienna, 2 Dec. 1879; *d* Vienna, 7 Apr. 1948). Austrian contralto. Originally an actress: début Lwów 1897, in Millöcker's *Sieben Schwalben*. Voice then discovered; studied with Materna. Graz, 1899-1900; Vienna, 1901-31 and 1936; Vienna V., 1933-4. Guest appearances in Paris, Budapest, Prague, etc. Bayreuth 1902, 1908, Erda; Salzburg 1922, 1925. After retirement taught in Vienna. Married the bass Alexander Haydter (1872-1919). (R)

Kiurina, Berta (*b* Linz, 19 Feb. 1882; *d* Vienna, 3 May 1933). Austrian soprano. Studied Vienna with Fischof and Geiringer. Début Vienna, O., 1905 Shepherd in *Tannhäuser*. Vienna, O., 1905-21, 1926-7. Guest appearances in Berlin, Budapest, Zurich, etc. Salzburg, 1906, Cherubino; Buenos Aires, C., 1928. Large repertory, from Queen of Night to Desdemona and Nedda, also Gilda, Eva, and the Empress (*Frau ohne Schatten*). Married to the tenor Hubert Leuer. Her records reveal an effortless and beautiful soprano voice. (R)

Klafsky, Katharina (orig. Katalin) (*b* Mosonszentjános, 19 Sept. 1855; *d* Hamburg, 22 Sept. 1896). Hungarian soprano. Joined chorus of Vienna Komische Oper, 1874, soon attracting attention. Début Salzburg 1875. Studied Berlin with Julius Hey; also introduced to Mathilde Marchesi, who gave her free tuition. Leipzig 1876-8; first local Brangäne. London 1882 with Angelo Neumann's company (Wellgunde and Waltraute). Hamburg 1886-95. Returned to London 1892, singing in

Wagner and in *Fidelio* at C.G. and D.L. under Mahler; again D.L. 1894 under her husband Otto *Lohse, making a great impression as Leonore, Agathe, Elsa, Brünnhilde, and Isolde. America 1895-6 with Lohse, as principal soprano and as conductor of Damrosch O.C. She sang 78 performances, and both artists were engaged for the 1896-7 season at the Met.; she died before she could take up the engagement, at the height of her powers.
Bibl: L. Ordemann: *Aus dem Leben und Wirken von Katharina Klafsky* (1903).

Klagenfurt. Town in Carinthia, Austria. Opera is given in the City T. (cap. 770), opened in 1910. The Opera company shares the season (September to August) with the drama company.

Klausenburg. See *Cluj.*

Kleiber, Carlos (*b* Berlin, 3 July 1930). German conductor. Son of conductor Erich Kleiber. Studied chemistry in Zurich; began musical studies Buenos Aires 1950; voluntary Korrepetitor La Plata, 1953; Munich, Gärtnerplatz, 1954-6; Vienna, Volk-Th., 1956-8; Düsseldorf, as conductor, 1958-64; Zurich, 1964-66; Stuttgart since 1966; Munich, N., since 1968; Bayreuth, 1974-6, *Tristan und Isolde*; Edinburgh Festival 1966, *Wozzeck*; London, C.G., 1974, *Rosenkavalier*. Milan, Sc., 1977, *Otello*. Small repertory also includes *Elektra, Carmen* and *Freischütz.* He has displayed a talent comparable to his father's; a perfectionist, he demands long rehearsal periods, and is not above cancelling a performance if dissatisfied. (R)

Kleiber, Erich (*b* Vienna, 5 Aug. 1890; *d* Zurich, 27 Jan. 1956). Austrian, later Argentinian, conductor. Studied Prague. Darmstadt 1912-18; Wuppertal 1919-21; Mannheim 1922-3; Generalmusikdirektor Berlin S.O. 1923-34. Guest conductor at many leading opera houses 1933-56, notably T. Colón, Buenos Aires, 1937-49; C.G. 1938 and 1950-3; Amsterdam 1933-8 and 1949-50. Kleiber's directorship of the Berlin Opera was one of the most brilliant periods in the theatre's history, with the world premières of *Wozzeck* and *Christophe Colomb* and the introduction of *Jenůfa* and *Shvanda* into the repertory. He resigned his Berlin post in 1934 at the time of the *Mathis der Maler* controversy (see *Hindemith*) and did not return to Germany again until 1950. He was reappointed to his old position at the S.O. in 1954 but again resigned as a protest against political interference. His contribution to the development of the English Company at London C.G., 1950-3, cannot be overestimated. He was beloved by all orchestras with whom he worked; and his eloquent stick technique enabled him to indicate to each player every shade of expression. (R)
Bibl: J. Russell: *Erich Kleiber* (1958).

Klein, Herman (*b* Norwich, 23 July 1856; *d* London, 10 Mar. 1934). English critic and teacher. Studied singing with Manuel Garcia. Taught privately and at the G.S.M. Began writing criticism in 1875. Critic of *The Sunday Times* 1881-1901; during part of this period the paper was owned by Augustus Harris, and Klein acted as an unofficial adviser to him as far as the engagement of singers at C.G. was concerned. 1902-9 critic of the *New York Herald.* His many publications include *The Reign of Patti* (1920); *The Art of Bel Canto* (1924); *Musicians and Mummers* (1925); *Great Women Singers of Our Time* (1931); and *The Golden Age of Opera* (1933).

Klein, Peter (*b* Zündorf, 25 Jan. 1907). German tenor. Studied Cologne. Cologne Opera chorus 1930-1; then after a period at Düsseldorf, Kaiserlautern, and Zurich he joined the Hamburg Opera, where he sang with success as Shuisky, Mime, Pedrillo, etc., 1937-41. Vienna S.O. 1934 and 1940, engaged from 1941; also sang regularly at Salzburg, where his Basilio, Valzacchi, Captain in *Wozzeck,* and Monsieur Taupe in *Capriccio* were much praised. London début C.G., 1947, with Vienna Company; returned regularly to sing Mime in *The Ring* until 1960. N.Y., Met., 1949-51, as Mime, Jacquino, David, Basilio, and Valzacchi. (R)

Klementyev, Lev (Mikhailovich) (*b* St Petersburg, 1 Apr. 1868; *d* Tiflis, 26 Oct. 1910). Russian tenor. After singing in operetta in Kharkov (1887) and St Petersburg, joined Kiev Opera 1888-9. Tiflis 1889-90. Moscow, B., 1892-1910. Created Bobilya in *The Snow Maiden,* and other parts. Repertory included Nero (Rubinstein), Raoul, Lensky, and Hermann in *Queen of Spades.* (R)

Klemperer, Otto (*b* Breslau, 14 May 1885; *d* Zurich, 6 July 1973). German conductor. Studied Frankfurt and Berlin. Début Berlin 1906 conducting the Reinhardt prod. of *Orpheus in the Underworld.* Recommended by Mahler to the German T., Prague, where he conducted 1907-10. Engagements followed at Hamburg 1911-12, Barmen, 1913-14; Strasbourg 1914-17; music director Cologne 1917-24; Wiesbaden 1924-7; Berlin 1927-33, first at the Kroll Opera, and then at the S.O. Awarded Goethe Medal 1933 and within a few months had to leave Nazi Germany. During his Berlin period he conducted the premières and first Berlin performances of many important works including *Cardillac, Neues vom Tage, Erwartung, Die glückliche Hand, Das Leben des Orest, From the House of the Dead,* and *Mavra,* as well as such standard repertory works as *Luisa Miller, Rosenkavalier, Tannhäuser,* and *Der fliegender Holländer.* Except for a period at the Budapest State Opera (1947-50) he conducted little opera in the post-war period, but

made a belated C.G. début, conducting and producing *Fidelio* in 1961; he returned to conduct and produce *The Magic Flute* 1962 and *Lohengrin* 1963. One of the great conductors of the century.
Bibl: O. Klemperer: *Minor Recollections* (1964); P. Heyworth (ed.): *Conversations with Klemperer* (1973).

Klenau, Paul von (*b* Copenhagen, 11 Feb. 1883; *d* Copenhagen, 31 Aug. 1946). Danish composer and conductor. The most successful of his seven operas was *Gudrun auf Island* (1924). Worked at Freiburg Opera 1907; at Stuttgart Court Opera 1908-14.

Klingsor. The evil magician (bass) in Wagner's *Parsifal*.

Klose, Margarete (Frida) (*b* Berlin, 6 Aug. 1902; *d* Berlin, 14 Dec. 1965). German mezzo-soprano. Studied Berlin with Marschalk and with Bültemann (whom she married). Concert début Berlin 1902. Début Ulm 1927, Young Gipsy (*Gräfin Maritza*). Mannheim 1927-31; Berlin, Stä. O., 1929, 1946-56, S.O. 1931-50; Bayreuth 1936-42; London, C.G., 1935, 1937; Buenos Aires 1950. One of the finest German mezzos of her day; especially distinguished in Wagner and Verdi. Her repertory also included Orfeo, the Kostelnička, Carmen, and Klytemnestra. Created Oona in Egki's *Irische Legende.* (R)

Kluge, Die (The Clever Girl). Opera in 6 scenes by Carl Orff; text by composer, after Grimm's story *Die Geschichte von dem König und der klugen Frau.* Prod. Frankfurt, 20 Feb. 1943, with Wackers, Gonszar, Staudenmeyer, cond. Winkler; Cleveland, Karamu House, 7 Dec. 1949; London, S.W., 27 July 1959 with Harper, cond. Priestman.

The King (bar.), tired of the wisdom of the Clever Girl (sop.), whom he married after she had successfully answered his riddles, sends her away, telling her she can take with her whatever she wants from the palace. She sets off down the road, and opens the trunk from which the king emerges, he being the one thing she wanted above all else. Delighted at her choice, he offers to take her back, if she promises not to be clever any longer.

Klytemnestra. Wife of Agamemnon, whom she murdered, then wife (mezzo) of Aegisth in Strauss's *Elektra.*

Knappertsbusch, Hans (*b* Elberfeld, 12 Mar. 1888; *d* Munich, 25 Oct. 1965). German conductor. Studied Cologne with Steinbach and Lohse. Début Mulheim 1911; after engagements at Bochum, Elberfeld, Leipzig, and Dessau was appointed Generalmusikdirektor Munich Opera in 1922, a position he had to relinquish in 1936 owing to his hostility to the Nazis. Vienna S.O. 1936-50. From 1951 he con-

ducted at Bayreuth; and he returned to Munich in 1954. He appeared as a guest conductor in Paris, Milan, Rome, and Zurich. Sole London appearance, C.G., 1937, *Salome*. Strauss and Wagner were Knappertsbusch's special study, and his *Parsifal* reading was generally considered the noblest of this century. Did much of his greatest work on very little rehearsal.
Bibl: R. Betz and W. Panofsky: *Knappertsbusch* (1958).

Knoch, Ernst (*b* Karlsruhe, 1 Aug. 1875; *d* New York, 20 Mar. 1959). German conductor. Studied Karlsruhe and privately with Mottl, whose assistant he was at Karlsruhe 1898-1901. Strasbourg 1901-7; Essen 1907-9; Cologne 1909-12. Worked at Bayreuth 1904-7 and joined the Quinlan Company to give the first Australian performances of *Tristan* and other works 1912. Conducted various touring companies in America and settled in New York as teacher in 1938.

Knot Garden, The. Opera in 3 acts by Tippett; text by composer. Prod. London, C.G., 2 Dec. 1970, with Barstow, Gomez, Minton, Tear, Herincx, Carey, Hemsley, cond. Davis; Evanston, N.W. University, 22 Feb. 1974, with Strauch, Jaffe, Evans, Kraus, Pollock, Cooper, Dickson, cond. Rubenstein (first Tippett opera in U.S.).

The analyst Mangus (bar.) has been invited by Faber (bar.) and Thea (mezzo) to treat their ward Flora (sop.), but quickly perceives that the real trouble lies in the marriage: Faber has grown too far outward, Thea too far inward, and they no longer meet in a true marriage. A homosexual couple arrive: they are the Negro writer Mel (bar.) and the musician Dov (ten.). A further arrival is Denise (sop.), Thea's sister and 'a dedicated freedom fighter' who has suffered torture. Mangus contrives a series of devices to set their difficulties to rights, including an elaborate charade based on *The Tempest*; the stage devices include the revolving of the symbolic knot garden of the title, in which they meet and play out their relationships. Eventually Mel leaves with Denise, and Faber and Thea find renewed marriage: Flora has found adulthood and independence, and Dov is left to set off upon a journey (recorded in Tippett's *Songs for Dov,* which arose out of the opera).

Knote, Heinrich (*b* Munich, 26 Nov. 1870; *d* Garmisch, 12 Jan. 1953). German tenor. Studied Munich with Kirschner. Début Munich, 1892, Georg in *Waffenschmied.* After several years as a Spieltenor began to sing heavier roles, developing into one of the leading Heldentenors of his day. Apart from a short period at Hamburg, he remained a member of the Munich ensemble until 1932, when he made his farewell appearance as Siegfried.

London, C.G., 1901, 1903, 1907–8, 1913 as Lohengrin, Walther, Siegfried, Tannhäuser, Erik, and Tristan; N.Y., Met., 1904–8, where in addition to Wagner roles he was heard as Assad in *The Queen of Sheba* and Manrico; returned U.S.A. with German Opera Company 1923–4 as Tristan and Rienzi. Extremely handsome, with a clear resonant voice and excellent diction. In New York he was compared favourably with both Jean de Reszke and Caruso. After retiring from stage taught singing in Munich. (R)
Bibl: J. H. Wagenmann: *Der 60 – Jährige deutsche Meistersänger, Heinrich Knote* (1930).

Knüpfer, Paul (*b* Halle, 21 June 1866; *d* Berlin, 4 Nov. 1920). German bass. Studied Sonderhausen, where he made his début 1885. Leipzig 1888–98; Berlin 1898–1920; Bayreuth 1901–12; London, C.G., 1909–14, where he was the first London Barber of Bagdad, Baron Ochs, and Gurnemanz. (R) Married the soprano **Marie Egli** (1872–1924), who appeared at C.G., also Darmstadt 1894–5, Berlin, H., 1895–8, Bayreuth 1902–7. (R)

Koanga. Opera in prologue, 3 acts, and epilogue by Delius; text by C. F. Keary, after George Washington Cable's novel, *The Grandissimes* (1880). Prod. Elberfeld, 30 Mar. 1904, with Kaiser, Whitehill, cond. Cassirer. London, C.G., 23 Sept. 1935, with Slobodskaya, Brownlee, cond. Beecham; Washington, 18 Dec. 1970, with Lindsey, Holmes, cond. Callaway. On a Mississippi plantation the mulatto Palmyra (sop.) spurns the slave-driver Simon Perez (ten.) and falls in love with Koanga (bar.), a prince of her own tribe. The planter Don José Martínez allows the wedding, during which Palmyra is abducted by Perez. Koanga quarrels with the planter and flees into the forest, where he and a voodoo priest invoke a plague on their enemies. But Palmyra is also afflicted. Koanga arrives in time to save her from Perez, whom he kills before being himself killed. Palmyra stabs herself with Koanga's spear.

Kobbé, Gustav (*b* New York, 4 Mar. 1857; *d* Long Island, 27 July 1918). American critic and writer. Studied Wiesbaden and New York. After editing *The Musical Review* served as critic on several New York papers including *The World*, which sent him to Bayreuth in 1882 for the first performance of *Parsifal*. Wrote several books, including a two-volume study of Wagner (1890) and the famous *Complete Opera Book* (1919), revised by Lord Harewood 1954 and enlarged 1976.

Kodály, Zoltán (*b* Kecskemét, 16 Dec. 1882; *d* Budapest, 6 Mar. 1967). Hungarian composer. His three stage works (though in separate numbers with dialogue) are a vital contribution to Hungarian national opera. *Háry János* (1926) draws strongly on Hungarian folk-lore and folk

music in manner; *Székely fonó* (The Spinning Room of the Székelys, 1932) is a 1-act Singspiel; *Czinka Panna* (1948) is an historical piece written to celebrate the centenary of the 1848 revolution, and makes greater use of dialogue. *Bibl:* L. Eösze: *Z. Kodály* (1962).

Kollo (orig. Kollodzievski), **René** (*b* Berlin, 20 Nov. 1937). German tenor. Son of operetta composer Willi Kollo. Studied Berlin with Elsa Varena. After period as a pop singer, and in operetta, made opera début Brunswick, 1965, Oedipus Rex. Düsseldorf 1967; Bayreuth since 1969, Steersman, Erik, Lohengrin, Walther, Parsifal, Siegfried. London, C.G., 1976 Siegmund, 1977 Max and Lohengrin. N.Y. Met., 1976, Lohengrin. Fine lyric tenor who has been persuaded to attempt Heldentenor roles, which he sings with great musicianship but an essentially light lyric voice. (R)

Köln. See *Cologne*.

Koltai, Ralph (*b* Berlin, 31 July 1924). Hungarian (later British) designer. Studied London, Central School of Arts and Crafts. London, C.G., *Tannhäuser* 1954, *Taverner* 1972; S.W., *Mahagonny, Ring*; E.N.O. and Scottish Opera; Munich 1974 *Fidelio*. Generally works in collaboration with Michael Geliot. Very much a contemporary designer; his early *Tannhäuser* (1954) was far ahead of his day. Makes great use of tubular effects and scaffolding; his *Ring* settings in grey and silver use other new materials.

Konetzni, Anny (*b* Ungarisch-Weisskirchen, 12 Feb. 1902; *d* Vienna, 6 Sept. 1968). Austrian soprano. First sang in chorus of V.O., but was dismissed for loss of voice. Studied Vienna Conservatory with Erik Schmedes, then Berlin with Stückgold. Début Chemnitz as contralto 1927. Berlin, S.O., 1931–6; Vienna, S.O., from 1933; London, C.G., 1935–9, 1951; N.Y., Met., 1934–5. Specialized in the Wagner and Strauss repertory. (R)

Konetzni, Hilde (*b* Vienna, 21 Mar. 1905). Austrian soprano. Sister of above. Studied Vienna Conservatory and Prague with Ludmilla Prochaska-Neumann. Début Chemnitz 1929, Sieglinde. Prague 1932–8; Vienna, S.O., from 1936. London, C.G., 1938 when she made her début during a performance of *Rosenkavalier* replacing Lehmann who became ill half-way through first act; sang Chrysothemis, Sieglinde, Donna Elvira, and Elisabeth at C.G. 1938–9. Returned in 1947 with the Vienna Company as Leonore in *Fidelio*, and appeared subsequently as Sieglinde (with her sister as Brünnhilde) and Gutrune. One of the most popular artists in Vienna, she possessed a very beautiful voice and a strong sense of Wagner style. Continued to appear in small parts well into the 1970s. (R)

König Hirsch (The Stag King). Opera in 3 acts by

263

Henze; text by Heinz von Cramer, after Gozzi's *fiaba, Re Cervo* (1762). Prod. Berlin, Stä. O., 23 Sept. 1956, with Pilarczyk, Fischer-Dieskau, cond. Scherchen. Revised and shortened as *Re Cervo*, Kassel 1963, cond. Henze; Santa Fé 4 Aug. 1965, with Shirley, Allen, cond. Baustian.

Abandoned in the forest as a child by the Governor (bass-bar.), the King (ten.) has been cherished by wild beasts. Grown up, he returns to claim his throne and choose a bride, but the Governor's scheming contrives that he shall renounce the crown and return to the forest from what he now believes to be a world of lies. After various adventures he enters the body of a stag, while the Governor takes his shape and returns to the city to initiate a reign of terror. But, driven by human longings, the Stag King returns to the city; the Governor is killed by his own assassins, and the King regains human form.

Königin von Saba, Die (The Queen of Sheba). Opera in 4 acts by Goldmark; text by Salomon Mosenthal. Prod. Vienna, Court Opera, 10 Mar. 1875, with Materna, Wild, Beck; N.Y., Met., 2 Dec. 1885, with Lilli Lehmann, Brandt, Stritt, Fischer, cond. Seidl; London, Kennington T., 29 Aug. 1910, with Woodall, Wheatly, Winckworth, cond. Goossens. The opera tells of the love of Assad (ten.), King Solomon's (bar.) favourite courtier, for the Queen of Sheba (mezzo), and of his banishment by the King when he rejects his betrothed Sulamith (sop.).

Königsberg. See *Kaliningrad.*

Königskinder (The Royal Children). Opera in 3 acts by Humperdinck; text by 'Ernst Rosmer' (Else Bernstein-Porges). Prod. N.Y., Met., 28 Dec. 1910, with Farrar, Jadlowker, Goritz, cond. Hertz; Berlin, H., 14 Jan. 1907, with Artôt de Padilla, Kirchoff, Hoffmann; London, C.G., 27 Nov. 1911, with Gura-Hummel, Langendorff, Wolf, Hofbauer, cond. Schalk.

The story of the Goose-girl (sop.) who falls in love with the King's son who comes to the woods disguised as a beggar. The Witch (con.), with whom the Goose-girl lives, brings about the lovers' deaths.

Konwitschny, Franz (*b* Fulnek, 14 Aug. 1901; *d* Belgrade, 27 July 1962). German conductor. Studied Leipzig. Stuttgart 1926–33; Freiburg 1933–7; Frankfurt 1937–45; Hanover 1945–6; Dresden 1953–5. Chosen to succeed Kleiber, when the latter resigned, as Generalmusikdirektor of the rebuilt Berlin S. O. 1955. London, C.G., 1959, conducting *The Ring.* (R)

Kónya, Sándor (*b* Sarkad, 23 Sept. 1923). Hungarian tenor. Studied Budapest. Début Bielefeld 1951, Turiddu. After engagements in Darmstadt, Stuttgart, and Hamburg he joined the Berlin Stä. O. in 1955. Bayreuth as Lohengrin 1958; Milan, Sc., 1960; San Francisco

1960-5; N.Y., Met., 1962-73; London, C.G., 1963 and subsequently. (R)

Korngold, Erich Wolfgang (*b* Brno, 29 May 1897; *d* Hollywood, 29 Nov. 1957). Austrian composer. Studied Vienna with Fuchs, Zemlinsky, and Grädener. Very precocious; he made his début as a stage composer with a ballet *Der Schneemann* (orch. Zemlinsky) aged 11. His first two (1-act) operas *Der Ring des Polykrates* and *Violanta* were produced at Munich when he was 19 (1916), but his greatest operatic success was with *Die tote Stadt* (1920). Lush and eclectic, his operas had a wide appeal in their day. He later lived in America and worked chiefly as a film composer; one of his films, *Give Us This Night,* included an original 1-act opera.
Bibl: R. Hoffmann: *E.W. Korngold* (1923).

Korrepetitor (*Ger.* rehearser). The term used in German-speaking opera houses for the member of the music staff who coaches the singers in their roles and is responsible for other musical tasks such as sub-conducting. See *Répétiteur.*

Košice. Town in Czechoslovakia. Opera is given in the State T., usually 3–4 times a week by a company of about 30 soloists.

Köth, Erika (*b* Darmstadt, 15 Sept. 1927). German soprano. Sang with a jazz orchestra in order to earn enough for her musical training. Won first prize in competition organized by Hessische Radio 1947, sharing it with Christa Ludwig. Début Kaiserslautern 1948, Philine (after radio début as Adele, from Darmstadt); Karlsruhe 1950–3; Munich and Vienna since 1953. London, C.G., with Munich Company, 1953 as Fiakermilli (*Arabella*) and Italian singer (*Capriccio*). A very high coloratura, excelling as Zerbinetta. *Lucia di Lammermoor* was specially revived for her in Munich in 1957. (R)

Koussevitzky, Serge (Alexandrovich) (*b* Vishny Volochek, 26 July 1874; *d* Boston, 4 June 1951). Russian conductor. Although primarily known as a symphonic conductor, he was one of the pioneers in introducing Russian opera to western Europe, conducting *Boris, Khovanshchina, Prince Igor,* and *The Queen of Spades* in Paris in 1921, and *The Snow Maiden* and other works in Barcelona the same year. He was responsible for the commissioning of Britten's *Peter Grimes* for the Berkshire Festival, although the première took place in London. (R)
Bibl: H. Leichentritt: *Serge Koussevitzky.* (1946).

Kovařovic, Karel (*b* Prague, 9 Dec. 1862; *d* Prague, 6 Dec. 1920). Czech composer and conductor. Studied Prague with Fibich. Conductor Brno 1885–6, Plzeň 1886–7. Conductor at the Prague N., 1900–20; greatly influenced evelopment of Czech opera, partly by the atholic choice of his repertory: he loved rench opera, and introduced Bizet, Massenet, nd Charpentier to Prague audiences, as well s works by Mussorgsky, Wagner, and Strauss. lso a brilliant if controversial conductor who id much to raise orchestral and singing standards in the ensemble. Particularly successful ith the operas of Smetana and Dvořák; less nthusiastic for new music. As a composer, he ad his greatest success with *Psohlavci* (The log-Heads, 1898), a patriotic work in the metana-Dvořák tradition and still popular.

ozlovsky,   Ivan   (Semyonovich)   (*b* Maryanovka, 24 Mar. 1900). Russian tenor. tudied Kiev with Muravyova. Début Poltava 920, Faust. Kharkov 1924, Sverdlovsk 1925; Moscow, B., 1926–54. Though he sang Italian, rench, and German roles (including Lohenrin), he was most famous in Russian opera, specially as Lensky, Berendey, and Vladimir *Prince Igor*). For the operatic ensemble which e founded (1938–41) he also produced opera, ncluding *Werther, Orfeo ed Euridice,* and rkas's *Katerina,* in which he took a leading ole. (R)

raków (Cracow). Town in Poland. The first pera libretto in Polish, Francesca Caccini's *La iberazione di Ruggero dall'isola d'Alcina,* was ublished here in 1628. The first private opera erformances were given in 1628, the first ublic ones by visiting companies, mostly Italan, from about 1780. In 1789 a Polish opera ompany was formed by Jacek Kluszewski, nd this survived until the beginning of the 9th cent. Occasional efforts to organize opera n a regular basis were made 1844–50 and 865–6, but from then until 1914 there were nly guest performances by companies from wów and elsewhere. In 1915 the Opera was ounded by Bolesław Wallek-Walewski; this xisted until 1924, and was revived 1931–9. After the Second World War, the Society of riends of Opera formed a company 1946–8, nder the direction of Walerian Bierdiajew. In 954 the repertory opera was organized by the Operatic Society, and a Municipal Music T. of Opera and Operetta was formed in 1958. The lirector, 1952–70, was Kazimierz Kord. A new pera house, T. Muzyczny, is under construcion, and is due to be opened *c*1980; it is to have wo auditoria (cap. 2,000).

rásová, Marta (*b* Protivín 16 Mar. 1901; *d* ráž, 20 Feb. 1970). Czech mezzo-soprano. tudied Prague and Vienna. Début Bratislava 924, Julia (*Jakobín*). Prague, N., 1927–70; uest appearances throughout Europe. Toured J.S.A. 1938–9 in concert. Repertory included boli, Amneris, Carmen, Kostelnička, the Witch n *Rusalka,* and many roles in Czech opera. Had beautiful voice and was a fine dramatic per-

former. Married to the composer Karel Jirák. (R)

Kraus, Alfredo (*b* Las Palmas, 24 Nov. 1927). Spanish tenor of Austrian descent. Studied Barcelona, Valencia, and Milan with Mercedes Llopart. Début Madrid 1954 in Zarzuela; opera début Cairo 1956, Duke (*Rigoletto*); London, Stoll T., 1957 Alfredo, C.G., 1959 Edgardo, 1974 Duke of Mantua; Milan, Sc., since 1959; Chicago; San Francisco; N.Y., Met., since 1962. Repertory includes Ottavio, Ferrando, Almaviva, Fernando (*Favorita*), Arturo, Des Grieux, Werther. Regarded by many as the best *tenore di grazia* since Schipa. (R)

Kraus, Ernst (*b* Erlangen, 8 June 1863; *d* Waldstadt, 6 Sept. 1941). German tenor. Studied Munich with Schimon-Regar, Milan with Cesare Galliera. Début Mannheim 1893, Tamino. Principal tenor Damrosch Opera Company 1896–9; Met. 1903–4. Leading tenor Berlin 1898–1924, Bayreuth every festival 1899–1909, Siegmund, Siegfried, Walther, Erik. London, C.G., 1900, 1907, 1910: first London Herod. After leaving the stage in 1924, taught in Munich. (R) His son **Richard Kraus** (*b* 16 Nov. 1902; *d* Kassel, 11 Apr. 1978) was a conductor. He has held posts in Hanover, Stuttgart, Halle, Cologne and at the Berlin Stä. (later D.) since 1953. (R)

Kraus, Otakar (*b* Prague, 10 Dec. 1909). Czech, later British, baritone. Studied Prague with Konrad Wallerstein, Milan with Fernando Carpi. Début Brno 1935, Amonasro; Bratislava 1936–9; then came to England. After war-time appearances in *Sorochintsy Fair* and with the C. R., joined the E. O. G. in 1946, creating Tarquinius in *The Rape of Lucretia,* and also singing Lockit, and the Vicar in *Albert Herring.* Netherlands Opera 1950–1; C.G. 1951-73 Created Nick Shadow in *The Rake's Progress,* Venice 1951, Diomede in *Troilus and Cressida* and King Fisher in *The Midsummer Marriage,* both at C.G. A fine Alberich, which he sang at Bayreuth 1960–2. Kraus was a first-rate singeractor and a master of make-up. Retired 1973, and now teaches. (R)

Krause, Tom (*b* Helsinki, 5 July 1934). Finnish baritone. Studied Vienna and Hamburg. Début Berlin, Stä., 1959, Escamillo; Hamburg since 1962; Bayreuth, 1962, Herald in *Lohengrin*; N.Y., Met., since '1967. Gly. 1963, Count (*Capriccio*). Created Jason in Křenek's *Der goldene Bock* (1964) and title-role in Searle's *Hamlet* (1968), both at Hamburg. Repertory also includes Don Giovanni, Count Almaviva, Guglielmo, Germont. (R)

Krauss, Clemens (Heinrich) (*b* Vienna, 31 Mar. 1893; *d* Mexico, 16 May 1954). Austrian conductor. Studied Vienna with Graedener and Heuberger. Début Brno 1913, *Zar und Zimmer-*

mann. After seasons in Riga (1913–14), Nuremberg (1915–16), and Stettin (1916–22) he went to Vienna 1922–4 as assistant to Schalk. Director of the Frankfurt Opera 1924–9; Vienna 1929–35; Berlin 1935–7. Generalmusikdirektor at Munich 1937–42. Krauss's leading singers, including Adele Kern, Viorica Ursuleac (whom he married), and Julius Patzak were faithful to him, and followed him from Vienna to Berlin and from Berlin to Munich. A close friend of Strauss, he conducted the premières of *Arabella* (Dresden 1933), *Friedenstag* (Munich 1938), *Capriccio,* for which he wrote the libretto (Munich 1942), and *Die Liebe der Danae* (Salzburg 1952). London, C.G., 1934 (*Arabella* and *Shvanda*); 1947 with the Vienna S.O. (*Salome* and *Fidelio*); 1949 Stoll T. (*Falstaff* and *Tosca*), and C.G. again 1951–3, *Tristan, Fidelio,* and *Meistersinger.* (R)
Bibl: O. von Pander: *Clemens Krauss in Munich* (1955).

Krauss, Felix von (*b* Vienna, 3 Oct. 1870; *d* Munich, 30 Oct 1937). Austrian bass. Studied Amsterdam with C. Van Zanten, Frankfurt with Stockhausen. Début in concert, Vienna 1896; stage début Bayreuth 1899, Hagen, appearing there until 1909 as Gurnemanz, King Mark, Landgrave. London, C.G., 1907. Professor Munich Conservatory 1908 and artistic director of the Bavarian State Opera. (R) His wife was **Adrienne Krausse-Osborne** (orig. Adrienne Eisbein) (*b* Buffalo, 2 Dec. 1873; *d* Zell am Ziller, 15 June 1951). American contralto. Studied Leipzig with Götze. Début Leipzig 1893, Mignon. Leipzig until 1908, then Munich. Bayreuth 1899–1909, Erda and Waltraute. London, C.G., 1907. Her most famous role was Carmen. (R)

Krauss, (Marie) **Gabrielle** (*b* Vienna, 24 Mar. 1842; *d* Paris, 6 Jan. 1906). Austrian soprano. Studied Vienna Conservatory with Marchesi. Début Berlin 1859, Mathilde (*William Tell*). Remained in Vienna until 1867, then sang in Italy and Russia. Paris, T.I., 1867–70; O., 1875, singing Rachel in *La Juive* at the opening performance of the present building (5 Jan.) and remaining there until 1887. Created a number of roles including Pauline in Gounod's *Polyeucte* and Katherine of Aragon in Saint-Saëns's *Henry VIII.* Her repertory further included Donna Anna, Valentine, Norma, Lucia, Gilda, Elsa, and Aida. Her acting powers were such that the French nicknamed her 'La Rachel chantante'.

Krefeld – Mönchen Gladbach. The first opera performances were given in Krefeld in 1794 in the theatre built in 1780. A new theatre opened in 1825 with *La Dame blanche;* it was enlarged in 1886 and destroyed in 1943. Olczewska was a member of the company 1917–20, Greindl 1936–8. After the war performances were given in the Aula of the Lyzeum. A new theatre (cap. 832) opened in October 1952 with *Lohengrin;* the present house opened in 1963 with *Don Giovanni.* In Mönchen Gladbach the first permanent opera house (cap. 753) was opened in 1959. The two companies joined forces in 1966. Robert Satanowski was music director 1969-76.

Krehbiel, Henry Edward (*b* Ann Arbor, 10 Mar 1854; *d* New York, 20 Mar. 1923). American critic. Studied law in Cincinnati. Music critic *Cincinnati Gazette* 1874–80; *New York Tribune* 1880–1923. Championed Wagner in the U.S.A. Prolific writer whose books included a history of opera in New York, entitled *Chapters of Opera* (1908), and *Studies in the Wagnerian Drama* (1891).

Křenek, Ernst (*b* Vienna, 23 Aug. 1900). Austrian, later American, composer. Studied Vienna with Schreker. His first stage work was the scenic canta *Die Zwingburg* (1924). His first opera, *Der Sprung über den Schatten* (1924) incorporates jazz in an atonal idiom. He worked in Kassel (1925–7), then lived in Vienna until leaving for America in 1937. His *Orpheus und Eurydike* (1926) came out in Kassel, as did his most famous work, the jazz opera *Jonny spielt auf* (1927), which aroused wide interest for the skill of its absorption of jazz techniques and some of the fashions of the contemporary world into a traditional framework. He attempted to follow this success up with three *Zeitopern,* then with a self-styled 'grand opera' *Leben des Orest* (1930). Adopting serial techniques, he wrote the large-scale music drama *Karl V,* a work which includes pantomime, film and play. Banned by the Nazis in 1934, it was eventually produced in Prague in 1938. Moved to America and made a reputation as a distinguished teacher. *Der goldene Bock* (1964) again showed Křenek's interest in the modern treatment of mythic subjects with a kind of comic fantasy on the search for the Golden Fleece. He has also written a TV opera, *Der Zauberspiegel* (1966). A brilliantly equipped musician, he has tried in his four principal periods to find some universally valid principle of contemporary composition and thus to achieve wide popularity for the art of opera without any sacrifice of artistic conscience.

Krenn, Fritz (*b* Vienna, 11 Dec. 1897; *d* Vienna 17 July 1964). Austrian bass. Studied Vienna with Forsten and Iro. Début Trieste 1917 Herald (*Lohengrin*). Vienna, V.O., 1917–18 Bratislava 1918–19; Vienna, S.O., 1919–25 1934–42, 1946–59; Wiesbaden 1925–7; Berlin S.O., 1927–43; London, C.G., 1935; N.Y., Met. 1951. Sang in the premières of *Cardillac* and *Neues vom Tage.* A distinguished buffo, also successful in Verdi, Wagner, and Strauss: his most famous role was Ochs. (R)

Kreutzer, Konrad (from 1799, Conradin) (*b* Messkirch, 22 Nov. 1780; *d* Riga, 14 Dec. 1849). German composer. Studied privately. His first stage work was an operetta, *Die lächerliche Werbung*, which was performed by students of the University of Freiburg im Breisgau where he studied law; he sang a leading tenor role in the work. Further studied with Albrechtsberger. The success of his 3-act opera *Konradin von Schwaben*, and *Feodora*, in Stuttgart in 1812, led to his appointment to succeed Danzi as court conductor there. In Vienna from 1822, he had a success with *Libusse* (1822) at the Kä., where he conducted 1822–7, 1829–32, and 1835–40; he also conducted at the J., 1833–5, and from this period dates his most successful opera, *Das Nachtlager von Granada* (1834). He was music director at Cologne 1840–2, and after many further travels settled in Riga with his daughter Marie, a singer. His music tapped a popular vein of light Romantic melody, though his operas were criticized for their lack of dramatic interest.

Kreutzer, Rodolphe (*b* Versailles, 16 Nov. 1766; *d* Geneva, 6 Jan. 1831). French violinist and composer. Studied with his father and Stamitz. Best known as a violinist (and the dedicatee of Beethoven's Op. 47 violin sonata). From 1790 he had a number of works produced at the T.I. and O.C., notably *Paul et Virginie* (1791) (remarkable in that Act 3 is virtually continuous) and *Lodoïska* (1791): the latter was initially rated above Cherubini's work of the same year. Continued to write many operas, the most successful being *Astyanax* (1801), *Aristippe* (1808), and *Abel* (1810): the latter was admired by Berlioz. In 1810 a fracture of his arm ended his solo career; but in 1816 he became second conductor of the O., chief conductor 1817–24, director 1824–6. His music became outdated in his own day, and his last opera, *Matilde* (comp. *c*1826–7), was rejected by the O.

Krips, Josef (*b* Vienna, 8 Apr. 1902; *d* Geneva, 13 Oct. 1974). Austrian conductor. Studied Vienna with Weingartner. Vienna, V.O., 1921; Dortmund 1925–6; Karlsruhe 1926–33; Vienna S.O. 1933–8, when he was dismissed by the Nazis. He conducted the first opera performance in Vienna after the war in 1945, and under his direction the Vienna S.O. was restored to its pre-war eminence in the years 1945–50. London début C.G. 1947 with Vienna Company (*Don Giovanni, Figaro,* and *Così fan tutte*); returned 1963, and again 1971-4. Chicago 1960, 1964; N.Y., Met., 1966-7, 1969-70. He played an important part in the resumption of the Salzburg Festival, where he had first conducted in 1935. (R)

Kroll Oper. See *Berlin*.

Krombholc, Jaroslav (*b* Prague, 30 Jan. 1918).

Czech conductor. Studied Prague with Novák and Talich. Prague N.T. 1940-4 and since 1945, where he is music director. London, C.G., 1959, *Boris Godunov*; 1961 *Bartered Bride*. E.N.O. 1978. *Don Giovanni.* (R)

Krull, Annie (orig. Marie Anna) (*b* Rostock, 12 Jan. 1876; *d* Schwerin, 14 June 1947). German soprano. Studied Berlin with Hertha Brämer. Début Plauen 1898; Dresden 1900-12, where she created Diemut (*Feuersnot*), Elektra, and Ulana in Paderewski's *Manru*. Mannheim and Weimar 1911-12; Schwerin 1914-15. London, C.G., 1910, Elektra. (R)

Krushelnytska (or Krusceniski), **Salomea** (Ambrosivna) (*b* Bilavyntsy (Pol., Biata), 23 Sept. 1873; *d* Lwów, 16 Nov. 1952). Russian (Ukrainian) soprano. The daughter of a priest, she first sang in choirs and amateur theatres. Studied Lwów with Wysocki; début Lwów 1893 in *La favorita*. Further studies Milan 1893-6 with Crespi, and Vienna. Warsaw Opera 1898-1902, then a triumphant international career, generally under the name of Krusceniski. Sang Cio-Cio-San at Brescia 1904 when *Butterfly* had its first success after its Milan Sc. fiasco. Sc. from 1906, first Elektra in Italy, and created title-role in Pizzetti's *Fedra*. Buenos Aires 1906-13. A repertory of more than 50 roles including Tatyana, Lisa, Isolde, Brünnhilde, Salome, Gioconda, and Aida. Last stage appearances Naples 1920, after which she sang only in concerts; subsequently taught at the M.V. Lysenko Conservatory, Lwów. Her records reveal a voice of great beauty, spanning a range of two-and-a-half octaves; also praised for her dramatic talents. (R)

Kubelík, (Jeroným) **Rafael** (*b* Býchory, 29 June 1914). Czech conductor and composer. Son of Jan Kubelík. Studied Prague with Talich. After a period with the Czech Philharmonic, appointed chief conductor Brno, 1939-41. Left Czechoslovakia 1948 when he went to Edinburgh to conduct *Don Giovanni.* S.W. 1954, *Káťa Kabanová.* Music director C.G. 1955-8, where his successes included *Otello, Jenůfa* (first stage perf. in England), and *Les Troyens.* Encouraged native singers, and tried to maintain the highest musical standards by keeping the cast of each opera intact throughout the season. Returned to C.G. 1970, *Jenůfa.* Guest appearances Hamburg, Munich. Music director N.Y., Met., from 1973 (the first in the company's history), but resigned in protest over cuts in the budget in 1974. San Francisco 1977. His five operas include *Cornelia Faroli*, of which he cond. the première, Augsburg 1966. (R)

Kullman, Charles (*b* New Haven, Conn., 13 Jan. 1903). American tenor of German birth. Studied Juilliard School and the American Conservatory, Fontainebleau, with Salignac. Début American Opera Company 1929, Pinkerton; Berlin 1931-4; London, C.G., 1934-5 and 1938; N.Y., Met., 1935-62. Salzburg 1934-6, Ferrando, Belmonte, Walther. Taught at Bloomington from 1956. (R)

Kundry. The enchantress (sop.) who tries to seduce Parsifal in Wagner's opera. Often sung by a mezzo.

Kunz, Erich (*b* Vienna, 20 May 1909). Austrian bass-baritone. Studied Vienna with Lierhammer and Duhan. Début Opava 1933, Osmin. After engagements in Plauen (1936-7) and Breslau (1937-41), came to Gly. in 1935 and sang in the chorus. Vienna S.O. since 1940. London, C.G., 1947 with Vienna Company as Leporello, Figaro, and Guglielmo, all of which parts he has sung with success at Salzburg and elsewhere in Europe. N.Y., Met., 1952-4; Bayreuth 1943-4 and 1951, as Beckmesser. In this role and as Papageno he had few equals, though his sense of comedy sometimes overcame his artistry. (R)

Kupper (-Herrmann), **Annelies** (Gabriele) (*b* Glatz, 21 July 1906). German soprano. Studied Breslau, where she made her début, 1935, Second Boy (*Magic Flute*). After seasons at Schwerin (1937-8) and Weimar (1938-9, 1940), joined Hamburg Opera 1940, remaining until 1946. Munich 1946-61. Bayreuth 1944 Eva, 1960 Elsa. London, C.G., 1953, Chrysothemis, then with Munich company. Created Danae at Strauss's request, Salzburg 1951. Retired 1961. Teaches in Munich. (R)

Kurpiński, Karol (Kazimierz) (*b* Włoszakowice, 6 Mar. 1785; *d* Warsaw, 18 Sept. 1857). Polish composer and conductor. Studied with his father, the local organist. After holding various appointments, became deputy conductor, and then principal conductor of the Warsaw Opera (1824-40). Founded and taught at his own schools of singing and drama, and founded the first Polish music journal, *Tygodnik muzyczny* (1820). Played an important part in Warsaw's concert life (he conducted Chopin's first concerts); also made an important contribution to the development of Polish opera. He wrote 24 stage works, of which nine survive: these include *Zamek na Czorsztynie* (The Castle of Czorsztyn, 1819), which has occasionally been revived. He married (1815) the soprano **Zofia Brzowska** (*b* Warsaw, 19 Jan. 1800; *d* Warsaw, 28 June 1879), who made her début aged 14 and sang soubrette roles at the Warsaw Opera.

Kurt, Melanie (*b* Vienna, 8 Jan. 1880; *d* New York, 11 Mar. 1941). Austrian soprano. Studied Vienna under Leschetitzky and appeared as a solo pianist 1897-1900, when she began to take singing lessons with Müller in Vienna. Début

Lübeck 1902, Leonore. Leipzig 1903-4, then followed two years' further training with Lilli and Marie Lehmann. Brunswick 1905-8; Berlin 1908-14; London, C.G., 1910 as Sieglinde and Brünnhilde and 1914 Kundry; N.Y., Met., 1915-17 as Isolde, Kundry, Brünnhilde, Pamina, Leonore, Fricka (*Rheingold*), Iphigénie in the first Met. performance of *Iphigénie en Tauride* and other roles. When America entered the war her contract was cancelled. Taught Berlin, Vienna, and New York from 1939. (R)

Kurwenal. Tristan's retainer (bar.) in Wagner's *Tristan und Isolde.*

Kurz, Selma (*b* Bielitz, 15 Nov. 1874; *d* Vienna 10 May 1933). Austrian soprano. Studied Vienna with Johannes Ress, Paris with Marchesi. Début Hamburg 1895 as mezzo, Mignon Frankfurt 1896-91. Engaged by Mahler for Vienna 1899 where she sang until 1929, first as a lyric-dramatic soprano, e.g. Sieglinde Elisabeth, and Eva, then as a coloratura, e.g Lucia, Gilda, and Violetta, London, C.G., 1904-7. Her remarkable trill, as well as her success in certain roles, is said to have aroused Melba's jealousy, and she did not reappear until 1924 (R) Her daughter, **Desi Halban-Kurz** (*b* Vienna 1912) had a short career in opera and concerts. (R)
Bibl: H. Goldmann: *Selma Kurz* (1933).

Kusche, Benno (*b* Freiburg, 30 Jan. 1916) German bass-baritone. Studied Karlsruhe with his mother, Freiburg with Fritz Harlan. Début Koblenz 1938, Renato. Augsburg 1939-44; Munich since 1946. London, C.G., 1952, Beckmesser, and 1953 with Munich company as La Roche. Gly. 1954, Leporello, 1963-4 La Roche N.Y., Met., 1972. One of the best character singers in post-war German opera. (R)

Kuznetsova, Maria (Nikolayevna) (*b* Odessa, 1880; *d* Paris, 26 Apr. 1966). Russian soprano, daughter of the artist Nikolay Kuznetsov, who painted the most famous portrait of Tchaikovsky. Studied St Petersburg with Tartakov. Début St Petersburg Conservatory, with Russo-Italian Company, 1904; M. 1905-13, Tatyana, Oxana, Juliette, Violetta, Butterfly, Berlin and Paris, 1908. London, C.G., 1909 Mimì, Marguerite, 1910, Manon. D.L. 1914 in ballet *Josephslegende.* Petrograd, Narodny Dom, 1915-16. Chicago 1916. In Russia, before the Revolution, one of the most admired and versatile sopranos, singing Elsa and Carmen as well as the Russian repertory. She escaped from Russia in 1918, disguised as a boy, hidden in a trunk in a Swedish ship. Stockholm and Copenhagen 1919; C.G. 1920. Later settled in Barcelona, where she acted as artistic adviser at the Liceo for Russian operas. (R)

L

Labia, Fausta (*b* Verona, 3 Apr. 1870; *d* Rome, 6 Oct. 1935). Italian soprano. Studied with Aldighieri. Début Verona 1893, Alice (*Robert le diable*). Stockholm 1893-5. Specialized in Wagner in Italy 1901-5; virtually retired on her marriage to the tenor Emilio Perea (*b* 1884). Buenos Aires 1912. She established a school of singing in Rome, and her *L'arte del respiro nella recitazione e nel canto* was publ. 1936. (R). Her daughter **Gianna Perea-Labia** (*b* 1908) had an Italian career in the 1930s and 1940s.

Labia, Maria (*b* Verona, 14 Feb. 1880; *d* Malcesine del Garda, 11 Feb. 1953). Italian soprano, sister of above. Studied with her mother and began carrer as concert singer; stage début Milan, T.d.V., 1900, a Geisha in *Iris*. Stockholm 1905, Mimì. Berlin, K.O., 1906-11, where she was a great success, especially in *verismo* roles: first Berlin Tosca, Martha (*Tiefland*). An actress of great emotional power, she was also a celebrated Salome, Thaïs, Fedora, and Carmen. Manhattan Opera Company 1908; Milan, Sc., 1912. Accused of espionage for Germany in 1914 and arrested. Resumed career after the war: first European Giorgetta, Rome 1919. From 1930 taught first in Warsaw, then Siena, finally at her own villa on Lake Garda; continued to sing, especially in *Quatro rusteghi*, until 1936. (R)
Bibl: M. Labia: *Guardare indietro: che fatica* (1950).

Labinsky, Andrey (Markovich) (*b* Kharkov, 1871; *d* Moscow, 8 Aug. 1941). Russian tenor. Orginally sang in chorus at St Petersburg, M.; then studied with Gabel. St Petersburg, M., 1897, then 1899-1912. Moscow, B., 1912-24. Created Vsevolod (*Kitezh*). Repertory included Sobinin (*Life for the Tsar*), Berendey (*Snow Maiden*), Lohengrin, Don José. From 1920 taught in Moscow. (R)

Lablache, Luigi (*b* Naples, 6 Dec. 1794; *d* Naples, 23 Jan. 1858). Italian bass of French and Irish parentage. Studied Naples with Valente: début Naples 1821 in Palma's *L'erede senza eredità*. Then followed a further period of study and a five-year engagement at Palermo. Milan, Sc., 1821, Dandini; Vienna 1824 (while there sang in Mozart's *Requiem* at Beethoven's funeral); London, H.M.'s, 1830, Geronimo (*Il matrimonio segreto*); Paris the same year; St Petersburg 1852. Sang regularly in Paris and London until 1856, and was one of the few singers who remained loyal to Lumley and H.M.'s at the time of the opening of C.G., though he went over to the latter house in 1854.

He created Riccardo in *I Puritani*, and Don Pasquale, and was their first interpreter in London. Also first London Podestà (*Linda di Chamounix*), Karl von Moor (*I masnadieri*), and Caliban (*La tempesta*). Famous as Leporello, Bartolo, Pollione, and Baldassare. His voice had a compass of two octaves (E-e). He was an enormous man – as Leporello he used to carry off Masetto under his arm. He was for a time Queen Victoria's singing teacher. His elder son, **Frederick**, also was a singer, and his daughter married the pianist Thalberg. His *Méthode de chant* did not add to his reputation. *Bibl:* F. Castil-Blaze: *Biographie de Lablache* (n.d.).

Labrocca, Mario (*b* Rome, 22 Dec. 1896; *d* Rome, 1 July 1973). Italian composer, administrator, and critic. Studied Parma with Respighi and Malipiero. Artistic director Florence Festival 1936-44; organized seasons of contemporary opera Milan, Sc., and Rome, T.R., 1942; administrator Venice, F., 1946-7 and 1959-73, and of Milan, Sc., 1947-9; director of Italian Radio 1949-58, during which period he arranged for Furtwängler to conduct *The Ring*.

La calunnia. See *Calunnia, La*.

Lachner, Franz (*b* Rain ober Lech, 2 Apr. 1803; *d* Munich, 20 Jan. 1890). German conductor. Studied Vienna; where he became conductor, Kä., 1826-34. From 1834 to 1836 he was at Mannheim and from 1836 until his death at Munich, becoming Generalmusikdirektor there in 1852. The real fame of the Munich Opera dates from his directorship. At first a great opponent of Wagner's music, he was persuaded to produce *Tannhäuser* in 1855 and *Lohengrin* in 1858. He was also a prolific composer and three of.his four operas were produced at Munich. His younger brother **Ignaz** (1807-1895) held appointments in Vienna, Stuttgart, Munich, Hamburg, Stockholm, and Frankfurt. A third brother **Vincenz** (1811-1893) conducted in Vienna and at Mannheim (1836-73); and conducted a German company at C.G. in 1842 which gave the first performance in England of *Les Huguenots* and performances of *Iphigénie en Tauride*, *La Vestale*, and other works.

Lachnith, Ludwig (*b* Prague, 7 July 1746; *d* Paris, 3 Oct. 1820). Bohemian composer. He was notorious as an arranger of famous operas to suit them to public taste. He made *The Magic Flute* begin with the finale and included Don Giovanni's 'Finch'han dal vino', arranged as a duet, as well as excerpts from other Mozart operas and from Haydn's symphonies: this entertainment was entitled *Les Mystères d'Isis* (1801). Reichardt and Berlioz were among those who protested, to little avail at first: the work had 134 performances. Lachnith also wrote some original operas.

Là ci darem la mano. Duet in which Don Giovanni (bar.) woos Zerlina (sop.) in Act 1, sc. 3, of Mozart's *Don Giovanni;* after hesitating, she succumbs.

Lacy, Michael (*b* Bilbao, 19 July 1795; *d* London 20 Sept. 1867). Irish violinist. He was a skilful if unprincipled adaptor of many famous operas for the London stage, among them a pasticcio jumbling Handel's *Israel in Egypt* and Rossini's *Mosè in Egitto* as *The Israelites in Egypt* (1833).

La donna è mobile. The Duke of Mantua's (ten.) aria in Act 3 of Verdi's *Rigoletto,* proclaiming his philosophy of fickleness. Hearing it again, sung in the distance, Rigoletto realizes that the body he has in a sack at his feet cannot be that of the Duke. One of the most famous of all arias, it was kept secret by Verdi until the day of the première. Also the title of an opera by R. Malipiero (1954).

Lady Macbeth of the Mtsensk District, The. Opera in 4 acts by Shostakovich; text by composer and A. Preis, after Leskov's story (1865). Prod. Leningrad, Maly T., 22 Jan. 1934, with Sokolova, Modestov, Balashov, Zasetsky, Adrianova, cond. Samosud; Cleveland (semi-staged) 31 Jan. 1935, with Leskaya, cond. Rodzinski; London, C.G., 2 Dec. 1963, with Collier, Howitt, Craig, Evans, Kraus, cond. Downes. Also known as *Katerina Izmaylova.* This opera unleashed the first serious attack on Shostakovich and on modernist art in general from the Russian Communist party. It originally had considerable success, including 83 performances in Leningrad and 97 in Moscow; then on 28 Jan. 1936 *Pravda* published a violent attack on the opera entitled 'Chaos instead of music', following this on 6 Feb. with a second article attacking Shostakovich's ballet *The Limpid Stream.* Being anonymous articles, these had the standing of official policy pronouncements. Not until 1963 was the work revived in Russia (Moscow, Stanislavsky T.), as *Katerina Izmaylova,* in a striking modern production.

Katerina Izmaylova (sop.), the wife of a merchant, takes one of his workmen as a lover. She gives her father-in-law rat-poison and, aided by her lover, strangles her husband. On their way to Siberia, the lover deserts her for one of the women convicts, and she kills her rival and herself.

Lagrange, Anne Caroline de (*b* Nancy, 24 July 1824; *d* Paris, 23 Apr. 1905). French soprano. Studied Paris with Bordogni. Amateur début Paris, T. Renaissance, 1840, in Flotow's *La Duchesse de Guise.* Further study in Italy with Mandanici and Lamperti. Professional début Piacenza 1842 in *Il bravo;* Milan, Sc., 1861; N.Y. 1855-8, where she was the first local Violetta. Repertory also included Rosina, Norma, Lucia, and Lucrezia Borgia.

Lakmé. Opera in 3 acts by Delibes; text by Gondinet and Gille, after the former's *Le Mariage de Loti.* Prod. Paris, O.C., 14 Apr. 1883, with Van Zandt, Talazac, and Cobalet, cond. Danbé, London, Gaiety T., 6 June 1885, with Van Zandt, Dupuy, and Carroul, cond. Bevignani, Chicago, Grand O.H., 4 Oct. 1883, but first full-scale U.S. prod. N.Y., Ac. of M., 1 Mar. 1886 with L'Allemand, Bartlett, Canddus, Stoddard cond. Thomas.

The opera, set in mid-19th cent. India, tells of the love of a British officer, Gerald (ten.), for Lakmé (sop.) (daughter of the Brahmin priest Nilakantha (bass)), which ends in Lakmé's suicide.

Lalande, Henriette. See *Méric-Lalande, Henriette.*

Lalo, Édouard (-Victoire-Antoine) (*b* Lille, 27 Jan. 1823; *d* Paris, 22 Apr. 1892). French composer. Studied Lille, Paris with Schulhoff and Crèvecoeur. Originally a violinist, beginning to compose chamber music; his first opera, *Fiesque,* failed to win the T.L. prize in 1866, which greatly discouraged him. However, the success of other instrumental works encouraged him to write another opera, and this proved to be his masterpiece, *Le Roi d'Ys* (1888). Though in the manner of grand opera, it is marked by Lalo's own personality, especially his capacity for elegant and charming melody and his vigorous sense of movement. His only other opera, *La Jacquerie,* was left with one act completed at his death; it was finished by Coquard, prod. 1895. Lalo married the singer Julie de Maligny; their son **Pierre Lalo** (1866-1943) was a well-known music critic.
Bibl: G. Servières: *Édouard Lalo* (1925).

L'altra notte. Margherita's (sop.) aria in Act 3 of Boito's *Mefistofele,* as she lies in prison and describes the drowning of her child.

La mamma morta. Madeleine de Coigney's (sop.) aria in Act 3 of Giordano's *Andrea Chénier,* in which she tells Gérard of the terrible death of her mother when their house was burned by the Revolutionary mob.

Lambert, Constant (*b* London, 23 Aug. 1905; *d* London, 21 Aug. 1951). English conductor, composer, and critic. Although primarily associated with the growth of ballet in Great Britain, in particular at S.W., he had a great love of Italian opera, and conducted *Manon Lescaut* and *Turandot* at C.G. before the Second World War, as well as *The Fairy Queen* (for which he arranged the score) and *Turandot* (1946-7). (R)

Lamento (*It* lament). A tragic aria common in early 17th cent. opera, usually placed immediately before the climax of the plot and often, the unexpected turn to the happy ending. The most famous is Monteverdi's from *Arianna* (1608), and is all that survives of the opera.

mmers, Gerda (b Berlin, 25 Sept. 1915).
erman soprano. Studied Berlin Hochschule
ith Lula Mysz-Gmeiner and Margaret
hwedler-Lohmann. After 15 years as a con-
rt and lieder singer made stage début
ayreuth 1955 as Ortlinde. Kassel 1955-70,
aking début as Marie in *Wozzeck,* following it
ith Elektra. Also appeared there as Senta,
ceste, the Singer in *Cardillac,* Medea, Isolde,
d Brünnhilde. When Goltz fell suddenly ill in
957, Lammers made an unheralded London
but at C.G. as Elektra, scoring one of the
eatest individual triumphs in post-war
ndon opera. Sang Dido in *Dido and Aeneas*
Ingestre Hall in 1958, and Kundry at C.G. in
959. N.Y., Met., 1961-62, Elektra. (R)

amour est un oiseau rebelle. Carmen's
ezzo) Habanera, in Act 1 of Bizet's *Carmen.*

moureux, Charles (b Bordeaux, 28 Sept.
834; d Paris, 21 Dec. 1899). French violinist
d conductor. For many years a member of
e Opéra orchestra; cond. O.C., 1876-7, O.,
877-9, resigning after a dispute about the
mpo of an aria in *Don Giovanni.* A pioneer
agnerian, he included long operatic excerpts
his famous series of concerts. He gave
stinguished performances in Paris of *Lohenrin* and *Tristan,* and lived to see Wagner's
use triumphant.

ampe, Johann Friedrich (b Saxony, c1703; d
dinburgh, 25 July 1751). German-English bas-
onist and composer. From 1725 he was in
ndon, where he played in the orchestra of
e King's T., and composed many works for
e Hm. His collaboration with Henry Carey
lminated in *The Dragon of Wantley* (1737), a
urlesque much appreciated by Handel. His
ife and Arne's were sisters, both accomp-
shed singers, and Lampe toured with them
ccessfully.

amperti, Francesco (b Savona, 11 Mar. 1811;
Como, 1 May 1892). Italian singing teacher.
ducated Milan Conservatory. With Masini
rected T. Filodrammatico, Lodi, whither stu-
ents came from all over Europe. Appointed
rofessor of singing at Milan Conservatory
850. His pupils included Albani, Campanini,
rtôt, Cruvelli, Sembrich, Stolz, and Wald-
ann, and he was a friend of Pasta and Rubini.
e based his teaching on the method of the old
alian school, and wrote several vocal studies
nd a treatise on singing. His younger son
iovanni (1839-1910) was also a teacher,
hose pupils included Bispham, Sembrich,
chumann-Heink, and Stagno. Writings
clude *The Technique of Bel Canto* (1905). His
der son, **Giuseppe** (1834-98), was an impre-
ario.

ampugnani, Giovanni Battista (b Milan, 1706;
Milan, 1781). Italian composer. He succeeded

Galuppi as composer at the King's T. in 1743,
where he produced two of his own operas; he
also shared the conducting at the Hm., with
Gluck among others. His works continued to be
produced in London and Milan, where he
played the harpsichord with Mozart in *Mitridate* in 1770. His 29 operas are for the most part
in the opera seria tradition, following the
example of Hasse; but he was admired for the
lightness and spirit of his arias, though Burney
observed in them 'new and difficult divisions'.

Lanari, Alessandro (b S. Marcello di Jesi, 1790;
d Florence, 3 Oct. 1862). Italian impresario.
Directed the fortunes of Milan, Sc., Venice, F.,
and finally Florence, P. (1823-8, 1830-5, 1839-
48, 1860-2). Commissioned Bellini's *Norma*
and *Beatrice di Tenda,* Donizetti's *L'elisir
d'amore* and *Parisina,* and Verdi's *Attila* and
Macbeth, as well as operas by Pacini and Mercadante. Known as 'the Napoleon of impresarios'.
Bibl: G. Monaldi: *Impresari celebri del Sec. XIX*
(1918).

Lancaster, Osbert (b London, 4 Aug. 1908).
British designer. Already well known as an
artist and cartoonist, Lancaster turned to opera
in 1952, designing *Love in a Village* for the
E.O.G. For Gly. he designed *The Rake's Progress* (first perf. in Britain), *L'italiana in Algeri,
La pietra del paragone, Falstaff, L'Heure Espagnole,* and *The Rising of the Moon.* He
also designed *Don Pasquale* for S.W. His settings and costumes are wittily and intelli-
gently observed, with a loving eye for detail.

Landgrave. Hermann, the Landgrave of
Thuringia (bass), in Wagner's *Tannhäuser.*

Langdon, Michael (b Wolverhampton, 12 Nov.
1920). British bass. Studied Vienna with Jerger,
Geneva with Maria Carpi, London with Otakar
Kraus. Joined C.G. 1948 as chorister; principal
singer from 1951; created Mr Ratcliffe (*Billy
Budd*), Recorder of Norwich (*Gloriana*), He-
Ancient (*Midsummer Marriage*), and sang in
first British *Wozzeck, Jenůfa, Katerina
Izmaylova, Moses and Aron, Die schweigsame
Frau.* His enormous repertory includes French,
German and Italian roles, and he has sung
Baron Ochs at most of the world's leading
opera houses. Created title role in Orr's *Her-
miston,* Edinburgh Festival 1975. Has a rich
bass voice and is a good actor and a master of
make-up. Director, National Opera Studio,
1978. (R)

Laparra, Raoul (b Bordeaux, 13 May 1876; d
Paris, 4 Apr. 1943). French composer. Studied
Paris with Gédalge, Massenet, and Fauré. Of
his operas, the most successful was *La
Habanera* (1908); he used Spanish and Basque
themes in his music.

Laporte (orig. Delaporte), **Pierre François** (*b* 1799; *d* nr Paris, 1841). French actor and operatic manager. Manager of King's T., London, 1828-31 and 1833-41. His management included the first performances in London of *Il pirata, La sonnambula, Anna Bolena, Norma, I Capuleti e i Montecchi, I Puritani, Beatrice di Tenda, L'elisir d'amore,* and *Lucrezia Borgia.* Among the singers he brought to London for the first time were Rubini, Grisi, Nourrit, Tamburini, Persiani, Mario, Lablache, and Pauline Viardot.

Largo (*It* broad). The name ('Handel's Largo') by which the *larghetto* aria 'Ombra mai fù' from Handel's *Serse* has become known in countless arrangements.

Largo al factotum. Figaro's (bar.) aria introducing himself in all his versatility and popularity in Act 1, sc. 1, of Rossini's *Il barbiere di Siviglia.*

Larrivée, Henri (*b* Lyons, 9 Jan. 1737; *d* Vincennes, 7 Aug. 1802). French bass-baritone. Début Paris, O., 1775 in *Castor et Pollux.* Greatly admired by Gluck, who wrote Agamemnon and Orestes for him in the two *Iphigénie* operas. His wife **Marie-Jeane Le Mière** (*b* Sedan, 29 Nov. 1733; *d* Paris, Oct. 1786) was a soprano who sang at the O., 1750-77.

Larsén-Todsen, Nanny (*b* Hagby, 2 Aug. 1884). Swedish soprano. Studied Stockholm, Germany, and Italy. Début Stockholm 1906, Agathe (*Freischütz*). Leading lyric soprano Stockholm 1907-33, by which time she had become a dramatic soprano and begun to specialize in Wagner. Milan, Sc., 1923-4, Isolde; N.Y., Met., 1924-7, Brünnhilde, Isolde, Kundry, Fricka, Leonore (*Fidelio*), Rachel (*La Juive*), and La Gioconda; London, C.G., 1927 and 1930, Brünnhilde; Bayreuth 1927-8, 1930-1. Continued to sing until the late 1930's, after which she taught in Stockholm. (R)

La Scala, Milan (rightly Teatro alla Scala). Built in 1778 by the architect Piermarini to replace the Royal Ducal T. that had been burned down two years previously, the theatre was named after Regina della Scala, wife of the Duke Barnabò Visconti of Milan, who had founded a church on the same site in the 14th century. It opened on 3 Aug. 1778 with Salieri's *Europa riconosciuta.* Every great Italian composer has written for La Scala – Rossini, Donizetti, Bellini, Verdi, and Puccini – and it has been the scene of the first performances of *La gazza ladra, Lucrezia Borgia, Norma, Otello, Falstaff, Madama Butterfly,* and *Turandot,* as well as many more works, some of which survived no more than a season. The Scala's most glorious periods were those under Toscanini's direction, 1898-1903, 1906-8, and 1921-9. During the first period Toscanini brought Wagner into the

Scala repertory and gave the first perfoc mances in Italy of *Salome, Louise,* and *Pellé et Mélisande;* during the third there were th premières of *Debora e Jaele* (Pizzetti), *Nero* (Boito), *Turandot, Belfagor* (Respighi), *La ce delle beffe* (Giordano), *I cavalieri di Ekebù* (Za donai), and some famous productions of *F staff, Boris Godunov, Rigoletto,* and *Lucia Lammermoor.* The company at this peric included Cobelli, Bruna Rasa, Dal Monte, Da Rizza, Raisa, Pampanini, Casazza, Supervi Pertile, Merli, Trantoul, Badini, Galeffi, Journe Pasero, and Stabile. The conductors who we associated with Toscanini at this time we Panizza, Guarnieri, Ghione, Gui, Santini, ar Votto.

After Toscanini's departure from the Scala 1929, owing to his quarrel with the Fascist two rather mediocre seasons followed; then the 1931-2 season *De Sabata began his lor association with the theatre, to be joined in th 1934-5 season by Marinuzzi. Despite Mu solini's attempt to turn the Rome O. into th premier theatre in Italy, the Scala continued set a standard of performance that few oth theatres could equal. The theatre was almo destroyed by bombs in Aug. 1943. By May 194 it had been rebuilt (cap. 3,600) and today loo much as it always had with its six tiers, four them boxes (146), all lined with red, the wa cream, gold, and maroon, and the beautiful 2 chandelier. The theatre reopened on 11 M 1946 with a concert conducted by Toscanir who had subscribed 100,000 lire to i rebuilding. The soloists included the vetera Stabile, Nessi, and Pasero, and a young nev comer, Renata Tebaldi.

De Sabata continued as musical and artist director until forced to retire by ill health 1954, after which Gavazzeni, Sanzogno, ar Votto were the chief conductors each seaso From 1952 to 1958 the presence of Callas in th Scala Company (she was called 'La Regi della Scala') led to the revivals of many lon neglected works, including *Anna Bolena, pirata,* and *Médée,* and splendid productio by Luchino Visconti of *La traviata, La vesta* and *La sonnambula.*

During the 1960s, premières included Pi zetti's *Clitennestra* and *Il calzare d'Argent* Falla's *L'Atlantida,* Rossellini's *Il linguaggio c fiori,* as well as the first performances in Italy *Les Troyens, Moses und Aron, A Midsumm Night's Dream, Mahagonny, Kateri Izmaylova, The Mines of Sulphur, From tl House of the Dead,* and *The Nose.*

In Dec. 1955 a chamber theatre, bu within the large Scala building and called I Piccola Scala (cap. 600), was opened. On i stage *Il matrimonio segreto, Così fan tutte,* buona figliuola, Don Pasquale, Il Signor Bru chino, Il campanello,* and works by mode composers are performed.

During the post-war period, 1946-1972, Antonio Ghiringhelli was the theatre's general administrator; in 1972 he was succeeded by Paolo Grassi, who appointed Massimo Bogianckino artistic director, and Claudio Abbado music director. This new triumvirate planned to change the theatre's image, aiming at democratizing the Scala and trying to attract a younger and wider audience. Bogianckino left in 1975 and Grassi in 1977. Claudio Abbado became artistic director in 1977, with Carlo Maria Badini as Sovrintendente.

The Scala Company has paid several visits abroad since the war, including London, C.G., in 1950 and 1976, Edinburgh in 1957, Moscow in 1964 and 1974, and Washington in 1976. *Bibl:* P. Cambiasi: *La Scala e la Canobbiana, 1778-1906* (1906); G. Marangoni and C. Vanbianchi: *La Scala* (1922); F. Armani: *La Scala, 1946-66* (1967); C. Gatti: *Il Teatro alla Scala* (1964).

Lassalle, Jean (-Louis) (*b* Lyons, 14 Dec. 1847; *d* Paris, 7 Sept. 1909). French baritone. Studied Paris Conservatoire and privately with Novelli. Début Liège 1868, St Bris (*Huguenots*). After appearances in the French provinces, Holland, and Belgium, was engaged for the Paris O. 1872), where he made his début as William Tell. He succeeded Faure as principal baritone and remained there for more than 20 years, creating leading roles in Reyer's *Sigurd*, Saint-Saëns's *Henry VIII*, Paladilhe's *La Patrie*, and other works. He sang at C.G. 1879-81 and 1888-93. Was the first London Alim (*Le Roi de Lahore*), and the Demon in Rubinstein's opera of that name. Greatly admired as Hans Sachs in the De Reszke performances of *Meistersinger*, and was also heard as the Dutchman and Telramund. N.Y., Met., 1891-2, 1893-4, 1896-7. Retired 1901 and spent the rest of his life as a teacher. (R)

Last Rose of Summer, 'Tis the. An old Irish air, *The Groves of Blarney,* for which Thomas Moore wrote new words; in this form it was used by Flotow for Lady Harriet's (sop.) song in Act 2 of *Martha*.

László, Magda (*b* Marosvásáhely, ?1919). Hungarian soprano. Studied Franz Liszt Academy of Budapest, and with Irene Stowaser and Ferenc Székelyhídi. Budapest Opera 1943-6, singing Elisabeth (*Tannhäuser*), Maria Boccanegra, &c. Went to Italy, where she created the role of the Mother in Dallapiccola's *Il prigioniero,* radio 1949 and Florence 1950. She sang the title roles in Gluck's *Alceste* (1953) and Monteverdi's *Poppea* (1962) at Gly., and in 1954 she created Cressida in Walton's *Troilus and Cressida* at C.G. Her wide repertory includes many modern roles. (R)

Lattuada, Felice (*b* Milan, 5 Feb. 1882; *d* Milan, 2 Nov. 1962). Italian composer. His operas, which are his most important works, include *La tempesta* (1922), *Sandha* (comp. 1915, prod. 1924), *Le preziose ridicole* (1929), *Don Giovanni* (comp. 1922, prod. 1929), *La caverna di Salamanca* (1938), and *Caino* (1957).

Latvia. In 1772 a German theatre was built in Riga, and the repertory included opera. This proved too small, and was replaced in 1782 by the Vitinghoff T., where Wagner was music director, 1837-9. In his first season he conducted 85 performances of 16 works, in his second 83 of 22 works; the scope of his activity strained the resources of Riga and the goodwill of the Intendant, Carl von Holtei. A larger theatre, proposed in 1829, was not built until 1860-3; burned down in 1882, it was rebuilt in 1887. The first, primitive attempt at a Latvian opera was *Spoka Stunda* (1890) by Jēkabs Ozols. A Russian theatre was built in 1902. In the same year the Latvian Jaunais Teatris opened with a largely French and Italian repertory; this closed in 1905 on suspicion of collaboration with the Russian revolutionaries. The first organized company was founded by Pavils Jurjaņš (1866-1947) and operated 1912-15. With national independence in 1918, the Nacionalā opera was founded on the basis of the old German theatre; this opened with *Tannhäuser* in 1919. This company became independent in 1922, national in 1927. The first true Latvian opera was *Baņjuta* (1920) by Alfreds Kalniņš (1879-1951), also the composer of *Salenieki* (The Islanders, 1926). Other early Latvian operas were *Uguns un Nakts* (Fire and Night, 1921) and *Spriditis* (1927) by Jānis Mediņš (*b* 1890), and *Vaidelote* (The Vestal, 1927) by his brother Jāzeps Mediņš (1877-1947). Other operas included *Hamlets* (1936) by Jānis Kalniņš (*b* 1904, son of Alfreds). The Liepajas Opera was founded in 1922, and the touring Celojoša Opera in 1929. Under Soviet domination, the opera became the Valsts Operas un Baleta Teatris; the repertory was similar to Russian repertories, with the addition of Latvian works including *Uz Jauno Krastu* (Towards the New Shore, 1955) and *Zalas Dzirnavas* (The Green Mill, 1957) by Margers Zariņš (*b* 1910). Riga also has an operetta theatre. After the war a number of exiled singers attempted to form a Latvian opera in Oldenburg.

Laubenthal, Rudolf (*b* Düsseldorf, 10 Mar. 1886; *d* Starnbergsee, 2 Oct. 1971). German tenor. Originally a doctor; turned to opera while in Berlin, studied with Lilli Lehmann. Début Berlin, Deutsches O., 1913. N.Y., Met., 1923-33 where he sang in the American premières of *Jenůfa* (Steva), *Die Aegyptische Helena* (Menelaos), *Shvanda* (Babinsky), as well as in other roles. In London he sang Wagner roles at C.G., 1926-30. (R)

Laura. Alvise's wife (mezzo sop.) and Enzo's lover in Ponchielli's *La gioconda*.

Lauretta. Schicchi's daughter (sop.) in Puccini's *Gianni Schicchi.*

Lauri-Volpi, Giacomo (*b* Rome, 11 Dec. 1892). Italian tenor. Originally a lawyer, then studied at the Accademia di Santa Cecilia, Rome, with Cotogni, and later with Enrico Rosati. Début (under name of Giacomo Rubini) Viterbo 1919, Arturo (*Puritani*); then under his own name, Rome 1920, Des Grieux (*Manon*) opposite Storchio. N.Y., Met., 1923-34, singing in 232 performances of 26 operas, including Calaf in the American première of *Turandot* and Rodolfo in the Met. première of *Luisa Miller*. London, C.G., 1925 (Chénier) and 1936 (Duke of Mantua, Radamès, and Cavaradossi). Chosen to sing Nerone (Boito) at the opening of the Rome O. and Arnold in *William Tell* in the centenary performance of that opera at Sc. His bright ringing tone, beautifully poised, with a superb legato and ringing top notes, made him one of the finest lyric-dramatic tenors of his day. In 1959 he was still making occasional appearances in Italy, and he took part in a gala at the T. Liceo, Barcelona, in 1972, singing 'Nessun dorma' to great enthusiasm. His writings include *L'equivoco* (1939), *Voci parallele* (1955), and *Misteri della voce umana* (1957). (R)

La vergine degli angeli. Leonora's (sop.) scene with chorus in Act 2, sc. 2, of Verdi's *La forza del destino*, in which she and the monks pray for her protection.

Lavrangas, Denis (orig. Dionysios) (*b* Argostoli, 17 Oct. 1864; *d* Razata, 30 July 1941). Greek composer. Studied Naples, and Paris with Delibes and Massenet. After conducting in France and Italy, returned to Greece 1894. Founded the National Opera of *Greece 1898. His own operas were in the repertory, incl. *Dido* (1909). His other operas include *Elda di Vorn* (1890), *La vita è un sogno* (1891), and *Fakanapas* (comp. 1935, prod. 1950).

Lawrence, Marjorie (*b* Dean's Marsh, Australia, 17 Feb. 1909). Australian soprano. Studied Melbourne and Paris with Cécile Gilly. Début Monte Carlo 1932, Elisabeth in *Tannhäuser*. Paris, O., 1933–8, where her roles included Alceste, Valentine in *Les Huguenots*, Salome, Brünnhilde, and Ortrud; N.Y., Met., 1935–41 where she shared the leading Wagner roles with Flagstad, and was also heard as Salome, Tosca, and Thaïs. At Mexico City in 1941 she was stricken with poliomyelitis during a performance of *Die Walküre*, but although she could not walk unaided thereafter, she appeared as Venus, Isolde, and Amneris in specially staged performances at the Met., Cincinnati, and Paris. She sang in a concert performance of Elektra in Chicago in 1947. Retired 1952. (R)
Bibl: M. Lawrence: *Interrupted Melody* (1949).

Lazaro, Hippolito (*b* Barcelona, 13 Aug. 1887; *d* Madrid, 14 May 1974). Spanish tenor. Studied Milan with Colli. Début Barcelona 1909 in operetta. London, Coliseum, and English provinces 1912 under name of Antonio Manuele. Genoa 1913, Folco in *Isabeau*, as a result o which Mascagni invited him to create Ugo in *Parisina* (Milan, 1913); also created title-role in Mascagni's *Piccolo Marat* (Rome 1921), and Giannetto in Giordano's *La cena delle beffe* (Milan, 1924). N.Y., Met., 1917–20; especially successful there in *I Puritani*. Many appearances in Latin America and Spain; after Spanish Civil War was briefly director of Barcelona, L. Farewell N.Y. concert 1940, but continued to make occasional appearances in Barcelona and Havana until 1950. (R)

Lazzari, Virgilio (*b* Assisi, 20 Apr. 1887; *d* Caste Gandolfo, 4 Oct. 1953). Italian, later naturalized American, bass. Studied Rome with Cotogni Début Vitale Light Opera Company 1908 as L'Incognito in Suppé's *Boccaccio*. After appearances in Rome and South America he went to the U.S.A., making his début at Springfield as Sparafucile. Chicago 1918–32, intermittently until 1936. N.Y., Met., 1933–50. Salzburg Festivals 1934-39 as Leporello, Bartolo, and Pistol. London, C.G., 1939, Leporello. A fine singing actor with a repertory of some 55 operas. His most famous role was Archibaldo in *L'amore dei tre Re* (R)

Lazzi (*It* of uncertain etymology, but probably deriving from *far azi*, abbreviation of *fare azione*: to perform an act; hence *l'azi* for theatrical acts or turns, and the spurious singular *lazo* or *lazzo*). The term for improvised acts in the course of a theatrical performance, above all in the *commedia dell'arte, when one of the troupe performs a turn by himself. These *lazzi* became greatly ritualized, and through the commedia dell'arte exercised a great influence on comic librettos and on absurd or farcical arias within them.

Lear (orig. Schulman), **Evelyn** (*b* Brooklyn, Jan. 1928). American soprano. Studied N.Y. Juilliard School, and Berlin. Début Berlin, Stä O., 1958, sang the Composer in *Ariadne au Naxos*; then became member of company. Sang Lulu in concert perf. of Berg's opera at the 1962 Vienna Festival at 3 weeks' notice; has since sung the part on stage with great success e.g. in Hamburg, London, and Munich. Created title role in Klebe's *Alkmene*, 1961, Jeanne in Egk's *Die Verlobung in San Domingo*, 1963 and Lavinia in Levy's *Mourning Becomes Electra*, 1967. London, C.G., 1965, Donna Elvira; S.W. with Hamburg Co. 1966, Lulu, Kansas City 1965, Cleopatra in *Giulio Cesare* Repertory also includes Poppea, Countess Almaviva, Fiordiligi, Marschallin, and Arabella. Married to baritone Thomas *Stewart. (R)

ebrun, Franziska (Danzi) (*b* Mannheim, 24 1ar. 1756; *d* Berlin, 14 May 1791). German sop-ano. Daughter of violinist Innocenz Danzi; wife f oboist and composer August Ludwig ebrun. Début Schwetzingen 1771, Sandrina in acchini's *La contadina in corte*; London, .ing's T., 1777; Milan, Sc., 1778, where she ang on the theatre's opening night in Salieri's *uropa riconosciuta*. Munich 1782–6 and 1789. Created leading roles in operas by Sacchini, .C. Bach, Alessandri, Rauzzini, etc. Her aughter **Rosine** (1783–1855) was a singer and ctress.

ecocq, Charles (*b* Paris, 3 June 1832; *d* Paris, 4 Oct. 1918). French composer. After initial difficulties he became established as one of the most successful operetta composers of his day. His sole attempt at a more serious vein, *Plutus* (1886), was a failure, and he returned to the long series of works in which his gay, untroubled style repeatedly delighted the Paris public. Of his 50-odd pieces, *La Fille de Mme Angot* (1872) was the most successful, running initially for 500 nights.

.effler-Burckhard, Martha (*b* Berlin 16 June 1865; *d* Wiesbaden, 14 May 1954). German soprano. Studied Dresden with Anna von Mei-chner and Paris with Viardot. Début Stras-bourg 1888. Breslau 1889-90, Cologne 1891-2, Bremen 1893-97; Weimer 1898-9; Wiesbaden 1900-1912; Berlin, H. 1915-18. Bayreuth 1906-8 as Kundry and Sieglinde; London, C.G. 1903, Brünnhilde; 1907 Leonore, Isolde; N.Y. Met. 1907-8 Brünnhilde (R)

Legend of Kleinzach, The. Hoffmann's (ten.) aria in the Prologue to Offenbach's *Les Contes d'Hoffmann*, telling the story of the dwarf at the court of Eisenach.

Legend of the Invisible City of Kitezh, The. See *Invisible City of Kitezh, The*.

Legros, Joseph (*b* Monampteuil, nr. Laon, 7 Sept. 1730; *d* La Rochelle, 20 Dec. 1793). French tenor and composer. Début Paris, O., 1764, as Titon in Mondeville's *Titon et l'Aurore*; con-tinued to sing there until 1783. Created five Gluck roles, Achilles (*Iphigénie en Aulide*), Admète (*Alceste*), Pylades (*Iphigénie en Tauride*), Cynire (*Écho et Narcisse*) and the tenor Orphée, as well as roles in operas by Monsigny, Philidor, Piccinni, and Grétry.

Lehár, Franz (*b* Komárom, 30 Apr. 1870; *d* Ischl, 24 Oct. 1948). Hungarian composer. After some early operas he turned to operetta, which included his greatest triumphs. *Die lustige Witwe* (The Merry Widow) (1905) is the most famous, but many others regularly appear in German operetta repertories. His appearance, after the deaths of the Strausses, Suppé, Zeller, and Millöcker, revived the apparently doomed tradition of operetta, and opened the way for Oscar Straus, Leo Fall, and Emmerich Kálman. Though less sparkling than Johann Strauss's, his operettas have comparable melodic charm, and his gentle waltzes are probably the ancestors of the modern dance-music slow waltz. His lavish use of dance, dominated always by the waltz, almost created a form of ballet-operetta. After 1925 Lehár's popularity began to decline, but thanks in part to the championship of Richard Tauber he made a remarkable recovery with operettas centring on the prin-cipal singers, though the plots now tended to have unhappy endings. From the latter period, the opera, *Giuditta* (1934) has been the most successful. His chief works are *Die lustige Witwe*, *Der Graf von Luxembourg* (1909), *Gipsy Love* (1910), *Frasquita* (1922), *Paganini* (1925), *Frederica* (1928), and *Das Land des Lachelns* (The Land of Smiles, 1929). (R) *Bibl*: B. Grun: *Gold and Silver* (1970).

Lehmann, Lilli (*b* Würzburg, 24 Nov. 1848; *d* Berlin, 17 May 1929). German soprano. Her father August Lehmann was a singer; her mother, Marie Loewe, had been leading sop-rano at Kassel under Spohr, and was harpist in the Prague National Theatre's orchestra at the time of her daughter's birth. Taught singing by her mother. Début Prague 1865, 1st Boy in *Zauberflöte*. After appearances in Danzig and Leipzig was engaged as lyric and coloratura soprano in Berlin 1870–85. In the first Bayreuth *Ring* (1876) sang Woglinde, Helmwige, and Woodbird. Début London, H.M.'s, 1880, Vio-letta and Philine; one of the Rhinemaidens in the first London *Ring*, 1882. She developed into a dramatic soprano and sang Isolde under Richter at C.G. 1884. American début 1885, N.Y., Met., as Carmen; between then and 1889 was heard in a variety of roles, including the first American Isolde and *Götterdämmerung* Brünnhilde. When she overstayed her leave from Berlin the Kaiser barred her from all German opera houses until 1891. In 1896 returned to Bayreuth as Brünnhilde, and in 1905 she sang in the Mozart Festival at Salz-burg, where she became the artistic director. Returned to the Met. in 1898–9 and C.G. in 1899 as Norma, Donna Anna, Leonore, Isolde. She continued to sing in Europe and was heard as Isolde in Paris in 1903 and in Vienna in 1909. Her recital work continued until the 1920's. She sang 170 roles in 119 operas in German, French, and Italian. As a teacher she had uncompromisingly high ideals. Her pupils included Geraldine Farrar and Olive Fremstad. Her writings include *Meine Gesangkunst* (translated into English by Richard Aldrich as *How to Sing*), *Mein Weg* (her autobiography), and *Studie zu Fidelio*. She was married to the tenor Paul Kalisch (1855–1946). (R) Her younger sister **Marie Lehmann** (*b* Hamburg, 15 May 1851; *d* Berlin, 19 Dec. 1931) was also a soprano. Though somewhat overshadowed by her sister, she was an active and respected artist. Début Leipzig 1867; member of companies in Hamburg, Prague, Cologne, and elsewhere. Vienna O. 1882–96. Sang with Lilli in the first Bayreuth *Ring* as Wellgunde and Ortlinde. Retired 1897. (R)

Lehmann, Lotte (*b* Perleberg, 27 Feb. 1888; *d* Santa Barbara, 26 Aug. 1976). German, later American, soprano. Studied Hochschule Berlin with various teachers and finally Mathilde Mallinger. Début Hamburg 1909, 3rd Boy in *Zauberflöte*. Vienna 1914–38, where she created the roles of the Composer in *Ariadne* and the Dyer's Wife in *Die Frau ohne Schatten.* The first Vienna Suor Angelica, Turandot, and Arabella; also created Christine in *Intermezzo* at Dresden. London, C.G., 1924–35 and 1938. The outstanding Marschallin of her day; also greatly admired as Sieglinde, Eva, Elsa, and Leonore. N.Y., Met., 1934–45, after which she continued to sing in concerts for another six years. Taught at Santa Barbara. Her sincerity, musicianship, and beautiful voice endeared her to audiences the world over. Leaving Vienna at the time of the *Anschluss,* she did not return until the opening of the S.O. in Nov. 1955, when she was greeted by the public and old singers as if she were Royalty. Returned to London in 1957 and 1959 to give masterclasses at the Wigmore Hall. Her writings include her autobiography *Anfang und Aufstieg* (translated *On Wings of Song*), *Singing with Richard Strauss,* a novel *Orplid, Mein Land* (Eternal Flight), and poems. (R)

Lehmann, Maurice (*b* Paris, 14 May 1895; *d* Paris, 17 May 1974). French producer and manager. After a period in the theatre, became producer at the Porte St-Martin, where he staged Pierné's *Fragonard* (1934), and then at the T. du Châtelet. After the liberation of France he was asked to reorganize the O. and O.C., which he did with the assistance of Reynaldo Hahn and Albert Wolff. Between 1951 and 1955 he was responsible for productions of *Oberon, The Magic Flute, L'Aiglon, Antar,* and *Les Indes Galantes* at the O.

Leider, Frida (*b* Berlin, 18 Apr. 1888; *d* Berlin, 4 June 1975). German soprano. Studied in Berlin and Milan. Début Halle 1915, Venus. Rostock 1916–18; Königsberg 1918–19; Hamburg 1919–23; Berlin S.O. 1923–40, continued to sing there until 1940; London, C.G., 1924–38; Chicago Opera 1928–32. N.Y., Met., 1933-4; Bayreuth 1928-38. Her rich and often beautiful voice and great dramatic intensity combined to make her the outstanding Brünnhilde and Isolde of the inter-war years. She also appeared in London as the Marschallin, Armide, and Donna Anna, and in Berlin in several Verdi roles. (R)
Bibl: F. Leider: *Das war mein Teil* (1959).

Leigh, Walter (*b* London, 22 June 1905; *d* nr Tobruk, 12 June 1942). English composer. Studied Berlin with Hindemith. With his melodic gift and expert craftsmanship, he raised the standard of English light opera in *The Pride of the Regiment* (1932), a clever parodistic piece, and *Jolly Roger* (1933), which originally ran for six months.

Leila. The Brahmin priestess (sop.) in Bizet's *Pêcheurs de perles.*

Leinsdorf (orig. Landauer), **Erich** (*b* Vienna, 4 Feb. 1912). Austrian, later American, conductor. Studied Vienna. Went to Salzburg in 1934 as Walter's assistant; assisted Toscanini there 1935–7. Engaged at the N.Y., Met., for the 1937–8 season, making his début in Jan. 1938 conducting *Die Walküre.* Succeeded Bodanzky as chief conductor of the German repertory there 1939, remaining until 1943. He returned as Bing's 'Musical Consultant' and conductor 1958–62 and as guest conductor since 1971. San Francisco, 1938–41, 1948, 1951, 1955, 1957. Music and artistic director of the N.Y. City Center 1956–7. Conducted *Meistersinger* at Bayreuth in 1959. (R)
Bibl: E. Leinsdorf: *Cadenza* (1976).

Leipzig. Town in Saxony, Germany. From the inauguration of the first opera house in 1693 until 1720, 100 operas were given. In the 18th cent. visited by Italian companies, but became the home of the German Singspiel. Standfuss's *Der Teufel ist los* was given there in 1752. In the early years of the 19th cent., it was an important operatic centre of Germany, with a repertory of the French and German works of the day. The *Seconda Company was based there. The city's reputation as a major intellectual and publishing centre (e.g. of the influential *Allgemeine musikalische Zeitung,* from 1798, which was dedicated to the cause of German opera) gave it also an important role in the development of Romantic opera. In 1833–45 and 1849–50 Lortzing was singer and conductor at Leipzig, and the premières of nearly all his works were given there.

Between 1876 and 1882, under the managership of Angelo *Neumann, Leipzig became the base of the Wagner company that gave the first *Ring* performances in London, Amsterdam, Brussels, Venice, and a number of other European cities. From 1878 to 1889 Artur Nikisch was the first conductor at Leipzig, and from 1886 to 1888 he was assisted by Mahler. Premières at Leipzig before 1914 included Lehár's *Kukuschka* (1896), Weingartner's *Orestes* (1902), and Ethel Smyth's *The Wreckers* (1906); there were also the first performances in Germany of *Oberon, The Kiss,* and Stanford's *Much Ado about Nothing.* Gustav Brecher was the music director (1923–33), the premières of Křenek's *Jonny spielt auf* (1927) and *Leben des*

Orest (1930) and of Weill's *Mahagonny* (1930) were given. In 1938 the Opera gave a 12-week Wagner Festival during which two complete cycles of the composer's works were given in chronological order, including *Die Hochzeit*, *Das Liebesverbot*, and *Die Feen*. The opera house was destroyed by bombs in 1943, and from 1945 to 1960 performances were given at the Dreilinden Theatre, now used for operetta. The opera house was rebuilt on its old site and opened on 8 Oct. 1960 (cap. 1,682), with *Die Meistersinger*, conducted by Helmut Seidelmann (1901–61) who had been appointed music director in 1951. He was succeeded by Paul Schmitz, Vaclav Neumann, and Rolf Reuter, with Joachim Herz, a Felsenstein pupil, as chief producer and opera director.Herz left in 1976. The theatre's orchestra is that of the Leipzig Gewandhaus. Premières since the end of the war include Blacher's *Die Nachtschwalbe* (1948), Schoeck's *Die Laune des Verliebten* (1949), Bush's *Wat Tyler* (1953), and *Guyana Johnny* (1966); as well as the first performances in Germany of Prokofiev's *The Duenna* and *War and Peace*, Butting's *Plautus in Nonnenkloster* (1959), and Hanell's *Griechische Hochzeit* (1969). Members of the ensembles since 1920 have included Margarete Bäumer, Irma Beilke, Hedwig Müller-Bütow, Rudolf Bockelmann, Frederick Dalberg, and August Seider.

Leise, leise. Agathe's (sop.) aria in Act 2 of Weber's *Der Freischütz*, in which she prays for protection for her lover Max.

Leitmotiv (*Ger* leading motive). A term first used by F.W. Jähns in his *Carl Maria von Weber in seinen Werken* (1871) to denote a short musical figure identifying a person, thing, event, or idea in music and above all in opera. The origins of the device are disputed, and its history is controversial. There are suggestions of it in Gluck and Mozart, and a more consistent use of a musical figure to represent a character or idea in various early German Romantic operas and especially those of Weber, e.g. Samiel's diminished 7ths in *Der Freischütz*, Eglantine's theme in *Euryanthe*. Though instances in Weber caused Jähns to coin the term, it has since been generally reserved for a rather more advanced use of the device, above all as first developed by Wagner. Taking the old *Reminiscence motive, Wagner showed how a subtle and intelligent use of it could not only recall characters or objects to mind, and further serve as a powerful structural force, but could convey to the listener an intricate understanding of how they change with the course of the drama, the musical modification or development expressing a new psychological or dramatic state. What are in *Das Rheingold* essentially Reminiscence motives are by *Die Walküre*, and above all by *Götterdämmerung*,

formed into a subtle expressive network of ideas working in the music. The Leitmotiv became an obsession with some of Wagner's followers, as it never had with him. His own preferred term (in 1867) was *Hauptmotiv*; he made use of other terms, but only once mentioned 'so-called Leitmotivs'.

Leitner, Ferdinand (*b* Berlin, 4 Mar. 1912). German conductor. Studied Berlin with Schnabel and Karl Muck. Assistant to Busch at Gly. 1935. Début as conductor Berlin 1943. Hamburg 1945–6; Munich 1946–7; music director Stuttgart 1947–69; Zurich since 1969. Guest appearances all over Europe and South America. (R)

Le Maure (Lemaure, Le more), **Catherine-Nicole** (*b* Paris, 3 Aug. 1704; *d* Paris, Jan 1787). French soprano. Chorus member of the O. 1719; début as soloist 1721, Astrée in Lully's *Phaéton*. Became the rival of Pélissier: Voltaire preferred 'Pélissier par son art; Lemaure par sa voix'. Continued to sing until 1743; and in July 1771 reappeared to inaugurate the new Colisée. Lully composed roles in several operas for her.

Lemeshev, Sergey (Yakovlevich) (*b* Knyazevo, 10 July 1902; *d* Moscow, 1977). Russian tenor. Studied Moscow with Raysky; first heard as Lensky in a student *Eugene Onegin* in 1920. Début Sverdlovsk 1926; Sverdlovsk and Tiflis 1926–31; Moscow, B., 1931–61. Excelled in the lyric repertory, and was a very popular artist especially as Lensky, the Duke of Mantua, Alfredo, and Roméo (Gounod). Also made films. Professor Moscow Conservatory; has produced opera in Moscow and Leningrad. (R)

Lemmens-Sherrington (orig. Sherrington), **Helen** (*b* Preston, 4 Oct. 1834; *d* Brussels, 9 May 1906). English soprano. Studied Rotterdam and Brussels. After singing in London in concerts she appeared at C.G. during the Royal English Opera season 1864–5 as Helvelyn and Rose in *Rose, or Love's Ransom*. From 1866 to 1868 she sang at the Royal Italian Opera, C.G., where her roles included Adalgisa, Donna Elvira, Elisabeth de Valois, Prascovia (*L'Étoile du Nord*), and Isabella (*Robert le Diable*). She was generally regarded as the leading English soprano of her day. Taught at Brussels Conservatoire after leaving stage. Married Belgian composer J. N. Lemmens (1823–81) in 1857.

Lemnitz, Tiana (*b* Metz, Lorraine, 26 Oct. 1897). German soprano. Studied Metz, and Frankfurt with Anton Kohmann. Début Heilbronn 1921, in *Undine*. Aachen 1922–8. Leading soprano Hanover 1928–34 and Berlin S.O. 1934–57, when she retired. C.G. 1936 and 1938. Sang leading roles in German, French, Italian, and Russian repertories, and her repertory ranged from Pamina to Sieglinde, Euridice to Aida, and

Micaëla to Jenůfa. Her Octavian was considered one of the best of its day, and her Pamina, in which her exquisite *pianissimo* was employed to the full, was hailed as the finest since that of Claire Dux. Retired 1957 (R)

Leningrad. Town in the U.S.S.R., formerly St Petersburg (1703–1914), then Petrograd (1914–24). The first theatrical productions were given soon after Peter the Great's foundation of the city, but the first opera to be performed was *La forza dell'amore e dell'odio* (1736) by the company of Francesco *Araia, who wrote several operas for the Court. In 1783 the Bolshoy T. (Grand T.) was opened, in which a mixed repertory included opera. Italian opera was given 1826–32, and 1840. In 1832 Nicholas I opened the Alexandrovsky T., built by Rossi. The Bolshoy was rebuilt in 1836, opening with Glinka's *A Life for the Tsar*: for many years this work opened every season, and by the end of the century had been given over 700 times. Rubini headed a company playing 1843–5; Government-supported opera then lasted until 1885. Opera was also given from 1855 at the T. Tsirk (Circus T.), opposite the B.: this was burnt down in 1859 and rebuilt by A. Cavos (son of the composer) as the Maryinsky T. in 1860. The influential conductor from 1863 (chief from 1869) to 1913 was Eduard *Nápravník. Premières included *La forza del destino* (1862) as well as most of the operas by the leading Russian composers of the day. From 1860 visiting French operetta and Italian companies played at the T. Mikhailovsky (built by Bryullov 1831–3, rebuilt by A. Cavos 1859). The three Imperial Theatres of St Petersburg were the Maryinsky, Mikhailovsky, and (for drama) Alexandrinsky.

At the Revolution there was more resistance to change in Petrograd than in Moscow, and the commissar, the enlightened Anatoly Lunacharsky, was obliged to bring pressure on the company to resume work. The Maryinsky re-opened in 1919 as the State Academic T. of Opera and Ballet (abbrev. as GATOB: in it some of the first Soviet operas were given in 1925), the Mikhailovsky in 1920 as the State Academic T. of Comic Opera, and the Maly T. in 1921 as the Little Petrograd Academic T., becoming in 1926 the State Academic Little Opera T. (abbrev. as MALEGOT). The latter was the home of most of the operatic experiments, and of the more advanced foreign works of the 1920s; but many smaller experimental groups flourished, among them the T. Komichesky Opery (from 1920), the T. Muzykalny Komedy, and the Palas-T. (for operetta). In 1922 an Opera Studio was established at the Conservatory, and here much enterprising and successful work was done; 1928–9 they toured clubs and factories, and even gave a season in Salzburg. In 1935 the State Academic T. was

renamed the Kirov Opera and Ballet T. While this theatre upheld a traditional style, experimental work continued at the Malegot, including new works and productions (e.g. a Meyerhold production of *The Queen of Spades*), until sharply interrupted by the 1936 attack on *Shostakovich's *The *Lady Macbeth of the Mtsensk District*. During the war the Kirov was evacuated to Perm, the Malegot to Orenburg, both returning in 1944. A group of artists who remained in the city formed an Opernobalety Kollektiv. After the war, the Kirov and Maly set about re-establishing their reputations, which have continued to be for the traditional with the former, the more experimental with the latter. In the early 1960s the Leningrad Conservatory opened a section to train musicians as opera directors: there is also an opera training section at the State Institute of T. Art.

See also *Russia*.

Lensky. A young poet (ten.), Onegin's friend and then adversary in Tchaikovsky's *Eugene Onegin*.

Leo, Leonardo (orig. Leonardo Ortensio Salvatore de) (*b* San Vito degli Schiavi, 5 Aug. 1694; *d* Naples, 31 Oct. 1744). Italian composer. Studied Naples with Provenzale and Fago. His more than 70 operas include some examples of opera buffa that were very popular in their day. An inheritor of the tradition of Alessandro Scarlatti, he brought great melodic liveliness to the comic genre; among his innovations were an added role for the chorus (in *Olimpiade* (1737), choruses in motet and da capo form, and greater harmonic range in the handling of recitative. His pupils included Jommelli and Piccinni.

Leoncavallo, Ruggero (*b* Naples, 8 Mar. 1857; *d* Montecatini, 9 Aug. 1919). Italian composer. Leoncavallo's ambitions are shown in his early *Chatterton* (1896) and in his scheme for a vast Wagnerian trilogy embracing the Renaissance in Italy; but his reputation continues to rest on a single 2-act opera, *Pagliacci* (1892), which immediately made him famous. The subsequent failure of *I Medici* (1893) discouraged him from continuing the trilogy. *La Bohème* (1897) contains some excellent ideas, and is in spirit close to Murger's original novel, but it has suffered from comparison with Puccini's work, with which it originally coincided. Apart from *Zazà* (1900), a work of sentimental charm which won praise from Fauré, Leoncavallo thereafter produced little to justify his own ambitions and his friends' hopes, certainly not *Der Roland von Berlin* (1904), commissioned in admiration for *I Medici* by Wilhelm II. He turned to a series of trivial operettas. In his final work, *Edipo Re* (1920), he attempted to recapture the grand manner of his youth. However, it is in the famous *Pagliacci* that the best of him is to be found. Here his strong dramatic flair and direct melodic appeal in the most vivid *verismo* manner, coupled to a certain originality of technique, find full expression. (R)

Leonora. (1) Donna Leonora di Vargas (sop.), in Verdi's *La forza del destino*. (2) Lady-in-waiting (sop.) to the Princess of Aragon, in Verdi's *Il trovatore*. (3) Oberto's daughter (sop.) in Verdi's *Oberto*. (4) The King's mistress (mezzo) in Donizetti's *La favorite*. Also operas by Mercadante (1844) and Fry (1845).

Leonore. Florestan's wife (sop.), known as Fidelio, in Beethoven's *Fidelio*; also the title of the opera's original version.

Leonore, ou L'Amour conjugal. Opera in 2 acts by Gaveaux; text by Jean Nicolas Bouilly. Prod. Paris, T. Feydeau, 19 Feb. 1798. Historically important as the first setting of the *Fidelio* story: others are by Paer (1804), Mayr (1805), and Beethoven (*Fidelio*, 1805), all based on Bouilly. Also opera by Champein (1781). See also below.

Leonore 40/45. Opera in 2 acts by Liebermann; text by Heinrich Strobel. Prod. Basel 26 Mar. 1952, with Schemionek, De Vries, Olsen, cond. Krannhals.

Huguette (sop.), a French girl, falls in love with Alfred (ten.), a German soldier whom she meets at a concert in occupied Paris during the 1940s. He deserts, and they meet again at the end of the war through the offices of her guardian angel, M. Emile (bar.).

Leonova, Darya (Mikhailovna) (*b* Vishny Volochuk, 21 Mar. 1829; *d* St Petersburg, 6 Feb. 1896). Russian contralto. Studied St Petersburg. Début St Petersburg 1852, Vanya (*Life for the Tsar*); having rehearsed the part with Glinka, she then had lessons from him, and may have been his mistress. She championed Russian music: she created the Princess in Dargomyzhsky's *Rusalka*, Serov's Rogneda, Vlasevnya in *The Maid of Pskov*, and the Hostess in *Boris Godunov*, also singing other roles including especially Orfeo, Azucena, and Ortrud. Toured Russia, China, U.S.A., and Western Europe, 1875–9. In her later years she championed Mussorgsky. She had a strong, clear voice with a range from g to c''', and was admired for her acting ability.
Bibl: V. Yakovlev: *D. M. Leonova* (1950).

L'Épine, Margherita de (*b* ?; *d* London 9 or 10 Aug. 1746). Italian or French-Italian soprano. Appeared in London from 1692 onwards at Lincoln's Inn Fields, D.L., and elsewhere. In 1710 sang in *Almahide* and in 1712 and 1713 in Handel's *Pastor Fido* and *Rinaldo*. Continued to appear until 1718 when she married Pepusch, to whom she is said to have brought a fortune of £10,000. Reputedly an ugly woman but a very fine musician.

Leporello. Don Giovanni's servant (bass) in Mozart's *Don Giovanni*.

Leppard, Raymond (*b* London, 11 Aug. 1927). English conductor and musicologist. Studied Cambridge. Music director Royal Shakespeare Company, Stratford-upon-Avon 1954; Gly. as répétiteur 1954–6; returned to Cambridge as lecturer in 1958 and began his exploration and editing of 17th-cent. and early 18th-cent. music, especially Monteverdi and Cavalli. Conducted his realization of *Il ballo dell'ingrate* Aldeburgh 1958; and at Gly. *L'incoronazione di Poppea* 1962, *Ormindo* 1967, *Calisto* 1969, and *Il ritorno d'Ulisse in patria* 1972. London, S.W., Monteverdi's *Orfeo* 1965, *Poppaea* 1971; C.G. Samson (Handel) 1958, *Nozze di Figaro*, and *Così fan tutte* 1972. Also conducted première of Maw's *The Rising of the Moon*, 1970. *Cunning Little Vixen* 1975. Santa Fe 1974, *Egisto*. His realizations, which include additions from other works and some original composition, have been very controversial and have been attacked for their lack of authenticity; nevertheless, like Beecham's Handel arrangements, they have served to introduce neglected music to a wide audience. (R)

Lermontov, Mikhail (Yuryevich) (*b* Moscow, 15 Oct. 1814; *d* Pyatigorsk, 27 July 1841). Russian writer. Operas on his works are as follows:
The Angel (1831): Koreshchenko (1900).
Vadim (1832–4): Aksyuk (*Pugachevtsy*, 1937); Kreitner (1952).
The Boyar Orsha (1835): Kashperov (1880); Krotkov (1898); Agrenev-Slavyansky (1910); Fistulari (?).
Hajji-Abrek (1835): Rubinstein (1858).
Masquerade (1835–6): Kolesnikov (*c*1890); Mosolov (1940); Denbsky (1941); Bunin (1944); Zeidman (1945); Y. Nikolayev (1946); Nersesov (1948); D. Tolstoy (1955); Artamov (1957).
The Tambov Treasurer's Wife (1837): Asafyev (1937).
The Song of the Merchant Kalashnikov (1837): Rubinstein (1880).
A Hero of Our Time (1840). Pt. 1 *Bela*: Gaygerova (1941); A. Alexandrov (1946). Pt. 2, *Princess Mary*: Dekhterev (1941).
The Demon (final version, 1841): Rubinstein (1875).
The Fugitive (1841): Avetisov (1943).
Tamara (1841): Bourgault-Ducoudray (1891); Wietinghoff-Scheel (1886); Rogowski (1918).
Also opera *Vengeance* (Rubinstein, 1850s).

Le Rochois, Marthe. See *Rochois*.

Lert, Ernst (Joseph Maria) (*b* Vienna, 12 May 1883; *d* Baltimore 30 Jan. 1955). Austrian manager, conductor, and critic. Studied Vienna with Adler and Mahler. Breslau, 1909, as producer and Dramaturg; Leipzig 1912–19; director of opera Basle 1919–20; general administrator Frankfurt 1919–23. Regular producer at Milan, Sc., 1923–29; N.Y., Met., 1929–31. Head of Opera School, Curtis Inst. Philadelphia, 1936–8 and of Peabody Inst., Baltimore, 1938–1953. Writings include *Mozart auf dem Theater* (1918) and a biography of Otto Lohse (1918).

Lescaut. Manon's cousin (bar.) in Massenet's *Manon* and brother (bar.) in Puccini's *Manon Lescaut.*

Le Sueur, Jean-François (*b* Drucat-Plessiel, 15 Feb. 1760; *d* Paris, 6 Oct. 1837). French composer. After early experience as a choirmaster, he went to Paris and studied with the Abbé Roze, continuing to work at Notre Dame and elsewhere; he was reproved for introducing an operatic style, and eventually dismissed. Turning to opera, with help and advice from Spontini, he began work on *Télémaque* (part prod. 1796), but made his début with *La Caverne* (1793). This made him, with Cherubini and Méhul, the most prominent composer of the Revolution. It is a powerful, indeed harsh work that well matched the temper of the times, and is formally pioneering in its successful reconciliation of elements from opera seria and buffa and opéra comique. *Paul et Virginie* (1794) and *Télémaque* followed; then, after a period at the Tuileries Chapel, he produced his greatest success, *Ossian, ou Les Bardes* (1804). The presence of Napoleon as patron helped to win the work favour, but Le Sueur's wide love of choral music tends to dominate the work and to give it the flavour of oratorio. Two works written with Persuis followed, and finally *Alexandre à Babylone* (1815, unprod.), in which Le Sueur anticipates the continuous manner of later 19th-cent. opera. A well-loved teacher; his pupils included Berlioz, whose effects of sonority and scoring he sometimes foreshadows even if he did not directly influence them.
Bibl: F. Lamy: *Jean-François Le Sueur* (1912).

Let's Make an Opera. Children's opera in 2 parts by Britten, text by Eric Crozier. Prod. Aldeburgh, Jubilee Hall, 14 June 1949, with E. Parry, Parr, Worthley, Lumsden, cond. Del Mar; St Louis, Kiel Auditorium, 22 Mar. 1950. In the first part the preparations for the opera are discussed by the children and grown-ups taking part and the audience is rehearsed for its part in four songs. The second part, *The Little Sweep,* tells of the rescue by a family of children of the sweep's boy Sammy; the audience providing comments with its songs.

Letter Duet. The Duettino 'sull'aria' between the Countess and Susanna (sops.) in Act 3 of Mozart's *Le nozze di Figaro,* in which the Countess dictates to Susanna the letter to be sent to

the Count, making the assignation that evening in the garden.

Letter Scene. A favourite scene in 17th-cent. opera in which a character reads out a letter brought to him. The device long survived; nowadays usually taken to refer to the extended scene for Tatyana (sop.) in Tchaikovsky's *Eugene Onegin,* in which she writes to Onegin declaring her love.

Levasseur, Nicolas (Prosper) (*b* Bresles, Oise, 9 Mar. 1791; *d* Paris, 7 Dec. 1871). French bass. Studied Paris with Garat. Début Paris, O., 1813, as Osman Pacha in Grétry's *La Caravane.* London, King's T., 1815–17 and again 1832 when he sang Bertram in the first London performance of *Robert le Diable.* Milan, S.C. in 1819–28. Principal bass at the Théâtre des Italiens, Paris, and 1828–53 again at the Opéra. Created many roles in Paris, including Bertram, Marcel (*Huguenots*), Zacharie (*Le Prophète*), Balthazar (*Favorite*), Don Juan (*Dom Sébastien*), Governor (*Ory*), Fürst (*Guillaume Tell*). Retired from the stage in 1853 but continued to teach at the Conservatoire until 1870.

Levasseur, Rosalie (Marie-Claude-Josephe) (*b* Valenciennes, 8 Oct. 1749; *d* Neuwied, 6 May 1826). French soprano. Début Paris 1766 in Campra's *Europe Galante.* Sang L'Amour in première of *Orphée,* as Mlle Rosalie. Her talents as a singer and actress were recognized by the Austrian Ambassador, Mercy-Argenteau, whose mistress she became. Resuming her own name, she succeeded Sophie Arnould as leading soprano at the Opéra, singing title role in first Paris *Alceste* (1776) and creating the title roles in Gluck's *Armide* (1777) and *Iphigénie en Tauride* (1779) as well as in works by Philidor, Piccinni, and Sacchini. Prima Donna at the Opéra until 1788.

Le Veau d'or. The song in praise of gold, sung by Méphistophélès (bass) in Act 2 of Gounod's *Faust.*

Levi, Hermann (*b* Giessen, 7 Nov. 1839; *d* Munich, 13 May 1900). German conductor. The son of a rabbi; studied Mannheim with Lachner and in Leipzig. After appointments at Saarbrücken (1859–61), Rotterdam (1861–4), and Karlsruhe (1864–72), became principal conductor at Munich (1872–96). Conducted first performance of *Parsifal* at Bayreuth; Wagner admired him greatly and was committed to him as the Munich conductor, but nearly wrecked the collaboration by crude behaviour especially over the notion of Levi as a Jew conducting a work that included the representation of Christian ritual. Their friendship and mutual admiration survived, and Levi conducted at Wagner's funeral. He edited new versions of Mozart's *Così fan tutte, Don Giovanni,* and *Figaro*: though now discredited, these were valuable in their day for the following they helped to win for Mozart at a time when his operas were little known and much misrepresented. He also translated Berlioz's *Les Troyens* and Chabrier's *Gwendoline* into German.

Bibl: E. Possart: *Erinnerungen an Hermann Levi* (1900).

Levine, James (*b* Cincinnati, 23 June 1943). American conductor. Studied Cincinnati, N.Y., Juilliard, with Morel. Assistant to Szell at Cleveland, 1964–70; N.Y. Met., since 1971, principal conductor 1972, music director since 1975. Cardiff, W.N.O., *Aida* 1970; Salzburg since 1976. Generally considered the most gifted young American conductor of recent years. (R)

Lewis, Richard (*b* Manchester, 10 May 1914). English tenor. Studied with T.W. Evans, R.M.C.M., and R.A.M. with Norman Allin. Début Gly. 1947, Male Chorus in *The Rape of Lucretia*; C.G. 1947, Grimes. Since then has sung regularly at Gly. (Don Ottavio, Ferrando, Idomeneo, Admète, Bacchus, Tom Rakewell, Florestan), and on numerous occasions at C.G. (Simpleton in *Boris*, Tamino, Alfredo, Hoffmann, Don José, and creating Troilus, Mark in *The Midsummer Marriage,* and Achilles in *King Priam*; Aaron in Schoenberg's *Moses und Aron,* which he also sang in Paris 1973). San Francisco 1955–60, 1962, 1965, 1968, where his roles have included Jason (*Médée*), Des Grieux, Jeník, Pinkerton, the Captain (*Wozzeck*), Tom Rakewell, Eisenstein, Alwa (*Lulu*), and Herod. An extremely versatile and intelligent artist. (R)

Lexington Theatre, New York. Built in 1913 on Lexington Avenue and 51st Street by Oscar *Hammerstein in an attempt to evade the contract he had signed with the Met. in 1910 which prevented him from giving opera in New York for ten years. It was then sold and became the scene of the Boston National Opera Company 1916 N.Y., season, the Chicago Opera's annual visits 1917–19, and the German Opera Company's 1923–4 seasons. Later became a cinema.

Lhérie (orig. Lévy), **Paul** (*b* Paris, 8 Oct. 1844; *d* Paris, 17 Oct. 1937). French tenor and baritone. Studied Paris with Obin. Début Paris, O.C., (as tenor) 1866 as Reuben in *Joseph*. Left after quarrel 1868, returning 1872. Created Benoit in *Le Roi l'a dit* and Don José (1875). Changed to baritone 1882, and sang Posa in the 1884 *Don Carlos* at Milan, Sc.; London, C.G., 1887, Rigoletto, Germont, Luna. Continued career until 1894 and then taught in Paris.

Libiamo, libiamo. *Brindisi,* or drinking song, sung by Alfredo (ten.) and Violetta (sop.) in Act 1 of Verdi's *La traviata.*

Liberec. Town in Czechoslovakia. Opera is given in the F.X. Salda T. about 3–4 times a week by a company of about 30 soloists. The company also gives a weekly performance at Jablonec; though it is one of the country's smaller theatres, they have staged *Rienzi, L'Africaine* (1967), and *War and Peace* (1967). The theatre was renovated in 1971.

Libretto (*It* little book). The name generally given to the book of the words of an opera. Though the earliest were some 8½ in. in height, the diminutive was always used and the term has been current in English since about the mid-18th cent. The first ever written was for Peri's *Dafne* at Florence in 1600; there have since been over 30,000. Early librettos usually began with a title page succeeded by a preface in which the writer made obsequious dedication to his patron, and then by a few words addressed to the reader. The *argomento* was a summary of the events preceding the action of the opera: these tended to increase in complexity, and even to take their place in the opera itself as a prologue (e.g. Verdi's *Il trovatore*). After the list of the characters in the opera came a catalogue of the scene changes, dances, perhaps also the scenic effects: this trait survives onto playbills of the English musical theatre of the 19th cent. Until about the end of the 18th cent. there would also be a *protesta,* in which the author affirmed his good Roman Catholic faith despite the pagan references to *numi, fati* etc.: this arose from the necessity of having the libretto approved in cities under Papal domination.

Essentially, a good libretto has always been a story, whether dramatic in origin or not, moulded to the needs of music drama. The sources of successful librettos have ranged from great dramatic masterpieces (*Othello* for Verdi) and great novels (*War and Peace* for Prokofiev) to sentimental novels (*Scènes de la vie de Bohème* for Puccini) and narrative poems (*Eugene Onegin* for Tchaikovsky), from heroic legend (most of Metastasio's librettos) to real-life incident (perhaps *Pagliacci,* Janáček's *Osud*), from metaphysics and questions of belief (*Parsifal*) to farce (most of Offenbach), from great painting (Hindemith's *Mathis der Maler,* Granados's *Goyescas*) to comic strip (Janáček's *Cunning Little Vixen*), from history or biography (*Rienzi,* and much French grand opera) to fairy tale (Russian opera in both categories). There are no rules of origin but a number of successful methods of their application, of which most composers have singled out conciseness and a capacity to depict human emotions in a dramatic context as prime but not exclusive virtues.

In the 17th and 18th cents. the established pattern of recitative, aria, and chorus made special, demands upon the librettist, and determined to course of the action. The argument about how much precedence music or words should have been raging ever since, and found operatic expression (if not resolution) in Strauss's *Capriccio*. Though conventions have naturally changed, with the virtues of formality and the contrasting virtues of freedom changing precedence, the vital element has remained dramatic potency as it charges a composer's imagination. Collaboration has not proved indispensable: Metastasio is the great example of a librettist, 27 of whose works did duty for 1,000 settings by 50 composers at least. At the other extreme, very fruitful results have come from the careful mutual planning of Quinault and Lully, Calzabigi and Gluck, Da Ponte and Mozart, Boito and Verdi, Gilbert and Sullivan, Hofmannsthal and Strauss. Berlioz, Wagner, Charpentier, and Menotti are among the most successful of those composers who have preferred to shape their own librettos, which further suggests that any rules must follow rather than precede example.

The popularity of published librettos is as steady as ever, and many opera lovers, if in lesser numbers outside Italy, still furnish themselves with copies both to study at home and to take to the performance. As candlegrease spots on the early specimens show, there is even an historical precedent for the now intolerable habit of trying to read the libretto with a light during the performance: in early days, with the audience expected to behave more informally and occasionally to consult its libretto to remind itself of the action on the stage, these so-called *cereni* (from *cero*: wax candle) were on sale at the door for use during the performance. Librettos were also, however, published as part of a poet's collected works, in well printed and handsomely bound editions. The translation of librettos became widespread during the development of national opera houses during the 19th cent., and some works have been given in many different languages – *Lohengrin* in at least 22, *Rigoletto* in at least 21 – and their librettos published. Gramophone companies now normally accompany complete opera sets with a full libretto (and, if necessary, translation), as well as preliminary synopses, notes etc., printing the original and the translation side by side as was normal practice at Covent Garden in Victorian times. Then, the libretto was still a natural part of a gentleman's equipment for the opera – palmy days when *Punch* imagined a young man saying:

A pound, dear father, is the sum,
    That clears the opera wicket:
Two lemon gloves, a lemon ice,
    Libretto, and your ticket.

Bibl: P. Smith: *The Tenth Muse* (New York, 1970).

Libuše. Opera in 3 acts by Smetana; text (orig.

German) by Josef Wenzig, trans. into Czech by Ervín Špindler. Prod. Prague, for the inauguration of the Czech National T., 11 Jun. 1881, with Reichová, Fibichová, Vávra, Lev, Čech, Stropnický, Hynek, Sittová, cond. Smetana.

The opera tells of the rivalry of two brothers, Chrudoš (bass.) and Štáhlav (ten.), for the love of Krasava. They are brought to trial before Libuše, (sop.) Queen of Bohemia, who is insulted by Chrudoš. The Queen abdicates in favour of a man who can rule with a rod of iron. The new king effects a reconciliation between the brothers.

Other operas on the subject are by J. F. Sartorio (1763–4), K. Kreutzer (1822), and Škroup (*Libušin Sňatek*, 1828: one of the first Czech operas). Also anon. opera *Praga nascente da Libussa e Primislao* (c1730).

Licenza (*It* permission). The final choral ode to the dedicatee of an opera or to the ruler before whom and by whose patronage the opera was given. Sometimes used in early 17th cent. opera, but particularly common in Vienna reform opera of the later 17th cent.

Licette, Miriam (*b* Chester, 9 Sept. 1892; *d* Twyford, 11 Aug. 1969). English soprano. Studied Milan and Paris with Marchesi, Jean de Reszke, Sabbatini. Début Rome 1911, Cio-Cio-San. Beecham Comp. 1916–20; B.N.O.C. 1922–8. Also appeared in important roles during C.G. International seasons 1919–29 (Marguerite, Mimì, Euridice, Desdemona, Donna Elvira, Gutrune). Much admired as Mozart singer and for her Louise and Juliette. (R)

Liebe der Danae, Die (The Love of Danae). Opera in 3 acts by Richard Strauss; text by Josef Gregor. Prod. Salzburg, 14 Aug. 1952, with Kupper, Gostic, Schoeffler, cond. Krauss. The work reached public dress rehearsal at Salzburg in 1944 (16 Aug., with Ursuleac, Taubmann, and Hotter, cond. Krauss), but then the theatres were closed by a decree of the Nazi minister Goebbels. London, C.G., 16 Sep. 1953, with Kupper, Vandenburg, Frantz, cond. Kempe; Los Angeles, Univ. of S. California, 10 Apr. 1964, with Weide, Gibson Riffel, cond. Ducloux.

Jupiter (bar.) desires to possess Danae (sop.) and assumes the form of Midas (ten.), who is also trying to win her. Midas refuses to give her up, and Jupiter deprives him of his golden touch and godly status. Danae and Midas then share an earthly life, and when Jupiter again appears to Danae and tries to tempt her with the promise of wealth she again rejects him. Impressed by her loyalty to Midas, Jupiter gives them both his blessing.

Liebermann, Rolf (*b* Zurich, 14 Sept. 1910). Swiss composer. He followed up the success of *Leonore 40/45* (1952) with *Penelope* (1954) and

The School for Wives (1955). His style extends from 12-note music to jazz, and though freely experimental is based on knowledge of practical effect. Intendant Hamburg Opera 1959-73, where he extended the repertory to include many 20th cent. works and commissioned several new ones. Paris, O., 1973-80, greatly raising the standard of performances.

Bibl: R. Liebermann: *Actes et Entractes* (1976).

Liebestod (*Ger* love-death). The term's first appearance in opera is probably in Hoffmann's *Undine* (1816), where it is used near the end of the work by Heilmann (a spirit). However, it is now always taken to refer to Isolde's death scene at the end of Wagner's *Tristan und Isolde*, beginning 'Mild und leise', though Wagner himself used it of the love duet in Act 2.

Liebesverbot, Das (The Ban on Love). Opera in 2 acts by Wagner; text by composer, after Shakespeare's drama *Measure for Measure* 1604–5). Prod. Magdeburg, 29 Mar. 1836, with Pollert, cond. Wagner; London, University College, 15 Feb. 1965, with Davies, Jenkins, Bentley, Kallipetis, cond. Badacsonyi.

Lied (*Ger* song). In German opera, the term has generally been used for a number rather simpler than an aria, sometimes interpolated by a character and outside the plot. The May song in Weber's *Euryanthe* is described as 'Lied mit Chor', though other numbers in the work are described as Aria, Romanze, etc.

Liederspiel (*Ger* song play). A German dramatic musical form, deriving from *Singspiel, and consisting of songs joined by dialogue. The composer who gave Liederspiel its most typical form was J. F. *Reichardt, who used the manner of German popular music in his songs. Subsequent composers, including F. H. Himmel, Carl Eberwein, and B. A. Weber, were successful, though to a lesser degree. Mendelssohn described his *Die Heimkehr aus der Fremde* (1829) as a Liederspiel, as did Lortzing his *Der Pole und sein Kind* (1832).

Liège. Town in Liège, Belgium. The Grand T. (cap. 1,246), whose architecture imitated that of the Opéra in Paris, opened in 1820 with Grétry's *Zémire et Azor*. Until 1914 the theatre had a permanent company of French and Belgian singers, and all operas were performed in French. Between the wars opera was given by visiting companies. From 1955 to 1965 the theatre was directed by André d'Arkor, who did much to raise its standards. From 1965 to 1967 the co-directors were Marcel Desimon and Raymond Rossius. The Opéra de Wallonie occupied the theatre 1967-74, also giving performances in Liège and other Belgian cities and in Luxemburg and France. From Sept. 1974 it has been the permanent home of the Centre Lyrique de Wallonie, under Rossius.

Lieto fine (*It* happy ending). The term used, especially in 17th cent. Italian opera, for the final turn of the plot towards a happy resolution. Often this took the form of the last-minute repentance of a tyrant, shown the error of his ways or cured of his 'madness' by divine intervention, so as to provide a joyful conclusion and to emphasize to the audience the benefits of liberty. The term and its particular application is said to have been the invention of Giacinto Cicognini, librettist of many works including Cavalli's *Giasone* (1649).

Life for the Tsar, A. Opera in 4 acts by Glinka; text by Baron Georgy Fyodorovich Rosen. Prod. St Petersburg, Bolshoy T., 9 Dec. 1836, with Stepanova, Petrova-Vorobyova, Leonov Petrov, cond. Cavos; London, C.G., 12 July 1887, with Albani, Scalchi, Gayarré, Devoyod, cond. Bevignani; San Francisco 12 Dec. 1936. Originally entitled *Ivan Susanin*, the work was renamed *A Life for the Tsar* by permission of Nicholas I following his visit to one of the rehearsals. Since the Russian Revolution, it has generally been known in Russia as *Ivan Susanin*.

The opera is set in Russia and Poland during the winter of 1612. News arrives of the Poles' defeat, while Antonida (sop.) thinks of her love for Sobinin (ten.). In the Polish camp soldiers vow to fight on, and decide to advance against the Russians on hearing that Romanov has been made Tsar. They compel Susanin (bass), a Russian, to guide them, but he leads them on a false trail and is killed. The new Tsar comes to Moscow; he praises his supporters and laments the death of Susanin.

Also opera by Cavos (1815).

Ligendza, Caterina (*b* Stockholm, 18 Oct. 1937). Swedish soprano. Daughter of the tenor Einar Beyron and the soprano Brita Hertzberg. Studied Vienna, Stuttgart with Trude Eipperle, and later Berlin with Greindl. Début 1963 Linz, Countess; Brunswick 1964-5; Saarbrücken, 1966; Geneva 1968 Brünnhilde (*Siegfried*); Salzburg Easter Festival 1969; Bayreuth 1971-7, Brünnhilde, Isolde. London, C.G., 1972 Senta; Vienna, S.O., 1973 Isolde; repertory also includes Verdi and Strauss roles. (R)

Lille. Town in Nord, France. Opera was first given in the auditorium of the Hôtel de Ville, which was burned down in 1700. Rebuilt with a 90,000 florin gift from Louis XIV, it opened again in 1718. A larger auditorium, opened in 1784 survived until 1903, when it was burned down. The T. in Sebastopol (cap. 2,000) was built to replace it. The present Grand T., built in 1919, was used by the Germans and not reopened for opera until 1934.

Lily of Killarney, The. Opera in 3 acts by Benedict; text by John Oxenford and Dion Boucicault, after the latter's drama *Colleen*

Bawn (1860). Prod. London, C.G., 8 Feb. 1862, with Pyne, Santley, Thirlwall, Harrison, cond. Mellon; Philadelphia 20 Nov. 1867.

Lincoln Center for the Performing Arts. The Arts complex in New York which houses the State T., home of the Metropolitan Opera House, and the New York City Opera, as well as Philharmonic Hall and the Juilliard School.

Lincoln's Inn Fields Theatre. The first theatre on the site was known as the Duke's T., 1661-73. The second theatre, 1695-1705, was the scene of the first public performance of *Dido and Aeneas* in 1700. The third theatre, built by Christopher Rich and opened by his son John Rich in 1714, was the scene of the first production of *The Beggar's Opera* (1728). It was the home of the Italian opera company set up in opposition to Handel, with Porpora as composer and Senesino as leading singer, 1733-4. Handel's last opera, *Deidamia,* was given there in 1741. It later became a barracks, then a warehouse, and its site is now occupied by the Royal College of Surgeons.

Lind, Jenny (orig. Johanna) (*b* Stockholm, 6 Oct. 1820; *d* Malvern, 2 Nov. 1887). Swedish soprano. Studied Stockholm. Début there 1838, Agathe. After three years went to Paris where she met with failure and suffered a temporary loss of voice. She then studied with Garcia and polished her technique. Meyerbeer recommended her to the Berlin Opera, where she made her début in 1844 as Norma, and then created the leading role in his *Feldlager in Schlesien*. After successful appearances throughout Germany, Scandinavia, and Vienna – where her Norma gained her 30 curtain calls, and where after her Amina the Empress threw one of her own bouquets on to the stage (an unprecedented action) – she was engaged by Lumley for H.M.'s Theatre in 1847 as a rival attraction to the stars assembled at the newly opened C.G. In her first London season she created the role of Amalia in Verdi's London opera *I masnadieri*. She continued to appear in opera for the next two seasons, making her final appearances on the operatic stage on 10 May 1849 as Alice in *Robert le diable*. In 1852 she married Otto Goldschmidt, the founder of the Bach Choir. Thereafter she sang only in oratorio and concert. She became Professor of Singing at the R.C.M. in 1883, and devoted much of her time to charitable causes and other good works. Her voice was remarkable for its purity, range (b to g^{ll}), agility, breath control, and sympathetic quality. She was known as the 'Swedish Nightingale' and has been the subject of nearly 20 books in English, German, and Swedish, of which H. E. Holland's and W. S. Rockstro's *Jenny Lind the Artist* (2 vols., London, 1891) and Joan Bulman's *Jenny Lind* (London, 1956) can be recommened.

Rockstro also published a short study on her method with a selection of the cadenzas and other ornaments she used (1894).

Linda di Chamounix. Opera in 3 acts by Donizetti; text by Rossi. Prod. Vienna, Kä., 19 May 1842 with Tadolini, Brambilla, Moriani, Varesi, Dérivis, Rovere; London, H.M.'s, 1 June 1843 with Persiani, Brambilla, Mario, Lablache; N.Y., P.O.H., 4 Jan. 1847, with Barili, Pico, Benedetti, Sanquirico, Beneventano, Riese, cond. Barili.

Linda (sop.) loves Charles (ten.), a nobleman disguised as a painter. Believing herself deserted, she goes mad, but he restores her to sanity by returning and reminding her of their love with an old song.

Lindholm (orig. Jonsson), **Berit** (Maria) (*b* Stockholm, 18 Oct. 1934). Swedish soprano. Studied Stockholm, where she made her début in 1963 as the Countess in *Figaro*. London, C.G., 1966 Chrysothemis, and since 1973 Isolde, Brünnhilde; Bayreuth 1967-74 as Venus, and Brünnhilde; San Francisco 1972, Brünnhilde. A Wagner soprano with a splendid voice and physique. (R)

Lindoro. (1) Isabella's lover (ten.) in Rossini's *L'italiana in Algeri*. (2) The name assumed by Count Almaviva in Rossini's *Il barbiere d' Siviglia*.

Lindpaintner, Peter (Josef) **von** (*b* Koblenz, 2 Dec. 1791; *d* Nonnenhorn, 21 Aug. 1856). German composer. Studied Munich with Winter. He became conductor at the new Isartortheater in Munich in 1812, then renewing his studies with Grätz. When the opening of the Munich Hoftheater put the Isartortheater in difficulties, he was forced to resign, and moved to Stuttgart; here he remained until his death, much admired as a conductor. His early operas are in Singspiel manner; later he became deeply interested in Romantic opera, to which he made an interesting contribution. *Der Bergkönig* (1825) shows the strong influence of Weber, especially of *Euryanthe* in the sensational use of tremolo and the appeal to the spirits of darkness. *Der Vampyr* (1828: on the same subject as Marschner's opera, but with different librettist) is still more Weber-like, particularly in its use of polacca rhythms, its chromatic harmony including copious diminished 7ths, a Cavatine in the manner of Aennchen, and a Bridesmaids' Chorus; but it also anticipates Wagner with its powerful use of running figures under tense triplets, its choral prayer (suggesting *Lohengrin*) when the heroine, Isolde, is abducted, and a final collapse of a palace in ruins. *Die Macht des Liedes* (1836) represents a reconciliation with Singspiel, and shows Lindpaintner's gift with simple song forms.

Linley, Thomas (b Badminton, 17 Jan. 1733; d London, 19 Nov. 1795). English singing teacher and composer. He wrote, mostly for Drury Lane, a large number of stage works under various headings – opera, pantomime, ballad opera, musical entertainment, musical farce, &c. The best known was The Duenna (1775), a composition and compilation of music for his son-in-law Sheridan's play, done in collaboration with his eldest son Thomas (b Bath, 5 May 1756; d Grimsthorpe, 5 Aug. 1778). A friend of Mozart, Linley jun. showed precocious musical gifts; he was drowned in a boating accident, leaving little more than a 3-act opera The Cady of Bagdad (1776), an oratorio, and some songs. His sister Elizabeth (b Bath, 5 Sept. 1754; d Bristol, 28 June 1792), Sheridan's wife, was a gifted soprano, as to a lesser degree were her sisters Mary (1758-87) and Maria (1763-84). Their brother Ozias (1765-1831) was an organist, and William (1771-1835) brought out three pieces at Drury Lane which became known as The Ring, before taking up an official post in India.

Lionel. The young farmer (ten.) in love with Lady Harriet in Flotow's Martha.

Lionel and Clarissa. Opera in 3 acts by Dibdin; text by Issac Bickerstaffe. Prod. London, C.G., 25 Feb. 1768; Philadelphia 14 Dec. 1772.

Lipkovskaya (orig. Marschner), Lydia (Yakovlevna) (b Babino, 10 May 1882; d Beirut, 22 Jan. 1955). Russian (Bessarabian) soprano. Studied St Petersburg with Iretskaya, Milan with Vanzo. Début St Petersburg 1907, Gilda. St Petersburg 1906-8, 1911-13. Boston 1909-11; Paris 1910; N.Y., Met., 1910-12; London, C.G., 1911-12, Susanna in Segreto di Susanna, Mimì, Gilda, Violetta. Sang with Russian O.C. in Paris in 1920s. Returned to sing in Russia 1927-9, Odessa 1941, Violetta. (R)

Lisa. The Countess's granddaughter (sop.), Hermann's lover, in Tchaikovsky's The Queen of Spades.

Lisbon (Port., Lisboa). Capital of Portugal. Opera was first heard there regularly in the 18th century. The Royal Opera di Tejo was opened on 31 Mar. 1755 with Pérez's Alessandro nell'Indie. Opera was given there, and at the T. d'Ajuda, until 1792, when a group of business men decided to erect an opera house which was a replica of the San Carlo in Naples. The T. San Carlos was designed by Jose da Costa and Silva, and opened on 30 June 1793 with Cimarosa's La ballerina amante. In Dec. 1794 the first opera to be sung in Portuguese there was heard, Moreira's A Vingança da Cigana. The oval-shaped auditorium (cap. 1,100) has 120 boxes arranged in 5 tiers with 12 boxes on each side; there are two balconies and a gallery. The history of the theatre has been that of a first-class Italian opera house

outside Italy, with occasional excursions into the French and German repertories. All the great singers of the last two centuries have appeared there. The theatre is now known as the National T. of San Carlos, being under state control with João de Freitas Branco as its artistic director.

Lisenko, Nikolay. See Lysenko, Mikola.

Lisinski, Vatroslav (orig. Ignacije Fuchs) (b Zagreb, bapt. 8 July 1819; d Zagreb, 31 May 1854). Yugoslav composer. Studied with Sojka and Wisner von Morgenstern. His first opera, Ljubav i zloba (Love and Malice, 1845), was also the first Croatian opera. Its success encouraged Lisinski to devote himself wholly to music, and he studied further in Prague with Kittl and Pitsch. Returning to Zagreb, he found it impossible to earn a living in music, and became a clerk. However, he left a second opera, Porin (comp. 1848-51, prod. 1897), in which he not only makes use of Croatian folk music but shows an awareness of Glinka's example in giving such ingredients a wider context, and further makes some use of Leitmotiv.
Bibl: F. Kuhač: Vatroslav Lisinski (1887, 2/1904).

Lisitsyan, Pavel (Gerasimovich) (Pogos Karapetovich) (b Vladikavkaz, 6 Nov. 1911). Russian (Armenian) baritone. Studied Leningrad. Début as actor, 1932; singing début Leningrad 1935. Leningrad, Maly T., 1935-7, Spendiarov O.C. 1937 in Armenian works, including title role in Chukhadjian's Arshak II. Moscow, B., from 1940. N.Y., Met., 1960, Amonasro. Repertory includes Onegin, Escamillo, Janusz (Halka), and many Russian roles. (R)

List (orig. Fleissig), Emanuel (b Vienna, 22 Mar. 1890; d Vienna, 21 June 1967). Austrian, later naturalized American, bass. After singing as boy chorister at Vienna W., touring Europe in a vocal quartet and America in vaudeville, studied in New York with Josiah Zuro. Début Vienna, V., 1922, Méphistophélès. Berlin 1923-33; London, C.G., 1925, 1934-36; N.Y., Met., 1933-50. Also sang at Bayreuth and Salzburg. Had a rich deep bass voice; especially noted for his interpretations of Hunding, Hagen, Pogner, and King Mark, and a distinguished Baron Ochs. (R)

Liszt, Ferenc (Franz) (b Raiding, 22 Oct. 1811; d Bayreuth, 31 July 1886). Hungarian composer, pianist, and conductor. His sole attempt at opera was Don Sanche (1824-5), a 1-act operetta written with the help of his teacher Paer. It was produced in Paris in 1825, and after four performances was forgotten (revived London, Oct. 1977). He became Kapellmeister at Weimar in 1848, and here he championed with characteristic generosity many composers, including Wagner, whose *Lohengrin* had its première under him in 1850, and Berlioz, whose *Benvenuto Cellini* he gave in the revised 3-act version in 1852. His position became difficult, partly for personal reasons, and matters came to a head over the première of Cornelius's *Der Barbier von Bagdad* in 1858; he was obliged to resign. His daughter Cosima married first Hans von *Bülow, then Wagner.

Lithuania. Opera was first given in Lithuania in the 17th cent., when it formed part of Poland and the Court T. of the Grand Dukes had a company of 90 directed by the Italian Marco Sacchi. For most of its history, Lithuanian theatre and opera were controlled by Polish nobles; the most famous theatre belonged to the Radziwiłłs, one of whom, Michał, wrote the text of Johann Holland's vaudeville *Agatka* (1784). The first public theatre was opened in Vilnius in 1785, and, despite the country's changing political fortunes, opera was performed (from 1805, organised by I. Frank). A German theatre existed in Vilnius, 1835-44, a Russian one from 1845. After the 1863 revolution, the Lithuanian theatre of Vilnius was closed, and many Lithuanians emigrated to America, where a number of musicians formed companies. Outstanding among them was Mikas Petrauskas (1873-1937), whose *Birute* (Vilnius, 1906: the first Lithuanian opera) was followed in America by operas and operettas in which he sometimes also sang: many other Lithuanian opera and operetta groups were formed in a number of American cities. In Lithuania, an opera company began at Kaunas in 1920 with *La traviata*: Petrauskas's brother Kipras (*b* 1885) was director, and Juzas Tallat-Kelpša (1889-1949) conductor. In 1922 this was amalgamated with the theatre as the Lietuvos Tautos Teatras (Lithuanian Nat. T.). The company made a considerable reputation; guest singers included Shalyapin and Kiepura, and guest conductors Coates and Malko. Lithuanian operas included *Trys Talismanis* (The Three Talismans, 1936) by Anastas Račiūnas (*b* 1905); *Egle Žalčiukaraliene* (Egle, the Snake Queen, 1918) by Mikas Petrauskas; and *Gražina* (1933, celebrating the 15th anniversary of the Lithuanian state) and *Radvila Perkunas* (1937) by Georgy Karnavičius (1884-1931).

On the Soviet occupation in 1941, an operetta theatre was formed in Kaunas, with a mainly Russian repertory. This was abandoned with the German advance in 1942, when an opera theatre was formed at Vilnius; the return of Soviet troops caused further emigrations, and various groups were then active in Germany. With the incorporation of Lithuania into the U.S.S.R., the capital was transferred to Vilnius, and with it the opera. In May 1959 a new company was formed at Kaunas, under Juozas

Indra (*b* 1918), with a wide repertory that has included new Lithuanian operas, e.g. *The Drowned Girl* by Vitolis Baumilas (*b* 1928) and the satirical *Franz Kruk* (1959) by Beniaminos Gorbulskis (*b* 1925). Other Lithuanian operas include *Dalya* (1959) by Balis Dvarionas (*b* 1904), *Prie Niemuno* (By the Niemen, 1960) by Abel Klenickis (*b* 1904), and *Sukeleliai* (The Rebels, 1957) by Julius Juzeliunas (*b* 1916).

Liturgical music drama. The name generally given to the medieval dramas, chiefly of the 12th and 13th cent., presenting Biblical stories in Latin, with monophonic music; they did not in fact form part of the liturgy. Favourite subjects included the story of Daniel and the miracles of various saints, especially St Nicholas. From the 14th to 16th cent. these plays developed into mystery plays, no longer directly connected with the church and church performance, and using the vernacular; music was used only incidentally, for fanfares, dances, etc., occasionally incorporating plainsong and popular songs. Though an earlier dramatic musical form, the liturgical music drama is not a true ancestor of opera; however the modern revival of a number of the works, such as the 13th cent. *The Play of Daniel,* has shown that they possess considerable dramatic and musical power.

Litvinne, Félia (orig. Françoise-Jeanne Schütz) (*b* St Petersburg, 11 Oct. 1860; *d* Paris, 12 Oct. 1936). Franco-Russian soprano. Studied Paris with Barthe-Banderali, Pauline Viardot, and Maurel. Début Paris, T.I., 1883, replacing Fidès Devriès as Maria Boccanegra. Six months later official début as Elvira (*Ernani*) under name of Litvinova. Appeared in various European cities and in N.Y. with Mapleson Company 1885-6; N.Y., Met., 1896-7; London, C.G., from 1899. The first Isolde in Paris (1899); the Brünnhilde of the first complete *Ring* at La Monnaie, Brussels (1903), and in Paris at the O. (1911). Her last operatic performances were in 1919 at Vichy, after which she continued to appear in concerts until 1924. She taught in Paris and her pupils included Nina Koshetz, Marcelle Denya, and Germaine Lubin. Her performance of Gluck's *Alceste* is said to have set a standard still not surpassed in our day. Her voice was brilliant and flexible and her singing impassioned. (R)
Bibl: F. Litvinne: *Ma Vie et mon art* (1933).

Liù. The slave girl (sop.) in love with Calaf in Puccini's *Turandot.*

Liverpool. Town in Lancashire, England. Largely dependent on touring companies over the years, having been visited by the C. R., C.G. S.W., Gly., and other groups. Flagstad sang her last Isolde on any stage in Liverpool with the C.G. Opera in 1951, and Beecham persuaded the Liverpool Festival authorities, the Arts

Council, and Covent Garden into allowing him to mount *The Bohemian Girl* there as part of Liverpool's contribution to the Festival of Britain the same year. Local amateur companies have contributed to the city's operatic life, notably the Liverpool Grand Opera Company which gave the first British performance of Bizet's *Ivan IV* in 1956, as well as productions of *Hérodiade, Macbeth, La gioconda,* and *Eugene Onegin.* In 1971 the Merseyside Arts Association, and the Vaughan Williams Trust helped the Liverpool University to stage the première of Elaine Murdoch's *Tamburlaine.*

Livorno (previously known in Eng. as Leghorn). Town in Tuscany, Italy. Short seasons are given at the T. Goldoni.

Ljungberg, Göta (*b* Sundsvall, 4 Oct. 1893; *d* Lidingö, 28 June 1955). Swedish soprano. Studied Stockholm with Bratt, and with Cahier, also London, Milan, and Berlin with Oscar Daniel. Début Stockholm 1918, Gutrune. London, C.G., 1924-9 where she created title role in Goossens's *Judith* (1929) and was praised as Salome and Sieglinde. N.Y., Met., 1932-5, creating Lady Marigold Sandys in Hanson's *Merry Mount* (1933), also Isolde and Brünnhilde. After retiring from the stage taught in New York for several years. (R)

Lloyd, Powell (*b* London, 6 May 1900). English tenor. Studied London, Morley College, and G.S.M. First appeared in small roles with the Old Vic Shakespeare Company, then became leading character tenor there and at S.W. Also sang the Witch in *Hänsel und Gretel* and Bartolo in *The Barber,* originally a mezzo-soprano and a bass role. Since 1941 has produced and designed sets for S.W., Dublin, W.N.O. Has also designed sets for a number of operas etc.

Lloyd, Robert (Andrew) (*b* Southend-on-Sea, 2 Mar. 1940). English bass. Studied Oxford and London U. Centre. Début London, Univ. College O. 1969, Minister in first perf. in England of Beethoven's *Leonore.* S.W. 1969-72; C.G. since 1972. Guest appearances Aix-en-Provence Festival, Paris, San Francisco, Boston, etc. Repertory includes Sarastro, Heinrich (*Lohengrin*), Fasolt, Banquo, and Monterone. (R)

Lockhart, James (Lawrence) (*b* Edinburgh, 16 Oct. 1930). Scottish conductor. Studied Edinburgh and London, RCM. Münster as répétiteur 1955-6; Munich 1956-7; Gly. 1957-9; London, C.G., 1959-60, 1962-8; S.W., 1961-2. Music director W.N.O. 1968-72; Kassel since 1972. First British-born conductor to hold position of music director in a German opera house. (R)

Loder, Edward (*b* Bath, 1813; *d* London, 5 Apr. 1865). English composer. Studied Frankfurt with Ries. Operatic début with *Nourjahad,* composed to a drama of Samuel Arnold's to open the new English O.H. (Lyceum) on 21 July

1834. Other works included *The Night Dancers* (1846), a ballad opera *Robin Goodfellow* (1848), *King Charles II* (1849), and *Raymond and Agnes* (1855). Loder's melodic gifts and command of vivid orchestration, and keen sense of drama when his librettos permitted, suggest that in more favourable conditions he might have achieved considerable stature as a composer of English Romantic opera. His sister **Kate** (*b* Bath, 21 Aug. 1825; *d* Headley, 30 Aug. 1904) was a pianist and composer; among her works is an opera *L'elisir d'amore.*

Lodoïska. Opera in 3 acts by Cherubini; text by Fillette-Loraux. Prod. Paris, T. Feydeau, 18 July 1791 (a fortnight before R. Kreutzer's opera on the same subject, Paris, C.-I., 1 Aug. 1791); N.Y. 4 Dec. 1826.

Lodoïska (sop.) is imprisoned in the castle of Dourlinski (bar.), who wants to marry her. She is in love with Floreski (ten.), who rescues her when the castle is attacked and destroyed by the Tartars under Titzikan (bar.).

Other operas on the subject are by Storace (pasticcio using Cherubini, Kreutzer, and Andreozzi, 1794), Mayr (1796), Caruso (1796), Paer (1804), Bishop (adapting Storace, 1816), Curmi (1846), and Succo (1849).

Lodoletta. Opera in 3 acts by Mascagni; text by Forzano, after Ouida's novel *Two Little Wooden Shoes* (1874). Prod. Rome, C., 30 Apr. 1917, with Storchio, Campioni, Molinari, cond. Mascagni; N.Y., Met., 12 Jan. 1918, with Farrar, Caruso, Amato, cond. Moranzoni.

Antonio (bass) gives Lodoletta (sop.) a pair of new red shoes. After his death she falls in love with a painter, Flammen (ten.), and follows him from Holland to Paris. She is afraid to enter his house, where a party is in progress, and dies in the snow. Flammen finds her and laments that he has always loved her.

Also opera on subject by Hubay (*Moharósza,* 1903).

Łódź. Town in Poland. Opera was first heard in 1860s in this newly built industrial town; Polish operas and lighter works were given by companies from Warsaw and abroad. An unsuccessful attempt to establish a permanent company was made in 1888. Even after 1918, operatic life was dependent upon guest performances. An operetta theatre was founded in 1946, and on 18 Oct. 1954 the Society of Friends of Opera inaugurated the Łódź Opera. The first directors were Władysław Raczkowski, Zygmunt Latoszewski 1961-72, Bogusław Madey from 1972. The new T. Wielki (cap. 1,300: the largest in Poland after Warsaw) opened on 19 Jan. 1967. Since then it has built up a fine reputation. Its singers have included Teresa Kubiak and Izabela Nawe; premières have included works by Twardowski, Czyż, and Kurpiński.

Loewe, Sophie (Johanna) (*b* Oldenburg, 24 Mar. 1815; *d* Budapest 28 Nov. 1866). German soprano. Daughter of the actor Ferdinand Löwe. Studied Vienna with Ciccimarra and Milan with Lamperti. Début Vienna, Kä., 1832, Elisabetta in *Otto mesi in due ore*. London 1841; Milan, Sc., 1841; created title-role in Donizetti's *Maria Padilla*; Venice, F., created Elvira in *Ernani* (1844) and Odabella in *Attila* (1846). Verdi said after the production of *Attila* that he 'never would have believed that a German could display such patriotic fire'. Retired 1848 on her marriage to Prince Ferdinand von Liechtenstein.

Loewenberg, Alfred (*b* Berlin, 14 May 1902; *d* London, 29 Dec. 1949). British musical historian of German birth. Studied Berlin and Jena. Emigrated to England 1934. His *Annals of Opera*: rev. ed. Zürich, 1954; London, 1978 is a monument of painstaking scholarship and research, containing details of some 4,000 òpera performances in chronological order. Essential to any student of operatic history.

Loge. The fire god (ten.) in Wagner's *Das Rheingold*.

Logroscino, Nicola (*b* Bitonto, bapt. 22 Oct. 1698; *d* ?Palermo, 1765). Italian composer. Studied Naples, with Durante. Settled in Naples about 1738 and became highly popular as a comic opera composer; he wrote opera seria, but excelled in comedy, contributing to the genre of 18th cent. Neapolitan opera an exceptional liveliness in the handling of the finale. Many of his later works were written in collaboration, some with Piccinni, who eventually captured his popularity.

Lohengrin. Opera in 3 acts by Wagner; text by the composer, after the anonymous German epic. Prod. Weimar, Court T., 28 Aug. 1850 with Agthe, Fastlinger, Beck, Von Hilde, Höfer, cond. Liszt; N.Y., Stadt T., 3 Apr. 1871, with Lichtmay, Friderici, Habelmann, Vierling, Franosch, Formes, cond. Neuendorff; London, C.G., 8 May 1875, with Albani, D'Angeri, Nicolini, Maurel, Seidemann, cond. Vianesi. Originally intended for production in Dresden, the opera was rejected because of Wagner's revolutionary activities. Liszt gave it, with an orchestra of only 38, in Wagner's absence in Switzerland; Wagner did not attend a performance until 1861 in Vienna.

King Henry the Fowler (bass), who has been visiting Antwerp to raise an army, holds court. He asks Frederick of Telramund (bar.) why the kingdom of Brabant is torn by strife. Telramund accuses his ward Elsa (sop.) of having murdered her young brother Gottfried in order to obtain the throne. Elsa describes a dream in which a knight in shining armour has come to defend her. The King's Herald (bar.) twice calls for a champion. A swan-drawn boat bearing a

knight in shining armour arrives. The knight (Lohengrin, ten.) bids the swan farewell, and agrees to champion Elsa, offering her his hand in marriage on condition that she will never ask him his name or origin. Lohengrin defeats Telramund, generously sparing his life.

In the courtyard of the castle in Antwerp, Telramund, who has been banned as a traitor by the King, and his wife Ortrud (sop.), are brooding on the state of events. Elsa appears on a balcony and sings a song to the night breezes. She descends, and Ortrud, offering her friendship, begins to sow distrust of Lohengrin in her mind. Dawn breaks, and processions form for the marriage of Elsa and Lohengrin. On the steps of the Cathedral, Ortrud accuses Lohengrin of having defeated Telramund by evil means, and then Telramund repeats his wife's accusations. Elsa assures the knight that she trusts him; but the seeds of suspicion have taken root.

A brilliant orchestral prelude and the celebrated Wedding March open the scene, which is set in Elsa's bridal chamber. Elsa's happiness gives way to hysteria and she demands to know her husband's name. Telramund and four of his followers break into the room to attack Lohengrin, who immediately kills Telramund. He bids the nobles to bear the body to the King, and tells Elsa that he will reveal his secret to them all.

The scene changes to the banks of the Scheldt. The King and court assemble, and Lohengrin tells them that he has come from the Temple of the Holy Grail in Monsalvat; his father was Parsifal, and Lohengrin is his name. He bids Elsa a sad farewell, and then turns to greet the swan which has brought the boat for him. Ortrud rushes on and reveals that the swan is in reality Gottfried, Elsa's brother. Lohengrin falls on his knees and prays. The swan becomes Gottfried, and a white dove of the Grail flies down and draws the boat away.

Lohse, Otto (*b* Dresden, 21 Sept. 1858; *d* Baden-Baden, 5 May 1925). German conductor. Studied Dresden with Richter, and originally cellist in Dresden Court Orchestra. Début as conductor Riga 1889. Music director at Hamburg 1893-5, where he met Katharina *Klafsky whom he married. Conducted Damrosch Company in U.S.A. 1895-6; London, D.L., 1894; C.G. 1901-4. Subsequently at Cologne (1904-11), Brussels (1911-14), and Leipzig (1912-23). His son **Georg Lohse** was a lyric tenor: Chemnitz 1913-14, and elsewhere.

Lola. Alfio's wife (mezzo) and Turiddu's lover in Mascagni's *Cavalleria rusticana*.

Lombardi alla prima Crociata, I (The Lombards at the First Crusade). Opera in 4 acts by Verdi; text by Solera. Prod. Milan, Sc., 11 Feb. 1843, with Frezzolini-Poggi, Ruggeri, Guasco, Severi,

Dérivis, Rossi, Marconi, Vairo, Gandaglia; London, H.M.'s, 12 May 1846, with Grisi and Mario; N.Y., P.O.H., 3 Mar. 1847 – first Verdi opera in U.S.A. A second version in French, under the title of *Jérusalem*, text by Royer and Vaëz, prod. Paris, O., 26 Nov. 1847, with Van Gelder, Duprez, Portheaut, Alizard, Bremont.

The opera tells of the rivalry of two brothers Arvino (ten.) and Pagano (bass) for the love of Viclinda at the time of the first Crusade, Pagano, in an attempt to abduct Viclinda and kill his brother, in error murders his own father. He is exiled to the Holy Land, where he lives as a hermit. Giselda (sop.), daughter of Arvino, who has accompanied her father on the Crusade, is captured by Acciano, tyrant of Antioch; she falls in love with his son Oronte (ten.). The couple escape, but Oronte is mortally wounded and before he expires is baptized by the Hermit. The latter leads the attack on Jerusalem and he too is wounded. He reveals his identity to Arvino and dies forgiven in his brother's arms.

London. Capital of Great Britain. Performances of opera began towards the end of the 17th cent. Many masques had been given earlier, and opera was inaugurated with *The Siege of Rhodes,* given at Rutland House in Sept. 1656 (music by various composers, now lost). Blow's *Venus and Adonis* was given during the 1680s, and many other works followed at the many theatres in the city. In 1689 Purcell's *Dido and Aeneas* was given in Chelsea. After his death, the history of opera in London became largely that of Italian opera. The first complete Italian opera to be sung in English was Bononcini's *Camilla* (1706), the first in Italian having been Greber's *Gli amori d'Ergasto* (1705). In 1710 Handel arrived in London, producing a long series of operas between *Rinaldo* (1711) and *Deidamia* (1741). Gluck, Galuppi, and Lampugnani also appeared in London during the 1760s. The first Mozart opera was heard in 1806, *La clemenza di Tito*; and his operas, together with Rossini's, dominated the London repertories during the 1820s. Another very popular work was *Der Freischütz,* of which six versions were current in the early 1820s; this led to the invitation to Weber to compose and conduct his *Oberon* in 1826. The work also helped to encourage native composers to write for London theatres. Italian opera remained very popular. Wagner was first heard regularly in the 1870s, the complete *Ring* in 1892. Opera grew rapidly after the turn of the century, and several new companies were formed to perform in many theatres. As London, with its long and powerful dramatic traditions, has always been well furnished with theatres, it is chiefly by way of their histories that the course of opera in the city is best followed. See *Adelphi T., Cambridge T., Camden Festival, Coliseum T., Covent Garden T., Dorset Garden T., Drury Lane T., Her Majesty's T., King's T., Lincoln's Inn T., London Opera Company, Old Vic T., Palace T., Pantheon T., Royal Italian Opera, Sadler's Wells T., Savoy T., Shaftesbury T., Strand T.*

London (orig. Burnstein), **George** (*b* Montreal, 30 May 1920). Canadian bass-baritone, administrator, and producer. Studied Los Angeles with Strelkitzer and Stewart, and later with Rosati and Novikova. Début (as George Burnson) Hollywood Bowl, 1941, Dr Grenvil in *La traviata.* After appearing in musical comedy and touring in concerts, he auditioned for Karl Böhm in 1949 and was engaged for the Vienna Opera, where he made his début in Sept. that year as Amonasro. N.Y., Met., 1951-66., where he was especially admired as Boris, Don Giovanni, and Scarpia. Bayreuth, 1951-64, Amfortas and Dutchman. First American artist to sing at Moscow B., 1960. Appointed music administrator, Kennedy Centre, Washington, 1968. Began producing opera in 1971, with *The Magic Flute* at the Juilliard School, N.Y., and the *Ring* in Seattle and San Diego, 1973-5. Director Opera Society of Washington since 1975. He had a rich and sonorous bass-baritone voice, an imposing stage presence, and was an intense actor. (R)

London Opera House. Built by Oscar *Hammerstein in 1911 and opened on 13 Nov. that year with Nouguès's *Quo Vadis?* Survived two seasons. Massenet's *Le Jongleur de Notre-Dame* and *Don Quichotte* and Holbrooke's *The Children of Don* were given their first London performances. Closed on 13 July 1912 and (as the Stoll T.) became a variety theatre and cinema. During the First World War a short season of Russian, French, and Italian opera, including the first English performance of *The Queen of Spades,* was given there under the direction of Vladimir Rosing, and then no opera was heard there again until the summer of 1949, when a season of Italian opera was given by Jay Pomeroy's company. Further seasons were given by Italian touring companies between 1952 and 1957; and it was also the scene of *Porgy and Bess* (1951), the Zagreb Opera visit (1955), and Honegger's *Jeanne d'Arc au Bûcher.* Later demolished.

Long Thursday. The name given to the non-subscription nights at the Royal Italian Opera, C.G., in the 1850s and 1860s, when complete acts of operas were given in addition to the evening's advertised programme. The entertainment often lasted until well after midnight – hence the name. A typical Long Thursday night would consist of *Norma* followed by the last act of *Lucia di Lammermoor,* with a ballet to round off the evening.

Loreley, Die. *Azione drammatica* in 3 acts by

Catalani; text by Zanardini and D'Ormeville. Prod. Turin, T.R., 16 Feb. 1890, with Ferni-Germano, Dexter, Durot, Stinco-Palermini, Pozzi, cond. Mascheroni; London, C.G., 12 July 1907, with Scalar, Kurz, Bassi, Sammarco, Journet, cond. Campanini; Chicago, 17 Jan. 1919, with Fitziu, Macbeth, Dolci, Rimini, Lazzari, cond. Polacco. Orig. entitled *Elda*, in 4 acts: prod. Turin, 31 Jan. 1880, with Garbini, Boulicioff, Barbacini, Athos, E. De Reszke, cond. Pedrotti.

Walther (ten.) is betrothed to Anna (sop.), but falls in love with the Loreley (sop.). At the wedding ceremony the Loreley appears and Walther rushes out to follow her. Anna dies of grief, and Walther throws himself into the Rhine because the Loreley continues to evade him.

Other operas on the subject are by Lachner (1846), Mendelssohn (unfin. 1847), Wallace (*Lurline*, 1860), Bruch (1863), Mohr (1884), Pacius (1887), Bartholdy (1887), E. Naumann (1889), and A. Becker (1898).

Lorengar, Pilar (orig. Pilar Lorenza Garcia) (*b* Saragossa, 16 Jan. 1928). Spanish soprano. Studied Barcelona. Début there as mezzo-soprano 1949. Soprano since 1951; operatic début Aix-en-Provence 1965 Cherubino; N.Y. 1955 (concert perf. of *Goyescas*), Met. since 1966; London, C.G., 1955, Violetta, and since 1964 as Donna Anna, Countess Almaviva, Fiordiligi, Eurydice and Alice Ford; Berlin, D., since 1958, in Mozart, Verdi, and Puccini repertory. Repertory also includes Eva and Mélisande. Although she sings dramatic roles such as Tosca and Nedda, her voice and temperament are better suited to the classical repertory. (R)

Lorenz, Max (*b* Düsseldorf, 10 May 1901; *d* Vienna, 12 Jan. 1975). German tenor. Studied Berlin with Grenzebach. Début Dresden 1927, Walther von der Vogelweide (*Tannhäuser*). Berlin, S.O., 1929–44; Vienna, S.O., 1929–33, 1936–44, 1954. N.Y., Met., 1931–4 and 1947–50. London, C.G., 1934 and 1937; Bayreuth 1933–9 and 1952. One of the finest Wagner tenors of his day, he was considered by the Viennese the best Otello since Slezak. (R)
Bibl: Walter Hermann: *Max Lorenz* (1976).

Lortzing, (Gustav) **Albert** (*b* Berlin, 23 Oct. 1801; *d* Berlin, 21 Jan. 1851). German composer, conductor, librettist, singer, and actor. Son of an actor; studied in Berlin with Rungenhagen, later by himself when obliged by his father's profession to travel frequently. He played children's parts on the stage both as actor and singer. His first opera, written in 1824 when he was almost 23, was *Ali Pascha von Janina* (prod. 1828), a vivid work which includes a strong vengeance aria making use of four trumpets. He then turned to comedy; *Die beiden Schützen* (1837) made a reputation later

confirmed with *Zar und Zimmermann* (1837). These two works, long popular in Germany, display his characteristic vein of light tunefulness (deriving from the manner of German popular song), his easy control of the stage, his light-hearted, sentimental approach to character, and a certain musical originality. *Caramo* (1839), *Hans Sachs* (1840), and *Casanova* (1841) proved less enduring. Nevertheless, *Hans Sachs* includes some attractive music, and is remarkable for some anticipations of Wagner's *Die Meistersinger*: there are similarities in the handling of the characters (Sachs as a dreamer), and in the dramatic sequence of events (a group of dances before the final scene) which are not wholly accounted for by the operas' common textual ancestry, and even one or two curious musical anticipations, as with the theme for Görg (David). *Der Wildschütz* (1842) was his greatest triumph, and it is still popular in Germany; it is characteristic of Lortzing's easy, attractive musical manner in drawing on the German feeling for the countryside which Weber had first aroused in opera.

Meanwhile he was also acting as producer, singer, and conductor; he worked as Kapellmeister in Leipzig 1844–5, but was forced to leave and suffered great difficulty in providing for his large family. *Undine* (1845) was a magic opera on the popular Romantic legend. It includes some striking stage effects: the conclusion, with rising waters and a palace crashing in ruins, appeared in other Romantic operas up to and including Wagner. The opera also includes some early use of true Leitmotiv. In 1846 Lortzing moved to Vienna, where *Der Waffenschmied* (1846) was given; this strengthened his popularity, and at the same confirmed the pattern of opera he had made his own – a lightly romantic comedy, to his own text, often turning on the disguise of an aristocrat as a workman, and expressed in engaging and tuneful songs culminating in rather stronger finales. *Zum Grossadmiral* (1847) followed in Leipzig; and Lortzing then attempted in *Regina* (comp. 1848; prod. 1899) an opera on the fashionable theme of revolution, discovering to his cost that the idea was in uneasy times found too subversive. He lost his post, but was nevertheless called to Leipzig to supervise his *Rolands Knappen*, an impressive work which has a heroine named Isolda and also contains some harmonic glimpses of *Tristan*. An appointment in Leipzig fell through, and in 1850 he moved to Berlin as conductor of a small theatre. Here his family lived in poverty despite the frequent performance of his works, and he died when about to be dismissed from even this humble post. His last work was *Die Opernprobe* (1851). His music has a simple charm that fits it well to the kind of romantic comedy he preferred. Though not a sophisticated composer, and sometimes an over-sentimental one, he was capable of some remarkably advanced strokes, and his works represent the most agreeable type of German comic opera.

Bibl: G. R. Kruse: *Albert Lortzing* (1899).

Los Angeles. Town in California, U.S.A. The first opera seasons in Los Angeles were given by various touring companies in the 1880s and 1890s, including the Abbott, Juch, and National Opera Companies. In 1897 the Del Conti Opera Company, which had been appearing in Mexico City, was brought to Los Angeles by L. E. Beyhmer and C. Modini, and gave the first performance in the United States of *La Bohème*. Beyhmer also brought the Metropolitan Opera from New York to the west coast for the first time in 1900. In 1906 the Lombardi (later the San Carlo) Company began its visits, and from 1914 until the end of the 1920s the Chicago Opera made 11 visits to Los Angeles. Among the many visiting companies during the 1920s were the Scotti Company and a Russian company with Shalyapin. In 1924 the Los Angeles Grand Opera Association was formed with Gaetano Merola as general director, and worked in close contact with the San Francisco Opera. In 1925 Merola withdrew and formed a rival company, the California Grand Opera Association. Two years later Merola rejoined the Los Angeles Grand Opera Association, and seasons were given at the Shrine Auditorium until 1932. From 1936 to 1965 the San Francisco Opera visited Los Angeles regularly at the close of the autumn San Francisco season. Opera has also been given from time to time in the Hollywood Bowl, a vast open-air arena, beginning with H. W. Parker's *Fairyland* in 1915. The Opera School of Los Angeles University gives interesting performances, and from 1946 to 1954 was under the direction of Carl Ebert.

In 1965 the Dorothy Chandler Pavilion (cap. 3,250) opened with the last Los Angeles season by the San Francisco Opera. The New York City Opera has given an annual seasonal each November since 1968. Various attempts to establish a permanent company in Los Angeles since 1965 have all failed.

Los Angeles, Victoria de (orig. Victoria Lopez Cima) (*b* Barcelona, 1 Nov. 1923). Spanish soprano. Studied Barcelona Conservatory, completing six-year course in three, and gaining every prize. First public appearance while still a student in Monteverdi's *Orfeo*. Debut Barcelona, T. Victoria, 1941, Mimì. Gained first place in International Festival, Geneva, 1947. In 1949 invited by B.B.C. to sing Salud in Falla's *La vida breve*. London, C.G., 1950–1, 1957, 1960–1 as Mimì, Cio-Cio-San, Nedda, Santuzza, Manon, Elsa; N.Y., Met., 1951–61. Bayreuth 1961–2, Elisabeth. Also appeared Milan, Sc.,

Paris, O., Vienna etc. She had one of the most beautiful soprano voices in the immediate post-war period and a charming stage presence; this made her one of the outstanding interpreters of Mimì and Manon. Her repertory also included Ariadne, Donna Anna, Agathe, Rosina, Melisande, and Marguerite. From the mid-1960s onwards she has devoted herself increasingly to concerts and recitals. (R)

Louise. *Roman musical* in 4 acts by Gustave Charpentier; text by composer. Prod. Paris, O.C., 2 Feb. 1900, with Rioton, Deschamps-Jehin, Maréchal, Fugère, cond. Messager – 950 perfs. by 1950; N.Y., Manhattan O., 3 Jan. 1908, with Garden, Bressler, Dalmorès, Gilibert, cond. Campanini; London, C.G., 18 Jun. 1909, with Edvina, Bérat, Dalmorès, Gilibert, cond. Frigara.

Louise (sop.) is in love with Julien (ten.), but her parents (mezzo and bass) refuse to allow them to marry. They set up house together, but when Louise's mother comes to tell her that her father is seriously ill she returns home to help nurse him back to health. The parents refuse to allow Louise to rejoin Julien; she quarrels with her father and he throws her out of the house, accusing the city of Paris of destroying his home.

Love in a Village. Ballad and pasticcio opera in 3 acts partly composed and partly compiled by Arne and Bickerstaffe. Prod. London, C.G., 8 Dec. 1762; Charleston, 10 Feb. 1766.

Love of the Three Oranges, The. Opera in 4 acts by Prokofiev; text by composer, after Gozzi's comedy (1761). Prod. Chicago, 30 Dec. 1921, with Koshetz, Pavloska, Mojica, Dua, Beck, Defrère, Cotreuil, cond. Prokofiev; Edinburgh, by Belgrade O., 21 Aug. 1962, with Miladinović, Čakarević, Z. Cvejić, Andrasević, Paulik, Djokić, Hejbalova, cond. Danon.

An opera is taking place in which a melancholy prince can only be cured by laughter. Every attempt is thwarted by Fata Morgana until she herself falls down and he laughs. He is now forced to find three oranges. He finds them in a kitchen and drags them with him into the desert. Each contains a princess. Two die of thirst; the third is helped by some of the stage-audience with a bucket of water. Eventually the prince and princess are united and the sorceress is confounded.

Lualdi, Adriano (*b* Larino, 22 Mar. 1885; *d* Milan, 8 Jan. 1971). Italian composer, conductor, and critic. In his operas, for which he wrote his own librettos, he revived older Italian forms. They include an intermezzo *Il cantico* (1915), an intermezzo giocoso *Le furie di Arlecchino* (1915), a dramatic scena *La morte di Rinaldo* (1920), and the puppet opera *Guerrin Meschino* (1920). Other operas include *La figlia* del Re (1922), Il diavolo del campanile (1925), and La granceola (1930).

Lübeck. Town in Schleswig-Holstein, Germany. The first opera performance was probably given in 1701. A permanent company was established in 1799. Opera is given in the theatre built in 1908 (cap. 1,012). Music directors have included Abendroth, Furtwängler, Berthold Lehmann, Christoph von Dohnányi, and Bernhard Klee. The first performances in Germany of Pizzetti's *Assassinio nel cattedrale* and Burian's *Marysa* were given there in 1961 and 1964.

Lubin, Germaine (*b* Paris, 1 Feb. 1890). French soprano. Originally studied medicine, then turned to music, studying in Paris with Martini, Isnardon, and Litvinne. In 1912 won three prizes for singing and joined O.C. same year; début Antonia (*Tales of Hoffmann*). Paris, O., 1914–44; London, C.G., 1937 as Alceste and Ariane, and 1939 as Isolde and Kundry. First French artist to sing Kundry and Isolde at Bayreuth. Had a beautiful voice and was an excellent actress. Her career was brought to a premature end after the war as a result of her collaboration with the Germans. (R)

Lucan. Marcus Annæus Lucanus (*b* Corduba, 3 Nov. 39; *d* Rome, 30 Apr. 65). Latin poet, the nephew of the younger Seneca, and the author of the *Pharsalia*. As Lucano, he appears in Monteverdi's *L'incoronazione di Poppea* in his role as Nero's friend (though later he suffered Seneca's fate of being commanded to commit suicide). His observation, 'The more that a good act costs us, the dearer it is to us', is quoted at the start of Bouilly's libretto for Cherubini's *Les Deux journées* as its moral.

Lucca, Pauline (*b* Vienna, 25 Apr. 1841; *d* Vienna, 28 Feb. 1908). Austrian soprano. Studied Vienna where she first sang in the chorus of the Court Opera. Début Olomouc 1859, Elvira in *Ernani*. Engaged Berlin 1861 on recommendation of Meyerbeer, with whom she studied several roles. London, C.G., 1863 as Valentine and was first London Selika. Her Marguerite, Cherubino, and Carmen were considered unsurpassed in their day. She sang in the United States 1872–4 and was leading soprano in Vienna 1874–89, when she retired. Her voice had a range of two and a half octaves (f'–c''''').
Bibl: A. Jansen-Mara and D. Weisse Zahrer: *Die Wiener Nachtigall* (1935).

Lucia di Lammermoor. Opera in 3 acts by Donizetti; Text by Cammarano, after Scott's novel, *The Bride of Lammermoor* (1819). Prod. Naples, S.C., 26 Sept. 1835, with Persiani, Duprez, Zappucci, Cosselli, Porto, Balestrieri, Rossi; London, H.M.'s, 5 Apr. 1838, with Persiani and Rubini; New Orleans 28 Dec. 1841,

with Julia Calvé and Auguste Nourrit.

Lucy Ashton (sop.) is in love with Edgar Ravenswood (ten.), an enemy of her family. Her brother Henry (bar.) persuades her to marry Lord Arthur Bucklow (ten.) by showing her a forged letter, supposedly written by Edgar. The wedding ceremony is interrupted by Edgar, who curses Lucy for betraying him. She goes mad, kills her newly-wed husband, and then dies. Edgar kills himself in grief.

Other operas on the subject are by Carafa (1829), Damse (1832), Brédal (1832), and Mazzucato (1834).

Lucio Silla. *Dramma per musica* in 3 acts by Mozart; text by Giovanni da Gamerra, with alterations by Metastasio. Prod. Milan, T.R.D., 26 Dec. 1772, with Morgnoni, De Amicis, Rauzzini, Suardi, Mienci, Onofrio; London, Camden T.H., 7 Mar. 1967, with Curphey, Bruce, Jenkins, Conrad, cond. Farncombe; Baltimore, Peabody Concert Hall, 19 Jan. 1968, with Perret, Winburn, Riegel, Gerber, cond. Conlin.

Other operas on the subject are by Anfossi (1774), J. C. Bach (1777), and Mortellari (1778).

Lucrezia Borgia. Opera in prologue and 2 acts by Donizetti; text by Romani, after Victor Hugo's tragedy (1833). Prod. Milan, Sc., 26 Dec. 1833, with Méric-Lalande, Brambilla, Pedrazzi, Mariani; London, H.M.'s, 6 Jun. 1839, with Grisi, Mario; New Orleans, American T., 11 May 1843, with Castellan, Maiocchi, Perozzi, Valtellina, Thames. Guissiner, cond. Mueller. When it was produced in Paris in 1840, Hugo protested and the work was withdrawn; the libretto was then rewritten, the title changed to *La inegata* and the action transferred to Turkey.

Alfonso suspects Lucrezia (sop.) of an affair with Gennaro (ten.); he is actually her son, though she alone knows it. When he is arrested she arranges his escape. She poisons some men who taunt her, only to find that she has also killed her son.

Ludikar (–Vyskočil), **Pavel** (*b* Prague, 3 Mar. 1882; *d* Vienna, 19 Feb. 1970). Czech bass-baritone. Studied Prague, and Paris with Lassalle. Début Prague, N., 1904, Sarastro. After appearances in Austria, Germany, and Italy, where he was the first Italian Ochs, he made his U.S. début with the Boston Civic Opera in 1913. N.Y., Met., 1926–32. Sang Figaro more than 110 times while with Hinshaw O.C. Director Prague N. 1935; created the title role in Křenek's *Karl V* in 1938. (R)

Ludwig II of Bavaria (*b* Nymphenburg, 25 Aug. 1845; *d* Lake Starnberg, 13 June 1886). Son of Maximilian II, he succeeded his father in 1864. He took only a sporadic interest in the affairs of state, and lived a partly withdrawn life. Devoting himself to the patronage of Wagner, he provided a home in Munich, appointed Bülow court pianist, allotted Wagner the Villa

Pellet on Lake Starnberg, and made plans for a festival theatre in Munich to house *The Ring*, engaging Semper for the purpose. Though the latter project was prevented by the government, Ludwig was instrumental in getting the Court Opera to give the premières of *Tristan* (1865), *Meistersinger* (1868), *Rheingold* (1869), and *Walküre* (1870). Wagner's autobiography *Mein Leben* was undertaken at Ludwig's request. Dissension followed Wagner's deception of Ludwig over his affair with Cosima, though Ludwig continued to provide support. Finally he helped Wagner with money to build the Bayreuth Festspielhaus (he lent 200,000 marks) and the Villa Wahnfried.
Bibl: W. Blunt: *The Dream King* (1970).

Ludwig, Christa (*b* Berlin, 16 Mar. 1928). German mezzo-soprano. Her parents, Eugenie Besalla and Anton Ludwig, were both singers at the Vienna V.O in the 1920s. Her father later became intendant at Aachen. She studied with her mother and Felice Hüni-Mihaček. Début Frankfurt 1946, Orlovsky. After engagements in Darmstadt, Hanover, and Hamburg, she sang Cherubino at Salzburg in 1954 and was engaged for the Vienna S.O. in 1955. N.Y., Met., since 1959. London, C.G., 1976, Carmen. As Octavian, the Composer, and Eboli, she established herself as one of the leading mezzo-sopranos of the day; then in 1962 sang successfully as Leonore in *Fidelio*. She went on to sing other soprano roles, including the Marschallin and the Dyer's Wife; also added Dido (*Troyens*) and Charlotte to her mezzo repertory. (R)

Ludwig, Leopold (*b* Ostrava-Vitkovice, 12 Jan. 1908). Austrian conductor. Studied Vienna. Début Jablonec 1929. Held appointments at Opava (1931), Brno, Oldenburg (1936–9), Vienna (1939–43), Berlin (Stä. O. 1943–50). Generalmusikdirektor 1950-71, Hamburg S.O. Has appeared as guest conductor all over Europe, including Edinburgh (1952 and 1956), Gly. (1959), San Francisco (1958– 68), and at the Colón. (R)

Luisa Miller. Opera in 3 acts by Verdi; text by Cammarano, after Schiller's tragedy, *Kabale und Liebe* (1784). Prod. Naples, S.C., 8 Dec. 1849, with Gazzaniga, Salvetti, Malvezzi, De Bassini, Selva, Salandri, Arati, Rossi, cond. Verdi; Philadelphia 27 Oct. 1852, with C. Richings, Bishop, P. Richings, Röhr, McKeon, cond. Cunningham; London, S.W., 3 June 1858.
The opera, set in the Tyrol in the early 18th cent., tells of the love of Luisa (sop.), daughter of an old soldier, Miller (bar.), for Rodolfo (ten.), son of Count Walter. Rodolfo is expected to marry Frederica (mezzo), Duchess of Ostheim, and when he refuses is imprisoned by his father. He also arrests Luisa's father and then gets his follower Wurm (bass) to make Luisa

write a letter to Rodolfo saying she is in love with someone else. When Rodolfo is released from prison, he makes Luisa confess that she wrote the letter, and poisons both himself and Luisa. Before the poison takes effect, Luisa reveals to Rodolfo that Wurm forced her to write the letter, and Rodolfo kills him.

Lully, Jean-Baptiste (orig. Giovanni Battista Lulli) (*b* in or nr Florence, 28 Nov. 1632; *d* 22 Mar. 1687). French composer of Italian birth. Studied privately; taken to France aged 11 or 12. He soon attracted the attention of Louis XIV and entered his service; became master of music at Court. In 1662 he became friendly with Molière and collaborated with him in many ballets until 1671. He produced his first French opera, *Les Fêtes de l'Amour et de Bacchus* in 1672. In the next 20 years he composed 20 operas to texts of every kind by *Quinault, establishing the tradition that was later to represent one side in the *Guerre des bouffons – the formal French overture, accompanied recitative strictly conforming to the rules of good declamation, and conventionally planned arias, with everything disciplined and elevated as befitted the entertainment of *Le Roi Soleil*.
In this careful attention to formality, there was a certain rigidity; but it is remarkable to what extent Lully makes this a strength, largely through his understanding of proportion allied to an acute stage sense and a melodic strength that is not only dignified but often elegant or touching or witty. Despite his Italian origins, both by birth and by artistic ancestry in the operas of Cavalli, Lully is with reason regarded as the founder of a French national opera, then known as *tragédie lyrique*. Apart from the elements already mentioned, this included an increased importance given to the chorus and an obligatory ballet. His operas are *Cadmus et Hermione* (1673), *Alceste* (1675), *Thésée* (1675), *Atys* (1676), *Isis* (1677), *Psyché* (1678), *Bellérophon* (1679), *Proserpine* (1680), *Persée* (1682), *Phaëton* (1683), *Amadis de Gaule* (1684), *Roland* (1685), *Armide et Renaud* (1686), *Acis et Galatée* (1686), and *Achille et Polyxène* (1687, with Colasse). Operas on him are by Isouard (*Lully et Quinault*, 1812), Larochejagu (*La Jeunesse de Lully*, 1846), Berens (1859), H. Hoffmann (*Lully*, 1889), and Peau (*La Jeunesse de Lully*), and he appears in Grétry's *Les trois ages de l'Opéra* (1778).
Bibl: H. Prunières: *Lully* (1910).

Lulu. Unfinished opera by Alban Berg; text by composer, after Wedekind's dramas *Erdgeist* (1895) and *Die Büchse der Pandora* (1901). Prod. Zurich, 2 June 1937, with Hadzič, Bernhard, Feichtinger, Baxevaux, Felier, Melzer, Stig, Emmerich, Monische, Frank, cond. Denzler; London, S.W., by Hamburg O., 1 Oct. 1962, with Lear, cond. Ludwig; Santa Fé, 7 Aug.

1963, with Joan Carroll, cond. Robert Craft. Completed version due Paris, O., 1979.

Lulu (sop.) is a *femme fatale* who destroys all her lovers – though there is little love in any of the transactions, except from the Countess Geschwitz (mezzo). Eventually she comes to London as a prostitute, and is killed by Jack the Ripper.

Also opera (after Wieland) by Mainzer (announced 1853).

Lumley (orig. Levy), **Benjamin** (*b* London, 1811; *d* London, 17 Mar. 1875). English opera manager. A lawyer by profession, he was the legal adviser to *Laporte, whom he succeeded as manager of H.M.'s in 1841. He remained manager of the theatre until 1852, when he was forced to close owing to lack of public support after the opening of C.G. Reopened the theatre in 1856 and retired in 1859. From 1850 to 1851 also manager of the T.I., Paris. During his management of H.M.'s gave the first performances in England of *Linda di Chamounix, La favorite, Maria di Rohan, Don Pasquale, Ernani, I due foscari, Attila, I Lombardi, Nabucco, Luisa Miller, La traviata, Il trovatore, and I masnadieri* (the latter commissioned by him from Verdi). He introduced several great singers to London, including Jenny Lind, Frezzolini, Cruvelli, Piccolomini, Tietjens, Staudigl, Giuglini, and Ronconi. His company further included Grisi, Mario, Persiani, Tamburini, and Lablache, it was his quarrel with the first four that led to the establishment of the Royal Italian Opera at C.G. His *Reminiscences of the Opera,* published in 1864, gives a vivid, if one-sided, picture of London operatic life in the 1840s and 1850s.

Lunn, Louise Kirkby (*b* Manchester, 8 Nov. 1873; *d* London, 17 Feb. 1930). English mezzo-soprano. Studied Manchester with J. H. Greenwood and R.C.M. with Visetti. Début, while still a student, D.L. 1893 as Margaret in Schumann's *Genoveva*. Appeared in Stanford's *Shamus O'Brien* at Opéra-Comique, London, 1896; then sang small roles at C.G. that summer. Carl Rosa 1897–9; C.G. regularly 1901–14 and 1919–22. N.Y., Met., 1902–3, 1906–8. In 1904 she sang Kundry in the first performance in English of *Parsifal* at Boston. At C.G. she was a famous Fricka, Brangaene, Ortrud, Amneris, and Delilah. She sang in the first English performances of *Hélène* and *Hérodiade* (Massenet), *Armide,* and *Eugene Onegin.* Her large rich voice, under superb control, ranged from g to b''. (R)

Lussan, Zélie de. See *De Lussan.*

Lustigen Weiber von Windsor, Die (The Merry Wives of Windsor). Opera in 3 acts by Nicolai; text by Mosenthal, after Shakespeare's comedy (1600–1). Prod. Berlin, Court, 9 Mar. 1849, with Tuczek, Zschiesche, cond. Nicolai; Philadelphia, 16 Mar. 1863; London, H.M.'s 3

May 1864 (as *Falstaff*), with Tietjens, Santley. Nicolai's last and most important opera, for some time exceeding even Verdi's *Falstaff* in popularity on German stages.

Very much the same plot as Verdi's *Falstaff,* but without Bardolph and Pistol, and with Slender and Master Page. The Wives are given German names: Frau Fluth (Alice), Frau Reich (Meg).

Lustige Witwe, Die (The Merry Widow). Operetta in 3 acts by Lehár; text by Viktor Léon and Leo Stein, after Meilhac's comedy *L'Attaché.* Prod. Vienna, W., 30 Dec. 1905, with Günther; London, Daly's T., 8 June 1907, with Lily Elsie; N.Y., New Amsterdam T., 21 Oct. 1907. The gay, complicated plot deals with the attempts of Baron Mirko Zeta (bass) to obtain the Merry Widow Hanna Glawari's (sop.) fortune for his impoverished country of Pontevedria by getting his young compatriot Danilo (ten.) to marry her.

Luxon, Benjamin (*b* Redruth, 24 Mar. 1937). British baritone. Studied London, G.S.M. with Walter Grünner. Début with E.O.G., 1963 U.S.S.R. tour as Sid (Albert Herring) and Tarquinius (*Rape of Lucretia*). Created title-role *Owen Wingrave* (B.B.C. TV 1971). C.G., since 1972, created Jester and Death in Davies's *Taverner*; Diomede in revival of *Troilus and Cressida* (1976). Gly. since 1972 as Ulysses (Monteverdi), Count Almaviva, Don Giovanni, Papageno; E.N.O. as Posa in *Don Carlos.* Repertory also includes Eisenstein, Wolfram, Onegin. A gifted singer and actor with a strong stage personality. (R)

Luzzati, Emanuele (*b* Genoa, 3 July 1921). Italian designer. Studied Lausanne and began career in the theatre in 1947; has since designed operas for most of the leading Italian opera houses, especially in collaboration with the producer Franco Enriquez, who brought him to Gly. in 1963 for *Die Zauberflöte.* Since then he has designed *Macbeth, Die Entführung aus dem Serail, Don Giovanni,* and *Così fan tutte* there, and *A Midsummer Night's Dream* for the E.O.G. Favours greens and blues in his designs, and uses moving panels and revolving pillars to simplify scene changes.

Lvov. Russian family of musicians and artists.

(1) **Nikolay** (Alexandrovich) (*b* Tver Govt., 1751; *d* St Petersburg, 1803) was a poet and architect who wrote the libretto for Fomin's *The Postdrivers* (1788). His great-nephew

(2) **Alexey** (Fyodorovich) (*b* Reval, 5 June 1798; *d* nr Kovno, 28 Dec. 1870) was a composer and violinist. Studied music before joining the army, and after holding several government appointments and acting as adjutant to the Tsar, was Director of the Imperial Court Chapel, 1837. He wrote the Russian national anthem, and also won an international

reputation as a violinist. His operas, none of which was very successful, are *Bianca und Gualtiero* (1844), *Undina* (1848) (to the libretto later used by Tchaikovsky), and *Boris the Headman* (1854).

Lyceum Theatre, London. Originally built in 1772 to house exhibitions and for concerts, it was converted into a theatre in 1792 by Dr Arnold, who wanted to perform operas and other musical entertainments there. He was unable to procure a licence until 1809, when the theatre housed the Drury Lane English Opera Company, after D.L. burned down. In 1812, Samuel Arnold was able to retain the licence and the theatre became known as the English Opera House. Rebuilt in 1815; 1816–30 again known as the English Opera House, it staged works by Bishop, Braham, Loder, and others. In 1824 *Freischütz* received its first English performance there as *Der Freischütz or the Seventh Bullet*; in 1828 the first perf. in English of *Così fan tutte* was given there under the title of *Tit for Tat, or The Tables Turned.* Burned down again in 1830; rebuilt and opened in 1834. A long series of English Romantic operas was inaugurated with Barnett's *The Mountain Sylph.* Balfe, who himself sang at the Lyceum in 1839, took over its management in 1840. In 1856 and 1857, while C.G. was being rebuilt, it housed Gye's C.G. company and became known as the Royal Italian Opera. Mapleson took the theatre for 1861, when he thought he had Patti under contract (which he did not), but nonetheless mounted the first English perf. of *Un ballo in maschera.* Seasons by the Carl Rosa Co. were given in 1876 and 1877, and again in the 1920s and 1930s. The Sc. Milan company under Faccio gave first perf. in England of *Otello* in 1889. In 1931 Beecham gave his last season of Russian opera there with Shalyapin as the chief attraction. In 1935 George Lloyd's *Ierin* was given its first production there. In 1945 the theatre became a dance hall.

Lyons (Fr. Lyon). Town in Rhône, France. An Académie Royale de Musique was opened in 1676, moving to a new theatre in 1689, then to another under Nicolas Levasseur. In 1707 the opera moved to the rue St. Jean, but various fires and other vicissitudes seriously affected the development of operatic life. The Grand T. was built by J.-G. Soufflot in 1754–6, rebuilt in its present form in 1831 (opened with *La Dame blanche*), and enlarged again in 1842 from a cap. of 1,800 to 3,000. Subsequently known as the T. Impérial, the Grand T. and now the Opéra Grand T. The first French *Meistersinger* was staged there, and much Wagner performed. In recent years, under Louis Erlo and with Theodor Guschlbauer as music director, the theatre has pursued an adventurous policy including productions of works by Dallapiccola, Berg, Martinů, and Weill.

Lysenko, Mykola (Vitalyevich) (*b* Hrynky, 22 Mar. 1842; *d* Kiev, 6 Nov. 1912). Russian (Ukrainian) composer. Studied with Panochini, Dimitryev, and Wilczek, Leipzig with Reinecke and Richter. His operas and operettas were very popular in his native Ukraine, and were admired by Tchaikovsky and Rimsky-Korsakov. Many of them are based on Gogol. They include *Christmas Eve* (comp. 1873, prod. 1883), *Natalka Poltavka* (1889), and *Taras Bulba* (comp. 1890; prod. 1924). Attempts by Tchaikovsky and others to have his works staged in Moscow were frustrated by his dislike of having them translated into Russian.

M

Maag, Peter (*b* St Gallen, 10 May 1919). Swiss conductor. Studied with Franz von Hoesslin and Ansermet. Début Biel-Solothurn 1943 as répétiteur and chorus master, conductor from 1945; début in opera, *Zauberflöte*. Düsseldorf 1952–4; Bonn 1954–9, where he conducted *La rappresentazione di anima e di corpo* and Schumann's *Genoveva*; Vienna, V., 1964; London, C.G., 1958 and 1977; Chicago, Lyric O., 1961; N.Y., Met., from 1974. After successful appearances in various Italian houses, including Venice and Parma, engaged as musical director Turin, T.R., 1974-6. A gifted Mozart conductor. (R)

Maas, Joseph (*b* Dartford, 30 Jan. 1847; *d* London, 16 Jan. 1886). English tenor. Studied Rochester, where he was a chorister in the cathedral, and later with San Giovanni in Milan. Début London, C.G., 1872 in *Babil and Bijou* (operetta). Opera début Kellog English Opera Company, U.S.A., 1873, Faust. C.R. 1878–81; London, H.M.'s 1880; and C.G. 1883 as Lohengrin; D.L. 1885, where he was the first Des Grieux (Massenet) in London. Also first English Rienzi (1879), Wilhelm Meister (*Mignon*), and Radamès (both 1880).

Maastricht. Town in Holland. The Zuid-Nederlandse Opera, founded 1948, gives 70 performances a year in Limburg, N. Brabant, and Zeeland.

Maazel, Lorin (*b* Paris, 6 March 1930). American conductor. Studied New York with Vladimir Bakaleinikoff and first appeared as child prodigy; invited by Toscanini to conduct N.B.C. orchestra. After further study in U.S.A. and Europe began adult career. Bayreuth, 1960, *Lohengrin*, 1968-9, *Ring*; N.Y., Met., 1962 *Don Giovanni*. Music director Berlin, D., 1965-71. London, C.G., 1978, *Luisa Miller*. (R)

Macbeth. Opera in 4 acts by Verdi; text by Piave, after Shakespeare's tragedy (1605–6). Prod. Florence, T. della Pergola, 14 Mar. 1847, with Barbieri-Nini, Rossi, Brunacci, Benedetti, Varesi, cond. Verdi; N.Y., Niblo's Garden, 24 Apr. 1850, with Bosio, Badiali, cond. Arditi; Dublin, 30 Mar. 1859, with Viardot, cond. Arditi; Gly. 21 May 1938, with Schwarz, Valentino, Lloyd, Franklin, cond. Busch (productions had previously been announced in London for 1861 and 1870). Prod. St Petersburg, 1855, as *Sivardo il sassone*. For the Paris première a new version was made by Verdi and Piave from the French translation of Nuittier and Beaumont, which includes the addition of Lady Macbeth's 'La luce langue' in Act 2, a new Exiles' Chorus, the opening and final choruses of Act 4, and the battle fugue. Prod. Paris, T.L., 19 Apr. 1865, with Rey-Balla, Montjaure, Ismael, Petit, cond. Deloffre.

A straightforward adaptation of Shakespeare's play, with Macbeth (bar.), Lady Macbeth (sop.), Banquo (bass), Macduff (ten.), and Malcolm (ten.).

Other operas on the subject are by Aspelmayr (1777), Bishop (1819), Chélard (1827), Taubert (1857), L. Rossi (*Biorn*, 1877), Bloch (1910), Gatty (20th cent., not prod.), Collingwood (1934), Goedicke (1944).

McCormack, (Count) **John** (*b* Athlone, 14 June 1884; *d* Dublin, 16 Sept. 1945). Irish tenor. Won gold medal for singing in 1904; then studied with Sabatini in Milan. Début Savona 1906 as Fritz; London, C.G., 1907 as Turiddu; N.Y., Manhattan Opera, 1909 as Alfredo. Sang with Boston, Philadelphia-Chicago, and N.Y. Met. Opera Companies. Created Lieut. Paul Merrill in Victor Herbert's *Natoma* (1911). Gave up opera after 1913, being on his own admission a poor actor, and devoted rest of his life to concert work. Repertory of 21 roles, of which the most famous were Don Ottavio, Rodolfo, Elvino, Edgardo, and the Duke of Mantua. His exquisite phrasing, impeccable breath control, and pure, limpid voice made him one of the outstanding singers of his day. (R)
Bibl: J. MacCormack: *John McCormack. His Life Story* (1919); R. Foxall: *John McCormack* (1963).

McCracken, James (John Eugene) (*b* Gary, 16 Dec 1926). American tenor. Studied New York with Walter Ezekiel and Mario Pagano. Début Central City 1952, Rodolfo. N.Y., Met., 1953-7 in small roles. After engagements in Bonn, Vienna, and Zurich, returned to U.S.A. to sing Otello in Washington. Met again from 1963 as leading tenor. London, C.G., since 1964 as Otello, Manrico, Florestan, Calaf. Repertory also includes Samson, Don José, Hermann in *Queen of Spades*. A huge, impressive figure on the stage, with a voice to match, and an exciting performer. Married to the mezzo-soprano Sandra Warfield. (R)

MacCunn, Hamish (*b* Greenock, 22 Mar. 1868; *d* London, 2 Aug. 1916). Scottish composer. Studied with Parry and Stanford; later worked in the C.R., conducting the first English-language *Tristan* 1898, also conducting with the Moody-Manners Opera Company and at C.G. in Beecham season, 1910. As a composer, he was basically German-influenced; and his talent, though distinctive, was not profound enough to reconcile this with the Scottish musical cause dear to his heart. The *rapprochement* is most successfully achieved in *Jeanie Deans* (1894) and to a lesser extent in *Diarmid* (1897).

He later moved away from Scottish interests, and two later light operas are unremarkable.

MacFarren, (Sir) **George** (Alexander) (b London, 2 Mar. 1813; d London, 31 Oct. 1887). English composer. Studied with Charles Lucas and at R.A.M., of which he was director from 1876. He had a number of his operas produced in London, the most successful being King Charles II (1849) and Robin Hood (1860); other operas are The Devil's Opera (1838), An Adventure of Don Quixote (1846), Jessie Lea (1863), and Helvellyn (1864). Knighted 1883. His wife **Natalia Macfarren** (orig. Andrae, b Lübeck 1827; d Bakewell, 9 Apr. 1916) was a contralto (she sang in King Charles II) and a gifted translator of opera and Lieder.

M'Guckin, Barton (b Dublin, 28 July 1852; d Stoke Poges, 17 Apr. 1913). Irish tenor. Studied Armagh, Dublin, and Milan. Appeared in concerts from 1874; stage début Birmingham with C.R. 1878. Remained with C.R. until 1887, creating Phoebus in G. Thomas's Esmeralda (1883), Orso in Mackenzie's Colomba (1883), Waldemar in G. Thomas's Nordissa (1887). The first Des Grieux (Massenet) in England (Liverpool). Appeared in U.S.A. 1887–8; rejoined C.R. 1889–96. (R)

McIntyre, Donald (b Auckland, N.Z., 22 Oct. 1934). New Zealand bass-baritone. Studied London, G.S.M. Début 1959, W.N.O., Cardiff, Zaccaria (Nabucco). London, S.W., 1960–66 including title-role in Attila, Caspar, and Mozart repertory; C.G., since 1967 as Pizarro, Wotan, Aegisthus, Jochanaan, Orestes, Golaud, Escamillo, Dutchman, Kothner, Kurwenal, Klingsor, Amfortas, Shaklovity; created Heyst in Bennett's Victory. Bayreuth since 1967 as Telramund, Wotan, Dutchman, Klingsor; guest appearances Milan, Hamburg etc. Has established himself as one of the leading Heldenbaritons of the 1970s. (R)

Macintyre, Margaret (b India, c1865; d London, Apr. 1943). English soprano. Studied London with Garcia. Début London, St George's Hall, 1885, Countess C.G. 1888–97. Her repertory included Donna Elvira, Senta, and Elisabeth. Created Rebecca in Sullivan's Ivanhoe at Royal English Opera (1891) and also appeared with success at Milan Sc. (she was the first Sieglinde there), and in St Petersburg and Moscow.

Mackerras, (Sir) (Alan) **Charles** (MacLaurin) (b Schenectady, New York, 17 Nov. 1925). Australian conductor. Descended on his mother's side from Menehem Mona, Jewish cantor of Canterbury, and from Isaac Nathan, the 'Father of Australian music'. Studied Sydney, N.S.W. Conservatory, and Prague with Talich. London, S.W., 1948–54 as staff conductor; conducted first British stage performance of Káťa Kabanová and 19 other operas. E.O.G.,

1955–60, including premières of Berkeley's Ruth and Britten's Noyes Fludde; Berlin (East) State Opera, 1961–3; Hamburg State Opera, 1965–70. Returned S.W. 1963 and conducted first British performances of The Makropoulos Case and From the House of the Dead and a new musical edition of Le nozze di Figaro in 1965, complete with appoggiaturas and decorations. London, C.G., as guest conductor since 1964; N.Y., Met., 1972; Paris, O., since 1973. Music director, S.W. (later E.N.O.) 1970–77. His catholic tastes, enthusiasm, and energy, coupled with his musicianship and scholarship, combine to make him one of the outstanding opera conductors of the day. (R)

Ma dall' arido stelo divulsa. Amelia's (sop.) aria opening Act 2 of Verdi's Un ballo in maschera, when she has come to a lonely spot to pick a herb to cure her love for Riccardo.

Madama Butterfly. Opera in 2 acts by Puccini; text by Giacosa and Illica, after David Belasco's drama (1900) on the story by John Luther Long, possibly based on a real event. Prod. Milan, Sc., 17 Feb. 1904, with Storchio, Zenatello, De Luca, cond. Campanini, when it was a fiasco. New version (three acts) prod. Brescia, Grande, 28 May 1904, with Krusceniski, Zenatello cond. Campanini; London, C.G., 10 July 1905 with Destinn, Caruso, Scotti cond. Campanini; Washington, 15th Oct. 1906, with Szamosy, Sheehan, Goff, cond. Rothwell.

Pinkerton (ten.), an American naval officer, falls in love with a young Japanese geisha girl, Cio-Cio-San (sop.), known as Butterfly, and goes through a ceremony of marriage with her, despite the warnings of the American Consul, Sharpless (bar.). Pinkerton goes back to America, but Butterfly waits for his return with their child 'Trouble' and her servant Suzuki (mezzo). Pinkerton returns with his new American wife and learns that he has a son. The grief-stricken Butterfly kills herself.

Madame Sans-Gêne. Opera in 3 acts by Giordano; text by Simoni after the drama by Sardou and Moreau. Prod. N.Y., Met., 25 Jan. 1915, with Farrar, Martinelli, Amato, cond. Toscanini; Turin, 28 Feb. 1915 with Farneti, Grassi, Stracciari, cond. Panizza. The story of Catherine Huebscher (the laundress, later Duchess of Danzig), Napoleon Bonaparte, and Lefèbvre. Also opera by Dłuski (1903).

Madamina. Leporello's (bass) *catalogue aria in Act 1, scene 2, of Mozart's Don Giovanni enumerating Giovanni's conquests to Donna Elvira.

Maddalena. Sparafucile's sister (mezzo) in Verdi's Rigoletto.

Madeira (orig. Browning), **Jean** (b Centralia, 14 Nov. 1918; d Providence, 10 July 1972). American mezzo-soprano. Studied Juilliard

School. Début Chautauqua, as Jean Browning, 1943, Nancy (*Martha*). N.Y., Met., 1948. Sang Carmen, Puerto Rico 1954, and in Vienna, Aix-en-Provence, Munich. London, C.G., 1955, Erda;•Bayreuth 1955; Salzburg 1956, Klytemnestra. Sang regularly in Munich and Vienna, returning to Met. 1956. Created Circe in Dallapiccola's *Ulisse*, Berlin 1968. Had a rich, dark voice and a compelling stage presence. (R)

Madeleine de Coigny. A noblewoman, heroine (sop.) of Giordano's *Andrea Chénier.*

Maderna, Bruno (*b* Venice, 21 April 1920; *d* Darmstadt, 13 Nov. 1973). Italian conductor and composer. Studied Venice with Malipiero, Milan with Pizzetti, and Vienna with Scherchen. Conducted premières of Nono's *Intolleranza* (Venice, 1960), Berio's *Passaggio* (Milan, 1963), and his own *Satyricon* (Holland 1973). Florence Festival 1964, 1970; Holland Festival, 1965–8 and 1973; Milan, Sc., 1967; N.Y., Juilliard School, 1970 *Il giuramento*, 1971 *La clemenza di Tito*; City Opera, 1972 *Don Giovanni*. As well as being expert in the modern repertory, he had a special interest in Monteverdi and Rameau. (R)

Madrid. Opera was first given in the private Royal theatres, initially in the Palacio Real Buen Retiro for Philip IV. At the Real Sitio del Buen Retiro, an island was used for for open-air performances. An Italian company gave performances in 1703 and 1708, then at the T. de los Canos del Peral. Philip V arranged for Farinelli to come and sing nightly to him as a cure for his melancholy. From 1740 the theatre ·gave performances in Spanish. The T. del Real Palacio was opened in 1849, the T. Real in 1850 with *La favorita*. Theatres that opened in the 19th cent. included the T. del Liceo, the T. del Instituto (1839) where zarzuela was given, the T. del Circo, originally for equestrian performances but also used by Italian singers, the T. del Museo, the T. del Variedades (1842), the Circo del Príncipe Alfonso (as an opera house renamed the Circo de Rivas (1863), where *zarzuelas of the *género chico* were given), and the T. Rossini (1864). The important T. de La Zarzuela opened in 1856. The T. Lírico opened in 1902 (with Chapi's *Circe*, with the intention of paying special attention to Spanish opera. Many of these and other theatres were later closed, but the principal theatres, e.g. the Teatro de la Zarzuela, continue to house short seasons, often with Italian singers as well as Spanish.

Madrigal opera, or **Madrigal comedy.** A dramatic sequence of madrigals, presenting a loosely knit plot in staged form. The most famous early example is Vecchi's *L'Amfiparnasso* (1594); though it was designed by Vecchi to appeal to the imagination through the ear and not the eye, it had some influence in determining the next stage of the experiments that led to opera. Menotti's *The Unicorn, the Gorgon, and the Manticore* is a modern attempt to revive the form.

Mad Scene. A scene in which the hero or heroine goes mad, generally with tragic results. It was a common feature of opera seria, as in Handel's *Orlando*, where the hero, *furioso*, suffers a vision of Hell in which the disturbance of his reason is expressed by irregular rhythms including the first use of quintuple rhythm (which Burney thought would have been intolerable in any sane context). Handel later makes satirical use of the convention in *Imeneo* as the heroine feigns madness. The Mad Scene was a common element in 19th cent. opera: the most famous is in Donizetti's *Lucia di Lammermoor* ('Ardon gl'incensi'), and others occur in his *Anna Bolena* and *Linda di Chamounix*, in Bellini's *I Puritani*, and in Thomas's *Hamlet*. This phase of the convention was satirized by Sullivan with Mad Meg in *Ruddigore*, and in Britten's *Midsummer Night's Dream*. Madness or mental derangement of one sort or another is also depicted in Strauss's *Elektra*, Berg's *Wozzeck*, Stravinsky's *The Rake's Progress*, and Britten's *Peter Grimes.*

Maestro (*It* master). A courtesy title given to composers, conductors, and even impresarios in Italy, sometimes more colloquially in other countries. In the 17th cent. the *maestro al cembalo* (at the keyboard) sat at the harpsichord, guiding the performance; by the end of the 18th cent. this function had been reduced to accompanying secco recitative, and it disappeared with the end of basso continuo. The *maestro di cappella* (of the chapel) was originally the equivalent of the German *Kapellmeister, with duties that included presiding as *maestro al cembalo*. The *maestro sostituto* (deputy) is a coach, répétiteur, and general musical assistant, now usually known as *maestro collaboratore* (in collaboration). The former term *maestro concertatore* (conductor) has now generally given way to *direttore* (*d'orchestra*). The only other musical official with the title *maestro* in an Italian opera house is normally the *maestro di coro* (of the choir).

Maeterlinck, Maurice (*b* Ghent, 29 Aug. 1862; *d* Nice, 6 May 1949). Belgian writer. Operas on his works are as follows:
La Princesse Maleine (1889): Lili Boulanger (unfin.).
Les Aveugles (1890): Achron (1919).
L'Intruse (1890): Pannain (1940).
Les Sept princesses (1891): Nechayev (1923).
Pelléas et Mélisande (1894): Debussy (1902).
Alladine et Palomides (1894): E. Burian (1923);
   Chlubna (1925); Burghauser (1944).

La Mort de Tintagiles (1894): Nouguès (1905); Collingwood (1950).
Ariane et Barbe-Bleue (1901): Dukas (1907).
Monna Vanna (1902): E. Ábrányi (1907); Février (1909); Pototsky (1926); Brânzeu (1934).
Soeur Béatrice (1902): Valasques (1900); Yanovsky (1907); Grechaninov (1912); Mitropoulos (1919); Laliberté (1920); Rasse (1944); Hoiby (1959); Marqués Puig.
Joyselle (1903): A. Cherepnin (1926).
L'Oiseau bleu (1909): Wolff (1919).

Magdalene. Eva's nurse (sop.) in Wagner's *Die Meistersinger*.

Magdeburg. City in Saxony, Germany. The first permanent theatre was built in 1795 with K.G. Dobbelin as music director. Wagner was conductor there 1834-6, and his *Das Liebesverbot* was produced there in 1836 for one night only. A new theatre (cap. 1,200) was opened in 1891 and destroyed during the Second World War. The present house, the Maxim-Gorki-Theater (cap. 1,109), opened in 1959. Lortzing's *Undine* was first prod. there in 1845 and Schubert's 1 act *Fernando* in 1918.

Maggio Musicale Fiorentino. The annual May Festival in Florence was established in 1933, largely due to the initiative of Vittorio *Gui, who had, in 1928, founded the Florence Orchestra round which the festival was built. Originally planned as a biennial event, it became a yearly festival in 1938, and has continued as such ever since, apart from a wartime interruption, 1943–7. Opera performed in the T. Comunale, T. Pergola, and in the Boboli Gardens is the chief attraction of the festival. Verdi and Rossini are the composers who have contributed most to the festival's success, though it has also been the organizers' aim to include works by Bellini, Cherubini, Donizetti, and Spontini, as well as by various contemporary composers, and by Mozart and Wagner, generally performed by visiting companies from Germany and Austria. Gui was succeeded as artistic director by Mario Labrocca 1936–44. Since the Second World War the festival has been directed by Parisi Votto, Francesco Siciliani, Roman Vlad, and Masimo Bogianckino. Premières have included Pizzetti's *L'Orseolo* (1935) and *Vanna Lupa* (1949), Frazzi's *Re Lear* (1939) and *Don Chisciotte* (1962), and Dallapiccola's *Volo di Notte* (1960), and *Il prigioniero*. First performances in Italy have included Bartók's *Bluebeard's Castle* (1938), Busoni's *Turandot* (1940), *Doktor Faust* (1942) and *Die Brautwahl* (1966), Ravel's *L'Enfant et les sortilèges* (1939), Purcell's *Dido and Aeneas* (1940), Handel's *Acis and Galatea* (1940) and *Orlando* (1959), Lully's *Armide* (1950), Spontini's *Olimpia* (1950) and *Agnese von Hohenstaufen* (1954), Schumann's *Genoveva* (1951), Rameau's *Les Indes galantes* (1953), Pro-

kofiev's *War and Peace* (1953), Tchaikovsky's *Mazeppa* (1954), Cherubini's *Les Abencérages* (1957), Janáček's *Káťa Kabanová* (1957), *Jenůfa* (1960), *Makropoulos Case* (1966), *The Excursions of Mr. Brouček* (1967), Britten's *Billy Budd* (1961), Hába's *Matka* (1964), Schoenberg's *Die glückliche Hand* (1964) and Shostakovich's *The Nose* (1964). In addition there have been important revivals of Cavalli's *Didone* (1952), Peri's *Euridice* (1960), De Gagliano's *Dafne* 1965, and Meyerbeer's *Robert le Diable* (1968) and *L'Africaine* (1971).
Bibl: L. Pinzauti: *Il Maggio Musicale Fiorentino* (1967).

Magic Flute, The. See *Zauberflöte, Die*.

Mahagonny. See *Aufstieg und Fall der Stadt Mahagonny*.

Mahler, Gustav (*b* Kalište, 7 July 1860; *d* Vienna, 18 May 1911). Austrian composer and conductor. Studied Vienna. Début as conductor Summer T., Bad Hall, 1880. Appointments followed at Ljubljana 1881; Olomouc 1882-3; Kassel 1884; Prague 1885 (where Seidl was first conductor and where Mahler gave notable performances of *The Ring*); Leipzig 1886-8 (under Nikisch); Budapest 1888-91 (as director – originally engaged for ten years, but he resigned after two owing to insuperable difficulties); Hamburg 1891-7; Vienna 1897-1907 (appointed conductor in May 1897, director July 1897, and artistic director Oct. 1897). Also conducted London, C.G., 1892, first *Ring* cycle at that theatre and other German works, and D.L.; N.Y., Met., 1907-10, including first American performances of *The Bartered Bride* and *The Queen of Spades*.
It was during his ten years at the Vienna S.O. that Mahler's true greatness as a conductor and director was revealed. He was an ardent perfectionist ('Tradition ist Schlamperei (slovenliness)' he said at the outset) and aimed always at the ideal performance. He built up an ensemble of singers who brought to the Vienna S.O. some of its greatest glories; they included Gutheil-Schoder, Kurz, Mildenburg, Weidt, Mayr, Slezak, Schmedes, Winkelmann, and Weidemann; his chief designer was Alfred Roller. Mahler's newly studied productions in Vienna included *The Ring*, *Figaro*, *Così*, *Entführung*, *Don Giovanni*, and *Zauberflöte* (these five for Mozart's 150th birthday celebrations), *Fidelio*, *Aida*, *Falstaff*, *Die lustigen Weiber*, *Louise*, *Der Corregidor*, *Taming of the Shrew* (Götz), and *Iphigénie en Aulide*. He had many enemies during his period in Vienna – he was Jewish, dictatorial, and he spent lavishly on productions – yet he succeeded in wiping out the deficit which the Opera had accumulated, and in raising the performances to a standard rarely if ever equalled anywhere in the world. His early operas were *Herzog Ernst von*

Schwaben (1877-9?, destroyed), *Die Argonauten* (c1880, destroyed), and *Rübezahl* (1881-3?, lost). He completed and scored Weber's *Die drei Pintos* (1888), and made new versions of *Euryanthe* (1903-4) and *Oberon* (1906), and of Mozart's *Figaro* (1908).
Bibl: H.-L. de la Grange: *Mahler* (1973).

Maid of Pskov, The (also sometimes known as *Ivan the Terrible*). Opera in 4 acts by Rimsky-Korsakov; text by composer, after Lev Mey's drama (1860). Prod. St Petersburg, M., 13 Jan. 1873, with Platonova, Leonova, Melnikov, Orlov, Solovev, Petrov, cond. Naprávník. Rev. 1877 and 1891-2; 3rd version prod. St Petersburg, Panayevsky T., 18 Apr. 1895, by members of St Petersburg Musical Society. New prologue, *Boyarynya Vera Sheloga*, for 2nd version, comp. 1876-7, prod. separately Moscow, Solodovnikov T., 27 Dec. 1898. London, D.L., 8 July 1913, with Brian, Nikolayeva, Petrenko, Andreyev, Alchevsky, Shalyapin, cond. Cooper. Apparently never prod. U.S.A., apart from prologue, N.Y., New Amsterdam T., 9 May 1922 by touring Russian company.

The Tsar (bass) terrorizes Novgorod; the inhabitants of Pskov unite against him and Olga (sop.) and her lover Tucha (ten.) are killed. She turns out to be bearing Tsar Ivan's daughter.

Maid of the Mill, The. Pasticcio in 3 acts arranged by Samuel Arnold; text by Bickerstaffe, after Richardson's 'series of familiar letters', *Pamela* (1740). Prod. London, C.G., 31 Jan. 1765 with Brent, Dibdin, Mattocks; N.Y., John St. T 4 May 1769. The first English work since Purcell in which concerted music was used to accompany stage action, and the first of Arnold's many stage pieces. It drew on music by 18 composers.

Maillart, Aimé (orig. Louis) (*b* Montpellier, 24 Mar. 1817; *d* Moulins, 26 May 1871). French composer. Studied Paris with Leborne and Halévy. Between 1847 and 1864 he composed six operas for Paris, including *Gastibelza* (1847, for the opening of Adam's T. Nat.) and *Les Dragons de Villars* (1856), given in Berlin (1860) as *Das Glöckchen des Eremiten* and in this form popular in Germany.

Mainz. Town in Rhineland-Palatinate, Germany. First performances of Singspiels given there in 1665. First permanent theatre built in 1767. In 1789 the first performance in German of *Don Giovanni* was given. In 1813 a new theatre (cap. 1,400) opened with *La clemenza di Tito* and opera was performed there until it was destroyed in 1942. The present house (cap. 1,100) opened in 1951, with Karl Maria Zwisler as music director; he was succeeded in 1967 by Helmut Wessell-Therhorn. First performances in Germany have included *The Cunning Little Vixen* (1927), Zandonai's *Giulietta e Romeo*

(1927), and Wolf-Ferrari's *La dama boba* (1939).

Maio, Gian Francesco de (known as Ciccio) (*b* Naples, 24 Mar. 1732; *d* Naples, 17 Nov. 1770). Italian composer. Studied with his father Giuseppe de Maio (*b* Naples, 6 Dec. 1697; *d* Naples, 18 Nov. 1771), a well-known opera composer, also with his uncle G. Manno and his great-uncle F. Feo. His operas were very popular and much praised in their day; Mozart spoke of their 'bellissima musica'. They went beyond the traditional opera seria format, handling the arias with greater freedom and loosening the distinctions between aria and recitative. One of his most important operas, *Ifigenia in Tauride*, prod. Mannheim, 1764, was pioneering in its adumbrations of some of Gluck's ideas. He was advanced in drawing material for his overtures from his operas.

Maiorano, Gaetano. See *Caffarelli*.

Maître de Chapelle, Le. Opera in 2 parts by Paer; text by Sophie Gay, after Duval's comedy *Le Souper imprévu* (1796). Prod. Paris, O.C., 29 Mar. 1821 with Boulanger, Martini, Fereol; London, C.G., 13 June 1845; New Orleans, 21 Nov. 1848. Paer's most successful work.

Makropoulos Affair, The (Cz., Věc Makropoulos). Opera in 3 acts by Janáček; text by composer, after Karel Čapek's drama (1922). Prod. Brno, 18 Dec. 1926, with Čvanová, Miřiovská, Otava, Pelc, Olšovský, Pour, Šindler, cond. Neumann; London, S.W., 12 Feb. 1964, with Collier, Dempsey, Herincx, cond. Mackerras; San Francisco 19 Nov. 1966, with Collier, Dempsey, Ludgin, cond. Horenstein.

The famous singer Emilia Marty (sop.) intervenes in a lawsuit concerning some events of 300 years previously and shows first-hand knowledge of the case. She proves to be the victim of a process, invented at that time, for prolonging life, and to be unable to die until she finds the formula. Others, convinced of the truth of her story, are eager to share the secret; but for her, life has grown to be an intolerable burden, every pleasure hopelessly staled. In the end the formula is burnt, and she dies.

Malanotte (-Montresor), **Adelaide** (*b* Verona, 1785; *d* Salò, 31 Dec. 1832). Italian contralto. Début Verona 1806. Created title-role in Rossini's *Tancredi* (Venice 1813). Career continued until 1821. Herold described her as 'superb in appearance' and said that she sang with 'perfect intonation and very refined taste. . . Habits unseemly in a *signorina* were attributed to her, such as that of over use of tobacco and brandies'. Her son, **Giovan Battista Montresor** (*b* Salò, c1800; *d* ?), made his début in Bologna 1824 in Sarti's *Giulio Sabino* and appeared in many theatres until 1860. Director and tenor, Italian Opera at Richmond Hill T., N.Y., 1832-3.

Appeared in Europe until mid-1840s, then taught in Bucharest.

Malatesta. Pasquale's friend (bar.) in Donizetti's *Don Pasquale.*

Malherbe, Charles Théodore (*b* Paris, 21 Apr. 1853; *d* Corneilles, 5 Oct. 1911). French musicologist and composer. Assistant archivist Paris, O., 1896; archivist 1898. Author of books on Wagner, Mozart, Auber, opéra comique, and the Salle Favart. Composer of several opéras comiques. Owner of a great collection of musical autographs, now in the Conservatoire.

Malheurs d'Orphée, Les (The Sorrows of Orpheus). Opera in 3 acts by Milhaud; text by Armand Lunel. Prod. Brussels, La M., 7 May 1926, with Bianchini, Thomas, cond. De Thoran; N.Y., T.H., 29 Jan. 1927 (concert), Humber Coll. 22 May 1958 (staged); London, St Pancras T.H., 8 Mar. 1960, with J. Sinclair, Cameron, cond. Fredman.

Orpheus is a chemist with animals for clients. He takes his lover Eurydice to the mountains where, in spite of all he and his animals can do to help her, she dies.

Malibran (orig. Garcia), **Maria** (Felicia) (*b* Paris, 24 Mar. 1808; *d* Manchester, 23 Sept. 1836). Spanish mezzo-contralto. Daughter of Manuel Garcia, with whom she studied. Appeared aged five at Naples in the child's role in Paer's *Agnese*. Début London, King's T., 1825, Rosina. During her first season sang Felicia in the London première of Meyerbeer's *Il Crociato in Egitto.* N.Y. 1825-6 with her father's opera company, singing in Mozart and Rossini works; while in N.Y. married François Eugène Malibran, from whom she was soon separated. Returned to Europe and enjoyed a series of unparalleled triumphs in Paris, London, Milan, Rome, Naples, and Bologna. In 1830 she formed an attachment with the Belgian violinist De Bériot, whom she married in 1836. In London in 1833 and 1834 she sang at C.G. and D.L. in English (Amina, Leonore in *Fidelio*); D.L. 1836, creating title role in Balfe's *The Maid of Artois.* Created Maria Stuarda, 1835, and famous for her Desdemona (Rossini).She was also a renowned Norma, in which character a statue of her by Geefs was erected in a mausoleum built by her husband in Laeken, Belgium. She died of serious injuries received when she was thrown from her horse in Apr. 1836. She concealed her injuries and insisted on singing at the Manchester Festival in Sept. that year. Her voice was that of a contralto with a soprano register added, but with an interval of dead notes in between, which she had learned to conceal with great skill. Its chief attraction seems to have lain in the unusual colour and extent of her voice, and in her excitable temperament. She has been the subject of several biographies and tributes, including Musset's famous *Stances* and Pougin's *Marie Malibran: The Story of a Great Singer* (London, 1911). Also the heroine of Robert R. Bennett's 3-act opera, *Maria Malibran* (1935).

Maliella. The heroine (sop.) in Wolf-Ferrari's *I gioielli della Madonna.*

Malipiero, Gian Francesco (*b* Venice, 18 Mar. 1882; *d* Treviso, 1 Aug. 1973). Italian composer. His great knowledge and love of old music has found practical expression in editorial work on complete editions of Monteverdi and Vivaldi, and has also deeply influenced his composing style. Though contemporary in spirit and outlook, he owes much in his technique to modal harmony, dislike of counterpoint or thematic development, and great rhythmic freedom following syllabic declamation. His long list of operas, many of which were first produced outside Italy, includes *Canossa* (1914), the trilogies *L'Orfeide* (1925) and *Il mistero di Venezia* (1932), seven nocturnes *Torneo notturno* (1931), *Giulio Cesare* (1936), *Antonio e Cleopatra* (1938), *Ecuba* (1941), *I capricci di Callot* (1942), *La vita è sogno* (1943), six novels in one drama *L'allegra brigata* (1950), *'tre atti con sette donne'*, *Mondi celesti e Inferni* (1950), *Il figliuol prodigo* (1953), *Venere prigioniera* (1957), and *Il capitan pavento* (1963).

Malipiero, Riccardo (*b* Milan, 24 July 1914). Italian composer and critic, nephew of the above. He has written one opera in the 12-note system, of which he is a firm advocate, *Minnie la candida* (1942), and an opera buffa, *La donna è mobile* (1954).

Mallinger (orig. Lichtenegger), **Mathilde** (*b* Zagreb, 17 Feb. 1847; *d* Berlin, 19 Apr. 1920). Croatian soprano. Studied Zagreb, Prague with Gordigiani and Vogl, Vienna with Lewy. Début Munich 1866, Norma. Created Eva (*Meistersinger*) 1868; Berlin Opera 1869-82, where in 1871 she became the rival of Pauline Lucca. Quarrels and intrigues resulted, culminating in a performance of *Figaro* (1872) in which they both appeared. Lucca was hissed on her entrance, as a result of which she broke her contract. Professor of singing Prague 1890-5, Berlin from 1895. Her pupils included Lotte Lehmann.

Malta. Island in the Mediterranean. In the middle of the 17th century masques were performed on Carnival days, mostly by the Knights of St John and their followers, in one of the great halls of the Auberges, generally that of Italy. In 1732 the T. Pubblico (later known as the T. Manoel, after Antonio Manuel de Vilhema, Grand Master of the Knights of St John) was opened, and is today the National T. of Malta. It was modelled on the T. San Cecilia of Palermo, and works by Jommelli, Piccinni,

Galuppi, Paisiello, and Cimarosa were heard there during the next 60 years. In 1796 Nicolo Isouard, the Maltese composer, returned home, and several of his works were given.

From 1798 to 1800 the island was occupied by the French, and works by Dalayrac and other French composers were produced. The British occupation followed, and opera was again given by Italian singers, generally from Naples and Palermo. These seasons lasted from Sept. until the following May, and the impresario was contrcted to mount 12 operas each season, of which five had to be new to Malta. By the 1860s 32 of Donizetti's operas had been staged, together with practically every one of Verdi's works up to that time. Opera proved so popular that a new theatre had to be built in Valetta. Designed by Edward Barry, the architect of Covent Garden, it opened on 9 Oct. 1866 with *I Puritani*, Jan. 1847; it burnt down in 1873 and was rebuilt by 1877, opening with *Aida*.

By the turn of the century many famous singers had been heard in Malta, including Albani, Bellincioni, and Scotti (who began his career in Malta in 1890 as Amonasro). From 1900 to 1939 the seasons were very similar to those of the larger Italian houses, with all works, including those of Strauss and Wagner as well as the Russian and French repertory, being sung in Italian. Relatively unfamiliar works by Giordano, Mulé, Zandonai, and others were heard in Malta, often within a few months of their premières in Italy. During World War II the Royal Opera was destroyed, and performances were given by local artists at the Manoel T. and elsewhere; these included *La figlia del sole* by Cervello (a sequel to *Madama Butterfly*). After the war Italian singers were heard again, and in 1961 opera returned to the Manoel T. The seasons of 1966-8 and 1972 were directly subsidized by the Italian government.

Four operas by the Maltese composer Carmelo Pace have been produced in recent years: *I martiri*, *Caterini Oesguanez*, *Angelica*, and *Ipogeana*; but rising costs and changing tastes have meant a general diminution in the amount of opera given each year in Malta.

Malten (orig. Müller), **Therese** (*b* Insterburg, 21 June 1855; *d* Neuzschieren, Saxony, 2 Jan. 1930). German soprano. Studied Berlin with Engel. Début Dresden 1873, Pamina; leading soprano there for 30 years. Bayreuth 1882, Kundry (alternating with Materna and Brandt), and until 1894; also heard there as Isolde. London, D.L., 1882, Leonore, Elsa, Elisabeth, Eva.

Mamelles de Tirésias, Les. *Opéra-bouffe* in 2 acts by Poulenc: text by Guillaume Apollinaire. Prod. Paris O.C., 3 June 1947, with Duval, Rousseau, cond. Wolff; Brandeis University, 13

June 1953; Aldeburgh 16 June 1958, with Vyvyan, Pears, cond. Mackerras. The surrealist plot deals with a husband and wife changing sexes; he produces 40,000 children before reverting to masculinity and advising his audience to proliferate.

Manchester. Town in Lancashire, England. The first theatre in Manchester was built in 1753 and in 1775 the first T. Royal was approved by Parliament. Opera was provided by touring companies and operatic excerpts in the 'Gentlemen's Concerts' until Hallé conducted a season of operas at the Theatre Royal in 1855, including *Fidelio, Don Giovanni, Der Freischütz, Robert le Diable, Les Huguenots, Lucrezia Borgia,* and *La favorite.* He followed this with concert performances at the Free Trade Hall of *Fidelio, Die Zauberflöte,* and Gluck's *Armide, Iphigénie en Tauride,* which he also took to London, and *Orfeo ed Euridice.* The performances of *Iphigénie* and *Orfeo* were the first in English. Opera was also provided by the Rouseby and Parepa-Rosa companies. The latter began its existence in England with a performance in Manchester of *Maritana* on 1 Sept. 1873. After Hallé's death opera was again only provided by touring companies and by ambitious amateurs, though in 1897 Cowen conducted a concert perf. of *Les Troyens à Carthage* after giving the first British concert perf. at Liverpool earlier in the same year. Between 1916 and 1919 Thomas Beecham presented an ambitious series of opera seasons at the New Queen's T., and it seemed as though Manchester would rival London as an operatic centre until Beecham's enforced withdrawal in 1920, when touring companies again took over. Since then amateur opera has flourished, and seasons have been given by C.G. and S.W., and Italian companies, at the Palace T., Opera House, and occasionally at the Hippodrome, Free Trade Hall, and suburban theatres. The following operas have had their first performances in Manchester: Loder's *Raymond and Agnes* (1855), Nicholas Gatty's *Duke or Devil* (1909), Campbell's *Thais and Talmaae* (1921), Holst's *At the Boar's Head* (1925), and Walter Leigh's *Jolly Roger* (1933). Foreign works performed for the first time in Britain at Manchester theatres include Bizet's *Djamileh* (1892) and *La Jolie Fille de Perth* (1917), Gluck's *Le Cadi dupé* (1893), and Puccini's *La Bohème* and *Le Villi* (both 1897).

Mancinelli, Luigi (*b* Orvieto, 6 Feb. 1848; *d* Rome, 2 Feb. 1921). Italian conductor and composer. Studied at Florence and led the cello sec tion at the Teatro della Pergola, Florence, an Rome, Ap., where in 1874 he was called on t fill the place of a drunk conductor in *Aida*. Afte engagements in various Italian cities, con ducted a concert in London in 1886; on th strength of this he was engaged by Harris a chief conductor at D.L., 1887, and C.G., 1888-1905, where he conducted the first performances in England of *Falstaff, Werther, Henri VIII* (Saint-Saëns), *Tosca, Much Ado About Nothing* (Stanford), as well as his own *Ero e Leandro* and many of the De Reszke Wagner performances in Italian. He was music director of the Theatre Royal, Madrid, 1888-95, and principal Italian conductor at the N.Y. Met. 1893-1903, directing the first Met. performances of *Werther, Falstaff, Samson et Dalila, Le Cid, Die Zauberflöte, La Bohème, Tosca,* and *Ernani.* As well as *Ero e Leandro,* his operas included *Isora di Provenza* and *Paolo e Francesca.*

The most important Italian conductor between Faccio and Toscanini, he anticipated the latter in his powerful authority, personal magnetism, and deep fidelity to the score. His Italianate Wagner performances were controversial, but were not without German admirers (including Weingartner). As a composer, he was more successful in creating atmosphere than character, and resisted *verismo* in favour of a classicism he associated with Boito (who in 1877 called him the ideal conductor of *Mefistofele*).

Mancini, Francesco (*b* Naples, 16 Jan. 1672; *d* Naples, 22 Sept. 1737). Italian composer. Studied Naples with Provenzale and Ursino. Scarlatti's most important contemporary in Naples; also made a considerable reputation abroad. His *Idaspe fedele* (1710) was, after the anonymous *Almahide* of the same year, the first opera in Italian in London. Though eclipsed by a younger generation, he continued writing: his *Trajano* (1723) represents the climax of the Neapolitan baroque pageant opera.

Mandini. Italian family of singers.
(1) **Paolo** (*b* Arezzo 1757; *d* Bologna, 27 Jan. 1842). Italian tenor. Début Brescia 1777. St Petersburg, 1795-1800; Moscow, 1797; Berlin. His brother
(2) **Stefano** made his debut as buffo bass in Venice, 1775. Vienna, 1784-88; created Count Almaviva in *Le nozze di Figaro.* Career continued until 1799 in Spain, Italy, and Russia. His wife
(3) **Maria** was the first Marcellina.

Mandryka. The rich landowner (bar.) who marries Arabella in Strauss's opera.

Manelli, Francesco (*b* Tivoli, 1595; *d* Parma, Sept. 1667). Italian composer and bass. In Feb. 1637 his *Andromeda* inaugurated the first public opera house in Italy, the T. San Cassiano in Venice. Manelli himself sang two parts on that occasion.

Manfredini-Guarmani, Elisabeth (*b* Bologna, 1790; *d* ?). Italian soprano. Début Bologna, 1809. Admired by Rossini, for whom she created Amira in *Ciro in Babilonia* (1812), Amenaide in *Tancredi* (1813), Aldimira in *Sigismondo* (1814), and Elisabetta in *Adelaide di Borgogna* (1817). She appeared with success at the Regio, Turin and Milan Sc. Stendhal commended her fine voice but found her 'weak in expression'.

Manfredo. Fiora's husband (bar.) in Montemezzi's *L'amore dei tre re.*

Manhattan Opera Company. The company established by Oscar *Hammerstein in 1906 at the Manhattan O.H., West 34th Street, New York. Opened on 3 Dec. 1906 with *I Puritani,* with Pinkert, Bonci, and Ancona, cond. Campanini (the music director). The first season included the N.Y. débuts of Renaud and Bressler-Gianoli and appearances by Calvé and Melba. The 1907-8 season saw the American premières of *Thaïs, Louise,* and *Pelléas,* all with Mary Garden; the 1908-9 season included the New York première of *Le Jongleur de Notre-Dame* and a revival of *Salome;* the 1909-10 season, the last, included the American premières of *Elektra* (in French), *Hérodiade, Sapho,* and *Grisélidis.* Other artists appearing with the company included Nordica, Tetrazzini, Schumann-Heink, Cavalieri, Zenatello, McCormack, Dalmorès. The company gave 463 performances of 49 operas during its four seasons; besides appearing in N.Y. gave weekly performances in Philadelphia in an opera house built by Hammerstein; and from 1908-10 the Philadephi Co. had its own chorus, orchestra and staff of conductors, giving four or five performances a week, the singers commuting between Philadelphia and New York. In addition, the Manhattan company visited Boston, Cincinnati, Pittsburgh, and Washington.

Its success was so great as to threaten the Met., which finally offered Hammerstein $1,200,000 if he undertook to refrain from giving opera in New York for ten years; he agreed to this proposal and signed a contract to that effect. He tried to break this in 1913 by building the Lexington T., but was restrained by legal action from giving performances.

The Manhattan O.H. was used for the Chicago Opera's N.Y. seasons and other organizations. It was later sold to a Masonic order.

Bibl: J. F. Cone: *Oscar Hammerstein's Manhattan Opera Company* (1964).

Manners, Charles (orig. Southcote Mansergh) (*b* London, 27 Dec. 1857; *d* Dublin, 3 May 1935). Irish bass and impresario. Studied Dublin and London and for a short time in Italy. Joined chorus of D'Oyly Carte Company 1881; début Savoy T., London, 1882, Private Willis (*Iolanthe*). Joined C.R. and then engaged C.G. 1890. Sang Gremin in English première of

Eugene Onegin (1892). In 1897 he established the *Moody-Manners Company with the soprano Fanny Moody, whom he had married in 1890. Appeared in U.S.A. 1893. Retired 1913.

Mannheim. Town in Baden-Württemberg, Germany. The Schlosstheater, designed by Bibiena, opened 1742 with Grua's *Meride*. Carlo Grua, Kapellmeister until 1753, was required to compose one new opera a year. Visitors included Hasse, Galuppi, and Jommelli; other distinguished Italians came at the invitation of Holzbauer, who was Kapellmeister 1753-78. Due largely to the excellence of the famous orchestra, Mannheim opera flowered 1760-70; and after a period when J. C. Bach's Italian operas were in favour, there was a turn towards German opera. Holzbauer's *Günther von Schwarzburg* had a celebrated triumph in 1777. In the same year the Nationaltheater was opened. But the transfer of the Court to Munich badly affected operatic activity, and only one opera a week could be given.

In the early 19th cent. matters improved, and opera enjoyed a particularly prosperous period under V. Lachner, 1837-72, and August Nassermann, 1895-1900. Music directors have included Weingartner (1889-91), Bodanzky (1909-15), Furtwängler (1915-20), Kleiber (1922-3), Elmendorff (1937-43). Works first perf. at Mannheim include Goetz's *Taming of the Shrew* (1874), Wolf's *Der Corregidor* (1896), Wellesz's *Alkestis*, and the first German *Rossignol*, *Prince Igor*, and *From the House of the Dead*; Nabucco was revived there in 1928 after long neglect. The Nationaltheater was bombed in 1943; the new Nationaltheater (cap. 1,200) opened in Jan. 1957 with *Der Freischütz*. Horst Stein was music director 1961-70.

Manon. Opera in 5 acts by Massenet; text by Meilhac and Gille, after Prévost's novel *Manon Lescaut* (1731). Prod. Paris, O.C., 19 Jan. 1884, with Heilbronn, Talazac, Taskin, cond. Danbé; Liverpool 17 Jan. 1885, with Roze, M'Guckin, cond. Goossens sen.; N.Y., Ac. of M., 23 Dec. 1885 with Hauk, Giannini, Del Puente, cond. Arditi. Ten years later, Massenet wrote a sequel, *Le Portrait de Manon* (1894). Other operas on the story by Auber (1856), Kleinmichel (1887), and Puccini (see below).

The Chevalier Des Grieux (ten.) falls in love with Manon (sop.), whom he meets as she stops at an inn in Amiens with her cousin Lescaut (bar.) on her way to a convent; the young lovers elope to Paris. De Brétigny (bar.), a friend of Lescaut, persuades Manon to go away with him. Des Grieux, in despair, decides to enter the priesthood, despite pleas from his father, the Count Des Grieux (bass). Manon comes and persuades Des Grieux to go off with her. At a gambling house Des Grieux is accused of cheating and Manon is arrested as a prosti-

tute and condemned to transportation. Des Grieux bribes an officer for permission to speak to her and tries to persuade her to run away with him. She is too weak to do so and dies in his arms.

Manon Lescaut. Opera in 4 acts by Puccini; text by Giacosa, Illica, Giulio Ricordi, Praga, and Oliva, after Prévost's novel (1731). Prod. Turin, T.R., 1 Feb. 1893, with Ferrani, Cremonini, Moro, cond. Pomé; London, C.G., 14 May 1894, with Olghina, Beduschi, Pini-Corsi, cond. Seppilli; Philadelphia, Grand O.H., 29 Aug. 1894, with Kört-Kronold, Montegriffo, cond. Hinrichs. *Manon Lescaut* was Puccini's third opera and first great success.

Des Grieux (ten.) falls in love with the young Manon (sop.) and they elope, thwarting the plans of the elderly roué Géronte (bass), who is planning to abduct her. Manon deserts Des Grieux and goes to live in splendour with Géronte, but the reappearance of Des Grieux awakens her former love. Géronte has her arrested and she is sentenced to be deported to Louisiana. Des Grieux persuades the captain of the ship to let him accompany her, and they are reunited in the desert near New Orleans, where she dies in his arms.

Manowarda, Josef von (*b* Kraków, 3 July 1890; *d* Berlin, 24 Dec. 1942). Austrian bass. Début Graz 1911. After engagements in Graz, Vienna V.O., and Wiesbaden, was engaged Vienna, S.O., 1919-42. In his initial season in Vienna he created the role of the Messenger in Strauss's *Die Frau ohne Schatten*. He sang at Salzburg from 1922; at Bayreuth in 1931, 1934, 1939 and 1942; and at the Berlin S.O. 1934-42. His most famous roles were King Philip, Osmin, King Mark, and Gurnemanz. (R)

Manrico. A troubadour, hero (ten.) of Verdi's *Il trovatore*.

Manru. Opera in 3 acts by Paderewski; text by Nossig, after Kraszewski's novel *The Cabin Behind the Wood* (1843). Prod. Dresden 29 May 1901; N.Y., Met., 14 Feb. 1902, with Sembrich, Scheff, Horner, Bispham, cond. Damrosch.

Against her mother's wishes, Ulana marries the gipsy Manru. She revives his love with a potion, but the gipsy girl Asa lures him back to his people. Ulana commits suicide and Manru, now chief of the tribe, is killed by Oros, the man he had deposed who himself loves Asa.

Mantelli, Eugenia (*b* c1860; *d* Lisbon, 3 March 1926). Italian mezzo-soprano. Début Treviso, 1883, Kalad (*Le Roi de Lahore*). N.Y., Met., 1894-7, 1898-1900 1902-3; first N.Y. stage Delilah and a famous Urbain, Amneris, and Ortrud. London, C.G., 1896, Brünnhilde in a French-language *Walküre*. Sang title-role in Mascagni's *Zanetto* under composer in N.Y., Manhattan Opera, 1902. After leaving Met. ran her own company 1903-4, and then appeared in variety, 1905-6. Last appearances Lisbon, 1910. (R)

Mantua (It. Mantova). Town in Lombardy, Italy. The first town after Florence to stage opera, though *feste teatrali* had been a feature at Court during the 16th cent. Monteverdi's *Favola d'Orfeo* was produced there in 1607 and his *Arianna* the following year. Other early operas premièred there include Gagliano's *Dafne* and Guarini's *L'idropica*. The singers at that time in the employ of Vincenzo Gonzaga (the Duke of Mantua) included Claudia Cattaneo (Monteverdi's wife), Lucrezia Urbana, Caterinuccia Martinelli, and Adriana Basile. In 1732 the Regio Ducale T. Nuovo, designed by F. Galli Bibiena and A. Galuzzi, opened with *Caio Fabrizio*. It was burned down in 1780(?); redesigned by Piermarini, it reopened in 1783 with Sarti's *Il trionfo della pace*. Vivaldi's *Candace* and *Semiramide* had their premières there in 1720 and 1732. The present Teatro Sociale, designed by L. Cannonica, opened in 1822 with Mercadante's *Alfonso ed Elisa,* and the T. Andreani opened in 1862 with *I masnadieri.*

Manzuoli (Manzoli), **Giovanni** (*b* Florence 1720; *d* Florence, c1780). Italian male soprano. Début Verona 1735 in Vivaldi's *Tamerlano.* Sang in Gluck's *Trionfo di Clelia* for opening of T. Comunale, Bologna (1763). London, 1764-5; admired by J. C. Bach, who wrote *Adriano in Siria* for him: also created title role in Mozart's *Ascanio in Alba* (1771); retired shortly after and taught in Florence. His pupils included Angelo Monanai and Celeste Coltellini.

Mapleson, (Col.) **James Henry** (*b* London, 4 May 1830; *d* London, 14 Nov. 1901). English impresario, popularly known as 'The Colonel'. Studied London, R.A.M. Sang at Verona 1854 as Enrico Mariani. Began his career as impresario 1861 when he took the Ly. after A. T. Smith, whose assistant he had been, abandoned Italian opera. Mapleson's first season included the English première of *Un ballo in maschera.* Managed H.M.'s, 1862-7; in 1868 he was at D.L.; in 1869 and 1870 he joined Gye at C.G. for the two famous 'coalition seasons' at that house; he was again at D.L. 1871-6, and in 1877 he reopened H.M.'s and continued to give seasons there until 1881. In 1885 and 1887 he gave his last seasons at C.G. and in 1887 and 1889 at H.M.'s. Promoted seasons at the Academy of Music, N.Y., 1878-96 and 1896-7, and he also took his company to other American cities.

Among the operas he produced for the first time in England were *Faust, Carmen, Ballo in maschera, La forza del destino, Vêpres siciliennes, Mefistofele,* and *Médée.* He also gave the first U.S. performances of *Carmen, Manon,* and *Andrea Chénier.* Singers he brought to London for the first time included Di Murska, Gerster, Nilsson, Scalchi, Trebelli, Hauk, Nordica; Campanini, Fancelli, Ravelli, Jean de Reszke (as a baritone), Del Puente, and Pandolfini. The *Mapleson Memoirs* (London, 1888; reissued, 1966, ed. Rosenthal) give an amusing and highly coloured account of his operatic activites.

Mapleson, Lionel (*b* London, 23 Oct. 1865; *d* New York, 21 Dec. 1937). Violinist and librarian of the Met., N.Y. Son of Alfred Mapleson, music librarian and secretary to Queen Victoria, and nephew of J. H. Mapleson. He amassed an invaluable collection of operatic mementoes (letters, autographs, programmes, Caruso caricatures, etc.), as well as the scores of all the operas given at the Met. since 1883, and the famous recordings on cylinders, made of a series of performances at the Met. early this century.

M'appari. Italian translation of Lionel's (ten.) aria 'Ach, so fromm' in Act 3 of Flotow's *Martha,* in which he sings of his hopeless love for Martha.

Mara (orig. Schmeling), **Gertrud** (Elisabeth) (*b* Kassel, 23 Feb. 1749; *d* Reval, 20 Jan. 1833). German soprano. Studied London and Leipzig. Début Dresden; then in 1771 engaged by Frederick II for life at the Berlin Opera; she broke her Berlin engagement, however, in 1780 and sang in Paris and Vienna. London début 1786 in *Didone abbandonata.* The following year scored great success as Cleopatra in Handel's *Giulio Cesare.* She sang at C.G. in 1790, earning special praise for her performance in Nasolini's *Andromaca.* Continued to appear in London until 1802, then Moscow 1802-12. Her voice ranged from g^l to e^{lll} and was of great beauty. She was an inferior actress.

Marais, Marin (*b* Paris, 31 Mar. 1656; *d* Paris, 15 Aug. 1728). French composer. Though most of his work is instrumental, Marais produced several operas in the Lully tradition: the most successful, partly for its famous representation of a storm, was *Alcyone* (1706).

Maŕák, Otakar (*b* Ostríhom (Esztergom), Hungary, 5 Jan. 1872; *d* Prague, 2 July 1939). Czech tenor. Originally intended to be a painter, but studied singing Prague Conservatory with Paršova-Zikešová. Début Brno, 1899, Faust. Prague, N., 1900-7, 1914–34; London, C.G., 1908 Don José, Turiddu, Canlo, H.M.'s, 1913 as first London Bacchus; Chicago 1914 Parsifal; guest appearances Vienna, Berlin, etc. Lost most of his money on a sound-film project in the early 1930s and went to U.S.A. to try and recoup his losses, but was soon reduced to selling papers on the streets of Chicago. Funds were raised to finance his return to Prague, but he died soon after returning home. Sang Canio in one of the first complete recordings of *Pagliacci* and was dubbed the Czech Caruso. Married the soprano Mary Cavanová. (R)

Marcel, Lucille (*b* New York, 1877; *d* Vienna, 22 June 1921). American soprano. Studied N.Y., Berlin, and Paris with Jean De Reszke. Début Paris, O.C., 1903, Mallika (*Lakmé*) as Mlle Marcelle. Engaged by Weingartner, whom she later married, for Vienna H., making début in title-role of *Elektra* in opera's first Vienna perf. 1909; Hamburg 1912-14; Boston Opera Company, 1912-14, Tosca, Marguerite, Aida, Desdemona, Eva, and first U.S. Djamileh. (R)

Marcellina. Rocco's daughter (sop.) in Beethoven's *Fidelio*.

Marcello. The bohemian painter (bar.) in Puccini's *La Bohème*.

Märchen (*Ger* tale, esp. fairy-tale). A title occasionally used for a Germany fairy opera.

Marchesi, Blanche (*b* Paris, 4 Apr. 1863; *d* London, 15 Dec. 1940). French soprano, daughter of Mathilde (below). Début Prague 1900, Brünnhilde. Sang with the Moody-Manners Company in England; later settled in London as a teacher. Her autobiography *A Singer's Pilgrimage* appeared in 1923. (R)

Marchesi (Marchesini), **Luigi Lodovico** (*b* Milan, 8 Aug. 1754; *d* Inzago, 14 Dec. 1829). Italian male soprano. Studied with Caironi and in Milan with Fioroni. Début Rome 1773, Giannetta in Anfossi's *L'Incognita perseguitata*. Turin 1782 in Bianchi's *Il trionfo della pace*; appointed Court Musician to King of Sardinia. After appearances in St Petersburg and Vienna, went to London in 1788 where he caused a sensation in Sarti's *Giulio Sabino*, especially among the women. Admired by Mount Edgcumbe, who found him 'incomparable in recitative and scenes of energy and passion... had he been less lavish of ornaments, which were not always appropriate, and possessed of a more pure and simple taste, his performance would have been faultless'. In 1796 refused to sing for Napoleon on his entry into Milan; but in 1800 was one of the first to greet him, with Mrs Billington and Grassini. In Venice involved in rivalry with Luisa Toldi, the Portuguese prima donna. Sang at opening of Teatro Nuovo, Trieste, 1801 in Mayr's *Ginevra di Scozia*, and continued to appear in Milan until 1806.

Marchesi de Castrone (orig. Graumann), **Mathilde** (*b* Frankfurt, 24 Mar. 1821; *d* London, 17 Nov. 1913). German mezzo-soprano and teacher. Studied in Vienna with F. Ronconi and in Paris with Garcia, who was so impressed by her abilities that when an accident forced him to give up teaching he handed over all his pupils to her. Began career as a concert singer, 1849. Married Salvatore Marchesi (below) 1852. Début Bremen 1852, Rosina. Professor of singing, Vienna, 1854-61 and 1869-78; Cologne Conservatory 1865-8. Set up own school in Paris 1861-5 and from 1881. Her pupils included Calvé, Di Murska, Eames, Gerster, Garden, Melba, and Sanderson. She wrote a method of singing and 24 books of exercises. Her memoirs *Marchesi and Music* appeared in 1897.

Marchesi, Salvatore (Cavaliere de Castrone, Marchese della Raiata) (*b* Palermo, 15 Jan. 1822; *d* Paris, 20 Feb. 1908). Italian baritone and teacher. Studied Palermo and Milan with Lamperti and Fontana. Début New York., Carlos in *Ernani*. Returned to Europe to study with Garcia. Held various teaching posts in Vienna and Cologne. Translated into Italian the librettos of *La vestale*, *Médée*, *Iphigénie*, *Lohengrin*, and *Tannhäuser*.

Marchetti, Filippo (*b* Bolognola, 26 Feb. 1831; *d* Rome, 18 Jan. 1902). Italian composer. Studied Naples with Lillo and Conti; also helped by Mercadante. The success of his first opera, *Gentile de Varano* (1856), in Naples was not matched by that of *La demente* (1856) in Turin and elsewhere, and the difficulties of finding a stage for his third opera *Il paria* (not prod.), coupled with the rise of Verdi, led him to withdraw from composition. He moved to Rome in 1862 and began work on *Romeo e Giulietta*, initially a failure in Trieste in 1865 but more successful in Milan in 1867. He fully regained his popularity with *Ruy Blas*, after a poor reception in Milan in 1869, when it was revived in Florence: the work then swept Europe and was even staged in New York. One of the only Italian operas apart from Verdi's to achieve real success in these years, it was followed by two more failures, *Gustavo Wasa* (1875) and *Don Giovanni d'Austria* (1880). Though of the second rank, Marchetti's work was intermittently popular in its day for its melodic charm (the duet 'O dolce voluttà' from Act 3 of *Ruy Blas* was long famous), and to some extent it anticipates *verismo*.

Marchisio, Barbara (*b* Turin, 6 Dec. 1833; *d* Mira, 19 Apr. 1919). Italian contralto. Studied Turin with L. Fabbrica. Début Madrid 1856, Rosina. Sang all over Europe with success, including Paris (1860) and London, H.M.'s (1862) being especially successful as Adalgisa and Arsace. Her sister **Carlotta** (1835-72) often appeared with her and Rossini wrote his *Petite Messe solennelle* for them. She later became a teacher and her pupils included Raisa and Dal Monte. Other members of the family included a brother **Antonio** (1817-1875), who wrote several operas, another brother, **Giuseppe** (1831-1903), a pianist admired by Liszt, and a nephew **Massimo** (1860-1948), who founded the school of church music in Turin.

Marcolini, Marietta (*b* Florence, *c*1780; *d*?). Italian mezzo-soprano. Début uncertain, but already singing in Venice 1800. Naples 1803-4; Rome 1807-8; Milan, Sc., 1809. Greatly admired by Rossini, whom she met in 1811, and who wrote roles for her in five operas: Ernestina in *Lequivoco stravagante* (1811), title-role in *Ciro in Babilonia* (1812), Clarice in *La pietra del paragone* (1812), Isabella in *L'italiana in Algeri*(1913), and title-role in *Sigismondo* (1814). Stendhal suggests that in 1813, she, 'a charming *buffa* singer, then in the flower of her genius and youth, not wanting to be in arrears with Rossini, sacrificed Prince Lucien Bonaparte to him'. Retired from the stage 1820.

Marcoux, Vanni (orig. Jean Émile Diogène) (*b* Turin, 12 June 1877; *d* Paris, 21 Oct. 1962). French bass-baritone. Studied Turin with Collino, Paris with Bryer. Début Bayonne 1889, Frère Laurent. After appearances in France and Belgium, sang London, C.G., 1905-14, where he was the first English Arkel (*Pelléas*) (he returned to sing Golaud in 1937); Boston 1912; Chicago 1913-14 and 1926-32, where he was the first American Don Quichotte (Massenet), a role he had created at Monte Carlo 1910, and Colonno in Février's *Monna Vanna*, which he created in Paris 1909. He had a repertory of 240 roles. Taught at the Conservatoire 1938-43; director Grand T., Bordeaux, 1948-51. Made a few appearances in Paris, O.C., in the post-war years as Don Quichotte. (R)

Maréchal, Adolphe (*b* Liège, 26 Sept. 1867; *d* Brussels, 1 Feb. 1935). Belgian tenor. Studied Liège. Début Tournai 1891. Paris, O.C., 1895-1907 where he created Julien in *Louise* (1901), Alain in *Grisélidis* (1901), Daniélo in Leroux's *La Reine fiammette* (1903). At Monte Carlo he created Jean in *Le Jongleur de Notre-Dame* (1902). London, C.G., 1902, Don José, Faust, Des Grieux. Lost his voice in 1907. (R)

Marenka. The heroine (sop.) of Smetana's *The Bartered Bride*.

Maretzek (orig. Mareček), **Max** (*b* Brno, 28 June 1821; *d* New York, 14 May 1897). Czech, later American, composer, conductor, and impresario. After playing the violin in various theatre orchestras, conducted in Germany and London. Engaged 1848 for Astor Place Opera House, N.Y., as conductor; later managed seasons there, the Ac. of M., and Niblo's Gardens. He presented a number of famous artists for the first time to the American public, including Hauk (1866), Ronconi, Tamberlik, Lucca, Di Murska, and Graziani, and introduced *Rigoletto, La traviata, Il trovatore, L'Africaine, Le Prophète, La Favorite, Linda di Chamounix,*

Don Pasquale, and *Roméo et Juliette* to the American public. He was a picturesque and colourful figure, and his managerial career was full of trouble, with orchestra and chorus often on strike.
Bibl: M. Maretzek: *Crotchets and Quavers, or Revelations of an Opera Manager in America* (1885), and *Sharps and Flats* (1870).

Marguerite. The heroine (sop.) of Gounod's *Faust*.

Marguerite de Valois. Henry IV's betrothed (sop.) in Meyerbeer's *Les Huguenots*.

Maria Antonia Walpurgis (*b* Munich, 18 July 1724; *d* Dresden, 23 Apr. 1780). German amateur composer, daughter of the Elector of Bavaria, later the Emperor Charles VII. Her most important works were two operas to her own librettos, *Il trionfo della fedeltà* (prod. 1754, after alterations and help by Metastasio and Hasse), and *Talestri, Regina delle Amazoni* (1760).

Maria di Rohan. Opera in 3 acts by Donizetti; text by Cammarano, after Lockroy's melodrama *Un Duel sous le cardinal de Richelieu* (orig. called *Il Conte di Chalais* and composed by Lillo 1839). Prod. Vienna, Kä., 5 June 1843 with Tadolini, Novarra, Guasco, Ronconi; London, C.G., 8 May 1847, with E. Ronconi, Alboni, Ronconi, cond. Costa; N.Y. 10 Dec. 1849, with Bertucca, Perrini, Forti, Salvatore Patti, Beneventano, Giubilei, cond. Maratzek.

Maria (sop.) is secretly married to Chevreuse (bar.), but later falls in love with the Count of Chalais (ten.), after interceding with him on behalf of her husband, who has been arrested for killing Richelieu's nephew. Chevreuse challenges Chalais to a duel and kills him; Maria too wants to die, but her husband decrees that she live a life of disgrace.

Maria Egiziaca. Opera in 1 act (3 episodes) by Respighi; text by C. Guastalla. Orig. prod. concert form N.Y., Carnegie Hall, 16 Mar. 1932, with Boerner, Eddy, cond. Respighi. First stage prod. Buenos Aires, C., 23 July 1933, with Dalla Rizza Domiani, cond. Marinuzzi; London (concert), Hyde Park Hotel, 11 Apr. 1937.

Maria Stuarda. Opera in 3 acts by Donizetti; text by Bardari after Schiller's tragedy (1800). Prod. under title of *Buondelmonte,* with libretto changed by Salatino, Naples, S.C., 18 Oct. 1834 with Ronzi de Begnis, Del Serre, Pedrazzi, Crespi, Porto; given in Donizetti's original form Milan, Sc., 30 Dec. 1835 with Malibran, Puzzi-Tosso, Reina, Marini, Novelli; N.Y., Carnegie Hall (concert perf.), 16 Nov. 1964 with Hoffman, Jordan, Traxel, Michalski, Metcalf, cond. Scherman; N.Y., City O., 7 Mar. 1972 with Sills, Tinsley, Stewart, Fredericks, Devlin, cond. Rudel; London, St Pancras T.H., 1 March 1966, with Landis, Jolly, Hillmann, Drake, cond. Gover.

Queen Elizabeth I of England (sop.) is in love with Leicester (ten.), who persuades her to visit Mary Stuart (mezzo or sop.), held prisoner at Fotheringhay. Mary insults Elizabeth, and the Queen eventually signs her death warrant. Leicester, who is in love with Mary himself, is sent to witness her execution.

Other operas on Mary Stuart are by P. Casella (1813), Sogner (1815), Attwood (1820), Mercadante (1821), Fétis (1823), Coccia (1827), Grazioli (1828), Niedermeyer (1844), Duprato (1850), Capecalatro (*David Riccio*, 1850), Canepa (*Davide Rizzio*, 1872), Palumbo (1874), Lavello (1895), Moore (1932), Fontrer (1972), Virani (1974), and Musgrave (1977).

Mariani, Angelo (*b* Ravenna, 11 Oct. 1821; *d* Genoa, 13 June 1873). Italian conductor. Studied Ravenna, and attracted the attention of Rossini with some of his works. Début Messina 1844–5. His Milan début in *I due foscari* (1846) so impressed Verdi that he was asked to conduct the première of *Macbeth*; this came to nothing, though he gave performances of *I Lombardi* and *Nabucco* so exciting that he was threatened with imprisonment for stirring up rebellion. He worked in Copenhagen 1847-8 (composing a Requiem for Christian VIII); Constantinople 1848-51; Genoa, C.F., 1852 (*Robert le diable*), where he made the orchestra the best in Italy. He first worked with Verdi in the theatre in 1857 (*Aroldo* at Rimini); they became close friends, and it was Mariani who suggested the Requiem to Verdi. In 1860 he moved to Bologna, opening a long series of Verdi performances with *Ballo* and also giving the Italian premières of *Lohengrin* (1871) and *Tannhäuser* (1872). His great contribution was, by unremitting attention to detail and thoroughness of preparation, to make opera more genuinely integrated as a total theatrical experience. Mariani's refusal, on grounds of health, to conduct the première of *Aida* in Cairo caused a breach with Verdi: the matter is fully discussed by Frank Walker in *The Man Verdi*.

Mariani, Luciano (*b* Cremona, 1801; *d* Castell'Arquato (Piacenza), 10 June 1859). Italian bass. Created Oroe (*Semiramide*), Rodolfo (*La sonnambula*), and Alfonso (*Lucrezia Borgia*). His sister **Rosa** (*b* Cremona 1799; *d* ?) often sang with him; début Cremona 1818. London, King's T., 1832. She created Arsace in *Semiramide*; Stendhal wrote that she was 'in my humble opinion, the finest contralto now living'.

Mariani-Masi, Maddalena (*b* Florence 1850; *d* Erba (Como) 25 Sept 1916). Italian soprano. Studied Florence and Vienna. Début Florence 1871. Milan, Sc. 1872, Agathe. Created title-role in *La gioconda* and Margherita and Elena in the revised version of *Mefistofele*. Taught Lina Cavalieri. Her sister **Flora Mariana de Angelis**

had a successful career as a contralto, 1871-90.

Marie. Wozzeck's mistress (sop.) in Berg's opera.

Marina. The Polish princess (mezzo) who marries the false Dmitry in Mussorgsky's *Boris Godunov*.

Marini, Ignazio (*b* Tagliuno (Bergamo), 28 Nov. 1811; *d* Milan, 29 Apr. 1873). Italian bass. Début probably 1832 Brescia. Milan, Sc., 1833-47; London, C.G., 1847-9; N.Y. 1850-2; London 1852; St Petersburg 1856-63, where he succeeded Lablache as leading bass. Created title-roles in Verdi's *Oberto* and *Attila*, and the first Vienna Silva in *Ernani*; when he took over this role at Milan Sc., Verdi wrote the Cabaletta to 'Infelice' for him. His repertory also included Rossini's Mosè and Mustaphà, and Oroveso. His wife, **Antonietta Rainieri-Marini**, created Leonora in *Oberto* and the Marchesa del Poggia in Verdi's *Un giorno di regno*.

Marino Faliero. Opera in 3 acts by Donizetti; text by E. Bidera, after Casimir Delavigne's tragedy (1829) and also Byron's tragedy (1821). Prod. Paris, T.-I., 12 Mar. 1835, with Grisi, Rubini, Tamburini, Lablache, Santini, Ivanoff; London, C.G., 14 May 1835, same Co.; New Orleans, Charles T. 22 Feb. 1842, with Salvatori, Ober-Rossu, Cecconi, Perozzi, cond. Repperti. Has been performed in Germany as *Antonio Grimaldi*.

Marinuzzi, Gino (orig. Giuseppe) (*b* Palermo, 24 Mar. 1882; *d* Milan, 15 Aug. 1945). Italian conductor and composer. Studied Palermo. Début there. After engagements throughout Italy, including Palermo where he conducted the first performance there of *Tristan* in 1909, went to the Colón, Buenos Aires. Here he conducted the first local performance of *Parsifal*, 1913. Conducted the première of *La rondine*, Monte Carlo, 1917. Succeeded Campanini at Chicago 1919-21. Chief conductor at Rome O. 1928-34; at Sc. (with De Sabata) 1934-44. London, C.G., 1934. He wrote three operas, *Barberina* (Palermo 1903), *Jacquerie* (Buenos Aires 1918) and *Palla de' Mozzi* (Milan 1932). His son **Gino Marinuzzi** (*b* New York, 1920) is a composer; he also conducts occasionally at Rome. (R)

Mario, Giovanni (orig. Giovanni Matteo, Cavaliere di Candia) (*b* Cagliari, 17 Oct. 1810; *d* Rome, 11 Dec. 1883). Italian tenor. Eloped with a ballerina in 1836 to Paris, where he studied with Bordogni and Poncharde. Début Paris, O., 1838, Robert le Diable. Italian Opera in Paris 1840. Début London, H.M.'s, 1839, Gennaro (*Lucrezia Borgia*); sang there until 1846; C.G. 1847-67, returning to make farewell in 1871. With Grisi, whom he married in 1844, Tamburini, and Lablache, he sang in the première of *Don Pasquale* (1843). He was the first London

Gennaro, Ernesto, Duke of Mantua, John of Leyden, and Roméo. Sang Don Giovanni as tenor, though otherwise an artistic singer. His voice was considered one of the most beautiful ever heard, and he sang with elegance and style. His handsome appearance and acting abilities made him the idol of Victorian operagoers. After his retirement he soon became poverty-stricken, and a Benefit concert was organized for him in London in 1880.
Bibl: Mrs. Godfrey Pearce (his daughter) and F. Hird: *The Romance of a Great Singer* (1910).

Marionette Opera-Theatre. See *Puppet Opera.*

Maritana. Opera in 3 acts by Wallace; text by Edward Fitzball, after the drama *Don César de Bazan* by D'Ennery and Dumanoir. Prod. London, D.L., 15 Nov. 1845; Philadelphia 9 Nov. 1846. Also operetta *Don César* by Dellinger (1885).

Marlowe, Christopher (*b* Canterbury, 6 Feb. 1564; *d* Deptford, 30 May 1593). English poet and dramatist. Busoni's *Doktor Faust* (1925) is based on his *Dr. Faustus* (?, entered Stationer's Register 1601); and he is the central figure of Mellers's *The Tragicall History of Christopher Marlowe* (comp. 1950-2).

Marmontel, Jean François (*b* Bort, 11 July 1723; *d* Abloville, 31 Dec. 1799). French dramatist, librettist, and critic. His many librettos include four for Rameau, seven for Grétry, and others for composers including Cherubini (*Démophoon,* 1788) and Zingarelli. His writings include important articles in the *Encyclopédie* and an *Essai sur les révolutions de la musique* (1777) in which he sided with Piccinni in the controversy against Gluck. His novel *Les Incas* (1773) was the basis of the operas *Cora* by Naumann (1782) and Méhul (1791). In his librettos, he initiated a number of ideas that were to prove attractive to his contemporaries and successors. His enthusiasm for Rousseau, whom he knew personally, marks his libretto *Huron* for Grétry (1768), with its adulation of the Noble Savage; he helped to give impetus to the interest in the medieval; and his story *Soliman Second,* made into a Favart libretto and then a verse play, helped to kindle interest in the Oriental. It even directly influenced a number of more famous librettos, including that of Mozart's *Seraglio,* in its characters, which number among them a Chief Eunuch named Osmin. However, his tragic ambitions were not matched by a comparable talent, and for all the range of his subjects his handling of them is conventional and emotionally limited.

Mârouf, Savetier du Caire (Mârouf, Cobbler of Cairo). Opera in 4 acts by Rabaud: text by Népoty, after a story in Mardrus's French version of *The 1,001 Nights.* Prod. Paris, O.C., 15

May 1914, with Davelli Jean Périer, Vieuille, cond. Ruhlmann; N.Y., Met., 19 Dec. 1917, with Alda, De Luca, Rothier, cond. Monteux.

The cobbler Mârouf (ten.) escapes his wife by going to sea. Shipwrecked, he is introduced by a friend to the Sultan (bass) as a wealthy merchant; he marries the Sultan's daughter (sop.) and rifles his treasury, continually promising that his caravans will soon arrive. The princess loves him even when he confesses to her, and they flee. A magic ring provides them with a palace, and the pursuing Sultan forgives Mârouf on finding him surrounded by wealth.

Marquise de Brinvilliers, La. Opera in 3 acts by Auber, Batton, Berton, Blangini, Boieldieu, Carafa, Cherubini, Hérold, and Paer; text by Scribe and Castil-Blaze. Prod. Paris, O.C., 31 Oct. 1831. The most famous of several collective works of the period.

Marriage, The. Unfinished opera by Mussorgsky; text after Gogol's comedy (1842). One act only completed in 1864; concert performance at Rimsky-Korsakov's house, 1906; stage performance with piano, St Petersburg, Suvorin School, 1 Apr. 1909; first full prod., Petrograd 26 Oct. 1917, rev. Rimsky-Korsakov. Also opera in 1 act by Martinů, with text by the composer, after Gogol. N.B.C. Television Opera, 7 Feb. 1953 with Stollin, Heidt, Gramm. cond. Adler; first stage performance, Hamburg 13 Mar. 1954, with Görner, Litz, Gura, Katona, Gollnitz, Marschner, Blankenheim, Roth, cond. Stein. The comedy turns on the difficulties of securing the marriage of the vain government clerk Podkolesin, under heavy pressure from the marriage broker Fiokla and from the lures of his friend Kochkarev.

Marriage of Figaro, The. See *Nozze di Figaro, Le.*

Marschallin (or **Feldmarschallin**). The Princess von Werdenberg (sop.) in Strauss's *Der Rosenkavalier.*

Marschner, Heinrich (August) (*b* Zittau, 16 Aug. 1795; *d* Hanover, 14 Dec. 1861). German composer. Studied Bautzen with Hering, Leipzig with Schicht. His early *Heinrich IV und d'Aubigné* (1820) was produced by Weber in Dresden, where he then settled, replacing Morlacchi as music director. On failing to gain the appointment to the German opera after Weber's death in 1826, moved to Leipzig, becoming Kapellmeister at the Stadttheater. Here he had successes with *Der Vampyr* (1828) and *Der Templer und die Jüdin* (1829). Moved to Hanover in 1830 as conductor of the Hoftheater. *Hans Heiling,* his greatest success and the work that established him as a major German national composer, was produced in Berlin in 1833. There followed *Das Schloss am*

Ätna in Leipzig (1836), *Der Bäbu* in Hanover (1838), *Kaiser Adolf von Nassau* in Dresden (1845), *Austin* in Hanover (1852), and posthumously, *Hiarne* in Frankfurt (1863). Despite his renown, his enthusiasm for German opera and his antagonism to the Italian tradition of the Hanoverian Court made his life there difficult; even the backing of Rossini failed to assure him a performance of *Hiarne* in Paris in the wake of the *Tannhäuser* débâcle.

Marschner occupies an important position in the history of German Romantic opera, absorbing much from the world of Weber but also contributing some original ideas to the tradition, and suggesting much to Wagner. Thus *Der Vampyr* takes much from *Der Freischütz*, and from the *Schauerromantik* of contemporary German drama, but anticipates *Der fliegende Holländer* in the handling of the accursed hero and his relationship with the pure heroine. Especially, Marschner here develops the idea of the character containing both good and evil, and divided against himself. *Der Templer und die Jüdin* reflects the more elevated manner of *Euryanthe* and anticipates much in *Lohengrin* and *Tannhäuser*, e.g. in the functional use of orchestration: Wagner much admired the character of Bois-Guilbert, typical of Marschner in the complex mixture of motives both good and evil. Marschner diverges from Weber in his attention to the examination of character at the expense of setting, theatrical effect, and incidental episodes, though his intentions are apt to be more subtle than his actual musical achievements. His disregard of comedy for its function of light relief led him to ignore this aspect of opera, and his one comic opera, *Der Bäbu*, was a failure. However, he explored greater use of chromatic harmony, greater expressive subtleties of scoring, and a more fluent movement between numbers and sections of the opera, that comes close to Wagnerian practice. Certain characteristics also caught Wagner's imagination, such as the liking for plunging into the middle of a drama, and certain details, such as the appearance of the Mountain Queen in *Heiling* in a situation and to a phrase that anticipates the *Todesverkündigung*.

However, Marschner did not really depart from the Singspiel structure, and was more concerned with extending the range of set forms and finding links between them than with annulling them. Only *Hiarne* is truly *durchkomponiert*; even *König Adolf von Nassau* is really a historical grand opera in the manner of Spontini, whom Marschner much admired and whom he had once hoped to succeed in Berlin. Often categorised as a bridge between Weber and Wagner, Marschner made his own positive and individual contribution to German Romantic opera.

Bibl: G. Münzer: *Heinrich Marschner* (1901).

Marseilles (Fr. Marseille). Town in Provence, France. The first opera given there was Gautier's *Le Triomphe de la paix* (1685). The Grand T. was opened in 1787 with Champein's *La Mélomanie*, and opera was given there regularly until it was destroyed by fire in 1919. The present theatre (cap. 1,786) was opened in 1924. Since 1945 the theatre has been subsidized by the Municipality, and artistic directors have included Leduc, Lefort, and Giovaninetti.

Martern aller Arten. Constanze's (sop.) aria in Act 2 of Mozart's *Die Entführung aus dem Serail*, in which she declares that neither torture nor death itself will make her yield to the Pasha. Written for Katharina Cavalieri.

Martha, oder Der Markt von Richmond. Opera in 4 acts by Flotow; text by W. Friedrich (Friedrich Wilhelm Riese), after Vernoy de St Georges's ballet-pantomime *Lady Henriette, ou La Servante de Greewich*, to which Flotow had contributed some music. Prod. Vienna, Kä., 25 Nov. 1847, with Anna Zerr, Schwarz, Erl, Formes, Just; London, D.L., 4 June 1849; N.Y., Niblo's Garden, 1 Nov. 1852, with Anna Bishop, Jacques, Guidi, Leach, Strini, Rudolph, cond. Bochsa. Parody *Martl* by Suppé (1848).

Lady Harriet (sop.), Maid of Honour to Queen Anne, is tired of court life, and so she and her maid Nancy (mezzo), disguise themselves as country girls. Under the names of Martha and Julia they go to Richmond Fair where they are hired as servants by two young farmers, Lionel (ten.) and Plunkett (bass). The two men fall in love with the girls; when the latter return to court life, Lady Harriet realises that she loves Lionel. A replica of Richmond Fair is set up in her own garden and there, once again, Lionel sees 'Martha' in her humble clothes and the two couples are happily united.

Martin, Frank (*b* Geneva, 15 Sept. 1890; *d* Naarden, 21 Nov. 1974). Swiss composer. Apart from his dramatic oratorio *Le Vin herbé* (1941), based on the Tristan legend, Martin's only opera is *Der Sturm* (1956), a word for word setting of *The Tempest* in Schlegel's translation. The poetry is sometimes allowed to stand unaccompanied, sometimes set in a *parlando* style resembling the technique of *Pelléas*. Also wrote opera *M. de Pourceaugnac* (1963).

Martin, Jean-Blaise (*b* Paris, 24 Feb. 1768 or 14 Oct. 1769; *d* Ronzières, 28 Oct. or 18 Oct. 1837). French baritone. Début Paris, T. Feydeau, 1789, in *Le Marquis de Tulipan*, singing in various theatres there including the O.C. until 1823; later also 1826, 1834, creating 14 roles. Subsequently taught at the Conservatoire. His voice was of extraordinary range and gave the name to the type of French baritone known as Baritone Martin. See *Baritone*.

Martinelli, Caterina (*b* Rome, 1590; *d* Mantua, 9 March 1608). Italian soprano. Known as 'La Romanina' or 'Caterinuccia'. Studied Rome with Arrigo Gabbino. Début aged 13 at Mantua, where she studied with Monteverdi. Created title-role in Da Gagliano's *Dafne*; died while preparing title-role of Monteverdi's *Arianna*.

Martinelli, Giovanni (*b* Montagnana, 22 Oct. 1885; *d* New York, 2 Feb. 1969). Italian tenor. Voice discovered by army bandmaster while on military service. Studied Milan. Début Milan, T.D.V., 1910, Ernani. Heard by Puccini who engaged him for European première of *La fanciulla del West* (Rome 1911). London, C.G., 1912-14, 1919, and 1937; N.Y., Met., 1913-46, during which time he sang in more than 50 operas, including the world première of *Madame Sans-Gêne*, the American premières of *Francesca da Rimini*, *La campana sommersa*, *Simone Boccanegra*, and *Goyescas*, and the first Met. performances of *Oberon* and *Gioielli della Madonna*. Late in his career he became a fine Otello and Eleazar, and in Chicago in 1939 he sang Tristan opposite Flagstad. His voice was sterling silver rather than golden, not very large in size but used with impeccable style and faultless technique. (R)

Martini, Andrea (*b* Siena 1761; *d* 1819). Italian male soprano. Début Rome 1780, where he sang mostly female roles in both serious and comic operas. Known also as Senesino, but should not be confused with the famous castrato of that name. When he sang in Cimarosa's *I due baroni di Rocca Azzura* in 1783, a poem, beginning with the words 'La tua voce soave', was written in his honour.

Martinů, Bohuslav (*b* Polička, 8 Dec. 1890; *d* Liestal, 29 Aug. 1959). Czech composer. His first opera was a 3-act comedy, *Voják a tanečnice* (The Soldier and the Dancer, 1928). Moving to Paris, he wrote *Les Larmes du couteau* (The Tears of the Knife, 1928), a 1-act jazz opera, and *Trois souhaits, ou Les Vicissitudes de la vie* (Three Greetings, 1929), a 3-act opera film also making use of jazz; *Le Semaine de bonté* (The Happy Week) of 1929 remained unfinished. *Hry o Marii* (The Miracle of Our Lady, 1935) consisted of a cycle of four mystery plays, and was produced in Brno, then Prague; this was followed by *Divadlo za bránou* (The Suburban Theatre, 1936) and a 1-act opera buffa, *Alexandre bis* (1937). Martinů's first great success on the stage was *Julietta* (1938), a successful interpretation of a play by Georges Neveux, concerning the relationship of reality and dream, and of reality and memory, in which Martinů's invariably fluent idiom achieves considerable lyrical intensity. This was followed by another Neveux play, *La Plainte contre inconnu* (Complaint against the Unknown) in 1953, left

unfinished. *Mirandolina* (1959) was an attempt to update the spirit of Goldoni. A serious work followed, *The Greek Passion* (1961), to an English libretto by the composer after Kazantzakis's novel *Christ Recrucified*, but the cumulative atmosphere of the original proved difficult to translate to the stage in short scenes lacking in true dramatic power. Martinů's last opera was *Ariadne* (1958), again after Neveux. However, he wrote three radio operas, *Hlas lesa* (The Voice of the Forest, 1937), *Veselohra na mostě* (Comedy on a Bridge, 1952), *Čím člověk žije* (What men live by, a pastoral opera after Tolstoy, 1953), and a TV opera, *Ženitba* (The Marriage, 1953). The pungent wit of *Comedy on a Bridge,* one of his most attractive works, has successfully transferred to the stage.
Bibl: M. Šafránek: *Bohuslav Martinů* (1944); B. Large: *Martinů* (1973).

Martín y Soler, Vicente (*b* Valencia, 18 June 1754; *d* St Petersburg, 30 Jan. 1806). Spanish composer. After a successful début with an opera in Naples, he went to Vienna, where he found in Da Ponte his ideal librettist (the admiration was reciprocated). The best known of their first three operas was *Una cosa rara* (1786), quoted by Mozart in the Supper Scene of *Don Giovanni*. He also had a great success with *L'arbore di Diana* (1787). In St Petersburg from 1788, he became Catherine II's Court composer, writing operas to two of her librettos. Went to London in 1794, where he again collaborated with Da Ponte, though less successfully. Returned to Russia about 1798, and spent his last years as a singing teacher. His lively, tuneful vein of opera buffa was very popular in his day, and he was compared to Cimarosa, Paisiello, and even Mozart.

Martyrs, Les. Opera in 4 acts by Donizetti; text by Scribe, after Corneille's tragedy *Polyeucte,* orig. composed to an Italian libretto by S. Cammarano, *Poliuto,* in 3 acts and written for Nourrit in Naples (rehearsed 1838) but banned by the censor. Prod. Paris, O., 10 Apr. 1840, with Dorus-Gras, Duprez, Massol, Dérivis, Wartel, Serda; New Orleans, T. d'Orléans, 24 Mar. 1846, with J. Calvé, Arnaud, Garry, Douvry, Mordant, cond. E. Prévost; London, C.G., 20 Apr. 1852, as *I martiri*, with Jullienne, Tamberlik, Ronconi, Marini, cond. Costa. For plot see *Poliuto*.

Mary Stuart. See *Maria Stuarda*.

Masaniello. See *Muette de Portici, La*.

Mascagni, Pietro (*b* Leghorn, 7 Dec. 1863; *d* Rome, 2 Aug. 1945). Italian composer and conductor. Studied Leghorn, and Milan Conservatory under Ponchielli. Unwilling to submit to the regular discipline of the Conservatory, he left to join a touring opera company as a con-

ductor; he then settled in Cerignola as a piano teacher. In 1890 he won first prize in a competition sponsored by the publishers Sanzogno with his 1-act *Cavalleria rusticana* (1890). This melodramatic *verismo* opera of love and hatred in Sicily speedily swept Europe and started the vogue for similar 1-act works. Despite the fact that Mascagni wrote more than a dozen other works, his fame rests soley on *Cavalleria*. *L'amico Fritz* (1891) contains some charming pastoral passages, but is very slight musically; *Iris* (1898) has an unattractive libretto but shows some originality in orchestration; *Le maschere* (1901) had a brief and stormy career (see below); *Isabeau* (1911), based on the story of Lady Godiva, enjoyed a short-lived success; and *Il piccolo Marat* (1921), which many musicians consider his best work, is very rarely played outside Italy. Mascagni was a not inconsiderable opera conductor and allowed himself to become the musical mouthpiece of Fascist Italy, composing his *Nerone* for the Milan Sc. with Mussolini in mind, and choral and orchestral works for various political occasions. As a result many Italian musicians, including Toscanini, broke off relations with him; and he spent the last few years of his life in comparative poverty and disgrace in a Rome hotel. (R).
Bibl: M. Morini (ed.): *Pietro Mascagni* (1964); A. Jeri: *Mascagni* (2/1940).

Maschere, Le (The Masks). Opera in a prologue and 3 acts by Mascagni; text by Illica. Prod. simultaneously in six Italian cities, 17 Jan. 1901. In Milan (Sc., with Brambilla, Carelli, Caruso, cond. Toscanini), Venice, Turin, and Verona it was hissed; in Genoa it was not allowed to be completed; only in Rome, where Mascagni conducted it, did it meet with any kind of favour. It is a commedia dell'arte opera, and has had a few revivals.

Mascheroni, Edoardo (*b* Milan, 4 Sept. 1852; *d* Como, 4 Mar. 1941). Italian conductor and composer. Début Leghorn 1883; Rome, Teatro Apollo, 1885-88, Milan, Sc., 1892-5, where he conducted the premières of *La Wally* and, at Verdi's request, of *Falstaff*. He also directed the first Scala performances of *Tannhäuser*, *Fliegende Holländer*, and *Walküre*. He then conducted in Germany, Spain, and South America. His *Lorenza* (libretto by Illica) was produced in Rome in 1901, and his *La Perugina* (libretto again by Illica) at Naples in 1909. His brother **Angelo** (1855-95), who studied in Paris with Delibes, was also a conductor and accompanied Patti on several of her tours.

Mascotte, La. Operetta in 3 acts by Audran; text by Duru and Chivot. Prod. Paris, B.-P., 28 Dec. 1880 (1,000 perfs. by 1885); N.Y., Abbey's Park Theatre, 5 May 1881; Brighton, 19 Sept. 1881. Audran's most popular work.

The farmer Rocco is sent the goose-girl Bettina by his brother as a mascot in the hope that it will cure his bad luck; this greatly delights Pippo, his shepherd, in love with Bettina. Prince Laurent appears, bewailing his ill luck, and persuades Bettina that she is of noble blood and must return to his castle; his daughter Fiammetta meanwhile tries to seduce Pippo. At Court, Laurent tries to keep Pippo from Bettina, for he knows that her secret as a mascot depends upon her virginity. Pippo is made to believe her about to marry the Prince, so he agrees to marry Fiammetta; but as the marriage is about to take place, Pippo turns to Bettina, and they escape through the window. War breaks out, and Pippo, with Bettina disguised as a boy by his side, has covered himself with glory; Laurent, on the other side, is out of luck, and rejected by his subjects he comes to the enemy's camp and finds Pippo. Eventually all is forgiven, and Pippo marries Bettina, in the expectation that her powers as a mascot will prove hereditary.

Masetto. The peasant (bar.) betrothed to Zerlina in Mozart's *Don Giovanni*.

Masini, Angelo (*b* Terra del Sole, nr Forlì, 28 Nov. 1844; *d* Forlì, 28 Sept. 1926). Italian tenor. Studied with Gilda Minguzzi. Début Finale Emilia 1867, Pollione. After appearances in the Italian provinces, Spain, St Petersburg, etc., was chosen by Verdi for the tenor role in the Requiem, which he sang in London, Paris, and Vienna under the composer's baton; also sang Radamès under Verdi in Paris. Engaged by Mapleson for London 1879, but owing to a misunderstanding never appeared, and was prevented by Mapleson from singing under any other management in London. Verdi offered to write an extended aria for him if he would create the role of Fenton in *Falstaff* – Masini refused. Had seven different ways of ending 'La donna è mobile'. Continued to sing until 1907.

Masini, Galliano (*b* Livorno, 1896). Italian tenor. Début Finale Emilia 1924, Cavaradossi. Leading tenor Rome O. 1930-50; also sang at Milan Sc., but with little success, though chosen by Mascagni to sing Turiddu in the 50th anniversary celebrations there of *Cavalleria rusticana*. Sang with much success Chicago 1937-8, and N.Y., Met., 1938-9. Loris (*Fedora*), Cavaradossi, and Edgardo were among his best roles. (R)

Maskerade. Opera in 3 acts by Nielsen; text by Vilhelm Andersen after a play by Holberg. Prod. Copenhagen, 11 Nov. 1906 with Ulrich, Møller, Knudsen, Neiiendam, Kierulf, Jerndoff, Mantzius, cond. Nielsen; London, B.B.C. 19 Mar. 1972; St Paul, Minn., 23 June 1972, with Neil, Williams, Atherton, Christeson, Beri, cond. Buketoff. Leander (ten.) and Leonora (sop.) meet at a masquerade and fall in love only to discover that the marriages arranged for each of them by their respective parents which they have resisted, is in fact to be between them.

Masnadieri, I (The Robbers). Opera in 4 acts by Verdi; text by Maffei, after Schiller's drama *Die Räuber* (1781). Prod. London, H.M.'s, 22 July 1847, with Lind, Gardoni, Coletti, Lablache, Corelli, Bouché, cond. Verdi; Rome, Teatro Apollo, 12 Feb. 1848; N.Y. 31 May 1860, with Olivieri, Guerra, Luisia, Mirandola.

Carlo (ten.) is disinherited by his father, Massimilian, Count of Moor (bass), through the machinations of his younger brother Francesco (bar.). Carlo forms a Robin-Hood-like band of robbers, is reunited with his beloved Amalia (sop.), and saves his father from starving to death in prison, but rather than let Amalia join him and the 'robbers' he stabs her to death in their presence.

Masque. A 16th and 17th cent. stage entertainment combining poetry, music, singing, dancing, and acting, normally setting mythological subjects in elaborate scenery. Originating as an entertainment by and for the Court in Italy and France, it reached England in the 16th cent., where the best writer of masques was Ben Jonson. He also developed the 'antimasque', an inserted scene of comedy comparable to the operatic *intermezzo. After the Civil War, the more complete dramatic form of opera superseded the masque, though it has occasionally been revived and has been included in operas, e.g. in Britten's *Gloriana*. Purcell's *The Fairy Queen* (1692) is virtually a series of masques.

Massé, Victor (*b* Lorient, 7 Mar. 1822; *d* Paris, 5 July 1884). French composer. Early successes, notably with *Les Noces de Jeannette* (1853), roused hopes that he would equal Auber's talent; but though always charmingly tuneful, his later pieces did not prove enduring. His most ambitious work was *Paul et Virginie* (1876); here the short lyrical numbers were the most effective. Massé was chorus master at the Paris O. 1860-76.

Massenet, Jules (*b* Montaud, Loire, 12 May 1842; *d* Paris, 13 Aug. 1912). French composer. Studied Paris Conservatoire with Ambroise Thomas. Prix de Rome 1863. On his return from Italy he completed his 1-act *La Grand'-Tante* which was produced at the Paris O.C., 1867. However, it was not until the production of *Le Roi de Lahore* in 1877 that his position on the French opera scene was firmly established. Of his 27 operas, *Hérodiade* (1881). *Manon* (1884), *Werther* (1892), *Thaïs* (1894), *Le Jongleur de Notre-Dame* (1902), and *Don Quichotte* (1910) have met the greatest popularity not only in France, but in Italy, in America, and, to some

extent, in England; however here the 'discreet and semi-religious eroticism' (d'Indy) of his works has not found favour. In America the works had a special success during the Hammerstein régime in N.Y., and in Chicago in the 1920s, when Mary Garden proved an ideal interpreter of many of them. When the operas are sung and produced tastefully and sincerely, the natural charm of Massenet's melodies, and his shrewd sense of the stage, can make a considerable appeal. In an attempt to perpetuate this type of opera, Massenet continued to repeat his musical clichés in his later works, *Chérubin* (1905), *Ariane* (1906), *Thérèse* (1907), *Bacchus* (1909), *Roma* (1912), *Panurge* (1913), *Cléopâtre* (1914), and *Amadis* (1922), the last three produced posthumously. *La Navarraise* (1894), a 1-act piece composed in *verismo* style as an answer to the success of Mascagni's *Cavalleria rusticana,* was written for C.G. None of these works enjoyed more than a *succès d'estime*. Massenet also orchestrated and completed Delibes's *Kassya*. From 1878 until his death he was professor of advanced composition at the Paris Conservatoire and among his pupils were Bruneau, Leroux, Pierné, Charpentier, and Rabaud.

Bibl: J. Harding: *Massenet* (1970).

Massol, Jean-Étienne August (*b* Lodère, 1802; *d* Paris, 30 Oct. 1887). French baritone. Studied Paris Conservatoire. Début Paris, O., Licinio in *La Vestale*, 1825. Remained at O. until 1845, first singing second tenor roles and creating Rodolphe in *Guillaume Tell,* Kalaf in Cherubini's *Ali Baba*, and De Nevers in *Les Huguenots,* then, as a baritone, Sévère in Donizetti's *Les Martyrs* and Abayaldo in his *Dom Sébastien*. In 1845 he joined the Brussels Company and appeared with them at D.L. in 1846 as De Nevers; London, C.G., 1848-50 as Alfonso (*Favorita*), De Nevers, Pietro (*Masaniello*); H.M.'s 1851. Returned Paris, O., 1850, remaining there until retirement 1858, creating Reuben in Auber's *L'Enfant prodigue* and Ahasuerus in Halévy's *Le Juif errant*. The tenor Roger relates in his *Carnet d'un tenor* that Massol did not understand Italian and 'uttered the most horrible jargon'.

Master Peter's Puppet Show. See *Retablo de Maese Pedro, El.*

Mastersingers of Nuremberg, The. See *Meistersinger von Nürnberg, Die.*

Masterson, Valerie (Margaret) (*b* Birkenhead, 3 June 1937). British soprano. Studied Liverpool and London with Gordon Clinton and Edoardo Asquez, and Milan with Saraceni. Début Salzburg, Landestheater, 1963, Frasquita (*Carmen*), also heard there as Nannetta and Fiorilla (*Turco in Italia*). D'Oyly Carte Company, 1966-70. S.W. (later E.N.O.) since 1970 in wide variety of roles, including Constanze, Adèle in

Comte Ory, and Fledermaus, Micaëla, Manon, Sophie, Gilda. London C.G., since 1974; created Second Soldier's Wife in Henze's *We Come to the River.* Aix-en-Provence 1974, 1976. Paris, O., 1978, Marguerite. Many appearances in French provinces. (R)

Mastilović, Danica (*b* Negotin, 7 Nov. 1933). Yugoslav soprano. Studied Belgrade with Nikola Cvejić and while a student (1955-9) sang at the Belgrade Operetta T. Engaged by Solti for Frankfurt Opera; début Tosca 1959. Sang there for ten years in the Italian repertory; particularly successful in Verdi. Since 1969 has gained a reputation in the Wagner-Strauss repertory. Chicago 1963 as Abigaille. London, C.G., 1973, 1975 Elektra. N.Y., Met., 1975 Elektra. Vienna, Munich, Bayreuth (from 1956), Paris, and Italian houses. Repertory includes Turandot, which she sang at Torre del Lago in 1974 to commemorate the 50th anniversary of Puccini's death. Her large and at times unwieldy voice is always excitingly use. (R)

Matačić, Lovro von (*b* Sušak, nr. Rijeka, 14 Feb. 1899). Yugoslav conductor and producer. Member of the Wiener Sängerknabern 1908-11; subsequently studied Vienna with Herbst and Nebdal. Cologne 1917 as 'voluntary' répétiteur to study with Gustav Brecher. Noví Sad 1919; Ljubljana 1924-6; Belgrade 1926-32 and 1938-42; Zagreb 1932-8; Vienna, V., 1942-5. Guest appearances Germany and Italy from 1954; Generalmusikdirektor Dresden, 1956-8, and joint appointment Berlin with Konwitschny same period. Frankfurt as Solti's successor 1961-6; Monto Carlo from 1974. Bayreuth, Munich, Vienna, Buenos Aires, and Italian opera houses. Produced many operas including *Orfeo, Incoronazione di Poppea, Parsifal,* and *Turandot.* (R)

Materna, Amalie (*b* St Georgen, 10 July 1844; *d* Vienna, 18 Jan. 1918). Austrian soprano. Début Graz, as soubrette 1864, in Suppé's *Light Cavalry.* Vienna, Karl T., in operetta: début Hofoper 1869 (Solika), remaining until 1897. First Bayreuth Brünnhilde 1876, and Kundry 1882. Sang under Wagner in concerts in London 1877. N.Y., Met., 1884-5, Elisabeth, Valentine, Rachel, and Brünnhilde in the first Met. *Walküre.* Joined *Damrosch's Company 1894. Had few equals in Wagner roles. After her retirement taught in Vienna.

Mathis, Edith (*b* Lucerne, 11 Feb. 1938). Swiss soprano. Studied Lucerne and Zurich with Elisabeth Basshart. Début Lucerne 1956, 2nd Boy (*Zauberflöte*). Cologne 1959-63; Berlin, D., since 1963; Gly., 1962 Cherubino; N.Y., Met., 1970; London, C.G., 1970, 1972 Susanna and Despina; Salzburg since 1960 Ninetta (*La finta semplice*), Cherubino, Marzelline, Sophie; Munich Festival as Pamina, Mélisande. Created Luise in *Der junge Lord* and Kathi in

Einem's *Der Zerrissene.* A sensitive and highly musical singer with a charming stage presence. Married to the conductor Bernard Klee. (R)

Mathis der Maler (Mathis the Painter). Opera in 7 scenes by Hindemith; text by composer, after Matthias Grünewald's life and his altar-piece at Colmar. Prod. Zurich 28 May 1938, with Hellwig, Funk, Stig, cond. Denzler; Edinburgh 29 Aug. 1952, with Wasserthal, Rothenberger, Ahlersmeyer, cond. Ludwig; Boston University 17 Feb. 1956, with Gay.

In the Peasants' War of 1542, Grünewald (bar.) leads the peasants against the Church. Losing faith in his cause, he escapes with Regina (sop.). He renounces the outside world in favour of his art. This portrayal of people rising against authority alarmed the Nazis, who despite protests by Furtwängler banned the scheduled 1934 Berlin première. Furtwängler was dismissed and Hindemith had to leave the country. A symphony drawing on music from the opera has become well known in the concert hall.

Matinsky, Mikhail (Alexeyevich) (*b* Pokrovskoye, 1750; *d* St Petersburg, *c*1820). Russian composer. Studied in Italy. He wrote the text and, probably with Pashkevich, the music of *The St Petersburg Bazaar* (1779), only surviving in its revised version *As you Live, so you are Judged* (1792), which makes much use of folk music and of the chorus (including seven wedding choruses) to give one of the earliest operatic pictures of Russian life.

Matrimonio Segreto, Il (The Secret Marriage). Opera in 2 acts by Cimarosa; text by Bertati, after the comedy *The Clandestine Marriage* (1766) by Colman and Garrick. Prod. Vienna, Burgtheater, 7 Feb. 1792, with Bussani, Bosello, Mandini, when the whole work was encored at the request of Leopold II; London, King's T., 11 Jan. 1794 with Pastorelli, Casentini, Braghetti, Rovedino, Morelli. N.Y., Italian O.H., 4 Jan. 1834. Cimarosa's most popular work frequently revived. Chosen to inaugurate La Piccola Scala 26 Dec. 1955.

The opera tells of the attempts of Geronimo (bass), a wealthy citizen of Bologna, to marry off his daughter Elisetta (sop.) to an English 'Milord', Count Robinson (bass). The latter prefers Geronimo's other daughter Carolina (sop.) who is secretly married to Paolino (ten.), a young lawyer and business associate of Geronimo. Geronimo's sister Fidalma (mezzo), who rules the household, is herself in love with Paolino. Carolina and Paolino plan an elopement, and after a bedroom scene of mistaken identities, all ends happily with the Count agreeing to marry Elisetta.

Also operas by Graffigna (1883) and Gast (*Der Löwe von Venedig,* prod. 1891 as *Die heimliche Ehe*).

Mattei, Stanislao (*b* Bologna, 10 Feb. 1750; *d* Bologna, 12 May 1825). Italian composer. He was Martini's successor at San Francesco in Bologna, and later became famous as a teacher, his pupils including Rossini, Morlacchi, Donizetti, and Bertolotti.

Matters, Arnold (*b* Adelaide, 11 Apr. 1904). Australian baritone. Studied Adelaide, then London. Début London, S.W., 1932, Valentine. S.W. until 1939, when he returned to Australia. S.W. 1947-53, where he was the first English Boccanegra. C.G. 1935-9 and 1946-53. At C.G. created Pilgrim in Vaughan Williams's *Pilgrim's Progress* (1951) and Cecil in Britten's *Gloriana* (1953). Returned to Australia in 1954 to work as teacher and producer. (R)

Mattheson, Johann (*b* Hamburg, 28 Sept. 1681; *d* Hamburg, 17 Apr. 1764). German organist, harpsichordist, singer, and composer. From 1696 he sang female parts at Hamburg, producing his first operas there from 1699. As well as singing in these, he would step down and accompany them from the harpsichord. Here he met and befriended Handel, from whom he learnt much. His eight operas and other compositions are overshadowed by his writings on music, which are lively and thoughtful if egotistical and not a little truculent.

Matzenauer, Margarete (*b* Temesvár, 1 June 1881; *d* Van Nuys, Cal., 19 May 1963). Hungarian contralto, also soprano. Studied Graz and Berlin. Début Strasbourg 1901, Puck (*Oberon*). Munich 1904-11; N.Y., Met., 1911-30. Also Bayreuth, London, C.G., and Colón. Until 1914 she was always described as a soprano, but as well as being especially distinguished in Wagner (Kundry, Brünnhilde, Isolde) and Verdi, she sang mezzo roles including Ortrud, Venus, Fricka, Fidès, and Laura (*Gioconda*). After 1914 she sang chiefly in contralto roles, including the Kostelnička in the American première of *Jenůfa*, and Eboli in the first Met. *Don Carlos*. (R)

Maurel, Victor (*b* Marseilles, 17 June 1848; *d* New York, 22 Oct. 1923). French baritone. Studied Paris with Vauthrot and Duvernoy. Début Paris, O., 1868, De Nevers (*Huguenots*), but made little impression and was only given small roles. After singing in St Petersburg, Cairo, and Venice (where he once substituted for the tenor in *Linda di Chamounix*) appeared at La Scala 1870 in première of *Il Guarany*, and later created Iago (1887) and Falstaff (1893), both at Verdi's request. London, C.G., 1873-9, 1891-5, and 1904, where he was the first London Telramund (1875), Wolfram (1876), and the first C.G. Dutchman (1877); N.Y., Ac. of M., 1873, and Met., 1894-6 and 1898-9, where he was the first Falstaff. Paris, O., 1879-94. He did not possess an exceptional voice, but used it with consummate art and displayed extraordinary dramatic abilities (he appeared on the straight stage for a period early in the century). He also studied painting, and designed the sets for *Mireille* at the Met. (1919). For a short time he had an operatic studio in London, and from 1909 until his death he taught in N.Y. He wrote three books on singing, one on the staging of *Don Giovanni*, and an autobiography, *Dix Ans de carrière* (1897), which was translated into German by Lilli Lehmann. (R)

Mavra. Opera in 1 act by Stravinsky; text by B. Kochno, after Pushkin's poem *The Little House at Kolomna* (1830). Prod. Paris, O., 3 June 1922, with Slobodskaya, De Sadowen, Belina, cond. Fitelberg (after private performance at the Hôtel Continental); Philadelphia, Ac. of M., 12 Dec. 1934, with Kurenko; Edinburgh, King's T., 21 Aug. 1956, by Hamburg S.O., with Muszely, Ast, Litz, Förster, cond. Ludwig.

Parasha (sop.) replaces her mother's cook with her lover, Vasily (ten.), who has disguised himself as a girl, 'Mavra'. But 'Mavra' is found shaving, and has to escape through the window.

Max. A huntsman (ten.), hero of Weber's *Der Freischütz*.

Maximowna, Ita (*b* Pskov, 31 Oct. 1914). Russian designer. Studied Paris and Berlin. Her designs for *L'incoronazione di Poppea* at Milan, Sc., *Fidelio* and *Don Giovanni* at Gly. and especially her work at Hamburg, Stuttgart and Munich in association with Gunther Rennert, have established her as one of the leading designers of the post-war period.

Maxwell Davies, Peter (*b* Manchester, 8 Sept. 1934). English composer. Studied Manchester with Richard Hall, Rome with Petrassi, Princeton with Sessions. Though he has experimented with music theatre and semi-staged dramatic music, e.g. *Revelation and Fall* (1968), *Eight Songs for a Mad King* (1969), and *Vesalii Icones* (1969), his only opera is *Taverner* (1962). Produced at C.G. in 1972, this is a study of the 16th cent. composer John Taverner and his relationship to the political issues of his day, expressed in music that draws on many resources, including those of post-Expressionism and the quotation of Taverner's own music.

May Night. Opera in 3 acts by Rimsky-Korsakov; text by composer, after Gogol's story (1831-2). Prod. St Petersburg, M., 21 Jan. 1880, with Slavina, Bichurina, Velinskaya, Stravinsky, Lody, Melnikov, Solovyov, Ende, cond. Naprávník; also used to reopen the M., renamed the Russian State O.H., Petrograd 12 Mar. 1917; London, D.L., 26 June 1914, with Petrenko, Smirnov, Andreyev, Belyanin, Ernst, cond. Steinberg.

Levko (ten.) and Hanna (mezzo) are in love, but his father the Mayor (bass) disapproves. Levko tells her the legend of Pannochka (sop.), who drowned herself to escape from her stepmother and became a *rusalka*: the stepmother was also drowned, but cannot be distinguished now from the good *rusalki*. Levko is furious to find his father later serenading Hanna. Great complications ensue at a drinking orgy of the Mayor, leading to his sister-in-law being mistaken for the Devil and nearly burnt. Near the castle by the lake, Levko is singing in praise of Hanna when the *rusalki* appear; in return for his identifying the disguised stepmother, they provide him with evidence that leads to the Mayor being outwitted and his own wedding to Hanna being celebrated.

Mayr, Richard (*b* Henndorf, Austria, 18 Nov. 1877; *d* Vienna, 1 Dec. 1935). Austrian bass-baritone. Studied medicine; then at 21, on the advice of Mahler, turned to music, studying at the Vienna Conservatory. Début Bayreuth 1902, Hagen. Vienna S.O. 1902-35; London, C.G., 1924-31; N.Y., Met., 1927-30. Although particularly renowned for his Gurnemanz and other Wagner roles, it is as Baron Ochs, in which role he has never been equalled, that he will always be remembered. At Salzburg he appeared with hardly less success as Leporello, Figaro, and Sarastro. In Vienna he created, among other roles, that of Barak in *Frau ohne Schatten*. (R)
Bibl: O. Kunz: *Richard Mayr* (1933).

Mayr, Simone (orig. Johannes Simon) (*b* Mendorf, 14 June 1763; *D* Bergamo, 2 Dec. 1845). Italian composer of German origin. Studied Bergamo with Lenzi, Venice with Bertoni. On the death of the patron who had supported him, he was urged by Piccinni to try his hand at opera, and his *Saffo* was prod. Venice 1794; its success led to many commissions, and he wrote 61 operas between then and 1824, including *Lodoïska* (1796), *Adelaide di Guesclino* (1799), *Ginevra di Scozia* (1801), *Alonso e Cora* (1804, rev. as *Cora*, 1815), *Elisa* (1801, to the same text as Cherubini's opera), and *Medea in Corinto* (1813). He also wrote a 1-act *L'amor coniugale*, (1805), to a text based on Bouilly's *Léonore*. Most of his operas were in buffo style, but he brought a new vividness of orchestration to opera buffa (including the regular use of a stage band) with the addition of harps to the orchestra and a novel virtuosity of wind writing; he also introduced orchestral numbers depicting storms, earthquakes, and so on. He also developed the chorus, with music of a variety that extended from church polyphony to double choruses and folk-like ensembles. His most celebrated work, *Medea in Corinto*, also makes striking advances in fluency between numbers. He wrote on music, especially a treatise on Haydn, and in 1805

founded a Conservatory in Bergamo where his pupils included Donizetti (whom he taught without charge for ten years). He died blind, greatly honoured by musicians who included Verdi, a mourner at his funeral; his influence on early 19th cent. Italian opera extended beyond Rossini, whose rise to some extent eclipsed him, to the composers of early Italian Romanticism, including Verdi.
Bibl: C. Scotti: *Simone Mayr* (1903).

Mazeppa. Opera in 3 acts by Tchaikovsky; text by composer and V. P. Burenin, after Pushkin's poem *Poltava* (1829). Prod. Moscow, B., 15 Feb. 1884, with Krutikova, Pavlovskaya, Korsov, Borisov, Usatov, Führer, Grigoryev, Dodonov, cond. Altani; Liverpool 6 Aug. 1888, with Winogradoff, cond. Truffi; Boston, O.H., 14 Dec. 1922, with Guseva, Valentinova, Radeyev, Karlash, Danilov, Alimov.

Maria (sop.), daughter of Kochubey (bass), loves Mazeppa (bar.) and rejects Andrey (ten.). When Mazeppa is refused her hand by Kochubey, he abducts her; Andrey offers to approach the Tsar with information about Mazeppa's treachery in siding with the Swedes. But the Tsar believes Mazeppa, and Kochubey is arrested; torture fails to break him or to discover his treasure. Maria is told of this and pleads with Mazeppa, who is absorbed in his plans to set up a separate state under his rule. Kochubey is led to execution. After the symphonic picture *The Battle of Poltava*, the last act shows Andrey pursuing the fleeing Swedes; however, he is shot by Mazeppa, and Maria, now gone mad, sings a lullaby over his body.

Other operas on the subject (those marked S based on Słowacki's drama, 1840) are by Maurer (1837), Campana (1850), Wietinghoff (1859), Pedrotti (1861), Pourny (1872), Jarecki (S, 1876), Pedrell (1881), Minchejmer (S, comp. 1885, prod. 1900), Grandval (1892), Koczalski (S, 1905), Nerini (1925).

Mazzinghi, Joseph (*b* London, 25 Dec. 1765; *d* Downside, 15 Jan. 1844). English composer of Corsican origin. From 1784 he was director of the King's T., for which he composed a number of popular operas.

Mazzoleni, Ester (*b* Sebenico, 12 March, 1883). Italian soprano. Studied Pisa and Trieste. Début Rome, C., Leonora, 1906. Milan, Sc., 1908 and subsequently; first Medea (Cherubini) there in Italy 1909, and particularly successful in Verdi repertory. Sang Aida at opening performance of the Verona Arena (1913). Retired 1926 and devoted herself to teaching in Palermo. (R)

Medea. In Greek legend, the sorceress who helped Jason to win the Golden Fleece, afterwards escaping with him. She prevented pursuit by casting the limbs of her brother behind her to delay the king, their father. Deserted by Jason, she killed his two children and poisoned his new wife: she then fled to Athens, where she married King Aegeus. Operas on her legend are by Cavalli (*Giasone*, 1649), Gianettini (*Medea in Atene*, 1675), Kusser (*Jason*, 1692), M.-A. Charpentier (1693), Salomon (*Médée et Jason*, 1713), Benda (1775), Vogel (*La Toison d'Or*, 1786), Cherubini (1797), Mayr (*Medea in Corinto*, 1813), Pacini (1843), Milhaud (1939), and others.

Médecin Malgré Lui, Le (The Doctor in Spite of Himself). Opera in 3 acts by Gounod; text a slight alteration of Molière's comedy (1666) by composer, Barbier, and Carré. Prod. Paris, T.L., 15 Jan. 1858 with Caye, Faivre, Lesage, Meillet, cond. Deloffre; London, C.G., 27 Feb. 1865; Cincinnati, 20 Mar. 1900. Gounod's first opéra comique and first wider success.

Médée (Medea). Opera in 3 acts by Cherubini; text by Hoffmann, after Corneille's tragedy (1635). Prod. Paris, T. Feydeau, 13 Mar. 1797 with Julie Legrand, Gaveaux, Dessaules: popular in Germany, especially in version with recitatives by Lachner (Frankfurt 1855). London, H.M.'s (with recits. by Arditi), 6 June 1865 with Tietjens, Santley. Not performed in Italy until 30 Dec. 1909 at Milan, Sc., with Mazzoleni, Frascani, Isalbanti. N.Y., T.H., 8 Nov. 1955 (concert); N.Y., 7 July 1973, with Niska, Bible, Cassilly, cond. Rudel. Callas's performance of the title role at the 1953 Florence Festival gave the opera a new lease of life. In Germany it has also been revived with Borkh and Lammers.

Medium, The. Opera in 2 acts by Menotti; text by composer. Prod. Columbia Univ., 8 May 1946; London, Aldwych Theatre, 29 Apr. 1948. The Medium, Madame Flora (con.), helped by her daughter Monica (sop.) and the mute Toby, cheats her clients. During a seance she feels a hand on her throat and confesses to her clients that she is a fraud. They refuse to believe her, but she loses her nerve, beats Toby and turns him out of the house; she then turns to the whisky bottle. Toby, in love with Monica, returns to find her and hides in a closet. A noise awakens Madame Flora, and seeing the closed curtain move she shoots at it, killing Toby. 'I've killed the ghost!', she screams.

Mefistofele. Opera in a prologue, 4 acts, and an epilogue by Boito; text by composer. Prod. Milan, Sc., 5 Mar. 1868 with Reboux, Spallazzi, Junca; but not a success. Revised and prod. Bologna 4 Oct. 1875 with Borghi-Mamo, Campanini, Nannetti. London, H.M.'s 6 July 1880 with Nilsson, Campanini, Nannetti; Boston, 16 Nov. 1880.

Unlike Gounod, in his *Faust* Boito based the opera on both parts of Goethe's work; thus after Marguerite's death comes the scene of the Night of the Classical Sabbath introducing Helen of Troy.

Mehta, Zubin (*b* Bombay, 29 Apr. 1936). Indian conductor. Studied Vienna with Swarowsky. Début Toronto, 1964, *Tosca*. N.Y., Met. 1965-71 conducting world première of Levy's *Mourning Becomes Electra* (1967) as well as *Aida*, *Carmen*, *Tristan und Isolde*, and other works; Milan, Sc., since 1974; London, C.G., since 1977, *Otello*, *Fanciulla del West*, and *Die Fledermaus*. Also appeared at Salzburg, Florence, Vienna. (R)

Méhul, Étienne-Nicolas (*b* Givet, 22 June 1763; *d* Paris, 18 Oct. 1817). French composer. Studied in the local abbey of Givet, later Paris with Edelmann. His first opera, *Cora* (1789), was unperformed; he followed this with *Euphrosine* (1790), an opéra-comique mixing serious and comic elements; it immediately became famous for its duet, 'Gardez-vous de la jalousie'. It was here that Méhul made his first steps in the development of dramatic motive, associating a specific phrase with jealousy and subsequently modifying it. The more severe *Stratonice* (1792) also contained a popular number, 'Versez tous vos chagrins'. Set in ancient times, it shows Méhul's care for achieving a vivid and individual setting that was to mark his operatic work; much of this he achieved by means of very carefully devised orchestration. *Le Jeune sage et le vieux fou* (1793) was a comedy, with an overture that like many others has featured in concert programmes.

With the establishment of the new political régime, Méhul was appointed to the Institut National de Musique in 1793, and his next opera, *Horatius Coclès* (1794), used a classical theme to make a contemporary political point. He was more successful with *Mélidore et Phrosine* (1794), in which he takes still further his use of motive, and with his other major work of the decade, *Ariodant* (1799), whose ambitious structure and chevaleresque setting to some extent anticipate Weber's *Euryanthe*. Meanwhile, in 1795, he had been granted a pension by the Comédie-Italienne, and in 1794 made a director of the Conservatoire. Possibly on the orders of Napoleon, with whom he had many contacts, he wrote *La Prise du pont de Lody* (1797), celebrating the Austrian defeat of 1796.

There followed a series of comedies, beginning with *Bion* (1800), and including the Ossianic opera *Uthal* (1806), in which Méhul's care for establishing an individual orchestral atmosphere shows in the total banishing of violins from the string ensemble. His last major success was *Joseph* (1807), a masterly work in which many of his gifts, including his melodic grace and his feeling for atmosphere and situation, are powerfully and movingly displayed. It was immediately successful, as much admired in Germany and other countries as in France, influencing a number of composers including Weber, and surviving in repertories well into the 20th cent. A few opéras-comiques followed, but Méhul never again gave himself so concentratedly to a dramatic subject. A Classic by training, his powerful Romantic impulses and his original and searching musical mind made him both successful and deeply respected in his own day, and a strong formative influence on German Romantic opera as well as on French Grand Opera.

Bibl: A. Pougin: *Méhul* (1889, 2/1893).

Mei-Figner, Medea. See *Figner, Medea Mei-*.

Meilhac, Henri (*b* Paris, 21 Feb. 1831; *d* Paris, 6 July 1897). French dramatist and librettist. Most of his librettos were written in collaboration, with Millaud for Hervé's *Mlle Nitouche*, with Gille for Massenet's *Manon* and Planquette's *Rip*; but by far the most important collaboration of his career was with Ludovic *Halévy. Their most famous libretto is certainly *Carmen*, for Bizet; but their most characteristic vein was operetta, especially as shown in Offenbach's *La Belle Hélène, Barbe-Bleue,* and *La Vie parisienne.* Frequently by means of a classical setting, they satirized contemporary society in the guise of mocking an old myth, also parodying some of the conventions of opera. At a time when the Paris O. enshrined the pomp of the most elevated manner of grand opera, Meilhac and Halévy provided the necessary corrective of laughter at human foibles and the shortcomings of society.

Mein Herr Marquis. Adele's (sop.) laughing song in Act 2 of J. Strauss's *Die Fledermaus,* in which, disguised at Orlofsky's party, she flirts with her employer Eisenstein.

Meistersinger von Nürnberg, Die (The Mastersingers of Nuremberg). Opera in 3 acts by Wagner; text by composer. Prod. Munich 21 June 1868, with Mallinger, Diez, Nachbaur, Schlosser, Betz, Hoelzel, Fischer, Bausewein, cond. Bülow; London, D.L., 30 May 1882, with Sucher, Schefsky, Winkelmann, Landau, Gura, Ehrke, Kraus, Koegel, cond. Richter; N.Y., Met., 4 Jan. 1886, with Seidl-Krauss, Brandt, Strift, Krämer, Fischer, Kemlitz, Lehmler, Staudigl, cond. Seidl.

In the Church of St Katherine in 16th-century Nuremberg, Walther von Stolzing (ten.) tries to attract the attention of Eva (sop.), daughter of the goldsmith Veit Pogner, who is with her nurse Magdalene (sop.). He learns that Eva will be betrothed next day to the winner of a singing contest held by the Guild of Mastersingers. Magdalene's admirer, the apprentice David (ten.), explains the rules to Walther. The Mastersingers gradually enter, led by Pogner (bass) and Beckmesser (bass-bar.), the small-minded town clerk who himself hopes to win Eva's hand. Hans Sachs (bass-bar.) the cobbler finally arrives, and the baker Fritz Kothner (bass) calls the roll. Pogner addresses the Masters and tells them of the contest. Walther is introduced as a candidate for the Guild; he is asked to tell of his background and training, and then invited to sing a trial song. Beckmesser is appointed marker, and enters a special box; Kothner reads the rules. Walther improvises a song about the spring and love, but soon Beckmesser's slate is full of the mistakes the knight has made. The meeting breaks up in disorder; only Sachs has seen something new and attractive in the song.

It is Midsummer Eve, and the apprentices are closing Sachs's shop. The cobbler himself sits under the elder tree and reflects on the events in the church. Eva makes her way from her house opposite Sachs's shop and questions him about the trial. Sachs, a widower, is himself half in love with Eva, but realizes that he is too old for her. He teases her and she rushes home in tears. Seeing the situation, Sachs resolves to help the young couple, who have met and planned to elope. Sachs prevents this by opening his widow and letting light stream across the roadway. Beckmesser now arrives to serenade Eva. When Beckmesser protests at Sachs's hammering, he is told that his shoes will not be ready unless work continues. Sachs suggests he act as a marker, hammering each time Beckmesser makes a mistake. Beckmesser agrees, seeing a figure in the window above – it is really Magdalene in Eva's clothes. The serenade and hammering wake the neighbours and apprentices. Beckmesser receives a drubbing, and in the tumult Sachs prevents Eva and Walther from running off, and takes the latter into his own house. The stage empties when the Night Watchman's horn sounds.

Sachs is musing over a large book. He does not hear the apologies proffered by David for his part in the riot. Left alone, he soliloquizes on the madness of the world, and the love of Walther and Eva. Walther comes to tell Sachs of a wonderful dream. Sachs writes this down, for it is a prize song – only the final stanza is lacking. While Sachs and Walther change into their festal robes, the aching Beckmesser enters. He sees the song, and believing it Sachs's, hastily pockets it. Sachs now returns and allows Beckmesser to keep the song. Eva appears, pretending that her shoes hurt, but really hoping to see Walther. While Sachs is attending to her shoe, Walther enters, and the sight of Eva inspires him to his final stanza. David and Magdalene are summoned, David is made a journeyman; the song is christened. All depart for the festal meadow. On the banks of the River Pegnitz the apprentices and guildsmen assemble. The apprentices dance with some girls. They are interrupted by the entrance of the Masters, who take their places on the stand. Sachs is acclaimed, and thanks the people. Beckmesser rises and makes a fiasco of the song. When the crowd laughs he accuses Sachs of having written it. Sachs disclaims authorship, but summons Walther to show how the song should be sung. Walther wins the prize and Eva's hand, but when Pogner moves to invest him with the insignia of the guild, he brushes the chain aside, still smarting under his previous rejection. Sachs comes forward and persuades Walther to accept the honour, explaining the purpose of the Mastersingers in preserving the art of German song. Eva takes the wreath that she had placed on Walther's head and puts it on Sachs's amid the acclamations of the people.

Other operas on the hero, Hans Sachs, by Gyrowetz (1834) and Lortzing (1840); the latter, partly through a play by Deinhardstein (1827), provided Wagner with some suggestions for his work.

Melani. Italian family of 10 musicians including 7 singers and 3 composers, all sons of Domenico Melani.

(1) **Jacopo** (*b* Pistoia, 6 July 1623; *d* Pistoia, 19 Aug. 1676). Italian composer. One of the pioneers of Italian comic opera; wrote several works for Florence.

(2) **Alto** (*b* Pistoia, 3 March 1626; *d* Paris, 1714). Italian male soprano and court musician to Mattia de'Medici; sang in France and Italy. Became a secret agent of Cardinal Mazarin, and from 1665–72 was under Louis XIV's protection.

(3) **Francesco Maria** (*b* Pistoia, 3 Nov. 1628; *d* Pistoia, 1663). Italian male soprano. In service of Sigismond of Austria 1657; Paris 1659 sang Amastri in Cavalli's *Serse*.

(4) **Bartolomeo** (*b* Pistoia, 6 March 1634; *d*?). Italian singer. Munich 1657–8; Florence, creating parts in operas by Jacopo; maestro di cappella at Pistoia from 1677.

(5) **Alessandro** (*b* Pistoia, 4 Feb. 1639; *d* Rome, Oct. 1703). Italian composer whose three operas were produced in Rome, Florence, and Bologna.

(6) **Domenico** (*b* Pistoia, 1630; *d* Florence 12 July 1693). Italian male soprano. Stockholm, 1652–54; Dresden 1654–85. There were four more brothers, Antonio, Nicola, Vincenzo, and Giacinto.

Melba, (Dame) **Nellie** (orig. Helen Porter Mitchell) (*b* Richmond, nr. Melbourne, 19 May 1861; *d* Sydney, 23 Feb 1931). Australian soprano. Studied Melbourne, Paris with Marchesi. Début Brussels, La M., 1887, Gilda. London, C.G., 1888, Lucia, successful but not triumphant; her great London triumphs began (in 1889) as Juliette. Appeared regularly at C.G. until 1914 (missing only the 1909 season), and continued 1919, 1922–4 (with B.N.O.C.), and

1926. N.Y., Met., 1893–7, 1898–9, 1900–1, 1904–5, and 1910–11. Also appeared with Damrosch's Company, Manhattan Company, and Chicago Opera in America; and elsewhere in Europe. Bemberg wrote *Elaine* for her, and Saint-Saëns *Hélène,* both of which roles she created. At first a high coloratura famous for her Rosina, Lucia, Gilda, Violetta, etc., she later sang such lyric roles as Marguerite, Mimì, and Desdemona. She was also heard as Aida, Elsa, Nedda (of which she was the first London interpreter), and even the *Siegfried* Brünnhilde, which was her one great failure. Her voice, which retained its freshness and purity to the very end of her career, originally had a compass from b♭ to f''', and her technique and brilliant and easy ornamentations were a source of admiration and wonder. Her acting abilities were somewhat restricted, and many people found her interpretations cold. She was indeed the *prima donna assoluta,* and at C.G. she had for many years the final word in the engagements of other artists and the castings of the operas in which she sang. She gave her name to an ice-cream and a kind of toast. A film was made of her life in 1953 with Patrice Munsel. (R) *Bibl:* N. Melba: *Melodies and Memories* (1925); John Hetherington: *Melba* (1967).

Melbourne. Town in Victoria, Australia. Like other Australian towns, Melbourne was long dependent on visits from the many companies which toured Australia; performances have normally been given in the Princess T. It has also been the home of the National Theatre movement. In 1959 the Sydney Meyer Music Bowl was opened (cap. 2,000, lawn seating for 30,000). The Victoria Opera Company has also been very active, in the face of great financial and other difficulties The Melba Memorial Centre opened 1973, and includes a theatre.

Melchior, Lauritz (orig. Lebrecht Himml) (*b* Copenhagen, 20 Mar. 1890; *d* Santa Monica, Cal., 19 Mar. 1973). Danish, later American, tenor, orig. baritone. Studied Copenhagen with Poul Bang; toured Denmark 1912 with Zwicki Opera Company as Germont. Joined Royal T., Copenhagen, 1913; 'official' début there as Silvio; continued to sing baritone roles for four years. Mme Charles Cahier, who appeared with him in a performance of *Trovatore,* suggested he should study tenor roles, which he did with Vilem Herold, making his second début in 1918 as Tannhäuser. Further study 1921–3 with Victor Beigel in London, Ernst Grenzebach in Berlin, Mildenburg in Munich, and Kittel in Bayreuth. London, C.G., 1924 as Siegmund, and 1926–39; Bayreuth 1924–31; N.Y., Met., 1926–50. His career as a Heldentenor was unique. He sang Tristan over 200 times: his large, ringing voice never tired, and his singing was always exciting, if sometimes lacking in musicianship. Sang in the first broadcast from the Marconi experimental station in London in 1920 in a programme with Melba. Appeared in several films, including *Luxury Liner* (1947) and *The Stars are Singing* (1952). (R)

Melis, Carmen (*b* Cagliari, 16 Aug. 1885; *d* Longone al Segrino. nr. Como, 19 Dec. 1967). Italian soprano. Studied Florence with Teresina Singer, Rome with Cotogni, Paris with Jean de Reszke. Début Novara 1905, Iris. N.Y., Manhattan O. 1909–10, Boston and Chicago. London, C.G., 1913 Tosca, Nedda, and Maliella, 1929 Tosca and Musetta. Milan, Sc., 1924–5: created Ginevra in *La cena delle beffe*. Frequently at Rome, T.R., as Manon Lescaut and Minnie. Repertory also included Thaïs, Marschallin, Mistress Ford, Adriana Lecouvreur, Zazà, and Fedora. Retired from stage 1935 and taught in Pesaro and Milan; her pupils included Tebaldi and Rita Orlandi-Malaspina. (R)

Mélisande. The heroine (sop.) of Debussy's *Pelléas et Mélisande*.

Mellon, Alfred (*b* London, 7 Apr. 1820; *d* London, 27 Mar. 1867). English conductor and composer. After playing in the orchestra at C.G. and elsewhere in London, became chief conductor for the *Pyne-Harrison Company. His *Victorine* was produced at C.G. in 1859.

Melnikov, Ivan (Alexandrovich) (*b* St. Petersburg, 4 Mar. 1829; *d* St. Petersburg, 8 July 1906). Russian baritone. Studied with Lomakin and in Italy with Repetto. Début St. Petersburg 1867, Riccardo *(Puritani)*. He created the title role in *Boris Godunov*, Don Juan in Dargomyzhsky's *The Stone Guest*, Tomakov in *Ivan the Terrible*, the title role in Rubinstein's *The Demon* and *Prince Igor*. He sang in all Tchaikovsky's operas except *Yolanta*, but Onegin was his least successful role and he relinquished it after five performances. He retired in 1890 and devoted himself to teaching.

Melodrama. A dramatic composition, or section of a composition, in which one or more actors recite to a musical commentary: if for one actor, the term 'monodrama' may be used, if two, 'duodrama' (as in the *duodramas of *Benda). The form became popular in the second half of the 18th cent. The first full-scale melodrama was Rousseau's *Pygmalion,* in which he tried 'to join the declamatory art with the art of music', alternating short spoken passages with instrumental music as a development of the *pantomime dialoguée.* The most successful examples of its power of heightening the dramatic tension are in the grave-digging scene in Beethoven's *Fidelio* and in the Wolf's Glen scene in Weber's *Der Freischütz.*

Mozart, who admired Benda, used melodrama in his *Zaide.* The form has retained some following in Czechoslovakia: Fibich wrote a trilogy *Hippodamia* (1890–1).

Melodramma. A 17th cent. term for opera, also used in later times.

Mendelssohn (-Bartholdy), **Felix** (*b* Hamburg, 3 Feb. 1809; *d* Leipzig, 4 Nov. 1847). German composer and conductor. Early in his career, Mendelssohn was interested in opera and hoped to develop a career as an opera composer. His failure to make a success in the genre in Berlin served to turn his attention away from the stage in the direction of oratorio) but Wagner records (in *Mein Leben*) a conversation which supports the view that he was to some extent a frustrated opera composer. His operas are as follows: *Die Soldatenliebschaft* (comp. 1820, prod 1962); *Die beiden Pädagogen* (1820); *Die wandernden Komödianten* (comp. 1822); *Der Onkel aus Boston* (1824); *Die Hochzeit des Camacho* (1827); *Die Heimkehr aus der Fremde* (1829); and the unfinished *Loreley* (comp. 1847). *Die Heimkehr* has been known in English as *Son and Stranger.*

Menotti, Gian Carlo (*b* Cadegliano, 7 Jul. 1911). American composer of Italian birth. His first surviving opera is *Amelia Goes to the Ball* (1937), in which his light fertility of invention admirably serves the buffo plot. A more powerful dramatic vein was attempted in *The Old Maid and the Thief* (1939) and *The Island God* (1942); and these were followed by a thriller, *The Medium* (1946), which often shares the bill with one of his most successful works, the entertaining *The Telephone* (1947). *The Consul* (1950) showed Menotti at his most theatrically powerful, though it was noticeable that the power and sincerity of the dramatic plea was sharply at odds with the sub-Puccini lyricism of the score. Experience gained in filming *The Medium* has stood Menotti in good stead in TV; *Amahl and the Night Visitors* (1951) is often shown at Christmas. *The Saint of Bleecker Street* (1954) marked a return to blood-and-thunder *verismo*; but *The Unicorn, the Gorgon, and the Manticore* (1956) was a satire, cast in *madrigal opera form, on the vagaries of social fashion. In *Maria Golovin* (1958) Menotti tackled the deeper theme of personal imprisonment: his hero is a blind man tormented by jealousy. A brilliantly skilled man of the theatre, quick and versatile, he has found it difficult to sustain the invention and the genuine theatrical power of his dramatic ideas with music that gives them proper operatic force. His later operas are *Labyrinth* (TV, 1963) and a 20th-cent morality, *The Last Savage,* prod. Paris, O.C., 1963. He was librettist for Barber's *Vanessa* (1958); in 1958 he also founded the successful Festival of Two Worlds in Spoleto, designed to give openings to young musicians.

Méphistophélès. The Devil (bass or bass-bar.) in Gounod's *Faust* and Berlioz's *La Damnation de Faust.*

Mercadante, (Giuseppe) **Saverio** (Raffaele) (*b* Altamura, nr. Bari, bapt. 17 Sept., 1795; *d* Naples, 17 Dec. 1870). Italian composer. An illegitimate child, he went to Naples aged about 11 and studied at the Collegio di S. Sebastiano with Furno and Tritto, later Zingarelli. Here he attracted the attention of Rossini, who may have encouraged him to take up opera: his *L'apoteosi d' Ercole* was well received in 1819. He followed this with others in quick succession, having his first great success with the seventh, *Elisa e Claudio,* in Milan (1821) and abroad. After failing to establish himself in Vienna, he renewed his success with *Caritea, Regina di Spagna* (or *Donna Caritea*) in Venice (1826). A proposed Spanish appointment having failed, he wrote *Ezio* for Turin (1827), returned to Spain for *I due Figaro* (comp. 1827, postponed on political grounds until 1835), and then moved to Lisbon and back to Cadiz and Madrid before settling in Italy in 1831. Here he had a triumph in Turin with *I Normanni a Parigi* (1832). Invited by Rossini to Paris in 1835, Mercadante experienced a failure with *I briganti,* despite the presence in the cast of Grisi, Rubini, Tamburini, and Lablache. But his contact with Meyerbeer's *Les Huguenots* gave him decisive encouragement for his next work, his most famous, *Il giuramento,* produced at Milan in 1837. The striking expansion in his style, coupled with the withdrawal from the scene of Rossini, Bellini, and Donizetti, led to further successes with *Le due illustri rivali* (1838), *Elena da Feltre* (1838), *Il bravo* (1839), and *La vestale* (1840). Appointed director of the Naples Conservatory (1840), he continued to compose busily, his operas including *Il reggente* (1843) and the successful *Orazi e Curiazi* (1846).

Having begun in the hey-day of Rossini, Mercadante's career extended well into the middle of Verdi's. His earliest operas are 18th cent. in manner, four of them deriving from Metastasio, and only later was he drawn to Cammarano and especially Romani, exchanging the manner of Rossini for lyrical melodrama and eventually, in *Il giuramento,* for a music drama of considerable breadth and originality. Though this, and his succeeding works, are a clear bridge to Verdi, they have a strength of their own: structurally and harmonically they are more fluent, more closely geared to the drama, while not losing a grasp on essentially Italian melody, and they impressed no less a judge of new music than Liszt. Verdi, who had been a victim of Mercadante's jealousy but for-

gave him, was fruitfully influenced. Though the later operas do not always maintain the ambition or the quality of his best work, Mercadante is an important pioneer of 19th cent. Italian music drama.
Bibl: B. Notarnicola: *Saverio Mercadante* (1945, 2/1949, 3/1951).

Merelli, Bartolomeo (*b* Bergamo, 19 May 1794; *d* Milan 3 (4?) April 1879). Italian manager and librettist. Studied law, later music with Mayr. One of his fellow students was Donizetti, for whom he later provided librettos of five operas including *Enrico di Borgogna* and *Zoraide di Franata.* 1826–30 managed a theatrical agency in Milan; 1830–35 managed seasons in Varese, Como and Cremona; from 1834 engaged singers for Carlo Visconti di Modrone at La Scala, Milan, whom he succeeded as director in 1836. Dismissed through public protest, 1846. Joined forces with Carlo Balochino, director of the Vienna Kä., 1836, and together they managed the theatre until 1848. He returned to Vienna 1853–5, and was again director of Sc. 1861–3. He also wrote librettos for Mayr, Vaccai, and Morlacchi, and was responsible for suggesting to Verdi the libretto of *Nabucco,* thus helping to bring Verdi back to opera. One of the great impresarios of the 19th cent. His son **Luigi** (1825–82) was also a manager and organised seasons in Vienna and St Petersburg in the 1860s; a younger son **Eugenio** was more successful, organizing tours throughout Europe, even to Edinburgh (1860). His last was to Dresden 1874. His singers included Patti and Trebelli.

Méric, Joséphine see *De Méric, Joséphine.*

Méric-Lalande, Henriette (*b* Dunkirk, 1798; *d* Chantilly, 7 Sept. 1867). French soprano. Daughter of Jean-Baptiste Lalande, French conductor with whom she studied. Début Nantes, 1814. After further study with Garcia in Paris and Bonfichi and Bandeali in Italy, appeared Naples, S.C., where she created Bianca in Bellini's *Bianca e Gernando* (1826); Milan, Sc., where she created Imogene in *Il pirata* (1827), Alaide in *La straniera* (1829), and Lucrezia Borgia (1833); at Parma she created the title-role in Bellini's *Zaira* (1829); London, Kings T., 1830. She retired 1836, but even at the time of her London début Chorley commented that 'she had arrived in England too late . . . and gave little satisfaction'.

Mérimée, Prosper (*b* Paris, 28 Sep. 1803; *d* Cannes, 23 Sep. 1870). French author. Operas on his works are as follows:
Le Carrosse du Saint-Sacrement (1829): Offenbach (*La Périchole,* 1868); Berners (1924); Busser (1948).
Matteo Falcone (1829): Zöllner (1894); Cui (1907).
La Vénus d'Ille (1837): Schoeck (1922); Wetzler

(*Die baskische Venus*, 1928).

Colomba (1840): Pacini (*La Fidanzata corta*, 1842); Grandjean (1882); Mackenzie (1883); Radeglia (1887); Büsser (1921).

Carmen (1845): Bizet (1875); Halffter (*La Muerte di Carmen*, 1930).

La Dame de Pique (translation of *Pushkin) (1849): Halévy (1850).

La Chambre bleu: Bouval (1902); Lazarus (1937).

Donna Urraca: Malipiero (1954).

Inès Mendo: Erlanger (1897).

L'Occasion: Durey (1920).

La Vénus d'Ille: Schoeck (1922); Wetzler 1928).

Merli, Francesco (*b* Milan, 27 Jan. 1887; *d* Milan, 12 Dec. 1976). Italian tenor. Studied Milan with Negrini and Borghi. Début Milan, Sc., 1916, Alvaro in Spontini's *Fernando Cortez*. London, C.G., 1926–30, where he was the first London Calaf; N.Y., Met., 1931–2. Sang regularly at Sc. and the Rome Opera, where in the mid-1930s he was a famous Otello, Dick Johnson, Samson, and Don José. Created title-role in Respighi's *Belfagor*. (R)

Merlo, Marisa. See *Morel*.

Mermaid Theatre. The name given the theatre built by Bernard Miles in the back garden of his London home, which was inaugurated in 1951 by a performance of *Dido and Aeneas* with Flagstad. Subsequently rebuilt in the City of London at Puddle Dock, but not used for opera.

Merola, Gaetano (*b* Naples, 4 Jan. 1881; *d* San Francisco, 30 Aug. 1953). Italian conductor and manager. Studied Naples Conservatory. Went to U.S.A. 1899 as assistant conductor at Met. Cond. Henry Savage and Hammerstein's Manhattan Company, of which he was also chorus master 1906–10, and London O. H. 1910–11. Toured U.S.A. with Naples S.C. Company, and then in 1923 became music director and manager of the San Francisco Company, remaining its director until his death. He raised the San Francisco Company to rank second only to the Met., bringing many famous artists to America for the first time. He collapsed and died while conducting an open-air concert with the San Francisco Symphony Orchestra. See *San Francisco Opera*.

Merrie England. Opera in 2 acts by German; text by Basil Hood. Prod. London, Savoy T., 2 Apr. 1902; N.Y., Hunter College, 13 Apr. 1956 (concert). The plot turns on the rivalry of the Earl of Essex and Sir Walter Raleigh for the favour of Queen Elizabeth I, who discovers that Raleigh's true affections are with Bessie Throckmorton, but whose attempts to have Bessie murdered are frustrated by a plot of Essex's.

Merrill, Robert (*b* Brooklyn, 4 June 1917). American baritone. Studied with his mother, Lillian Miller Merrill, a former concert singer, and later Samuel Margolis in N.Y. Début Trenton 1944, Amonasro. Won Met. Auditions of Air, 1945, and made début there 1945 as Germont. Sang Posa in *Don Carlos* on opening night of the Bing régime, Met. 1950. He was subsequently dismissed by Bing in Apr. 1951 when he failed to keep his engagements on the Met. tour through filming in Hollywood; reinstated the following season. London, C.G., 1967, Germont. Chosen by Toscanini to sing Germont and Renato in his broadcasts and recordings of *La traviata* and *Un ballo in maschera*. (R)

Bibl: R. Merrill: *Once More from the Beginning* (1965).

Merriman, Nan (*b* Pittsburg, 28 Apr. 1920). American mezzo-soprano. Studied Los Angeles with Alexia Bassian and Lotte Lehmann. Début Cincinnati 1942, La Cieca. Chosen by Toscanini for his broadcasts and recordings of *Orfeo* (title role), *Falstaff* (Meg), *Rigoletto* (Magdalena), *Otello* (Emilia). Sang Baba the Turk in the British première of *The Rake's Progress* and Laura in Dargomyzhsky's *The Stone Guest*, Piccola Scala 1958. (R)

Merry Widow, The. See *Lustige Witwe, Die*.

Merry Wives of Windsor, The. See *Lustigen Weiber von Windsor, Die*.

Messa di voce (*It* placing of voice; *Fr*, *son filé*; *Ger*, *Schwellton*). The art of swelling and diminishing tone on a single note. First mentioned by Caccini in the preface to *Le nuove musiche* (1601), it acquired great importance in the age of bel canto as a demonstration of vocal skill and control.

Messager, André (Charles Prosper) (*b* Montluçon, 30 Dec. 1853; *d* Paris, 24 Feb. 1929). French composer and conductor. Studied Paris, with Fauré, Saint-Saëns, and others. Organist at St Sulpice, then conducted in various theatres and began writing operettas and ballets (including *Les Deux pigeons*, 1886). The success of *La Basoche* (1890) as successor to Sullivan's *Ivanhoe* at the English O.H. (1891) led to *Mirette* (1891), though his most popular works were *Madame Chrysanthème* (1893), *Les P'tites Michu* (1897), and *Véronique* (1898). Coming under Wagner's influence in the 1880s, he made a name as a Wagner conductor; he was also music director of the O.C. 1898–1903, during which time he conducted the première of *Pelléas et Mélisande* (1902). He was manager of the Grand Opera Syndicate at C.G. 1901–7, Director of the Opéra 1907–14, music director of the O.C. again 1919–20. After the war, when he toured N. and S. America, he gave more time to composition; his operettas include *Monsieur Beaucaire* (prod., with Maggie Teyte, 1919). As a conductor, he did much to introduce Wagner into France, and is also famous for his support of Russian music and Mozart; he revived Gluck and Rameau, as well as encouraging his contemporaries and introducing Charpentier's *Louise* and Massenet's *Grisélidis*. At C.G. he conducted a wide repertory that included premières of Saint-Saëns's *Hélène* and Massenet's *Le Jongleur de Notre-Dame*. His music is unfailingly elegant and deft, with a theatrical flair and tunefulness that are the product of much musical learning lightly worn.

Bibl: M. Augé-Lanibé: *André Messager* (1951).

Messel, Oliver (*b* Cuckfield, 13 Jan. 1904). English designer. Studied with Tonks at the Slade School, London. Began to work for theatre in 1926. Designed scenery and costumes for the Herbert-Korngold *Helen* (1931); later ballets for S.W., and C.G. His *Magic Flute* at C.G. (1947) was a brilliant success; he also designed *The Queen of Spades, Samson* (Handel) for C.G., and many operas for Gly. including *Ariadne auf Naxos, Idomeneo, Comte Ory,* and *Rosenkavalier.*

Metaphor aria (or **Simile aria**). A term used for arias in opera seria in which the singer takes a metaphor or simile, illustrated by the music, to illustrate a dramatic or emotional situation. Characteristic examples in Metastasio, in whose librettos they abound, are when the singer compares himself to a raging lion, a steersman in a storm, a turtle-dove awaiting his mate, or (in *Sosarme*) compares another singer to a deranged butterfly. The merit of the convention was to provide singers with a vivid excuse for virtuosity, the composer with a chance to display his powers of illustration. A celebrated later example, containing in its genuine emotion a touch of parody of the convention, is Fiordiligi's 'Come scoglio' in Mozart's *Così fan tutte.*

Metastasio (orig. Trapassi), **Pietro** (*b* Rome, 3 Jan. 1698; *d* Vienna, 12 Apr. 1782). Italian poet and librettist. He published his first work at 14, and for long enjoyed the protection of the singer Marianna Benti-Bulgarelli (known as 'La Romanina'). From 1730 he lived in Vienna, where most of his dramas were written. Of his huge output, some texts were used as often as 60 or 70 times: *Artaserse* was set 40 times in a century, and Hasse set all his librettos. His contemporaries ranked him high as a poet, and his aim was to purify and elevate the opera seria libretto. To this end, he abolished certain 17th cent. elements, in particular excessive use of pageantry and stage machinery, recourse to the supernatural (though not the mythical or divine), and the interpolation of comedy into tragic subjects. His success lay in his skill in providing elegant, charming verse, marked by a vivid gift for imagery especially in providing

*metaphor arias, within a framework wholly approved by fashion: intricate plots and elaborate speeches served classical subjects in which a social structure and standard of conduct deriving from classical example was glorified. Only the aristocracy could mingle with the gods, and neither group reveals any but the most detached, formalised emotions, their utterances dependent on situation and effect rather than character. The rigidity of this convention, of which Metastasio was the greatest master though not the inventor, served to stress only the merits of conformity; and when the *intermezzo began to provide an earthier, more human contrast, this soon told against Metastasian heroes, pointing fatally to their artificiality. It was against the abuses of Metastasian opera – above all, the halting dramatic progress, the plot continually being arrested to make way for demonstrations of vocal skill – that Gluck rebelled. An operetta on Metastasio is by L. Dall'Argine (1903). For a virtually complete list of settings of Metastasio's librettos, see *Enciclopedia dello spettacolo*, Vol. VII, col. 501–5. The following is a list of his operatic librettos, with date of first setting: *Siface* (1723), *Didone abbandonata* (1724), *L'Impresario delle Canarie* (1724), *Siroe* (1726), *Catone in Utica* (1728), *Ezio* (1728), *Semiramide* (1729), *Alessandro nell' Indie* (1729), *Artaserse* (1730), *Demetrio* (1731), *Issipile* (1732), *Adriano in Siria* (1732), *L'Olimpiade* (1733, *Demofoonte* (1733), *La clemenza di Tito* (1734), *Achille in Sciro* (1736), *Ciro riconosciuto* (1736), *Temistocle* (1736), *Zenobia* (1740), *Attilio Regolo* (written 1740, comp. 1750), *Antigono* (1743), *Ipermestra* (1744), *Il re pastore* (1751), *L'Eroe cinese* (1752), *Nitteti* (1756), *Il Trionfo di Clelia* (1762), *Romola ed Ersilia* (1765), *Ruggiero* (1771).

Metropolitan Opera Auditions of the Air. A series of weekly radio programmes instituted in 1936 by the A.B.C. Network in New York to audition singers for the Met. Among those who have won contracts at the Met. as a result of these broadcasts (now discontinued) are Arthur Carron, Frank Guarrera, Margaret Harshaw, Raoul Jobin, Robert Merrill, Patrice Munsel, Risë Stevens, Regina Resnik, Eleanor Steber, Teresa Stratas, and Leonard Warren.

Metropolitan Opera Guild. An organization founded in 1935 under the presidency of Mrs. Augustus Belmont, to help sell subscriptions for the Metropolitan Opera. This membership has increased from 2,000 to more than 60,000, and its activities include performances for schools and other educational institutions; the publication of a weekly magazine during the season, *Opera News,* which prints articles and other features about the weekly Saturday afternoon broadcasts from the Met.; and the issuing of gramophone records. It also provides funds to finance at least one new production a season and sponsors regional auditions for young singers as well as the Central Opera Service.

Metropolitan Opera House. New York's leading opera house formely stood on Broadway between 39th and 40th Streets. In the second half of last century opera was given at the *Academy of Music, and a number of rich New York business men, unable to get boxes there, decided to finance another opera house in New York and subscribed $800,000 for this purpose. The Met. (cap. 3,615) opened on 22 Oct. 1883 with *Faust* under the management of Henry Abbey. This first season resulted in heavy losses, and the management was taken over by the stockholders who appointed Leopold *Damrosch as artistic director. He died before the end of his first season and was succeeded by his son Walter *Damrosch, whose régime lasted until the end of the 1890–1 season. During this time all operas were sung in German, and the American premières of most of the later Wagner works were given.

Abbey returned to the management in 1892 and was joined by Maurice *Grau and Edward Schoeffel until 1898. Grau was manager 1898–1903, and Heinrich Conried 1903–8. During the Grau régime the company included the De Reszkes, Eames, Lilli Lehmann, Nordica, Sembrich, Schumann-Heink, Ternina, Maurel, Plançon, and Van Dyck; and then Conried brought Caruso, Farrar, and Fremstad to the company, as well as Mahler and Mottl as conductors. He enraged Bayreuth by giving the American première of *Parsifal* some ten or more years before the copyright expired, and public opinion in New York by mounting *Salome*.

Conried was succeeded by *Gatti-Casazza, whose management lasted until 1935. The first seven of his seasons were distinguished by the presence of Toscanini as chief conductor, and the period included the world premières of *La fanciulla del West*, Humperdinck's *Königskinder*, and Giordano's *Madame Sans-Gêne*, and the American premières of *The Queen of Spades, Boris Godunov, Le donne curiose, Der Rosenkavalier*, and *L'amore dei tre Re*. The company was strengthened by the débuts of Destinn, Alda, Tetrazzini, Bori, Hempel, Martinelli, Amato, and Renaud. Among Toscanini's colleagues as conductors were Hertz, Mahler, and Polacco.

After Toscanini there came a whole host of conductors, the most important of whom were Bodanzky, Moranzoni, Serafin, and Wolff. This period saw the débuts of Galli-Curci, De Luca, Ponselle, Gigli, Pinza, Lauri-Volpi, Muzio, Jeritza, Rethberg, Edward Johnson, Tibbett, Melchior, Grace Moore, Pons, and then, during the last three Gatti-Casazza seasons, Schipa, Leider, Olszewska, Lehmann, and Flagstad. As well as the Puccini *Trittico*, premières of a number of American works were given, and the first American performances of works by Strauss, Janáček, Křenek, Respighi, and others.

From 1935 to 1950 Edward *Johnson was the company's general manager. He encouraged American artists, and his régime saw the emergence of Leonard Warren, Dorothy Kirsten, Jan Peerce, Richard Tucker, Helen Traubel, Blanche Thebom, Patrice Munsel, and Margaret Harshaw. He also strengthened the conducting staff by engaging Beecham, Walter, Busch, Stiedry, Szell, and Reiner. This was the period, too, of great Wagner performances with Flagstad, Lawrence, Varnay, Traubel, Melchior, Svanholm, Schorr, Janssen, Berglund, Kipnis, and List.

After Johnson's retirement the general manager was Rudolf *Bing, who modernized stage techniques and brought in producers from the theatre, including Alfred Lunt, Margaret Webster, and Tyrone Guthrie. There were more performances of opera in English, including successful excursions into the realms of operetta–*Fledermaus, La Périchole*, and *The Gipsy Baron* – as well as *The Rake's Progress, Wozzeck*, and Barber's *Vanessa*. The Italian repertory fared particularly well with Callas, Tebaldi, Milanov, De los Angeles, Di Stefano, Del Monaco, Campora, Björling, Bergonzi, Siepi, and Valletti, and still more American artists established themselves, including Dobbs, Elias, Peters, Rankin, Resnik, Hines, Merrill, Tozzi, and Uppmann. The new Met. (cap. 3,800) opened in the Lincoln Center with Barber's *Antony and Cleopatra*, 16 Sept. 1966. In 1972 Göran Gentele was appointed as Bing's successor, but was killed in a car crash a few weeks before taking up his post. In the same year Kubelík became music director, but resigned in 1974. Anthony Bliss was appointed executive director in 1975 with James Levine as music director and John Dexter director of productions.

Bibl: I. Kolodin: *The Metropolitan Opera* (1966).

Meyer, Kerstin (b. Stockholm, 3 Apr. 1928). Swedish mezzo-soprano. Studied Stockholm, Royal Academy Music, with Arne Sunnegard and Andrejeva von Skilonde, N.Y. with Paola Novikova, and Rome, Siena and Salzburg. Début Stockholm 1952, Azucena. Member of Stockholm Opera ever since. N.Y., Met., 1960–2; Gly. since 1961, where she created Carolina in original version of *Elegy for Young Lovers* and Elisabeth in *The Rising of the Moon*, and sang Claire Zachanassian in first English production of *The Visit of the Old Lady*; London, C.G. 1960, Dido (Berlioz) and subsequently Octavian and Clytemnestra. Hamburg S.O.; created Mrs. Arden in Goehr's *Arden* must Die, Mrs Claiborne in Schuler's The Visitation, and Gertrude in Searle's Hamlet; also created Agave in The Bassarids (Salzburg 1966). One of the most intelligent modern singing actresses, especially successful in contemporary works but also a fine interpreter of Ottavia, Orfeo, Dorabella, and Fricka. (R)

Meyerbeer, Giacomo (orig. Jakob Liebmann Beer) (b Vogelsdorf, nr Berlin, 5 Sept. 1791; d Paris, 2 May 1864). German composer of Jewish parentage. His career was largely pursued in France, and he can claim to be one of the creators of French grand opera. He studied in Berlin, and was a child prodigy at the piano. He subsequently studied composition under the Abbé Vogler at Darmstadt, at which time his first two operas were written – Jephthas Gelübde (Munich, 1812), and Wirt und Gast, oder Aus Scherz, Ernst (Stuttgart, 1813). The first, more oratorio than opera, was a failure; the second, a comic work, was accepted for Vienna under the title of Alimelek, where it was a complete fiasco. In Vienna he pursued his career as a pianist; but, still hankering after the opera stage, he sought the advice of Salieri, who suggested that he should go to Italy to study the human voice. In Venice in 1815 he fell under the spell of Rossini's Tancredi, and immediately began to write Italian operas – Romilda e Costanza (Padua, 1817), Semiramide riconosciuta (Turin, 1819), Emma di Resburgo (Venice, 1819), Margherita d'Anjou (Milan 1820), L'Esule di Granata (Milan, 1822), and Il Crociato in Egitto (Venice, 1824)–all of which were immediately successful throughout Italy.

He was entreated by Weber to give up Italian opera, but it was to France rather than to Germany that he turned. He was so attracted by Paris, where he went for the first performance of his Crociato in 1826, that he made his home there. The next few years were spent in assimilating French art, history, and character. His collaboration with Scribe began at this time, and the first result of their partnership was the highly successful Robert le Diable (Paris, 1831), in which Meyerbeer's German technique, Italian melodies, and newly found French spirit, coupled with brilliant staging and singing, brought unprecedented success to the Paris Opéra. This was followed in 1836 by Les Huguenots, the grandest of all French grand operas, which despite its pomposity and musical weaknesses can still impress when properly staged and sung. In 1838 he began work on L'Africaine, which was put aside in favour of Ein Feldlager in Schlesien, written for Jenny Lind (Berlin, 1844), and Le Prophète (Paris, 1849). He was Generalmusikdirektor in Berlin 1842-9, where he conducted his own operas and those in which Lind sang. He was also responsible for the Berlin production of Rienzi

(1847), and succeeded in getting the Berlin Opera to accept Der fliegende Holländer. Despite these services, and the influence that his French operas obviously had on Wagner's early style, Meyerbeer was bitterly attacked in Das Judentum in der Musik. L'Étoile du Nord, partly based on Ein Feldlager, was produced in Paris in 1854, Le Pardon de Ploërmel (or Dinorah) in 1859. Both these works, successful at the time, were, in essence, French opéras comiques, a genre in which the composer was not really happy. In 1863 he returned to Paris for rehearsals of L'Africaine, on which he had been working on and off for nearly 25 years. He was already in bad health, and he fell seriously ill on 23 Apr., dying ten days later. L'Africaine was finally produced in Apr. 1865. Despite its original length – more than six hours – and the protracted period spent on its composition, this is generally considered his finest work.

Though essentially an assimilative composer, Meyerbeer left a distinctive mark upon opera. His love of effect, and his striving for success, led him often merely to make the maximum impression as easily as possible by well-tried devices. Yet he could, at moments of intense dramatic excitement, as with the Blessing of the Daggers in Les Huguenots, create music worthy of the situation; and his love of stage spectacle – deriving from the conventions of *Grand Opera and the Paris audiences' love of pomp – led him to produce music of much grandeur. Thus his talent is justly associated with processions, coronations, church scenes, splendid gatherings, and the ensembles of great singers in the roles of eminent historical personages. Fétis wrote that 'All that his works contain – characters, ideas, scenes, rhythm, modulation, instrumentation – all are his and his only'. His influence on Wagner has been exaggerated: Wagner himself acknowledged that he owed much to Meyerbeer's approach to the stage, but he derived much also from the other composers, especially Auber, who worked with success in the Opéra, and in turn exercised some influence on Meyerbeer himself.

Bibl: J. Kapp: Giacomo Meyerbeer (8/1932).

Mexico. The first opera written in Mexican was Partenope (1771), by P. Manuel Zumaya. This was followed by Manuel de Aremán's El extranjero (1806). Meanwhile, the T. Coliseo was opened in 1733, and presented various musical entertainments, including Paisiello's Il barbiere di Siviglia (1806). Activity began to increase considerably in the early 19th cent., and Italian opera was given great popularity by the visit of Garcia's company in 1830. Opera by Mexican composers quickly followed. Cenobio Paniagua's (1821-82) Catalina de Guisa (1859) was very popular, his Piero d'Abano (1863) less so. Melesio Morales (1838-1908) wrote Romeo *y Julieta* (1863), and the first Mexican opera to be staged abroad, in Florence, *Ildegonda* (1866). The first true Romantic was Aniceto Ortega, whose music was influenced by Beethoven and Weber and whose *Guatimotzin* (1871) was on a national subject. At this period zarzuela also became popular. Gustavo Campo (1863-1934), an important teacher, organiser, and writer, encouraged a feeling for Wagner, and himself wrote *El rey poeta* (1901), influenced by his friends Massenet and Saint-Saëns.

Italian opera continued to be popular. In 1887 a pirated version was given of Verdi's *Otello*, orchestrated by P. Vallère from the vocal score. This was the first performance outside Italy; the genuine version followed in 1890. After the 1910 revolution, foreign companies virtually ceased to visit Mexico, though some open-air performances were given in bull-rings by, among others, Caruso and Ruffo, to audiences of 25,000. During the 1930s opera was again in decline, though in 1934 the Palacio de las Bellas Artes, begun 1910, was finally opened. A local company performed there in 1935. In 1941 the first steps to establish a permanent company were taken by Franz Steiner, with his fellow Viennese refugees Karl Alwin and William Wymetal. The first production was *Die Zauberflöte*, with European and Mexican singers. Conductors who came during the war included Beecham, Kleiber, and Horenstein. In 1943 the contralto Fanny Anitua founded the Opera Nacional, where Callas made her N. American début; this went bankrupt in 1953. In 1955 it was re-founded.

Mezza voce (*It* half voice). The direction to sing at half power, with consequently muted expression.

Mezzo-soprano (*It* half-soprano). The middle category of female (or artificial male) voice. In Italy the mezzo-soprano differs from the soprano chiefly in that a few notes are missing at the top of the tessitura, and in that the voice has a darker quality. In Germany it is a more distinctly different voice, with a tessitura of about g-bb''.

Miami. Town in Florida, U.S.A. Opera is performed in both the Miami Beach Auditorium (cap. 3,700) and the Dade County Auditorium (cap. 2,500) by the Opera Guild of Greater Miami, founded in 1941 by Arturo Di Filippi, a tenor, who himself participated in some of the company's early performances. He was succeeded as director on his death in 1975 by Lorenzo Alvary, who resigned in 1976, to be succeeded by Robert Hermann, for many years Bing's assistant at the N.Y. Met. Emerson Buckley has conducted most of the performances since 1950. The repertory is generally popular with star guest singers in the leading roles.

Micaëla. Don José's peasant sweetheart (sop.) in Bizet's *Carmen*.

Micheau, Janine (*b* Toulouse, 17 Apr. 1914; *d* Paris, 18 Oct. 1976). French soprano. Studied Toulouse and Paris. Début Paris, O.C., 1933, La Plieuse (*Louise*); first O.C., Zerbinetta and Anne Trulove. At the O., 1936-56, where she has created Creuse in Milhaud's *Médée* (1940) and Manuela in his *Bolivar* (1950). London, C.G., 1937, Micaëla; San Francisco 1938, Mélisande; Chicago 1946, Violetta and Micaëla. (R)

Michele. A Seine bargee (bar.), Giorgetta's husband, in Puccini's *Il tabarro*.

Mi chiamano Mimì. Mimì's (sop.) aria in Act 1 of Puccini's *La Bohème*, in which she describes herself.

Midsummer Marriage, The. Opera in 3 acts by Tippett; text by composer. Prod. London, C.G., 27 Jan. 1955, with Sutherland, Leigh, Dominguez, Lewis, Lanigan, Kraus, cond. Pritchard.

The plot concerns the quest of two young people, Mark (ten.) and Jenifer (sop.), for each other in marriage, which they cannot achieve until they have more completely found themselves; they match with a secondary pair of lovers, the uncomplicated Bella (sop.) and Jack (ten.), in an acknowledged analogy with the couples of *The Magic Flute*. Jenifer's father is a businessman who resists their betrothal. The action is pitched between the practical and the mythical and magical, with mundane details (King Fisher and his secretary) acted out against the background of a timeless English midsummer with mysterious overtones (the presence of the seer Sosostris, and a group of Ancients). The action includes, centrally in the second Act, the Ritual Dances which illustrate conflict between the sexes in ballet terms. Eventually Mark and Jenifer achieve the fuller understanding that gives them the true condition for marriage.

Midsummer Night's Dream, A. Opera in 3 acts by Britten; text by composer and Peter Pears, after Shakespeare's comedy (*c*1593-4). Prod. Aldeburgh, 11 June 1960, with Deller, Vyvyan, Cantelo, Thomas, Hemsley (acting, sung by Joseph Ward), Maran, Pears, Brannigan, Lumsden, Kelly, Byles, Massine, cond. Britten; San Francisco 10 Oct. 1961, with Oberlin, Costa, Evans, cond. Varviso.

The plot follows Shakespeare closely, with the characters separated musically into three groups: the fairies Oberon (counter-tenor), Tytania (coloratura sop.), and Puck (speaking role, acrobat); the lovers Lysander (ten.) and Demetrius (bar.), initially both in love with Hermia (mezzo), who is in love with Lysander, and Helena (sop.), in love with Demetrius; and the rustics, Bottom (bass-bar.), Quince (bass),

Flute (ten.), Snug (bass), Snout (ten.), and Starveling (bar.). The high sounds of the fairies' voices (often associated by Britten with the exceptional or strange) is reinforced by the chorus of fairies, led by Cobweb, Peaseblossom, Mustardseed, and Moth (trebles). The playlet of *Pyramus and Thisbe* in Act 3 parodies various devices of Romantic opera.

Mignon. Opera in 3 acts by Thomas; text by Barbier and Carré, after Goethe's novel *Wilhelm Meisters Lehrjahre* (1795-6). Prod. Paris, O.C., 17 Nov. 1866, with Galli-Marié Gabel, Achard, Bataille; London, D.L., 5 July 1870, with Christine Nilsson; New Orleans, 9 May 1871.

Lothario (bass), a wandering minstrel, is searching for his long-lost daughter. A band of gipsies arrive and try to make one of their number, Mignon (mezzo), dance. She refuses and they start to beat her. She is rescued by Wilhelm Meister (ten.), who engages her as his servant and then falls in love with her. Later she is saved from a burning castle by Wilhelm who, with Lothario, nurses her back to health. Lothario, who had lost his memory when Mignon was first kidnapped, now remembers that he is Count Lothario, and recognizes Mignon as his long-lost daughter Sperata.

Mikhailov, Maxim (Dormidontovich) (*b* Koltsovka, 25 Aug. 1893; *d* Moscow, 30 Mar. 1971). Russian bass. Studied Kazan. Archdeacon in Russian Church in Moscow 1924-9. Made several concert tours 1929-32; Moscow, B., from 1932, début as Zaretsky in *Onegin.* His roles included Khonchak, Pimen, Chub (*Cherevichki*), Varlaam, and Gremin. (R)

Mikhailova, Maria (Alexandrovna) (*b* Kharkov, 1866 or 1871; *d* Leningrad, ?). Russian soprano. Studied St Petersburg, Rapgov School, with Groening-Wilde, Paris with Saint–Yves Bax, and Milan with S. Ronconi. Début St Petersburg, M., 1892, Marguerite de Valois. Member of the M. until 1912; repertory included Ludmilla, Antonida (*Life for the Tsar*), Tamara (*The Demon*), Micaëla, Juliette, Lakmé, Olympia, Gilda, Elena, Musetta, Nannetta (first in Russia); created Electra in Taneyev's *Oresteia.* Appeared in Moscow, Kiev, and other Russian cities. All trace of her vanished after a concert tour with Alexander Alexandrovich in 1913 or 1914. The archives of the M. contain a plea to the authorities in 1921 to have her granted an 'academic allowance' of supplementary rations; there were unconfirmed reports that she was still alive in Leningrad in the late 1930s, others that she died between 1915 and 1917. She was a prolific recording artist and her performances on disc reveal a most beautiful voice allied to a skilled technique and fine sense of style, especially in the French repertory. (R)

Milan (It. Milano). Town in Lombardy, Italy. As well as at *La Scala, opera has been given at the Teatro della Cannobiana (cap. 2,000), the T. Carcano, the T. Lirico, and the T. Dal Verme, and also at other smaller theatres. The Cannobiana was founded at the same time as La Scala and was built on land given free to the city by Maria Theresa. It opened in 1779 with a double bill comprising Salieri's *Fiera di Venezia* and *Il talismano.* In 1807 it gave hospitality to La Scala and continued to be used for opera and ballet fairly regularly until the 1860s. The most famous première staged there was probably Donizetti's *L'elisir d'amore* in 1832. In 1894 it was demolished and replaced by the Teatro Lirico, which was built by Edoardo Sonzogno, the publisher. The theatre opened in 1894 with Samara's *La martire.* In 1897 Caruso made his Milan début there in the première of Cilea's *L'arlesiana.* The same composer's *Adriana Lecouvreur,* Giordano's *Fedora,* and Leoncavallo's *Zazà* also enjoyed their premières there, and it was also the scene of the first Italian performances of *Werther, Thaïs, Louise,* and *La Prise de Troie.* In 1938 the Lirico was destroyed and was rebuilt the following year. After the bombing of La Scala it served as the home of the Scala company for several seasons. It is now a cinema.

The Carcano was opened in Sept. 1803 with Federici's *Zaira.* It was the scene of the first Milan performances of Verdi's *La battaglia di Legnano* in 1859, of the first concert of Wagner's music (given in Milan under Faccio in 1883), and of the first Italian performance of *Manon* in 1893. The premières of Donizetti's *Anna Bolena* in 1830 and *La sonnambula* the following year were also given there.

The Dal Verme was built in 1872 to replace the Politeama Ciniselli, which had been opened in 1864 in the square opposite the Palazzo Dal Verme. It opened with *Les Huguenots* but was primarily the home of drama, though the premières of Puccini's *Le Villi* (1884), Leoncavallo's *Pagliacci* (1892), and Zandonai's *Conchita* (1911) were all given there. It was also the scene of the famous Toscanini concerts during the First World War. It became a cinema in 1930.

Milanov (orig. Kunc), **Zinka** (*b* Zagreb, 17 May 1906). Yugoslav soprano. Studied Zagreb and then three years with Ternina; later with Kostrenčić, Carpi in Prague, and Stueckgold in New York. Début Ljubljana 1927, Leonora (*Trovatore*). From 1928 to 1935 leading soprano Zagreb, where she sang more than 350 performances, all in Croatian, including Sieglinde, the Marschallin, Rachel, and Minnie. Prague, German Theatre, 1936. Following year sang in Verdi *Requiem* at Salzburg under Toscanini. This led to her engagement at the Met., where she made her début in Dec. 1937 as Leonora.

Except for a short break for the 1947-8 and
1949-50 seasons she was leading dramatic
soprano there until her farewell in 1966; has
also sung with the Chicago and San Francisco
Operas, and at the Colón, Buenos Aires.
London, C.G., 1956-7. In Verdi roles she had
few equals in the 1940s and 1950s, possessing
one of the most exquisite soprano voices of the
day, capable of beautiful *pianissimo* singing.
(R)

Milde, Hans Feodor (*b* Petronell, Vienna, 13
Apr. 1821; *d* Weimar, 10 Dec. 1899). German
baritone. Studied with Hauser and Manuel
Garcia. Member of the Weimar company
during the whole of his career. Created Telramund in *Lohengrin* (1850). His wife, **Rosa
Agathé-Milde** (1827-1906), was likewise a
member of the Weimar Company and was the
first Elsa. Their son **Franz** (1855-1929) sang at
Weimar (1876-8) and Hanover (1878-1906), and
from 1906-26 taught in Munich. Another son,
Rudolf (1859-1927), sang mostly at Dessau,
and from 1921-9 taught in Berlin.

Mildenburg, Anna von. See *Bahr-Mildenburg.*

Milder-Hauptmann, Pauline Anna (*b* Constantinople, 13 Dec. 1785; *d* Berlin, 29 May 1838).
Austrian soprano. Came to the notice of
Schikaneder, who urged her to study with
Tomaselli and then Salieri. Début Vienna 1803
as Juno in Süssmayr's *Der Spiegel von Arka-
dien.* Created Leonore in *Fidelio* (1805). Went
to Berlin 1812; was engaged there 1816-31, but
left following a quarrel with Spontini. Greatly
admired for her interpretation of Gluck's
Iphigénie, Alceste, and Armide. Her voice was
very powerful. (Haydn told her it was 'like a
house'.) She was praised for her clarity and
simplicity, though she was often inaccurate
and was a poor actress.

Mildmay, Audrey (*b* Hurstmonceaux, 19 Dec.
1900; *d* Glyndebourne, 31 May 1953). English
soprano. Formerly member of C.R.; toured
U.S.A. with *Beggar's Opera* then in 1931 married John *Christie and inspired him to build an
opera house at Glyndebourne and launch a festival there in 1934. She was heard as Susanna,
Zerlina, and Norina. After the war she and
Rudolf Bing conceived the idea of the *Edinburgh Festival. (R)

Milhaud, Darius (*b* Aix-en-Provence, 4 Sep.
1892; *d* Geneva, 22 June 1974). French composer. Studied Aix, and Paris with Dukas,
Gédalge, Widor, and D'Indy. One of the group
Les Six. Technically a very well equipped composer, and willing to produce music for almost
any occasion, he always responded to the
demands of the work in hand. His shorter stage
pieces, which include three children's operas,
are remarkable for their certainty of touch, and
at least once – in *Christophe Colomb* (1930) –

he matched himself impressively to a large
theme. *Le Pauvre matelot* (1927) is a simple
little Cocteau *pièce noire* using slender
resources to maximum effect, while *Christophe Colomb* musters an army of devices
including cinema and a Greek chorus for the
staging. His *Bolivar* (1943) enjoyed only a
succès d'estime in Paris (1950), but *David*
(1954), written for the 3,000th anniversary of
Israel, has subsequently been performed at
Milan Sc. and in Los Angeles. He also set the
little known third play of Beaumarchais's
Figaro trilogy, *La Mère coupable* (1966).

Miller, Jonathan (*b* London 21 July 1934).
English producer. Début with New O. Co.
(S.W.) 1974 *Arden Must Die* (Goehr); Kent O.
snce 1974 *Così fan tutte, Orfeo* (Monteverdi),
Rigoletto, Eugene Onegin; Gly. 1975, *Cunning
Little Vixen;* E.N.O. 1978 *Figaro.* A gifted and
stimulating producer who strips opera of its
inessentials.

Millico, Giuseppe (*b* Terlizzi, nr Bari, 20 Jan.
1739; *d* Naples, 1 Oct. 1802). Italian male soprano and composer, known as 'Il Moscovita'.
Heard by Gluck in 1769 who engaged him to
create Paris in his *Paride ed Elena* in Vienna the
same year; became singing teacher of Gluck's
niece Marianna. London 1772-4 in Sacchini's *Il
Cid* and *Tamerlano* and other works. Settled in
Naples in 1780; became Maestro di Capella to
the Royal Chapel, in which capacity he gave
lessons to Lady Hamilton. Collaborated with
Calzabigi and became much admired as a composer of several operas including *La pieta
d'amore, La Zelinda,* and *L'avventura benefica.*
According to Mrs Thrale his quaint English
pronunciation resulted in his singing the words
'I come my Queen to chaste delights' as 'I comb
my Queen to chase the lice'.

Millöcker, Karl (*b* Vienna, 29 Apr. 1842; *d*
Baden, nr Vienna, 31 Dec. 1899). Austrian composer. Studied Vienna, joining the Theater an
der Josephstadt as a flautist, then on Suppé's
recommendation becoming conductor in Graz.
Here he produced his first operettas, before
moving back to Vienna. In 1868 he became conductor of the German Theatre in Budapest;
returned to the Vienna W. as second conductor
in 1869. Continued writing operettas; *Das ver-
wunschene Schloss* (1878) and *Apajune der
Wassermann* (1880) were fairly successful, but
Der Bettelstudent (1882) conquered Vienna.
After *Gasparone* (1884) he lost his touch,
though he had some success with *Der arme
Jonathan* (1890). Though an immensely skilled
musician, he lacked something of the essential
melodic verve which distinguished his contemporaries in Viennese operetta, Strauss and
Suppé; but *Der Bettelstudent* is still popular in
the German and Austrian operetta repertory.

Milnes, Sherrill (*b* Downers Grove, 10 Jan.

1935). American baritone. Studied Drake University and with Andrew White and Hermanus Baer. Début 1960 as Masetto with Boris Goldovsky's company. After engagements in Baltimore and other American cities, 1960-65, including Rupprecht in the U.S. première of *The Fiery Angel* in September 1965, he joined the Met., making his début there as Valentin in *Faust*. Created Adam Brandt in Levy's *Mourning Becomes Electra* (1967), and soon established himself as leading baritone in the Italian repertory. London, C.G., since 1971 as Renato, Don Carlos, Di Luna, Macbeth; Vienna since 1970. Salzburg 1977, Don Giovanni. Although often regarded as Warren's successor as a Verdi baritone, his voice is thinner and more incisive, and his acting more vital. (R)

Milton, John (*b* London, 9 Dec. 1608; *d* London, 8 Nov. 1674). English poet. Operas on his works are as follows:

Paradise Lost (1667): Le Sueur (*Le Mort d'Adam*, 1809 – also based on Klopstock and the Book of Genesis); Spontini (unfin., begun 1838); Rubinstein (1856, prod. 1875).

Samson Agonistes (1671): Handel (*Samson*, 1743).

Spontini's *Milton* (1804) is based on the poet's life and provided material for his *Das verlorene Paradies*; a projected *Miltons Tod* did not materialise.

Mime. The Nibelung dwarf (ten.), brother of Alberich, in Wagner's *Ring*.

Mimì. A seamstress (sop.), heroine of Puccini's *La Bohème*.

Mingotti. Italian family of impresarios.

(1) **Pietro** (*b* ?, 1702; *d* Copenhagen, 28 Apr. 1759) and his brother

(2) **Angelo** (*b* ?; *d* ?) first formed companies in Dresden and Stuttgart, then travelled widely in Germany. They were among the most successful of all the travelling impresarios of the age, and did much to introduce Italian opera to parts of Europe, especially Germany. They were in Brno 1732-6, Graz 1736 (where they built the first public theatre); then divided the company. In 1740 Angelo was in Hamburg; in 1741 Pietro was in Pressburg, returning to Graz and then going to Prague. Both brothers were able to recruit fine singers, including Cuzzoni. Failing to establish himself in Prague, Pietro moved to Linz, though he continued to tour. Angelo continued working in Graz, and also visited Prague, Leipzig, and Dresden. In 1746 Pietro built a wooden theatre in the Zwinger in Dresden. In 1747 Caterina Valentini (*b* Naples, 16 Feb. 1722; *d* Neuburg, 1 Oct. 1808), Italian soprano and sister of the composer Michaelangelo Valentini, married Pietro, taking the professional name

(3) **Regina Mingotti**. She had studied with Porpora. Début Dresden 1747, Porpora's

Filandro. It was at this stage that Gluck worked with the company. Regina now became a fierce rival of Faustina Bordoni; though Hasse sought to diminish her reputation by compelling her to sing a notoriously difficult part, she triumphed, but left Dresden in disgust. In 1748 the brothers visited Leipzig, and Pietro went on to Copenhagen, where, apart from further tours, he remained, living to see the decline of Italian opera there. Angelo moved to Bonn, where he may have worked with Beethoven's father. Regina also appeared in England where she sang in works by Jommelli, etc. Her quarrels with Vaneschi at the Hm. rivalled the Bordoni-Cuzzoni fights. In the musical satire *Lethe* (1775), Kitty Clive mimicked her.

Minnie. A saloon proprietress (sop.), heroine of Puccini's *La fanciulla del West.*

Minton, Yvonne (*b* Sydney, 4 Dec. 1938). Australian mezzo-soprano. Studied Sydney with Marjorie Walker, and in London with Henry Cummings and Joan Cross. Won International vocalist competition at 'S Hertogenbosch, Holland, 1961. Début 1964, Lucretia. After appearances with the Handel Opera Company, New Opera Company, and other fringe groups made her Covent Garden debut in 1965 as Lola (*Cavalleria rusticana*), since when she has sung there regularly as Orpheus, Dorabella, Cherubino, Marina, Octavian, Geneviève, Helen (*King Priam*), Mistress Page, Olga, Marfa (*Khovanschina*), Dido. Created Thea in *The Knot Garden* (1970). Cologne Opera since 1970. Chicago 1970; Israel Festival, Delila, 1972; N.Y., Met., 1973. Australian Opera 1972-3. Bayreuth since 1974. Repertory also includes Sextus, Waltraute, and Brangäne. Has a beautiful lyric mezzo-soprano voice, natural dramatic gifts, and a lovely stage presence. (R)

Miolan-Carvalho, Marie (Caroline Felix) (*b* Marseilles, 31 Dec. 1827; *d* Puys, Seine-Inférieure, 10 July 1895). French soprano. Studied Paris Conservatoire under Duprez. Début Brest, 1849, Isabella (*Robert le Diable*). Paris, O.C., 1849, Lucia, singing there until 1855; T.L. 1856-67, creating Marguerite (*Faust*), Baucis, Juliette, and Mireille. London, C.G., 1859-64 and 1871-2, where she was the first London Dinorah. She also sang with success in Berlin and St Petersburg. She married the impresario Léon *Carvalho.

Bibl: E. Accoyer-Spoll: *Mme. Carvalho* (1885).

Mira, o Norma. The duet between Norma (sop.) and Adalgisa (sop.) in Act 2 of Bellini's *Norma*, in which Adalgisa pleads with Norma not to give up her children.

Mireille. Opera in 3 (orig. 5) acts by Gounod; text by Carré, after Mistral's poem *Mireio* (1859). Prod. Paris, T.L., 19 Mar. 1864, with

Miolan-Carvalho, Faure-Lefevre, Morini, Ismael, Petit, cond. Deloffre; London, H.M.'s, 5 July 1864, with Tietjens, Trebelli, Giuglini, Santley, Junta, cond. Arditi; Philadelphia, Ac. of M., 17 Nov. 1864 (2 acts), in full at Chicago 13 Sept. 1880.

The opera takes place in Arles and tells of the love of Mireille (sop.) for Vincent (ten.); this is opposed by Mireille's father Ramon (bass), and complicated by a rival for Mireille's affections in the bull-tender Ourrias (bar.). The original 5-act version ended tragically with Mireille's death. The revised version ends with Vincent and Mireille happily united.

Mir ist so wunderbar. The canon quartet in Act 1 of Beethoven's *Fidelio* in which Leonore, Marcellina, Jacquino, and Rocco express their conflicting emotions.

Miserere. Properly the opening word of Psalm LI (L in the Vulgate). In opera, the scene for Leonora (sop.), Manrico (ten.), and chorus in Act 4 of *Il trovatore*.

Mistress Quickly. See *Quickly, Mistress.*

Mitropoulos, Dimitri (*b* Athens, 1 Mar. 1896; *d* Milan, 2 Nov. 1960). Greek conductor and composer. Studied Athens, Brussels, Berlin with Busoni. Répétiteur Berlin S.O., 1921-5. Conducted several opera performances in Athens, but did not conduct opera again until the 1950s when he directed concert performances of *Wozzeck* and *Elektra* with the New York Philharmonic. N.Y., Met., 1954-60, including première of *Vanessa*. Conducted *Wozzeck* at Milan Sc., and *Elektra* at Florence Festival. His opera *Sœur Béatrice* was produced at the Athens Conservatory 1920. (R)

Miura, Tamaki (*b* Tokyo, 1884; *d* Tokyo, 26 May 1946). Japanese soprano. Studied Tokyo with Junker, and Germany with Petzold and Sarcoli. Début Tokyo 1909, Eurydice. London O.H., 1915 Cio-Cio-San. U.S.A., San Carlo Co. 1923-5, after which she formed own campany, known as the Salmaggi or Manhattan Opera Company 1926-27. Created Messager's *Madame Chrysanthème,* Chicago, 1920, and Aldo Franchetti's *Namiko San,* Chicago, 1925. Repertory included Manon, Marguerite, Mimì, Iris, and Santuzza. The first Japanese-born singer to make an international career. (R)

Mlada. Opera in 4 acts by Rimsky-Korsakov; text by composer, based on text for earlier opera to be written with Borodin, Cui, and Mussorgsky. Prod. St Petersburg, M., 1 Nov. 1892.

Mocchi, Walter (*b* Turin, 1870; *d* Rio de Janeiro, July 1955). Italian impresario. His first operatic ventures were at Florence in 1906, followed a year later by a successful season at the T.L., Milan. He then took an Italian company to South America, and for many years was responsible for the great seasons in Buenos Aires at the Teatro Colón and Teatro Coliseo. Formed Società Teatrale Internazionale e Nazionale (S.T.I.N.), and controlled the seasons at the Costanzi in Rome, the Massimo in Palermo, and the San Carlo in Naples, as well as Bari and Parma. From 1911 to 1926 the Constanzi, Rome, was under the artistic direction of his wife, the soprano Emma *Carelli.

Mödl, Martha (*b* Nuremberg, 22 Mar. 1912). German soprano, orig. mezzo-soprano. Studied Nuremberg. Début Remscheid 1942, Hänsel. Düsseldorf 1945-9 as mezzo. Hamburg State Opera from 1949, also appearing regularly in Vienna. London, C.G., 1949-50, 1953, 1959 and 1966, Carmen, Brünnhilde, Clytemnestra. N.Y., Met., 1956-60. Began to sing dramatic soprano roles 1950-1 and was engaged to sing Kundry, Bayreuth, 1951; since then as Isolde, Brünnhilde, Sieglinde, and Gutrune. Leonore in *Fidelio* at opening of Vienna State Opera. Her voice, with its warm and beautiful lower register, was always at the service of highly individual and intense artistry. (R)

Bibl: W. Schäfer: *Martha Mödl* (1967).

Moffo, Anna (*b* Wayne, 27 June 1935). American soprano. Studied Philadelphia, Curtis Inst. with Eugenia Giannini-Gregory, and Rome with Luigi Ricci and Mercedes Llopart. Début Spoleto, 1955, Norina. Aix-en-Provence, 1956 Zerlina; Milan, Sc., 1957 Nannetta, Chicago 1957; N.Y., Met., since 1959 in wide variety of roles including Pamina, Luisa Miller, Juliette, Mélisande, the four soprano roles in *Hoffmann,* and Violetta. London, C.G., 1964 Gilda. Has appeared in Vienna, Salzburg, Berlin, and elsewhere. Her talent, musical and dramatic, has not always been wisely deployed, and she was persuaded to appear in roles for which she was not suited, in both the theatre and recording studio, leading to a vocal breakdown in 1974-5. By 1976 she was able to resume her career. (R)

Moïse. See *Mosè in Egitto.*

Moldavia. A musical theatre was opened in Kishinev in 1933; in 1955 this became the Pushkin National Opera and Ballet T. Though operas had previously been written by Moldavian composers, notably *Zhar-Ptitsa* (The Fire Bird, 1926) by Evgeny Koka (1893-1954), the first Moldavian national opera was the historical opera *Grozovan* (1956) by David Gerschfeld (*b* 1911), who also write *Aurelia* (1958). Other Moldavian operas include *Kasa Mare* (1968) by Mark Kopitman (*b* 1929); *Klop* (The Bug, 1963) by Edward Lazarev (*b* 1935); an operetta *Na Beregu Urala* (On the Edge of the Urals, 1943) by Solomon Lobel (*b* 1910); and a children's fairy-tale opera *Koza s Tremya Koz-*

Myatamy (Koza with the Three Kids, 1967) by Zlata Tkach (*b* 1929).

Molière (orig. Jean-Baptiste Poquelin) (*b* Paris, 15 Jan. 1622; *d* Paris, 17 Feb. 1673). French dramatist. Operas on his works are as follows:
Les Précieuses ridicules (1659): Galuppi (1752); Blanchard (*c*1830s); Mériel (1877); Galliera (1901); Goetzl (1905); Seymour (1920); Zich (1924); Behrend (1928); Lattuada (1929); Bush (*If the cap fits*, 1956).
Sganarelle (1660): Arcais (1871); Grosz (1925); Wagner-Régeny (1929); Kaufmann (1958); Zito (1972); Pasatieri (*Il Signor deluso,* 1974); V. Archer (1974).
L'École des maris (1661): Allessandri (*Il Vecchio geloso,* 1781); Bondeville (1936).
L'École des femmes (1662): Liebermann (1955); Mortari (1959).
Le Mariage forcé (1664): F. Hart (1928).
La Princesse d'Élide (1664): Laverne (1706); Galuppi (*Alcimena,* 1749).
L'Amour médécin (1665): Berton (1867); Poise (1880); Wolf-Ferrari (1913); Herberigs (1920); Bell (1930); Bentoiu (1964).
Le Médécin malgré lui (1666): Desaugiers (1792); Gounod (1858); Poise (1887); Veretti (1927); Behrend (1947); Kaufmann (1958).
Le Sicilien (1666): Kospoth (*Adrast und Isidor,* 1799); Preu (1779); Levasseur (1780); Miča (1781); Mézeray (1825); Joncières (1859); Cadaux (mid-19th cent.); K. H. David (1924); Letorey (1930).
Tartuffe (1667): Haug (1937); Kosa (1952); Eidens (20th cent.); Benjamin (1964).
L'Avare (1667): Burghauser (1950).
Amphitryon (1668): Grétry (1786); Oboussier (1948).
Georges Dandin (1668): Mathieu (1877); Sebastiani (1893); D'Ollone (1930).
M. de Porceaugnac (1669): Orlandini (1727); Hasse (1727); Jadin (1792); Mengozzi (1793); Alani (1851); Franchetti (1897); Bastide (1921); Martin (1963).
Le Bourgeois gentilhomme (1670); Hasse (*Larinda e Vanesio,* 1726); Esposito (1905); Gargiulo (1947); Hlobil (1972). See also *Ariadne auf Naxos.*
L'Idylle comique (1667): Cabaner (1879).
Le Malade imaginaire (1673): Thern (*A képzett beteg,* mid 19th cent.); Napoli (1939); Dupérier (1943); Haug (*Le Malade immortel,* 1946); L. Miller (1970); J. Paner (*Zdrarý nemocný,* 1970).
Also Veretti (*Il medico volante*), Dibdin (*Dr Ballardo,* 1770), Galuppi (*Le virtuose ridicole,* 1752), Locke (*Psyché,* 1675), Isouard (*Les Deux avares,* 1801), J. Kaffka (*So prellt man alte Füchse,* late 18th cent.).

Molinari-Pradelli, Francesco (*b* Bologna, 4 July 1911). Italian conductor. Studied Bologna and Rome with Molinari. Début as symphonic conductor 1937, then began to conduct at all the leading Italian opera houses, from 1942. London, C.G., 1955, 1960; San Francisco 1957-66; N.Y., Met., 1966-73. Vienna since 1959. (R)

Mombelli. Italian family of singers.
(1) **Domenico** (*b* Villanova, 17 Feb. 1751; *d* Bologna, 15 Mar. 1835). Tenor and composer. Sang mostly in Italy 1780-1816, especially in Naples, where he was considered second only to the elder Davide; also appeared in Vienna, Madrid, and Lisbon. From 1816 taught singing in Florence and Bologna. In 1805 became friendly with Rossini, who described him as 'an excellent tenor'; created Demetrio in Rossini's first opera, *Demetrio e Polibio.* His own compositions included *Didone* (1776). His first wife
(2) **Luisa** (or Luigia) **Laschi** (-Mombelli) (*d* 1791) created Countess Almaviva in Mozart's *le nozze di Figaro.*
(3) **Vincenza Vigarnò** (-Mombelli), second wife of Domenico, niece of Boccherini, and sister of choreographer Salvatore Vigano. Wrote libretto for Rossini's *Demetrio e Polibio* in which two of her and Domenico's daughters also appeared:
(4) **Ester** (*b* 1794) and
(5) **Anna** (*b* 1795). Rossini relates that one was 'a contralto, one a soprano; they got a bass to join them and without any outside help, gave opera performances in Bologna, Milan, and other cities'. Ester also created Madame Cortene in *Il viaggio a Reims* (1825) and was successful in *La cenerentola*; she created Zoraide (1822) and Gilda in *L'ajo nell'imbarazzo* (1824) for Donizetti. A son,
(6) **Alessandro,** taught singing at the Bologna Liceo.

Monaco. See *Monte Carlo.* Also Italian for Munich.

Mona Lisa. Opera in 2 acts by Schillings; text by Beatrice Dovsky. Prod. Stuttgart 26 Sept. 1915 with Hedy Iracema-Brügelmann, Forsell; N.Y., Met., 1 Mar. 1923 with Kemp, Bohnen, cond. Bodanzky.
A traveller (bar.) and his young wife (sop.), on their honeymoon in Florence, visit a Carthusian monastery, where a lay brother (ten.) tells them the story of Mona Lisa, the beautiful wife of Francesco del Giocondo, and her love for Giovanni de Salviati. This story forms the main part of the opera, and ends with Francesco shutting Giovanni in a cupboard where he suffocates; when her husband opens the cupboard, Mona Lisa pushes him into it and locks the door. In the opera's epilogue, the traveller and his wife are revealed as the modern counterparts of Giocondo and Mona Lisa, while the lay-brother is Giovanni.

Mon cœur s'ouvre à ta voix. Dalila's (mezzo-sop.) aria in Act 2 of Saint-Saëns's *Samson et Dalila.*

Mond, Der (The Moon). Opera in 3 acts by Orff; text by composer, after Grimm. Prod. Munich 5 Feb. 1939 with Patzak, cond. Krauss. N.Y., C.C., 16 Oct. 1956 with Kelly, Treigle, cond. Rosenstock.

The narrator (ten.) tells the story of four boys (tenor, two baritones, and bass) who steal the moon, each taking a quarter to their graves. The world grows dark and the four stick the pieces of the moon together and hang it up as a lamp; this wakes up all the dead, who create such a tumult that it is heard in heaven, so St Peter descends to the underworld, takes the moon away, and hangs it up on a star.

Mondo della luna, Il (The World on the Moon). Opera in 3 acts by Haydn; text by Goldoni (first set by Galuppi 1750, also by Piccinni, Paisiello, and others). Prod. Esterháza 3 Aug. 1777. Revived, in incomplete form, London Opera Club, Scala T., 8 Nov. 1951, cond. Pritchard; N.Y., Greenwich Mews Playhouse, 7 June 1949. Restored by Robbins Landon, performed Holland Festival 24 June 1959, with Adani, Alva, Cortis. cond. Giulini, and subsequently elsewhere. The plot concerns the discomfiture of a father who opposes his daughter's marriage: a quack astrologer leads him to suppose that he has been transported to the Moon, where he is led to reform.

Monelli, Raffaele (b Fermo, 5 Mar. 1782; d S. Benedetto del Tronto, 14 Sept. 1859). Italian tenor. Studied Fermo with Giordaniello. Pursued career in Italy 1808-20. Created Bertrando in Rossini's *L'inganno felice* and Dorvil in his *La scala di seta*. His brother **Savino** (b Fermo, 9 May 1784; d Fermo, 5 June 1836), also a tenor, also studied with Giordaniello. Created Giannetto in Rossini's *La gazza ladra* and Adalberto in his *Adelaide di Bergogna*; Don Ramiro in Donizetti's *Chiara e Serafina* (1822) and Enrico in his *L'ajo nell'imbarazzo* (1824).

Mongini, Pietro (b Rome, 29 Oct. 1828; d Milan, 27 Apr. 1874). Italian tenor. Leading tenor London, H.M.'s 1860s and 1870s. Succeeded *Giuglini and also sang at C.G. 1869-70. Created Radamès at Cairo, and was a notable Manrico, Arnold (*William Tell*), and John of Leyden (*Le Prophète*); the first London Arrigo (*Vespri siciliani*).

Moniuszko, Stanisław (b Ubiel, 5 May 1819; d Warsaw, 4 June 1872). Polish composer, the most important figure in the development of Polish national opera. His first work, after some early operettas, was *Halka* (1848), which on its eventual production in Warsaw was joyfully welcomed as a representative national opera; it is still extremely popular in Poland. Standing half-way between the old tradition of separate numbers and the new music drama, *Halka* makes use of an idiom that is recognizably Polish (without drawing on folk music) as well

as of most Romantic opera clichés. His later works were less successful, though *Straszny dwór* (The Haunted Manor, 1865) is said to contain fine music. The failure of his last two works hastened his death.
Bibl: W. Rudziński: *Stanisław Moniuszko* (1961).

Monna Vanna. Opera in 4 acts by Février; text by Maeterlinck. Prod. Paris, O., 10 Jan. 1909 with Bréval, Muratore, Marcoux, cond. Vidal; Boston, 5 Dec. 1913 with Garden, Muratore, Marcoux, Ludikar, cond. Caplet. Maeterlinck's play was also adapted for opera by Emil Abrányi.

Prinzivalle (ten.), commander of the Florentine army that is besieging Pisa, offers to lift the siege if Monna Vanna (sop.), wife of the Pisan commander Guido (bar.), comes to his tent. Guido refuses, but his wife is prepared to sacrifice herself to save Pisa. Prinzivalle discovers that he has known Monna as a child, and respects her love for Guido. The siege is lifted, but Guido refuses to believe his wife is innocent and has Prinziballe thrown into prison. This act turns Monna against her husband, and she obtains the key to Prinzivalle's dungeon and declares her love for him: together they escape.

Monnaie, Théâtre Royal de la. See *Brussels*.

Monostatos. Sarastro's black slave (ten.) in Mozart's *Die Zauberflöte*.

Monpou, Hippolyte (b Paris, 12 Jan. 1804; d Orléans, 10 Aug. 1841). French composer. His comic operas include *Les Deux Reines* (1835), *Le Luthier de Vienne* (1836), *Le Piquillo* (1837, to a libretto by the elder Dumas), *Le Planteur* (1839), and *Lambert Simnel* (1841, to a Scribe libretto).

Monsigny, Pierre Alexandre (b Fauquembergue, 17 Oct. 1729; d Paris, 14 Jan. 1817). French composer. Encouraged by the success of *Les Aveux indiscrets* (1759), he devoted himself to regular composition and already in *Le Cadi dupé* (1761) showed considerable operatic mastery. He produced about an opera a year, generally simple pastoral comedies which gave scope to his melodic charm and sensitive response to situations, though the form of the works was mostly an alternation of chansons and speech. In *Le Roi et le fermier* (1762) he attempted to improve the content of his operas by subtler musical techniques, and by introducing social and political overtones into the plots. *Rose et Colas* (1764) is more in folk style; but *Le Déserteur* (1769), in its dramatic power and its strong pathos, represents a new maturity in opéra-comique, finally abandoning the manner of the *comédie mêlée d'ariettes* and achieving proper dramatic and musical unity. Without losing his characteristic

charm of expression, Monsigny strengthened his melodic style further in *La Belle Arsène* (1773), and again in *Félix* (1777 – his last opera). Having made a number of important developments in opera, including thematic relationships such as those between final choruses and overtures, he was thereafter content to rest upon his laurels and not to challenge the rising generation of composers who owed much to him.
Bibl: P. Druilhe: *Monsigny* (1955).

Montagnana, Andrei (*b* Montagna,?). Italian bass. London 1731-8, singing first for Handel and then Porpora. Both composers wrote arias for him to be inserted in their operas. Created roles in several of Handel's operas, including *Ezio, Sosarme,* and *Orlando.*

Monte Carlo. Capital of the Principality of Monaco. The Grand T. (cap. 600), designed by Charles Garnier, was opened in 1879, and enjoyed its greatest days under the management of Raoul Gunsbourg from 1892 to 1951. It was the scene of many important premières, including Massenet's *Le Jongleur de Notre Dame* (1902) and *Don Quichotte* (1910), Fauré's *Pénélope* (1913), and Ravel's *L'Enfant et les sortilèges* (1925), and also the scene of famous performances by Patti, Melba, Caruso, and Shalyapin. The season usually lasts from Jan. to Apr., and includes popular works in the French and German repertory and Italian works sung by prominent artists.
Bibl: T. Walsh: *Monte Carlo Opera, 1879-1909* (1975).

Montecilli, Angelo Maria (*b* Milan, c1710; *d* Dresden, 1764). Italian male soprano. After appearances (notably in female roles) in Italy he came to London, where, Burney records, he made a powerful effect on English audiences.

Montemezzi, Italo (*b* Vigasio, 4 Aug. 1875; *d* Vigasio, 15 May 1952). Italian composer. Studied Milan, but mainly self-taught in composition. As a composer he stands closer to Boito than to his *verismo* contemporaries. His works have enjoyed more success abroad than in Italy, though the Turin production of his first opera, *Giovanni Gallurese* (1905), made so good an impression that it was given 17 times in its first season. His masterpiece is *L'amore dei tre Re* (1913), a work which in Italy has been compared to *Pelléas*; however, the true influence is that of Wagner, and in *La nave* (1918) that of Strauss. His eclectic late-Romantic style is also shown in his other operas, *Hellera* (1909), *La notte di Zoraima* (1931), and *L'incantesimo* (1943).

Monterone. The nobleman (bass) who curses Rigoletto in Verdi's opera.

Monteux, Pierre (*b* Paris, 4 Apr. 1875; *d* Hancock, 1 July 1964). French conductor. Studied Paris Conservatoire. Viola player at the Paris O.C.; cond. Paris, O., 1913–14; N.Y., Met., 1917–19, 1953–6, conducting American premières of *The Golden Cockerel, Mârouf,* and *La Reine Fiammette,* and between 1953 and 1956 authoritative performances of *Manon, Faust, Orfeo, Hoffmann,* and *Samson et Dalila.* (R)
Bibl: D. Monteux: *It's All in the Music* (1965).

Monteverdi, Claudio (*b* Cremona, ? May 1567; *d* Venice, 29 Nov. 1643). Italian composer. His first opera was *La favola d'Orfeo* (1670), which magnificently united the instrumental and vocal traditions of the day with the new dramatic recitative proposed by the *Camerata. A further group of operas composed for a festival at Mantua celebrating a ducal marriage included *Arianna* (1608), of which only the wonderful Lamento survives. Moving to Venice, he continued to write dramatic works, among them *Il combattimento di Tancredi e Clorinda* (1624). Twelve operas for Parma and Mantua were lost in the sack of Mantua; this and the ensuing plague may have precipitated his admission to holy orders (1632). The opening in 1637 of the first public opera house, the San Cassiano in Venice, rearoused his interest in opera. The rest of his life was largely taken up with a series of works in which he laid the foundations of later Neapolitan opera. It has been questioned whether *Il Ritorno d'Ulisse in Patria* (1641) is entirely his work; *L'Incoronazione di Poppea* (1642), though only a year later, is certainly a work of greater mastery, and has indeed come belatedly to be recognized as one of the masterpieces in the history of opera.

Monteverdi inaugurated the bel canto and buffo styles, with recitativo secco; but his true genius was as a composer who, at the dawn of opera, perceived the essentials of music drama and embodied them in music of extraordinary inventive fluency yet close artistic control, of an expressive range that can encompass both tragedy and wit and can illuminate subtleties of character in a few strokes, of an emotional truthfulness that has in the long history of opera never been excelled. His convictions found a gifted advocate in the writings of his brother **Giulio Cesare Monteverdi** (*b* Cremona, 31 Jan. 1573; *d* ?).
Bibl: L. Schrade: *Monteverdi* (1950, 2/1964).

Monti, Anna Maria (*b* Rome, 1704; *d* ?). Italian soprano. Sometimes called Marianna (but not to be confused with her cousin of that name – see below). Début when only 13 in Falco's *Lo imbruoglio d'amore*; appeared regularly in Naples until 1782. Her sister **Laura** made her début in Naples in 1726 and often appeared with the bass Gioacchino Corrado in the *intermezzi giocosi* of Hasse and Pergolesi. Created Auletta's *La locandiera*, Naples 1783, which was so successful that the Queen requested that all the intermezzi be revived.

Monti, Marianna (*b* Naples, 1730; *d* Naples, 1814). Italian soprano, cousin of above. Début Naples 1746 in small roles, and ended her career in 1780 as *prima buffa assoluta,* having sung with success in operas by Logroscino, Anfossi, Traetta, Paisiello, Cimarosa, and her brother **Gaetano** (1750–1816), who composed a dozen or more operas.

Montreal. Town in Canada founded in 1682. Economic, political, religious and social factors combined against early development of cultural life before the end of the 18th cent. The first opera to be heard was Dibdin's *The Padlock,* on 2 June 1786. In the following years there were local productions of *The Poor Soldier* by Shield (1787), *Les Deux chasseurs et la laitière* by Duni (1789), and the première of an original work by Joseph Quesnel, *Colas et Colinette* (1790).

Throughout the 19th cent. Montreal was frequently visited by touring companies which gave the standard repertory, including works by Bellini, Donizetti, and Rossini, to which were later added some of the works of Wagner; *Der fliegende Holländer* (1871), *Lohengrin* (1888), *Parsifal* (1905), and *Die Walküre* (1905). In 1910 a permanent company was formed and many famous singers were engaged. The Montreal Grand Opera Company enjoyed great critical acclaim, and also appeared in Toronto, Ottawa, and Quebec City, and in Rochester, U.S.A. Unfortunately the cost of the venture was not met by local financial support and the Company collapsed in debt in 1913. It was succeeded by the National Opera Company of Canada, 1913–14, after which no further attempt was made to establish a permanent company.

Opera performances have continued to originate as special events by particular organizations. The Montreal Festival began its summer performances in 1936 and for the following thirty years usually produced an annual opera. It gave the first performances in Canada of *Pelléas et Mélisande, Ariadne auf Naxos,* and Pizzetti's *Assassinio nella cattedrale.* Beecham participated in the 1942 and 1943 festivals, conducting performances of *Figaro, Roméo et Juliette,* and *Tristan und Isolde.* In 1941 the Opera Guild of Montreal was formed by Pauline Donalda, who had enjoyed a career in Europe as a leading singer and later as a teacher. The Guild produced one opera each year until Donalda's death in 1969, mounting, for example, *Boris Godunov, Falstaff,* and *The Golden Cockerel* as well as many other familiar works.

In 1964 the Montreal Symphony Orchestra under Zubin Mehta began to stage two or three operas each season in its new home, the Salle Wilfred Pelletier at the Place des Arts. In 1971 the Provincial Government set up L'Opéra du Québec. It was not intended to be a permanent company, but to organize operatic activity with government support. It operated chiefly in Montreal and Quebec, and ceased in 1975.

Expo '67, the World's Fair which was held in Montreal in 1967, brought to the city over a few months an array of opera and performers unequalled anywhere up to that time. In addition to productions by the Montreal Symphony Orchestra and the Canadian Opera Company of Toronto, there were visits by the full companies of the Bolshoy Opera, the English Opera Group, the Hamburg State Opera, La Scala, the Royal Stockholm Opera, and the Vienna State Opera.

Moody, Fanny (*b* Redruth, Cornwall, 23 Nov. 1866; *d* Dundrum, Ireland, 21 July 1945). English soprano. Studied privately. Début Liverpool 1887, Arline (*Bohemian Girl*), with C.R. Company. Leading soprano with C.R. until 1898, when with her husband Charles *Manners, whom she had married in 1890, she formed the Moody-Manners Company. She was the first Tatyana in England (1892) and created Rosalba in Pizzi's opera of that name (1902) and Militza in McAlpin's *The Cross and the Crescent* (1903).

Moody-Manners Company. Formed by the bass Charles *Manners and his wife Fanny *Moody in 1898 and lasting until May 1916. Manners awarded prizes for English operas and produced several new works. At the height of touring opera's popularity in Great Britain there were two companies numbering 175 and 95 respectively. The singers included Florence Easton, Enid Cruickshank, Philip Bertram, Harry Brindle, Maria Gay, Zélie de Lussan, John Coates, Joseph O'Mara, Philip Brozel, and E. C. Hedmont. Richard Eckhold and Hamish McCunn were the chief conductors.

Moore, Douglas (*b* Cutchogue, N.Y., 10 Aug. 1893; *d* Greenpoint, 25 Jul 1969). American composer. Of his operas, the *Devil and Daniel Webster* (1938) and the folk opera *The Ballad of Baby Doe* (1956) have proved the most successful, and are regularly performed in America.

Moore, Grace (*b* Slabtown, 5 Dec. 1901; *d* Copenhagen (in air crash), 26 Jan. 1947). American soprano. Studied locally. After appearances in night clubs and musical comedy went to Europe for further study with Richard Berthélemy. Début Paris 1928. N.Y. Met., 1928, Mimì; sang there 1928–32, 1935–6, 1937–46; London, C.G., 1935. Also sang Paris, O.C., 1929, 1938, and 1946, when she appeared as Louise, having studied the role with Charpentier. Her most famous roles, apart from Mimì and Louise, were Manon, Tosca, and Fiora. She became known outside the opera house by her films (*One Night of Love,*

Love Me For Ever, and *New Moon).* Her glamour and personality more than her voice and acting abilities made her a great favourite. (R)
Bibl: G. Moore: *You're only human once* (1944).

Moore, Thomas (*b* Dublin, 28 May 1779; *d* nr Devizes, 28 Feb. 1852). Irish poet and musician. Active as a poet and arranger of songs which had an enormous popularity in their day, especially when sung by him. He wrote the libretto of a comic opera, *The Gypsy Prince* (1801) for Michael Kelly, and in 1811 produced an opera of his own, *M.P., or The Blue Stocking.* His *Lalla Rookh,* a story with four interpolated narrative poems, provided the texts for operas by C.E. Horn (1818), Kashin (*The One-Day Reign of Nourmahal),* Spontini (*Nourmahal,* 1822), F. David (1862), and Rubinstein (*The Veiled Prophet,* 1881). His *The Light of the Harem* was set as an opera by A.G. Thomas (1879).

Morel (orig. Merlo), **Marisa** (*b* Turin, 13 Dec. 1914). Italian soprano and producer. Studied Turin. Début Milan, Sc., 1933, Musetta. After further appearances at Sc. and other Italian opera houses, and at the N.Y., Met., 1938–9, she formed her own company in 1941 for the production of Mozart operas and gave performances at Aix-en-Provence, Paris, Ch. É., and elsewhere in Europe. Artists who participated in her productions included Suzanne Danco, Tatiana Menotti, Giulietta Simionato, Fernando Corena, Marcello Cortis, Petre Munteanu, Marko Rothmüller, and Heinz Rehfuss; and the conductors Ackermann, Ansermet, Böhm, and Krannhals.

Morena (orig. Meyer), **Berta** (*b* Mannheim, 27 Jan. 1878; *d* Rottach-Egern, 7 Oct. 1952). German soprano. Her great beauty attracted the painter Lenbach, who persuaded her to study in Munich with Röhr-Brajnin. She further studied with Regina de Sales, and was encouraged by Ternina and made her début at Munich 1898 as Agathe, remaining a member of the Munich Opera until 1924. N.Y., Met., 1908–11 and 1924–5; Chicago 1912; London, C.G., 1914. A distinguished Brünnhilde and Isolde. (R)
Bibl: L. A. Vogl: *Berta Morena und ihre Kunst* (1919).

Morère (orig. Couladère), **Jean** (*b* Toulouse, 6 Oct. 1836; *d* Paris, Feb 1887). French tenor. Studied Toulouse with Paul Laget. Début Paris, Oct. 1861, Manrico; remained there until 1869, and created title-role in *Don Carlos* (1867); Brussels, La M., 1865–6, 1869–70. Became insane in 1871.

Morgenlich leuchtend. The opening words of Walther von Stolzing's (ten.) Prize Song in Act 3 of Wagner's *Die Meistersinger von Nürnberg.*

Moriani, Napoleone (*b* Florence, 10 Mar. 1806 (or 1808); *d* Florence, 4 Mar. 1878). Italian tenor. Studied with C. Ruga. Début Milan, Sc., 1832 in concert; Pavia, 1833 in Pacini's *Gli Arabi delle Gallie.* Especially successful in the Donizetti repertory, creating Enrico in *Maria di Rudenz* (1818) and Carlo in *Linda di Chamounix* (1842). Also successful in Bellini and became the first outstanding Verdi tenors. Verdi wrote the *romanza* 'O dolore! ed io vivea' for him to sing in the Scala production of *Attila,* and they remained on good terms despite his relationship with Giuseppina Strepponi. London, H.M.'s 1844–5. Lost his voice suddenly in 1847. According to Chorley, 'his voice was superb and richly strong, with tones full of expression as well as force . . . but either he was led away by bad taste or fashion into drawling and bawling, or he had never been thoroughly trained'. Mendelssohn speaks more than once of him as 'my favourite tenor, Moriani'.

Morison, Elsie (*b* Ballarat, 15 Aug. 1924). Australian soprano. Studied Melbourne and London, R.C.M., with Clive Carey. Début London, Albert Hall, 1948, *Acis and Galatea.* London, S.W., 1948–54, and C.G. 1953–62. Sang Blanche in English première of *The Carmelites,* and Anne Trulove in *The Rake's Progress* for Glyndebourne, where she has also sung Zerlina and Marcellina (*Fidelio*). In 1955 created title-role in Arwel Hughes's *Menna* for the W.N.O.C. (R)

Morlacchi, Francesco (Giuseppe Baldassare) (*b* Perugia, 14 June 1784; *d* Innsbruck, 28 Oct. 1841). Italian composer and conductor. Studied Perugia with his uncle, L. Mazzetti, then with L. Caruso, finally with Zingarelli and Mattei. His first opera was *Il poeta in campagna* (1807): the success of this, *Il ritratto* (1807), especially *Il corradino* (1808) led to commissions from Rome for *La principessa per ripiego* (1809) and *Le Danaidi* (1810), and from Milan. In 1810 he succeeded Josef Schuster as Kapellmeister in Dresden, where he did much to improve standards, setting a fine example as a musician and as a virtuoso conductor and showing a capacity for selecting and training singers into an ensemble. His vanity and deviousness were exacerbated by the rivalry with Weber, who arrived at the German opera in 1817. His operas for Dresden included *Il nuovo barbiere di Siviglia* (1816), *La simplicetta di Pirna* (1817), *Tebaldo e Isolina* (1820), *La gioventù di Enrico V* (1823), *Il Colombo* (1828), and *Il rinnegato* (1823). Of the first of these, Weber remarked 'the fellow has little musical knowledge, but he has talent, a flow of ideas, and especially a fund of good comic stuff in him'. The operas' greatest strength is in their handling of voices, especially in comic scenes; latterly Morlacchi showed an increasing response to German influences in his greater enterprise with orchestration, revealing some

awareness of the work of Weber (with whom his relationship had improved). He also wrote a number of operas for Italy. He was one of the last important Italian composers to work as Kapellmeister in German theatres, and the closure of the Italian Opera in Dresden in 1832 was a step towards ending the supremacy of Italian opera in Germany.
Bibl: G. Ricci des Ferres-Cancani: *Francesco Morlacchi* (1958).

Moscow. Capital of Russia and the U.S.S.R. Though Italian opera troupes visited Moscow from 1731, the first opera house in Russia was the Operny Dom (Opera House), opened in 1742 with *La clemenza di Tito.* In 1759, Locatelli opened another Operny Dom, which gave opera alternately with Russian drama. The opening of the Petrovsky T. in 1780 by P. Urusov and the English ex-acrobat Michael Maddox was a major step: here most of the early Russian operas were given. When it burned down in 1805, the independent theatres at which opera was also given absorbed the company.

In 1824 there opened the Maly T. (Little T.), so-called to distinguish it from the Bolshoy T. (Grand T.), which was built by O. Bove on a project by A. Mikhailov and opened in 1825. The Maly was primarily a dramatic theatre, but in the Bolshoy a mixed repertory included works by Verstovsky and Glinka. Reconstructed by A. Cavos (son of the composer) after a fire in 1853, the new theatre opened in 1856 (cap. 2,000) and was reserved for opera and ballet. This was the home of a rising generation of great singers and saw the premières of many important Russian operas of the second half of the century. The production style (echoing French taste, as so much in Russian art) favoured an elaborate manner with large crowd scenes, histrionic gestures, and elaborately detailed sets, and this survives as a characteristic of the theatre. Among the most successful designers was Victor Vasnetsov. As all the Imperial Theatres were a crown monopoly until a decree of Alexander III in 1882, no independent reform movement developed until the end of the century. In 1897 Savva Mamontov (1841–1918) opened his Moskovskaya Chastnaya Russkaya Opera (Moscow Private Russian Opera), re-organized in 1899 as Tovarishchestvo Chastnoy Opera (Private Opera Society) under *Ippolitov-Ivanov: among the distinguished singers it attracted was *Shalyapin, and the enterprising production style served as a widely-admired corrective to the official Bolshoy style. In 1904 this closed and was succeeded by the Zimin Opera T., which worked (from 1908 at the Solodovnikov T., later Filial T.) under Ippolitov-Ivanov and Emil *Cooper: this arrangement lasted until 1917, though the company survived until 1924.

At the Revolution, the Bolshoy was temporarily directed by the tenor Leonid *Sobinov. The theatre was re-organized, re-opening in April 1918 and also taking over the Filial T. In the same year Konstantin *Stanislavsky began working with the studio, which became the Stanislavsky Opera Studio in 1924 and was re-organized in 1926 and as the Stanislavsky O. H. in 1928. The theatre known from 1926 as the Nemirovich-Danchenko Music Theatre was founded in 1919; it specialized at first in opéra comique and operetta, and later turned to the classics and to new Soviet works. Stanislavsky died in 1938, and the two groups were united in 1941, with *Nemirovich-Danchenko himself directing until his death in 1943. Though neither director had staged anything at the Bolshoy, their influence on the replacement of a fossilized style by vivid acting and staging was vital. The Stanislavsky-Nemirovich-Danchenko T. is Moscow's second opera house, where it still is that the more adventurous productions may be seen. Opera is also given, on a panoramic scale, in the vast Kremlin Palace of Congresses. See also *Russia.*

Mosè in Egitto (Moses in Egypt). *Azione tragica-sacra* in 3 acts by Rossini; text by Tottola, after Francesco Ringhieri's tragedy, *Sara in Egitto* (1747). Prod. Naples, S.C., 5 Mar. 1818, with Colbran, Funk, Manzi, Benedetti, Nozzari, Cicimarra, Remorini, Chizzola (the famous *preghiera* 'Dal tuo stellato soglio' was added for the 1819 revival); London, H.M.'s, 23 Apr. 1822, as *Pietro l'Eremita,* with Camporese, De Begnis, Zucchelli; N.Y., Masonic Hall, 22 Dec. 1832. Revised as grand opera, in 4 acts, as *Moïse et Pharaon, ou Le Passage de la Mer Rouge,* text by Balocchi and Jouy, Paris, O., 26 Mar. 1827, with Cinti-Damoreau, Mori, Nourrit, Dupont, Levasseur, L.–Z. and H.–B. Dabadie; London, C.G., 20 Apr. 1850, as *Zora,* with Castellan, Vera, Tamberlik, Tamburini; N.Y., Ac. of M., 7 May 1860, with Path, Strakova, Brignoli, Sasia, Ferri.

Onto the Old Testament story of Moses (bass) leading the Hebrews from Egypt across the Red Sea into the Promised Land, has been added a sub-plot of the love of Amenophis (ten.), son of Pharaoh (bar.), for Anaide (sop.), Moses's sister.

Other operas on Moses include that by Orefice (1905); see also below.

Moses und Aron. Opera in 2 acts (3rd uncompleted) by Schoenberg; text by composer, after the Book of Exodus. Prod. Zurich 6 June 1957, with Fiedler, Melchert, cond. Rosbaud; London, C.G., 28 June 1965, with Robinson, Lewis, cond. Solti; Boston, Back Bay T., 30 Nov. 1966, with Gramm, Lewis, cond. McConathy.

Moses (speaking role) receives the word of God, but lacks the gift of communication possessed by his less visionary brother Aron (ten.).

While he is on Mount Sinai receiving the Ten Commandments, Aron encourages the Hebrews to erect a Golden Calf, as a tangible object they, as a simple people, can worship. The subsequent orgy is interrupted by Moses's return from Sinai: appalled, he shatters the tables of stone and resolves to be released from his mission. The second act ends with him sinking to the ground mourning, 'O word, thou word, that I lack'. The (unset) third act was to show Moses triumphant in the desert.

Mosonyi (orig. Brand), **Mihály** (orig. Michael) (*b* Boldogasszonyfalva, bapt. 4 Sept. 1815; *d* Pest, 31 Oct. 1870). Hungarian composer, bass player, and writer on music. During his first period he was entirely Germanic in his musical ideas; *Kaiser Max auf der Martinswand* (comp. 1856–7) was promised performance by Liszt but postponed and eventually abandoned: extensive revisions were planned, but Mosonyi had meanwhile turned his attention to Hungarian music. He Magyarized his name in 1859, but continued to champion Wagner and Liszt while also working by example and precept for Hungarian national music. His opera *Szép Ilonka* (Fair Helen, 1861) was, in his words, 'written entirely in the Hungarian idiom to the exclusion of all foreign elements'. His third and last opera, *Álmos* (1862, prod. 1934) attempted to reconcile the two strains in his idiom; it is a Romantic opera incorporating Hungarian elements into a Germanic technique.

Mother, The (Cz., Matka). Opera in 10 scenes by Alois Hába; text by composer. Prod. Munich 17 May 1931. The first quarter-tone opera. Also title of operas by Stanley Hollier (1954, after Hans Andersen) and Khrennikov (1956, after Gorky).

Mother of Us All, The. Opera in 3 acts by Virgil Thomson; text by Gertrude Stein. Prod. New York, 7 May 1947 with Dow, Blakeslee, Mowland, Horne, Rowe. The opera tells the story of Susan B. Anthony, American feminist leader and leading woman suffragette. Other historical characters appear, including Ulysses S. Grant, Andrew Jackson, and Daniel Webster.

Motif, motive. See *Leitmotiv*.

Mottl, Felix (*b* Unter-Sankt-Veit, 24 Aug. 1856; *d* Munich 2 July 1911). Austrian conductor and composer. Studied Vienna, where his teachers included Bruckner. One of Wagner's assistants at the first Bayreuth Festival, 1876, and subsequently conducted there 1888–1902. At Karlsruhe, 1891–1904, he raised the standard of performance to considerable heights, and gave there the first complete performance of *Les Troyens* (on two consecutive nights, Dec. 1890) as well as a revised version of Cornelius's *Der Barbier von Bagdad* (1884). London, C.G.,

1898–1900; N.Y. 1903–4; Munich 1903–11 (director from 1907). Collapsed and died while conducting *Tristan*. Composed three operas and edited the vocal scores of all Wagner's works. Married soprano Zdenka *Fassbender.

Mount Edgcumbe, Earl of (Richard Edgcumbe) (*b* Plymouth, 13 Sept. 1764; *d* Richmond, Surrey, 26 Sept. 1839). English writer and composer. His *Reminiscences*, published anonymously in 1825, with three further editions, bringing them up to 1834, contain an account of Italian opera in London from 1773 and have proved an amusing and valuable source-book. His *Zenobia* was produced for the Benefit of Banti at the King's Theatre in 1800.

Mozart, Wolfgang Amadeus (*b* Salzburg, 27 Jan. 1756; *d* Vienna, 5 Dec. 1791). Austrian composer. It was, on the whole, into his piano concertos and operas that Mozart poured his most intense and personal music. If in the concertos we sense him, through the medium of his favoured instrument, in a special relation to his art, it is to the operas that we turn for his vivid, shrewd reflection of the world's aspirations and follies. Goethe's comparison of Mozart to Shakespeare is not merely one of stature: they both belong to the category of artists whose sensibilities, ungoverned by reforming zeal, are at the disposal of everything mankind has to show. We may further compare Mozart to Chaucer, the unobtrusive figure in the crowd cherishing every detail of the busy scene.

Mozart was born into an age still dominated by Italian opera. Leaving aside two early stage pieces, the sacred play *Die Schuldigkeit des ersten Gebotes* and the Latin comedy *Apollo et Hyacinthus*, his first opera is *La finta semplice* (1796). It is a stock Goldoni opera buffa, fluently imitating the best models. *Bastien und Bastienne* (1768) does use a German text, but is scarcely more advanced in its agreeable reflection of the Rousseau-inspired village comedy. *Mitridate, Re di Ponto* (1770) is an opera seria of not much more scope, though it was successful enough to draw a commission for the serenata *Ascanio in Alba* (1771). In *Lucio Silla* (1772) there are traces of a maturer Mozart beginning to show themselves intermittently, and *La finta giardiniera* (1775), again to a routine *buffo* plot, is charming in places and interesting for the first signs of Mozart's symphonic approach to opera. Yet the festival play *Il Re pastore* (1775) is once more a string of arias. With the unfinished *Zaide* (1779) there is a clear step forward. 'I prefer German opera, even though it means more trouble for us', he wrote a few years afterwards; and there is in this Singspiel the seed of much that was to flower so richly not only in *Die Entführung*, whose plot it anticipates, but in *Die Zauberflöte*. Turning back to opera seria, Mozart now produced his first great stage masterpiece,

Idomeneo (1781). 'There is a monumental strength and a white heat of passion that we find in this early work of Mozart's and shall not find again', wrote Dent. Opera seria in form, it already possesses that most typically Mozartian quality, the power to transcend old forms without breaking them; for though the conventions are observed and influences (principally of Gluck) are present, *Idomeneo* looks directly forward across the later operas to Wagnerian music drama itself. *Die Entführung aus dem Serail* (1782) is a much simpler construction, a musical play with set numbers that charmingly illuminate the situations. *L'oca del Cairo* and *Lo sposo deluso* (both 1783, unfin.) are unimportant; *Der Schauspieldirektor* (1786), though slight, entertainingly guys the opera world.

With *Le nozze di Figaro* (1786) we enter upon the four late masterpieces. Mozart does not set the spinning intrigues of Beaumarchais's *folle journée* as social satire, but responds to the brilliantly contrasted figures with music of a new compassion and perception. The opera is an enormous advance on its predecessors: moving at a heightened pace, it none the less explores situation and character more fully, and whether in the beautiful set arias or in the great symphonic finales, this riotous harlequinade never loses contact with each of the human beings it creates. With *Don Giovanni*, musically and dramatically a less satisfactory structure, revolving round the possessed central figure are characters familiar to every age; and the music's power of simultaneously facing tragedy and comedy severs almost the last connexions, still present in *Figaro*, with set types. This increased world of experience and understanding was next brought to bear upon an anecdote with, for title, the tavern catchphrase *Così fan tutte* (1790). Yet Mozart cannot help bringing the six participants into our affections by giving them complete musical characters; and in so doing he transforms a practical joke into a ruefully humorous comment on human failings. *Così* is insincerity and cynicism transcended into great art, qualities that roused the gravest Victorian misgivings and produced various bowdlerizations. The last masterpiece was also Mozart's strangest and most inspiring work – *Die Zauberflöte* (1791). To some it is but a muddled pantomime, redeemed (as the opera seria, *La Clemenza di Tito* (1791) was to a lesser extent) by some ravishing musical numbers. But for any who look further, Mozart's feeling for the brotherhood of many-sided man, and his lifelong care for the truthful observation of human behaviour, are now turned to spiritual ends. The absurd, contradictory fantasy mysteriously becomes a vessel for Mozart's innermost religious longings. He is the playful Papageno, but also the hero Tamino, whose quest transforms itself from simple amorous adventure to a journey, through rigorous self-chastening, towards an absolute truth.

Operas on him by Riotte (*Mozarts Zauberflöte*, 1820), Lortzing (*Scenen aus Mozarts Leben*, comp. 1832), Flotow (*Die Musikanten*, 1887), M. Anzoletti (*La fine di Mozart*), Rimsky-Korsakov (see below), and Reynaldo Hahn (1925).
Bibl: E. J. Dent: *Mozart's Operas* (1913, 2/1947); A. Einstein: *Mozart* (1946); W. Mann: *The Operas of Mozart* (1977).

Mozart and Salieri. Opera in 2 acts by Rimsky-Korsakov; text a setting of Pushkin's 'little tragedy' (1830). Prod. Moscow, private opera company, 7 Dec. 1898, with Shkafer, Shalyapin, cond. Truffi; London, R.A.H., 11 Oct. 1927, with Ritch, Shalyapin, Lavretsky, cond. Coates; Forest Park, Pa., 6 Aug. 1933. Pushkin's original concerns the jealousy felt by talent, however exceptional, for the unpredictable and disruptive gift of genius; the opera follows the plot closely, with Salieri (bar.) deciding that only by poisoning Mozart (ten.) can he preserve the even course of art.

Mravina (orig. Mravinskaya) **Evgeniya** (Konstantinovna) (*b* St Petersburg, 16 Feb. 1864; *d* Yalta, 25 Oct. 1914). Russian soprano. Studied St Petersburg with Pryanishnikov, Berlin with Désirée Artôt. Début Italy 1885. St Petersburg, M., 1886–98, Antonida (*Life for the Tsar*), Lyudmila, Tatyana, also in operas by Gounod, Meyerbeer (Marguerite de Valois), Verdi (Gilda, Violetta), Wagner (Elsa), and others; created Fornarina in Arensky's *Raphael*. A woman of great beauty, with a fine stage presence and a lucid, well-produced voice, she was also an intelligent actress and did much to bring new dramatic standards onto the Russian operatic stage.

Much Ado About Nothing. Opera in 4 acts by Stanford; text by J. Sturgis, after Shakespeare's comedy (1598–9). Prod. London, C.G., 30 May 1901, with Adams, Brema, Hyde, Coates, Bispham, Griswold, Plançon, cond. Mancinelli.

Muck, Karl (*b* Darmstadt, 22 Oct. 1859; *d* Stuttgart, 3 Mar. 1940). German conductor. Studied Leipzig and began career as professional pianist. Chorus master, Zurich; subsequently conductor there and at Salzburg, Graz, and Brno. Engaged by Neumann for Prague 1886. Cond. Neumann's Wagner Company in first performances of *The Ring* in Moscow and St Petersburg 1889. Berlin S. O., 1892–1912 (Generalmusikdirektor from 1908). During his period in Berlin he conducted 1,071 performances of 103 operas, of which 35 were novelties. London, C.G., 1899; Bayreuth 1901–30, where he was generally considered the greatest conductor of *Parsifal* of his generation. (R)

Mudie, Michael (*b* Manchester, 3 Dec. 1914; *d* Brussels, 27 Apr. 1962). English conductor. Studied London, R.C.M. Conductor C.R., 1935–9; S.W., 1946–53, when ill health forced him to retire from active music-making. He conducted the first performance in England of *Simone Boccanegra*, and was regarded as one of the most promising opera conductors of his day. (R)

Muette de Portici, La (The Dumb Girl of Portici). Opera in 5 acts by Auber; text by Scribe and Delavigne. Prod. Paris, O., 29 Feb. 1828, with Damoreau, Nourrit, Dabadie, Dupont, Prévost; London, D.L., 4 May 1829, as *Masaniello;* N.Y., Park T., 9 Nov. 1829, with Sharpe, Wheatley, Barry, Barnes, Ruchings, Chapman. The opera, based on historical events in Naples in 1647 when the fishermen rose against their Spanish oppressors, sparked off the Belgian revolt after a performance in Brussels on 25 Aug. 1830. Other operas on the subject by Carafa (1831), Pavesi (1831), and Napoli (1953).

Mugnone, Leopoldo (*b* Naples, 29 Sept. 1858; *d* Naples, 22 Dec. 1941). Italian conductor and composer. Studied Naples, and began career by writing a comic opera, *Il dottore Bartolo Salsapariglia,* prod. when he was 12. When 16 he directed a season of comic opera at F. Venice, Cond. the premières of *Cavalleria rusticana* (1890) and *Tosca* (1900). Milan, Sc., from 1890. London, C.G., 1905, 1906, 1919, and 1924, where he conducted the first London performances of *Adriana Lecouvreur, Fedora,* and *Iris.* N.Y., Manhattan O., 1922. Beecham considered him the best Italian opera conductor of his period.

Mulhouse (Ger. Mülhausen). Town in Haut-Rhin, France. The T. Municipal (opened 1868) had a resident company until the Franco-Prussian war (1871). It then passed into German hands, and after 1884 French-language performances were not resumed until 1900. Since 1946, it has become one of the best operatic centres in France. From 1946 to 1948 Roger Lalande was the theatre's director, and staged there the first production in France of Britten's *Rape of Lucretia,* as well as the première of Büsser's *Roxane.* Lalande was succeeded by Pierre Deloger from the O. C., and under his administration there were several premières including Paul Bastide's *Jeanne d'Arc,* Tomasi's *L'Atlantide,* and Michel-Maurice Lévy's *Moïse,* as well as the first performances in French of *Boris* and *The Consul,* and the first local performances of *Così fan tutte, Angélique, La vida breve, L'Aiglon,* and *Le Roi malgré lui.* Since 1973 it has been part of the *Opéra du Rhin.* Among singers who made their débuts at Mulhouse were Lily Pons and Fanély Révoil.

Müller, Maria (*b* Teresienstadt (Litoměřice), 29 Jan. 1898; *d* Bayreuth, 13 Mar. 1958). Austrian soprano. Studied Vienna with Schmedes and New York with Altglass. Début Linz 1919, Elsa. After engagements in Prague and Munich, N.Y., Met., 1925, remaining until end of 1934–5 season. In N.Y. the first Dorota (*Schvanda*), Mariola (*Frau Gherardo*), and Maria (*Simone Boccanegra*). Berlin (S. and Stä.O.) 1926–43; 1950–2; London, C.G., 1934 and 1937; Bayreuth 1930–9; Salzburg 1931–4. In addition to her Wagner roles, in which she was greatly admired, she sang with success as Jenůfa, Iphigénie, and Reiza. Her voice was warm and vibrant, and her acting abilities above the average. (R)

Müller, Wenzel (Václav) (*b* Trnava, 26 Sept. 1767; *d* Baden, nr Vienna, 3 Aug. 1835). Austrian composer and conductor of Bohemian origin. Learnt many instruments as a youth, and began to compose; moved to Johannesberg and studied with Dittersdorf. He joined the Brno theatre as a violinist in 1782; also composed a Singspiel, *Das verfehlte Rendezvous.* Moved to Vienna; became Kapellmeister at the L. before he was 19. Greatly improved musical standards, working very hard as conductor and composer: his first great success was *Das Sonnenfest der Brahminen* (1790), equalled by *Das Neusonntagskind* (1793). As the National Singspiel no longer operated, he was able to give the L. a position of great importance in Viennese musical life, and his own, very popular, works of this period include *Kaspar der Fagottist oder Die Zauberzither* (1791), *Die Schwestern von Prag* (1794, *Die zwölf schlafenden Jungfrauen* (1797), *Das lustige Beilager* (1797), and the exceptionally successful *Die Teufelsmühle am Wienerberg* (1799). Later operas were less successful; and in 1807 he moved to the German Opera in Prague, with his daughter, the soprano Therese *Grünbaum (1785–1870).

Müller left in 1813, having been less successful than in Vienna at raising standards. But back at the L. in Vienna, he resumed activities with much success; he wrote many popular Singspiels, parodies, and Possen, including *Tankredi* (1817), and several works with Raimund, *Der Barometermacher auf der Zauberinsel* (1823), *Die gefesselte Phantasie* (1828), and notably *Der Alpenkönig und der Menschenfeind* (1828), some of which interested the young Wagner.

Müller was the most successful of all early 19th cent. Viennese popular composers, and a few of his works with Raimund remain in the local repertory. Though early in his career he showed greater operatic ambitions, writing extended finales, it was in simpler songs and ensembles that he was most at ease. Witty and satirical numbers were his strong point, but he could also write in a more tender, reflective

vein that charmed his audiences.
Bibl: L. Raab: *Wenzel Müller* (1928).

Mullings, Frank (*b* Walsall, 10 Mar. 1881; *d* Manchester, 19 May 1953). English tenor. Studied Birmingham. Début Coventry 1907, *Faust*. Denhof Company 1913; Beecham Company 1916–21; B.N.O.C. 1922–6. Created Hadyar in *Naïl* (De Lara) and Apollo in *Alkestis* (Boughton). A distinguished Tristan, Siegfried, Parsifal, and Tannhäuser. His greatest role was Otello, for which his imposing stature and acting ability, coupled with a robust voice, ideally suited him. (R)

Munich (Ger. München). Town in Bavaria, Germany. The first recorded opera performance was that of Macchioni's dramatic cantata *L'arpa festante* in Aug. 1653. Opera was given in the Herkules-Saal of the Residenz. J.K. Kerll came to Munich and inaugurated the Opernhaus am Salvatorplatz with his *Oronte* in 1656. This was one of the first opera houses in Germany, and survived until 1822. Kerll was succeeded by Ercole Bernabei 1674–87. An important period began when Agosto Steffani emerged as an opera composer with *Marco Aurelio* in 1681; this development was interrupted when the Court was transferred to Brussels in 1692, but resumed under Pietro Torri in 1701. The new Residenztheater was built by Cuvilliés 1752–6. The premières of Mozart's *La finta giardiniera* (1775) and *Idomeneo* (1781) were given here. Carl Theodor ordered the cessation of Italian operas in 1787, and a period of cultivation of German opera followed. There were many works by Danzi and Fränzl; Winter's *Das unterbrochene Opferfest* (1766) was one of the most popular operas of its day. Singspiel was given in the old Opernhaus.

Under Maximilian I, Joseph Maria Babo revised the repertory to develop Singspiel and French opera as genres; Weber's *Abu Hassan* was premièred in 1811. The Hof und Nationaltheater, built to plans by Karl von Fischer, opened in 1818 (burnt down 1823, rebuilt 1825, bombed 1943). Ludwig I closed the Isartor T., where Lindpaintner had worked 1812–19, and again abolished Italian opera. Under Franz Lachner (1836–68) the Munich opera achieved new fame; a number of operas were premièred, and Wagner, Meyerbeer, Rossini, Verdi, Bellini, and many others introduced into the local repertory. From 1860, Ludwig II's relationship with Wagner made Munich a centre of musical history. The première of *Tristan und Isolde* was given in 1865, that of *Die Meistersinger* in 1868, and many other Wagner performances, including a private one of *Parsifal* for the King. Hans von Bülow was music director 1867–9, Franz Wüllner 1869–71, Hermann Levi 1872–96, Mottl 1903–11, Walter 1911–22, Knappertsbusch 1922–34, Clemens Krauss 1937–44, Ferdinand Leitner 1944–6,

340

Georg Solti 1946–52, Rudolf Kempe 1952–4, Ferenc Fricsay 1955–9, Keilberth 1959–68, Sawallisch from 1971.

Karl von Perfall was an influential Intendant 1867–93, as was his successor Ernst von Possart 1894–1905. Munich's Strauss tradition dates from 1919, when performances of his works became a feature of the season and of annual summer festivals. Strauss had been Kapellmeister there 1886–9 and 1894–8, and both *Friedenstag* (1938) and *Capriccio* (1942) were first performed there.

The Prinzregententheater (cap. 1,012) was built by Possart on the Bayreuth model: intended originally for Wagner, it was opened in 1901 with *Meistersinger*. It was the permanent home of the Bavarian State Opera 1945–63. The Nationaltheater was rebuilt 1963. The Residenztheater has been rebuilt on modern lines, but Cuvilliés's rococo auditorium of the Residenz has been reconstructed in the Alter Residenz, opened 1958. The Staatstheater am Gärtnerplatz (cap. 932) opened 1865. Since 1945 it has been Munich's second opera house. It was extensively rebuilt 1968–9, and reopened 1969 with Rameau's *Platée*. Many other important works have had their premières at Munich in modern times, and most important German singers have sung with the company.
Bibl: H. Friess and R. Goldschmidt: *Nationaltheater, München* (1963)

Münster. Town in North Rhine Westphalia, Germany. Münster was long dependent upon the visits of Italian travelling companies. The architect Wilhelm Lipper built a Komödienhaus which opened in 1775 and survived until 1889, and a permanent ensemble was established in 1782. The repertory included works by Grétry, Gluck, and Mozart. Under Pichler 1818–41 the repertory developed and Lortzing's first opera, *Ali Pascha von Janina*, was premièred in 1828. Opera was also given during the 19th cent. by the Essen company. Lortzing settled in the city 1827–33, and the new theatre opened in 1900 bore his name. It was bombed in 1941 and a new house (cap. 956) opened 1956 with *Zauberflöte*. Hans *Rosbaud began his career there. The first German *Gloriana* was given there 1968.

Muratore, Lucien (*b* Marseilles, 29 Aug. 1878; *d* Paris, 16 July 1954). French tenor. Studied Marseilles as horn-player. Began career on straight stage and appeared opposite Réjane and Sarah Bernhardt. Studied voice Paris Conservatoire. Début Paris, O.C., 1902, Le Roi in Hahn's *La Carmélite*. Paris, O., 1905–11; Boston 1913; Chicago 1913–22; never at C.G. Created more than 30 roles including Thésée in *Ariane*, title role in *Bacchus*, Lentulus in *Roma*, all by Massenet, Prinzivalle in Février's *Monna Vanna*, Edmond in Missa's *Miguette*. For seven years was mayor of Biot. In 1943 he settled in Paris and was manager of the O.C. at time of liberation. He was famous as a teacher and his pupils include Kenneth Neate. He was an impressive actor and a skilful vocalist. (R)

Murska, Ilma di. See *Di Murska.*

Musetta. Marcello's lover (sop.) in Puccini's and Leoncavallo's *La Bohème.*

Musgrave, Thea (*b* Edinburgh, 27 May 1928). Scottish composer. Studied Edinburgh, and Paris with Boulanger. Her operas are the 1-act *The Abbot of Drimock* (1955), *The Decision* (1967), *The Voice of Ariadne* (1974), and *Mary Queen of Scots* (1977). A very intelligent and resourceful composer, she has shown, particularly in the last two works, an enterprising and original grasp of dramatic problems.

Musical Comedy. A form of light opera in which romantic and comic elements predominate, set to music whose principal aim is to frame the plot with tuneful numbers. Characteristic composers of musical comedy in England, where the term and the genre had a particular vogue between the wars, are Lionel Monckton, Montague Phillips, Noël Coward, Ivor Novello, and Vivian Ellis. In its abbreviation as Musical, the term has been particularly applied to American works, especially those written for Broadway. The first successful American-written operetta was Willard Spencer's *The Little Tycoon* (1886); but the genre first began to develop in the 20th cent. with the work of George M. Cohan, and was taken forward with works by Friml, Romberg, and Jerome Kern (to books by P.G. Wodehouse, Guy Bolton, and Oscar Hammerstein II), among many others; the enormous success of Hammerstein-Kern's *Show Boat* (1927) really established the musical play, or Musical in the modern sense. Outstanding composers of musicals have been George Gershwin, Richard Rodgers, Frederick Loewe, Frank Loesser, Irving Berlin, Cole Porter, Kurt Weill, and Leonard Bernstein. Though loosely applied to both musical play and musical comedy, each a distinct and thriving branch of the American musical theatre, the term Musical is usually reserved for the play in which music serves the plot with song and dance.

Music drama. The name given to works in which the musical and dramatic elements are (or are intended to be) entirely unified, with every other consideration (such as opportunities for display by singers) subjugated to this end. The term first came into general use with Wagner: he realized in his later works the ideal to which German opera had been groping for over a century. See also *Dramma per musica.*

Music Theatre. A term for works in which musical and dramatic elements are involved, not necessarily representationally. Thus instrumentalists may be costumed and on the stage, or a musician may use a mask, or a group of musicians operate in semi-dramatic conventions. Originally an attempt, deriving from Brecht, to infuse a new kind of dramatic immediacy into opera, it has been taken up by a number of younger composers, especially Goehr, Birtwistle, and Maxwell Davies, with works in which a dramatic convention rather than a full staging is used, partly for reasons of economy but fundamentally in the wish to explore new relationships between music and drama.

Mussorgsky, Modest (*b* Karevo, 21 Mar. 1839; *d* St Petersburg, 28 Mar. 1881). Russian composer. Mussorgsky only completed one opera, his masterpiece *Boris Godunov*. His three earliest projects were *Han d'Islande* (1856), after Victor Hugo; *Oedipus in Athens* (1858–61), of which there survives only a choral scene, later to be incorporated in *Salammbô, Mlada,* and *Sorochintsy Fair,* and some other choruses; and *St. John's Eve* (1858), after Gogol. *Salammbô* (1863–6), after Flaubert, is also unfinished, and remains interesting chiefly for its lyrical elements and for a tough realism which hints at *Boris.* The latter quality is developed in the first and only completed act of *The Marriage* (1909), after Gogol, a lively comedy of manners that further exercised Mussorgsky's gift for realistically inflected musical speech and characterization, for the first time by way of *Leitmotiv.*

Mussorgsky was by now growing interested in an opera on Pushkin's *Boris Godunov*: the original version was completed by 1870. Here the lyrical and realistic elements are fully developed and balanced. Though *Boris* has antecedents in Romantic opera, in Meyerbeer, and more immediately in *Dargomyzhsky's *Stone Guest,* it is a unique and original product of them. The personal tragedy of Tsar Boris is played out against a living backcloth of the Russian people: there is not only intense individual characterization but a feeling for corporate emotions in boyars, foreign nobles, and peasants that gives the opera much of its Russian quality and extraordinary violence of impact. The subject suited Mussorgsky's talents ideally – his acute dramatic flair, his gift for reflecting broad and subtle detail in music, his humane and national sympathies. When he revised the opera in 1871–2 he softened his portrait of Boris and generally heightened the romantic elements, sacrificing thereby some of the work's grim strength.

While negotiating the production of *Boris* in 1870, Mussorgsky began a new opera, *Bobil*: one scene was later inserted in *Khovan-*

shchina. He also collaborated with Rimsky-Korsakov, Borodin, and Cui in a projected opera-ballet, *Mlada* (1872), using parts of the *Oedipus* music and *Night on the Bare Mountain.* He began planning another historical opera, *Khovanshchina* (1872–80). This is less dramatic or sharply characterized than *Boris,* but it contains moving and powerful scenes.

Work on *Khovanschina* was interrupted by yet another project destined to remain unrealized, the comedy *Sorochintsy Fair* (1874–80), after Gogol. This draws heavily on Ukrainian folk-music. For the last project, *Pugachevshchina* (1877), he had begun noting down Kirghiz, Transcaucasian, and other tunes.

Bibl: M. D. Calvocoressi: *Modest Mussorgsky* (1956).

Mustafà. The Bey of Algiers (bass) in Rossini's *L'Italiana in Algeri* and *Il Turco in Italia.*

Muti, Riccardo (*b* Naples, 28 July 1941). Italian conductor. Studied Naples, S. Pietra a Maiella with Vitale, Milan with Votto. Won Guido Cantelli prize 1967. After conducting concerts, made opera début 1961 Florence, conducting *Puritani,* followed by *Cavalleria rusticana, Pagliacci, Masnadieri,* and *L'Africaine*; quickly established himself as one of the most gifted of conductors of his generation. Salzburg, 1971, *Don Pasquale*; Vienna, 1973, *Aida.* London. C. G., 1977. Artistic director Florence Festival since 1977 (R)

Muzio, Claudia (*b* Pavia, 7 Feb. 1889; *d* Rome, 24 May 1936). Italian soprano. Her father was stage manager at C.G. and Met. for many years. Studied Turin with Casaloni, and Milan with Viviani. Début Arezzo 1910, Manon. London, C.G., 1914; N.Y., Met., 1916–22 and 1933–4 (created Giorgetta, *Tabarro,* 1918, and was first American Tatyana and first Met. Loreley and Madeleine de Coigny); Chicago 1922–31. Great favourite at Buenos Aires, Colón, and Rome Opera. Besides Giorgetta, created Baronessa di Carini (Mulè), Melenis (Zandonai), and Cecilia (Refice). Her greatest roles were Violetta, Desdemona, and Madeleine de Coigny. She possessed a beautiful voice and a moving warmth of personality. (R)

Mysliveček, Joseph (known in Italy as Venatorini) (*b* Prague, 9 Mar. 1673; *d* Rome, 4 Feb. 1781). Bohemian composer. Studied Prague with Habermann and Seeger; went to Venice in 1763 to study opera composition with Pescetti. His first opera, *Medea* (1764), was so successful in Parma that he was invited to Naples, where he had an even greater success with *Bellerophon* (1767). Some 30 operas followed, especially for Rome, Naples, Bologna, Milan, and Florence; his popularity became such that he was known to the Italians, who could not pronounce his name, as 'il divino Boemo' and as Venatorini (hunter–its Italian equivalent). In 1773 he wrote *Erifile* for Munich; but he met with success only in Italy, whither he then returned. Subsequent successes included *Demofoonte* (1775), *Ezio* (1775), and *Olimpiade,* (1778) all to Metastasio texts, like many of his operas. Though he was admired, and personally liked, by Mozart, and praised by singers for his understanding of the voice, he accepted without demur the conventions of opera seria and did little more than fill them elegantly.

Bibl: R. Pečman: *Joseph Mysliveček und sein Opernepilog* (1970).

N

Nabucodonosor (Nebuchadnezzar) – more commonly, **Nabucco**. Opera in 4 acts by Verdi; text by Solera, after the drama by Anicet-Bourgeois and Francis Cornue, *Nabucodonsor* (1836). Prod. Milan, Sc., 9 Mar. 1842, with Strepponi, Bellinzaghi, Ruggeri; Miraglia, Marconi, Ronconi, Dérivis, Rossi, London, H.M.'s, as *Nino*, 3 Mar. 1846, with Sanchioli, Corbari, Fornasari, Botelli; N.Y., Astor Opera House, 4 Apr. 1848, with Truffi, Amalia Patti, Beneventano, Rossi.

The opera tells of the Babylonian captivity of the Hebrews and of Nabucco's (bar.) madness, recovery, and subsequent conversion to the faith of Jehovah, despite the opposition of his daughter Abigaille (sop.).

Also opera by Ariosti (1706).

Nachbaur, Franz (Ignaz) (*b* Giessen, 25 Mar. 1830; *d* Munich, 21 Mar. 1902). German tenor. Studied Stuttgart with Pišek and Milan with Lamperti. Début Passau 1857. Basel 1857, Cologne 1859, Hanover 1859-60, Prague 1860-3, Darmstadt 1863-8, Munich from 1868. Guest appearances Vienna, Mainz, Leipzig, Dresden, Wiesbaden. Created Walther and Froh. London, D.L., 1882, Adolar. Also Rome 1878, Lohengrin; Moscow 1887.

Nacht in Venedig, Eine (A Night in Venice). Operetta in 3 acts by Johann Strauss II; text by 'F. Zell' (Camillo Walzel) and Genée. Prod. Berlin, Friedrich-Wilhelm-Städtisches Theater, 3 Oct. 1883 for opening of theatre; N.Y. 24 Apr. 1884; London, Cambridge T., 25 May 1944.

The old senator Delaqua (bass), decides to marry his ward Barbara (sop.), who is being wooed by both Delaqua's nephew, Enrico (ten. or spoken role), and the Duke of Urbino (ten. or bar. Martin). The plot is further complicated by the fact that Annina, who had been brought up by the same nurse as Barbara, changes clothes with her during the Venetian Carniaval, while Ciboletta (sop.), engaged to Pappacoda (bar.), pretends she is Barbara. By the end of the opera Caramello (ten.), the Duke's barber, has married Annina, and Enrico has married Barbara.

Nachtlager von Granada, Das (The Night Camp of Granada). Opera in 2 acts by Konradin Kreutzer; text by K. J. Braun von Braunthal, after Kind's drama. Prod. Vienna, J., 13 Jan. 1834; London, Prince's T., 13 May 1840; N.Y. 15 Dec. 1862. Kreutzer's most popular work.

Disguised as a hunter, the Crown Prince of Spain is granted a night's rest by shepherds, who decide however to kill and rob him when they find him kissing the shepherdess Gab-

riela. She is loved by, and loves, Gomez, but is also being pursued by Vasco. She appeals to the 'hunter', who promises to intercede for her with the Crown Prince; and when she and Gomez, having found the Prince's followers, expose the plot, he reveals himself and joins her and Gomez in betrothal.

Nadir. A fisherman (ten.), Zurga's friend and rival for Leïla's love in Bizet's *Les Pêcheurs de perles*.

Naldi, Giuseppe (*b* Bologna 2 Feb. 1770; *d* Paris, 14 Dec. 1820). Italian bass. Début probably Milan 1789. Milan, Sc., 1796; Lisbon 1803-6; London, 1806-18, where he was the first London Don Alfonso, Papageno, Figaro (both Mozart and Rossini), and Leporello. Considered an excellent actor with humour and good artistic judgement. Mount-Edgecumbe described his voice as 'weak and uncertain'. Died in Garcia's apartment in Paris when attending a trial of a newly-invented cooking-kettle which accidentally burst. His daughter **Carolina Naldi**, (1809–76), made her début in Paris in 1819 and appeared there with success in the Rossini and Bellini repertory until her marriage in 1824 to Count di Sparri.

Nancy, Town in Vosges, France. The first theatre, built 1708 by Grand Duke Leopold, opened with Desmorest's *Le Temple d'Astrée*. The Pavillon de la Comédie staged opera from 1850 until it was burnt down in 1906. The present Grand Théâtre (cap. 1310) was opened in 1919 with *Sigurd*.

Nannetta. Ford's daughter (sop.) and Fenton's lover in Verdi's *Falstaff*.

Nantes. Town in Loire-Atlantique, France. Opera is given at the Grand T. Graslin (opened 1788). The first performance in France of Massenet's *Hérodiade* was given there in 1883. Since 1973 the administrator has been René Tarrasson and the music director Jésus Etcheverry. Productions are exchanged between Nantes, Avignon, Tours, and Rouen.

Nantier-Didiée (orig. Nantier), **Constance** (*b* St-Denis, 16 Nov. 1831; *d* Madrid, 4 Dec. 1867). French mezzo-soprano. Studied Paris with Duprez. Début Turin 1849, Giunia in Mercadante's *La vestale*. London, C.G., 1853-64. U.S. tour 1855-6. Ly. 1856-7. At C.G., first London Maddalena (*Rigoletto*) and Ascanio (*Cellini*) and first C.G. Ulrica and Siebel: Gounod wrote 'Si le bonheur a souri' for her. Also Paris, St Petersburg (where she created Preziosilla), Madrid. Chorley thought her better in supporting roles than as a principal.

Naples (It. Napoli). Town in Campania, Italy. Opera came late to Naples, in 1651. The Viceroy, Conte d'Ognatte, invited the 'Accademia dei Febi Armonici' under the direction of

Antonio Generoli from Rome to perform. The company included Angelica Generoli, Caterina Gabrielli, Angela Visconti, Francesco Sarleti, and Francesco Cirillo. It performed privately in a small theatre built in the Royal Park, and gave *Il Nerone, overo L'incoronazione di Poppea*, with music by Monteverdi and additions by Cirillo. On 3 Apr. 1654 the first public performance of opera took place at the Teatro di San Bartolomeo, when Cirillo's *L'Orontea, Regina d'Egitto* was produced. By the end of the 17th cent. Naples had supplanted Venice as the centre of opera in *Italy, and in 1737 the San Bartolomeo was replaced by the Teatro *San Carlo. By the middle of the 18th cent. opera buffa had developed under Pergolesi and Jommelli, and then Galuppi, Paisiello, Cimarosa, Fioravanti, etc. To meet the demand for this new kind of entertainment, three more theatres were built: T. dei Fiorentini (1709-1820), T. Pace (1724-49), and the Teatro Nuovo (1724-1828). The T. Fondo (today the T. Mercadante) opened in 1779, and the T. D. Ferdinando in 1790. Many famous singers, including Farinelli, Caffarelli, Gizziello, Mingotti, Carolina Bassi, Lablache, De Lucia, Scotti, Caruso, and Stignani, were born in Naples.
See *Neapolitan opera.*

Napoli, Jacopo (*b* Naples, 26 Aug. 1911). Italian composer. Studied Cons. S. Pietro, Naples, where he eventually became director. His comic operas, which use Neapolitan songs, include *Il malato immaginario* (1939), *Miseria e nobiltà* (1945), and *Un curioso accidente* (1950), and have enjoyed a limited success. His *Masaniello* (1953) was awarded one of the prizes in La Scala's Verdi competition.

Nápravník, Eduard (*b* Býšt, 24 Aug. 1839; *d* Petrograd, 23 Nov. 1916). Czech conductor and composer. Studied with Půhonný and Svoboda, then in Prague with Blazek and Pitsch, also with Kittl. Recommended to Prince Yusupov, he moved to Russia as director of the Prince's private orchestra. When this was disbanded on the emancipation of the serfs in 1863, he worked at the St Petersburg M., becoming assistant conductor 1867, conductor 1869. His four operas were produced at the M.: they are *Nizhegorodtsy* (1868), *Harold* (1886), *Dubrovsky* (1895), and *Francesca da Rimini* (1902). Though praised in their day, by Tchaikovsky among others, these were less important than to his reputation than his work as a conductor. He was a well-trained, hard-working, efficient conductor, somewhat dry but unfailingly clear in detail, and for all his lack of emotion a faithful servant to the operas of the rising generation of Russian composers. He conducted over 4,000 performances during his career, and among 80-odd works he introduced were Tchaikovsky's *The Oprichnik, Vakula the Smith, The Maid of Orleans, The Queen of*

Spades, and *Yolanta,* Dargomyzhsky's *The Stone Guest,* Mussorgsky's *Boris Godunov,* Rubinstein's *The Demon,* and Rimsky-Korsakov's *May Night, The Maid of Pskov,* and *The Snow Maiden.* He did much, almost single-handed, to raise the standard of performance and of company discipline in Russia, also concerning himself with improving the lot of singers and musicians.
Bibl: V. Walter: *Eduard Nápravník* (1914).

Nash, Heddle (*b* London, 14 June 1896; *d* London, 14 Aug. 1961). English tenor. Studied London and Milan with Giuseppe Borghatti. Début Milan 1924, Almaviva. London, Old Vic and S.W., from 1925; B.N.O.C.; C.G. 1929-39 and 1947-8; Gly. 1934-8; C.R. during war years; New Opera Company 1957-8. A cultured Mozart singer, his Ottavio being compared to McCormack's, and an incomparable David in *Meistersinger.* Created Dr. Manette in Benjamin's *Tale of Two Cities.* His lyrical voice had great natural charm. (R) His son **John Heddle Nash** (*b* London, 30 March 1928) is a baritone who has sung with the S.W. and C.R. Companies. (R)

Nathan, Isaac (b Canterbury, 1790; d Sydney, 15 Jan. 1864). Australian composer of Polish descent. After a career in England which included collaboration with Byron (*Hebrew Melodies*) and staging, and singing in some of his own operettas, he was ruined financially and forced to emigrate to Australia. Here his many activities culminated in the composition of the first two Australian operas, *Merry Freaks in Troublous Times* (comp. 1843, never fully staged), a comic opera on Charles II, and *Don John of Austria* (1847), a Spanish historical opera. Both are in the style of contemporary English ballad operas. See *Mackerras, Charles.*
Bibl: Catherine Mackerras: *The Hebrew Melodist* (1963).

National Broadcasting Company Television Opera (N.B.C.). Formed in New York 1949-50 with Samuel Chotzinoff as producer and Peter Herman Adler as music and artistic director and launched with a performance of Weill's *Down in the Valley* Jan. 1950. Between then and Jan. 1964 it gave performances of many operas, including the first in the U.S.A. of *Billy Budd, War and Peace,* and *Dialogues des Carmélites.* It commissioned Menotti's *Amahl and the Night Visitors* and Hollingsworth's *La Grande Bretèche,* and gave the world première of Martinů's *The Marriage.* It was also responsible for the controversial Auden-Kallman version of *The Magic Flute* in the Mozart bicentenary year. In 1956 the N.B.C. Opera Company toured 47 American cities, and in 1957-8 55 cities, with *Figaro, Traviata,* and *Butterfly.* The performance of *Carmen* in Oct. 1953 was the first opera to be televised in colour.

Naudin, Emilio (*b* Parma, 23 Mar. 1823; *d* Bologna, 5 May 1890). Italian tenor of French parentage. Studied Parma, and Milan with Giacomo Panizza. Début Cremona 1843 in Pacini's *Saffo*. London, D.L., 1858 and subsequently H.M.'s and C.G. where he sang regularly 1863-72, and where he was the first London Don Carlos. A famous Vasco da Gama (which he had created in Paris 1865), Fra Diavolo, and Masaniello. Sang Lohengrin in the English provinces and Tannhäuser in Moscow (1877).

Naumann, Johann Gottlieb (*b* Blasewitz, 17 Apr. 1741; *d* Dresden, 23 Oct. 1801). German composer. Studied Italy with Tartini and Padre Martini among others. Returned to Dresden as Court composer of sacred music, revisited Italy, composing *Achille in Sciro* for Palermo (1767) and *Alessandro nell' Indie* for Venice (unfin.1768). After further successes, especially in Venice, settled in Dresden as Kapellmeister. Also visited Stockholm; produced three Swedish operas, *Amphion* (1778), *Cora och Alonzo* (1782), and *Gustav Vasa* (on a sketch by Gustav III, 1786); also composed Italian works for Dresden. In Copenhagen he produced *Orpheus og Euridice* (1786); based on Calzabigi's libretto for Gluck, this was the first large-scale Danish opera. Declined an offer to remain in Copenhagen and returned to Dresden as Oberkapellmeister. Further Italian operas included *Protesilao* for Berlin (with Reichardt, 1789), and – his most successful work – *La dama soldata* for Dresden (1791). His last opera was *Aci e Galatea* (1801).

With Hasse and Graun, Naumann was one of the last composers of Neapolitan opera in Germany. However, in his Scandinavian operas particularly he is closer to Gluck, reflecting a French influence and making some use of motivic technique. His more pompous operas for Berlin and his lighter ones for Dresden were more Italianate and virtuosic in manner. An enterprising orchestrator; his later works anticipated some of the characteristics of Romantic opera. His international career gave prestige to Dresden, where his chief loyalties lay; he was the most important opera composer in the city between Hasse and Weber.
Bibl: R. Engländer: *Johann Gottlieb Naumann als Opernkomponist* (1922).

Navarini, Francesco (*b* Citadella, 1853; *d* Milan, 23 Feb. 1923). Italian bass. Studied Milan with Giuseppe Felix and Carlo Boroni. Début Ferrara, 1876, Alfonso (*Lucrezia Borgia*). Sang in most Italian opera houses; Milan, Sc., 1883-1900, creating Lodovico (*Otello*) and roles in opera by Gomez and Franchetti. London, D.L., 1887; C.G., 1888; St Petersburg, Moscow, Paris, Madrid, etc. U.S.A. with Mascagni's company 1902 as Il cieco (*Iris*). Had enormous repertory including leading bass roles in

Wagner, and French and Italian operas. His exceptional height (6ft.6in.) and fine powerful voice made him one of the most imposing bass singers of his day, especially distinguished in such roles as Marcel (*Huguenots*), Grand Inquisitor (*Don Carlos*), Pogner, and Silva (*Ernani*). (R) (Not to be confused with the bass Vittorio Navvarrini (? – 1916), who was a soloist and then a chorister in various American companies.)

Navarraise, La (The Girl from Navarre). *Episode lyrique* in 2 acts by Massenet; text by Jules Claretie and Henri Cain, after the former's story *La cigarette*. Prod. London, C.G., 20 June 1894, with Calvé, Alvarez, Plançon, Gilibert, cond. Flon; Paris, O.C., 3 Oct. 1895, with Calvé, Jérôme, Bouvet, Mondaud Carbonne, Belhomme, cond. Danbé; N.Y. Met., 11 Dec. 1895, with Calvé, Lubert, Castelmary, Plançon. Massenet's only *verismo* opera.

Anita (sop.) is in love with Araquil (ten.), but his father opposes the match as Anita has no dowry. In order to get some money, Anita decides to help General Garrido (bar.), who is leading the royalist troops against the Carlist enemy, Zuccaraga. When Araquil learns of this he follows Anita to Zuccaraga's camp, but is killed; Anita goes mad.

Neapolitan Opera. An 18th-cent. school of opera to which many important composers made contributions, including A. Scarlatti, Porpora, Leo, Feo, Vinci, Logroscino, Pergolesi, Terradellas, Jommelli, Anfossi, Traetta, Guglielmi, Piccinni, Sacchini, Tritto, Paisiello, Cimarosa, and Hasse. Though many of these were born, educated, or worked in Naples, the genre did not belong exclusively to the city, nor even to Italy; some composers worked as far afield as St Petersburg or Lisbon. The type was characterised by a use of Metastasian texts, with the number of characters set and the musical make-up based on the alternation of recitative and da capo aria, with occasional duets but few ensembles. Later in the 18th cent. this adherence to the rules of *opera seria gave way before foreign demands and influences, especially French. Opera buffa also flourished in Naples in the 18th cent. as a type, being marked by a particular swiftness and vivacity.

Nedda. Canio's wife (sop.) in Leoncavallo's *Pagliacci*.

Neefe, Christian Gottlob (*b* Chemnitz, 5 Feb. 1748; *d* Dessau, 26 Jan. 1798). German conductor and composer. Studied Chemnitz, and Leipzig with Hiller. In Leipzig he wrote his first Singspiels; then succeeded Hiller as conductor of Abel Seyler's theatrical company. When this failed financially, he joined Grossmann's company and became court organist at Bonn (during this period he taught Beethoven). He moved to Dessau as music director for the

1796-7 season. Married the soprano Maria Zink (1751-1821). Their three daughters **Louise**, **Felice**, and **Gretchen** were singers, who appeared together in Lichtenstein's *Bathmendi* in 1798; his son **Hermann** was a scene painter, who provided the décor for Schubert's *Die Zauberharfe*.

Neefe won a considerable following in his day for his Singspiels, especially *Adelheit von Veltheim* (1780), which in its handling of a Turkish subject is a forerunner of Mozart's *Entführung*. He was much admired for his melodic gifts and neatness of characterization.

Negrini, Carlo (Villa) (*b* Piacenza, 24 June 1826; *d* Naples, 14 March 1865). Italian tenor. Studied Milan. After a period in the chorus, début as soloist, Milan, Sc., 1847 in *Due foscari*. Created Gabriele Adorno in *Simone Boccanegra* (Venice 1857) and Glauco in Petrella's *Jone* (Milan, 1858).

Neher, Caspar (*b* Augsburg, 11 Apr. 1897; *d* Vienna, 30 June 1962). German designer and librettist. Studied Munich with Pasetti and Vienna with Roller. Designer at the Kroll Oper, Berlin, in Klemperer régime 1924-8, then Städtische Oper with Ebert 1931-3, designing *Macbeth, Ballo in maschera,* and other works. Wrote and designed *Die Bürgschaft* (Weill). Neher's designs for *Macbeth* have also been seen in England (Glyndebourne) and N.Y., Met., and his *Wozzeck* at C.G., Salzburg, Vienna, and N.Y. Also provided the librettos for Einem's *Agamemnon* and Wagner-Régeny's *Der Günstling, Die Bürger von Calais,* and *Johanna Balk.*

Neidlinger, Gustav (*b* Mainz, 21 Mar. 1910). German bass-baritone. Studied Frankfurt. Début Mainz 1931. Hamburg 1936-50; Stuttgart since 1950; Bayreuth since 1952. London, R.F.H., with Stuttgart Company, 1955; C.G. 1963, Telramund, 1965, Alberich. N.Y., Met., 1973. Bayreuth until 1975. (R)

Nelusko. The slave (bar.) in Meyerbeer's *L'Africaine.*

Németh, Mária (*b* Körmend, 13 Mar. 1897; *d* Vienna, 28 Dec. 1967). Hungarian soprano. Studied Budapest with Georg Anthes and Géza László, Milan with Giannina Russ, Naples with De Lucia, and Vienna with Kaschowska. Début Budapest 1923, Sulamith (*Königin von Saba*). At first sang lyric and coloratura roles, then became a dramatic soprano. Vienna, S.O., 1925-46; London, C.G., 1931. One of the finest Turandots, Toscas, and Donna Annas of the inter-war years. Her dramatic soprano voice, coupled with her training as a coloratura soprano, enabled her to sing Constanze and Queen of Night as well as Amelia, Aida, and even the *Siegfried* Brünnhilde. (R)

Nemico della patria. Gérard's monologue in

Act 3 of Giordano's *Andrea Chénier,* accusing Chénier of being an enemy of the Revolution.

Nemirovich-Danchenko, Vladimir (Ivanovich) (*b* Ozurgety, 23 Dec. 1858; *d* Moscow, 25 Apr. 1943). Russian (Georgian-Armenian) producer. Studied Moscow. Together with *Stanislavsky, he founded the Moscow Arts T. in 1898. Its revolutionary choice of works and methods influenced the staging of opera in Russia and eventually abroad. In 1919 he founded a Musical Studio, which became in 1926 the Nemirovich-Danchenko Musical Theatre. Bolder in his opera productions even than in the straight theatre, he was one of the first producers to conceive of the 'singing actor' (his phrase). Though admired for his productions of operetta, e.g. of Offenbach and Lecocq, it was in his avant-garde productions that his work was at its most characteristic, e.g. a very popular version of *Carmen* known as *Carmencita and the Soldier* (1924), Knipper's *North Wind* (1930), and the Moscow version in 1934 of Shostakovich's *The Lady Macbeth of Mtsensk*. He also staged a famous production of *La traviata* (1934).

Nemorino. The peasant hero (ten.) of Donizetti's *L'elisir d'amore.*

Neri, Giulio (*b* Turilla di Siena, 21 May 1909; *d* Rome, 21 Apr.1958). Italian bass. Studied Florence with Ferraresi. Sang in *Barbiere*, Rome 1928, but real début Rome, T. delle Quattro Fontane, 1935, as comprimario. By 1938 had established himself as leading bass at Rome, T.R., and appeared there regularly until shortly before his death. London, C.G., 1953 as Oroveso and Ramfis; guest appearances in Barcelona, Munich, Buenos Aires, Rio, etc. His enormous repertory included Wagner and Verdi. A famous Basilio, Mefistofele (Boito), and Grand Inquisitor. (R)

Nerone (Nero). Opera in 4 acts by Boito; text by composer. Music left unfinished at composer's death and completed by Tommasini and Toscanini. Prod. Milan, Sc., 1 May 1924, with Raisa, Pertile, Galeffi, Journet, Pinza, cond. Toscanini.

The opera is a series of pictures of Imperial Rome at the time of Nero (ten.), in which the decadent civilization, corrupted by Oriental influences represented by Simon Mago (bar.) and Asteria (sop.), is contrasted with the new world of Christianity, symbolized by Fanuel (bar.) and Rubria (mezzo). The opera includes the scene of the burning of Rome.

Also opera in 3 acts by Mascagni; text by Targioni-Tossetti, after Pietro Cossa's comedy (1872). Prod. Milan, Sc., 16 Jan. 1935, with Rasa, Carosio, Pertile, Granforte, cond. Mascagni.

Nessi, Giuseppe (*b* Bergamo, 25 Sept. 1887; *d*

Milan, 16 Dec. 1961). Italian tenor. Studied Bergamo with Vezzani and Melli. Début Saluzzo 1910, Alfredo, but on Serafin's advice became character tenor. Milan Sc. leading comrimario tenor 1921-59. London, C.G., 1927-37 and again with Sc. 1950. Created Gobrias in *Verone*. Pang, Donna Pasqua (*Il campiello*), and many roles in modern Italian works. An inimitable Bardolfo (which he sang at Salzburg under Toscanini), Goro, Spoletta, and Missail *Boris*). (R)

Jessler, Victor (Ernst) (*b* Baldenheim, 28 Jan. 1841; *d* Strasbourg, 28 May 1890). German composer and conductor. The success of his early *Fleurette* decided him to devote himself entirely to music. After producing several more operas, he became chorus master at Leipzig in 1870. Nine years later he took over the conductorship of the Carola T. and produced his first wider success, *Der Rattenfänger von Hameln* (1879). A still greater triumph followed in 1884, *Der Trompeter von Säckingen*. None of his later works won a comparable success; its sentimental harmonies and catchy melodies illustrating a popular legend made *Der Trompeter* enormously fashionable.

Nessun dorma. Calaf's (ten.) aria in Act 3, scene 1, of Puccini's *Turandot,* sung while Pekin is searched all night to find someone who can tell Turandot Calaf's name.

Nesterenko, Evgeny (Evgenyevich) (*b* Moscow, 8 Jan. 1938). Russian bass. Studied Leningrad with Vasily Lukanin. Début Leningrad, Maly T., 1963 as Gremin. Moscow , B., since 1971. Guest appearances Vienna, Milan, Paris, Wiesbaden, etc. Repertory includes Ruslan, Boris, Konchak, Kutuzov, Méphisophélès, Don Basilio, Philip. In the long line of distinguished Russian basses, possessing a voluminous, rich bass voice and strong dramatic gifts. (R)

Nestroy, Johann Nepomuk (Eduard Ambrosius) (*b* Vienna, 7 Dec. 1801; *d* Graz, 25 May 1862). Austrian playwright, actor, producer, and singer. Abandoned the study of law for singing; appeared aged 17 as a bass in Handel's *Alexander's Feast*. Stage début in Vienna, Kä., aged 20 as Sarastro. In 1823 he moved to Amsterdam, extending his repertory particularly to include comic roles, in which he subsequently specialized appearing in various cities. Settled in Vienna again in 1831. A very popular actor-dramatist; his range included figures of the Viennese popular theatre (e.g. Kasperl) and roles in local and French operetta, though he is most associated with parts in his own plays: he played 880 different parts. He wrote a series of highly popular opera parodies, e.g. of Rossini, Meyerbeer, and Wagner (*Tannhäuser*, 1857, and *Lohengrin*, 1859). He included songs in his own plays, almost always for himself; his favourite composer was Adolf Müller (41 of his plays). His name is forever associated with the witty, irreverent, gay Viennese musical play that was almost operetta.
Bibl: W. Yates: *Nestroy* (1972).

NET opera. See *Television Opera*.

Neues Deutsches Theater. See *Prague*.

Neues vom Tage (News of the Day). Opera in 3 parts by Hindemith; text by Schiffer. Prod. Berlin, Kroll, 8 June 1929, with Stückgold, Kalter, Cavara, Krenn, Ernster, cond. Klemperer. The last of Hindemith's operas to be produced in Germany until after the Hitler régime. It was revised by Hindemith and heard in Naples 1954, and again in Germany (Cologne) 1956; Santa Fé, New Mexico, 12 Aug. 1961 with Willauer, Bonazzi, Driscoll. The opera burlesques the antics of the gutter press, which is exploiting an innocent and unhappy married couple in order to provide sensational 'copy'.

Neumann, Angelo (*b* Vienna, 18 Aug. 1838; *d* Prague, 20 Dec. 1910). Austrian baritone and impresario. Studied with Sessi. Début Berlin, H., 1859. Vienna 1862-76. Director of Leipzig Opera 1876-82; Bremen Opera 1882-5; Prague, Landestheater, 1885-1910. Formed a touring company based on Leipzig to take Wagner's operas, including *The Ring*, to London, Paris, Rome, St Petersburg, &c. He wrote a volume of reminiscences, *Erinnerungen an R. Wagner* (1907).

Neumann, František (*b* Přerov 16 Jul. 1874; *d* Brno, 25 Feb. 1929). Czech conductor and composer. Studied Leipzig. Prague 1906-19; Brno 1919 until his death; conducted premières of Janáček's *Šárka, Káťa Kabanová, The Cunning Little Vixen*, and *The Makropoulos Case*, and Brno premières of *Jenůfa* and *Mr Brouček*. His compositions include 8 operas.

Neumann, Václav (*b* Prague, 29 Sep. 1920). Czech conductor. Studied Prague Conservatory. Début Prague 1948, (concert) replacing the indisposed Kubelík. After engagements in Carlsbad and Brno, engaged by Felsenstein for Berlin, K.O., 1956. Music director Württembergische Staatsoper, Stuttgart 1969-72. Conducted première of Cikker's *Play of Love and Death,* Munich 1969. (R)

Nevada (orig. Wixom), **Emma** (*b* Alpha, Cal., 7 Feb. 1859; *d* Liverpool, 20 June 1940). American soprano. She took her name from Nevada City, the nearest town of any size. Said to have appeared in public at the age of three to sing 'The Star-Spangled Banner'. Studied Berlin, and Vienna with Marchesi. Début London, H.M.'s, 1880, Amina; Milan, Sc. 1881; Paris O.C., 1883-4; N.Y., Ac. of M., 1884-5. Married Dr. Raymond Palmer, in Paris in October

1885 (given away by Ambroise Thomas); thereafter she only sang opera in Europe, though she returned to the U.S.A. for concert tours. Continued to sing opera until 1907 (last appearance Berlin K.O., Rosina); then she appeared in concerts until 1910. An especially fine Bellini singer; her medallion is alongside those of Pasta and Malibran on the composer's statue in Catania. Ambroise Thomas and Mathilde Marchesi were god-parents of her daughter Mignon (see below).

Nevada, Mignon (b Paris, 14 Aug. 1886; d Long Melford, 25 June 1971). English soprano, daughter of above, with whom she studied. Début Rome 1908, Rosina. London, C.G., 1910 in Beecham season. Sang elsewhere in Europe including Sc. and Paris, O.C. (R)

Neway, Patricia (b Brooklyn, 30 Sept. 1919). American soprano. Studied N.Y. with Gesell. Début Chautauqua Summer Opera 1946, Fiordiligi. Female Chorus in *The Rape of Lucretia* on its N.Y. production (1948-9), created Magda Sorel in *The Consul* (1950), Leah in Tamkin's *The Dybbuk* (N.Y. 1951); also sang Marie in *Wozzeck* there. Iphigénie at Aix Festival 1952; Tosca, and Katiusha in Alfano's *Risurrezione*, which was revived for her at Paris, O.C. Created title role in *Maria Golovin* (1958). (R)

Newman, Ernest (orig. William Roberts) (b Liverpool, 30 Nov. 1868; d Tadworth, 6 July 1959). English critic. While still in commerce studied music and philosophy, writing *Gluck and the Opera* (1895) and *A Study of Wagner* (1899). On staff of Midland Institute of Music, Birmingham 1903-5; critic *Manchester Guardian* 1905-19; *Observer* 1919-20; *The Sunday Times* 1920-58. Newman's great love was opera, and Wagner in particular. His *Wagner as Man and Artist, Wagner Nights, Fact and Fiction about Richard Wagner,* and above all the four-volume *Life of Richard Wagner* form an authoritative and valuable collection of works on the composer in English. Newman also translated most of Wagner's operas, and his versions of *Tannhäuser* and *Meistersinger* have been used at post-war C.G.

New Opera Company, London. Originally a part-amateur and part-professional group, founded in Cambridge in 1957 to stimulate interest in contemporary opera by promoting first performances of British works and first performances in Great Britain of 20th-cent. operas. In 1960-63, and again from 1973, the company worked in close co-operation with the S.W. organization. Premières since 1957 have included Benjamin's *A Tale of Two Cities* (1957) and *Tartuffe* (1964), Joubert's *In the Drought* (1959) and *Under Western Eyes* (1969), Gordon Crosse's *Purgatory* (1966), Thea Musgrave's *The Decision* (1967), and Elizabeth Lutyens's *Time off? Not a ghost of a*

chance (1972) and *Infidelio* (1973). First English stage performances have included Egk's *De Revisor* (1958), Dallapiccola's *Il Prigioniero* (1959), Orff's *Die Kluge* (1959), Schoenberg's *Erwartung* (1960), Henze's *Boulevard Solitude* (1962), Prokofiev's *Fiery Angel* (1965), Hindemith's *Cardillac* (1970), Shostakovich's *The Nose* (1973), Goehr's *Arden Must Die* (1974) Szymanowski's *King Roger* (1975), Ginastera's *Bomarzo* (1976), and Martinů's *Julietta* (1978) Leon Lovett is the company's music director and Anthony Besch director of productions.

New Opera Company, New York. A short-lived organization founded by Mrs Lytle Hull in 1941 with Fritz Busch as its music director. Performances of *Così fan tutte* and *Macbeth* based on the Gly. productions of the 1930s were given, as well as *The Queen of Spades, La Vie parisienne, Sorochintsy Fair,* and *Die Fledermaus.* Singers who began their careers with the company include Regina Resnik, Jess Walters, Martha Lipton, Winifrid Heidt, and Virginia MacWatters. The conductors, in addition to Busch, were Antal Dorati, Herman Adler, Emil Cooper, Erich Korngold, and Fritz Stiedry.

New Orleans. Town in Louisiana, U.S.A. In Le Spectacle de la Rue St Pierre, opened in 1791, short operas and plays were performed by a company from France. In May 1796 Grétry's *Sylvain* was performed; works by Méhul and Boieldieu were also given, for the first time in America. In 1806-10, under the management of Louis Tabary, there were at least 351 performances of 76 operas by 32 composers. Other important houses in New Orleans were the T. de la Rue St Philippe which opened Jan. 1808 with Méhul's *Une Folie.* It was also under the management of Tabary and functioned until 1832, when it was sold and turned into a school. At the T. d'Orléans, opened in Nov. 1809, the auditorium included the novel feature of *loges grillés* (latticed boxes) for people in mourning and for others who did not wish to be seen by the rest of the audience. It remained the leading theatre in New Orleans until 1859 when its manager, Charles Boudousquie, left to build his own opera house. It burnt down in 1813, but was quickly rebuilt; in February 1854 the galleries collapsed, killing many people. It was the scene of the first American performances of many important works including *Les Huguenots, Le Prophète, Lucia di Lammermoor, Don Pasquale, La Juive,* and *Guillaume Tell.* When Boudousquie left it quickly deteriorated, and closed during the Civil War. In 1866 the entire company, on its way from France for its reopening, drowned when the S.S. *Evening Star* sank. The theatre itself burnt down shortly afterwards.

The French Opera House, built by Boudousquie and designed by James Gallier Jr, was erected in six months. It was said to be superior any theatre in North America and only equalled by a handful in Europe. It opened 1 Dec. 1859 with *Guillaume Tell*. Patti, aged 17, sang there in *Martha* in 1860, and in the title-role in *Dinorah* in March 1861; this was the first of many American premières including *Le Roi de Lahore, Le Cid, Hérodiade, Samson et Dalila, Siberia*, and *Adriana Lecouvreur*. Most leading European singers appeared there until it closed in 1913. In 1919 it was purchased by William R. Irby, who presented it to Tulane University with funds for its restoration. Its planned reopening in December 1919 never took place, as the theatre burnt down on the night of 2 Dec.

The city remained without permanent opera (though various touring companies did pay visits) until 1943, when Walter Loubart founded the New Orleans O.H. Association. Walter Herbert was music director 1944-54; Renato Cellini 1954-64; and Knud Andersson since 1964. Performances were given in the unsuitable New Orleans Auditorium until 1973, when the New Orleans T. for the Performing Arts opened. Many artists made their American débuts in New Orleans, including Vinay, Treigle, and Domingo. Richard Tucker sang his only stage performance of Eléazar in *La Juive* there in October 1973. Recent seasons have seen a return to the city's French operatic traditions with revivals not only of *La Juive* but also of *Les Huguenots, Thaïs, Roméo et Juliette*, and *Les Pêcheurs de perles*.

Bibl: H. Konen: *Music in New Orleans, 1797-1841* (1966).

New Theatre, New York. Built by Heinrich Conried on Central Park West, between 63rd and 64th Streets; opened in 1909 as a home for drama and the opéra comique repertory not suitable for the Met. During the 1909-10 season *Don Pasquale, Alessandro Stradella, Fille du Mme Angot, The Bartered Bride, Zar und Zimmermann* etc. were performed. Renamed the Century T. in 1913, it became the home of the short lived Century Opera Company (Otto Kahn was on its board), which gave opera in English at low prices. Gallo's San Carlo Company gave its New York seasons there 1922-3 and 1925-6. The theatre was demolished in 1930.

New York. Town in U.S.A. During the first half of the 18th cent. ballad operas were heard. In 1752 the first theatre built for musical entertainment was opened, and in 1767 the John Street T. was opened. There in Mar. 1794 was performed Hewitt's *Tammanny, or the Indian Chief*, one of the earliest of American operas. In 1796 Carr's *The Archers, or Mountaineers of Switzerland* was given there; this is the first American opera of which parts of the music are extant. In 1798 the Park T. was opened and it was there that the first Italian

opera in New York was heard, Rossini's *Il barbiere di Siviglia*, given by Garcia's company in 1828. Other theatres in New York in which opera was heard in the last century included the Astor Place O.H., the Broadway T., Italian O.H., Richmond Hill Theatre, and the Stadt Theatre. See also *Academy of Music, Castle Gardens, City Center, Damrosch Opera Company, Juilliard School, Lexington Theatre, Lincoln Center, Manhattan Opera, Metropolitan Opera Auditions, Metropolitan Opera Guild, Metropolitan Opera House, National Broadcasting Company, New Opera Company (New York), New Theatre (New York), New Theatre (New York), New York City Opera, Niblo's Garden, Palmo's Opera House, Park Theatre.*

New York City Opera. A company founded in Feb. 1944 by the late Mayor La Guardia and Newbold Morris, former president of the New York City Council, originally housed at the City Center. The aim was 'to present opera with the highest artistic standards, while maintaining the civic and democratic ideas of moderate prices, practical business planning and modern methods'.

László Hálász was the music director 1944-51, when he was dismissed on the grounds that his conduct was 'a threat to the prosperity and advancement of the City Center'. He was succeeded by Joseph Rosenstock, who resigned in 1956; next came Erich Leinsdorf, who resigned after one season. Since 1957 the music director has been Julius Rudel.

The initial seasons of the company were short and the repertory popular; but gradually the length of the seasons, both spring and autumn, was extended first to six or eight weeks, and then to two or three months. In February 1966 the company moved to the State T., Lincoln Center, and opened its new season with Ginastera's *Don Rodrigo*. It has become a serious rival to the Metropolitan, offering an interesting repertory of classical and contemporary works, often in controversial productions by Frank Corsaro, Tito Capobianco, Sarah Caldwell, and others. Guest conductors have included Bernardi, Keene, and Märzendorfer, and singers have included Sills, Bible, Domingo, Quilico, Treigle, and many young American singers.

Since 1949 the company has staged more than 150 operas and given successful seasons devoted to American operas. World premières include Still's *The Troubled Island* (1949), Tamkin's *The Dybbuk* (1951), Copland's *The Tender Land* (1954), Kurka's *The Good Soldier Schweik* (1958), Weisgall's *Six Characters in Search of an Author* (1959), Floyd's *The Passion of Jonathan Wade* (1962), Beeson's *Lizzie Borden* (1965), and Menotti's *The Most Important Man* (1971). First U.S. stage performances include *Quatro rusteghi* (1951), *Bluebeard's*

Castle (1952), Einem's *Der Prozess* (1953) and *Danton's Tod* (1966), Martin's *Der Sturm* (1956), Orff's *Der Mond* (1956), Strauss's *Die schweigsame Frau* (1958), Egk's *Der Revisor* (1960), Prokofiev's *The Fiery Angel* (1965), and Ginastera's *Don Rodrigo* (1966). Since moving to the State Theatre there have also been interesting productions of *Giulio Cesare*, *L'incoronazione di Poppea*, Donizetti's 'Tudor' operas, *Mefistofele*, *The Makropoulos Case*, Delius's *A Village Romeo and Juliet*, Henze's *Der junge Lord*, in which Rudolf Bing played the non-singing role of Sir Edgar, and Musgrave's *Voice of Ariadne*.

New Zealand. In 1954 a New Zealand O.C. was founded by Donald Munro to tour all over the country. After some short works (in English, recruiting local choruses), the company gave its first full-length production, *The Consul*, in 1957. Other productions followed, and the company benefited greatly from the experience of the growing number of New Zealand singers who began to make international careers but returned to sing with the company. In 1962 Anthony Besch went to New Zealand to produce *Carmen* with Joyce Blackham.

Nezhdanova, Antonina (Vasilyevna) (*b* Krivaya Balka, 29 June 1873; *d* Moscow, 26 Jun. 1950). Russian soprano. Studied Moscow with U. Masetti. Début Moscow, 1902, Antonida (*Life for the Tsar*); soon became leading soprano at Bolshoi and sang regularly in St Petersburg, Kiev, and Odessa. Paris, Ch. E., 1912, Gilda, with Caruso and Ruffo. Remained in Moscow after Revolution as leading coloratura at the B. Taught singing in Moscow from 1936; professor at Conservatory from 1943. Repertory included Rosina, Juliette, Lakmé, Tatyana; she also sang Elsa, Desdemona, and Tosca. (R)

Niblo's Garden. Originally a summer resort in New York, built by William Niblo at the corner of Broadway and Prince Street. In 1828 Niblo built the Sans Souci T. there, and it and its two successors, later known as Niblo's Garden, were the scene of various opera seasons until 1895; these included Shireff's English Company (1838), the New Orleans French Company (1840), and the Havana Italian Company (1848 and 1850). Important seasons were also given there in 1853 by a company that included Sontag, Badiali, and Pozzolini, and in 1858 by Strakosch's company, with Gazzaniga, Pauline Colson, and Marcel Junca. The theatre, which had a capacity of 1,700 with standing room for another 1,000, closed in 1895.

Nice. Town in Alpes-Maritimes, France. In 1776 the Marquis Alli-Maccarini financed the building of a wooden theatre which opened the following year as the T. Maccarini. In 1792 it was taken over by the state and renamed the T. de la Montagne and then Le T. Municipal. In

1826 the city purchased the theatre and demolished it, replacing it with a new opera house, designed on the model of the San Carlo in Naples, and named the T. Royale. 1828-59 housed French and Italian companies. In 186 the theatre was renamed the T. Imperial; reverted to the title Municipal in 1871. In March 1881 the first performance in France of *Lohengrin* took place, and two days later, before planned performance of *Lucia di Lammermoor*, the house burnt down with man deaths. A new theatre was opened in February 1885 (cap. 1,230); the directors have included Gunzbourg, Salignac, Aquistapace, Ancel, Luccioni, and Aymé. It was the scene of the first performance in France of *Otello* with Tamagno (1891) and the premières of Massenet's *Marie Magdalene* (1903), De Lara's *Sanga* (1906) Nouguès's *Quo Vadis* (1909), and Falla's *L vida breve* 1913. Antonio De Almeida has bee music director since 1976.

Niccolò. See *Isouard.*

Nicholls, Agnes (Lady (Hamilton) Harty) (Cheltenham, 14 July 1877; *d* London, 21 Sept 1959). English soprano. Studied London R.C.M., with Visetti. Début London, Ly., 1895 Dido (Purcell). London, C.G., 1901-8, and subsequently with the Denhof, Beecham, and B.N.O.C. Companies. Sang Sieglinde and Sieg fried Brünnhilde in the English *Ring* under Richter 1908, and was also a famous Donn Elvira. (R)

Nicklausse. Hoffmann's friend (mezzo), i Offenbach's *Les Contes d'Hoffmann.*

Nicolai, (Carl) **Otto** (Ehrenfried) (*b* Königsberg 9 Jun. 1810; *d* Berlin, 11 May 1849). Germa composer and conductor. He ran away from a unhappy home, and was helped in his studies in Rome by friends; by 1837 he was Kapell meister and singing master at the Vienna Ka He returned to Rome in the following year. Hi first opera, *Rosomonda d'Inghilterra*, wa written for Turin in 1838, but given in Trieste a *Enrico II* in 1839. He followed this with a Scot opera, *Il templario* (1840), *Gildippe ed Odoard* (1840), and *Il proscritto* (1841). In 1841 becam Hofkapellmeister in Vienna; moved to Berlin i 1847 as director of the Royal Opera. Here h produced the work by which he remain famous, *Die lustigen Weiber von Windso* (1849). In it the German tradition of comi opera is fertilized by the grace and fluenc Nicolai had learnt in Italy: despite Verdi's *Fa staff*, on the same subject, it has remaine popular in Germany as one of the best-loved o repertory operas, and is occasionally revive abroad.

Bibl: H. Mender: *Otto Nicolai* (1911)

Nicolini (orig. Nicolas), **Ernest** (*b* Saint-Malo 23 Feb. 1834; *d* Pau, 19 Jan. 1898). French

tenor. Studied Paris Conservatoire. Début
Paris, O.C., 1857 in Halévy's *Mousquetaires de
la Reine*. Sang in Italy as Nicolini. London, C.G.,
1866 and again from 1872 to 1884, where he
was the first London Lohengrin, Pery (Gomes's
Il Guarany), and Radamès. He appeared frequently opposite Patti, whom he married in
1886.

Nicolino (real name Nicolò Grimaldi) (*b* Naples,
Apr. 1673; *d* Naples, 1 Jan. 1732). Italian male
contralto. After making his name in Italy, he
went to London in 1708, making his dèbut in
Scarlatti's *Pirro e Demetrio*. His success was
enormous—in *The Spectator* Addison went so
far as to call him 'the greatest performer in
dramatic music that is now living, or that ever
appeared upon a stage'. Praised equally for his
acting and his singing. Handel's original
Rinaldo and Amadigi. He returned to Italy in
1731 to rehearse Pergolesi's first opera,
Salustia, but died before the première.

Nicolò. See *Isouard*.

Nielsen, Carl (August) (*b* Nørre Lyndelse, 9
Jun. 1865; *d* Copenhagen, 2 Oct. 1931). Danish
composer. Studied Copenhagen, with Gade
and others. His reputation rests chiefly on his
symphonic music, though his two operas have
won praise. *Saul og David* (1902) is an
imposing work of his first maturity, and was initially controversial. *Maskarade* (1906) is a
comedy that won for itself a position comparable to that of *Halka* or *The Bartered Bride* as a
national opera.

Niemann, Albert (*b* Erxleben, Magdeburg, 15
Jan. 1831; *d* Berlin, 13 Jan. 1917). German
tenor. Début Dessau 1849 in chorus and small
roles. Trained by Schneider Rusch, and later
Duprez in Paris. Solo début Dessau 1851, 1st
Captain (*Le Prophète*). After engagements at
Stuttgart, Königsberg, Stettin, and Hanover,
became a member of the Berlin H. 1866-88.
Chosen by Wagner to sing Tannhäuser in Paris
(1861). Siegmund at Bayreuth 1876. London,
H.M.'s, 1882, where he was the first London
Siegmund. N.Y., Met., 1886-8, as the first
American Tristan, Siegfried (*Götterdäm-
merung*), and Cortez in Spontini's *Fernando
Cortez*.
Bibl: A. Sternfeld: *Alfred Niemann* (1904).

Niering, Josef (*b* ? ; *d* Frankfurt 27 June 1891).
German bass. Breslau 1869; Danzig 1869-72;
Darmstadt 1874-7; Bremen 1877-8; Frankfurt
1878-88. Hunding at first Bayreuth Festival
1876.

Nietzsche, Friedrich (Wilhelm) (*b* Röcken, 15
Oct. 1844; *d* Weimar, 25 Aug. 1900). German
philosopher, poet, and amateur composer. His
interest in music expressed itself chiefly in his
writings on Wagner, who greatly influenced his
*Die Geburt der Tragödie aus dem Geiste der

Musik (1872). At first an ardent Wagnerian,
believing in Wagner personally and as a genius
of fundamental artistic and historical importance; published his *Richard Wagner in
Bayreuth* (1876) after the first Bayreuth Festival. Later he became disillusioned with
Wagner, and published three monographs
attacking him: *Der Fall Wagner* (1888),
Götzendämmerung (1888), and *Nietzsche
contra Wagner* (1889).

Nightingale, The. Musical fairy tale in 3 acts by
Stravinsky; text by composer and Stepan
Mitusov, after Hans Andersen's story. Prod.
Paris, O., 26 May 1914, with Dobrovolska, Pet-
renko, Andreyev, Brian, Varfolomeyev,
Gulayer, Belialin, cond. Monteux; London,
D.L., 18 Jun. 1914, same cast cond. Cooper;
N.Y., Met., 6 Mar. 1926, with Talley, Bourskaya,
Errolle, Didur, cond. Serafin.
   The famous nightingale (sop.), whose song
thrills all, sings to a poor fisherman (ten.). The
imperial court arrives in search of the bird, who
agrees to sing for the Emperor (bar.).
   The nightingale refuses any reward save the
pleasure of seeing tears of emotion in the
Imperial eyes. A mechanical nightingale
arrives from the Emperor of Japan, but a comparison is prevented by the real bird's
disappearance. The mechanical bird is
installed at the royal bedside.
   Death (con.) sits by the Emperor's bed, but
promises to return the crown when the nightingale returns and sings. This it does, and the
Emperor's strength returns.
   Also opera by Gallas-Montbrun (1959).

Nilsson, (Märta) **Birgit** (*b* Karup, 17 May 1918).
Swedish soprano. Studied with C. Blennon and
in Stockholm with Joseph Hislop and Arne
Sunnegaardh. Début Stockholm 1946, Agathe.
Royal Opera, Stockholm, since then, where she
gradually built up a large repertory of Wagner
and Verdi roles. Glyndebourne 1951 as Elettra
(*Idomeneo*); her major international career
dates from 1954-5 when she sang Brünnhilde
and Salome at Munich. Since then she has
established herself as the leading Wagner soprano of the day, singing at Bayreuth, Vienna,
London, Chicago, and New York. She created a
sensation at Sc. as Turandot in 1958 and has
often returned there in the Wagner and Strauss
repertory. Ernest Newman, writing about her
C.G. début as Brünnhilde in 1957, said he considered himself lucky to have lived long enough
to hear so promising a young Brünnhilde. Her
vocal and dramatic abilities .continued to
develop, and by the mid-1960s she had no
rivals in the Wagner repertory and seemed to
possess inexhaustible vocal reserves. (R)

Nilsson (orig Törnerhjelm), **Christine** (orig.
Kristina) (*b* Sjöabol 20 Aug. 1843; *d* Stockholm,
22 Nov. 1921). Swedish soprano. Studied

Stockholm and Paris, where her teachers included Delle Sedie. Début Paris, T.L., 1864, Violetta. London, H.M.'s 1867, and subsequently C.G. and D.L. until 1881; the first London Ophélie in *Hamlet* (which she had created in Paris in 1868), Margherita, and Elena in *Mefistofele*. N.Y., Ac. of M., 1870-4, where she was the first N.Y. Mignon, in which role she was considered incomparable. Sang Marguerite on opening night of Met., N.Y., 1883. Her voice was sweet and brilliant and encompassed two and half octaves from g to d'''; she possessed great personal charm and beauty.
Bibl: M. Löfgren: *Kristina Nilsson* (1944).

Nissen, Hans Hermann (*b* nr. Danzig, 20 May 1893). German bass-baritone. Studied Berlin with Raatz-Brockmann. Début Berlin, Volksoper, 1924, Caliph (*Barbier von Bagdad*). Munich State Opera 1925-67. London, C.G., 1928; Chicago 1930-2; N.Y., Met., 1938-9; Salzburg and Bayreuth, Sachs. Sang as guest artist in Vienna, Berlin, and elsewhere in Europe. An outstandingly fine Wotan and Hans Sachs of the inter-war years. (R)

Niun mi tema. The opening words of Otello's (ten.) death scene in Act 4 of Verdi's *Otello*.

Noble, Dennis (*b* Bristol, 25 Sept. 1899; *d* Spain, 14 Mar. 1966). English baritone. Educated as chorister Bristol Cathedral. After First World War sang a Prologue to the silent film of *The Prisoner of Zenda* in London: heard by Pitt who invited him to audition for C.G. Début there 1924, Marullo (*Rigoletto*). Sang there regularly until 1938 and again 1947; also with B.N.O.C. and C.R. Companies; Cleveland U.S.A., 1935-6. Created Sam Weller in Coates's *Pickwick*, Achior in *Judith*, and Don José in *Don Juan de Mañara*, both by Goossens. (R)

Nobles seigneurs, salut! The page Urbain's (sop.) song in Act 1 of Meyerbeer's *Les Huguenots*. Originally a soprano role, later sung by a mezzo-soprano.

Non mi dir. Donna Anna's (sop.) aria in Act 2 of Mozart's *Don Giovanni*, in which she bids Ottavio speak no more about his hopes of marrying her so soon after her father's death.

Non più andrai. Figaro's (bar.) aria in Act 1 of Mozart's *Le nozze di Figaro*, describing to the reluctant Cherubino his impending transformation from civilian to military life. It is also the last of the three numbers played by Don Giovanni's private band at supper in the penultimate scene of *Don Giovanni*, in recognition of the tune being so well-known – too well-known, according to Leporello.

Non so più. Cherubino's (sop.) aria in Act 1 of Mozart's *Le nozze di Figaro*, declaring his bewilderment at the novel excitement of desire he feels burgeoning within him.

Noni, Alda (*b* Trieste, 30 Apr. 1916). Italian soprano. Studied Trieste and Vienna. Début Ljubljana 1937, Rosina. Vienna S.O. 1942-6; London, Cambridge T. 1946, Norina opposite Stabile, in first performance in London of opera in Italian after 1939. Gly. 1949-53. Originally a high coloratura, she was chosen by Strauss for Zerbinetta in the special 80th birthday *Ariadne* performance in Vienna in 1944. She became one of the best Italian soubrettes of the day; her repertory included Blonde, Despina, Oscar, and Nannetta. (R)

Nono, Luigi (*b* Venice, 29 Jan. 1924). Italian composer. Studied with Scherchen and Maderna. In 1961 his opera *Intolleranza 1960* was given a stormy première in Venice; his left-wing views expressed in the work aroused a demonstration from a Neo-Fascist group, Ordine Nuovo. A gifted and sensitive composer, with a feeling for drama in his music, he has not followed up this work with further operas.

No! pazzo son! guardate. Des Grieux's (ten.) aria in Act 3 of Puccini's *Manon Lescaut*, beseeching the ship's captain to allow him to accompany Manon on her journey into exile.

Nordica, Lillian (orig. Lillian Norton) (*b* Farmington, 12 May 1857; *d* Batavia, 10 May 1914). American soprano. Studied Boston and Milan. Début Milan T. Manzoni. 1879, Donna Elvira. After appearances in Germany and Russia, during which time she was heard as Marguerite and Ophélie (roles which she had studied with their composers), made American début N.Y., Ac. of M., with Mapleson's Company 1883. London, C.G., 1887-93; N.Y., Met., 1891-1910 (intermittently); Bayreuth (first American artist engaged there) 1894 as Elsa; then became famous as Brünnhilde and Isolde, which she sang in London and N.Y. Such was her vocal training that she was able to sing Brünnhilde one night and Violetta the next. Her singing was beautiful in both dramatic and florid roles. (R)
Bibl: I. Gluckers; *Yankee Diva* (1963).

Norena, Eidé (orig. Kaja Hansen) (*b* Horten, 26 Apr. 1884; *d* Lausanne, 19 Nov. 1968). Norwegian soprano. Studied Oslo, Weimar, London with Raimund von zur Mühlen, and Paris. Début Oslo 1907, Amour (*Orphée*). Married Egil Eidé 1909, taking his name as her stage Christian name. Engaged by Toscanini for Milan, Sc., 1924, Gilda. London, C.G., 1924-5, 1930-1, 1934, 1937. Chicago 1926-8; N.Y., Met., 1933-8. Had a beautiful and excellently trained voice, and sang with impeccable taste. Her most succesful roles were Desdemona, Gilda, Violetta, Juliette, and the three soprano roles in *Contes d'Hoffmann*. (R)

Norina. The young widow (sop.) in Donizetti's *Don Pasquale*.

Norma. Opera in 2 acts by Bellini; text by Romani after Soumet's tragedy (1831). Prod. Milan, Sc., 26 Dec. 1831, with Pasta, Grisi, Donzelli, Negrini; London, King's T., 20 Jun. 1833, with Pasta, De Méric, Donzelli, Galli; New Orleans 1 Apr. 1836, with Pedrotti, Montressor, Rosa.

Norma (sop.), a Druid priestess who has had two children by Pollione (ten.), a Roman proconsul, finds that he has transferred his affections to another young priestess, her friend Adalgisa (sop. or mezzo). Norma tries to persuade him to renounce Adalgisa and return to her; when he refuses she confesses her own guilt publicly and is condemned to death. Pollione, moved by her action, asks to die with her.

Norway. Opera was slow to develop in Norway, and was for a long time dependent upon visiting companies such as the *Mingotti troupe. The first Norwegian opera was Waldemar Thrane's (1790-1828) *Fjeldeventyret* (A Mountain Adventure, 1824), which although heard in a concert performance was not staged until 1850; it had no immediate successor. The first professional local performances were given in 1858. In 1870 Martin Andreas Udbye's (1820-99) *Junkeren og Flubergrosen* (The Knight and the Fluberg Sprote), more operetta than opera, was produced and was the first Norwegian national musical work for the stage since Thrane's opera. A plan by Bjørn Bjørnson, the novelist and playwright, for Grieg to collaborate with him and write a major national opera came to nothing, and *Olaf Trygvason* remained unfinished. Its three scenes were heard in concert form at Christiania (Oslo) in 1889 and were staged in 1908, sharing the bill with the première of Olsen's *Lajla*. Johannes Haarklou's (1847-1925) five operas include *Fra gamle Dage* (Of Olden Days, 1870) and *Marisagnet* (Mary's Legend, 1910). Ole Olson (1850-1927) wrote three operas to his own texts, *Stig Hvida* (1876), *Lajla* (1893), and *Stallo* (1902), as well as *Svein Uroed* (1880), and *Klipperoerne* (1905). Christian Sinding (1956-1941) wrote *Der heilige Berg* (The Mountain, prod. in Dessau in 1914 and in a concert perf. in Oslo in 1931 with Flagstad), and *Titandrod* (unprod.). Gerhard Schjelderup (1859-1933) and Sigwardt Apestrand (1856-1941) composed most of their works to German texts and they were produced in Germany, though eventually heard in Norwegian translations in Norway. Catharinus Elling (1858-1942) wrote *Kosakkerne* (The Cossacks, 1897). More recently, opera composers have included Arne Eggen (1881-1955) with *Liti Kjersti* (Little Christina, after Hans Andersen, 1933), *Olav Liljekrans* (after Ibsen, 1940), and *Cymbeline* (1951); and Ludvig Paul Irgens Jensen (1894-1969) with *Kong Badvines Armring* (1935), *Driftekaren, Mennesket,* and *Robin Hood*

(1945); his oratorio *Heimferd* (1930) was adapted as an opera in Oslo (1947). Most of the country's operatic activity took place in Oslo, but Ole Bull, the violinist, founded the Norse Theatre in Bergen and attempted to establish regular opera there, and opera performances have alternated with drama. Distinguished Norwegian singers include Ivar Andrésen, Kirsten Flagstad, Karl Oestvig, Ellen Gulbranson, Eidé Norena, Ingrid Bjoner, Aase Nordmo-Løvberg, Edith Thalaug, and Ragnar Ulfung. See also *Oslo*.

Nose, The. Opera in 3 acts by Shostakovich; text by A. Preis, A. Zamyatin, G. Yonin, and composer, after Gogol's story (1835), with extracts and suggestions from other works by Gogol and using Smerdyakov's song from Dostoyevsky's *The Brothers Karamazov*. Prod. Leningrad, Maly T. 12 Jan. 1930, cond. Samosud; Santa Fe, 11 Aug. 1965; London, S.W. by New O.C., 4 Apr. 1973, with Harrhy, Winfield, Dickerson, Oliver, Opie, cond. Lovett.

Major Kovalyov (bar.) loses his nose (ten.), which begins to lead a life of its own and even masquerades as a state councillor, treating its former owner with disdain. Eventually it is arrested and returned. The events are a mixture of fantasy and reality, designed as a satire on philistinism, and the roles include one of the highest tenor parts in the repertory, that of the Police Inspector, a tenor required to sing a series of d''s and e''s.

Noté, Jean (*b* Tournai, 6 May 1859; *d* Brussels, 1 Apr. 1922). Belgian baritone. Studied Ghent. Début Ghent 1884. Engagements in Lille, Brussels, Lyons, Marseilles. Paris, O., 1913-1922. N.Y., Met., 1908-9. Created many roles in Paris including Amarat in Dupont's *Antar*. The O.'s first Donner and Alberich (*Siegfried*). Repertory included Nelusko, Hamlet, Beckmesser, Wolfram, and Rigoletto. (R)

Nothung ! Nothung ! Siegfried's (ten.) forging song in Act 1 of *Siegfried*: *Nothung* – 'Needful' – is the name of the sword.

Nougès, Jean (*b* Bordeaux, 25 Apr. 1875; *d* Paris, 28 Aug. 1932). French composer. His early operas were produced at Bordeaux, but he made his name with *Quo Vadis?* (1909) in Nice, which quickly became so well known that it was chosen for the opening of the London O.H. on 13 Nov. 1911, though its shallowness may have contributed to the failure of this venture. None of his later operas approached its popularity.

Nourrit, Adolphe (*b* Paris, 3 March 1802; *d* Naples, 8 March 1839). French tenor. Son of above. Despite father's opposition, studied voice (secretly) with Garcia. Début Paris, O., 1821 as Pylades in *Iphigénie en Tauride* with his father as Orestes. Set a standard in singing

and helped re-establish the Paris O., as a centre of artistic interest. Greatly admired by Rossini, for whom he created Néocles in *Le Siège de Corinthe* (1826), Aménophis in the French version of *Mosè* (1827). For Meyerbeer he created the title-role of *Robert le Diable* (1831) and Raoul in *Les Huguenots* (1836); also created Masaniello in Auber's *La Muette de Portici* and Eléazar in *La Juive*. In 1837, when Duprez was engaged by the Paris Opéra instead of him, he became so upset that he left for Italy. Although well received in Naples and elswhere in Italy, he suffered from severe melancholia and killed himself by throwing himself from his hotel window. In Paris he was 'Professeur de déclamation' at the Conservatoire. He wrote the words of 'Rachel quand du Seigneur' in *La Juive*, and suggested the abrupt and pathetic close to the Act 4 love-duet in *Les Huguenots*. He also wrote the scenarios of several ballets danced by Taglioni and Fanny Elssler and composed a march, *La Parisienne*, to verses by Casimir Delavigne. His brother **Auguste** (1808-1853) was also a tenor, who became director of theatres in Amsterdam, the Hague, and Brussels, and subsequently taught singing.
Bibl: M.L. Quicherat: *Adolphe Nourrit, sa vie (3 vols, 1867);* E. Boutet de Monvel: *Un artiste d'autrefois: Adolphe Nourritt* (1903).

Nourrit, Louis (*b* Montpellier, 4 Aug. 1780; *d* Baunoy, 23 Sept. 1831). French tenor. Studied Montpellier, and Paris with Guichard and Garat. Début Paris, O., 1803 Renaud in *Armide*, and remained there until his retirement in 1826. During whole of Paris career carried on business as a diamond merchant.

Novák, Vitězslav (*b* Kamenice, 5 Dec. 1870; *d* Skuteč, 18 Jul. 1949). Czech composer. Studied Prague, with Dvořák and others. His affinity with the German Romantics was later supplemented by a passionate love of his native country: deliberately avoiding the example of Smetana and Dvořák, he invites comparison, in his exploration of the springs of human behaviour and his boundless love of nature, with Janáček. But where Janáček's inflexible devotion to truth led him to mistrust too much tampering with the raw material, Novák was always ready to mould and polish his material. After the comic *Zvíkovský rarášek* (The Imp of Zvíkov, 1915), his characeristic irony softened. *Karlštejn* (1916) is a patriotic gesture, *Lucerna* (The Lantern, 1923) one of sympathy to his oppressed countrymen. *Dědův odkaz* (The Grandfather's Heritage, 1926) marks a return to his devotion to Slovak scenery.
Bibl: V. Štěpan; *Vitěslav Novák* (1946).

Novara. Town in Novara, Italy.The first opera was produced there in 1695, *Antemio in Roma* with music by G. Besozzi, Erba, and Battistini. The Teatro Nuovo opened in 1779 with Sarti's

Medonte, Re d'Epiro. In 1973 the theatre was renamed the T. Coccia, after the Neapolitan conductor who was the city's Maestro di musica. In 1883 the theatre was virtually rebuilt, largely as it is today. Short popular seasons are given in spring and autumn.

Novello, Clara (Anastasia) (*b* London, 10 Jun. 1818; *d* Rome, 12 Mar. 1908). English soprano. Fourth daughter of Vincent Novello. Studied London, Paris, and Milan. After several years on the concert platform, made her stage début Padua 1841, Semiramide; became a lifelong friend of Rossini. Sang widely in Italy. London, D.L., 1843.
Bibl: A. Mackenzie-Grieve: *Clara Novello* (1955).

Novi Sad (Neusatz). Town in Vojvodina, Yugoslavia. It was an early centre of Hungarian opera, whose conductor introduced opera to Belgrade 1829. The Serbian National T. was founded 1864. A private company, founded in Belgrade in 1900, settled here 1911. The company re-formed after 1945.

Novotná, Jarmila (*b* Prague, 23 Sept. 1907). Czech soprano. Studied Prague with Destinn; début Prague 1926, Violetta. After further studies in Milan joined Berlin S.O. 1928. Vienna 1933-8; Salzburg 1935-7, 1949 N.Y., Met., 1939-54. One of the most aristocratic artists of her day, remembered for her Octavian and Donna Elvira. Also sang Pamina, Violetta, Eurydice, Manon, and the Czech repertory. Created title role in Lehár's *Giuditta*. (R)

Noyes Fludde. Miracle play in one act by Britten; text part of the Chester Miracle Play. Prod. Orford, Parish Church, 18 June 1958, with Brannigan, Parr, cond. Mackerras; N.Y., James Memorial Chapel, 16 Mar. 1959.
The Voice of God (speaker) tells Noye (bar.) to build an ark and thus save his family, Mrs Noye (sop.) and their children and wives (boy and girl trebles), from the Flood. Animals process in pairs into the Ark, and the Flood rises. Eventually Noye releases a dove, which finds dry land; the Ark's occupants leave. The score, which is for a children's orchestra including recorders and bugles as well as a professional group, also involves the congregation with the use of three hymns, 'Lord Jesus, think on me', 'Eternal Father, strong to save', and 'The Spacious Firmament on High' (to Tallis's Canon).

Nozzari, Andrea (*b* Vertova, nr. Bergamo, 1775; *d* Naples, 12 Dec. 1832). Italian tenor. Studied Bergamo with Petrobelli. Début 1794, probably Pavia. Appeared in Rome, Milan, and Paris. Engaged 1811-25 by Barbaia for Naples. Created nine roles in Rossini operas: Leicester (*Elisabetta, Regina d'Inghilterra*), Otello Rinaldo (*Armida*), Agorante (*Ricciardo e Zoraide*), Pirro (*Ermione*), Rodrigo di Dhu (*La donna del lago*), Osride (*Mosè*), Paolo Erisso

(*Maometto II*), Antione (*Zelmira*). After retiring he taught singing; his pupils included Rubini. Carpani said he 'was more a baritone than a tenor, but gifted with uncommon strength and with a wise extension of voice'.

Nozze di Figaro, Le (The Marriage of Figaro). Opera in 4 acts by Mozart; text by Lorenzo da Ponte, after Beaumarchais's comedy *La Folle Journée, ou Le Mariage de Figaro* (1778, prod. 1784). Prod. Vienna, B., 1 May 1786, with Laschi, Storace, D. Bussani, M. Mandini, Gottlieb, S. Mandini, Benucci, F. Bussani, Kelly, cond. Mozart; London, Hm., 18 June 1812, with Dickens, Catalani, Bianchi, Fischer, Naldi, Rigli; N.Y., Park T., 10 May 1824, arr. Bishop, with Johnson, Holman, Jones, Pearman (Bishop's version was made in 1819).

Figaro (bar.) is to marry Susanna (sop.) and is preparing the rooms allotted to them by the Count (bar.), whose roving eye has lit upon Susanna. Figaro is in further difficulties, having signed a contract promising to marry Marcellina (con.) if he cannot repay some money borrowed from her. She and Bartolo (bass) consider how he may be trapped, and there is naturally great tension between her and Susanna. The page Cherubino (sop.) is about to be banished for flirting; he sings about his susceptible nature, and hurriedly hides when the Count enters in search of Susanna. The arrival of the priest Basilio (ten.) sends the Count also into hiding, but they are both discovered. Cherubino is ordered off to the army.

The Countess laments the loss of her husband's love, and Figaro and Susanna plan to re-arouse it by means of jealousy and ridicule. Cherubino enters with a love song for the Countess, but has to hide in a neighbouring room when the Count enters. He emerges when the Count goes in search of tools to break the door, and escapes through the window while Susanna takes his place. She baffles the Count by blithely emerging; but the gardener has seen Cherubino's escape and disaster is only averted by Figaro's claiming that it was he who jumped from the window.

The Count tries to win Susanna by threatening to make Figaro marry Marcellina, and she pretends to yield. But Marcellina and Bartolo turn out to be Figaro's parents. The Countess, still mourning the loss of love, arranges a rendezvous between the Count and Susanna in which she will take Susanna's place. The marriage formalities of Figaro and Susanna are attended to.

In the garden, Susanna and the Countess appear in each other's clothes. Figaro, believing that Susanna is to yield to the Count, jealously hears a serenade actually meant for him. Cherubino has an appointment with Barbarina (sop.) but tries to kiss 'Susanna'. He is routed by the Count, who makes approaches to his own wife, as he then discovers to his horror and remorse. She forgives him, and all ends well.

Also operas by Tarchi (a version of Mozart 1787), Dittersdorf (1789), and L. Ricci (new libretto by G. Rossi, 1838). See also *Figaro*.

Nuittier (orig. Truinet), **Charles-Louis-Étienne** (*b* Paris, 24 Apr. 1828; *d* Paris, 24 Feb. 1899). French librettist and writer on music. Collaborated (especially with A. Beaume) on librettos, e.g. for Offenbach, Guiraud, Lecocq, and Hervé; also translated numerous works, including operas by Weber, Wagner, and Verdi, for the T.–L. and elsewhere. Archivist at the Opéra, whose collection he systematized and greatly enriched, from 1866. Also published several valuable books on opera, notably *Les Origines de l'opéra français*.

Number Opera. The name given to an opera written in separate numbers, that is, arias, duets, trios, ensembles, choruses, etc., separated by spoken dialogue or recitative. The normal form until the early 19th cent., it survived especially in France and Italy, but in Germany was gradually replaced, after Mozart's tendency to link sections into a larger whole, by operas in which the music was increasingly continuous. Wagner strongly opposed number opera, insisting on music forming a dramatic whole with the text. In the 20th cent. the number opera has been revived e.g. by Hindemith, Stravinsky, and Weill.

Nuremberg (Ger Nürnberg). Town in Bavaria, Germany. *Seelewig*, generally regarded as the first extant German opera, was performed privately in 1644. A Komödienhaus was opened in 1668, and much used by travelling Italian companies. Opera did not greatly flourish until the early 19th cent. With the opening of the Stadttheater in 1833, matters improved and many important singers visited the city. Wagner and Verdi entered the repertory from 1858. The present opera house (cap. 1,456) was opened in 1905, damaged during the Second World War, and reopened 1945. Robert Heger, Fritz Stiedry, and Rudolf Hartmann have worked there, also Trude Eipperle, Jaro Prohaska, and Heinrich Schlusnus. Hans Gierster has been music director since 1965.

O

Obbligato (*It* obligatory). Strictly a term for an instrumental part that cannot be omitted. (It is often used, however, for a part that may be omitted.) In vocal music, it is essential but subordinate to the voice, e.g. the corno di bassetto obbligato in Vitellia's 'Non più di fiori' in Act 2 of Mozart's *La clemenza di Tito*.

Ober, Margaret Arndt- (*b* Berlin, 15 Apr. 1885; *d* Bad Sachs, 17 Mar. 1971). German mezzo-soprano. Studied Berlin with Benno Stolzenberg, and with Arthur Arnot (whom she married). Début Frankfurt 1906, Azucena. Berlin 1907-44; N.Y., Met., 1913-17, first local Octavian, and Eglantine in Toscanini's revival of *Euryanthe* (1914). Interned in America during First World War and in 1919 resumed her career in Berlin with great success. First Berlin Kostelnička under Kleiber. (R)

Oberon. Opera in 3 acts by Weber; text by James Robinson Planché, after William Sotheby's translation (1798) of Wieland's *Oberon* (1780), which is in turn based on a 13th cent. *chanson de geste, Huon de Bordeaux.* Prod. London, C.G., 12 Apr. 1826, with Paton, Goward, Cawse, Vestris, Braham, Fawcett, Bland, Isaacs, cond. Weber; Leipzig 23 Dec. 1826; N.Y., Park T., 20 Sept. 1826, with Austin, Wollack, Sharpe, Horn, Richings.

Oberon (ten.) has vowed not to meet Titania again until he has found a faithful pair of lovers. With some supervision and help from Puck (sop.), and provision of a magic horn that can summon aid, Sir Huon (ten.) is sent to Bagdad to rescue Reiza (sop.) in expiation of a crime against Charlemagne. He does so, with his squire Sherasmin (bar.), who rescues Reiza's attendant Fatima (sop.). After being shipwrecked, captured by pirates, and sold in slavery to the Emir of Tunis, they survive and are restored to Charlemagne's favour; Oberon accepts their proof of faithfulness.

Other operas on the subject are by Kunzen (*Holger Danske*, 1789 – the principal 18th cent. Danish opera), Wranitzky (1789 – very successful until replaced by Weber's opera), and Hanke (*Hüon und Amande*, 1794). Also opera by Grosheim (*Titania*, 1792) and Dessauer (19th cent., unprod.). See also *Midsummer Night's Dream*, and *Shakespeare*.

Oberspielleiter (*Ger* senior producer). The name given to the chief resident producer of an opera company. He might sometimes also be the Generalintendant.

Oberto, Conte di San Bonifacio. Opera in 2 acts by Verdi; text by Piazza, revised by Solera.

Prod. Milan, Sc., 17 Nov. 1839, with Rainieri-Marini, Shaw, Sacchi, Salvi, Marini; London, St Pancras T.H., 8 Apr. 1965 (concert), with Edwards, Sinclair, Pilley, Robinson, Ruta, cond. Head; N.Y., Amato T., 18 Feb. 1978. Libretto reset by Graffigna and prod. Venice as *I Bonifazi ed i Salinguerra* (1842).

Leonora (sop. or mezzo), daughter of Count Oberto (bass), has been seduced by Riccardo (ten.), who now wants to marry Cuniza (cont.). Oberto kills Riccardo in a duel and leaves Italy for ever.

Also opera on same plot by F. Ricci, *Corrado d'Altamura* (1841).

Obratsova, Elena (Vasilyevna) (*b* Leningrad, 19 Mar. 1939). Russian mezzo-soprano. Studied Leningrad with Grigoryev. Début Moscow, B., 1963 Marina. Many guest appearances in Eastern and Western Europe including Milan, Sc., Vienna, Hamburg etc. as Adalgisa, Charlotte, Eboli, Ulrica. N.Y., Met., with Bolshoy Co., 1975 as Marina, Countess in *Queen of Spades,* Helen Bezukhova in *War and Peace*; and from 1977. San Francisco 1975 Azucena. Repertory also includes Carmen, Delila, Rosina, and roles in contemporary Russian works. Has a deep, rich mezzo and a dynamic stage personality. One of the most exciting Russian singers to have emerged in the 1970s. (R)

Obukhova, Nadezhda (Andreyevna) (*b* Moscow, 6 Mar. 1886; *d* Feodosiya, 15 Aug, 1961). Russian mezzo-soprano Studied Moscow with Masetti. Début Moscow, B., 1916, Pauline (*Queen of Spades*). Leading mezzo, B., until 1943; her roles included Orfeo, Dalila, Carmen, and Amneris, also Fricka and Erda but she was especially successful in the Russian repertory, particularly in Rimsky-Korsakov's operas. (R)

Oca del Cairo, L' (The Goose of Cairo). Opera in 2 acts by Mozart; text by Varesco. Comp. 1783, unfin. Prod. Paris, F.-P., 6 June 1867, with Armand, Géraizer, Mathilde, Laurent, Bonnet, Masson; London, D.L., 12 May 1870 with Lewitzky, Sinico, Gardoni, Gassier, cond. Arditi.

O Carlo, ascolta. The introduction to Posa's (bar.) death aria in the last act of Verdi's *Don Carlos.*

Ocean! thou mighty monster. Reiza's (sop.) aria in Act 2, scene 3 of Weber's *Oberon,* first apostrophizing the ocean and then hailing the boat she believes to be coming to her rescue.

Ochs von Lerchenau, Baron. The Marschallin's boorish cousin (bass) in Strauss's *Der Rosenkavalier.*

O cieli azzurri. The introduction to Aida's (sop.) aria in Act 3 of Verdi's *Aida.* Sometimes known as the Nile Aria.

Octavian. Count Rofrano (sop. or mezzo), the

Rose Cavalier in Strauss's *Der Rosenkavalier.*

O du mein holder Abendstern. Wolfram's (bar.) song to the evening star in Act 3 of Wagner's *Tannhäuser.*

Odysseus (Lat., Ulysses). In Homer's *Iliad* and *Odyssey,* the Greek hero, most nimble-witted of the leaders of the army before Troy, who on the fall of the city was condemned to long years of wandering, and after many adventures (including those on the island of *Circe) returned to his native Ithaca. Here he found his wife *Penelope waiting faithfully for him; and after killing her importunate suitors with the help of his son *Telemachus, he claimed her back. Most operas on his legend deal with his return to Ithaca, and therefore overlap with those dealing with Penelope as their main subject: for the latter, see *Penelope.*

Operas on the subject are as follows: Monteverdi (*Il ritorno d'Ulisse in patria,* 1641); Sacrati (*Ulisse errante,* 1644); Gandio (*Ulisse in Feazia,* 1681: according to Fétis, staged using the carved figures of the Teatro San Mosé in Venice); Accaciuoli (*Ulisse in Feaccia,* 1681); Pollarolo (*Ulisse sconosciuto in Itaca,* 1698); G. Porta (1725); D. G. Treu (*Ulisse e Telemacco,* 1726); Sciroli (*Ulisse errante,* 1749); G. F. Maio (1769); Gazzaniga (*Il ritorno d'Ulisse a Penelope,* 1781); Giordani (*Il ritorno d'Ulisse,* 1782); F. Alessandri (*Il ritorno d'Ulisse a Penelope,* 1790); F. Basili (*Il Ritorno d'Ulisse,* 1798); ?Perrino (*Ulisse nell'isola di Circe,* 1805); Mayr (*Il Ritorno d'Ulisse,* 1809); Dallapiccola (1968).
See *Circe, Telemachus.*

Oedipus Rex (King Oedipus). Opera-oratorio in 2 acts by Stravinsky; text by Cocteau, after Sophocles's tragedy (*c*435-425 B.C.), trans. into Latin by Daniélou. Prod. Paris, Th. S.B., 30 May 1927, as oratorio; first stage prod. Vienna 23 Feb. 1928; Boston 24 Feb. 1928 (concert) and N.Y. 21 Apr. 1931 (stage), cond. Stokowski; London, Queen's Hall, 12 Feb. 1936 (concert), with Slobodskaya, Widdop, Williams, Walker, cond. Ansermet; and Edinburgh (by Hamburg Company), 21 Aug. 1956 with Ilosvay, Melchert, Pease, Van Mill, cond. Ludwig.

The Narrator describes how Oedipus was doomed from birth to the horror of killing his father and marrying his mother. Though Oedipus (ten.), Jocasta (sop.), Creon (bassbar.), and Tiresias (bass) enact their roles, the chorus is static, and the dramatic metaphor is somewhere between opera and oratorio.

Oestvig, Karl (*b* Oslo, 17 May 1889; *d* Oslo, 21 July 1968). Norwegian tenor. Studied Cologne with Steinbach and Walter. Début Stuttgart 1914; here he created Giovanni in Schillings's *Mona Lisa.* Vienna, S.O., 1919-27, where he created the Emperor in *Frau ohne Schatten.* Berlin, S.O. till 1926, Stä. O. 1927-30. Retired 1932; taught singing and produced opera in Oslo. Director Oslo Opera 1941. A distinguished Lohengrin, Parsifal, and Walther. Married soprano Maria Rajdl. (R)

Offenbach, Jacques (orig. Jakob) (*b* Cologne, 20 June 1819; *d* Paris, 5 Oct. 1880). German, later French, composer and conductor. Son of a Cologne synagogue cantor from Offenbach originally named Eberst; studied with J. Alexander and B. Breuer, then Paris with Vaslin, also having lessons from Halévy. Played the cello in the orchestra of the O.C., and began writing light musical pieces for the stage. In 1850 became conductor of the T. Français; then rented the T. Marigny in the Champs-Elysées and opened it as the Bouffes-Parisiens in 1855: his performances were a success of the Exhibition, and included works by Adam and Delibes as well as himself and others. For the winter he gave up his position at the T. Français and moved to the T. Comte. He organised a competition which attracted 78 entries and was won by Bizet and Lecocq with their settings of *Le Docteur Miracle.* In 1857 his company visited London. Enlarging his range, he wrote *Orphée aux enfers* (1858), then *Barkouf* (1860) for the O. He resigned from the B.-P. in 1862. His reputation was by now international, and he helped to encourage J. Strauss II to write operetta. His greatest successes belong to this period: *La Belle Hélène* (1864), *Barbe-Bleue* (1866), *La Vie parisienne* (1867), *La Grande Duchesse de Gérolstein* (1867), and *La Périchole* (1868). After the war of 1871, the new mood in Paris was against his frivolous manner. However, he continued to write, and to tour (with especial success in America, 1876), and at his death was working on *Les Contes d'Hoffmann* (unfin. 1880, completed at his request by Guiraud).

A brilliant man of the theatre, with a flair for epitomizing the wit of his day, Offenbach discovered a style which appealed irresistibly to the French taste of the 1860s. His pieces satirize the classics or contemporary politics and society, sometimes by reference one to the other, and with especial allusion to the modes and manners of the Second Empire. Similarly, familiar music is often pressed into service in absurd situations or made ludicrous by association with unexpected words. The impeccable *boulevardier* manner and exhilarating high spirits conceal the skill of these captivating pieces; they also distract attention from the lack of a true lyrical gift such as Johann Strauss could display. That he never lacked melodic appeal is shown not only in the frothiest of the operettas but also in *Les Contes d'Hoffmann,* though structural slackness and a lack of real musical substance weaken this, his one attempt at a larger-scale serious work. At his best, his melodic manner could be touching (as with John Styx's aria in *Orphée aux enfers*, 'Quand j'étais roi de Béotie') as well as hilarious (the famous concluding Galop in the same work). There is, moreover, a recurrent cynicism and fatalism concealed beneath the Second Empire merriment which led Mauriac to write of *La Grande Duchesse de Gérolstein*, 'The laughter I hear in Offenbach's music is that of the Empress Charlotte, gone mad.'

Ohms, Elisabeth (*b* Arnhem, 17 May 1888; *d* Marquardstein, Dec. 1974). Dutch soprano. Studied Amsterdam with Morello, Van Oort, and Rose Schönberg, Frankfurt with Eduard Bellwidt, and Berlin with Max Barth. Début Mainz 1921; Munich, N., 1922-36, where she was particularly successful in Wagner, and was the first Munich Turandot and Aegyptische Helena. London, C.G., 1928-9, 1935, Venus, Ortrud, Brünnhilde, and Isolde; N.Y., Met., 1930-32; Bayreuth 1931, Kundry. Chosen by Toscanini to sing Fidelio and Kundry at Sc., Milan, 1927-9. Married the painter and designer Leo Pasetti. (R)

O Isis und Osiris. Sarastro's (bass) prayer to the Egyptian gods in Act 2 of Mozart's *Die Zauberflöte*.

Olczewska, Maria (orig. Marie Berchtenbreitner) (*b* Ludwigsschwaige bei Donauwörth, nr Augsburg, 12 Aug. 1892; *d* Klagenfurt, 17 May 1969). German mezzo-soprano. Studied Munich with Karl Erler. Originally operetta singer; opera début Krefeld 1917, Page in *Tannhäuser*. Leipzig 1918-20; Hamburg 1920-23, where she created Brigitte in *Tote Stadt*; Vienna, S.O., 1921-2; Munich 1923-5; Vienna, 1925-30. London, C.G., 1924-32, leading mezzo in Wagner repertory, also Amneris, Carmen, and Orlofsky; Chicago 1928-32; N.Y., Met., 1933-5. Professor Vienna Conservatory from 1947. Had a rich and beautiful voice and was a fine actress. Married (later divorced) Emil *Schipper. (R)

Oldenburg. Town in Lower Saxony, Germany. The first permanent theatre opened in 1883 with Auber's *La Neige*. Until 1921 opera was generally given by the Bremen company. Julius Köpsch was music director 1921-8. Johannes Schüler pursued an adventurous policy 1928-32, giving performances of *Neues vom Tage* and *Wozzeck* (first production after Berlin première). The old theatre, damaged during the war, was completely renovated in 1961.

Old Vic, The (properly The Royal Victoria Hall). The theatre in the Waterloo Road in south London, birth-place of the English opera company which later had its home at *Sadler's Wells. Built originally in 1818 by Joseph Glossop, an English impresario, who, as Giuseppe Glossop, was the impresario of the

Scala, Milan, and the San Carlo, Naples, where he married one of the singers. Their son Augustus Glossop Harris was the father of Augustus *Harris, manager of C.G. 1888-96, thus providing a generally unknown link between four famous opera houses. The Royal Coburg Theatre, as the Royal Victoria Hall was previously known, opened in 1818; it was renamed the Royal Victoria Hall in 1833. In 1880 its lease was acquired by the social reformer Emma Cons and it was renamed the Royal Victoria Coffee Hall. Opera was first heard there in the form of excerpts in costume. Emma Cons was succeeded in 1898 by her niece Lilian *Baylis, who developed the theatre's opera along with its Shakespearian repertory, opera being given on two nights a week and on alternate Saturday matinées. Even works like *Tristan und Isolde* were heard, with the score drastically reduced by Charles Corri, the theatre's excellent music director. After the First World War Lilian Baylis decided that *Figaro* should be newly produced and invited the soprano Muriel Gough to undertake the task; she demurred, and suggested instead Clive Carey, who accepted and urged Lilian Baylis to accept a new translation by Edward J. Dent. This was the beginning of the Dent-Carey Mozart revival in England, and of the move towards sensible and singable translations. By 1931, when S.W. was opened, the repertory included *La forza del destino*, *Aida*, *Otello*, *Samson et Dalila*, *Tannhäuser*, and *Lohengrin*. The singers at that time included Joan Cross, Edith Coates, Winifred Kennard, Rose Morris, Constance Willis, Sumner Austin, Arthur Cox, Tudor Davies, Henry Brindle, Powell Lloyd, Booth Hitchin, and Henry Wendon. Lawrance Collingwood became one of the conductors, and there were also evenings of ballet under the direction of Ninette de Valois and conducted by Constant Lambert. No opera was given at the Old Vic after 1935.
Bibl: E. J. Dent: *A Theatre for Everybody* (1945).

Olghina (-Yozeforiez), Olga N. (*b* ?; *d* ?). Russian soprano. St Petersburg, M., 1889-94; Milan, Sc., 1893-4 Manon Lescaut; London, C.G., 1894 where she was the first London Manon Lescaut and Nannetta. Appearances in Moscow, Warsaw, Helsinki, until the early 1900s. Not to be confused with Olga Olghini, mezzo-soprano active in the 1860s and 1870s, or Olga F. Olghina, Russian coloratura soprano, active in the 1920s and 1930s.

Olivero, Magda (*b* Saluzzo, 25 Apr. 1914). Italian soprano. Début Turin 1933, Lauretta (*Schicchi*). Distinguished as much for her acting as for her singing as Adriana Lecouvreur, Liù, Violetta, Suor Angelica, and Minnie. Married 1941, returned to stage in the 1950-1 season as Adriana, having promised Cilea that she would do so. London, Stoll, 1952, Mimì; Edinburgh Festival 1963, *Adriana Lecouvreur.* Continued to sing with great success during the 1950 and 1960s, and in 1967 made a belated U.S. début in Dallas as Cherubini's *Medea.* N.Y., Met., 1975, Tosca. (R)

Olomouc (*Ger.* Olmütz). Town in Czechoslovakia. Opera is given in the Oldřich Stibor T. (cap. 750) 3-4 times a week by a company of about 30 soloists.

O luce di quest'anima. Linda's (sop.) aria in Act 1 of Donizetti's *Linda di Chamounix* in which she sings of her love for Arthur.

Olympia. The Doll (sop.), Hoffmann's first love, in Offenbach's *Les Contes d'Hoffmann.*

Olympians, The. Opera in 3 acts by Bliss; text by J. B. Priestley. Prod. London, C.G., 29 Sept. 1949, with Grandi, Coates, Johnston, Franklin, Glynne, cond. Rankl. The story concerns the adventures of the Olympian gods, now reduced to a group of travelling players but restored to their former glory for one night of each year.

Olympie. Opera in 3 acts by Spontini; text by M. Dieulafoy and C. Brifaut, after Voltaire's tragedy (1762). Prod. Paris, O., 22 Dec. 1819, with Albert, Branchu, Nourrit, Dérivis, cond. R. Kreutzer. Revived in Berlin (trans. E.T.A. Hoffmann) 14 May 1821, with Schulz, Milder, Blume, Bader, cond. Spontini. Failed owing to rival popular support for Weber's *Der Freischütz,* though occasionally revived until 1870. Revived Florence, 1950.

Olympie (sop.), daughter of Alexander the Great, wants to marry Cassandre (ten.), but Statire (mezzo), Alexander's widow, opposes the choice, as she believes Cassandre murdered her husband. Antigone (bass) also wants to marry Olympie; he is mortally wounded in a battle with Cassandre's army and before he dies confesses that it was he who murdered Alexander. Olympie and Cassandre are reunited, and Statire succeeds to the throne. Also opera by C. Conti (1829).

O'Mara, Joseph (*b* Limerick, 16 July 1864; *d* 5 Aug. 1927). Irish tenor. Studied Milan with Moretti. Début London, Royal English O.H., 1891 in title role of Sullivan's *Ivanhoe.* Sang at C.G. and D.L., during Harris's management became leading tenor Moody-Manners O.C. Also sang with Beecham O.C., and formed his own O'Mara O.C. Often sang in Wagner, and had a repertory of nearly 70 parts. Roles he created included the title-role of Stanford's *Shamus O'Brien.* Retired 1926. (R)

Ombra mai fù. Serse's (male sop.) aria in Act 1 of Handel's *Serse,* apostrophizing the tree that gives him shade. Though marked *larghetto,* it has become irrevocably known as Handel's Largo.

Ombra scene. In early opera, a scene taking place in Hades, or one in which a ghost or shade (*ombra*) is conjured up. Latterly this was often allied to a *Slumber scene, in which the sleeping hero was addressed, usually in warning or reproach, by a ghost. Though originating in 17th cent. opera (and a regular feature of Orpheus operas), the effect has proved tenacious: among the most celebrated, and powerful, ombra scenes are those in Berlioz's *Les Troyens.*

O Mimì, tu più non torni. The duet between Rodolfo (ten.) and Marcello (bar.) in Act 4 of Puccini's *La Bohème.*

O mio babbino caro. Lauretta's (sop.) appeal to her father to allow her to marry Rinuccio in Puccini's *Gianni Schicchi.*

O mio Fernando. Leonora's (mezzo) aria in Act 3 of Donizetti's *La Favorite* in which she sings of her love for Fernando.

O namenlose Freude. The duet of reunion for Leonore (sop.) and Florestan (ten.) in Act 2, scene 1, of Beethoven's *Fidelio.*

Oncina, Juan (*b* Barcelona, 15 Apr. 1925). Spanish tenor. Studied Barcelona with Capsir. Début Barcelona, 1946, Des Grieux (Massenet). Sang widely in Italy 1946-52, establishing himself as a leading exponent of Rossini, Donizetti, etc. Glyndebourne 1952-61, especially successful as Ramiro, Lindoro, Almaviva, and Ory. Has latterly sung heavier Verdi and Puccini roles. His voice is inclined to whiteness; he is a charming and witty artist. (R) Husband of the soprano Tatiana Menotti.

Onegin (orig. Hoffmann), **Sigrid** (Elisabeth Elfriede Emilie) (*b* Stockholm, 1 June 1889; *d* Magliaso, 16 June 1943). Swedish contralto. Daughter of a German father and a French mother, and married first to a Russian pianist and composer named Eugene Onegin (the professional name of E. Lvov). Studied Frankfurt, Munich, and Milan with Schröder-Kaminsky, Weiss, Siems, Di Ranieri. Début Stuttgart 1912, Carmen, where she created Dryade in *Ariadne auf Naxos*; London début same role 1913, as Lilli Hoffmann-Onegin. Munich 1919-22; Berlin 1926-33; N.Y., Met., 1922-4; London, C.G., 1927. Possessed a voice of great power and range, and was famous as Lady Macbeth, Eboli, Orfeo, Fricka, Brangäne, and Fidès in *Le Prophète.* (R)
Bibl: F. Penzoldt: *Sigrid Onegin* (1929).

O paradiso. Vasco da Gama's (ten.) apostrophe to the island of Madagascar in Act 4 of Meyerbeer's *L'Africaine.*

O patria mia. Aida's Nile Aria. See *O cieli azzurri.*

Opava. Town in Czechoslovakia. Opera is given in the Zdeněk Nejedlý Silesian T. 3-4 times a week by a company of about 20 soloists. The company also tours to Krnov.

Open-air opera. During the summer, *al fresco* (or *all'aperto*) performances of opera are regularly to be seen and heard in many countries. In some cases classical arenas are used (most notably at Verona); other attempts have been made with specially constructed stages, the audience being seated in the open; still others have made use of the natural architecture or scenery for their setting. The principal problem has always been of balance, not only in projecting voices adequately but also in siting the orchestra effectively; it is also difficult to achieve a satisfactory illusion with an art that, even more than the theatre, depends on the conventions of the actual opera house.

One of the earliest recorded open-air performances was at Regensburg by Schikaneder's company of Hartmann's *Balders Død* (1788). In the 20th cent., especially with the development of festivals, there have been many such performances. Those in Italy include the regular series at the Verona Arena, beginning in 1913 with the work still most associated with and most appropriate to its vast size, *Aida,* and also the seasons at the Terme di Caracalla in Rome, given since 1937. Venice has seen *Cavalleria rusticana* in the Piazza San Marco, and *Aida* on the Lido. In Florence, opera is given in the Boboli Gardens.

In France, similar use has been made of ancient arenas and theatres in a number of southern towns such as Arles, and especially Orange, where from 1899 performances of opera have included works by Méhul (*Joseph*), Wagner, Saint-Saëns, and others. An excellent and comfortable open-air theatre has been built for the performances at the Aix-en-Provence Festival. In earlier times, performances of works by Lully were given in the gardens at Versailles.

In Germany, open-air opera has been given in Augsburg at the Rote Tor, and in Munich at Schloss Nymphenburg. Summer performances of *Der Freischütz* are given by the lake at Eutin, Weber's birthplace, and at Rathen, a forest amphitheatre up the Elbe from Dresden. At *Zoppot the Zoppoter Waldoper gave Wagner performances, as well as works by other composers, 1909-39 in a magnificent forest amphitheatre with splendid acoustics. Performances on a specially constructed stage floating on the lake are given at Bregenz in Austria. In Czechoslovakia, productions have included those of Smetana's *The Bartered Bride* at Divoká Sárka, near Prague, in 1913, and of *The Kiss* at his birthplace, Litomyšl, in 1952. In Hungary open-air performances have been given at various sites in Szeged and in

Budapest. In Jugoslavia, opera is given in the open at Dubrovnik.

In America, an annual opera season was given at the Cincinnati Zoo with artists from the Met. until 1970, and several successful opera seasons were given by a company based on the Chicago Opera at Ravinia Park, 1910-31; since 1957 the Santa Fe Opera has given open-air performances. There are also, as in other countries, performances attached to summer schools. Though the English climate is not conducive to open-air opera, there have been university performances, and an attempt was made before the war in Scarborough. The London County Council has sponsored occasional performances in London parks. Performances at Hintlesham have been given in the open air. Holst's *Savitri* is probably the only opera intended primarily for open-air performance.

Opera (*It* work; an abbreviation of *opera in musica*). A drama to be sung with instrumental accompaniment by one or more singers in costume; *recitative or spoken dialogue may separate set musical numbers.

Opéra, Paris. Officially entitled the Académie de Musique, like other French theatres and companies on their foundation; 'Opéra' is generally taken to refer to the Paris theatre and company.

On 28 June 1669, Robert Cambert and the Abbé Pierre Perrin obtained a Royal privilege from Louis XIV to perform 'académies d'opéra ou réprésentations en musique et en langue françoise, sur le pied de celles d'Italie'. They joined with the Marquis de Sourdéac as producer and Beauchamps as ballet-master to recruit singers in the Languedoc. In 1670 they rented the Salle du Jeu de Paume de la Bouteille for five years. Guichard converted it to a theatre, inaugurated on 3 Mar. 1671 with Cambert and Perrin's *Pomone.* Profiting by dissensions, Lully secured the patent from Perrin in Mar. 1672. Together with his librettist Quinault, he had produced 17 grand operas at the Palais-Royal by his death in 1687, setting a style whose grandeur and formality exercised an enduring influence on the Opéra. However, the *tragédie lyrique which he inaugurated was not notably developed by his immediate successors, such as Destouches and Campra. In 1733 Rameau made his début at the O. with *Hippolyte et Aricie;* 24 of his operas were produced by 1760. In 1763 the theatre was destroyed by fire, and the new theatre at the Tuileries was inaugurated with Rameau's *Castor et Pollux* in 1764. The O. returned to the Palais-Royal in 1769 (renovated, cap. 2,500).

The reign of Gluck began with the performance of *Iphigénie en Aulide* in 1774; the arrival of Piccinni, representing a more Italianate manner in opposition to Gluck's theatrical reality, precipitated a famous controversy. In June 1781 the Palais-Royal again burnt down, and the O. transferred to the Salle des Menus-Plaisirs. The new house at Porte-St-Martin was opened by Marie Antoinette in October 1781. In 1794 the theatre moved again to the Salle Montansier in the rue de Richelieu (cap. 1,650). After various changes of name and organization during the Revolution and its aftermath, the Opéra was established on a firmer footing, with the title Académie Imperiale de Musique. The repertory was widened, though the traditional French emphasis on ballet remained.

In 1807, the era of Spontini opened with the performance of *La vestale*. Together with Cherubini, he set a style of *Grand opera that marked the Opéra for many decades. In 1820 it moved to the Salle Favart, then in 1822 to the theatre in the rue Lepeletier (cap. 1,954). Gaslight was first used in Isouard's *Aladin, ou la Lampe merveilleuse* (1822). Operas by Rossini, Donizetti, Auber, Weber, Meyerbeer, Hérold, Halévy and others joined those of Spontini and Cherubini, in grandiose stagings by *Cicéri and *Daguerre. This was the period in which the Paris Opéra dominated Europe as a theatre, setting a grand style and imposing powerful standards, to which composers from all countries were drawn. Spectacle was all-important; a second-act ballet was virtually obligatory; dialogue was forbidden (so that for works with dialogue, recitatives had to be written, e.g. by Berlioz for Weber's *Der Freischütz*, in 1841). In 1849 Meyerbeer's *Le Prophète* was staged with electric lighting. Verdi's works were taken into the repertory, the style of the Opéra affecting several of them (e.g. *Don Carlos*). In 1861 Wagner's *Tannhäuser* was a notorious fiasco. Among the singers of this great period in the theatre's history were Cinti-Damoreau, Falcon, Viardot, Nourrit, Duprez, Marie Sass, and Faure.

In 1873 the O. again burnt down. Charles Garnier's sumptuous theatre was planned in 1867, but delayed by the Franco-Prussian War. It eventually opened on 5 Jan. 1875 (cap. 2,156). It remains one of the largest and grandest theatres in the world. Massenet and Gounod were among the most important composers, and Wagner was reintroduced after the *Tannhäuser* disaster. Even Berlioz had a hearing, though it was not until the 20th cent. that a version of *Les Troyens* was staged. The theatre housed a number of important Russian seasons, as well as developing its own repertory along traditional lines. After the Second World War, a number of re-organizations took place, most radically in 1971 with the appointment of Rolf Liebermann as administrator and Georg Solti as music adviser: the new régime was inaugurated with a performance of *Le nozze di Figaro* at Versailles in 1973. It was

further re-organized as an international house, on the system of the Met. and C.G, no longer as an ensemble house. With the closure of the O.C. in 1972, spoken dialogue was admitted for the first time with works from the other theatre's repertory. Charles Mackerras and Julius Rudel were appointed chief guest conductors. Liebermann was due to be succeeded by Bernard Lefort in 1980. The building now seats 2,131: the stage, the largest in the world, is 100' wide and 112' deep.

Bibl: O. Meslin: *L'Opéra de Paris* (1975).

Opera-ballet. A form that arose in France, where dance has, ever since the early *ballet de cour* and its incorporation into opera by Lully, been an important ingredient of opera. The first important opera-ballet was Campra's *L'Europe galante* (1697), in which the dramatic content was minimal and dancing, choral, and scenic elements paramount. A famous example of the genre was Rameau's *Les Indes galantes* (1735).

Opera buffa (*It* comic opera). A term for the Italian comic opera that developed, from the short comic scenes that ended the acts in *opera seria, via the *intermezzo, into a form in its own right. The chief contrast with opera seria is the use of a comic subject with characters drawn from everyday life. The earliest independent examples of opera buffa were Mazzocchi's *Chi soffre spere* (1639) and Abbatini's *Dal male il bene* (1653), both to texts by Giulio Rospigliosi (later Pope Clement IX). Opera buffa did not necessarily contain spoken dialogue, though this was a requisite of the French equivalent, *opéra-bouffe*. The latter term is used with special reference to the works of Offenbach and those in similar vein.

Opéra comique (*Fr* comic opera). Despite its literal meaning, 'comic opera' conveys a false impression of this vague but generally accepted term. The French themselves understand different things by it according to the date of its use. Beginning in the early 18th cent. with farces and satires using spoken dialogue with well-known airs (*vaudevilles), the genre developed into the *comédie mêlée d'ariettes; thence, in the early 19th cent., it drew closer to serious opera, handling serious or Romantic themes, as in Boieldieu's *La Dame blanche*, Auber's *Fra Diavolo*, etc., later Bizet's *Carmen*. By this stage, the most marked difference between opéra comique and serious opera was the former's retention of spoken dialogue; the banning of all dialogue at the Opéra further ensured the distinction between works performed there and works belonging to the Opéra-Comique.

Opéra-Comique, Paris. Paris's second opera house, originally the home for French musical pieces with spoken dialogue. In 1715 an agreement between the *comédiens* and the director of the Académie Royale de Musique resulted in the setting up of the Institution known as the Opéra-Comique. Its success was so great that the Académie had it closed in 1745, but it was reopened seven years later by Monet at Saint-Germain. In 1762 it joined the Comédie-Italienne and had its home in the rue Mauconseil, and in 1783 moved to the rue Favart, where it was known first as the Comédie-Italienne, then the Théâtre de la rue Favart, and finally as the Opéra-Comique; it is sometimes colloquially called the Salle Favart. In 1791 a rival company was established at the rue Feydeau. This ended in ruin and both houses were closed in 1783: the companies then amalgamated.

During the early days of the new régime, works by Dalayrac, Méhul, Auber, and Boieldieu were produced. In 1840 the theatre saw the première of *La Fille du régiment,* and in 1866 of *Mignon.* After the closing of the *Théâtre-Lyrique and the assumption by Carvalho of the Comique's management, the theatre entered a successful period with the premières of *Hoffmann, Lakmé,* and *Manon.* In 1887 the building was destroyed by fire, and the company carried on at the Théâtre Sarah Bernhardt until the opening of the present building (cap. 1,750) on 7 Dec. 1898, with Albert Carré as manager. During his régime *Louise, Pelléas et Mélisande, Ariane et Barbe-Bleue,* and *L'Heure espagnole* were produced. After Carré the directors were Gheusi and Isola (1914-18), Carré and Isola (1919-25), Masson and Ricou (1925-31), Masson (1931-2), Gheusi (1932-6), 1936-9 joint administration with that of the Opéra under Rouché assisted by Mariotte, Busser (1939-40), Max d'Ollonne (1941-4), Muratore (1944), Désormière, Jamin, Musy Rousseau (1944 – after the Liberation), Wolff (1945-6), Malherbe (1946-8), Bondeville (1948-51), Beydts (1952-3), Agostini (1953-9), Lamy (1959-62). A. M. Julien was appointed joint Administrator of both the Opéra and the Opéra-Comique in 1959. He was succeeded by Georges Auric in 1962 and René Nicoly, 1969-71. The theatre closed in April 1972 and reopened as 'Opéra Stadio de Paris' in Jan. 1973 under the direction of Louis Erlo. The Opera Studio moved to Lyons in 1976, and the O.C., under Liebermann, opened with the old name Salle Favart in Dec. 1976.

Opéra du Rhin. An operatic organization based on Strasbourg, but also giving performances in Colmar and Mulhouse. It was formed in 1972 with a company of more than 300 singers, dancers, musicians, and technical and administrative staff, with Alain Lombard as joint music director with Frédéric Adam. It made a promising start with its production of *Der Freischütz.* Lombard resigned at the end of the first season, but was re-appointed as artistic

director from October 1974, with Nathaniel Merrill as principal producer and Ignace Strasfogel as principal conductor.

Opera for All. A small group founded in 1949 by the Arts Council of Great Britain, to take opera to small towns, and even villages, throughout the country. The initial group of six members had by 1966-7 expanded into three groups of 12 members each, touring a mini-bus, one based on the London Opera Centre, one on the Welsh National Opera, one on Scottish Opera. By 1974, the Scottish and Welsh group had expanded into large autonomous ensembles, and Opera for All's London-based group remained the only one to retain the original name. Artists who gained their early experience with Opera for All include Josephine Barstow, Patricia Kern, Josephine Veasey, Keith Erwen, William McAlpine, and Richard Van Allan.

Opéra-lyrique (*Fr* lyric opera). A term used for a style of opera that flourished in 19th-cent. France in distinction to *grand opera and *opéra-comique. In general, it was shorter and less rich in choral, scenic, and other effects than the former, while avoiding the spoken dialogue of the latter. Beginning in the late 18th and early 19th cent., it developed e.g. in the works of Gounod and Thomas, and later Massenet, as a genre in which, on the whole, romantic elements were handled with a clarity, simplicity, and elegance that was at once more intense than opéra-comique in its more literally comic manifestations, and yet lighter in treatment than the most profound serious opera.

Opera semiseria (*It* semi-serious opera). A term originating in the second half of the 18th cent. for a work in which serious and comic elements were mingled. It was established as a genre by Piccinni's *La buona figliuola* (1760), in which serious arias were joined to a comic finale. The work had immediate successors in operas by Piccinni himself, by Cimarosa (*Il matrimonio segreto*), and by Paisiello (*Nina*); it also influenced Mozart, in the delicate balance of comic and serious elements in *Così* and *Figaro,* and in rather different fashion in the *dramma giocoso, Don Giovanni.*

Opera seria (*It* serious opera). The principal operatic form of the 17th and early 18th cent., in particular associated with the librettos of Zeno and Metastasio. Elaborate da capo arias, designed to give singers the utmost opportunity for display, were set in a framework of pageantry; mythological or classical subjects prevailed, with emotions formalized and the existing moral, social, and religious order celebrated in the close relationship of gods and nobles. When it became too rigid, it prompted a reaction in *opera buffa. Also the subject of a *commedia per musica* by Gassmann, to a text by Calzabigi (1796). See also *Neapolitan Opera*.

Opera Workshop. The term used in the U.S.A. or operatic study and preparation groups. It does not apply to the major activities of opera departments in the universities and academies, though the phrase is used to describe more elementary work in their opera departments. Some opera workshops resemble a local operatic society, and engage professional directors to prepare annual productions on a grand scale. Three out of every five performances of opera in the U.S.A. are sung by students, and many premières and first American performances of contemporary works have been given by these groups. In the 1957–8 season 228 workshops were listed in *Opera News*, ranging from Indiana University, which stages an annual *Parsifal*, and the Music Academy of the West, where Lotte Lehmann staged *Der Rosenkavalier*, to Louisiana State University, where *Fidelio* and Monteverdi's *Orfeo* were staged, and the University of Minnesota, which staged *Dido and Aeneas, The Magic Flute, The Telephone*, and a concert version of *The Tender Land* (Copland).

Operetta, opérette (*It, Fr* little opera). Originally used in the 17th cent. for a short opera, the term became associated by the 19th cent. with comic opera, to describe a play with an overture, songs, interludes, and dances.

Opernball, Der (The Opera Ball). Operetta in 3 acts by Heuberger; text by Léon and Waldeberg, after the farce *Les Dominos roses* by Delacour and Hennequin. Prod. Vienna, W., 5 Jan. 1898, with Dirkens; N.Y. 24 May 1909, with Morena, Bartet, Beria. Heuberger's most successful work.

Ora e per sempre addio. Otello's (ten.) farewell to his past glories in Act 2 of Verdi's *Otello*.

Orchestra pit. The space before and below the stage which contains the opera orchestra. The covered pit at Bayreuth (Wagner's 'mystic gulf') allows an exceptionally faithful balance without any visual distraction to the audience. Most opera houses are now built with pits in sections of variable height to assist the balance of different operas.

Orefice, Giacomo (*b* Vienna, 27 Aug. 1865; *d* Milan, 22 Dec. 1922). Italian composer. Studied Bologna with Mancinelli, offering *L'Oasi* as his graduation exercise. His operas include *Chopin* (1901), based on the composer's life and using his music, and *Il Mosè* (1905), his most successful work. He taught at the Milan Conservatory from 1909, and was active as a music critic, doing much to encourage interest in older music and to raise standards in editions: he himself made versions of Monteverdi's *Orfeo* and Rameau's *Platée*. His own technically proficient operas are of the **verismo* school.

Orest (or Orestes). Elektra's brother (bass-bar.) in Strauss's *Elektra*.

Orfeide. Operatic triptych by Malipiero; text by composer, comprising (1) *La morte delle maschere*, (2) *Sette canzoni*, and (3) *Orfeo, ovvero L'ottava canzone*. Pt. 2 prod. Paris, O., 10 Jul. 1920, with Lapeyrette, Noel, Duclos, cond. Grovlez. First complete prod., Düsseldorf 31 Oct. 1925, with Nettesheim, Schilp, Domgraf-Fassbänder, cond. Orthmann.

Orfeo. For Monteverdi's opera, see *Favola d'Orfeo, La*. See also *Orpheus*.

Orfeo ed Euridice. *Azione teatrale per musica* in 3 acts by Gluck; text by Calzabigi, after the classical legend. Prod. Vienna, B., 5 Oct. 1762, with Bianchi, Guadagni, Clavaran, cond. Gluck; London, King's T., 7 Apr. 1770, with Guadagni, Zamparini; N.Y., Winter Garden, 25 May 1863, with Vestvali, Rotter, Geary. French version, translated by Moline and with the title role transposed for tenor, prod. Paris 2 Aug. 1774, with Legros, Arnould, Levasseur, cond. Francoeur. Revised by Berlioz and prod. Paris 1859, with Viardot, Sass, cond. Berlioz. See also *Orpheus*.

Orff, Carl (*b* Munich, 10 July 1895). German composer. After his studies in Munich he began his career as a répétiteur and then conductor at Mannheim and Darmstadt. In 1920 he resumed his studies with Kaminski and in 1926 began his career as a composer with his first realization of Monteverdi's *Orfeo* (a second followed in 1931 and a third in 1941). Orff has tried to free opera from what he considers the exaggerations that had accrued to it by the beginning of the present century; this he does by returning to elementary rhythm and popular folk-song. He eschews counterpoint and thematic development and regards opera, as Wagner did, as a *Gesamtkunstwerk*. In *Carmina Burana* (1937), *Catulli Carmina* (1943), and *Trionfi dell'Afrodite* (1953) he uses Latin texts, and unashamedly appeals to the most primitive levels of emotion in his musical setting of them. *Der Mond* (1939) is a Bavarian fairy-tale and contains some of the composer's more lyrical music, as does *Die Kluge* (1943), his most successful work. *Die Bernauerin* (1947) is a Bavarian folk play with music, and *Antigonae* (1949) is an austere setting of the Sophocles tragedy in Hölderlin's translation. Later works are *Oedipus der Tyrann* (1959), *Ludus de Nato Infante Mirificus* (1960), *Prometheus* (1968), and *De Temporum Fine Comoedia* (1973).
Bibl: A. Liess: *Carl Orff* (1966).

Orgeni, Aglaja (orig., Anna Maria von Görger St. Jörgen) (*b* Roma Szombat, 17 Dec. 1841; *d* Vienna, 15 Mar. 1926). Hungarian soprano. Studied Baden-Baden with Pauline Viardot.

Début Berlin 1865, Amina. London, C.G., 1866, Violetta, Lucia, Martha. Sang extensively in Europe and was greatly admired for her elegant style. Taught at Dresden 1886–1914, where she became the first woman Royal Professor in 1908; and in Vienna from 1914. Her pupils included Erika Wedekind and Edyth Walker.

Orlandi, Elisa (*b* Macerata, 1811; *d* Rovigo, 1834). Italian mezzo-soprano. Created Jane Seymour (*Anna Bolena*) and Eleanora (*Il furioso all'isola di San Domingo*) for Donizetti. She died suddenly while waiting to make her entrance as Adalgisa in *Norma*.

Orlando. Opera in 3 acts by Handel; text by Grazio Bracioli (first composed by Ristori, 1713), after Ariosto's *Orlando furioso* (1516). Prod. London, Hm., 7 Feb. 1733, with La Strada, Senesino. Other operas on the subject are by Steffani (1691), D. Scarlatti (1711), Ristori (1713), Bioni (1724), Pollarolo (1725), and Vivaldi (1727). Revived Abingdon, 1959. See also *Ariodante*.

Orlofsky. The Russian prince (con., sometimes ten.) in Johann Strauss's *Die Fledermaus.*

Ormindo. Opera in 3 acts by Cavalli; text by Giovanni Faustini. Prod. Venice, S.C., 1644. New version by R. Leppard, prod. Glyndebourne 16 June 1967, cond. Leppard; N.Y., Juilliard School, 24 Apr. 1968.

Ornamentation. The art of decorating a melodic line, expected by the composer and improvised according to certain customs or rules by the singer. From early days, opera composers intended singers to demonstrate their musical and technical skill by embellishing the melodic line, and wrote with this in mind. Throughout the 17th and 18th cent. no singer would have performed a musical line as it was written down by the composer, and modern revivals of works of this period should take this into account. However, what had begun as a co-operative creative enterprise between composer and interpreter eventually deteriorated into unmusical and egotistical display by singers. Gluck and later composers tended to restrain and then suppress singers' excesses. The practice of the appoggiatura in recitative remained the custom; for composers normally wrote the appoggiatura, which would usually appear at the end of phrases of recitative, as a harmony note, so as to indicate the harmony to the singer, while expecting him to make the suitable melodic inflection. A simple, and common, instance is of a phrase ending on the tonic chord with two repeated notes (written), which the singer executes as the supertonic followed by the tonic. There was also a complicated system of signs, known in French as *agréments,* abandoned by Rossini in

favour of an accurate writing-out of the notes required.

Oroveso. The High Priest of the Druids (bass) in Bellini's *Norma.*

Orphée aux Enfers (Orpheus in the Under world). *Opéra-féerie* in 4 acts by Offenbach text by Crémieux and Halévy, possibly from a German scenario by Cramer. Prod. Paris, B.-P 21 Oct. 1858 (2 acts); Paris, Gaité, 7 Feb. 187 (4 acts), with Tautin, Leonce, Tayan, Désiré N.Y., Stadt T., ? Mar. 1861 (in German), with Scheller, Fr. & Herr Meaubert, Krilling, Klein London, Hm., 26 Dec. 1865, adapted by Planche as *Orpheus in the Haymarket.*

In this burlesque on the Greek gods, Orpheus is depicted as a music teacher in Thebes, married to Eurydice. Orpheus is in love with the shepherdess Chloe, Eurydice with the shepherd Aristeus – actually Pluto in disguise Orpheus calls on Jupiter to help him ge Eurydice back from the underworld, but Pluto himself has fallen in love with her and takes her as a Bacchante. Orpheus is quite happy to return to Chloe.

Orpheus. In Greek mythology, the poet and singer who could charm wild animals with the beauty of his music. When his wife Eurydice died, he followed her to Hades and won her back by his art, on the condition that he should not turn to look at her until he reached the world again. At the very last moment his loving anxiety overcame him, and turning, he saw her snatched back to Hades. His grief turned him against all other women, and he was torn to pieces by Maenads in Thrace. The fragments of his body were collected by the Muses and buried at the foot of Olympus. The story firs appears in early Greek writings; it is set down by Virgil in the Fourth Georgic. The legend came to have deep religious significance, but i was principally the account of Eurydice's rescue and its failure that first drew opera composers, together with the theme of the musician imposing order upon the natural world by the exercise of his art.

Operas on the subject are as follows: Peri (*Euridice,* 1600, the first opera to survive); Caccini (1602); Monteverdi (1607); Anon. (*Il pianto d'Orfeo,* Florence 1608); Belli (1616); Land (1619); Anon. (*La morte d'Orfeo,* Bologna 1622); Anon. (*La favola d'Orfeo,* Recanat 1633); Schütz (1638); Rossi (1647); D'Aquino (1654); Loewe (1659); Sartorio (1672); Di Dia (1676); Della Torre (1677); Draghi (1683) Krieger (1683); Sabadini (*Amore spess inganna,* 1689); Kuhnau (1689); L. and J. B Lully (1690); Anon. (*Orfeo,* Rome 1694); var ious (*Orfeo, ossia Amore spesso inganna* Bologna 1695); Anon. (? partly Sartorio) (*Orfe a torto geloso,* Turin 1697); various (*Le finezz d'amore,* 1698); ?R. Goodson (1698); Campra

1699); Keiser (Pt. 1, *Die sterbende Euridice*, 699; Pt. 2, *Die verwandelte Leyer des Orpheus*, 1966); Anon. (*Orpheus und Euridice*, Naumburg 1701); Anon. (*Orfeo a torto geloso*, Genoa 1706); various (masque, *Orpheus*, London 1707); Keiser (revision and conflation of operas of 1699, above, 1709); Fux (1715); Telemann (1726); Anon. (*Orfeo ed Euridice*, Karlsruhe 1729); Hasse, Vinci, Araia, Porpora (pasticcio, *Orfeo*, London 1736); Wagenseil (1740); Ristori (1750); Graun (1752); Gluck (1762); Gluck, Guglielmi, J. C. Bach, Guadagni (pasticcio, London 1770); J.C. Bach, Gluck and others (pasticcio, Naples 1774); Tozzi (1775); Bertoni (1776); Torelli (1781); Benda (1785); Monfossi, J.C. Bach, Gluck, Handel, and others (pasticcio, London 1785); Naumann (1786); Bertoni (from opera of 1776) and Reichardt (1788); Amendola (1788); Winter (1789); Trento (1789); Haydn (*L'anima del filosofo*, comp. 1791, prod. 1951); Paer (1791); Lamberti (1796); Morolin (1796); Bachmann (1798); Canabich (1802); Kanne (1807); Sampieri (1814); Bodard (1887); De Azevedo e Silva (1907); Malipiero (trilogy, *L'*Orfeide*, 1918–22); Křenek (1926); Milhaud (*Les Malheurs d'Orphée*, 1926); Casella (*La favola d'Orfeo*, 1932).

Comic versions, parodies, etc., are as follows: Barthélemon ('Musical burletta' by Garrick, 1767); various (parody of Gluck, *Roger Bontemps et Javotte*, Paris 1775); Dittersdorf operetta, *Orpheus der zweite*, from opera *Die Liebe in Narrenhaus*, Hamburg 1788); Deshayes (*Le Petit Orphée*, 1792); Kauer parody, 1813); Offenbach (1858); Michaelis Posse mit Gesang', *Orpheus auf der Oberwelt*, 1860); Konradin (operetta, *Orpheus im Dorfe*, 1867); Casiraghi and Offenbach (parody in Milanese dialect, after Offenbach, *Orfeo in Fioron*, 1871); Casiraghi and Offenbach parody in Milanese dialect, re-working of *Orfeo in Vioron, Orfeo o La musica dell'avenire*, 871); Selim ('commedia lirica', *Orphée et Pierrot*, 1902); Offenbach and Vicente operetta, reduction of Offenbach, *Anda la fiosa!* 1907).

Orpheus in the Underworld. See *Orphée aux Infers.*

Ortrud. Telramund's wife (mezzo) in Wagner's *Lohengrin.*

Oscar. The page (sop.) to King Gustavus (or Riccardo) in Verdi's *Un ballo in maschera.*

Oslo. Capital of Norway. In 1790 King Frederik V of Denmark visited Christiania (Oslo) accompanied by ministers and ambassadors of several countries. To entertain his guests the King brought with him an Italian opera company with Gluck as its conductor and the performances they gave constituted the first operas to be heard in Norway. In the early 19th cent., the Mingotti company included Oslo on its tours, and Singspiels were given at the Strømberg T. in 1827. Operas were performed at the Christiania T. from 1837, with visits from Italian, Danish, and Swedish companies; there were also some performances by local artists. The first professional troupes performed in 1858 with Thrane's *Fjeldeventyret*. In 1873 Ludvig Josephson directed the company, but this broke up when the theatre burnt down in 1877. In 1883-6 Olefine Moe and Matilda Lundstrøm gave performances at the Tivoli T.; and in 1890 Bjørn Bjørnson gave *Faust* and *Carmen*, also Haarklou's *Fra gamle Dage* (1894) and Olsen's *Lajla* in 1908. The National T. opened in 1899 and included opera in its repertory. The first theatre devoted exclusively to opera opened in 1918, but was forced to close three years later after giving only 26 works; opera was then given again in other theatres in a mixed repertory. In 1950 the Norsk Operaselskap, founded by Jonas and Gunnar Brunvoll, with Istvan Pajor as music director and financially supported by the City of Oslo, began operations; this became the Den Norske Opera in November 1957 with the government, the city and the Opera Foundation as joint shareholders. Kirsten Flagstad was appointed administrator, and its first season in February 1959 opened with *Tiefland*, the opera in which Flagstad herself had made her debut in Oslo in 1913. Øivin Fjelstad was music director. Flagstad was forced to retire by ill health in 1960 and was succeeded by Odd Grüner-Hegge, artistic director of the Oslo Philharmonic. By the end of the first ten years of its existence the company had built up a repertory of 40 operas and seven operettas, and had given a total of 1,290 performances in Oslo and 329 on tour. Lars Runsten succeeded Hegge as general administrator in 1969, and was followed by Gunnar Brunvoll in 1973; Runsten, however, remained an artistic director. Martin Turrovsky became music director in 1975 and has succeeded in raising musical standards in a striking manner. The repertory has continued to expand and includes several contemporary Norwegian works, and guest appearances by foreign singers, conductors and producers have become a regular feature. From August 1978 Aase Nordmo-Løvberg became general administrator.

Osmin. The steward (bass) in charge of the seraglio in Mozart's *Die Entführung aus dem Serail.*

Osnabrück. Town in Lower Saxony, Germany. Opera was performed by visiting companies in the 18th cent. Local performances were also given of Singspiel, opéra comique, and opera buffa; in 1797 performances were given of *Die Zauberflöte* and *Così fan tutte*. Through private subscription a permanent theatre was built in the Waisenhof; this was taken over by the city in 1882. The Theater am Domhof opened 1909. During the 1920s Ernst Pabst was chief producer, and notable productions of works by Křenek, Korngold, and Hindemith were staged. The theatre was bombed in 1945, reopened 1950.

O soave fanciulla. The opening words of the love duet for Rodolfo (ten.) and Mimì (sop.) in Act 1 of Puccini's *La Bohème*.

O souverain! ô juge! Rodrigo's (ten.) prayer in Act 2 of Massenet's *Le Cid*.

Ossian. A near-legendary Gaelic bard of the 3rd cent. whose 'rediscovered' works were a sensation of the 1760s: they were in fact the work of James Macpherson, but despite Dr Johnson's denunciations and the eventual exposure of the fraud, the fashion swept Europe and kindled the first enthusiasm for Scotland as a country of Romanticism. Operas on Ossianic subjects are by Barthélémon (*Oithona*, 1768); Shield (*Oscar and Malvina*, 1791); Le Sueur (*Ossian*, 1804: written at the suggestion of Napoleon and dedicated to him); Méhul (*Uthal*, 1806: famous for its omission of violins from the score to suggest a mysteriously dark Northern atmosphere); Winter (*Colmal*, 1809); J. G. Kastner (*Oskars Tod*, 1833); Sobolewski (*Comala*, 1858, at Weimar cond. Liszt); Carrillo (*Ossian*, 1903); Corder (*Nordisa*, 1904); Bainton (*Oithona*, Glastonbury 1915); I. Whyte (*Comala*, 20th-cent.). A verse of Ossian provides the text for 'Pourquoi me réveiller', the aria which Werther sings in Massenet's opera as he remembers happier days when he had translated it for Charlotte.

Osten, Eva Plaschke von der (*b* Insel, Heligoland, 19 Aug. 1881; *d* Dresden, 5 May 1936). German soprano and producer. Studied Dresden with August Iffert. Début Dresden 1902, Urbain (*Huguenots*). Leading soprano Dresden 1902–27; created Octavian, first Dresden Ariadne, Kundry, Louise, Maliella, and many other roles. Berlin, K.O., as regular guest from 1906; sang title-role in first German performance of *Zazà* (1908). London, C.G., 1913–14; first London Octavian and Kundry, and at H.M.'s, 1913, first London Ariadne. U.S.A. 1924 with German Opera Company. Farewell as *Walküre* Brünnhilde 31 July 1927 with her husband **Friedrich *Plaschke** as Wotan. Also a famous Tatyana and Tosca. After retiring worked as producer at Dresden, and was assistant producer for the première of *Arabella* (1933). (R)

Ostrava. Town in Czechoslovakia. Opera is given in the Zdeněk Nejedlý State T. 3 to 4 times a week by a company of about 20 soloists. The theatre was reconstructed in 1945 and substantially rebuilt and enlarged in 1972.

Ostrčil, Otakar (*b* Smíchov, Prague, 25 Feb.

1879; *d* Prague, 20 Aug. 1935). Czech composer. Studied with Fibich. Though initially teacher of modern philology in Prague, Ostrč also composed fluently from early years, and i 1914 became Dramaturg and conductor at th Vinohradské divadlo: here he introduced littl known operas by his contemporaries Foerst and Zich, also by Mozart, Weber, Berlioz, an Halévy. From 1909 he was conductor at th National Theatre; director from 1920 (when h conducted the première of *Mr. Brouček*). He he gave cycles of operas by Smetana (192 1927, 1934), Fibich (1925), and Dvořák (1929 He also introduced many new works, e.g. b Janáček (whom he befriended), and conducte the Prague première of *Wozzeck*. His ow idiom shows him to be a follower of Smetar and Fibich: his operas are *Rybáři* (Th Fishermen, unfin. 1894); *Jan Zhořelecl* (comp. 1898); *Cymbelin* (unfin. 1899); *Vlas skon* (The Death of Vlasta, 1904); *Kunálovy o* (Kunal's Eyes, 1908); *Poupě* (The Buds, 1911 *Legenda z Erinu* (The Legend of Erin, 1921 and his most successful work, after Tolsto *Honzovo království* (Johnny's Kingdom, 1934

Ostrovsky, Alexander (Nikolayevich) (Moscow, 12 Apr. 1823; *d* Shchelikovo, 14 Jur 1886). Russian playwright. Operas on his worl are as follows:

Don't Live as you Like (1854): Serov (*Th Power of Evil*, 1863, text partly b Ostrovsky).

The Storm (1860): Kashperov (1867, text b Ostrovsky); Janáček (1921); Asafye (1940); Trambitsky (1943); Rocca (1952 Dzerzhinsky (1955); Pushkov (1962).

A Dream on the Volga (1865): Blaramber (1865); Tchaikovsky (*The Voyevoda*, 1869 Arensky (1890).

Tushino (1867): Blaramberg (1895).

The Forest (1871): Kogan (1954).

The Snow Maiden (1873): Rimsky-Korsakc (1882).

A 17th Century Comedian (1873): Blaramber (*Skomorokh*, 1887).

The Girl Without a Dowry (1879): Novyk (comp. 1945); D. Frankel (1959); Asafye (n.d.).

O'Sullivan, John (*b* Cork, 1878; *d* Paris, 28 Ap 1955). Irish tenor. Studied Paris. Début Genev 1911, Sigurd. After engagement in the Frenc provinces sang at the Paris O. 1914, 1916–1 1922, 1930–2. Raoul, Parma 1922 and C.l 1927. Chicago 1919–20. His excellent top note suited him especially to such roles as Arnol Manrico (Verona Arena, 1926), and Raol Much admired and championed by Jame Joyce. (R)

Otello. (1) Opera in 3 acts by Rossini; text b Marchese Francesco Beria di Salsa, aft Shakespeare's tragedy (1604–5). Prod. Naple

. del Fondo, 4 Dec. 1816; with Colbran, Nozari, David Manzi, Benedetti, Ciccimarra; London, King's T., 16 May 1822, with Camporese, Curioni; N.Y., Park T., 7 Feb. 1826, with Malibran, Garcia.

(2) Opera in 4 acts by Verdi; text by Boito, after Shakespeare's tragedy (1604–5). Prod. Milan, Sc., 5 Feb. 1887, with Pantaleoni, Tamagno, Maurel, cond. Faccio; N.Y., Ac. of M., 16 Apr. 1888, with Eva Tetrazzini, Marconi, Galassi, cond. Campanini; London, Ly., 5 July. 889, with Cataneo, Tamagno, Mauriel, cond. Faccio.

The plots of both operas follow Shakespeare closely, though they omit the Venetian first act.

terra, addio. The closing duet between Radamès (ten.) and Aida (sop.) in Act 4 of Verdi's *Aida* in which they bid farewell to life on earth.

Otto, Teo (*b* Remscheid, 4 Feb. 1904; *d* Frankfurt, 9 June 1968). German designer. Studied Kassel, Paris, and the Bauhaus in Weimar. Engaged by Klemperer for the Kroll Opera, Berlin, 1927, and appointed chief designer of the Berlin State Theatres, 1931. Left Germany 1933, worked mostly in Zurich in the theatre until 1945. Designed opera productions Salzburg, Vienna, Zurich, etc. N.Y. Met., *Tristan* (1960); London, C.G., *Figaro* (1963); and sets for the film of *Rosenkavalier.* He favoured real materials to give 'tactile excitements to the set' rather than the painted scenic object. Professor of stage design at the Düsseldorf Academy of Fine Arts.

Ottone. Opera in 3 acts by Handel; text by Nicola Francesco Haym (altered from Pallavicino's text for Lotti's *Teofane,* 1719). Prod. London, Hm., 23 Jan. 1723, with Cuzzoni (her début), Robinson, Senesino, Boschi, Berenstadt, Durastanti. Revived Handel Opera Society, 1971.

O tu che in seno agli angeli. Alvaro's (ten.) aria in the first scene of Act 3 of Verdi's *La forza del destino* which he sings on the battlefield, remembering Leonora, whom he believes dead.

Otvos, Gabor (*b* Budapest, 21 Sept. 1935). Hungarian conductor. Studied Budapest and Italy; worked in Venice, F., 1957–8 and Trieste, 1958–61. First conductor Frankfurt 1967–72; music director Augsburg from 1972. N.Y. City Opera 1970, conducted first N.Y. perf. of *Makropoulos Case;* N.Y., Met., from 1971.(R)

Oudin, Eugène (Espérance) (*b* New York 24 Feb. 1858; *d* London, 4 Nov. 1894). American baritone. Studied law at Yale, then turned to singing. Debut N.Y., Wallack's T., 1886 in Roger's *Joséphine vendue par ses soeurs.* London, Royal English O. H., 1891, where he created the Tempter in Sullivan's *Ivanhoe*; first

Onegin in London and High Priest in *Samson et Dalila* (concert perf.). St. Petersburg 1893–4 as Wolfram, Telramund, Albert (*Werther*). Died in artist's room at Queen's Hall after appearing in a Richter concert. He married the soprano Louise Parker.

Overture. From the Italian *overtura,* opening, the word normally used for the instrumental prelude to an opera, oratorio, play, ballet, or other work; later a concert work unconnected with the stage.

The earliest operas usually began with little more than a flourish of instruments, e.g. the Toccata opening Monteverdi's *Orfeo* (1607), and sometimes had no overture at all. More elaborate introductions began with the sinfonias that open the three acts of Landi's *Il Sant' Alessio* (1632); and a familiar form in Venetian opera was the canzona overture, usually cast with an introductory slow movement in duple rhythm and a fast movement in triple rhythm. This became the model for the French overture systematized by Lully, which consisted of a slow, grandiose introduction, followed by a faster section in imitative or even strictly fugal style, and possibly concluding with a dance or some slower passage. The Italian overture, introduced in the late 17th cent. by Alessandro Scarlatti, consisted of three more strictly divided sections, an allegro, followed by an adagio, and concluding with another allegro: this was usually known as a sinfonia. This division was one of nomenclature rather than nationality: it was possible for an Italian opera to be prefaced with a French overture, as in the case of Handel.

The idea of using material from the opera in the overture began in the first part of the 18th cent., e.g. in Rameau's *Castor et Pollux* (1735); despite earlier suggestions, it did not become accepted practice until Gluck, whose overtures may prepare for the first scene or set the mood of the opera. Mozart continued the practice, setting the mood in *Don Giovanni* and *Die Zauberflöte* or using some elements that recur, and in *Così fan tutte* using a motto theme to represent the words of the title. Beethoven took this principle of thematic anticipation further in the three *Leonore* overtures he wrote for *Fidelio*; and it reached its climax in Weber, who (taking its cue from Spohr's *Faust*) made his later overtures virtually synopses of the ensuing opera, while adhering to sonata form. In Italy the overture was still designed chiefly to hush talkers and admit late-comers, only incidentally attempting to compose the audience's mind for the opera indiscriminately, e.g. Rossini's overture to *Aureliano in Palmira,* which was re-used for the tragedy *Elisabetta, Regina d'Inghilterra* and the comedy *Il barbiere di Siviglia.* Wagner, though he came to prefer the term *Vorspiel* (prelude) at first pursued

Weber's methods; later he composed still more subtle introductions to his dramas, preparing the audience thematically and psychologically for what was to come. The *verismo* composers on the whole preferred the brief introduction that had latterly become Verdi's habit, while Strauss sometimes even raised the curtain directly on the drama. In French grand opera, the overture usually took the form of a freely composed selection of the most important tunes in the opera. Light composers have generally remained faithful to this potpourri style of overture.

O welche Lust. The prisoners' chorus in Act 1 of Beethoven's *Fidelio,* praising the sun and freedom as they emerge from their cells for exercise.

Owen Wingrave. Opera in 2 acts by Britten; text by Myfanwy Piper, after Henry James's story (1892). Written for TV and prod. B.B.C.-TV and NET (U.S.) 16 May 1971, with Harper, Vyvyan, Fisher, Baker, Pears, Luxon, Shirley-Quirk; London C. G., 10 May 1973, with almost same cast, cond. Bedford: Santa Fe, 9 Aug. 1973.

Owen (bar.), the last of a family with military traditions, rejects his studies for the Army with Spencer Coyle (bass-bar.) because of his pacifist convictions, thus affronting both his family, in particular his aunt Miss Wingrave (sop.) and his grandfather Sir Philip (ten.), and also his betrothed, Kate (mezzo). Despite the sympathy of Coyle, they reject him, and to prove his courage to Kate he agrees to spend a night in the haunted room of the family seat. He is found dead in the morning.

Oxford. English university town. Apart from Sir Hugh Allen's productions of *Fidelio* and *Der Freischütz,* shortly before the First World War, there was no opera at Oxford until the University Opera Club came into being as a result of the 1925 performance of Monteverdi's *Orfeo.* For this, J. A. Westrup made a complete transcription of the 1615 edition of the score in the Bodleian Library. In 1927 *L'Incoronazione di Poppea* had its first stage performance in England. From 1928 to 1933 Sumner Austin was music adviser. During this period productions included *The Bartered Bride, May Night* and *The Devil and Kate* (first in England). In 1930, 1931, and 1932, Hans Strohbach, one of Germany's leading producers, came to Oxford to supervise the productions. Between 1933 and 1939 the productions included *Iphigénie en Aulide, Castor and Pollux,* and *Master Peter's Puppet Show.* There were no performances during the war years, but since 1947 the annual productions have included *Idomeneo, Iphigénie en Tauride, Les Troyens,* Wellesz's *Incognita* (première), *Hans Heiling* (first in England), *Macbeth, Ernani, The Fair Maid of Perth, The Secret, Oedipus Rex, L'Enfant et les sortilèges* (English première), *Khovanshchina, Ruslan and Lyudmila, Mitridate Eupatore, Armide,* and *Rosinda* (Cavalli). Artists who have started at Oxford include the singers John Kentish, David Galliver, Doreen Murray, Thomas Hemsley, and Heather Harper; the conductors Trevor Harvey and Robert Irving; the producer Anthony Besch, and the administrator Robert Ponsonby.

In 1967 and 1968, as part of Lina Lalandi's festivals, productions of Rossini's *L'inganno felice* and *Adina* were given; and in 1971 the short-lived Oxford Opera produced Gluck's two *Iphigenie* operas in the same week.

P

Pacchierotti, Gasparo (*b* Fabriano, bapt. 21 May 1740; *d* Padua, 28 Oct. 1821). Italian male soprano. Began singing secondary parts at Venice, Vienna, and Milan before age of 16; successful in principal roles from 1769. Sang in opening performance of La Scala, Milan, in Salieri's *Europa riconosciuta*. His fame spread quickly through Italy and heralded him on his arrival in London in 1778, where he triumphed. After a long and brilliant career, he retired to Padua in 1792, after singing Alceo in Paisiello's *I giuochi d'Agrigento*, which opened La Fenice, Venice, reappearing only for the benefit of Napoleon in 1796.

Pace, pace, mio Dio. Leonora's (sop.) aria in the last scene of Verdi's *La forza del destino* in which she prays for peace of soul.

Pacini, Giovanni (*b* Catania, 17 Feb. 1796; *d* Pescia, 6 Dec. 1867). Italian composer. Son of Luigi Pacini, the first Geronio in *Il turco in Italia*; began to study singing with Marchesi at the age of 12, and also worked at composition with Mattei and Furlanetto. His first opera, *Don Pomponio* (1813), was not produced, but his second, *Annetta e Lucindo*, was given in 1813. He continued to pour out operas (14 comedies in four years); his first real success was an opera semiseria, *Adelaide e Comingio,* in Milan (1817). In 1820 he went to Rome, where his easy Rossinian manner enabled him to help out Rossini himself by composing three numbers for *Matilde di Shabran*. Many works followed; his Naples début was with *Alessandro nell'Indie* (1824), which had 70 consecutive performances, and in 1825 he became music director of the Naples S.C. By now he was one of the most successful opera composers in Italy, though threatened by the growing reputation of Bellini and Donizetti: realizing this, he withdrew to found a music school at Viareggio to which he devoted himself after the failure of *Carlo di Borgogna* (1835). He made a come-back after the death of Bellini and the retirement of Rossini with *Saffo* (1840), the most successful work in his new, more careful style and indeed his masterpiece. He continued to write successful works, including *La fidanzata corsa* (1842), *Maria Tudor* (1843), *Medea* (1843), *Lorenzo de' Medici* (1845), and *Bondelmonte* (1845); but with the rise of Verdi he was once more eclipsed.

In his early works Pacini took Rossini as his model, believing this to be the natural and successful way to write Italian opera, and even copied Rossini's move towards a more serious manner. He was well aware of this, and of his

carelessness; he relied on a fluency and dexterity which won him the respect of Rossini and Bellini, above all for his skill in writing singable melodies. He was known, from his energetic melodic vein, as *il maestro della cabaletta*, and it is in *cabaletta sections that his most characteristic music is to be found. In his middle works, he tried to improve on earlier weaknesses in harmony and orchestration; he helped to unify aria, ensemble, and chorus in the years before Verdi. For his pupils he wrote some theoretical treatises, and he also left an entertaining autobiography.
Bibl: G. Pacini: *Le Mie memorie artistiche* (1805).

Padilla (y Ramos), Mariano (*b* Murcia, 1842; *d* Auteuil, nr Paris, 23 Nov. 1906). Spanish baritone. studied Florence, with Mabellini and Ronconi. London, H.M.'s, 1881, Hoël (*Dinorah*). Also sang at C.G., and was heard as Don Giovanni in Prague in the centenary performance of Mozart's opera. Married soprano **Désirée *Artôt** in Sèvres 1869 shortly after she had refused Tchaikovsky. Their daughter was Lola Artôt de Padilla.

Padmâvatî. *Opéra-ballet* in 2 acts by Roussel; text by Louis Laloy, after an event in 13th cent. Indian history. Prod. Paris, O., 1 June 1923, with Lapeyrette, Laval, Franz, Rouard, Fabert, cond. Gaubert; London, Coliseum, 6 July 1969 (concert), with Gorr, Berbié, Chauvet, Souzay, cond. Martinon.

The Mogul sultan Alaouddin (bar.) proposes an alliance with Ratan-sen, (ten.), King of Tchitor. He is well received, but demands Ratan-sen's wife Padmâvatî (mezzo) as a condition; to this Ratan-sen reluctantly consents. A Brahmin (ten.) who later asks for her to be handed over is torn to pieces, and the crowd riots. Alaouddin defeats Ratan-sen in battle, but rather than have the sin of betraying her rest on her husband's conscience, Padmâvatî stabs him. She therefore has to die on his funeral pyre.

Padre Guardiano, Il. The abbot (bass) in Verdi's *La forza del destino*.

Padre nobile (*It* noble father). The former term for a role, normally taken by a senior member of a company, representing a figure of dignity and authority, paternal either literally or metaphorically. Historically it was a descendant of the *magnifico* of the commedia dell'arte. A famous instance is the elder Germont in Verdi's *La traviata*. Despite the French usage *père sérieux* as virtually interchangeable with *père noble*, the role could include comic elements.

Padua (*It* Padova). Town in Veneto, Italy. The scene of the first Italian *sacra rappresentazione, La passione e morte di Cristo*, in 1243

369

and of many theatrical and musical entertainments in the 16th cent. During the early days of opera, Padua almost rivalled Venice. Pio Enea II degli Obizzi built the T. degli Obizzi in 1652, which with the T. dello Stallone (built 1642) was the scene of most opera performances in Padua. In 1751 the T. Nuovo opened with Galuppi's *Artaserse*, and towards the end of the 18th cent. performances were also given at the T. del Piato della Valle. When the Obizzi family died out, the theatre passed into the hands of the Duke of Modena and was successively renamed the T. Già degli Obizzi, Vecchio, Nuovissimo, and finally Dei Concordi. The,T. Nuovo was rebuilt in 1847, and in 1884 renamed the T. Verdi; it gives short winter seasons.

Paer, Ferdinando (*b* Parma, 1 June 1771; *d* Paris, 3 May 1839). Italian composer. Studied Parma with Ghiretti, and won early success with operas in Italian cities, especially with *Griselda* (1796), a Boccaccio opera in the semiseria manner that he particularly cultivated. As director of the Vienna Kä. (1797-1801), he came to know Beethoven. The most striking successes of this period were *Camilla* (1799) and *Achille* (1801). He was in Dresden 1801-6: semiseria works included *Leonora* (1804), to the plot used by Beethoven. In 1806 he was taken up by Napoleon, becoming *maître de chapelle* in Paris, 1807, and later director of the O.–C. and (1812) the T.I. His most successful Paris work was *Le Maître de chapelle* (1821). In 1824 Rossini (who had made his stage début singing the boy Adolfo in *Camilla*) joined him at the T.I. in what was to prove a troublesome partnership.

Paer was expert in matching the taste of the day with fluent, singable melody, and this gave him a dominating position in Italian music at the start of the 19th cent., and won him his many European appointments over the heads of local composers. His style was enriched by his contacts with Viennese music, and he even had some influence on Beethoven; but his real contribution is as a composer of *semiseria opera and *Rescue opera, in which the mingling of a serious theme with often delightful elements of light relief is agreeably expressed in music of great fluency and operatic efficiency.

Pagliacci (Clowns). Opera in 2 acts (orig. 1 act) by Leoncavallo; text by composer. Prod. Milan, T. d V., 21 May 1892, with Stehle, Giraud, Maurel, Ancona, cond. Toscanini; London C. G., 19 May 1893, with Melba, De Lucia, Ancona, Green, cond. Bevignani; N.Y., Grand Opera House, 15 June 1893, with Kört-Kronold, Montegriffo, Campanari, Averill, cond. Hinrichs.

In the Prologue, Tonio (bar.) tells the audience that the story they are about to see is a real one about real people. Canio (ten.) the leader of a travelling troupe of players, warns that if he were to find his wife Nedda (sop.) unfaithful, she would pay dearly for it. Tonio makes advances to Nedda but she repulses him; however, he overhears Nedda and her lover Silvio (bar.) planning to run away together, and he hurries to bring Canio back from the village inn. Canio gives vent to his grief; and in the play put on for the villagers (in which he takes the part of Pagliaccio, Nedda that of Colombine, and Beppe (ten.) that of Harlequin), he finds the situation so like reality that he stabs first Nedda, and then Silvio, who rushes to her aid.

Pagliughi, Lina (*b* Brooklyn, 27 May 1907). Italian soprano. Heard in a concert by Tetrazzini, whose protegée she became. Subsequently studied in Milan with Bavagnoli. Début Milan, T. Nazionale, 1927, Gilda. Milan, Sc., 1930-31, 1937-8, 1940, 1947; London, C.G., 1938, Gilda. Toured Australia 1932. Sang all over Italy and was greatly admired for her singing of Bellini, Donizetti, and Rossini. Possessed a pure, limpid voice, and an excellent technique. The latter part of her career was mostly devoted to recording and singing for the Italian radio until 1956. (R) Married the tenor Primo Montanari (1895-1972). (R)

Paisiello, Giovanni (*b* Taranto, 9 May 1740; *d* Naples, 5 June. 1816). Italian composer. Studied with Durante, and Naples with Abos (1755-9). His first successes were in opera buffa, beginning with *Il ciarlone* (1764), *I francesi brillanti* (1764), *Demetrio* (1765), *Le finte contesse* (1766), and *La frascatana* (1774). He was admired as a rival to Piccinni in Naples, later also as a rival to Cimarosa and Guglielmi. In 1776 he went to St Petersburg at the invitation of Catherine the Great; he helped to establish Italian opera at the Russian Court, and composed *Lucinda ed Armidoro* and *Nitteti* (1777). A series of popular works followed culminating in *Il barbiere di Siviglia* (1782), which became so popular in Italy as to prejudice the public against the setting by Rossini that was to oust Paisiello's work. In Italy again after 1784, he became *maestro di cappella* at Naples, writing among other works *L'amor contrastato* (or *La molinara*: 1788), a very popular work, including the aria 'Quant'è più bello' and the duet 'Nel cor più non mi sento' taken for variations by Beethoven (WOO 69 and 70), the latter also by Paganini. A private entertainment in Vienna, influenced by *La molinara*, led Wilhelm Müller to write his cycle of poems *Die schöne Müllerin*, used by Schubert. Other popular works of these years included *Nina* (1789) and *I zingari in fiera* (1789). He sided with Napoleon in the disturbances of 1799, and, out of favour at the Bourbon Restoration, went to Paris. He returned to Naples, but the Bourbons did not forgive his previous actions and he died in comparative poverty. His 100-odd operas are distinguished for their ease and accomplishment rather than for profundity, though his elegant melodic manner is capable of much sensitivity, and his feeling for the orchestra is vivid.

Bibl: E. Faustini-Fasini: *Opere teatrali di Giovanni Paisiello* (1940).

Palace Theatre, London. Originally the Royal English Opera House (cap. 1,500), built by Richard D'Oyly Carte, opened in January 1891 with Sullivan's *Ivanhoe*. In 1945 *Gay Rosalinda* (a version of *Fledermaus*) and in 1947 Zeller's *Vogelhändler* was staged, conducted by Richard Tauber. A short Italian season was given in 1955, and performances of *La finta semplice* were given by a company from Salzburg in 1956.

Palazzesi, Matilde (*b* Montecarotto, 1 Mar. 1802; *d* Barcelona, 3 July. 1842). Italian soprano. Studied Pesaro with Giacomo Solarto. Début Dresden 1824, in title-role of Rossini's *Zelmira*. Remained in Dresden as member of the Italian Opera until 1833; especially successful in Rossini repertory as Countess Almaviva and Donna Elvira. Sang at Milan, Sc., and other Italian houses; Barcelona 1841-2, where she sang in the first performance there of a Verdi opera, *Oberto*. Repertory included works by Bellini, Donizetti, Spontini, Mercadante, and Morlacchi; Rossini's *Cenerentola* was thought 'too deep for her'. She married the flautist and composer Angelo Savinelli (1800-1870).

Bibl: B. Padovano: *Matilde Palazzesi* (1953).

Palco (*It.,* stand or platform). In theatrical usage, box. The terms for special boxes in Italy are *palco reale* (or *ducale, governativo, elettorale*), Royal box; *palco di proscenio,* stage box; *palco di pepiano,* a box on stage level; *palchettone,* a large central box, perhaps originally the Royal box, used for general or special purposes; *palco della vedova,* 'widow's box', a box so placed as to afford a view of the stage while concealing its occupants from the rest of the audience.

Palermo. Town in Sicily. Opera was first heard there in 1658 when the Teatro dello Spasimo was opened with a version of Cavalli's *Serse.* From 1693 to 1726 operas (including works by Alessandro Scarlatti, born in Palermo) were performed at the T. di Santa Cecilia. In 1726 a second opera house was built, the T. Santa Lucia, at first devoted to comic opera; in 1809 it was reconstructed and named the Real T. Carolino. There Donizetti conducted, 1825-6, and composed his *Alahor in Granata* for the season. From 1829 to 1830 Balfe sang there as leading baritone and composed his *I rivali di se stesso.* Here, too, several operas appeared

under different guises because of censorship difficulties: *I Puritani* was given as *Elvira ed Arturo, Ernani* as *Elvira d'Aragona,* and *Giovanna d'Arco* as *Orietto di Lesbo.*

In May 1848, by decree of the Sicilian Parliament, the theatre was renamed the Real Teatro Bellini. Much later, it became a cinema, and burnt down in 1964. In 1864 the local authorities decided to build a municipal opera house, the Teatro Politeama Garibaldi, which was opened in June 1874 with Bellini's *I Capuleti e i Montecchi;* it became the city's chief opera house until May 1897, when the Teatro Massimo (cap. 2,500) opened with *Falstaff,* conducted by Mugnone. The stage of the Massimo was, after the Paris Opéra, the largest in Europe until the reopening of the Vienna Opera. It became an *Ente Autonomo* in 1935. Leoncavallo's *La Bohème,* rechristened *Mimì Pinson,* had its first performance there in the composer's revised version in 1913, but otherwise there have been few premières there this century. Yet since the war the repertories have been among the most interesting and adventurous of any Italian opera house.

Palestrina. *Musikalische Legende* in 3 acts by Pfitzner; text by composer. Prod. Munich, N., 12 June 1917 with Karl Erb in the title role and Ivogün, Krüger, Kuhn, Brodersen, Feinhals, Schützendorf, Bender, cond Walter. Never performed in Great Britain or America: Act 1 only, N.Y., Mannes Coll., 26 May 1970. The opera tells how Palestrina (ten.) saved the art of contrapuntal music for the Church in the 16th century through his *Missa Papae Marcelli.* The second act, which depicts the Council of Trent, introduces the excellently drawn character of Cardinal Borromeo (bass-bar.). Also opera by Sachs (1886).

Pallavicino (Pallavicini), **Carlo** (*b* Salò, 1630; *d* Dresden, 26 Jan. 1688). Italian composer. He worked as Visekapellmeister in Dresden 1666, Kapellmeister 1672; moved to Venice in 1673-4, returned to Dresden in 1687. His 22 known operas include *La Gerusalemme liberata* (1687, for Venice). He was regarded as an ingenious and capable composer, a prominent representative of the later Venetian school. His son **Stefano Benedetto Pallavicino** (*b* Padua, 21 Mar. 1672; *d* Dresden, 16 Apr. 1742) was a librettist who wrote for Stefani, Lotti, Hasse, and Ristori, among others.

Palmo's Opera House, New York. A theatre situated in Chambers Street, west of Broadway, which was built by Ferdinand Palmo, a New York restaurateur of Italian birth. It opened in Feb. 1844 with the New York première of *I Puritani.* In July that year Cinti-Damoreau appeared there in a number of operas. In 1848 it was renamed Burton's Chambers Street T., and no more opera was heard there. Many of Palmo's former patrons, however, joined together and raised a subscription which resulted in the building of the Astor Place O. H., which opened 1847 with *Ernani*. In 1859 it was converted into the Mercantile Library.

Pamina. The Queen of Night's daughter (sop.), heroine of Mozart's *Die Zauberflöte*.

Pampanini, Rosetta (*b* Milan, 2 Sept. 1896; *d* Corbola, 2 Aug. 1973). Italian soprano. Studied with Emma Molaioli. Début Rome 1920, Micaëla. After four further years of study, second début at Biella as Mimì; there she came to the notice of Toscanini, who engaged her for Butterfly at Sc. Sang there regularly until 1937. London, C.G., 1928, 1929, 1933; Chicago 1931-2. Sang Mimì in a special performance of *Bohème* under Mascagni outside Puccini's villa at Torre del Lago 1930. Other famous roles were Desdemona, Iris, and Liù. She retired in 1942: her pupils included Amy Shuard and Victoria Elliott. (R)

Pandolfini, Angelica (*b* Spoleto, 21 Aug. 1871; *d* Lenno, 15 July 1959). Italian soprano, daughter of the baritone Francesco Pandolfini (see below). Studied piano, and singing Paris with Jules Massart. Début Modena, 1894, Marguerite. After appearances in Italian provinces, Malta, and elsewhere; engaged Milan, Sc., 1897-99, 1906. Created Adriana Lecouvreur, Milan, T.L., 1902, and sang in *Figlia di Jorio*, Sc., 1906. Especially famous in *verismo* repertory, which she sang in Italy, Portugal, and Spain until 1908. Retired on her marriage. (R)

Pandolfini, Francesco (*b* Termini Imerese, Palermo, 22 Nov. 1836; *d* Milan, 15 Feb. 1916). Italian baritone. Studied Florence with Felice Ronconi and Vannuccini. Début Pisa, 1859 in *Gemma di Vergy*. Milan, Sc., 1871, where he was first Amonasro in Italy, and created Arnoldo in Ponchielli's *I Lituani* (1874); London, C.G., 1877, 1882. Farewell perf. Rome, 1890 as Alfio.

Panerai, Rolando (*b* Camp Bisenzio, 17 Oct. 1924). Italian baritone. Studied Florence with Frazzi, Milan with Armani and Giulia Tess. Début Naples 1947, Faraone (*Mosè*). One of the leading Italian baritones of the 1950s and 1960s. Sang at Barcelona and Lisbon, as well as in Italy and at the Aix and Salzburg Festivals (esp. as Figaro and Guglielmo). London, C.G., 1960, Figaro (Rossini). (R)

Panizza, Ettore (*b* Buenos Aires, 12 Aug. 1875; *d* Buenos Aires 27 Nov. 1967). Argentinian conductor of Italian descent. Studied Milan. Début 1890. London, C.G., 1907-14, 1924; Milan, Sc., as Toscanini's assistant, 1916-17, 1921-9, and then 1930-32, 1946-8; N.Y., Met., 1934-42; Buenos Aires, C., 1908 (his own *Aurora*), 1921-

67. In London he conducted the first performances of Franchetti's *Germania*, Erlanger's *Tess*, Zandonai's *Conchita* and *Francesca da Rimini*. He conducted the first Scala performances of the *Trittico*, *Khovanshchina* (first in Italy), *Sly* (Wolf-Ferrari), *Tsar Saltan* (first in Italy), *La vedova scaltra*, *Mârouf*, and *Segreto di Susanna*. His own operas, including *Aurora* (1908) and *Bisanzio* (1939), had some success in South America.

Pantaleoni, Adriano (*b* Udine, 7 Oct. 1837; *d* Udine, 18 Dec. 1908). Italian baritone, son of composer Luigi Pantaleoni (*d* 1872). Studied Udine and Milan; leading baritone Milan, Sc., 1871-7 and 1896, especially praised for his Verdi perfs. London, H.M.'s; U.S.A. 1879. After leaving stage taught singing at Udine and Trieste.

Pantaleoni, Romilda (*b* Udine, 1847; *d* Milan, 20 May 1917). Italian soprano, sister of above. Studied Milan with B. Prati, L. Rossi, Lamperti. Début Milan, T. Carcano, 1868 Foroni's *Margherita*. Turin, 1875, Margherita (*Mefistofele*). Chosen by Verdi to create Desdemona (1887). First Scala Santuzza (1891); also created Tigrana in Puccini's *Edgar* and Ponchielli's *Marion Delorme*. Said to have possessed a magnetic stage personality; often compared to Duse.

Pantheon. A building in Oxford Street, London, opened in Jan. 1772 and used mostly for concerts and appearances by singers including Aguiari and Giorgi-Banti. After the destruction of the King's T. in 1789 it was adapted as a theatre and used to house Italian opera 1791-2. In 1812 it became the home of a company composed of singers from the King's who had quarrelled with the management; and in 1813 there was a short-lived attempt to establish an English opera company there.

Pantomime (Gr. παντόμιμος, imitation of everything). A dramatic entertainment in which the artists express themselves in dumb show. The old intermezzos often included a pantomime part (e.g. the mute servant Vespone in Pergolesi's *La serva padrona*) since most of the singers were needed for the main opera.

The *Pantomime dialoguée* was a kind of melodrama with a patchwork score, popular at the end of the 18th cent.

Papageno and **Papagena.** The birdcatcher, Tamino's attendant (bar.), and his lover (sop.) in Mozart's *Die Zauberflöte*.

Parable Aria. see *Metaphor Aria*.

Pardon de Ploërmel, Le. See *Dinorah*.

Parepa-Rosa, Euphrosyne (*b* Edinburgh, 7 May 1836; *d* London, 21 Jan. 1874). Scottish soprano, daughter of the soprano Elizabeth *Seguin and Demetrius Parepa, Baron de Boyescu, a Wallachian boyard. Début, when

16, Malta; London, Ly., 1857, Elvira (*Puritani*). U.S. tours 1863-8 with Maretzek's company; 1869-72 with De Vivo company which was called the Parepa-Rosa Opera; she married Carl Rosa in 1867 and became principal soprano of her husband's company. Her voice was powerful and of pleasing quality with an extensive range. After her death her husband founded the Parepa-Rosa scholarship at the R.A.M., London.

Pareto, Graziella (*b* Barcelona, 15 May 1889). Spanish soprano. Studied Milan with Vidal. Début Barcelona, 1906, Micaela. After engagements in South America, St Petersburg, and Italian provinces, engaged Milan, Sc., 1914, Gilda. London, C.G., 1920, Leila, Norina, Violetta. Chicago O.1921-2 in N.Y., then 1923-5; Salzburg 1931, Carolina, Rosina. Beecham considered her the finest coloratura soprano of the period immediately after the First World War. (R)

Paride ed Elena (Paris and Helen). Opera in 5 acts by Gluck; text by Calzabigi. Prod. Vienna, B., 3 Nov. 1770 with Schindler, Kurz, Millico; N.Y., Town Hall, 15 Jan. 1954 (concert), by American Opera society; Birmingham, Barber Institute, 13 May 1971, with Browning, M. Smith, Manning, cond. Keys.

Paris (ten.) lands in Greece to claim the fairest woman in the country as reward for having chosen Venus in his famous Judgement. He woos Helen, at first unsuccessfully, and is eventually ordered to leave; but as he does so she confesses love, and they flee together, braving the condemnation of Pallas Athene, but comforted by the support of Cupid (who has helped them, disguised as Erasto).

Parigi, o cara. The opening words of the duet in Act 3 of Verdi's *La traviata*, in which Alfredo (ten.) suggests to the dying Violetta (sop.) that they resume their life together far from the bustle of Paris.

Paris. Capital of France. The first opera given in Paris was an unknown work at the Palais Royal in Feb. or Mar. 1645, referred to in a letter written by the singer Atto Melani to Prince Matthias de' Medici. The first known Italian opera performed in Paris was Sacrati's *La finta pazza* given at the Salle du Petit Bourbon in Dec. 1645. The first French work was Dassoucy's *Andromède* given at the Petit Bourbon in Feb. 1650, which is regarded as the forerunner of French opera. Between 1660 and 1800 opera was performed in Paris in some 22 different theatres including the Académie de Musique (the Opéra) and the Opéra-Comique. Other theatres in which opera was given in Paris during this period included the Colisée the T. de Monsieur, and the Odéon. Between 1800 and the period just after the First World War the number of theatres in which opera was

performed increased to about 30 and included the Théâtre Italien, the Bouffes-Parisiens (the scene of the production of many of Offenbach's works), the T. Lyrique, the Trianon-Lyrique, the Gaîté Parisienne, the T. Lyrique de la Renaissance (for which Messager wrote *Madame Chrysanthème* as the opening piece), the Marigny, the Eden, the T. du Châtelet (where Strauss's *Salome* had its first Paris performance), and the T. des Champs-Élysées. In more recent times there has been little or no opera except at the two national theatres, and the O.C. ceased to function as such in 1972. Since 1957 there has been an annual summer festival covering all the arts under the general title of the T. des Nations, and opera performances have been given by leading ensembles from all over the world including the Berlin K.O. the Berlin Stä. O., Gly., the Leipzig Opera, the Belgrade Opera, the Frankfurt Opera, and S.W.

In addition to the theatres mentioned above, opera has also been given in Paris in many other theatres including the Athénée-Musicale, Lyrique-Dramatique, Nouveau-T., Monacey, T. du Château d'Eau, Fantaisies-Parisiennes, T. Lyrique de la Gaîté, T. de la Demoiselle Montausier, Opéra Populaire, T. des Arts, T. du Vaudeville Ghesui.

See also *Bouffes - Parisiens, Opéra, Opéra-Comique, Théâtre des Champs-Elysées, Théâtre-Italien*, and *Théâtre-Lyrique*.

Pari siamo. The opening words of Rigoletto's (bar.) monologue in Act 1, scene 2, of Verdi's opera.

Parisina. Opera seria in 3 acts by Donizetti; text by Felice Romani, after Byron's verse tale *Parisina* (1816), 'grounded on a circumstance mentioned in Gibbon's *Antiquities of the House of Brunswick*'. Prod. Florence, P., 17 Mar. 1833, with Ungher, Sacchi, Duprez, Cosselli, Porto; New Orleans, Charles St. T., 5 Jun. 1837, with Pantanelli; London, H.M.'s, 1 Jun. 1838, with Grisi.

Stella de Tolomei (mezzo) has an illegitimate son by Nicolò d'Este (bar.). When Nicolo deserts his mistress to marry Parisina Malatesta (sop.), his now grown-up son Ugo (ten.) consents to live with them. Ugo and Parisina fall in love, and after a year's passionate intrigue are discovered and sentenced to death. Stella comes to visit her son in prison, but he refuses to see her.

Also operas by Keurvels (1890) and Mascagni (1913, text by D'Annunzio).

Park Theatre, New York. Three theatres of this name have occupied a site in Park Row, near Ann Street, N.Y. The first opened in Jan. 1798 with *As You Like It*; the second, opened in 1825, was the scene of the first Italian opera season in the U.S.A. given by Manuel Garcia's company. Until it was destroyed by fire in 1848 it staged

373

the first U.S. performances of many operas including *Le nozze di Figaro, Don Giovanni, Il barbiere di Siviglia, La cenerentola, La sonnambula, L'elisir d' amore,* and *Ernani.* A third theatre was also burnt down.

Parlamagni, Antonio (*b* 1759; *d* Florence, 9 Oct. 1838). Italian basso buffo. After appearances in Rome (1789-90) and Florence (1795-6) sang in Milan, Sc., 1797, and Venice. Rossini wrote Macrobio in *La pietra del paragone* and Isidoro in *Matilde di Shabran* for him; in the latter he appeared with his daughter Annetta, who created Edoardo.

Parlando (*It* speaking). A direction to let the tone of the voice approximate to that of speech. The term *parlato* (*It* spoken) is used synonymously, but also to distinguish the spoken sections in opera with dialogue.

Parma. Town in Emilia, Italy. Its musical tradition dates from the 15th cent. In 1618, on the orders of Ranuccio Farnese, a theatre designed by Aleotti of Argenta, holding 4,500 and made entirely of wood, was erected in the armoury of the Rilotta Palace. The T. Farnese, as it was called, opened on 21 Dec. 1628 with a 'torneo' entitled *Mercurio e Marte,* with music by Monteverdi and text by Claudio Achillini, to mark the wedding of Duke Odoardo Farnese to Margherita de' Medici. Between then and 1732 magnificent performances were given there of works by various composers. The theatre closed in October 1732 with a performance to honour Carlo di Borbone, Infante of Spain. After this the theatre was abandoned. It was damaged by bombs in 1944 and rebuilt in the 1950s; with the Teatro Olimpico at Vicenza it is one of the two oldest theatres in Italy.

Several other theatres were built in Parma in the 17th cent. including the T. del Collegio dei Nobili (1600), the T. della Rocchetta (1674), the T. di Corte (1689), and the T. Ducale, the predecessor of the present T. Regio. The Ducale (cap. 1,200) had four tiers of boxes, 112 in all, and opened in 1688 with *Teseo in Atene;* its last performance, in 1828, was of Rossini's *Zelmira.* It was the scene of the premières of several of Paer's operas (he had been born in Parma), including *Agnese.* In *c*1688-1828 the Parma public had the reputation of being the most difficult in Italy. In 1816 the tenor Curioni was arrested for daring to insult the audience who had protested at his poor performance; a similar fate awaited the impresario of the 1818 season who was jailed for 'offending the public sensibilities' with his poor choice of artists and repertory. During the reign of Marie-Louise the present Teatro Regio came into being (cap. 1,300); it was designed after La Scala, Milan, and like its model is decorated in white, gold, and red velvet. The Regio opened in May 1829 with Bellini's *Zaira.* Verdi, who was born in

nearby Le Roncole, became identified with Parma; and between 1843, when his *Nabucco* was performed there, and 1951, the year of the 50th anniversary of his death, 1,382 performances had been given there of all his operas, except for *Un giorno di regno* and *Il Corsaro.* *Les Vêpres siciliennes* received its first performance in Italy at the Regio under the title of *Giovanna di Guzman.*

Appropriately Parma has become the home of the Institute of Verdi Studies founded in 1959 under the direction of Mario Medici. Parma was also the birthplace of Toscanini, who played the cello in the orchestra of the Regio while still a student, and of Cleofonte Campanini, who conducted there often and was responsible for organizing the 1914 singing competition which discovered both Gigli and Merli. It was at Parma, too, that Tebaldi studied, and began her career.

Bibl: C. Alcari: *Il Teatro Regio di Parma* (1924); M. Corradi-Cervi: *Cronologia del Teatro Regio di Parma, 1728-1948* (1955).

Parmeggiani, Ettore (*b* Rimini, 17 Aug. 1895; *d* Milan, 28 Jan. 1960). Italian tenor. Début Milan, T.d.V., 1922, Cavaradossi. Notable in Wagner roles during inter-war years, including Siegmund, Lohengrin, and Parsifal, all of which he sang at the Sc. Here in the 1950s he organized and led the claque. (R)

Parmi veder le lagrime. The Duke of Mantua's (ten.) aria in Act 2 of Verdi's *Rigoletto,* in which he regrets the loss of Gilda.

Parody. It was common in the 18th and 19th cent. for parodies of the most popular operas of the day to be staged, generally at the same time as the original. In the case of Weber's *Der Freischütz,* an anonymous German parody *Samiel, oder Die Wunderpille* was produced in 1824, and even translated into Danish and Swedish; another of the same year was the English version, ostensibly by 'Septimus Globus Esq.,' entitled '*Der Freischütz,* a new muse-sick-all and see-nick performance from the new German uproar. By the celebrated Funny-bear.' This was given in London and Edinburgh. Many other composers were given these elaborate backhanded compliments. The last major figure to be so parodied seems to be Wagner. *Tannhäuser* had a number of parodies, including one by Carl Binder, with music praised for its aptness, to a text by Nestroy (1857); Binder also wrote a *Lohengrin* parody with Nestroy (1859). Another *Tannhäuser* parody was a French one of 1861 entitled '*Ya-mein-Herr,* Cacophonie de l'avenir, en 3 actes, entr'acte mêlée de chants, de harpes, et de chiens savants.' One of the last parodies of all is probably *Tristanderl und Süssholde* (1865), produced in Munich before *Tristan und Isolde* itself. See also Scutta.

Parr, Gladys (*b* Bury, Lancs., 3 Jan. 1892). English contralto. Studied R.A.M., London. Has sung with C.R., B.N.O.C., S.W., and at C.G., where she was heard during international seasons in the 1920s as Magdalene in *Meistersinger*. She sang with the English Opera Group, creating Miss Pike (*Albert Herring*) and Mrs. Noah (*Noyes Fludde*). Her performances were marked by clear diction and dramatic ability. (R)

Parsifal. *Bühnenweihfestspiel* (sacred festival drama) in 3 acts by Wagner; text by composer, principally after Wolfram von Eschenbach's poem, *Parzival* (early 13th cent.). Prod. Bayreuth 26 July. 1882, with Materna, Winkelmann, Reichmann, Scaria, Hill, Kindermann, cond. Levi; N.Y., Met., 24 Dec. 1903 (infringing the Bayreuth copyright, which did not expire until 31 Dec. 1913), with Ternina, Burgstaller, Van Rooy, Blass, cond. Hertz; London, C.G., 2 Feb. 1914, with Eva von der Osten, Hensel, Bender, Knüpfer, cond. Bodansky.

The Bayreuth copyright was also broken by performances in English in Boston and elsewhere in the U.S.A. 1904-5, in Amsterdam 1905, in Zurich 1903, and in Buenos Aires and Rio de Janeiro 1913.

In a forest near a lake at Monsalvat in the kingdom of the Grail, Gurnemanz (bass) and his two Esquires arouse themselves from sleep and offer up their morning prayers. They are interrupted by the wild entry of Kundry (sop.) who comes with balsam for the suffering Amfortas (bar.), who is carried in on a litter on his way to bathe his wounds. Gurnemanz relates to his Esquires how Amfortas, son of Titurel, who had entered the magic garden of the magician Klingsor armed with the Sacred Spear, had been seduced by Kundry and wounded by Klingsor, who had seized the Sacred Spear. The wound will only heal at the touch of the Spear, now in Klingsor's possession, and the only person who can gain possession of it is a 'Pure Fool made wise through pity'. Cries are now heard, and an unknown youth (Parsifal, ten.) is dragged in having killed a swan. In reply to Gurnemanz's questions it is clear that this youth may be the 'Pure Fool', and he is taken back to the castle to witness the unveiling of the Grail by Amfortas. Having failed to understand the ceremony, he is driven from the hall by the angry Gurnemanz.

Klingsor (bar.) summons Kundry and instructs her to seduce Parsifal, whom they have both recognized as the only possible redeemer of Amfortas and Kundry. In Klingsor's magic garden the Flower Maidens tempt Parsifal, but he remains indifferent. Kundry calls him by his name and recalls for him memories of his childhood and his mother. As she kisses him on the lips all is revealed to him: 'Amfortas! the wound!' he cries. Realizing the nature of Amfortas's temptation, he becomes 'wise through pity'; while Kundry changes from temptress to suppliant as she recognizes that her one chance of salvation is now at Parsifal's hands. Klingsor hurls the Sacred Spear at him, but it remains suspended in mid-air over his head. He seizes the Spear and as he makes the sign of the Cross, Klingsor's domain falls in ruins.

Many years have passed. Gurnemanz, now grown old, is a hermit, and the repentant Kundry comes to draw water for him. A knight in black armour approaches; it is Parsifal. He is recognized by Kundry but not by Gurnemanz, who chides him for coming armed onto holy ground on Good Friday. The knight kneels in prayer. Gurnemanz recognizes first the Sacred Spear, then Parsifal. After Kundry has bathed the knight's feet and dried them with her hair, Gurnemanz anoints Parsifal as the new King of the Holy Grail. His first task is to baptize Kundry. The three make their way to the Hall of the Grail where the funeral of Titurel is about to take place. The knights call on Amfortas to uncover the Grail, but he is unable to do so. He tears open his tunic and displaying his wound, asks the knights to kill him. Parsifal enters the hall and, touching the wound with the Spear, heals it. As the knights pay homage to their new King, Parsifal raises the Grail aloft; a white dove hovers over his head, and Kundry falls lifeless.

Pasero, Tancredi (*b* Turin, 11 Jan. 1893). Italian bass. Studied with Pessina. Début Vicenza 1917, Rodolfo (*Sonnambula*). N.Y., Met., 1929-33; London, C.G., 1931. Leading bass at Milan, Sc., 1926-52. Sang regularly in all the leading Italian opera houses, South America, Spain, and Portugal. Possessed a large, resonant voice: at home in Italian, French, German, and Russian repertory. Notable roles included Boris, Mefistofele, Gurnemanz, and Verdi bass parts. (R)

Pashkevich, Vasily (Alexeyevich) (*b* 1742; *d* 20 Mar. 1797). Russian composer. Played the violin in the opera at St Petersburg in 1763, then worked in various capacities in the Imperial Theatres. An important pioneer of Russian opera. Possibly the author of *Anyuta* (1772); became well known with *Neschastye ot karoty* (Misfortune from a Carriage, 1779): unlike many early nationalist operas, this includes only one folk song. *Skupoy* (The Miser, probably based on Molière's *L'Avare*, 1782) looks forward to later Russian opera in its use of natural speech rhythms; and other developments in Russian opera are anticipated in *Fevey* (1786), to a libretto by Catherine the Great, which makes use of a fairy subject and includes exotic elements, also in one song using the technique of a repeated melody against a changing background which was to be developed by Glinka. Other operas include *Nachalnoye upravlenye Olega* (The early reign of Oleg, with Sarti and Cannobio, text by Catherine, 1790) and *Fedul s detmi* (Fedul and his Children, text by Catherine, 1792).

Pasini, Camilla (*b* Rome, 6 Nov. 1875; *d* Rome, 29 Oct. 1935). Italian soprano. Sister of Lina. Studied Rome. Début Rome, T. Nazionale, Inez (*Africaine*). Created Musetta, Turin 1896. Retired 1905. A third sister, **Enrica**, had a brief career as a mezzo-soprano.

Pasini, Laura (*b* Gallarate, nr Milan, 28 Jan 1894; *d* Rome 6 Sept. 1942). Italian soprano (orig. pianist, concert in Rome 1912). Studied Milan and Rome. Début Milan, Teatro Eden, 1922, Zerlina in *Fra Diavolo*. Rome 1921-3; Milan, Sc., 1923-6 and 1930-1; sang in first Italian performance of *Le Rossignol* under Stravinsky. Career continued until 1934, after which she taught singing at Cagliari. (R)

Pasini (-Vitale), **Lina** (*b* Rome, 8 Nov. 1872; *d* Rome 23 Nov. 1959). Italian soprano. Studied Rome; début Milan, T. d. V., Jan 1893 as Cecilia in Cilea's *Tilda*. Also sang Suzel, Iris, Micaela, Mimì, and Gretel. Became a leading Italian Wagner soprano, and one of the first Kundrys in Italy. Much acclaimed in South America. Last appearance Naples 1928 as Kundry. Married the conductor Edoardo *Vitale. (R)

Paskalis, Kostas (*b* Livadia, 1 Sept. 1929). Greek baritone. Studied Athens Conservatory. Début Athens 1951, Rigoletto. Vienna, S.O., since 1958; Gly., as Macbeth, 1964-5, Don Giovanni 1967; N.Y., Met., 1965-7; London, C.G., 1969, 1971-2. Created Pentheus (*Bassarids*), Salzburg 1966. An intense singer and actor. (R)

Pasta (orig. Negri), **Giuditta** (*b* Saronno, nr Milan, 28 Oct. 1797; *d* Blevio, nr Lake Como, 1 April 1865). Italian soprano. An almost legendary figure, the creator of Norma, Amina, Beatrice di Tenda, Ugo (Donizetti), and Anna Bolena. Studied Como with Bartolomeo Lotti, and Milan with Asioli. Début Brescia 1815, in small roles, as Giuditta Negri. Paris, T.I., 1815 with tenor Pasta, whom she married. London, K., 1817, début as Telemachus in Cimarosa's *Penelope*, followed by Cherubino, Despina, and Servilia, all with little success. After a period of further study in Milan with Scappa, second début 1819, Milan, Filodrammatici, in Scappa's *Le tre Eleonore*. Her real fame dates from the 1821 season in Paris, when between June and November she scored great successes as Desdemona (Rossini), Donna Anna, and Romeo (Zingarelli); her splendid soprano voice, ranging from a to d''', her gifts for dramatic interpretation, and the poignancy of her singing, created a sensation. Even at the height of her powers, however, her voice was

not equal throughout its range and on off-nights she received adverse criticism. Reappeared London 1824 as Desdemona (Rossini), and continued to appear regularly in London, Paris, and St. Petersburg until 1837. In 1840 she reappeared at St. Petersburg, being offered 200,000 francs; and in 1850 she unwisely returned to London with little or no voice left. Maria Ferranti Giulini's *Giuditta Pasta e i suoi tempi* (Milan 1935) is the most recent study of this singer. Chorley in his *Thirty Years' Musical Recollections* gives some vivid descriptions of Pasta's London performances.

Pasticcio (*It* pie). A play with airs, ensembles, dances, and other movements assembled from one or more composers. These were grouped together, not according to their original intention, so as to provide the audience with the maximum number of its favourite tunes in the briefest space of time, or to furnish a dramatic situation or song with music that more or less fitted. It was a genre particularly popular in the 18th cent. A vintage example is *Thomyris* (D.L., 1707), for which Pepusch wrote recitatives, and adapted and arranged airs by Bononcini. Scarlatti, Gasparini, and Albinoni. See also *Castil-Blaze, Lacy, Lachnith*.

Pastor Fido, Il (The Faithful Shepherd). Opera in 3 acts by Handel; text by Rossi, after Guarini's pastoral play (1585). Prod. London, Hm., 22 Nov. 1712, with Valeriano, Pilotti, Schiavonetti, Marguerita, Barbier, Urbani, Leveridge.

Pastorale. A stage piece on a legendary or pastoral subject. Originally without music, the genre spread through Europe from Italy; in France it was first given music and then found a place as an early form of opera. *La Pastorale en musique* (1659) and *Pomone* (1671) by Perrin and Cambay are regarded as the earliest French operas. The slender plots allowed ample scope for the ballet and spectacle always beloved of the French.

Paton, Mary Ann (*b* Edinburgh, Oct. 1802; *d* Chapelthorpe, 21 July 1864). Scottish soprano. After singing in concerts, made stage début London, Hm., 1822, Susanna. C.G. same year; created Reiza (*Oberon*) there 1826 and was highly praised by Weber. Sang C.G., D.L., and King's T. until 1844. Visited U.S. (N.Y. 1833-6, 1840-1) and subsequently with her husband, the tenor Joseph Wood: Her voice, ranging from a to d'''' or e'''', was notable for its purity, brilliance, and sweetness. Her personal beauty was much admired, and there are numerous portraits of her by Lawrence, Newton, and others.

Patter song. A comic song in which the greatest number of words, delivered rapidly in conversational style, are fitted into the shortest space of time, with the music generally merely supporting their inflexion. From Haydn and Mozart to Sullivan the patter song has had a firm place in comic opera.

Patti, Adelina (*b* Madrid, 19 Feb. 1843; *d* Craigy-Nos Castle, Wales, 27 Sept. 1919). Italian soprano. Her parents, Salvatore Patti and Caterina Barilli, were both singers, who took their daughter to N.Y. when very young, where she made her first public appearance in concert in 1850. Studied singing with her brother-in-law Strakosch, and piano with her sister Carlotta. Stage début N.Y. 1859 as Lucia, under the stage name of the 'Little Florinda'. London, C.G., 1861 as Amina, from which her fame dates. Hailed as Grisi's successor, she sang Zerlina in Grisi's last *Don Giovanni* in London. She appeared regularly in London and Paris, and occasionally in Italy and America. She sang in 25 consecutive seasons at C.G., where she sang some 30 roles in works by Rossini, Bellini, Donizetti, Verdi, Gounod, and Meyerbeer. The first London Aida and Juliette. The most highly paid singer of her day (200 guineas a performance at C.G., $5,000 in America), she had a clause in her contract excusing her from rehearsal and stipulating the size in which her name was to appear on posters. She was essentially a coloratura soprano, though she sang many lyric roles including Marguerite and Leonora (*Trovatore*) and even dramatic ones like Aida. Her voice ranged from c to f''' and was amazingly even and flexible. She was unrivalled for beauty and purity of tone, though her interpretations were said to lack temperament and she possessed only an average musical intelligence. She was married three times, her second husband being the tenor *Nicolini. (R) Her sister **Carlotta Patti** (1835-89) confined her singing career to the concert platform. *Bibl:* H. Klein: *The Reign of Patti* (1920).

Pattiera, Tino (*b* Ragusa, 27 June 1890; *d* Čavtat, nr Ragusa, 24 Apr. 1966). Yugoslav tenor. Studied Vienna with Horboucky Ranieri. Début Dresden, March 1916, Manrico. Dresden 1916-41; Berlin, S.O., 1924-9 (joint contract with Dresden); Chicago 1920-1. Played leading part in the German Verdi renaissance of 1920s; repertory also included Hermann, Andrea Chénier, Bacchus, and Tannhäuser. A handsome man with a fine stage presence and thrilling and beautiful *lirico-spinto* voice. Taught in Vienna from 1950 until shortly before his death. (R)

Patzak, Julius (*b* Vienna, 9 Apr. 1898; *d* Rottach, 26 Jan. 1974). Austrian tenor. Studied conducting with Franz Schmidt; turned to singing 1926. Début Reichenberg (Bohemia) 1926, Radamès. Brno 1927-8; Munich, N., 1928-45; Vienna, S., 1945-60; London, C.G., 1938, Tamino, 1947 (with Vienna Company),

Florestan, Herod, 1951-4 including Hoffmann (in English), and Florestan which, with Pfitzner's Palestrina, was considered his greatest role. His voice was never outstanding, but his style, intelligence, musicianship, superb enunciation, and complete identification with his role combined to make him one of the great singers of his day. Created roles in Pfitzner's *Das Herz* and Orff's *Der Mond*. (R)

Pauer, Jiří (*b* Libušin, 22 Feb. 1919). Czech composer. Studied Prague with Šín and Hába. Director Prague Opera 1953-5. His works include the successful *Zuzana Vojířová* (1959).

Pauly, Rosa (orig. Rose Pollak) (*b* Eperjes, 15 Mar. 1894; *d* Tel Aviv, 14 Dec. 1975). Hungarian soprano. Studied Vienna with Rose Papier. Début Hamburg 1918, Aida. Gera 1919-21; Karlsruhe 1921-2; Cologne, 1922-6; first German Káťa Kabanová; Mannheim 1926-7; Berlin, Kroll, 1927-31, as leading dramatic soprano of Klemperer's company: her roles there included Leonore in *Fidelio*, which opened the theatre, Donna Anna, Senta, Carmen, and parts in Křenek's *Diktator* and Hindemith's *Neues vom Tage*. Berlin, S.O., as Marie, Jenůfa, Elektra. Vienna, S.O., 1922-9 and 1932-8; London, C.G., 1938, Leonore, Elektra; N.Y., Met., 1938-40 Elektra, Venus, Ortrud. Guest appearances in Italy, Argentina, Mexico, Chicago, San Francisco, etc. Last appearances Buenos Aires under Kleiber 1943 as Gutrune and Elektra. The most famous Elektra of her day; also an outstanding Dyer's Wife in *Frau ohne Schatten*, and Helena in *Aegyptische Helena*. Much admired by Strauss, who was unable to prevent the Nazis from forbidding her to sing first in Germany, then in Austria. Lived in Israel from 1946. (R)

Pauvre Matelot, Le (The Poor Sailor). Opera in 3 acts by Milhaud; text by Cocteau, based on a newspaper report of an actual event. Prod. Paris, O.C., 16 Dec. 1927 with Sibille, Legrand, Vieulle, Musy, cond. Lauweryns; Philadelphia, Ac. of M., 1 Apr. 1937; London, Fortune T., 1 Oct. 1950 with Vyvyan, Servent, Loring, Wallace, cond. Renton. A sailor (ten.) returns home after a long absence and is not recognised by his wife (sop.). He tests her fidelity by pretending to be her husband's rich friend, and showing her jewels to prove his wealth tries to make love to her. When he is asleep the wife murders him and steals the jewels in order to help pay for her husband's voyage back home.

Pavarotti, Luciano (*b* Modena, 12 Oct. 1935). Italian tenor. Studied with Pola and Campogalliani. Début Reggio Emilia 1961, Rodolfo. London, C.G., 1963 Rodolfo, and subsequently Tonie (*Fille du régiment*), also Elvino, Alfredo, Duke of Mantua, Edgardo; Glyndebourne, 1964, Idamante; Milan, Sc., 1966, Romeo in *I Capuletti e i Montecchi* and subsequently.

Toured Australia with Sutherland, 1965. N.Y., Met., since 1968. Specializes in bel canto repertory; has a fine technique and a voice of considerable beauty. (R)

Pavesi, Stefano (*b* Casaletto Vaprio, 22 Jan. 1779; *d* Crema, 28 July. 1850). Italian composer. Studied Naples with Piccinni, but was expelled from the Conservatory for his republican sympathies; later studied with Gazzaniga. His first opera, *Un avvertimento ai gelosi* (1803), was followed by about 70 others. Director, Vienna Court Opera, 1826-30. One of the most active and prolific Italian composers before the advent of Rossini; he had a distinctive melodic invention and handled the orchestra expertly. *Ser Marcantonio* (1810), on a subject similar to that of *Don Pasquale*, was repeated on 54 consecutive evenings; *La fiera* (1804), *La festa della rosa* (1808), and *Fenella, o La muta di Portici* (1831), were also successful.

Pearl Fishers, The. See *Les Pêcheurs de perles*.

Pears, (Sir) Peter (*b* Farnham, 22 June 1910). English tenor. Studied R.C.M., London, and later with Elena Gerhardt. After singing with B.B.C. Chorus and Singers, and being a member of the Glyndebourne Chorus (1938), made stage début London, Strand Theatre, 1942, Hoffmann; S.W., 1943-6; E.O.G., 1946-76; C.G. guest appearances since 1947. At S.W. sang in Italian repertory, Tamino, Vašek, and created title role in *Peter Grimes* (1945), since when he has been particularly associated with Britten's music, creating Male Chorus (*Lucretia*), Albert Herring, Vere (*Budd*), Essex (*Gloriana*), Quint (*Turn of the Screw*), Flute (*A Midsummer Night's Dream*), the Madwoman (*Curlew River*), Sir Philip Wingrave (*Owen Wingrave*), and Aschenbach (*Death in Venice*); also created Pandarus in Walton's *Troilus and Cressida*. Belated N.Y. opera début, Met., 1974, Aschenbach. Knighted 1978. An exceptionally intelligent and musical artist. (R)

Pêcheurs de perles, Les (The Pearl Fishers). Opera in 3 acts by Bizet; text by Eugène Cormon (Pierre-Étienne Piestre) and Michel Carré. Prod. Paris, T.-L., 30 Sept. 1863, with Léontine de Maësen, Morini, Ismaël, Guyot, cond. Deloffre; London, C.G., 22 Apr. 1887 (as *Leila*), with Föhström, Garulli, Lhérie, Miranda; Philadelphia 23 Aug. 1893. Much admired by Berlioz, who wrote that 'it does M. Bizet the greatest honour'.

Zurga (bar.) is chosen chief by his tribe of fishermen in ancient Ceylon. His friend Nadir (ten.) returns, and after long estrangement caused by falling in love with the same priestess they are reconciled. A new priestess, Leila (sop.) appears to offer her prayer and she and Nadir recognize each other. She is under a vow of chastity, with death as penalty. In a ruined temple she tells the high priest Nourabad

(bass) how she risked death to save a fugitive and was given a gold chain. Later he finds Nadir and Leila embracing, and denounces her to the people and to the enraged Zurga. She pleads for Nadir, and, having failed, charges Zurga to give her mother her chain, which Zurga recognizes as one he had long ago given to a child who saved his life. He helps the lovers to escape by firing the village, but is himself killed.

Pécs. Town in southern Hungary. Touring companies first performed there in 1800, and the first permanent company was formed in 1881. The National. T. (cap. 820) opened in 1959, and tours western Hungary.

Pederzini, Gianna (*b* Vò di Avio, 10 Feb. 1903). Italian mezzo-soprano. Studied Naples with De Lucia. Début Messina 1923, Preziosilla. Milan, Sc., 1930-43, 1956-7; Rome, 1939-52; London, C.G., 1931, Preziosilla, Maddalena; Buenos Aires., T.C., 1937-9, 1946-7. One of the outstanding mezzos of the inter-war years. Her roles included Carmen, Mignon, and the Rossini heroines. During the 1950s and 1960s sang the title role in Menotti's *The Medium*, the Countess in *The Queen of Spades*, and Mistress Quickly, all roles for which her highly developed dramatic talents suited her admirably. Created Prioress in *Dialogues des Carmélites*, Milan, Sc., 1957. (R)

Pedrazzi, Francesco (*b* Bologna, early 19th cent.). Italian tenor. Son of tenor Luigi Pedrazzi. Studied with Giuseppe Tadolini. Début Pisa 1828. Parma, 1828-9; Milan, Sc., 1832-41; created Gennaro in *Lucrezia Borgia* and Viscardo in Mercadante's *Giuramento*. Pest 1845; Vienna 1846. Noted for his interpretations of Rossini and Donizetti.

Pedrell, Felipe (*b* Tortosa, 19 Feb. 1841; *d* Barcelona, 19 Aug. 1922). Spanish composer. Pedrell's position as the father of Spanish music drama rests on his foundation of a Spanish national style. This took its inspiration from folk music and from the major achievements of centuries of great artistic development in non-dramatic musical spheres. His most serious studies were folk music and Victoria. The first operas he produced led to him being misunderstood as a Spanish Wagnerian. There is a note of studiousness in his operas, which, though they contain much fine music, inhibits their wide acceptance. They include *L'ultimo Abenzerragio* (1874), *Quasimodo* (1875), *Cleopatra* (1875), *Mazeppa* and *Il Tasso a Ferrara* (1881), *Los Pirineos* (1902), and some zarzuelas. Pedrell is most significant for his direct influence on his pupils (who include Falla and Roberto Gerhard) and indirect influence in encouraging Spanish musical self-confidence.
Bibl: G. Tebaldini: *Felipe Pedrell ed il dramma lirico spagnuolo* (1897).

Pedrillo. Belmonte's servant (ten.), in Mozart's *Die Entführung aus dem Serail.*

Pedrotti, Carlo (*b* Verona, 12 Nov. 1817; *d* Verona, 16 Oct. 1893). Italian composer and conductor. Studied Verona with Foroni. Two early operas were unproduced, but *Lina* (1840) and *Clara di Mailand* (1840) were successful. This led to his appointment to the Italian opera at Amsterdam, where he wrote two more operas, *Matilde* (1841) and *La figlia dell'arciere* (1844). Back in Verona (1845-68) he wrote a number of further works, chiefly *buffa* or *semiseria*, that won him his fame. His first international success came with *Fiorina* (1851), followed by the even greater success of *Tutti in maschera* (1869). Turin 1868 as director of the T.R., exercising an important influence on the development of the city's musical life. His interest in Wagner led to a sensational performance of *Lohengrin* in 1876; he also introduced to Italy a number of important works by French composers (including Massenet and Gounod) and gave some premières of Italian works (including Catalani's first opera, *Elsa*, 1880), thus winning the T.R. an Italian reputation to rival that of La Scala. However, this energetic activity left him little time for composition, even when he left Turin in 1882 to direct the Liceo Musicale at Pesaro. His operas were popular in their day above all for their tunefulness, lightness of touch, and expert construction. Intelligent enough to see that he had outlived his own style, he latterly discouraged performance of his operas. He continued to be influential as a conductor; he trained in Turin the orchestra of Toscanini's first successes.

Bibl: T. Mantovani: *Carlo Pedrotti* (1894).

Peerce, Jan (orig. Jacob Pincus Perlemuth) (*b* New York, 3 June 1904). American tenor. Began musical career as a violinist in dance bands, &c., and sometimes sung vocal refrains. This led to an engagement at Radio City Music Hall 1933-9. Opera début Baltimore, 1939 Duke of Mantua. Leading tenor N.Y., Met., 1941-66. Chosen by Toscanini for his broadcast performances of *Bohème, Fidelio, Traviata,* and *Ballo in maschera,* which were also recorded. Has sung with most American opera organizations as well as in Russia, Germany, and Holland Festival. (R)

Pélissier (or Pellissier), **Mlle** (*b* ?1706 or 1707; *d* Paris, 21 Mar. 1749) French soprano. Début Paris, O., 1722. Sang at O. until 1741; created leading roles in operas by Rameau, including *Castor et Pollux, Indes Galantes, Dardanus,* and *Les Fêtes d'Hébé.* Considered the successor to Le Rochois.

Pelléas et Mélisande. Drame lyrique in 5 acts, 12 *tableaux,* by Debussy; text a slight alteration of Maeterlinck's tragedy (1892). Prod. Paris,

O.C., 30 Apr. 1902, with Mary Garden, Gerville-Réache, Périer, Dufranne, Vieuille. cond. Messager; N.Y., Manhattan O.C., 19 Feb. 1908 with Garden, Gerville-Réache, Dufranne, Arimondi, Crabbé, cond. Campanini; London, C.G., 21 May 1909, with Rose Féart, Bourgeois, Warnery, Vanni-Marcoux, Bourbon, Crabbé, cond. Campanini.

Golaud (bar.), grandson of King Arkel of Allemonde (bass), takes home a mysterious girl, Mélisande (sop.), he has found weeping in the forest. Geneviève (mezzo), mother of the half-brothers Pelléas (ten.) and Golaud, reads Arkel a letter from Golaud to Pelléas describing his meeting and marriage with Mélisande. Arkel accepts this marriage. Pelléas comes to tell of a summons he has had from a sick friend, but Arkel reminds him that he should stay with his own sick father, who lies upstairs. Mélisande and Geneviève are joined by Pelléas in the castle gardens and watch a ship departing.

Playing with her wedding ring, Mélisande loses it down a well; Pelléas advises her to tell Golaud the truth. Golaud, thrown from his horse at the moment the ring fell, is being tended by Mélisande. He notices the ring's absence, and tells her to go and search in the grotto by the seashore, where she says she lost it. Pelléas and Mélisande explore the grotto. Frightened by three sleeping beggars, they abandon their pretended search.

Mélisande drops her long hair from her window, and it is fondled by Pelléas. They are surprised by Golaud. Golaud shows Pelléas the stagnant castle vaults. Golaud warns Pelléas to let Mélisande alone. Golaud questions little Yniold (sop.), son of his former marriage, about Pelléas and Mélisande and holds him up to the window to tell what he sees: they are sitting together.

Pelléas plans to leave, on his father's advice. Golaud enters and in jealous fury seizes Mélisande's hair and hurls her to and fro. In the park, Yniold is trying to lift a large stone. Pelléas comes to say good-bye to Mélisande, but they declare their love as the castle gates shut. Golaud appears and strikes down Pelléas; Mélisande flees, pursued by Golaud.

Arkel, Golaud, and the Physician wait by Mélisande's bed, where she is dying, having given birth to a child. Golaud, repentant but still jealous, questions her about her love for Pelléas—was it a 'forbidden' love. The castle servants enter, and fall on their knees as Mélisande dies without answering Golaud.

Penelope. In Homer's *Odyssey,* the wife of Odysseus, who waited faithfully for his return from the Trojan War, rejecting all advances from suitors during his long travels, and was finally reunited with him. Operas on her story are as follows:

(1) Opera in 3 acts by Fauré; text by René Fauchois. Prod. Monte Carlo, 4 Mar. 1913, with Bréval, Raveau, Rousselière, Bourbon, cond. Jehin; London, R.A.M., 20 Nov. 1970 with Lees, Adams, Roberts, Bottone, cond. Lloyd-Jones.

(2) Opera semiseria in 2 parts by Liebermann; text by Heinrich Strobel, a modern adaptation of the legend based on an actual incident of the Second World War. Prod. Salzburg, Festspielhaus, 17 Aug. 1954, with Goltz, Schock, Böhme, cond. Szell.

Other operas by Draghi (1670); Pallavicino (1685); ?Niccolini (?1685); Keiser (1702); Chelleri (1716); F. Conti (1724); Galuppi (1741); Gazzaniga (1781); Piccinni (1785); Cimarosa (1795). See *Odysseus*.

Pepusch, John Christopher (*b* Berlin, 1667; *d* London, 20 July 1752). English composer of German birth. He arrived in London in 1700 and joined the orchestra of D.L., also making some arrangements of operas. His best-known work is his arrangement of *The Beggar's Opera* (1728), though he also composed music for a number of masques while music director at Lincoln's Inn Fields T. Married Margherita de l'*Épine.

Perez, Davide (*b* Naples, 1711; *d* Lisbon, 30 Oct. 1778). Italian composer. Studied Naples 1723-33, with Mancini. His first opera, *La nemica amante*, was given in Naples, 1935; then followed *Siroe* (1740). He worked in Palermo till 1748, then writing *La clemenza di Tito* (1749) for Naples and *Semiramide* (1750) for Rome; thereafter he had successes in many Italian towns. He then went to Lisbon, where he had a triumph with *Demofoonte* (1752), and with his most important work, *Solimano* (1757). He wrote *Ezio* (1755) for London. Though not very highly regarded by his contemporaries and by some later historians (e.g. Burney and Fétis), he served to introduce the style of *Neapolitan opera to Portugal, and helped by his own success to encourage opera there.

Perfect Fool, The. Comic opera in 1 act by Holst; text by the composer. Prod. London, C.G., 14 May 1923 by B.N.O.C., with Teyte, Thornton, Ellis, Parker, Hyde, Collier, cond. Goossens; Wichita, 20 Mar. 1962. The opera, which parodies opera conventions and the music of Wagner and Verdi, enjoyed much success originally, but has rarely been performed since the 1920s.

The plot concerns the wooing of the Princess (sop.) by a (Verdian) Troubadour (ten.) and a (Wagnerian) Traveller (bass); she is eventually won by the Perfect Fool (speaking part), who has no interest in her.

Pergola, Teatro della. See *Florence*.

Pergolesi, Giovanni Battista (*b* Jesi, 4 Jan. 1710; *d* Pozzuoli, 16 Mar. 1736). Italian composer. His first opera, *Salustia* (1731), was performed in Naples with an unnamed intermezzo of his, and failed; but *Lo frate 'nnamorato* succeeded there (1732). *Il prigionier superbo* (1733) is now forgotten, apart from its association with the most famous of all intermezzos, *La serva padrona*. The same pattern was repeated with *Adriano in Siria* (1734) and its intermezzo *La contadina astuta*. *L'Olimpiade* (1735), despite its quality, was a failure, but the opera buffa *Flaminio* (1735) was a considerable success. Pergolesi's greatest talent lay in comic opera: though he wrote some expressive music in opera seria, helping to enrich the tradition with arias of considerable sensitivity to words, it was in the intermezzos and in opera buffa that his natural wit and freshness found most complete expression.

Bibl: G. Radiciotti: *G.B. Pergolesi: vita, opere ed influenza su l'arte* (1910).

Peri, Jacopo (*b* Rome, 20 Aug. 1561; *d* Florence, 12 Aug. 1633). Italian composer. Studied Florence with Cristofano Malvezzi, becoming a musician at the Medici court and winning fame as a singer (nicknamed Il Zazzerino, from his long golden hair). He became a prominent member of the *Camerata, and his *Dafne* (1597) is considered the first opera: most of the music is lost. He took the part of Apollo himself at the first performance, and later that of Orpheus in the first performance of his *Euridice* (1600). This work, in the novel *stile recitativo*, proved the validity of the new art form, and showed some of the possibilities later to be fulfilled by greater artists. None of Peri's subsequent works matched the success of *Euridice*, but he and his great rival *Caccini are the founding fathers of opera.

Périchole, La. *Opéra bouffe* in 3 acts by Offenbach; text by Meilhac and Halévy, after Mérimée's drama, *Le Carrosse du Saint Sacrement* (1829). Prod. Paris, T., des Variétés, 6 Oct. 1868, with Schneider, Legrand, Dupuis, Grenier, Lecomte, Bondelet, Bac; N.Y., Pike's O.H., 4 Jan. 1869, with Irma, Rose, Aujac, Leduc, Lagriddou; London, Princess's T., 27 June 1870.

A gypsy street singer, La Périchole (sop.), and her partner and lover Piquillo (ten.), come to Lima. Don Andres (bar.), the viceroy of Peru, is charmed by La Périchole and engages her as a lady in-waiting. After many intrigues and complications, including an escape from the local prison, the lovers are re-united.

Périer, Jean (-Alexis) (*b* Paris, 2 Feb. 1869; *d* Neuilly, 6 Nov. 1954). French baritone. Studied Paris Conservatoire with Taskin and Bussine. Début Paris, O.C., 1892, Monostatos. N.Y. Manhattan O.H., 1907-8. Created many roles in Paris, including Pelléas, Landry in Messager's *Fortunio*, Ramiro in *L'Heure espagnole*, and Mârouf. Was the first Sharpless in France. (R)

erlea, Jonel (orig. Ionel) (*b* Ograda, 13 Dec.)00; *d* New York, 29 July 1970). Romanian onductor. Studied Munich with Beer-Valdbrunn and Kotana (1918-20), and Leipzig 'ith Lohse, Martinsen, and Graener (1920-23). ébut in concert Bucharest, 1919; Korrepetitor eipzig 1922-3; Rostock 1923-5. Opera début luj, 1927, *Aida*. Cond. Bucharest 1928-32,)36-44; director Bucharest Opera, 1929-32,)34, 1936. Vienna, Stuttgart, Breslau, and erlin guest appearances from 1935. Gave first erformances in Bucharest of many works, cluding *Meistersinger*, *Falstaff*, *Rosen-* avalier (all in Romanian). Milan, Sc., and other alian houses 1945-58; conducted first perfs. in aly of *Capriccio* (Genoa, 1953), *Boulevard Sol-* ude (Naples, 1954), *Mazeppa* (Florence, 954), and Tchaikovsky's *Joan of Arc* (1956), as vell as premières of works by Bianchi, Bucchi, nd Rota. N.Y., Met., 1949-50; Aix Festival 958. Taught conducting at Manhattan School f Music, N.Y., 1952-69. (R)

ernet, André (*b* Rambervillers, 6 Jan. 1894; *d* aris, 23 June 1966). French bass. Studied aris with Gresse. Début Nice 1921. Leading ass Paris O., 1928-45 (except for 1931, when e moved to the O.C. over salary dispute) and 948, where he was much admired as Boris, on Quichotte, Méphistophélès, and Don iiovanni. Created leading roles in a number of ontemporary operas, including Milhaud's *Maximilien*, Hahn's *Marchand de Venise*, and nesco's *Oedipe*. Sang the Father in the film of *ouise* with Grace Moore, made under the lirection of Charpentier. (R)

er pietà. Fiordiligi's (sop.) aria with horn bbligato in Act 2, scene 2, of Mozart's *Così fan* utte, her resistance weakening to the dvances of her sister's disguised lover.

errin, Emilie Cesare (*b* Paris ?; *d* Paris ?). rench administrator. Succeeded Basset as lirector of the Paris O.C. 1848, remaining there intil 1857 and returning from 1862 to 1876. His vo periods of management saw the produc-ion of many new works, including Thomas's e Caïd (1849), *Mignon* (1866), Massenet's first opera, *La Grand' Tante* (1867), Bizet's)jamileh (1872), Saint-Saëns's first opera, *La* 'rincesse jaune (1872), Le Roi l'a dit (1873), and :armen (1876), as well as works by Halévy, Adam, Massé, Auber, and Offenbach.

errin, Pierre (*b* Lyons, *c*1620; *d* Paris, 25 Apr. 675). French librettist. Assumed the title of Abbé. The first important French librettist, and he founder of the *Académie Royale de Musique et de Danse (the Paris *Opéra). Previ-ously, he had written an opera for Cambert for erformance at the small Royal theatre at Issy La Pastorale d'Issy, 1659), 'in an attempt to evolve a genre of opera simpler than the cur-ent forms of Italian opera'. He abandoned the alexandrines of the French classical theatre in favour of short lyric verses. His success led Louis XIV to consider the foundation of a national opera, and in 1669 letters patent were granted to Perrin for the formation of the Académie. In 1671 the first French opera, Cam-bert's *Pomone* (text by Perrin), was publicly given. But financial difficulties and malprac-tices led to his imprisonment, and he died in poverty, having sold his letters patent to Lully. Though a mediocre versifier, Perrin is remem-bered as a founder of French opera, and also for his influence, directly on *Quinault and later on the pastoral operas and writings of *Rous-seau, in developing a simpler and more popular style that reflected folk influence.

Perron (orig. Pergamenter), **Karl** (*b* Frank-enthal, 3 June 1858; *d* Dresden, 15 July 1928). German bass-baritone. Studied Berlin with Hey, Munich with Hasselbasch, Frankfurt with Stockhausen, and acting with Possart. Début Leipzig 1884, Wolfram. Leipzig, 1884-91. Dresden, 1892-1924, where he created Jocha-naan, Orestes, and Ochs, and was the first Dresden Onegin. Bayreuth 1889-1904, Amfortas, Wotan, Marke, and Daland; also a famous Don Giovanni.

Persephone. See *Proserpine*.

Persiani (orig. Tacchinardi), **Fanny** (*b* Rome, 4 Oct. 1812; *d* Paris, 3 May 1867). Italian soprano. Her father was the tenor Nicola Tacchinardi, who was also her teacher. In 1832 she made her début Leghorn 1832 in Fournier's *Fran-cesca da Rimini*. Donizetti wrote Lucia for her, which she created in 1835. London, H.M.'s, 1838 as Amina, and sang there until 1846. Then from 1847 to 1849 at C.G., which theatre she helped establish as the Royal Italian Opera, her husband putting up much of the money. A great favourite in Paris 1837-48. Also in Paris 1858. Her voice was of great range (b to f'''); her singing was brilliant and clear; and she was capable of the most dazzling displays of ornamentation. In 1830 she married the com-poser **Giuseppe Persiani** (?1799/1805-1869). His best known opera was *Ines de Castro* (1835), one of Malibran's last roles. He and his wife were well-known as teachers in Paris.

Persichini, Venceslao (*b* Rome, 1827; *d* Rome 19 Sept. 1897). Italian composer and teacher. Taught at Santa Cecilia, Rome; his pupils included Battistini, Magini-Coletti, and De Luca.

Pertichino (*It* understudy). The term used for the character in opera who during a recitative or aria remains silent or makes occasional interjections. The common dramatic function is to provide a listener, reacting suitably, for a singer's narration: an example is Ines listening to Leonora's 'Tacea la notte' in Act 1 of Verdi's

Il trovatore. The term was common in the 18th cent. but gradually fell into disuse (though it remained as a dramatic function) towards the end of the 19th cent.

Pertile, Aureliano (*b* Montagnana, 9 Nov. 1885; *d* Milan, 11 Jan. 1952). Italian tenor. Studied with Orefice. Début Vicenza 1910, Fra Diavolo. A further period of study followed in Milan with Manlio Bavagnoli. Milan, Sc., 1918, and leading tenor 1921-37; N.Y., Met., 1921-2; London, C.G., 1927-31. At Sc. was Toscanini's favourite tenor; created the title roles in Boito's and Mascagni's *Nerone* and Wolf-Ferrari's *Sly*. His last years were spent as professor of singing at the Milan Conservatory. His voice was not one of intrinsic beauty, but the great intensity of his singing and acting, his integrity, and his intelligence made him one of the most respected artists of the 1920s and 1930s. (R)

Peru. The first Peruvian opera was *Atahualpa* (1877) by the Italian composer Carlo Enrico Pasta. *Ollanta* (1900) by José Maria Valle is on a national subject. Opera is given at the T. Municipal in Lima.

Pesaro. Town in Marche, Italy. Opera was first given at the T. del Sole in 1637-1816; it was then replaced by the T. Nuovo, which opened in June 1818 with Rossini's *La gazza ladra* with the composer (a native of Pesaro) at the harpsichord. The theatre was renamed the T. Rossini in 1855, and has been the scene of various seasons given in commemoration of the composer. The first performances of Mascagni's *Zanetto* (1896) and Zandonai's *La via della finestra* (1919) were given there. Directors of the Liceo Musicale Rossini (founded 1882) have included Pedrotti, Mascagni, Zandonai, Alfano, Liviabella, and Fiume. The Centro di Studi Rossiniani was founded in 1940.

Peter Grimes. Opera in 3 acts by Britten; text by Montagu Slater, after Crabbe's poem *The Borough* (1810). Prod. London, S.W., 7 June 1945, with Cross, Coates, Pears, R. Jones, Donlevy, Brannigan, cond. Goodall; Stockholm, 21 Mar. 1946, with Sundström, Bergstrom, Svanholm, G. Björling, cond. Sandberg; Tanglewood 6 Aug. 1946, with Manning, W. Horne, Pease, cond. Bernstein.

Peter Grimes has been the most successful of all modern English operas, and its appearance immediately after the war was exciting not only as a revelation of Britten's full talent but as a sign of new growth in English opera.

In a little fishing village in Suffolk, Peter Grimes (ten.) has lost an apprentice at sea in suspicious circumstances. He is acquitted at the inquest, but warned not to take another apprentice. Ellen Orford (sop.), the schoolmistress, alone stands by him, and helps him to get another boy. Later she discovers that the boy has been ill-treated and she quarrels with

Peter. He takes the boy to his hut on the cliff to but they have been overheard, and popul feeling rises to such a pitch that the entire v lage sets out after him. Peter and his apprenti hear the mob coming, and as they descend b another route the boy falls to his death dov the cliff. Three days later Grimes turns up in th village at dawn, exhausted. Balstrode (bar.) retired sea captain, advises him that the on way to escape the village now is to sail his bo out to sea and sink in it. This Peter does as th village comes to life for another, ordinary day

Peter Ibbetson. Opera in 3 acts by Deem Taylor; text by composer, and Constance C lier, after the latter's play founded on Georg du Maurier's novel (1892). Prod. N.Y., Met., Feb. 1931, with Bori, Johnson, Tibbett, con Serafin. One of the most successful America operas before Menotti.

Peter Ibbetson (ten.) murders his tyrannic uncle, Colonel Ibbetson (bar.), and is impri oned for life in Newgate. In prison he succumb to dreams and visions, and he conjures up h past, including memories of his childhoo sweetheart, Mary, now Duchess of Towe (sop.). After nearly 40 years in prison, he lears that she has died, and losing the will to live h also dies; the prison walls disintegrate an Peter, young once more, finds Mary waiting fo him.

Peter the Great (Tsar Peter I of Russia) (Moscow, 9 June 1672; *d* St Petersburg, 8 Fe 1725). Operas on him, usually taking as subje the period he spent working in the shipyards Saardam in Holland, are as follows: Grét (*Pierre le grand*, 1790); Shield (*The Czar*, 1790 Weigl (*Die Jugend Peter des Grossen*, 1814 Lichtenstein (*Frauenoert, oder der Kaiser a Zimmermann*, 1814); Bishop (*The Bu gomaster of Saardam*, musical drama, 1818 Pacini (*Il Falegname di Livonia*, 1819); Vacc (*Pietro il grande*, 1824); Donizetti (*Il bo gomastro di Saardam*, 1827); Mercadant (1827); Flotow (*Pierre et Cathérine*, 1829 Lortzing (**Zar und Zimmermann*, 1837); Fro doni (1839); Meyerbeer (*L'Étoile du nor* 1854); Arapov (?1949); Lourié (1958).

Petrassi, Goffredo (*b* Zagarolo, nr Palestrin 16 July 1904). Italian composer. Studied Rom with Bustini. His operas form a comparativel minor part of his output, though *Il cordovan* (1949) and especially *Morte dell'aria* (1950 were successful. The latter is based on an inc dent, early in this century, when a would-b bird-man fell to his death from the Eiffel Towe (a grim little piece of film has recorded th affair). Petrassi was Intendant of F., Venic 1937-40.

Petrella, Clara (*b* Milan, 28 Mar. 1914). Studie Milan with her sister Micaela Petrella and with Giannina Russ. Début Alessandria 1939, Liù

Milan, Sc., 1941 in Doenisch's *Soleida*, and regularly from 1947, creating leading roles in Pizzetti's *Cagliostro* and *La figlia di Jorio*. Scored great success as Maliella in first revival in Italy for many years of *I gioielli della Madonna* (Rome, 1954). Sang Manon Lescaut, 25th anniversary of Rome Teatro Reale. Created Anna in Rossellini's *Il vortice* (Naples, 1958). During 1950s and 1960s considered one of the best singing-actresses in Italy and was dubbed 'the Duse of singers'. (R)

Petrella, Errico (*b* Palermo, 10 Dec. 1813; *d* Genoa, 7 Apr. 1877). Italian composer. Studied Naples, e.g. with Bellini and Zingarelli. When only 15 he wrote, against the will of his teachers, an opera *Il diavolo color di rosa*, which had a great success; for this, he was expelled from the Conservatory. He continued to write operas, until a quarrel in 1839 interrupted his career; he resumed it in 1851 with the successful *Le precauzioni*, then with *Elena di Tolosa* (1852) and *Mario Visconti* (1854), the latter rivalling even Verdi's *Il trovatore* in the same season. Taken up by the firm of Lucca as rival to Ricordi's Verdi, he wrote a number of well-received works, of which the most widely publicized was *I promessi sposi* (1869). Though his music had an appeal in its day, his success was ephemeral, with subjects that really demanded greater imaginative control than he could give them; but though old-fashioned towards the end of his time, he did command a lyrical manner in the central Italian tradition.

Petrograd. See *Leningrad*.

Petrov (orig. Krause), **Ivan** (Ivanovich) (*b* Irkutsk, 29 Feb. 1920). Russian bass. Studied Moscow, Glazunov School, with Mineyev. Début Moscow, B. Filial, 1943, Capulet. Guest appearances throughout Europe including Paris, O., 1954, Boris. Roles include Don Basilio, Ruslan, Kochubey, Dosifey, Méphistophélès, Philip. (R)

Petrov, Osip (Afanasyevich) (*b* Elizavetgrad, 15 Nov. 1806; *d* St Petersburg, 12 Mar. 1878). Russian bass. First sang in church choir, then with various local troupes (Zhurakhovsky's and Stein's: sang in Cavos's *Cossack Poet*, 1826). Heard by the St Petersburg director Lebedev singing in Kursk, and engaged: début St Petersburg, M., 1830, Sarastro, and worked there until 1878. One of the greatest of all Russian basses, he at once set an example for Russian composers of the emerging nationalist school and became one of their finest interpreters. He was accordingly sought out to create most of the important bass parts of new operas performed in St Petersburg in the period: these included Ivan Susanin, Ruslan, the Miller (*Rusalka*), Leporello (*Stone Guest*), Ivan (*Maid of Pskov*), Varlaam, the Mayor (*Vakula the Smith*), and many others, especially in works

by Rubinstein and Serov. A close friend of Mussorgsky, whose theories of realism greatly influenced his dramatic ideals. His voice ranged from B♭ to g♯.
Bibl: E. Lastochkina: *Osip Afanasyevich Petrov* (1950). V. Stasov: *Osip Afanasyevich Petrov* (1952).

Pfitzner, Hans (Erich) (*b* Moscow, 5 May 1869; *d* Salzburg, 22 May 1949). German composer. Studied Frankfurt with Knorr and Kwast, Wiesbaden with Riemann. Cond. Mainz 1894-6, Berlin 1903-6, Strasbourg 1908-18 (director 1910-16). A great admirer of Wagner and Schopenhauer, he expressed dislike for modernistic tendencies in music and became a fervent nationalist. His operas have enjoyed little success outside Germany; even there, the general public has not been unanimous in its acceptance of his operas, though the much respected *Palestrina* (1917) has become a regular feature of the Munich Summer Festivals, and may also be heard regularly in Vienna. His other operas are *Der arme Heinrich* (1895), *Die Rose vom Liebesgarten* (1901), *Christelflein* (1906, rev. 1917), and *Das Herz* (1931).

Pforzheim. Town in Baden-Württemberg, Germany. Opera was given by travelling companies in the 18th cent. The present City T., (cap. 437) opened in 1948, and has staged premieres of works by Eastwood, Rivière, Chailly, and Sauguet.

Philadelphia. Town in Pennsylvania, U.S.A. The first opera heard there was *Flora or Hob in the Well*, a ballad opera by an unknown composer, on 7 May 1754 at Plumsted's Warehouse. Most opera in the first half of the 19th cent. took place at the Chestnut Street Theatre, known as 'Old Drury'. The first 'grand' opera given there was *Der Freischütz* in 1825. A French company from New Orleans appeared there annually 1827-31, and the Havana Italian Opera Company gave the first Italian opera there, Mayr's *Che originali*, in 1829. *Norma* had its first American performance there in 1841, in an English translation by J.R. Fry. Fry's brother, the composer William H. Fry, wrote the 'first publicly performed grand opera written by a native American', *Leonora*, with a libretto by J.R. Fry and based on Lytton's *The Lady of Lyons*; it had its first performance on 4 June 1845 and was given 16 times in the 1845-6 season.

The Philadelphia Academy of Music, opened Jan. 1857, is the oldest opera house in continuous use in the U.S.A. In 1859 Edward, Prince of Wales, travelling incognito as Baron Renfrew, attended a performance given in his honour – he was 19; and Patti, aged 16, sang in *Martha*. Up to the end of the century many works had their first U.S. performances in Philadelphia including *Luisa Miller*, *Faust* (in

German), *Die lustigen Weiber von Windsor,
Der fliegende Holländer* (in Italian), *Pagliacci,
Cavalleria rusticana, L'Amico Fritz, Les
Pêcheurs de perles,* and *Manon Lescaut.*

Companies which have functioned in
Philadelphia include a Philadelphia O. that
gave performances in English under Gustav
Heinrichs 1891-6, under Damrosch 1896-7, and
Damrosch and Ellis 1897-9. The Metropolitan
O. appeared regularly there 1899-1961 (except
1934) giving weekly performances, generally
on Tuesday evenings, at the Academy of
Music. In 1910-14 the Chicago Grand O.C. was
known as the Chicago-Philadelphia Grand O.,
as financial support came from both cities, and
the company gave a two to three month season
in Philadelphia. During this time a number of
works had their first U.S. performances,
including Herbert's *Natoma,* Goldmark's *The
Cricket on the Hearth,* and Franchetti's *Cristoforo Colombo;* the seasons by the Chicago-
Philadelphia C. were given in the Metropolitan
O.H., built by Hammerstein in 1908 to house
the performances of his Manhattan Company,
and originally known as the Philadelphia Opera
House.

The Philadelphia Civic O., founded in 1923
with Alexander Smallens as music director,
was renamed the Philadelphia Lyric O.C. in
1958; it gave a number of first U.S. performances including Korngold's *Der Ring des
Polycrates* and Strauss's *Feuersnot* and
Ariadne auf Naxos. The Pennsylvania Grand
O.C., under the artistic direction of Franco
Pelosi, was active 1927-30, and gave the U.S.
première of *Khovanshchina* and the Philadelphia première of *The Demon;* this company
developed into the Philadelphia La Scala C.,
and then into the Philadelphia Grand O.C. The
Lyric and the Grand finally merged into the
Philadelphia O.C., under the artistic direction of
Carl Suppa, in March 1975.

Other important if short-lived operatic enter-
prises included the Philadelphia Grand O.,
1926-32, which launched the careers of Helen
Jepson, Rose Bampton, Nino Martini, and
John Charles Thomas, and the Philadelphia
Orchestra O.C., 1930-5, which gave the
American premières of *Die glückliche Hand,
Wozzeck* (in collaboration with the Philadelphia
Grand), *Mavra,* and *Iphigénie en Aulide;*
Stokowski, Goossens, and Reiner conducted
several performances. In 1938 the Philadelphia
O.C. was founded by David Hocker, with
Sylvan Levin as music director, to give opera in
English; it gave the première of Menotti's *The
Old Maid and the Thief.* The Curtis Institute has
staged student and semi-professional perfor-
mances, and gave the première of Menotti's
Amelia al ballo in a double bill with the first
American performance of *Le Pauvre matelot.*

Philidor (orig. Danican), **François André** (*b*

Dreux, 7 Sept. 1726; *d* London, 24 Aug. 1795).
French composer. Studied with Campra. His
proficiency as a chess-player – he toured as a
master and published a study of the game –
was one facet of a gift for calculation that made
him the first truly learned composer of *opéras
comiques.* His operas include *Blaise le savetier*
(1759), *Le Maréchal ferrant* (1761); *Le Sorcier*
(1764: the first occasion on which a composer
was accorded a curtain call), *Tom Jones* (1765),
Ernelinde (1767), and *Le Bon fils* (1773). He did
much to develop the art of opéra comique, both
by the greater character he gave to melody and
his richer harmonic palette (especially in
modulation) and by novelties he introduced,
such as the unaccompanied canon quartet in
Tom Jones. He also had vivid imitative powers,
and brought into his scores the sounds of a
hammer, or a donkey, or other effects to under-
line the text wittily; and he gave the orchestra a
more powerful expressive role in ostensibly
light works.

Bibl: G. Allen: *The Life of Philidor* (1858).

Philip II. The King of Spain (bass) in Verdi's *Don
Carlos.*

Piacenza. Town in Piacenza, Italy. Opera was
first given at the T. di Palazzo Gotico in 1644,
where Cavalli's *Coriolano* had its première in
1669. Other theatres were T. delle Saline and T.
della Cittadella. The T. Comunale opened in
1834 with Mayr's *Zamori o L'eroe delle Indie.*

Piave, Francesco Maria (*b* Murano, 18 May
1810; *d* Milan, 5 Mar. 1876). Italian librettist. A
close friend of Verdi; provided the libretto of
*Ernani, La forza del destino, Macbeth, Simone
Boccanegra , Rigoletto, La traviata, Il corsaro,
Stiffelio, Aroldo,* and *I due Foscari.* Also wrote
librettos for Balfe, Mercadante, Ricci, and
others. A complaisant colleague, he saw his
role as servant to Verdi's demands, and was
prepared to listen to, and answer, the most
detailed instructions about versification.

Piccaver, Alfred (*b* Long Sutton, 15 Feb. 1884; *d*
Vienna, 23 Sept. 1958). English tenor. Studied
N.Y. Début Prague 1907, Roméo; then studied
Milan and Prague. Leading tenor Vienna 1910-
37, where he sang in the first performances in
Austria of *La fanciulla del West* and *Il tabarro;*
Chicago 1923-5; London, C.G., 1924. Possessed a large velvety voice which he used
with skill; noted for the smoothness of his
legato and expansive phrasing. From 1937 until
1955 lived in London, taking a few pupils, and
returned to Vienna for the reopening of the
S.O. in 1955 as an honoured guest, remaining
there as a teacher until his death. (R)

Picchi, Mirto (*b* S. Mauro, Florence, 15 March
1915). Italian tenor. Studied Milan. Début
Milan, Palazzo dello Sport, 1946, Radamès.
London, Cambridge T., 1947-8 Duke of Mantua,

Cavaradossi, Rodolfo; C.G., 1952-3 Pollione; Edinburgh Festival, 1949 Riccardo (*Ballo in maschera*). Has sung in most leading opera houses. In addition to a vast classical repertory, created leading roles in works by Pizzetti, Castro, Lizzi, Testi etc. First Italian Billy Budd and an admired Grimes. A highly musical performer and gifted actor. Retired from stage 1974; last role, Basilio in *Figaro*, Milan, Sc. (R)

Piccinni, Niccolò (*b* Bari, 16 Jan. 1728; *d* Passy, 7 May 1800). Italian composer. Studied Naples with Leo and Durante. He made his début in 1754 with *Le donne dispettose*, quickly following this success up with a series of operas that culminated in *La cecchina, ossia La buona figliuola* (1760). By far the most successful opera buffa of its day in Italy, *La buona figliuola* (as it is generally known) led to a number of imitations, and is still sometimes revived in Italy. *L'Olimpiade* (1768) followed. Rivalry with Anfossi upset Piccinni, but he continued composing, then left for Paris. His first French opera, *Roland* (1778), was not finished when there broke out the famous Gluck-Piccinni feud, one fostered not by the composers but by their supporters. Paris was soon ranged in two camps. An enterprising director arranged for them both to compose an *Iphigénie en Tauride*, but Piccinni's (1781), though containing many beauties, could not rival Gluck's. After Gluck's departure a new rival arose in Sacchini, and though *Didon* (1783) proved Piccinni's best opera, his star was on the wane. At the Revolution he returned to Naples (1789), where he was involved in political trouble. He was fêted on his return to Paris in 1789, but never regained his old position.

With Paisiello, Cimarosa, and Guglielmi, Piccinni represents the last great generation of the Neapolitan school. His strengths lay in his mastery of detail: he could write a gentle, elegiac vein of melody entirely his own, and he brought a new fluency into the handling of orchestral accompaniments to arias; certain harmonic characteristics. such as an effective use of major-minor relationships, impressed many later Italian composers, including Bellini. *La buona figliuola* is a milestone of Italian comic opera, especially in giving prominence to emotional arias, but also in a number of innovatory details such as the introduction of Rondo finales (among the first in Italian opera). Nevertheless, Piccinni's strength lay in his contribution, to a traditional framework, of apt and telling details and sensitively handled incidents: he did not, like Gluck, command a strong overall view of opera as drama. It has been well said that his art was of the kind that adapts itself to its age, where Gluck's is the art to which the age must adapt itself.

His son **Luigi** (*b* Naples, 1766; *d* Passy, 31 Aug. 1827) wrote a number of French and Ital-

ian operas for Paris and Naples. His grandson (illegitimate son of his elder son Giuseppe) **Louis Alexandre** (*b* Paris, 10 Sept. 1779; *d* Paris, 24 Apr. 1850) was accompanist at the T. Feydeau and (1802-6) at the Opéra: he wrote over 200 stage works, including 25 comic operas (performed at various Paris theatres: *Alcibiade solitaire* was given at the O., 1824). *Bibl*: A. Della Corte: *Piccinni* (1928).

Piccola Scala, La. See *La Scala*.

Piccolo Marat, Il. Opera in 3 acts by Mascagni; text by Forzano and Targioni-Tozzetti. Prod. Rome, C., 2 May 1921 with Dalla Rizza, Lazaro, Franci, Badini, cond. Mascagni. Prod. in several countries outside Italy, and revived in Italy from time to time. One of Mascagni's more successful works. An opera about the fanatics who terrorized Paris after the assassination of the revolutionary Jean-Paul Marat by Charlotte Corday.

The Prince Jean-Charles de Fleury (ten.), in order to free his mother from prison, joins the revolution and becomes known as the Piccolo Marat (the 'little' Marat). With the help of his lover Mariella (sop.) and the Carpenter (bar.), they force the President of the revolutionary council (bass) to sign a release order for the imprisoned princess, and all escape to freedom.

Piccolomini, Marietta (*b* Siena, 15 Mar. 1834; *d* Poggio Imperiale, 23 Dec. 1899). Italian soprano. Studied Florence with Rosa Mazzarelli and Raimondi. Début Florence, Teatro Pergola, 1852, Lucrezia Borgia; London, H.M.'s 1856, Violetta in English première of *Traviata*; was the first interpreter of Luisa Miller in London 1858, and Arline in the Italian version of *The Bohemian Girl*. U.S.A. 1858. Married the Marchese Gaetani della Fargia in 1860 and retired from the stage, apart from one appearance at Lumley's Benefit at D.L., 1863. Admired more for her beauty and histrionic abilities than for her voice, which aroused much adverse criticism.

Pierné, Gabriel (*b* Metz, 16 Aug. 1863; *d* Ploujean, 17 July 1937). French composer. His long list of works includes eight operas, of which the most successful have been *La Coupe enchantée* (1895) and *On ne badine pas avec l'amour* (1910). Also wrote opera, *Sophie *Arnould* (1927).

Pietra del Paragone, La (The Touchstone). *Melodramma giocoso* or *opera buffa* in 2 acts by Rossini; text by Luigi Romanelli. Prod. Milan, Sc., 26 Sept. 1812, (Rossini's first opera for Sc.); with Marietta, Marcolini, Zerbini, Fei, Vasoli, Galli, Bonoldi, Parlamagni, Rossignoli Hartford, Hart Coll. of Music, 4 May 1955, with Kallisti, Dippe, De Vita, Verduce, Stuart, cond. Paranov; London, St Pancras T.H., 19 Mar.

1963, by Group Eight, with Clark, Bainbridge, Sarti, Robertson, Hammond-Stroud, Mangin, Wicks, cond. Fredman.

The wealthy Count Asdrubale (bar.) puts to the test three young widows who want to marry him. Disguising himself, he produces a document declaring the Count bankrupt. Only Clarice (mezzo) remains loyal. She then in turn tests the Count, disguising herself as her twin brother and threatening to remove Clarice. All ends happily.

Pilarczyk, Helga (*b* Schöningen, nr Brunswick, 12 Mar. 1925). German soprano. Studied Hamburg and Hanover. Début Brunswick 1951 (mezzo-sop.), Irmentraud (*Der Waffenschmied*). Hamburg Opera 1954-1967, where she specialized in modern roles—the Woman in *Erwartung*, Marie in *Wozzeck*, Lulu, etc.—as well as in Verdi and Strauss. Gly., 1958; London, C.G., 1958; Holland Festival; U.S.A., Washington, 1962. Chicago, 1964. One of the most intelligent and intensely dramatic artists of the day. (R)

Pilgrims' Chorus. The chorus of pilgrims on their march to and from Rome in Acts 1 and 3 of Wagner's *Tannhäuser.*

Pilgrim's Progress, The. Morality in 4 acts by Vaughan Williams; text by composer, after Bunyan's allegory (Pt. 1, 1674-9; Pt. 2, 1684). Prod. London, C.G., 26 Apr. 1951, with Matters, Te Wiata, Walker, E. Evans. cond. Hancock. Pilgrim's journey towards the Heavenly City is shown in a series of scenes depicting his most famous encounters, one of which, that with the Shepherds of the the Delectable Mountains, Vaughan Williams had set as a 1-act, 'pastoral episode' in 1922 and later incorporated into the main work.

Pimen. A monk (bass) in Mussorgsky's *Boris Godunov.*

Pini-Corsi, Antonio (*b* Zara, June 1858; *d* Milan, 22 Apr. 1918). Italian baritone. Début Cremona 1878, Dandini. Chosen by Verdi to create Ford in *Falstaff* at Sc. 1893. London, C.G., 1894-6, 1902-3; N.Y., Met., 1909-14 where he sang in the first performances of *La fanciulla del West* (Happy), *Königskinder* (Inn-keeper), and other works, and in the American premières of *Le donne curiose, L'amore medico,* and *Germania.* His Bartolo, Pasquale, Leporello, etc. were considered the finest of his day. (R) His brother **Gaetano Pini-Corsi** (*b* Empoli, 1860) made his début Empoli 1881, Ernesto. After a successful career in leading roles assumed character roles, and became noted for his Mime, David, and Cassio. Created Goro (*Butterfly*). At a Festival in 1883 in Sampierarena, he sang Manrico, his brother Count Luna, and their respective wives Leonora and Azucena.

Pinkerton. The American naval lieutenant (ten.) in Puccini's *Madama Butterfly.*

Pinto, Amalia (*b* Palermo, 1878; *d* Palermo, 21 June 1946). Italian soprano. Studied Rome. Début Brescia, 1899 Gioconda. Milan, Sc., from 1900 as Gioconda, Brünnhilde, Isolde, Tosca, and Queen of Sheba. Created Ricke in Franchetti's *Germania* (1902). Retired 1914 and lived in Palermo, where she taught. (R)

Pinza, Ezio (orig. Fortunio) (*b* Rome, 18 May 1892; *d* Stamford, Conn., 9 May 1957). Italian bass. Studied Bologna. Début Soncino 1914, Oroveso, then four years of military service; real début Rome 1920, Comte Des Grieux. Milan, Sc., 1921-4; N.Y., Met., 1926-48; London, C.G., 1930-9. Generally regarded as the greatest Italian bass of the inter-war years, possessing a beautiful, noble, basso-cantante voice, an imposing stage presence, and great dramatic ability. Chosen by Bruno Walter to sing Don Giovanni and Figaro at Salzburg 1934-7; was the first Met. Fiesco (*Boccanegra*), Gaudenzio (*Signor Bruschino*), and Chervek (*Sorochintsy Fair*). Appeared in every major opera house in the world, and had a repertory of more than 95 roles; sang Don Giovanni more then 200 times, and sang more than 750 times in 50 operas during his engagement with the Met. In 1949 appeared in *South Pacific* and then in *Fanny,* and made a number of films. (R) His daughter **Claudia** (sop.) had a brief career in the 1940s.

Pipe of Desire, The. Opera in 1 act by Converse; text by George Edward Burton. Prod. Boston 31 Jan. 1906, with Cushingchild, Deane, Townsend, cond. Goodrich. The first American opera to be prod. at the Met., 18 Mar. 1910, with Homer, Martin, Whitehill, cond. Hertz.

A magic pipe belonging to the Elf King (bass) is selfishly used by Iolan (ten.) and brings disaster to himself and to his lover Naoia (sop.). The King pipes, and they die.

Piper, John (*b* 13 Dec. 1903). English painter. One of the founder members of the E.O.G. in 1947 (with Benjamin Britten and Eric Crozier). Some of his designs for the Group, for Gly., C.G., and S.W., have been among the best to be seen in England since the war. His sets for Britten's operas—*The Rape of Lucretia, Albert Herring, Billy Budd, Gloriana, The Turn of the Screw, A Midsummer Night's Dream, Owen Wingrave,* and *Death in Venice* – have been particularly distinguished. Those for *The Magic Flute* at C.G., *Don Giovanni* at Glyndebourne, and *The Pearl Fishers* at S.W. were less so. His wife **Myfanwy** has acted as librettist for Britten with three excellent texts for *The Turn of the Screw, Owen Wingrave,* and *Death in Venice.*

Pirata, Il (The Pirate). Opera in 2 acts by Bellini; text by Romani. Prod. Milan, Sc., 27 Oct. 1827, with Méric-Lalande, Rubini, Tamburini, cond. Lavigna; London, H.M.'s, 17 Apr. 1830, same cast – first Bellini opera in London; N.Y., Richmond Hill T., 5 Dec. 1832, with Pedrotti, Verducci, Montressor, Fornasari, Placci, Sapignoli, cond. Rapetti.

Imogene (sop.), married against her will in a useless attempt to save her father's life, is deserted by her lover and accused of adultery by her husband. He is killed by the man she loves, who is then condemned to death. Imogene then loses her reason.

Pirogov. Family of Russian singers.

(1) **Alexander** (Stepanovich) (*b* Ryazan, 4 July 1899; *d* Moscow, 26 June 1964). Russian bass. Studied Moscow with Vasily Tyutyunnik. Sang in choir 1919-22. Moscow, Z., 1922-4; B., from 1924. His roles included Boris, Méphistophélès, Ivan the Terrible (*Maid of Pskov*), Ivan Susanin, Ruslan, Pestel (*The Decembrists*), etc. (R)

(2) **Grigory** (*b* Ryazan, 1885; *d* Leningrad, 20 Feb. 1931), his brother, was also a bass. Studied Moscow with Medvedyev and Donsky. Began singing in Rostov, Shumsky's Co. Début Moscow, B., 1908, Caspar; B., 1908-20, also singing St Petersburg, M., 1909-10. Possessed a voice of very wide range, and sang Marcel (*Huguenots*) as well as Escamillo, Boris, Dodon, Marcel, etc. Sang in Berlin, Paris, Pest, Riga, Copenhagen, and elsewhere. A famous Russian Wotan. Retired 1930.

(3) **Alexey** (stage name, Pirogov-Okskin) (*b* 21 Feb. 1895) was another brother who studied Moscow with Donsky; worked in Tashkent and Sverdlovsk, and Novosibirsk, also sang at the B., 1931-48: his roles included Boris, Varlaam, Pimen, Dosifey, and Soviet works. A fourth brother, **Mikhail** (*b* ?, 29 Dec. 1887; *d* ? 1933) was also a bass who sang with the Moscow Z., 1922-3, Ivan Khovansky etc.

Bibl: I. Remezov: G.S. Pirogov (1951).

Pisaroni, Benedetta Rosamunda (*b* Piacenza, 16 May 1793; *d* Piacenza, 6 Aug. 1872). Italian soprano, later contralto. Studied with four male sopranos, Moschini, Marchesi, Velluti, and Pacchierotti. Début Bergamo 1811, *La rosa bianca e la rosa rossa*; mezzo début 1814 Padua. A serious illness affected her high notes, and after a brilliant career as a soprano she developed her lower register so successfully that she became known as the first Italian contralto. She was so conscious of the facial disfiguration she had suffered as a result of smallpox that she always warned impresarios by sending them her picture. A fine actress as well as a fine singer, excelling in the Rossini repertory. Created Zomira in *Ricciardo e Zoraide* (1818), Malcolme Graeme in *La donna del lago* (1819), and Andromaca in *Ermione* (also 1819). London 1829. Retired from the stage in the early 1830s (last appearances

Milan, 1831, Piacenza, 1832) when she found her popularity waning. Last concert, Piacenza, February 1835.

Pischner, Hans (*b* Breslau, 20 Feb. 1914). German pianist and administrator. Studied Breslau. Director Weimar Hochschule for Musik 1947-56. Minister for Culture D.D.R., 1956-63; general administrator, Berlin State Opera, since 1963.

Pistocchi, Francesco Antonio (*b* Palermo, 1659; *d* Bologna 13 May 1726). Italian male contralto and composer. Studied Bologna. His first opera, *Capricci puerili*, was prod. Bologna, 1667. Début as singer 1675, Ferrara. After appearances in Parma and Vienna he opened a singing school in Bologna in 1705, which became the most famous in Italy; his pupils included Bernacchi, Pasi, Mirelli, and Fabri.

Pitt, Percy (*b* London, 4 Jan. 1870; *d* London, 23 Nov. 1932). English conductor. Studied Leipzig and Munich. Apptd. music adviser and assistant conductor C.G., 1902; music director Grand Opera Syndicate 1907-24; collaborated with Richter in the production of the English *Ring* (1908-9); Beecham Opera Company 1915-18. Artistic director B.N.O.C. 1920-4, after which he devoted most of his time to the B.B.C. Conducted the first C.G. performances of *Bastien und Bastienne*, *L'Enfant prodigue*, *Ivanhoe*, *Joseph*, *L'Heure espagnole*, *Thérèse*, *Khovanschchina*, *The Goldsmith of Toledo*, and *Fête galante*. (R)

Bibl: I.D. Chamier: *Percy Pitt of Covent Garden and the B.B.C.* (1958).

Pixérécourt, (René-Charles) **Guilbert de** (*b* Nancy, 22 Jan. 1773; *d* Nanay, 25 July 1844). French playwright. The father of the French *mélodrame*, with its insistence on moral subjects; he also influenced the librettos of his time, both by his example and as director of the O.C. 1822-7. His *mélodrames* make skilful use of music to heighten dramatic tension, and were deliberately designed for popular appeal with their stereotyped innocent heroine, virtuous hero, evil villain, etc; 'I wrote for those who could not read'. Donizetti's *Chiara e Serafina* and *Otto mesi in due ore* and Meyerbeer's *Margharita d'Anjou* are based on his plays. Also had some influence on the later Romantic drama (Dumas and Hugo) and thence on Romantic opera.

Pixis, Johann Peter (*b* Mannheim, 10 Feb. 1788; *d* Baden-Baden, 22 Dec. 1874). German pianist and composer, son and pupil of Friedrich Wilhelm Pixis. One of the most brilliant and successful pianists of his time, and the composer of much virtuoso piano music; he also wrote four operas, *Almazinde* (1820), *Der Zauberspruch* (1822), *Bibiana* (1829), and *Die Sprache des Herzens* (1836). His adopted daughter **Francilla** (orig. Göhringer) (*b* Lichtenthal, 1816, *d* ?) was a contralto who made her début in Karlsruhe 1834 and appeared in Munich, Leipzig, Milan, Berlin, Paris, and London; she was particularly successful in Naples, where Pacini wrote *Saffo* for her.

Pizarro. (1) The evil prison governor (bar.) in Beethoven's *Fidelio*. (2) Francisco Pizarro (*c*1478-1578), Spanish conqueror of Peru, hero of a number of operas.

Pizzetti, Ildebrando (*b* Parma, 20 Sept. 1880; *d* Rome, 13 Feb. 1968). Italian composer. After studying at Reggio Emilia and Parma he began to show an interest in the theatre, and his early attempts at opera included *Sabina* (1897), *Giulietta e Romeo* (1899), and *Il Cid* (1902), which he entered for the Sonzogno competition for 1-act operas. Between 1903 and 1907 he started work on a number of opera projects and abandoned them–*Sardanapalo* (Byron), *Mazeppa* (Pushkin), and *Aeneas* (Virgil) were all begun. In 1905 he came under the influence of D'Annunzio and composed some incidental music for his tragedy *La Nave*. Soon afterwards he began work on the same author's *Fedra*, based on the Greek tragedy, which was produced at Milan Sc. in 1915. The libretto is wordy and the music not as free and expressive as in his later works. Thereafter he provided his own librettos for all his operas except *Ifigenia* (1950, for which he collaborated with A. Perrini), *La figlia di Jorio* (1954, for which he adapted D'Annunzio's play), *L'assassinio nella cattedrale* (1958, for which Alberto Castelli adapted T.S. Eliot), and *Il calzare d'argento* (1961, for which Riccardo Bacchelli wrote the text). *Debora e Jaele* (1922) is generally regarded as the best example of his conception of music-drama. *Lo straniero* (1930) and *Fra Gherardo* (1928) are both conceived in the same spirit. In his later works Pizzetti exhibits a tendency to the *arioso* type of opera–*Orsèolo* (1935), *L'Oro* (1938-42 but not produced until 1947), *Vanna Lupa* (1949), *Ifigenia* (his radio opera–1950), *Cagliostro* (1953), and *La figlia di Jorio* and *L'assassinio nella cattedrale* mentioned above. These last two works have enjoyed success outside Italy. He announced that he was closing his career with *Clittenestra* (1965).
Bibl: G.M. Gatti: *Pizzetti* (1951).

Pizzi, Pier Luigi (*b* Milan, 15 June 1930). Italian designer. Studied Milan School of Architecture. Began designing opera in 1952, since when has designed productions for most leading opera houses in Europe and America, including *The Queen of Spades* for Glyndebourne, *Walküre* and *Siegfried* for Milan, Sc., and *Guillaume Tell* and *Orfeo* for Florence. Began producing opera, 1977.

Plaichinger, Thila (*b* Vienna, 13 Mar. 1868; *d*

Vienna, 17 Mar. 1939). Austrian soprano. Studied Vienna with Gänsbacher, Dustmann, and Mampe-Babbrigg. Début Hamburg 1893; after engagements at Strasbourg and Munich was leading soprano at Berlin 1901-14; London, C.G., 1904 as Isolde, Venus, and Ortrud, 1910 as Elektra, of which role she was the first interpreter in Berlin. She sang small roles at Bayreuth in 1896 and 1897. After leaving the stage she taught in Berlin and Vienna. (R)

Planché, James Robinson (*b* London, 27 Feb. 1796; *d* London, 29 May 1880). English theatrical writer. Translated many operas for the English stage, including works by Rossini, Auber, Marschner, Bellini (*Norma*), Hérold, Offenbach, and Mozart (*Magic Flute* and *Marriage of Figaro*). His version of Weber's *Der Freischütz* led Kemble to engage him as the librettist for *Oberon*. The form this took reflects not only Planché's assessment of the contemporary English musical theatre, and what would be acceptable, but his own interest in pantomimes and in historical costume. His *Recollections and Reflections* (2 vols., 1872) give a detailed picture of the theatrical life of his day.

Plançon, Pol (*b* Fumax, 12 July 1854; *d* Paris, 11 Aug. 1914). French bass. Studied Paris with Duprez and Sbriglia. Début Lyons 1877, St Bris; Paris 1880, Opéra from 1883 to 1893; London, C.G., 1891-1904; N.Y., Met., 1893-1908. He created Don Gormas in *Le Cid*, Francis I in Saint-Saëns's *Ascanio* in Paris, Garrido in *La Navarraise*, Francis in *Much Ado About Nothing* (Stanford), and the King in *Princess Osra* (Bunning) at C.G. He was the most admired Méphistophélès of his day, and was also at home in the German and Italian repertory. His voice was a true bass of enormous range, smooth and even and extremely flexible. His runs and trills were said to be the envy of many a soprano. (R)

Planquette, (Jean) **Robert** (*b* Paris, 31 July 1848; *d* Paris, 28 Jan 1903). French composer. Studied Paris with Duprato. After trying to earn a living by making arrangements and by playing the piano in cafés, he had some 1-act operettas performed at the Eldorado Music Hall and the Délassements-Comiques; then achieved his greatest success with *Les Cloches de Corneville* (1877: 400 consecutive performances at the Folies Dramatiques). He wrote *Rip van Winkle* for London (1882), following this with *Nell Gwynne* (1884), and adapting other works for the English stage. Among his later works *Mam'zelle Quat'sous* (1897) is outstanding, but on the whole they were not well received. A careful and stylish composer, with a lively melodic vein, he lacked the ease and variety of invention to keep his name before a public notorious for tiring quickly of anything lacking novelty.

Plaschke, Friedrich (orig. Bedřich Plaške) (*b* Jaroměř, 7 Jan. 1875; *d* Prague, 4 Feb. 1952). Czech bass-baritone. Studied Prague with Leontine von Dötscher and Ottilie Sklenář-Mala, and Dresden with Karl Scheidemantel. Début Dresden 1900, Herald in *Lohengrin*. Member of Dresden company until 1937, where he created Pöschel in *Feuersnot* (1901), 1st Nazarene in *Salome* (1903), Arcesius in *Die toten Augen* (1916), Altair in *Aegyptische Helena* (1928), Waldner in *Arabella* (1933), and Sir Morosus in *Schweigsame Frau* (1935); he was also the first Dresden Barak. Bayreuth 1911; London, C.G., 1914 Amfortas, Kurwenal, and Sachs; U.S.A. with German O., 1923, Kurwenal and Telramund. (R) Married the soprano Eva von der *Osten. (R)

Plovdiv. Town in Bulgaria. Long dependent on visiting Italian companies, which from the 1880s (F. de Lucia, 1889) played in the Luxembourg T. and Bulgarian T.; interest in them led to the formation of a local society (1896). In 1920 the tenor Alexander Krayev (1885-1958) formed an operatic group which began with Hadjigeorgyev's *Takhir Begovitsa*. In 1922 the Plovdiv City Opera was organized: it began with *La Juive*. Seasons continued until the war. The Plovdiv National Opera was formed in 1953, and began with *The Bartered Bride*; it has developed a good international repertory.

Plzeň (Ger., Pilsen). Town in Czechoslovakia. Opera is given in the J.K. Tyl T. (cap. 1,000) 3-4 times a week by a company of about 30 soloists.

Poggi, Antonio (*b* Castel S. Pietro, Bologna, 1806; *d* Bologna, 15 Apr. 1875). Italian tenor. Studied with Celli-Corticelli and Nozzari. Début Paris 1827, Giacomo in *Donna del lago* (a fiasco); then Bologna Dec. 1827 as Peter the Great in Pacini's *Il falegname di Livonia*; Milan, Sc., 1834-6 and 1845; created Carlo VII in Verdi's *Giovanna d'Arco*; Vienna, K., 1835-40. Married the soprano *Frezzolini 1841-6.

Pogner. The goldsmith, Eva's father (bass), in Wagner's *Die Meistersinger*.

Poisoned Kiss, The. Romantic extravaganza in 3 acts by Vaughan Williams; text by Evelyn Sharp, after Richard Garnett's story *The Poison Maid* in the collection *The Twilight of the Gods* (1888). Prod. Cambridge 12 May 1936, with Field-Hyde, Ritchie, Jones, Dunn, cond. Rootham; N.Y., Juilliard School, 21 Apr. 1937.

The fantastic plot turns on the rivalry of a sorcerer and an empress; his daughter Tormentilla (sop.) has been brought up on poisons so that when she meets the empress's son Amaryllus (ten.) she will kill him with her kiss. In the end the sincerity of their love defeats the plot.

Poissl, Johann Nepomuk von (*b* Haukenzell, 15 Feb. 1783; *d* Munich, 17 Aug. 1865). German composer. Studied Munich with Danzi and Vogler. His first opera was the comic *Die Opernprobe* (1806), but his first real successes were the serious *Antigonus* (1808) and the *dramma eroico, Ottaviano in Sicilia* (1812). Meanwhile he had met Weber in 1811, from whose friendship and championship he greatly benefited. He continued his operatic career with *Athalia* (1814) and *Der Wettkampf zu Olympia* (1815); their success did not bring him much material reward, and he was further disappointed of hopes of an appointment to Darmstadt, for which he composed the successful *Nittetis* (1817) and *Issipile* (unprod.). In 1823 he gained a court appointment in Munich, and in 1825 became director of the Court Theatre; but the theatre lost money and he was forced to resign in 1832. Though he seldom staged his own operas, he did reopen the Nationaltheater after the 1823 fire with *Die Prinzessin von Provence* (1825), and later produced his *Untersberg* (1829) and *Zaide* (1843). He died in poverty.

Poissl is important as a transitional figure between Mozart and Weber, and was one of the first German composers to make a constructive attempt to move away from Italian and French example in favour of a continuously-composed German opera. Weber praised *Der Wettkampf* and *Athalia* for their melodic qualities, commending the latter as a national achievement. Poissl was ahead of his time in writing most of his own librettos, and he published criticism and essays on theatre organization.

Polacco, Giorgio (*b* Venice, 12 Apr. 1874; *d* New York, 30 Apr. 1960). Italian conductor. Studied St Petersburg, Venice and Milan. Assistant C.G., 1890, *Cavalleria rusticana*. Début London, Shaftesbury T., 1893, replacing an indisposed Arditi in a performance of Orfeo. After engagements throughout Italy, and appearances in Brussels, Lisbon, Warsaw etc., he conducted the Italian première of *L'Attaque du moulin* (Milan 1898) and the première of *Zazà* (Milan 1900). Engaged seven seasons at Rio, where he conducted local premières of *Bohème*, *Chénier, Tosca*, and *Boris*. Toured U.S. 1911-2 with the English production of *La fanciulla*. N.Y., Met., 1912-17, during which period he conducted 342 performances. Chicago Opera 1918-19, 1921-30, directing many memorable performances of French operas with Mary Garden, as well as the Italian and German repertory. London, C.G., 1913-14 and 1930. Forced by ill health to retire at the height of his powers.

Poland. Opera was first given in Poland in 1613, when Prince Stanisław Lubomirski invited an Italian company to perform at his residence at

Wiśnicz. In 1625, Prince Władisław Zygmunt visited the Grand Duchess of Tuscany, and operas were given in his honour including the première of Francesca Caccini's *La liberazione di Ruggero dall'isola d'Alcina* (the first opera by a woman). This may have been heard in Poland soon afterwards: certainly a Polish translation was published in Kraków in 1628. The Prince was crowned Władisław IV in 1632, and founded an Italian company with Margherita Cattaneo as prima donna; it included some young Poles. About twelve operas, probably adaptations, were performed and published, including one by a Polish composer, Piotr Elert, *La fama reale* (1633). The librettos were mostly written by Virgilio Puccitelli, and the music to some of the operas was by Marco Sacchi.

Frederick Augustus, Elector of Saxony, was crowned Augustus II in 1697; he did almost nothing for his new country's art, but he did bring in his retinue an ensemble directed by J.C. Schmidt and Jacek Różycki. In 1700 a company of 60, formed in Paris at his request by Angelo Costantini, was brought, under Deschallières; other companies also toured Poland. In 1725 the Operalnia (Opera T.) opened in Warsaw; this was the first public theatre in Poland. Augustus II was crowned in 1733, and at once showed his enthusiasm for opera. He provided heavy subsidies, and twice weekly performances were given with an orchestra of over 100. Many Metastasian operas were performed; the company included *Hasse and *Bordoni. From *c.*1725 private operas were also established in the residences of some Polish nobles, e.g. in Nieświtz, Ołyka, Słuck and Białystock, performing mostly French and Italian works.

The first growth of Polish national opera dates from the second half of the 18th cent. and the reign (1764-95) of Poland's last king, the enlightened and intelligent Stanisław August Poniatowski, who summoned artists of every kind to Warsaw and vigorously encouraged the arts throughout the country. The opening of the first public theatre in Warsaw in 1765, under Karol Tomatis, encouraged the popularity of opera; and, from 1776, opera seria was added to the prevailing opera buffa. The first Polish opera was *Nędza Uszczęśliwiona* (Sorrow Turned to Joy) by Maciej Kamieński (1734-1821) with a text by Wojciech Bogusławski: produced in 1778, this consisted of 11 airs and two duets. In 1779 the Teatr Narodowy (National T.) was opened with Audinot's *Le Tonnelier*, sung in Polish. In the same year there followed Kamieński's *Zośka* and *Prostota Cnotliwa* (Virtuous Simplicity), and *Nie każdy śpi, co chrapi* (Not all who snore are asleep) by Gaetano (also known as Kajetan Majer, *d* 1792).

Despite the three partitions of Poland at the end of the 18th cent., Polish texts began

superseding foreign ones, due largely to 'the father of the Polish theatre', Wojciech Bogusławski (1757-1829). An actor, producer, and singer (he was the first Antek in *Nędza Uszczęśliwiona*) who also directed the theatre, 1782-4 and 1799-1814, he translated many librettos and wrote others, including *Krakowiacy i Górale* (The Krakowians and the Highlanders, 1794) by Jan Stefani (1746-1829): in 4 acts, this was the first full-scale Polish opera, and was based on peasant life. In the period of national difficulties which followed, Bogusławski staged excellent productions of foreign works; while Józef Elsner (1769-1854) wrote a long series of Polish operas, including *Andromeda*: this was given on 14 Jan. 1807 before Napoleon, who followed the performance with a French translation. Other operas by Elsner, mostly on Polish historical themes, which became popular included *Leszek Biały* (King Leszek the White, 1809), *Król Łokietek czyli Wiśliczanki* (King Łokietek or The Women of Wiślica, 1818), and *Jagiełło w Tenczynie* (King Jagiełło at Tenczyn, 1820). In 1810 Karol Kurpiński (1785-1857) was appointed to the opera: of his 26 operas the most important were *Jadwiga, Królowa polska* (Jadwiga, Queen of Poland, 1815) and *Zamek na Czorsztynie* (The Castle of Czorsztyn, 1819). Though Italianate in manner, his operas as well as his personal efforts helped to maintain a Polish opera independent of Russian influence. He introduced works by himself, Elsner, Mozart, Rossini, later Weber, Auber, Donizetti, Bellini, and eventually Verdi. *Moniuszko's *Halka* was first given in Wilno in 1848, but kept out of Warsaw by the director Tomasz Nidecki; when Giovanni (Jan) Quattrini took over in 1852, he immediately staged the work, which was hailed as Poland's first great national opera. It set an example in its skilful, somewhat Weberian use of national melodic contours and folk customs in music of much freshness and charm. In Moniuszko's period as music director (1858-72), many new Polish works were introduced, such composers as Stanisław Duniecki (1839-70), Gabriel Rozniecki (1815-87), Ignacy Feliks Dobrzyński (1807-67), Adam Minchejmer (Münchheimer) (1830-1904), and Moniuszko himself. In the decade 1858-67, despite a difficult year in 1863 following the Revolution, some 40 new operas appeared, the most important being Moniuszko's own *Straszny Dwór* (The Haunted Castle, 1865). Wagner was first heard, under Cesare Trombini. New composers included Władysław Zeleński (1837-1921), whose four operas included *Konrad Wallenrod* (1885) and *Goplana* (1896); and Ludomir Różycki (1884-1953), conductor at the Lwów Opera, whose *Bolesław Śmiały* (Bolesław the Bold, 1909) and *Meduza* (1912) show an ability to reconcile post-Wagnerian and *verismo* methods within a Slavonic manner, and whose most important work was *Eros i Psyche* (1917). Dominating these, however, was Karol *Szymanowski, whose sumptuous post-Romantic manner finds expression in *Hagith* (comp. 1913, prod. 1922) and culminates in *Król Roger* (King Roger, 1926).

After the First World War, there followed a period of intense activity in Warsaw, Poznań, Lwów, Kraków, and Katowice; many famous singers came as guests. In composition, however, it was a reactionary period, and throughout the 1930s only about 30 new Polish operas appeared, among them works by Henryk Opieński (1870-1942), Tadeusz Joteyko (1872-1932), Witold Maliszewski (1873-1939), Piotr Rytel (1884-1970), and Ludomir Różycki (*b* 1884). After the Second World War, activity greatly increased. Warsaw's T. Wielki, burned in 1939 and bombed in 1944, re-opened in 1946; and outside the capital there are now nine companies, as well as 10 operetta theatres. 19th cent. Polish opera remains popular in repertories that concentrate on Italian and Russian opera but are increasingly catholic in taste. The first post-war Polish opera was *Bunt żaków* (The Students' Rebellion, 1951) by Tadeusz Szeligowski (1896-1963), who followed this with other works. Other contemporary composers include Witold Rudziński (*b* 1913: *Chłopi* (The Peasants), 1974), Tadeusz Baird (*b* 1928: *Jutro* (Tomorrow), 1966), Romuald Twardowski (*b* 1930: *Tragedyja albo Rzecz o Janie i Herodzie* (The Tragedy or the Affair of John and Herodias), 1966), and Krzysztof *Penderecki (*b* 1933: *Diabły z Loudun* (The Devils of Loudun), 1969). See *Gdańsk, Kraków, Łódź, Poznań, Warsaw, Wrocław.*

Poliuto. Opera seria in 3 acts by Donizetti; text by Cammarano, after Corneille's tragedy *Polyeucte* (1640). Composed in 1838 for Nourrit, for production in Naples, but not passed by censor: rehearsed by Ronzi de Begnis, Nourrit, Barroilhet, Finocchi. New 4-act version as grand opera, with French text by Scribe, prod. Paris, O., 10 Apr. 1840 as *Les Martyrs*, with Dorus-Gras, Duprez, Massol, Dérivis. Retranslated into Italian as *I martiri* by Bassi, prod. Lisbon 15 Feb. 1843; London, C.G., 20 Apr. 1852, with Julienne, Tamberlik, Ronconi; New Orleans 24 Mar. 1846. After Donizetti's death performed in Italy in original 3-act version, Naples, S.C., 30 Nov. 1848.

Polyeucte (Poliuto, ten.) has become a secret convert to Christianity, and is arrested and condemned to death. His wife Pauline (Paolina, sop.) although still in love with Severus (Severo, bar.), the Roman Proconsul, decides to join her husband and die with him.

Pollak, Anna (*b* Manchester, 1 May 1912). English mezzo-soprano of Austrian origin. Studied Holland and Manchester, and began career on straight stage. Studied with Joan Cross who engaged her for S.W. in 1945. Début London, Princes T., with S.W. Opera, 1945, Dorabella; and remained member of Company until 1961. Created Lady Nelson (*Nelson*), Mrs Strickland (*Moon and Sixpence*). E.O.G. 1946, creating Bianca in *Rape of Lucretia* and the title role in Berkeley's *Ruth*. Appeared Holland Festival, Gly. and C.G. (R)

Pollak, Egon (*b* Prague, 3 May 1879; *d* Prague, 14 June 1933). Austrian conductor. Studied Prague; began career there as chorus master, Landestheater. Bremen 1905-10 as first Kapellmeister; Leipzig 1910-12; Frankfurt 1912-17; Hamburg 1917-31. London, C.G., 1914; Chicago 1915-16, 1929-32; Buenos Aires, T.C., 1928; Vienna, S.O., 1932-3. Conducted première of *Die tote Stadt*, Hamburg 1920. Was greatly admired for his readings of Wagner, Strauss, and D'Albert. Collapsed and died while conducting a performance of *Fidelio*. (R)

Pollini, Bernhard (orig. Baruch Pohl) (*b* Cologne, 16 Dec. 1838; *d* Hamburg, 27 Nov. 1897). German tenor, baritone, and impresario. Début as tenor, Cologne, 1957 in *Puritani*. Later toured with an Italian company, singing leading baritone roles and becoming its manager. Director of Lwów (Lemberg) Opera, *c*.1865, and for several years impresario of the Italian Opera in St Petersburg and Moscow. Director of Hamburg Opera 1874-1897, also managing the Altona and Thalia Theatres there. Worked in close co-operation with Mahler in Hamburg, responsible for taking the Hamburg company to London in 1892, when Mahler conducted the *Ring* and other operas at Covent Garden.

Pollione. The Roman proconsul (ten.) in love with Adalgisa but loved by Norma, in Bellini's *Norma*.

Polly. Ballad opera in 3 acts by Gay, with music arranged by Pepusch and Arnold. Prod. London, Little Hm., 19 June 1777; N.Y., Cherry Lane, 10 Oct. 1925. The preface to the libretto is dated 1729, but owing to the intervention of the Lord Chamberlain (possibly at the instigation of Walpole, who had been lampooned in the previous *Beggar's Opera*), the piece was not then performed.

Polovtsian Dances. Dances in Act 2 of Borodin's *Prince Igor*, with which Khan Konchak entertains Igor.

Pomo d'oro, Il (The Golden Apple). *Festa teatrale* in 5 acts, with prologue, by Cesti; text by Sbarra; designs by Ludovico Burnacini. Prod Vienna, Carn. 1667. Composed for the wedding of Leopold I and the Infanta Margherita (12 Dec. 1666); perhaps the most elaborate opera production ever staged; the cost of the décor alone was estimated at 100,000 Reichsthaler.

The music for Act 5 is lost; the rest has been published in a modern edition. In the same season Cesti's *Le disgrazie d'amore* was given, for which Leopold himself wrote the prologue.

Ponchard. French family of singers and composers.

(1) **Antoine** (*b* Boussu, Péronne, 1758; *d* Paris, Sep. 1827). Composer, and from 1803 director of the Grand T., Lyons.

(2) **Louis-Antoine-Eléonore** (*b* Paris, 31 Aug. 1787; *d* Paris, 6 Jan. 1866). French tenor and composer. Son of above, Studied with Garat. Début Paris, O.C., 1812, where he sang until 1837, taking part in many first performances; created George Brown (*Dame blanche*). Brussels, Toulouse, Bordeaux. From 1819 taught at the Paris Conservatoire; his pupils included Faure, Roger, Mario, Stoltz, and Dabadie.

(3) **Marie Sophie Collault-Ponchard** (*b* Paris, 30 May 1792; *d* Paris 19 Sept. 1873). French soprano. Wife of (2). Début Paris, O., 1914, Iphigénie (*Aulide*) ; O.C., 1818-36, taking part in first performances of works by Auber and Hérold; created Queen in *Le Pré aux clercs*. First singer to be awarded the Legion d' Honneur.

(4) **Charles Marie Auguste-Ponchard** (*b* Paris 17 Nov. 1824; *d* Paris 26 Apr. 1891). French tenor. Son of (2) and (3). Début Paris, O., 1847, Léopold in *L'Ame en peine*; O.C., 1847-71, and as producer 1872-90, staging the premières of *Carmen, Manon,* and *Lakmé*. Taught singing at the Paris Conservatoire from 1872. Married Mlle D'Halbert 1848; she had a career in Italy as D'Albert.

Ponchielli, Amilcare (*b* Paderno Fasolaro, 31 Aug. 1834; *d* Milan, 17 Jan. 1886). Italian composer. Studied Milan with Frasi and Mazzucato, and composed his first operatic music, with fellow-students, for *Il sindaco babbeo* in 1851. Conducted at the T. Carcano, Milan, 1860. His first opera was *I promessi sposi* (1856), followed by *Bertrando dal Bormio* (rehearsed but not prod., 1858), *La savoiarda* (1861), and *Roderico, Re dei goti* (1861). A revised version of *I promessi sposi* was successful in 1872, as was the Ricordi commission for La Scala, *I lituani* (1874). But Ponchielli's greatest, and only enduring, triumph was *La Gioconda* (1876). His dramatic instinct here finds its best outlet: *Boito's libretto combines many features of French grand opera and Italian Romantic melodrama, in a way that suited the composer's gift for agreeable, warm music. The work's musical and dramatic styles were already exhausted in opera; but it contains celebrated passages, including the arias 'Cielo e mar' and 'Suicidio', and the Dance of the Hours ballet. In his other operas Ponchielli toyed with exotic styles, Slavonic in *I lituani* and Oriental in a later work, *Il figliuol prodigo* (1880). His last work, *Marion Delorme* (1885), is

closer to opéra comique in style. Another opera, *I mori di Venezia,* was composed in 1879 but not discovered (and scored) by Arturo Cadore until 1902 (prod. 1914). In 1874 Ponchielli married the soprano Teresina *Brambilla.

Bibl: A. Damerini: *Amilcare Ponchielli* (1940).

Poniatowski, Józef (Michał Xawery Franciszek) (Prince of Monte Rotondo) (*b* Rome, 20 Feb. 1816; *d* Chislehurst, 3 Jul. 1873). Polish composer and tenor. Great-nephew of Stanisław August, King of Poland 1764-95. Studied Florence. Début Florence in title role of his own *Giovanni di Procida* (1839). Went to Paris, then followed Napoleon III into exile in England. His 13 operas, written for Italy, France, and England, include *Ruy Blas* (1843), *La sposa d'Abido* (1848), *Pierre de Médicis* (1890), *L'Aventurier* (1865), and *Gelmina* (1872, composed for Patti).

Ponnelle, Jean-Pierre (*b* Paris, 19 Feb. 1932). French designer and producer. Studied art and music in Paris. Invited by Henze, whom he knew from his student days, to design *Boulevard Solitude* (for its 1952 première in Hanover) and *König Hirsch* (1956); designed productions in Germany, Italy, and U.S.A. 1952-9; he was then conscripted into the French army. Began producing plays after his release in 1961; first opera production *Tristan und Isolde*, Düsseldorf, 1962. He has since produced and designed in the world's leading opera houses works including *Così fan tutte, Le nozze di Figaro,* and *Il barbiere di Siviglia* at Salzburg; *Pelléas et Mélisande* in Munich; *Don Pasquale* at Covent Garden; *L'italiana in Algeri* at the Met., N.Y.; *La Cenerentola* in San Francisco; a Mozart cycle in Cologne; and a Monteverdi cycle in Zurich. A highly gifted painter and producer whose work exhibits great originality, charm, and style, though occasionally he has been tempted to overload the stage and action with too much detail.

Pons, Lily (orig. Alice Josephine Pons) (*b* Draguignan, 16 Apr. 1904; *d* Dallas, 13 Feb. 1976). French, later American soprano. Studied Cannes with Dyna Beumer. Concert début May 1917; Paris T. des Varietés, 1924, *Azaïs.* Formal début Mulhouse, 1927, Lakmé. After further appearances in the French provinces was heard by Maria Gay and Zenatello, who recommended her to Gatti-Casazza at the Met., N.Y. Début there 3 Jan. 1931, Lucia, and sang there until 1961. London, C.G., 1935, Rosina; Chicago, San Francisco, etc. There were few coloratura sopranos in her time; she achieved considerable success in a repertory of less than a dozen roles, though in France she also sang Cherubino, Blonde, Gretel, Mimì and other parts. Her voice, while limited in colour, was flexible and appealing in quality, and her charm and vivacity were considerable. She also made a number of films. (R)

Ponselle (orig. Ponzillo), **Rosa** (b Meriden, Conn., 22 Jan. 1897). American soprano. Born of immigrant Neapolitan parents, she first sang in public when in her early teens, first in local cinemas, and then in vaudeville with her sister Carmella. Studied N.Y. with William Thorner, then with Romani. Heard by Caruso, who suggested that Gatti-Casazza engage her to sing Leonora in *La forza del destino*, in which role she made her N.Y. début at the Met., 15 Nov. 1918. Sang Met. 1918-37; London, C.G., 1929-31; Florence, Maggio Musicale, 1933. Her rich dramatic soprano voice, beautifully covered and even in scale throughout its range, of a dark exciting quality, made her one of the greatest singers of the century. For her the Met. revived *La vestale, Norma, La Gioconda*, and other works. She sang her first Violetta at C.G. 1930. In 1935 she sang Carmen, which was not an unqualified success; and two years later she retired, while still at the height of her powers. She now lives and teaches in Baltimore. Artistic director, Civic O., since 1954. (R) Her sister **Carmela Ponselle** (b 7 June 1888; d New York, 13 June 1977) 1924-8, 1930-5 appeared with various small companies, including Maurice Frank, Pittsburgh, etc. at the N.Y. Met., 1924-32 and sang Amneris, Azucena, Santuzza, etc. (R)

Ponticello (*It* little bridge). The term used by the bel-cantists for the join between the chest and head registers.

Ponziani, Felice (b ? ; d c1826) Italian basso buffo. Created Leporello (Prague, 1787), and 1792-8 appeared regularly in Venice, after which he seems to have vanished from the operatic scene.

Popp, Lucia (b Uhorska Ves, 12 Nov. 1939). Czech soprano. Studied Bratislava, and Vienna with Amy Hurovsky. Début Bratislava Opera, while still a student, Queen of Night; Vienna, W., 1963, Barbarina; Vienna, S., since 1963; Cologne, since 1967; London, C.G., since 1966 as Oscar, Gilda, Despina, Sophie, Aennchen; N.Y., Met., 1967, 1969, 1970. Repertory also includes Zerlina, Queen of Night, Pamina, Ilia, and Sextus (*Giulio Cesare*). An attractive voice with a winning stage personality combine to make her one of the most attractive artists of her kind today. (R)

Porgi amor. The Countess's (sop.) aria in Act 2 of Mozart's *Le nozze di Figaro*, lamenting that she has lost her husband's love.

Porgy and Bess. Opera in 3 acts by Gershwin; text by Du Bose Heyward and Ira Gershwin, after the drama *Porgy* by Du Bose and Dorothy Heyward. Prod. Boston, Colonial T., 30 Sep. 1935, with Brown, Mitchell, Duncan, Elzy, Bubbles, Buck, Matthews, Harvey, Dowdy, Davis, Coleman, Johnson, cond. Smallens; London, Stoll T., 9 Oct. 1952, with Price, Warfield, Colbert, Dowdy, Calloway, McCurry, cond. Smallens.

Porgy (bar.), a cripple, and Crown (bass), a stevedore, compete for the love of Bess (sop.). She is lured to New York by the gambler, Sportin' Life (ten.). Porgy kills Crown and follows Bess to New York.

Poro. Opera in 3 acts by Handel; text an adaptation of Metastasio's *Alessandro nell'Indie*, trans. Samuel Humphreys. Prod. London, King's T., 2 Feb. 1731, with Strada, Senesino, Merighi, Bertolli, Fabri Comaro,. Revived Abingdon, 1966.

Porpora, Nicola (Antonio) (b Naples, 17 Aug. 1686; d Naples, 3 Mar. 1768). Italian composer and singing teacher. Studied Naples with Greco. His first opera, *Agrippina* (1708), was to a text reworked by Cardinal Grimani from Handel's opera of that name; this was followed by *Flavio Anicio Olibrio* (1711) and *Basilio, Re d'oriente* (1713). A famous teacher; his pupils included Farinelli, Caffarelli, and (though unsuccessfully) Hasse. He also taught Metastasio, whose libretti for him include *Didone abbandonata* (1725), *Siface* (1725), *Siroe* (1727), *Ezio* (1727), *Semiramide riconosciuta* (1729), *Issipile* (1733), and *Temistocle* (1743). He went abroad to take up various appointments as director of music and teacher: Vienna (1725), Venice (1726), and London (1733-6): his London operas included *Arianna in Nasso* (1733), *Enea nel Lazio* (1734), *Polifemo* (1753), *Ifigenia in Aulide* (1735), and *Mitridate* (1736). After the success of Handel's *Atalanta* he was forced to leave the King's T., and returned to Italy; Naples (1739), then Venice (1742). He took up an appointment in Dresden in 1747, but was forced to leave by intrigues organized by Faustina Bordoni; went to Vienna 1752, where Haydn was his pupil and accompanied his lessons. Finally returned to Italy: Naples 1758, Venice 1759, and Naples again 1760, where he died in poverty.

As a great singing teacher, Porpora tended to write operas in which the voice was the end rather than the means; but he wrote elegantly and with virtuosity for the finest singing techniques of the day, and though no match for Handel in London he showed a keener sense of the dramatic force of virtuoso singing than many of his minor contemporaries.

Portamento (*It* carrying). The smooth carriage of the voice from one note to another.

Portland. Town in Oregon, U.S.A. The first opera performance in the Northwest Pacific, was in summer 1867 at the Oro Fino T. when the Bianchi Opera company arrived by steamer from San Francisco and opened their season with *Il trovatore*. The New Market T., which opened in 1875, and the Marquam Grand O.H. in 1890, housed seasons by the Emma Juch Grand Opera Company and other touring companies. In 1913 the Chicago Grand Opera Company visited the city and returned on several occasions until 1931. Portland's first resident company was founded in 1917 under the direction of Roberto Corruccini and lasted until his death in 1923. 1918-48 the San Carlo Opera Company visited Portland virtually every year. In 1964 the Portland Opera Association was established, and since 1968 has given its performances in the Portland Civic Auditorium. It has given more than 100 performances during its first ten years of existence; Henry Holt was music director 1964-66, Herbert Weiskopf 1966-70, and Stefan Minde since 1970. In addition to popular works, Minde has given the first local performances of *Ariadne auf Naxos*, *Der Freischütz*, *La rondine*, and in November 1975, the first U.S. performance of Křenek's *Das Leben des Orest*.

Portugal. Though popular dramas with music, especially the form known as *vilhancico*, were familiar in Portugal from the Middle Ages, Portuguese opera began in 1733, when the *Vida de Don Quichote de la Mancha* by A. J. da Silva and *La pazienza di Socrate* by Francisco António de Almeida were given. The former was in Portuguese; the music is lost. Other operas by Almeida are preserved. Works by António Leal Moreira (*d* 1819) were also given. The first important composer, was M.A. da Fonseca Portugal, whose first work, *A Casa de pasto*, was given in 1784. He spent eight years in Italy, then returned and later went to Rio de Janeiro with the Royal family. Opera did not advance greatly during the 19th cent., despite the activity of Francisco de Sá Noronha (1820-81), José de Arneiro (1838-1903), Miguel Ángel Pereira, Francisco de Freitas Gazul, and Augusto Machado. The latter attempted to resist the prevalent Italian influence with elements of French opera. The father of Portuguese Romantic opera was Alfredo Keil (1850-1907): his *Serrana* (1899) drew on folk elements. His work was developed by Ruy Coelho (*b* 1891) with a number of operas to Portuguese texts. There was also an attempt by various 19th cent. composers to develop an indigenous strain of Portuguese operetta on the basis of popular music drama. A number of modern Portuguese composers have written opera, and their works are included in the Lisbon repertory. See *Lisbon*.

Portugal, Marcos Antonio de Fonseca (orig. Ascençao; also known as Portogallo) (*b* Lisbon, 24 Mar. 1762; *d* Rio de Janeiro, 7 Feb. 1830). Portuguese composer. He wrote five Portuguese operettas 1785-92, including the popular *A castanheira* (1787), and became director of the Siltre T. In 1792 went to Naples;

composed 20 operas for Italy, of which the most successful were *La confusione nata dalla somiglianza* (1793), *Cinna* (1793), *Rinaldo d'Asti* (1794), *Lo spazzacamino principe* (1794), *La vedova raggiratrice* (1794), *Demofoonte* (1794), *Gli avventurieri* (1795), *Zulema e Selimo* (1796), *La donna di genio volubile* (1796), *L'inganno poco dura* (1796), *Il ritorno di Serse* (1797), *Le donne cambiate* (1797), and *Fernando nel Messico* (1797). Director of Royal Opera in, Lisbon, 1799, and of San Carlos, 1800; here he engaged Catalani 1801-6. When court fled to Brazil, he first stayed in Lisbon but then followed (1810); opened the T. São João in Rio de Janeiro in 1811. Illness prevented him from returning to Lisbon with the Court in 1821. He wrote in all some 35 Italian operas and 21 Portuguese comic operas. They are in conventional Neapolitan style, and though he also wrote in Portuguese he did less for his country's national opera as a founder of a new style than by his international reputation as a successful composer and conductor.

Posse (*Ger* buffoonery, farce). A form of popular theatrical entertainment which flourished especially in the late 18th and early 19th cent. Above all a Viennese form, though also found in different aspects in a number of other German cities, including Hamburg, and also Berlin, where the manner tended to be more realistic than in the generally fantastic comedies of Vienna. Local colour was important (*Lokalposse*) as was magic (*Zauberposse*); often the two were combined in plots that dealt with the intrusion of magic into normal life, perhaps by transferring an ordinary Viennese citizen to fairyland. This device was particularly popular with the most famous of all Viennese popular theatre authors, Ferdinand *Raimund (1790-1836), in *Der Alpenkönig und der Menschenfeind* (1828) and others. It was also typical of the Viennese *Zauberposse* to touch on moral and general issues while keeping to a comic and fantastic narrative. Some authors provided songs more or less of their own composition (adapted folk-melody, original song-melody); others drew on composers including Riotte, Drechsler, Wenzel Müller, and Konradin Kreutzer. The *Zauberposse*, especially in the hands of Raimund, was enormously popular and influenced a number of dramatists and composers, including Wagner.

Postillon de Longjumeau, Le. Opera in 3 acts by Adam; text by De Leuven and Brunswick. Prod. Paris, O.C., 13 Oct. 1836, with Prévost, Ray, Clollet, Henri; London, St James's T., 13 Mar. 1837; N.Y., Park T., 30 Mar. 1840. Adam's most popular opera outside France. A centenary performance was given at Longjumeau in May 1936.

Chapelou (ten.), the postillion of the title, possesses a fine voice, and is engaged by De

Courcy (bar.), the manager of the royal amusements, to sing at Fontainebleau. Under the name of St-Phar he becomes a great singer, and promises marriage to the rich Madame de Latour (sop.). She is none other than Madeleine, whom he had previously married when he was a postillion and she the hostess of a village inn. All ends happily.

Adaptation by Oudrid y Segura, *El postillón de la Rioja* (1856). Also opera by P.A. Coppola (1838).

Pougin, Arthur (orig. François Auguste Arthur Paroisse-Pougin; pseudouym Pol Dax) (*b* Châteauroux, 6 Aug. 1834; *d* Paris, 8 Aug. 1921). French writer and critic. Published biogaphies of Rossini, Bellini, Meyerbeer, Verdi, Auber, and others, and of singers including Dugazon, Malibran, Favart, and Grassini.

Poulenc, Francis (*b* Paris, 7 Jan. 1899; *d* Paris, 30 Jan. 1963). French composer. Studied with Koechlin. The greater part of his music was not for the theatre. *Le Gendarme incompris*, a *comédie-bouffe* (1920), was not followed until 1944, by the witty satire *Les Mamelles de Tirésias* (1944). However, *Dialogues des Carmélites* (1957) is a deeply felt religious opera written in a simple lyrical style. *La Voix humaine* (1958), text by Cocteau, is a 45-minute monologue for soprano.

Bibl: H. Heil: *Francis Poulenc* (1958).

Pourquoi me réveiller? Werther's (ten.) aria in Act 3 of Massenet's *Werther*, in which the poet sings a song of tragic love from the verses of Ossian which in happier days he had translated with Charlotte.

Poveri fiori. Adriana Lecouvreur's (sop.) aria from Act 4 of Cilea's *Adriana Lecouvreur*, which she sings as she looks at the faded bunch of violets (now poisoned by her rival the Princesse de Bouillon) that she had given Maurizio.

Poznań. Town in Poland. Opera was first given in Poznań towards the end of the 18th cent. During the 19th cent. seasons were given by visiting companies, including the T. Narodow from Warsaw, under Wojciech Bogusławski, and from Kraków and elsewhere. In 1875 the T. Polski was founded as a permanent repertory theatre which still exists and until 1918 was the principal encouragement to opera. Poznań was under Prussian domination 1795-1918, and opera was also given by German companies. On 31 Aug. 1919 the T. Wielki was founded, and was maintained until 1 Sept. 1939. During the war, a German company played in the theatre (until 1944). The Poznań Opera (cap. 950) opened on 2 June 1945; in 1919 it was renamed the Stanisław Moniuszko O.H. Between the wars, the Poznań Opera was the only company to perform without interruption and to main-

tain the highest artistic standards. Its most successful periods were 1922-9 (under Piotr Stermich-Valcrociata), 1933-9 and 1945-8 (under Zygmunt Latoszewski), 1949-54 (under Walerian Bierdiajew), and 1963-9 and from 1976 (under Robert Satanowski). In 1919-69, 435 stage works by 147 composers of all countries and periods were given, including 22 premières of Polish works and 30 premières in Poland of foreign works including *Jenůfa*, *Così fan tutte*, *Prince Igor*, Gluck's *Alceste*, *Les Vêpres siciliennes*, and Handel's *Giulio Cesare*.

Prague (Cz. Praha). Capital of Czechoslovakia from 1918, formerly capital of Bohemia. A *commedia pastorale cantata* by G.B. Buonamente and Cesare Gonsaga was given by a Mantuan company for the Coronation of Ferdinand II in 1627. Among other Italian works performed in succeeding years was Draghi's *La patienza di Socrate con due moglie* (Carn. 1680). The first opera theatre was built at Jeleni Příkop on the Hradčany in 1681. Visiting companies included that of Johann Friedrich Sartorio, who gave *La Libussa* with music by Bartolomeo Bernardi probably in 1703 or 1704; performances were given in the Regnard House on the Malá Strana, rebuilt by Sartorio. Most performances were given in the Hradčany, the citadel of Prague, during the Court's residence. In 1723 Fux's *Costanza e fortezza* was produced for the 4,000 visitors to the Coronation of Charles VI in a vast specially constructed amphitheatre at Jeleni Příkop, with room for 1,000 performers. The sumptuous staging was by *Galli-Bibiena. A private opera theatre, giving Italian works, was built in the Na Poříčí quarter by Count František Šporck. From 1738 opera was also given at the theatre V Kotcích, then at Count Thun's theatre in the Malá Strana.

The first permanent opera theatre in the city was the Kotce T. Visiting companies included those of the *Mingottis, a troupe which gave *La serva padrona*, under Nicolini, and a group giving performances of Gluck under Locatelli (1750-2). In 1767-72 Giuseppe Bustelli gave operas by the expatriate Czechs *Mysliveček and Koželuh. After a period in which Singspiel predominated, Pasquale Bondini revived Italian opera at the Thun T. in the Malá Strana with works that included Sarti's *Fra due litiganti il terzo gode*. The theatre in Kotce closed in 1783, and the Thun T. burnt down in 1794. In 1783 Count Nostic opened the Nostické národní divadlo, which was long the centre of Prague operatic life (cap. 1,129): here, Mozart conducted *Figaro* in 1786, and the première of *Don Giovanni* in 1787. Weber was Intendant 1813-16, in charge of a German company. In 1798 the theatre was bought by the state and renamed the Královské Stavovské divadlo (State T.); it was enlarged in 1834, and has since 1949 been known as the Tylovo divadlo (Tyl T.). As an overflow house, the Novoměstské divadlo (or Zabranskí divadlo (Surburban T.)) was opened in 1858 (cap. 3,000): opera was given 2-3 times a week.

Since another theatre was clearly required, a newly formed theatrical association built the Prozatímní divadlo (Provisional T.), in 1862 (cap. 900). Its methods and resources were primitive: most of its singers were amateurs, and the orchestra of 18 had also to work in cafés. The first original Czech opera heard there was Skuherský's *Vladimir, bohů zvolenec* (Vladimir, the Elect of God, 1863). Smetana was director, and six of his operas were produced here, as were the first stage works of Dvořák and Fibich. Practical and political disputes delayed its replacement, and the laying of the foundation stone of the new theatre in 1868 was a national event. In 1881 the Národní divadlo (National T.), incorporating the Provisional T., was opened with Smetana's *Libuše*; but shortly aferwards the theatre was completely gutted by fire. Nevertheless, money was quickly found for another theatre, which opened in 1883 (cap. 1,598). Chief conductors have included Adolf Čech (1883-1900), Karel Kovařovic (1900-20), Otakar Ostrčil (1920-35), Václav Talich (1935-44 and 1947-8), Otakar Jeremiáš (1945-7 and 1948-51), Zdeněk Chalabala (1953-62), and Jaroslav Krombholc since 1963. Important premières included Schoenberg's *Erwartung* (1924).

Meanwhile, replacing the Novoměstské divadlo, the German minority of Prague built the Neues Deutsches T., which opened in 1887 (cap. 1,554); the company was directed by Angelo *Neumann and Alexander Zemlinsky (1911-27), first of a line of distinguished German musicians who have developed their careers in Prague, including Seidl, Mahler, and Klemperer. After 1945 the theatre became first the Velká Opera 5. května (Grand opera), then in 1949, as filial of the National T., the Smetanovo Divadlo (Smetana T.). Opera has also been given at the Městské divadlo (Vinohradské divadlo) opened in 1907; particularly during the Intendantship of Otakar Ostrčil (1913-19) this was a pioneering centre of modern opera. Operetta has been given in various theatres but especially in the Variété-Opereta na Karliné and the Velká Opereta. In 1934 Emil Burian opened, in the Mozarteum, an avant-garde theatre called D34 (D from *divadlo*, theatre, 34 from 1934).

Pré aux clercs, Le. Opera in 3 acts by Hérold; text by Planard, after Mérimée's novel *Chronique du règne de Charles IX* (1829). Prod. Paris, O.C., 15 Dec. 1832, with Ponchard, Casimir, Massy, Thénard, Lemonnier, Féreol, Gent; London, Adelphi T., 9 Sept. 1833; Baltimore, Holliday St. T. 14 Oct. 1833, but poss. earlier in New Orleans.

The opera tells how Marguerite de Valois (mezzo) brought about the marriage between Isabelle de Béarn (sop.) and the young Baron de Mergy (ten.).

Preetorius, Emil (*b* Mainz, 21 June 1883; *d* Munich 27 Jan. 1973). German scenic artist. After working as a book illustrator, he was suggested to Bruno Walter by Thomas Mann in 1912 as designer for the Munich production of *Iphigénie en Aulide*. Worked in Berlin, Dresden and Madrid in the 1920s; Bayreuth 1932-41, designing *The Ring, Meistersinger, Tristan, Lohengrin*, and *Fliegende Holländer*; sets for the latter seen at Covent Garden, 1937-8 and 1950. Regarded at Bayreuth as a reformer, but elsewhere as a traditionalist.
Bibl: W. Rüdiger: *Emil Preetorius* (1943).

Preghiera (*It* prayer). An aria or chorus of quiet and reverent character in which the singer or singers make a prayer to God or to supernatural powers. Designed to display mastery of soft vocalization and simple line, it became a very popular ingredient of Italian opera, especially in the 19th cent., and thence of French and German opera. An early example, if not the first, is in Salieri's *Tarare*. A famous instance is Desdemona's 'Ave Maria' in Verdi's *Otello*; others are Rienzi's *Gebet* (*preghiera*) 'Allmächt'ger Vater' in Wagner's opera, and Huon's 'Ruler of this awful hour' in Weber's *Oberon*. The *preghiera* could be treated with considerable fluency, especially by Verdi: choral *preghiere* occur in *Aroldo* ('Angiol di Dio'), *La forza del destino* ('Padre eterno Signor'), and *Aida* ('O tu che sei d'Osiride') and a *preghiera* is built into the finales of *Luisa Miller* and Act 2 of *Aroldo*.

Prelude (from Lat *praeludium*, something played before another work). There is no clear distinction between prelude and overture, though in general the former may be shorter and may also run directly into the opera (or act of an opera) which it introduces.

Prendi, l'anel ti dono. Elvino's (ten.) aria in the opening scene of Bellini's *La sonnambula* as he places the ring on Amina's finger.

Preobazhenskaya, Sofya (Petrovna) (*b* St Petersburg, 27 Sept. 1904). Russian mezzo-soprano. Studied Leningrad with Zaitseva and Ershov. Leningrad, Kirov C., 1924-48. Salzburg 1928-30. Roles include Martha, Joan of Arc, Countess (*Queen of Spades*), Azucena, Amneris, Lel, Waltraute, Marina. Taught Leningrad Conservatory 1948-53. (R)

Près des remparts de Séville. The Seguidilla in Act 1 of Bizet's *Carmen*, sung by Carmen (mezzo) as she tempts Don José to release her and accompany her to Lillas Pastia's inn.

Pressburg. See *Bratislava*.

rêtre, Georges (*b* Waziers, 14 Aug. 1924). French conductor. Studied Douai, Paris Conservatoire, and with Cluytens. Début Marseille, 1946, *Samson et Dalila*. Marseilles 1946-8; Lille 1948-50; Toulouse 1951-4; Lyons 1955; Paris, O.C., 1956 *Mignon, Capriccio*. Première of *Voix humaine* there, 1959; Paris, O., since 1959. Chicago 1959; San Francisco 1963-; N.Y. Met., 1964-7; London, C.G., 1965, 1976; Milan, Sc., since 1965. (R)

revitali, Fernando (*b* Adria, 16 Feb. 1907). Italian conductor. Studied Turin. Assisted Gui in organizing the Florence Orchestra and Festival 1928-35. Genoa, C.F., 1935-6, incl. *Elisir* with Schipa. Director Radio Italiana Orchestra 1936-3, and responsible for many fine radio opera performances, including the Verdi cycle of 1951. Rome, Buenos Aires, Milan, Sc., 1942 947-8. Naples 1957 Conducted the premières of many modern works, including Ghedini's *Re Hassan* (Venice 1939) and the same composer's *Le Baccanti* (Sc. 1948), Dallapiccola's *Volo di notte* (Florence 1940) as well as revivals of Busoni's *Turandot* and *Doktor Faust*. (R)

révost (d'Exiles), **Antoine-François**, Abbé (*b* esdin, 1 Apr. 1697; *d* Chantilly, 23 Nov. 1763). French writer. His *L'Histoire du Chevalier Des Grieux et de Manon Lescaut* (1731), vol. 7 of his *Mémoires d'un homme de qualité*, was the source of the following operas: Auber (1856); Kleinmichel (*Das Schloss de l'Orme*, 1883); Massenet (1884; a sequel, *Le Portrait de Manon*, appeared in 1894); Puccini (1893); more distantly, Henze (*Boulevard Solitude*, 952).

révost, Henri (*b* ?1858; *d* ?). French tenor. Début Paris, Château d'Eau, 1881, Manrico. Engaged by Mapleson for U.S. tour, 1881-2, Manrico, Arnold; London C.G., 1887, Manrico; Arnold, Hinrich's French Opera Co. U.S.A., 895-7. Guest appearances Italy, Hungary, South America. Small repertory of twelve roles, including Franchetti's Asrael, which he sang under Mahler in Budapest.

rey, Hermann (*b* Berlin 11 July 1929). German baritone. Studied Berlin with Günther Baum and Harry Gottschalk. Début Wiesbaden 1952, Second Prisoner (*Fidelio*). Hamburg, S.O., 953; Vienna and Berlin, S., 1956; Munich since 1959; Vienna and Berlin, S., 1956; Munich since 1959; Salzburg since 1959, Baber *Schweigsame Frau*), Guglielmo, Papageno, Figaro (Rossini), Count Almaviva. Bayreuth 965-7, Wolfram; N.Y., Met., 1960-1, 1964-7, 969-70; San Francisco 1963; Chicago 1971. Edinburgh Festival (with Munich Opera) 1965, Storch; London, C.G., since 1973. Created Aleton in Křenek's *Pallas Athene weint* (Hamburg 1955). Repertory includes many roles in talian repertory. Has a beautiful lyric baritone

voice, a fine technique, and an engaging stage personality. (R)

Preziosilla. The gipsy girl (mezzo) in Verdi's *La forza del destino*.

Price, Leontyne (*b* Laurel, Mississippi, 10 Feb. 1927). American soprano. Studied Juilliard School where she sang Mistress Ford in a student performance of *Falstaff*. Chosen by Virgil Thomson to sing in a revival of *Four Saints in Three Acts* in N.Y. and Paris; and then from 1952 to 1954 sang Bess in *Porgy and Bess*. San Francisco 1957 (Madame Lidoine in American première of *Carmélites*), 1958-9; Chicago 1959, Thaïs and Liù; Vienna since 1958, Pamina and Aida; London, C.G., 1958-9, Aida; Salzburg 1960, Donna Anna and subsequently; N.Y., Met., since 1960; Milan, Sc., since 1962. Created Cleopatra in Barber's *Antony and Cleopatra* at opening of new Met., 1966. Especially admired in Verdi. (R)

Price, Margaret (Berenice) (*b* Tredegar, 13 Apr. 1941). Welsh soprano. Studied London, T.C.L. Début W.N.O., 1964, Cherubino; returned 1969-71 as Nannetta and Amelia Boccanegra. London, C.G., 1964, 1968, and since 1970 as Pamina, Countess, Donna Anna, Fiordiligi, and Marzelline; Glyndebourne 1968, 1971, 1972, Constanze and Fiordiligi; San Francisco 1969-70; Chicago 1972; Cologne and other German houses since 1971; Vienna, 1973; Paris, O., since 1973. B.B.C.-TV opera as Salud and Tatyana. Has a rich, creamy voice and a secure technique; one of the most admired Mozart singers of the 1970s. (R)

Prigioniero, Il (The Prisoner). Opera in prologue and 1 act by Dallapiccola; text by composer, after Villiers de l'Isle-Adam's *La Torture par espérance* (1883) and Charles Coster's *La Légende d'Ulenspiegel*. Prod. Florence, T.C., 20 May 1950 with Laszlo, Binci, Colombo, cond. Scherchen; London, S.W., 27 July 1959 with Raisbeck, Young, Cameron, cond. Lovett; N.Y., Juilliard School, 15 Mar. 1951.

The gaoler (ten.) speaks kindly to the prisoner (bar.) as 'brother'. Finding his cell door open, the prisoner escapes, past monks who seem not to notice him, into the garden, where he is enfolded in the arms of the Grand Inquisitor (ten.). The worst torture has been hope.

Prima Donna. Opera in 1 act by Benjamin; text by Cedric Cliffe. Prod. London, Fortune T., 23 Feb. 1949 with Perilli, Maclean, Hughes, James, cond. Benjamin; Philadelphia 5 Dec. 1953.

Set in 18th-century Venice, the opera includes a comic duet between rival prima donnas 'La Filomela' and Olimpia, who try to outdo one another in a scene from *Ariadne desolata* much in the manner of *Le cantatrici villane*.

Prima donna (*It* first lady). The name given to the leading female singer in an opera, or the principal soprano of an opera company. Less commonly, *primo uomo* is used for the principal male singer.

Prima la musica e poi le parole (First the music and then the words). *Divertimento teatrale* in 1 act by Salieri; text by Casti. Prod. Vienna, Kä., 11 Feb. 1786. Prod. in English, Brooklyn College, 18 Nov. 1967; London, St John's, 11 June 1978. The libretto is a witty, often sarcastic, dialogue between a composer and a poet about the respective standing of their arts in opera. The phrase, representing an argument as old as opera, is also used as the dramatic peg for Strauss's *Capriccio*.

Prince Igor. Opera in a prologue and 4 acts by Borodin; text by composer after a sketch by Stasov. Music completed by Rimsky-Korsakov and Glazunov. Prod. St Petersburg, M., 4 Nov. 1890, with Olgina, Dolina, Slavina, Melnikov, Koryakin, Stravinsky, Ugrinovich, cond. Nápravník; London, D.L., 8 June 1914, with Kuznetsov, Petrenko, Andreyev, Shalyapin, cond. Steinberg; N.Y., Met., 30 Dec. 1915, in Italian, with Alda, Perini, Amato, Didur, cond. Polacco.

The opera tells of the capture of Prince Igor (bar.), with his son Vladimir (ten.), by the Polovtsians led by Khan Konchak (bass), who entertains his captive like a Royal guest, treating him to a display of oriental dances. He offers to let Igor go free if he promises not to fight the Polovtsians again. Igor refuses, but manages to escape and rejoin his wife Yaroslavna (sop.). Igor's son Vladimir remains behind in the Polovtsian camp, having fallen in love with the Khan's daughter Konchakovna (mezzo), whom he is allowed to marry.

Prinzregententheater. See *Munich*.

Prise de Troie, La. See *Troyens, Les*.

Pritchard, John (*b* London, 5 Feb. 1921). English conductor. Gly. as répétiteur, 1947, where he became chorus master. Schooled by Fritz Busch, who gave him *Don Giovanni* and some performances of *Figaro* to conduct in 1951. Since then has conducted at Gly. regularly, Mozart, Rossini, *Ariadne auf Naxos*, *Capriccio*, and the English première of Henze's *Elegy for Young Lovers*, Einem's *Visit of the Old Lady*, and Strauss's *Intermezzo*. Music director Gly. 1968-77. C.G. since 1952, when he opened the season with a new production of *Un ballo in maschera*; he has directed the premières of *Gloriana*, *Midsummer Marriage* and *King Priam*, and revivals of *The Trojans* and *Wozzeck* as well as works in the French, German, Italian, and Russian repertories. Vienna State Opera 1952-3, 1964-5; Ingestre 1958-9; Salzburg, 1966; N.Y., Met., since 1971; San Francisco since 1970. Apptd. chief conductor Cologne, from 1 Jan. 1978. (R)

Probe (*Ger* trial, rehearsal). Thus *Beleuchtungsprobe* (lighting rehearsal), *Hauptprobe* (main rehearsal), *Generalprobe* (final (dress) rehearsal). For *Rheingold* some German opera houses call a *Schwimmprobe* for the Rhinemaidens. See also *Prova, Répétition, Sitzprobe*.

Procter-Gregg, Humphrey (*b* Kirby Lonsdale, Westmorland, 31 July 1895). English producer, translator, and administrator. Studied Cambridge and London, R.C.M., with Stanford. Responsible for several productions at the College Opera School. Stage manager and designer for B.N.O.C., Carl Rosa, C.G., Touring Companies 1922-33, and responsible for many B.B.C. studio operas 1941-5, often providing new translations, including *Prince Igor*, *Dalibor*, *Falstaff*, *Manon Lescaut*, *Louise*. Director C.R. 1957-8, and Touring Opera 1958. Director of the London Opera Centre 1963-4.

Prodaná Nevěsta. See *Bartered Bride*.

Prodigal Son, The. Church parable in 1 act by Britten; text by William Plomer, after Luke xv 11-32. Prod. Orford Parish Church, 10 June 1968, with Pears, Tear, Shirley-Quirk, Drake, cond. Britten; Katonah 29 June 1969, with Lankson, Velis, Clatworthy, Metcalf, cond. Rudel.

The Father (bass-bar.), his Elder Son (bar.) and Younger Son (ten.) work in the fields, but the Younger Son is lured by the Tempter (ten.), the Abbot in the dramatic fiction) to demand his inheritance and leave for the city. Here he is robbed by Parasites, and eventually returns to his home, where he is welcomed by his father and in the end reconciled with his brother.

Producer (in America, General Stage Director; in Germany, *Spielleiter*; in Italy, *Regista*; in France (and often Germany and elsewhere) *Régisseur*). The term is a comparatively modern one and did not appear on programmes regularly until after the First World War.

When opera was in its infancy, the ballet master probably instructed the chorus in its movements; and the stereotyped gestures of certain Italian singers, recalling the old conventions of mime, may derive from this. With the development of opera buffa in the 18th century, the principal basso buffo often took over the stage direction – a habit that survived throughout the last century (as with Tagliafico at C.G.) and can even today be found in small companies. Mozart was one of the first musical stage directors who not only rehearsed his operas from the pit, but controlled his singers; he was followed by Weber and Spohr in Germany and in Italy by Verdi, who generally supervised every detail of production. But it was Wagner who recognized fully the importance of staging – in his conception of the

Gesamtkunstwerk, or 'unified work of art'; and not only the modern singing actor but many other developments in stage technique and production stem from him. The principles he laid down for Bayreuth, which were carried on by his widow and son, came to be generally accepted by conductors, producers, and singers in Germany. In Vienna it was Mahler who demonstrated the virtues of a musician as producer; in Italy it was Toscanini.

Soon men of the theatre began to find their way into the opera house. The Munich Hofoper ntendant early this century, Ernst von Possart, was a considerable actor. Max Reinhardt was summoned by Strauss a week before the première of *Der Rosenkavalier* to help with Act 3, and subsequently produced many operas. Carl Ebert, originally one of Germany's finest actors, came to opera through Fritz Busch. Günther Rennert and Walter Felsenstein began their careers in the straight theatre. John Gielgud, Peter Brook, Tyrone Guthrie, Sam Wanamaker, Peter Hall, and John Dexter have all produced opera in England. Italy's film revival after the war gave us Visconti and Zeffirelli, masters of elaborate veristic opera production, and the Italian theatre produced Giorgio Strehler and Edoardo de Filippi. Some designers have also turned their hands to production, notably Jean-Pierre Ponnelle and Filippo Sanjust. There was a trend during the 1970s for conductors to stage their own productions, and notable in this field have been Karajan and Peter Maag; Klemperer also produced *Fidelio* and *Die Zauberflöte* in the early 1960s. Certain singers, including Gobbi, Hotter, Geraint Evans, and Regina Resnik have also produced opera. Ballet has once more contributed a fine producer in Margherita Wallmann. Mention should also be made of Russia, where the reforms of Konstantin *Stanislavsky (1863-1938) touched opera as they did everything else in the theatre.

Prohaska, Jaro (*b* Vienna, 24 Jan. 1891; *d* Munich, 28 Sept. 1965). Austrian bassbaritone. Member of the Wiener Sängerknaben, then studied Vienna with Otto Müller. Début in concert 1920; stage début Lübeck 1922. Nuremberg 1925-32; Berlin, S.O., 1932-53; Bayreuth 1933-42. A notable Wotan, Sachs, Amfortas, and Dutchman of the inter-war years. (R)

Prokofiev, Sergey (Sergeyevich) (*b* Sontsovka, Ekaterinoslav, 23 Apr. 1891; *d* Moscow, 5 Mar. 1953). Russian composer. Wrote his first opera at the age of nine (*The Giant*), at least three others during adolescence, and seven mature works that are fully characteristic of him.

The first to survive, *The Gambler* (1929), is both comedy and study of obsession: it first revealed Prokofiev's full lyricism and his fascination with abnormal states of mind. The *Love of the Three Oranges* (1921) represents a change of course; the treatment is basically anti-Romantic, and Gozzi's fantastic comedy provides the composer with the opportunity for some pungent and wittily grotesque music. *The Fiery Angel* (1922-5, prod. 1955) is a very different matter. Here the fantastic strain in Prokofiev is turned to horrific purposes. Based on Bryusov's novel of possesion and sorcery, the opera has its grotesque elements, but is an openly Romantic, expressionistic work of violent dramatic power. Prokofiev thought it his best opera.

But Soviet critics condemned these last two works for their qualities of parody and expressionism, and welcomed the returning prodigal with a chorus of only slightly reserved praise for *Semyon Kotko* (1940). Back in Russia after two decades of exile, Prokofiev quite sincerely hastened to prove himself a true Soviet citizen with this opera, based on *I, Son of the Working Class,* Katayev's novel of the closing stages of the Revolution in the Ukraine. Less successful when consciously attempting the broad gestures required to express bluff, optimistic Communist emotions, the work also finds room for some lyrical love music and some vividly colourful ensembles of true operatic mastery. 'Socialist realism' is abandoned in *The Duenna* (1940-1, prod. 1946; based on Sheridan, and known also as *Betrothal in a Monastery*). The simplicity here is not artificial, and the composer responds unaffectedly to the subject with some of his most charmingly accomplished music. *War and Peace* (1941-2; prod. 1946) could hardly avoid a return to the spacious manner; it is made with an expertness that may have quickly become Prokofiev's second nature in the face of political pressure, and has distinct grandeur. *The Story of a Real Man* (1948) was written in a tone of apology after the notorious Zhdanov tribunal had condemned leading Soviet composers for 'formalism' and other supposed vices, but failed to please even the authorities for whom it was designed.

Bibl: I. Nestyev: *Prokofiev* (1957, trans. 1960).

Prompter (in France and Germany *Souffleur,* in Italy *Maestro suggeritore*). Unlike in the straight theatre, where the prompter only intervenes when the actor forgets his words or cue, the prompter in the opera house helps the performers by giving them the opening words of every phrase a few seconds in advance. In Italian opera houses the prompter also relays the conductor's beat, which he sees reflected in a kind of driving mirror, or by means of closed-circuit TV, to the singers on the stage. In Strauss's *Capriccio* we meet one of these characters in the person of M. Taupe ('Mr. Mole'). Extra prompters are sometimes concealed on the stage. In the last act of *Tristan* *und Isolde* there is sometimes one lying under Tristan's couch. The **Prompter's box** (It *buca*) is a little cupboard-like compartment wherein the prompter is seated, placed generally in the middle of the footlights and covered over so that he is invisible to the audience. Some producers make use of the Prompter's box in their productions. Figaros have been known to place a foot on it to sing 'Aprite un po' quegl'occhi', and Papagenos and Papagenas to sit on it for their duet. Some temperamental Italian singers have been known to hiss rude remarks at the prompter for having failed to give them a cue in a loud enough voice, and the ensuing aria has even become a duet. On one occasion a singer helped the prompter to find his place in the score.

Prophète, Le. Opera in 5 acts by Meyerbeer; text by Scribe. Prod. Paris, O., 16 Apr. 1849, with Viardot, Castellan, Roger, Levasseur, cond. Girard; London, C.G., 24 July 1849, with Viardot, Hayes, Mario, Tagliafico, cond. Costa. New Orleans 1 Apr. 1850 with Devries, Tabon-Bessin, Duluc, Scott. The opera is based on an historical episode during the Anabaptist rising in Holland in the 16th century; the real John of Leyden was Jan Neuckelzoon, born in 1509, who had himself crowned in Münster in 1535, when the city became the scene of orgy and cruelty.

The plot describes the love of John of Leyden (ten.) for Bertha (sop.), whom Count Oberthal (bar.), ruler of Dordrecht, desires for himself. The opera ends with the palace of Münster being set on fire and the powder magazine blowing up, killing the Anabaptists, who have turned against John; he is now joined in death in the blazing palace by his mother Fidès (mezzo).

Proserpine (Greek, Persephone). In Latin and Greek mythology the daughter of Jupiter (Zeus) and Ceres (Demeter) who was carried off by Pluto (Hades) to become his wife and rule over the shades. Ceres, goddess of agriculture, did not allow the earth to produce until Mercury (Hermes) had rescued Proserpine. Even after her rescue she was bound to return to the underworld for a third of the year–she thus represents the seed-corn, hidden in the ground and bursting forth to nourish men and animals. Operas on her legend are as follows. Monteverdi (1630, lost); Ferrari (1641); Colonna (1645); Lully (1680); Sacrati (1696); Asioli (1785); Paisiello (1803); Winter (1804); Saint-Saëns (1887); Bianchi (1938); J.J. Castro (1951).

Prospectus. The name given to the booklet issued by the managements of the large opera houses (especially C.G., and H.M.'s in the Gye-Mapleson era, and still issued by the Met.) announcing the coming season's plans. The C.G. prospectuses of the 1850s, 1860s etc. generally contained promises of new works and artists, many of which never appeared. The managements themselves indulged in self-eulogy, and the nobility and gentry were invited to take up subscriptions for the season. The German theatres issue their seasonal prospectus (*Spielplan*) well in advance, the Italian houses their *Indiscrezioni* rather nearer the beginning of each season.

Protesta (It protest, declaration). The affirmation printed in many 17th and 18th cent. Italian librettos to the effect that, while using such figurative terms as 'Fate' or other pagan usages, the author was a faithful Roman Catholic; this was often necessary, especially in the Papal States, in order to obtain the Church's *Imprimatur*.

Prova (It trial, rehearsal). The *prova generale* is the dress rehearsal to which members of the public and often critics are admitted. Both terms are currently used in many opera houses.
See also *Probe, Répétition*.

Pryanishnikov, Ippolit (Petrovich) (*b* Kerch, 26 Aug. 1847; *d* Moscow, 11 Nov. 1921). Russian baritone and producer. Studied St Petersburg 1873-4, then Milan. Sang in Italy 1875-7. St Petersburg, M., 1878-86 (début as the Demon). Singer and producer Tiflis 1886-9, Moscow 1892-3; some perfs. cond. Tchaikovsky, who much admired him. Created Lionel (*Maid of Orleans*), Mizgir (*Snow Maiden*); first St Petersburg Onegin, Mazeppa. Productions include first Moscow *Stone Guest, Igor, May Night*; translated and prod. *Pagliacci*. Taught Baklanov, Mravina, Slavina, and Nikolay Figner.

Puccini, Giacomo (*b* Lucca, 22 Dec. 1858; *d* Brussels, 29 Nov. 1924). Italian composer. Puccini's four immediate paternal ancestors were opera composers, and he received his first instruction at Lucca, where the family had always lived. His name won him a subsidy to study at Milan, where at the suggestion of his teacher, Ponchielli, he wrote his first opera, the 1-act *Le Villi* (1883). Rejected by a prize committee, the work was recommended by Boito and produced at Milan in 1884. Though it is a number opera, bound by many conventions and influences, something of the later skill in handling ensembles and the orchestra already appears. This was one of the few operas by his juniors to win the admiration of the aged Verdi. *Edgar* (1889) was a notorious failure, largely because of its libretto; yet it contains some impressive strokes and certainly shows the composer's dramatic growth.

With *Manon Lescaut* (1893) we reach the first work of his mastery. Some elements–the choral scenes, for instance–are already fully mature; some are still developing; but the unevenness and certain failures of characterization are less noticeable than the fresh impulse and generous invention of the music.

In *La Bohème* (1896) the apprenticeship is complete. Puccini's voice is fully his own, though it is used to describe a foreign city, Paris. The characterization is more certain, deeper, lighter; there is a richer attention to detail and the melody of dialogue. Above all, perhaps, there is a deceptive casualness of method and raciness of incident that, concealing the immaculate craftsmanship, ideally mirror the gay, shiftless existence of the Bohemians.

Tosca (1900), based on Sardou's morbid thriller, has a darker intensity of feeling and a more powerful dramatic flow. The characters are more strongly, even violently, depicted, and dense use of *Leitmotiv* in a widened and tenser harmonic idiom provides the method for Puccini's clash of lurid personality and situation.

With *Madama Butterfly* (1904), Puccini turned to a play by David Belasco (a kind of American Sardou) and back to what was now established, as Mosco Carner has shown, as the typical Puccini heroine–the 'little girl' whose love involves tragic guilt that must be expiated. But the lessons of Tosca had been learnt: the *Leitmotive* (some based on genuine Japanese tunes) are more fluently and expressively used; the musical idiom is subtler in its penetration of a small, precious, remote world hemmed with conventions.

In *La fanciulla del West* (1910), Puccini tackled exoticism of the geographically opposite sort in a superficially similar manner but showed his concern to modernize his idiom. Belasco's jumble of a plot – Wagnerian redemption in a mining camp – concerned the composer less than its strange and striking situations; the lack of lyrical scenes and the blankness of the characters – which partly account for the work's neglect – are largely compensated for by the vitality of the action, the expansive musical vision of the Californian setting, and the brilliant craftsmanship.

Resemblances to Verdi's opera caused *La rondine* (1917) to be dubbed 'the poor man's Traviata'; Puccini was unhappy about this operetta from the start, and certainly his invention flagged – though not his accomplishment, as is shown in the crowd scenes. Harmonically it continues the *Fanciulla* advance and even foreshadows *Turandot*.

Il Trittico (1918) follows the unusual but successful plan of contrasting in one evening a lurid thriller, *Il Tabarro*, a sentimental tragedy, *Suor Angelica*, and a comedy, *Gianni Schicchi*. These 1-act pieces gain from the contrast, but each is successful in its own right. *Tabarro* is dark, evocative work, compact but rich in atmosphere, harmonically tense and economical in structure, perceptively relating the weary lives of the characters to the river on which they live and toil. *Angelica* is a gentle work, largely low-pitched in tension and, despite a sympathetic evocation of the cloister's quiet, not escaping the charge of dramatic flatness. *Schicchi* is a brilliant farce, racy and bitingly witty, deftly scored, creating its own atmosphere as surely as its companion works.

Turandot (1926) begun in 1921, was to remain unfinished: it has been suggested that the task of showing fulfilled love was beyond Puccini. Yet here he was able to give rein, in an unusually sympathetic operatic framework and with long-mastered technique, to elements that form the basis of his style–the passionately heroic (Calaf), the 'little girl' pathetic (Liù), the comic-grotesque (the Masks), and the exotic (the Chinese setting). There is, moreover, a structural mastery that places *Turandot* at the peak of Puccini's achievement; while a plot both plainer and crueller than that of *Tosca* grows from fairy-tale thriller to tragedy and love story in one. Puccini has had no successor, and he was a much more limited artist than his great predecessor, Verdi. Though he was at pains to modernize his style, he is instinctively a 'late' artist.

Bibl: M. Carner: *Puccini* (1958, 2/1975).

Puppet opera. The popularity of puppet theatres throughout history, and the virtuosity of the puppeteers in some countries (notably Czechoslovakia), has led their managers to attempt opera from time to time. The first première given by puppets was probably of Ziani's *Damira placata* (Venice 1680). Haydn wrote several puppet operas for Esterháza, one of which, *Philemon und Baucis*, has been given in London. In our own century the Teatro dei Piccoli in Rome has staged opera performances with singers behind the stage. Falla's *El Retablo de Maese Pedro* requires a puppet theatre which performs to live singers; the puppets are eventually attacked by Don Quixote, who becomes confused about their reality. At the first performance all, including Quixote, were puppets. The Salzburg Marionettentheater has given opera performances, and the Hogarth Puppets have staged *El Retablo* (Ingestre 1957).

Purcell, Henry (*b* London, *c*1659; *d* London, 21 Nov. 1695). English composer. It is clear from the one work of Purcell which may properly be classed as an opera, *Dido and Aeneas*, that the fashion of the day which deflected his dramatic powers into extravagant stage spectacles (such as the Dryden-Davenant version of *The Tempest*) deprived England of its greatest operatic composer. Purcell himself regretted the inferior position of music among the stage effects, especially in the light of Italian and French opera. *Dido* itself is a great operatic masterpiece–one of such dramatic potency and such depth of human understanding as to make its uniqueness a tragedy.

Bibl: J. Westrup: *Purcell* (2/1965).

Puritani, I (rightly, *I Puritani di Scozia*–The Puritans of Scotland). Opera in 3 acts by Bellini; text by Pepoli, after the play *Têtes Rondes et Cavaliers* by Ancelot and Saintine, in its turn derived from Scott's novel *Old Mortality* (1816). Prod Paris, T.I., 25 Jan. 1835, with Grisi, Rubini, Tamburini, Lablache; London, King's T., 21 May 1835, with same cast; Philadelphia, Chestnut St. T., 22 July 1843 - records of première lost, but perf. a few weeks later by same company incl. Ester Corsini, Perozzi, Calvet, Valtelina.

The opera is set in Plymouth at the time of the Civil War. Queen Henrietta (mezzo), widow of Charles I, is held prisoner in a fortress whose Warden is the Puritan Lord Walton (bass). His daughter Elvira (sop.) is in love with Lord Arthur Talbot (ten.), a Cavalier, and permission for the two to wed has been given. Arthur helps Henrietta to escape by dressing her in Elvira's bridal veil. Elvira, thinking she has been betrayed, loses her reason, which is restored when Arthur is reunited with her. Arthur is pardoned by the victorious Cromwell.

Pushkin, Alexander (Sergeyevich) (*b* Moscow, 26 May 1799; *d* St Petersburg, 29 Jan. 1837). Operas on his works are as follows:

The Triumph of Bacchus (1818); Dargomyzhsky (1848).

Ruslan and Lyudmila (1820): Glinka (1842).

The Captive of the Caucasus (1821): Alyabyev (unfin., c1820); Cui (1883); Popova (1929).

The Fountain of Bakhchiserai (1823): Mêchura (*Marie Potocka*, 1871; Fyodorov (1895); Zubov (1898); Ilyinsky (1899); Parusinov (1912); Krylov (1912); Arkhangelsky (1915); Smetanin (*Khan Girey*, 1935); Shaposhnikov (1940).

The Gipsies (1824): Wielhorski (1838); Kashperov (1850); Lishin (1876, unfin.); Morosov (1892); Konius (1892); Rakhmaninov (*Aleko*, 1893); Zubov (1894); Juon (1896); Sacchi (1899); Ferretto (1899); Mironov (?1900); Shäfer (1901); Siks (1906); Galkauskas (1908); Leoncavallo (1912); Shostakovich (lost); Kalafaty (1941); Shakhmatov (1949); Snatokov (1952).

The Bridegroom (1825); Blüm (1899).

Count Nulin (1825): Lishin (1876); Zubov (1894); Strelnikov (1938); Koval (comp. 1949, unfin.)

Boris Godunov (1825); Mussorgsky (1874) (historical subject also previously set by Mattheson, 1710).

Scene from 'Faust' (1825): Asafyev (comp. 1936).

The Negro of Peter the Great (1827, unfin.): Arapov (*The Frigate 'Pobeva'*, comp 1958); Lourié (1958).

Eugene Onegin (1828); Tchaikovsky (1879).

Poltava (1829): Vietinghoff-Scheel (*Mazeppa*, 1859); Sokalski (1859, unfin.); Du Bois (late 19th cent); Tchaikovsky (*Mazeppa*, 1884).

The Snowstorm (1830): Dzerzhinsky (*Winter Night*, 1946).

Mistress into Maid (1830): Larionov (1875); Zajc (*Lizinka*, 1878); Ekkert (1911); Spassky (1923); Biryukov (1947); Kovner (1948); Dukelsky (1958).

The Tale of the Parson and his Man Balda (1830): Karagichev (1931); Bakalov (comp. 1937).

The Little House at Kolomna (1830): Solovyov (1899, unfin.); Stravinsky (*Mavra*, 1922).

The Shot (1830): Strassenburg (1936).

The Post Master (1830): Kryukov (1940); Reuter (*Postmeister Wyrin*, 1947).

The Undertaker (1830): Yanovsky (1923); Admoni-Krasny (1935).

A Feast in Time of Plague (1830): Cui (1901); Rechmensky (1927); Lourié (1933); Tarnopolsky (1937); Dodnov (1930); Asafyev (1940); Goldenweiser (1942).

The Stone Guest (1830): Dargomyzhsky (1872); Malipiero (1963).

Mozart and Salieri (1830); Rimsky-Korsakov (1898).

The Covetous Knight (1830): Rakhmaninov (1906); Kryukov (1917).

Roslavev (1831): Bagrinovsky (*1812,* comp 1927).

The Tale of Tsar Saltan (1831); Rimsky-Korsakov (1900); Nikolsky (1913); Nasedkin (1950s).

Rusalka (1832); Dargomyzhsky (1856); De Maistre (1870); Alexandrov (1913); Stepanov (1913).

Angelo (1833); Kuznetsov (1894).

Dubrovsky (1833): Nápravník (1894); Napoli (1974).

The Tale of the Fisherman and the Fish (1833): Polovinkin (1934); Gibalin (1936); Parchomenko (1936); Manukyan (1937); Croses (1942).

The Bronze Horseman (1833): Asafyev (1942).

The Dead Princess (1833): Vessol (1909); Mittelstädt (1913); Krasev (1924); Weisberg (1936); Emelyanova (1939); Kotilko (1946); Chernyak (1947); Zybin (1949).

The Queen of Spades (1834): Halévy (distantly: 1850); Suppé (1865); Tchaikovsky (1890).

The Captain's Daughter (1834): Cui (1911); Katz (1941).

The Golden Cockerel (1834): Drasev (1907); Rimsky-Korsakov (1909).

Also: Kreitner: *The Death of Pushkin* (1937, unfin.: uses settings of seven Pushkin poems);

PYNE

Shekhter: *Pushkin in Exile* (1958). Prokofiev planned an opera on Pushkin and Glinka.

Pyne, Louisa (*b* ?, 27 Aug. 1832; *d* London, 20 Mar. 1904). English soprano. Studied with George Smart. Début Boulogne 1849, Amina; appeared Princess's Theatre, D.L., Hm., and C.G. Toured U.S.A., 1854-6. On her return to England joined *Harrison in formation of the Pyne-Harrison Opera Company, giving seasons at the Ly., D.L., and C.G. 1858-64, during which time she created leading roles in *Satanella, Lurline, Bianca, Lily of Killarney, Armourer of Nantes, Blanche de Nevers*, etc. Said to have possessed a soprano voice of beautiful quality and great flexibility.

Q

Quadri, Argeo (*b* Como, 23 Feb. 1911). Italian conductor. Has conducted in all the leading Italian opera houses. London, C.G., 1956; Vienna, V.O., 1957-75, where he has conducted very many performances of the Italian and French repertory. Directed Verdi commemoration performances of *La traviata* at Busseto 1951, and Puccini performances at Viareggio of *La fanciulla del West* and *Madama Butterfly*. (R)

Quadrio, Francesco Saverio (*b* Ponte in Valtellina, 1 Dec. 1695; *d* Milan, 21 Nov. 1756). Italian author and theorist. Volumes 2 and 3 of his seven-volume *Della storia e della ragione d'ogni poesia* (1749) discuss opera, oratorio, and cantata. Probably the first writer to recognise and discuss the relationship between poetry and music in the theatre. His ideas were put into practice by Goldoni. Provided valuable comments on many of the singers active at the time especially the *castrati*.

Quaglio. German (orig. Italian) family of scene-designers who were active from the early 18th to the 20th cent. They generally worked in pairs and made an important contribution to the visual aspect of German Romantic opera. Of the 6 generations, 15 members of the family were active as designers.
(1) **Giulio I** (*b* Laino, 1601; *d* Vienna , after 1668). A fresco painter who occasionally worked for the stage.
(2) **Giulio II** (*b* Laino, 1668; *d* Laino, 3 July 1751). Son of (I). Not active in the theatre.
(3) **Giulio III** or Giovanni Maria I (*b* Laino, c.1700; *d* Vienna, 1765). Known as G. Quaglio, he was the son or nephew of (2) and father of (5). Designed operas for Viennese Court, making considerable use of transparent drops. Among his designs were those for Gluck's *Cinesi* (1754), *Orfeo* (1762), and *Telemacho* (1762).
(4) **Carlo** (*b* ?; *d* ?). Son of (3). Worked in Vienna and Warsaw (1766-7).
(5) **Lorenzo I** (*b* Laino, 25 May 1730; *d* Munich, 7 May 1804 or 5). Worked in Mannheim, Schwetzingen, designing works by Salieri, Galuppi, Hasse, and Paisiello. Dresden, 1769; designed new Ducal Theatre at Zweibrücken 1775-6, and new Schlosstheater at Mannheim (with Alessandro Bibiena). Munich from 1781; designed the sets for première of *Idomeneo*. His designs are preserved in the Theatre Museum, Munich, and the Uffizi Gallery, Florence.
(6) **Martin** (*b* ?; *d* ?). Son of Giovanni Maria I. Worked at Mannheim with his brother and later at Kassel.

(7) **Domenico I** (*b* Laino, 1708, *d* Laino 1773). Son of (3) or (2). Worked in Milan, Salzburg, and Vienna.
(8) **Giuseppe** (*b* Laino, 1747; *d* Munich, 23 Jan. 1828). Son of (7). Second designer at Mannheim and Schwetzingen, also worked at Ludwigsburg, Speyer, and Frankfurt. Designed Redoutensaal in Mannheim. His designs in Munich include those for *Don Giovanni*, *Zauberflöte*, and *Freischütz*.
(9) **Giulio IV** (*b* Laino, 1764; *d* Munich, 27 Jan. 1801). Son of (7). Worked in Mannheim (1770), Munich (1778), Zweibrücken, and Dessau, where he collaborated with Pozzi and Koch in constructing the Hoftheater. Returned Munich 1799, and from 1800 until his premature death was director of productions there.
(10) **Giovanni Maria II** (*b* Mannheim, 1772; *d* Munich, 1813). Son of (5). Worked in Munich and Mannheim but mostly engaged on military work.
(11) **Angelo I** (*b* Munich 13 Aug. 1784; *d* Munich 2 Apr. 1815). Son of (8). Worked in Munich 1801-15.
(12) **Domenico II** (*b* Munich, 1 Jan. 1787; *d* Hohenschwangau, 9 Apr. 1837). Son of (8). Munich 1803-14.
(13) **Lorenzo II** (*b* Munich, 19 Dec. 1793; *d* Munich, 15 Mar. 1869). Son of (8).
(14) **Simon** (*b* Munich, 23 Oct. 1795; *d* Munich, 8 Mar. 1878). Son of (8). Succeeded his brother (12) in 1814 and his father in 1828, at the Hoftheater. Most prolific of the family. One of the first designers to use built scenery in 1839; designed more than 100 productions between 1828 and 1860, including the first Munich *Fidelio* and *Freischütz*, scenes for *Lohengrin* (1858) and *Tannhäuser* (1855); these were highly realistic and clearly anticipated pre-First World War design at Bayreuth.
(15) **Angelo II** (*b* Munich, 13 Dec. 1829; *d* Munich 5 Jan. 1890). Son of (14). Worked with his father in Munich from 1849 and designed the first *Meistersinger*, *Tristan und Isolde*, *Rheingold*, *Walküre*, and important productions of *Oberon* and Gluck's *Armida*, all of which revealed a flair for epic architecture. The courtyard at Ludwig's castle of Neuschwanstein is supposedly based on Act 2 of Angelo's 1867 Munich *Lohengrin*. Dresden, 1865-1880; also worked in Prague and St Petersburg. Designs in the Munich Theatre Museum and Ludwig II Museum at Herrenchiemsee.
(16) **Franz** (*b* Munich, 22 Apr. 1844; *d* Wassenburg, 19 Feb. 1920). Son of (14).
(17) **Angelo III** (*b* Munich, 11 June 1877; *d* Munich, 20 Mar. 1917). Son of (16).
(18) **Eugen** (*b* Munich 3 Apr. 1857; *d* Berlin 24 Sept 1942). Son of (15). Worked with his father in Munich and later in Berlin, Stuttgart, and Prague until 1923.

Quand'ero paggio. Falstaff's (bar.) arietta in

Act 2 of Verdi's *Falstaff* in which he recalls the days when he was a slender young page to the Duke of Norfolk.

Quando le sere al placido. Rodolfo's (ten.) aria in Act 2 of Verdi's *Luisa Miller*, in which he recalls his love for Luisa.

Quanto è bella! Nemorino's (ten.) aria in the opening scene of Donizetti's *L'elisir d'amore*, which he sings as he looks on the beautiful young Adina.

Quatro Rusteghi, I (The Four Curmudgeons). Opera in 3 acts by Wolf-Ferrari; text by Pizzolato, after Goldoni's comedy. Prod in German as *Die vier Grobiane*, Munich 19 Mar. 1906, with Bosetti, Matzenauer, Tordek, Gever, Koppe, Walter, Sieglitz, Geis, Bender, Bauberger, cond. Mottl; London, S.W., as *The School for Fathers*, 7 June 1946 with Gruhn, Jackson, Hill, Iacopi, Glynne, Franklin, cond. Robertson; N.Y., C.C., as *The Four Ruffians*, 18 Oct. 1951, with Faull, Yeend, Russell, Scott, Mayer, Pease, cond. Halasz.

The opera tells of the efforts of four boorish husbands to keep their womenfolk in order, and of the women's stratagems to allow Lucieta (sop.), daughter of Lunardo (bass), to see Filipeto (ten.), son of Maurizio (bass), before their wedding, despite the opposition of the men. The Intermezzo is one of the composer's most delightful little pieces.

Queen of Night, The. Sarastro's evil adversary (sop.), Pamina's mother, in Mozart's *Die Zauberflöte*.

Queen of Shemakha, The. The Queen (sop.) in Rimsky-Korsakov's *The Golden Cockerel.*

Queen of Spades, The. Opera in 3 acts by Tchaikovsky; text by Modest Tchaikovsky, with suggestions and contributions from the composer, after Pushkin's story (1834). Prod. St Petersburg, M., 19 Dec. 1890, with M. Figner, Dolina, Piltz, Olgina, Slavina, N. Figner, Yakovlev, Melnikov, Vasilyev, Frey, Kondaraki, cond. Nápravník; N.Y., Met., 5 Mar. 1910, with Destinn, Meitschik, Slezak, Forsell, Didur, cond. Mahler; London, London O.H., 29 May 1915, with Nikitina, Krasavina, Rosing, Bonell, Kimbell, cond. Gurevich.

The opera tells of the love of Hermann, a young officer, for Lisa, granddaughter of the old Countess, once a gambler known as the Queen of Spades, who is said to possess the secret of winning at cards. Hermann goes to the Countess's bedroom at night to obtain the secret from her so as to win enough money to marry, but so terrifies her that she dies without speaking. Her ghost appears to him and reveals the secret: 'Three, seven, ace.' As Hermann

becomes obsessed with winning, Lisa drowns herself. He wins on the first two stakes he makes–3 and 7. He then stakes all on the third card, which he thinks will be the ace, but which is the Queen of Spades; at the same time the Countess's ghost appears, and Hermann, losing his reason, kills himself.

Other operas on the subject by Halévy (1850) and Suppé (1865).

Querelle des Bouffons. See *Guerre des Bouffons.*

Questa o quella. The Duke of Mantua's (ten.) aria in the opening scene of Verdi's *Rigoletto* in which he declares that all women attract him.

Quickly, Mistress. A lady of Windsor (mezzo) who decoys Falstaff to his two disastrous rendezvous, in Verdi's *Falstaff*, and in Vaughan Williams's *Sir John in Love.*

Qui la voce. The opening words of Elvira's (sop.) Mad Scene in Bellini's *I Puritani.*

Quinault, Philippe (*b* Paris, 3 Jun. 1635; *d* Paris, 26 Nov. 1688). French dramatist and librettist. Though an established dramatist by the time he turned to opera, he was able to modify his technique with great skill to the requirements of opera and of his famous, and demanding, collaborator, *Lully. As servant of the composer who was directly subject to the King, Louis XIV, he wrote formal scenes, expressing stereotyped noble sentiments, in verse whose stateliness and grace reflected the Court's expression of Royal *gloire* (frequently remarked upon in a special Prologue). Thus, despite their often tremendous adventures, Quinault's heroes seem to express above all the weaker emotions. Love is generally idyllic. The chief influences on Quinault were Romantic novels and the melodramatic Spanish tragedies; he made much use of scenic effects and pantomime or dance sequences, all marked by the frequent intervention of the miraculous. Quinault's development of *tragédie lyrique* for Lully was a crucial influence on later French opera, and had an important effect on the manner of *Grand opera.

Quodlibet (*Lat* what pleases). A kind of musical game of the 16th, 17th, and early 18th cent., involving extempore juxtaposition of different melodies. The three dances in the Act 1 finale of Mozart's *Don Giovanni* form a quodlibet. In the 19th cent. German theatre it came to mean the confections made of the favourite pieces of many composers which were interpolated in plays at the Theater an der Wien, rather in the same way that Arne and Arnold put together *Love in a Village* and *The Maid of the Mill.*

R

Raaff, Anton (b Gelsdorf, bapt. 6 May 1714; d Munich, 28 May 1797). German tenor. Studied for the priesthood, then sent by Elector Clemens August to study singing in Munich with Ferrandini and in Bologna with Bernacchi. Returned to Germany 1742; also sang in Vienna 1749, Italy 1752, Lisbon and Madrid 1755 with Farinelli, with whom he went to Naples 1759. Sang at Court of Carl Theodor, Mannheim 1770 and on its move to Munich, 1778. In Mannheim Mozart wrote a concert aria for him, and in 1781 the part of Idomeneo; there is a charming account in Mozart's letters of how carefully he tried to suit Raaff, then 64 and by his own admission unable to sustain notes as well as formerly. 'I like an aria to fit a singer as perfectly as a well-made suit of clothes', Mozart wrote; and 'Fuor del mar' in *Idomeneo* was written to make the most of Raaff's qualities.

Rabaud, Henri (Benjamin) (b Paris, 10 Nov. 1873; d Paris, 11 Sept. 1949). French composer and conductor. Studied Paris with Gédalge and Massenet. Conducted Paris O., 1908–18, Director 1914–18. Director Paris Conservatoire 1920–40. His operas are *La Fille de Roland* (1904), *Mârouf* (1914), *L'Appel de la mer* (after Synge's *Riders to the Sea*, 1924), *Roland et le mauvais garçon* (Roland and the Bad Boy, 1934), *Martine* (1947), *Les Jeux de l'amour et du hasard* (The Games of Love and Chance, 1954; completed by Busser and D'Ollone).

Rabelais, François (b Chinon, c1494; d ? Paris, ? 9 Apr. 1553). French writer. Operas on his works are as follows.
Pantagruel (1532): Grétry (*Panurge dans l'île des lanternes*, 1785); Planquette (*Panurge,* 1895); Terrasse (*Pantagruel,* 1911); Massenet (*Panurge,* 1913); Sutermeister (*Séraphine,* 1959)
Gargantua (1534): Mariotte (1935).
? *L'Isle sonante* (1562): Monsigny (1767).
Also opera *Rabelais* by Ganne (1892).

Rachel, quand du Seigneur. Éléazar's (ten.) aria in Act 4 of Halévy's *La Juive,* in which the Jewish goldsmith sings of his conflicting emotions, torn as he is between letting Rachel die at the hands of the Christians or saving her life by telling Cardinal Brogni that she is in fact the latter's daughter.

Rachmaninov. See *Rakhmaninov.*

Racine, Jean (b La Ferté-Milon, 21 Dec. 1639; d Paris, 21 Apr. 1699). French poet and dramatist. Operas on his works are as follows:
Alexandre (1665): Méreaux (1783).

Andromaque (1667): Grétry (1780); Rossini (*Ermione,* 1814).
Britannicus (1669): Graun (1751).
Bérénice (1670): Magnard (1911).
Bajazet (1672): Hervé (*Les Turcs,* parody of Racine, 1869).
Mithridate (1673): Graun (1750); Scheinpflug (1754); Gasparini (1767); Mozart (1770).
Iphigénie en Aulide (1675): Graun (1748); Gluck (1774).
Phèdre (1677): Lemoyne (1786).
Esther (1688): Meyerowitz (1957).
Athalie (1691): Handel (1720); Poissl (1814); Weisgall (1964).

Radamès. The leader of the Egyptian army (ten.), hero of Verdi's *Aida.*

Radamisto. Opera in 3 acts by Handel; text by Nicolo Haym, altered from *L'amor tirannico,* attrib. Domenico Lalli. Prod. London, King's T., 27 Apr. 1720, with Durastini, Montagnana. Revived Handel Opera Society, 1960.

Radford, Robert (b Nottingham, 13 May 1874; d London, 3 Mar. 1933). English bass. Studied London, R.A.M., with Randegger. Concerts from 1899; stage début London, C.G., 1904, Commendatore. Sang Hagen and Hunding in English *Ring* under Richter, and subsequently became leading member of the Beecham and B.N.O.C. companies; a founder and director of the latter. First Boris in English, greatly admired in Wagner and Mozart. (R) His daughter **Winifred Radford** sang at Gly. 1934–8. (R)

Radio opera. In the early days of the century an aria from *Carmen* sung by Mariette Mazarin was broadcast from the Manhattan Opera, and in 1910 parts of *Cavalleria rusticana* (Destinn, Riccardo Martin) and *Pagliacci* (Caruso, Amato) were broadcast from the Met. The first European broadcast of a complete opera was *Hänsel und Gretel* (C.G., 6 Jan. 1923). Two years later a New York station began weekly opera broadcasts, and on 7 Sept. the first regular American opera performance was relayed (*Aida* at the Met.). The first transatlantic opera broadcast was from Dresden to America (*Fidelio,* 16 Mar. 1930). The first opera written for broadcasting was Walter Goehr's *Malpopita* (Berlin, 1930). Skilton's *Sun Bride* was also first performed in 1930. Another early radio opera was Cadman's *The Willow Tree* (1933). In 1939 N.B.C., New York, commissioned Menotti's *The Old Maid and the Thief,* and in 1943 Montemezzi's *L'incantesimo.* Saturday afternoon live broadcasts from the Metropolitan, N.Y., sponsored by Texaco, are also taken by stations all over the U.S.A. and Canada and, linked with the Metropolitan Opera Guild's magazine *Opera News,* form a strong link between the opera public outside New York and the Metropolitan.

Since the Second World War opera broadcasts in Europe have become a regular feature. The B.B.C.'s Third Programme (later Radio 3), the Italian Radio's third network, and the French Radio's music programme all plan special series of opera broadcasts, either live or recorded from opera houses and festivals, in the studio, or on tapes borrowed from one another, including works that otherwise would be rarely or never performed for economic reasons. The B.B.C.'s survey of French opera 1974–5 and the Italian Radio's Verdi cycle 1950–51 were especially noteworthy. Most companies commission new works from time to time, and these have included Henze's *Elegy for Young Lovers,* Dallapiccola's *Il prigioniero,* and Sutermeister's *Die schwarze Spinne.* See also *Television Opera, British Broadcasting Corporation.*

Raimondi, Gianni (*b* Bologna, 17 Apr. 1923). Italian tenor, studied with Melandri and Barra-Caracciolo. Début Budrio, 1947, Pinkerton. London, Stoll T., 1953; Milan, Sc., since 1955; N.Y., Met., 1965–9; San Francisco 1957–8. Especially successful in Donizetti and early Verdi roles; more recently has assumed heavier roles including Pollione, Gabriele Adorno, and Arrigo. (R)

Raimondi, Ruggero (*b* Bologna, 3 Oct. 1941). Italian bass. Studied Rome with Edwige Ghibaudo, Teresa Pediconi, and Piervenanzi. Début Spoleto, 1964, Colline. Rome, O., since 1965; Milan, Sc., since 1970; N.Y., Met., since 1970–1; Gly., 1969, Don Giovanni; London, C.G., Fiesco, 1972. Repertory also includes Attila, Procida, Padre Guardiano, and other Verdi bass roles, Boris Godunov, and Mosè. Has a beautiful *basso-cantante* voice and a handsome stage presence. (R)

Raimund, Ferdinand (*b* Vienna, 1 June 1790; *d* Pottenstein, 5 Sept. 1836). Austrian dramatist, actor, and producer. Spent all his life in the theatre, working especially in the Vienna J. and L. A popular actor, but especially remembered for his brilliant series of magic comedies with music by, among others, Wenzel Müller, Drechsler, Riotte, and Konradin Kreutzer. He also wrote tunes for them himself. His subjects frequently treat the humour of situation and local allusion, such as the effect of transferring an ordinary Viennese citizen to fairyland. In these classic examples of the *Posse, he won wide popularity, especially with *Der Alpenkönig und der Menschenfeind* (1828). Other great successes included *Der Diamant des Geisterkönigs* (1824) and *Das Mädchen aus der Feenwelt* (1826).
Bibl: D. Prohaska: *Raimund and Vienna* (1970).

Rainforth, Elizabeth (*b* ? 23 Nov. 1814; *d* Bristol, 22 Sept. 1877). English soprano. Studied London with George Persy and T.

Cooke, and later with Crivelli. Début London, St James's 1836, Mandane (*Artaxerxes*). C.G., 1838–43, then D.L., created Arline (*Bohemian Girl*), 1843. Repertory also included Susanna, Countess Almaviva, Lodoïska, and Zerlina (*Fra Diavolo*).

Raisa, Rosa (orig. Rose Burchstein) (*b* Białystok, 23 May 1893; *d* Los Angeles, 28 Sept. 1963). Polish soprano. Fled from Poland during a pogrom and reached Naples. Studied there with Eva Tetrazzini and Marchisio. Début Parma 1913, Leonora (*Oberto*); Baltimore Nov. 1913, Mimì; Chicago 1913–37, sang in American premières of *Isabeau, La nave,* and *La fiamma.* London, C.G., 1914 and 1933; Milan, Sc., 1916, 1923–6 – first Asteria (*Nerone*) and Turandot. A thrilling singer and actress; greatly admired as Norma, Tosca, and Maliella. (R) Married the baritone **Giacomo Rimini** (1887–1952), who sang in Milan, London, Chicago, and elsewhere; they set up a school of singing in Chicago in 1937. (R)

Rake's Progress, The. Opera in 3 acts and epilogue by Stravinsky; text by W. H. Auden and Chester Kallman, after Hogarth's eight engravings (1735). Prod. Venice, F., 11 Sept. 1951, with Schwarzkopf, Tourel, Rounseville, Kraus, cond. Stravinsky; N.Y., Met., 14 Feb. 1953, with Gueden, Thebom, Conley, Harrell, cond. Reiner; Edinburgh, 25 Aug. 1953, by Gly. Company, with Morison, Merriman, Lewis, Hines, cond. Wallenstein.

Tom Rakewell (ten.) leaves Anne Trulove (sop.) to go to London when Nick Shadow (bar.) appears with news of sudden wealth. His physical pleasures palling, Tom is easily tempted by Shadow, now his servant, first to marry the fantastic bearded lady Baba the Turk (mezzo) and then to place his trust in a fake machine for turning stones into bread. He goes bankrupt, and all his effects are sold. The year and a day stipulated by Shadow for their association being at an end, Shadow reveals himself as the Devil and claims Tom's soul. But Shadow suggests a gamble for Tom's soul, and Tom wins; Nick sinks into the ground, but makes Tom mad. The final scene finds Tom in Bedlam, believing himself to be Adonis; Anne now takes her last leave of him. In the Epilogue the characters point the moral: 'For idle hearts and hands and minds the Devil finds a work to do.'

Rakhmaninov, Sergey (Vasilyevich) (*b* Oneg, 1 Apr. 1873; *d* Beverly Hills, 28 Mar. 1943). Russian composer and pianist. His first opera, *Aleko* (1893), was championed by Tchaikovsky and its first production won some approval. Though immature, being written as a student exercise, it contains some impressive music, and was revived for Shalyapin. *The Miserly Knight* (1906), like *Aleko* based on

Pushkin, is a stronger work, late Romantic in language influenced by both Tchaikovsky and Wagner, but also suggesting Bartók's rich manner in *Duke Bluebeard's Castle.* Written for an all-male cast, the opera is cast in three scenes, the central one consisting of a superb monologue for the Knight, intended for Shalyapin. For *Francesca da Rimini* (1906), Rakhmaninov had a poor libretto by Modest Tchaikovsky, and the work has not been successful. Apart from an uncompleted setting of Maeterlinck's *Monna Vanna* (1906), Rakhmaninov never returned to opera.
Bibl: G. Norris: *Rakhmaninov* (1976).

Ralf, Torsten (*b* Malmö, 2 Jan. 1901; *d* Stockholm, 27 Apr. 1954). Swedish tenor. Studied Stockholm with Forsell and Berlin with Hertha Dehmlow. Début Stettin 1930, Cavaradossi; Frankfurt 1933–5; Dresden 1935–44 – created Apollo in Strauss's *Daphne*; London, C.G., 1935–9 and 1948; N.Y., Met., 1945–8. Especially successful as Parsifal, Lohengrin, and Walther, and also in Verdi repertory (Radamès and Otello). (R) His elder brother **Oscar** (*b* Malmö, 3 Oct. 1881; *d* Stockholm, 3 Apr. 1964) was leading tenor of the Stockholm Opera 1918–30, where he sang Wagner and Verdi; sang Siegmund at Bayreuth (1927) and Tristan in Paris; toured U.S.A. 1925. Translated more than 40 operas into Swedish. (R)

Rameau, Jean-Philippe (*b* Dijon, 25 Sept. 1683; *d* Paris, 12 Sept. 1764). French composer. Studied with his father, Jean Rameau, organist in Dijon, and in Italy. After three *opéras comiques* for the Fair at St Germain, he wrote his first *opéra tragi-lyrique, Samson,* in 1733: it was unperformed, and the music was later used for *Zoroastre* (1749). There followed the *tragédie, Hippolyte et Aricie* (1733). This met with a doubtful reception despite the enthusiasm of his supporters, among them Campra; but the public recovered more quickly than musicians, and in quick succession popular successes followed for *Les Indes galantes* (1735), *Castor et Pollux* (1737), and *Dardanus* (1737).

Thereafter Rameau's success was assured, though he remained controversial. He came to represent the French tradition in the *Guerre des bouffons – ironically when his first works had been accused of Italianism, which remains present in his operas, though the chief influence was that of Lully. His development of Lully's recitative was his most notable contribution to the tradition; far greater flexibility of treatment, with devices carefully catalogued and labelled as befitted a great theorist, allowed increased subtlety of characterization. French classical opera remained formal and ornate in his hands, but he brought to it a new power, vividness, and excitement; and if the forms often recall those

of Lully, the treatment has a modernity that looks far forward. In the last 30 years of his life, he wrote 25 full-length operas and a number of shorter pieces; it was upon some of the reforms in these that Gluck was able to base his more radical reform of opera. Rameau's developments include the descriptive overture (as in *Zoroastre*), the design of a complete act as a dramatic unity, a restraint on singers and on the da capo aria and hence a greater musical interest given to arioso and recitative, and the development of the role of the orchestra in illustrating and commenting. It was the novel richness of style to which these trends led that caused so much controversy among musicians: Gluck declared of a Rameau opera that it *'puzza di musica'* ('stinks of music'); of *Hippolyte et Aricie,* Rousseau observed that Rameau, 'wished to substitute harmonic speculations for the delight of the ear', while Campra remarked that it contained, 'enough music for ten operas', and went on the prophesy that 'this man will drive us all from the stage'.
Bibl: C. Girdlestone: *Rameau* (1957).

Ramfis. The High Priest (bass) in Verdi's *Aida.*

Rammentatore (*It* prompter). An alternative term for *maestro suggeritore,* or *prompter, in Italian opera houses.

Ranalow, Frederick (*b* Dublin, 7 Nov. 1873; *d* London, 8 Dec. 1953). Irish baritone. Studied London, R.A.M., with Randegger. Leading baritone Beecham Company, where his Figaro, Papageno, and Sachs were highly regarded. In 1922–3 he sang Macheath in the long run of *The Beggar's Opera* at the Lyric, Hammersmith, more than 1,500 times. (R)

Rance, Jack. The Sheriff (bar.) in Puccini's *La fanciulla del West.*

Ranczak, Hildegard (*b* Vitkovice, 20 Dec. 1895). Czech soprano. Studied Vienna. Début Düsseldorf, 1918. Düsseldorf 1918–22. Cologne 1923–5; Stuttgart 1925–7; Munich 1927–1944, 1946–9. London, C.G., 1936, Salome; Paris O., 1937, Octavian. Member of the famous Clemens Krauss Munich ensemble; created Clairon (*Capriccio*). Also a distinguished Dyer's Wife, Aithra (*Aegyptische Helena*) and Zdenka, and a famous Carmen. (R)

Randegger, Alberto (*b* Trieste, 13 Apr. 1832; *d* London, 18 Dec. 1911). Italian, later British, conductor, composer, and teacher. After holding appointments in Brescia and Venice, became professor of singing, R.A.M., 1868. Cond. C.R. 1879–85; D.L. and C.G. 1887–98. His comic opera *The Rival Beauties* was produced at Leeds in 1864.

Rankl, Karl (*b* Gaaden, 1 Oct. 1898; *d* St Gilgen, 6 Sept. 1968). Austrian, later British, conductor and composer. Studied Vienna with Schoenberg and Webern. Vienna, V.O., 1924, conducting *Der Bettelstudent.* After appointments in Reichenberg and Königsberg, became Klemperer's assistant at the Kroll Opera, Berlin, 1928–31; Wiesbaden, 1931–2; Graz, 1932–7; Prague, 1937–9, where he conducted the première of Křenek's *Karl V.* Appointed music director of new English Company at C.G., London, 1946, a position he held until 1951; his work in building up the new opera company was invaluable, though his conducting of Wagner and Verdi did not meet with general approval. At his best in Strauss. Music director, Elizabethan Opera Trust, Australia, 1958–60. His opera *Deirdre of the Sorrows* was one of Festival of Britain prizewinning works 1951, but has never been produced. (R)

Rape of Lucretia, The. Opera in 2 acts by Britten; text by Ronald Duncan, based on André Obey's play *Le Viol de Lucrèce* (1931), in turn based on Shakespeare's poem *The Rape of Lucrece* (1594) and on Livy's history *Ab Urbe Condita Libri,* I, 57-9 (*c* 26 B.C.-17 A.D.). Prod. Gly., 12 July 1946, with Cross, Ferrier, Pears, Kraus, cond. Ansermet; Chicago, 1 June 1947, with Resnik, Kibler, Kane, Rogier, cond. Breisach.

With a male (ten.) and female (sop.) Chorus commenting and eventually drawing a Christian moral, the opera relates the story of the proud, self-destroying Tarquinius (bar.). He rides from the camp where news has come of the Roman wives' infidelity to make an attempt on the virtue of the sole exception, Lucretia (mezzo), wife of Collatinus (bass). Claiming hospitality, he later enters her room and rapes her. Unable to bear the burden of her shame, she kills herself next day in the presence of her urgently summoned husband.

Rappresentazione (*It* representation). A species of acted oratorio, forerunner of opera. See below.

Rappresentazione di anima e di corpo, La (The Representation of the Soul and the Body). Stage oratorio by Emilio de' Cavalieri; text by Agostino Manni. Prod. Rome, S. Filippo Neri, Feb. 1600; Cambridge, Girton College, June 1949; University of N. Dakota, 23 Feb. 1966. The characters represent not only man's soul and body, but various human attributes.

Rasa, Lina Bruna (*b* nr Padua, 24 Sept. 1907). Italian soprano. Studied Padua with Tabarin, Palumbo, Milan with Manilo and Bavagnoli. Début Genoa 1925, Elena (*Mefistofele*). Created Doll Tearsheet in Wolf-Ferrari's *Sly* and Atte in Mascagni's *Nerone* at Sc. Became Mascagni's favourite interpreter of Santuzza, and recorded the role under him for *Cavalleria rusticana*'s 50th anniversary. Also sang Tosca and Isabeau with success. Forced to retire through ill-health while at the height of her powers. (R)

Rasi, Francesco (*b* Arezzo, *c*1575; *d* ?). Italian singer and composer. He was associated with the *Camerata; sang in some of the first operas, including Peri's *Euridice,* and composed an opera, *Ati e Cibele,* for the wedding of the Duke of Mantua and Catherine de' Medici in 1617 (lost). He may also have sung the title-role in Monteverdi's *Orfeo.*

Rataplan. An onomatopoeic word for the sound of a drum. Used for the name of solos and ensembles in operas by Donizetti (*Fille du régiment*), Meyerbeer (*Huguenots*), Verdi (*Forza del destino*); also a trio in Sullivan's *Cox and Box.* Also a Singspiel by Pillwitz (1830).

Ratisbon. See Regensburg.

Rautavaara (Rautawaara). Family of Finnish musicians.

(1) **Väinö** (*b* Ilmajoki, 21 June 1872; *d* Helsinki, 11 Nov. 1950) was a singer who taught in Helsinki.

(2) **Eino** (*b* Ilmajoki, 14 Mar. 1876; *d* Helsinki, 7 Aug. 1939), brother of (1) was a baritone who studied in Italy, Paris, and Berlin. 1911–24 leading baritone Helsinki opera.

(3) **Aulikki** (Terttu) (*b* Vaasa, 2 May 1906) is a soprano, daughter of (1); studied in Helsinki with her father and in Berlin with Olgar Eisner. Début Helsinki, 1932. Gly. 1934–8, Countess Almaviva, Pamina; Salzburg, 1937 (R).

(4) **Einojuhani** (*b* Helsinki, 9 Oct. 1928) is a composer, son of (2). Studied Helsinki and U.S.A. with Copland and Sessions. His works include the operas *Kaivos* (The Pit, 1963) and *Apollo and Marsyas* (1973).

Rauzzini, Matteo (*b* Camerino, 1754; *d* Dublin, 1791). Italian singer, composer, and teacher. Début Munich 1771. Composed three operas, also one in collaboration with Rust; followed his brother Venanzio to England, then settled in Dublin as a teacher.

Rauzzini, Venanzio (*b* Camerino, 19 Dec. 1746; *d* Bath, 8 Apr. 1810). Italian male soprano, composer, and teacher. Brother of the above. Début Rome, T. della Valle, 1765. Sang in Munich, Dresden, Vienna, and in Milan, where he appeared in the première of *Lucio Silla* by Mozart, who also wrote 'Exsultate, jubilate' for him. Went to London 1774 and remained in Britain for the rest of his life. Five of his operas were produced in London, five in Munich. They include *Astarto* (1769), *L'Eroe cinese* (1770), and *Pompeo* (1773) for Munich, *Creusa in Delfo* (1783), *La Regina di Golconda* (1784), and *La vestale* (1787) for London. Best remembered as a teacher, his pupils including Braham, Storace, Incledon, Mara, Kelly, and Mrs Billington. Buried in Bath Abbey.

Ravel, Maurice (*b* Ciboure, 7 Mar. 1875; *d* Paris, 28 Dec. 1937). French composer. His two operas are unique contributions to the art.

L'Heure espagnole (1907) and *L'Enfant et les sortilèges* (1925) are both masterpieces in miniature, calling for elaborate resources but focusing them shrewdly on two themes especially suited to the composer – the first a cynical, farcical romp with ample local colour, the other a touching story of innocence rediscovered that finds room for a rich array of amusing characterization in the furniture and animals that harry the child. Ravel is known to have contemplated at least three more serious subjects – *The Sunken Bell* (he was working on this as late as 1914), *Jeanne d'Arc,* and *Don Quixote.*
Bibl: H. Stuckenschmidt: *Ravel* (1969).

Ravenna. City in Emilia, Italy. Opera was first performed in the 17th cent. At the beginning of the 18th cent. the T. dell'Industria opened, and in 1726 the first performance of Vivaldi's *Armida al campo d'Egitto* was given there. Performances were also given in the T. Communitativo, later, the T. Vecchio. In 1852 the T. Alighieri opened, and has remained the leading theatre for opera. Performances are also given at the T. Angelo Mariani and T. Luigi Rosi.

Ravinia. A suburb of Chicago where an annual summer opera festival was given in a semi-outdoor pavilion in a park from 1910 to 1931. The first festival consisted of seven performances of *Cavalleria rusticana*; in subsequent years scenes and acts from operas were given, but gradually the season was lengthened until in the 1920s it lasted ten weeks. The company included Bori, Pareto, Raisa, Rethberg, Lauri-Volpi, Schipa, and Martinelli.

Rebikov, Vladimir (Ivanovich) (*b* Krasnoyarsk, 31 May 1866; *d* Yalta, 1 Oct. 1920). Russian composer. Studied Moscow with Klenovsky, and Berlin. His operas include *In the Storm* (1894), the fairy-tale opera *Yolka* (after Dostoyevsky, Hans Andersen, and Gerhard Hauptmann, 1903), and *Narcissus* (after Ovid, 1913). Essentially a lyrical composer, he won international success with *Yolka* (known in Germany as *Der Christbaum*), though *In the Storm* is a more advanced, Expressionist work.

Re Cervo, Il. See *König Hirsch.*

Recitative. The name given to the declamatory portions of opera, in which the plot is generally advanced, as opposed to the more static or reflective lyrical settings. In *recitativo secco* the notes and rhythm follow the verbal accentuation, with only the slenderest accompaniment, usually on a harpsichord, perhaps with cello. In *recitativo stromentato* or *accompagnato* (probably introduced by Rovettino in 1663) the accompaniment is fuller and musically more elaborately organized. The distinction between recitative and aria is clear-cut in most 17th and 18th-century opera, especially in opera seria. Recitative is virtually absorbed into other forms by Gluck; Mozart often preserves it, but he also foreshadows, in the range and expressiveness of his recitative, the eventual breakdown of the convention. A striking example is the recitative to 'Mi tradì' in *Don Giovanni*, though already in *Idomeneo,* despite its opera seria framework, the recitative has an exceptional freedom and expressive range.

Recondita armonia. Cavaradossi's (ten.) aria in Act 1 of Puccini's *Tosca* in which he contrasts the dark beauty of his beloved Tosca with the fair beauty of the Countess Attavanti, the model for his painting of the Magdalen.

Reeves, Sims (orig. John) (*b* Shooters Hill, Kent, 26 Sept. 1818; *d* Worthing, 25 Oct. 1900). English tenor. Studied with his father. Début as baritone, Newcastle 1838, in *Guy Mannering.* Studied further in London with Cooke, Paris with Bordogni, Milan with Mazzucato. Milan, Sc., 1846 as Edgardo; London, D.L., 1847, same role. Created Lyonnel in Balfe's *Maid of Honour* (1848); H.M.'s from 1848, where he sang Faust in the English première of Gounod's opera, Huon, and other roles. The latter part of his career was devoted to oratorio.
Bibl: S. Reeves: *His Life and Recollections* (1881); H. S. Edwards: *Sims Reeves* (1888).

Refice, Licinio (*b* Patrica, 12 Feb. 1883; *d* Rio de Janeiro, 11 Sept. 1954). Italian composer. Studied Rome, Santa Cecilia, with Boezi, Falchi, and Renzi. Ordained 1910. Most of his music is for the Church, but he also wrote two operas, *Santa Cecilia* (a mystery play, 1934) and *Margherita da Cortona* (1938). He died while conducting a performance of *Santa Cecilia.*
Bibl: E. Mucci: *Licinio Refice* (1955).

Regensburg. Town in Bavaria, Germany formerly known as Ratisbon. Opera was first performed by travelling companies in the 17th cent. Schikaneder was director of the theatre 1786-9, Ignaz Walter 1804-22. The old theatre burnt down in 1849; a new one opened 1852 (cap. 608), which was taken over by the city 1859. In 1888-1935 opera was lavishly supported by the Prince of Thurn und Taxis. The theatre was bombed in 1944, reopened 1955.

Reggio Emilia. Town in Emilia-Romagna, Italy. Opera is given at the T. Municipale (cap. 1,600), opened in 1857 with Achille Peri's *Vittore Pisani.* The beautiful auditorium designed by Costa has 106 boxes.

Regie. The term used in German opera houses for 'production'.

Régisseur. The French and German term for the *producer of an opera.

Regnava nel silenzio. Lucia's (sop.) aria in Act

1, scene 2, of Donizetti's *Lucia di Lammermoor*, in which she recounts to Alisa the legend of the fountain.

Reichardt, Johann Friedrich (*b* Königsberg, 25 Nov. 1752; *d* Giebichenstein, 26 June 1814). German composer. As Kapellmeister to Frederick the Great from 1776 he introduced various reforms that won him an unpopularity which, in some part due to his vanity, dogged him all his life. His music shows more intelligence and liberal-mindedness than talent; but he found a vigorous champion in Mendelssohn, and has its place in the history of German opera for the originality of his Singspiels.

Reicher-Kindermann, Hedwig (*b* Munich, 15 July 1853; *d* Trieste, 2 June 1883). German mezzo-soprano, later soprano. Daughter of the baritone August *Kindermann. Studied Vienna and Hamburg. Début Munich 1871, Countess in *Wildschütz*. Appeared in Wiesbaden, Karlsruhe, and Berlin; Bayreuth – sang Erda and Grimgerde in the first *Ring* (1876). Joined Neumann's company in Leipzig, 1880. London, H.M.'s, 1882 – sang Fricka in the first London *Ring* and Brünnhilde in the second. Married the actor Emanuel Reicher.

Reichmann, Theodor (*b* Rostock, 15 Mar. 1849; *d* Marbach, Bodensee, 22 May 1903). German baritone. Studied Berlin, Prague, and Milan with Lamperti. Début Magdeburg 1869. After engagements in Berlin, Strasbourg, Hamburg, and Munich, joined Vienna Opera in 1883, remaining there until 1889, returning from 1893 to 1903. Created Amfortas, Bayreuth 1882, and also sang Sachs and Wolfram there. London, C.G., 1884 and 1892, in Wagner; and N.Y., Met., 1889-91, where in addition to the German repertory he sang French and Italian roles: an admired William Tell.

Reina, Domenico (*b* Lugano, 1797; *d* Lugano 29 July 1843). Italian tenor. Studied Milan, with Boile. Début Milan, Sc., 1829, Ilio in Rossini's *Zelmira*. Sc. 1831, 1833-6, where he created Arturo in *La straniera*, Leicester in *Maria Stuarda*, and Tamas in *Gemma di Vergy*; he also sang Pollione to Pasta's Norma and was greatly admired by Bellini. London, K., 1923 in first London perfs. of Rossini's *Riccardo e Zoraide, Mathilde di Shabran*, and *La donna del lago*.

Reine de Saba, La (The Queen of Sheba). Opera in 4 acts by Gounod; text by Barbier and Carré. Prod. Paris, O., 28 Feb. 1862 with Mme Guéymard, Belval, Guéymard; Manchester, 10 Mar. 1880; New Orleans, 12 Jan. 1899.

Adoniram (ten.), a Hebrew sculptor, is in love with Balkis (sop.), the Queen of Sheba; she leaves King Solomon (bass) to join him only to find that he has been killed.

Reiner, Fritz (*b* Budapest, 19 Dec. 1888; *d* New York, 15 Nov. 1963). Hungarian, later American, conductor. Studied Budapest. Conducting début (*Carmen*) as Chorus Master, Budapest Comic Opera, 1909. After engagements in Ljubljana and Budapest, first conductor in Dresden 1914-21. In U.S.A., 1922-35, mostly conducting concerts; returned to opera 1934, conducting Philadelphia Orchestra in *Tristan, Rosenkavalier, Falstaff*, and other works. London C.G., 1936-7, conducted Flagstad's London début as Isolde; N.Y., Met., 1949-53, first U.S. perf. of *Rake's Progress*; San Francisco 1936-8. (R)

Reinhardt, Delia (*b* Elberfeld, 27 Apr. 1892; *d* Arlesheim 3 Oct. 1974). German soprano. Studied Frankfurt with Strakosch and Hedwig. Début Breslau 1913. Munich, 1916-23; N.Y., Met., 1922-4; London, C.G., 1924-9; Berlin, 1924-33. Sang Octavian in the famous Lehmann-Schumann-Mayr-Bruno Walter performances of *Der Rosenkavalier;* repertory included Eva, Elsa, Desdemona, and Pamina. (R)

Reinhardt (orig. Goldmann), **Max** (*b* Baden bei Wien, 9 Sept. 1873; *d* New York, 30 Oct. 1943). Austrian producer, administrator, and actor. Although primarily a man of the theatre, he influenced operatic production by collaborating with Roller for the première of *Der Rosenkavalier* and played a major part in the founding of the Salzburg Festival. His spectacular productions of *Les Contes d'Hoffmann, La Belle Hélène,* and *Die Fledermaus* in Berlin in the 1920s set a standard for future producers.

Reining, Maria (*b* Vienna, 7 Aug. 1903). Austrian soprano. Vienna State Opera 1931-3 and 1937-56: London, C.G., 1938; Chicago 1938; N.Y., C.C., 1949. Chosen by Toscanini to sing Eva at Salzburg (1937); was heard there regularly until 1953, being especially successful as Arabella and the Marschallin. (R)

Reinking, Wilhelm (*b* Aachen, 18 Oct. 1896). German designer. Studied Karlsruhe, Danzig, and Münster. First work for theatre *Meistersinger,* Würzburg, 1925. Engaged by Ebert for Berlin, S.O., 1931. Hamburg, 1937; Vienna 1941; since 1946 has designed for most leading European theatres and festivals.

Reinmar (orig. Wochinz), **Hans** (*b* Vienna, 11 Apr. 1895; *d* Berlin, 7 Feb. 1961). Austrian baritone. Studied Vienna, and Milan with Vanzo. Début Olomouc 1919, Sharpless. Nuremberg 1921-2; Zurich 1923-5; Dresden 1926; Hamburg 1926-31; Berlin, Stä O., 1928-45 and 1952-61; Munich 1945-6, 1950-7; Berlin, S.O., 1948-52; Berlin, K.O., 1952-61. Bayreuth 1939-41 as Donner, Gunther, and Amfortas; Salzburg 1942-3, Mandryka. A famous Macbeth, Boris, and Iago. One of the best German singing actors of his day. (R)

Reiss, Albert (*b* Berlin, 22 Feb. 1870; *d* Nice, 19 June 1940). German tenor. Originally an actor, he was discovered by Pollini who engaged him for Königsberg, where he made his début in 1897 as Ivanov (*Zar und Zimmermann*). After engagements in Poznań, Wiesbaden, and Munich, engaged for N.Y., Met., 1901, remaining there until 1920. London, C.G., 1902-5, 1924-9. One of the finest of Mimes, Davids, and Valzacchis. In New York he created many small roles including the Broom-maker in *Königskinder* and Nick in *La fanciulla del West*. (R)

Reissiger, Carl Gottlieb (*b* Belzig, 31 Jan. 1798; *d* Dresden, 7 Nov. 1859). German composer and conductor. Studied Leipzig with Schicht, Vienna with Salieri, Munich with Winter, and in Italy. Succeeded Weber as music director of the German Opera in Dresden, 1826; later he became Hofkapellmeister and also directed the Italian Opera in place of Morlacchi. A vigorous supporter of Weber and of Beethoven, he also championed Wagner and prepared the première of *Rienzi* (1842). Though a capable musician, he lacked a distinctive talent as a composer: his operas mingle French and Italian styles and classical and Romantic elements. The most successful was *Die Felsenmühle* (1831).

Reiza. Haroun al Raschid's daughter (sop.), heroine of Weber's *Oberon*. Known as Rezia in German translation.

Reizen, Mark (Osipovich) (*b* Zaitsevo, 3 July 1895). Russian bass. Studied Kharkov. Début there 1921, Boris; Leningrad 1925-30; Moscow, B., 1930-54. Guest appearances throughout Europe. Roles include Boris, Dosifey (*Khovanshchina*), Gremin (*Onegin*). (R)

Remedios, Alberto (*b* Liverpool, 27 Feb. 1935). English tenor. Studied with Edwin Francis, Hislop, and at R.C.M. with Carey. London, S.W., since 1955; Frankfurt, O., 1968-70; London, C.G., 1966, Dmitri, Erik, 1970 Mark (*Midsummer Marriage*), 1978 Bacchus; San Francisco, 1973. Developed into leading *Heldentenor*, singing Walther, Lohengrin, Siegmund, and Siegfried in the London Coliseum *Ring*. Repertory also includes Bacchus, Max, Faust (Berlioz and Gounod), Aeneas, and Otello. Sings Wagner with an Italianate and apparently tireless voice. (R)

Reminiscence Motive. A short theme identified with a person, place, object, or idea in an opera, which can then be re-introduced so as to recall its subject at a later stage of the drama. It is distinct from *Leitmotiv in that it does not normally change its shape very markedly, since its

function is to represent, rather than to suggest dramatic progress. It was a feature of opera particularly at the end of the 18th cent. and in the early years of the 19th cent., before the development of Leitmotiv as a stronger structural and expressive force. An example is the chord sequence for the Statue in Hérold's *Zampa*. In German, *Reminiscenzmotiv* or *Erinnerungsmotiv*.

Renard. *Histoire burlesque chantée et jouée* in 2 parts by Stravinsky; text by composer, after Russian folk tales, translated into French by C. F. Ramuz. Prod. Paris, O., 18 May 1922, with Fabert, Dubois, Narcon, Mahieux, cond. Ansermet; N.Y., 2 Dec. 1923. Played by clowns, dancers, or acrobats, with singers (T.T.B.B.) placed in the orchestra.

The fox persuades the cock down from his perch by preaching to him; but the cat and the goat rescue him. Renewing his efforts, the fox again lures the cock into his reach, and he is rescued again, just in time, by the others suggesting that Mrs Fox is being unfaithful.

Renato. Amelia's husband (bar.) in Verdi's *Un ballo in maschera*.

Renaud (orig. Cronean), **Maurice** (*b* Bordeaux, 24 July 1861; *d* Paris, 16 Oct. 1933). French baritone. Studied Paris and Brussels. Début Brussels, La M., 1883, remaining there until 1890 and 1908-14; Paris, O. and O.C., 1890-1902; London, C.G., 1897-1904, and London Opera House 1911; N.Y., Manhattan Opera, 1906-10; Met., 1910-12. Created High Priest in Reyer's *Sigurd* and Hamilcar in same composer's *Salammbô* in Brussels; in Paris was the Opéra's first Telramund, Alberich, Beckmesser, Chorèbe, and Méphistophélès (Berlioz); in London the first Henry VIII (Saint-Saëns), Hares (*Messaline*), Herod (*Hérodiade*); in America the first Athanael. Although his voice was remarkable for neither range nor volume, it was of excellent quality and used with great skill. This, with his remarkable dramatic abilities and masterful make-up and costuming, made Renaud one of the most distinguished French singers of his day. (R)

Rennert, Günther (*b* Essen, 1 Apr. 1911). German producer and Intendant. Studied Germany and Argentina. Began producing for the cinema 1933; 1935-9 at Wuppertal, Frankfurt (where he came under the influence of Felsenstein), and Mainz; Königsberg 1939-42; Berlin 1942-4; Munich 1945, where he produced the *Fidelio* with which the Staatsoper resumed its post-war activities in 1945; Intendant, Hamburg 1946-56, then guest producer at Stuttgart, Hamburg, Milan, Gly. (artistic counsellor 1960-68), etc. London, C.G., 1952 (*Ballo*) and 1954 (*Hoffmann*). N.Y., Met., since 1960. Intendant Munich, Bavarian S.O., 1967-76. A cosmopolitan with wide tastes, Rennert's productions are marked by humanity and deep understanding. His crowd movements and lighting are impressive. He is one of the finest producers in Western Germany. During his time as Intendant the Hamburg opera became the leading ensemble in Germany. His brother **Wolfgang** (*b* 1922) has had a considerable career as a conductor.

Re pastore, Il (The Shepherd King), *Dramma per musica* in 2 acts by Mozart; text by Metastasio. Prod. Salzburg 23 Apr. 1775, with Consoli; London, St Pancras Town Hall, 8 Nov. 1954, with Ilse Wolf, J. Sinclair, Young, cond. Ucko. Metastasio's story of the Royal shepherd was first set by Bonno in 1751; it was also used by Gluck (1775), and at least ten other composers.

The plot concerns an episode in the life of Alexander the Great (Alessandro). After conquering Sidon, he decides to place on the throne a distant descendant of the Royal house, Aminta (sop.), who was brought up as a shepherd, and loves Elisa (sop.), a shepherdess of noble Phoenician descent. Tamiri (sop.), an exiled princess, is in love with Agenore (ten.), a Sidonian noble and friend of Alessandro (ten.). Alessandro sends Agenore to offer Aminta the throne of Sidon and he is thus reunited with Tamiri. But Elisa and Aminta fear that fate may ruin their happiness. Agenore persuades Aminta that as a king he cannot marry a shepherdess, and Alessandro, on hearing that Tamiri has been found, decides that Aminta shall marry her; Agenore renounces her. In the end, rather than lose Elisa, Aminta gives up the throne, and Alessandro, impressed by their loyalty, makes them King and Queen of Sidon, promising to conquer new territory for Agenore and Tamiri.

Répétiteur (*Fr* rehearser). The member of an opera house's music staff who coaches singers in their roles. In German theatres he is called *solo répétiteur* or *Korrepetitor*; in Italy, *maestro collaboratore*; in England, coach (though the French word is as commonly used).

Répétition (*Fr* rehearsal). The *répétition générale* is the final dress rehearsal, usually attended by critics and other guests. See *Probe, Prova.*

Rescue opera. The name given to an opera in which an essential part of the plot turns on the rescue of the hero or heroine from prison or some other threatening situation. Examples are to be found at various times in the 18th cent., but it developed into a recognizable genre with the French Revolution and the closer involvement of opera with real-life situations, often highly dramatic. The first Revolutionary rescue opera was Berton's *Les Rigueurs du cloître* (1790), concerning the

repression of monasticism. Dalayrac's *Camille* (1791) involves the rescue of a girl from a haunted ruined castle; he also wrote *Léhéman, ou La Tour de Neustadt* (1801). In Le Sueur's *La Caverne* (1793) the heroine is held prisoner by brigands. Cherubini's *Les Deux journées* (1800, to a libretto by Bouilly greatly prized by Beethoven) is set in the time of the Thirty Years War but has contemporary allusions in its theme of the rescue of innocent aristocrats from arrest. Bouilly's libretto *Léonore* (1798) concerns the rescue of the hero more exclusively in its first setting by Gaveau than in Beethoven's *Fidelio* (1805), in which the genre is raised to the level of the ideal of freedom.

Residenztheater. See *Munich.*

Resnik, Regina (*b* New York, 30 Aug. 1922). American mezzo-soprano (formerly sop.). Studied N.Y. with Rosalie Miller. Début N.Y., New Opera Company, 1942, Lady Macbeth; after appearances in Mexico and N.Y., C.C., joined Met. 1944; London, C.G., 1957-72. As a soprano at the Met. she created Delilah in Rogers's *The Warrior,* and was the first N.Y. Ellen Orford; Female Chorus in American première of *Rape of Lucretia,* and appeared at Bayreuth as Sieglinde; as a mezzo-soprano created the Baroness in *Vanessa* and has appeared with success as Carmen, Amneris, Mistress Quickly, and Herodias. Her rich voice is allied to a good dramatic sense and vivid stage personality. In 1971 she began to produce opera: *Carmen,* Hamburg; *Elektra,* Venice and elsewhere; *Falstaff,* Warsaw. (R)

Respighi, Ottorino (*b* Bologna, 9 July 1879; *d* Rome, 18 Apr. 1936). Italian composer. While a violist in the St Petersburg opera orchestra, he studied composition with Rimsky-Korsakov; later worked in Berlin with Bruch. His first operas, the comic *Re Enzo* (1905) and *Semirâma* (1910) (*Marie-Victoire,* 1909, was unprod.), made his name and led to his appointment to the Conservatory in Rome, where he settled. Of the operas which followed, *Belfagor* (1923), *Maria Egiziaca* (1932), and *La fiamma* (1934) have had the greatest success. In them his sumptuously scored, sensuous music perhaps makes its richest effect; dramatic tension never came naturally to him. Keenly interested in the music of his early predecessors (he has reworked Monteverdi's *Orfeo*), Respighi reverted in last opera, *Lucrezia* (1937), to a principle of dramatic recitative echoing the 17th century. His wife, **Elsa Respighi Olivieri Sangiacomo** (*b* Rome, 24 Mar. 1894) was a concert singer and has also composed two operas: *Alcesti* (1941) and *Samurai* (1945), and wrote her husband's biography (1954).

Bibl: R. de Renzis: *Respighi* (1935).

Reszke, de. See *De Reszke.*

Retablo de Maese Pedro, El (Master Peter's Puppet show). Opera in 1 act by Falla; text by composer after Cervantes's novel *Don Quixote* (1615). Prod. Seville, T. San Fernando (concert), 23 Mar. 1923, with Redondo, Segura, Lledo, cond. Falla; Paris, Princesse Edmond de Polignac's house, 25 June 1923 (in French) with Dufranne, Salignac, Peris, cond. Golschmann, Wanda Landowska as harpsichordist; Clifton, 14 Oct. 1924, with Tannahill, Goody, Cranmer; New York, 29 Dec. 1925.

The piece was originally intended for performance with puppets taking all the parts, double-sized for the human beings. A boy narrator (treble) introduces the puppet show to an audience including Don Quixote (bass or bar.) and Sancho Panza (silent). The interaction of fiction and reality characteristic of *Don Quixote* takes the form of the boy telling the story of Don Gayferos rescuing the fair Melisendra from the Moors, subject to interruptions from Don Quixote and Master Peter himself (ten.). Eventually Don Quixote becomes confused about the reality of the puppets, and leaping forward, beheads the Moors and destroys the puppet show.

Rethberg (orig. Sättler), **Elisabeth** (*b* Schwarzenburg, 22 Sept. 1894; *d* New York, 6 June 1976). German, later American, soprano. Studied Dresden with Otto Watrin. Début Dresden 1915, Arsena (*Zigeunerbaron*); N.Y., Met., 1922-42; London, C.G., 1925, 1934-9. Also appeared in Salzburg, Milan, and elsewhere in Europe. Created title role in Strauss's *Aegyptische Helena* (1928), and sang Rautendelein in the American première of Respighi's *La campana sommersa*. Equally at home in the Italian and German repertory, she was generally considered the finest Aida of her day and was famous as Desdemona, Amelia, Sieglinde, Elsa, and Elisabeth. She possessed a lyric-dramatic soprano voice of great beauty. (R)

Reuss-Belce (orig. Baumann), **Luise** (*b* Vienna, 24 Oct. 1862; *d* Aichach, nr Augsburg, 5 Mar. 1945). Austrian soprano and producer. Studied Vienna with Joseph Gänsbacher. Début Karlsruhe, 1881, Elsa; Karlsruhe 1882-97, Cassandre; Wiesbaden 1897-1901; Bayreuth 1882, Flowermaiden in first *Parsifal*; 1896-1912, Fricka, Gutrune, Eva; London, C.G., 1893, Sieglinde; 1900, Fricka; Dresden 1900-11; N.Y., Met., 1901-3 Elisabeth, Brünnhilde, Fricka, Gutrune, Iolanthe in first U.S. *Der Wald*. Berlin; D., 1916-25 as producer. Taught in Dresden and Berlin. (R)

Reutter, Hermann (*b* Stuttgart, 17 June 1900). German composer. His operas, on ambitious themes, are to his own distinguished literary texts and are marked by a feeling for the human voice which he developed as accompanist to a number of eminent German singers, among them Karl Erb. His greatest success was *Dr Johannes Faust* (1936); his other operas include *Odysseus* (1942), *Don Juan und Faust* (1950), and *Die Witwe von Ephesus* (1954).

Revisor, Der. Opera in 5 acts by Egk; text by composer, after Gogol's story *The Government Inspector* (1836). Prod. Schwetzingen, by Stuttgart Opera, 9 May 1957, with Sailer, Plümacher, Stolze, Wunderlich, Ollendorf, cond. Egk; London, S.W. (New Opera Company), 25 July 1958, with Clarke, Peters, Young, Platt, cond. Lovett; N.Y., City Opera, 19 Oct. 1960, with Brooks, Kobart, Crain, Beattie, cond. Egk.

Khlestakov (ten.), a penniless civil servant, is mistaken for the Government Inspector and lavishly entertained by the Mayor (bass), his wife (mezzo), and daughter (sop.).

Reyer (orig. Rey), (Louis-Étienne-) **Ernest** (*b* Marseilles, 1 Dec. 1823; *d* Le Lavandou, 15 Jan. 1909). French composer and critic. Studied privately, largely self-taught. Made an early reputation with his works, including two opéras comiques, *Maître Wolfram* (1854) and *La Statue* (1861), and an opera, *Erostrate* (1862). However, his most famous work was *Sigurd* (1884), a success he almost equalled with *Salammbô* (1890). Though *Sigurd* is Wagnerian in subject matter, and Reyer was a great admirer of Wagner (as of Berlioz and Weber), his work is not greatly coloured by any of their influences. His music does not reveal great individuality, but reflects the intelligence and independence of mind which made him a witty and forceful critic. He defended Wagner and Berlioz eloquently, and travelled widely (he was among those who went to Cairo for the première of *Aida*) in the course of his work.
Bibl: E. Reyer: *40 ans de musique* (1909); H. de Curzon: *Ernest Reyer* (1924).

Rezia. See *Reiza*.

Rezniček, Emil Nikolaus von (*b* Vienna, 4 May 1860; *d* Berlin, 2 Aug. 1945). Austrian composer and conductor. He held many conducting posts, including Mannheim (1896-9), Warsaw (1907-8), Berlin, K.O. (1909-11). Of his operas, the best known are *Donna Diana* (1894) and *Till Eulenspiegel* (1902); comic subjects found the quickest response in him, though he also wrote *Die Jungfrau von Orleans* (1887), *Holofernes* (1923), and other serious works.
Bibl: M. Chop: *Emil Nikolaus von Rezniček* (1920).

Rheingold, Das. See *Ring der Nibelungen, Der*.

Riccardo Primo. Opera in 3 acts by Handel; text chiefly by P. A. Rolli. Prod. London, King's T., 11 Nov. 1727, with Cuzzoni, Faustina, Senesino, Boschi. Revived Handel Opera Society, 1964.

Ricci, Federico (*b* Naples, 22 Oct. 1804; *d* Conegliano, 10 Dec. 1877). Italian composer. Studied Naples, with Zingarelli and Raimondi, also with Bellini and his brother **Luigi** (*b* Naples, 8 July 1805; *d* Prague, 21 Dec. 1859). Apart from works written in collaboration with his brother, Federico had successes with *La prigione d'Edimburgo* (1837), *Luigi Rolla* (1841), and *Corrado d'Altamura* (1841). The latter, based on the same plot as Verdi's *Oberto*, led to other commissions; but his serious operas fared less well than his comedies. *Il marito e l'amante* (1852) was successful in Vienna, but *Il paniere d'amore* (1853) failed and he decided to accept a post in St Petersburg; he moved in 1869 to Paris, where he had some success with the *opéra-bouffe*, *Une Folie à Rome* (1869) and other works. His gift for comedy distinguishes him from his brother. The most famous of their collaborations was *Crispino e lo comare* (1850). A younger brother, **Egidio Gaetano**, became an impresario in Naples, then in Copenhagen (1850), where he married the soprano Amalie Luzio. Luigi's son **Luigino** (*b* Trieste, 27 Dec. 1852; *d* Milan, 10 Feb. 1906) was a composer whose operas included *Frosina* (1870), *Cola di Rienzi* (1880), and *Don Chischiotte* (1887).
Bibl: L. de Rada: *I fratelli Ricci* (1878).

Ricciarelli, Katia (*b* Rovigo, 18 Jan. 1946). Italian soprano. Studied Venice with Iris Adami-Corradetti. Début Mantua, 1969, Mimì. Prizes at the Parma Competition for Young Singers (1970) and the Italian Radio's New Verdi Voices Competition (1971) led to engagements all over Italy including Venice, F., in *Il corsaro*, Rome, O., in *Giovanna d'Arco*. Milan, Sc., since 1973, London, C.G., since 1974; Chicago 1973 in *Due foscari*. Large repertory includes Caterina Cornaro, Lucrezia Borgia, Maria de Rohan, Imogene (*Il pirata*), Giulietta (*Capuleti e i Montecchi*), and Puccini and Verdi roles, as well as operas by Gluck and Cherubini. A gifted and dedicated singer with a beautiful voice. (R)

Rich, John (*b* London, *c*1682; *d* London, ?1761). English producer and manager. As manager of Lincoln's Inn Fields T., introduced *The Beggar's Opera* to London, which proved so successful that he decided to build another theatre – the first Covent Garden T. – in 1732.

Richard, Cœur de Lion. Opera in 3 acts by Grétry; text by Sedaine. Prod. Paris, C.I., 21 Oct. 1784 with Rosalie, Colombe, Dugazon, Philippe, Clairval; London, C.G., 16 Oct. 1786; Boston 23 Jan. 1797.

Blondel, Richard's minstrel, wanders in search of his King disguised as a blind singer. Helped by an English knight and by Marguerite of Flanders, he manages first to make contact with the imprisoned King, by means of his Romance 'Une fièvre brûlante', and then to

rescue him. Grétry consciously designed the Romance, which appears nine times in the opera in various melodic and rhythmic transformations, as a form of motive; and it became a much-admired example in the later development of Leitmotiv.

Also opera by Shield (1786).

Richter, Hans (*b* Györ, 4 Apr. 1843; *d* Bayreuth, 5 Dec. 1916). Austro-Hungarian conductor. Studied Vienna, where he was choirboy in the Court Chapel. Horn-player Kärntnerthor T. 1862-6. Worked with Wagner at Triebschen 1866-7, making fair copy of *Meistersinger* score. Wagner recommended him to Bülow as chorus master for Munich. Cond. Munich 1868-9, making his début with *Guillaume Tell*. In 1868 in Munich he also sang, at short notice, the part of Kothner in the sixth performance of *Die Meistersinger*. Prepared and conducted Belgian première of *Lohengrin* 1870; Budapest 1871-5; Vienna 1875-1900 (music director 1893-1900); Bayreuth 1876-1912, where he conducted the first *Ring*; London, D.L., 1882, conducting first performances in England of *Tristan* and *Meistersinger*; C.G. 1884, where he was instrumental in bringing Lilli Lehmann to London, and C.G. 1903-10, where, after his production of *The Ring* in English, his attempts to found a permanent English national opera in association with Percy *Pitt were thwarted by the implacable attitude of the Grand Opera Syndicate at H.M.'s 1880. He was regarded in his day as the authoritative interpreter of Wagner and the German classics. (R)

Ricordi. Italian (orig. Spanish) family firm of music publishers, founded in 1808 by
(1) **Giovanni** (1785-1853). The firm scored its first success with the publication of Mosca's *I pretendenti delusi*, and has handled the works of Rossini, Bellini, Donizetti, Verdi, Boito, Catalani, Puccini, Zandonai, Montemezzi, Pizzetti, Respighi, Menotti, and Poulenc.
(2) **Giulio** (1840-1912) exercised a notable force on Italian opera. Himself a minor composer (his single opera, *La secchia rapita*, was to a text by Renato Simoni, later *Turandot*'s librettist), he combined a shrewd musical judgement in his choice of composers with ruthless business acumen in furthering their and the firm's interests. Though, it is true, he attacked Toscanini and rejected the works of Bizet, Leoncavallo, and Mascagni, he championed Verdi with a fervour that was based on personal friendship and belief in Verdi's supremely Italian genius (Wagner was an enemy so vile that Ricordi even continued the attacks after acquiring the composer's operas with Lucca's stock in 1887). Ricordi quickly recognized Puccini as the 'Crown Prince' to Verdi, and helped him incalculably in his early career. Librettos were bought in case Puccini might use them, and Ricordi came near to sharp prac-

tice when he and Illica persuaded Franchetti, who had the rights to *Tosca*, that this was a poor subject and thus won it for Puccini. 'Don Giulio' became for Puccini 'the only person who inspires me with trust, and to whom I can confide what is going through my mind'. He was the first to advertise operas with illustrated posters (starting with *La Bohème*), and these were later used for the early editions of the vocal scores.

His son (3) **Tito** (1865-1933) was impulsive and dictatorial; as *Tosca*'s producer he showed the importance of good acting and realistic scenery in *verismo* opera, but his treatment of Puccini was less tolerant than his father's, and their relations deteriorated. Puccini even contemplated a London publisher for one projected opera. When Tito left the firm in 1919, Puccini patched up their quarrel. The firm retains many of Verdi's and Puccini's original scores, and controversy over discrepancies between these and the published versions even reached the Italian Senate in 1961.

Ridderbusch, Karl (*b* Recklinghausen, 29 May 1932). German bass. Studied Essen. Début Münster, 1961. Essen, 1962-5; Deutsche Oper am Rhein since 1965; guest appearances Hamburg, Vienna, Munich, Berlin, Milan; Bayreuth since 1967; Salzburg Easter Festival since 1967; N.Y., Met., 1967-9; London, C.G., 1971 Fasolt, Hunding, Hagen; 1973 Landgrave. Repertory also includes Daland, Sachs, Rocco, Boris, and Ochs. A powerfully built man with a capacious voice and an effective style with Wagner in particular. (R)

Riders to the Sea. Opera in 1 act by Vaughan Williams; text, J. M. Synge's tragedy (1904). Prod. London, R.C.M., 30 Nov. 1937, with Olive Hall, Smith-Miller, Steventon, Coad, cond. Sargent; Cleveland, 26 Feb. 1950.

The setting is the west coast of Ireland, where Maurya (con.) has lost her husband and four sons at sea. A fifth is also discovered to have been drowned when her daughters Cathleen (sop.) and Nora (sop.) identify some clothes brought in; and when her last son, Bartley (bar.) in turn is claimed by the sea as he is riding some horses to a fair, her grief finally turns to resignation and peace. Other operas on the subject are by Rabaud (*L'Appel de la mer*, 1924) and Betts (1955).

Rienzi (orig. *Cola Rienzi, der letzte der Tribunen*). Opera in 5 acts by Wagner; text by the composer, after Mary Russell Mitford's drama (1828) and Bulwer Lytton's novel (1835). Prod. Dresden, Hofoper, 20 Oct. 1842, with Wüst, Schröder-Devrient, Tichatschek, Dettmer, Wächter, cond. Reissiger; N.Y., Ac. of M., 4 Mar. 1878, with Pappenheim, Hüman, Adams, Wiegand, cond. Menetzek; London, H.M.'s, 27 Jan. 1879, with Crosmond, Vanzini,

Maas, Olmi, cond. Carl Rosa.

Set in 14th-century Rome, the opera tells of the struggle between the Orsinis and the Colonnas. Paolo Orsini (bass) attempts to abduct Irene (sop.), sister of Cola Rienzi (ten.), but is interrupted by Stefano Colonna (bass), whose son Adriano (mezzo) appears to defend Irene. Rienzi, the papal legate, appears, and encouraged by Cardinal Raimondi (bass) urges the people to resist the tyranny of the nobles. The nobles swear allegiance to Rienzi as tribune, but they plot to murder him and almost succeed. Condemned to death, they are spared through Adriano's intercession; but when they break their oath of submission, the people rise and kill them. However, the people in turn prove disloyal to Rienzi, and Adriano also tries to kill him. Rienzi is excommunicated, and Adriano now warns Irene of her brother's danger. She finds him at prayer in the Capitol, and refusing to flee with Adriano, remains with him as the mob fire the Capitol; Adriano rushes into the flames to perish with them.

Other operas on the subject are by John Barnett (1828, based only on Mitford), Conrad (1839), A. Peri (1862), Kashperov (1863), Lucilla (1872), Persichini (1874), and L. Ricci (1880).
Bibl: J. Deathridge: *Wagner's Rienzi* (1977).

Riga. See *Latvia*.

Righetti-Giorgi, Geltrude (*b* Bologna, 1793; *d* Bologna, 1862). Italian contralto. Studied Bologna. Début Bologna 1814, as Geltrude Righetti. Decided to retire from stage on her marriage soon after to Luigi Giorgi, but was persuaded by Rossini to return; created Rosina in 1816, followed by *Cenerentola* (1817). Continued to sing until 1836. Spohr found her voice 'full, powerful, and with extensive range'; her vocal technique was said to be flawless.

Righini, Vincenzo (*b* Bologna, 22 Jan. 1756; *d* Bologna, 19 Aug. 1812). Italian composer. His early operas included one on the Don Juan subject (1777; ten years before Mozart's). Many other works were well received in Germany and Austria, where he held conducting posts. He married first the contralto Anna Maria Lehritter (1762-83), then the singer Henrietta Kneisel (1767-1801). He also made a reputation as a singing teacher.

Rigoletto. Opera in 3 acts by Verdi; text by Piave, after Hugo's drama *Le Roi s'amuse* (1832). Originally entitled *La Maledizione*. Prod. Venice, F., 11 Mar. 1851, with Brambilla, Saini, Mirate, Varesi, Ponz, Damini, cond. Marès; London, C.G., 14 May 1853, with Bosio, Mario, Ronconi; N.Y., Ac. of M., 19 Feb. 1855, with Bertucca-Maretzek, Bolcioni, Barili. Also performed, variously censored, as *Viscardello* (Rome 1851, Bologna 1852), *Clara di Perth* (Naples 1853), and *Lionello* (Naples 1858).

The licentious Duke of Mantua (ten.) has

been paying court, disguised as a student, to Gilda (sop.), who unknown to him is the daughter of his court jester, Rigoletto (bar.). When Rigoletto, who has unwittingly helped in the abduction of Gilda, learns she has been seduced by the Duke, he plans to have him killed by the professional assassin, Sparafucile (bass). Sparafucile's sister Maddalena (mezzo), pleads that his life be spared, and Gilda, who has overheard their conversation, sacrifices her own life in order to save the Duke.

Rijeka (It. Fiume). Town in Croatia, Yugoslavia. First theatre built 1765, closed by government, 1797. Zajc took over direction, 1895. Present theatre built 1885. Company re-formed, 1946.

Rimsky-Korsakov, Nikolay (Andreyevich) (*b* Tikhvin, 18 Mar. 1844; *d* St Petersburg, 21 June 1908). Russian composer. With two exceptions, all Rimsky-Korsakov's operas are on Russian themes; mythology attracted him especially, as did fantastic subjects. Only *The Maid of Pskov* (1873) and *The Tsar's Bride* (1899) treat conventional human emotions. His gift for harmonic and orchestral colour, coupled with his love of legend and fairy-tale, drew him more to the type of opera of which *May Night* (1880) was the first – an old folk-tale involving supernatural elements, played out in a colourful setting. Thus he delighted in ballets or set numbers that could release his imagination and unshackle his virtuoso technique from story-telling or delineation of character.

In *The Snow Maiden* (1882), fairy and human worlds impinge; but the heroine's dilemma is made touching more by Rimsky-Korsakov's demonstration that these are hopelessly irreconcilable than by anything beyond the very simplest characterization of the Maiden. *Christmas Eve* (1895) reveals this weakness the more vividly when compared with Tchaikovsky's setting (*Vakula the Smith*, 1874). This and *Mlada* (1892) were regarded as studies for *Sadko* (1898), in which he wholly responds to the excitement and colour of the story; his already spectacular technique was now affected by a slight Wagner influence (*The Ring* had had its St Petersburg première in 1888-9) and a wish to strengthen his feeling for Russia's past by use of a special type of bardic declamation. But the next work, *Mozart and Salieri* (1898), was a neo-classical opera (the first ever), based on Pushkin's 'little tragedy' on the rumour that Mozart had been poisoned by his rival. *Kashchey the Immortal* (1902) is a fairy-tale with dark undercurrents, musically presaging *The Firebird* of Rimsky-Korsakov's pupil Stravinsky, it has been suggested. This has a high craftsmanship and an appeal to both intellect and ear which in *The Invisible City of Kitezh* (1907) are augmented by a warm human feeling and a touching quality of lyricism. *Tsar Saltan* (1900) and *The Golden Cockerel* (1909)

combine the old fantastic elements with a sharp vein of satire; that much is left obscure is of little importance in a setting where no problems except those of virtuosity engage the composer and where the listener's delight is never touched by deeper reflections.
Bibl: N. Rimsky-Korsakov: *My Musical Life* (1909, trans. 1924).

Rinaldo. Opera in 3 acts by Handel; text by Rossi, after a sketch by Aaron Hill from Tasso's first epic (1562). Prod. London, Hm., 24 Feb. 1711, with Boschi, Girardeau, Schiaronetti, Nicolini, Valentini (the first of Handel's operas for England). Houston, 16 Oct. 1975, with Horne, Rogers, Mandac, Ramey, cond. Foster.

Ring des Nibelungen, Der (The Ring of the Nibelung). A stage-festival play for three days and a preliminary evening (*Ein Bühnenfestspiel für drei Tage und einen Vorabend*) – sometimes called a tetralogy – by Wagner; text by the composer, based on the Nibelung Saga. Prod. Bayreuth, Festspielhaus, 13, 14, 16, 17 Aug. 1876, with Betz (Wotan), Grün (Fricka), Elmblad (Donner), Engelhardt (Froh), Vogl (Loge), Haupt (Freia), Reichenberg (Fafner), Eilers (Fasolt), Hill (Alberich), Schlosser (Mime), Jaide (Erda), Niemann (Siegmund), Scheffzky (Sieglinde), Niering (Hunding), Unger (Siegfried), Materna (Brünnhilde), L. Lehmann (Woodbird), Siehr (Hagen), Gura (Gunther), Weckerlin (Gutrune), Brandt (Waltraute), L. and M. Lehmann, Lammert (Rhinemaidens), Jachmann-Wagner, Scheffzky, Grün (Norns), Haupt, L. and M. Lehmann, Weckerlin, Amann, Lammert, Reicher-Kindermann, Jachmann–Wagner (Valkyries), cond. Richter. The separate operas were produced as follows:

Das Rheingold (The Rhine Gold). Prologue in 1 act to the trilogy *Der Ring des Nibelungen*. Prod. Munich, 22 Sept. 1869, with Sophie Stehle, Vogl, Schlosser, Nachbaur, Kindermann, Fischer, Baussewein, cond. Wüllner; London, H.M.'s, 5 May 1882, with Reicher-Kindermann, Vogl, Schlosser, Scaria, Burger, Wiegand, Schelper, Eilers, Biberti, cond. Seidl; N.Y., Met., 4 Jan. 1889, with Moran-Olden, Alvary, Sedlmayer, Mittelhauser, Fischer, Beck., Grienaues, Mödlinger, Weiss, cond. Seidl.

Die Walküre (The Valkyrie). Music-drama in 3 acts. Prod. Munich, Hofoper, 26 June 1870, with Stehle, Teresa Vogl, Kaufmann, Vogl, Kindermann, Bausewein, cond. Wüllner; N.Y., Ac. of M., 2 Apr. 1877, with Pappenheim, Canissa, Listner, Bischoff, Preusser, Blum, cond. Neuendorf; London, H.M.'s, 6 May 1882, with Reicher-Kindermann, Vogl, Riegler, Niemann, Scaria, Wiegand, cond. Seidl.

Siegfried. Music-drama in 3 acts. Prod. Bayreuth, Festspielhaus, 16 Aug. 1876; London, H.M.'s, 8 May 1882, with Therese Vogl,

Vogl, Schlosser, Scaria, cond. Seidl; N.Y., Met., 9 Nov. 1887, with Lehmann, Alvary, Ferenczy, Fischer, cond. Seidl.

Götterdämmerung (The Twilight of the Gods). Music-drama in 3 acts. Prod. Bayreuth, Festspielhaus, 17 Aug. 1876; London, H.M.'s, 9 May 1882, with Therese Vogl, Schreiber, Reicher-Kindermann, Vogl, Wiegand, Biberti, Schelper, cond. Seidl; N.Y., Met., 25 Jan. 1888, (incomplete, without Norns or Waltraute scenes) with Lehmann, Seidl-Krauss, Niemann, Robinson, Fischer, cond. Seidl.

The *Ring* is an allegory, and tells of the struggle for power between the Nibelung dwarfs, the Giants, and the Gods.

In *Rheingold,* the Nibelung dwarf Alberich (bass-bar.) renounces love so that he may steal the Rhinegold, guarded by the Rhine-maidens, and by forging himself a Ring from it become master of the world. Wotan (bass-bar.), ruler of the gods, has engaged the giants Fasolt and Fafner (basses) to build Valhalla for the gods; unable to pay for it he has promised them Freia (sop.), goddess of youth. Loge (ten.), the fire god, persuades Wotan to accompany him to Nibelheim where by a trick Wotan obtains the Ring and the Rhinegold from Alberich; he intends to pay the giants with the gold and to keep the Ring himself. Alberich curses the Ring. The giants see the Ring on Wotan's finger and demand it as well as a magic helmet, the Tarnhelm. Wotan at first refuses, and the giants prepare to drag Freia away. Wotan's wife Fricka (mezzo) urges her husband to give the giants the Ring. Erda (con.), the earth goddess, warns Wotan of the consequences of retaining the Ring. He adds it to the gold, whereupon Fasolt and Fafner quarrel. Fafner kills Fasolt and takes away the gold, the Tarnhelm, and the Ring. The gods, watched cynically by Loge, enter Valhalla as the curtain falls.

[In order to defend Valhalla, Wotan begets with Erda nine warrior daughter Valkyries, who bear the bodies of dead heros to Valhalla, where they are revived and help defend the castle. But in order to restore the ring to the Rhinemaidens and rid the gods of the curse, Wotan has to beget human children. He descends to earth and begets Siegmund and Sieglinde, hoping that the former will one day kill Fafner and restore the ring to the Rhine-maidens. The pair are separated, Sieglinde being married to Hunding (bass) and Sieg-mund driven to lead a wandering life of hardship.]

In *Die Walküre,* Siegmund (ten.) is forced to shelter in Hunding's hut. He and Sieglinde (sop.) feel a mysterious attraction. Sieglinde shows him the sword Nothung that Wotan had left embedded in the trunk of the tree growing in Hunding's hut to be withdrawn by a hero. He pulls the sword out and rushes off with Sieglinde. Fricka, the guardian of marriage vows,

forces Wotan to side with Hunding in the latter's coming combat with Siegmund. But Brünnhilde (sop.), Wotan's favourite Valkyrie, disobeys him and sides with Siegmund. Wotan intervenes and Siegmund is killed, the sword Nothung being shattered by Wotan's spear. Brünnhilde gathers the fragments and entrusts them to Sieglinde, who will soon bear Siegmund's child – the hero Siegfried. Brünnhilde is punished by being put to sleep on a fire-girt rock, through which one day a hero will come to claim her. The curtain falls on the magic fire.

[Sieglinde has died giving birth to Siegfried. The boy has been brought up by the dwarf Mime, brother of Alberich. Mime's cave is in the forest close to the cave where Fafner, who by means of the Tarnhelm has changed himself into a dragon, guards the treasure. Mime hopes to weld the fragments together so that Siegfried can kill Fafner: he means thereby to gain the Ring himself.]

In *Siegfried,* Wotan, disguised as a Wanderer, visits Mime (ten.) and prophesies that the sword will be forged by a hero. Mime recognizes Siegfried (ten.) as this hero and plans to kill him when it is done. Siegfried successfully forges the sword Nothung, and with Mime sets out to seek Fafner. After Siegfried has aroused and killed Fafner (bass), he burns his finger in the dragon's blood. Sucking it, he finds he can understand the language of the birds, one of which (sop.) warns him of Mime's treachery and then tells him of the sleeping Brünnhilde. Siegfried kills Mime, and with the Ring and Tarnhelm follows the bird to the Valkyrie's rock. The Wanderer, although he has told Erda that he longs only for the end, tries to bar his path, but Siegfried shatters his spear with Nothung and, making his way through the fire, awakens Brünnhilde and claims her as his bride.

In *Götterdämmerung,* the Three Norns (con., mezzo, sop.) prophesy the end of the gods. Siegfried gives Brünnhilde the Ring, and leaving her, goes to seek adventure. He comes to the Hall of the Gibichungs, where Alberich's son Hagen (bass) lives with his half-brother Gunther (bar.) and his half-sister Gutrune (sop.). Hagen plans Siegfried's death, and by giving him a drug to make him forget Brünnhilde, arranges for him to marry Gutrune, and to fetch Brünnhilde as Gunther's bride; thus Hagen will have the Ring. To Brünnhilde comes her sister Waltraute (mezzo), who urges her to return the Ring to the Rhine-maidens. Brünnhilde refuses. Siegfried, wearing the Tarnhelm and in the guise of Gunther, penetrates the fire again, and overcoming Brünnhilde, tears the Ring from her finger and takes her back, an unwilling bride for Gunther. Hagen summons the Gibichungs for the double wedding ceremony. Gunther leads on Brünnhilde, unrecognized by the drugged Siegfried. Seeing the

Ring on Siegfried's finger, she accuses him of treachery. With Gunther and Hagen she plans Siegfried's death.

Siegfried is resting on the banks of the Rhine, and the Rhine-maidens plead with him to return the ring. Hagen, Gunther, and the huntsmen now arrive. Siegfried is asked to relate his adventures. Hagen gives him a second drug to restore his memory, and he speaks of his love for Brünnhilde. Hagen spears him in the back. Siegfried's body is carried back to the Gibichung Hall, and in a quarrel over the Ring, Gunther is killed by Hagen. When the latter approaches the dead Siegfried to remove the ring, Siegfried's hand rises in the air. Brünnhilde orders a funeral pyre to be built for Siegfried, and taking the Ring from his finger places it on her own. On her horse, Grane, she plunges into the flames. The hall collapses, the Rhine overflows, and as Hagen tries to snatch the Ring from Brünnhilde, he is dragged below the waters by the Rhine-maidens. Valhalla rises in flames, and as the kingdom of the gods is destroyed, a new era of love dawns.

Rinuccini, Ottavio (*b* Florence, 20 Jan. 1552; *d* Florence, 28 Mar. 1621). Italian librettist. A member of the *Camerata; one of the first librettists in the new style. His text for Peri's *Favola di Dafne* was made in 1594, that for *Euridice* (set by Peri and Caccini) in 1600, that for *Arianna* (set by Peri and Monteverdi) in 1608. He also wrote the text for Monteverdi's *Il ballo delle ingrate* (1608). The ideals of the Camerata impelled him to seek simplicity in his work; a disciple of Tasso, he turned above all to the manner and technique of the pastoral play for his example.

Rio de Janeiro. Capital of Brazil. Among various attempts to organize opera in the 18th cent. were a Casa de Opera founded (also conducted and directed) by P. Ventura in 1767 which was burned down in 1770 or 1771; and a newly founded but short-lived Casa de Opera organized by Luiz de Ferreira. Visiting Italian companies played at the Real T. di São João, opened in 1813, which burnt down in 1815, but this was quickly rebuilt. Many other theatres were built in the first decades of the 19th cent., many of them housing occasional opera, including the T. Provisório (opened 1852 with Verdi's *Macbeth*; demolished 1875), the T. Lirico, and two operetta houses, the Fénix Dramática and the Alcazar Lyrique. The T. Municipal was opened in 1909. Visiting Italian seasons were given by, among others, Mascagni; Toscanini made his début in Rio.

Riotte, Philipp Jakob (*b* St Wendel, 16 Aug. 1776; *d* Vienna, 20 Aug. 1856). German composer and conductor. Studied Offenbach with André. Music director at Gotha *c*1805–6; moved to Vienna to the Court Opera (1818–20)

and then the W. (1824–6). A popular composer of Singspiels in his day. *Der Berggeist* (1818) and *Die Wildschützen* (1820) were particularly successful; he also wrote some operas, including *Piedro und Elmira* (1805) and *Nur-redin, Prinz von Persien* (1825), and parodies, including the successful *Staberl als Freischütz* (1826).

Rise and Fall of the City of Mahagonny. See *Aufstieg und Fall der Stadt Mahagonny*

Risurrezione (Resurrection). Opera in 4 acts by Alfano; text by Cesare Hanau, after Tolstoy's novel *Resurrection* (1900). Prod. Turin, V.E., 30 Nov. 1904, with Magliulo, Mieli, Scandiani, cond. Serafin; Chicago, 31 Dec. 1925, with Garden, Ansseau, Baklanoff, cond. Moranzoni.

Katusha (sop.) meets and falls in love with Prince Dimitri (ten.), by whom she becomes pregnant. He has to join his regiment and fails to keep a rendezvous with her at a railway station. Katusha committs a murder and is sentenced to be deported to Siberia; Dimitri follows her there and obtains a free pardon for her; but she rejects him in favour of Simonson (bar.) a fellow convict.

Rita. Opera in 1 act by Donizetti; text by Vaëz. Prod. Paris, O.C., 7 May 1860, with Faure-Lefèbvre, Warot, Barielle; N.Y., Hunter College, 14 May 1957; London, National School of Opera, 12 Dec. 1962. A charming trifle about Rita (sop.), proprietress of a Swiss inn, her husband Beppe (ten.), and her admirer Gasparo (bar.).

Ritorna vincitor. Aida's (sop.) aria in Act 1 of Verdi's *Aida,* in which she sings of her conflicting emotions: she has joined in the Egyptian cries bidding Radamès to return victorious, only to realize that he is leading the army against her own father and kinsfolk.

Ritornello (*It* little return, refrain). In 17th-cent. Italian,opera, an instrumental section added to an aria which served the expressive function of summarizing the emotional content. Occasionally the term was applied to opening instrumental sections, as with that to Orfeo's 'Vi ricorda' in Monteverdi's opera. Apart from the sinfonia, the ritornello was the only instrumental piece in early opera.

Ritorno d'Ulisse in patria, Il (The Return of Ulysses to his Country). Opera in prologue and 5 acts by Monteverdi; text by Badoaro. Prod. Venice, S. Cass., Feb. 1641; London, St Pancras Town Hall., 16 Mar. 1965, with Bainbridge, Dinoff, Sarti, Kentish, Dickerson, McKinney, McCue, cond. Marshall; Washington, 18 Jan. 1974, with Von Stade, Allen, Stillwell, Gramm, cond. Gibson.

The opera relates the events of the closing books of *The Odyssey,* with added comments from the gods and from allegorical figures (Human Fragility, Time, Fortune, and Love:

these appear as a prologue, and are sometimes omitted). Penelope laments the continued absence of Ulisse to her nurse Ericlea. After a discussion of men's sins between Giove and Nettuno, Ulisse is put ashore on Ithaca and encouraged by Minerva to reclaim his palace, given over to the suitors of his wife Penelope. Eumete, his herdsman, is taunted by the jester Iro, and then welcomes the disguised Ulisse, who revives his hopes of his master's return. Eumete then welcomes Ulisse's son Telemaco, also returning home, and there is a joyful reunion, while Eumete tells Penelope that Ulisse may soon appear. The suitor Antinoo mocks Ulisse, disguised as a beggar, who first wins a contest with the suitors by being able to string his bow, and then turns it upon them. Penelope's fear that he may not truly be Ulisse is overcome by Ericlea, and they join in a love duet. The distribution of the voices varies in different editions.

Ritter. Professional name of the French musical family Bennel.

(1) **Cécile Ritter-Ciampi** (*b* La Cabrière, 22 Nov. 1859; *d* St Briac, 1939) was a soprano. Studied with Carvalho and Carlotta Patti. Created Virginia in Massé's *Paul et Virginie* (1876). Married tenor Ezio Ciampi-Cellai (1855–1927).

(2) **Gabrielle Ritter-Ciampi** (*b* Paris, 2 Nov. 1886; *d* Paris, Jan. 1975) was also a soprano, daughter of above. Studied with her parents. Début Paris, 1917, Virginie. O.C., from 1919; first local Fiordiligi and Constanze. Taught singing in Paris. One of the best French Mozart singers between the wars. (R)

Robert le Diable (Robert the Devil). Opera in 5 acts by Meyerbeer; text by Scribe. Prod. Paris, O., 21 Nov. 1831, with Cinti-Damoreau, Dorus-Gras, Nourrit, Levasseur, and Taglioni dancing, cond. Habeneck; London, D.L., 20 Feb. 1832; N.Y., Park T., 7 Apr. 1834 (Rophino Lacy's version), with Mrs Wood, Sharpe, Harrison, Wood, Clarke, Placide, Blakeley, Haydn.

In 13th-cent. Palermo, Robert, Duke of Normandy (ten.), the son of a mortal and a devil, falls in love with the Princess Isabella (sop.). Disguised and under the name of Bertram (bass), the Devil tries to gain Robert's soul; he prevents Robert from winning Isabella in a tournament, and Robert is then willing to use diabolical means. At a midnight orgy with ghostly nuns, Robert acquires a magic branch with which he gains access to Isabella; but she persuades him to break it. Robert denounces his father the Devil, and he is married to Isabella.

Other operas on the subject are by J. Barnett (1829), Casimiro (1842). Parodies include A. Müller's *Robert der Teufel* (1833), Damse's *Robert Birbanduch* (1844). Also J. G. Kastner (*Les Nonnes de Robert le Diable*, comp. 1845).

Roberto Devereux, ossia Il Conte d'Essex. Opera in 3 acts by Donizetti; text by Cammarano, after F. Ancelot's tragedy *Élisabeth d'Angleterre*. Prod. Naples, S.C., 29 Oct. 1837 with Ronzi de Begnis, Granchi, Basadonna, Barroilhet, Barrattini, Rossi, Benedetti; London 24 June 1841 with Grisi, Rubini, Tamburini; N.Y., Astor Place O.H., 15 Jan. 1849, with Truffi, Amalia Patti, Benedetti, S. Patti, Rossi-Corsi, Giubilei, cond. Maretzek.

The Earl of Essex (Robert Devereux, ten.), although loved by Queen Elizabeth (sop.), is in love with Sara (sop. or mezzo), Countess of Nottingham. Essex is accused of treason and sentenced to death by the Queen.

Robertson, James (*b* Liverpool, 17 June 1912). English conductor. Studied Cambridge, Leipzig, and London, R.C.M. Gly, music staff, 1937–9; C.R., chorus master and conductor, 1938–9; music director, 1938–9; music director, S.W. 1946–54, when he conducted the English premières of *The School for Fathers* (*Quatro rusteghi*) and Sutermeister's *Romeo and Juliet*, as well as the S.W. premières of *Werther* and *Don Pasquale*. Director, London Opera Centre, 1964-78. (R)

Robin, Mado (*b* nr Tours, 29 Dec. 1918; *d* Paris, 10 Dec. 1960). French soprano. Discovered by Ruffo, who sent her to study with Giuseppe Podestà. Won first prize in the 'Concours des soprani', Paris, O., 1937; but owing to the war did not make stage début until 1945, when she sang Gilda. Appeared in Brussels, Liège, French provinces, San Francisco. Her voice was extremely flexible and she is said to have been able to reach the highest note ever emitted by a singer–c''''. Her most famous roles were Lucia and Lakmé. (R)

Robin Hood. Opera in 3 acts by Macfarren; text by Oxenford. Prod. London, H.M.'s, 11 Oct. 1860, with Lemens-Sherrington, S. Reeves, Santley. The earliest celebrations of the hero seem to date from 16th-cent. May Day feasts. Among many early masques and ballad operas on the subject are works by Watts, Mendez, and Shield. Also operas by Baumgarten (1786), Dietrich (1879), Holmes, and De Koven (1890).

Robinson, Anastasia (*b* c1695; *d* Southampton, April 1755). English soprano. Studied with Croft, Sandoni, Lindelheim. After a concert career, début London 1714, King's T., in a pasticcio, *Creso*. Created leading roles in several Handel operas, including *Amadigi*, *Floridante*, *Ottone*, *Giulio Cesare*, and *Flavio*. According to Burney her salary was 'said to be £1,000, and her emoluments by Benefits and presents were estimated at nearly as much more'. Had a fine voice of extensive compass, but uncertain intonation. Left the stage in 1724 on her marriage to the Earl of Peterborough, who did not publicly acknowledge the marriage until 1735. Her sister, **Margaret**, studied with Buononcini and Rameau, but suffered from excessive stage fright and did not appear in public, though she may have been the Miss Robinson Jr who appeared at Drury Lane in 1729 as Ariel in *The Tempest*.

Robinson, Forbes (Peter) (*b* Macclesfield, 21 May 1926). English bass. Began professional life as schoolmaster; won Mario Lanza competition 1952 and studied Milan, Sc. School. London, C.G. since 1954 (début Monterone); created title-role *King Priam* (1962) and Moses (speaking role) in British première of *Moses und Aron*; first British Don Giovanni at C.G. since Santley, and an impressive Claggart in *Billy Budd*. Guest appearances with Scottish and Welsh Opera, Berlin, Zurich, Buenos Aires, etc. Repertory of more than 70 roles includes Pizarro, Figaro, Boris, Dodon, Kecal, Swallow, and others. One of the best singing-actors in the post-war British operatic scene. (R)

Rocca, Lodovico (*b* Turin, 29 Nov. 1895). Italian composer. His two most famous works are *Il Dibuk* (1934) and *Monte Ivnor* (1939), which have established him as a composer in the *verismo* tradition. Director, Turin Conservatory, 1940–60.

Rocco. The gaoler (bass) in Beethoven's *Fidelio*, Marzelline's father and Leonore's employer.

Rochois (orig. Le Rochois), **Marthe** (*b* 1650; *d* Sartrouville-sur-Seine, 9 Oct. 1728). French soprano. Protégée of Lully. Début Paris, O., 1678; remained there until 1697, creating leading roles in Lully's *Proserpine, Persée, Armadis, Armide, Acis et Galathée*. Retired from stage 1698.

Rode, Wilhelm (*b* Hanover, 17 Feb. 1887; *d* Munich, 2 Sept. 1959). German bass-baritone. Début Erfurt 1908 Herald (*Lohengrin*). After engagements in Mannheim, Breslau, and Stuttgart, joined Munich Opera in 1922, where he remained until 1934, also appearing in Vienna, Prague, Budapest, and Dresden. London, C.G., 1928. Salzburg 1929–32, Pizarro, Almaviva. Intendant Deutsches Opernhaus, Berlin, 1934–44 continuing to sing Sachs, Wotan, Dutchman, etc. Considered by some critics to be the finest Heldenbariton between the wars. (R)

Rodelinda. Opera in 3 acts by Handel; text by Salvi, altered by Haym. Prod. London, Hm., 13 Feb. 1725, with Cuzzoni, Dotti, Senesino, Pacini, Boschi, Borrosini; Northampton, Mass., Smith College, 9 May 1931. Also set by Perti (1710), Canuti (1724), Nelvi (1726), Cordans (1731), and Graun (1741).

Rodolfo. The poet (ten.), one of the bohemians, hero of Puccini's *La Bohème.*

Rodrigo. The Marquis of Posa (bar.) in Verdi's *Don Carlos*. Also opera in 3 acts by Handel; text anon. Prod. Florence 1707 or 1708.

Rodziński, Artur (*b* Split, 2 Jan. 1892; *d* Boston, 27 Nov. 1958). Polish conductor. Studied Vienna with Schalk. Début Lwów 1920; Warsaw Opera 1924–8. Then emigrated to U.S.A., conducting mostly concerts though he did conduct the American première of *The Lady Macbeth of the Mtsensk district* (1935) and performances of Wagner and Strauss in Cleveland and Chicago. He emerged after the war as a prominent opera conductor in Europe. In Florence he conducted the first Western performance of Prokofiev's *War and Peace*, and also appeared at Milan, Sc., Rome, and Naples. (R)

Roger, Gustave (*b* Paris, 17 Dec. 1815; *d* Paris, 12 Sept. 1879). French tenor. Studied Paris with Martin. Début Paris, O.C., 1838, Georges in Halévy's *L'Éclair*. Paris, O., 1849–59, where he created John of Leyden in *Le Prophète* and other roles; London, C.G., 1847. In 1859 injured in hunting mishap and had right arm amputated. Continued at O.C. until 1862; then guest appearances in Brussels, Prague etc. until 1868. Professor, Paris Conservatoire, from 1868 till his death.
Bibl: G. Roger: *Le Carnet d'un ténor* (1880)

Roi David, Le (King David). *Psaume dramatique* in 2 parts by Honegger; text by René Morax. Prod. Mézières, T. du Jorat, 11 June 1921; N.Y. 26 Oct. 1925; London, R.A.H., 17 Mar. 1927. Honegger's first dramatic work.

Roi de Lahore, Le (The King of Lahore). Opera in 5 acts by Massenet; text by Gallet. Prod. Paris, O., 27 Apr. 1877 with Joséphine de Reszke, Salomon, Lassalle, cond. Deldevez; London, C.G., 28 June 1879, with Turolla, Gayarré, Lassalle, cond. Vianesi. New Orleans Dec. 1883.

King Alim (ten.) and his minister Scindia (bar.) love Sita (sop.). Scindia kills Alim, who is allowed by a god to return as a beggar. Sita kills herself so as to join him in Paradise.

Roi d'Ys, Le (The King of Ys). Opera in 3 acts by Lalo; text by Blau. Prod. Paris, O.C., 7 May 1888, with Deschamps-Jehin, Simonnet, Talazac, Bouvet, Cobalet, cond. Danbé; New Orleans 23 Jan. 1890; London, C.G., 17 July 1901, with Pacquot, Adams, Jerome, Seveilhac, Plançon, cond. Flon.

Mylio (ten.) is to be married to Rozenn (sop.), but her sister Margared (mezzo) loves him too. On the wedding night Margared jealously lets the sea in on the town. She kills herself in remorse; the town is saved by its patron saint.

Roi l'a dit, Le (lit., The King has commanded it). Opera in 3 acts by Delibes; text by Gondinet. Prod. Paris, O.C., 24 May 1873, with Priola,

Lhérie, Ismael, cond. Deloffre; London, Prince of Wales's, 1 Dec. 1894; Iowa, University of Iowa, 29 Apr. 1967.

Having claimed to possess a son, the Marquis de Montecontour is compelled to produce a peasant boy pretender, who promptly embarrasses the Marquis by taking advantage of the situation. He is got rid of and marries his girl, while the Marquis is consoled for the loss of his 'son' with a dukedom.

Roi malgré lui, Le (The King in spite of himself). Opera in 3 acts by Chabrier; text by De Najac and Burani. Prod. Paris, O.C., 18 May 1887, with Isaac, Mezevay, Bouvet, Fugère, cond. Danbé. Revived 1929 in revised version by Albert Carré, with Brothier, Guyla, Bourdin, Musy, cond. Masson.

Henri de Valois (bar.), about to be crowned King of France, learns from Minka (sop.), his betrothed, that there is a plot to kill him. He disguises himself as his friend De Nangis (ten.) and joins the plotters. De Nangis comes to the camp and is mistaken for Henri. The plot is foiled and the lives of both men are spared. Henri is finally crowned king of France and Poland.

Roller, Alfred (b Vienna, 10 Feb. 1864; d Vienna, 21 June 1935). Austrian designer and artist. Worked with Mahler in Vienna, where his designs for Wagner, Mozart, and Beethoven operas were greatly admired. He also designed the scenery and costumes for the premières of *Rosenkavalier* (Dresden 1911) and *Frau ohne Schatten* (Vienna, 1919), and for many of the productions at Salzburg.

Roman, Stella (orig. Florica Vierica Alma Stela Blasu) (b Cluj, 25 Mar. 1904). Romanian soprano. Studied Cluj with Pfeiffer and Bucharest with Cosma, Vulpescu, and Pessione, Milan with Narducci and Poli-Randaccio, Rome with L. Ricci. Début Piacenza, 1932. Rome, 1936–40, and other Italian theatres; created Cordelia in Alberto Ghislanzoni's *King Lear* (1937) and Regan in Frazzi's *Re Lear* (1939); Empress in first Sc. *Frau ohne Schatten* (1940). N.Y., Met., 1940-50 in Italian repertory, also Chicago, San Francisco. An uneven but exciting singer. (R)

Romance, Romanza, Romanze (*Fr, It, Ger* romance). In opera, an aria, generally amorous or soliloquizing, normally intended less for display than aria proper, and thus lacking ornamentation, cadenzas, etc. However, the distinction is not precise: Verdi used the terms almost interchangeably. Examples are Matilde's 'Sombres forêts' in Rossini's *Guillaume Tell*, Radamès's 'Celeste Aida' in Verdi's *Aida*, and Pedrillo's 'Im Mohrenland gefangen war' in Mozart's *Die Entführung aus dem Serail*.

Romanelli, Luigi (b Rome, 21 July 1751; d

Milan, 1 Mar. 1839). Italian librettist. Used his wide literary and linguistic knowledge to organize a systematic but adaptable set conventions for operatic use. Though basically a classicist, he did treat the medieval and exotic subjects that were becoming an important part of Romantic feeling. Composers who used his librettos included Fioravanti, Mayr, Mercadante, Nicolini, Pacini, Rossini (*La pietra del paragone*), and Weigl.

Romani, Felice (b Genoa, 31 Jan. 1788; d Mongelia, 28 Jan. 1865). Italian librettist. Originally a lawyer, he turned to literature and provided more than 100 libretti for Mayr, Vaccai, Rossini, Donizetti, Bellini, and others. Among the well-known operas for which he wrote texts are *Norma, Il pirata, La sonnambula, L'elisir d'amore, Lucrezia Borgia, Il Turco in Italia,* and *Un giorno di regno.*

Romani, Pietro (b Rome, 29 May 1791; d Florence, 6 Jan. 1877). Italian composer. He wrote two operas, but is better known for his aria 'Manca un foglio', which replaced 'A un dottor' in *Il barbiere di Siviglia* in 1816 and is still found in some vocal scores.

Romania. The first opera performances were given at Sibiu, 1722, by one of the many Italian companies that toured the country. Another played in Bucharest, 1787; a German company visited Iaşi, 1795. Romania's long struggle for national opera took place almost exclusively in *Bucharest. Early Romanian operas include *Braconierul* (The Poacher, 1833) and *Zamfira* (1834) by Ion Wachmann (1807–63), who conducted the Theodor Müller Company in Timişoara and Bucharest (1931–5); *Baba-Hîrca* (1848) by Alexander Flechtenmacher (1824–98), who conducted at the T. Naţional in Iaşi, 1844–7, later in Bucharest; *Verful cu Dor* (The Summit of Desire, 1879) by Liubicz Skibinski (?–?), text by 'Carmen Sylva' (Queen Elizabeth of Romania), given by an Italian company. The first foreign opera given in Romanian was Boieldieu's *Jean de Paris;* the first libretto published in Romanian was *Norma.* The first opera season with performances in Romanian was given in 1885–6 under George Stephănescu (1843–1925); he also translated librettos, wrote polemic articles, composed operettas (beginning with *Peste Dunăre,* 1880), and founded a school of singing whose pupils included Hariclea Darclée. Other important works included *Candidatul Linte* (Candidate Linte, 1877) and *Crai nou* (New World, 1877) by Ciprian Porumbescu (1853–83); *Olteanca* (The Girl from Olt, 1880, in collaboration with Gustav Otremba) and *Petru Rares* (comp. 1889, prod. 1900) by Eduard Caudella (1841–1924). The Tennyson opera *Enoch Arden* (1906) by Alexis Catargi (1876–1923), a pupil of D'Indy and Enescu who was also a diplomat, and *La*

Şezătoare (The Vigil, 1908) by Tiberiu Brediceanu (1877–1968), whose long career
included posts conducting opera in Cluj (from
1919) and, in his seventies, directing the
Bucharest Opera (1941–4), were both successful. With the development of a national opera
in the 1920s, encouragement was given to new
Romanian works. Some of the more important
were *Năpasta* (The Disaster, 1928) and *Constantin Brâcoveanu* (1935) by Sabin Drăgoi
(1894–1968), who conducted opera in Cluj and
Timişoara, and whose work reflects his studies
in folk music; *Marin Pescarul* (1934) by Marţian
Negrea (*b* 1893), a pupil of Franz Schmidt;
Mona Vanna (1934) by Nicolae Brânzue (*b*
1907), a prominent opera conductor; *O noapte
furtunoasă* (A Stormy Night, 1935), by Paul
Constantinescu (1909–63); and settings of
Chekhov, *La drumul mare* (1932), and Musset,
Cu dragostea nu se glumeşte (On ne badine
pas avec l'amour, 1941) by Constantin Nottara
(1890–1951). Since the Second Word War,
opera has greatly developed and spread and
many composers have been encouraged to
write for the newly opened opera houses:
there are theatres in Braşov, Constanţa, Galaţa,
Oradea, and Oraşul. See also *Bucharest, Cluj,
Iaşi* and *Timişoara.*

Romanza, Romanze See *Romance.*

Rome (It. Roma). Capital of Italy. The first
operas here were private entertainments for
the nobility. Agazzari's *Eumelio,* written in a
fortnight and performed by pupils of the
Seminario Romano early in 1606, is probably
the earliest opera. Works by M. A. Rossi, Vittori,
Mazzocchi, and Marazzoli were given in various palaces and houses of the nobility. In 1632
Landi's *Il S. Alessio,* with libretto by G. Rospigliosi (later Pope Clement IX), inaugurated the
Great Hall of the Palazzo Barberini. The opera
was repeated in 1634 for the visit of Alexander
Charles, brother of King Władisław IV of
Poland. Works presented at the Barberini
Palace included Mazzocchi's and Marazzoli's
Chi soffre, speri (1639) the first comic opera,
libretto by Rospigliosi. Marazzoli's *La vita
umana, overo Il trionfo della pietà* (1656) was
the last opera produced there, staged in
honour of Queen Christina of Sweden, to
whom the score is dedicated. Count Giacomo
d'Albert from Queen Christina's court was
authorized by Clement IX to build the first
public opera house in Rome in 1669, the T.
Torre di Nona (better known as the T.
Torinona). This opened 1761 with Stradella's
Lesbo e Ceffea. Closed 1776, as Clement IX's
successors looked on opera less favourably.
Reopened 1690; demolished on instructions of
Pope Innocent XII 1697. Rebuilt 1733, burnt
down 1781, rebuilt 1787. Altered 1795 (22 rows
of seats in the stalls and 174 boxes), and
reopened as T. Apollo. Staged premières of

Rossini's *Mathilde de Shabran,* conducted by
Paganini, *Il trovatore, Un ballo in maschera,*
and Donizetti's posthumous *Duca d'Alba;* and
the first Rome performances of twelve of
Verdi's operas. Pulled down 1889 to make way
for an embankment on the banks of the Tiber,
Lungo Tevere Torre di Nona.

Other Rome opera houses included the T.
Caprinaca, opened as a private theatre 1679
(189 private boxes), and to the public 1695. In
1711–47 staged mostly opera seria, but from
1754 its repertory was mostly of comic opera.
Continued to function until 1881. The site is
now occupied by a cinema. The T. delle Dame
was built in 1717 by Count d'Alibert's son, and
devoted for almost a century to opera seria.
The T. Valle was originally a wooden structure
erected in the courtyard of the Palazzo Caprinaca by Domenico Valle. Opened in 1727. It
staged the première of Rossini's *La Cenerentola,* and three of Donizetti's works. From c1840
it became a theatre and was used by visiting
companies to Rome, including those of Duse,
Bernhardt, and Rachel. The T. Argentina was
built 1731–2 by the Duke Sforza-Cesarini, with
186 boxes. Opened with Sarro's *Berenice,* and
premièred *Il barbiere di Siviglia, I due Foscari,*
and *La battaglia di Legnano,* as well as the first
Rome performances of *Ernani, Macbeth,
Alzira,* and *Rigoletto* under the title of *Viscardello.* Remained one of Rome's leading opera
houses until the building of the *Costanzi in
1880. Continued to give occasional seasons of
opera, and housed the main Rome opera
season 1926–7, when the Costanzi was being
modernized as T. Reale dell'Opera. Now
mostly used as a concert hall for the Accademia
di Santa Cecilia.

The T. Costanzi was built by Domenico Costanzi, a rich builder, designed by Achille Sfon-
drini (cap. 2293). Opened 27 Nov. 1880 with
Semiramide; the first act was interrupted for
the Royal March as King Umberto and his wife
arrived late; the King left long before the end,
but the Queen remained. In 1888 the music
publisher Edoardo Sonzogno took over the
management, and announced his second
competition for a one-act opera: *Cavalleria rusticana* won and was first performed there May
1890. Other Mascagni operas premièred at the
Costanzi were *L'amico Fritz, Iris, Lodoletta,* and
Il piccolo Marat. Also staged first performances
of *Tosca* and Zandonai's *Giulietta e Romeo.*
From 1911–25 directed by the soprano Emma
*Carelli. In 1926 taken over by the city of Rome,
enlarged and completely renovated,
reopening as the T. Reale dell'Opera on 28
February 1928 with Boito's *Nerone.* Gino
Marinuzzi was the chief conductor 1928–34,
Tullio Serafin 1934–43 (also artistic director).
Mussolini hoped to make the Rome O. the best
in Italy, challenging La Scala. Leading Italian
singers were enticed back from the Met-

ropolitan, and Gigli, Lauri-Volpi, Caniglia, Cigna, and Stignani were members of the regular ensemble. Serafin's achievements included cycles of *The Ring* in Italian, with almost exclusively Italian singers, Verdi cycles in 1940 and 1941, a Rossini cycle in 1942, and a cycle of contemporary opera, which included the first perfomance in Italy of *Wozzeck*, surprisingly given during the German occupation although long banned in Nazi Germany.

Since the end of the Second World War there have been productions of many contemporary works, including *Mathis der Maler*, *The Rape of Lucretia*, and *Boulevard Solitude*, all in their first performances in Italy, and visits from foreign companies. Massimo Bogianckino was artistic director 1963–8, during which period the T. dell'O., as it had been called since 1946, produced some of the best opera in Italy; Bruno Bartoletti was appointed permanent conductor, Giulini and Gui made frequent appearances, and Visconti was one of the regular producers. Mario Zafred succeeded Bogianckino in 1968–74. Gioacchino Tomasi was appointed artistic director in 1976. Other operas premièred at the Rome O. include Pizzetti's *Lo straniero* (1930), Refice's *Cecilia* (1934), Malipiero's *Ecuba* (1941), Alfano's *Dottor Antonio* (1949), Rossellini's *Uno sguardo dal ponte* (1961), and Chailly's *L'idiota* (1970).

Bibl: A. Ademolo: *I teatri di Roma nel secolo XVII* (1888).

Romeo and Juliet. See *Capuleti e i Montecchi*, *Giulietta e Romeo*, and below.

Roméo et Juliette. Opera in 5 acts by Gounod; text by Barbier and Carré, after Shakespeare's tragedy (1594–5). Prod. Paris, T.L., 27 Apr. 1867, with Cavallo, Michot, Barré, Cazaux, cond. Deloffre; London, C.G., 11 July 1867, with Patti, Mario, Cotogni, Taliafico, cond. Costa; N.Y., 15 Nov. 1867, with Hauk, Pancani, Dominici, Medici, cond. Bergman. Voices: Roméo (ten.), Juliette (sop.), Mercutio (bar.), Friar Lawrence (bass). Parody, *Rhum et Eau en Juillet* by Dejazet (1867). For other operas on the subject, see *Shakespeare*.

Romer, Emma (*b* ?, 1814; *d* Margate, 11 Apr. 1868). English soprano. Studied with George Smart. Début London, C.G., 1830, Clara (*The Duenna*). Continued to appear at C.G. until 1848, and at D.L. and the English Opera House. In 1852 took over the Surrey T. where she produced opera in English with a strong company of native singers. Her most famous role was Amina.

Romerzählung. Tannhäuser's (ten.) long narration of his pilgrimage to Rome in the last act of Wagner's opera.

Ronald (orig. *Russell), (Sir) **Landon** (*b*

London, 7 June 1873; *d* London, 14 Aug. 1938). English conductor and composer. Studied R.C.M. Engaged by Mancinelli as *maestro al piano* at C.G., 1891, subsequently touring with Augustus Harris's company, and conducting some performances at D.L. Toured as Melba's accompanist, and played for Patti when she recorded in 1905. (R)

Ronconi. Italian family of singers.

(1) **Domenico** (*b* Leninara, nr Rovigo, 11 July 1772; *d* Milan 13 Apr. 1839). Italian tenor. Début Venice, 1797. St Petersburg, 1801–5; Milan, Sc., 1808, creating roles in operas by Mosca, Orlandi, and Lamberti. Vienna, Italian Opera, 1809, where he was also director; Paris, 1810; after a further period in Italy, sang at Munich H., 1819–29, where he also produced. In 1829 opened a school for singing in Milan.

(2) **Giorgio** (*b* Milan, 6 Aug. 1810; *d* Madrid, 8 Jan. 1890). Italian baritone, son of above. Studied with his father. Début Pavia, 1831, Valdeburgo (*La straniera*); Rome, T. Valle, 1833, where he created Cardenio (in Donizetti's *Il furioso all'isola di San Domingo*), and title-role in *Torquato Tasso* – both in 1833; also created roles in Donizetti's *Pia de' Tolomei* (Venice, 1837), *Maria di Rudenz* (Venice, 1838), *Maria Padilla* (Milan, 1841), and *Maria di Rohan* (Vienna, 1843). At Sc. created title-role in *Nabucco*. London H.M.'s, 1842, Enrico, Belcore and other roles; C.G., 1847–66, principal roles in the first English performances of *Poliuto*, *Rigoletto*, *Maria di Rohan*, and *Due Foscari*; greatly admired in other parts including Figaro, Iago (both Rossini), and Podestà (*Gazza ladra*). Chorley wrote a description of his Doge in *Due Foscari*: 'he possessed such wonderful dramatic powers, that one virtually forgot his vocal limitations, a compass of barely more than one octave, inferior in quality, weak and habitually out of tune'. St Petersburg, 1850–60; N.Y., 1866–72. Returned to Europe and opened singing school in Granada; appointed professor of singing at Madrid Conservatory 1874. Married the soprano **Giovannina Giannoni**, who sang in London, 1837, 1842–3 and 1847 as Elguerra Ronconi, with only moderate success. Their daughter, **Antonietta**, had a short career as a soprano.

(3) **Felice** (*b* Venice, 1811; *d* St Petersburg, 10 Sept. 1875). Italian teacher, second son of (1). Studied with his father. Appointed professor of singing, Würzburg 1837. Also held appointments in Frankfurt, Milan (1844–8), London, and St Petersburg. Author of a method of teaching singing; composed several songs.

(4) **Sebastiano** (*b* Venice, May 1814; *d* Milan, 6 Feb. 1900). Italian baritone. Third son of (1). Studied with his father. Début Lucca, 1836, Torquato Tasso. Generally sang same repertory as Giorgio. London, H.M.'s, 1860, Rigoletto, Masetto etc. Sang for some 35 years in Europe

and America, after which he taught singing in Milan.

Rondine, La (The Swallow). Opera in 3 acts by Puccini; text by Adami, translated from a German libretto by A.M. Willner and H. Reichert. Prod. Monte Carlo, 27 Mar. 1917, with Dalla Rizza, Ferraris, Schipa, Huberdeau, cond. Marinuzzi; N.Y., 10 Mar. 1928, with Bori, Fleischer, Gigli, Ludikar, cond. Bellezza; London, Fulham Town Hall (Opera Viva), 9 Dec. 1965, with Doyle, Morgan, Gloster, Allum, cond. Head. Intended as an operetta for Vienna, the work was kept from production by the war, and the composer decided to set the libretto rather differently.

The opera, set in Paris and Nice during the Second Empire, tells of the love of Magda (sop.), mistress of the wealthy Parisian Raimbaud (bar.), for Ruggero (ten.), a young man of aristocratic family. Her moral scruples overcome her, and she renounces him.

Ronzi, Giuseppina. See *De Begnis.*

Rooy, Anton (orig. Antonius Maria Josephus) **Van** (*b* Rotterdam, 1 Jan. 1870; *d* Munich, 28 Nov. 1932). Dutch bass-baritone. Studied Frankfurt with Stockhausen. Début Bayreuth, 1897, Wotan; London, C.G., 1898–1913; N.Y., Met., 1898–1908, first U.S. Jochanaan, 1907. Amfortas in N.Y. première of *Parsifal* in 1903, which resulted in his being banned from Bayreuth. An extremely serious and sensitive artist, he was considered the finest Sachs, Kurwenal, and Wotan of the first decade of this century. (R)

Ros, Maria (orig. Maria Asunción Aguilar) (*b* Alicante, 16 May 1895; *d* Burjasot, Sept. 1970). Spanish soprano and teacher. Début Alicante, 1915. Sang with great success in South America, Spain and Monte Carlo, but retired from stage on her marriage to Giacomo Lauri-Volpi. Repertory included Rosina, Gilda, Violetta, Sophie. Pupils included Lily Pons and Franco Corelli. (R)

Rosa, Carl (orig. Karl Rose) (*b* Hamburg, 22 Mar. 1842; *d* Paris, 30 Apr. 1889). German conductor and impresario. After touring Europe and America as a solo violinist, he met the soprano Euphrosyne *Parepa whom he married and with whom he set up the Parepa-Rosa Opera Company, which after his death was renamed the *Carl Rosa Opera Company.

Rosalinde. Eisenstein's wife (sop.), heroine of J. Strauss's *Die Fledermaus.*

Rosbaud, Hans (*b* Graz, 22 July 1895; *d* Lugano, 30 Dec. 1962). Austrian conductor. Studied Frankfurt. Held appointments before the war in Frankfurt, Mainz, Münster, and Strasbourg. Chief conductor of the Aix-en-Provence Festival 1947–59. Directed memor-

able performances of Schoenberg's *Erwartung* and *Von Heute auf Morgen* at the 1958 Holland Festival; conducted both radio and stage premières of *Moses und Aron*. Renowned for his understanding and able performance of modern music. (R)

Rosenberg, Hilding (Constantin) (*b* Bosjökloster, 21 June 1892). Swedish composer and conductor. Studied Stockholm R.A.M. with Ellberg, then in Germany, again in Stockholm with Stenhammar. Assistant conductor Stockholm Opera 1932-4, then conductor. His operas, which have won a following in Sweden, include the following: *Resan till Amerika* (Journey to America, 1932); *Marionetter* (Marionettes, 1939); *Lycksalighetens ö* (The Island of Happiness, 1945); a fourpart opera-oratorio *Josef och hans bröder* (Joseph and his Brothers, after Thomas Mann, 1945-8); and *Hus med dubbel ingång* (The House with Two Entrances, after Calderón, 1970).
Bibl: M. Pergament: *Hilding Rosenberg* (1956).

Rosenkavalier, Der (The Knight of the Rose). Opera in 3 acts by Richard Strauss; text by Hugo von Hofmannsthal. Prod. Dresden, Hofoper, 26 Jan. 1911, with Siems, Von der Osten, Nast, Perron, cond. Schuch; London, C.G., 29 Jan. 1913, with Siems, Von der Osten, Dux, Knüpfer, cond. Beecham; N.Y., Met., 9 Dec. 1913, with Hempel, Ober, Case, Goritz, cond. Hertz.

The Princess of Werdenberg, known as the Feldmarschallin (sop.), has been having an affair with the young Count Octavian (sop. or mezzo). The Princess's cousin, Baron Ochs (bass), arrives to announce his marriage to the much younger Sophie von Faninal (sop.), and to ask for a young Cavalier to take the traditional Silver Rose to her. Octavian, who has spent the night with the Marschallin, is forced, so as to prevent discovery, to dress himself up as a young maid, whom Ochs immediately pursues. Sophie and Octavian fall in love at first sight; Sophie is repelled by the manners and age of Ochs and tells her father, Faninal (bar.) that she will not marry him. Octavian hatches a plot to discredit Ochs, and disguising himself again as the Marchallin's maid ('Mariandl'), arranges a rendezvous with Ochs at a disreputable inn. The Marschallin arrives, reminds Ochs of his rank, given the young couple her blessing, and Octavian walks out of her life with Sophie.

Rosenstock, Joseph (*b* Kraków, 27 Jan. 1895). Polish conductor. Studied Kraków and Vienna with Schreker. Stuttgart 1921–2; Darmstadt 1925–7; Wiesbaden 1927–8. Invited to succeed Bodanzky at the Met. 1929, but after a few performances resigned. Mannheim 1930–3; music director Jewish Kulturbund, Berlin,

425

1933–6, after which he left Germany. Tokyo 1936-41. N.Y., C.C., 1948–55; Cologne 1958–9. Returned to the Met. 1960. (R)

Rosina. Bartolo's ward (mezzo) in Rossini's and (sop.) in Paisiello's *Il barbiere di Siviglia*.

Rosing, Vladimir (*b* St Petersburg, 23 Jan. 1890; *d* Los Angeles, 24 Nov. 1963). Russian tenor. Teachers included Jean de Reszke and Sbriglia. Début in concert with Heifetz 1910; stage début, St Petersburg 1912, Lensky. Directed and participated in season at London Opera House, 1915, in which he sang Herman in the English première of *The Queen of Spades*. In 1936, in collaboration with Albert Coates, he organized the British Music-Drama Opera Company, which survived for only one season, at C.G. In 1923 organized American Opera Company, financed by Eastman School, which included S. Fisher, Votipka, Kullman, and toured U.S. for six years giving opera in English. In 1939 founded the California O. Association. Later joined staff of N.Y. City O. and produced. (R)

Rossellini, Renzo (*b* Rome 2 Feb. 1908). Italian composer and critic. Studied Rome with Sallustio, Setaccioli, and Molinari. Held teaching appointments at Varese and Pesaro, and was critic of *Il messagero*. His operas, which are in the tradition of Zandonai, Respighi and Alfano, include *La guerra* (Naples 1956), *Il vortice* (Naples 1958), *Uno sguardo dal ponte*, after Arthur Miller's play *A View from the Bridge* (Rome 1961), *Il linguaggio dei fiori* (Milan 1963), and *L'Anonce faite à Marie* after a play by Claudel (Paris 1970). His brother is the producer Roberto Rossellini.

Rossi, Gaetano (*b* Verona, 18 May 1774; *d* Verona, 25 Jan. 1855). Italian librettist. Wrote over 120 librettos for numerous composers, including Carafa, Coccia, Donizetti (2, incl *Linda di Chamounix*), Mayr, Mercadante, Meyerbeer (4, incl. *Il Crociato in Egitto*), Nicolai, Pacini, and Rossini (*La cambiale di matrimonio, La scala di seta, Tancredi,* and *Semiramide*). He drew on a wide range of sources and put into operatic currency many of the themes of Romanticism. His plots were often taken from classical or historical drama, and embraced the fashionable Spanish, Nordic, and English subjects as well as more traditional material; and his techniques contributed to the loosening of set forms characteristic of the reforms of early 19th-cent. opera.

Rossi, Lauro (*b* Macerata, 19 Feb. 1812; *d* Cremona, 5 May 1885). Italian composer. Studied Naples with Zingarelli, Furno, and Crescentini. His first opera was a comedy, *La contessa villane* (1829), followed by the successful *Costanza e Oringaldo* (1830) (with Raimondi). The further success of three more comedies

attracted the attention of Donizetti, who recommended him to the Rome T. Valle (1831–3). *La casa disabitata* (1834) was so successful that Malibran arranged for Barbaia to commission *Amelia* (1834) for her; but through Malibran's insistence on being allowed to dance in a *pas de deux* with the ballerina Mathis, the opera was hissed. Rossi then toured Mexico, producing *Giovanna Shore* there (1836); he returned to recover from yellow fever in 1843.

Settling in Milan, he revived *La casa disabitata* in 1843 as *I falsi monetari*; it gained a place in the repertory and restored his fame. He also became head of the Milan Conservatory; he moved to a similar post in Naples in 1870. Here he was unpopular, and in 1880 retired to Cremona. His last opera, *Biorn* (1877), was a version of *Macbeth* transferred to Norway, and written for London: it failed, and the music is lost. He was always more successful in comedy, and was considered by some Donizetti's natural successor.

Rossignol, Le. See *Nightingale, The.*

Rossi-Lemeni, Nicola (*b* Istanbul, 6 Nov. 1920). Italian bass. Born of an Italian father and Russian mother (Xenia Lemeni Makedon, teacher of singing at Odessa). Début Venice 1946, Varlaam; Milan, Sc., since 1947; San Francisco 1951–3; N.Y., Met., 1953–4; London, C.G., 1952. Although noted for his interpretations of the Russian repertory (especially Boris), and Méphistophélès (Gounod and Boito), he has been extremely successful in such diverse roles as Gruenberg's Emperor Jones and Bloch's Macbeth. His imposing stage presence and dramatic abilities compensate for some vocal inequalities. Married to the soprano Virginia *Zeani. Since 1965 he has also produced opera. (R)

Rossini, Gioacchino (*b* Pesaro, 29 Feb. 1792; *d* Paris, 13 Nov. 1868). Italian composer. Rossini's parents were both musicians, his father a town trumpeter, his mother a singer of *seconda donna* parts. By the age of 15, he had learnt the violin and harpsichord and had often sung in public. In 1806 he entered the Bologna Conservatory, and during his student years wrote an opera, *Demetrio e Polibio* (staged 1812). His first professional works for the stage were *La cambiale di matrimonio* (1810), *L'equivoco stravagante* (1811), and *L'inganno felice* (1812) – all *buffo* operas – and *Ciro in Babilonia* (1812), his first serious work, which like the comic *La scala di seta* (1812) was a failure.

However, *La pietra del paragone* (1812), written for the soprano Marcolini who had procured him its commission for La Scala, was a success. It was in the finale of this work that the public first heard the famous Rossini *crescendo*; they had already learnt to enjoy the pace and verve of his tunes. Four works for Venice followed between Nov. 1812 and May 1813; *L'occasione fa il ladro*, *Il Signor Bruschino*, *Tancredi*, and *L'italiana in Algeri*. *Tancredi* first made his name known outside Italy, and contains the warmest love music he ever wrote: in it there is a new approach to the handling of the orchestra, especially the use of woodwind to add expressiveness to the vocal line. *L'italiana*, dashed off in just over three weeks, was Rossini's first great success in the field of opera buffa, and remains one of the best examples. A failure now came with *Aureliano in Palmira* (1813); the overture and part of the first chorus survive in *Il barbiere di Siviglia*. *Il turco in Italia* (1814) at first suffered from comparison with *L'Italiana*; and after these two failures Rossini returned from Milan to Venice, where he suffered a third failure with *Sigismondo* (1814) – some of its music is also to be found in *Il barbiere*.

Rossini was now engaged by Barbaia as music director of both the Naples Opera houses, the T. San Carlo and the T. del Fondo. For the former he wrote *Elisabetta, Regina d'Inghilterra*, in which for the first time recitatives were accompanied by strings and ornaments written out in full. Elisabetta was sung by Isabella Colbran, who was to become Rossini's wife. Several more operas were now written for Naples, including *Otello* (1816), the tragic ending of which so distressed the public that a happy ending had to be provided for Rome; *Armida* (1817), another work of considerable musical power; *Mose in Egitto* (1818), revived for Paris nine years later as *Moïse*; *La donna del lago* (1819); and *Maometto II* (1820), revised for Paris as *Le Siège de Corinthe*. During Rossini's Naples engagement his commissions included *Il barbiere di Siviglia* (1816), which, after a stormy première at which the supporters of Paisiello's *Barbiere* were out in force, came to be accepted as one of the great masterpieces of comic opera. Other commissions included *La Cenerentola* (1817), which again made use of the coloratura contralto (or mezzo-soprano) which Rossini had first used in *L'italiana*; *La gazza ladra* (1817); *Bianca e Faliero* (1819); *Mathilde di Shabran* (1821); and *Semiramide* (1823), one of Rossini's longest and most ambitious works. He was now approaching his 31st birthday; he was the most popular and prolific composer of his day, having in the 10 years since *Tancredi* composed some 25 operas. Stendhal declared, 'The glory of the man is only limited by the limits of civilization itself, and he is not yet 32.'

Semiramide closed Rossini's Italian period, and after visits to Vienna, where he met Beethoven, and London, where he conducted and sang in concerts with his wife, he settled in Paris as director of the Théâtre Italien for six months. There his *Il viaggio a Reims*, a stage cantata with a ballet, was produced in 1825. Written for the extravagant coronation of Charles X, it lasted three hours and was written for 15 voices – at the première these included Pasta, Cinti, Levasseur, Graziani, Donzelli, and Bordoni. He retained Paer at the theatre as *maestro al cembalo*, engaged the young Hérold as chorus master, and introduced Meyerbeer to Paris with *Il Crociato in Egitto*. He was then appointed Composer for the King and Inspector General of Singing for all Royal institutions. This opened the doors of the Opéra to him, and after revising *Maometto II* and *Mosè in Egitto*, he produced his *Le Comte Ory* (1823) and *Guillaume Tell* (1929). *Tell* was his crowning achievement in opera, with which (according to Hanslick) 'a new era for opera began, and not only in France'. It was to have been the first of five works for the Opéra in ten years; but the 1830 revolution dethroned Charles and the new government set aside the contract, allowing (after much litigation) only an annuity that was attached. *Tell* was Rossini's last stage work, though he lived for another 39 years, composing two religious works and a host of trifles (the so-called *péchés de vieillesse*). He died on Friday, 13 Nov. 1868, and was buried near Cherubini, Chopin, and Bellini. In 1887 his body was handed over to the city of Florence for reburial, when there was a procession of more than 6,000 mourners, four military bands, and a chorus of 300 which sang the Prayer from *Mosè*, to such effect that the crowd in front of the Church of Santa Croce cheered until it was encored.

Bibl: H. Weinstock: *Rossini* (1968).

Rostand, Edmond (*b* Marseilles, 1 Apr. 1868; *d* Paris, 2 Dec. 1918). French playwright. Operas on his works are as follows:
Les Romanesques (1894): F. Hart (1918).
La Princesse lointaine (1895): Montemezzi (unfin.); Witkowski (1934); Barberis (*Domniţa din depărtări*, 1948).
Cyrano de Bergerac (1897): Damrosch (1913); Alfano (1936).
L'Aiglon (1900): Honegger and Ibert (1937).
Also opera *Colombine* (Yanovsky, 1907).

Rostock. Town in Rostock, Germany. Travelling companies visited from 1606, and Singspiel was popular until the end of the 18th cent. The Hoftheater was opened 1751, and Italian and German companies gave seasons. The new Schauspielhaus opened in 1786, giving, among many Singspiels, Mozart's *Entführung* (1786) and *Zauberflöte* (1795). Seasons were also given by visiting companies from Schwerin. *Der Freischütz* was given 1822; the first Wagner opera was *Tannhäuser*, 1854. The theatre burnt down in 1880, and performances were given in the Thaliatheater. The Stadttheater opened in 1895, and enjoyed an important period of growth under W. Kaehler, 1897–9. Visiting conductors included Nikisch, and singers included Lilli Lehmann. The theatre was bombed in 1942. Reopened, it has has played an important part in the life of the city, and has given a number of premières, including works by Wagner-Régeny.

Roswaenge (orig. Rosenving le-Hansen), **Helge** (*b* Copenhagen, 29 Aug. 1897; *d* Munich, 19 Jun. 1972). Danish tenor. Début Neustrelitz 1921, Don José. After engagements in Altenburg, Basle, Cologne, joined Berlin State Opera 1929, remaining there until 1945; returned there 1949; Vienna 1936–58; London, C.G., 1938; Bayreuth 1934–6, Parsifal; Salzburg 1933–9, where he was an admired Huon, Tamino, and Florestan. Generally considered in his prime one of the finest lyric-dramatic tenors in central Europe. He continued to appear until the late 1960s with great success as Calaf, Radamès, Manrico, etc. (R)
Bibl: H. Roswaenge: *Mach' es besser, mein Sohn* (1963).

Rota, Nino (*b* Milan, 3 Dec. 1911). Italian composer. Studied Milan with Orefice and later Pizzetti, and in Philadelphia with Scalera and Reiner. Held teaching posts in Taranto and Bari. Composed much music for the cinema and radio. His operas are tuneful and unashamedly popular and include *Il cappello di paglia di Firenze* (The Italian Straw Hat) (Palermo 1955); *La notte di un nevrastenico* (Milan 1959), and *Aladino e la lampada magica* (Naples 1968).

Rothenberger, Anneliese (*b* Mannheim, 19 June 1924). German soprano. Début Coblenz as straight actress 1942. Hamburg Opera 1946–74. Vienna since 1956. Has appeared at N.Y., Met., Gly. Salzburg, etc. A charming and versatile artist, she has sung in many modern works, including *Lulu*, and is an outstanding Sophie, Zdenka, and Adele. (R)

Rothmüller, (Aaron) Marko (*b* Trnjani, 31 Dec. 1908). Yugoslav baritone. Studied Zagreb and Vienna (composition with Berg and singing with Steiner). Début Hamburg 1932, Ottokar (*Freischütz*); Zurich 1935–47; London, C.G., 1939 and 1948–55; New London Opera Company 1947–8; Edinburgh and Gly. Festivals 1949–52, being especially successful as Macbeth; N.Y., C.C., 1948–52; Met. 1959–60, 1964–5; also appeared Vienna, Berlin, etc. Wozzeck (which he sang in the C.G. production under Kleiber 1951), Rigoletto, and Scarpia were his chief roles; in them his fine singing and musical characterization were at their best. Teaches singing, Bloomington, U.S.A. Wrote *Die Musik der Juden* (1951; trans. 1954). (R)

Rouen. Town in Seine-et-Marne, France. Opera has been performed there since 1776, firstly in the T. de la Montagne, renamed T. des Arts 1794. Boieldieu's first opera, *La Fille coupable*, was produced there 1793. The theatre was destroyed by fire in April 1876. Rebuilt and opened in Sept. 1882 with *Les Huguenots*; staged the first productions in France of *Salammbô* (1890), *Samson et Dalila* (1900), and *Thérèse* (1909). Destroyed by bombs in June 1940. After the liberation, opera was given at the T. Cirque. The present T. des Arts opened Nov. 1962, and under the direction of André Cabourg pursues an adventurous artistic policy.

Rouleau, Joseph (*b* Matane, Quebec, 28 Feb. 1929). Canadian bass. Studied Montreal with Donalda, later with Singher and Mario Basiola. Début Montreal, 1955, Philip (*Don Carlos*). New Orleans, 1955. London, C.G., since 1957. Many appearances in France and with Scottish Opera. Large repertory includes Don Quichotte, the General in Prokofiev's *The Gambler* and Bishop Tache in Somers's *Louis Riel*, which he created in Toronto (1967). Has a dark, voluminous bass voice and an imposing stage presence. (R)

Rousseau, Jean-Jacques (*b* Geneva, 28 June 1712; *d* Ermenonville, 2 July 1778). Swiss philosopher, composer, author, and writer on music. Produced his first opera, *Les Muses galantes*, in 1742; declared highly uneven by Rameau. His most important composition was *Le Devin du village* (to his own text), produced with great success in 1752. Siding with the Italians in the *Guerre des Bouffons, he then published his important *Lettre sur la musique française* (1753), expounding his musical beliefs and taking a strong stand for melody as a form of heightened speech. His other writings on music include the *Dictionnaire de musique* (? 1767). *Pygmalion* (1775) uses orchestral interludes between speeches; he also left parts of an opera, *Daphnis et Chloé*, and six new arias for *Le Devin*. Musically he never acquired great technical skill: *Le Devin* is very simple, standing almost entirely by its melodic charm. But his effect on Romanticism, especially on musicians, was incalculable. His stand for personal sensibility and emotion as a guide (evinced in the *Confessions*), coupled with his belief in natural virtues and the qualities to be found in unspoiled, natural people, exercised a potent influence on the early Romantics.

Bruni wrote a sequel to his *Pygmalion* (*Galatée*, 1795). Operas on him include Dalayrac's *L'Enfance de Jean-Jacques Rousseau* (1794) and Bruni's *Le Mariage de Jean-Jacques Rousseau* (1794). Also operetta based on Rousseau, *Pygmalion* by Kurpiński (1808).

Roussel, Albert (*b* Tourcoing, 5 Apr. 1869; *d* Royan, 23 Aug. 1937). French composer. Roussel's major stage work, the opera-ballet *Pad-*

mâvatî (1923), is based on an Indian legend. He found in Oriental music the means for liberating and developing his own idiom – there ensued a greater flexibility and muscularity of melody, an increased harmonic palette, and a subtler rhythmic sense. His other operas are *La Naissance de la lyre* (1923) and *Le Testament de la Tante Caroline* (1936).
Bibl: B. Deane: *Albert Roussel* (1961).

Rousselière, Charles (*b* St Nazair, 17 Jan. 1875; *d* Joue-les-tours, 11 May 1950). French tenor. Studied Paris with Vaguet. Début Paris, O., 1900, Samson. Paris, O., 1900–1912; Monte Carlo 1905–14, created leading tenor roles in Mascagni's *Amica* (1905), Saint-Saëns's *L'Ancêtre* (1906), and Fauré's *Pénélope* (1913); also created title-role in Charpentier's *Julien,* Paris, O.C., 1913. N.Y., Met., 1906–7; Buenos Aires, first Parsifal there 1914. Roles included Max, Manrico, Radamès, Siegmund, Loge. After retiring from stage taught singing in Paris. (R)

Rovere, Agostino (*b* Monza, 1804; *d* New York, 10 Dec. 1865). Italian bass. Studied Milan. Début Pavia 1826. Began career in serious roles, then developed into leading *basso buffo*. Milan, Sc., 1831-44, 1846-7, 1856-7; Vienna, 1839, 1842-5, where he created Boisfleury in *Linda di Chamounix* (1842); London, C.G., 1847-8, Bartolo, Leporello, Dulcamara, Mustafà, Magnifico.

Royal Italian Opera. The name given to certain London theatres and companies occupying them during the 19th cent. including H.M.'s, C.G., Ly., and D.L., when all operas, irrespective of the original language, were sung in Italian.

Roze, Marie (orig. Hippolyte Ponsin) (*b* Paris, 2 Mar. 1846; *d* Paris, 21 June 1926). French soprano. Studied Paris Conservatoire with Mocker and Auber. Début Paris, O.C., 1865 in Hérold's *Marie.* London, D.L., 1872, H.M.'s, 1873-81; and also appeared on C.R. U.S. tours 1877-8, 1880-1. Much admired as Marguerite, Carmen and Manon, of which she was the first interpreter in London. She married Mapleson's son; their son **Raymond Roze** (1875-1920) organized a season of opera in English at C.G., 1913, in which his *Joan of Arc* was produced.

Rozkošný, Josef (Richard) (*b* Prague, 21 Sept. 1833; *d* Prague, 3 June 1913). Czech composer. His first opera, *Mikuláš,* was to a text by Smetana's librettist Karel Sabina; few of the remainder were successful, apart from the Romantic *Svatojanské proudy* (or *Vltavská víla,* The Vltava Nymph, 1871), which is notable as one of the fairy-tale operas in a genre later to be distinguished by Dvořák, and *Stoja* (1884), which is the first Czech *verismo* opera.

Rubato (*It.* robbed). The art (sometimes the abuse) of hurrying or slowing the pace in varying degrees for expressive effect.

Rubinelli, Giovanni (*b* Brescia, 1753; *d* Brescia, 1829). Italian male contralto. Début Stuttgart, 1770, in Sacchini's *Calliroe.* Returned to Italy 1774, appearing with success in Naples, Milan, Venice, and Rome. London, 1786-7; further appearances in Milan and Vicenza until 1800. Kelly admired him as 'an excellent actor as well as a sound musician'; but Burney and Mount-Edgcumbe had reservations.

Rubini, Giovanni Battista (*b* Romano, nr Bergamo, 7 Apr. 1794; *d* Romano, 2 Mar. 1854). Italian tenor. Studied Bergamo, and Naples with Nozzari. Début Pavia 1814. After 11 years of increasing success in Italy, went to Paris 1825, where his appearances in Rossini's *Cenerentola, Otello,* and *La donna del lago* caused a sensation. His successes were repeated in London 1831-43 and in St Petersburg, where he received the equivalent of over £20,000 a season. The tenor roles in *Il pirata, La sonnambula, I Puritani,* and in Donizetti's *Anna Bolena* were composed for him. His voice was sweet, yet capable of organ-like power and volume, and extended from e to b' with an extension of falsetto register to f' and g'. He was the first great singer to make extensive use of the musical sob. He was thoroughly identified with his roles. Wagner, who heard him as Don Ottavio in Paris in 1840, thought Rubini found 'the task of playing this Mozartian role a very thankless one', and compared his singing of 'Il mio tesoro' to a trapeze-artist's display. He married Mlle Chomel in 1819, who sang under the name of La Comelli. A portrait of him by Manet hangs in the Kröller-Müller Museum near Otterloo. He published *12 lezioni di canto* and *'L'addio',* a collection of 6 songs.
Bibl: C. Traini: *Il cigno di Romano* (1954).

Rubinstein, Anton (*b* Vekhvotinets, 28 Nov. 1830; *d* Peterhof, 20 Nov. 1894). Russian pianist and composer. His 20 operas embrace local legends, Oriental subjects (*Feramors,* 1863), heroic opera (*The Maccabees,* 1875, and *Nero,* 1879), Russian pieces (*The Merchant Kalashnikov,* 1880), and religious opera-oratorio (*Moses,* 1887, and *Christus,* 1888). The most important was *The Demon* (1875), which in its Frenchified manner supported Rubinstein's contention that Russian composers must imitate Western modes; its lurid, romantic story ensured it wide popularity.

Rudel, Julius (*b* Vienna, 6 Mar. 1921). Austrian, later naturalized American, conductor. Studied Vienna, and New York, Mannes School of Music. After conducting small operatic groups in New York, joined the City Center as a répétiteur in 1943; first opera conducted for company, *Zigeunerbaron,* November 1944. Music and artistic director New York City Opera since 1957, where he has been responsible for a progressive policy and several seasons devoted to contemporary American opera. Music director Kennedy Center, Washington 1971-6; Paris, O., since 1972; guest appearances Hamburg, Stuttgart etc. Conducted première of *Bomarzo* (1967). (R)

Ruffo, Titta (orig. Ruffo Cafiero Titta) (*b* Pisa, 9 June 1877; *d* Florence, 6 July 1953). Italian baritone. Studied Rome with Persichini, and Milan with Casini. Début Rome 1898, Herald (*Lohengrin*). London, C.G., 1903; Chicago 1912-14; N.Y., Met., 1922-29. Possessed one of the largest and at the same time most beautiful baritone voices of his day. Superb in Verdi roles. De Luca considered him 'not a voice, but a miracle', and recorded that he could still sing a♭' in 1951. Also famed for his Scarpia, Tonio, and Hamlet. (R)
Bibl: T. Ruffo: *La mia parabola* (1937, rev. by his son 1977).

Rusalka. (1) Opera in 3 acts by Dvořák; text by Jaroslav Kvapil, based largely on De la Motte Fouqué's *Undine,* with additions from Hans Andersen's *The Little Mermaid* and suggestions from Hauptmann's *The Sunken Bell.* Prod. Prague, N., 31 Mar. 1901, with Maturová, Ptak, Kuratová, Kliment, Bradachová, Hájková, cond. Kovařovic; London, Peter Jones T., 9 May 1950; S.W. 18 Feb. 1959, with Hammond, Stuart, Denise, Pollak, Craig, J. Ward, Glynne, cond. Tausky; Chicago, Sokol Slav Hall, 10 Mar. 1935, with Mashir, Valentinova, Daen, Bujanovsky, Karlash, Tulchinov.
(2) Opera in 4 acts by Dargomyzhsky; text by composer, after Pushkin's dramatic poem (1832). Prod. St Petersburg, Circus T., 16 May 1856, with O. Petrov, Bulakhova, Bulakhov, Leonova, Lileyeva, Gumbin, cond. Lyadov; Seattle 23 Dec. 1921; London, Ly., 18 May 1931, with Slobodskaya, Pozemkovsky, Shalyapin, cond. Steiman.
The water sprite Rusalka (sop.) falls in love with a Prince (ten.), and with the help of the witch Ježibaba (mezzo) becomes human so as to marry him. But she must remain silent, and when the Prince tires of her and proves unfaithful, a condition of her becoming human is violated and she dies together with the remorseful Prince.
In Dargomyzhsky's opera, Natasha (sop.), daughter of a Miller (bass), is betrayed by the Prince (ten.) and drowns herself in the stream. She becomes a water sprite who lures men to their death. When the Prince marries, he hears her cries every time he approaches his bride. Wandering by the stream, he meets a child who reveals herself as his daughter. The Miller hurls the Prince into the stream, where he joins Natasha, now the Rusalka, and their child.
Other operas on the subject are by Czerwiński (1874), Blaramberg (1888), and A. Alexandrov (1913).

Ruse. Town in Bulgaria. A Ruse Operatic Society was formed in 1914; re-formed in 1919, it gave Ivanov's *Kamen i Tsena* and Hadjigeorgyev's *Takhir Begovitsa.* Regular professional opera began when the Ruse National Opera opened 1949, with *La traviata.* In 1954 the company visited Sofia, and has also toured Romania. The theatre was reconstructed in 1956 (cap. 670).

Ruslan and Lyudmila. Opera in 5 acts by Glinka; text by V. Shirkov and others, after Pushkin's poem (1820). Prod. St Petersburg, B., 9 Dec. 1842, with O. Petrova, Stepanova, Petrova, Lileyeva, Baikov, Tosi, Leonov, Marcel, Likhansky, cond. Albrecht; London, Ly., 4 June 1931, with Lissichkina, Yurenev, Kaydanov, cond. Steiman; New York, T.H., 26 Dec. 1942 (concert); Boston, 5 Mar. 1977, with Scovotti, Evans, Moulson, Braun, Tozzi, cond. Caldwell.
Lyudmila (sop.) disappears from a feast for her three suitors, the knight Ruslan (bar.), the poet prince Ratmir (con.), and Farlaf (bass), a cowardly warrior. Her father Svyetozar (bass) promises her to the one who can find her. Ruslan learns that she has been stolen by the dwarf Chernomor (silent role), and is warned by the good fairy Finn (ten.) against the wicked fairy Naina (mezzo), who advises Farlaf to wait until Ruslan has captured Lyudmila and then abduct her. Ruslan meets a gigantic head on a battlefield, and killing it discovers a magic sword. In Naina's palace, Ruslan is rescued from sirens by Finn. He defeats Chernomor, but only with the aid of a magic ring from Finn can he awaken Lyudmila.

Russell, Henry (*b* London, 14 Nov. 1871; *d* London, 11 Oct. 1937). English impresario and teacher. Son of the singer and composer of the same name (1812-1900). His novel method of vocal teaching attracted the attention of Melba, who sent him some of her best pupils. He organized the 1904 autumn season at C.G., bringing most of the Naples S.C. Company; and the following summer presented a season at the new Waldorf T. (now the Strand), London, with a company that included Bonci, De Lucia, Ancona, and Pini-Corsi. He took this company to New Orleans 1906, then to Boston, where in 1909 he organized the Boston Opera Company, of which he was the general manager until 1914; he took the Boston Company to Paris in 1914. His brother was better known as Landon *Ronald. Memoirs, *The Passing Show* (1926).

Russia. Though various theatrical entertainments with songs and dances were given in the 17th cent., no true operatic influence was felt until the opening up of Russia to the West by Peter the Great. The first Italian opera troupes to arrive were those of Tommaso Ristori and Johann Keyser, and the first opera performed in Russia was the former's *Calandro* (Moscow, 1731). Other Italian companies came 1733 and 1734, and the excellent company under Francesco *Araia 1735. His *La forza dell' amore e dell'odio* (St Petersburg, 1736) was a great success, and two more works followed. German Singspiel probably made its first appearance in Russia in 1740.

The Empress Elizaveta Petrovna (reigned 1741-61), with her love of Italy, further encouraged opera, which soon began to put down Russian roots. The first opera in Russian was *Tsefal i Prokris* (Cephalus and Procris, 1755), an opera seria by Araia. Peter III sent for Galuppi and Tartini, and this invitation, renewed by Catherine the Great, inaugurated a century-long dynasty of Italian composers in Russia: Araia, 1735-40, 1742-59, 1762; Manfredini, 1759-66; Galuppi, 1765-8; Traetta, 1768-76; Paisiello, 1776-83; Sarti, 1784-6 and 1792-6; Cimarosa, 1787-91; the Spanish Martín y Soler, 1788-94; Cavos, 1798-1840. French opéra comique was first staged in the 1750s, English opera (Dibdin's *The Padlock*) 1771. By the end of the century some 100 operas had been written by Russians, the first being *Anyuta* (1772 – music lost, but perhaps by Vasily Pashkevich, 1796-1867). The first whose music has completely survived is Zorin's *Pererozhdenye* (Rebirth, 1777). The first three significant Russian operas all date from 1779: they are *Melnik koldun* (The Miller a Magician) by Mikhail Sokolovsky (1756-?), *Sanktpeterburgsky Gostinny Dvor* (The St Petersburg Bazaar) by Mikhail Matinsky (1750-1820) and *Neschastye ot Kareta* (The Misfortunes of Having a Carriage) by Pashkevich. Another outstanding work of the period was *Sbitenshchik* (The Sbiten [a drink] Seller, 1784) by the Czech Anton Bullandt (*d* 1821).

Pashkevich's third opera was *Fevey* (1786), to a text by Catherine the Great herself. As an admirer of the Encyclopedists, she believed in opera's role as social commentary; and her librettos include the patriotic *Nachalnoye Upravlenye Olega* (The First Government of Oleg, music by Pashkevich, Canobbio, and Sarti 1789), also domestic homily and political satire, as in her attack on Gustav III during the Swedish war, *Gore Bogatyr Kosometovich* (The False Hero Kosometovich, music by Soler, 1789). Other successful works were by Mathias Stabhinger (e.g. *Shchastlivaya Tonya* (Lucky Tonya) and *Baba Yaga,* both 1786), and especially by *Fomin and *Bortyansky.

Paul I severely censored and restricted opera, but with Alexander I's accession in 1801 interest was renewed, in a French direction. A fashion for German fairy opera followed, and successful examples were written by Stepan Davydov (1777-1825), part-composer of the popular *Lesta* (from 1803), by Alexey Titov (1769-1827) (at least 13), and especially by

Caterino *Cavos and Alexey *Verstovsky. At this time true singers emerged, replacing actors who sang. But it is with *Glinka that Russian opera, indeed Russian music, attains maturity. After Alexander II's accession in 1855 steps were taken to improve the training of composers and singers, with the foundation of the Conservatories of St Petersburg (1861) and Moscow (1864); and the strong influence of their respective founders, the brothers Anton and Nikolay *Rubinstein, gave a lead to such diverse composers as *Serov, *Dargomyzhsky, and *Tchaikovsky, and the Slavophile group dubbed by the critic Vladimir Stasov the *moguchaya kuchka* ('mighty handful'), *Balakirev, *Mussorgsky, *Rimsky-Korsakov, *Borodin, and *Cui. After this great flowering of Russian opera, and of a school of singers to meet and encourage its demands, there was a brief recession in the 20th cent. Interest turned elsewhere, despite the work of Rakhmaninov, Arensky, Grechaninov, Rebikov, and others. The line of lyrical, Italian-inspired operas was consciously re-invoked, and closed, by Stravinsky in *Mavra* (1922).

After the Revolution, opera was threatened by Lenin's doubts about its importance in the social priorities, and by its aristocratic associations; but largely through the able arguments of Boris Asafyev, opera was viewed as based on national music and folk images, thus forming a foundation for the development of a Soviet operatic style. A reluctance to take opera seriously on the part of stage directors was overcome, and *Stanislavsky, *Nemirovich-Danchenko, Kommisarzhevsky, and Meyerhold were all persuaded to apply their talents to opera by the arts commissar, Elena Malinovskaya. Fruitful contact between the Moscow Arts T. and the Bolshoy led to the evolution of true actor-singers, though both Stanislavsky and Nemirovich-Danchenko preferred to work in their own studios. New life was infused into old productions, with more attention given to intelligent acting and expressive staging, less to vocal display; and the more able-minded singers, including Shalyapin and Ershov, were encouraged to produce operas in which they appeared. Sometimes, for lack of original Revolutionary operas, new librettos were provided for old works: *Les Huguenots* became *The Decembrists; Tosca* became *Into Battle for the Commune.* New Western operas were also introduced, including works by Schreker and Berg (*Wozzeck,* Leningrad 1927). The first attempts at genuinely modern Soviet opera, vigorously advocated by Asafyev, were *Za Krasny Petrograd* (For Red Petrograd), by Arseny Gladkovsky and E. Prussak, Andrey Pashchenko's *Orliny Bunt* (Eagles in Revolt), and Vasily Zolotaryov's *Dekabristy* (The Decembrists, all 1925).

The quarrel between restraint and adventure

came to a head, inevitably, not over the many mediocre works that followed but over a major talent. *Shostakovich's *Nos* (The Nose, 1930) aroused both enthusiasm and opposition: the opposition was intensified with *Lady Macbeth of the Mtsensk district* (1934). This precipitated a notorious *Pravda* article 'Chaos instead of music' (28 Jan. 1936) and the establishment of a hard, probably Stalin-inspired line which preferred Ivan Dzerzhinsky's *Tikhy Don* (The Quiet Don, 1934). Even *Prokofiev, though interested in working for Soviet opera, found it virtually impossible to satisfy the new demands, and his operas were misunderstood by officials; the willingness of lesser composers to toe the line assured their works of careers, but usually short ones. Great difficulties confronted composers anxious to reconcile an ideology they often did not entirely share, to their artistic integrity. Initial success was sometimes followed by violent rejection, e.g. *Velikaya Druzhba* (The Great Friendship, 1947), by Vano Muradeli (1907-70). The nadir of State intervention was reached at the notorious 1948 Congress (repudiated ten years later) at which leading Soviet composers were abused by the minister Andrey Zhdanov. Since then there has been cautious evolution; but despite enthusiasm for opera in Russia, the excellence of the singers' training, and the generous facilities available, few Soviet operas have found a secure place in world repertories. Among the Soviet composers most successful within the U.S.S.R. are Ivan Dzerzhinsky, Tikhon Khrennikov (*b* 1913) (*V Buryu* (Into the Storm) 1939), Vissarion Shebalin (*b* 1902) (*Ukroshchenye Stroptivoy* (The Taming of the Shrew) 1957), Dmitry Kabalevsky (*b* 1904) (*Colas Breugnon,* 1938, and *Nikita Vershinin,* 1955) and Yury Shaporin (1887-1966) (*Dekabristi* (The Decembrists) 1953). A younger generation includes Kyril Molchanov (*b* 1922), Alexander Kholminov (*b* 1925), Alexey Nikolayev (*b* 1931), Rodion Shchedrin (*b* 1932), and Sergey Slonimsky (*b* 1932).

The principal opera houses of Russia are in Chelyabinsk (opened 1956), Gorky (Pushkin T., opened 1935), Kuybyshev (opened 1931), *Leningrad, *Moscow, Novosibirsk (Glinka T., opened 1945), Perm (Tchaikovsky T., first season 1894), Saratov (seasons from 1860s, first company 1890, Cheryshevsky T. opened 1928), and Sverdlovsk (Lunacharsky T., orig. opened 1912). An important and valuable feature of post-Revolutionary Russia has been the encouragement given to the republics that became part of the *U.S.S.R.

Ruth. Opera in 1 act by Berkeley; text by Eric Crozier, after the Book of Ruth. Prod. London, Scala, 2 Oct. 1956, with Pollak, Pears. The plot keeps fairly close to the Biblical story, with Ruth (sop.) following Naomi (sop.) into the fields of Boaz (ten.), whom she marries.

Other operas on the subject by Duni (*Les Moissonneurs,* 1708), Ippolitov-Ivanov (1887).

Rysanek, Leonie (*b* Vienna, 14 Nov. 1926). Austrian soprano. Studied Vienna with Jerger and later with the baritone Rudolf Grossmann Début Innsbruck 1949, Agathe. Sang Saarbücken 1950-52; Munich since 1952; Vienna since 1954; London, C.G., 1953-5, 1959, and 1963; San Francisco since 1957; N.Y., Met., since 1959. Sang Sieglinde in the first post-war Bayreuth Festival, and later heard there as Elsa and Senta. Her rich voice with its strong upper register makes her an excellent Empress (*Frau ohne Schatten*), Aegyptische Helena, and Danae; and has also been admired in Verdi roles and as Salome. (R) Her sister **Lotte Rysanek** (*b* 18 Mar. 1928) is a lyric soprano in Vienna. (R)

S

Saarbrücken. Town in Saar, Germany. Three theatres, built in the Baroque palace of the last Prince of Nassau-Saarbrücken, were destroyed during the French Revolution. In 1897 the Neue T. (cap. 450, enlarged to 700 in 1912) opened with *Mignon*. From 1919 until 1922 it was run in conjunction with the theatre at Trier under the direction of Heinz Tietjen. The Gau-T., Saarpfalz (cap. 1,056, enlarged to 1,132), which opened in 1938 with *Der fliegende Holländer*, was destroyed in 1945 and rebuilt 1947.

Sabata, Victor de. See *De Sabata*.

Sacchini, Antonio (*b* Florence, 14 June 1730; *d* Paris, 6 Oct. 1786). Italian composer. After early successes in Italy, he came to London and there produced 17 operas in which his skilful vocal writing won him great popularity. He became even more popular in Paris, where he later settled, though the failure of his masterpiece, *Œdipe à Colone* (1785), to be chosen for Fontainebleau, owing to political pressure, broke his heart and hastened his death. Later it was to have 583 performances in 57 years at the Paris O. Burney called him a 'graceful, elegant and judicious composer', and the fluency of his music, coupled with his ability to match it to local taste and individual singers, won him a success in his day that for lack of more solid or personal gifts has not proved enduring.

Sachs, Hans (*b* Nuremberg, 5 Nov. 1494; *d* Nuremberg, 19 Jan. 1576). The cobbler (bass-bar.) in Wagner's *Die Meistersinger von Nürnberg*. He is also the hero of Lortzing's *Hans Sachs* (1840), which is based on the Deinhardstein play drawn on by Wagner. Also Singspiel by Gyrowetz, *Hans Sachs im vorgerückten Alter* (1834), and three *Hans-Sachs Spiele* by Behrend (1949).

Sachse, Leopold (*b* Berlin, 5 Jan. 1880; *d* Englewood Cliffs, 3 Apr. 1961). German, later American administrator and producer, former bass. Studied Cologne, Vienna, and Milan with Selva. Début as singer Kiel, 1906; Strasbourg, 1907-8. Intendant, Münster, 1907; Halle, 1914-19; Hamburg State Opera, 1922-35, producing *Doktor Faust, Jenůfa, Leben des Orest, Jonny spielt auf, Palestrina, Intermezzo*, and *Aegyptische Helena*. Forced to leave Germany in 1935. Met., N.Y., 1935-45, producing most of the Wagner repertory, *Rosenkavalier, Hoffmann*, and other works. N.Y. City Opera, stage director 1945. Taught Juilliard and Academy of Vocal Arts, Philadelphia.

Sack, Erna (Eva Weber) (*b* Berlin, 6 Feb. 1898;

d Wiesbaden, 2 Mar. 1972). German soprano, formerly contralto. Studied Prague, and Berlin with Oscar Daniel. Début Berlin, Stä. O, 1925. After engagements in Bielefeld, Wiesbaden, and Breslau, joined Dresden State Opera 1935, where she created Isotta in *Schweigsame Frau* (1935). London, C.G., 1936 with Dresden company, Zerbinetta (under Strauss); Chicago, 1937, Lucia and Rosina. Had a voice of phenomenal range, for which Strauss wrote several cadenzas in Zerbinetta's arias. A 'Protektionskind' of the Nazi Kulturpolitik. After the Second World War made several concert tours. (R)

Sacra rappresentazione. See *Rappresentazione*.

Sadko. Opera-legend in 7 scenes by Rimsky-Korsakov; text by composer and V. I. Belsky, after folk legends. Prod. Moscow, private theatre, by Solodovnikov company, 7 Jan. 1898, with Sekar-Rozhansky, Rostovsteva, Strakova, Alexanov, Karklin, I. Petrov, Negrin-Schmidt, Bedlevich, cond. Esposito; N.Y., Met., 25 Jan. 1930, with Bouraskaya, Swarthout, Johnson, Diaz, Basiola, Ludikar, cond. Serafin; London, Ly., 9 June 1931, with Lissichkina, Sadoven, Pozemkovsky, Ritch, Petrov, cond. Goossens.

The wanderings of the minstrel Sadko (ten.) bring him to Volkhova (sop.), Princess of the Sea, who promises him that his net will be filled with golden fish. He wagers to a crowd that he can catch the golden fish; succeeds; and sets sail with some companions. Becalmed, they throw gold overboard to pacify the King of the Sea (bass); but his daughter Volkhova tells Sadko that one of the company must be sacrificed. Sadko is set adrift on a raft and sinks to the sea bed, where his song wins him Princess Volkhova's hand. At the wedding Sadko's singing so excites the sea that many ships sink; this brings down the anger of St Nicholas, who orders Sadko back to land. On the shore of Lake Ilmen Sadko bids farewell to Volkhova, who is transformed into the river that bears her name.

Sadler's Wells. Theatre in north London, home of the former Sadler's Wells Opera. Originally a place of entertainment in the grounds of one Sadler, who in 1683 discovered in his garden a well whose waters were drunk for medicinal purposes. In 1765 the first theatre was built and saw musical performances by Braham, the Dibdins, and others. Opera was occasionally performed there in the mid-19th century, including the British première of *Luisa Miller* (1858). It later became a music hall before falling into disuse.

In Mar. 1925 a move was set on foot to turn the old theatre into an Old Vic for north London and some £70,000 was raised during the next five years. The theatre (cap. 1,650) was opened under the management of Lilian *Baylis on 6

Jan. 1931. At first opera and ballet alternated with Shakespeare; in 1934, however, Sadler's Wells became the exclusive home of the opera and ballet companies. Between then and 1939 the repertory was enlarged and included the English premières of *The Snow Maiden, Tsar Saltan,* the original *Boris,* the first performance in English of *Don Carlos,* productions of *Valkyrie, Mastersingers, The Devil Take Her* (Benjamin), *The Boatswain's Mate* (Smyth), *Eugene Onegin,* and the *Travelling Companion* (Stanford). Singers included Joan Cross, Edith Coates, Janet Hamilton-Smith, Ruth Naylor, Sumner Austin, Arthur Cox (Carron), Redvers Llewellyn, Powell Lloyd, Arnold Matters, Henry Wendon, and John Wright; conductors were Warwick Braithwaite and Lawrance Collingwood; and producers Clive Carey, Sumner Austin, and J. B. Gordon. Guest appearances were made by many distinguished British artists, including Noël Eadie, Florence Easton, Florence Austral, Miriam Licette, Heddle Nash; Beecham, Barbirolli, Coates; and the German producer Strohbach. The 1939-40 season took place at Rosebery Avenue, but then the company concentrated on touring, though short seasons were given at the New T. in London by a reduced company under the direction of Tyrone Guthrie. Later the company was built up again and Joan Cross assumed its direction. By the end of the war there had been several new productions including a successful *Bartered Bride* and *Così fan tutte,* and artists new to the public had included Elisabeth Abercrombie, Victoria Sladen, Owen Brannigan, and Peter Pears.

On 7 June 1945 the company returned to its home in north London with the première of *Peter Grimes.* Joan Cross then resigned to work with the E.O.G. and at the Opera School, and Clive Carey took charge for the 1946-7 seasons. In 1948 Norman *Tucker began his association with the theatre. James Robertson was music director 1946-54, Alexander Gibson 1957-9, Colin Davis 1961-5. The postwar period included the premières of Hopkins's *Lady Rohesia,* Berkeley's *Nelson,* Gardner's *The Moon and Sixpence,* and Bennett's *Mines of Sulphur,* the British premières of *I quatro rusteghi* (*The School for Fathers*), *Simon Boccanegra, Kát̀a Kabanova, Romeo and Juliet* (Sutermeister), *Rusalka* (Dvořák), *The Cunning Little Vixen* and *The Makropoulos Affair* (Janáček), and *Mahagonny,* and first productions at Sadler's Wells of *Shvanda, The Consul, Martha, Don Pasquale, The Flying Dutchman, The Merry Widow, Duke Bluebeard's Castle, Cenerentola, Oedipus Rex, Ariadne auf Naxos, Idomeneo, Love of the Three Oranges, Girl of the Golden West, Der Freischütz,* and *L'Enfant et les sortilèges.* Many of the singers were later heard at C.G. and elsewhere; they include Victoria Elliott, Anna Pollak, Amy Shuard; Charles

Craig. James Johnston, Howell Glynne, David Ward, and Owen Brannigan. The producers have included Denis Arundell, Basil Coleman, George Devine, Powell Lloyd, and Tyrone Guthrie, with Glen Byam Shaw as director of productions since 1962. In 1958 the theatre was threatened with a financial crisis, averted by amazing public and press response. Elements of the Carl Rosa Touring Company were taken over by Sadler's Wells, which became responsible for most of the provincial touring opera in Great Britain, there being two full companies available.

Not the least encouraging aspect of the spontaneous public warmth towards S.W. in the 1958 crisis was the sign that a stable opera company providing sound repertory performances week in week out can claim the loyalty of a public normally regarded as only intermittently opera-loving. Whereas C.G.'s function since the war has mainly been to house larger works generally with international casts, S.W. concentrated on developing a stable opera company formed almost exlusively of British singers, singing in English, and on building up a large, well-balanced repertory in which modern works feature alongside established favourites. S.W. could cast from strength, with several singers available for each role. The theatre is now used by visiting companies (opera and ballet) all the year, and seasons have been given by the English Opera Group, the Handel Opera Society, the Welsh and Scottish Operas, the D'Oyly Carte Company, and ensembles from abroad.

In the summer of 1961 the new plans for a National T. included a proposed move from Sadler's Wells to the projected South Bank site: these plans were eventually abandoned and the company moved to the Coliseum T. in Aug. 1968. Norman Tucker had resigned in 1966 and was succeeded by Stephen Arlen (1966-72). Lord Harewood was appointed managing director in April 1972. Charles Mackerras was music director from 1970; he was succeeded by Sir Charles Groves in 1977. At the Coliseum the company has introduced a number of productions of an adventurous theatrical nature, such as Berlioz's *Damnation de Faust,* Prokofiev's *War and Peace,* Penderecki's *The Devils,* and Henze's *The Bassarids.* It has also added to its superb *Meistersinger* an English *Ring,* in a translation by Andrew Porter; these performances were the occasions of the rediscovery of Reginald *Goodall as a great Wagner conductor. In 1974 the company was renamed English National Opera. On 15 Nov. 1978 a separate company, English National Opera North, opened in Leeds (Grand T.), with David Lloyd-Jones as music director.

Bibl: D. Arundel: *The Story of Sadler's Wells* (1965, 2/1978).

Sainete. A genre of Spanish comic opera, portraying scenes from everday life often in the form of low comedy. *Sainete* composers included Antonio Soler and Blas Laserna.

Saint-Aubin, Jean Charlotte Schroeder (*b* Paris, 9 Dec. 1764; *d* Paris, 11 Sept. 1850). French soprano. Started career as child actress, charming Louis XV with her talent. Début Paris, O., 1786 in *Colinette à la cour*. Comédie Italienne 1787-1808; from then on one of the five members of the management; retired from the board at same time as Dugazon. Continued to appear occasionally after her 'official' farewell in 1808 as Mme Bebonent in *Les Prisonniers*. Her singing was said to be 'always intelligent and in tune' and her acting 'refined and graceful'. Her two daughters Cécile (*b* 1785) and Alexandrine (*b* 1793) were both singers; the former, under the name of Mme Duret created several roles in operas by Isouard; she was his favourite singer.

Saint-Huberty, Antoinette Cécile (Anne-Antoinette Clavel) (*b* Strasbourg, 15 Dec. 1756; *d* Barnes, London, 21 July 1813). French soprano. After engagements in Berlin and Strasbourg, studied with Gluck and created Melissa in his *Armide* in 1777; principal soprano Paris, O., from 1781, creating leading roles in Piccinni's *Didone* (1783), Sacchini's *Chimère* (1783), and Salieri's *Danaïdes* (1784). Greatly admired as Alcestis; retired from stage in 1790. Mount-Edgecumbe found her 'less violent and extravagant in her singing than the generality of French singers. . . In truth and force of expression she was unequalled; her declamation was impassioned, her byplay terrible, and her silence eloquent'.
Bibl: E. de Goncourt: *Mme Saint-Huberty* (1885).

St Petersburg. See *Leningrad*.

Saint-Saëns, Camille (*b* Paris, 9 Oct. 1835; *d* Algiers, 16 Dec. 1921). French composer. His numerous works include 12 operas, of which *Samson et Dalila* (1877) is the only outstanding example. Here Saint-Saëns's unfailing craftsmanship and fluency are supplemented by a genuine sense of characterization for the two principals and, if not a very potent dramatic flair, the ability to create a unique and consistent emtional world. It was, no doubt, these qualities which led Liszt to secure it for production at Weimar. His last three operas were written for Monte Carlo.
Bibl: J. Harding: *Saint-Saëns and his Circle* (1965).

Salammbô. Opera in 5 acts by Reyer; text by Camille du Locle, after Flaubert's novel (1862). Prod. Brussels, La M., 10 Feb. 1890, with Rose Caron, Sellier, Renaud, Sentein, cond. Baerwolf; New Orleans 25 Jan. 1900, with Pacary, Layolle, Bonnarde, Bouxmann, cond. Vianesi.
Matho (ten.) has stolen a sacred veil from the shrine of the Carthaginian goddess Tamit. He is condemned to die at the hands of Salammbô (sop.), who has fallen in love with him. She kills herself in his place, and Matho stabs himself.
Other operas on the subject are by Fornaris, Massa (1886), Morawski-Dąbrowa (?early 20th cent.), Hauer (part perf., radio, 1930), Cuscinà (1931), Stoyanov (1940), and Casavola (1948).

Salce, salce. Desdemona's (sop.) Willow Song in Act 4 of Verdi's *Otello*.

Saléza, Albert (*b* Bruges, Basses-Pyrénées, 28 Oct. 1867; *d* Paris, 26 Nov. 1916). French tenor. Studied Paris Conservatoire. Début Paris, O.C., 1888, Mylio (*Le Roi d'Ys*). Sang with great success in Paris, Brussels, Monte Carlo; Nice, where he was Aeneas in *La Prise de Troie*; London, C.G., 1898-1902; N.Y., Met., 1899-1901, and 1904-5. Continued to sing in Paris until 1911. His Roméo and Faust were compared with Jean de Rezke's; also a fine Don José and Otello. (R)

Salieri, Antonio (*b* Legnano, 18 Aug. 1750; *d* Vienna, 7 May 1825). Italian composer. Studied with his brother Francesco, and Venice with Pescetti, later Vienna with Gassmann. His first opera was the comedy *Le donne letterate* (1770), and his success led to his appointment as Kapellmeister of the Italian Opera in Vienna on Gassmann's death. He wrote *Europa riconosciuta* for the opening of Milan, Sc. in 1778. For the new German Opera in Vienna he wrote *Der Rauchfangkehrer* (1781), and for a celebration at Schönbrunn, at which Mozart's *Der Schauspieldirektor* was also given, *Prima la musica e poi le parole* (1786). Gluck suggested him as a suitable composer for an opera for Paris; Salieri had by now been much impressed by Gluck's reforms, and under his supervision composed *Les Danaïdes* (1784). After writing two more operas for Paris, he returned to Vienna and increased his renown with the opera buffa *La grotta di trionfo* (1785). Back in Paris, *Les Horaces* was a failure, but *Tarare* (1787) an enormous success. Written to a text by Beaumarchais (who also contributed a lively preface on the importance of words in opera), this was an ambitious, and musically impressive, work: its text was frequently revised in the succeeding years (initially by Da Ponte as *Axur*), chiefly in order to reflect changing social principles through Revolution and Empire. In 1801 the Trieste opera house opened with *Annibale in Capua,* his last Italian opera; his last German one was *Die Negersclaven* (1804).
Salieri has survived in opera as the villain of Rimsky-Korsakov's *Mozart and Salieri*, a piece which, like Lortzing's pasticcio *Szenen aus*

Mozarts Leben, perpetuates the charge that he poisoned Mozart, but which really treats the envy of talent confronted by genius. Salieri has long been acquitted of the former charge; as to the latter, he failed to influence the Emperor in Mozart's favour and even intrigued against him. However, he did help Mozart's son, as he had also greatly helped Gassmann's family; he also gave generous aid to improverished musicians, and retained the devotion and respect of many important musicians, especially his pupil Beethoven. His work as a conductor and on behalf of opera composers won him great respect, as did his eminence as a teacher and theorist. His own operatic style is in the conventions of the day, in some works not without grandeur; his silence after 1804 was due to his dislike of the changes coming over the art.

Bibl: G. Magnani: *Antonio Salieri* (1934).

Salignac, Thomas (orig. Thomas Eustace) (*b* Générac, Gard, 19 Mar. 1867; *d* Paris, 1945). French tenor. Studied Marseilles and Paris with Duvernoy. Début Paris, O.C., 1893. N.Y., Met., 1896-1903; London, C.G., 1897-9, 1901-4. From 1905 to 1914 he was again at the O.C., creating leading roles in operas by Laparra, Milhaud, and Massenet. Created title role in *Mârouf,* Brussels 1919. In 1923 created title-role in Falla's *El retablo de Maese Pedro* at the Princesse de Polignac's private theatre in Paris. He was director of the Nice Opéra 1914, and of a French *opéra comique* company that toured Canada and the U.S.A. 1926. Professor of singing Fontainebleau 1923, of elocution Paris Conservatoire 1924. Founded the periodical *Lyrica* 1922 which he edited until 1939, organized the Congrès Du Chant 1925, and singing competitions in 1933 and 1937. (R)

Salimberi, Felice (*b* Milan, *c*1712; *d* Ljubljana, Aug. 1755). Italian male soprano. Studied with Porpora. Début Rome, 1731 in Hasse's *Caio Fabrizio.* 1745-50 court singer to Frederick the Great; sang with success at Dresden in Hasse's operas. In 1751 went to Torre del Greco (Naples) to take the cure, and died on the return journey. Generally considered one of the finest singers of his time, with a beautiful and expressive voice of great range.

Salmhofer, Franz (*b* Vienna, 22 Jan. 1900; *d* Vienna, 22 Sept. 1975). Austrian conductor and composer. A descendant of Schubert on his mother's side, he studied in Vienna with Schreker and Schmidt. Cond. Vienna, B., 1929-39; S.O. 1945; director V.O. from 1955. His *Dame im Traum* (1935), *Ivan Tarassenko* (1938, revised 1946), and *Das Werbekleid* (1943) have enjoyed success in Vienna.

Salome. Opera in 1 act by Richard Strauss; text, Oscar Wilde's tragedy (1893) in the German translation of Hedwig Lachmann.

Prod. Dresden, Court, 9 Dec. 1905, with Wittich, Chavanne, Burrian, Perron, cond. Schuch; N.Y., Met., 22 Jan. 1907, with Fremstad, Weed, Burrian, Van Rooy, cond. Hertz; London, C.G., 8 Dec. 1910, with Ackté, Metzger, E. Krauss, Whitehill, cond. Beecham.

During a banquet Jochanaan (John the Baptist) (bar.) proclaims – from the cistern where he is imprisoned – the coming of the Messiah. He is brought out for Salome (sop.) to see, and repels her fascinated advances: he urges her not to follow the ways of her mother Herodias (mezzo). He is taken back to the cistern. Herod (ten.) asks Salome to dance; she agrees on condition that he will grant her a wish. After her Dance of the Seven Veils she demands the head of Jochanaan, which Herod is forced to have brought to her. She fondles and kisses it until the revolted Herod orders his soldiers to crush her with their shields.

Other operas on the subject are by Chichetti, Pierrotti, Giacomo Puccini (1741), Yanovsky (1912), and Lupi (1952).

Saltzmann-Stevens, Minnie (*b* Bloomington, Ill., 17 Mar. 1874; *d* Milan, 25 Jan. 1950). American soprano. Studied Paris with J. de Reszke. Début London, C.G., 1909 Brünnhilde in English *Ring,* and other Wagner roles 1910-13; Bayreuth 1911-13, Sieglinde and Kundry; also appeared in Berlin and Frankfurt and finally Chicago, 1914-16. Her highly promising career came to a premature end during the First World War through illness. (R)

Salut, demeure. Faust's (ten.) apostrophe to Marguerite's home in Act 2 of Gounod's *Faust.*

Salvi, Lorenzo (*b* Ancona, 4 May 1810; *d* Bologna, 16 Jan. 1879). Italian tenor. Début Naples, S.C., 1830. Milan, Sc., 1939-42 created title-role in *Oberto* (1839) and Riccardo (*Giorno di regno*) (1840); London, C.G., 1847-50, mostly in the Donizetti and Bellini repertory; N.Y., Castle Gardens and Niblo's Garden. Married the soprano Adelina Spech.

Salvini-Donatelli (Lucchi), **Fanny** (*b* Florence, *c*1815; *d* Milan, June 1891). Italian soprano. Began career as actress; operatic début Venice, T. Apollo, 1839, Rosina. Vienna 1842; London, D.L., 1858. Created Violetta (Venice, 1853). Highly regarded as Verdi interpreter in *Macbeth, Due Foscari, Ernani,* and *Il corsaro.*

Salzburg. Town in Austria. Birthplace of Mozart and venue of an annual summer festival. The first opera performance north of the Alps, Caneggi's *Andromeda,* was given there in 1618. Operas were given soon after in the garden of Schloss Hellbrunn, and then from the early 18th cent. in the gardens of Schloss Mirabell, where the young Mozart's *Apollo et Hyacinthus* was produced in 1767; his *Sogno di Scipione* was produced there in 1772. The first

Mozart festivals were held from 1877 to 1910, and included concerts and operas under Richter, Mottl, Mahler, Strauss, Muck, and Schalk. Lilli Lehmann arranged two *Don Giovanni* performances in 1901, in which she sang Donna Anna, and in 1906 there were performances of *Don Giovanni* and *Figaro* under Mahler in the Roller settings, with Mayr as Figaro.

In 1917 the Salzburg 'Festspielhausgemeinde' was formed with Hofmannsthal, Reinhardt, Schalk, and Strauss as artistic directors. In 1922 four Mozart operas were given at the Stadttheater under Strauss and Schalk, with Kurz, Rethberg, Schumann, Tauber, Jelger, and Mayr among the singers. In 1922 the Festspielhaus was opened, but not used for opera until 1927, when Schalk conducted *Fidelio* with Lotte Lehmann. Clemens Krauss, Strauss, and Bruno Walter were the principal conductors, and the singers included the best of the Vienna and Munich Opera ensembles and several guest artists. Mozart and Strauss filled most of the repertory, with often *Fidelio* or a work by Gluck or Weber. Toscanini conducted *Falstaff, Fidelio, Meistersinger,* and *Zauberflöte,* 1935-7. After the Anschluss, Toscanini and Walter were replaced by Fürtwangler, Karl Böhm, and Gui. Strauss's *Liebe der Danae* was planned for 1944 but was only given a public dress rehearsal; its Salzburg production was in 1952.

The Festival was resumed in 1946 and has included premières of *Dantons Tod* (Einem, 1947), *Antigonae* (Orff, 1949), *Romeo und Julia* (Blacher, 1950), *Der Prozess* (Einem, 1953), *Penelope* (Liebermann, 1954), *Irische Legende* (Egk, 1955), *Julietta* (Erbse, 1959), and the European premières of *The School for Wives* (1957) and *Vanessa* (1958). In 1949 the old riding school (Felsenreitschule) was used for opera for the first time, staging *Die Zauberflöte, Orfeo,* and *Antigonae;* then *Idomeneo, Don Giovanni, Fidelio, Elektra, Don Carlos,* and *Simon Boccanegra* until 1961. Herbert von Karajan was artistic director of the festival, 1957-60, and again from 1964. In 1960 the new Festspielhaus, which cost almost three and a half million pounds to build, was opened with *Der Rosenkavalier.* It adjoins the old Festspielhaus, and seats 2,160. The stage, the largest in the world, is 135' wide, 120' high, and 70' deep, and in order to accommodate it, a large part of the 160' high Möchsberg, behind the theatre, had to be blasted out to a depth of 50'. The architect was Clemens Holzmeister. Since 1960 premières have included Wagner-Régeny's *Das Bergwerk zu Falun* (1961), Henze's *The Bassarids* (1966), and Orff's *De Temporum fine comoedia* (1973). An Easter Festival, under the musical and artistic direction of Karajan, was inaugurated in 1966, since when there have been outstanding produc-

tions of the *Ring, Fidelio, Tristan und Isolde,* and *Die Meistersinger von Nürnberg.*
Bibl: J. Kaut: *Festspiele in Salzburg* (1965).

Sammarco, (Giuseppe) **Mario** (*b* Palermo, 13 Dec. 1867; *d* Milan, 24 Jan. 1930). Italian baritone. Studied Palermo and Milan. Début Palermo 1888, Valentine. Milan, Sc., and other Italian houses from 1896; London, C.G., 1904, Scarpia, and then regularly until 1914, and in 1919; N.Y., Manhattan, 1908-10; Philadelphia-Chicago 1910-13. Created Gérard, Cascart (*Zazà*), Worms (*Germania*) in Italy, Alvardo in Herbert's *Natoma* and Don Fulgenzio in Parelli's *The Lovers' Quarrel* in Philadelphia; and was the first C.G. Alec (*Tess*), Conte Gil (*Segreto di Susanna*), Raffaele (*Gioielli della Madonna*), and Zamor in Camussi's *Dubarry.* He had a voice of great beauty and evenness, covering a range of two octaves. (R)

Samson et Dalila. Opera in 3 acts by Saint-Saëns; text by Lemaire, after Judges 14-16. Prod. Weimar (in German) 2 Dec. 1877, with Dengler, Müller, Ferenczy, cond. Liszt; N.Y. 25 Mar. 1892 (concert); New Orleans 4 Jan. 1893, with Mounier, Reynaud, Hourdin; London, C.G., 25 Sept. 1893 (concert), 26 Apr. 1909, with Kirkby Lunn, Fontaine, Davey, cond. Frigara. First French performance Rouen 3 Mar. 1890; Paris, T. Eden, 31 Oct. 1890, O. not until 23 Nov. 1892, then 500 perfs. in 30 years.

Samson (ten.), the Hebrew warrior, leads a revolt against the Philistines. Delilah (mezzo), the Philistine temptress, is urged by the High Priest of Dagon (bar.) to seduce Samson and discover the secret of his strength. Samson reveals to her that it lies in his hair, which Delilah cuts off, thus rendering him powerless. He is taken prisoner by the Philistines, and his eyes are put out. Brought to the Temple of Dagon, where he is mocked by his captors, he prays to God for the return of his strength and brings down the Temple, thus killing himself and his enemies.

Other Samson operas are by Graupner (1709), Handel (dramatic oratorio, perf. 1743), Tuček (1803), Basili (1824), C. Conti (19th cent.), and Szokorlay (1973).

San Antonio. Town in Texas, U.S.A. The first opera peformances were given at the theatre on the Alamo Plaza in the early 1880s by touring companies, including the Carleton, Faust, Tuck, and Campanini. In 1901 the Metropolitan Opera from New York gave a single performance of *Lohengrin* on 5 Nov. with Sembrich as Elsa. During the 1920s there were short visits by the Chicago O., including such rarities as *Risurrezione* with Garden and *Norma* with Raisa. In 1944 Baccaloni's touring company gave a sold-out performance of *Il barbiere di Siviglia* in the Municipal Auditorium (cap. 5,800). Since 1945 an annual 'Grand Opera Festival' has been given, under the direction of Max Reiter, founder of the San Antonio Symphony Orchestra. He was succeeded in 1950 by Victor Alessandro. Three or four popular operas are performed each year with leading U.S. and European singers.

San Carlo, Naples, Teatro di. Built in 270 days to replace the old St Bartholomew T., the San Carlo was opened on 4 Nov. 1737 with Sarro's *Achille in Sciro*. The first building was enlarged in 1777 and again in 1812 and was destroyed by fire in Feb. 1816; it was the scene of the production of many works by the Neapolitan school of composers – Pergolesi, Piccinni, Paisiello, Scarlatti, Cimarosa, Jommelli, and Spontini. It was also a 'singers' theatre', where vocal gymnastics and rivalry between the artists were the rule rather than the exception. The behaviour of its audience is said to have been the worst in Italy – as the noise on the stage rose so did that in the auditorium. In 1810 Domenico *Barbaia became the theatre's manager, and soon after commissioned Rossini to write for the San Carlo and invited him to become music director of the smaller T. del Fondo. The operas Rossini wrote for Naples included *Elisabetta Regina d'Inghilterra, Mosè, Otello, Armida, La donna del lago,* and *Maometto II.* Barbaia also discovered and encouraged Bellini and Donizetti: the former's *Bianca e Fernando* was staged in 1826 and the latter's *Lucia di Lammermoor* in 1835. Verdi's relations with the San Carlo were not of the happiest, with the failures there of his *Oberto* and *Alzira,* and censorship troubles which resulted in *La traviata* being given as *Violetta, Rigoletto* as *Clara di Pert* and later *Lionello,* and *Les Vêpres siciliennes* as *Batilde di Turenna* and *Giovanna di Sicilia.* His *Attila* and *Luisa Miller,* however, received successful premières there.

The present theatre (cap. 3,500) was designed by Nicolini and built in 1816 in six months. It underwent extensive alterations in 1844. In 1929 the stage was modernized and a new foyer added. An air-raid in 1943 caused some destruction in the theatre but not enough to interrupt opera. The theatre came under the management of the British Forces during the Allied occupation, and became the most popular opera house among the Allied troops, so much so that the San Carlo Company was invited to give the first opera performances at Covent Garden after the war in the autumn of 1946. Until 1975, under the direction of Pasquale di Costanzo, the theatre pursued an adventurous artistic policy and enjoyed a reputation in Italy second to that of La Scala; but since Costanzo's death no suitable successor has been appointed. Modern works that have been produced at the San Carlo since 1948 include Honegger's *Judith*, Hindemith's

Neues vom Tage, Berg's *Wozzeck,* Henze's *Boulevard Solitude,* Prokofiev's *The Gambler, The Duenna,* and *Semyon Kotko,* Einem's *Der Prozess,* Shostakovich's *Lady Macbeth of the Mtsensk District,* and most of Rossellini's operas.

Performances of chamber operas have been given in the Teatro della Corte, in the adjoining Royal Palace, and summer open-air performances of opera and operetta at the Arena Flegrea.

Bibl: Cento anni di vita del T. San Carlo 1848-1948 (1948).

San Carlo (Touring) Company, U.S.A. A company founded in 1919 (disbanded 1955) by the impresario Fortune *Gallo (1878-1970) which gave popular-priced opera throughout America. There were seasons in New York and Chicago as well as in smaller cities. Its repertory was a popular one. Many of its singers later became famous, including Jean Madeira, Dorothy Kirsten, Eugene Conley, and the conductor Rescigno. In addition many famous singers have appeared with the ensemble as guest artists. An attempt was made in 1974 to revive the company in Florida.

Bibl: F. Gallo: Lucky Rooster (1971).

Sanderson, Sibyl (*b* Sacramento, 7 Dec. 1865; *d* Paris, 15 May 1903). American soprano. Studied Paris Conservatoire and privately with Marchesi and Sbriglia. Début The Hague 1888, *Manon* (as Ada Palmer). Massenet, who fell under her spell, wrote *Esclarmonde* and *Thaïs* for her; and Saint-Saëns composed *Phryné* for her. Neither in London (C.G. 1891) nor N.Y., (Met., 1894-5 and 1901-2) did she repeat her Paris successes. Her voice ranged from g to g'''. Her personal beauty and dramatic talent were not the least of her attractions. Massenet described her as the 'ideal Manon' and an 'unforgettable Thaïs'.

San Diego. Town in California, U.S.A. Operas were given by touring companies in the late 19th cent. and up to the late 1930s. In 1950-62 the San Francisco Opera paid an annual visit; in 1963 the San Diego Opera Guild began plans to establish a local company to perform in the new Civic T. (cap. 2,945); it started in 1965 with *La Bohème,* under the direction of Walter Herbert. In addition to popular operas, the company has staged the first U.S. performance of Henze's *The Young Lord* (1967), the première of Alva Henderson's *Medea* (1972), and productions of *The Rake's Progress, Don Quichotte, Der Mond, Help, Help, the Globolinks!,* and *A Village Romeo and Juliet.* In 1974 a start was made on the *Ring,* sung in Andrew Porter's English translation and produced by George London. Tito Capobianco was appointed artistic director in 1974.

Sandunova, Elizaveta (Semyonovna) (*b* St

Petersburg, 1772 or 10 Sept. 1777; *d* Moscow, 3 Dec. 1826). Russian mezzo-soprano. Professionally known as Uranova by command of Catherine the Great, after the recently discovered planet Uranus. Début St Petersburg, Hermitage, 1790 in Martín y Soler's *Arbore di Diana*. Very popular and one of the finest Russian singers of the early 19th cent. Retired 1823.

San Francisco. Town in California, U.S.A. Opera was first given in 1852 at the Adelphi T. by the Pellegrini Company with *La sonnambula*, followed by *Norma* and *Ernani*. Opera was performed in eleven different theatres, including The Baldwin T., the Civic Opera House, and the Auditorium. Mapleson's company paid several visits from 1879, followed by the National Opera under Theodore Thomas, the Emma Juch Company, the Del Conte Company, and the Damrosch Company. The Metropolitan first visited San Francisco in 1890, with Tamagno in *Otello*, *L'Africaine*, and *Trovatore*, and Patti in *Semiramide*, *Sonnambula*, *Martha*, *Traviata*, and *Lucia*. In 1900 the Met. brought a complete *Ring*; in 1906 the season was only two days old when the famous earthquake struck the city – a few hours previously, Caruso, Fremstad, and Journet had been singing in a performance of *Carmen*.

The idea of a San Francisco Company was first proposed in 1909 by Gateano Merola, conductor of W. A. Edwards's International Opera Company; and the large Italian population of the city tried to raise funds for this purpose. Merola returned in 1919 and 1920 with the touring San Carlo Company, and remained to found the San Francisco Opera in 1923 after a short summer season in the Stadium of Stanford University, consisting of *Pagliacci*, *Carmen*, and *Faust* (with Martinelli as leading tenor). Until 1932 the annual autumn seasons were given in the Civic Auditorium; the repertory was popular and leaned heavily on Italian and French works, though *Tristan und Isolde* was given in 1927 and *Salome* in 1931; a few novelties, including Vittadini's *Anima allegra*, Giordano's *La cena delle beffe*, *Mârouf*, and *L'Enfant et les sortilèges*, were also heard. During this period singers included Homer, Jeritza, Muzio, Rethberg, Ansseau, De Luca, Didur, Gigli, Journet, Lauri-Volpi, Martinelli, Pinza, Schipa, and Scotti. In 1932 the War Memorial Opera House (cap. 3,252) opened with *Tosca* (Muzio, D. Borgioli, Gandolfi); it has been the home of the company ever since. Merola continued as general director until his death in 1953; the repertory was mostly popular, with an emphasis on Italian works, sung by leading singers, often from the Met. Artists who made their U.S. débuts in San Francisco include Favero, Novotna, Simionato, Tebaldi, Baccaloni, Del Monaco, and Gobbi,

before they were engaged by the Met. German operas were better represented from the 1930s onwards, first with Flagstad, Melchior, Schorr, and List, and then with Traubel, Varnay, Djanel, Lehmann, Janssen, and Svanholm.

Merola was succeeded in 1953 by Kurt Adler, who had been on the music staff since 1943 and Merola's assistant since 1949. His régime has included the first U.S. performances of *Jeanne d'Arc au bûcher*, *Frau ohne Schatten*, *Dialogues des Carmélites*, *Troilus and Cressida*, *A Midsummer Night's Dream*, *Carmina Burana*, *The Makropoulos Case*, *The Visitation* (Schuler), *The Visit of the Old Lady*, and Massenet's *Esclarmonde* and the U.S. débuts of Gencer, Jurinac, Nilsson, Margaret Price, Rysanek, Schwarzkopf, Sciutti, Silja, Te Kanawa, Geraint Evans, Glossop, Richard Lewis, Stuart Burrows, and Ingvar Wixell. Many artists sang roles for the first time in San Francisco, including Martinelli's first Otello, Tibbett's first Iago, Geraint Evans's first Wozzeck, Bjoerling's first Riccardo (*Ballo*), Collier's first Minnie, Horne's first Eboli, Kirsten's first Louise, Sutherland's first Mary Stuart, and Jess Thomas's first Tristan. San Francisco was also the scene of Lehmann's last Marschallin, Schorr's 200th Hans Sachs, and Journet's 100th Méphistophélès. Regular conductors have included Reiner, Steinberg, Ludwig, Stein, Suitner, Cleva, Molinari-Pradelli, Patanè, Pritchard, and Bonynge. Until 1965 the company gave annual seasons at the Shrine Auditorium in Los Angeles after the San Francisco season. In 1961 a Spring Opera Company was founded to give popular operas with young American singers; gradually contemporary American works were added to this company's repertory and new production styles were encouraged.

Bibl: A. J. Bloomfield: *The San Francisco Opera* (1962, 3/1978).

Sanjust, Filippo (*b* Rome, 9 Sept. 1925). Italian designer and producer. Collaborated with Visconti, London, 1958, *Don Carlos* and subsequently. Designed *Bassarids*, Salzburg, 1966. First own production, *Zauberflöte*, Frankfurt, 1968. London, Col., 1970, *Semele*. Worked in Hamburg, Berlin, and Amsterdam. Has designed and produced such diverse works as *L'incoronazione di Poppea*, *Lohengrin*, and *Lulu*. More remarkable as designer than producer.

Sanquirico, Alessandro (*b* Milan, 27 July 1777; *d* Milan, 12 Mar. 1849). Italian designer. The leading Italian scene designer of his day, at Milan Sc. from 1817 to 1832, where he designed many premières including *Norma*, *Il pirata*, and *La gazza ladra*, as well as many works by Mercadante, Pacini, and Donizetti. In 1829 he redecorated the interior of the Sc. His designs, most of which can be seen at the Sc.

Museum and elsewhere in Milan, reveal an impressive neo-classical style and later a warmer Romantic one.

Santa Fe. Town in New Mexico, U.S.A. The Santa Fe company, founded in 1957 by John Crosby, gives an annual summer festival in an outdoor auditorium. It has established itself as a leading cultural and musical institution and has staged the premières of Floyd's *Wuthering Heights* (1958), Levy's *The Tower*, Berio's *Opera* (1970), and Villa-Lobos's *Yerma* (1971); the first stage performance of Schoenberg's *Jakobsleiter* (1968) and first production since the 17th cent. of Cavalli's *Egisto*; and the first U.S. performances of *Lulu*, *König Hirsch*, *Boulevard Solitude*, *The Bassarids*, *Neues vom Tage*, *Cardillac*, *The Nose*, *Daphne*, *Help, Help, the Globolinks!*, *The Devils of Loudun*, *Melusine*, and *Owen Wingrave*. Young U.S. and British singers, including Frederica von Stade, Rita Shane, Kiri Te Kanawa, Pauline Tinsley, George Shirley, Stuart Burrows, Don Garrard, and Richard Stilwell have regularly appeared. The original theatre burnt down in 1967 a few hours after the first U.S. performance of *Cardillac*, but the season continued at the local High School. A new theatre opened a year later with *Madama Butterfly*.

Santi, Nello (*b* Adria (Rovigo), 22 Sept. 1931). Italian conductor. Studied Padua. Début Padua, T. Verdi, 1951, *Rigoletto*. Zurich since 1959; Salzburg 1960; London, C.G., 1960, *Traviata*; N.Y., Met., 1962-5. Salzburg 1960, *Don Carlos*. Guest appearances Hamburg, Munich, Vienna etc. Considered a good 'singers' conductor'. (R)

Santini, Gabriele (*b* Perugia, 20 Jan. 1886; *d* Rome, 13 Nov. 1964). Italian conductor. Début 1906. Assistant to Toscanini at Sc., Milan, 1925-9; Rome, Opera, 1929-32, and 1945-1962 where he was music director until 1962. Also conducted in Buenos Aires, Chicago, and London. (R)

Santley, (Sir) **Charles** (*b* Liverpool, 28 Feb. 1834; *d* London, 22 Sept. 1922). English baritone. Studied Milan with Nava, London with Garcia. Début Pavia 1857, Dr Grenvil (*Traviata*); London, C.G., 1859, Hoël (*Dinorah*) in Pyne-Harrison English season; joined Mapleson's company 1862; first English Valentine 1863, pleasing Gounod so much that he composed 'Even bravest heart' for the following year's revival. Sang title role in *Der fliegende Holländer* in first London production of any Wagner opera. Joined company of Gaiety T. 1870, when heard in *Zampa, Zar und Zimmermann*, *Fra Diavolo*; Carl Rosa 1875-6. Also sang in America, Milan, Sc., and Barcelona. Knighted 1907; farewell at C.G., 23 May 1911 in Dibdin's *The Waterman*. Though not gifted with a beautiful voice, he sang with great expression and was especially effective in dramatic roles. (R)
Bibl: C. Santley: *Reminiscences of My Life* (1909); J. Mewburn Levien: *Sir Charles Santley* (1930).

Sanzogno, Nino (*b* Venice, 13 Apr. 1911). Italian conductor and composer. Studied with Malipiero and Scherchen. Has conducted at Milan, Sc., since 1941, where he has been associated with modern works including *Arlecchino*, *Oedipus Rex*, *Le Pauvre matelot*, *The Consul*, *David*, *Troilus and Cressida*, *The Fiery Angel*, and *Dialogues des Carmélites*. He also has a great affection for Scarlatti, Cherubini, Piccinni, Paisiello, Cimarosa, and Donizetti, and has conducted their works at La Piccola Scala. He conducted the opening performance there in Dec. 1955, and appeared with the company at Edinburgh in 1957. Appointed permanent conductor at Sc., 1962. (R)

São Paulo. Town in Brazil. Opera has been given regularly since 1874, first at the T. Provisorio, then 1876-97 at the T. São José, with occasional performances at the Doliteama Naçional, and 1901-9 at the T. Santana. The T. Municipal opened 12 Sept. 1907 with *Hamlet*, and has been the home of opera there ever since. The companies, mostly of Italian artists, who had been appearing in Buenos Aires and Rio, generally went on to São Paulo every autumn, and most of the great names among Italian opera singers appeared there. As well as the popular Italian and French repertory, works by South American composers have been staged, including Arroyo's *Amor de Perdicão*, Mignone's *O Contratador dos diamantes,* and several works by Gomes.
Bibl: P. De Oliveira Castro Cerquena: *Un século de Opera en São Paolo* (1954).

Sapho. Opera in 5 acts by Massenet; text by Henri Cain and Arthur Bernede after Daudet's novel (1884). Prod. Paris, O.C., 27 Nov. 1897, with Calvé (who studied the role with Daudet), Wyns, Lepestre, Gresse, Jacquet, Dufour, cond. Danbe; N.Y., Manhattan O., 17 Nov. 1909, with Garden, D'Alvarez, Dalmores, Dufranne, Leroux, cond. De La Fuente; London, Camden Town Hall, 14 March 1967, with Andrew, Domzolski, De Peyer, Christiansen, Lennox, Olegario, cond. Gover.
The opera tells of the unhappy love of Fanny Legrand (sop.), who has been posing as artist's model for a statue (or painting) of Sapho, and a country youth, Jean Gaussin.
A record exists of Massenet accompanying Georgette Leblanc in a scene from the opera.

Saporiti, Teresa (*b* ? 1763; *d* Milan, 17 March 1869). Italian soprano. Engaged by Bondini, 1782, and toured with his company in Germany. Prague 1787 – created Donna Anna. After appearances in Italy, engaged in 1795 by

Astaritta for St Petersburg: also appeared in Moscow.

Saraceni, Adelaide (*b* Rosario, Argentina, 25 Nov. 1895). Argentinian soprano. Studied Pesaro with Edvige Ghibaudo. Début Argenta, 1919, Rosina. Milan, Sc. 1928-32, and all leading Italian houses until 1935. Created Rosaura (*Vedova scaltra*). Repertory included Adina, Susanna, Cio-Cio-San, Liù, Adriana Lecouvreur and Violetta. After retiring from stage, taught singing in Milan. (R)

Sarastro. The priest of Isis (bass) in Mozart's *Die Zauberflöte*.

Sardou, Victorien (*b* Paris, 5 Sept. 1831; *d* Paris, 8 Nov. 1908). French dramatist. He first made his name as a writer of comedies; later turned to historical dramas (e.g., *La Tosca*, 1887), in which he developed a characteristic theme of dark, passionate stories set against a background of war or political tension. He wrote a number of roles for Sarah Bernhardt, and two, *Robespierre* and *Dante*, for Henry Irving. Wrote the libretto for *Le Roi Carotte* (1872) for Offenbach and *Les Barbares* (1901) for Saint-Saëns; best remembered for the operas based on his works, in which many different composers found his strong situations, vivid characters, and lavishly developed scenes a powerful stimulus to music. Operas on his works are as follows:
Piccolino (1861): Grandval (1869); J. Strauss II (*Karneval in Rom*, 1873); Guiraud (1876).
Les Près-St Gervais (1862): Lecocq (1874).
La Bataille d'amour (1863): Vaucorbeil (1863).
Don Quichotte (1864): Renaud (1895).
Le Capitaine Henriot (1864): Gevaert (1864).
Patrie! (1869): L. Rossi (*La Contessa di Mons*, 1874); Paladilhe (1880). The subject was also contemplated by Verdi.
Rabugas (1872): De Giosa (1882).
Les Merveilleuses (1873): Félix (1914).
La Haine (1874): Solovyov (*Cordelia*, 1885).
Les Noces de Fernande (1878): Deffès (1878); Millöcker (*Der Bettelstudent*, 1882).
Fédora (1882): Giordano (1898).
La Tosca (1887): Puccini (1900).
Madame Sans-Gêne (1893): Caryll (*The Duchess of Dantzic*, 1903); Giordano (1915); Długi (early 20th cent.); Petit (1947).
Gismonda (1894): Février (1918).
La Fille de Tabarin (1901): Pierné (1901).
Les Barbares (1901): Saint-Saëns (1901).
La Sorcière (1903): D'Erlanger (1912).
Fiorella (1905): Webber (1905).

Sargent, (Sir) **Malcolm** (*b* Stamford, 29 Apr. 1895; *d* London, 3 Oct. 1967). English conductor. Although primarily a concert conductor, Sargent worked with the B.N.O.C., directing the first performances of *Hugh the Drover* and *At the Boar's Head* in 1924. D'Oyly Carte Company 1926-8, 1951; C.G., 1936,

Louise; première of *Troilus and Cressida*, 1954. (R)

Šárka. (1) Opera in 3 acts by Janáček; text by Julius Zeyer, after his own drama (1887). Orig. version 1887, rev. 1888, 1918, final version rev. Chulba, prod. Brno, 11 Nov. 1925, with Pirková, Flögl, Oslovský, V. Šindler, cond. Neumann.

After the death of Libuše, her husband Přemysl (bass) plans to dispense with her council of women. They revolt, under Šárka (sop.), who falls in love with the warrior hero Ctirad (ten.); nevertheless she brings about his death, eventually hurling herself on to his funeral pyre.

(2) Opera in 3 acts by Fibich; text by Anežka Schulzová, after the Czech legend. Prod. Prague, N., 28 Dec. 1897.

Sarti, Giuseppe (*b* Faenza, bapt. 1 Dec. 1729; *d* Berlin, 28 July 1802). Italian composer. His fame spread so early that at 24 he was invited to Denmark as director of opera. He did not finally return to Italy for over 20 years, and then after a brilliant nine years he left for St Petersburg. Here he collaborated in one of the earliest Russian operas, *The First Government of Oleg* (1790), to a text by the Empress Catherine II, who had appointed him. He founded a school of singing in the Ukraine, and later he became head of the St Petersburg Conservatory. He died on the way to Italy after 18 years in Russia. Sarti's operas are forgotten now, apart from the single air 'Come un agnello' from *Fra due litiganti*, which Mozart made Don Giovanni's private band play. Some 75 in number, they are well written for voices and have a certain stage flair.

Sass (Sasse), **Marie Constance** (*b* Oudenaarde, 26 Jan. 1834; *d* Auteuil, Paris, 8 Nov. 1907). Belgian soprano. Studied Ghent with Gevaert, Paris with Ugalde, Italy with Lamperti. Début Venice 1852, Gilda. Paris, T.L., 1859; Paris O., from 1860 – created Selika in *L'Africaine* (1865), Elisabeth de Valois in *Don Carlos* (1867); Elisabeth in first Paris *Tannhäuser* (1861); Milan Sc., 1869-70 – Cecilia in Gomez's *Il Guarany*. For a period she sang as Marie Sax, but Adolphe Sax brought a law-suit against her and she subsequently sang only as Sass or Sasse. Her temperamental behaviour at the rehearsals and première of *Don Carlos* so incensed Verdi that he refused to allow her to create Amneris. In 1864-7 she was married to the bass *Castelmary. Retired from stage 1877 and taught singing for a time; died in great poverty.
Bibl: M. Sass: *Souvenirs d'une artiste* (1902).

Sass, Sylvia (*b* Budapest, 12 July 1951). Hungarian soprano. Studied Budapest with Ferenc Revhegyi. Début Budapest, 1971, Frasquita. Scottish Opera, 1975, Desdemona; London,

C.G., 1976, Giselda (*Lombardi*), 1977 Violetta, N.Y. Met. 1977, Tosca. Aix Festival, 1976, Violetta. Guest appearances in Cologne, Hamburg, Munich, etc. A highly talented *lirico-spinto*, with exceptional vocal and dramatic gifts and a powerful stage personality. (R)

Satie, Erik (orig. Alfred Eric Leslie) (*b* Honfleur, 17 May 1866; *d* Paris, 1 July 1925). French composer. His stage works include a puppet operetta *Geneviève de Brabant* (1899) and two operettas, *Pousse l'amour* (1905) and *Le Piège de Méduse* (1913).

Sauguet, Henri (*b* Bordeaux, 18 May 1901). French composer. The most substantial of his five operas is a 4-act setting of *La Chartreuse de Parme* (1939), for which he composed music more substantial than that in his usual smart metropolitan style and tackled a large subject with the devotion it demands. His dextrous and eminently civilized *Les Caprices de Marianne* was prod. Aix-en-Provence 1954.

Saul og David. Opera in 4 acts by Nielsen; text by Einar Christiansen, after I Samuel. Prod. Copenhagen, Royal T., 28 Nov. 1902, with Dons, Lendrop, Hérold, Cornelius, Simonsen, Nissen, Müller, cond. Nielsen; London, Collegiate T., 23 Feb. 1977, with Gail, Hillman, Masterson-Smith, Doghan, McDonnell, Francis, cond. Wolfenden.

In this version of the Biblical story, Saul (bar.) is cast as a complex, questioning figure in contrast to the more straightforward David (ten.). The events encompass David falling in love with Saul's daughter Michal (sop.), the narrated defeat of Goliath, and the return of Jonathan (ten.) with news of the victory over the Philistines, Saul's jealousy of David, and David's eventual accession as King.

Savage, Henry (*b* New Durham, 21 Mar. 1859; *d* Boston, 29 Nov. 1927). American impresario. Originally a dealer in real estate, he was forced to take over the Castle Square T., Boston, when a lessee failed in 1897. He proved a successful manager, and in 1900 collaborated with Grau in forming the Grau-Savage Metropolitan English Grand Opera Company. In 1904-5 he presented *Parsifal* in English throughout the U.S.A., and in 1906-7 and 1911 he made similar tours with Puccini's *Madama Butterfly* and *La fanciulla del West.*

Savitri. Opera in 1 act by Holst; text by composer, after an episode in the *Mahabharata*. Prod. London, Wellington Hall, by London School of Opera, 5 Dec. 1916, with Corran, Pawlo, Cook, cond. Grunebaum; first public prod. London, Lyric T. Hammersmith, 23 June 1921, with Silk, Steuart Wilson, Clive Carey, cond. Arthur Bliss; Chicago, Palmer House, 23 Jan. 1934, with Witwer, Colcaire, Schmidt, cond. Krueger. Also opera by Zumpe

(unfin. 1903, completed Rössler 1907).

Savoy Operas. The name given to the operettas by *Gilbert and *Sullivan, from the theatre at which many of them were first produced.

Savoy Theatre, London. Theatre built by Richard D'Oyly Carte to house the Gilbert and Sullivan operas, opened in October 1881 with *Patience.* Three seasons of opera were organized by Marie Brema, 1910-11; she sang the title-role in Gluck's *Orfeo.* The present theatre (cap. 1,122) opened in Oct. 1941, and celebrated the centenary of the beginning of the Gilbert and Sullivan collaboration with a complete cycle of the Savoy operas in Mar. 1975.

Sawallisch, Wolfgang (*b* Munich, 26 Aug. 1923). German conductor. Début Augsburg 1947; remained there until 1953, progressing from répétiteur to first Kapellmeister. Generalmusikdirektor Aachen 1953-7; Wiesbaden 1957-9; Cologne 1959-63. Bayreuth 1957-62, conducting new productions of *Tristan* (1957), *Holländer* (1959), and *Tannhäuser* (1961). Generalmusikdirektor Bavarian State Opera since 1971. (R)

Sayão, Bidu (orig. Baldwina de Oliveira) (*b* Rio de Janeiro, 11 May 1902). Brazilian soprano. Studied Rio with Theodorini, Nice with Jean de Reszke. Début Rome, Costanzi, 1926, Rosina. After engagements in Rome, Milan, Naples, and Buenos Aires she went to the U.S.A.: Washington 1936, Lakmé; N.Y., Met., 1937-51, where her best roles included Manon, Juliette, Mélisande, Mimì, and Zerlina. Farewell performances Rio 1958. (R) Married the baritone Giuseppe Danise (1883-1963). (R)

Sbriglia, Giovanni (*b* Naples, 23 June 1829; *d* Paris, 20 Feb. 1916). Italian tenor and teacher. Début Naples, S.C., 1853. Toured Canada, U.S.A., and South America with Teresa Parodi's company in the 1860s. Settled in Paris 1875 as teacher: pupils included the De Reszkes, Nordica, Plançon, and Sibyl Sanderson.

Scala, Teatro alla. See *La Scala.*

Scala di seta, La (The Silken Ladder). Opera in 1 act by Rossini; text by Foppa, after the play *L'Échelle de soie* by François-Antoine-Eugène de Planard and possibly a libretto from it made for Gaveaux (1808). Prod. Venice, S. Moisè, 9 May 1812, with (probably) Cantarelli, Nagher, Monelli, Del Monte, De Grecis, Tacci; London. S.W., by T. dell'Opera Comica, Rome, 26 Apr. 1954, with Tuccari, Lollin, Bernardi, Catalani, Dolciotti, cond. Morelli; San Francisco, O., 18 Feb. 1966.

The silken ladder of the title is used nightly by Dorvil (ten.) to rejoin his wife Giulia (sop.), whom he has secretly married, but who is living in the house of her father Dormont (bass).

Scala Theatre, London. Opened in September 1905; the scene of the London Opera Festival 1929-30, which included the first stage performance in London of Monteverdi's *Orfeo* conducted by J. A. Westrup, *Giulio Cesare,* and *Der Freischütz* under Beecham. After the Second World War several semi-professional and 'fringe' operatic organizations staged performances there, including The Revival Opera Company, which gave *Les Huguenots* in 1959. The E.O.G. gave its 10th anniversary season there in 1956; this included the première of Berkeley's *Ruth.* The theatre was closed in 1969 and has since been demolished.

Scalchi, Sofia (*b* Turin, 29 Nov. 1850; *d* Rome, 22 Aug. 1922). Italian mezzo-soprano. Studied with Boccabati. Début Mantua 1866, Ulrica. London, C.G., 1868, Azucena, regularly until 1890. Toured U.S.A. 1882-3, 1884-5 with Mapleson Company, N.Y., Met., 1883 (Siebel at opening of theatre) and 1891-6 – the first American Mistress Quickly, La Cieca, and Emilia. Although she spent more than 20 years at C.G., she created no important roles there; heard as Amneris, Arsace, Urbain, etc. Her voice was of great volume and ranged from f to b'', with an amazing command of coloratura that enabled her to sing soprano cadenzas. It was very uneven, however: she was said to have four registers. Retired 1896.

Scandiani, Angelo (*b* Venice, 1872; *d* Milan, 24 June 1930). Italian baritone and administrator. Noted for his Méphistophélès in *La Damnation de Faust.* Administrator of Milan, Sc., 1919-29. London, C.G., 1906-8, Escamillo, Valentine, and Verdi-Puccini repertory; Buenos Aires, T. Colón, 1916, Hans Sachs. (R)

Scaria, Emil (*b* Graz, 18 Sept. 1838; *d* Blasewitz, nr Dresden, 22 July 1886). Austrian bass. Studied Graz, Vienna, and London with Garcia. Début Pest 1860, St Bris (*Huguenots*). Leipzig 1863-4; Dresden 1864-72; Vienna 1873-86. Created Gurnemanz (1882) and was a notable Wotan, of which he was the first interpreter in London at H.M.'s 1882. Toured U.S.A. 1884. Hanslick wrote that his 'carefully deadened high notes form a great contrast to the vigorous notes of his lower and middle register'. He died insane.

Scarlatti, (Pietro) **Alessandro** (Gaspare) (*b* Palermo, 2 May 1660; *d* Naples, 24 Oct. 1725). Italian composer. His first opera, *Gli equivoci nel sembiante,* produced at Rome when he was 19, won him the patronage of Queen Christina of Sweden and the encouragement to follow up his success. From 1702 he composed several operas for Ferdinando de' Medici in Florence; but he was dropped by the Prince in the year in which he wrote his finest work,

Mitridate Eupatore (1707). He was now at the height of his fame in Naples, where the major part of his career was spent; a brief period in Rome working for a now no less admiring audience followed before his final return to Naples in 1722 or 1723.

This is the bare outline of the career of one of the great figures of operatic history. Compelled as he was by the conditions of his age to please a long list of princes and bishops, his feat in establishing himself as a father of classicism in music is considerable. Needing a ready mould for music, he firmly established the da capo aria and the so-called Italian *overture; he also made rich use of accompanied recitative for powerful dramatic effects and established the *secco* recitative conventions. His best work was for Ferdinando de' Medici: *Mitridate Eupatore* is a great classical document. The poetic dignity found here was never quite matched again, but Scarlatti's mastery subsequently allowed a loosening of the da capo aria's strictness. His style became less rigidly contrapuntal, more enterprisingly harmonic. Towards the end of Scarlatti's life, Rome caught the passion for opera so wholeheartedly as to overcome ecclesiastical objections and provide an audience capable of appreciating the master in its midst. Scarlatti had now rallied all his powers, and the works of this last period show both brilliance and emotional depth expressed with a complete technical resource. Only one of his 70-odd surviving operas (the total was 115) is wholly comic, *Il trionfo dell'onore* (1718); and even this succeeds chiefly in the scenes where Scarlatti was guying what he understood best – heroic figures in tragic predicaments. He has inevitably been more revered by musicologists than by amateurs, for whom opportunities of seeing his operas are very rare; he has also been reproached with categorizing forms too firmly and so playing into the hands of singers and their embellishments. His best work shows a dignity of invention as well as a logical mastery of musical means that justify his lofty reputation. His son **Domenico** (*b* Naples, 26 Oct. 1685; *d* Madrid, 23 July 1757) is remembered now as a great keyboard composer, though he began his career in opera. In 1709, after various travels and studies, Domenico became composer to Queen Maria Casimira of Poland's court in Rome, for which he wrote seven operas.

Scarpia. The corrupt police chief (bar.) in Puccini's *Tosca.*

Scena (from *Gr* σκηνή: stage). A solo operatic movement of primarily dramatic purpose, less lyrical or formally composed than an aria, though very similar. One of its greatest examples is Leonore's 'Abscheulicher' in Beethoven's *Fidelio.*

Scenario (*It* scenery). An outline libretto indicating the characters and number and type of scenes. In German, *Scenarium* means a complete libretto with detailed indications of scenery and setting.

Schack (orig. Žak), **Benedikt** (*b* Mirovice, 7 Feb. 1758; *d* Munich, 11 Dec. 1826). Bohemian-German tenor and composer. Début Schikaneder's company, in Paisiello's *La frascatana* (1786); first Tamino (30 Sept. 1791, when his wife Elisabeth Weinhold sang one of the Three Ladies and he himself played the eponymous flute); first to sing Don Ottavio and Almaviva in German (5 Nov. and 28 Dec. 1792); said to be one of the singers of the unfinished Requiem to Mozart on his death-bed. He also wrote five operas.

Schalk, Franz (*b* Vienna, 27 May 1863; *d* Edlach, 2 Sept. 1931). Austrian conductor. Studied with Bruckner. Début Liberec 1886; Graz 1889-95; Prague 1895-8; Berlin 1899-1900; Vienna from 1900, where he succeeded Gregor as director in 1918, and shared first conductorship with Strauss 1919-24; when differences arose between them and Strauss resigned, leaving Schalk in control until his death. One of the founders of the Salzburg Festival. London, C.G., 1898, 1907, and 1911, when he conducted the English première of *Königskinder* and three highly successful *Ring* cycles. N.Y., Met., 1898-9. (R)

Schauspieldirektor, Der (The Impresario). *Komödie mit Musik* in 1 act by Mozart; text by Gottlieb Stephanie jr. Prod. Vienna, Schönbrunn Palace, 7 Feb. 1786 (in same bill as Salieri's *Prima la musica e poi le parole*), with Lange, Cavalieri, Adamberger; London, St James's T., 30 May 1857; N.Y. 9 Nov. 1870, with Lichtmay, Römer, Hölzel, Himmer, Rohbeck, Himmer.

The plot describes the rivalries between two prima donnas, Madame Silberklang (sop.) and Madame Herz (sop.): each offers a sample of her ability, the former in sentimental vein, the latter with a brighter rondo. They then come to blows over which of them deserves the higher salary, and try to outsing each other in a trio with M. Vogelsang (ten.) in the presence of the long-suffering Impresario (speaking part). Various revisions have been made, including one that turns the singers into Aloysia Lange, Katharina Cavalieri, and Valentin Adamberger, and the impresario into Mozart himself.

Scheff, Fritzi (*b* Vienna, 30 Aug. 1879; *d* New York, 8 Apr. 1954). Austrian soprano. Daughter of the soprano Anna Jaeger (-Scheff). Studied with her mother, in Munich with Schröder-Hanfstaengl, Frankfurt Conservatory. Début Frankfurt, 1897, Martha. Munich, H., 1897-1900; London, C.G., 1900-3 where her Zerlina, Musetta, and Nedda were much admired; N.Y.,

Met., 1900-3. Elsa, Asa in Paderewski's *Manru* earning the nickname of the 'Little Devil of the Opera' from the composer. Then turned to operetta and musical comedy, starring on Broadway in *Boccaccio, Giroflé-Girofla, Mlle Modiste*, then in plays, notably *Arsenic and Old Lace*. (R)

Scheidemantel, Karl (*b* Weimar, 21 Jan. 1859; *d* Weimar, 26 Jan. 1923). German baritone. Studied with Borchers and Stockhausen. Début Weimar 1871, Wolfram, and sang there until 1886; Dresden 1886-1911; Bayreuth 1886-92 as Amfortas, Sachs, Wolfram; London, C.G., 1884 as Kurwenal and Rucello in Stanford's *Savonarola*, 1899 as Sachs. In Dresden created Urok in Paderewski's *Manru*, Kunrad in *Feuersnot*, and Faninal. 1911-20 taught in Weimar; from 1920 to 1922 director, Dresden Landesoper. Produced a new text for *Così fan tutte* 1909 under the title of *Dame Kobold*, and his translation of *Don Giovanni* (1914) won the prize of the Deutscher Bühnenverein. Two books on singing, *Stimmbildung* (1907) and *Gesangsbildung* (1913). (R)

Scheidt, Robert vom (*b* Bremen, 16 Apr. 1879; *d* Frankfurt, 10 Apr. 1964). German baritone. Studied Cologne. Début Cologne, 1897. Hamburg, 1903-12; Frankfurt 1912-40. Created Tamare in Schreker's *Die Gezeichneten* (1918), and Vogt in his *Schatzgräbers* (1920). Bayreuth 1904, Biterolf, Donner, Klingsor. (R) His brother, **Julius** (1877-1948) was a leading baritone in Berlin, D., (1915-24), and Hamburg (1924-30); a sister, **Selma** (1874-1959) was a leading soprano. Weimar 1900-25. (R)

Schenk, Johann Baptist (*b* Wiener Neustadt, 30 Nov. 1753; *d* Vienna, 29 Dec. 1836). Austrian composer. Studied with Wagenseil. From 1794 he was music director for Prince Auersperg. He wrote many Singspiels, of which by far the most popular, was *Der Dorfbarbier* (1796), which was a success all over Germany and Austria. Beethoven took some counterpoint lessons with him.

Schenk, Otto (*b* Vienna, 2 June 1930). Austrian producer and administrator. Studied Vienna at the Reinhardt Seminar. Began career as actor and theatre producer; first opera production, *Zauberflöte*, Salzburg Landestheater. Vienna, S.O., since 1962, where his *Lulu* and *Fidelio* were much admired. Salzburg, Munich, Milan, Sc., London C.G., *Ballo in maschera* (1975). Often collaborates with conductors Claudio Abbado and Carlos Kleiber, and designer Jürgen Rose. Prefers 'people' to 'concepts' in his productions.

Scherchen, Hermann (*b* Berlin, 21 June 1891; *d* Florence, 12 June 1966). German conductor. Originally viola player in Berlin Philharmonic, he made his conducting début in 1911, collaborating with Schoenberg. Although primarily a symphonic conductor, he made a number of appearances in the opera house, generally conducting contemporary works, of which he was a great champion: premières of Dallapiccola's *Il prigioniero*, Florence 1950; Dessau's *Das Verhör des Lukullus*, Berlin 1951; Henze's *Konig Hirsch* Berlin 1956; performances of *Von Heute auf Morgen, Salome*, Prokofiev's *The Gambler* at Naples, and *Mavra, Hin und Zurück* and Blacher's *Abstracte Oper No. 1* in Berlin. Adapted Webern's second cantata for the stage, and conducted its première in Naples 1958 as *Il cuore*. (R)

Scherman, Thomas (*b* New York, 12 Feb. 1917). American conductor. Studied Columbia University, and conducting with Carl Bamberger and Max Rudolph. Début Mexico National Opera 1947; in same year organized New York Little Orchestra Society, which has given many important concert performances of opera including *Ariadne auf, Naxos, L'Enfant et les sortilèges, Goyescas, Iphigénie en Tauride, The Makropoulos Case*, and *Euryanthe*. (R)

Schiavazzi, Piero (*b* Cagliari, 14 Mar. 1875; *d* Rome, 25 May 1949). Italian tenor. Studied Pesaro. Début S. Giovanni Persicheto 1899, Rodolfo. Created Mateo in Zandonai's *Conchita* (1911). London, C.G., 1912, Mateo. Admired in Mascagni repertory, especially Osaka (*Iris*) and Amica. Guest appearances South America. Retired 1924 and taught singing in Rome. (R)

Schikaneder, Emanuel (orig. Johann Schikeneder) (*b* Straubing, 1 Sept. 1751; *d* Vienna, 21 Sept. 1812). German theatre manager, singer, actor, and playwright. After an early life as a wandering musician, he became manager of the Vienna Kä., where he also appeared. Took over the theatre at Regensburg briefly before returning to manage a small Vienna theatre in the suburb of Wieden, for which Mozart set his libretto *Die Zauberflöte*; the success of the opera, with Schikaneder as Papageno at the première (30 Sept. 1791), made the fortunes of the theatre. In 1800 he partnered a merchant in opening the T. an der Wein, near the T. auf der Wieden, and continued as manager until 1806. Other composers who set his librettos include Schack (the first Tamino), Süssmayr, Paisiello, Seyfried, and Winter; *Vestas Feuer* (1805), intended for and begun by Beethoven, was set by Weigl.

Schiller, Friedrich von (*b* Marbach, 10 Nov. 1759; *d* Weimar, 9 May 1805). German poet and playwright. Operas on his works are as follows:

Die Räuber (1782): Mercadante (1836); Verdi (*I masnadieri*, 1847); Zajc (*Amelia*, 1860); Klebe (1957).

Fiesco (1783): Lalo (comp. 1866).

Kabale und Liebe (1783): Verdi (*Luisa Miller*, 1849).

Don Carlos (1787): P. D. Deshayes (1799); Nordal (1843); M. Costa (1844); Bona (1847); Ferrari (1854); Moscuzza (1862); Ferrara (1863); Verdi (1867).

Der Handschuh (1798): Polgar (1973).

Der Taucher (1798): Reichardt (1811).

Die Bürgschaft (1798): Schubert (1816, unfin.); Lachner (1828); Hellmesberger (comp. 1851).

Wallenstein (1799): Seyfried (1813); Adelburg (*c*1872); Musone (1873); Denza (1876); Ruiz (1877); Weinberger (1937); Shabelsky (1950); Zafred (1965).

Das Lied von der Glocke (1799): D'Indy (1912).

Maria Stuart (1800): Donizetti (1834, as *Buondelmonte*); Lavello (1895).

Die Jungfrau von Orleans (1801); Vaccai (1827); Balfe (1837); Vesque von Püttlingen (1840); Verdi (1845); Langert (1861); Tchaikovsky (1881); Rezniček (1886).

Die Braut von Messina (1803): Vaccai (1839); Orzen (1840); Bonawitz (1874); Fibich (1884).

Wilhelm Tell (1804): Carr (*The Archers*, 1796); Rossini (1824).

Der Gang nach dem Eisenhammer (xxxx): B. A. Weber (1810); Schoenfeld (1832); K. Kreutzer (1837); Terry (1861).

Turandot (1804): Vesque von Püttlingen (1838); Busoni (1917); Puccini (1926).

Demetrius (1805, unfin.): Joncières (1876); Dvořák (1882).

Schillings, Max von (*b* Düren, 19 Apr. 1868; *d* Berlin, 24 July 1933). German composer, conductor, and manager. Studied Bonn and Munich where he came under the influence of Strauss. Assistant stage director, Bayreuth 1892, and chorus master there 1902. Stuttgart 1908-18, first as assistant to Intendant, then, conductor, and from 1911 Generalmusikdirektor; ennobled by the King of Württemberg when the new Stuttgart Opera opened 1912; Intendant, Berlin 1919-25. U.S.A. 1924 and 1931 with German Opera Company. His operas include *Ingwelde* (1894), *Moloch* (1900), and *Mona Lisa* (1915). (R) Married the soprano Barbara *Kemp 1923. (R)

Schinkel, Karl Friedrich (*b* Neuruppin, 13 Mar. 1781; *d* Berlin, 9 Oct. 1841). German architect and designer. Studied Berlin. Began working as a scene designer for Wilhelm Gropius, 1807-15, then engaged at the Königliche T., to design *Zauberflöte*; this was a famous production, and he remained at the theatre until 1832. Also designed some of Spontini's operas at the Hofoper: for these works, his grasp of architectural design and ability to handle large structures was particularly appropriate (*La vestale*, 1818; *Olimpie*, 1821). He attempted to make his designs functional to the drama, and gave the stage a new sense of space and grandeur; but a certain rigidity limited his achievement.

Schipa, Tito (Raffaele Attilio Amedeo) (*b* Lecce, 2 Jan. 1889; *d* New York, 16 Dec. 1965). Italian tenor. Began career as composer of piano pieces and songs, studying singing later with Piccoli in Milan. Début Vercelli 1911, Alfredo; after appearances in the Italian provinces, engaged Rome 1914 and Buenos Aires. Milan, Sc., 1915, and in same year chosen by Toscanini for his season at Dal Verme, Milan, singing Alfredo and Fenton. Created Ruggero in Puccini's *La rondine,* Monte Carlo, 1917. Chicago Opera 1919-32 and subsequently; N.Y., Met., 1932-5 and 1940-1; San Francisco from 1924. Continued to appear at La Scala, Rome, etc., until 1950, and later in the Italian provinces. Never appeared in opera in England. He possessed a magnificent vocal technique and impeccable taste and style. His voice, which was not large, commanded a wide range of tone colour; his phrasing was aristocratic, his enunciation model. Gigli said of him, 'When Schipa sang we all had to bow down to his greatness.' (R)
Bibl: T. Schipa: *Si confessa* (1961).

Schipper, Emil (*b* Vienna, 19 Aug. 1882; *d* Vienna, 20 July 1957). Austrian bass-baritone. Studied Vienna and Milan with Guarinto. Début Prague 1904, Telramund. Linz, Vienna, V., 1912-15; Munich 1916-22, Vienna 1922-40; London, C.G., 1924-8; Chicago 1928-9. Also appeared at Salzburg and Munich Festivals and in South America. Excelled in Wagner and Strauss. Married to mezzo Maria *Olczewska. (R)

Schippers, Thomas (*b* Kalamazoo, 9 Mar. 1930; *d* N.Y., 16 Dec. 1977). American conductor. Studied Curtis Institute, Philadelphia, and with Olga Samaroff. Début N.Y. 1948 with Lemonade Company. Conducted première of *The Consul* (1950) and Copland's *The Tender Land* (1954); became associated with Menotti, also conducting his *Amahl and the Night Visitors, The Saint of Bleecker Street,* and at the Festival of Two Worlds, Spoleto. N.Y., Met., 1953, conducted première of Barber's *Antony and Cleopatra* which opened new Met. at Lincoln Center in 1966; Milan, Sc., 1967, *Assiedo di Corinto;* Bayreuth 1963, *Meistersinger;* London, C.G., 1968, *Elektra.* (R)

Schira, Francesco (*b* Malta, 21 Aug. 1809; *d* London, 15 Oct. 1883). Italian composer and conductor. After early successes with operas in Milan and Lisbon, became music director at the Princess's in London. Succeeded Benedict at D.L., 1844-7; cond. C.G., 1848; D.L., 1852. The good reception given his operas in London was far exceeded by the success of *Selvaggia* in Venice (1875).

Schlosser, Max (*b* Amberg, 17 Oct. 1835; *d* Utting am Ammersee, 2 Sept. 1916). German

tenor. After an early career in opera, operetta, and drama in Zurich, St Gallen, and Augsburg, left stage and became a baker. Urged by a friend to sing for Perfall, Intendant of Munich opera, who suggested he study David for première of *Meistersinger;* he did this and then sang for Bülow and Wagner, and created David, later Mime at Bayreuth. Munich 1868-1904. Toured with Neumann's company and sang Mime in first *Ring* perfs. in many European cities including London H.M.'s 1882. Repertory also included Max, Almaviva, Lionel, Tonie (*Fille du Régiment*), and the baritone role of Beckmesser. Farewell perf. as Nightwatchman in *Meistersinger* (1904).

Schlusnus, Heinrich (*b* Braubach, 6 Aug. 1888; *d* Frankfurt, 18 June 1952). German baritone. Studied Frankfurt and Berlin with Louis Bacher. Début Hamburg 1915, Herald (*Lohengrin*), Nuremberg 1915-17; Berlin S.O., 1917-51; Chicago 1927-8; Bayreuth 1933. In Germany he established himself as the leading Verdi baritone in the years between the wars. (R)
Bibl: E. Naso: *Heinrich Schlusnus–Mensch und Sänger* (1957).

Schmedes, Erik (*b* Gjentofte, nr Copenhagen, 27 Aug. 1866; *d* Vienna, 23 Mar. 1931). Danish tenor, formerly baritone. Studied in Paris with Artôt, Berlin with Rothmühl, Vienna with Riess. Début Wiesbaden 1891, Herald (*Lohengrin*). Dresden as baritone 1894-7, then further study with Iffert. Début as tenor Siegfried. Vienna 1898-1924; Vienna 1898, Bayreuth 1899-1902, 1906, Parsifal and Siegfried. N.Y., Met., 1908-9. One of the great singers of the Mahler period in Vienna; an admired Florestan and Palestrina. Retired 1924 and taught singing in Vienna. (R)

Schmidt-Isserstedt, Hans (*b* Berlin, 5 May 1900; *d* Hamburg, 28 May 1973). German conductor. Studied with Schreker. After appointments in Barmen-Elberfeld, Rostock, and Darmstadt, engaged Hamburg 1935 as first Kapellmeister. Berlin, Deutsches Opernhaus, 1943. Gly. 1958; London, C.G., 1962. Composed *Hassan gewinnt* (1928). (R)

Schmitt-Walter, Karl (*b* Gernersheim am Rhein, 29 Dec. 1900). German baritone. Studied Nuremberg, and Munich with Richard Trenk. Début Oberhausen 1921. After engagements in Nuremberg, Saarbrücken, and Dortmund, was at Wiesbaden 1929-34, Berlin, D., 1934-50, Munich State Opera 1950-61. Salzburg 1949, Papageno; Bayreuth 1956-61, Beckmesser; London, C.G., with Munich company 1953, Count in *Capriccio;* Edinburgh Festival with Stuttgart Opera, 1958 Count Ebenbach (*Wildschütz*). An elegant, aristocratic singer and actor. Professor of singing, Munich Academy of Music since 1957. (R)

Schneider, Hortense (*b* Paris, 20 April 1833; *d* Paris, 6 Aug. 1920). French soprano. Début

Paris 1855, in Offenbach's *Violoneux*. Sang with success at B.P., Palais Royal, and other theatres. Created title roles in Offenbach's *Belle Hélène*, *Grande Duchesse*, and *La Périchole*.

Schneider-Siemssen, Günther (*b* Augsburg, 7 June 1926). German designer. Studied Munich with Preetorius. Bremen 1954-62; Vienna State Opera since 1962; London, C.G. *Ring* 1964-6; Salzburg since 1965, *Boris*, *Don Giovanni*, *Otello*, *Frau ohne Schatten*, and all Karajan's Easter Festival productions. N.Y., Met., since 1967, *Ring*, *Tristan*. Is adept both at producing traditional settings and using modern techniques with sparse scenery, and what he likes to call 'painting with light'.

Schnorr von Carolsfeld, Ludwig (*b* Munich, 2 July 1836; *d* Dresden, 21 July 1865). German tenor, son of the painter Julius Schnorr von Carolsfeld. Studied Dresden, Leipzig, and Karlsruhe with Eduard Devrient, where he made his début 1853. After engagement at Wiesbaden, Frankfurt, Mainz, and Düsseldorf, became leading tenor at Dresden 1860-5. Wagner, who had heard him sing Lohengrin, insisted on his creating Tristan, Munich 1865. Died shortly afterwards of rheumatic fever and heart failure.

Schnorr von Carolsfeld (orig. Garrigues), **Malvina** (*b* Copenhagen, 7 Dec. 1832; *d* Karlsruhe, 8 Feb. 1904). Danish soprano. Wife of above. Created Isolde opposite her husband. After his death sang in Hamburg and Karlsruhe, then taught.
Bibl: C. H. Garrigues: *Ein ideales Sängerpaar* (1937).

Schoeck, Othmar (*b* Brunnen, 1 Sept. 1886; *d* Zurich, 8 Mar. 1957). Swiss composer. His sensitivity to poetry and love of the human voice led him to express himself most fully in song and in opera. Some early stage works included a comic opera *Don Ranudo* (1919), and this period culminated in *Venus* (1919). Turning away from his first Romantic manner, he purged and refashioned his style to suit what he felt to be modern requirements; his success is shown in *Penthesilea* (1927), regarded as the peak of his achievement. Two later operas, *Massimilla Doni* (1937) and *Das Schloss Dürande* (1943), have also won wide respect.

Schoeffler, Paul (*b* Dresden, 15 Sept. 1897; *d* Amersham, Bucks., 21 Nov. 1977). German later Austrian, baritone. Studied Dresden with Staegemann, Berlin with Grenzebach, Milan with Sammarco. Début Dresden 1925, Herald (*Lohengrin*), remaining there until 1938; Vienna, S.O., 1938-65. London, C.G., 1934-9 and 1949-53; N.Y., Met., 1949-53 and 1954-6 Bayreuth 1943-4 Sachs; Salzburg 1938-41, 1947, 1949-65 and in Italy. Starting his career as

a lyric baritone, he graduated into the Wagner repertory, coming to be regarded as an outstanding post-war Hans Sachs. Among the roles he created were Danton in Einem's *Dantons Tod* and Jupiter in *Liebe der Danae*. Also appeared in the first Salzburg performance of *Capriccio* as La Roche. (R)

Schoenberg, Arnold (*b* Vienna, 13 Sept. 1874; *d* Los Angeles, 13 July 1951). Austrian composer. Schoenberg's four operas cover the major part of his creative life. *Erwartung* (1909, prod. 1924) was one of the first works in which tonality was definitely abandoned; *Von Heute auf Morgen* (1930) was the first 12-note opera; *Moses und Aron* (two acts finished 1932, resumed 1951; prod. 1957) was left unfinished by the composer, though the extant two acts have proved complete enough to be capable of providing an overwhelming experience in performance.

In making use of only one character, a woman, for *Erwartung*, Schoenberg is able to follow with extraordinary depth of penetration the nightmare journey of her mind; there is no characterization (no thematic development), but a full world of the woman's crazing mind is explored. *Die glückliche Hand* (1913, prod. 1924) again uses one character, with mimed parts and a chorus; it concerns the quest for truth of the artist, whose *glückliche Hand* is his individual, specially favoured touch. *Von Heute auf Morgen* belies the suspicion that 12-note comic opera is a contradiction in terms: it is a brilliantly observed comedy of a witty and determined woman keeping hold of her husband – satirical, farcical, yet underpinned with deep understanding and optimism.

Moses und Aron did not reach the stage until 1957. Schoenberg's largest opera, it is also his fullest expression of the quest theme that absorbed him so deeply. It concerns communication between God and Man, and the distortion suffered by pure truth (received by Moses) when it undergoes exposition (by Aaron) in terms comprehensible to Man. Schoenberg's religious nature and his artist's concern over communication were profoundly touched by this theme, and the opera has by its emotional power done much to overcome prejudices against the composer. Wrote the libretto for Zemlinsky's *Sarema* (1897).
Bibl: K. Wörner: *Gotteswort und Magie* (1959, trans. as *Schoenberg's 'Moses and Aron'*, 1963).

Schöne, Lotte (orig. Charlotte Bodenstein) (*b* Vienna, 15 Dec. 1891; *d* Paris, 22 Dec. 1977). Austrian soprano. Studied Vienna with Johannes Rees, Luise Ress, and Maria Brossement. Début Vienna, V.O., 1912, a Bridesmaid in *Freischütz*; S.O., 1917-26 Berlin 1925-33. Sang regularly at Salzburg 1922-35, where her best roles included Zerlina, Despina, and

Blondchen. London, C.G., 1927, where she was the first London Liù. Settled in Paris 1933, becoming a French citizen and appearing as guest at O. and O.C., where she sang Mélisande in 1933. Returned to Germany 1948 as guest in Berlin. Retired 1953. (R)

School for Fathers, The. See *Quatro rusteghi, I.*

Schorr, Friedrich (*b* Nagyvárad, 2 Sept. 1888; *d* Farmington, Conn., 14 Aug. 1953). Hungarian, later American, bass-baritone. Studied Vienna, and after singing small roles with the Chicago Opera 1912, made official début at Graz as Wotan, same year. Graz 1914-16; Prague 1916-18; Cologne 1918-23; Berlin 1923-31; N.Y., German Grand Opera Co., 1923; N.Y., Met., 1924-43; London, C.G., 1924-33; Bayreuth 1925-33. Guest appearances at many other leading operatic centres. Considered by many the greatest Wotan of the 1920s and 1930s, and also an outstanding Sachs and Dutchman. In N.Y. sang Daniello in the American première of *Jonny spielt auf* and the title role in *Shvanda*. In his prime his voice was opulent, noble, and dramatic, capable of ravishing beauty in *mezza voce* passages. (R)

Schramm, Friedrich (*b* Frankfurt, 26 Jan. 1900). German producer. Studied law. Stage director, Darmstadt 1921; Breslau 1923; Duisburg 1924; Düsseldorf 1926; Basle 1934 and 1939-50 and again from 1962; Prague 1937. Generalintendant, Wiesbaden 1951-62. Produced the first post-war Wagner performances and *Fidelio*, C.G., 1947-51. His father **Hermann Schramm** (1871-1951) was a well-known German *Spieltenor* who sang David at Bayreuth (1899), and sang at Frankfurt 1900-33; returned Frankfurt 1946, Eisenstein.

Schreier, Peter (*b* Meissen, 29 July 1935). German tenor. Studied Leipzig with F. Polster, Dresden with Winkler. Member of the Kreuzchor in Dresden, and sang as one of the three Genii in *Zauberflöte* in 1944 just before the closing of the old Semper O. House. Début Dresden, 1959, 1st Prisoner (*Fidelio*). Dresden, S.O., 1959-63; Berlin, S.O., since 1963; N.Y., Met., 1968; Vienna S.O., since 1967; Salzburg since 1967 as Tamino, Ferrando, Loge, David; London, S.W., with Hamburg State Opera 1966, Ferrando. Large repertory also includes Sextus, Leukippos, Flamand, and Lensky. Gifted singer and actor; considered by many an outstanding Mozart singer, in the line of Tauber and Wunderlich. (R)

Schreker, Franz (*b* Monaco, 23 Mar. 1878; *d* Berlin, 21 Mar. 1934). Austrian composer. Studied Vienna with Fuchs and Grädener. His first serious opera, *Der ferne Klang* (1912), made a powerful impression on his own generation; Schoenberg quoted passages of it in his *Harmonielehre*, and Berg, who made

the piano score, was influenced (in *Wozzeck*) by its use of set forms. Three operas followed – *Das Spielwerk und die Prinzessin* (1913), *Die Gezeichneten* (1918), which at last won Schreker a wider success, and *Der Schatzgräber* (1920), establishing him as an avant-garde leader. But this position was challenged by the reaction against late Romanticism that followed the war, and his operas were less and less well received. His position as director of the Berlin Hochschule (1920-32) was taken from him by the Nazis, and the ensuing sharp decline in his fortunes hastened his death. His best work has real power, and – despite such diverse influences as Wagner and Debussy, Puccini and Strauss – an original if limited world of its own.
Bibl: F. Bayerl: *Franz Schrekers Opernwerk* (1928).

Schröder-Devrient, Wilhelmine (*b* Hamburg, 6 Dec. 1804; *d* Coburg, 26 Jan. 1860). German soprano. Daughter of Friedrich Schröder (1744-1816), the first German Don Giovanni, and the actress Sophie Schröder, née Bürger (1781-1868). Appeared in ballet and drama (e.g. as Ophelia), in Hamburg and Vienna; then studied singing in Vienna with Giuseppe Mozatti. Début as singer, Kä., 20 Jan. 1821 (Pamina). Made a great impression, notably on Weber when he conducted her as Agathe; he thought her the best of all Agathes, and said that she had revealed more than he had believed the role to contain. Her greatest truimph was as Leonore in Nov. 1822. She had been rehearsed by Beethoven, who promised to write an opera for her. This was her greatest role, and her performance inspired Wagner to write a famous letter to her declaring that she had roused him to his sense of vocation as an opera composer. She sang in Dresden 1822-47, where she married the actor Karl Devrient (divorced 1828). Her most famous roles now were Donna Anna, Euryanthe, Reiza, Norma, Romeo, Valentine, and Rossini's Desdemona. Berlin 1828. Paris 1831-2. London, King's, 1832, Leonore, Donna Anna, Lady Macbeth (*Macbeth* by Chelard, the conductor of the season); 1833, Agathe, Euryanthe, Pamina, Desdemona; 1837, Leonore, Amina, Norma. Despite a decline in her vocal powers, she successfully created Adriano (*Rienzi*), Senta, and Venus; she also sang Gluck's Iphigenia (*Aulide*). Her last appearance was in Riga, 17 Dec. 1847. She remarried twice.

Though deficient in vocal technique (as Berlioz forcefully observed in his *Memoirs*), she was a powerful and moving actress, dubbed 'The Queen of Tears' when seen to weep on stage. Her Leonore was by every contemporary account the greatest of the age: Moscheles preferred her to Malibran. At a time when few singers gave serious attention to acting, she revealed new possibilities to composers, including Weber and above all Wagner, who includes a detailed tribute to her in *Über Schauspieler und Sänger* (dedicated to her memory). The first great singing actress.

Bibl: C. Hagemann: *Wilhelmine Schröder-Devrient* (1904).

Schröder-Feinen, Ursula (*b* Gelsenkirchen, 21 July 1936). German soprano. Studied Gelsenkirchen with Maria Helm. Joined chorus Gelsenkirchen Opera 1958 and began career there as operetta singer 1961 in *Vogellhänder*; a week later replaced a sick colleague as Aida. Her roles at Gelsenkirchen (1961-8) included Cleopatra, Alcestis, Oscar, Bess (*Porgy and Bess*), Leonore, Chrysothemis, Salome, and Turandot. Düsseldorf, Deutsche Oper am Rhein, 1968-72, where she added Elektra, Kundry, and Brünnhilde to her repertory. N.Y., Met., since 1970; Bayreuth since 1971 as Senta, Ortrud, Brünnhilde, Kundry; Salzburg since 1975 as Dyer's Wife and Ortrud; Edinburgh Festival with Berlin, D., 1975, Salome. Paris, O., 1976-7 Brünnhilde in Solti *Ring*. Guest appearances Milan, Naples, Amsterdam, Prague, etc. One of the most exciting talents to have emerged in Germany in the late 1960s; proved herself to be in the great German *Hochdramatische* tradition, with a warm voice and personality. (R)

Schubert, Franz (Peter) (*b* Vienna, 31 Jan. 1797; *d* Vienna, 19 Nov. 1828). Austrian composer. Studied with Ružička and Salieri. Schubert's operas fall into three categories. Most of them are Singspiels (six completed); one of the completed works is a melodrama; three completed works are true operas. All his life he was fascinated by opera, but by the time of his early death he had not yet made the medium distinctively his own. His first opera, *Des Teufels Lustschloss* (comp. 1813-14), is a 3-act work based on Kotzebue, which for all its naive Romantic nonsense impressed Salieri with its music: this includes a charming drinking song and some admirably scored numbers, including melodrama, that have a certain fluency of movement between them. In 1815 came four Singspiels. *Der vierjährige Posten* is a slight, amusing piece in simpler style. *Ferrando* (prod. 1918) is rather weightier, and includes a most imaginative aria for the heroine that makes skilful use of orchestral effects. *Claudine von Villa Bella* (unfin.) is less striking; but *Die Freunde von Salamanca* (prod. 1928) shows, in the absence of the text, a greater sense of music interacting with the plot, and includes an excellent chorus of winegrowers.

In 1816 came *Die Bürgschaft* (unfin.). This was followed in 1819 by a Singspiel, *Die Zwillingsbrüder* (prod. 1820), and then in 1821 to 1823 his three most important operatic

works. Schubert himself set most store by *Alfonso und Estrella* (comp. 1822, prod. 1954), his most lyrical and most Romatic opera. Next came *Die Verschworenen* (also known as *Der häusliche Krieg,* comp. 1823, prod. 1861), an amusing little 1-act Singspiel transferring the situation of Aristophanes's *Lysistrata* to the time of the Crusades, with the women on sexual strike in order to keep their husbands at home: there are some charming separate numbers, and a witty dramatic contrast between the male and female marches. *Fierrabras* (comp. 1823, prod. 1897) shows a more mature promise, however: though it occasionally has an insecure grasp of dramatic timing and a tendency to let movements bulk too large for their dramatic role, it has the capacity to use a plot based on rather feeble Romantic gestures for some advanced music that includes a suggestion of Leitmotiv. It is a freely composed work, including elements of Singspiel and of melodrama within the framework of a full-scale opera: there are only three actual arias in the opera, and many more scenes which merge swiftly and easily into one another. Had he lived to write further operas, he might well have found a way of putting his greatest gifts into the form: *Fierrabras* certainly indicates the possibility.

Bibl: G. Abraham (ed.): *Schubert* (1946) (incl. chapter by A. Hyatt King on the stage music); A. Hutchings: *Schubert.*

Schubert, Richard (*b* Dessau, 15 Dec. 1885; *d* Oberstaufen, 24 Oct. 1958). German tenor, formerly baritone. Studied with Rudolf von Milde. Début Strasburg, 1904 as baritone. After a further period of study with Vanzo in Milan and with Nietan in Dresden, engaged as tenor, Nuremberg 1910-13; Wiesbaden, 1913-17; Hamburg, 1917-21; Vienna, S., 1920-29. Chicago 1921-22, *Tannhäuser,* Tristan. Retired 1938 and taught at Mannheim and Heidelberg. (R)

Schuch, Ernst von (*b* Graz, 23 Nov. 1846; *d* Dresden, 10 May 1914). Austrian conductor. Studied Graz and Vienna. Début Breslau 1867. After engagements in Würzburg, Graz, and Basle, went to Dresden in 1872, becoming court conductor in 1873, and remaining there until 1914. Ennobled by the Emperor of Austria 1877. Generalmusikdirektor Dresden Opera from 1882, raising it to great heights. Conducted the first performances of *Feuersnot, Salome, Elektra,* and *Rosenkavalier,* and memorable performances of *The Ring* and other Wagner operas. Was instrumental in introducing Puccini into the repertory there. He married the soprano **Clementine Proska** (orig. Procházka) (1850-1932) who became the leading coloratura soprano at Dresden 1873-1898. She was a Marchesi pupil and sang Aennchen and Eva in London at C.G., 1884.

Their daughter **Liesel von Schuch** (*b* 1891) was a coloratura soprano who sang in Dresden and Vienna.
Bibl: F. von Schuch: *Richard Strauss, Ernst von Schuch und Dresdens Oper* (1953).

Schuh, Oscar Fritz (*b* Munich, 15 Jan. 1904). German producer. After holding positions in Gera, Hamburg, and elsewhere, was appointed Oberspielleiter of the Vienna Opera, where his productions of Mozart operas and *Wozzeck* were famous. For several years he was director of the Berlin Kurfürstendamm T., from which position he resigned in 1959 to become Generalintendant of the Cologne Opera, remaining there until 1962.

Schüler, Johannes (*b* Vietz/Neumark, 21 June 1894; *d* Berlin, 3 Oct. 1966). German conductor. Studied Berlin. Début Gleiwitz 1920. Held appointments at Königsberg, Oldenburg, Halle, Essen, Berlin, S.O., 1936-49. Generalmusikdirektor, Hanover 1949-60, where he built up a very large repertory including *Wozzeck, Mathis der Maler, Volo di Notte, Jenůfa,* and *From the House of the Dead.* (R)

Schumann, Elisabeth (*b* Merseburg, 13 June 1885; *d* New York, 23 Apr. 1952). German soprano. Studied Berlin, Dresden, Hamburg. Début Hamburg 1909, Shepherd (*Tannhäuser*); Hamburg, 1912-19; N.Y., Met., 1914-15; Vienna 1919-37; London, C.G., 1924-31. Sang regularly at Salzburg and Munich Festivals. Left Austria after the *Anschluss* and settled in U.S.A., teaching singing at the Curtis Institute. She possessed a voice of pure silvery clarity. Her Sophie has rarely been equalled, and in Mozart soubrette roles (Susanna, Zerlina, Blondchen) and as Adele she was incomparable. (R)
Bibl: E. Puritz: *The Teaching of Elisabeth Schumann* (1956).

Schumann, Robert (*b* Zwickau, 8 June 1810; *d* Endenich, 29 July 1856). German composer. Schumann's one opera, *Genoveva* (1850), includes some agreeable music but reveals his inability to think in dramatic terms; there is no real characterization, and the effects are invariably muffled, in part through the composer's scorn of all he thought cheap in Italian opera.

Schumann-Heink (orig. Rössler), **Ernestine** (*b* Lieben, 15 June 1861; *d* Hollywood, 17 Nov. 1936). Czech, later American, contralto. Studied Graz and Dresden, where she made her début 1878, Azucena as Tini Rössler. Hamburg 1883-98; engaged on a ten-year contract Berlin 1898, but purchased her release in order to sing regularly in America. Chicago 1898; N.Y., Met., 1899-1903, then most seasons until 1932; London, C.G., 1892 (Erda, Fricka, Waltraute in first C.G. *Ring*), 1899-1900; Bayreuth

1896-1906. Created Klytemnestra in *Elektra*. Repertory of 150 roles; she also sang on Broadway in a comic opera, *Love's Lottery* (1904) and as Katisha in *The Mikado* in 1931. After her retirement from the stage, she appeared in the film *Here's to Romance* (1935). (R)
Bibl: M. Lawton: *Schumann-Heink, the Last of the Titans* (1928).

Schuster, Ignaz (*b* Vienna, 20 July 1779; *d* Vienna, 6 Nov. 1835). Austrian actor, singer, and composer. Studied Vienna with Eybler and Volkert. Became known as a comic actor and singer from 1801 at the L. From 1804 also wrote music for light theatrical pieces. In 1813 created the role of Staberl in Bäuerle's *Die Bürger von Wien,* making of it one of the last standard comic figures of the Viennese popular theatre (such as the long-established Kasperl and Hanswurst). In 1818 he appeared in the title-role of his own *Die falsche Primadonna* (a title altered by the censor from *Die falsche Catalani*); the work was long popular. The emergence of *Raimund did not diminish his popularity, despite his jealousy of the younger man. He was also known as a church musician, and composed music for Beethoven's death and acted as coffin-bearer at the funeral.

Schützendorf. German family of singers.
(1) **Gustav** (*b* Cologne, 1883; *d* Berlin, 27 Apr. 1937). Baritone. Studied Cologne and Milan. Debut Krefeld then N.Y., Met., 1922-35. He was a successful Alberich, Beckmesser, and Faninal. (R)
(2) **Leo** (*b* Cologne, 7 May 1886; *d* Berlin, 16 Dec. 1931). German bass. Brother of the above. Studied Cologne with d'Arnals. Début Düsseldorf, 1908. Krefeld 1909-12; Darmstadt 1913-17; Wiesbaden 1917-19; Vienna 1919-20; Berlin, S., 1920-29 – created Wozzeck and made 445 appearances in 47 roles including Ochs, Boris, Beckmesser, Alberich, and Méphistophélès. Appeared in *Bettelstudent* with Alpar and Pattiera without obtaining leave from the S.O. and was accordingly dismissed. This led to a persecution mania and a breakdown resulting in his death in 1931. (R) In addition to Gustav, he had two more brothers who were singers:
(3) **Alfons** (*b* Vught, nr Hertogenbosch, 25 May 1882; *d* Weimar, 1946). German bass-baritone. Studied Cologne with Walter. Début Düsseldorf. Bayreuth 1908-12, Donner, Klingsor, Telramund; London, C.G., 1910, Wotan, Gunther. (R)
(4) **Guido** (*b* Vught, 22 Apr. 1880; *d* Apr. 1967). German baritone. Sang in Strasburg, Krefeld, Bremen, often under the name of Guido Schützendorf an der Mayr. In 1919 he made a film of *Der fliegende Holländer.* (R) A performance of *Meistersinger* in Bremen during World War I featured Alfons as Sachs,

Leo as Beckmesser, Gustav as Pogner, and Guido as Kothner – the only occasion all 4 brothers sang together.
Bibl: E. Schützendorf: *Kunstenblut, Leo Schützendorf und seine Brüdern* (1943).

Schwanda the Bagpiper. See *Shvanda the Bagpiper.*

Schwarzkopf, Elisabeth (*b* Jarocin, nr Poznań, 9 Dec. 1915). German soprano. Studied Berlin with Lula Mysz-Gmeiner and Ivogün. Début Berlin, Stä. O., 1938, Flower-maiden. Remained in Berlin until 1942, first singing small roles, then graduating to Musetta, Susanna, and Zerbinetta, in which part she made her Vienna début 1942. Sang coloratura roles there until 1947, when she became a lyric soprano. London, C.G., 1947, with Vienna S.O., Donna Elvira; 1948-51, member of permanent company singing in English; returned 1959 as Marschallin. Salzburg 1947, Milan, Sc., 1948-63; San Francisco 1955; Chicago 1959; N.Y., Met. 1964-6. Created Anne Trulove (*Rake's Progress*) 1951. Awarded the Lilli Lehmann medal by Mozart Society of Salzburg, and the Italian *Orfeo d'Oro*. Married Walter Legge, artistic director of the Philharmonia Orchestra and Columbia Records. Farewell stage. perf., Marschallin, Brussels, 1972. (R)

Schweigsame Frau, Die (The Silent Woman). Opera in 3 acts by Richard Strauss; text by Stefan Zweig, after Ben Jonson's drama *Epicœne* (1609). Prod. Dresden, 24 June 1935, with Cebotari, Sack, Kremer, Ahlersmeyer, Plaschke, cond. Böhm; N.Y., C.C., 7 Oct. 1958, with Carroll, Moody, Alexander, Beattie, cond. Herrmann; London, C.G., 20 Nov. 1961, with Holt, Vaughan, Macdonald, J. Ward, D. Ward, cond. Kempe.

Sir Morosus (bass), a retired English admiral, cannot abide noise of any kind. His nephew, Henry (ten.) is secretly married to Aminta (sop.), and both are members of a group of travelling actors. With the help of the Barber (bar.), they arrange a mock marriage between Morosus and 'Timida', the silent woman, actually Aminta in disguise. Once married, she emerges like Norina in *Don Pasquale* as a noisy termagant. Morosus gives the young people his blessing and begins to adopt a more mellow attitude to life.

Other operas on the subject are by Salieri (*Angiolina*, 1800) and Lothar (*Lord Spleen*, 1930).

Schwerin. Town in Mecklenburg, Germany. The first opera performances were given in the 18th cent. in the Schlosstheater: Rösler wrote *Das Winzerfest der Hirten* (1792) for Ludwigslust. I.C.C. Fischer opened the Ballhaustheater 1788; this burnt down in 1831, and was rebuilt in Schinkel style in 1836. Performances of *Don Giovanni* were given in 1790, and the catholic repertory that developed included French opéra comique. Under Flotow, who was Intendant 1855-63, a high standard was maintained: among visitors was Jenny Lind, singing Bellini. This level was continued under Alois Schmitt, A. von Wolzogen (1867-83), and Karl von Ledebur (1894-1913), the latter organizing some distinguished Gluck performances. The Staatstheater opened 1886. Herman Zumpe was music director 1897-1901; he, and his successor Willibald Kaehler, gave attention to Wagner and to other contemporary works. An operetta ensemble was formed in 1918. In 1936 Pfitzner conducted his *Der arme Heinrich* there. Particular attention is now given to Slavonic opera.

Schwetzingen. Town in Baden-Württemberg, Germany. Since 1956 there has been an annual festival in the beautiful rococo theatre of the Castle, including premières of works by Egk, Henze (*Elegy for Young Lovers*), Fortner, Reutter, Klebe, and Reimann, also the first German *Turn of the Screw.* There have been revivals of works by Monteverdi, J. C. Bach, Campra, Galuppi, Handel, Purcell, Rameau, and Gluck.

Scio (LeGrand), **Julie-Angélique.** (*b* Lille, 1768; *d* Paris, 14 July 1807). French soprano. Début 1786 under the name of Mlle Grécy. After engagements in Montpellier, Avignon, and Marseilles, married the violinist Etienne Scio (1766-1796) who took her to Paris; début at the O.C., 1792, then O., where she created title-role in *Medée* (1797) and Constance in *Les Deux journées* (1800) as well as roles in works by Le Sueur, Dalayrac, Berton, etc. Said to have been a gifted singer with strong dramatic ability.

Scipione. Opera in 3 acts by Handel; text by P. A. Rolli, after Zeno's *Scipione nelle Spagne* (originally written in 1710, probably for Caldara). Prod. London, Hm., 23 Mar. 1726, with Cuzzoni, Baldi, Senesino, Boschi. Revived Handel Opera Society, 1967.

Sciutti, Graziella (*b* Turin, 17 Apr. 1932). Italian soprano. Studied Rome. Début Aix-en-Provence 1951, Lucy (*The Telephone*). Here she often sang as Susanna, Zerlina, and also created Marianne in Sauguet's *Les Caprices de Marianne*. Gly. 1954-9; London, C.G., 1956-62; Milan, Sc., since 1956, especially at the Piccola Scala where she has proved a delightful Despina, Norina, Cecchina (*La buona figliuola*), etc.; Salzburg 1958-66. Her vivacity and pointed phrasing and diction make her an outstanding soubrette. Produced and sang in *Voix humaine*, Gly. 1977. (R)

Scott, (Sir) **Walter** (*b* Edinburgh, 15 Aug. 1771; *d* Abbotsford, 21 Sept. 1832). Scottish novelist and poet. Operas on his works are as follows:

The Lady of the Lake (1810): Bishop (*The Knight of Snowdoun*, 1811); Rossini (*La donna del lago*, 1819); Lemière de Corvey (Rossini pasticcio 1825); Vesque von Püttlingen (1829).

Waverley (1814): Holstein (*Die Gastfreunde*, 1852, rev. as *Die Hochländer*,1876); Dulcken (*MacIvor*, ?1865).

Old Mortality (1817): Bishop (*The Battle of Bothwell Brigg*, 1820); Bellini (*I Puritani*, distantly, 1835).

The Black Dwarf (1817): C. E. Horn (*The Wizard*, 1817).

Rob Roy (1818): Blanchard (*Diane de Vernon*, 1831); Curmi (1833); Flotow (1836); De Koven (1894); Grieve (1950).

The Heart of Midlothian (1818): Bishop (1819); Carafa (*La Prison d'Édimbourg*, 1833); Ricci (*La prigione d'Edimburgo*, 1838); Berlijn (*Le Lutinn de Culloden*, comp. *c*1848); MacCunn (*Jeanie Deans*, 1894).

The Bride of Lammermoor (1819): Adam (*La Caleb de Walter Scott*, 1827); Carafa (*Le nozze di Lammermoor*, 1829); Rieschi (1831); Damse (1832); Bredal (*Bruden fra Lammermoor*, 1832); Mazzucato (*La fidanzata di Lammermoor*, 1834); Donizetti (*Lucia di Lammermoor*, 1835).

The Abbot (1820): Fétis (*Marie Stuart en Écosse*, 1823).

The Legend of Montrose (1820): Bishop (1820).

Ivanhoe (1820): Rossini (pasticcio, 1826, in Scott's presence); Marschner (*Der Templer und die Jüdin*, 1829); Pacini (1832); Nicolai (*Il Templario*, 1840); Sari (1863); Pisani (*Rebecca*, 1865); Castegnier (*Rébecca*, *c*1882); Ciardi (1888); Sullivan (1891); Lewis (1907).

Kenilworth (1821): Auber (*Leicester*, 1823); Donizetti (*Elisabetta al castello di Kenilworth*, 1829); Damse (1832); Weyse (*Festen paa Kenilworth*, 1836); Seidelmann (1843); Schira (rehearsed 1848); Badia (*Il Conte di Leicester*, 1851); Caiani (1878); De Lara (*Amy Robsart*, 1893); Klein (1895); Schiuma (1920).

Peveril of the Peak (1822): C. E. Horn (1826).

Quentin Durward (1823): Laurent (1848); Gevaert (1858); Maclean (comp. 1893, prod. 1920).

Redgauntlet (1824): Gomis (*Le Revenant*, 1833).

The Talisman (1825): Bishop (1826); Pacini (1829); Adam (*Richard en Palestine*, 1844); Balfe (1874).

Woodstock (1826): Flotow (*Alice*, 1837).

The Highland Widow (1827): Grisar (*Sarah*, 1836).

Tales of a Grandfather (1828): Rossini (pasticcio, *Robert Bruce*, 1846).

The Fair Maid of Perth (1828): Bizet (1867); Lucilla (1877).

Bibl: J. Mitchell: *The Walter Scott Operas* (1977).

Scotti, Antonio (*b* Naples, 25 Jan. 1866; *d* Naples, 26 Feb. 1936). Italian baritone. Studied Naples with Triffani Paganini. Début Malta 1889, Amonasro. After nine seasons in Italy, Spain, and South America, engaged for Scala 1898, as Hans Sachs. London, C.G., 1899, Don Giovanni, singing there regularly until 1910 and 1913-14. N.Y., Met., 1899-1933. First London Scarpia and Sharpless; a fine Falstaff and Iago. First N.Y. Scarpia and many others. Though not large, his voice was of great beauty, and used with rare artistry. His acting was outstanding. (R)

Scottish Opera. The company was founded in 1962 by Alexander Gibson, conductor of the Scottish National Orchestra. Its first season in Glasgow consisted of six performances, three each of *Madama Butterfly* and *Pelléas et Mélisande*. Under Gibson and with Peter Hemmings as general administrator, the company had given 800 performances of more than 50 operas by the end of the 1974-5 season. Its policy has been to perform neglected masterpieces, which, as far as Scotland was concerned, included *Boris Godunov*, *Otello*, and *Falstaff* as well as small-scale works such as *The Turn of the Screw* and *Albert Herring*. It has also mounted very successful productions of *The Trojans* and *The Ring*. Until 1975 performances were chiefly given in the King's Theatre, Glasgow, with shorter seasons in Edinburgh, Aberdeen, and other Scottish towns, as well as visits to a few northern English cities, including Leeds and Newcastle upon Tyne. From 1967 the company began to appear at the Edinburgh Festival, where it has been heard in *The Rake's Progress*, *The Trojans*, *Peter Grimes*, *Elegy for Young Lovers*, *Alceste*, *Macbeth* and Robin Orr's *Hermiston*; it has also given the premières of Orr's *Full Circle*; Hamilton's The *Catiline Conspiracy* and Musgrave's *Mary, Queen of Scots*. Leading British and foreign artists appear regularly with the company, and a number of Scottish-born singers have developed their careers with Scottish Opera. In the autumn of 1975 the company moved into its permanent home at the refurbished T. Royal, Glasgow, which became the first city in Great Britain to have opened its own opera house since the Second World War. In 1977 Hemmings was succeeded as general administrator by Peter Ebert.
Bibl: C. Wilson: *Scottish Opera* (1970).

Scotto, Renata (*b* Savona, 24 Feb. 1933). Italian soprano. Studied Milan with Ghirardini and Llopart. Début Savona, 1952. Violetta. Milan, Sc., since 1953. London, Stoll, 1957, Mimì, Adina, Violetta, Donna Elvira; Edinburgh 1957, Amina (*Sonnambula*), successfully replacing

Callas at final performance; London, C.G., 1962-71; N.Y., Met., since 1965. After 1970 she turned increasingly to the lirico-spinto repertory. (R)

Scribe, Eugène (*b* Paris, 25 Dec. 1791; *d* Paris, 21 Feb. 1861). French librettist. His enormous productivity of librettos – his complete works comprise 76 volumes – led to references to the 'Scribe factory'; but his brilliant sense of the stage is confirmed by the frequency with which the best composers of the age turned to him. The list, with the numbers of librettos used, includes the following. Adam (7), Auber (38), Audran (1), Bellini (1, *Sonnambula*), Boieldieu (4, incl. *La Dame blanche*), Cherubini (1), Cilea (1, *Adriana Lecouvreur*), Clapisson (6), Donizetti (5 incl. *Elisir d'amore* and *Favorite*), Gatzambide (1), Gomis (1), Gounod (1), Grisar (1), Halévy (6, incl. *La Juive*), Hérold (2), Kastner (1), Kovařović (1), Lavrangas (1), Macfarren (1), Meyerbeer (5, incl. *L'Africaine, Les Huguenots*, and *Le Prophète*), Moniuszko (1), Offenbach (2), Rossi (1), Rossini (2 incl. *Le Comte Ory*), Setaccioli (1), Södermann (1), Suppé (1), Verdi (2, *Vêpres Siciliennes* and *Ballo in maschera*), Zandonai (1), and Zimmermann (1).

Scutta, Andreas (*b* Vienna, 1806; *d* Prague, 24 Feb. 1863). Austrian composer. He took up music after acting in Rossini's *Mosè* at the W.; then studied singing. Lost his voice, so returned to acting; also composed the music for many farces and parodies. His 30-odd scores for the L., W., and J. include many parodies, among them *Robert der Wau Wau* (1833, parody of *Robert le Diable*). His greatest original success was *Eisenbahnheiraten* (1844), a setting of Nestroy. He married Therese Palmer, who had created Isouard's *Cendrillon* aged 13.

Searle, Humphrey (*b* Oxford, 26 Aug. 1915). English composer. His first opera was a 1-act setting of a Gogol story, *The Diary of a Madman* (1958): a Berlin Festival commission, this made use of electronic music as well as a normal orchestra. *The Photo of the Colonel* (1964) was a setting of Ionesco, a comedy making extensive use of rapid parlando for the singers with the burden of the commentary in the orchestra. *Hamlet* (1968) matches some contemporary operatic techniques to Shakespeare's tragedy, and provides some ingenious music.

Seattle. City in Washington, USA. First musical stage production was an operetta version of *Uncle Tom's Cabin* in the early 1870s. The usual touring companies provided opera until the founding of a permanent company 1964, which performs in the Opera House (cap. 3,100), built during the 1962 World Fair. Glynn Ross is the company's artistic director. Until

1967 the repertory comprised popular works; in 1968 Ward's *The Crucible* was produced, followed by the première of Floyd's *Of Mice and Men* (1970), and Pastieri's *The Black Widow* (1972), as well as a complete *Ring* in both German and English since 1972 as an annual summer festival.

Sebastian, George (orig. György Sebestyén) (*b* Budapest, 17 Aug. 1903). Hungarian conductor. Studied Budapest with Kodály and Munich with Bruno Walter, where he worked as a coach. Répétiteur, N.Y., Met., 1923–4, as Georg Sebestyen. Leipzig 1924–7; Berlin, Städtische Opera, 1927–31; San Francisco 1944–7; chief conductor, Paris O., 1947–73, especially in the German repertory. Frequent appearances in French provinces and in Geneva. (R)

Secret, The (Cz., *Tajemstvi*). Opera in 3 acts by Smetana; text by Eliska Krásnohorská. Prod. Prague, Cz., 18 Sept. 1878 with Sittová, Fibichová, Vávra, Čech, Mareš, Lev; Oxford 7 Dec. 1956 with C. Hunter, Baker, D. Minton, Reynolds, N. Noble, cond. Westrup.

The plot concerns the separation through pride and poverty of two lovers, Rose (con.) and Councillor Kalina (bar.), who after many vicissitudes, including their mockery by the ballad singer Skřivanek, discover one another when Kalina, seeking a promised treasure, follows an underground passage that leads him into Rose's house.

Sedaine, Michel-Jean (*b* Paris, 4 July 1719; *d* Paris, 17 May 1797). French librettist. Originally a stonemason, then an architect; wrote vaudevilles for the O.C. after the *Guerre des Bouffons. His first successes were comédies mêlées d'ariettes, in the style of Favart, but as in his text for Philidor's *Blaise le savetier* (1759), with greater attention to the detail of the action and the setting. His text for Monsigny's *On ne s'avise jarmais de tout* (1761) was an example for Beaumarchais in his *Barbier de Séville*. The realism of his plots and incidents (as opposed to the idealized pastoral convention) impressed his contemporaries, despite the poor quality of his actual verse: his greatest strength is his instinctive grasp of theatrical character and situation. His librettos for Monsigny's *Le Deserteur* (1769) and Grétry's *Richard Coeur de Lion* (1784) transform the *larmoyant* element from being merely a touch of colour for the *ingénu*, into the atmosphere of the whole drama, and subdue the comic element: their mixture of comic and serious disconcerted audiences, but was influential on *Rescue opera, and even on Romantic opera. Two more important librettos were for Grétry's *Raoul Barbe-Bleue* (1789) and *Guillaume Tell* (1791). Sedaine helped to increase the importance of comic opera, and hence to give the Opéra-Comique a new stature vis-à-vis the Opéra.

Sedie, Enrico delle. See *Delle Sedie.*

Seefehlner, Egon (*b* Vienna, 3 June 1912).
Austrian administrator. Studied Vienna. After a
business and literary career, he was appointed
secretary-general of the Wiener Konzert-
hausgesellschaft, 1946-51. Vienna S.O. 1954-
61 as assistant to Böhm and then Karajan.
Berlin, D., 1961-72 as assistant general
administrator; general administrator 1972-5.
Vienna S.O., same post, from 1975.

Seefried, Irmgard (*b* Köngetried, 9 Oct. 1919).
German soprano of Austrian parentage.
Studied Augsburg and Munich. Début Aachen,
Priestess (*Aida*), remaining there until 1943;
Vienna since 1943. Chosen by Strauss to sing
the Composer (*Ariadne*) in his 80th birthday
celebrations. London, C.G., with Vienna Company 1947; N.Y., Met. 1953. Appeared regularly
at Salzburg as Pamina, Susanna, and Zerlina. In
the 1960s she began to spend more time on the
concert platform, and only added two roles to
her repertory after 1953 – Blanche (*Dialogues
des Carmélites*) and Cleopatra (*Giulio Cesare*).
Gifted with a warm and beautiful voice and an
engaging personality. (R)

Segreto di Susanna, Il (*Susanna's Secret*).
Opera in 1 act by Wolf-Ferrari; text by Enrico
Golisciani. Prod. Munich (*as Susannas
Geheimnis*) 4 Dec. 1909, with Tordek,
Brodensen, cond. Mottl; N.Y., Met., (by
Philadelphia-Chicago Co.), 14 Mar. 1911, with
White, Sammarco, cond. Campanini; London,
C.G., 11 July 1911, with Lipkowska, Sammarco,
cond. Campanini.
  A slight but charming curtain-raiser about a
jealous husband, Count Gil (bar.), who, smel-
ling tobacco in the house, suspects his pretty
wife Susanna (sop.) of secretly entertaining a
lover. Susanna's secret is that she herself
smokes.

Seguin, Arthur (*b* London, 7 Apr. 1809; *d* New
York, 9 Dec. 1852). English bass. Sang in
English opera at C.G. and D.L. and in Italian
opera at the King's T. between 1831 and 1838.
N.Y. 1838, where he became popular and
formed his own company, the Seguin Troupe.
Probably the only opera singer to be elected a
chief by one of the Indian tribes, being given a
name meaning 'the man with the deep mellow
voice'. The career of his wife **Ann** (orig. Childe)
(*b* London, 1814; *d* New York Aug. 1888) coincided with his own. His sister **Elizabeth** (*b*
London, 1815; *d* London, 1870) was a soprano,
and the mother of Euphrosyne *Parepa.

Seidl, Anton (*b* Pest, 7 May 1850; *d* New York,
28 Mar. 1898). Hungarian conductor. Studied
Leipzig. Engaged as chorus master, Vienna
1872, by Richter, who introduced him to
Wagner. Remained with Wagner till 1876,
helping him prepare the score of the *Ring*.

Wagner recommended him to Neumann at
Leipzig, where he became first conductor
1879–82; then conducted Neumann's Wagner
Company on its great tour of Europe 1883.
Bremen 1883–5, where he married the soprano
Auguste Krauss. N.Y., Met., 1885–92, 1893–7,
conducting first American performances of
*Meistersinger, Tristan, Rheingold, Siegfried,
Götterdämmerung.* London, H.M.'s 1882, first
English *Ring*; C.G., 1897. Bayreuth, 1897, *Par-
sifal.* Died suddenly at the height of his career.

Seidl-Kraus, Auguste (*b* Vienna, 28 Aug. 1853;
d Kingston, N.Y. 17 July 1939). Austrian sop-
rano. Wife of above. Studied with Marchen
Début Vienna, H., 1877 in small roles. First
Vienna Wellgunde and Waldvogel. Leipzig
1881–2. Joined Neumann's Wagner company
and married its conductor Seidl. Bremen 1883.
London, H.M.'s 1882; N.Y., Met. 1884, Elsa; first
American Sieglinde, Eva, Waldvogel, and
Gutrune.

Seinemeyer, Meta (*b* Berlin, 5 Sept. 1895;
d Dresden, 19 July 1929). German soprano.
Studied Berlin with Grenzebach. Début there
1918. N.Y. with German Company 1923, Eva;
Dresden 1925–9; London, C.G., 1929, Sieglinde
and Eva. Established herself as one of the finest
lyric-dramatic sopranos, especially in Verdi, in
her few seasons at Dresden; Leonora in the
Forza del destino there which began the Verdi
revival in Germany. (R)

Selika. The African queen (sop.) in Meyerbeer's *L'Africaine.*

Sellner, Gustav Rudolf (*b* Traunstein, 25 May
1905). German producer and administrator.
Studied Munich. Début as opera producer, Kiel
1945. After engagements in Oldenburg,
Hanover, and other cities, Intendant Darmstadt, 1957–61; Berlin, D., 1961–72. Staged premières of *Junge Lord, Bassarids, Alkmene*
(Klebe), *Prometheus* (Orff).

Selva, Antonio (*b* Padua, 1824; *d* Padua, Sep.
1889). Italian bass. Début Padua, 1842, Zaccaria. Paris, T.I., 1865–7; Madrid 1852–3,
1864–74. Specialized in Verdi repertory;
created Silva in *Ernani* and Count Walther in
Luisa Miller. After retiring from stage taught
singing; pupils included Rusche-Endorf,
Novara, and Sachse.

Sembrich, Marcella (orig. Prakseda Marcellina
Kochańska) (*b* Wiśniowczyk, 15 Feb. 1858; *d*
New York, 11 Jan. 1935). Polish soprano. Took
her mother's maiden name. Began career as a
child pianist and violinist. Sang to Liszt, who
urged her to study singing, which she did with
Rokitansky and Lamperti. Début Athens 1877,
Elvira (*Puritani*). Dresden 1878–80; London,
C.G., 1880–4 and 1895, scoring great success
as Lucia, Marguerite de Valois, Amina. N.Y.,
Met., 1883–4 and 1898–1909, where she was

heard in more than 30 roles, of which Violetta was her favourite. Her voice, which ranged from c' to f''', was of great beauty and brilliance, and her technique was superb. From 1924 taught at the Curtis Institute, Philadelphia, and at the Juilliard School, N.Y. (R)

Semele. Masque, or musical drama, by Handel; text a version of Congreve's drama (1710), orig. libretto for John Eccles about 1707. Prod. London, C.G., 10 Feb. 1744, with Elisabeth Duparc (La Francescina), Young, Avolio, Beard, Sullivan, Reinhold; 1st stage prod. Cambridge 10 Feb. 1925 (Arundell version); Evanston, N.W. University., Jan. 1959, cond. Thor Johnson.

Semiramide. Opera in 2 acts by Rossini; text by Rossi, after Voltaire's tragedy *Sémiramis* (1748). Prod. Venice, F., 3 Feb. 1823, with Colbran, Mariani, Spagna, Galli, Sinclair; London, Hm., 15 July 1824, with Pasta; New Orleans, St. Charles T., 19 May 1837, with Marozzi, Pantanelli, Badioli, Fornasari, Candi, cond. Gabici.

Semiramis (sop.), Queen of Babylon, and her lover Assur (bar.) murder the king. She later falls in love with a young man who turns out to be her son Arsace (mezzo). She receives a mortal blow Assur intends for Arsace, who then kills Assur and becomes king.

There are some 65 operas on the subject, including those by Aldrovandini (1701), Destouches (1718), Porpora (1724), Vinci (1729), Porpora (1729), Vivaldi (1723), Hasse (1747), Gluck (1748), Perez (1749), Galuppi (1749), K. H. Graun (1754), Fischietti (1759), Sacchini (1762), Bernasconi (1765), Bertoni (1767), Sarti (1768), Paisiello (1773), Mortellari (1784), Salieri (1784), Gyrowetz (1791), Borghi (1791), Cimarosa (1799), Catel (1802), Nicolini (early 19th cent.), Meyerbeer (1819), M. Garcia (1828), Respighi (1910).

Sempre libera. The *cabaletta* to Violetta's (sop.) aria 'Ah! fors' è lui' in Act 1 of Verdi's *La traviata*.

Seneca. Lucius Annaeus Seneca the Younger (*b* Corduba, *c*.4BC; *d* Rome, 12 Apr. 65), the Stoic philosopher, appears in Monteverdi's *L'incoronazione di Poppea* as a bass, in his historical role as Nero's mentor who accepts with dignity the command to commit suicide.

Senesino (orig. Francesco Bernardi) (*b* Siena, whence his stage name, *c*1680; *d* Siena, *c*1750). Italian male mezzo-soprano. Studied with Bernacchi at Bologna. Believed to have sung at Genoa *c*1709 and Naples *c*1715, though Angus Heriot in his book on castrati (1956) says his name first appears in a cast list at Venice 1714 in Pollarolo the elder's *Semiramide*. Dresden 1719: here he was heard by Handel, who engaged him for London, where he made his début in Nov. 1720 in Bononcini's *Astarto*,

remaining with Handel's company until 1728. Re-engaged by Handel 1730, but broke with him in 1733 and went over to Porpora's rival company at Lincoln's Inn Fields, remaining there until 1737. Returned to Italy and engaged Naples, S.C., 1738–9. Created leading roles in Handel's *Ottone, Flavio, Giulio Cesare, Tamerlano, Rodelinda, Scipione, Alessandro, Admeto, Riccardo, Siroe, Tolomeo, Poro, Ezio, Sosarme*, and *Orlando*. Senesino's voice was a mezzo-soprano, or according to some a contralto, of great beauty, and was considered by many people superior to Farinelli's in quality. A contemporary critic describes it as 'clear, penetrating, and flexible, with faultless intonation and a perfect shake'.

Andrea Martini (1761–1819) and Giusto Ferdinando *Tenducci were also known as Senesino.

Senger-Bettaque, Katherine (*b* Berlin, 2 Aug. 1862; *d* ?). German soprano. Studied Berlin with Heinrick Dorn. Début Berlin H., 1879 in Rubinstein's *Feramors*. After engagements in Leipzig, Rotterdam, Bremen, and Hamburg, joined Munich H., 1893–1906; Stuttgart, 1906–9. As Kathi Bettaque sang Eva in first Bayreuth *Meistersinger* (1888), and Flower Maiden; London, C.G., 1892 Freia, Sieglinde, Gutrune, and Venus; N.Y. Met., 1888–9 and 1904–5; also sang heavier roles including Ortrud, Brünnhilde, and Leonore with little success. (R)

Senta. Daland's daughter (sop.), the heroine of Wagner's *Der fliegende Holländer*.

Senta's Ballad. The 'Legend of the Flying Dutchman' sung by Senta (sop.) to her friends in Act 2 of Wagner's opera.

Serafin, Tullio (*b* Rottanova di Cavarzere, 8 Dec. 1878; *d* Rome, 2 Feb. 1968). Italian conductor. Studied Milan, played violin in Scala Orchestra. Début Ferrara 1900. Turin 1903; Milan, Sc., 1902 as assistant to Toscanini, 1910–14, 1918, 1939–40, 1946–7; London, C.G., 1907, 1931, 1959, 1960; N.Y., Met., 1924–34; C.G. 1952; Rome 1934–43, chief conductor and artistic director; Chicago 1956–8. Reappointed Rome Opera, 1962. At the Met. conducted world premières of *The Emperor Jones, The King's Henchman, Merry Mount*, and *Peter Ibbetson*, as well as the American premières of *La cena delle beffe, Turandot, La vida breve*, and *Sorochintsy Fair*. At the Scala he directed the premières of Montemezzi's *La nave* and the first stage performance in Italy of *Peter Grimes*. During his Rome directorship he conducted many premières and revivals of old works. Under the German occupation of Rome he gave a season of contemporary opera including *Wozzeck* and Dallapiccola's *Volo di notte*. Has championed many young artists, and did much to help Ponselle and then Callas in their formative years, launching the latter as a dramatic coloratura. Coached Joan Sutherland for her C.G. Lucia. (R) His wife the Polish soprano **Elena Rakowska** (1878–1964) sang soprano roles at Sc., the Met., and the Colón, Buenos Aires. She was especially successful in Wagner. (R)

Seraglio, The. See *Entführung.*

Serenade (It. *serenata*, evening song, from *sera*, evening). By origin, a song sung under his lady's window by a lover, with or without instrumental accompaniment, which might in opera be provided by himself (as in Don Giovanni's 'Deh, vieni') or by a hired band (as in Almaviva's 'Ecco ridente in cielo' in *Barbiere*.) The term was soon applied to any instrumental piece of light nature.

Serenata (*It* *serenade). The term used for a serenade, but also used in the 18th cent. for a short operatic piece performed, probably in the evening, to celebrate Royal birthdays and other occasions in a room with a small amount of scenery. A famous example is Handel's *Acis and Galatea* (1720).

Serov, Alexander (Nikolayevich) (*b* St. Petersburg, 23 Jan. 1820; *d* St. Petersburg, 1 Feb. 1871). Russian composer and critic. Studied St Petersburg, initially following a career in the civil service, though composing in his spare time and, through his friendship with Stasov, taking a correspondence course with Joseph Hunke. In the early 1850s he completed an opera on Gogol's *May Night.* He became an ardent advocate of Liszt and Wagner, paving the way for Wagner's 1865 Russian visit with articles and organizing the first Russian *Tannhäuser* in 1868; he was not, however, himself influenced by Wagner. A quarrelsome man and a sharp critic, he broke with Balakirev over the latter's objections to his *Judith,* and was also at odds with both the Slavophile and Westernizer groups of Russian composers: he was patronized by the Grand Duchess Helena Pavlovna, who helped over the production of *Judith* (1868). Its tremendous success established Serov both artistically and materially, and enabled him to marry the pianist and composer Valentina Bergmann (whose *Uriel Acosta* was prod. Moscow 1885). He followed this with the still more successful *Rogneda* (1865), a historical drama that rivalled the success of *Der Freischütz* in Germany (70 performances at the St. Petersburg M., 1865–70). His last opera was *Vrazhya Sila* (The Power of Evil, unfin. 1871, completed Solovyov).

Greatly influenced by French opera (Gounod, Halévy, and especially Meyerbeer) and by Verdi, Serov also assimilated much that had been evolved by Glinka and Dargomyzhsky; and in turn he influenced a later generation. Mussorgsky admired his naturalistic handling of crowd scenes, and in *Boris Godunov* he reflects not only this but also the potent effect of a hallucination scene and of the essentially Russian figure of the holy simpleton. Tchaikovsky, another admirer, was impressed by Serov's handling of dances and folk choruses, though in this he was more directly influenced by Glinka; and Rimsky-Korsakov consciously took over some of his effects. His many original and intelligent ideas were not well held together, but he left some fine music and he proved successful in his own day and influential on the next generation.

Serpette, Henri (*b* Nantes, 4 Nov. 1846; *d* Paris, 3 Nov. 1904). French composer. Failing to realize his early ambitions as a serious composer, he took to writing operettas for the B.-P., where from 1874 he produced at regular intervals light pieces whose charm of manner won them great popularity.

Serse (Xerxes). Opera in 3 acts by Handel; text from a libretto by Minato, written for Cavalli in 1654 and revised for Bononcini in 1694. Prod. London, Hm., 15 Apr. 1738, with Francescina, Lucchesina, Caffarelli, Montagnana; Northampton, Mass., 12 May 1928, with Garrison, Ekberg, F. Martinelli, Kullman, Dickenson, Meyer, Marsh, cond. Josten. Revived Handel Opera Society, 1970.

Though set in ancient Persia, it makes use of some London street songs. Handel's only opera containing a purely comic character, it includes the famous *larghetto* aria 'Ombra mai fù', which was satirical by intent but is now invariably taken seriously as 'Handel's Largo'.

Other operas on the subject are by Cavalli (1654), Förtsch (1689), and Bononcini (1694).

Serva Padrona, La (The Maid Mistress). *Intermezzo in 2 parts to the opera *Il prigionier superbo* by Pergolesi; text by Federico. Prod. Naples, S.B., 28 Aug. 1733; London, Hm., 27 Mar. 1750; Baltimore, 13 June 1790.

The most famous of all intermezzos describes how Serpina (sop.) lures her master Uberto (bass) into marrying her by pretending to leave with a ferocious soldier, in fact another servant, Vespone (silent role).

Text also set by Paisiello, prod. Tsarkoye Selo 10 Nov. 1781 with De Bernucci, Marchetti. Other operas on the same text are by Predieri (1732), Abos (1744), and, in modified form, P.A. Guglielmi (1790).

Sessi, Marianna (*b* Rome, 1776; *d* Vienna, 10 Mar. 1847). Italian soprano. Vienna, 1793–5. Sang in opening performances at F., Venice, 1792, in Paisiello's *I giuochi d'Agrigento*. Temporarily left stage on her marriage in 1795, but returned in 1804 and continued to sing until 1836. Appeared with success in operas by Mayr, Zingarelli, and Mozart. Her two sisters, **Imperatrice** (*b* Rome 1784; *d* Florence 25 Oct.

1808), and **Anna Maria** (*b* Rome 1790; *d* Vienna, 9 June 1864), both had successful careers in Italy and Vienna.

Se vuol ballare. Figaro's (bar.) aria in Act 1 of Mozart's *Le nozze di Figaro,* in which he promises to pit his wits against those of the count.

Seyfried, Ignaz (Xaver) **von** (*b* Vienna, 15 Aug. 1776; *d* Vienna, 27 Aug. 1841). Austrian composer, conductor, and writer. Studied with Albrechtsberger, Winter, and possibly Mozart. He conducted in Schikaneder's Freihaustheater, writing many operas for it and the W., beginning with *Der Friede* (1797). A friend of Beethoven, he conducted the 1808 première of *Fidelio.* His own music, much performed in his day, includes Biblical music dramas, e.g. *Saul* (1810), *Abraham* (1817), *Die Makabäer* (1818), and *Noah* (1819). He also made many arrangements, among them the popular *Rochus Pumpernickel* (1809, with Haibel). He wrote a number of parodies, and his own *Idas und Marpissa* (1807) was parodied in 1818 by Perinet and Tuczek: both were successful. His pupils included Suppé.

's Gravenhage. See *The Hague.*

Shacklock, Constance (*b* Sherwood, Nottingham, 16 Apr. 1913). English mezzo-soprano. Studied London, R.A.M., with Frederic Austin. Début London, C.G., 1947, Mercedes (*Carmen*). Member of company until end of 1955–6 season, singing leading roles in German, French, and Italian repertory. Admired by Kleiber, who invited her to Berlin to sing Brangäne, one of her best roles; also a successful Octavian and Amneris. Appeared in Holland, Russia, and Australia. (R)

Shaftesbury Theatre, London. Built in 1888, it was the scene of Lago's last season of Italian opera in London in 1891, which included the first performance in England of *Cavalleria rusticana.* The first seasons by the Beecham Company were given there in 1916; these included the premières of Stanford's *The Critic* and Smyth's *Boatswain's Mate.* The theatre was bombed in 1941.

Shakespeare, William (*b* Stratford-on-Avon, bapt. 26 Apr. 1564; *d* Stratford-on-Avon, 23 Apr. 1616). English poet and dramatist. Operas on his works are as follows (the dates of the first seasons are those suggested by Sir Edmund Chambers):
Henry VI, pts. 2 and 3 (1590–1): None.
Henry VI, pt. 1 (1592–3): None.
Richard III (1592–3): Meiners (1859); Canepa (1879); Salvayre (1883).
The Comedy of Errors (1592–3): Storace (*Gli Equivoci,* 1786); Bishop (1819); Lorenz (*c*1890); Krejči (*Pozdvižení v Efesu,* 1946).
Titus Andronicus (1593–4): None.
The Taming of the Shrew (1593–4): Braham

and others (1828); Goetz (1874); Samara (1895); Maclean (*Petruccio,* 1895); Le Rey (1895); Silver (1922); Bossi (*Volpino il calderaio,* 1925); Wolf-Ferrari (1927: the induction only); Persico (1931); Clapp (1946); Porter (*Kiss me, Kate,* 1948); Giannini (1953); Groth (1954); Shebalin (1957); Eastwood (1960); Argento (1967).
Two Gentlemen of Verona (1594–5): None.
Love's Labour's Lost (1594–5): Folprecht (1926); A. Beecham (publ. 1936); Nabokov (1973).
Romeo and Juliet (1594–5): Benda (1776); Schwanenberger (1776); Marescalchi (1789); Rumling (1790); Dalayrac (1792); Steibelt (1793); Zingarelli (1796); B. Porta (1809); P. G. Guglielmi (1810); Vaccai (1825); Torriani (1828); Bellini (*I Capuleti e i Montecchi,* 1830); Storch (1863); Morales (1863); Marchetti (1865); Gounod (1867); Mercadal (1873); H.R. Shelley (publ. 1901); D'Ivry (*Les Amants de Vérone,* 1878); Campo (1909); Backworth (1916); Ferroni (early C20); Zandonai (1922); Sutermeister (1940); Malipiero (1950); Blacher (1950); Fribec (1954); Gaujac (1955); Fischer (1962); Mullins (1965); Zanon (1969); Matuszczak (1970).
Richard II (1595–6): None.
A Midsummer Night's Dream (1595–6): Purcell (*The Fairy Queen,* 1692); Leveridge (*Pyramus and Thisbe,* masque, 1716); Lampe (*Pyramus and Thisbe,* 1745); J. C. Smith (*The Fairies,* 1755); E. W. Wolf (*Die Zauberirrungen,* 1785); Alyabyev (*Volshebnaya noch,* comp. 1839); Manusardi (1842); Suppé (1844); Roti (1899); De Boeck (1902); Huë (1903); Mancinelli (comp. 1917); Vreuls (1925); Arundell (1930); Doubrava (comp. 1948); Delannoy (*Puck,* 1949); Britten (1960).
The Merchant of Venice (1596): Just (1787); Pinsuti (1873); Deffès (*Jessica,* 1898); Foerster (*Jessika,* 1905); Alpaerts (Shylock, 1913); Radò (Shylock, comp. 1914); Taubmann (*Porzia,* 1916); Carlson (1920); A. Beecham (1922); Laufer (publ. 1929); Laviolette (1929); Hahn (1935); Brumagne (1938); Castelnuovo-Tedesco (1961).
King John (1596–7): None.
Henry IV, pts. 1 and 2 (1597–8): Pacini (*La Gioventù di Enrico V,* 1820); Mercadante (*La Gioventù di Enrico V,* 1834); Holst (*At the Boar's Head,* 1925).
Much Ado About Nothing (1598–9): Berlioz (*Béatrice et Bénédict,* 1862); A. Doppler (1896); Puget (1899); Podesta (*Ero,* 1900); Stanford (1901); Mojsisovics (*c*1930); Hahn (1936); Heinrich (1956).
Henry V (1598–9): Boughton (*Agincourt,* Dramatic Scene, 1924).
Julius Caesar (1599–1600): Seyfried (1811); Robles (late C19); Malipiero (1936); Klebe (1959).
As You Like It (1599–1600): Veracini

(*Rosalinda*, 1744); F. Wickham (*Rosalind*, 1938); Jirko (1969).

Twelfth Night (1599–1600): Steinkühler (*Cäsario*, 1848); Rintel (1872); Taubert (*Cesario*, 1874); Weis (*Viola*, 1892); Hart (*Malvolio*, 1913); Smetana (*Viola*, unfin., prod. 1924); Farina (1929); Kusterer (1932); Holenia (*Viola*, 1934); De Filippi (*Malvolio*, 1937); Shenshin (1940); Gibbs (comp. 1947).

Hamlet (1600–1): Caruso (1789); Andreozzi (1792); Mercadante (1822); Maretzek (1840); Buzzolla (1848); Zanardini (1854); Stadtfeld (1857, prod. 1882); Moroni (1860); Faccio (1865); Thomas (1868); Hopp (1874); Hignard (1888); Keurvels (1891); Marescotti (1894); Grandi (1898); Heward (comp. 1916, unfin.); J. Kalniņš (1936); Szokolay (1969); Horky (*Jed z Elsinoru*, 1969, distantly); Engelmann (1969); Bentoiu (1971).

The Merry Wives of Windsor (1600–1): Papavoine (*Le Vieux coquet*, 1761); Philidor (*Herne le chasseur*, comp. 1773); Ritter (1794); Dittersdorf (1796); Salieri (*Falstaff*, 1799); Horn 1823); Balfe (*Falstaff*, 1838); Nicolai (1849); Adam (*Falstaff*, 1856); Verdi (*Falstaff*, 1893); Vaughan Williams (*Sir John in Love*, 1929).

Troilus and Cressida (1601–2): Zillig (1951).

All's Well That Ends Well (1602–3): F. David (*Le Saphir*, 1865); Audran (*Gillette de Narbonne*, 1882); Castelnuovo-Tedesco (*Giglietta di Narbona*, 1959).

Measure for Measure (1604–5): Wagner (*Das Liebesverbot*, 1836).

Othello (1604–5): Rossini (1816); Verdi (1887); Zavodsky (1945); Machavariani (?1963).

King Lear (1605–6): Séméladis (1854); Gobatti (1881); Reynaud (1888); Cagnoni (1890); G. Cottrau (1913); Ghislanzoni (1937); Frazzi (1939); Pogodin (1955); Durme (comp. 1957); Reimann (1968).

Macbeth (1605–6): Asplmayr (1777); Chélard (1827); Verdi (1847); Taubert (1857); L. Rossi (*Biorn*, 1877); E. Bloch (1910); Gatty (1920); Daffner (1930); Collingwood (1934); Goedicke (1944); Halpern (1965); Koppel (1970).

Antony and Cleopatra (1606–7): Kaffka (1779); Sayn-Wittgenstein-Berleburg (1883); Yuferov (publ. 1900); Ardin (1919); Malipiero (1938); Barber (1966); Bondeville (1973).

Coriolanus (1607–8): Baeyens (1941); Sulek (1958); Cikker (1973).

Timon of Athens (1607–8): ?Leopold I (1696).

Pericles (1608–9): Cottrau (comp. c. 1915).

Cymbeline (1609–10): R. Kreutzer (*Imogène*, 1796); Sobolewski (*Imogene*, 1833); O. van Westerhout (1892); Missa (*Dinah*, 1894); A. Eggen (1951).

A Winter's Tale (1610–11): C.E. Barbieri (*Perdita*, 1865); Bruch (*Hermione*, 1872); Nešvera (*Perdita*, 1897); Bereny (1898); Zimmermann (1900); Goldmark (1908).

The Tempest (1611–12): Locke, Humphrey, and others (1674); Purcell (1695); J.C. Smith (1756); Asplmayr (1781); Rolle (1784); Fabrizi (1788); Hoffmeister (1792); Winter (1798); W. Müller (1798); Fleischmann (*Die Geisterinsel*, 1796); Reichardt (*Die Geisterinsel*, 1798); Zumsteeg (*Die Geisterinsel*, 1798); Haack (*Die Geisterinsel*, ?1798); Ritter (1799); Caruso (1799); Hensel (1799); Emmert (1806); Kanne (1808); Riote (1833); Alyabyev (c 1835); Raymond (comp. c 1840); Kunz (1847); Halévy (1850); Nápravnik (1860); Duvernoy (1880); D. Jenkins (1880); Frank (1887); Urspruch (1888); Fiblich (1895); Ángyal (c 1900); Delfante (1900); De Angelis (1905); Farwell (*Caliban*, masque, 1916); Hale (publ. 1917); Gatty (1920); Lattuada (1922); Canonica (*Miranda*, 1937); Sutermeister (*Die Zauberinsel*, 1942); Atterberg (1948); Martin (1956); Sulek (1969).

Henry VIII (1612–13): None.

Two Noble Kinsmen (1612–13): None.

Also: Logar (*Four Scenes from Shakespeare*) and Zelinka (*Spring with Shakespeare*, 1955). Operas in which Shakespeare appears are by Lillo (*La Gioventù di Shakespeare*, 1851), Benvenuti (*Guglielmo Shakespeare*, 1861), and Serpette (*Shakespeare*, 1899). In Thomas's *La Songe d'une nuit d'été* (1850), Shakespeare, Queen Elizabeth, and Falstaff all appear.

Shalyapin, Fyodor (Ivanovich) (*b* Kazan, 11 Feb. 1873; *d* Paris 12 April 1938). Russian bass. Of a humble peasant family, he had little formal education, though he studied briefly with the tenor Dmitri Usatov in Tiflis 1893. After singing in choirs and touring with a minor theatrical company, together with Gorky, he joined Semyonov-Smarsky's company in Ufa in 1890, making his formal début in December of that year as the Stolnik in *Halka*. After appearances in Baku, Batum, and Kutaisi, he was engaged for Tiflis 1893–4, singing bass and baritone roles including both Valentin and Méphistophélès in *Faust*; St. Petersburg, Panayev's company, 1894, successful as Bertram in *Robert le Diable*; St Petersburg, M., 1895–6; left after disagreements with management over production and acting. Joined Mamontov's Company in Moscow 1896; remained until 1899, and had great personal success as Ivan Susanin, Ivan the Terrible, Dosifey, Boris, Holofernes in Serov's *Judith*, and created Salieri in Rimsky-Korsakov's *Mozart and Salieri*. Moscow, B., 1899, continuing to appear there until 1920; Milan, Sc., 1901 (first appearance outside Russia), Mefistofele (Boito), 1904, 1908, 1912, 1929, 1930, 1933, as Méphistophélès, Don Basilio, Ivan the Terrible, Boris; Monte Carlo, 1905–1937, most above roles as well as Rubinstein's Demon, Philip in *Don Carlos*, Colline, the Mad Miller, title role in Massenet's *Don Quichotte* (which he created), and works by Gunsbourg; N.Y., Met., 1907–8 as Mefistofele, Don Basilio, Leporello, when his realistic acting and robust vocalisation were not to the liking of American audiences; more successful when he returned 1921–29. London after a private concert 25 July 1905 at the house of Mrs Potter Palmer), D.L., 1913 and 1914 in Sir Joseph Beecham's Russian seasons, appearing in the first London *Boris Godunov, Khovanschina, Ivan the Terrible,* and *Prince Igor*; C.G. 1926, 1928, 1929; Lyceum, 1931, Mad Miller in first London *Rusalka*. Last stage appearance Monte Carlo, 1937, as Boris. Made a film of *Don Quichotte* (director Pabst, music Ibert) 1933. Considered unrivalled as a singing actor. Wrote two books of memoirs, *Pages from my Life* (1926) and *Man and Mask* (1932). (R)

Shaporin, Yury (Alexandrovich) (*b* Glukhov, 8 Nov. 1889; *d* Moscow, 9 Dec. 1966). Russian composer. Studied St Petersburg. His only opera, *The Decembrists* (1953), is based on the Revolutionary incident of 1825, and has won approval in Russia for its heroic sentiments and optimistic' musical style.

Sharpless. The U.S. Consul (bar.) in Puccini's *Madama Butterfly*.

Shaw, (George) **Bernard** (*b* Dublin, 26 July 1856; *d* London, 2 Nov. 1950). Irish dramatist, novelist, and critic. Wrote regular music criticism for *The Hornet* (1876–7), under the pseudonym of 'Corno di Bassetto' for *The Star* (1880–90), and for *The World* (1890–94). He had an intimate knowledge of the subjects he wrote about, especially Italian opera. He was always highly personal in his approach, often devastatingly witty, and was allowed to make an essay of each occasion. Shaw remains the most intelligent and entertaining journalist music critic in English letters. The fundamental seriousness of his passion for music is openly displayed in *The Perfect Wagnerite* (1898, 4/1922), a closely argued thesis on a Socialist theory of *The Ring*. This is still one of the most important studies of Wagner's music to have appeared in English: Shaw's miscellaneous criticisms, well worth re-reading today, were reprinted as *Music in London 1890–4* (3 vols, 1932), *London Music in 1888–9 as heard by Corno di Bassetto* (1937), and *How to Become a Musical Critic* (1960).

Music, especially opera, also permeates Shaw's plays. This extends from many scattered references, such as the prize-fighter Cashel Byron comparing his battles to those of Wagner ('a game sort of composer') and the love of music shown by many of his characters, to the basing of *Man and Superman* on *Don Giovanni*; also to Shaw's insistence that his plays were conceived as operas without music,

with duets, trios, etc., and with casting for actors with high or low voices to match their roles and provide effective vocal contrasts. Operettas on his works are by O. Straus (*Der tapfere Soldat*, 1908, after *Arms and the Man*) and Lilien (*Die grosse Katharina*, 1932, after *Great Catherine*). The musical *My Fair Lady* (1956), music by Loewe, is based on *Pygmalion*.

Shaw, Glen Byam (*b* London, 13 Dec. 1904). English producer. After a career as actor and producer in the straight theatre turned to opera in 1962 when appointed director of productions at S.W. Since then he has staged many notable productions for S.W./E.N.O. including *Idomeneo, Così fan tutte,, The Rake's Progress, Duke Bluebeard's Castle,* and notably (with John Blatchley) *The Ring*. His work is marked by an economy of movement and a concentration on the essentials of the character.

Shaw, Mary (orig. Postans – also known as Mrs. Alfred Shaw) (*b* Lea, Kent, 1814; *d* Hadleigh Hall, Suffolk, 9 Sept. 1876). English contralto. Studied London, R.A.M. After several years of concert and oratorio work, début Novara 1839 in *Semiramide* and *La donna del lago*. Created Cuniza in Verdi's *Oberto*, Milan, Sc., 1839. London, C.G. and D.L., from 1842, being especially successful as Arsace, Fidalma, and Malcolm Graeme (*Donna del lago*). Her career came to a premature close when her husband's serious illness caused her to have a breakdown, and lose her voice.

Shepherds of the Delectable Mountains, The. See *Pilgrim's Progress, The.*

Sheridan, Margaret (*b* Castlebar, 15 Oct. 1889; *d* Dublin, 16 Apr. 1958). Irish soprano. Studied London, R.A.M., and Milan with Tina Scagnamilio. Début Rome 1918, Mimì. London, C.G., 1919, 1925–30; Milan, Sc., 1921–4. Sang the role of Olimpia in Respighi's *Belfagor* at Sc.: first London Iris (Mascagni). Chosen by Toscanini to sing in *La Wally* at Sc. 1922. (R)

Sheridan, Richard Brinsley (*b* Dublin, 30 Oct. 1751; *d* London, 7 July 1816). English dramatist. Operas on his works are as follows. *St Patrick's Day* (1775): S. Hughes (1947). *The Duenna* (1775): Linley sen. & jun., songs & c. for original production; Bertoni (*La Governante*, 1779); Bell (1939); Prokofiev (1946); Gerhard (comp. 1948, radio perf. 1949). *School for Scandal* (1777): Klenau (1926). *The Critic* (1779): Stanford (1916).

Sherrington, Helen. See *Lemmens-Sherrington.*

Shevelev (orig. Shevyukhin), **Nikolay** (Artemyevich) (*b?*,1869 or 18 Dec. 1874; *d?*,12 Dec. 1929). Russian baritone. After singing in choirs, studied in Milan (1889–96) with Signoretti. Moscow, Mamontov's Company, 1896–1903; Moscow, Z., 1908–13, 1922–4; Tiflis, 1919–22. Guest appearances Prague, Berlin, etc. Created Gryaznoy in *Tsar's Bride* and Messenger in *Tsar Saltan*; repertory also included title role in *The Demon*, Onegin, Mazeppa, Mizgir, Nelusko, Rigoletto, Escamillo, Sachs, and Gérard. After leaving the stage taught in Tiflis. His records reveal a beautiful and powerful voice but a coarse style. (R)

Shield, William (*b* Whickham, 5 Mar. 1748; *d* Brightling, 25 Jan. 1829). English composer. Originally a violinist, he played in orchestras at the Italian Opera in London, 1772; principal viola 1773–91. Composer to C.G. 1778–91 and 1792–7. Wrote more than 50 light operas, including *The Flitch of Bacon* (1778) and *Robin Hood* (1784). Himself a gifted melodist, he also introduced many songs by English and foreign composers into his stage pieces.

Shirley, George (*b* Indianapolis, 18 April 1934). American tenor. Studied Wayne University and with Therny S. Georgi. Début Woodstock, N.Y., 1959., Eisenstein. Milan T. Nuovo, 1960 Rodolfo. Won N.Y., Met., Auditions of the Air 1961; N.Y. Met., 1961; San Francisco, Santa Fe, Caramoor; Spoleto. Glyndebourne 1966-74 Tamino, Lord Percy (*Anna Bolena*), Idomeneo. London, C.G., since 1967 Don Ottavio, David, Pelléas, Loge. Sang in first U.S. *König Hirsch*, and first N.Y. *Indes Galantes, Aroldo, Doktor Faustus*. A highly gifted and sensitive singer, whose performances show intelligence and complete musical integrity. (R)

Shirley-Quirk, John (*b* Liverpool, 28 Aug. 1931). British baritone. Studied with Roy Henderson. Début Gly., 1961, Doctor in *Pelléas*. E.O.G. 1964–76, creating the baritone roles in Britten's the Church Parables, Coyle (*Owen Wingrave*), baritone roles in *Death in Venice*. Scottish O. 1962, 1969–70, and subsequently, Don Alfonso, Don Giovanni, Arkel, Gregor Mittenhofer (*Elegy for Young Lovers*). London, C.G., 1973; created Lev in Tippett's *The Ice Break* (1977). Repertory also includes Onegin, Dark Fiddler (*Village Romeo*), Death (*Savitri*). A thoughtful and sensitive artist. (R)

Shostakovich, Dmitry (Dmitriyevich) (*b* St Petersburg, 25 Sept. 1906; *d* Moscow, 9 Aug. 1975). Studied Petrograd with Steinberg. His first opera, *The Nose* (1930), after Gogol, gave scope to his considerable satirical abilities, in this case at the expense of the old Russian régime. Its experimental eccentricities were one of the causes of the reaction by the Communist Party that led to the formulation of 'Socialist Realism' as an artistic principle in 1932. Influenced by foreign contemporaries (Hindemith) as well as Russian contemporaries

(Prokofiev and Stravinsky) and predecessors (Mussorgsky and Dargomyzhsky), the work ingeniously uses a modern form of Russian musical declamation of the kind for which many Russian composers had sought. In 1932 Shostakovich also completed *The Lady Macbeth of Mtsensk*; in 1934 it became the first opera to be produced under the new rules in which the goal was 'the complete musical expression of the ideas and passions motivating Soviet heroes' (Stalin). Its first success was followed by an equally violent reaction, probably Stalin-inspired, and it was denounced in a notorious *Pravda* article 'Chaos instead of music' (28 Jan. 1936). Shostakovich's deep and warmly expressed sympathy for his heroine, Katerina Izmaylova (the title of the revised version, 1959) is expressed in contrast to brilliant, if shallow, alienating satire for the other characters. *Moscow, Cheremushky* (1959) is a local-joke operetta on the housing question, and remained the only further engagement with original opera of a composer richly gifted with the dramatic talent to have contributed immeasurably to the Soviet operatic stage. He also made new versions of Mussorgsky's *Boris Godunov* (1940) and *Khovanshchina* (1960, also used for a film).
Bibl: D. Rabinovich: *Dmitry Shostakovich* (1950).

Shuard, Amy (*b* London, 19 July 1924; *d* London, 18 Apr. 1975). English soprano. Studied London, T.C.M. Début Johannesburg 1949, Aida. London, S.W., 1949–55; C.G. 1954–74. Leading British dramatic soprano of the 1960s. Sang title-roles in first English stage performances of *Káťa Kabanová* and *Jenůfa*; was also an impressive Aida, Amelia, Santuzza, Lady Macbeth, Elektra, and Magda (*The Consul*). In 1958 acclaimed as the finest Turandot since her teacher Eva Turner; first English-born C.G. Brünnhilde, 1964; Elektra, 1965. Subsequently invited to Vienna, Buenos Aires, San Francisco, and Milan. Retired 1974 (R)

Shuisky. A scheming boyar (ten.) in Mussorgsky's *Boris Godunov*.

Shvanda the Bagpiper (Cz., *Švanda dudák*) Opera in 2 acts by Weinberger; text by Miloš Kareš and Max Brod, after the folk tale by Tyl. Prod. Prague, N., 27 Apr. 1927, with Novák, Kejřová, Nordenová, Schütz, Koslíková, Munclingr, Pollert, Lebeda, Hruška, cond. Ostrčil; N.Y., Met., 7 Nov. 1931, with Müller, Laubenthal, Schorr, cond. Bodanzky; London, C.G. 11 May 1934, with Ursuleac, Kullmann, Schoeffler, cond. Krauss. Weinberger's most successful opera.

Babinsky (ten.) persuades Shvanda (bar.) to try to win Queen Ice Heart (mezzo) by means of his piping. Finding Shvanda is already married, she orders his execution, but he is saved by his music and by Babinsky. A rash promise lands him in Hell, whence he is again rescued by Babinsky, who cheats the Devil (bass) at cards.

Other operas on the subject by Hřímaly (1896), Weis (1905), and Bendl (1906).

Siberia. Opera in 3 acts by Giordano; text by Illica. Prod. Milan, Sc., 19 Dec. 1903, with Storchio, Zenatello, De Luca, Pini-Corsi, cond. Campanini; New Orleans, 13 Jan. 1906 (in French), with Galli-Sylva, Lucas, Mezy, Baer, Régis, Bourgeois, cond. Rey; London, Fulham T.H., 8 Dec. 1972, by Hammersmith Municipal O., with Doyle, O'Neil, Metcalfe, Corner, cond. Vandernoot.

Vassili (ten.), in love with Stephana (sop.), mistress of Prince Alexis, has wounded him in a duel, and for this is exiled to Siberia; there he is joined by Stephana. They attempt to escape together, but are shot at by guards; Stephana is fatally wounded, but before she dies she persuades Gleby (bar.), Commandant of the camp, to free Vassili.

Sibiriakov, Leo (b St. Petersburg, 1869; d Antwerp, Oct. 1942). Russian bass. Début St. Petersburg 1895. Boston O. C., 1910–11, Don Basilio, Mephistophélès; London, C.G., 1911. After the First World War emigrated to Belgium, where he taught in Antwerp; still made occasional appearances in Paris, Brussels etc. Sang Pimen in Brussels in 1938. (R)

Siebel. A village youth (mezzo), in love with Marguérite, in Gounod's *Faust*.

Siege of Rhodes, The. Opera by Locke and others; text by William D'Avenant. Prod. London, Rutland House, Sept. 1656. According to the preface of *The Fairy Queen* (1695), 'That Sir William D'Avenant's *The Siege of Rhodes* was the first Opera we ever had in England, no Man can deny; and is indeed a perfect Opera. . .'. The music has been lost.

Siegfried. See *Ring des Nibelungen*. Also the young hero (ten.) in Wagner's *Siegfried* and *Götterdämmerung*.

Sieglinde. Hunding's wife and Siegmund's sister, later lover (sop.), in Wagner's *Die Walküre*.

Siegmund. Sieglinde's brother and lover (ten.) in Wagner's *Die Walküre*.

Siehr, Gustav (b Arnsberg, 17 Sept. 1837; d Munich, 18 May 1896). German bass. Studied with Heinrich Dorn and Julius Krause. Début Neustrelitz 1863. Prague 1865–70; Wiesbaden 1870–81; Munich 1881–96. Created Hagen, Bayreuth, 1876, and alternated with Scaria as Gurnemanz in the first series of *Parsifal* performances in 1882, repeating the same role in 1883, 1884, 1886, 1889; also King Mark (1886).

Siems, Margarethe (b Breslau, 30 Dec. 1879; d Dresden, 13 Apr. 1952). German soprano. Studied with Orgeni, a pupil of Viardot and Marchesi. Début Prague 1902, Marguerite de Valois. Dresden 1908–19; London, C.G., 1913; D.L. 1914. Created Chrysothemis (*Elektra*), Marschallin (*Rosenkavalier*), Zerbinetta (*Ariadne*). First London Marschallin, in which role Strauss considered her ideal. She could also sing the coloratura roles of Bellini and Donizetti, and also sang Aida, Amelia, Venus, and even Isolde. Took up a teaching appointment in Berlin 1920, and taught in Dresden and Breslau (where she gave her farewell performance, Marschallin, 1925) until 1940. (R)

Siena. Town in Tuscany, Italy. Here in the 1930s Count Guido Chigi-Saracini founded the Accademia Chigiana, where every Sept. the Settimana Chigiana is held. Performances are given at the Teatro dei Rozzi and Teatro dei Rinnovati; this latter dates from 1753, and was adapted by Bibiena from the ancient hall of the Grand Council of the republic. Operas revived have included Vivaldi's *L'Olimpiade*, Scarlatti's *Il filosofo di campagna*, and works by Cimarosa, Cherubini, Sacchini, and Donizetti.

Siepi, Cesare (b Milan, 10 Feb. 1923). Italian bass. Self-taught. Début Schio, nr Venice, 1941, Sparafucile. Career interrupted by war, when he became an active anti-Fascist and had to take refuge in Switzerland. Resumed career Venice 1945. Milan, Sc. 1946-58; London, C.G., 1950, 1962-73, as Don Giovanni and Philip. N.Y., Met., 1950-74; Salzburg 1953-8. In N.Y. he has sung Boris and the Verdi bass roles with considerable success. (R)

Siface (orig., Giovanni Francesco Grossi) (b Uzzanese Chiesina, 12 Feb. 1653; d nr Ferrara, 29 May 1697). Italian male soprano. He acquired his stage name from the part of Syphax in Cavalli's *Scipione Africano*, in which he excelled at Venice in 1678. His admirers during his English visit (from 1679) included Pepys, Evelyn, Burney, and Purcell, whose pretty harpsichord piece 'Sefauchi's Farewell' laments his departure for Italy. He was murdered by the postillion while travelling between Bologna and Ferrara.

Si, fui soldato. Chénier's (ten.) defence of his actions in the revolutionary tribunal in Act 3 of Giordano's *Andrea Chénier*.

Signor Bruschino, Il; ossia Il figlio per azzardo. *Farsa giocosa* in 1 act by Rossini; text by Foppa, after a French comedy by De Chazet and Ourry. Prod. Venice, S. Moisè, late Jan. 1813, with Pontiggia, Nagher, Raffanelli, Del Monte, Berti, De Grecis; N.Y., Met., 9 Dec. 1932, with Fleischer, Tokatyan, Windheim, De Luca, Pinza, cond. Serafin; Orpington, Kent Opera Group, 14 July 1960 cond. Langford. Occasionally revived in Italy.

Sofia (sop.), ward of Gaudenzio (bass), is being forced to marry Bruschino's (bar.) son, whom she has never seen. Her lover, Florville (ten.), passes himself off as Bruschino's son, and when Bruschino himself arrives, he helps the plot along for his own reasons.

Signore, ascolta. Liù's (sop.) plea to Calaf in Act 1 of Puccini's *Turandot*.

Sigurd. Opera in 5 acts by Reyer; text by Du Locle and Blau. Prod. Brussels, La M., 7 Jan. 1884 with Rose Caron, Deschamps-Jehin, Jourdain, Devries, Renaud, cond. Dupont; London, C.G., 15 July 1884 with Albani, Fursch-Madi, Jourdain, Devoyod, Soulacroix, E. de Reszke, cond. Bevignani; New Orleans, French O.C., 24 Dec. 1891, with Baux, Duvivier, Priolaud, Paulin, Guillemot, Bordeneuve, cond. Warnots. The libretto is based on the Nibelung legend.

Si j'etais roi (If I were King). Opera in 3 acts by Adam; text by d'Ennery and Brésil. Prod. Paris, T.L., 4 Sept. 1852; N.Y. 29 Nov. 1881, with Colson, Dulaurens, Debrinay, De la Grave, Graat, Dutasta, Crambade; Newcastle 20 Feb. 1893.

Silja, Anja (*b* Berlin, 17 Apr. 1940). German soprano. Studied with her grandfather Egon von Rijn. Début aged 10 in concert in Berlin. Stage début Brunswick, 1955, Rosina. Stuttgart, since 1955; Bayreuth 1960-66, Senta, Elsa, Eva, Elisabeth, Venus, Freia, Isolde. Greatly influenced by Wieland Wagner and appeared in his productions of *Wozzeck, Lulu, Otello, Salome* and *Elektra*, as well as in Wagner. London, C.G., 1969 Leonore under Klemperer; 1970 Cassandra; 1972 Senta; 1975 Marie. San Francisco, 1968, 1970-71; Chicago. A vivid and forceful singing actress. (R)

Silken Ladder, The. See *Scala di Seta, La.*

Sills, Beverly (orig. Belle Silverman) (*b* Brooklyn, 25 May 1929). American soprano. Studied N.Y., with Estelle Liebling. Début Philadelphia 1947, Frasquita. San Francisco 1953 as Helen of Troy (*Mefistofele*) and Donna Elvira; N.Y., City O., since 1955; Milan, Sc., 1969 Palmira in *L'assedio di Corinto*; London, C.G. 1970 Lucia; N.Y., Met., 1975, Palmira. Repertory of more than 60 roles including Cleopatra (Handel), Queen of Shemakha, Manon, Violetta; especially noted as Anna Bolena, Elizabeth in *Roberto Devereux*, and Maria Stuarda. Also sings with success in contemporary American operas. Possibly the most popular U.S. soprano since Grace Moore. At her best a singing-actress in the Callas manner, though her voice is whiter in quality. (R)

Silva. Don Ruy Gomez de Silva, a Spanish grandee and Ernani's rival (bass) in Verdi's *Ernani.*

Silveri, Paolo (*b* Ofena, nr Aquila, 28 Dec. 1913). Italian baritone. Studied Florence and Rome, Accademia di Santa Cecilia with Stracciari. Début Rome, as bass, 1939, Schwarz (*Meistersinger*); from 1944 baritone (first role, Germont). London, C.G., 1946 with Naples Company, 1947-9 as member of permanent company, 1950 with Scala Company; N.Y., Met., 1950-3. Tenor début Dublin 1959, Otello. Reverted to baritone roles again 1960. As a baritone enjoyed a short but brilliant career, especially in Verdi and Puccini roles. Since 1970 has taught singing in Rome. (R)

Silvio. A villager, Nedda's lover (bar.), in Leoncavallo's *Pagliacci.*

Simile aria. See *Metaphor aria.*

Simionato, Giulietta (*b* Forlì, 15 Dec. 1910). Italian mezzo. Studied Rovigo with Lucatello and Palumbo. Won first prize, Bel Canto Competition, Florence, 1933, and during next five years sang small roles in Florence, Padua, Milan, Sc., regularly 1939-66; Edinburgh Festival 1947, Cherubino; C.G. 1953, Adalgisa, Amneris, Azucena and 1964; Chicago 1954; N.Y., Met., 1949. As well as singing the usual mezzo repertory, made a great success in Rossini roles and as Jane Seymour in Donizetti's *Anna Bolena* and Romeo in Bellini's *I Capuleti e i Montecchi.* Her voice was a coloratura mezzo of great agility, with a warm characteristic timbre in its lower reaches; and she had a charming stage presence. In 1962 she sang the soprano role of Valentine in the Scala revivial of *Les Huguenots.* Farewell performance, Piccola Scala 1966, Servilia in *La clemenza di Tito.* (R)

Simon Boccanegra. Opera in a prologue and 3 acts by Verdi; text by Piave, based on the drama by António Garcia Gutiérrez. Prod. Venice, F., 12 Mar. 1857 with Benduzzi, Negrini, L. Giraldoni, Echeverria – libretto revised Boito, prod. Milan, Sc., 24 Mar. 1881, with D'Angeri, Tamagno, Maurel, and E. de Reszke, cond. Faccio; N.Y., Met., 28 Jan. 1932, with Rethberg, Martinelli, Tibbett, Pinza, cond. Serafin; London, S.W., 27 Oct. 1948, with Gartside, Johnston, Matters, Glynne, cond. Mudie.

Boccanegra (bar.), a corsair, has had a child by Maria, daughter of the patrician Fiesco. Boccanegra is elected Doge of Genoa, and discovers that his beloved Maria has died. Twenty-five years later, Fiesco, under the assumed name of Andrea, is plotting against the Doge, with the help of Gabriele Adorno (ten.) who is in love with Fiesco's adopted daughter Amelia (sop.) – in reality Boccanegra's long-lost daughter. Boccanegra visits Andrea and tries to persuade him to agree to a marriage between Amelia and Paolo (bar.), leader of the plebeian party. Amelia's true identity is revealed and father and daughter are reunited. Gabriele thinks that

Amelia is Boccanegra's mistress, but when he learns the truth joins Boccanegra in his fight against the plotters; but already Paolo has poisoned Boccanegra's wine. The dying Boccanegra and Fiesco, who has been captured for his part in the plot, are reconciled; and Boccanegra proclaims Gabriele the new Doge.

Simoneau, Leopold (*b* Quebec, 3 May 1918). Canadian tenor. Studied N.Y. with Paul Althouse. Début Montreal 1943, Basilio (*Figaro*). Paris, O., 1947-9; Aix-en-Provence 1950; Glyndebourne 1951 and subsequently; London, R.F.H., with Vienna Company, 1954; Chicago 1954. Outstanding in Mozart, as Wilhelm Meister in *Mignon*, and as Nadir. After retiring from stage taught in Montreal. In 1971 appointed artistic director of the newly-formed O. du Québec, but resigned after differences with the board. (R)

Sinclair, Monica (*b* Somerset, 1926). English mezzo. Studied London, R.A.M. and R.C.M. Début C.R. 1948, Suzuki. London, C.G., since 1949; Glyndebourne since 1954. Successful in Handel Opera Society's productions, in Lully's *Armide* in France, and *Alcina* in Venice. A most intelligent and musical singer. (R)

Singher, Martial (*b* Oloron-Sainte-Marie, 14 Aug. 1904). French baritone. Studied Paris Conservatoire with Gresse. Début Amsterdam 1930, Pylade (*Iphigénie en Tauride*). Paris, O., 1930-9; London, C.G., 1937; N.Y., Met., 1943-59. Equally at home in French, German, and Italian repertory, he has been praised in N.Y. for his Mercutio, Pelléas, Amfortas, Figaro, and the four roles in *Hoffmann*. (R)

Singspiel (*Ger* song-play). A term for a German opera in which musical numbers are separated by dialogue. Though such works were written in the 17th cent., e.g. Staden's *Seelewig* (1644), the term was first regularly applied to dramas with music in the early 18th cent. An early example was Keiser's *Croesus* (1710). The influence of French opéra comique and especially of English ballad opera helped to develop Singspiel as a genre of comic opera with spoken dialogue, especially with the translation *c*1750 of Coffey's ballad operas *The Devil to Pay* (1728) and *The Merry Cobbler* (1735) by C. F. Weisse as *Der Teufel ist los* and *Der lustige Schuster*, with new music by J. C. Standfuss. Both texts were then reset by J. A. Hiller, one of the most important Singspiel composers; he followed these with many more (e.g. *Die Jagd*, 1770), making the genre particularly distinctive in Leipzig. From here it spread to Berlin, where one of the prominent Singspiel composers was Benda (*Der Jahrmarkt*, 1775). In Vienna, Haydn wrote a Singspiel *Der krumme Teufel* (lost); and other composers active included *Umlauff (*Die Bergknappen*, 1778), *Dittersdorf (*Doktor und Apotheker*, 1786),

*Schenk (*Der Dorfbarbier*, 1796), Mozart (*Die Entführung aus dem Serail*, 1782), and Schubert (several early works, including *Die Freunde von Salamanca*, comp. 1815, and *Die Zwillingsbrüder*, 1820). The popular and romantic nature of many of the Singspiel texts, and the easily approachable nature of the music, made Singspiel (especially that of North Germany) one of the ancestors of German Romantic opera. *Der Freischütz* (1821) shows its Singspiel ancestry; but the real apotheosis of the Singspiel was with Mozart's *Magic Flute* and Beethoven's *Fidelio*.

Sì, pel ciel marmoreo giuro! The vengeance duet between Otello (ten.) and Iago (bar.) in Act 2 of Verdi's *Otello*.

Si può? The prologue to Leoncavallo's *Pagliacci*, in which the singer, generally Tonio (bar.), asks the audience to listen to his exposition of the situation.

Sir John in Love. Opera in 4 acts by Vaughan Williams; text selected by composer from Shakespeare's *The Merry Wives of Windsor* (1600-1), *Love's Labour's Lost* and *Much Ado About Nothing*, and from Thomas Middleton, Ben Jonson, Thomas Campion, *Gammer Gurton's Needle*, Christopher Marlowe, John Fletcher, Psalm 137, George Peele, Nicholas Udall, Philip Sidney, Richard Edwards, Philip Rosseter, Thomas Campion, and the song 'Greensleeves'. Prod. London, R.C.M., 21 Mar. 1929, with Walmsley, Kennedy, Warde, Herbert, Leyland White, Hemming, Holmes, Hancock, Moore, Evers, Mansfield, Rickard, Bamfield Cooper (chorus of fairies and imps incl. Imogen Holst), cond. Sargent; N.Y., Univ. of Columbia, 20 Jan. 1949, with Kovey, Dettens, Symes, Witwer, Wheeler, Hester, Lalli.

The plot follows the story of the Merry Wives of Windsor and their discomfiture of Falstaff (bar.). A number of the minor characters are given larger parts than in Verdi's or Nicolai's operas, as part of the composer's attempt to fill out the vivid English background to the comedy.

Siroe. Opera in 3 acts by Handel; text by Metastasio, altered by Haym. prod. London, King's T., 17 Feb. 1728, with Cuzzoni, Faustina, Senesino, Boschi; revived Halle 1962.

Sitzprobe (*Ger.* sitting rehearsal). The term for the first complete rehearsal of an opera, when soloists and chorus join with the orchestra, generally in the auditorium, with the singers sitting either in the stalls or on chairs on the stage. The term has been adopted in English opera houses. Known in Italian opera houses as *prova all'italiana*.

Škroup, František Jan (*b* Osice, 3 June 1801; *d* Rotterdam, 7 Feb. 1862). Bohemian composer.

After studying law, he was drawn into the movement for Czech national opera, first as an amateur and then as a professional répétiteur, conductor, and composer. With Josef Chmelenský as librettist, and basing his ideas on the established tradition of Czech Singspiel, he wrote the first Czech opera, *Dráteník* (The Tinker), and took the title role at the very successful première on 2 Feb. 1826. He then became Kapellmeister at the Stavovské T., where he introduced many new works, latterly including some by Wagner and Verdi. His own subsequent operas were unsuccessful, largely because he proved unwilling or unable to advance from the simple, charmingly naive Singspiel of *Dráteník* to answer the demands of new expressive ideals.

Bibl: J. Plavec: *František Škroup* (1941).

Slavina, Mariya (Alexandrovna) (*b* ?, 5 June 1858; *d* Paris, 1951). Russian mezzo-soprano. Studied St Petersburg with Everardi. Début St Petersburg, M., 1879, Amneris. Created Hanna in Rimsky-Korsakov's *May Night* (1880), Konchakovna in *Prince Igor* (1890), Clytemnestra in Taneyev's *Oresteia* (1895), and the Countess in *The Queen of Spades* (1890); her repertory also included Amneris, Carmen (first Russian), Olga, Fidès. Left Russia in 1917; eventually settled in Paris, where she taught singing.

Slezak, Leo (*b* Krásná Hora, 18 Aug. 1873; *d* Tegernsee, 1 June 1946). Austrian tenor. Studied Paris with Adolf Robinson and J. de Reszke 1908-9. Sang as a youth in chorus of Brno Opera; début there 1896, Lohengrin. Berlin 1898-9; Vienna 1901-12, 1917-27, where he made 936 appearances in 44 roles; London, C.G., 1900, 1909; N.Y., Met., 1909-13 – sang in the American première of *The Queen of Spades*. A man of imposing physique and voice. His Otello, Raoul (*Hugenots*), Radamès, and Lohengrin were much admired; in all he had a repertory of 66 parts. Possessed a great sense of humour: he once so convulsed the chorus at the Met. during *Aida* that they were fined by the management (Slezak paid the fine). After leaving the stage he appeared in several films, and wrote a number of books including *Song of Motley: Being the Reminiscences of a Hungry Tenor*. (R) His son **Walter** has appeared in several American films and in *Fledermaus*, N.Y., Met; and his daughter **Margarete** (1901-53) was a soprano, who sang mostly at the Berlin D. (R)

Slobodskaya, Oda (*b* Vilno, 28 Nov. 1888; *d* London, 30 July 1970). Russian soprano. Studied St Petersburg with Iretskaya. Début there, Narodny Dom, Sept. 1917, Lisa (*Queen of Spades*). Went to Paris 1922, where she created Parasha in Stravinsky's *Mavra*. London, Ly., 1931; C.G., 1932, 1935; Savoy 1941, Khivrya (*Sorochintsy Fair*). Also sang

with success at Milan, Sc., and Buenos Aires, Colón. She sang in first London stage performance of Delius's *Koanga* and Dargomizhsky's *Rusalka*, and title-role in first broadcast performance of *The Queen of Spades*. Operetta career as Odali Careno, Coliseum and Palladium, 1930-32. (R)

Slumber scene. A stock scene in 17th cent. Italian opera, in which a character is, or falls, asleep on the stage. The character may fall asleep to a lullaby (e.g. Poppea, to Arnalta's lullaby, in Monteverdi's *L'incoronazione di Poppea*) or simply through exhaustion (e.g. Giustino, over his plough, in Legrenzi's *Giustino*). He or she may then risk murder (as in *Poppea*), or talk in his sleep revealing secret feelings, either of hatred for a tyrant or love for the astonished beloved who has meanwhile arrived, or wake to overhear some plot, or be warned by a friendly shade of a course to pursue (a device that survives into the *Ombra scene).

Sly. Opera in 3 acts by Wolf-Ferrari; text by Forzano, developed from an idea in the Induction of Shakespeare's comedy *The Taming of the Shrew* (1593-4). Prod. Milan, Sc., 29 Dec. 1927, with Llopart, Pertile, Rossi-Morelli, Badini, cond. Panizza; London, BBC broadcast, 11 Dec. 1955, with Sladen, Vandenburg, Hemsley, R. Jones, cond. Kempe.

Smallens, Alexander (*b* St Petersburg, 1 Jan. 1889; *d* Tucson, 24 Nov. 1972). Russian, later American, conductor. Studied N.Y. and Paris. Boston 1911-14, Chicago 1919-22, Philadelphia 1924-31. Cond. premières of *Four Saints in Three Acts* and *Porgy and Bess*, and U.S. premières of *Iphigénie en Aulide*, *Feuersnot*, *Ariadne auf Naxos*, *Hin und Zurück*, and *The Invisible City of Kitezh*. Toured Europe with *Porgy and Bess* 1952-3. (R)

Smareglia, Antonio (*b* Pola, 5 May 1854; *d* Grado, 15 Apr. 1929). Italian composer. Studied Milan with Faccio, and was early associated with Boito. His first opera was the successful *Preziosa* (1879), followed by *Bianca di Cervia* (1882) and *Re Nala* (1887: a failure, destroyed by the composer). His next two operas were given sumptuous premières, *Il Vassallo di Szigeth* (1889) in Vienna under Richter, *Cornil Schut* (1893) in Dresden under Schuch. Various repeats in other German towns followed; the former opera was admired by Brahms. *Nozze istriane* (1895 – his finest work) was given first in Trieste, then (in Czech) in Prague and (in German) in Vienna. Smareglia's last operas, to texts by Silvio Benco, are *La Falena* (1897), *Océana* (1903), and *Abisso* (1914). Toscanini, who had introduced *Océana*, commissioned him to finish Boito's *Nerone*, but owing to many difficulties, above all the blindness that forced him to dictate his last two operas, only one act was finished.

In his own region of Trieste, Smareglia is still admired, though elsewhere in Italy his Wagnerian tendencies have militated against his acceptance (at the Sc. première of *Lohengrin* in 1873 he came to blows with an anti-Wagnerian). His style in fact reflects only the earlier Wagner, and was thought Wagnerian chiefly for its reliance on the orchestra and for its symphonic qualities: he is in many respects closer to the *verismo* composers, including Mascagni, and his last works show the influence of Strauss (who conducted some of his music).
Bibl: M. Smareglia: *Antonio Smareglia* (1934).

Smart, Sir George (*b* London, 10 May 1776; *d* London, 23 Feb. 1867). English conductor and teacher. Although primarily a concert conductor, he was closely connected with C.G. in the 1820s, and accompanied Kemble to Germany to engage Weber as the theatre's music director and to commission *Oberon*. He was much sought after as a teacher, and Sontag and Lind studied with him in London. Weber died in his house.
Bibl: H. and C. Cox: *Leaves from the Journals of Sir George Smart* (1907).

Smetana, Bedřich (*b* Litomyšl, 2 Mar. 1824; *d* Prague, 12 May 1884). Czech composer. His life coincided with the resurgence of Czech nationalism after the relaxation of the Austrian hegemony, and he became and has remained an outstanding musical spokesman for his country. The reawakening of artistic interest after the Austrian defeats by Italy in 1859 led to the establishment of a Provisional Theatre in 1862; Smetana immediately started work on his first patriotic opera, *Braniboři v Čechach* (The Brandenburgers in Bohemia 1862-3), produced there in 1866. Its success was eclipsed by *Prodaná nevěsta* (The Bartered Bride, 1866), which as well as remaining a national symbol for the Czechs has become Smetana's best-known opera throughout the world. *The Bartered Bride,* with its cheerful folk pleasures and vividly painted rustic types, was succeeded by the loftily heroic *Dalibor* (1868). The works typify two kinds of national feeling, but there were many who felt that with *Dalibor's* massive style and thematic transformations, too much of Wagner had possessed Smetana. *Libuše* (1872, prod. 1881) is a 'solemn festival tableau'; in the marriage of the foundress of Prague to a wise peasant it attempts to combine the different appeals of its pedecessors. *Dvě vdovy* (The Two Widows 1874) is a complete contrast – a delightful and successful attempt at transferring a French drawing-room comedy to a Czech milieu. *Hubička* (The Kiss, 1876) and *Tajemství* (The Secret, 1878) are both dramas of Czech life with music of great charm and sympathy overcoming somewhat strained librettos. *Čertova stěna* (The Devil's Wall, 1882) suffers from a muddled libretto, and was finished despite Smetana's sufferings from aural and mental ill health; its music has won high praise. He worked on *Viola,* a version of Shakespeare's *Twelfth Night,* from 1874 to 1884 without finishing more than 365 bars. All his previous operas feature in Czech repertories.
Bibl: B. Large: *Smetana* (1970).

Smirnov, Dmitry (Alexeyevich) (*b* Moscow, 19 Nov. 1882; *d* Riga, 27 Apr. 1944). Russian tenor. Début St Petersburg, under name of Solovyov, Hermitage 1903, with Mamontov's company as Gigi in Esposito's *Camorra*. Subsequently studied Moscow with E. K. Pavlovskaya. Moscow, Bolshoy, from 1904, début in *Ruslan and Lyudmila* at same perf. at which Rakhmaninov made his as a conductor; Leningrad, M., from 1907. Paris with Diaghilev company; Monte Carlo; Brussels; N.Y., Met., 1910-12; London, D.L., in Beecham's season 1914 as Levko in *May Night*. Left Russia after the Revolution but returned there for concert tour 1929. Taught London, 1935-7, Athens 1937-41. His repertory included roles in French and Italian as well as Russian opera; much admired by Puccini as Luigi in *Tabarro*. Made film of *Peter the Great* in Berlin, *c*1928. The soprano Lydia Smirnova-Maltseva was his wife. The most admired Russian tenor of his generation. (R)

Smyth, (Dame) **Ethel** (*b* London, 23 Apr. 1858; *d* Woking, 9 May 1944). English composer. Her output includes six operas – *Fantasio* (1898), *Der Wald* (1902), *The Wreckers* (1906), *The Boatswain's Mate* (1916), *Fête galante* (1923), and *Entente cordiale* (1925). Brought up in days when Germany reigned musically supreme, she studied in Leipzig and had the first three of her operas produced in Germany. In her music, her own breezy Englishry blows through a late German Romantic scene: for all the local colour of their setting, and the use of English ballads, the structure and much of the music of *The Wreckers,* and still more those of *The Boatswain's Mate,* reveal this. Her entertaining series of memoirs conveys considerable relish for the long struggle against suspicion of a woman who composed, and did so with a robust professionalism that took men's breath away.
Bibl: C. St. John: *Ethel Smyth* (1959).

Snow Maiden, The. 'Spring tale' in prologue and 4 acts by Rimsky-Korsakov; text by composer, after Ostrovsky's drama (1873) on a folktale. Prod. St Petersburg, M., 10 Feb. 1882, with Kamenskaya, Stravinsky, Velinskaya, Bichurina, Makarova, Pryanishnikov, Schröder, Vasilyev, Koryakin, Solovyov, cond. Nápravník; N.Y., Met., 23 Jan. 1922, with Bori, D'Arle, Delaunois, Harrold, Laurenti, Rothier, cond. Bodansky; London, S.W., 12 Apr. 1933, with Dyer, Cross, Coates, Davies, Austin, Kelsey, cond. Collingwood.

The Snow Maiden (Snegurochka) (sop.), who is safe from the sun only so long as she renounces love, begins the life of a mortal with Bobyl (ten.) and Bobylikha (mezzo). She is attracted to the singer Lel (con.), who resists her; but Mizgir (bar.), come to marry Kupava (sop.), falls in love with her, in vain. Tsar Berendey (ten.), asked to judge the Snow Maiden's actions, is impressed by her beauty and promises a reward to anyone who can win her love. At a feast, Lel prefers Kupava to her, and she flees from Mizgir. She appeals to her mother, Spring (mezzo), and then greets Mizgir lovingly. But the warmth of love is fatal to her; she dies, and Mizgir throws himself into the lake.

Sobinov, Leonid (Vitalyevich) (*b* Yaroslavl, 7 June 1872; *d* Riga, 14 Oct. 1934). Russian tenor. After studying law, turned to singing and studied Moscow with Dodonov and Santagano-Gorchakova. Début Moscow 1893-4 at Shelaputinsky T. under name of Sobonni in small roles. Bolshoy 1897, Sinodal (*The Demon*); St Petersburg, M., where his Lensky was thought better than Figner's; Milan, Sc., 1904-6, 1911. Director Moscow, B., 1917-18. Singing career continued until 1933, when he celebrated his 35 years as a singer at a gala perf. at the Bolshoy. Excelled in such diverse roles as Romeo, Lohengrin, Orfeo, and Werther. (R)

Söderström, Elisabeth (*b* Stockholm, 7 May 1927). Swedish soprano. Studied Stockholm with Mme Skildonz. Début Stockholm, 1947 Bastienne. Stockholm, Royal O., since 1950; Gly. since 1957 as Composer, Octavian, Susanna, Elisabeth Zimmer (*Elegy for Young Lovers*), Countess (*Capriccio*), Tatyana, Christine (*Intermezzo*); London, C.G., 1960 with Royal Swedish Opera as Daisy Doody (*Aniara*) and Morgana (*Alcina*), then Countess, Fiordiligi, Mélisande. N.Y., Met., 1959-64. Repertory also includes Marschallin, Marie (*Wozzeck*), Governess (*Turn of the Screw*), Emilia Marty (*Makropoulos Case*), Jenůfa. One of the finest singing actresses of the 1960s and 1970s; her singing is sensitive and musicianly. (R)

Sofia. Captial of Bulgaria. After the liberation of Bulgaria from the Turks in 1878, efforts were made to establish opera in the capital. The moving spirits in the foundation of the Dramatichesko-Operna Trupa in 1890 were Dragomir Kazakov (1866-1948), Ivan Slavkov, and the conductor and pianist Angel Bukorest-lyev (1870-1850). The first performance, conducted by Bukorestlyev, was given in the hall of the cultural society, Slavyanska Beseda, in 1891, and consisted of excerpts from *Die lustige Weiber von Windsor* and *Trovatore*; a second performance of excerpts followed in the same year. Bulgarian singers returning from foreign training formed the Bulgarska Opera Druzhba (Bulgarian Operatic Association) in 1907: the leaders were Kazakov, the bass Ivan Vulpe (1876-1929) and his wife the soprano Bogdana Gyuseleva-Vulpe (1878-1932), and especially the tenor Konstantin Mikhailov-Stoyan (1853-1914), son of Russian emigré parents, who had been a distinguished Bolshoy soloist and had sung with Shalyapin before settling in Bulgaria. Performances were given in the Naroden T. (National T.) in 1908. By 1910 a talented group of well-trained singers had gathered in Sofia, among them the tenor Panayot Dimitrov (1882-1941), the basses Ivan Vulpe and Georgy Donchev (1884-1936) (principal teacher of the next generation), the soprano Christina Morfova (1889-1936), and the tenor Stefan Makedonski (1885-1952). In that year, 1910, they gave the first important season of Bulgarian opera, and its success was immediately followed up.

The Opera T. survived with difficulty during the war; it received a subsidy for the first time in 1922, and was made the Darzhavna Narodna Opera (National State Opera). A strong company was built up; its repertory consisted chiefly of Russian and Italian opera, with an increasing number of native works. A new theatre was built after the Second World War and the repertory was further extended. In 1966 the company gave performances in Western Europe. As well as achieving a high artistic standard, the Sofia Opera has produced a number of distinguished singers, notably Boris *Christoff and Nikolay *Ghiaurov. In 1975 Dimiter Petkov succeeded Dimiter Uzunov as director.

The first efforts to form an operetta company date from the early years of this century, but it was not until 1912 that Angel Zlatkarov succeeded in forming a company of 30 which gave performances at the Odeon. Other theatres which staged operetta were the Korona, the Renaissance, and the Svoboden; here a repertory was given drawn chiefly from Vienna and Paris. The success of this genre with the public led to the foundation in 1922 of the Kooperativen Opereten T.; though on the outskirts of the city, it attracted large audiences. In 1944 the theatre was renamed the Khudozhestven Opereten Teatar (T. of Operetta Art). The Darzhaven Musikalen T. was rebuilt and nationalised in 1948 (dir, Stefan Makedonski, whose name it assumed on his death). Standards are comparatively old-fashioned, but the repertory, divided chiefly between Viennese, Russian, French, and Bulgarian operetta, remains full and varied, and audiences exceedingly enthusiastic.

Sola, perduta, abbandonata. Manon Lescaut's (sop.) final aria leading to her death scene in Act 4 of Puccini's *Manon Lescaut*.

Soldaten, Die. Opera in 4 acts (15 scenes) by Zimmermann; text by the composer from the drama by Jakob Michael Reinhold Lenz (1776). Prod. Cologne, 15 Feb. 1965, with Edith Gabry, De Ridder, Brokmeier, Nicolai, cond. Gielen; Edinburgh Festival, 21 Aug. 1972, by Deutsche Oper am Rhein, with Gayer, De Ridder, Runge, Rintzler, cond. Wich. Total theatre, with jazz, film, speech, electronic music, ballet, etc. all used to the full.

Marie (sop.), who is engaged to Stolzius (bar.), is seduced by the Baron Desportes (ten.), a high-ranking army officer; degraded, she becomes the soldiers' whore.

Soldiers' Chorus. The chorus sung in Act 4, scene 3, of Gounod's *Faust* to the words 'Gloire immortelle de nos dieux'.

Solenne in quest'ora. The duet in Act 3, scene 2, of Verdi's *La forza del destino* between Alvaro (ten.) and Carlo (bar.) in which they swear eternal friendship.

Solera, Temistocle (*b* Ferrara, 25 Dec. 1815; *d* Milan, 21 Apr. 1878). Italian librettist and composer. Ran away from boarding school in Vienna and joined a travelling circus; eventually arrested by the Austrian police in Hungary. Admired as a poet by *Merelli; was given the libretto of Verdi's *Oberto* to refashion, and was Verdi's favourite librettist for three years, working for him on *Nabucco* (partly plagiarized, it seems), *I Lombardi, Giovanna d'Arco*, and *Attila*; with the latter not quite completed, Solera left for Spain to follow his wife, the singer Teresa Rosmini. His subsequent adventures include periods as a manager in Madrid, Queen Isabella's lover, editor of a religious magazine in Milan, secret courier between Napoleon III and the Khedive of Egypt (for whom he also reorganized the police force), and various other pursuits, before he fell on hard times. He died in poverty and neglect. His librettos suited Verdi at this period, in their bold theatrical effects and vigorous, unsubtle verse. He composed four operas to his own texts: *Ildegonda* (1840), *Il contadino d'Agliate* (1841), *Genio e sventura* (1843), and *La hermana de Pelayo* (1845).

Solti, (Sir) Georg (*b* Budapest, 21 Oct. 1912). Hungarian, later naturalized British, conductor. Studied Budapest with Dohnányi and Kodály. Conductor Budapest 1933-9. Worked with Toscanini, Salzburg, 1937. In Switzerland during war years. Music director, Munich State Opera 1947-52 and Frankfurt 1952-61. San Francisco 1953; Chicago 1956-7. Edinburgh, with Hamburg Opera, 1952; Gly. 1954; London, C.G., 1959: music director 1961-71. Built up the

Royal Opera to a high musical and artistic level. Paris, O., 1973, as musical adviser. One of the best Verdi, Wagner, and Strauss conductors of the day; also specializes in modern scores. (R)

Somers, Harry (*b* Toronto, 11 Sept. 1925). Canadian composer. His major theatrical work, and one of the finest operas by a Canadian, is *Louis Riel* (1967), commissioned for the Canadian O.C. in Toronto. The work deals with the inflammatory situation which arose in Canada in 1869 when Riel, the visionary Métis leader in Manitoba, came into conflict with Sir John A. Macdonald, the Prime Minister. Riel was eventually executed for treason in 1885 but recent views have grown increasingly sympathetic towards him. The text, by Mavor Moore and Jacques Languirand, is in both French and English as appropriate to the characters and situations. Somers's score is an eclectic but personal and original blend of contemporary European techniques and a distinctly Canadian musical heritage. The Canadian O.C. produced *Louis Riel* in Toronto and Montreal in 1967, and again in Toronto in 1968, and it has been broadcast nationally on both radio and television. Somers is also the composer of two one-act operas, *The Fool* (1953) and *The Homeless Ones* (1955), both with texts by Michael Fram.
Bibl: R. Murray Schafer: *The Public of the Music Theatre — Louis Riel: A Case Study,* (1972).

Somigli, Franca (orig. Marin Bruce Clark) (*b* Chicago, 1901; *d* Trieste, 14 May 1974). American-Italian soprano. Studied violin in U.S.A., then singing Milan with Mario Malatesta, Votto, and Storchio. Début Rovigo, 1926, Mimì. Milan, Sc., 1933-44; Rome, T.R., 1934-43; Salzburg, 1936-9, Alice Ford. Buenos Aires, T.C., 1936-9; N.Y., Met., 1937. Created Conterina in Pizzetti's *L'Orseolo*. Particularly distinguished in the Wagner and Strauss repertory, including Salome, Marschallin, Arabella, Sieglinde, and Kundry. Married to the conductor **Giuseppe Antonicelli** (*b* Castrovillari, 29 Dec. 1896) who was director of the Teatro Giuseppe Verdi, *Trieste, 1937-45 and 1953-72, and who conducted at Covent Garden, N.Y. Met., and Milan, Sc.

Son lo spirito che nega. Mefistofele's (bass) aria in Act 1 of Boito's *Mefistofele*.

Sonnambula, La (The Sleepwalker). Opera in 2 acts by Bellini; text by Romani. Prod. Milan.T.C., 6 Mar. 1831, with Pasta, Taccani, Baillou-Hilaret, Rubini, Crippa, L. Mariani, Biondi; London, King's, 28 July 1831, with Pasta, Rubini, Santini; N.Y., Park T., 13 Nov. 1835, with Paton, Wood, Brough, cond. Penson.

In a quiet little Swiss village, early in the 19th cent., Amina (sop.), foster-daughter of Teresa (mezzo), owner of the mill, is to become betrothed to Elvino (ten.), a young farmer. Lisa (sop.), the proprietress of the local inn and herself in love with Elvino, gladly entertains the handsome Count Rodolfo (bass), the lord of the castle recently returned to the village. Amina, unknown to her lover and friends, is a sleepwalker, and she enters the Count's bedroom by night and is discovered asleep in his room. The distraught Elvino is now ready to marry Lisa, but the Count tries to prevent this by explaining sleepwalking. The villagers scoff; but at that moment Amina is seen walking in her sleep along the edge of the roof (in some prods., the insecure bridge over the mill stream, which collapses once she is safely across). Elvino gives her the ring he had taken back after she was discovered in the Count's bedroom, and Amina awakens to find Elvino ready to marry her.

Also opera on same text by Antoni (*Amina*, 1825). Other somnambulism operas by Piccinni (*Il sonnambulo*, 1797), Paer (*La sonnambula*, 1800), L. Ricci (*Il sonnambulo*, 1829), and Miceli (*Somnambule*, 1870).

Sontag, Henriette (Gertrud Walpurgis, orig. Sonntag) (*b* Coblenz, 3 Jan. 1806; *d* Mexico City, 17 June 1854). German soprano. Daughter of a comedian and actress, she made her first public appearances at Darmstadt aged six. Studied Prague Conservatory. Début when 15 as Princess in Boieldieu's *Jean de Paris*. Vienna from 1822. In 1823 heard in *La donna del lago* by Weber, who immediately offered her title role in *Euryanthe*. Berlin 1825, Paris 1826, London 1828. Her marriage to Count Rossi interrupted her stage career. Returned to stage after the political unrest of 1848 had impaired their fortunes. Died of cholera caught in Mexico, 1854. Her voice, which she used with exquisite taste and charm, was a clear, bright soprano reaching e'''. Her execution was said to have been unsurpassed by any singer of her time – some thought she even excelled Catalani. Her most famous roles were Donna Anna, Susanna, Rosina, Semiramide, and Amina. She created Miranda in Halévy's *La tempesta* at H.M.'s (1850).

Bibl: T. Gautier: *L'Ambassadrice* (1850); E. Pirchan: *Henriette Sontag* (1946).

Sonzogno, Edoardo (*b* Milan, 21 Apr. 1836; *d* Milan, 14 Mar. 1920). Italian publisher. His firm was founded at the end of the 18th cent. by G. B. Sonzogno. He began to publish French and Italian music in 1874. Established a series of competitions for new works in 1883, the second contest of 1888 being won by Mascagni's *Cavalleria rusticana*. Opened the Teatro Lirico Internazionale in Milan, 1894.

Soot, Fritz (*b* Neunkirchen, 20 Aug. 1878; *d* Berlin, 9 June 1965). German tenor. After a career as an actor at Karlsruhe, Hoftheater,

1901-7, studied singing Dresden with Scheidemantel. Début Dresden Hofoper 1908, Tonio (*La fille du régiment*). Dresden 1908-18: created Italian Singer in *Rosenkavalier*. Stuttgart 1918-22; Berlin, S.O., 1922-44, 1946-52; Berlin, Stä. O., 1946-48. Created Drum-major in *Wozzeck*, and roles in operas by Schreker and Pfitzner; first Berlin Laca and Mephistopheles (Busoni). London, C.G., 1924-5 Siegmund, Siegfried, Tristan, Walther, and Aegisthus. Also a famous Otello and Palestrina. (R)

Sophie. Faninal's daughter (sop.), the heroine of Strauss's *Der Rosenkavalier*.

Soprano (from It. *sopra* above). The highest category of female (or artificial male) voice. Many subdivisions exist within opera houses: the commonest in general use (though seldom by composers in scores) are given below, with examples of roles and their approximate *tessitura*. These divisions often overlap, and do not correspond exactly from country to country. In general, distinction is more by character than by *tessitura*, especially in France: thus, the examples of the roles give a more useful indication of the different voices' quality than any attempted technical definition.

German: dramatischer Sopran (Brünnhilde: g–c'''); lyrischer Sopran (Arabella: b♭–c♯'''); hoher Sopran or Koloratur Sopran (Zerbinetta, Queen of the Night: g–f'''); Soubrette (Blonde, Aennchen: b♭–c''').

Italian: soprano drammatico (Tosca: g–c'''); soprano lirico (Countess, Mimì: b♭–c'''); soprano lirico spinto (Butterfly, Desdemona: a–c♯'''); soprano leggiero (Norina, Despina: g–f''').

French: soprano dramatique (Valentine, Alceste: g–c'''); soprano lyrique (Lakmé: b♭–c♯'''); soubrette (Zerline in *Fra Diavolo*: b♭–c'''); soprano demicaractère (Manon, Casandre: a–c♯'''); *Dugazon, divided as jeune Dugazon (Bérénice in Thomas's *Psyché*), première Dugazon (Djelma in Auber's *Le Premier jour de bonheur*), forte première Dugazon (La Comtesse in Thomas's *Raymond*), and mère Dugazon (Mistress Bentson in *Lakmé*); *Falcon (Alice in *Robert le Diable*: b♭–c♯''').

See also *Castrato, Mezzo-soprano*.

Sorochintsy Fair. Opera (unfinished) by Mussorgsky; text by composer, after Gogol's story (1831-2). Mussorgsky completed only the prelude, the market scene and part of the sequel, most of Act 2, a vision scene adapted from *A Night on the Bare Mountain*, an instrumental hopak, and two songs. The first editors were Lyadov (1904) and Karatygin (1912). A version from these editions, with Rimsky-Korsakov's version of *A Night on the Bare Mountain*, and additions from other hands, prod. Moscow, Free T., 21 Oct. 1913, with Makarova-Shevchenko, Milyavskaya, Monakhov, Draculi, Karatov, cond. Saradjev. Version by Cherepnin prod. Monte Carlo, 17 Mar. 1923, with Luart, MacCormack, cond. Cherepnin. N.Y., Met., 29 Nov. 1930, with Müller, Bouraskaya, Jagel, Pinza, cond. Serafin; London, Fortune T., 17 Feb. 1934. In addition to these a version by Shebalin was published 1933.

Cherevik (bass) has brought his daughter Parasya (sop.) to the Fair, where she meets her lover Gritzko (ten.) and obtains her father's consent to their betrothal. His wife Khivrya (mezzo) disapproves, but she is discovered to have taken a lover, the Priest's Son (ten.), and eventually all ends happily for the young couple.

Other operas on the subject by Yanovsky (1899), Ryabov (1936), and V. Alexandrov.

Sosarme, Re di Media. Opera in 3 acts by Handel; text an altered version of Noris's *Alfonso Primo*. Prod. London, Hm., 15 Feb. 1732, with Strada, Senesino, Bagnolesi, Bertolli, Montagnana. Revived Abingdon, 1970.

Sotin, Hans (*b* Dortmund, 10 Sept. 1939). German bass. Studied with Wilhelm Hezel, and Hamburg with Dieter Jacob. Début Essen, 1962, Police Commissioner (*Rosenkavalier*). Essen 1961-4, Hamburg since 1964; Bayreuth since 1971, Landgrave, Mark, Pogner, Gurnemanz. N.Y., Met., 1972; Glyndebourne, 1968, Sarastro; London, C.G. 1974, Hunding. At Hamburg appeared in premières of works by Blacher, Einem, Klebe, Kelemen, Penderecki, and Steffen. One of the most talented singing actors on the German stage. (R)

Sotto voce (*It* below the voice). A direction to sing softly or 'aside'.

Soubrette (*Fr* from Old Fr., *soubret*, cunning or shrewd). Used in opera for such roles as Serpina, Despina, Susanna, etc. — the cunning servant girl; then, more generally, to designate a light soprano comedienne, such as Marzelline (*Fidelio*), Adele (*Fledermaus*). In Italian opera the term *servetta* is used. See *Damigella, Soprano*.

Souez (orig. Rains), **Ina** (*b* Windsor, Col., 3 June 1908). American soprano. Studied Denver with Florence Hinman and Milan with Sofia del Campo. Début Ivrea, 1928, Mimì. London, C.G., 1929, 1935; Gly. 1934-39, Fiordiligi and Donna Anna; N.Y., New O.C., 1941, Fiordiligi. After the war became a singer with Spike Jones and His City Slickers. (R)

Souffleur. See **Prompter.**

Soulacroix, Gabriel (*b* Villeneuve-sur-Lot), 11 Dec. 1853; *d* Paris, Aug. 1905). French baritone. Studied Toulouse and Paris. Début Brussels, M., 1878, Bellamy in *Les dragons de Villars*. Paris, O.C., 1885-94, where he created Morot

(*La Basoche*); was first Paris Ford; Paris, Gaîté-Lyrique; Monte Carlo, 1902, creating Le Prieur in *Le Jongleur de Notre-Dame;* London, C.G., 1881-4, 1898, Figaro (Rossini), Escamillo, Mercutio. (R)

Souliotis, Elena (*b* Athens, 28 May 1943). Greek soprano. Brought up in Buenos Aires. Studied Milan with Mercedes Llopart. Début Naples, S.C., 1964, Santuzza. Chicago, 1966, Elena (*Mefistofele*); N.Y., Met., 1969, Lady Macbeth; London, C.G., 1969, 1972, 1973, Lady Macbeth, Abigaille, Santuzza. An exciting but undisciplined singer whose early promise has not been fulfilled. (R)

South Africa. The first operas heard in Cape Town were the more popular British operas by Dibdin, Storace, etc. in the early years of the 19th century. The first serious opera was an amateur production of *Der Freischütz* (1831). In the 1870s touring companies began to visit South Africa and seasons were given at Johannesburg and elsewhere, among them the C.R., Moody-Manners, and Quinlan Companies. An annual opera season in Johannesburg grew out of the 'Music Fortnight' established in 1926, and visiting artists from Europe augmented local talent. In the Cape Town University, Erik Chisholm gave a number of outstanding opera performances, and in 1956 the Eoan Group, composed entirely of coloured singers, gave its first opera season.

Sovrintendente (*It* superintendent). The administrator of an Italian opera house—not necessarily the artistic or music director.

Soyer, Roger (*b* Paris 1 Sept. 1939). French bass. Studied Paris with Georges Daum and Georges Jouatte. Début Paris O., 1962, in small roles. Aix Festival, 1965, and subsequently as Pluto in *Orfeo* (Monteverdi), Don Giovanni, Don Basilio, Arkel; Wexford, 1968, in *Jolie fille de Perth;* Edinburgh Festival, Don Giovanni, 1973. At Paris O. has sung in many new productions since 1973, including Procida (*Vêpres siciliennes*), Don Giovanni, and Méphistophélès. More a bass-baritone than a true bass, he is in the tradition of Faure and Journet. (R)

Spain. Popular musical dramas were common in Spain from the Middle Ages, especially with religious subjects; the first Spanish opera is to Calderón's text *Celos aun del ayre matan* (1660), with music by Juan Hidalgo. Calderón was also the author of the text for the first *zarzuela, El Jardín de Falerina* (1684). However, developments were halted by the restraint placed on native opera by Philip V in favour of Italian opera. In the 18th cent. a number of Spanish composers wrote operas in Italian, notably Martin y Soler and Terradellas. The history of 18th cent. Spanish opera is largely that of struggle for supremacy between zarzuela and Italian-modelled serious opera. Then a Royal decree of 1800 forbade all operas except those sung in Spanish by Spaniards; translations of foreign works were still preferred, though these now included French opéra comique. Ramón *Carnicer wrote a number of popular and pioneering operas; in contrast to this genre, in the 19th cent. there developed a rivalry between two versions of zarzuela, the *género grande* and the *género chico*. Great influence was exercised by Felipe *Pedrell, and in the early years of the 20th cent. Spanish works were given at the T. Real (which closed, however, in 1925). Despite the continuing difficulties, Spanish operas of European popularity were composed by *Albéniz (*Pepita Jimenez*, 1896) and *Granados (*Goyescas*, 1916), and by *Falla, whose greatest stage work was for ballet, but who wrote *La Vida Breve* (1913), *El retablo del Maese Pedro* (1923) and the huge, long-neglected, unfinished *L'Atlantida*. See *Barcelona, Madrid*.

Spani, Hina (orig. Higinia Tuñon) (*b* Puán, 15 Feb. 1896; *d* Buenos Aires, 11 July. 1969). Argentinian soprano. Studied Buenos Aires, and with Montasi in Milan. Début Milan, Sc., 1915, Anna (Catalani's *Loreley*). Sang regularly in Italy until 1934; Buenos Aires, C., 1915-40. Created title role in first stage performance of Respighi's *Maria Egiziaca* (Colón 1934), as well as in a number of South American works. Her 70 roles ranged from Ottavia in Monteverdi's *L'Incoronazione di Poppea* to Verdi's Lady Macbeth. One of the finest lyric-dramatic sopranos of the inter-war period. (R)

Sparafucile. The professional assassin (bass) in Verdi's *Rigoletto*.

Spech-Salvi, Adelina (*b* Milan, 18 Aug. 1811; *d* Bologna, Aug 1886). Italian soprano. Studied with her father, the tenor Giuseppe Spech. Début London, 1825, Isolier (*Comte Ory*), at Malibran's suggestion. Successful career in Italy, especially Naples, S.C., where she created Eleonora d'Este (*Torquato Tasso*); a successful Norma and Amina. After retiring from stage, taught singing in Bologna. Married the tenor Lorenzo *Salvi.

Spetrino, Francesco (*b* Palermo, 2 July 1857; *d* Rome, 27 July 1948). Italian conductor and composer. Studied Palermo. Appeared with success in Italy 1876-93; Warsaw Opera, 1894-7; Vienna, H., 1904-8, where he conducted the first *Madama Butterfly* outside Italy, 1907; N.Y. Met., 1908-9. Abandoned career during First World War. Composed 2 operas and ballets; responsible for one of the several Italian translations of *Parsifal*.

Spieloper (*Ger* opera-play). A type of 19th cent. light opera, resembling *Singspiel, with a

comic subject and spoken dialogue, e.g. some of Lortzing's works.

Spielplan (*Ger* performance plan). The published *prospectus of the season's repertory. Also a monthly publication giving programmes in all German opera houses.

Spieltenor (*Ger* acting tenor). A light tenor in a German company who plays such character roles as Mime, David, and Pedrillo. See *Tenor*.

Spinning Chorus. The chorus sung by Senta's friends in the opening of Act 2 of Wagner's *Der fliegende Holländer*.

Spinto (*It* pushed). The description given to a voice, almost always tenor, of particular vigour and attack; the description may also be qualified, e.g. *tenore lirico spinto*.

Spirto gentil. Fernando's (ten.) aria in the last act of Donizetti's *La favorita* in which he sings of his love for Leonora.

Split (It. Spalato). Town in Dalmatia, Yugoslavia. The first theatre was built in the 17th cent. The Italians twice disbanded the company, and in 1859 built a theatre for their visiting companies. The first local opera was given in 1921, on the foundation of the National Dalmatian T., but the administration moved to Šarajevo. The post-war company gives indoor and summer festival performances in Diocletian's palace.

Spohr, Louis (*b* Brunswick, 5 Apr. 1784; *d* Kassel, 22 Oct. 1859). German composer and violinist. Studied Seesen, with Riemenschneider and Dufour, Brunswick with Kunisch and Dufour. His first stage work, *Die Prüfung* (1806), was an operetta which received a concert performance during his leadership of the ducal band at Gotha; its successor, *Alruna* (1808), was rehearsed at Weimar, when it won Goethe's admiration, but was not performed. The first production he achieved was of *Der Zweikampf mit der Geliebten* (1811); this was followed in 1816 by *Faust*.

Faust is a landmark in Romantic opera; it is, indeed, often claimed as the first true representative of the genre. The overture's use of leading themes from the opera was one of many devices admired by Weber, who conducted the première and whose review of it contains a remarkable formulation of the aims of German opera; he writes of 'a few melodies, carefully and felicitously devised, which weave through the whole work like delicate threads, holding it together intellectually'. Spohr strengthened this aspect of the work when he revised it in 1852, adding recitatives.

The work's popularity was, at the time, exceeded by that of *Zemire und Azor* (1819), given at the Frankfurt Opera during Spohr's two years as conductor, 1817-19. Here, the system of Reminiscence Motive and Leitmotiv is taken even further, and the theme of redemption through love, barely hinted at in *Grétry's treatment, achieves new significance. In other ways, too, the work is an anticipation of Wagner, e.g. in the atmospheric use of harmony and orchestration.

Among Spohr's operatic plans was an idea for the subject of *Der Freischütz*; he abandoned this, without later regrets, on learning that it was being set by Weber, who recommended him for the post of Hofkapellmeister at Kassel. Here he remained for the rest of his life, becoming Generalmusikdirektor in 1847. His greatest operatic success was *Jessonda* (1823). Spohr and his audiences were fascinated by the characteristically Romantic idea of an Oriental subject: he was here also able to give his lyrical gift, and above all his mastery of chromatic music, their fullest effect in a dramatic framework. He also gave a new fluency to recitative, making it almost continuous arioso, and loosened the set forms of aria, until he had virtually achieved the *Durchkomponierung* of Wagner.

Other works which followed were *Der Berggeist* (1825), *Pietro von Albano* (1827), and *Der Alchymist* (1830). Suggestions of *Tristan und Isolde*, remarkable in *Jessonda*, are taken further in these, especially with the *Durchkomponierung* of *Der Berggeist* and the advanced chromatic harmony of *Der Alchymist*. He also contributed to *Der Matrose* (1839), written in collaboration with Hauptmann, Grenzebach, and Baldewein. In 1842 he became the first musician of importance to support Wagner, when he produced *Der fliegende Holländer* at Kassel only five months after the Dresden première. He later staged *Tannhäuser*, but was frustrated by the Elector in his attempts to follow this with *Lohengrin* (another work influenced by *Jessonda*). The last of his operas was *Die Kreuzfahrer* (1845).

Bibl: L. Spohr: *Selbstbiographie* (1860-1; trans. 1865, 1878).

Spoleto. Town in Umbria, Italy. Opera was given from 1667 in the 17th cent. T. Nobile, which was reconstructed in 1830 as the T. Caio Melisso. The T. Nuovo opened in August 1864 with operas by Verdi and Petrella, with Stolz and Isabella Galletti. In 1958 Menotti established the Festival of Two Worlds, which gives young European and American artists chances to appear in productions by Menotti himself and Visconti. Thomas Schippers was music director 1958-70; he was succeeded by Christopher Keene. Schippers and Visconti were responsible for Donizetti's *Duca d'Alba* (1959), *Salome* (1961), and *Manon Lescaut* (1973); Schippers and Menotti collaborated on *Bohème* (1960), *Carmen* with the young Verrett and George Shirley (1962), and *Don Giovanni*

(1967). Other productions have included Donizetti's *Furioso all'isola di San Domingo* (1967), Mercadante's *Il giuramento* (1970), *Lulu*, produced by Polranski (1974), and Salieri's *Prima la musica, dopo le parole* (1974).

Spoletta. The police agent (ten.) in Puccini's *Tosca*.

Spontini, Gasparo (*b* Maiolati, 14 Nov. 1774; *d* Maiolati, 24 Jan. 1851). Italian composer and conductor. After early local teaching, studied Naples. He soon received a commission from a visiting German opera director. The successful outcome, *Li Puntigli delle donne* (1796), was immediately followed by five more works. When the Neapolitan Court moved to Palermo before the advancing French in 1798, Spontini took on Cimarosa's post as conductor and in 1800 produced three deft Neapolitan operas. Shortly afterwards he left for Paris, where his light style was unsuited to the special demands of opéra comique; but with the carefully composed *Milton* (1804), he won a success that carried his name to Germany and Austria. One of *Milton's* librettists was Étienne de Jouy, who, understanding better than the composer himself where his gifts lay, provided for *La Vestale* (1807) a text that fully released Spontini's talent and thus led to his recognition as one of the leading opera composers of the day.

Spontini intensified selected features of Gluck, Cherubini, and Méhul, and put them to novel use in his serious operas. These abound in processions, rituals, oath-takings, ceremonies and other imposing stage effects with choral groupings and tableaux. Spontini loved grandiose effects and striking dramatic contrasts; his calculated *coups de théâtre* suceed because of his sense of dramatic continuity and timing and his grasp of large-scale dramatic effect. *La Vestale* is Gluck's *tragédie lyrique* adapted to the taste of Empire audiences.

The Empress Joséphine's patronage carried Spontini through all opposition; and after the constant rewriting that was his habit, *La Vestale* triumphed in 1807. For *Fernand Cortez* the librettist was again Jouy, the patron now Napoleon (who felt that the subject might influence opinion more favourably in the Spanish Wars). A more polished work, its success was even greater. *Cortez* is a grand historical pageant filled with tableaux, including a cavalry charge, the burning of the Spanish fleet, a heroine who plunges into a lake, and other effects; the choruses of Spaniards and Aztecs are central characters, and the ballets are more functional than before in opera.

In 1810 Spontini took over the Théâtre-Italien, and at the Odéon formed a distinguished and enterprising ensemble before his dismissal in 1812; his restoration in 1814 was brief and again controversial, for his undoubted gifts were allied to a somewhat overbearing personality. A few minor pieces followed before *Olympie* (1819), another *tragédie lyrique* which again included much spectacle – processions, a Bacchanal, a battle, an apotheosis. Though carefully composed over a long period, it was not well received in its first form in 1819, but assiduous revision brought success in Paris and in Berlin, where Spontini was now summoned. Much impressed, Frederick William III of Prussia engaged him for the Berlin Court Opera, where he worked in uneasy co-operation with the Intendant, Brühl. His temper and pomposity quickly caused difficulties, and when the imposing spectacle of *Olympie* was succeeded in a few weeks by the thrilling new experience of Weber's *Der Freischütz* in 1821, Berlin was divided, the Court siding with Spontini's grandiose Italianate works, Brühl and the public preferring the new German Romantic opera. Spontini's painstaking method of composition prevented him from producing as much as was required of him. In *Nurmahal* (1822) and *Alcidor* (1825) he had to compete with German Romantic opera for Berlin, though actually they are closer in nature to French *opéra-féerie*. *Alcidor* in particular hardened the division of public opinion, and Spontini could not rally his scattering admirers even by a conscientious attempt at a German opera, *Agnes von Hohenstaufen* (1829). This was more continuously composed, building up large formal complexes and lengthening the finale to cover much of an act; in its nature and structure Spontini attempted to regain a hold on German audiences by way of a historical drama.

The sympathies of the new king who succeeded in 1840 lay elsewhere, but Spontini hastened his own downfall; though fairly, even generously treated, he felt obliged to leave. He made occasional return visits to Germany: on one of them, he conducted at Dresden a *Vestale* prepared by Wagner, who greatly admired much in Spontini and especially his command as a conductor. He spent most of his remaining years, however, in Paris, before returning to his native village.

Bibl: A. Ghislanzoni: *Gasparo Spontini* (1951).

Sprechgesang (*Ger* speech-song). A term used initially by Schoenberg and Berg for a form of musical declamation in which the actual pitch of the notes is indicated but the voice falls or rises in a manner somewhere between true speech and true song. An earlier version, known as *Sprechstimme* (*Ger* speaking voice) is used by Humperdinck in *Königskinder* (1910).

Sprezzatura (*It* scornfulness). The term used by Caccini for a 'nonchalant' manner of singing, presumably indicating a very free rubato.

Staatsoper (*Ger* state opera).

Stabile, Mariano (*b* Palermo, 12 May 1888; *d* Milan, 11 Jan. 1968). Italian baritone. Studied Rome, Santa Cecilia, with Cotogni. Début Palermo 1909, Amonasro. Milan, Sc., from 1922, when he sang Falstaff in the opening performance of Toscanini's third and greatest Scala régime; London, C.G., 1926-31; Glyndebourne 1936-9 and 1948 (Edinburgh); Cambridge and Stoll Theatres 1946-8; Chicago 1924-5; Salzburg 1935-9. Created title role in Respighi's *Belfagor*, and the Barber in the first Italian performance of *Die schweigsame Frau*. His repertory of some 60 parts also included Hamlet, Don Giovanni, Don Alfonso, Figaro (Mozart and Rossini), Malatesta (*Don Pasquale*), Iago, and Scarpia. As Falstaff, which role he was still singing with great success in 1961, he has not been surpassed in our day. His voice was never exceptional, but his style, elegance, phrasing, musicality – in short, his qualities as a singing actor – combined to make his performances unforgettable. (R)

Stabreim (*Ger* alliteration). The system of giving cohesion to verse, and also suggesting contacts in meaning, by alliterating key words in a line and perhaps also an adjacent line. Originating in early English verse (e.g. *Piers Plowman*) and German verse, it was taken up again and cultivated for use in mythic opera by Wagner, especially in *Tristan* and *The Ring*, e.g. (Wotan to the disobedient Brünnhilde):

Was sonst du warst,
Sagte dir Wotan.
Was jetzt du bist,
das sage dir selbst.

What once you were
Wotan decided.
What now you are
you decide for yourself.
(*Walküre*, III, 2).

Here, the effect is not only assonant: a distinction is suggested between the 'w' sounds associated with Wotan and the roles and privileges formerly conferred upon Brünnhilde, and the 's' sounds associated with her disobedient separation from Wotan's will. The device was taken up by Wagner's followers; but attempts to transfer it to English have not been successful, whether in translations of Wagner (e.g. by H. and F. Corder) or in original librettos (e.g. by Holst in *Sita*).

Stade, Frederica von (*b* Somerville, 1 June 1945). American mezzo-soprano. Studied New York, Mannes School with Engelberg. Début N.Y., Met., 1970, Third Boy in *Zauberflöte*. Paris, O., 1973, Cherubino. Glyndebourne, 1973, Cherubino; London, C.G., 1975, Rosina. Salzburg. Santa Fe, Holland Festival, etc. Repertory includes Sextus, Adalgisa, Penelope (Monteverdi), Composer, Octavia, and

Mélisande. Created Nina in Pasatieri's *The Seagull* (Houston, 1974). One of the most gifted young American singers of the 1970s. (R)

Städtische Oper (*Ger* city opera).

Stage design. Although the masques and other forms of elaborate entertainment which were the forerunners of opera often required elaborate scenery (Angelo Poliziano's *Orfeo* produced at Mantua in 1472 had scenery painted by Raphael), the first operas do not appear to have had it, and not until the spectacular performances staged in Cardinal Barberini's palace in Rome (*c.* 1630-50), and the establishment of the Court theatres shortly after, did stage spectacles become the fashion.

It was in these Court theatres, with their tiers of boxes, that the stage became separated from the audience by means of the proscenium frame. This, together with the two-dimensional flat scenery, was an entirely new concept. The perspective painting which characterized much Renaissance art was seized upon by the theatre designers, and splendid two-dimensional scenery characterized the magnificent baroque productions of opera. Cesti's *Pomo d'Oro*, performed in Vienna in 1668 for the marriage of the Emperor Leopold I to Margaret of Spain, had 23 different sets, designed by Lodovico Burnacini (1636-1707), who worked for the Imperial Court in Vienna.

The *Bibiena family descended from Giovanni Maria Galli (1619-65), a native of Bibiena in Tuscany, produced several generations of theatrical architects. Giuseppe Galli-Bibiena (1696-1757) worked almost entirely in Vienna; Ferdinando (1657-1743) and the two brothers Bernardino and Fabrizio Galliari were the designers at the old Ducal Theatre in Milan, and can be said to have set the pattern for Italian stage scenery. The Galliari brothers were also the first scene painters at La Scala, and they were followed by Pietro Gonzaga, whose daring use of colour and contrasts in light and shade in the Canaletto manner, in the days of rather poor stage lighting, brought, according to his contemporaries, 'the sun on to the stage'. Alessandro Sanquirico, whose settings for Rossini and Bellini at La Scala are still quoted as models of their kind, Carlo Ferrario, who was Verdi's favourite designer, and Antonio Rovescalli continued to paint splendid and sumptuous settings for La Scala and other Italian houses. Without stage towers, scenery had to be moved on and off the stage by means of grooves; it was not until the large reconstructions of 1919-21 that La Scala had a stage tower, being previously limited to 6-7 productions a season. More recently Alessandro and Nicola *Benois, Giorgio De Chirico, Gianni Ratto, Salvatore Fiume, Pier Luigi Pizzi, Ezio Frigerio, and Piero Zuffi, and the producers Franco *Zeffirelli, Luchino, Filippo *Sanjust,

and *Visconti, who like to design their own settings, can be cited as the best of this century's Italian stage designers.

In France, the greatest advance over the old Italian system of flats was made by *Cicéri and *Daguerre. Their work had antecedents: the chemist Lavoisier had experimented in redirecting light on stage sets by means of reflectors as early as 1781; and one Col. Grobet published a treatise in 1809 calling for the abolition of painted scenery and footlights, for the dimming of house lights during the performance, and the use of relief in décor. In 1820 M.J.A. Borgnis, a professor of mechanics, proposed a more sophisticated use of lighting and of stage machinery. But it was at the Paris O. in the 1820s and 1830s that these pioneering efforts were given proper artistic realization by Cicéri and Daguerre. They evolved a style, expressive of the ideals of *Grand Opera and matching the tastes of the newly wealthy audience, which made powerful use of three-dimensional scenery and vivid lighting effects. The effect of their work was to colour a whole style of opera presentation, and thus of composition, throughout the 19th century, and even into the 20th at the Paris O.

In Germany and elsewhere in Central Europe, Italian models were long copied and Italian designers imported. However, pioneering efforts at developing three-dimensional sets, with vivid use of perspective, were made in Frankfurt by the Italian Giorgio Fuentes (1756-1821), especially with his famous staging of Mozart's *Titus* (1799). His work was greatly admired by Goethe, who tried to obtain him for the Weimar theatre. Karl Friedrich Schinkel's famous *Zauberflöte* designs (1816) and those of Karl von Gropius for *Der Freischütz* (1821) (both Berlin), Eugen Quaglio's splendid scenery for Mozart and Wagner in Munich in the middle of the century, and Johann Kautsky's Wagner settings in Vienna (1860-90) were among the landmarks in the development of German scenic design. But it was really with the advent of Alfred Roller (1854-1935) in Vienna, during Mahler's time, Leo Pasetti in Munich in the 1920s and 1930s, Adolf Mahnke and Hans Strohbach in Dresden during the same period, and Caspar Neher at various German opera houses from the 1920s, that German stage design developed its individual modern style. This has seen great interest in experiment, as with the staging of Schoenberg's *Die glückliche Hand* with its famous lighting 'crescendo', and in the use of distortion, suggestion, and symbolism.

These modern trends were greatly influenced by the writings and designs of Edward Gordon Craig and Adolphe *Appia early this century. Present-day Bayreuth, where sets and lighting have been designed by the producers Wieland and Wolfgang Wagner, is the logical development of this type of scenery. Throughout Germany there emerged in the post-war period a number of scenic designers who, if they did not completely adopt the Bayreuth style, were clearly influenced by the methods of the Wagner brothers. These included Helmut Jürgens, Alfred Siercke, Ita Maximovna, Teo Otto, and Günther Schneider-Siemssen and the French-born Jean-Pierre *Ponnelle.

With the increase in operatic activity in Great Britain, much of the scenery at Covent Garden, and Sadler's Wells and Glyndebourne in the period has been the work of native artists including Oliver Messel, John Piper, Leslie Hurry, Osbert Lancaster, and Malcolm Pride. Covent Garden made great use of the French designer Georges Wakhevitch during the 1940s and 1950s, and even employed Salvador Dali to design a highly controversial *Salome* (1949). In the early 1960s the work of Visconti and Zeffirelli became increasingly familiar at Covent Garden.

More recently the producer-designer 'team' has become a familiar feature of the British operatic scene: thus Peter Hall's productions at Covent Garden and Glyndebourne were nearly always designed by John Bury; those of John *Copley by Stefanos Lazaridis (at both C.G. and the ENO); while Anthony *Besch has worked with John Stoddart. Other designers whose work has often been seen in recent years include Josef Svoboda (C.G.), Ralph Koltai (C.G., ENO, Scottish and Welsh Opera) Timothy O'Brien (ENO), David Hockney (Glyndebourne), and Ponnelle (C.G. and Glyndebourne).

This producer-designer system has become widespread, and settings by Svoboda for productions by John Dexter can be seen in New York, Hamburg and Paris; Maximovna works regularly with Rennert, wherever he happens to be producing; Ezio Frigerio with Giorgio Strehler; Robert O'Hearn with Nathaniel Merrill; Max Bignens with Jorge Lavalli; and the late Rudolf Heinrich regularly worked with Felsenstein and Joachim Herz. The French producer Patrice Chéreau, who was responsible for the controversial centenary *Ring* at Bayreuth in 1977, always works with Richard Peduzzi.

In the United States scenery was generally copied from European models until the mid-1930s. However, Joseph *Urban created unit sets at the Boston Opera as early as 1914, while Robert Edmond Jones (a disciple of Max Reinhardt), Boris Anisfeld, and Mstislav Dobuzhinsky all designed for American companies. The arrival in the U.S.A. of a number of refugees from the opera houses of Hitler's Germany, including Herbert Graf and Leopold Sachse, brought a fresh breath of life. Graf engaged Donald Oenslager, a Broadway artist,

to design sets for *Tristan* in Philadelphia, and later *Salome, Otello,* and *Die Entführung aus dem Serail* at the Metropolitan. Influenced by Appia and by Robert Edmond Jones, Oenslager brought the ideas of a theatre to the opera stage. Harry Horner was another straight theatre designer to come to opera; he has worked for the San Francisco Opera and the Metropolitan. Eugen Berman, a neo-Baroque designer, responsible for some fine work at the Metropolitan and the City Center, was invited to design *Così fan tutte* for the Piccola Scala in Milan. Rolf Gérard's many designs for the Metropolitan also deserve mention.

The later years of the Bing regime at the Metropolitan saw the engagements of several European designers including Marc Chagall, Cecil Beaton, Heinrich, Maximovna, Otto, and Zeffirelli. Chicago and San Francisco have likewise relied heavily on European designers.

Attempts have been made in most operatic countries in the use of slide-projections on to the cyclorama (sky-cloth) in order to dispense with heavy scenery and canvases; and the elaborate slide-projection technique of the Czech 'Magic Lantern' was tried for Nono's *Intolleranza* at Venice in 1961.

The 1970s have seen simpler and cheaper and less representational types of setting, in which platforms, gauzes, and subtle lighting have been used more and more. And though there will always be a place for realistic settings, designs seem to have reached a happy compromise between the often extravagant and realistic scenery of the 1950s and 1960s and the sparse Bayreuth style of Wieland Wagner. *Bibl:* V. Mariani: *Storica della scenografia Italiana* (1930); M. Allévy: *La Mise en scène en France dans la première moitié du 19e siècle* (1938); Tafuri: *Teatri e scenografie* (1976); H. Gollob: *Musik und Bühneninszenierung* (1956); R. Hainaux: *Stage Design throughout the World since 1960* (1972).

Stagione (*It* season). The *stagione lirica* is the opera season at any Italian theatre. The *stagione* system (as opposed to the repertory system) has come to mean putting on one opera for a series of performances within a few weeks with the same cast throughout its run.

Stagno (orig. Vincenzo Andrioli), **Roberto** (*b* Palermo, 1840; *d* Genoa, 26 Apr. 1897). Italian tenor. Studied Milan, with Lamperti. Début Lisbon, S.C., 1862, Rodrigo in Rossini's *Otello.* First made his name deputizing for Tamberlik in Madrid in *Robert le Diable,* 1865, a work that remained his speciality. Moscow, B., 1868, with Désirée Artôt. He was always very popular in Madrid, and was also successful in Buenos Aires (from 1879), where he sang in the local première of Verdi's *Otello* in 1888. He was also popular in Italy, singing in Rome, Naples, and Florence (1884). N.Y., Met., 1883-4; Paris, T.I.,

1884. In 1886, in Buenos Aires, he married Gemma *Bellincioni; he then turned towards *verismo* roles, creating Turiddu in *Cavalleria rusticana*.
Bibl: B. Stagno-Bellincioni: *Roberto Stagno e Gemma Bellincioni* (1945).

Stanford, (Sir) **Charles** (*b* Dublin, 30 Sep. 1852; *d* London, 29 Mar. 1924). Irish composer. Stanford's passionate interest in establishing English opera expressed itself in ten completed works, which have suffered neglect despite vigorous championship; high claims have been made particularly for *Shamus O'Brien* (1896), *Much Ado About Nothing* (1908), and *The Travelling Companion* (1925), and also for *The Critic* (1916).

Stanislavsky (orig. Alexeyev), **Konstantin** (Sergeyevich) (*b* Moscow, 17 Jan. 1863; *d* Moscow, 7 Aug. 1938). Russian producer. Famous as actor and producer and director of the Moscow Arts Theatre, and as developer of a new realism in acting; Stanislavsky also did much for opera. From 1885, with Tchaikovsky, Taneyev, Jürgenson, and Tretyakov, he was one of the directors of the Russian Musical Society. With Vladimir *Nemirovich-Danchenko, he founded the Moscow Arts T. in 1898, whose revolutionary choice of works and methods were also to influence the staging of opera in Russia and eventually abroad. He also sang in operetta with Savva Mamontov's opera company. In 1918 he founded the O. Studio of the Bolshoy T., opening in 1919 with an act of *Eugene Onegin*; this separated from the B. in 1920. Stanislavsky proposed to use the theatrical discoveries of the Moscow Arts T. to refresh the tradition of staging opera in Russia, and hoped to develop a style of singing in which words and their meaning would be given new dramatic importance; to this he brought great system and powers of persuasion. His productions included *Werther* (1921), *Onegin* (1922), and *Il matrimonio segreto* (1925). In 1926 he moved his theatre to the Dimitrovsky T. The last production he supervised completely was *May Night* (1928). Becoming ill, he was obliged to conduct his rehearsals by summoning the cast to his bedside and even by use of the telephone. He organised a new Operatic-Dramatic Studio in 1938: the last production in which he took a personal part was *Madama Butterfly* (1938). Bibl: C. Stanislavsky and P. Rumyantsev: *Stanislavsky on Opera* (trans. 1975).

Stara Zagora. Town in Bulgaria. Opera was first given under the auspices of the important local music society 'Kaval' in 1919, but the first full-scale performance was that of *Atanasov's *Gergana* in 1925. A new company was formed in 1928. The Stara Zagora National Opera opened in 1946 and, beginning with Dargomyzhsky's

Rusalka and other Slavonic works, has developed an international repertory.

Stasov, Vladimir (Vasilyevich) (*b* St. Petersburg, 14 Jan. 1824; *d* St. Petersburg, 23 Oct. 1906). Russian critic. His influence on the development of Russian national opera was enormous, and his opinion and practical encouragement was valued by all his contemporaries. He wrote valuable studies of Glinka, Mussorgsky, Borodin, Cui, and Rimsky-Korsakov.

Staudigl (orig. Koppmayer), **Gisela** (*b* Vienna, ?; *d*. ?). Austrian mezzo-soprano. Studied Vienna with Marchesi; debut (in concert), Vienna 1879. Hamburg, 1882-3; Karlsruhe, 1883-4; Bayreuth 1886-92, Brangäne in first Bayreuth *Tristan*, Magdalene; Met. O. tour 1886, Adriano and Queen of Sheba; Damrosch C. 1897-8; guest appearances Berlin, Munich, Leipzig, etc.

Staudigl, Joseph (*b* Wöllersdorf 14 Apr. 1807; *d* Döbling, 28 Mar. 1861). Austrian bass. After studying medicine, joined chorus of Vienna Kä.; then sang secondary roles. Established himself when he replaced a sick colleague as Pietro (*Masaniello*). Theater an der Wien 1845-8; Vienna Opera 1848-54; London D.L., 1841, Caspar, Sarastro, Lysiart; C.G., with German Company, 1842, when he sang Marcel in English première of *Les Huguenots.* Oroveso in first English performance of *Norma* 1843; H.M.'s 1847, where he sang Bertram in *Robert le Diable* at Jenny Lind's English début. His son **Josef** (1850-1916) was a bass-baritone who became principal baritone at the Met. N.Y., 1884-6, where he was the first American Pogner. He subsequently appeared at Bayreuth, Berlin, and Hamburg. Sang Don Giovanni under Richter, Salzburg 1886.

Steber, Eleanor (*b* Wheeling, 17 July 1916). American soprano. Studied Boston with W. Whitney, N.Y. with Althouse. Won Met. Auditions of the Air 1940, making début there same year as Sophie. Member of Met. until 1966, 1969-70, where she graduated from Sophie to the Marschallin; created title role, *Vanessa*, 1958. Gly. (Edinburgh) 1947. Bayreuth 1953; Florence 1954, Minnie. Highly regarded in Mozart, Verdi, and Puccini, and as Marie (*Wozzeck*). (R)

Steffani, Agostino (*b* Castelfranco, 25 July 1654; *d* Frankfurt, 12 Feb. 1728). Italian composer and diplomat. His early career was spent in Germany, where he held appointments and had operas produced at Munich and Hanover. From 1696 he was successful as a diplomat, winning high honours for his services. He continued writing operas, which were universally admired in their day and won respect for their composer's contrapuntal skill.

Stehle, Sophie (b Hohenzollern-Sigmaringen, 15 May 1838; d nr. Hanover, 4 Oct. 1921). German soprano. Début Munich 1860, as Emmeline in Weigl's *Schweizerfamilie*; there she created Fricka (*Rheingold*) 1869, and Brünnhilde (*Walküre*) 1870; the first Munich Senta and Marguerite (*Faust*).

Stehle-Garbin, Adelina (b Graz, 1860; d Milan, 24 Dec. 1945). Austrian, later Italian soprano. Studied Milan. Début Broni, 1881, Amina. After appearances in Bologna, Florence, Venice, etc., engaged for Milan, Sc., 1890, created Adin in Gomez's *Condor* (1891), Walter in *La Wally* (1892), Nannetta in *Falstaff* (1893), Maria in Mascagni's *Guglielmo Ratcliff*, and Mathilde in *Silvano* (1895); also first Nedda, Milan, T. d. V. (1892). Appeared with success in Vienna, Berlin, St. Petersburg, etc., often with her husband Edoardo *Garbin, in *Bohème*, *Fedora*, *Adriana Lecouvreur*, and *Manon*. Studied as a *soprano leggiero*, but developed into a *lirico-spinto*; one of the first great *verismo* singers. (R)

Stein, Horst (b Elberfeld, 2 May 1928). German conductor. Studied Cologne with Günther Wand. Wuppertal as répétiteur, 1947-51; Hamburg, 1951-55, 1961-3; Berlin, S.O., 1955-61; Generalmusikdirektor Mannheim 1963-70; Generalmusikdirektor Hamburg, 1972-; San Francisco 1964-8; Bayreuth since 1969, *Ring* and *Parsifal*; guest appearances Vienna, Paris, Buenos Aires (R)

Steinberg, William (orig. Hans Wilhelm) (b Cologne, 1 Aug. 1899; d New York, 16 May 1978). German, later American, conductor. Studied Cologne. Cologne 1920, as Klemperer's assistant; Prague 1925–9; Generalmusikdirektor Frankfurt 1929–33, where cond. première of Schoenberg's *Von Heute auf Morgen* (1930); then removed by the Nazis. 1933–6 music director of Jewish Culture League, Germany. San Francisco 1944-8; N.Y., Met., 1965. His Wagner, Strauss, and Verdi performances were highly regarded. (R)

Stella, Antonietta (b Perugia, 15 Mar. 1929). Italian soprano. Studied Perugia. Début Spoleto 1950, Leonora (*Trovatore*). Swiftly took her place as a leading Italian soprano. Milan, Sc., 1953-63; London, C.G., 1955; N.Y., Met., 1956-60. (R)

Stendhal (orig. Henri Beyle) (b Grenoble, 23 Jan. 1783; d Paris, 23 Mar. 1842). French writer. His musical biographies include essays on Mozart, Haydn, and Metastasio, though his best-known work is the entertaining *Life of Rossini* (1824). His novel *La Chartreuse de Parme* (1839) was set as an opera by Sauguet (1939).

Stephens, Catherine (b London, 18 Sept. 1794; d London, 22 Feb. 1882). English soprano.

Studied London. Début Pantheon 1812, small roles. C.G. 1813, as Mandane in Arne's *Artax-erxes*, singing there regularly until 1822; then at D.L. Polly, Donna Anna, and the Countess Almaviva were her best roles. Married the Earl of Essex 1838.

Stevens, Risë (b New York, 11 June 1913). American mezzo-soprano and administrator. Studied N.Y., with Anna Schoen-René, and later Salzburg with Gutheil-Schoder and Graf, and Prague with Schick. Début in operetta chorus Brooklyn Little Theatre Co., March 1931; N.Y., Opera-Comique, 1931. After three years at Juilliard Sch., where she sang her first Orpheus, was offered a contract at N.Y., Met., which she refused, choosing instead to audition in Europe. Prague 1936-8 Mignon, Orpheus, Octavian. N.Y., Met., 1938-61. Glyndebourne 1939 and 1955 Cherubino and Dorabella. Buenos Aires, Colón, 1938–40 Octavian, Orpheus, Delilah. Milan, Sc., 1954, creating Herodiade in Mortari's *Figlia del diavolo*. Made several films, including *The Chocolate Soldier* and *Going my Way*. Repertory also included Carmen, Laura in *Gioconda* and Orlofsky. A gifted and attractive singing actress. General manager of the short-lived Met. National Touring C. 1964-66. President Mannes College of Music, N.Y. since 1975. (R)
Bibl: K. Crichton: *Subway to the Met.* (1959).

Stewart, Thomas (b San Saba, Texas, 29 Aug. 1926). American baritone. Studied Juilliard School, N.Y. Début while still a student in first U.S. perf. of *Capriccio* as La Roche (1954). After appearances as a bass with New York City Opera and Chicago, went to Europe on a Fulbright Scholarship in 1956. Berlin, D., since 1958; London, C.G., 1960, 1963-4, 1972, 1974, 1978, as Escamillo, Gunther, Don Giovanni, Dutchman, and Golaud. Bayreuth 1960-72 as Guther, Wotan, Amfortas, Wolfram, and Dutchman. Nuremberg, Hans Sachs, 1971. N.Y., Met., since 1966; San Francisco 1971 as Onegin to his wife Evelyn *Lear's Tatyana. More a lyric than a dramatic baritone, he nonetheless has sufficient volume for the heroic Wagner roles (R).

Stich-Randall, Teresa (b West Hartford, Conn., 24 Dec. 1927). American soprano. Studied Hartford School of Music. Sang Aida when 15. Appeared in première of Virgil Thomson's *The Mother of Us All* (1947) and first American *Mac-beth* (Bloch). Sang Priestess in *Aida* and Nannetta in *Falstaff* under Toscanini for N.B.C., 1949-50. Won Lausanne singing contest 1951; and after a year at Basle, joined Vienna State Opera 1952. Aix-en-Provence 1953-72. Chicago 1955; N.Y., Met., 1961. (R)

Stiedry, Fritz (b Vienna, 11 Oct. 1883; d Zürich, 8 Aug. 1968). Austrian, later American, conductor. Studied Vienna. Recommended by

Mahler to Schuch, who engaged him for Dresden, 1907–8. First conductor Berlin 1914, remaining there until 1923; Vienna, V.O., 1924–8; Berlin, Stä. O., 1928-33, succeeding Walter as chief conductor 1929, and collaborating with Ebert in the famous *Macbeth* and *Boccanegra* productions of that period; also conducted the première of Weill's *Die Bürgschaft* and Schoenberg's *Die glückliche Hand*. Forced to leave Germany by the Nazis, he conducted in Russia 1933-7; N.Y., New O.C., 1941; Chicago 1945-6; Met. 1946-58, where he was the principal Wagner conductor and also conducted important Verdi revivals. Glyndebourne 1947, *Orfeo*; London, C.G., 1953-4 preparing and conducting the new *Ring*, and *Fidelio*. (R)

Stierhorn (*Ger* bull horn). A medieval war-horn required by Wagner off-stage in *Walküre* (Act 2) and *Götterdämmerung* (Acts 2 and 3); played by trombonists.

Stiffelio. Opera in 3 acts by Verdi; text by Piave, after the play by Émile Souvestre and Eugène Bourgeois, *Le Pasteur, ou L'Évangile et le foyer* (1849). Prod. Trieste, T. Grande, 16 Nov. 1850, with Gazzaniga-Malaspina, De Silvestrini, Fraschini, Dei, Petrovich, Colini, Reduzzi, cond. Verdi; London, Collegiate T., 14 Feb. 1973, with Conoley, Thomas, Kale, Lyon, Anderson, Seed. Dean, cond. Badacsonyi; Boston, 17 Feb. 1978 with Mosso, Oostwoud, Ellis, Fleck, cond. Caldwell. Unsuccessful: revised as *Aroldo*.
Stiffelio (ten.), a Protestant minister, finds his wife Lina (sop.) has been unfaithful to him. Her father, Stankar (bar.), is determined to prevent him from discovering the identity of the seducer, Raffaele (ten.), and instead challenges Raffaele to a duel. Stiffelio prevents the duel, discovers the truth and offers to divorce his wife. Stankar kills Raffaele, and Stiffelio publicly forgives Lina from the pulpit of his church.
In *Aroldo*, Stiffelio becomes Aroldo, an Englishman returning from the crusades; Lina is renamed Mina, and the final scene of forgiveness takes place on the banks of Loch Lomond.

Stignani, Ebe (*b* Naples, 10 July 1904; *d* Imola, 5 Oct. 1974). Italian mezzo. Studied Naples with Agostino Roche. Début Naples, S.C., 1925, Amneris. Milan, Sc., 1925-56, where her Eboli, Adalgisa, Laura (*Gioconda*), Azucena, and Leonora (*Favorite*) set a standard. London, C.G., 1937, 1939, 1952, 1955, 1957; San Francisco 1938, 1948. Her rich voice ranged from f to c''' and could compass dramatic soprano roles. Her acting was nearly all in the voice, though she moved with dignity on the stage. Farewell appearance, Azucena, London, D.L., 1958. (R)

Stile rappresentativo (*It* representative style). The term used by the first opera composers for

their new effort to represent dramatic speech in music.

Still, William Grant (*b* Woodville, 11 May 1895). American composer. His nine operas have met with success in U.S.A., his *Troubled Island* being given by the N.Y. City Opera in 1949 and *A Bayou Legend* by Opera South, Jackson, Miss., an all-black company, in 1974.

Stockholm. Capital of Sweden. Opera was first given during the reign of Queen Christina (1644-54). In the mid-18th century permanent French and Italian companies were established, and German companies paid visits. Queen Lovisa Ulrika built a theatre at Drottningholm (1754; burnt down 1762; reopened 1766); this still preserves stage machinery, a curtain, and some 30 18th-century stage sets used in the present annual summer seasons.
On his accession in 1771, Gustav III dismissed the resident French troupe at the Stockholm Opera and set about the creation of a Swedish opera. The old Bollhus (Ball House) was put in order and opened in 1773 with *Thetis och Pelée*, based on a text by the King and set to music by Uttini (the former chief Drottningholm composer). This was later parodied in *Petis och Thelée* (1779) by Stenborg, who also wrote the first Swedish historical opera, *Konung Gustav Adolfs Jakt* (1777). But also in 1773 the Swedish opera had given Gluck's *Orphée et Euridice* before the Paris première – a prized scoop. It was Gluck who formed the model for the busy operatic activity Gustav stimulated in the succeeding years. The crowning achievement was Naumann's *Gustav Vasa* (1786) based on a text by the King. In 1782 Gustav had opened the first Royal Opera House (pulled down in 1890 to make way for the present building); various other opera houses of the day were headed by the Munkbroteater, directed by Stenborg. This was bought by Gustav IV Adolf in 1799 and combined with the Arsenalsteater that had been set up in the Makalös Palace (founded 1793, burnt down 1825). Gustav's assassination in his own opera house (see Scribe's *Gustavus III ou Le Bal masqué*, set by Verdi) meant the eclipse of the arts for some 20 years.
The various 19th-century composers who attempted opera are now forgotten, even in Sweden, though the works of Rangström were noted as possessing an individuality lacking in those of, for instance, Stenhammar and Hallén. Swedish opera owes its renaissance largely to Rosenberg, whose example has been successfully followed by Blomdahl and Bäck. But foreign opera continued to flourish in the 19th century: a succession of able directors guided the opera house's destinies, and Swedish singers, among them Jenny Lind and Christine Nilsson, began to take their places on the

international scene. The present Royal Opera House (cap. 1,264) was opened in 1898 with parts of Berwald's *Estrella de Soria*. Hallén's *Waldmarsskatten* (1899) was the first opera specially written for the new building. By 1907 Stockholm had heard its first *Ring*, and a fine Wagner tradition soon developed. Famous Swedish Wagner singers have included Larsen-Todsen, Branzell, Wettergren, Thorborg, Svanholm, Berglund, Sigurd Björling, Nilsson, Berit Lindholm, and Helge Brilioth. John Forsell was director 1924-39, Harald André 1939-49, Berglund 1949-54, Svanholm 1954-63, Gentele 1963-71, Bokstedt from 1971. During the 1930s and the war the opera benefitted from the presence of Leo Blech and Issay Dobrowen. The company's 200th anniversary was celebrated in 1973 with the première of Werle's *Tintomara.*

In 1964 an annexe to the opera house, the Rotundan, was opened for performances of opera in the round: the first production was Werle's *Drömmen om Thérèse*. Further important singers who began their careers in Stockholm include Göta Ljungberg, Kerstin Meyer, Elisabeth Söderström, Jussi Björling, Nicolai Gedda, Ragnar Ulfung, Torsten Ralf, and Ingvar Wixell. In 1959 the company visited the Edinburgh Festival, bringing Blomdahl's *Aniara* and their interesting 'historical' version of *Un ballo in maschera*; they also gave these in London, C.G., 1960. The house was closed 1974-5 for modernization. See also *Drottningholm, Göteborg.*

Bibl: K. Ralf (ed.): *Operan 200 År* (1973); K. Ralf (ed.): *Kungliga Theatern i Stockholm 1773-1973* (1974).

Stockman, David (*b* Göteborg, 30 Nov. 1879; *d* Stockholm, 2 Dec. 1951). Swedish tenor. Studied Breslau with H. Hoffmann. Début Stockholm 1906, Wilhelm Meister. Leading tenor, Stockholm O. until 1940; first Swedish Mârouf, Chénier, Hermann, and Gennaro. Repertory also included Raoul, Roméo, Lohengrin, Tristan, and Parsifal. Considered the finest Swedish tenor before Björling, but spent his whole career in Stockholm. (R)

Stoltz, Rosine (orig. Victoire Noël) (*b* Paris, 13 Feb. 1815; *d* Paris, 28 July 1903). French mezzo. Studied Paris. First sang in public, under the name of Rosine Niva in concert, then Brussels 1832 as Mlle Ternaux, then as Mlle Héloïse Stoltz, Lille 1833. Her fame dates from her Rachel in *La Juive*, Brussels 1836 (where she married Lescuyer, the theatre's manager), opposite Nourrit, who recommended her to the Paris O. Début here in same role in 1837, remaining for ten years. Created Leonora (*La favorite*), Teresa (*Benvenuto Cellini*), Zaida in Donizetti's *Don Sebastiano* and works by Halévy. She formed a liaison with the Paris Opéra's manager Leon Pillet, and through him

influenced the engagements of new singers, causing great hostility; after a series of attacks in the Press she resigned from the Opéra in 1847. She answered some of the attacks made on her in three pamphlets. She then became the mistress of the Brazilian Emperor Dom Pedro, who invited her to make four tours of Brazil, 1850-9, at the salary of 400,000 fr. a season. Her last appearances were in 1860 at Lyons. She married several times, becoming a Baroness, Countess of Kestchendorf, and Princess of Bassano. Biographies include Gustav Bord's *Rosine Stoltz de l'Académie Royale de Musique* (1909).

Stolz, Teresa (orig. Terezie Stolzová) (*b* Kostelec, 2 June 1834; *d* Milan, 23 Aug. 1902). Bohemian soprano. Studied Prague with G. Neruda, Trieste with Ricci, and Milan with Lamperti. Début Tiflis 1857; sang also in Odessa and Constantinople till 1863. Italy from 1863; Bologna 1864, Mathilde (*Tell*), conducted by Angelo Mariani, whose mistress she became. Milan, Sc., 1865. First Italian Elisabeth de Valois (*Don Carlos*), 1867; first Italian Leonora (revised *Forza*), 1868; first Italian Aida, 1872; first soprano in Verdi's Requiem, 1874. Frequently sang Verdi's heroines, also Alice (*Robert le Diable*), Rachel (*La Juive*). She broke with Mariani in 1871, and in 1872 formed an association with Verdi close enough to distress Giuseppina Verdi: the matter is fully discussed in Frank Walker's *The Man Verdi.* Her voice was described as 'vigorous, flexible, dramatic, limpid, clear, brilliant', and ranged from g to c'''.

Her elder twin sisters **Francesca** (Františka, known as Fanny) (*b* Kostelec, 13 Feb. 1826; *d*?) and **Ludmila** (Lidia) (*b* Milan, *c*1810; *d*?) both had successful careers as sopranos, and both became mistresses of the composer Luigi Ricci and mothers of his children. The son of Fanny and Ricci, **Luigi Ricci-Stolz** (1852-1906) was a conductor and composer. Teresa's greatnephew **Robert Stolz** (1882-1975) was a composer who studied with Fuchs and Humperdinck and conducted at the Vienna, W., 1907. His many operettas include *Mädi* (1932), *Zwei Herzen im Drei-vierteltakt* (1933), *Wild Violets* (1937), and *Frühling im Prater* (1949).

Stolze, Gerhard (*b* Dessau, 1 Oct. 1926). German tenor. Studied Dresden with Willy Bader and Rudolf Dietrich. Début Dresden 1949, Moser (*Meistersinger*). Bayreuth 1951-69, Vienna since 1957. London, C.G., 1960. An outstanding Mime, David, Herod, and Captain (*Wozzeck*); also as character tenor specializes in contemporary works; created title role in Orff's *Oedipus der Tyrann* and Satan in Martin's *Le Mystère de la Nativité*, and sang Oberon in *A Midsummer Night's Dream*. (R)

Stolzing, Walther von. See *Walther von Stolzing.*

STRAKOSCH

Stone Guest, The. Opera in 3 acts by Dargomyzhsky; text, Pushkin's drama (1830). Prod. St Petersburg, M., 28 Feb. 1872, with Platonova, Llina, Komissarzhevsky, Melnikov, O. Petrov, cond. Nápravník; Evanston, N.W. Univ., 3 Dec. 1968 (scenes only); revived Florence, 1954.

This version of the Don Juan story tells how Juan (ten.), accompanied by his servant Leporello (bass), invites the statue of the Commandant (bass), husband (*sic*) of Donna Anna (sop.), to supper. The statue keeps the appointment, and Juan sinks to Hell (in Pushkin's original, together with Donna Anna, his last conquest).

Storace, Ann (Selina) (orig. Nancy) (*b* London, 1766; *d* London, 24 Aug. 1817). English soprano of Italian descent. Début as Cupid in her teacher Rauzzini's *Le ali d'amore* (1776); further studies in Venice and appearances in Italy. From 1784 soprano at Imperial Theatre, Vienna; first Susanna in *Figaro* 1786. Continued a successful career in England from 1788. Toured with Braham and bore him a son. Her greatest triumphs were in comic opera, where her liveliness and acting abilities could compensate for a harsh tone. Her brother **Stephen** (*b* London, 4 Jan. 1763; *d* London, 19 Mar. 1796) joined her in Vienna and became friendly with Mozart. His numerous operas were successful in their day for their astute use of popular airs and their skilful provision for effective parts for his sister, Michael Kelly, and other singers. His *Gli equivoci*, based on *The Comedy of Errors*, has had several revivals in the 1970s.

Storchio, Rosina (*b* Venice, 19 May 1872; *d* Milan, 22 July 1945). Italian soprano. Studied Milan with A. Giovanni and G. Fatuo. Début Milan, T.d.V., 1892, Micaëla. Sc., from 1895. Chicago 1920-1; N.Y., Manhattan O., 1921. Created Zazà, Butterfly, Lodoletta, Stefana (*Siberia*), Musetta (Leoncavallo's *Bohème*). Considered by Toscanini one of the finest lyric sopranos of her day. (R)

Story of a Real Man, The. Opera in 3 acts by Prokofiev; text by the composer and Mira Mendelson, after Boris Polevoy. Prod. Moscow, B., 7 Oct. 1960. The opera, originally in four acts, was performed privately at the Kirov, T., Leningrad on 3 Dec. 1948, but was rejected by the Soviet authorities following Zhdanov's attack on Prokofiev. It was subsequently reduced to three acts and not produced until seven years after Prokofiev's death. Set in Russia in 1942, it tells of the airman Aleksey whose plane is shot down and who has both his legs amputated after wandering 18 days in the frozen forest. When told of another pilot who continued to fly after losing a leg, he resolves to return to service, although forbidden to by the doctors. He is eventually reunited with his lover Olga.

Stracciari, Riccardo (*b* Casalecchio, nr Bologna, 26 June 1875; *d* Rome, 10 Oct. 1955). Italian baritone. Studied Bologna. Début Bologna, Marcello, 1898. Milan, Sc., from 1904 to 1906; London, C.G., 1905; N.Y., Met., 1906-8; Chicago 1917-19; San Francisco 1925. Continued to sing in Italy until 1944. Considered the finest Figaro (Rossini) in the 1920s and 1930s, and sang the role more than 900 times. Also admired in Verdi. Taught in Rome, S. Cecilia, 1940-5, his pupils including Silveri, Sved, and Christoff. Farewell, Milan, 1944. (R)

Strada (Del Pò), **Anna** (Maria). (*b* Bologna, ?; *d* Naples before 1773). Italian soprano, known as La Stradina. Début Milan *c*1720. Venice, 1722-4, in operas by Vivaldi and Orlandini; Naples, 1724-6, in works by Leo, Vinci, Porpora, etc. In Naples, she met the impresario Aurelio Del Pò, whom she married. Engaged by Handel for London 1729, and remained loyal to him until 1738 (when she left England after a quarrel with Heidegger). Created leading roles in his *Lotario, Partenope, Poro, Ezio, Sosarme, Orlando, Ariodante, Alcina, Atlanta, Arminio, Giustino,* and *Berenice*. It was thanks to his patient help that she triumphed over the disadvantages of succeeding Cuzzoni and Bordoni, and of an appearance that led to the nickname 'Pig'. After her return to Italy, appeared in Vicenza and Naples, retiring from the stage 1741.

Stradella, Alessandro (*b* Montefestino, bapt. 4 Oct. 1642; *d* Genoa, 25 Feb. 1682). Italian composer. Sang as a boy in the choir of San Marcello, then studied with Bernabei. Went to Venice and Florence 1666, Vienna 1670, and was composing for Rome theatres in 1671-2. He also worked at the Turin T.R. and in Genoa at the T. Falcone, where he produced his *La forza d'amor paterno* (1678) and *La gare dell'amor heroico* (1679), as well as some intermezzi. His career was filled with amorous adventures, which nearly led to his murder for the abduction of a nobleman's mistress; he actually was murdered for an affair of which his mistress's brothers disapproved. His operas give evidence of a serious, original talent, especially in his interest in extending the length of arias or in linking several for one character. Influenced the Neapolitan school headed by Alessandro Scarlatti.

His adventurous life is the subject of operas by Marchi (*Il cantore di Venezia*, 1835), Niedermeyer (1837), Flotow (1844), and Moscuzza (1850).

Strakosch, Maurice (orig. Moritz) (*b* Zidlochovice, 1825; *d* Paris, 9 Oct. 1887). Czech impresario. Studied Vienna and toured Europe and America as pianist. Married Carlotta Patti, and managed Adelina Patti's concert tours.

Undertook first opera season, N.Y. 1857; Chicago 1859; Paris 1873-4; Rome, Ap., with his brother Max, 1884-5. Often stood in for Patti at rehearsals. Autobiography, *Souvenirs d'un Impresario* (1887). His brother **Ferdinando** (*b*?; *d* Paris, 1902) was at various times director of the opera houses of Rome, Florence, Barcelona, and Trieste. Another brother **Max** (1834-1892) collaborated with him in 1884-5 directing seasons at the T. Apollo, Rome; took over management of the N.Y. Academy of Music from him on his death.

Strand Theatre, London. Built by the Shubert Brothers of New York; opened as the Waldorff Theatre (cap. 1,092) in May 1905 with a season of Italian opera organized by Henry Russell. In March 1942 a company of British and refugee musicians gave a season of *Les Contes d'Hoffmann* conducted by Walter Susskind.

Straniera, La (The Foreigner). Opera in 2 acts by Bellini; text by Romani. Prod. Milan, Sc., 14 Feb. 1829, with Méric-Lalande, Ungher, Reina, Tamburini; London, King's T., 23 June 1832, with A. Tosi, Gioa–Tamburini, Donzelli, Tamburini; N.Y., Italian O.H., 10 Nov. 1834, with Clementina and Rosina Fanti, Fabi, Porto, Monterasi, Sapignoli, cond. Boucher.

Arturo (ten.), who is betrothed to Isoletta (sop. or mezzo) falls in love with Alaide (sop.) who is thought to be a witch. Discovering her with Valdeburgo (bar.), who is her brother, he suspects that she is betraying him and challenges his supposed rival to a duel; Valburgo is seen to drown (though in fact he does not), and Alaide is accused of his murder, although Arturo is prepared to take the blame. Valdeburgo is found to be alive, and insists that Arturo marry Isoletta. Alaide is revealed as the unlawful wife of the French King, and in his grief Arturo kills himself.

Strasbourg (Ger. Strassburg, Fr. Strasbourg). Town in Bas-Rhin, France. The first opera house was built in 1701 in the Place Broglie, and performances were given by visiting companies; it burnt down in 1799 and the Church of Saint-Étienne was converted into a temporary theatre. A new opera house, built on the site of the old one, opened in May 1821 with Grétry's *Fausse Magie,* and flourished until its destruction in 1870 during the Franco-Prussian war. Viardot sang Fidès and Orpheus there, and Galli-Marié made her début in 1859. The present theatre (cap. 1,229) was opened in 1873, and until 1919 was under German direction; Otto Lohse, Hans Pfitzner, Klemperer, and Szell were successive music directors. When the city was returned to France, Paul Bastide was appointed music director, and continued until 1938. During World War II Hans Rosbaud was music director. Bastide returned in 1945 and built up a new ensemble and repertory. In 1972

a reorganization took place, and Strasbourg, Mulhouse, and Colmar joined forces to form the Opéra du Rhin. Alain Lombard was appointed artistic and music director from 1974, with Ignace Strasfogel as first conductor and Nathaniel Merrill as chief producer. Premières have included works by Rabaud, Delannoy, Martinon, and Françaix; first performances in France have included *Béatrice et Bénédict, Don Procopio, Peter Grimes, Duke Bluebeard's Castle, The Queen of Spades, Mathis der Maler, Wozzeck, Lulu, The Love of the Three Oranges, Il prigioniero, Jenůfa, Elegy for Young Lovers, The Mines of Sulphur* and *The Visit of the Old Lady.*

Stratas, Teresa (orig. Anastasia Strataki) (*b* Toronto, 26 May 1938). Canadian soprano of Greek parentage. Studied Toronto with Irene Jessner. Début Toronto, 1958, Mimì. N.Y., Met., since 1959; where she created Sardula in Menotti's *Last Savage* (1959) and has sung a wide variety of roles including Lisa, Cherubino, Despina, Mimì, and Liù. Created title-role in Glanville-Hicks's *Nausicaa,* Athens Festival, 1960, and Queen Isabella in Falla's *Atlantida,* Milan, Sc., 1962. London, C.G., 1961 Mimì, 1976-7 Susanna; Salzburg, 1972–3, Susanna. Guest appearances Paris, Munich, Hamburg, Berlin, etc. Repertory also includes title-role in *Giovanna d'Arco,* which she sang in its first U.S. perf., N.Y. 1966 (concert), Tatyana, Mélisande, and Violetta. Has a *lirico spinto* voice of individuality and a keen sense of the stage. (R)

Straus, Oscar (*b* Vienna, 6 Apr. 1870; *d* Bad Ischl, 10 Jan. 1954). Austrian composer. Studied in Berlin with Grädener and Bruch. After holding various conducting appointments (incl. Hamburg and Berlin), moved to America in 1928; returned to Austria shortly before his death. He wrote for Berlin, but his first real success was in Vienna with *Ein Walzertraum* (1907) and *Der tapfere Soldat* (1908: based on Shaw's *Arms and the Man,* and given in London as *The Chocolate Soldier*). He also wrote a number of successful operettas for London and New York.

Strauss, Johann (Baptist) (II) (*b* Vienna, 25 Oct. 1825; *d* Vienna, 3 June 1899). Austrian composer, eldest son of Johann Strauss (I). Studied Vienna, including with Drechsler. Though widely popular as 'the Waltz King', he also gave Viennese operetta its classic form. The popularity of Offenbach's *opéras bouffes* had led managements to encourage composers, especially Suppé, to rival these with Viennese works, and the Theater auf der Wien turned to Strauss. Chief among his many triumphs was *Die Fledermaus* (1874). In this, to the exuberance and wit of Offenbach is added a peculiarly Viennese hedonism and sentimentality, expressed not only in numbers of Offenbach-ian verve (such as the Champagne song, an idea which the librettist Haffner took from Lortzing's *Rolands Knappen*) but also in the waltz rhythm, which had been made Viennese property by the Strausses. *Der Zigeunerbaron* (1885) is a more carefully worked mixture of comic opera and operetta, and includes a strong Romantic element; and it was this which formed the manner of Viennese operetta in its first classic phase. Other successful operettas include the first, *Indigo und die vierzig Räuber* (1871), *Cagliostro in Wien* (1875), *Eine Nacht in Venedig* (1884), the more serious *Ritter Pázmán* (1892), and *Wiener Blut* (1899). Strauss was at one time influenced by Liszt and Wagner, insisting on conducting the latter's music in Vienna, and in a few of his waltzes reflecting Lisztian and Wagnerian tendencies, to the grave displeasure of Hanslick.

Strauss, Richard (*b* Munich, 11 June 1864; *d* Garmisch-Partenkirchen, 8 Sept. 1949). German composer and conductor. His father, Franz Strauss, was a leading horn player at the Munich Opera, and is said to have modified the original version of Siegfried's horn call into a more playable shape at Wagner's request. The younger Strauss's reputation as a composer and conductor was made in the concert hall, and several of his most celebrated tone-poems had been written by the time of his first appearances as an opera conductor (he directed *Tannhäuser* at Bayreuth in 1894) and his first opera, *Guntram* (1894). *Feuersnot* appeared at Dresden in 1900: it is a rich score whose sumptuous love music has made the closing scene (the first of many successful closing scenes) fairly familiar in the concert hall.

Salome followed in 1905, bringing with it the most violent storm of controversy Strauss had yet encountered in a hectic career. Wilde's drama remains to this day a horrifying study in necrophily which Strauss did nothing to modify. The role of the orchestra here reaches a new importance: there is more than flippancy in Strauss's fabled exhortation, 'Louder! louder! I can still hear the singers.' It is a score designed for physical shock in every way; its loudness, its harmonic violence, the garishness of the orchestration, the morbid sweetness of the melody all intensify the sensual horror of the story to stifling-point.

Elektra, which followed in 1909, was the first product of Strauss's long and active collaboration with Hugo von Hofmannsthal. Though even more brutal in its emotional onslaught than *Salome*, there is ampler scope for the development not only of character but of genuine tragedy as distinct from neurotic horror. Over the whole score looms the figure of the murdered Agamemnon, his name pronounced by the orchestra in one of the principal *Leitmotive*; and except in the questionable dance finale the invention is even stronger and more precise in characterization than with *Salome*.

After *Elektra*, Strauss turned his back on these extremes of violence with the warm comedy *Der Rosenkavalier* (1911). The period Viennese setting, the comic licentiousness of Baron Ochs, the ardent love scenes, the lively ensembles, above all the bitter-sweet ending with the radiance of young love given an added dimension by the Marschallin's renunciation of Octavian to Sophie – these elements in the story tapped Strauss's richest humanity, and the score, long, elaborate, and densely lush as it is, remains simple and direct in its appeal to the heart.

Ariadne auf Naxos (1912) began life as a one-act opera to be played after Hofmannsthal's shortened German version of Molière's *Le Bourgeois gentilhomme*, for which Strauss furnished incidental music. But the problems of assembling a cast of actors and singers on the same evening soon persuaded the authors to make their second, and better-known, version (1916), in which the events preparatory to the performance of *Ariadne* become a separate operatic Prologue. This new form brings forward one of Strauss's most moving characters, the young Composer whose ideals are affronted by the insult to music of telescoping comedy and tragedy at the master of the house's orders. There is later a brilliant coloratura aria for the comedienne Zerbinetta and a prolongedly radiant conclusion for Ariadne's ascension in the arms of Bacchus.

Die Frau ohne Schatten (1919) was the work by which Hofmannsthal set most store. It was intended as a complex psychological allegory, a kind of modern *Magic Flute*; but Strauss's talent was planted too firmly on the theatrical boards to allow him to follow his librettist's flights of intellectual fancy despite his many beautiful passages and ambitious ideas.

The autobiographical interest that had marked Strauss's work both in the concert hall (*Ein Heldenleben, Sinfonia Domestica)* and intermittently in the theatre (*Feuersnot*) became the spur for a complete opera with *Intermezzo* (1924); this was based on a real-life domestic incident.

Strauss's language was by now established, and remained more or less constant for the rest of his life: inspiration waxed – notably in his very last years, with a group of concert works including his moving requiem for the bombed Munich Opera, *Metamorphosen* – and also waned, but there was little further development. Admirers have readily been found for the later operas, which are regularly revived in Germany and occasionally elsewhere, but it is upon *Salome, Elektra, Rosenkavalier,* and *Ariadne* that his reputation really rests. *Die aegyptische Helena* (1928) was a classical *jeu d'esprit* piece, *Arabella* (1933) another Viennese comedy. The latter was also his last collaboration with Hofmannsthal, who had died in 1929. *Die schweigsame Frau* (1935), with Stefan Zweig after Jonson's *Epicœne*, includes some of the old but less expert handling of love and comic misunderstanding, with an especially touching prolonged curtain to the second act. The Nazis prevented any further collaboration with Zweig, and Strauss now turned to Josef Gregor, with whom he wrote three operas, *Friedenstag* (1938), *Daphne* (1938), and (on a libretto partly sketched by Hofmannsthal) *Die Liebe der Danae* (comp. 1938-40, prod. 1952).

His last opera, *Capriccio* (1942), on an idea of his own developed by Clemens Krauss, is a dramatization of the old argument as to whether words or music should take priority in opera. The question had long occupied Strauss. In *Salome* and *Elektra* the decision is clearly for the music. The Prologue to the second version of *Ariadne* is closer to heightened conversation, with the music keeping pace; and *Intermezzo* reserves its musical outbursts chiefly for the interludes. None of the subsequent works resolves the question; nor indeed can *Capriccio*. It is a mellow work, stating the words-music dilemma rather than really arguing it, and it ends on a note of irresolution: the Countess, who represents opera, cannot choose between her two suitors, the poet Olivier and the composer Flamand.

As a conductor, Strauss had a reputation second to none in German opera, both in his own music and in that of other men's, especially Mozart's. His gestures were notoriously discreet, almost unobtrusive, the effects he obtained clear, lucid, and eloquent. He conducted at the Munich H. (1886-9), in Weimar (1889-94), in Berlin at the H. and later S. (1898-1919), directing 1,192 performances including 200 of his own works; again as guest (until 1939), in Vienna as co-director with Schalk 1919), directing 1,192 performances including Munich, Milan Sc., London C.G., Buenos Aires C., and elsewhere. (R)
Bibl: W. Mann: *Richard Strauss: a Critical Study of the Operas* (1964); N. Del Mar: *Richard Strauss* (Vol. 1, 1962; Vol. 2, 1969; Vol. 3, 1972).

Stravinsky, Fyodor (Ignatyevich) (*b* Rechitsky, 20 June 1843; *d* St Petersburg, 4 Dec. 1902). Russian bass. After youthful appearances, studied St Petersburg Conservatory with Everardi, 1869-73. Kiev 1873-6; St Petersburg, M., 1876-1902. A fine singing actor, with a range of two octaves and a strong, rich voice, who was famous for the scrupulous and intelligent study of the musical and dramatic aspects of his roles. These included Basilio, Bartolo

(*Barbiere*), Mephistopheles (Gounod and Boito), Marcel, Gessler, Holofernes (Serov's *Judith*), the Miller (*Russalka*), Varlaam, Rangoni, Orlik (*Mazeppa*), Skula (Prince Igor), and Andrey Dubrovsky (Nápravník). Stasov praised him as a worthy sucessor to *Petrov as Farlaf. Created Tchaikovsky's Royal Highness (*Vakula the Smith*), Dunois (*Maid of Orleans*), and Mamirov (*Sorceress*: Tchaikovsky told Nadezhda von Meck that, 'his performance should be a model for all future productions'). Also created King Frost (*Snow Maiden*); and it was at Rimsky-Korsakov's special request that he sang Varlaam.
Bibl: V. Bogdanov-Berezovsky: *Fyodor Stravinsky* (1961).

Stravinsky, Igor (Fyodorovich) (*b* Oranienbaum 17 June 1882; *d* New York, 6 Apr. 1971). Russian, then French, then American composer. Studied with Rimsky-Korsakov. His first opera, *The Nightingale*, both covers and concludes the period of his early spectacular, lavishly composed stage works. The first act was written in Russia in 1909; the last two were completed in Switzerland in 1914. In between came the three great early ballets, *The Firebird*, *Petrushka*, and *The Rite of Spring*. Stravinsky was the first to recognize the perils of returning to a half-finished work after such experiences, and agreed only under pressure to do so. The change of idiom is theoretically justified by the contrast between the scenes in the forest with the child who loves the nightingale's song and the later ornate luxury of the Chinese court; but the stylistic and technical development is sharp, and despite great beauties the opera as a whole cannot manage the impossible task of bestriding two separate worlds.

Most of Stravinsky's later stage works reflect a doubt about traditional opera and place the singers in a special position with regard to the action. *L'Histoire du soldat* (1918) has speech and acting but no singing, though to some extent it sets a precedent for modern chamber music theatre. *Les Noces* (1914-17; finally prod. 1923), a ballet with songs and choruses, was the first result, and the composer's ambiguous feelings towards the stage were further revealed in his next dramatic work. This was *Renard*, described as 'Une histoire burlesque chantée et jouée', which gave the action to dancers and placed the singers (all male) in the orchestra. Written in 1916-17, it was not performed until 1922, in the same programme as the more conventionally operatic *Mavra* (1922). Based on a Pushkin story, this is a careful reaction against Wagner's 'inflated arrogance' in the form of a modern opera buffa 'because of a natural sympathy I have always felt for the melodic language, the vocal style, and conventions of the old Russo-Italian opera'. There is no recitative, but a succession of arias and ensembles with simple accompaniment figures, reminiscent of classical opera buffa.

Oedipus Rex (1927) again places the singers on the stage, but in the interest of preserving the impersonal and universal sense of tragedy that led to the choice of a dead language, Latin, for the libretto, all are masked: the chorus is confined to one position and the soloists are allowed only formal entries and restricted gestures and movements. A speaker using the audience's language introduces each of the six episodes which make up the 'opera-oratorio'. Despite the wide variety of influences, the music has a powerful artistic unity, and a precise expression and conviction of purpose.

Two ballets, *Apollon Musagète* and *Le Baiser de la fée*, followed before Stravinsky resumed his highly individual relationship with the lyric stage in *Persephone* (1934); this is a 'melodrama' for reciter, tenor, chorus, dancers, and orchestra, nearer to sung ballet than danced opera. Two more ballets, *Jeu de cartes* and *Orpheus*, separate this from Stravinsky's next opera, *The Rake's Progress* (1951) (a later opera on the rebirth of the world after atomic or cosmic disaster, with Dylan Thomas, was forestalled by the poet's death). Here the influences, again diverse, are consciously exposed, and help to set the old Hogarth moral tale in a fantastic framework. Yet the enigmatic shifts of emotional emphasis do create a curiously sympathetic figure of the puppet hero, and the final scene among the twitching lunatics of Bedlam drew from Stravinsky some of the most humanly compassionate music he had ever written. *The Flood* (1962), a setting of part of the York miracle play, is a slighter work in Stravinsky's neo-Webern manner. (R)
Bibl: E. White: *Stravinsky* (1966).

Strehler, Giorgio (*b* Trieste, 14 Aug. 1921). Italian producer. After working in the theatre during the 1940s, turned to opera in 1948. Début Milan, Sc., with *The Love of Three Oranges* and *La traviata*. Staged first perfs. in Italy of *Lulu*, Honegger's *Judith*, Prokofiev's *Fiery Angel*. Salzburg Festival since 1965, artistic consultant there since 1972.

Streich, Rita (*b* Barnaul, 18 Dec. 1920). German soprano, born of Russian and German parents. Studied Augsburg, Berlin with Maria Ivogün and Erna Berger, and with Domgraf-Fassbänder. Début Aussig (Ústi nad Labem) 1943, Zerbinetta. Berlin State Opera 1946-50, Städtische Oper 1950; Vienna 1953; London, with Vienna Co., 1954; San Francisco 1957; Glyndebourne 1958. Excels in Mozart and Strauss (Queen of Night, Constanze, Zerbinetta, and Sophie). (R)

Strepponi, Giuseppina (orig. Clelia Maria Josepha) (*b* Lodi, 8 Sept. 1815; *d* Sant'Agata,

14 Nov. 1897). Italian soprano. Her father **Feliciano** (1797-1832) was a composer and conductor, whose *L'Ulla di Bassora* was prod. Milan, Sc., 1831. She studied Milan. Début Adria, T. Orfeo, 1834 in Ricci's *Chiara di Rosemberg*. Sang in Trieste, 1835, in Rossini's *Mathilde di Shabran* with such success that engagements followed in Vienna, Rome, Florence, Venice, and elsewhere, often with the tenor Napoleone Moriani and the baritone Giorgio Ronconi. Milan, Sc., 1839 and 1842; largely responsible for the first production of Verdi's *Oberto*, and created Abigaille, 1842. Had two illegitimate children, and retired (after various returns as Abigaille) finally in 1846. She opened a singing school in Paris in the same year. She began living with Verdi in 1848, moved with him to his new house at Sant'Agata in 1849, and finally married him in 1859. Her warmth of character and her strong practical nature gave Verdi much, and theirs was a very happy marriage.
Bibl: M. Mundula: *La moglie di Verdi* (1938); F. Walker: *The Man Verdi* (1962).

Stretta (*It* tightening or squeezing). The passage at the end of an act, ensemble, aria, in which the tempo is accelerated to make a climax.

Stride la vampa. Azucena's (mezzo) narrative in Act 2, scene 1 of Verdi's *Il trovatore*.

Striggio, Alessandro (II) (*b* ? Mantua, *c*1573; *d* Venice, July 1630). Italian librettist, son of the composer (especially of madrigals) Alessandro Striggio (*c*1530-95). He is famous as Monteverdi's first librettist, for *Orfeo* (1607). He is thought to have wanted a tragic ending, which Monteverdi overruled in favour of the *deus ex machina.

Strong, Susan (*b* Brooklyn, 3 Aug. 1870; *d* London, 11 March 1946). American soprano. Studied London, R.C.M. with Francis Korbay. Début London 1895 with Hedmont Co., Sieglinde. London C.G., 1895, 1897, 1899-1900, 1902, Elsa, Sieglinde, Brünnhilde, Venus, Donna Anna, Aida; N.Y., with Mapleson Co., 1896; Met. 1896-1901; guest appearances, Naples, Vienna. After retiring from stage opened a laundry in London. (R)

Stünzner, Elise (*b* Altenburg, 10 Jan. 1886; *d*?). German soprano. Studied Leipzig, and Dresden with Dora Erl. Debut Altenburg, 1908, Shepherd (*Tannhäuser*). Member of Dresden ensemble 1909-35. Created the Milliner (*Rosenkavalier*) and Mother in D'Albert's *Mr. Wu*. Chosen by Strauss in 1930 to sing Salome in the 25th anniversary of the opera's première; also sang Diemut (*Feuersnot*), Octavian, and Composer. Farewell appearance as Elisabeth (*Tannhäuser*), 1935, after which she taught in Leipzig and Dresden. (R)

Stuttgart. Town in Baden-Württemberg, Germany. Permanent company established 1696; first opera given was probably *Amalthea* by the director, Theodor Schwartzkopf. Under Johann Cousser opera developed fruitfully 1698-1704. After a stagnant period, new interest grew after a visit by a company under Riccardo Broschi, brother of Farinelli. Singers who appeared at this time included Cuzzoni. The Hoftheater was inaugurated 1750 with Graun's *Artaserse,* and renovated 1758. Ignaz Holzbauer was Intendant from 1751, and gave works by Hasse and Galuppi. 1753-69 Jommelli developed operatic life and raised standards; during this period a number of smaller theatres were opened. Antonio Sacchini succeeded him in 1770, and the first signs of interest were shown in developing German opera. The Kleines T., was opened in 1812 (cap. 1,200). Franz Danzi and J. H. Knecht worked at the Hoftheater; they were succeeded in 1812 by Konradin Kreutzer, and then Hummel, who revised the repertory to include works by Méhul, Spontini, Boieldieu, and others. Lindpainter was appointed 1819, and remained until his death in 1856. The Wilhelminatheater opened in 1840. A distinguished period followed, especially under the Intendant Putlitz. The Wilhelminatheater was destroyed by fire in 1902.

The present theatre (cap. 1,400) opened in 1912, and six weeks later Strauss's *Ariadne auf Naxos* had its first performance there. Max von Schillings was music director 1911-18; his *Mona Lisa* has its première in 1915. Fritz Busch was director 1920-22, and conducted premières of works by Hindemith; also a Pfitzner cycle, and works by Stravinsky and Schreker. He was succeeded by Carl Leonhardt, 1922-37; and Herbert Albert 1937-44. The company included, 1912-44, Onegin, Teschemacher, Erb, Eipperle, Domgraf-Fassbänder, Oestvig, Suthaus, and Fritz Windgassen. The theatre closed in 1944-5, but after the war a new ensemble was quickly built up. In 1946 the German première was given of *Mathis der Maler,* then the première of Orff's *Die Bernauerin.* Leitner was music director 1947-69, Vaclav Neumann 1969-72, Silvio Varviso from 1972. Walter Erich Schaefer was Intendant 1949–72. Wieland Wagner and Rennert worked regularly with Leitner, and the post-war company included Grace Hoffmann, Res Fischer, Martha Mödl, Anja Silja, Gustav Neidlinger, Wolfgang Windgassen (director at the time of his death in 1974), and Fritz Wunderlich. The large repertory includes many 20th cent. works, and all Wagner's works (except the first two operas) and nearly all Strauss's. There have also been premières of works by Mihalovic, Egk, and Burt, and the German premières of works by Stravinsky, Janáček, Weill, and Cikker.

Bibl: B. Krauss: *Das Stuttgarter Hoftheater* (1908).

Sucher (orig. Hasselbeck), **Rosa** (*b* Velburg, Bavaria, 23 Feb. 1847; *d* Eschweiler, nr. Aachen, 16 Apr. 1927). German soprano. Studied Munich. Début Trier. Sang in Danzig, Berlin, and Leipzig, where she married the conductor Josef Sucher, 1877, after which their careers in Germany coincided: Hamburg 1878-90, Berlin, H., London, D.L., 1882, where she was the first London Isolde and Eva, also singing Euryanthe, Elsa, Senta, and Elisabeth; C.G., 1892, Brünnhilde and Isolde; Bayreuth 1886-94; N.Y., Met., 1895, with Damrosch Co. Farewell performance, Berlin 1903, Sieglinde. Lived in Vienna from 1908 and taught singing. Autobiography, *Aus meinem Leben* (1914).

Suchoň, Eugen (*b* Pezinok, 25 Sept. 1908). Slovak composer. Studied with Kafenda and Novák. His opera *Krútňava* (The Whirlpool, 1949) is one of the most highly regarded modern native operas in Czechoslovakia; it is an attempt to follow up Janáček's example in the use of speech patterns. The work has had many productions, including in Germany and Austria. Also wrote *Svätopluk* (1960).

Suggeritore. See *Rammentatore.*

Suicidio! La Gioconda's (sop.) dramatic monologue in the last act of Ponchielli's *La Gioconda* in which she contemplates suicide.

Suitner, Otmar (*b* Innsbruck, 16 May 1922). Austrian conductor. Studied Salzburg with Clemens Krauss. Innsbruck, Landestheater, 1942-44; music director Kaiserslautern, 1957-60; Dresden S.O., 1960-4; Berlin, S.O., since 1964. Bayreuth 1966-7; San Francisco since 1969. Specializes in Mozart, Wagner, and Strauss. (R)

Suliotis, Elena. See *Souliotis.*

Sullivan, (Sir) **Arthur** (*b* London, 13 May 1842; *d* London, 22 Nov. 1900). English composer. His first stage works were to librettos by F. C. Burnand, a one-act farce, *Cox and Box* (1867), and the two-act *Contrabandista* (1867). The first collaboration with W.S. Gilbert came in 1871 with *Thespis,* most of which is lost. In 1875 the impresario Richard D'Oyly Carte persuaded them to work together again on a piece to precede Offenbach's *La Périchole:* the result was the successful *Trial by Jury,* unique in their output as being the only operetta without spoken dialogue. In the same year Sullivan collaborated with B. C. Stevenson on *The Zoo.* It had a few performances, but Sullivan soon decided to join forces with Carte and Gilbert, and a theatre was taken.

Their first production was *The Sorcerer* (1877), which ran for 175 nights. This was followed by the immensely successful *H.M.S. Pinafore* (1878) and *The Pirates of Penzance*

(1880), which established the pattern of what have become known as the Savoy Operas, from the theatre to which Carte transferred in 1881. Selecting venue and target carefully, Gilbert contrived successions of ingeniously whimsical or paradoxical situations in verse whose wit and brilliance of invention has rarely been matched: the chief reproaches against him are a certain mawkishness and his notoriously cruel handling of the middle-aged spinsters who recur as a fixation in many of the operettas. Sullivan brought to these admirable librettos many apt qualities. Above all, his quick melodic ear responded to the lilt and patter of Gilbert's rhythms, and gave them new and often unexpected expressive twists: an outstanding example is the treatment of 'Fair Moon' in *H.M.S. Pinafore*. Harmonically he was less original and occasionally matches Gilbert's sentimentality too well; but his melodic brilliance extends to a contrapuntal ingenuity that enabled him to combine tunes of different character with satisfying musical and dramatic effect. The essence of his success as an operetta composer, however, was almost more in his vivid sense of parody and the sure instinct with which he seized and both guyed and used his models. Sometimes the parody is direct: more often he fastens on a composer (e.g. Handel) or form (e.g. madrigal) and absorbs as much of it as is needed to start his own invention running. His technical learning and wide knowledge of music stood him in good stead here.

Patience (1881) turns these devastating gifts on the current cult of the aesthetic, and in particular upon Oscar Wilde: the quality of the invention is proved by the work's continuing popularity long after the target has vanished. *Iolanthe* (1882) is a skilful mixture of fairy-tale and satire on the peerage; but in *Princess Ida* (1884), 'a respectful perversion of Tennyson's *Princess*', the combination of satire (on women's rights) and never-never-land court romp is less happily managed by Gilbert. Sullivan, however, provided for it some of his most ambitious and original operetta music, by which the piece has amply justified its revivals. A return to formula came with *The Mikado* (1885), which was pure never-never-land, spiced as ever with topical allusions, though it took its impulse from the Victorian cult of *japonaiserie*. It was at once a brilliant success, running for 672 nights, and has remained the most popular of the series. *Ruddigore* followed in 1887, a comedy on country life with ghostly goings-on that reach their climax in one of Sullivan's finest extended scenes, the so-called 'Ghosts' High Noon'. *The Yeomen of the Guard* (1888) was an attempt to break out into a more genuinely operatic manner; though it remains a vintage Gilbert and Sullivan operetta, it includes some of Sullivan's best numbers and

successfully creates a pervading sense of grimness in the dominating presence of the Tower of London. *The Gondoliers* (1889) reverts, brilliantly, to the former type of success, and is further notable for the skilfully handled long introductions and finales without spoken dialogue.

During its run, Sullivan quarrelled with Gilbert and, having already failed in his much-cherished attempt to write a successful grand opera, *Ivanhoe* (1891), collaborated with Sidney Grundy in the operetta *Haddon Hall* (1892). Reconciliation with Gilbert followed, and the 13th Gilbert and Sullivan operetta ensued, *Utopia Limited* (1893) – a satire which fails partly through trying to fire at too many targets in Victorian England at once. Together the partners remodelled Sullivan's old *Contrabandista* as *The Chieftain* (1895), and then produced a new piece, *The Grand Duke* (1896), their last.

Sullivan went on to write *The Beauty Stone* (1898) to a text by Pinero and Comyns Carr; and with *The Rose of Persia* (1899) it was hoped he had found his new Gilbert in Basil Hood. They began work on *The Emerald Isle*; after Sullivan's death in 1900 it was completed by Edward German (1901).

Bibl: G. Hughes: *The Music of Arthur Sullivan* (1960).

Suor Angelica. Opera in 1 act by Puccini; text by Forzano: part 2 of *Il Trittico*. Prod. N.Y., Met., 14 Dec. 1918, with Farrar, Perini, cond. Moranzoni; Rome, C., 11 Jan. 1919, with Dalla Rizza, Sadowen, cond. Marinuzzi; London, C.G., 18 June 1920, with Dalla Rizza, Royer, cond. Bavagnoli.

Sister Angelica (sop.) has taken the veil in expiation of a love affair that has produced a child. News comes to her from her aunt (con.) of its death. Praying for forgiveness, she commits suicide, but this second sin is forgiven when the Virgin and Child appear to her in a vision.

Suppé, Franz von (orig. Francesco Ezechiele Ermenegildo Suppe Demelli) (*b* Split, 18 Apr. 1819; *d* Vienna, 21 May 1895). Austrian composer of Belgian descent. Studied as a boy with a bandmaster, Ferrari, and with Cigala, later Vienna with Seyfried and Sechter. Conductor Vienna, J., 1840-5; W., 1845-62; L. from 1865. Inspired by the success of Offenbach's operettas, especially *Ba-ta-clan*, in Vienna, he began the long series of works that was to give Viennese operetta its first classic form. His greatest successes in this manner were *Die schöne Galatea* (1865), under the influence of Offenbach's classical parodies, and *Die leichte Kavallerie* (1866), a piece with a contemporary Austrian military setting. In a rather more ambitious manner, he had further success with *Fatinitza* (1876) and especially with his masterpiece, *Boccaccio* (1879). Here he comes closest to true opera, without sacrificing his typical melodic elegance and charm, his neat characterization, or his ability to develop musical ideas wittily and at some length. He had little success after *Boccaccio*; he was overshadowed by Johann Strauss.

Susanna. (1) Figaro's bride (sop.) in Mozart's *Le nozze di Figaro*. (2) Wife (sop) of Count Gil in Wolf-Ferrari's *Il segreto di Susanna*. (3) An Old Believer (sop.) in Mussorgsky's *Khovanschina*.

Süssmayr, Franz Xaver (*b* Schwanenstadt, 1766; *d* Vienna, 16 Sept. 1803). Austrian composer. After early studies, had some lessons with Mozart and with Salieri. Helped Mozart with the Prague production of *La clemenza di Tito*; best known for his work in completing Mozart's *Requiem*. Also conductor at the Vienna Kä. from 1795, where he produced a number of his own works; also composed operas for Prague, including *Il Turco in Italia* (1794). Süssmayr began with works in the Singspiel vein of Hiller; he then came under the strong influence of Mozart, and after the success of Cimarosa's *Il matrimonio segreto* (1792) he turned to Neapolitan opera buffa.

Sutermeister, Heinrich (*b* Feuerthalen, 12 Aug. 1910). Swiss composer. Claiming Italian opera (especially Verdi's last works) and Orff as influences, he has deliberately set himself to write simple, melodic, modern operas without sacrificing character or quality. *Romeo und Julia* (1940) has won wide acceptance. Other works are *Die Zauberinsel* (1942), *Raskolnikoff* (1948), *Die schwarze Spinne* (1936, rev. 1949), *Titus Feuerfuchs* (1958), *Séraphine* (1959), and *Madame Bovary* (1967), as well as radio and T.V. operas. Professor at Hanover Hochschule für Musik since 1965.

Suthaus, Ludwig (*b* Cologne, 12 Dec. 1906; *d* Berlin, 7 Sept. 1971). German tenor. Studied Cologne. Début Aachen 1928, Walther. Stuttgart 1933-41; Berlin, S.O., 1941-9; Berlin Stä. O., 1950-65; Vienna from 1948; London, C.G., 1952-3; San Francisco 1953, 1956; Bayreuth 1943 and subsequently. A powerful Tristan and Siegmund; much admired by Furtwängler. (R)

Sutherland, Joan (*b* Sydney, 7 Nov. 1926). Australian soprano. Studied Sydney, and London, R.C.M. with Clive Carey. Début Sydney, Judith (Goossens). London, C.G., 1952, First Lady (*Magic Flute*). Created Jenifer in Tippett's *Midsummer Marriage* (1955), and the New Prioress in first English *Carmelites*. Her Gilda and Israelite Woman in Handel's *Samson* prepared the way for her highly successful Lucia (1959), which established her as one of the leading dramatic coloraturas of the day, and led to appearances in Italy, France, Austria, and U.S.A. in the Rossini-Bellini-Donizetti repertory. N.Y., Met., since 1961. Also scored great success as Alcina and Rodelinda for Handel Opera Society. Visited Australia with her own company 1965 and again in 1974, when she sang all four soprano roles in *Hoffmann* for Australian Opera at the new Sydney Opera House. Her husband Richard *Bonynge conducts most of her performances. (R)
Bibl: E. Greenfield: *Joan Sutherland* (1972).

Suzel. A farmer's daughter (sop.), heroine of Mascagni's *L'amico Fritz*.

Suzuki. Cio-Cio-San's faithful servant (mezzo) in Puccini's *Madama Butterfly*.

Svanholm, Set (*b* Västeras, 2 Sept. 1904; *d* nr Stockholm, 4 Oct. 1964). Swedish tenor, formerly baritone. Studied Stockholm with Forsell. Début Stockholm 1930, Silvio (*Pagliacci*). Sang baritone roles for a few years and then renewed his studies. Second début 1936, Radamès. First Wagner roles 1937, Lohengrin and Siegmund. Salzburg 1938; Vienna, S.O., 1938-42; Bayreuth 1942; N.Y., Met., 1946-56; London, C.G., 1948-57. Intendant Stockholm Opera 1956-63. The leading Tristan and Siegfried during the first decade after the Second World War. In Sweden he has also sung in the Italian repertory, notably Otello and Radamès; created Peter Grimes there. His musicianship, intelligence, and dramatic intensity compensated for rather a dry tone and small stature. (R)

Sved, Alexander (orig. Sandor) (*b* Budapest, 28 May 1906). Hungarian baritone. Studied Budapest, and Italy with Sammarco and Stracciari. Début Budapest 1928, Count Luna. Vienna 1936-9, 1950 and V.O., 1958; London, C.G., 1936; N.Y., Met., 1940-50. Also sang in Italy, where his Rigoletto, Tell, Boccanegra, and Macbeth were much admired. (R)

Svoboda, Josef (*b* Čáslav, 10 May 1920). Czech designer. Leading designer, Prague O., since 1948. London, C.G., *Frau ohne Schatten* (1967), *Pelléas et Mélisande* (1969), *Nabucco* (1972), *Tannhäuser* (1973), *Ring* (1974-6). Creator of the 'Laterna Magica', which combines cinema projection on multiple screens. Makes great use of gauzes, lights, and staircases.

Swarthout, Gladys (*b* Deepwater, 25 Dec. 1900; *d* Florence, 7 July 1969). American mezzo. Studied Chicago and Italy with Mugnone. Début St Louis, 1924, Mercedes. N.Y., Met., 1929-45, especially successful as Carmen and Mignon; created Plentiful Tewke in Hanson's *Merry Mount* (1934), and sang Niejata in first U.S. performance of *Sadko* (1930). Left stage in 1940 but continued to sing in concerts until 1954. Made several films. Married the baritone Frank Chapman (1900-1966). (R)
Bibl: G. Swarthout: *Come soon, Tomorrow* (1945).

Sweden. See *Stockholm*.

Switzerland. Opera did not develop in Switzerland until the composer Meyer von Schauensee (1720-89), who had served as a soldier in Italy, produced some of his operas in Lucerne, beginning with *L'Ambassade de Parnasse* (1746). Though his work was appreciated, little followed. Swiss-born composers including Rousseau, Du Puy, Schnyder von Wartensee, Stuntz, and in our own time Honegger and Liebermann, chose to work abroad. However, foreign composers did work in Switzerland, notably Wagner during his years of exile, and a number of Romantic composers chose Swiss subjects, including Cherubini (*Elisa*), Rossini (*Guillaume Tell*), Bellini (*La sonnambula*), and Catalani (*La Wally*). Important Swiss composers have included Volkmar Andreae, Othmar Schoeck, Frank Martin, Willy Burkhard, and Rolf Liebermann. See *Basle, Bern, Geneva, Zurich*.

Sydney. Town in New South Wales, Australia. Even Sydney was for many years dependent on the various companies that toured Australia, and the struggle to establish a permanent company in a permanent home properly equipped for opera has been a long, complicated, and difficult one. In 1952 the New South Wales O.C. joined with the National T. Opera Company of Melbourne; this merger, after various difficulties, was completed under the auspices of the Elizabethan Theatre Trust in 1954. In 1955 Warwick Braithwaite was briefly music director of the Sydney opera; and in the same year the N.S.W. State government announced an international competition for the design of a new Sydney Opera House. This was won by a Dane, Joern Utzon, whose design immediately became the centre of controversy because of the many problems attendant upon its construction and especially the soaring costs (finally over $100 m.). In 1967 the large hall, intended for opera, was redesigned as a concert hall (cap. 2,700) and the smaller hall became the opera theatre (cap. 1,530). In July 1970 the old opera theatre, Her Majesty's, burnt down, destroying most of Australian O.'s equipment, scores, etc. The new Opera House was officially opened on 20 Oct. 1973 by the Queen, but the first public performance was on 28 Sept., *War and Peace* conducted by the music director of Australian Opera, Edward Downes. He was succeeded in that post by Richard Bonynge, 1976.

Szeged. Town in Hungary. Touring companies

first performed there 1800. The National T. (cap. 1,029) opened in 1883. The present company was formed and conducted by Viktor Vaszy in 1945, and tours S.E. Hungary. Since 1959 summer festivals, under Vaszy, and with leading singers from Hungary and abroad, have given a prominent place to Erkel's operas.

Szekely, Mihály (*b* Jászberény, 8 May 1901; *d* Budapest, 22 Mar. 1963). Hungarian bass. Studied Budapest with Géza László. Début Budapest, 1923, Ferrando (*Trovatore*). N.Y., Met., 1946-50; Glyndebourne 1957-62. An outstanding 'dark-voiced' bass, especially successful in Wagner and as Bluebeard (Bartók), which he sang in Paris and at the Holland Festival as well as in Budapest. (R)

Széll, Georg (orig. György) (*b* Budapest, 7 June 1897; *d* Cleveland, 30 July 1970). Hungarian, later American, conductor. Studied Vienna, Leipzig with Max Reger. After appearing as a child prodigy pianist, persuaded by Strauss to take up conducting. Strasbourg 1917. After appearances in Strasbourg, Darmstadt, and Düsseldorf, First Kapellmeister, Berlin, S.O., 1924-9; Generalmusikdirektor, Prague, German Opera, 1929-37; N.Y., Met., 1942-6 – his conducting of Wagner and Strauss was highly praised. Salzburg 1949-64, where he conducted the world premières of Liebermann's *Penelope* (1954) and *School for Wives*, and Egk's *Irische Legende* (1955). (R)

Szenkár, Eugen (orig. Jenő) (*b* Budapest, 9 Apr. 1891; *d* Düsseldorf, 25 March 1977). Hungarian conductor. Studied Budapest. Prague, Landestheater, 1911-13; Altenburg 1916-20; Frankfurt 1920-3; Berlin, Volksoper, 1923-4; Generalmusikdirektor Cologne, 1924–33. Returned to Germany 1950; Mannheim 1951-2; Generalmusikdirektor, Düsseldorf, 1952-6. (R)

Szymanowski, Karol (Maciej) (*b* Timoshovka, 6 Oct. 1882; *d* Lausanne, 29 Mar. 1937). Polish composer. Studied with his father and with Neuhaus. Hopes of having his first opera, the 1-act *Hagith* (comp. 1913), produced in Vienna under his friend Fitelberg were not realized, and the work was eventually produced in Warsaw in 1922. *Król Roger* (King Roger, 1926) is an ambitious attempt at handling the theme of the enticements and perils of Dionysos in a setting of the conflict between Christianity and paganism in 17th cent. Sicily; it has aroused much admiration for the skill with which it handles a modern Romantic language in dramatic terms.

T

Tabarro, Il (The Cloak). Opera in 1 act by Puccini; text by Adami, after Didier Gold's tragedy *La Houppelande* (1910). Prod. as Part 1 of *Il trittico*, N.Y., Met., 14 Dec. 1918, with Muzio, Crimi, Montesanto cond. Moranzoni; Rome, C., 11 Jan. 1919, with M. Labia, Di Giovanni, Galeffi, cond. Marinuzzi; London, C. G., 18 June 1920, with Dalla Rizza, Burke, Gilly, cond. Bavagnoli

The Seine bargee Michele (bar.) suspects his wife Giorgetta (sop.) of unfaithfulness, but tries to win her back by reminding her of how she used to shelter under his cloak. She has arranged a meeting with her lover, the bargehand Luigi (ten.), who mistakes Michele's lighting of his pipe for the signal that the coast is clear. Michele kills him and covers the body with his cloak. When Giorgetta appears, Michele tells her to come under the cloak again; then he reveals Luigi's body and flings her down on top of her dead lover.

Tableau (*Fr* picture). In international usage, a stage 'picture' in which the action is frozen for a picturesque display. The *tableau général,* popular in the late 18th- and early 19th-cent. French theatre, was usually a statuesque representation of the dénouement or of a particularly dramatic scene. Tableaux were also a feature of some German theatrical traditions: they were popular in Dresden, and Weber originally planned to raise the curtain in the overture to *Euryanthe* on a tableau of the ghost scene.

Tacchinardi, Niccolò (*b* Leghorn, 3 Sept. 1772; *d* Florence, 14 Mar. 1859). Italian tenor. Début 1804 Leghorn and Pisa. Sang at celebrations of Napoleon's coronation as King of Italy. He triumphed as Don Giovanni (transposed for tenor), Paris 1811. Retired 1831, and became a distinguished teacher, his pupils including his daughter Fanny (Tacchinardi) *Persiani and Frezzolini.

Tacea la notte placida. Leonora's (sop.) romantic soliloquy in Act I, scene 2 of Verdi's *Il trovatore,* leading into the cabaletta 'Di tale amor'.

Taddei, Giuseppe (*b* Genoa, 26 June 1916). Italian baritone. Début Rome 1936, Herald (*Lohengrin*); London, Cambridge T., 1947; San Francisco 1957; Salzburg 1948; then in most Italian theatres. One of the leading dramatic and character baritones of the post-war period being especially gifted in Verdi roles, as Scarpia, and in buffo parts. (R)

Tadjikistan. Not until the absorption of Tadjikistan into the USSR in 1924 was there any organized musical life. The foundation of the Ayny Opera and Ballet Theatre in Dushanbe in 1937 was largely the work of an Armenian, Sergey Balasanian (*b* 1902), who also wrote the first Tadjik national operas: these are *Schurishi Vose* (The Revolt of Vose, 1939), *Kovay Ochangar* (Kovay the Smith, 1941), and *Bakhtyor va Nisso* (1954). Other Tadjik operas include *Takhir i Zukhra* (1945) and *Nevesta* (The Bride, 1946) by Alexander Lensky (*b* 1910). The first national opera by a Tadzhik was *Pulat i Gulru* (1957) by Sharafiddin Sayfiddinov (*b* 1929), followed by *Bozgasht* (The Return, 1967) by Yankhel Sabzanov (*b* 1929).

Tadolini, Eugenia (Savonari) (*b* Forlí, 1809; *d* Naples,?). Italian soprano. Wife of the composer Giovanni Tadolini (1785-1872). Studied with Favi and Grilli. Début Parma 1829, Giulietta (Vaccai's *Giulietta e Romeo*). Milan, Sc., 1833. Much admired by Donizetti, and created his Linda di Chamounix (1842) and Maria di Rohan (1843). First Italian Paolina in *Poliuto* (1848) and Leonore in *La favorite* (1848); also created title-role in Verdi's *Alzira* (1845), but was rejected by him for Lady Macbeth as her voice was too beautiful and she 'sang to perfection'. London, H.M.'s 1848, London; not a success.

Tagliabue, Carlo (*b* Mariano Comense, 12 Jan. 1898; *d* Monza, 6 Apr. 1978). Italian baritone. Studied with Gennai and Guidotti. Début Lodi 1922, Amonasro. Milan, Sc., 1930-55; London, C. G., 1938, 1946; Stoll T. 1953; N.Y., Met., 1937-9. Sang at most of the world's leading theatres; a fine Verdi baritone, also admired as a Wagnerian in Italy. Created Basilio in Respighi's *La fiamma*. Retired 1958. (R)

Tagliafico, (Dieudonné) **Joseph** (*b* Toulon, 1 Jan. 1821; *d* Nice, 27 Jan. 1900). French bass-baritone of Italian descent. Studied Paris with Piermarini and Lablache. Début Paris 1844; London, C.G., on opening night of first Royal Italian Opera Season as Oroe (*Semiramide*), singing there every season until 1876; 1877-82 stage manager. Also sang regularly in Russia, France, and U.S.A., and was music critic of *Le Ménestrel,* in which he wrote under the name of 'De Retz'. Appeared in the first performances in England of many operas, including *Le Prophète, Benvenuto Cellini, Il trovatore* (as Ferrando), *Rigoletto* (as Sparafucile), *Roméo et Juliette,* etc. He married the soprano **Cotti,** who as **Mme Tagliafico** sang both at C.G., and H.M.'s in *comprimario* roles.

Tagliavini, Ferruccio (*b* Barco, 14 Aug. 1913). Italian tenor. Studied Parma with Branucci, Florence with Amedeo Bassi. Début Florence 1938, Rodolfo. Established himself as the leading Italian lyric tenor during the war years. Buenos Aires, Colón, 1946-7; N.Y., Met., 1946-54; London, C.G., 1950 with Scala Co., 1955-6;

Stoll 1953; D.L., 1958. At his best Tagliavini had few contemporary equals as a *bel canto* singer and was an outstanding post-war Nemorino and Elvino. Other roles in which he excelled were the Duke of Mantua, Fritz (Mascagni), Edgardo, Werther, and Cavaradossi. Retired 1965, last appearance Werther, in Venice. Married to the soprano (later mezzo) **Pia** *Tassinari. (R)

Taille. The French term used for a tenor-range voice, between *basse* and *haute-contre,* in opera from Lully to Rameau. It was also sometimes subdivided into *haute-taille* (or *première*) and *basse-taille* (or *concordant*), the latter approximating to a baritone.

Tajo, Italo (*b* Pinerolo, 25 Apr. 1915). Italian bass. Studied Turin with Nilde Stinchi Bertozzi. Début Turin, T.R., 1935, Fafner. Gly., chorus and small roles, 1935. Milan, Sc., 1940-1, 1946-56. Rome, T.R., 1939-48, including Doctor in first performance in Italy of *Wozzeck.* Edinburgh Festival, 1947, Figaro and Banquo; London, Cambridge T., 1947-8, Basilio, Leporello, Pasquale. San Francisco 1948-50, 1952-3, 1956. N.Y., Met., 1948-50. Created several roles in Italy in works by Bucchi, Lualdi, and Tosatti, and was first Samuel in Milhaud's *David,* Ivan in first performance in Italy of Shostakovich's *The Nose,* and Calchas in Walton's *Troilus and Cressida.* Replaced Pinza in *South Pacific* on Broadway 1956-7, also appeared in *Kiss me, Kate,* and made three films. A most accomplished buffo performer, but also successful as Méphistophélès, Philip, and Boris. Since 1966 has taught singing at the Cincinnati Conservatory. (R)

Talazac, Jean-Alexandre (*b* Bordeaux, 6 May 1851; *d* Chaton, Paris, 26 Dec. 1896). French tenor, Studied Paris Conservatoire. Début Paris, T.L., 1877; Paris, O.C., 1878-90 – created Hoffmann, Des Grieux; first Paris Samson at the opening of the Théâtre Eden, October 1890; London, C.G., 1889 as Alfredo, Faust and Nadir in *Les Pêcheurs de perles,* of which Shaw wrote that his 'figure offered a terrible temptation to the hungry shark'.

Tale of Tsar Saltan, The. See *Tsar Saltan.*

Tale of Two Cities, A. Opera in prologue and 3 acts by Benjamin; text by Cedric Cliffe, after Dickens's novel (1859). Prod. London, S.W. (New Opera Company), 23 July 1957, with Harper, Packer, Kentish, Nash, Cameron, cond. Lovett; San Francisco, State College, 2 Apr. 1960.

Tales of Hoffmann, The. See *Contes d'Hoffmann, Les.*

Talich, Václav (*b* Kroměříž, 28 May 1883; *d* Brno, 16 Mar. 1961). Czech conductor. After appointments in Odessa and Tiflis as a violinist

and in Prague and Ljubljana as conductor, became conductor, Plzeň Opera 1912-15. From 1935 took over administration of National Opera, Prague, where he initiated important reforms. Discharged after disagreements 1945; restored 1947; removed from this post and others 1948 but restored to favour in 1954. (R)

Talvela, Martti (*b* Hiitola, 4 Feb. 1935). Finnish bass. Studied Stockholm with Carl M. Ochmann. Début Stockholm, 1960, Sparafucile. Stockholm Opera, 1961-2; Berlin, S.O., since 1962; Bayreuth 1962-70, Titurel, Fasolt, Hunding, Hagen, Daland, King Mark; Salzburg Easter and Summer Festivals; N.Y., Met., 1968-9, 1974-5; London C.G., 1970, 1972-3, Hunding, Hagen, Dosifey, Gurnemanz. Artistic director Savonlinna Festival, Finland, since 1973. A very powerfully built man, with a powerful voice. (R)

Tamagno, Francesco (*b* Turin, 28 Dec. 1850; *d* Varese, 31 Aug. 1905). Italian tenor. Studied Turin with Pedrotti and Milan with Vannuccini. Début Palermo 1869. Turin, 1872-3 in secondary tenor roles, when his powerful voice attracted attention as Neacro in *Poliuto.* His fame dates from his Riccardo (*Ballo*) at Palermo, Jan. 1874. Milan, Sc., 1877-87, 1901, creating Azael in Ponchielli's *Il figliuol prodigo* (1880), Adorno in the revised *Boccanegra* (1881), Didier in Ponchielli's *Marion Delorme* (1885), and the title-role in *Otello* (1887), having been specially chosen by Verdi, at Sc. He also sang Ernani, Don Carlos, Radamès, John of Leyden, Faust, and Arnold. London, Ly., 1889, in first London *Otello*; C.G., 1895, 1901, Raoul, John of Leyden, Manrico, Otello, Radamès, and Hélion in De Lara's *Messaline.* Chicago, 1889-90; N.Y., Met., 1891, 1894-5, Monte Carlo Opera 1894, 1896-1901, 1903, where as well as roles already mentioned he sang Samson, Count Leicester in De Lara's *Amy Robsart,* Don José, Jean in *Hérodiade,* and Alfredo (opposite Melba). Final appearances Milan, T.d.V., 1904 in Act 3 of *Poliuto* and a concert at Ostend, Aug. 1904. The greatest *tenor di forza* of all time. His voice was virile and of seemingly limitless power, and it is said that the extraordinary facility of his upper range was such that he found it easier to sing certain pieces a semitone or a tone higher. (R)
Bibl: M. Corsi: *Tamagno* (1937).

Tamberlik, Enrico (*b* Rome, 16 Mar. 1820; *d* Paris, 13 Mar. 1889). Italian tenor (though Silva in his *Historia do Teatro Brasileira* says he was Romanian, orig. Nikita Torna). Studied Naples with Zirilli and Borgna; Bologna with Guglielmi, and Milan with De Abela. Début Rome, Ap., Dec. 1837, Arnold. London, C.G., 1850, *Masaniello* and regularly until 1864, again in 1870; H.M's., 1877. N.Y., Ac. of M., 1873-4 and tour of U.S.A. with Maretzek's company. Also appeared in Paris, St. Petersburg, and Madrid. Created Alvaro in *La forza del destino*. First London Manrico and Cellini, and a famous Otello (Rossini), John of Leyden, and Florestan. His rich, strong voice extended to a powerful c'' – he was the first to employ the *'ut de poitrine'*. He sang with taste, was a singularly handsome man, and a good actor.

Tamburini, Antonio (*b* Faenza, 28 Mar. 1800; *d* Nice, 9 Nov. 1876). Italian baritone. Studied with Aldobrando Rossi and B. Asidi. Sang in chorus at Faenza when 12. Début Cento 1818 in Generali's *La contessa di colle erboso*. From 1824 to 1832 appeared in all the important Italian theatres. London from 1832; Paris the same year, where his phenomenal technique earned him the name of 'Le Rubini des basse-tailles'. In Paris he sang Riccardo in the world première of *I Puritani* and Malatesta in *Don Pasquale*; in Milan, Valdeberg in Bellini's *La straniera*. Among the many roles he created for England were Riccardo, Alfonso (*Lucrezia Borgia*), the Earl of Nottingham (*Roberto Devereux*), Enrico (*Lucia*), Malatesta, Faone in *Sapho* (first Gounod opera in London). Also a famous Don Giovanni. One of the *vieille garde* which sparked off the 'Tamburini row' leading to the establishment of a second Italian opera house in London in 1847 at Covent Garden. Last public appearance 1859. His voice was full and round, encompassing two octaves. He married the mezzo **Marietta Goja** (1801-66), and their daughter married the tenor Italo Gardoni. Their son **Salvatore Tamburini** sang in St Petersburg 1847-9.

Tamerlano. Opera in 3 acts by Handel; text by Agostino Piovene, first set by Gasparini (1710), adapted by Haym. Prod. London, King's T., 31 Oct. 1724, with Cuzzoni, Dotti, Senesino, Paccini, Boschi. Revived Halle 1952.

Tamino. A Japanese [*sic*] prince (ten.), the hero of Mozart's *Die Zauberflöte*.

Tancredi. *Melodramma eroico* in 2 acts by Rossini; text by Rossi, after Tasso's poem *Gerusalemme liberata* (1575) and Voltaire's *Tancrède* (1760). Prod. Venice, F., 6 Feb. 1813 with Malanotte, Manfredini, Todran, Bianchi; London, 4 May 1820, with Belocchi, Corri, Torri, Angrisani; N.Y., Park T., 31 Dec. 1825, with Malibran, Barbieri, Garcia, Crivelli, Angrisani, cond. Étienne. Rossini's first world success and first opera to be translated.

Returning from exile in Sicily, Tancredi (mezzo) prevents the marriage of his beloved Amenaide (sop.) to Orbazzano (bar.). The latter, however, intercepts a letter from her to Tancredi, which he alleges is being sent to the Saracen Chief, the enemy of the Sicilians. Amenaide is thrown into prison and condemned to death unless a champion will fight for her honour. Tancredi agrees to be her champion, although believes her guilty of treason. He wins the duel, leads the Sicilians to victory and finally learns that Amenaide was falsely accused. The lovers are reunited. An alternative tragic ending to the opera, composed for the 1813 production at Ferrara, has recently been rediscovered.

Taneyev, Sergey (Ivanovich) (*b* Vladimir, 25 Nov. 1856; *d* Dyudkovo, 19 June 1915). Russian composer, Studied Moscow with Langer and Hubert, and especially with Tchaikovsky and N. Rubinstein. His only operatic work is the trilogy *Oresteia* which he began in 1887 and finished in 1894 (prod. St Petersburg, 1895). His painstaking approach is shown in a letter to Tchaikovsky describing how he laid out the entire work in outline before planning acts, then scenes, then numbers, and finally composing the notes; and the music, with its dependence upon contrapuntal techniques, reflects more care and skill than imagination. This 'trilogy' is really a 3-act opera, and was unusual for its time in Russia in turning away from fairy-tale and realism to classical mythology, drawing upon the methods of French grand opera to reflect the grandeur of the ancient world.
Bibl: N. Bazhanov: *Taneyev* (1971).

Tanglewood. See *Berkshire Festival*.

Tango, Egisto (*b* Rome, 13 Nov. 1873; *d* Copenhagen, 5 Oct. 1951). Italian conductor. Studied Naples. Début Venice 1893. N.Y., Met., 1909. Budapest 1913-19; Vienna Volksoper, 1919-25; Royal Opera, Copenhagen, 1927-32, and music director from 1932. Conducted first perf. in Rome of *Rosenkavalier* (1911), and première of *Duke Bluebeard's Castle* (1918).

Tannhäuser und der Sängerkrieg auf Wartburg. Grand Romantic opera in 3 acts by Wagner; text by the composer. Prod. Dresden 19 Oct. 1845 with Johanna Wagner, Schröder-Devrient, Tichatschek, Mitterwurzer, Dettmer, cond. Wagner; N.Y., Stadt T., 4 Apr. 1859, with Sidenburg, Pickaneser, Pickaneser, Lehmann, Graff, cond. Bergmann; London, C.G., 6 May 1876, with Albani, D'Angeri, Carpi, Maurel, Capponi, cond. Vianesi. Revision, known as Paris version, Paris, O., 13 Mar. 1861 (withdrawn by Wagner after three performances), with Saxe, Tedesco, Niemann, Morelli, Cazaux, cond. Dietsch; N.Y., Met., 30 Jan. 1889, with Bettaque, Lilli Lehmann, Kalisch, Grienauer, Fischer, cond. Seidl; London, C.G., 15 July 1895, with Eames, Adini, Alvarez, Maurel, Plançon, cond. Mancinelli. The revision was dictated by the rule of the Opéra that foreign works must be in French (trans. Charles Truinet), and by the rigid convention that there must be an Act 2 ballet. Wagner insisted on opening with the new 'ballet' (the Venusberg music), for which the Opéra's resources were evidently incompetent. The main agents in whistling the work off the stage were the members of the Jockey Club.

In the Venusberg, Tannhäuser (ten.) sings in praise of the pleasures offered him by Venus (mezzo-sop.). But he longs to return to the world, and when he names the Virgin, the Venusberg disappears and he finds himself in the valley of the Wartburg where a young shepherd (sop.) is singing. A group of pilgrims pass on their way to Rome, and then horns herald the Landgrave Hermann (bass), Wolfram (bar.) (Tannhäuser's close friend), and other knights. They welcome Tannhäuser after his year's absence, and he decides to return with them on hearing how sad Elisabeth, the Landgrave's niece, has been since his departure.

Elisabeth (sop.), happy at Tannhäuser's return, greets the Hall of Song in the Wartburg Castle. Tannhäuser will not tell her where he has been. The knights and guests enter for the contest of song. The Landgrave announces the theme as love. Wolfram sings of a pure selfless love. Tannhäuser follows with an outburst in praise of Venus. The knights threaten Tannhäuser, but Elisabeth intervenes. Tannhäuser promises atonement; he is banished to seek absolution from the Pope and joins the pilgrims.

Several months later Elisabeth is praying in the valley of the Wartburg that Tannhäuser may be forgiven. When she sadly returns home, Wolfram prays to the evening star to guide and protect her. Tannhäuser staggers in, distraught at the Pope's refusal of absolution: he can now only return to Venus. A funeral procession approaches: Elisabeth has died of a broken heart. Tannhäuser sinks beside her bier, and he too dies. Pilgrims arrive from Rome bearing the Pope's staff, which has sprouted leaves in token that God has forgiven Tannhäuser.

Parody by Binder (1857), also anon. *Tannhäuser, oder Die Keilerei auf der Wartburg* (1855). Other operas on the subject are by Mangold (1846, reworked as *Der getreue Eckart,* 1892; ends happily with Tannhäuser's marriage), Giménez (zarzuelas, *Tannhauser el estanquero* and *Tannhauser cesante,* 1890).

Tarare. Opera in prologue and 5 acts by Salieri; text by Beaumarchais. Prod. Paris, O., 8 June 1787; London, Ly., 15 Aug. 1825. Salieri's most important work, even more successful in Da Ponte's Italian version *Axur, Re d'Ormus* (Vienna, B., 8 Jan. 1788, wedding of Archduke Francis II). Beaumarchais's preface 'To Opera subscribers who want to like opera' is a lively and interesting defence of the librettist's position. Another opera on the subject is by Mayr (*Atar,* 1812).

Tarchi, Angelo (*b* Naples, *c* 1759; *d* Paris, 19 Aug. 1814). Italian composer. Studied Naples with Sala. His many operas became popular on European stages. The most successful of the Italian works was *Ariarte* (1786). He also wrote six French comic operas, of which the most successful was *D'Auberge en auberge* (1800), and re-composed acts 3 and 4 of Mozart's *Figaro.* He was in London in 1789, in Paris from 1797. A fluent representative of Neapolitan *opera buffa* who wrote very agreeably for the voice.

Tárogató. A conical-bored clarinet associated to the point of national symbolism with the Hungarians. Sometimes used for the second of the shepherd's tunes in Act 3 of *Tristan und Isolde* where Wagner specifies a *Holztrompete* (wooden trumpet). Mahler's introduction of a tárogató at Budapest was followed at Bayreuth by Richter.

Taskin, (Émile-) Alexandre (*b* Paris, 18 Mar. 1853; *d* Paris, 5 Oct. 1897). French baritone. Studied Paris. Début 1875 Amiens in Halévy's *Les Mousquetaires de la Reine;* from 1879 to 1894 one of the finest artists in the Opéra-Comique company. When the O.C. caught fire on 25 May 1887, during a performance of *Mignon,* he saved many lives through his calmness and bravery, and was decorated by the government. Created Phorcas in Massenet's *Esclarmonde,* 1889.

Tassinari, Pia (*b* Faenza, 15 Sept. 1909). Italian mezzo-soprano, formerly soprano. Studied Bologna with Vezzani. Début Casale Monferrato 1929, Mimì. Milan, Sc., 1931-7, 1945-6; Rome, O., 1933-43 and 1951-2; N.Y., Met., 1947-8. In the 1930s was considered one of the leading lyric sopranos in Italy. Later her darkening voice led her to assuming mezzo roles such as Carmen and Charlotte (*Werther*). She met her husband, the tenor *Tagliavini, during the war, and often sang with him in *Tosca, Bohème, Faust, Werther, L'Amico Fritz,* and *Manon.* (R)

Tasso, Torquato (*b* Sorrento, 11 Mar. 1544; *d* Rome, 23 Apr. 1595). Italian poet. Among the 80 or so operas on his masterpiece *Gerusalemme liberata* (1575) (generally under this title or as *Armida*) are those by Monteverdi (*Il combattimento di Tancredi e Clorinda* 1624); M. A. Rossi (*Erminia sul Giordano* 1633); Lully (1686); Pallavicino (1687); Moratelli (*Erminia de' Boschi* 1687); *Erminia al campo* 1688); Campra (*Tancrède* 1702; parodies, *Pierrot Tancrède* and *Arlequin Tancrède* 1729); Handel (*Rinaldo* 1711); Philip of Orléans (1711); Schürmann (1722); Traetta (1761); Jommelli (1770); Anfossi (1770); Sacchini (1772); Gluck (1777; parodies, *L'Opéra de Province* 1777; and *Mme Terrible* 1778); Winter (1780); Haydn (1784); Zumsteeg (1785); Zingarelli (1786); Häffner

(*Renaud* 1801); Righini (two 2-act operas, 1803; parody, *Jérusalème Déshabillée* 1812); Rossini (*Tancredi* 1813, *Armida* 1817); Dvořák (1904). Earliest work based on Tasso, Lasamino's madrigal opera *Novellette* (1594), after *Aminta*. Tasso's erratic career is the subject of Donizetti's * *Torquato Tasso* (1833). Also opera *La Mort de Tasse* by Garcia (1821).

Tatar Republic. The Musa Djalil Opera and Ballet T., was opened in Kazan in 1939. The principal Tatar opera composer is Nazib Zhiganov (*b* 1911): his operas include *Kachkin* (The Fugitive, 1939), *Irek* (Freedom, 1940), *Altynchech* (The Golden-haired Girl, 1941), the patriotic *Ildar* (1942), the folk legend opera *Tyulyak* (1945), *Namus* (Honour, 1950) and *Dakalil* (1957). Other Tatar composers include Mansur Musafarov (*b* 1902), whose operas are *Galya Banu* (1940) and *Zulkhabire* (comp. 1943), and the musical comedy composer Jaudat Faysy (*b* 1910).

Tatyana. The heroine (sop.) of Tchaikovsky's *Eugene Onegin*.

Tauber, Richard (orig. Ernst Seiffert (Denemy)) (*b* Linz, 16 May 1892; *d* London, 8 Jan. 1948). Austrian, later British, tenor. Studied Freiburg with Carl Beines. Début Chemnitz (where his father was Intendant) 1913, Tamino. Dresden 1913-26; Vienna 1926-38, with periods of absence in operetta in Germany and England. London, C.G., 1938-9, and 1947 with Vienna S.O. Also sang at Salzburg and Munich Festivals. As a Mozart tenor he was unequalled between the wars, and could still sing an impeccable Ottavio in 1947, when he made his last appearance as a guest with his old Vienna colleagues at C.G. Had a repertory of more than 60 roles, and was particularly associated with the works of Lehár from *Paganini* onwards. The first German Calaf (Dresden 1926), and also admired as Jeník, Rodolfo, etc. His voice had a highly individual timbre, sweet in quality and immaculately managed. Tauber also conducted and composed operettas, songs, and orchestral suites. (R)
Bibl: C Castle and D. Napier-Tauber: *This was Richard Tauber* (1971).

Tauberová, Marie (*b* Vysoké Mýto, 28 Apr. 1911). Czech soprano. Studied Vienna with Ferdinand Rebay and Milan with Carpi. Début Prague, 1936, Gilda, and member of ensemble ever since. Guest appearances Monte Carlo, Vienna, Berlin, Edinburgh (with Prague Company). Married to conductor Jaroslav Krombholc (R)

Taucher, Curt (*b* Nuremberg, 25 Oct. 1885; *d* Munich, 7 Aug. 1954). German tenor, Studied Munich with Heinrich Hermann. Début Augsburg, 1908, Faust. Chemnitz, 1911-14; Hanover, 1915-20; Dresden, 1920-34. N.Y.,

Met., 1923-7; London, C.G., 1932. Created Menelaus in *Aegyptische Helena*, title role in Weill's *Der Protagonist*. (R)

Taylor, Deems (*b* New York, 22 Dec. 1885; *d* New York, 3 July 1966). American composer and critic. *The King's Henchman* (1927) led to a Met. commission for *Peter Ibbetson* (1931), also successful. *Ramuntcho* (comp. 1937) was prod. Philadelphia, 1942.

Tchaikovsky, Pyotr (Ilyich) (*b* Votkinsk, 7 May 1840; *d* St Petersburg, 6 Nov. 1893). Russian composer. Tchaikovsky declared that to refrain from writing operas was a heroism he did not possess; from his youth the stage fascinated him. Seeing a performance of *Don Giovanni*, he wrote, decided him to devote himself to music; throughout his life he returned to opera. His first serious attempts at composition came after the shock of his mother's death in 1854, when he wrote to a relation for a libretto for a 1-act opera to be called *Hyperbole*. Nothing came of this, but other early pieces included a scene of Pushkin's *Boris Godunov* (1863-4, lost).

His first completed opera was *The Voyevoda* (1869), to a text partly by Ostrovsky; he later abandoned it, keeping the best music, and passed the subject on to *Arensky for his *A Dream on the Volga*. He then worked on *Undine*, but when it was rejected by the St Petersburg Imperial Theatres he destroyed it, again keeping some of the best music for re-use (e.g. a love duet for an Adagio in *Swan Lake*). His first surviving completed opera is *The Oprichnik* (1874), which contains a good deal of the *Voyevoda* music. Though he had not here found his individual touch, there are some good numbers in the work, some apt use of motives, and passages in which convention gives way to genuine feeling.

Hearing *Carmen* in Paris in 1876 renewed his impetus to write opera, especially in the work's association of love with a harsh fate, expressed in music of unfailing clarity and grace; and in the same year, his attendance as a special correspondent at the first Bayreuth Festival gave him an admiration for Wagner but no attraction to his methods. In *Vakula the Smith* (1876) he takes a much stronger operatic position, and develops a more personal vein of dramatic music. Though it lacks the comic realism and subtlety of character needed by the plot, the work is well written, with some attractive lyrical love music and some delightful dances, and a neat contrast between peasant vigour and urban, aristocratic grace. It was later revised as *Cherevichki* (The Little Shoes, also known as *Oxana's Caprices*, 1887).

These virtues find full expression in his masterpiece, *Eugene Onegin* (1879). Haunted by the predicament of Tatyana in her rejection by the subsequently repentant Onegin, he began work on the famous Letter Scene. He described the work as 'lyrical scenes', and hoped to get far from operatic convention as he knew it; his response to Pushkin's poem is subtle and sensitive. Bringing together a tragic story of frustrated love, scenes of Russian urban and country life, a feeling for the music and also for Russian folk music, *Onegin* touched on a great deal close to Tchaikovsky's nature, and it drew from him his freshest and most lyrical operatic music. Where the characters of *Vakula* are vivid types, those of *Onegin,* especially in the tenderly drawn portrait of Tatyana, are real human characters.

Turning from Russian subjects, Tchaikovsky next set a version of *The Maid of Orleans* (1881), drawing on a text based on a translation of Schiller. Again he was drawn above all to the heroine, and began by setting the scene of her narrative to the Dauphin and Count and her acclamation in Act 2. His intention was to conquer the Paris Opéra, and the work is thus cast in Grand Opera vein, with touches of Gounod and Massenet and with the pervading influence of Meyerbeer in its grandiose crowd scenes, processions, court ceremony, and battle scene. However, despite some fine strokes and effective passages, he is unable to give real emotional life to Joan; as he wrote in another context, 'Medieval dukes and knights and ladies captivate my imagination but not my *heart,* and where the heart is not touched there can't be any music.'

Mazeppa (1884) returns to a Russian subject; again Tchaikovsky began by composing a central, crucial scene so as to achieve immediate emotional identification with the characters: this was the Act 2 duet. The work exhibits some familiar Russian operatic characteristics in music, such as the suffering heroine, the intransigent old man, and the use of dances, and these are now fluently handled; but though there are delightful episodes and some striking dramatic ideas, he fails to characterize the agonised Maria and the harsh, impressive Mazeppa. Once again, Tchaikovsky cannot fully enter into the characterization of figures so remote from his own emotional world, and so provides them with music that portrays them only partially. The finest parts of the opera are the minor episodes.

There was still less chance of success with *The Sorceress* (1887), to a confused plot that drew on inconsistent musical characterization, with the tenor part French in manner, the bass Russian, and the central character of the 'Sorceress' herself, the woman of overwhelming spirit and attraction, made by turns sentimental and dull; it is, again, in some of the dances and choruses and incidental moments that the most successful music is to be found.

The influence of *Carmen* is also seen in *The Queen of Spades* (1890), another Pushkin set-ting. Mozart, too, is evoked in some scenes invoking the rococo past of Catherine the Great's Petersburg and its French elegance. The opera is permeated with the sense of Fate which obsessed Tchaikovsky, operating, as in *Carmen,* within a convention of lyrical elegance; and though the work is inconsistent, above all in juxtaposing Mozartian grace with Wagnerian chromatic intensity in the scenes of horror, this reflects Tchaikovsky's own character, and draws from him some of his finest operatic music.

Tchaikovsky's last opera was the 1-act *Yolanta* (1892), originally commissioned as a double bill with the ballet *The Nutcracker.* The remoteness of the medieval setting pleased him, and he was drawn to the touching idea of a blind heroine whose defect has been kept from her. It has much delicacy and grace, with some curiously Wagnerian juxtapositions in the harmony, and a tendency to place the main interest in the orchestra. For all the excellent music and impressive aspects of his lesser-known operas, it is above all in *Eugene Onegin* that Tchaikovsky's gift for the operatic stage finds full expression.

Bibl: J. Warrack: *Tchaikovsky* (1973); D. Brown: *Tchaikovsky* (vol. 1, 1979)

Tear, Robert (*b* Barry, 8 Mar. 1939). Welsh tenor. Studied Cambridge. St Paul's Cathedral chorister. Début E.O.G., 1963, Male Chorus (*Lucretia*), and subsequently other roles in Britten operas; created Misael in *Burning Fiery Furnace.* W.N.O., 1968, Jacquino, Simpleton (*Boris*); London, C.G., since 1970; created Dov (*The Knot Garden*), also sang Lensky, Jacquino, Paris (*King Priam*), Golitsyn, Froh, Eisenstein, Grimes. (R)

Tebaldi, Renata (*b* Pesaro, 1 Feb. 1922). Italian soprano. Studied Parma with Branucci and Campogalliani, and Pesaro with Carmen Melis. Début Rovigo 1944, Elena (*Mefistofele*). Chosen by Toscanini for reopening of Scala 1946. Milan, Sc., 1949-54 and 1959-60 London, C.G., with Sc. Co., 1950 and 1955. San Francisco 1950; Chicago 1955-69; N.Y., Met., 1954-73, after which she devoted herself increasingly to concerts. One of the outstanding postwar sopranos, she possesses a voice whose exquisite quality conceals great reserves of power; even when singing at extreme dynamics her voice retained its characteristic glowing beauty. Especially impressive in Verdi and Puccini and as Madeleine de Coigny and Adriana Lecouvreur. (R)

Bibl: V. Seroff: *Renata Tebaldi* (1961).

Tedeschi, Giovanni (Amadori) (*b* Ronciglione (Viterbo), *c* 1715; *d* ?). Italian male soprano. Studied with Bernacchi. Début Rome, 1735 in Duni's *Nerone.* Rome 1735-8; Venice and other leading Italian theatres from 1739 with Raaff.

Berlin 1754-5; Naples – became impresario of S.C., 1765. Returned to Rome and opened a school of singing.

Te Kanawa, Kiri (*b* Gisborne, New Zealand, 6 Mar. 1944). New Zealand soprano. Descended on her mother's side from Arthur Sullivan. Studied London Opera Centre, and with Vera Rosza. Camden Festival 1969, Elena (*Donna del lago*); London, C.G., since 1970, Flower Maiden, Xenia, Countess, Desdemona, Amelia Boccanegra, Marguerite, Micaela, Fiordiligi; San Francisco, Gly., N.Y., Paris etc. Has a rich, creamy soprano voice and beautiful stage presence. (R)

Telemachus. In Homer's *Odyssey*, the son of *Odysseus and *Penelope. After helping his father to kill his mother's suitors, he is said to have visited the island of *Circe (in some versions of the legend, Calypso), marrying either her or her daughter Cassiphone. He later killed Circe and fled to Italy, w..ere he founded Clusium. Many operas on his story concern the Circe or Calypso episode, and therefore overlap with those dealing with Circe as their main subject: for the latter, see *Circe*.

Operas on the subject are as follows: Campra (1704); Destouches (1714); A. Scarlatti (1718); Gluck (1765); Bertoni (*Telemacco ed Euridice nell'isola de Calipso*, 1777); Mayr (*Telemacco all'isola di Calipso*, 1797); Le Sueur (*Télémaque dans l'île de Calypso*, 1796); Sor (1797); Hoffmeister (*Der Königssohn von Ithaka*, 1800); Boieldieu (1806); Bishop (ballad opera, 1815).

Telemann, Georg Philipp (*b* Magdeburg, 14 Mar. 1681; *d* Hamburg, 25 June 1767). German composer. Virtually self-taught. Of his 40-odd operas, some half dozen were successful in his own day. The best-known is the intermezzo *Pimpinone* (1725), which anticipates Pergolesi's *La serva padrona* (1733) in its command of opera buffa style. *Sokrates* (1721), his first Hamburg opera, also aroused respect for its anticipation of classical style.

Telephone, The. Opera in 1 act by Menotti; text by composer. Prod. N.Y., Heckscher T., 18 Feb. 1947 with Cotlow, Kwartin, cond. Barzin; London, Aldwych T., 29 Apr. 1948, with Cotlow, Rogier, cond. Balaban.

Ben's (bar.) proposals of marriage are repeatedly frustrated by Lucy's (sop.) devotion to her telephone; eventually he leaves and successfully makes contact by ringing her from a call-box.

Television opera. The first television experiments in opera took place in the B.B.C. in 1936 when scenes from Albert Coates's *Pickwick* were broadcast. During the three years before World War II, the B.B.C. gave 20 or more TV operas in either full or shortened versions,

including the first performance in England of Busoni's *Arlecchino*, as well as works by Handel, Méhul, Falla, Dibdin, and others. The first U.S. TV opera was in March 1941, when *Pagliacci* (shortened) was televised from Radio City. In November 1948 the opening night of the Met. season (*Otello*) was televised live. TV opera was resumed in England in 1946 with *The Beggar's Opera*, since when it has become a regular feature, either in the form of studio productions, including *The Mines of Sulphur, Peter Grimes, Billy Budd, Eugene Onegin, Falstaff, La traviata,* and *Der fliegende Holländer,* or of performances from opera houses, especially Gly. and C.G., either live or telerecorded. In addition works have been commissioned or specially written for British television, including Britten's *Owen Wingrave*, Crosse's *Purgatory,* Tate's *Dark Pilgrimage,* and Bliss's *Tobias and the Angel.*

In 1949 the N.B.C. in New York formed its Television Opera Theatre under the direction of Samuel Chotzinoff and Peter Hermann Adler, beginning with Weill's *Down in the Valley* and ending in Jan. 1964 with *Lucia di Lammermoor*. During its 15 years it commissioned operas from Dello Joio, Foss, Menotti, and others; Menotti's *Amahl and the Night Visitors* was the first TV opera to be commissioned. It also gave the first U.S. performances of a number of works, including *Billy Budd* and *War and Peace.* In 1969, with a grant from the Ford Foundation, National Education Television formed the N.E.T. Opera Theatre, under the artistic direction of Peter Hermann Adler, and during its first season gave the first U.S. performance of *From the House of the Dead.*

In Europe it has become customary, especially in Italy and Germany, to pre-record with the singers miming at the time of filming. The Germans sometimes go further and substitute actors. Colour television has helped to make opera more convincing on TV, but the small area of the screen, and the generally inferior sound of the loudspeaker, have been inhibiting factors. Recently, however, the B.B.C. have simultaneously broadcast some of their TV operas in stereo on sound radio.

Telramund. Friedrich von Telramund (bar.), a Count of Brabant in Wagner's *Lohengrin*.

Templer und die Jüdin, Der (The Templar and the Jewess). Opera in 3 acts by Marschner; text by W.A. Wohbrück, after Scott's *Ivanhoe* (1820). Prod. Leipzig, 22 Dec. 1829; London, Prince's T., 17 Jun. 1840; N.Y., Stadt. T., 29 Jan. 1872, with Fabbri-Malden, Rosetti, Bernard, W. Formes, C. Formes, Zschiche, Weinlich, Müller, Dickhoff, Habelmann, Weisheit.

Templeton, John (*b* Riccarton, 30 July 1802; *d* New Hampton, 2 July 1886). Scottish tenor. Début Worthing, 1828. Dermot in *The Poor Sol-*

dier, London, D.L.,1831; first English Raimbaut (*Robert le Diable*) 1832; first English-born Don Ottavio 1833, at short notice. Became 'Malibran's tenor', singing beside her in *Sonnambula*, D.L., 1833, and often subsequently; a wooden actor, till Malibran coached him. Took principal tenor roles in first performances in English of *Cheval de bronze* (1836), *Zampa* (1836), *Siege of Corinth* (1836), *Magic Flute* (1838), *La favorite* (1843), and many others. Retired 1852.

Tender Land, The. Opera in 2 acts by Copland; text by Horace Everett. Prod. N.Y., City Opera, 1 Apr. 1954 with Carter, Newton, Treigle, cond. Schippers. Revised version, Berkshire Music Centre, 2 Aug. 1954; Cambridge, Arts T., 26 Feb. 1962, by Cambridge University Opera Group, with Wells, Westwood, Ford.

A harvester falls in love with the daughter of a Midwest farmer. When he fails to keep a promise to elope with her, she goes out into the world alone.

Tenducci, Giusto Ferdinando (*b* Siena, *c* 1736; *d* Genoa, 25 Jan. 1790). Italian male soprano (sometimes known as Senesino but not to be confused with the great *Senesino). Studied Naples. Début Venice, 1753, in Bertoni's *Ginevra*. Naples 1757-8, London 1758. After successes in London, attracted attention in Dublin, by his singing in some adaptations of his own, and by eloping with a councillor's daughter. Sang (with Mrs Billington) in his own version of Gluck's *Orfeo*, then in London in the original. Mozart wrote a song for him. Back in London 1768-91 (except for a period in 1776, when he was forced to leave to escape imprisonment for debt); director of the Westminster Abbey Festival 1784-91. Last stage appearance 1785 as Orfeo. Published various compositions, including three operas, and a treatise on singing.

Tenor (*It tenore* holding: in early times the voice which held the plainsong). The highest category of natural male voice. Many subdivisions exist within opera houses: the commonest in general use (though seldom by composers in scores) are given below, with examples of roles and their approximate *tessitura*. These divisions often overlap, and do not correspond exactly from country to country. In general, distinction is more by character than by *tessitura*, especially in France: thus, the examples of the roles give a more useful indication of the different voices' quality than any attempted technical definition.

German: Heldentenor (Huon, Bacchus: c-c''); Wagnerheldentenor (Siegfried: c-b♭'); lyrischer Tenor (Max: c-c''); Spieltenor (Pedrillo, David: c-b♭'); hoher Tenor (Brighella, *Rosenkavalier* tenor: c-c'').

Italian: tenore (Radamès: c-c''); tenore

spinto (Rodolfo: c-c''); tenore di forza (Otello: c-c''); tenore di grazia (Nemorino: c-d''); tenorbuffo (Dickson in *La Dame blanche*: c-b♭').

French; ténor (José: c-c''); ténor-bouffe (Paris in *La Belle Hélène*: c-c''); Trial (Torquemada in *L'Heure espagnole*) See also *Castrato, Countertenor*.

Tenuto (*It* held). A direction to hold notes for their full value, or very slightly longer. Consistently taken by singers as an invitation to hold them, especially if high ones, for as long as they please.

Teodorini (orig. De Monzuru), **Elena** (*b* Craiova, 25 Mar. 1854; *d* Bucharest, 27 Feb. 1926). Romanian soprano. Both her parents were actors; her father studied Italy with Salvini and Rossi. Studied the piano in Milan with Ratti and gave recitals at the age of eight; studied singing with Sangiovanni. Début Cuneo, 1877, Condé in *Maria de Rohan*. After appearances in Florence, Milan, Warsaw, had a further period of study in Bucharest 1877-8, mostly in mezzo roles; Milan, T.d.V., Amelia, Rachel, also Rosina, Amneris, and Preziosilla. Milan, Sc., 1880-82 and 1892-3 as Valentine, Hérodiade, Lucrezia Borgia, created Bianca in Smareglia's *Bianca di Cervia*. London, C.G., 1886, Gioconda, Valentine, Donna Anna. Created leading role in Gastaldoni's *Mala Pasqua*, based on the same subject as *Cavalleria rusticana*, Rome, 1890 – her only attempt at a *verismo* role. Appeared in South America, Lisbon, Bucharest, until 1900. 1909 founded Academia Teodorini in Buenos Aires. Settled in Brazil 1916 and taught there until 1923; one of her pupils was Bidu Sayão. Returned to Bucharest 1924 and appointed professor of singing at State Conservatory 1925. (R)

Ternina, Milka (*b* Vezišče, 19 Dec. 1863; *d* Zagreb, 18 May 1941). Croatian soprano. Studied Zagreb with Ida Winterberg and Vienna with Gänsbacher. While a student at Zagreb, début as Amelia 1882. Leipzig 1883-4; Graz 1884-6; Bremen 1886-9; Munich 1890-99; U.S. with German Opera Company, 1896; Met. 1899-1904; Bayreuth 1899, Kundry; London 1898-1906, where she was the first London Tosca. In N.Y. created Kundry in the 'pirate' production of *Parsifal* and was accordingly banned from Bayreuth; also the first N.Y. Tosca. Considered the greatest Isolde of her day and the finest Leonore (*Fidelio*) since Tietjens. She had a repertory of 85 roles: she possessed a flawless vocal method, a beautiful voice, and great dramatic temperament. Henry James found her singing 'a devastating experience'. Was forced by paralysis to retire at the height of her powers in 1916.

Terradellas, Domingo Miguel Bernabé (known in Italy as Domenico Terradeglias) (*b* Barcelona, bapt. 13 Feb. 1713; *d* Rome, 15 May

1751). Spanish composer. Studied Naples with Durante. After writing operas for Italy, he also visited London, where his *Mitridate* (1746) was successful, his *Bellerofonte* (1747) less so. Then returned via Paris to Rome. Began as a characteristic product of the first Neapolitan school, making little attempt to amend its typical forms and gestures. Later developed much greater fluency and originality, especially in his last opera, *Sesostri* (1751).

Tervani, Irma (*b* Helsinki, 4 June 1887; *d* Berlin, 29 Oct. 1936). Finnish mezzo-soprano. Daughter of soprano Emmy Strömer-Ackté (1850-1924), and sister of Aïno Ackté. Studied with mother, in Paris with Duvernoy, and in Dresden. Début Dresden, 1908, Delilah. Remained there as leading mezzo until 1932. Carmen, which she sang opposite Caruso, was her most famous role. (R)

Teschemacher, Marguerite (*b* Cologne, 3 Mar. 1903; *d* Wiessee, 19 May 1959). German soprano. Studied Cologne. Début Cologne 1922, Micaela. Aachen 1924-6; Dortmund 1926-8; Mannheim 1928-30; Stuttgart 1930-4; Dresden 1934-46 created title-role in Strauss's *Daphne*, Miranda in Sutermeister's *Zauberinsel*, and sang the Countess in the first Dresden *Capriccio*; Düsseldorf 1948-52; London, C.G., 1931 and 1936. Admired as Jenůfa and Minnie (*La fanciulla*). (R)

Teseo. Opera in 3 acts by Handel; text by Nicola Haym. Prod. London, Queen's T. 21 Jan. 1713, with La Pilotti, La Margarita, Barbier, Valeriano, Valentini, Schiavonetti.

Tesi-Tramontini, Vittoria (*b* Florence, 13 Feb. 1700; *d* Vienna, 9 May 1775). Italian contralto. Studied Florence with Redi and Bologna with Campeggi. Début Parma 1716. Dresden 1719; Milan 1727; Vienna 1749, where she settled and taught. Considered an outstanding Handel singer by Quantz, who described her as 'a contralto of masculine strength'.

Tess (orig. Tesscorolo), **Giulia** (*b* Verona 9 Feb. 1889; *d* Milan, 17 Mar. 1976). Italian soprano, formerly mezzo-soprano. Début Prato (as Giulia Tessi) 1904. Prague 1909, as Giulia Tessaroli. After a successful career as a mezzo, she was advised by Battistini to become a soprano, and was engaged by Toscanini for La Scala 1922 where she created Jaele in Pizzetti's *Debora e Jaele*. Was a famous Salome and Elektra and also a fine interpreter of lighter roles in operas by Wolf-Ferrari. Sang the Composer in Strauss's *Ariadne* and title role in Honegger's *Judith* in their first performances in Italy. In 1940 she began teaching at the opera school in Florence, and after 1946 taught at Sc. Her pupils included Barbieri and Tagliavini. In the 1940s and 1950s she produced operas at Sc. and other Italian theatres. Married conductor Giacomo Armani; their son Giuseppe Armani was for many years head of La Scala Press Office.

Tessitura (*It* texture). A term indicating the approximate average range of a piece of music in relation to the voice for which it is written. Thus we say that Zerbinetta's aria in *Ariadne auf Naxos* has a particularly high tessitura.

Tetrazzini, Eva (*b* Milan, Mar. 1862; *d* Salsomaggiore, 27 Oct. 1938). Italian soprano. Studied Florence with Ceccherini. Début Florence 1882, Marguerite. N.Y., Ac. of M., 1888, first American Desdemona; London, C.G., 1890. Married the conductor Campanini. Sister of Luisa (below).

Tetrazzini, Luisa (*b* Florence, 29 June 1871; *d* Milan, 28 Apr. 1940). Italian soprano. Studied Florence and with her sister. Début Florence as L. Tetrazzini-Scalaberni 1890, Inez (*L'Africaine*). After nearly 15 years of appearances in Italy and South America, made first real success with a company from Mexico at San Francisco 1904. London, C.G., 1907, creating sensation as Violetta and Lucia; and regularly 1907-12; N.Y., Manhattan Co., 1908-10; Met. 1911-12. Abandoned the stage during world War I, but continued to give concerts until 1934. She had brilliant voice above the stave, and a phenomenal coloratura technique; her singing of staccato passages and ornamentation was likewise greatly admired. She barely attempted to act. At the height of her fame was paid $3000 a performance and is said to have earned 5 million dollars during her career; but died in poverty. (R)
Bibl: L. Tetrazzini: *My life of Song* (1921); L. Tetrazzini: *How to Sing* (1925).

Teyte (orig. Tate), (Dame) **Maggie** (*b* Wolverhampton, 17 Apr. 1888; *d* London 26 May 1976). English soprano. Studied London, R.C.M., and Paris with J. de Reszke. Concert début as Tate, with Paderewski, Monte Carlo 1 Feb. 1907. Début Monte Carlo 1907, Tyrcis in Offenbach's *Myriame et Daphné*. Paris, O.C., 1907-11 where she created Glycère in Hillemacher's *Circe*, and in 1908 sang her first Mélisande. London, C.G., 1910, 1914, 1922-3, 1930, 1936-8; Chicago 1911-14; Boston 1915-17. Created the Princess in Holst's *The Perfect Fool*. An outstanding Mélisande (which she studied with Debussy), Butterfly, Cherubino, and Hänsel. In 1948 reappeared as Mélisande in N.Y., and sang Belinda to Flagstad's Dido at the Mermaid Theatre, London 1951. (R)
Bibl: M. Teyte: *Star on the Door* (1958).

Thaïs. Opera in 3 acts by Massenet; text by Louis Gallet, after Anatole France's novel (1890). Prod. Paris, O., 16 Mar. 1894, with Sybil Sanderson, Alvarez, Delmas, cond. Taffanel; N.Y., Manhattan O., 25 Nov. 1907, with Garden,

Dalmores, Renaud, cond. Campanini; London, C.G., 18 July 1911, with Edvina, Gilly, Darme, cond. Panizza.

Set in 4th-cent. Egypt, the opera tells how the monk Athanaël (bar.) converts the courtesan Thaïs (sop.), who becomes a nun, but loses his heart to her, and hence his own soul.

Thalberg, Zaré (orig. Ethel Western) (*b* Derbyshire, 16 Apr. 1858; *d* London, 1915). English soprano. Not the daughter of the Austrian pianist, but a pupil who took his name. Studied Paris, Milan. Début London, C.G., 1875, Zerlina, singing there five seasons and scoring a success as Susanna, Adina, etc. Lost her voice in 1881, and as Ethel Western acted in Shakespeare in Edwin Booth's company, retiring in the 1890s.

Theater an der Wien. Successor to the Theater auf der Wieden. Built by *Schikaneder with funds provided by the merchant Zitterbarth, opened 13 June 1801 (cap. 1,232) with Teyber's *Alexander* (text by Schikaneder). Scene of the premières of *Fidelio* (1805), *Der Waffenschmied* (1846), *Die Fledermaus* (1874), and other operettas by Strauss, Millöcker, and Lehár. Under the management of Barbaia (1821-2), saw the Viennese premières of many Rossini works. Scene of Jenny Lind's Vienna triumphs (1846-7) in *Norma*, *Sonnambula*, *Huguenots*, *Freischütz*, and *Ein Feldlager in Schlesien*. The international fame of *The Bartered Bride* dates from its first performance in German at this theatre in 1893; and in October 1897 *La Bohème*, the first Puccini opera in Vienna, was produced there. From 6 Oct. 1945 to 1954 it became the home of the Vienna State Opera while the Opera House was being rebuilt. Purchased by the city of Vienna in 1961, it was entirely renovated and reopened a year later on 30 May 1962 with *Die Zauberflöte*. Bernstein conducted a new production of *Fidelio* there on 24 May 1970 to commemorate the 200th anniversary of Beethoven's birth, and it is now the official theatre of the annual Vienna Festival.

Theater auf der Wieden. Built in 1787 by Schikaneder in one of the courts of the Freihaus, and granted royal privilege by the Emperor, hence sometimes known as the Kaiserlichkönigliches privilegiertes Theater auf der Wieden; was the scene of the first production of *Die Zauberflöte*. It closed on 12 June 1801.

Théâtre de la foire (*Fr* fairground theatre). The name given to the theatres, and hence to the works performed in them, of the two great Paris fairs of the 16th cent. the Foire St-Germain (held Feb.-Apr.) and the Foire St-Laurent (Aug.-Sep.). The musical entertainments given there, originally very primitive, consisting of hardly more than allusive use of popular tunes, were an important ancestor of *opéra-comique.

Théâtre des Champs-Élysées. Paris Theatre (cap. 2,000) opened in 1913 with a series of special performances of *Benvenuto Cellini* and *Der Freischütz* conducted by Weingartner. It was the scene of Diaghilev's 1913 season and other Russian opera seasons in the 1920s and 1930s, of a Mozart season in 1924, and of a visit by the Bayreuth ensemble in 1929. From Nov. 1936 to Feb. 1937 it offered house-room to the Opéra while the latter's home was being redecorated, and has staged occasional seasons by visiting foreign companies in the post-war period.

Théâtre-Italien or **Théâtre des Italiens.** Italian companies performed in Paris as far back as 1570, during the reign of Charles IX. The T. Ventadour, the home of the Opéra-Comique 1829-32, housed an Italian company headed by Rubini. Lablache etc. in 1828; and from 1841 to 1871 was the centre of Italian opera in Paris, opening on 2 Oct. 1841 with *Semiramide*. During autumn and winter each year there appeared a strong company which included such singers as Grisi, Persiani, Mario, Lablache, and Tamburini–in fact the company that performed each spring and summer in London. Indeed, from 1850 to 1852 *Lumley directed both Her Majesty's Opera in London and the T. des Italiens in Paris. The most famous première at the Italiens was probably *Don Pasquale* in 1843 with Grisi, Mario, Lablache, and Tamburini. After 1871 a number of attempts were made to restart Italian opera at the Ventadour (*Aida*, 1876) and then, after the theatre had been sold to the Bank of France in 1879, performances were staged at other theatres. Patti gave a series of performances at the T. des Nations in 1881, and in Nov. 1883, in the same auditorium, the T. Italien began a series of performances with the French première of *Simone Boccanegra* with Maurel in the title role, E. de Rezke as Fiesco, and conducted by Faccio. The project failed after a few months.

Théâtre Lyrique. Operatic enterprise in Paris, inaugurated 21 Sept. 1852, as successor to the Opéra-National, which had opened on 15 Nov. 1847 with Maillart's *Gastibelza*. *Carvalho was director 1856-60 and 1862-8, during which periods the theatre enjoyed its greatest artistic triumphs, with the premières of Gounod's *Le Médecin malgré lui* (1858), *Faust* (1859), *Philémon et Baucis* (1860), *Mireille* (1864), and *Roméo et Juliette* (1867), Bizet's *Les Pêcheurs de perles* (1863) and *La Jolie fille de Perth* (1867), and Berlioz's *Les Troyens à Carthage* (1863). The theatre had been rebuilt between 1860 and 1862 and reopened in that year with a special *Hymne à la Musique* composed by Gounod and sung by an ensemble that included Miolan-Carvalho, Viardot, and Faure.

Carvalho was succeeded by Pasdeloup, whose management lasted until 1870. In 1874 the theatre was again rebuilt (cap. 1,243) and was renamed the T. des Nations, and between 1887 and 1898 it was the home of the Opéra-Comique. The following year it became the T. Sarah-Bernhardt, and in 1968 the Théâtre de la Ville. Like them it has been used for occasional seasons by visiting foreign companies.

Thebom, Blanche (*b* Monessen, Pa., 19 Sept. 1918). American mezzo of Swedish parents. Studied with Matzenauer and Edyth Walker. Début Philadelphia with Met. Co., 1944 Fricka. N.Y. Met. 1940-67. Gly. 1950, Dorabella; London, C.G., 1957-8, Dido in *Les Troyens*. After retiring from Met. in 1967 was appointed general manager of the short-lived Atlanta O.C. (1968). (R)

The Hague. Town in Holland. Visiting Italian and French companies brought opera in the 17th and 18th cent. and it was staged more regularly thoughout the 19th cent. Opera was given at the Koninklijke Nederduitsche Schouwburg, also (1874-1918) as the Gebouw voor Kunsten en Vetenschappen. Since the inception of the *Holland Festival in 1947, many performances have been given.

Theodorini, Elena. See **Teodorini, Elena.**

Thieving Magpie, The. See *Gazza Ladra, La.*

Thill, Georges (*b* Paris, 14 Dec. 1897). French tenor. Studied Paris, and Naples with De Lucia. Début Paris, O., 1924, Nicias (*Thaïs*); London, C.G., 1928, 1937; N.Y., Met., 1931-2. Also sang in Italy and South America. Remained leading tenor of Paris O. until after the war. Successful as Roméo, Don José, Julien (*Louise*), as well as in Italian and German parts. Created roles in operas by Gunsbourg, Rabaud, Lazzari, and others. Last stage appearance 1953 at O.C., as Canio; sang Julien in film version of *Louise* with Grace Moore (1938). (R)

Thillon, Sophie Anne (orig. Anna Hunt) (*b* Calcutta or London, 1819; *d* Torquay, 5 May 1903). English soprano. Studied France with Bordogni, Tadolini, and Claude Thillon, whom she married. Début Paris, T. de la Renaissance, 1938, in title role of Grisar's *Lady Melvil*. O.C. from 1840, where she created Mathilde in Auber's *La Neige* and Caterina in *Les Diamants de la couronne*; London, D.L., 1845-6, created Stella in Balfe's *The Enchantress*; San Francisco 1853-4. Last stage appearance 1855, Ly. London.

Thoma. See *Vogl.*

Thomas, (Charles Louis) **Ambroise** (*b* Metz, 5 Aug. 1811; *d* Paris, 12 Feb. 1896). French composer. Studied at home and in Paris with Zimmerman and Dourlen, also with Kalkbrenner and Barbereau, later with Le Sueur. 1837-43

wrote nine stage works: the most successful was the first, the opéra-comique *La Double échelle* (1837). Then wrote a series of opéras-comiques, having great success with *Le Songe d'une nuit d'été* (1850); in the line of Auber, these are both more lively and more consciously Romantic, though not very markedly individual. Always prone to follow the leads of more distinctive (or more successful) composers, he produced *Psyché* (1857) in imitation of Gounod's classically inspired *Sapho*, *Le Carneval de Venise* (1857) in imitation of Massé, and – after a failure with *Le Roman d'Elvire* (1860) and then a pause – his greatest triumph, *Mignon* (1866) in imitation of Gounod's *Faust*. He then went on to repeat the success with *Hamlet* (1868) in imitation of Gounod's *Roméo et Juliette*. His last two operas were failures – *Gille et Gillotin* (comp. 1859, prod. 1874, an operetta) and *Françoise de Rimini* (1882). A distinguished and greatly respected Professor at the Paris Conservatoire, Director from 1871. *Bibl:* H. Delaborde: *Notices sur la vie et oeuvre d'Ambroise Thomas* (1896).

Thomas, Arthur Goring (*b* Ratton Park, 20 Nov. 1850; *d* London, 20 Mar. 1892). English composer. Studied Paris with Durand, London with Sullivan and Prout, later with Bruch. *The Light of the Harem* (1879) brought a C.R. commission which produced his best-known and most successful work, *Esmeralda* (1883), after Hugo's *Notre-Dame de Paris. Nadeshda* followed in 1885. A comic opera, *The Golden Web*, was prod. in 1893. One of the few English composers of his day with a real, if limited, operatic talent.

Thomas, Jess (*b* Hot Springs, 4 Aug. 1927). American tenor. Studied Stanford. Début San Francisco, 1957, Major-domo (*Rosenkavalier*) and since 1965; Karlsruhe, 1958; Munich since 1961; Bayreuth 1961-9, 1976; Salzburg, 1965, Bacchus; London, C.G., 1969-71, Walther and Tristan; N.Y. Met. since 1963, singing Caesar in Barker's *Antony and Cleopatra*, which opened new house at Lincoln Center. Sang Kaiser in *Frau ohne Schatten* at opening performance of rebuilt National T. Munich, 1963. Highly intelligent artist and capable Wagner singer, if not a natural *Heldentenor*. (R)

Thomas, Theodore (*b* Essen, 11 Oct. 1835; *d* Chicago, 4 Jan. 1905). German, later American conductor. Originally leader of orchestra at N.Y., Ac. of M.; took over perf. of *La Juive* in 1858. Music director of the American O. 1885. His greatest successes were in the concert hall.

Thomson, Virgil (*b* Kansas City, 25 Nov. 1896). American composer and critic. Studied initially with Nadia Boulanger; during a later stay in Paris, 1925-32, befriended by Satie and Gertrude Stein, both of whom influenced his work. *Four Saints in Three Acts* (1928) and *The*

Mother of Us All (1947), both to texts by Stein, show the more diatonic, elliptical, and detached side of his talent, together with great charm. Chief music critic, *New York Herald Tribune*, 1940-54; one of the liveliest and most penetrating of modern critics.

Thomyris, Queen of Scythia. Opera in 3 acts arr. from Scarlatti, Bononcini, Steffani, Gasparini, and Albinoni by Pepusch; text by Peter Motteux. Prod. London, D.L., 1 Apr. 1707. First true example of a London *pasticcio*, very popular in its day.

Thorborg, Kerstin (*b* Venjan, 19 May 1896; *d* Dalarna, 12 Apr. 1970). Swedish mezzo. Studied Stockholm; début there 1924, Ortrud. Stockholm Opera 1924-30; Nuremberg 1930-1; Prague 1932-3; Berlin 1933-5; Vienna 1935-8; Salzburg 1935-7; London, C.G., 1936-9; N.Y., Met., 1936-50. Considered by Newman the greatest Wagner mezzo he had seen or heard. Repertory included Ortrud, Fricka, Brangäne, Kundry, Klytemnestra, Orpheus, and roles in Italian opera. (R)

Thornton, Edna (*b* Bradford, 1875; *d* Worthing, 15 Jul. 1964). English contralto. London, C.G., 1905-10 and 1919-23. Leading member of Quinlan, Beecham, and B.N.O. Companies and admired specially in Wagner. Chosen by Richter as Erda and Waltraute in English *Ring* (1908-9). Also a distinguished Amneris and Dalila. Sang in première of *The Perfect Fool*. (R)

Tibbet, Lawrence (*b* Bakersfield, Cal., 16 Nov. 1896; *d* New York, 15 July 1960). American baritone. Studied New York with Frank la Forge. Début N.Y., Met., 1923 as Monk (*Boris*). Fame dates from his Ford in *Falstaff* revival, 1925. Remained at Met. until 1950; London, C.G., 1937, and guest appearances in Paris, Vienna, and Prague. In N.Y. created baritone roles in *Peter Ibbetson*, *The King's Henchman*, *The Emperor Jones*, *Merry Mount*, *In a Pasha's Garden*, and *Caponsacchi*, as well as in the first Met. performances of *Simon Boccanegra* (title role), *Peter Grimes* (Balstrode), *Khovanshchina* (Ivan Khovansky). At C.G., created title role in Goossens's *Don Juan de Mañara*. Excelled as Scarpia and Iago. A vivid and exciting actor, he made a number of films, including *The Rogue Song* and *The New Moon*, starring with Grace Moore in the latter. (R)

Tichatschek (orig. Tichaček, **Joseph** (Aloys) (*b* Teplice u Broumova (Ober-Weckelsdorf), 11 July 1807; *d* Dresden 18 Jan. 1886). Bohemian tenor. Abandoned medicine for singing and studied Vienna with Cicimarra. Joined chorus of Kä., 1830; then chorus inspector; began singing small roles. Official solo début Raimbaut, 1833. Graz 1835-7; Vienna 1837-8; Dresden 1838-72, principal tenor. In Dresden was befriended and coached by Schröder-

Devrient. Created Rienzi (1842) and Tannhäuser (1845), and was highly regarded by Wagner. He had difficulty with the passage in the Act 2 finale of *Tannhäuser*, beginning 'Zum Heil den Sündigen zu führen' and Wagner had to cut it from the first production. London, D.L., 1841, as Adolar and Robert le Diable.

Tiefland (Lowland). Opera in prologue and 3 acts by D'Albert; text by Rudolf Lothar, after the Catalan play *Terra Baixa* by Angel Guimerá. Prod. Prague, German T., 15 Nov. 1903, with Alföldy, Foerstel, Aranyi, Hunold, cond. Blech; N.Y., Met., (revised version) 23 Nov. 1908, with Destinn, L'Huilier, Schmedes, Feinhals, cond. Hertz; London, C.G., 5 Oct. 1910, with Terry, Teyte, Coates, Radford, cond. Beecham.

A German *verismo* opera of passion and murder. It tells of the betrayal of Martha (sop.) by her employer Sebastiano (bar.), a rich landowner who gives her to the shepherd Pedro (ten.) on condition that he leaves the mountains for the lowlands. She eventually confesses her past to Pedro, and when Sebastiano tries to take her back, Pedro strangles him and returns to the hills with Martha.

Tietjen, Heinz (*b* Tangier, 24 June 1881; *d* Baden-Baden, 30 Nov. 1967). German conductor and producer, born of German father and English mother. Trier, as cond. and prod., 1904-7, as Intendant 1907-22. Intendant Saarbrucken 1919-22. Breslau 1922-4; Berlin, Städtische Oper, 1925-30; Generalintendant, Berlin, Preussisches Staatsheater, 1927-45; artistic irector, Bayreuth, 1931-44, where he conducted *The Ring*, *Meistersinger*, and *Lohengrin*. Intendant, Berlin, Stä. O. 1948-54; Hamburg 1954-9. London, C.G., prod *Der fliegende Holländer* (1950) *Parsifal*, and *Meistersinger* (1951). His Wagner productions were traditional but never old-fashioned. In 1958 he combined with Wieland Wagner in a production of *Lohengrin* at Hamburg, Wagner producing, Tietjen conducting; returned to Bayreuth to conduct 1959. (R)

Tietjens, Therese (Carolina Johanna Alexandra) (*b* Hamburg, 17 July 1831; *d* London, 3 Oct. 1877). German soprano of Hungarian parents, and possibly Dutch origin. Studied Hamburg with Schmidt and Vienna with Dellessie and Babing. Début Hamburg 1848; Erma (*Le Maçon*); Frankfurt 1850-3; Vienna 1853-9; London, H.M.'s 1858, Valentine (*Huguenots*). Regularly in London (H.M.'s, D.L., C.G.,) until 1877, making her home there. N.Y., Ac. of M., 1874, 1876. First London Medea, Elena (*Vêpres siciliennes*), Amelia (*Ballo*), Leonora (*Forza*), Marguerite (*Faust*), Mireille. In her day unsurpassed as Norma, Donna Anna, Lucrezia Borgia, and Agathe. Could also sing Semiramide, Fidès (*Le Prophète*), and Ortrud, her only Wagner role, of which one critic wrote

'Her scolding of Telramund would have made Fricka's lecture to Wotan sound like gentle chiding'. Wagner wrote to her on 26 May 1864 offering her the first Isolde and even suggesting that cuts could be made. Her voice, which extended from c' to d''', was powerful, rich, and pure, and of great flexibility. In the first period of her English career she was tall and elegant on the stage; later she became extremely stout. She collapsed on stage during her last performance, as Lucrezia Borgia (H.M.'s 1877), a few months before her death.

Timişoara (Hung. Temesvar). Town in Romania. Transylvania was for long a centre of German culture, and opera (especially Mozart) was given in the early 19th cent., e.g. by Theodor Müller's company, conducted by Ion Wachmann, 1831-5. The present O.H. opened in 1947, and gave over 2,000 performances in its first ten years.

Tinsley, Pauline (Cecilia) (*b* Wigan, 27 Mar. 1928). British soprano. Studied Manchester, London with Joan Cross, Roy Henderson, and Eva Turner. Début 1961 London, Philopera, Desdemona (Rossini). W.N.O. since 1962 as Abigail, Lady Macbeth, Turandot, Aida, Elektra; London, S.W. later E.N.O. since 1963, as Leonora (*Forza*), Leonore, Queen Elizabeth (*Maria Stuarda*); C.G., since 1965, mostly in small roles, but Santuzza 1976; Santa Fe 1969 Anna Bolena; N.Y., City Opera, 1971 Queen Elizabeth. Repertory also includes Elettra (Idomeneo), Donna Elvira, Amelia, Elvira (*Ernani*), Lady Billows. Possesses a large, bright dramatic soprano and an exciting stage personality. (R)

Tippett, (Sir) **Michael** (Kemp) (*b* London, 2 Jan. 1905). English composer. Studied London with Charles Wood and R. O. Morris. His deep humanity, richly stocked mind, and fascination with elaborate concepts and literary and other allusions give his operas a common lyrical exuberance, for all the differences.

The Midsummer Marriage (1955) is a quest opera, taking *The Magic Flute* as artistic reference, and treating Tippett's lifelong absorption (first articulated as artistic reference in the oratorio *A Child of Our Time*) with the reconciliation between the dark and light sides of human nature before proper spiritual and emotional growth is possible. Here, the dramatic metaphor is centred on a couple who must achieve this before a true marriage is possible; and it is expressed in some of Tippett's most rich, ecstatic, haunting, and myth-invoking music. *King Priam* (1962) turns not only to an existing myth, that of the Trojan War, but also to a sparer and more sculptural idiom. The declared subject is 'the mysterious nature of human choice'; the plot is sharply dramatic, includes some stunning *coups de théâtre* (such

as the close of Act 1 on Achilles's wrath) and some tender lyrical exchanges (as that between Achilles and Priam who have both to take Hector's body), and is direct in its dramatic impact. In *The Knot Garden* (1970), suggesting *Cosi fan tutte* as his example, Tippett returned to his reconciliation theme; here his subject is a marriage which has gone wrong, and his characters are set in a psychological, but dramatically and musically expressed, maze, whose solution is the peace of a renewed emotional bond. The music draws on both the richness of Tippett's first opera and the spareness of his second, finding a new subtlety and grace of expression. His fourth opera, *The Ice-Break* (1977), enlarges the reconciliation theme to wider issues, and brings into an operatic framework the divisions, acute but (the opera suggests) not impossible to heal, between East and West, Black and White, old and young, past and present.

Bibl: M. Tippett: *Moving into Aquarius* (1959, R/1974); I. Kemp (ed.): *Michael Tippett: A Symposium on his 60th Birthday* (1965).

Titov, Alexander (Nikolayevich) (*b* St Petersburg, 23 July 1769; *d* St Petersburg, 20 Nov. 1827). Russian composer and violinist. Most of his works are for the stage, and based on a Mozartian idiom. About a dozen operas survive, including a 1-act comedy, *Yam, or The Post Station* (1805). This proved so popular that Titov wrote two sequels, *Posidelky, or The Sequel to Yam* (1808) and *Devichnik, or Filatkin's Wedding* (1809). His brother **Sergey** (1770-1825) wrote an opera *The Peasants* (1814).

Todesverkündigung. The announcement of death made to Siegmund (ten.) by Brünnhilde (sop.) in Act 2 of Wagner's *Die Walküre*.

Tofts, Catherine (*b* ?; *d* Venice, 1756). English soprano. The first singer of English birth to sing in Italian opera in England (1705), when she was heard in *Arsinoe, Camilla, Rosamond, Thomyris,* and *Love's Triumph*. Her salary of £500 was higher than any other paid in the Italian company of that time. Cibber wrote that 'the beauty of her finely proportioned figure and the exquisitely sweet, silver tone of her voice, with that peculiar rapid swiftness of her throat, were perfections not to be imitated by art or labour'.

Tolomeo. Opera in 3 acts by Handel; text by N. F. Haym. Prod. London, King's T., 11 May 1728, with Bordoni, Cuzzoni, Senesino, Baldi. Revived Halle 1963; Abingdon, 1973.

Tolstoy, (Count) **Lev** (Nikaloyevich) (*b* Yasnaya Polyana, 9 Sept. 1828; *d* Astapovo, 20 Nov. 1910). Russian writer. Although he played the piano, and could be deeply moved by music, Tolstoy was deeply suspicious of music's power to affect men's moral judgement, as he suggested in *The Kreutzer Sonata*. His dislike of opera (apart from *Don Giovanni* and *Der Freischütz*) is evident from his mockery in *War and Peace*; he tried to persuade Tchaikovsky not to persist with the form. He disliked Beethoven's music, and was unsympathetic to Russian music except for folk songs, which he admired uncritically for their reflection of the simple peasant life he venerated. Operas on his works are as follows:

War and Peace (1869): Prokofiev (1946).

Anna Karenina (1877); Sassano (1905); Granelli (1906); Malherbe (1914); Hubay (1923); Robbiani (1924); Hlobil (1962, prod. 1972).

How Men Live (1881); Martinů (1952).

The Tale of Ivan the Jester (1885): Ostrčil (*Honzovo království*, 1924).

The Two Old Men (1885): Fibich (*Bloud*, 1936).

Ivan and the Drum (1888): Reti (1933).

Resurrection (1899): Alfano (1904); Hristić (1912); Cikker (1962).

What for? (1906): Strelnikov (Beglets, 1934).

Tomasi, Henri (*b* Marseilles, 17 Aug. 1901; *d* Avignon, 13 June 1978). French composer and conductor. Studied Paris with Paul Vidal and began career as music director of Paris Radio (1930-35). Music director Monte Carlo O. 1946-50. His operas include *Don Juan de Mañara* (1952, prod. Munich 1958), *L'Atlantide* (1954), *Sampiero Corso* (1956), and *Le Silence de la mer* (1967).

Tonadilla (*Sp.* a little tune; diminutive of *tonada*, deriving from *tono*, polyphonic song). A short comic opera, which reached its greatest popularity in the 18th cent., consisting of solo songs and sometimes choruses, separated by dialogue, on a Spanish popular subject. There were usually two to four characters; in *tonadillas generales* there might be up to ten. The duration varied according to the number of characters; tonadillas for four characters seldom exceeded 20 minutes. Like the Italian **intermezzo*, it originated as an interlude between acts of a play or a serious opera, and later acquired independence. The mature stage of the genre was initiated by Luis Mison (?-1766) in *La mesonera y el arriero*; he wrote many extremely popular tonadillas. Towards the end of the 18th cent. the genre began to take on some of the characteristics of Italian opera; it began to die out in its original form towards the mid-19th cent. Other important tonadilla composers were Pablo Esteve (*c*1730-?) and Blas Laserna (1751-1816). A singer of tonadillas is a *tonadillera*.

Tonio. The clown (bar.) in Leoncavallo's *Pagliacci*.

Töpper, Hertha (*b* Graz, 19 Apr. 1924). Austrian mezzo-soprano. Studied Graz. Début there

1945, Ulrica; Munich since 1952; London, C.G., 1953, with Munich O., as Clairon in first London *Capriccio*; 1958, Octavian; Bayreuth 1951-2, 1960; San Francisco, 1960, Octavian; N.Y., Met., 1962. An elegant and musicianly singer, admired in Mozart, Wagner, and Strauss. (R)

Toreador's Song. Escamillo's (bar.) rousing account of the thrills of the bull ring in Act 2 of Bizet's *Carmen*.

Toronto. Town in Canada. The first operas given at Toronto were Coleman's *The Mountaineers* and Storace's *No Song, No Supper* in 1825, when the town, of fewer than 1,700 inhabitants, was still mainly a garrison town and administrative capital of Upper Canada. During the following years of growth to a commercial centre, visiting singers and small troupes appeared with increasing frequency; in the second half of the century most of the great singers who travelled in America sang there including Henriette Sontag, Jenny Lind, and Adelina Patti (generally in concerts). Full-scale productions date from July 1853, when Rosa Devries sang the title-role in a visiting production of *Norma* conducted by Luigi Arditi.

Semi-staged versions of *Lucrezia Borgia* were given in 1853, and of *Il trovatore* and *La sonnambula* in 1866, but little progress was made in resident production of opera until 1867, when the Holman English Opera Troupe leased the Royal Lyceum and installed itself as the city's permanent company for both plays and opera. They had appeared in the city before, but now the Holman family settled permanently in Canada, first in Toronto and, after 1873, at London, Ontario. In 1867-80 the company gave innumerable performances of about 35 different operas and operettas.

Visiting companies, including the Strakosch Company, English O.C., the Emma Abbott Company, the Kellogg Opera Company, a troupe headed by Melba (1895), by Sembrich (1901), and the N.Y., Met., continued regularly to present major artists in leading roles. Productions of local origin were sporadic until 1929, when Sir Ernest Macmillan organized the Conservatory Opera Company, which opened at the Regent T. with *Hansel and Gretel*. Owing to the financial crisis of the 1930s, it never developed. In 1934 Harrison Gilmour, a wealthy financier married to a singer, organized the Opera Guild of Toronto and produced a few operas, including *Faust*, *Aida*, *Tannhäuser*, and *Lohengrin*, until 1941.

After the war an Opera School was set up in 1946 as part of the Royal Conservatory of Music, with Arnold Walter as administrative director and Nicholas Goldschmidt as music director. They were joined in 1948 by Herman Geiger-Torel as stage director. The Royal Conservatory Opera Company, formed in 1950, presented three professional productions in the Royal Alexandra T. This Opera Festival was so successful that it gradually severed ties with the Conservatory and grew into the Canadian Opera Company, with Geiger-Torel as general director.

Since 1964 the School has occupied its own fully equipped modern theatre and workshops, and since 1969 has been a department of the Faculty of Music, University of Toronto. Although mainly a teaching organization, the Opera School produces several programmes of excerpts each year and two complete operas. Its major productions since 1964 have included *Pelléas et Mélisande, Dialogues des Carmélites, Ariadne auf Naxos, The Rake's Progress, Hamlet* (Humphrey Searle – North American première), *Iphigénie en Tauride, Il Turco in Italia,* and *Deirdre* (by Healey Willan – stage première). Since 1953 Ernesto Barbini has been music director of the School, and also acts as music adviser to the Canadian Opera Company.

The activities of the Canadian Opera Company during its first decade, when its seasons were given at the Royal Alexandra T. (cap. 1,700), were confined to productions of popular operas in short seasons in either spring or autumn. In 1961 the company moved to the O'Keefe Center (cap. 3,200), where it mounts six or seven operas each autumn. *Die Walküre* was the first Wagner opera staged by the company in 1962 and gradually other Wagner works and operas by Strauss were added to the repertory. The seventeen performances per season in 1961 and 1962 gradually increased to 36 in 1973 and 1974, and average attendances rose from 2,600 per performance to almost full houses. Every prominent Canadian singer has appeared with the Company, as well as leading guests from abroad. Since 1958, when the Canadian Arts Council asked the company to take *The Barber of Seville* on tour, a special touring group has travelled each year throughout Canada and also in the U.S.A. Geiger-Torel died in 1976 and was succeeded by Lofti Mansouri.

Torquato Tasso. Opera in 3 acts by Donizetti; text by Jacopo Ferretti, after Giovanni Rosini's drama *Tasso,* and Goethe's drama *Tasso* (1789). Prod. Rome, T. Valle, 9 Sept. 1833, with Spech, Carocci, Lauretti, Ronconi, Rinaldi; London, H.M.'s, 3 Mar. 1840 with De Varny, Coletti. Given in Naples 1835 under title of *Sordello il trovatore.*

A complicated plot that involves the poet Tasso (ten.), in love with the Duchess Eleonora (sop.), sister of the Duke of Ferrara (bass). Tasso's rival, Don Gherardo (bass), believes that Tasso loves another Eleonora, with whom he himself is in love – Eleanora di Scandiano (mezzo); he steals a poem that Tasso has written in praise of his Eleonora. Plots and counter-plots lead to the Duke declaring Tasso mad and having him confined to an asylum for seven years. When he is released he learns that Eleanora has died, and his mind really does now give way; but he is urged to think of his future glory and to return to his poetry.

Torresella, Fanny (*b* Tiflis, 1856; *d* Rome 2 May 1914). Italian soprano. Daughter of conductor Antonio Torresella. Studied with her father. Début Trieste, 1876. Career continued until 1909 in Italy and South America – first Buenos Aires Musetta and a specialist in the French repertory. Important in the development of the Italian vocal tradition from the *soprano drammatico d'agilità* of the 19th cent. to the *soprano lirico leggiero* of the 20th. (R)

Tosca. Opera in 3 acts by Puccini; text by Giacosa and Illica, after Sardou's drama *La Tosca* (1887). Prod. Rome, C., 14 Jan. 1900, with Darclée, De Marchi, Giraldoni, cond. Mugnone; London, C.G., 12 July 1900, with Ternina, De Lucia, Scotti, cond. Mancinelli; N.Y., Met., 4 Feb. 1901, with Ternina, Cremonini, Scotti, cond. Mancinelli.

Cavaradossi (ten.), a painter and republican, aids Angelotti (bass), the consul of the former Roman Republic, who has escaped from prison. Tosca (sop.), a singer and Cavaradossi's lover, jealously believes that Cavaradossi is having an affair with the beautiful Marchese Attavanti. The cruel and lustful police chief, Baron Scarpia (bar.), plays on Tosca's jealousy and also her love for Cavaradossi, whom he has had arrested and tortured. The cries of her lover break down Tosca's resistance and she reveals Angelotti's hiding place. Scarpia tells her she only can save her lover's life by giving herself to him, and in exchange he will arrange a mock execution for Cavaradossi. Tosca agrees, but seeing a knife on Scarpia's supper table, seizes it and kills him. She hurries to join Cavaradossi to tell him of the mock execution he must go through. The shots ring out and Cavaradossi falls dead; Scarpia has tricked Tosca. But his murder has been discovered, and, distraught, she jumps from the battlements of the Castel Sant'-Angelo.

Toscanini, Arturo (*b* Parma, 25 Mar. 1867; *d* New York, 16 Jan. 1957). Italian conductor. Studied Parma Conservatory, and began career as cellist. On the second night of an Italian opera season in Rio de Janeiro (25 Jan. 1886) he was called on by members of the company to replace the regular conductor, against whom the public had demonstrated, and directed *Aida* (from memory) with great success. Back in Italy, he was engaged to conduct Catalani's *Edmea* at Turin. In 1892 he conducted the première of *Pagliacci* at the Dal

Verme in Milan, and in 1896 that of *La Bohème* in Turin, where during the same season he introduced *Götterdämmerung* to Italy. He was summoned to the Milan Sc. in 1898 as principal conductor, and remained there until 1902, when he left after demonstrations against him for refusing to allow Zenatello an encore in *Un ballo in maschera*. He returned to Sc. in 1906-8 and 1921–9 (for details of premières, etc., during these periods, see *La Scala*).

From 1908 to 1915 Toscanini conducted at the other great centre of his influence, the Met. New York, whither he went with *Gatti-Casazza. Here he gave the world premières of *La fanciulla del West* and *Madame Sans-Gêne* and the first performances in America of *Boris Godunov, Ariane et Barbe-Bleue, Armide,* and *L'amore dei tre Re.* After he left the Sc. in 1929, owing to the growing tension between himself and the Fascists, his only other operatic appearances were at Bayreuth (1930-1) and Salzburg (1934-7), where his performances of *Falstaff* and *Fidelio* became celebrated. Between 1944 and 1954, however, he gave concert performances of a number of operas including *La traviata, Aida, Falstaff,* and *Un ballo in maschera* for the N.B.C. in New York, all of which were recorded and issued commercially. He also conducted the opening concert at the restored Sc. in May 1946, and a Boito commemorative performance in June 1948.

Toscanini's great love was always Italian opera. He had, at his special request, played the cello in the première of *Otello,* and later won Verdi's friendship and admiration; he championed Puccini; he remained all his life faithful to lesser Italian works, even naming his daughter Wally after the heroine of Catalani's opera (which he especially admired). Yet he also introduced Italians to operas from the German repertory, and revived, among other neglected works, Gluck's *Orpheus*. His genius rested perhaps above all on his uncanny ability to identify himself with the composer's intentions and his intense personal magnetism in persuading players and singers to share his vision. Verdi and Puccini both paid tribute to his insight into their music. A certain tyranny went with this. Though acutely humble about his art, he was an autocrat in the opera house, ruling singers, management, and audience despotically in the service of music. Especially in his later days, he sometimes dominated singers too ruthlessly; but his refusal of encores, his intolerance of personal vanities, and his celebrated fits of temper were based on a love of music that at times seemed almost too intense for him to bear.

Biographies include *Toscanini* by Howard Taubman (1951), *Il maestro* by Luciana Frassati (1967), and *Toscanini* by George Maek (1974); his work, with special reference to his many records, is studied in *Toscanini and the Art of*

Orchestral Performance by Robert C. Marsh (1956). (R)

Tosi, Piero Francesco (*b* Bologna 1647, or Cesena 1653; *d* Faenza, April 1732). Italian castrato and singing teacher. Studied singing with his father, Giuseppe Felice Tosi, and sang with success in Italy and Germany. Settled in London 1692; gave regular concerts and became a much sought-after and respected teacher of singing. His *Opinioni de' cantori antichi e moderni o siano osservazioni sopra il canto figurato* was published Bologna 1723, and translated into English by Galliard 1742, German by Agricola 1757, and French by Lemaire 1757. Reprinted in Italy 1905 and 1933, and in England in 1906. His theories on voice are still highly regarded by teachers of *bel canto*. He wrote that 'good taste was fast disappearing and the profession was suffering from a precipitous decline'. He emphasized four requirements of his pupils: beauty of tone; agility; correct intonation; and study of the text.

Toten Augen, Die (The Blind Eyes). Opera in prologue and 1 act by D'Albert; text by M. Henry. Prod. Dresden 5 Mar. 1916, with Forti, Taucher, Plaschke; Chicago 1 Nov. 1923, with Gernter-Fischer, Hutt, Lattermann.

Myrtocle (sop.), blind wife of the Roman proconsul Arcesius (bar.), miraculously recovers her sight, only to discover how ugly Arcesius is, and believes that the handsome Captain Galba (ten.) is the man to whom she had been married. He is secretly in love with her, but when she discovers the truth, all her love for Arcesius returns, and she prays to become blind again. She gazes on the bright sun, and once again her eyes lose their sight.

Tote Stadt, Die (The Dead City). Opera in 3 acts by Korngold; text by Paul Schott, after G.-R.-C. Rodenbach's novel *Bruges-la-morte* (1892). Prod. simultaneously 4 Dec. 1920 in Hamburg with Munchow, Olczewska, Schubert, Degler, cond. Pollak, and in Cologne with J. Klemperer, Rohr, Schröder, Renner, cond. Klemperer; N.Y., Met., 19 Nov. 1921, with Jeritza, Telva, Harrold, cond. Bodanzky. Korngold's greatest success.

Paul is mourning his dead wife Marie (sop.), and sees her once again in the person of the dancer Marietta (sop.). She proves unfaithful to him, and in his dream he strangles her with her own hair.

Tottola, Leone Andrea (*b* ?; *d* Naples, 15 Sept. 1831). Italian librettist. The poet of the Neapolitan theatre at a time when opera buffa still flourished, his busy, not to say hasty, pen was at the service of many different composers. Although his work sometimes lacked technique and taste, he sensed the impact of the novel ideas of Romanticism, and had some influence in impressing these on his composers. His subjects include many which became the stock in trade of Romanticism, such as the Biblical, Oriental, and medieval, German legend, and English novels (including Scott). His librettos include *Adelson e Salvini* for Bellini, seven for Donizetti (including *Gabriella di Vergy* and *Il castello di Kenilworth*), six for Rossini (including *La donna del lago*), and many others for Pacini, Mercadante, Guglielmi, Fioravanti, Mayr, and others.

Toulouse. A theatre has existed since the 16th century as part of the Hôtel de Ville and was originally called Le Logis de l'Écu. In 1687, Francine, Lully's son-in-law, was authorised by the King to create an Académie Royale de Musique d'Opéra, and in 1737 a new theatre was built which belonged to the Capitouls, the 12 elected consuls who also administered the city, hence the later name T. du Capitole. It opened on 11 May 1737 under the direction of Mlle. Dejardin, directress of the Paris O. A new theatre was built 1817-18 and opened on 1 October 1818 with *Les Jeux de l'amour et du hasard* and *Le Souper de Madélon*; it was completely redesigned in 1835 and again in 1880, and burnt down in 1917. The present T. du Capitole (cap. 1,550) was opened in 1923 and renovated and modernized in 1950. The tenor Louis Izar (1895-1971) was administrator 1948-68. Michel Plasson has been music director since 1974, and in 1975 it was agreed to share productions, etc. with the Grand T., Bordeaux. Famous singers who were born in Toulouse include Victor Capoul, Pedro Gailhard, Antonin Trantoul, Janine Micheau, and Jane Berbié.

Tourel (orig. Davidson), **Jennie** (*b* Russia, 26 June 1900; *d* New York, 23 Nov. 1973). French-Canadian mezzo-soprano of Russian parentage. Studied Paris with Anna El-Tour, an anagram of whose name she adopted professionally. Début Paris, O. Russe C., 1931, Polovtsian Maiden in *Prince Igor*; Chicago 1931, Lola, also small roles in Moret's *Lorenzaccio* and Hamilton Forest's *Camille*. Paris, O.C., 1933-9, Carmen, Cherubino, Mignon, Charlotte, Djamileh. N.Y., Met., 1937, Mignon, and 1943-7. Admired as Djamileh, Adalgisa, Rosina (original keys). N.Y., City O., 1941-2, Lisa. Created Baba the Turk (*Rake's Progress,* 1951). Her voice ranged from g' to c''', and she possessed an excellent technique. After retiring from the stage, she taught at the Juilliard School, N.Y. Sang Duchess of Crakentorp in *Fille du régiment,* Chicago, 1973. (R)

Touring opera. An opera company without a permanent home, giving performances in a different theatre each week or fortnight. In Great Britain, the *Carl Rosa, *Moody-Manners, Beecham, and *British National Opera companies were formerly the leading

touring companies; in America, the *San Carlo.

Tours are also made by permanent companies, sometimes in the form of a part of the regular company or a cadet branch of it. C.G. ceased its touring activities in the mid-1960s. S.W., later E.N.O., undertakes long periods of regional touring each year, as do other British companies. The Gly. Touring C. was founded in 1967 as a nursery for young British artists, and to a lesser extent the E.O.G. performs a similar function. In the U.S.A. the Met. makes a large-scale annual tour. Germany and Italy have more numerous and widely dispersed centres, and therefore do not tour, though major companies such as those of Berlin, Milan, Munich, Vienna, etc., make prestige trips abroad.

Toye, Geoffrey (*b* Winchester, 17 Feb. 1889; *d* London, 11 June 1942). English conductor and composer. Studied London, R.C.M. Governor of S.W. 1931; managed the opera company there until 1934; managing director, C.G., 1934-6, resigning after differences with Beecham and other members of the board following the engagement of Grace Moore (1935) and other moves to popularize opera.

Tozzi, Giorgio (*b* Chicago, 8 Jan. 1923). American bass-baritone of Italian origin. Studied Milan with Lorandi. Début Chicago, Mid-West O.C., 1945. N.Y., Ziegfield T., 1949, Tarquinius (*Rape of Lucretia*). Then went to London for the musical *Tough at the Top.* After further study in Milan appeared in Italy, including Milan, Sc., 1954. N.Y., Met since 1955, where he created the Doctor in *Vanessa* (1958) and has been most successful as Figaro, Sarastro, Gremin, and Sachs. (R)

Traetta, Tommaso (*b* Bitonto, 30 Mar. 1727; *d* Venice, 6 Apr. 1779). Italian composer. Studied Naples with Durante and Leo. His first opera, *Farnace* (1751), brought commissions for six more operas, and his fame quickly spread. As well as producing a long series of operas throughout Italy, he wrote two works for Vienna. He succeeded Galuppi as Catherine II's court musician from 1768 until 1775, when he was able to endure the Russian climate no more. He then visited London without displacing Sacchini from favour. Highly praised by good judges in their day for their dramatic flair, and notable as an influence on early Gluck, Traetta's works are now neglected.
Bibl: A. Nuovo: *Tommaso Traetta* (1939).

Tragédie Lyrique The term coined by *Quinault and *Lully, and first used by them for *Cadmus et Hermonie* (1673), for a genre of opera which would make use of tragic mythological or epic subjects, with great attention to clarity of declamation and naturalness of action. It was, nevertheless, much criticized, even in its heyday, for the high-flown and exaggerated treatment of its subjects in its reflection of the *gloire* essential to Louis XIV's Court entertainment. It became a stilted convention, anticipating many of the rigid features of opera seria and laying itself open to vigorous parody by *Favart. The term fell into disuse in the early 19th cent.; it had long been applied in a much more general way by Lully's successors from Rameau to Gluck and then Grétry, Gossec, and others.

Transposition. The term for the notation or performance of a piece of music in a key different from its original. Opera singers, particularly those of ripening years, may often require an aria to be transposed down, usually to accommodate their top notes (a typical example is Manrico's 'Di quella pira'), even during a complete performance when it may make nonsense of the composer's key structure.

Trantoul, Antonin (*b* Toulouse, 21 Feb. 1887; *d* Marseilles 31 Aug. 1966). French tenor. Studied Toulouse and Paris with Jean de Reszke. Début 1911, Nîmes, Des Grieux. Paris, O.C., 1920-24; O., 1923-5; Milan, Sc. 1925-9, especially successful as Don Carlo, Otello, and Nerone (Boito). (R)

Traubel, Helen (*b* St Louis, 20 June 1899; *d* Santa Monica, 28 July 1972). American soprano. Studied St. Louis and sang in concerts from 1925 to 1934. Engaged N.Y., Met., to create Mary in Damrosch's *The Man Without a Country* (1934) at the composer's request. Real success dates from 1939, when she sang Sieglinde. When Flagstad left the Met. in 1941, Traubel became the leading Wagner soprano, remaining there until 1953, when she and Bing disagreed over her night-club appearances. She sang in Buenos Aires, Rio, and Mexico. American critics compared her with Nordica. She also wrote detective stories, including *The Potomaine Canary* and *The Metropolitan Opera Murders.* Her autobiography, *St. Louis Woman,* appeared in 1959. (R)

Traubmann, Sophie (*b* N.Y., 12 May 1867; *d* N.Y., 16 Aug. 1951). American soprano. Studied N.Y. with Fürsch-Madi, and Paris with Viardot and Marchesi. She was also coached for Wagner roles by Cosima Wagner. Début N.Y., Ac. of M., Venus; Met., 1888-1902, where she was the first American Woglinde, and Margiana (*Barbier von Bagdad*). London, C.G., 1892.

Traurigkeit ward mir zum Lose. Constanze's (sop.) aria in Act 2 of Mozart's *Entführung aus dem Serail,* bewailing her imprisonment.

Travelling Companion, The. Opera in 4 acts by Stanford; text by Henry Newbolt, after Hans Andersen's fairy tale. Prod. Liverpool 30 Apr. 1925.

Travesti (Fr. past part. of *travestir* to disguise). The term used to describe such roles as Cherubino, Octavian, Orlofsky, Siebel, etc., which although sung by women are male characters. The English term is 'breeches part', or 'trouser-role', from the German *Hosenrolle.*

Traviata, La (The Wayward One). Opera in 3 acts by Verdi; text by Piave, after the drama *La Dame aux camélias* (1852) by Dumas *fils,* after his novel (1848) based on his own experiences. Prod. Venice, F., 6 Mar. 1853, with Salvini-Donatelli, Graziani, Varesi, cond. Mares; London, H.M.'s, 24 May 1856, with Piccolomini, Calzolari, Benevenuto, cond. Bonetti; N.Y., Ac. of M., 3 Dec. 1856 with La Grange, Brignoli, Amodio, cond. Maretzek.

Alfredo Germont (ten.) falls in love with the beautiful courtesan, Violetta Valery (sop.), known as the Lady of the Camelias. She is aware that she is dying from consumption. Finding a man she truly can love for the first time in her life, she leaves her demi-monde life and goes to live with Alfredo in the country. There she is visited by Alfredo's father, Giorgio Germont (bar.), who has come to ask her to give up Alfredo: his daughter's engagement is threatened by the scandal of the association. She agrees to make the sacrifice and returns to her former protector, the Baron Douphol (bar.). Alfredo publicly insults Violetta at a party given by Flora Bervoix (mezzo); he is challenged to a duel by the Baron and is also disowned by his father. He eventually learns the truth about Violetta's sacrifice and returns to find her dying.

Trebelli (orig. Gloria Caroline Gillebert or Le Bert, of which Trebelli is almost the reverse), **Zélia** (*b* Paris, 1834; *d* Étretat, 18 Aug. 1892). French mezzo-soprano. Studied with Wartel. Début Madrid 1859, Azucena; appeared in Germany, where she was compared with Alboni. London, H.M.'s 1862, as Maffeo Orsini (*Lucrezia Borgia*); C.G. 1868-71, 1881-2, 1888. Much admired in *travesti* roles. First Met. Carmen, 1884. Married the tenor Alessandro Bettini (1825-98): their daughter Antoinette sang first under her own name, then as Antonia Dolores.

Treble. The term for the higher of the two categories of girls' and unbroken boys' voice (the lower being alto). The two leading parts in Britten's *The Turn of the Screw,* Miles and Flora, are for trebles.

Treigle, Norman (*b* New Orleans, 6 Mar 1927; *d* there, 16 Feb. 1975). American bass. Studied New Orleans. Début New Orleans, 1947, Lodovico. New York, City O., 1953–72 in many operas, including title-roles in *Giulio Cesare, Mefistofele, Don Giovanni,* and *Boris Godunov.* Created Olun Blitch in Floyd's *Susannah* and title-role in same composer's *Passion of Jonathan Wade*; also sang title-role in first U.S. performance of *Il prigioniero.*

London, C.G., 1974 Méphistophélès in the first perf. of *Faust* there for 36 years. A tall, gaunt man, with a true bass voice with a cutting edge and a highly individual style of acting. (R)

Treptow, Günther (*b* Berlin, 22 Oct. 1907). German tenor. Début Berlin, Deutsches Opernhaus, 1936. Steersman (*Der fliegende Holländer*); Berlin, Städtische Oper, 1936-42, 1945-50; S.O. since 1955; Vienna 1947-55; Bayreuth, 1951-2; N.Y., Met., 1950-1; London, C.G., 1953. One of the few true Heldentenors of the post-war period, admired as Siegmund, Siegfried, and Tristan; repertory also included Florestan, Steva, and Otello. (R)

Treviso. Town in Veneto, Italy. The T. Communale opened in 1763 and has been rebuilt several times. It staged the first performance in Italy, after La Scala, of *Boris Godunov* in 1909. Lay empty for many years, but was restored in 1961, and since 1967 has been the scene of an annual autumn festival. Armando Gatto is the music director. In 1974 a Puccini Festival was organized to commemorate the 50th anniversary of his death; every one of his operas was staged.

Trial. The term, derived from Antoine *Trial traditionally applied at the Paris O.C. to a tenor of dramatic rather than vocal excellence, specializing in comedy – e.g. Le Petit Vieillard (Arithmetic) in Ravel's *L'Enfant et les Sortilèges*. See also *Tenor.*

Trial, Antoine (*b* Avignon, 1736; *d* Paris, 5 Feb. 1795). French tenor. Début Paris, T.I., 1764, O.C., for 30 years. A fervent supporter of the Revolution, who after the death of Robespierre was forced by the mob to sing the 'Reveil du Peuple' on his knees, and then had to resign; he went mad and committed suicide. His wife Marie Jeanne Milon (1746-1814) sang under the name of Mandeville. Their son Armand-Emmanuel (1771-1803) was a composer and accompanist. See also below.

Trier. Town in Rhineland-Palatinate, Germany. An opera house was opened in the former monastery in the Viehmarkt in 1802. As well as French opéras comiques, including works by Méhul and Boieldieu, German opera was given. Tietjens was an influential director there until 1922. The theatre was destroyed in the Second World War, rebuilt 1962–4 (cap. 622). The company gives performances in Saarlautern, St Wendel, Neunkirchen, and Dijon.

Trieste. Free city at the head of the Adriatic, capital of the Friuli-Venezia Giulia region; originally Italian, then French, Austrian, and now Italian. The first opera given there was *Serpilla e Bacocco* (Orlandini) in 1730 in the Palazzo Del Comune, where, in 1751, the first theatre, the T.S. Pietro, was opened (cap. 800). An imperial decree of 1760 turned this into the Cesario

Regio T. San Pietro. Operas by Pergolesi, Piccini, Cimarosa, Galuppi, Salieri, and Paisiello were given there with leading singers of the day. Da Ponte and his mistress, Ferrarese, lived for a time in Trieste, and persuaded leading Mozart singers from Vienna and Prague to appear, including Calvesi, Baglioni, Fantozzi, Micelli, and Mandini. In 1800 the T. S. Pietro closed with a performance of Zingarelli's *Giulietta e Romeo* with Catalani as Romeo. A new and larger theatre was planned, designed by Antonio Selva, architect of F., Venice, and Matteo Pertsch, a pupil of Piernarini; it opened on 21 Apr. 1801 as the T. Nuovo, with Mayr's *Ginevra di Scozia*, specially commissioned for the occasion. The Nuovo was renamed Grande (1821), Comunale (1861), and finally T. Comunale Giuseppe Verdi (1901).

In the first half of the 19th-cent., performances were given of most Rossini, Bellini, and Donizetti operas, with leading Italian singers. On 26 Oct. 1848 Verdi's *Il corsaro* received its première, and on 16 Nov. 1850 his *Stiffelio* – both were failures. The Trieste public was adventurous, and many French works were given there for the first time in Italy, including *La muette di Portici* and *Mignon*; Wagner's operas have also enjoyed great popularity in Trieste – the Angelo Neumann-Seidl performances of the *Ring* in 1883 given at the Teatro Politeama Rossetti (opened in 1883) drew an average audience of 1,000 a night, a record at that time for Wagner operas in Italy.

In 1936 the T. Giuseppe Verdi became an Ente Autonomo, with Giuseppe Antonicelli as Sovrintendente. The new régime began on 9 Jan. 1937 with *Otello*; Antonicelli remained director until 1945, was reappointed in 1951, and finally retired in 1968. Strauss's operas have been very popular in Trieste and Smareglia's operas are also successful. During the post-war period there have been seen distinguished productions of *Dialogues des Carmélites*, *Peter Grimes*, and *The Fiery Angel*, as well as operas by Pizzetti, Petrassi, Mortari, Zafred, etc. Raffaelo de Banfield was appointed artistic director in 1972. Open-air performances, mostly of operetta, are given at the Castello San Giusto.
Bibl: V. Viva and others: *Il Comunale di Trieste* (1962).

Trionfo d'Afrodite. *Concerto scenico* by Carl Orff; text by composer, after Catullus, Sappho, and Euripides. Part 2 of the 'Trionfi' triptych (the other two parts being. *Carmina Burana* and *Catulli Carmina*). Prod. Milan, Sc., 14 Feb. 1953, with Schwarzkopf, Gedda, cond. Karajan.

The work is divided into separate sections: a song to the evening star while awaiting the bride and groom, the wedding procession, the bride and groom, a song to Hymen, games and songs outside the bridal chamber, the song of the newly-weds in the bridal chamber, and a chorus in praise of Eros.

Trionfo dell'onore, Il (The Triumph of Honour). Opera in 3 acts by A. Scarlatti; text by F.A. Tullio. Prod. Naples, T. dei Fiorentini, 26 Nov. 1718; Loughton 23 July 1937; N.Y., Alma Gluck T., 11 Nov. 1954. The first surviving example of a Neapolitan comic opera.

Tristan und Isolde. Opera in 3 acts by Wagner; text by composer, after Gottfried von Strassburg's *Tristan* (*c* 1210), in turn based on Thomas of Britain's *Tristran* (*c* 1150), in turn based on a lost earlier version of the old legend. Prod. Munich, Court, 10 June 1865, with Malvina and Ludwig Schnorr von Carolsfeld, Deinet, Mitterwurzer, Zottmayer, cond. Bülow; London, D.L., 20 June 1882, with Sucher, Brandt, Winkelmann, E. Kraus, Gura, Landau, cond. Richter; N.Y., Met., 1 Dec. 1886, with Lilli Lehmann, Brandt, Nieman, Robinson, Fischer, cond. Seidl.

Tristan (ten.) is taking Isolde (sop.) to be King Mark's bride. He refuses through his squire Kurwenal (bar.) to see her on the ship. She describes to Brangäne how he was wounded in winning her from her betrothed, but healed by her (she will not admit love). She orders Brangäne to prepare poison for her and Tristan, but Brangäne substitutes a love potion. They drink it and become aware of their love.

Isolde takes advantage of her husband Mark's absence hunting with Melot (ten.) to meet Tristan. In the great love duet they sing of their passion and how it can only flourish in night. Melot causes them to be surprised, but the king is too grief-stricken to show anger at Tristan's betrayal. Isolde answers Tristan that she will follow wherever he goes; he is attacked by Melot and allows himself to be wounded.

In Tristan's castle in Brittany, Kurwenal tries to cheer his sick master, who thinks only of Isolde. The repeated sad strain of a shepherd's pipe tells that Isolde, sent for by Kurwenal, is not in sight. When the shepherd's joyful tune announces her ship, Tristan excitedly tears off his bandages, and dies in her arms. A second ship brings Mark and Melot, and Kurwenal dies killing Melot, unaware that they come to pardon Tristan. In her Liebestod, Isolde sings of the love which she can only now fulfil in the deeper night of death at Tristan's side.

Trittico, Il. The 'triptych' of operas by Puccini, *Il *Tabarro, *Suor Angelica, and *Gianni Schicchi.

Troilus and Cressida. Opera in 3 acts by Walton; text by Christopher Hassall, after Chaucer's poem (*c* 1385). Prod. London, C.G., 3 Dec. 1954, with László, Lewis, Pears, Kraus, cond. Sargent; San Francisco, 7 Oct. 1955, with Kirsten, Lewis, McChesney, Weede, cond.

Leinsdorf. Revised and shortened by Walton with Cressida's role transposed to mezzo-sop. range for Janet Baker and produced London, C.G. 12 Nov. 1976.

Cressida (sop., in second version mezzo), daughter of the High Priest of Troy, Calkas (bass), is turned from her intention of becoming a priestess by the love of Troilus (ten.), abetted by her uncle Pandarus (ten.). When Calkas goes over to the Greeks, she is exchanged for their prisoner Antenor (bar.), and agrees to marry Diomede (bar.). Troilus comes to find her and is stabbed in the back by Calkas when fighting Diomede, who orders his body to be returned to Troy and Cressida to remain in the Greek camp as a harlot; she kills herself over Troilus's body.

Trompeter von Säckingen, Der (The Trumpeter of Säckingen). Opera in 4 acts by Nessler; text by Rudolf Bunge, after Von Scheffel's poem (1854). Prod. Leipzig, 4 May 1884 with Jahns, Marion, Schelper, Grengg, cond. Nikisch. N.Y., 23 Nov. 1887, with Seidl-Kraus, Meissinger, Ferenczy, Von Milde, Robinson, Fischer, cond. Seidl; London, D.L., 8 July 1892, with Bettaque, Schumann-Heink, Landau, Litter, Reichmann, Wiegand, cond. Feld.

Set just after the Thirty Years' War, the opera describes the secret love of the trumpeter Werner for Maria, whose parents wish her to marry Damian. Werner gives Maria trumpet lessons, but their love is discovered. However, Damian proves to be a simpleton, and moreover a coward when the city is attacked. Werner is wounded in his heroic defence of the city; a mole on his arm reveals he is of noble birth and he is now permitted to marry Maria.

Troppau. See *Opava.*

Troutbeck, (Rev.) **John** (*b* Blencowe, 12 Nov. 1832; *d* London, 11 Oct. 1899). English translator. His English translations of opera include *Così fan tutte, Entführung,* Gluck's two *Iphigenias* and *Orfeo,* Götz's *Taming of the Shrew,* and *Der fliegende Holländer.*

Trovatore, Il (The Troubadour). Opera in 4 acts by Verdi; text by Cammarano, after the drama *El Trovador* by Gutiérrez. Prod. Rome, Ap., 19 Jan. 1853, with Penco, Goggi, Baucardé, Guicciardi, cond. Angelini; N.Y., Ac. of M., 2 May 1855, with Steffanone, Vestvali, Brignoli, Amodeo, cond. Maretzek; London, C.G., 10 May 1855, with Ney, Viardot, Tamberlik, Graziani, cond. Costa.

The notoriously confused action takes place in Spain at the beginning of the 15th century during the civil war caused by the rebellion of the Count of Urgel against the King of Aragon. The leader of the King's army is the Count Di Luna.

Act 1, scene 1. Ferrando (bass), an old retainer of Di Luna, tells the soldiers how, many years previously, the Count's young brother had been kidnapped by a gipsy whose mother had been burned as a witch by the Count's father. It was believed that the stolen child was burned by the gipsy.

Scene 2. In the palace garden that night Leonora (sop.), lady-in-waiting to the Queen of Aragon, tells her companion Inez (sop.) of her love for the troubador Manrico, who nightly serenades her, and who is the leader of the rebel army. Di Luna (bar.), himself in love with Leonora, enters the garden. Leonora, hearing the voice of Manrico (ten.), rushes out, but mistakes Di Luna for her lover. Manrico now enters, and the two men prepare to fight.

Act 2, scene 1. Several months later in the gipsy camp, Manrico, who was wounded by Di Luna, is being nursed by Azucena (mezzo), whom he believes to be his mother. She relates how her mother had been burned at the stake, and how in her madness she had thrown the wrong child into the flames (she had in fact killed her own child, and Manrico is Di Luna's brother, though no one but Azucena knows this). A messenger brings news that Leonora, believing her lover dead, is to enter a convent. Manrico hurries off to prevent this.

Scene 2. Di Luna and his followers assemble outside the Jerusalem Convent to abduct Leonora. They are thwarted by Manrico, who takes Leonora to the castle of Castellor.

Act 3, scene 1. A military encampment. Di Luna and his men are besieging Castellor. Azucena is found lingering near the camp. Ferrando recognizes her; she says she is Manrico's mother. Di Luna condemns her to be burned.

Scene 2. Preparations are being made in the castle for Manrico's marriage to Leonora. Learning from his retainer Ruiz (ten.) that Azucena is to die, Manrico hurries off to rescue her.

Act 4, scene 1. Manrico has been captured trying to rescue Azucena. Leonora comes to the palace hoping to see him and prays that her love will ease his suffering. Monks chant a Miserere and Manrico sings of his longing for death. Leonora pleads with Di Luna for Manrico's life. He agrees to spare Manrico on condition that Leonora gives herself to him. She consents. Di Luna goes to order Manrico's release, and Leonora drinks poison from a ring.

Scene 2. Manrico tries to comfort Azucena, reminding her of their home in the mountains. Leonora arrives to tell Manrico that he is free. When he learns the price of his freedom he curses her. But already the poison is working, and Di Luna enters to see Leonora die in her lover's arms. He orders Manrico's execution – and as Manrico dies, Azucena tells him triumphantly that he has killed his own brother. 'Mother, you are avenged!' she cries as the curtain falls.

Cortesi's *Il trovatore* (1852) is to a different plot.

Troyanos, Tatiana (*b* New York, 12 Sept. 1938). American mezzo-soprano. Studied N.Y., Juilliard School with Hans Heinz. Début N.Y., C.C., 1963, Hippolyta (*Midsummer Night's Dream*). Hamburg since 1965, where she created Jeanne in *The Devils of Loudun* (1969); London C.G., since 1969, Octavian, Carmen, Composer (with Bavarian State Opera). Sang title-role in *Ariodante* at opening of Kennedy Centre, Washington, 1971. Repertory also includes Poppea, Charlotte, Jocaste. An intense vocal and dramatic performer. (R)

Troyens, Les (The Trojans). Opera in 5 acts by Berlioz; text by composer after Virgil's *Aeneid* (*c* 27–19 B.C.). Composed 1856–8. To achieve a performance, Berlioz was obliged in 1863 to divide the work into 2 parts: Acts 1 and 2 into *La Prise de Troie* (The Capture of Troy) (3 acts), prod. Karlsruhe, 6 Dec. 1890 with Reuss, Harlacher, Oberländer, Cordes, Heller, Nebe, cond. Mottl; Acts 3, 4, and 5 into *Les Troyens à Carthage* (The Trojans at Carthage) (5 acts, with added prologue), prod. Paris, T.L., 4 Nov. 1863), with Charton-Demeur, Monjauze, Cabel, De Quercy, Petit, Peront, cond. Deloffre. The complete work was first prod. Karlsruhe, 6–7 Dec. 1890, with in addition Mailhac, Plank, Rosenberg, Guggenbühler, cond. Mottl; Glasgow, 18–19 Mar. 1935, with Jenny Black, Booth, Pugh, McCrone, Morrison, William Dickie, Moir, W. Noble, Reid, Graham, cond. Chisholm; Boston, O.H., 27 Mar. 1955 (much shortened), cond. Goldovsky; San Francisco, O.H., 1966 (shortened), with Crespin as Cassandra and Dido; N.Y., Met., 1973, with Verrett (Cassandra and Dido), Blegen, Dunn, Vickers, Riegel, Quilico, Macurdy, cond. Kubelík.

In the following synopsis, the original arrangement is preserved, with the act divisions of the second version given in brackets.

Act 1 (*Troy*, 1). The Greeks have abandoned their camp, leaving behind the wooden horse. The forebodings of Cassandra (sop. or mezzo), daughter of Priam (bass), are disbelieved even by her lover Choroebus (bar.). (*Troy,* 2) The celebrations of peace are interrupted by Aeneas (ten.), who brings news that the priest Laocöon, who mistrusted the horse, has been devoured by serpents: the horse is thereupon dragged into the city to propitiate Athene.

Act 2 (*Troy,* 3). Hector's ghost (bass) tells Aeneas to flee from Troy and found a new city in Italy. The priest Pantheus (bass) describes the burning of Troy by Greeks who have hidden in the horse. In the Temple of Vesta, Cassandra tells the women of Choroebus's death and Aeneas's escape. As the Greeks rush in, the women stab themselves.

Act 3 (*Carthage,* 1). At Carthage, festivities are in progress. Queen Dido (sop. or mezzo) states her intention of remaining single in devotion to her dead husband: her sister Anna (con.) tries to shake this resolve. The poet Iopas (ten.) reports the arrival by sea of strangers. Aeneas's son Ascanius (sop.) successfully begs Dido for hospitality. When her minister Narbal (bass) brings news of invasion, Aeneas, hitherto disguised, steps forward and offers help. (*Carthage*, 2) In a symphonic interlude (Royal Hunt and Storm), Dido and Aeneas are driven into a cave where they make love.

Act 4 (*Carthage*, 3). Aeneas is fêted in Dido's gardens. Narbal's apprehensions over Aeneas's impending conflict between love and duty are seen to be justified as Dido allows her firm resolve to weaken. Mercury exhorts Aeneas to voyage on to Italy.

Act 5 (*Carthage*, 4). The ghosts of Trojan heroes add their exhortations to depart, and Aeneas, now deaf to Dido's pleas, sets sail. (*Carthage*, 5) On hearing this, Dido, distraught with grief, decides to die; prophesying the glory of Rome, she kills herself on Aeneas's sword.

Tsar Saltan, The Tale of. Opera in a prologue and 4 acts by Rimsky-Korsakov; text by V. I. Belsky, after Pushkin's poem (1832). Prod. Moscow, Solodovnikov T., 3 Nov. 1900, with Mutin, Tsvetkova, Rostavtseva, Veretennikova, Strakhova, Sekar-Rozhansky, Zabela, Shkafer, Shevelyov, Levandovsky, cond. Ippolitov-Ivanov; London, S.W., 11 Oct. 1933, with Cross, Kennard, Palmer, Coates, Wendon, Kelsey, Austin, Hancock, cond. Collingwood; N.Y., St. James's T., 27 Dec. 1937, as *The Bumble Bee Prince* (in English).

Tsar Saltan (bass) marries Militrisa (sop.), whose sisters Tkachikha (mezzo) and Povarikha (sop.) cause her and her son Prince Guidon (ten.) to be thrown into the sea in a cask, by telling the Tsar that she has produced a monster. Washed up on an island, Guidon rescues a swan fleeing from a hawk: it turns out to be a disguised princess (sop.). Turned by her into a bee, he goes to find the Tsar; when the sisters try to dissuade the Tsar from visiting the island, Guidon stings them mercilessly. Back on the island, he frees the princess from her enchantment, and when the Tsar arrives she restores his wife to him.

Tsar's Bride, The. Opera in 3 acts by Rimsky-Korsakov; text from L.A. Mey's drama (1849), additional scene by I.F. Tyumenev. Prod. Moscow, Private opera society, 3 Nov. 1899, with Mutin, Zabela-Brubel, Shevelyov, Tarasov, Sekar-Rozhansky, Rostovtseva, Shkafer, Gladkaya, Strakhova, cond. Ippolitov-Ivanov; Seattle 6 Jan. 1922; London, Ly., 19 May 1931, with Vechov, Antonovich, Sadoven, Victorov, Yurenev, Kaydanov, cond. Steiman

Marfa (sop.), chosen by Tsar Ivan the Terrible as his bride, is loved both by Lykov (bass),

whom she loves, and the *oprichnik* Gryaznoy (bar.), who tries to win her with a love potion. Gryaznoy's mistress Lyubasha (mezzo) substitutes poison, and Marfa goes mad on learning, as she lies dying in the Kremlin, that the Tsar has had Lykov beheaded for the crime. Gryaznoy kills Lyubasha.

Tucker, Norman (*b* Wembley, 24 Apr. 1910). English theatre director. Studied London, R.C.M. Joint director S.W., with James Robertson and Michael Mudie, Jan. 1948–June 1953; with Robertson, June 1953–June 1954; sole director 1954–66. Translated *Simone Boccanegra*, *Kaťa Kabanová*, *The Cunning Little Vixen*, *The Makropoulos Case*, *Werther*, *Romeo and Juliet* (Sutermeister), *Luisa Miller* (with Tom Hammond), and the *Don Carlos* (including some drastic rearrangement) used by the company. (See also *Sadler's Wells*.) After several years he returned to opera, translating Einem's *Visit of the Old Lady* for Gly. (1973).

Tucker, Richard (orig. Reuben Ticker) (*b* New York, 28 Aug. 1913; *d* Kalamazoo, 8 Jan. 1975). American tenor. Studied N.Y., with Althouse, Martino, Borghetti, and Wilhousky. Début N.Y., Salmaggi Company, 1943 Alfredo. Joined Met. 1945, debut as Enzo (*Gioconda*) and leading tenor there until his death, singing more than 600 performances of some 30 roles in Italian and French repertory; also as Alfred (*Fledermaus*) and Lensky. London, C.G., 1958, Cavaradossi. Verona Arena 1947, Enzo in performance of *La gioconda* in which Callas made her Italian début. Chosen by Toscanini to sing Radamès in the N.B.C. performance 1949. Returned to Italy; Manrico, Florence 1969; Milan, Sc., 1969, as Rodolfo (*Luisa Miller*). Achieved his ambition of singing Eléazar in *La Juive*, New Orleans, 1973. (R)

Tudoran, Ionel (*b* Baragtii de Vede, 24 June 1913). Romanian tenor. Studied Iaşi; début there in 1936 as Roland in Ziehrer's *Landstreicher*. Cluj, 1937-48; leading tenor Bucharest Opera, 1948-63. Guest appearances Czechoslovakia, Germany, Russia. Retired 1963 and taught Bucharest Conservatory 1963–73. Roles included Faust, Don José, Cavaradossi, Otello. Had a very beautiful voice and was considered the finest Romanian tenor since Gorzavescu. (R)

Turandot. (1) Opera in 3 acts by Puccini, completed by Alfano; text by Adami and Simoni, after Gozzi's drama (1762), possibly after *The Arabian Nights*. Prod. Milan, Sc., 25 Apr. 1926, with Raisa, Zamboni, Fleta, cond. Toscanini; N.Y., Met., 16 Nov. 1926, with Jeritza, Attwood, Lauri-Volpi, cond. Serafin; London, C.G., 7 June 1927, with Scacciati, Schoene, Merli, cond. Bellezza.

The cruel Princess Turandot (sop.) poses

three riddles for her suitors to answer; if they fail they are beheaded. The unknown Prince Calaf (ten.) succeeds in answering them and challenges her to discover his name by morning, in which case he will forfeit his life. Turandot tortures the slave-girl Liù (sop.), Calaf's faithful companion, in an attempt to discover the name of the Prince; but Liù, rather than reveal it, kills herself. Turandot, realising what true love really is, accepts Calaf's hand.

(2) Opera in 2 acts by Busoni; text by composer, after Gozzi. Prod. Zurich, Stadttheater, 11 May 1917, with Enke, Smeikal, Richter, Pieroth, cond. Busoni; New York, Little Orch. Soc., 10 Oct. 1967, with Kuhse, cond. Scherman; London, Cockpit T., 8 Mar. 1978.

Other operas on the subject are by Blumenroeder (1810), Danzi (1817), Reissiger (1835), Vesque von Püttlingen (1838), Lövenskjow (1854), Jensen (*Die Erbin von Monfort,* 1864-5, adapted after his death to a *Turandot* libretto by his daughter), Bazzini (1867), Rehbaum (1888), Neumeister (1908).

Turcano (–Bercescu), **Lucia** (*b* Bucharest, 1913). Romanian soprano. Studied Bucharest with Elena Saghin and Demetru-Braziliu. Début Bucharest 1939, Marguerite. Bucharest Opera 1939-46 as Countess Almaviva, Agathe, Elsa, Aida, Tosca, etc.; also created Princess Ruxandra in Zirra's *Alexandra Lăpuşneanu.* Vienna Volksoper (as Lucia Bercescu) 1942-5. Milan, Sc., Abigaille in opening night of first full season at rebuilt theatre, and regularly until 1949 as Gioconda and Turandot; then appeared all over Italy in those roles and as Norma, Tosca, and Aida. N.Y., Salmaggi's C., 1949-50, City O. 1950, and Philadelphia. Returned to Romania 1963. Teaches in Bucharest.

Turco in Italia, Il (The Turk in Italy). Opera in 2 acts by Rossini; text by Romani. Prod. Milan, Sc., 14 Aug. 1814, with Maffei-Festa, Carpano, David, Galli, Pacini, Vasoli, Pozzi; London, H.M.'s, 19 May 1821, with Giuseppina and Giuseppe de Begnis; N.Y., Park T., 14 Mar. 1826, with Malibran, Barbieri, Garcia, Garcia jun., Crivelli, Rosich, Angrisani.

The opera is artificial to a degree, with the poet Prosdocimo (bar.) manipulating the intrigue between Donna Fiorilla (sop.), the dissatisfied wife of Don Geronio (bass), and Selim Damelec (bass) of Erzerum, the eponymous Turk.

Other operas on the subject are by Seydelmann (1788), Süssmayr (1794). Irish burlesque by S. Lover, *Il Paddy Wack in Italia* (1841).

Turgenev, Ivan (Sergeyevich) (*b* Oryol, 9 Nov. 1818; *d* Bougival, 3 Sep. 1883). Russian writer. His association with Pauline Viardot led to collaboration in her operettas *Trop de femmes* (1867), *Le Dernier sorcier* (1867), and *L'Ogre*

(1868). Operas based on his works are as follows:

The Parasite (1847): Dall'Olio (*Pasquino,* late 19th cent.).

A Sportsman's Sketches (1847–51): *The Singers:* Goldenweiser (1945).

Yermolay and the Miller's Wife: Goldenweiser (1945).

Asya (1857): Ippolitov-Ivanov (1900).

A Nest of Gentlefolk (1858): Rebikov (comp. 1816); Bagadurov (1919).

The Torrents of Spring (1871): Goldenweiser (1955).

The Song of Triumphant Love (1881): Harteveld (1895); Simon (1897).

Clara Milich (1882): Kastalsky (comp. 1907, prod. 1916).

The Dream (1876): K. H. David (1928).

Also *Vadim* by Kreitner (1952), *Il pane altrui* by Orefice (1907).

Turiddu. A young soldier (ten.), hero of Mascagni's *Cavalleria rusticana.*

Turin (*It* Torino). Town in Piedmont, Italy. The first opera performed there was *Zalizura,* by Sigismondo d'India, in 1611, in the Court T. of the Royal Ducal Palace. From 1638 performances were given at the T. delle Feste, and from 1740 at the new T. Regio, designed by Benedetto Alfieri, which opened on December 26 that year with Peo's *Arsace,* with Carestini in the title-role. Alfieri also designed the T. Carignano (cap. 1,000), Turin's second opera house, opened in 1753. Many operas were written for the Regio during the 18th and early 19th cents., including works by Gluck (*Poro*), Jommelli, G. Scarlatti, Galuppi, Traetta, Paisiello, Martin y Soler, Cherubini, Cimarosa, Gazzaniga, Zingarelli, Meyerbeer (*Semiramide riconosciuta*), Mercadante, and Nicolai (*Il templario*), sung by the greatest singers of the day.

The rise of the Scala, and various crises in the 1850s and 1860s, dimmed the Regio's splendour. Carlo Pedrotti took over in 1865, and during his 15 years reign the Regio became one of the leading operatic institutions in Italy, rivalled only by the Scala. Pedrotti conducted every production, and Verdi's operas in particular were strongly cast. Catalani's *Elda* had its première in 1880, and Massenet's *Roi de Lahore* had its first performance in Italy in 1878. After Pedrotti's departure there were seasons conducted by Faccio and Mascheroni. From 1895 to 1898, and again 1905-6, Toscanini was music director; he had already had great success in Turin at the Carignano in 1886. Catalani's *Loreley,* Puccini's *Manon Lescaut,* and *La Bohème* had their world premières at the Regio in 1890, 1893, and 1896, and Zandonai's *Francesca da Rimini* in 1914. The Regio was closed from 1901 to 1905 for modernization, and on 22 Dec. 1906 Strauss conducted the first Italian performance of his *Salome.*

There followed a series of fine Wagner performances, productions of lesser-known French works, and the first European perf. of Giordano's *Madame Sans-Gêne*. Toscanini's return to the Sc. in Milan, and the turning of the T. Costanzi in Rome into the T. Reale dell'Opera, both contributed to the artistic decline of the Regio in the 1920s and early 1930s, though there were some fine Wagner performances in this period, including the *Ring,* in Italian, conducted by Busch in 1936. On the night of 8–9 February 1936 the Regio was destroyed by fire. Performances continued at the T. Vittorio Emanuele, the T. Carignano, and the T. della Moda (later the T. Nuovo). Plans for the rebuilding of the Regio were announced in 1963 and eventually designs by Carlo Mollino and Marcello Zavelani Rossi were approved. The new Regio opened on 10 April 1973 with *I vespri siciliani,* produced by Callas and Di Stefano. Fulvio Vernizzi was appointed artistic director; he was succeeded in 1974 by Peter Maag.

The Rossini revival began in 1925 with *L'italiana in Algeri* with Conchita Supervia at the T. di Torino (the former T. Scribe) under the artistic direction of Guido Gatti and Vittorio Gui; the seasons 1925-7 included the first perfs. in Italy of *Ariadne auf Naxos, L'Heure espagnole,* and Malipiero's *Sette canzoni,* as well as the première of Gui's own *La fata malerba,* and Alfano's *Madonna Imperia.*

Italian Radio (formerly E.I.A.R., now R.I.A.), based on Turin, has given many outstanding performances of opera.
Bibl: V. Mazzoni and others: *Il Teatro Regio di Torino* (1970).

Turkey. The first operatic performances were given by a visiting Italian company 1797. Italian opera seasons took place at various theatres, especially the T. Naum, 1840-70. The composer Tigran Chukhadjian (1837-98), notable for his work as a pioneer of opera in *Armenia, also helped by his presence and example to initiate Turkish national opera; his works were given by Turkish operetta groups, especially that of Arshag Khachaturyan 'Benliyan' (1865-1923), which was active until 1910. A Turkish musical comedy, *Shaban,* by Vittorio Radeglia, was given at the Vienna Volksoper in 1918, and another by the Turkish composer Vedi Saba, *Kenan Çobanlari.* Operetta flourished in the 1930s at the Şehir Tiyatrosu T., especially the works of Kemal Reşit Rey, composer of *Köyde bir Facia* (1929) and *Yan Marek* (1932), and of Muglis Sabahattin (1890-1947), composer of *Asaletmeap* (The Noble), *Aşk Ölmez* (Love is Immortal) and *Aşk Mektebi* (The School for Love). The true founder of Turkish opera is Adnan Saygun, from whom Kemal Ataturk commissioned for the Shah of Persia's visit in 1934 the opera *Özsoy,* on a Turko-Persian legend. He also wrote *Taş Bebek* and *Kerem*

(1952). There is also an opera *Van Gogh* by Nevit Kodalli. See *Ankara, Istanbul.*

Turkmenistan. An opera studio was started in 1937, and the Makhtumkuly Turkmen Opera and Ballet T. opened in Ashkhabad in 1941, inaugurated with the first Turkmen opera, *Zokhre i Takhir,* by Andryan Shaposhnikov (*b* 1887); his subsequent operas include the very popular *Shasenem i Garib* (1944) and *Ayna* (1957). Another opera on a Turkmen subject was *Farkhad i Shirin* (1936) by Victor Uspensky (1879-1949). The Turkmen composer Velimuhammed Mukhatov (*b* 1916), who has collaborated with Shaposhnikov, has written *Ganly Saka* (The Bloody Watershed, 1964). The first opera written unaided by a Turkmen composer was *Song* (1964) by Aman Agajikov (*b* 1937). In 1948 Ashkhabad was destroyed by an earthquake. Reconstruction began quickly, and a new Opera and Ballet T. was opened in 1950.

Turner, (Dame) **Eva** (*b* Oldham, 10 Mar. 1892). English soprano. Studied London, R.A.M. Joined chorus Carl Rosa 1916; début Page, *Tannhäuser,* soon after. Sang with company until 1924, studying with Richard Broad and developing into a fine dramatic soprano. Auditioned in London by Panizza, 1924, who sent her to Milan to sing for Toscanini. Scala début 1924, Freia. Established herself as leading dramatic soprano and considered by Alfano as the ideal Turandot. London, C.G., 1928-30, 1933, 1935-9, 1947-8. Also Chicago, Buenos Aires, Lisbon, etc. Taught singing, Univ. of Oklahoma, 1950-9; London, R.A.M., since 1959. Her voice, of enormous proportions in its prime, ranged from g to d''' and was admirably suited to the dramatic soprano roles in Verdi and Wagner. (R)

Turn of the Screw, The. Opera in prologue and 2 acts by Britten; text by Myfanwy Piper, after Henry James's story (1898). Prod. Venice, F., 14 Sept. 1954 by English Opera Group, with Vyvyan, Cross, Mandikian, Pears, Hemmings, Dyer, cond. Britten; London, S.W., 6 Oct., 1954 by same cast; N.Y., College of Music (Kaufmann Concert Hall), 19 Mar. 1958.

The Governess (sop.), sent to look after two children in a country house run only by an old housekeeper Mrs. Grose (sop.), comes to realize that they are visited by the evil ghosts of two former servants Miss Jessel (sop.) and Peter Quint (ten.); more, that the children cherish the relationship. In fighting this she has first to convince the housekeeper, and having persuaded her to take the girl away, battles with the ghost who haunts the boy and wins – only to find him dead in her arms. The 'screw' of the title is represented by a theme that 'turns' through 15 variations, interludes between the 8 scenes of each act.

Tutte le feste. The opening words of Gilda's

(sop.) account to her father of her betrayal by the Duke in Act 2 of Verdi's *Rigoletto*.

Two Widows, The (Cz., Dvě vdovy). Opera in 2 acts by Smetana; text by E. Zungel, after Pierre Mallefille's comedy *Les Deux veuves* (1860). Prod. Prague, 27 Mar. 1874, with Sittová, Saková, Vávra, Čech, Lauannová, Šára, cond. Smetana. New version, with recitatives replacing dialogue, prod. Prague, 15 Mar.

THE TWO WIDOWS

1878; New York, Sokol Hall, 23 Oct. 1949; London, G.S.M., 17 June 1963, cond. Thorne.

The two widows Karolina (sop.) and Anežka (sop.) live on the former's estate. Their game-keeper Mumlal (bass) brings in a poacher, Ladislav (ten.), who proves to be the neighbouring landowner. Anežka is soon in love with him, but will not admit it; so Karolina forces her hand by pretending herself to appropriate him.

U

Uberti, (orig. Hubert) **Antonio** (b Verona, 1697; d Berlin 20 Jan. 1783). Italian male soprano of German parentage; known as Il Porporino, because he was Porpora's favourite pupil. From 1741, in the service of Frederick the Great, for whom he wrote arias and songs. 'My voice belongs solely to God and the King of Prussia.' Taught Gertrud Mara.

Udine. Town in Italy, capital of Friuli. The first public theatre was built in 1681 and demolished in 1756 because of its close proximity to the Cathedral. In 1770 the T. Nobile was opened, renamed the T. Sociale in 1852, and later the T. Puccini. After the second World War it became a cinema, and was closed in 1963. Opera is now given in the new T. Comunale.

Udite, udite, o rustici. Dulcamara's (bass) aria in Act 1 of Donizetti's L'elisir d'amore, in which he advertises his quack's wares.

Ugalde (orig. Beaucé), **Delphine** (b Paris, 3 Dec. 1829; d Paris, 19 July 1910). French soprano. Studied with her mother, with Moreau-Sainti, and probably with Cinti-Damoreau. Début Paris, O.C., 1848, Angela in Auber's Domino noir, until 1858 sang at O.C., T.L., and B.P. London, H.M.'s. 1851. Created roles in works by Auber, Thomas, and Massé. Married the impresario Barcollier, and for a period managed B.P. with him; sang in an operetta of her own composition, Halte au moulin, in 1867; retired in 1871 and devoted herself to teaching. Her pupils included her daughter, Marguerite Ugalde (1862-1940), and Marie *Sass.

Uhde, Hermann (b Bremen, 20 July 1914; d Copenhagen, 10 Oct. 1965). German bassbaritone. Studied Bremen with Philip Kraus. Début Bremen, 1936, Titurel. Bremen 1936-8; Freiburg 1938-40; Munich 1940-3; Hague, German Opera, 1942-4, where he sang his first baritone roles. Conscripted into German army and captured by Americans. Resumed career 1947, Hanover; Hamburg, 1947-50; Vienna, S.O. 1950-51; Munich, 1951-60; Bayreuth, 1951-7 and 1960 as Gunther, Klingsor, Telramund, Holländer, and Rheingold Wotan; Salzburg, 1949, 1950, and 1960, where he created Creon in Orff's Antigonae and Elis in Wagner-Régeny's Das Bergwerk zu Falun; also Tarquinius in first perf. there of Rape of Lucretia (1950). London, C.G., 1953 with Munich C. as Mandryka, and 1954-60; sang Telramund and Hoffmann villains in impeccable English, as well as Gunther in German. N.Y., Met., 1955-60; sang Wozzeck (in English), Grand Inquisitor, and other roles. Highly intelligent

artist and fine musician. Collapsed and died on stage during a performance of Bentzon's Faust III at Royal T. Copenhagen. (R)

Ukraine. From early days Ukrainian composers played a crucial part in Russia's operatic history. In 1739 a singing school opened in Glukhovo, the birthplace of Mazim Berezovsky (1745-77), who sang in opera in St. Petersburg when only 14 and wrote the first Russian opera to be produced in Italy (Demofoonte, 1773), and of Dmitry *Bortnyansky (1751-1825), who also produced operas in Italy, later returning to Russia. A few small, privately-run opera troupes were formed, and musical numbers were often inserted in popular dramas (e.g. Natalka Poltavka, 1819). But the first attempt at opera was Zaporozhets a Dunayem (The Cossack across the Danube, 1863) by Semyon Gulak-Artemovsky (1813-73), a pupil of Glinka and a fine baritone,. The first major Ukrainian composer was Mykola Lysenko (1842-1912). His operas, mostly based on Gogol, include Risdivyana Nich (Christmas Eve, 1875), a new setting of Natalka Poltavka (1889) and the 'heroic opera' Taras Bulba (comp. 1890, prod. 1924). Other Ukrainian operas of the period include Mayskaya Noch (May Night, 1876) and Osada Dubno (The Siege of Dubno, comp. c.1884) by Pyotr Sokalsky (1832-87); Kupalo (comp. c.1892, prod. 1929) by Natal Vakhnyanin (1841-1908); Katerina (1899) by Nikolay Arkas (1853-1904); and Branka Roxolana (1912) by Denis Sichinsky (1865-1912). The first Operatic Society in Greater Russia was organised at Kiev in 1889 by the singer Ippolit *Pryanishnikov: this gave a Moscow season in 1892-9.

In Kiev, opera was given in the Gorodski (City) T. (opened 1851); this was rebuilt in 1901, as the Liebknecht Opera T., and is now the Shevchenko Opera and Ballet T. (opera has been sung in Ukrainian since 1924). In Kharkov an opera house was opened in 1874, where the first Ukrainian operas were given. This became the Lysenko National State Opera and Ballet T. in 1924; since 1945 it has been the Lysenko Opera and Ballet T. The wide repertory includes foreign as well as Russian and Ukrainian works. There is also a flourishing operetta theatre. In Dnyepopetrovsk (until 1926, Ekaterinburg), an opera house was opened in 1928; during the war this was destroyed, and the company evacuated to Krasnyoyarsk. Besides this company, working in the reconstructed theatre, there are several important semi-professional groups. There is an opera house in Odessa (1809), and some touring companies. The Franko T. in Lvov was opened in 1940. Post-Revolutionary operas have included Schchors (1938) by Boris Lyatoshinsky (b 1894); and Perekop (1939) by Mikhail Tyts (b 1898), Vsevolod Rybalchenko (b

(1904), and Yuly Meytus (*b* 1903); the last-named also composed the widely-performed *Molodaya Gvardia* (1947). Since the war there have been five opera houses in the Ukraine. More recent successful operas have included *Bogdan Khmelnitsky* (1951) by Konstantin Dankevich (*b* 1905); *Gibel Eskadry* (1967) by Vitaly Gubarenko (*b* 1934); *Lesnaya Pesnaya* (Forest Song, 1958) by Vitaly Kireyko (*b* 1926); *Milana* (1957) by Georgy Mayboroda (*b* 1913); and Meytus's *Bratya Ulyanovy* (The Ulyanov Brothers, 1967), claimed as the first 'philosophical-psychological' drama, with Lenin as its hero.

Ulfung, Ragnar (*b* Oslo, 28 Feb 1927). Norwegian tenor. Studied Oslo, and Milan with Minghetti. Début Oslo 1950 (in concert); stage début in 1952, The Magician (*The Consul*). Bergen 1954-5; Gothenberg 1955-8; Stockholm, Royal Opera, since 1958. London, C.G., 1960 (with Stockholm Opera Company), 1963, 1970, 1972, 1974-6. Created title role in *Taverner,* also heard as Don Carlos, Herod, and Mime. San Francisco, 1967 as Chuck in Schuler's *Visitation*; and 1969-71; Santa Fe. Sang title-role in Bergman's famous production of *Rake's Progress* in Stockholm. (R)

Ulisse. Opera in a prologue and 2 acts by Dallapiccola; text by composer. Prod. Berlin, D., 29 Sept. 1968 as *Odysseus*, with Gayer, Hillebrecht, Madeira, Driscoll, Melchert, Saedén, cond. Maazel; London, B.B.C. studio perf., 20 Sept. 1969 (in English), with Gayer, Bernard, Madeira, Driscoll, English, Reich, cond. Maazel. The opera follows Homer's account of Odysseus's return after the Trojan wars and tells, in a series of flashbacks, of his adventures.

Ulm. Town in Baden-Württemberg, Germany. In the early 17th-cent. travelling companies visited the city; performances were given by the Ulm musician J.B. Braun 1656-67. Singspiel became very popular, and by the end of the century a local form had developed, known as Docken-Komödie. The Komodienhaus opened in 1781, but was bombed in 1944; the City T. (cap. 815) opened in October 1969. Heger was Kapellmeister 1908-9 and Karajan music director 1928-34.

Ulrica. The fortune-teller (mezzo) in Verdi's *Un ballo in maschera*; in the opera's Swedish setting, she is Mme Arvidson.

Umlauff (Umlauf), Ignaz (*b* Vienna, 1746, *d* Vienna, 8 June 1796). Austrian violinist, composer, and conductor. Played at the Court T. 1772, and became Kapellmeister of the German Singspiel 1778, deputy Kapellmeister under Salieri at the Court T. 1789. When the Emperor Joseph organized the national Singspiel, Umlauff opened it with *Die Bergknappen*

(1778). Other successes were *Die Apotheke* (1778), *Die pucefarbenen Schuhe* (1779), *Das Irrlicht* (1782), and others. Though basically simple in structure and popular in appeal, his stage works show a distinct originality in both their comic effects and in the Romantic tinges in some of the harmony.

Una donna di quindici anni. Despina's (sop.) aria in Act 2, scene 1, of Mozart's *Così fan tutte*, describing the wiles of love to her mistresses.

Una furtiva lagrima. Nemorino's (ten.) aria in Act 2 of Donizetti's *L'elisir d'amore*, in which he sees by a tear in Adina's eye that she loves him.

Un'aura amorosa. Ferrando's (ten.) aria in Act 1, scene 3 of Mozart's *Così fan tutte*, in which he sentimentally describes Dorabella's love.

Una voce poco fa. Rosina's (mezzo, often transposed to sop.) aria in Act 1, scene 2, of Rossini's *Il barbiere di Siviglia*, recalling the serenading voice of Almaviva that has awakened her love.

Un bel dì vedremo. Butterfly's (sop.) aria in Act 2 of Puccini's *Madama Butterfly*, in which she sings of Pinkerton's hoped-for return.

Un dì all'azzurro spazio. Andrea Chénier's (ten.) aria in Act 1 of Giordano's opera, in which the poet denounces the selfishness of those in authority. Sometimes known as the 'Improvviso'.

Un dì felice. The opening words of the love duet between Violetta (sop.) and Alfredo (ten.) in Act 1 of Verdi's *La traviata*.

Undine. The heroine of a popular Central European folk legend. Conceived by Paracelsus as one of the elemental spirits, she is the spirit of the waters: created without a soul, she can only gain it by marrying a mortal and bearing him a child, though she must thereby take on all the penalties of humanity. The legend was given great popularity among the Romantics by Friedrich de la Motte Fouqué's tale (1811). She is the German equivalent of the Slav *Rusalka. (1) Opera in 4 acts by Lortzing; text by composer, after De la Motte Fouqué's tale. Prod. Magdeburg 21 Apr. 1845; N.Y. 9 Oct. 1856, with Johanssen, Pidcaneser, Weinlich.

Hugo (ten.), accompanied by his squire Veit (ten.), falls in love with Undine (sop.) and returns to Court with her, though Veit has told Kühleborn (bar.), her father and a powerful water spirit, that he fears Hugo will desert her for Berthalda (sop.). Undine discloses her fairy nature to Hugo, and Berthalda is revealed as being really the child of Undine's foster-father Tobias (bass). Though protected by Undine, Berthalda seduces Hugo, and Undine returns to her kingdom; but he cannot forget her, and when Veit opens a sealed well she returns from it to claim him, as husband in her own realm. (2) Opera in 3 acts by E.T.A. Hoffmann; text by composer, after De la Motte Fouqué's tale. Prod. Berlin, Royal O.H., 3 Aug. 1816.

Other operas on the legend are by Lvov (1848), Semet (1863), and Rogowski (comp. 1920). See also *Donauweibchen*.

Unger, Georg (*b* Leipzig, 6 Mar. 1837; *d* Leipzig, 2 Feb. 1887). German tenor. Studied theology, then singing with Julius Hey. Début Leipzig 1867. Heard at Mannheim by Richter, who recommended him to Wagner – created Siegfried, Bayreuth 1876. London, R.A.H., in Wagner series 1877. Remained at Leipzig until 1887. The first Wagner Heldentenor.

Unger-Sabatier, Caroline (orig. Karolina: also known as Ungher) (*b* Székesfehérvár, 28 Oct. 1803; *d* Florence, 23 Mar. 1877). Hungarian contralto. Studied Vienna with Aloysia Weber, Lange, and Vogel, and Milan with D. Ronconi. Début Vienna 1821, Tancredi. Sang in first perfs. of Beethoven's Missa Solemnis and 'Choral' Symphony. Naples, 1825, created Marietta in Donizetti's *Il borgomastro di Saardam*; Milan, Sc., 1828, created Isoletta in Bellini's *La straniera*. Created title-roles in Donizetti's *Parisina* (Florence 1833), Antonia in his *Belisario* (Venice 1836), and title-role in *Maria Rudenz* (Venice 1838), as well as Bianca in Mercadante's *Due illustri rivali* (Venice 1838). Sang with great success in Paris, Vienna, Dresden, etc., but only appeared in concert in England, at Crystal Palace (1869). In 1841 she married the writer François Sabatier (1818-91) and retired from the stage, but continued to sing in concerts as Unger-Sabatier. Rossini said that she possessed 'the ardour of the South, the energy of the North, brazen lungs, a silver voice, and golden talent'; Fétis praised her dramatic ability and intelligence. She composed many songs.
Bibl: F. Margit: *Unger-Sabatier* (1941).

United States of America. For many years, America saw little but ballad opera (*The Beggar's Opera* was given in New York in 1750) and Italian opera given by visiting companies. The first native American opera was *The Disappointment or The Force of Credulity*, referred to in 1767 as 'a new American comic opera' (not performed, however). A musical comedy *The Temple of Minerva* was given in 1781 in the presence of Washington; the music, now lost, was by Francis Hopkinson, one of the signatories of the Declaration of Independence. The first American opera whose music survives was *The Archers* (1796), on the William Tell legend, by Benjamin Carr (1768-1831), a composer of English birth. Later in the same year, and also in New York, *Edwin and Angelina* by Victor Pelissier was given; he was a Frenchman who had settled in America in 1792 and went on to write other operas. John Bray wrote *The Indian Princess* (1808). A step

forward from these works came with *Enterprise* (1822), by Arthur Clifton (probably a pseudonym for the Italian-born Philip Anthony Corri). The first opera written by a native American seems to have been *The Saw Mill, or A Yankee Trick* (1824), by Micah Hawkins (1777-1825): this is virtually a ballad opera. The arrangements of C.E. *Horn introduced Americans to operatic music in mutilated forms. The first true opera season was in *New Orleans.

Many distinguished Italian artists were by now visiting America, some bringing their own companies, e.g. Garcia and Da Ponte; and by the middle of the 19th cent., opera was virtually synonymous with Italian opera. In 1861, Lincoln attended a performance of *Un ballo in maschera,* in the Boston version. The popularity of Italian opera, however, set up a reaction among American musicians, though William Henry Fry was unable to escape the influence in *Leonora* (1845). Others who attempted a more independent American national opera included George Frederick Bristow (1825-98) with *Rip Van Winkle* (1855), Dudley Buck (1839-1909) with *Deseret, or A Saint's Affliction* (1880), John Knowles Paine (1839-1906) with *Azara* (1901), and Silas Gamaliel Pratt (1846-1916) with *Zenobia* (1883). Despite the failure of this work, Pratt went on to campaign for native American opera, and in 1884 organized a Grand O. Festival; but he met with little success, partly through his extravagant claims for his own work.

Towards the end of the 19th cent. a German influence was added, as major German operatic artists crossed the Atlantic. In 1911 the Met. organized a prize, won by Horatio Parker with *Mona* (1912). Many American operas now joined the German and Italian repertory at the Met. and in other major American theatres. However, the fashion for European music and the difficulty of forming a true native tradition long resulted in foreign works being regarded as intrinsically superior, and hence in American composers either seeking European training or settling in Europe in the hope of achieving productions, e.g. Louis Adolf Coerne (1870-1922) with *Zenobia,* Bremen 1905.

A national tradition of operetta grew up early and developed into the classic American form, musical comedy. A number of musicians of European origin, either first or second generation Americans in the great waves of immigration, or refugees from persecution, contributed to this genre; operetta composers (e.g. Friml and Romberg) gave an example that was the basis for the original American achievements of Rodgers, Loewe, Kern, and above all Gershwin, whose *Porgy and Bess* (1935) remains a unique example of a masterpiece of opera based on popular American musical idioms. Other composers who returned from a European training (often Parisian) included Marc

Blitzstein (*b* 1905) with *The Cradle Will Rock* (1937), Virgil *Thomson (*b* 1896) with *Four Saints in Three Acts* (1934), and Aaron *Copland. Others who achieved success before and soon after the Second World War include Gian Carlo *Menotti, Douglas *Moore, Lukas *Foss, Samuel *Barber, Leonard *Bernstein, and Carlisle *Floyd. Their contemporaries and juniors have contributed to one of the richest operatic cultures in the world.

See also *Baltimore, Berkshire Festival, Bloomington, Boston, Caramoor, Central City, Chautauqua, Chicago, Cincinnati, Dallas, Detroit, Fort Worth, Hartford, Houston, Jackson, Kansas City, Los Angeles, Miami, San Antonio, San Carlo Touring Company, San Diego, San Francisco, Santa Fe, Seattle, Washington.*

Unterbrochene Opferfest, Das (The Interrupted Sacrifice). Opera in 2 acts by Winter; text by F.X. Huber. Prod. Vienna, Kä., 14 June 1796; London, Hm., 28 May 1834. Winter's most successful opera, very popular on German stages in the early 19th cent. and appearing regularly until the end of the century; also translated into several other languages and given abroad, (English version, music arr. Hawes, Ly., 7 Aug. 1826).

Uppman, Theodor (*b* San José, 12 Jan. 1920). American baritone. Studied Curtis Institute with Steuart Wilson, University of California with Ebert. Début Stanford Univ. 1946, Papageno. London, C.G., 1951-2, created title role in Britten's *Billy Budd.* N.Y., Met., since 1953: sang Pelléas under Monteux, Papageno under Walter. (R)

Urban, Joseph (*b* Vienna, 26 May 1872; *d* New York, 10 July 1933). Austrian architect, stage designer, and producer. After studying in Vienna and successfully executing many commissions, including remodelling an Esterházy palace and building the Tsar's bridge across the Neva in St Petersburg, was engaged as designer and producer of the Boston Opera 1912-14. Designed the sets for many of the Met.'s most successful productions in the interwar years, as well as for Vienna and C.G. In his production of *Don Giovanni* at Boston, with Weingartner in 1913, he set Don Giovanni's death in the cemetery.

Urbani, Valentino (known in England as Valentini or Valentino) (*b* 1660; *d* ?). Italian male contralto. Entered service of the Duke of Mantua during the 1680s and appeared at Parma and Piacenza in operas by Sabadini. Continued to sing in Italy until 1703, when he went to London. Here he was the first castrato to establish himself over a long period; appeared in Scarlatti's *Pirro e Demetrio,* Bononcini's *Almahide,* and Handel's *Rinaldo, Pastor fido,* and *Teseo.* Returned to Italy in 1715 and con-

tinued to sing until 1719, but as a *tenore leggiero.*

Urlus, Jacques (*b* Hergenrath, nr. Aix-la-Chapelle, 9 Jan. 1867; *d* Noordwijk, 6 July 1935). Dutch tenor. Studied Amsterdam with Cornélie van Zanten. Début Amsterdam 1894, Beppe. Leipzig 1900-17; London, C.G., 1910, 1914, 1924; Bayreuth 1911-12; Boston 1912; N.Y. Met., 1913-17. U.S. tour with German O.C. 1922-3. Berlin, Volksoper, 1923-4. Last appearance, Tristan, Amsterdam, 1932. One of the leading Heldentenors of his day, much admired as Tristan and Parsifal; repertory also included Tamino, Raoul, Faust, Don José, Samson, and Otello. (R)
Bibl: J. Urlus: *Mijn loopbaan* (1930).

Ursuleac, Viorica (*b* Czernowitz (Cernăuţi), 26 Mar. 1894). Romanian soprano. Studied Vienna, and Berlin with Lilli Lehmann. Début Zagreb 1922, Charlotte; Cernăuţi 1923-4; Vienna, V.O., 1924-7; Frankfurt 1927-30; Vienna, S.O., 1930-5; Berlin, S.O., 1935-37; Munich, 1937-44. London, C.G., 1934. Salzburg Festivals 1930-4 and 1942. Created Arabella, Maria in Strauss's *Friedenstag,* and the Countess in his *Capriccio;* also sang title-role in *Liebe der Danae* at the public dress rehearsal of this work at Salzburg, 1944. Considered by Strauss as his ideal soprano – he called her 'die Treueste aller Treuen'. Created leading roles in works by Křenek, Weill, and D'Albert; also successful as Senta, Sieglinde, and (in Germany and Austria) in Verdi. Wife of Clemens *Krauss. Her recordings, commercial and private, do not do justice to her art. (R)

Uruguay. Spanish light operas and tonadillas were given in Montevideo from the end of the 18th cent. A music school was opened in 1831, soon followed by the Sociedad Filarmonica; the first complete opera given in the capital was Rossini's *L'inganno felice,* 1830, by the Tanni family. The T. Solís was opened in 1856, with a musical repertory based on the Spanish light repertory. Opera was mostly given by visiting Italians. The first Uruguayan opera was *La parisina* (1878) by the amateur T. Giribaldi (*b* 1858). National opera was more securely founded by Eduardo Fabini (1883-1950), who in 1903 founded the conservatory and other organizations, before retiring to devote himself to composition. New operas included *La cruz del sur* (1920) by Alfonso Broqua (1867-1946), *Ardid de Amor* (1917) and *La guitarra* (1924) by Carlos Pedrell (1878-1941) and *Paraná Guazú* by Vincent Ascone (*b* 1897). Seasons are given in Montevideo.

U.S.S.R. (Union of Soviet Socialist Republics). See *Armenia, Azerbaijan, Bashkiria, Belorussia, Buryat Mongolia, Estonia, Georgia, Kazakhstan, Kirghizistan, Latvia, Lithuania, Moldavia, Russia, Tadjikistan, Tatar Republic,*

Turkmenistan, Ukraine, Uzbekistan, Yakutsk.

Ústí nad Labem (Ger. Aussig). Town in Czechoslovakia. Opera is given 3–4 times a week in the State T. (cap. 900), modernized in 1947, by a company of about 20 soloists. The company also tours neighbouring industrial towns, including Karlovy Vary, Mariánzké Lázně, and in the Most district.

Uthal. Opera in 1 act by Méhul; text by J.M.B. Bins de Saint-Victor, *'imité d'Ossian'*. Prod. Paris, O.C., 17 May 1806. Famous for the original effect whereby, in order to create a dark and mysterious 'Ossianic' effect, Méhul omitted violins from the orchestra.

Uzbekistan. A Russian opera house was opened in Tashkent in 1918. The first Uzbek musical theatre opened in 1929, the Naroy

Opera and Ballet T. in 1948. The first Uzbek opera was *Buran* (The Snowstorm, 1939) by Mukhtar Ashrafy (*b* 1912) and Sergey Vasilenko (1872-1956), who collaborated again in *Veliky Kanal* (The Great Canal, 1940). Other works of these years include *Leyla i Mejnun* (1940) by Reinhold Glière (1875-1956) and Talib Sadykov (*b* 1907); *Ulugbek* (1942), on a 15th-cent. subject, by Alexey Kozlovsky (*b* 1905); and *Farkhad i Shirin* (1940) by Victor Uspensky (1879-1949) and Georgy Mushal (*b* 1909). Later Uzbek operas include the comedies *Svetly Put* (The Bright Path, 1951), *Prodelky Maisary* (Maisary's Tricks, 1959) and *Pisma Zukhry* (Zukhry's Letters, 1964) by Solomon Yudakov (*b* 1916). Minasay Leviey (*b* 1912), Dany Zakirov (*b* 1914), and Boris Gyenko (*b* 1917) have written a number of musical comedies for the Tashkent Operetta T.

V

Vaccai, Nicola (*b* Tolentino, 15 Mar. 1790; *d* Pesaro, 6 Aug. 1848). Italian composer and singer. Studied with Jannaconi and Paisiello. Produced his first opera, *I solitari di Scozia,* in 1815; then, after two failures in Venice, became a singing teacher. After the success of *Giulietta e Romeo* (1825) in Milan, he went to Paris as a teacher, and on to London as a composer. Back in Italy from 1836, he wrote further operas and a cantata on the death of Malibran. The penultimate scene of *Giulietta* was often substituted for the last scene of Bellini's *I Capuleti e i Montecchi.* He also wrote a *Metodo pratico di canto italiano per camera* (*c*1833), which is still respected. A follower of Rossini, who praised him, Vaccai lacked the distinctive melodic talent of Donizetti and Bellini, but in his own day many of his operas were appreciated for the sympathetic understanding of the voice and their neat melodic manner.
Bibl: G. Vaccai: *Vita di Nicola Vaccai scritta dal figlio . . .* (1882).

Vakula the Smith. Opera in 4 acts by Tchaikovsky; text by Yakov Polonsky, after Gogol's story *Christmas Eve* (1832). Prod. St Petersburg, M., 6 Dec. 1876, with Komissarzhevsky, Matchinsky, Petrov, Melnikov, Vasilyev, Bichurina, Raab, Ende, Stravinsky, Dyuzhikov, cond. Nápravník. Revised in 1885 as *Cherevichki* (The Little Boots – also known in Western Europe as *Oxana's Caprices*), prod. Moscow, B., 31 Jan. 1887, with Usatov, Streletsky, Dodonov, Matchinsky, Khokhlov, Vasilyevsky, Klimentova, Svyatlovskaya, cond. Tchaikovsky; N.Y., Met., 26 May 1922, with Mashir, Valentinova, Svetlov, Gorlenko, Koslov, Busanovsky.

The witch Solokha (mezzo) is approached by the amorous Devil (bar.); as he flies off, he raises a storm and steals the moon so as to revenge himself on her son Vakula (ten.), who has made an ugly painting of him; this hinders Vakula, who is trying to make his way to court Oxana (sop.). When her father Chub (bass) comes home with his friend Panas (ten.), both drunk, Vakula throws them out but is himself thrown out by Oxana, though privately she admits she loves him. In Solokha's hut, the Devil hides in a sack when the mayor (bass), then the schoolmaster (ten.), and then Chub arrive; each in turn hides in a sack. Vakula staggers off with the sacks. Oxana demands a pair of *cherevichki* (high-heeled leather boots) belonging to the Tsaritsa, and Vakula flies off on the Devil's back to St Petersburg, where he is granted the *cherevichki*; he returns to claim Oxana.

Another opera on the subject is by Afansayev, written for the competition won by Tchaikovsky in 1875 (unprod.).

Valdengo, Giuseppe (*b* Turin, 24 May 1914). Italian baritone. Studied Turin with Michele Accoriuti. Début Alessandria, 1936, Sharpless. Milan, Sc. 1939. During the war oboist in an army band; resumed career in 1945. N.Y., 1946-8; C.C., Met. 1946-54. Gly. 1955. Chosen by Toscanini to sing Iago and Amonasro for N.B.C., 1947 and 1949, coached by him for Falstaff 1950. Played the part of Antonio *Scotti in the film *The Great Caruso.* (R)
Bibl: G. Valdengo: *Ho cantato con Toscanini* (1962).

Valentine. (1) Marguerite's brother (bar.) in Gounod's *Faust.* (2) St Bris's daughter (sop.) in Meyerbeer's *Les Huguenots.*

Valero, Fernando (*b* Seville, 6 Dec. 1854 or 1857; *d* St Petersburg, Feb. 1914). Spanish tenor. Studied with Salazar and Tamberlik. Début Madrid 1878, Lorenzo in *Fra Diavolo.* Milan, Sc., 1883-95, especially successful in the French repertory; first Nadir in Italy. London C.G., 1890; 1901. N.Y., Met., 1891. Nicknamed 'il piccolo *Gayarre'. Continued career until 1902, then went to St Petersburg, where he taught singing. (R)

Valleria (orig. Schoening), **Alwina** (*b* Baltimore, 12 Oct. 1848; *d* Nice, 17 Feb. 1925). American soprano. Studied London with Arditi. Début St Petersburg 1871, Linda di Chamounix. London, D.L., 1873, Martha; 1877-8; and C.G. 1879-82. The first London Micaëla and the first to sing Elisabeth (*Tannhäuser*) in English in London. Created title roles in Mackenzie's *Colomba* (1833), and Goring Thomas's *Nadeshda* (1885). N.Y., Ac. of M., 1879.

Valletti, Cesare (*b* Rome, 18 Dec. 1922). Italian tenor. Studied Rome, and with Schipa. Début Bari 1947, Alfredo. London, C.G., 1950, with Scala Company as Fenton; 1958 as Alfredo; Milan, Sc., 1950-5; N.Y., Met., 1953-62. Admired in Rossini, Wolf-Ferrari, Donizetti, and Mozart roles. Retired 1968. (R)

Vallin, Ninon (Eugénie) (*b* Montalieu-Vercien, 8 Sept. 1886; *d* Lyons, 22 Nov. 1961). French soprano. Studied Lyons with Mauvarnay, and Paris with Mme Héglon. Began career as concert singer in Debussy's *La Demoiselle élue* and *Le Martyre de Saint Sébastien.* Heard by Carré, who engaged her for the O.C. 1912: début as Micaëla. Sang under name of Vallin-Pardo (1913-19). Created several roles in operas by D'Erlanger and Leroux, and sang the title role in Respighi's *Maria Egiziaca* in its Paris première. Sang with success in Milan, Sc., San Francisco, and Buenos Aires, C. The leading Louise, Manon, and Charlotte of her day; sang all three *Hoffmann* heroines. Sang Eurydice in Monteverdi's *Orfeo* at Orange in 1937. In 1956-9 Professor of singing at Montevideo Conservatory. (R)

Valzacchi. An Italian intriguer (ten.), crony of Annina, in Strauss's *Der Rosenkavalier.*

Vampyr, Der. (1) Opera in 2 acts by Marschner; text by W. A. Wohlbrück, after the story *The Vampyre* (1819) attrib. Byron (actually by John Polidori), by way of a French *mélodrame* by Nodier, Carmouche, and De Jouffroy (1820), trans. L. Ritter (1822). Prod. Leipzig, Stadttheater, 29 Mar. 1828, with Röckert, Devrient, Streit, Höfler, Genast, Gay, Von Zieten, Vogt, Reinecke, Fischer, cond. Marschner; London, Ly., 25 Aug. 1829.

Lord Ruthven (ten.) has become a vampire, and must postpone the claiming of his soul by Satan with the sacrifice of three young girls. He destroys Janthe (sop.), and is killed, but revives supernaturally in the moonlight through the help of Aubry (bar.), to whom he entrusts his secret. He further seduces and kills Emmy (sop.), who is fascinated by vampires, and nearly succeeds in claiming Aubry's betrothed Malvina (sop.) as his third victim, but is denounced by Aubry just as the clock strikes.

(2) Opera by Lindpaintner; text by C. M. Heigel on same source as Marschner's opera. prod. Stuttgart 21 Sept. 1828.

Other vampire operas are by Palma (*I vampiri,* 1812) and M. Mengal (*Le Vampire,* 1826).

Van. For names with this prefix, see the following word (except for next entry).

Van Allan, Richard (orig. Alan Philip Jones) (*b* Nottingham, 28 May 1935). English bass. Studied Birmingham School of Music and with David Franklin and Jani Strasser. Gly. Chorus 1964; solo début Gly. 1966, Priest and Armed Man (*Zauberflöte*), and subsequently created Colonel Jowler in Maw's *Rising of the Moon* (1970). E.N.O. since 1969: C.G. since 1971. Guest appearances Paris, Wexford, Boston, San Diego, etc. Repertory includes Figaro, Don Giovanni, Leporello, Don Alfonso, Zaccaria, Padre Guardiano, Ochs. Versatile and gifted singing-actor. (R)

Vancouver. Town in Canada. A gala production of *Lohengrin* was given on 9 February 1891, only five years after the city was established. The performance starred Emma Juch, and inaugurated the opera house which the Canadian Pacific Railway had built at its western terminus. This continued to be the scene of theatrical entertainment, although only rarely of opera, until it was sold in 1912 to a vaudeville chain.

Opera achieved no degree of permanence in Vancouver until 1958, when the Vancouver International Festival, under the direction of Nicholas Goldschmidt, began to present an opera each summer until 1968. The list of standard works was varied with some more unusual ones (*La fanciulla del West, Macbeth*). The Festival presented the North American première of Britten's *A Midsummer Night's Dream* (1961), and the North American débuts of Gunther Rennert, and of Joan Sutherland as Donna Anna in *Don Giovanni* (1958).

In 1959 the Vancouver O. Association was formed, with Irving Guttman as artistic director. It gave its first performances in 1960 in the new Queen Elizabeth Theatre and has continued to mount three or four operas each year. In addition to major Canadian singers, outstanding singers from abroad are frequently engaged, among them Marilyn Horne (*Norma,* 1963; *L'italiana in Algeri,* 1965), Regina Resnik (*Carmen,* 1965), and Joan Sutherland (*Norma,* 1963; *Lucia,* 1967; *Lucrezia Borgia,* 1972). In 1974 Richard Bonynge succeeded Guttman as artistic director.

Vanna Lupa. Opera in 3 acts by Pizzetti; text by composer. Prod. Florence, T.C., 4 May 1949 with Pederzini, Annaloro, Petri, cond. Pizzetti. Tells of the political ambition and the spirit of revenge which characterizes Vanna Ricci, nicknamed Lupa (mezzo), and the love of freedom displayed by her son Vieri (ten.). Both die in following the courses they have set themselves.

Vanzo, Vittorio (Maria) (*b* Padua, 29 Apr. 1862; *d* Milan 13 Dec. 1945). Italian conductor and composer. Studied Milan with Ronchetti-Monteviti, Angeleri, and Bazzini. Début 1883, Bologna, *Lohengrin.* Conducted first perf. in Italy of *Walküre* (Turin 1891), and first *Götterdämmerung,* at Milan Sc., 1897. Moscow, B., 1897. Buenos Aires, *c*1899. Retired 1906 and devoted himself to composition and teaching singing in Milan. His operas include *Edipo Re* (1893).

Varady, Julia (*b* Siebenbürgen (now Oradia), ?). Romanian soprano. Studied Cluj and Bucharest Conservatory with Arta Florescu. Cluj State Opera 1960-70; her roles included Liù, Judith, Fenena, and Santuzza; Frankfurt, 1970-2 as Antonia, Elvira, Fiordiligi, Elisabeth, and Saffi; Munich since 1972, especially successful as Vitellia, Donna Elvira and Giorgetta; Edinburgh Festival, 1974, Alcestis. A gifted and highly temperamental singing actress. (R)

Varesi, Felice (*b* Calais, 1813; *d* Milan, 13 Mar. 1889). French-Italian baritone. Début Varese 1834 in Donizetti's *Furioso all'isola di San Domingo.* Became leading Verdi singer and created title roles in his *Macbeth* and *Rigoletto,* also the first Germont, a part he thought unworthy. London, H.M.'s, 1864. Married soprano Cecilia Boccabadatti Gazzudo. Their daughter **Elena** (1844-1920) sang at D.L. in 1873 and 1875; sang Zerlina there opposite Jean de Reszke's Don Giovanni. Retired to Chicago, where she opened a singing school.

Varlaam. The drunken monk (bass) in Mussorgsky's *Boris Godunov.*

Varna. Town in Bulgaria. A Varna Opera Soceity was founded in 1920 under Presiyan Dyukmedzhev; performances of *La traviata* and *The Demon* were given. Out of this, a permanent company was formed known in 1930 as the Varna Civic Opera, with Zlaty Atanasov as conductor; this closed at the end of 1931. Three years later another enterprise was launched, and lasted until 1935. After the war, a civic company was formed and began operations in 1947 under the tenor Petar Baychev (1887-1960) in the National T.; performances were also given in the summer festivals. The company has developed a good repertory, and has visited Sofia.

Várnay, (Ibolyka) **Astrid** (Maria) (*b* Stockholm, 25 Apr. 1918). American soprano of Austrian and Hungarian parentage. Her father was Alexander Várnay (1889-1924), Austrian singer and stage manager of the first opera company founded in Oslo, her mother a coloratura soprano, Maria Yavor (*b* 1889). She studied with her mother, and Herman Weigert, whom she married in 1944. Début N.Y., Met., 1941, Sieglinde, substituting at a few hours' notice for Lotte Lehmann. Remained at Met. until end of 1956 season, establishing herself as leading Wagner-Strauss soprano, but also singing occasionally in Verdi operas and creating Telea in Menotti's *The Island God.* London, C.G., 1948-9, 1951, 1958-9, 1968; Bayreuth 1951-68; Florence Festival 1951, as Lady Macbeth. Despite a less than perfect vocal technique, her intense, passionate singing and acting made her the finest Wagnerian dramatic soprano between Flagstad's retirement and the emergence of Birgit Nilsson. After 1962 began to sing mezzo-character roles equally successfully, including Herodias, Clytemnestra, Kabanicha, the Kostelinička, and title-role in *Visit of the Old Lady. (R)*
Bibl: Berndt W. Wessling: *Astrid Varnay* (1965).

Varviso, Silvio (*b* Zurich, 26 Feb. 1924). Swiss conductor. Studied Zurich, and Vienna with Clemens Krauss. Début St Gallen, 1944, *Die Zauberflöte.* Basel, 1950-58 (music director from 1956). San Francisco 1959-61, where he conducted first U.S. perf. of *A Midsummer Night's Dream*; N.Y., Met., 1962, 1968-9. Gly. 1962-3, *Figaro, Ariadne auf Naxos*; London, G.C., since 1961 in Strauss and Mozart repertory; also conducted new prod. there of *Bohème*, 1974. Music director Stockholm, Royal Opera, 1965-72. Appointed Royal Court Conductor by King; the second foreigner to

hold title (first being Leo Blech). Stuttgart Opera, Generalmusikdirektor since 1972. Bayreuth 1969-74 *Fliegende Holländer, Lohengrin, Meistersinger.* Appointed music director, Paris, O., from 1981. A sensitive and polished musician, though his interpretations are apt to lack fire. (R)

Vasco da Gama. The hero (ten.) of Meyerbeer's *L'Africaine.* Also the title of a pasticcio by E. Bianchi (1792) and an opera by Himmel (1801).

Vašek. The shy son (ten.) of Micha in Smetana's *The Bartered- Bride.*

Vasoli, Pietro (*b* ?; *d* ?). Italian bass. Created Don Pacuvio (*Pietra del Paragone*), Licinio (*Aureliano in Palmira*), and Prosdocimo (*Turco in Italia*). Stendhal, writing of his performance in *Turco*, commented, 'the generosity of the audience even embraced poor old Vasoli, an ex-grenadier from Napoleon's army of Egypt, but now almost blind, and as a singer, hardly even third-rate, who made his undying reputation in the aria "ombretta sdenosa del Missipipì" '.

Vaudeville (Fr of doubtful etymology. Poss. from *Vaux de Vire*, the songs sung in the valleys (*vaux*) near Vire at the start of the 15th cent. by Olivier Basselin. Alternatively, from *voix de ville*; catches sung about town in the 16th cent. were known as vaudevilles). Originally a song with a short text, usually amorous or lyrical, which was early taken into comedies with music. By the early 18th cent. it had become the chief type of song in opéra comique, street tunes frequently appearing on the stage for their familiarity as well as their merit. By *Le Mariage de Figaro* (completed 1778), Beaumarchais was concluding with a *vaudeville final* in which each character sang a verse. The most celebrated operatic example is in Mozart's *Die Entführung.* In the 19th cent., the name was given to short comedies using popular songs. In the 20th cent., the term has generally been applied to light musical comedy or cabaret.

Vaughan Williams, Ralph (*b* Down Ampney, 12 Oct. 1872; *d* London, 26 Aug. 1958). English composer. Vaughan Williams turned to opera six times during his long life, and set considerable store by these works. The first, *Hugh the Drover* (1924), is a ballad opera reflecting his earlier discovery of English folk-song as the basis for his musical language; it is in manner closer to the early nationalist operas of Smetana than to its contemporaries, and was clearly intended to perform a similar service for the re-foundation and emancipation of English opera. That it did not do so was largely due to its belatedness, in historical terms, and the inevitable artificiality, in 1924, of a pastoral idyll set in the Napoleonic Wars; this does not vitiate the considerable charm and vigour of much of the score. In *Sir John in Love* (1929), the folk influence is more fully absorbed, and, boldly challenging Verdi and Nicolai, Vaughan Williams attempts to give the character of Falstaff particular strength by the Englishness of the setting. However, by attempting to set the characters in a 'real' Windsor, abandoning the conventions of the Elizabethan verse drama which Boito ingeniously replaced with those of opera buffa, Vaughan Williams makes the actions seem less real, and cruder; for all the beauty of some of the settings, there is insufficient compensation in the use of much English poetry apart from Shakespeare and English folk-song.

Riders to the Sea (1937) abandons these preoccupations in favour of a word-for-word setting of Synge's tragedy, drawing on a style that owes something to Wagner and something to *verismo*, but that is also deeply characteristic of the composer. This is his operatic masterpiece. *The Poisoned Kiss* (1936) turns to a modern musical comedy, but suffers from a facetious text which has prevented the wider hearing of some of the composer's most delightful and satirical music.

Of all his operas, the work closest to Vaughan Williams's heart was *The Pilgrim's Progress* (1951). Already in 1922 he had set an episode, *The Shepherds of the Delectable Mountains*: the completion of the whole work, which he always insisted was intended for the opera house and not for cathedral performance, was an important event in his life. Inevitably uneven, given its long gestation, and suffering in places from an awkwardness in handling so large-scale an opera, it contains powerful scenes, and is a moving statement of faith.

With *Holst, Vaughan Williams did much to pioneer a revival in English opera; and quite apart from their individual achievements, which are coming to be more fully appreciated, it is certain that without them the way would have been less clear for the post-1945 revival initiated by *Peter Grimes*.
Bibl: U. Vaughan Williams: *R.V.W.* (1964); M. Kennedy: *The Works of Ralph Vaughan Williams* (1964).

Veasey, Josephine (*b* London, 10 July 1930). British mezzo-soprano. Studied London with Audrey Langford. London, C.G., chorus 1948-50; Opera for All 1950-1; London C.G., since 1954, graduated from small roles such as Shepherd Boy in *Tannhäuser*, Mercedes, Emilia, and Suzuki, to Carmen, Eboli, Fricka, Waltraute, Venus, Octavian, and Dido (Berlioz). Gly. 1969, Charlotte. Salzburg, Milan, Sc., and N.Y., Met., as Fricka in the Karajan *Ring*. Paris, O., as Dido. Has a beautiful high mezzo voice. (R)

Veau d'or, Le. Méphistophélès's (bass) mocking song to the crowd in Act 2 of Gounod's *Faust*.

Vecchi, Orazio (*b* Modena, bapt. 6 Dec. 1550; *d* Modena, 19 Feb. 1605). Italian composer. His operatic importance is due to *L'Amfiparnasso*, a 'comedia harmonica' prod. at Modena in 1594. This attempt to set the *commedia dell'arte* figures to music was not meant to be staged, and so the work can at most rank as a 'pre-opera'; it has, however, been staged in modern times.

Vedernikov, Alexander (Filippovich) (*b* Mokino, Kirov region, 23 Dec. 1927). Russian bass. Studied Moscow with Alpert-Khasina. Début Leningrad, Kirov, 1955. Moscow, B., since 1957, where he has sung leading bass roles in the Russian repertory, including Boris, Pimen, Varlaam, Ivan Susanin, Dosifey, Konchak etc. Appeared with Bolshoy Company in Paris, Milan, New York. Milan, Sc., 1977-8, Philip and Inquisitor, and Massimilione (*Masnadieri*). Has rather light bass voice of beautiful quality. (R)

Vedrai, carino. Zerlina's (sop.) aria in Act 2, scene 1, of Mozart's *Don Giovanni,* in which she comforts Masetto after his beating from Giovanni.

Velluti, Giovanni Battista (*b* Montolmo (Macerata), 28 Jan. 1780; *d* Sambruson di Dolo (Venice), 22 Jan. 1861). Italian male soprano. Studied Ravenna with Calpi and Bologna with Mattei. Début Forlì 1800. After appearances in Rome and Naples, opened 1808-9 Milan season at Scala, creating title-role in Nicolini's *Coriolano* opposite Colbran, and appearing in new works by Federici and Lavigna; created Arsace in *Aureliano in Palmira* there 1813. Rossini was infuriated by his lavish embroideries of the music on the grounds that they quite obscured the melody. Velluti vowed never to sing Rossini's music again; but later they became great friends. Continued to sing in Italy, especially Venice, where he created Armando in Meyerbeer's *Crociato in Egitto*, a role specially composed for him (1824). He made his English début in same role, 1825, opposite Malibran and Caradori, when an audience unused to castrati (the last having sung at the King's Theatre in 1800) was both fascinated and shocked. Entrusted with management of King's for 1826, appearing in Morlacchi's *Tebaldo ed Isolina* and as Arsace. His popularity declined and his managements ended following financial quarrels over extra pay for the chorus. Returned to London 1829 and appeared in concerts; was heard by Mendelssohn, who found his singing distasteful. The last great castrato: in his great days his voice was said to be sweet and full, smoothly produced, but of little emotional range.

Veneziani, Vittorio (*b* Ferrara, 25 May 1878; *d* Ferrara, 14 Jan. 1958). Italian composer and chorus master. Studied Bologna with Martucci. Chorus master Venice, Turin, and Bologna. Engaged for Sc. by Toscanini 1921, remaining there until 1938 when the racial laws compelled him to leave the country. Returned to Sc. 1945, remaining there until his retirement in 1954. He trained the Scala chorus into the most magnificent ensemble of its day. His works include *La leggenda del lago* (1911). (R)

Vengeance aria. An aria, common in 18th and 19th cent. opera, in which a character gives vent to his determination to avenge a wrong. It served a useful purpose in giving a singer a powerful dramatic number, marked by forceful declamation and vigorous coloratura. Though there are many examples of female Vengeance Arias, of which the most famous is the Queen of Night's *Der Hölle Rache* in Mozart's *Die Zauberflöte*, it is a genre especially associated with male singers, and above all with baritones or basses usually taking the parts of villains. The most celebrated is perhaps Pizarro's 'Ha! welch' ein Augenblick' in Beethoven's *Fidelio,* though the most influential example in early Romantic opera was Dourlinski's 'Oui! pour mon heureuse adresse' in Act 3 of Cherubini's *Lodoïska.*

Venice (It. Venezia). Town in Italy. The first opera performance in Venice was Monteverdi's *Proserpina rapita,* given at the Palazzo Mocenigo Dandolo (now the Danieli Hotel) to celebrate the marriage of Giustiniana Mocenigo to Lorenzo Guistinian, in 1630. The first public opera house in the world opened in Venice in 1637 with a performance of Mannelli's *Andromeda;* this was the T. San Cassiano, originally a private theatre built by the Tron family at the beginning of the 17th cent. It was destroyed by fire in 1629; when it was rebuilt the Tron family decided to open its doors to the public, thus introducing an art, hitherto only experienced by the aristocratic families, to a wider public. It remained open until c1800 and staged the first performances of Monteverdi's *Ritorno d'Ulisse* and several works by Cavalli. The success of the San Cassiano led to the opening of other public opera houses in Venice:

T. SS. Giovanni e Paolo. Considered the finest theatre in Venice at the time, it was opened in Jan. 1639 with Sacrati's *Delia.* Staged the first performances of Monteverdi's *L'incoronazione di Poppea* and of works by Cavalli, Cesti, Rovetta, and others. From 1658 Marco Faustini was the director, and he introduced operas by Luzzo and Ziani, as well as Cavalli's *Scipione.* After the death of Faustini the theatre was managed by Grimani and Morich. It closed in 1748 and was demolished.

T. S. Moïse. Built by the San Barnaba branch of the Giustinian family and opened in 1640 with Monteverdi's *Arianna*; gave opera regularly until 1818. Staged the first performances of operas by Vivaldi, Paisiello, Galuppi, Anfossi, and many others. Rossini's first opera, *La cambiale del matrimonio,* was produced there in 1810, followed by his *L'inganno felice, La scala di seta, L'occasione fa il ladro,* and *Signor Bruschino.* After 1818 it became a marionette theatre, and when rebuilt was known as the T. Minerva. Today it is partly a shop and partly an apartment house.

T. Novissimo. Opened in 1641 with Sacrati's *La finta pazza,* and continued to give opera until 1647. Mentioned by Evelyn in his diaries of 1645 and 1646.

T. SS Apostoli (sometimes known as the S. Aponal). Opened in 1649 with Cesti's *Orontea*; continued to give opera until 1687.

T. S. Appollinare. Opened in 1651 with Cavalli's *Oristeo*; continued to give opera until 1660. Demolished in 1690; today a poor-house occupies the site.

T. S. Samuele. Opened in 1655 for comedy, not opera, but from 1710 operas regularly performed there, especially opera buffa. Gave the first performances of many operas by Porpora, Galuppi, Piccinni, etc. and saw the triumphs of Carestini, Tenducci, Medici, and De Sanctis. It was reconstructed in 1748 after a fire, and continued to give opera until 1894.

T. S. Salvatore. The oldest theatre in Venice still standing (known today as the T. Goldoni). Built by the Vendramin family, it opened in 1661 with Castrovillari's *Pasife.* Renamed the T. S. Lucca in 1799, the T. Apollo in 1833, and the T. Goldoni in 1875. Staged the premières of Cavalli's last two operas; Pasta sang Norma there. Goldoni wrote more than 60 plays for the theatre.

T. S. Angelo. Built by two leading Venetian families, the Capelli and Marcelli, and situated on the Grand Canal. It opened in 1676 with Freschi's *Elena rapita da Paride.* Staged the first performances of several operas by Vivaldi, who was the theatre's impresario in the 1720s and 1730s, and was satirized in Benedetto Marcello's *Il teatro alla moda.* It continued to stage operas by Hasse, Albinoni, Lampugnani, and others until the end of the 18th cent.

T. S. Giovanni Grisostomo. Built by Grimani, on the site of houses owned and occupied by Marco Polo, it opened in 1678 with Pallavicino's *Vespasiano.* Galuppi was connected with the theatre 1749-56. Towards the end of the 18th cent., it was renamed the Emoroniti, and entered a period of decline. In 1835 Malibran performed there in *La Sonnambula*; at the end of the first act garlands of flowers were flung onto the stage and songbirds released from cages in the upper-tier boxes; Malibran refused her fee of 4,000 Austrian lire and told the impresario, Giovanni Gallo, to use the money to help the theatre. From that night the theatre was called the T. Malibran. It is now a cinema.

T. S. Fantino. Opened in 1699 with Pignatta's *Paolo Emilio*. Active until 1720.

T. S. Benedetto. Opened in 1755 with Cocchi's *Zoë*. Damaged by fire 1774; it reopened in 1784 as the T. Venier. By 1800, 146 works had had their first performances there. Rossini's *L'Italiana in Algeri* had its première there in 1813, his *Eduardo e Cristina* in 1819, and Meyerbeer's *Emma di Resburgo* the same year. It was renamed the T. Rossini in 1868; today it is a cinema.

Three other theatres gave opera: the T. S. Margherita, the T. S. Girolamo, and the T. Pepoli.

T. La Fenice. Venice's most famous opera house. It was planned as successor to the burnt down T. S. Benedetto, the 'Phoenix' that arose from the ashes (though not on the same site). It was planned by a syndicate made up of Venetian patricians, citizens, and merchants, who chose Gianantonio Selva to design it. He was not popular, and obstacles were put in his way. On the theatre's facade he inscribed the word 'Societas', from which the witty Venetians formed an acrostic: 'Sine Ordine Cum Irregularitate Erexit Theatrum Antonius Selva' ('without method and irregularly Antonius Selva built the theatre'). La Fenice opened on 16 May 1792 with Paisiello's *I Giuochi d'Agrigento*. It was the scene of the premières of Rossini's *Tancredi*, *Sigismondo*, and *Semiramide*, Bellini's *I Capuleti e i Montecchi* and *Beatrice di Tenda*, and Donizetti's *Belisario*. The first Fenice was destroyed by fire in Dec. 1836, and a second theatre was built on the same site to the ground plan of the original architect in less than a year, opening on 26 Dec. 1837. This theatre staged the premières of Verdi's *Ernani*, *Attila*, *Rigoletto*, *Traviata*, and *Simone Boccanegra*.

The theatre underwent alterations in 1854 and in 1938; in the latter year it was opened as an Ente Autonomo. In recent years the season has lasted from December to the end of May, with supplementary seasons during the summer, and some opera in the Venice Festival. It staged the world premières of *The Rake's Progress* (1951), *The Turn of the Screw* (1954), and *Intolleranza* (1961). Since 1968 the regular winter-spring seasons have included important revivals of Mercadante's *Le due illustri rivali*, Verdi's *Il corsaro* and *Giovanna d'Arco*, and Spontini's *Fernand Cortez*, as well as productions of contemporary works by Rossellini, Rota, Malipiero, and Dallapiccola. The theatre remained closed during the 1974-5 season because of a financial crisis. The auditorium seats 1,500, and with its dazzling chandelier, its 96 boxes, and blue, cream, and gold decorations is considered by many the

most beautiful opera house in the world.

Bibl: S. T. Worsthorne: *Venetian Opera in the Seventeenth Century* (1954); various: *La Fenice* (1972); H. T. Muran: *Venezia e il melodrama nel seicento* (1976).

Venus. The goddess of love (sop.) in Wagner's *Tannhäuser*. See also below.

Venus and Adonis. Opera in prologue and 3 acts by Blow; text by unknown author. Prod. London c1684, when Venus was sung by Mary Davies, mistress of Charles II, and Cupid by Lady Mary Tudor, their daughter; Cambridge, Mass., 11 Mar. 1941.

Vêpres Siciliennes, Les (The Sicilian Vespers). Opera in 5 acts by Verdi; text by Scribe and Duveyrier. Prod. Paris, O., 13 June 1855, with Cruvelli, Guéymard, Bonnehée, Obin, cond. Dietsch; London, D.L., 27 July 1859, with Tietjens, Mongini, Fagotti; N.Y., Academy of Music, 7 Nov. 1859 with Colson, Brignoli, Ferri, Junca, cond. Muzio.

Specially commissioned for the Great Exhibition in Paris of 1855, the opera tells of the occupation of Sicily by the French during the 13th century, and the efforts of the Sicilians to remove them. The climax of the work is the slaughter of the unarmed French by Sicilian patriots, the signal for which is given by the ringing of the vesper bell to mark the wedding of the Duchess Elena (sop.), sister of Frederick of Austria and a Sicilian patriot, to Arrigo (ten.), son of Guy de Montfort (bar.), the French governor of the island.

Also operas by Barth (1841) and Lindpaintner (1843).

Verdi, Giuseppe (*b* Le Roncole, 10 Oct. 1813; *d* Milan, 27 Jan. 1901). Italian composer. Born of humble parents, Verdi owed his first musical education to the local organist and his first advancement to Antonio Barezzi, a wealthy Busseto music-lover. He studied under Ferdinando Provesi, music director of the Busseto church, music school, and Philharmonic Society, deputizing for his teacher and conducting some of his own music. Barezzi soon arranged for him to go to Milan, where he failed the entrance exam to the Conservatory; returning to Busseto he assumed, amid fierce controversy, the post of *maestro di musica* and settled down as the husband of Barezzi's daughter Margherita.

In this year, 1836, Verdi completed his first opera, *Rocester*; this is lost, but some of its music may have been incorporated into *Oberto, Conte de San Bonifacio* (1839), which already shows typical Verdian traits. This was staged partly through the good offices of the young soprano who took the lead, Giuseppina Strepponi. Verdi was promptly offered a contract for three more operas by the Scala's manager, Merelli; but the death of his wife and two children, as well as the failure of *Un giorno di regno* (1840), so seriously depressed him that he tried to cancel the contract. *Un Giorno de regno* (subtitled *Il finto Stanislao*) was Verdi's only comic opera before *Falstaff*, of which it contains certain curious foretastes such as the duet for the soprano/tenor lovers over a male trio.

Merelli, ever sympathetic, tempted Verdi to resume work with the libretto for *Nabucodonosor* (usually abbreviated as *Nabucco*) (1842); and the result was his first masterpiece. Though modest in harmonic and rhythmic invention, the work has an exuberance and warmth in its tunes, a firm dramatic structure, and a deep sense of humanity (it contains three strikingly mature pieces of characterization) that still keep it on the stage. *Nabucco* triumphed; and as with a number of the operas that followed, the theme of an oppressed people was taken as symbolic by Italians suffering under Austrian domination.

Neither *I Lombardi alla Prima Crociata* (1843) nor *Ernani* (1844), though originally successes, measures up to *Nabucco*. *I Lombardi* is something of an anthology of operatic clichés, given life by Verdi's greater experience in handling accompaniments and the scoring: there is a 'Jerusalem' chorus that rivals *Nabucco's* famous 'Va pensiero'. *Ernani* is still more vigorous in patriotic expression, and is notable for the splendidly drawn figure of the vengeful Da Silva.

All the leading theatres were now demanding Verdi's services, and opera followed opera in quick, even hasty, succession. *I due foscari* (1844) contains more than a foretaste of *Traviata, Rigoletto,* and *Simon Boccanegra*; it is also notable for Verdi's first use of leading motives, and for winning Donizetti's opinion, 'This man is a genius'. It is a finer work than either *Giovanna d'Arco* (1845) (which had a short career despite Patti's appearances), *Alzira* (1845), or even *Attila* (1846), though the latter's robustness won it success at the time. Verdi later referred to this period as his 'years in the galleys', but they were years that established his popularity.

Macbeth (1847, rev. for Paris 1865) reaffirms Verdi's genius. It was the first-fruit of his lifelong admiration for Shakespeare, and its occasional weaknesses are flecks on the surface of a conception that is nobler and more intense than anything of his that had gone before. In dramatic force and characterization it overshadows *I masnadieri* (1847, in London with Jenny Lind), which is notable for a beautiful prelude and the soprano/baritone Tomb Scene in Act 2, presaging much in *Forza*, as well as for some original scoring and the now familiar melodic verve: a certain dark forcefulness is *Macbeth's* chief legacy, though *I masnadieri* makes its own bequests to the

Requiem, *Trovatore,* and *Traviata*. *Il corsaro* (1848) has little distinction; *La battaglia di Legnano* (1849) survives occasionally by virtue of its vivid music of love and action – it contains another superb piece of characterization, in the brief but dominating appearance of Barbarossa. The same year saw *Luisa Miller,* a much finer work which exploits the darker side of Verdi's genius: the last act introduces a new, flowing style that is markedly an advance on the first two acts' more conventional manner. *Stiffelio* (1850) has been regarded as something of a relapse, chiefly through the baffling situations, for Verdi's first audience, of the almost Ibsenesque libretto: a good revival might well show otherwise.

Meanwhile, in Paris, Verdi had again met Giuseppina Strepponi. They became companions and eventually (1859) man and wife. Her influence was wholly good: the mellowing and relaxation which came over his art, and the fulfilment of all the promise hitherto glimpsed on the whole intermittently, was undoubtedly hastened by her presence. In 1851 came the first work of complete genius, *Rigoletto*. The characterization is bolder, subtler, and (especially as regards Rigoletto) extraordinarily original; and the remaining conventional elements are masterfully harnessed to the dramatic scheme. The famous quartet is still an outstanding example of the great opera composer's ability to express contrasting emotions in a single piece of music.

After *Rigoletto, Il trovatore* (1853) is really a regression to the simple accompaniments and superbly vehement or pathetic tunes of *Nabucco*. In a sense it is the last early Verdi opera, though it comes in the centre of his middle period. This is crowned by *La traviata* (1853). At first a notorious fiasco, it has long since been accepted as a great masterpiece. The old blunt divisions are smoothed into a more flexible language that ideally matches the subject; while the tunes achieve new subtlety in expressing complex and finely shaded states of mind. Reliance on the conventional forms of Italian opera was increasingly cramping Verdi's style: *Traviata* represents a liberation, and by it he achieves new heights as a composer.

Verdi returned to Paris in 1853 for *Les Vêpres siciliennes,* written to Scribe libretto. This was produced in 1855; it is a lengthy, uncharacteristic piece which has never achieved more than occasional revival. Back in Busseto, he revised *Stiffelio* (whose music he had already used to a knightly libretto, *Guglielmo von Wellingrode,* to satisfy the Roman censors) as *Aroldo*; this had a new fourth act. He also opened negotiations for what he hoped would be *King Lear,* a project that haunted him all his life. During another visit to Paris he began work on *Simone Boccanegra,* which was produced

Venice in 1857 – unsuccessfully, largely owing to complexity of plot; a rescue operation by Verdi and Boito in 1881 presented the work's very fine episodes in a better light. It is a dark, imposing work, unequal but highly regarded for its particular atmosphere and for its noblest passages.

The beginning of 1859 saw *Un ballo in maschera* (q.v. for summary of its many censorship disputes). There are traces of Verdi's knowledge of Meyerbeer, but unlike *Les Vêpres siciliennes*, *Ballo* absorbs them, enlarging thereby the Verdian vocabulary rather than straining it. This is also a more deftly contrapuntal work, and one which shows greater skill in developing themes.

Verdi's name had long been associated with the Risorgimento as an artist of revolt – his operas were read as political gestures for liberty, and his very name was used as an acrostic slogan: 'Viva VERDI' meant 'Viva Vittorio Emanuele, Re D'Italia'. In 1859 Napoleon III drove the Austrians out of Lombardy; Verdi represented Busseto at the assembly in Parma and then, pressed by Cavour, became a member of the new Italian Parliament. During his Parliamentary career (1861-5) he found time for only one opera, *La forza del destino* (1862). Written for St Petersburg, this is again Verdi in dark mood. It is, moreover, implausible dramatically and disjointed musically: the contemporary cult of the *Schicksalstragödie*, or Fate Tragedy, was unsuited to Verdi. Individual scenes and arias are fine enough to sustain much admiration for the work; while hints of the great comic opera that lay within Verdi are underlined in the characterization of the Friar Melitone.

Macbeth was revised in 1864-5 and presented in Paris, where Verdi agreed to write *Don Carlos* (1867). Once again the demands of French Grand Opera are felt, but this is an incomparably greater work than *Vêpres*. It is a long opera, grand and subtle, filled with highly original strokes of character and carrying forward its action largely in the duets which express clashes and developments of relationship. Verdi wrote no more majestic opera.

Aida (1871), first performed at the Cairo Opera House, is purely Italian and embodies grandeur rather than majesty. The spectacular elements are part of the plot and so of the music, but Verdi was master enough now to place them firmly as the background against which his characters unfold their tragedy. Indeed, it is out of the contrast of public pomp and private emotion that *Aida* is composed: it was a design that matched the composer's gifts splendidly and drew some of his finest music.

But *Otello* (1887) excels even *Aida*. For this, the influence of Boito, who gave up his own composition to write librettos for Verdi, is largely responsible. Despite recurrent differences, he understood Verdi well, and as a composer himself, not only as a man of literary ability, he provided an ideal libretto. The fusion of aria and recitative into a single expressive language, varying its tension but hardly its nature, is complete. Melody is still supreme, but it is melody infinitely adaptable to situation and character, capable of running on in narration or bearing the weight of powerful expression, as the swift-moving drama demands. It is an opera abounding in sudden phrases whose curve illuminates what once needed an aria.

Falstaff (1893) is a fruit of the same collaboration in Verdi's beloved Shakespeare. It is swift-paced and genial, but also sharp: Verdi's ingenuity and his canny knowledge of human nature seemed to become heightened in his old age, but there is nothing of an old man's gentleness in his amused and affectionate jabs at his hero. Jealousy, tragic in *Otello*, becomes an object of laughter in *Falstaff*, and human fallibility is the source of wit, not regret. The score flashes with brilliance, yet there is a lyricism and sense of fantasy which give, it a peculiar grace. All Verdi's skills are present, refined and sharpened, and all his delight in humanity. For the Verdi-lover it is an extraordinarily moving moment when, at the end of opera, this comedy that ends the whole great series of operas, Falstaff turns to us in the audience and in the last fugal chorus reminds us that all the world's a stage.

Bibl: F. Walker: *The Man Verdi* (1962); J. Budden: *The Operas of Verdi* (vol. 1, 1973; vol. 2, 1978).

Vergnet, Edmond-Alphonse-Jean (*b* Montpellier, 4 July 1850; *d* Nice, 25 Feb. 1904). French tenor. Studied violin, Montpellier and Paris, and played in orchestra of T.L., Paris until 1870. Studied voice, Paris with Saint-Yves Bax. Début Paris, O., 1874, Raimbaud. Appeared in Italy, including Milan, Sc., where he created Admeto in Catalani's *Dejanice* (1883); toured U.S.A. with Van Zandt 1885-6. London, C.G., 1881-2 Radamès, Belmonte, Faust, Wilhelm Meister. H.M's. 1886. Paris, O., 1875-93, first Samson at O. Brussels, La M., created Jean in *Hérodiade* (1881) and Shanhabari (*Salammbô*) 1890, Dominique (*L'Attaque du moulin*), and Zarastra in *La Mage* (Massenet). Repertory also included Florestan, Lohengrin, John of Leyden, Vasco, and Romeo.

Verismo (*It* realism). The term describing the realistic or naturalistic school of Italian opera that flourished briefly in the late 19th and early 20th cent., typified by Mascagni, Leoncavallo, Giordano, Puccini, and Zandonai. Librettos were drawn not from moral, heroic, or idealistic subjects, but from the '*squarcio di vita*', the 'slice of life' announced by Tonio in the prologue to *Pagliacci*. As that pioneer work shows, the slice of life chosen may well include violent episodes and a heightened emotional approach to everyday life. This in turn made the sharp concentration of 1-act form effective: in response to the success of *Cavalleria rusticana* and *Pagliacci*, Massenet wrote an effective piece of French *verismo* in *La Navarraise*. Puccini's *La Bohème*, a subtler extension of *verismo*, in turn found its echo in some French operas, notably Charpentier's *Louise*.

Verni, Andrea (*b* Rome ? *d* Parma, Aug. 1822). Italian bass. Début Rome, prob. 1790; Milan, Sc., 1800-16 as buffo bass. Created Don Magnifico (Rome, 1817) and Gilberto in Donizetti's *Enrico di Borgogna* (Venice, 1818). His wife was the soprano Antonia Tognoli Verni; and other members of the family, who were singers, included Giacomo, Maria, and Pietro.

Veron, Louis Desiré (*b* Paris, 1798; *d* Paris, 1867). French administrator and critic. Founded the *Revue de Paris* (1839) and was director of the Opéra 1831-6.

Verona. Town in Veneto, Italy. First opera given under auspices of the Accademia Filarmonica 1549, *Il geloso*, with music by Canigiani, Bonzanini, and Brusasorzi. Religious dramas by Barba, Gazzaniga, Jommelli and others given in churches and small theatres during the 18th cent., and secular works in the T. dei Temperati. The T. Filarmonico, designed by Francesco Galli Bibiena, opened in 1732 with Vivaldi's *La fida ninfa*; destroyed by fire in 1749, reopened in 1754 with works by Hasse and Perez. It was in this theatre that the 14-year old Mozart performed in 1770 on his first visit to Italy. The Filarmonico continued to give opera with leading singers and conductors until bombed in Feb. 1945. Opera was also performed in the T. dell'Accademia Vecchia, the T. Nuovo (or Rena), the T. del Territorio, the T. Morando, the T. Leo di Castelnuovo, and the T. Ristori.

In 1856 and 1859 the famous Roman Arena had been used to stage performances of opera by Rossini and Donizetti; in 1913 summer opera in the Arena, as given today, came into being, due to the enterprise of the tenor Giovanni *Zenatello, his future wife Maria Gay, and the impresario Ottone Rovato. Serafin's advice was sought, and after acoustic tests, weather hazards, and various problems, *Aida* was staged on 10 August 1913, before an audience that included Puccini, Mascagni, Pizzetti, Zandonai, Montemezzi, and Illica. There have been summer seasons of opera ever since (except for 1915-18 and 1940-45). Athough the majority of the operas performed there have been spectacular ones such as *La Gioconda*, *Turandot*, *Mefistofele*, and *La forza del destino*, there have also been successful productions of more intimate works including *Manon*, *La traviata*, and *La Bohème*. Most leading singers and conductors of Italian opera have appeared there.

Véronique. Operetta in 3 acts by Messager; text by Van Loo and Duval. Prod. Paris, B.P., 10 Dec. 1898, with Sully, Tariol-Bauge, Périer, Regnard; London, Coronet T., 5 May 1903; N.Y., Broadway T., 30 Oct. 1905, with Gordon, Vincent, Maitland, Rea, Fitzgerald.

Verrett, Shirley (*b* New Orleans, 31 May 1931). American mezzo-soprano. Studied Chicago with Anna Fitziu, and N.Y., Juilliard School, with Mme. Székély-Fresche. Début Yellow Springs, Ohio, 1957 in *Rape of Lucretia*. N.Y., City O., 1958, in Weill's *Lost in the Stars*; Spoleto, 1963 as Carmen. London, C.G., since 1966 as Ulrica, Azucena, Eboli, Amneris, Orpheus, and Carmen; N.Y., Met., since 1968. Milan, Sc., since 1969. San Francisco, 1972, Selika in *L'Africaine*. Paris, O., 1973. A greatly-gifted vocal and dramatic artist, with a high mezzo-soprano voice. Repertory also includes Dido (*Troyens*), Elisabeth (*Maria Stuarda*), Adalgisa, Leonora (*Favorite*), and more recently Norma, Lady Macbeth, Amelia, and Tosca. (R)

Versailles. Palace built by Louis XIV to the south-west of Paris. Although Lully wrote operas and ballets for Louis XIV which were produced here, there was originally no permament theatre, and temporary stages were erected either in the gardens or in various rooms and courtyards of the Palace. The indoor make-shift theatres were always too small for opera, which was generally given outdoors during the summer. The famous opera house at Versailles, designed by Ange-Jacques Gabriel, was commissioned by Louis XV in 1748; after many delays due to lack of money, foreign wars, etc., the theatre was eventually completed for the celebrations of the marriage of the Dauphin (the future Louix XVI) and Marie Antoinette, and opened on 16 May 1770 with a grand banquet, followed on May 17 with Lully's *Persée* with Sophie *Arnould.

Opera continued to be performed there until the Revolution, when the theatre became the meeting-place of the Club des Jacobins; its furniture and decorations were plundered. Restored 1837 by Louis-Philippe and reopened with scenes from *Robert le Diable* with *Falcon and *Duprez, and a special ballet by Scribe with music by Auber, danced by the Elssler sisters. In 1848 Berlioz conducted a concert with 450 performers taking part; Queen Victoria and Prince Albert were entertained there in August 1855; and in 1864 the King and Queen of Spain saw a performance of Lully's *Psyché*. During the 1870s the theatre became the seat of the National Assembly, and of the Third Republic as proclaimed there in January 1875, after which the theatre fell into disuse until 1952, when a campaign was launched for its restoration. On 9 April 1957, Queen Elizabeth II and Prince Philip were entertained there by President Coty; the programme included the Acte des Fleurs from *Les Indes galantes*. Later that summer Monteverdi's tercentenary was celebrated, and in 1958 Gluck's *Orphée* was performed by the company of the Opéra Comique. Rolf *Liebermann's régime as general administrator of the Paris O. opened there on 30 March 1973 with *Le nozze di Figaro*, conducted by Solti. Works that had their premières at Versailles include Rameau's *Platée*, Grétry's *Aucassin et Nicolette*, and Sacchini's *Oedipe à Colonne*.

Verschworenen, Die (The Conspirators). Opera in 1 act by Schubert; text by Castelli, on the idea of Aristophanes's comedy *Lysistrata* (411 B.C.). Prod. Frankfurt, 29 Aug. 1861; N.Y., 16 June 1877; London, R.C.M., 20 June. 1956.

The Crusaders' wives go on sexual strike until their husbands forswear war, as in Aristophanes's original. A touchy political censor insisted that the title be changed to *Der häusliche Krieg* (Domestic War).

Verstovsky, Alexey (Nikolayevich) (*b* Seliverstovo, 1 Mar. 1799; *d* Moscow, 17 Nov. 1862). Russian composer. The son of a land-owner; abandoned engineering studies in St Petersburg to study music with Steibelt and Field. Wrote music for various vaudevilles; then took up a full-time career in the theatre when appointed Inspector of Theatres in Moscow in 1825. In 1842 became Director of all the Moscow theatres, exercising a powerful and beneficial influence until his retirement in 1860.

His first opera, *Pan Twardowski* (1828), met with little success. A Romantic Singspiel in the manner of *Der Freischütz*, it draws on some Weberian ingredients (a pact with the Devil, the *Preciosa* gypsy atmosphere) but is constructed of short, effective songs that show no influence of German Romantic opera. *Vadim* (1832) includes some consciously Russian characteristics. His greatest success was *Askold's Tomb* (1835), which was given some 600 times in Russia during the 19th cent. and in 1869 became the first Russian opera to be performed in America. Even this work, despite an incantation scene modelled on the Wolf's Glen scene in *Der Freischütz*, is essentially a collection of individual songs, which for all their appeal do not create characters or atmosphere except of the most rudimentary kind. It was the use of popular Russian elements in the songs and choruses, and strokes such as the introduction of folk instrument players, that won the operas such an enthusiastic following. His later operas were *Longing for the Homeland* (1839), *Chur Valley* (1841), and *Gromoboy* (1858). *Bibl:* B. Dobrokhotov: *A. N. Verstovsky* (1949).

Verurteilung des Lukullus. Opera in 12 scenes by Dessau; text by Brecht. Prod. Berlin, S.O., 17 Mar. 1951 as *Das Verhör des Lukullus* with Goerlich, Hülgert, Meyer-Krämer, Soot, cond. Scherchen. Withdrawn by East German authorities on political grounds and revised by composer same year. London B.B.C. (original version) translated by Geoffrey Dunn, 26 Mar. 1953. cond. Scherchen. Third version Berlin S.O., 1965, prod. by Dessau's wife, Ruth Berghaus; Cambridge 29 Jan. 1970, with Jonic, Walden, Lloyd, cond. Beaumont.

In the underworld, Lucullus (ten.) must stand trial before being allowed to enter the Elysian Fields. He pleads his cause by recounting his military victories, but the jury reject this; the ravages of war that resulted from his victories condemn him.

Vespri siciliani, I. See *Vêpres siciliennes, Les*.

Vestale, La (The Vestal Virgin). Opera in 3 acts by Spontini; text by Étienne de Jouy. Prod. Paris, O., 16 Dec. 1807, with Branchu, Maillard, Laintz, Lays, Dérivis; London, King's T., 2 Dec. 1826; New Orleans 17 Feb. 1828.

The opera tells of the love of the Roman captain Licinio (ten.) for Giulia (sop.), who becomes a Vestal Virgin while her lover is in Gaul. He breaks into the temple to win her back, and she allows the holy fire to become extinguished. She is condemned to death, but as she is being led to execution a flash of lightning rekindles the fire and she is spared; she is reunited with Licinio.

Other operas on the same libretto by Pucitta (1810) and Guhr (1814, new setting of Spontini text). Also operas by Vento (1776), Giordani (1786), Rauzzini (1787), Pavesi (*Arminia*, 1810), Pacini (1823), Mercadante (1841); opera buffa, *Les Petites vestales*, by Rey (1900).

Vesti la giubba. Canio's (ten.) aria closing Act 1 of Leoncavallo's *Pagliacci*, bewailing his duty to put on his motley and to clown, though his heart be breaking.

Vestris (orig. Bartolozzi), **Lucia Elizabeth** (*b* London, 3 Jan. or 2 Mar. 1787; *d* London, 8 Aug. 1856). English contralto. The wife of Auguste Armand Vestris, *maître de ballet* of the King's Theatre, she studied singing with Corri, and made her début on the occasion of her husband's Benefit in July 1815 as Proserpina in Winter's *Il ratto di Proserpina*. She sang with success at the Italian Opera in Paris and regularly at the King's T, 1821-5. The first London Pippo in *La gazza ladra*, Malcolm Graeme in *La donna del lago*, Edoardo in *Matilde di Shabran*, and Emma in *Zelmira*. She created Fatima in Weber's *Oberon* at C.G., 1826. Subsequently she managed the Olympic, C.G., and Lyceum Theatres, and appeared in English versions of *Norma*, *Figaro*, etc. She is even known to have sung the title role in *Don Giovanni* and

Macheath in *The Beggar's Opera*. She left Vestris in 1838 and married Charles Matthews.

Viaggio a Reims, Il (The Journey to Rheims). Opera in 2 acts by Rossini; text by Balochi. Prod. Paris, T.-I., for coronation of Charles X, 19 June. 1825. A complete failure: despite a cast that included Pasta, Cinti-Damoreau, Levasseur, and Donzelli, it only lasted three nights. Most of the music was re-used for *Le Comte Ory* in 1828; revived, without most of the *Ory* additions, Paris, T.-I., 26 Oct. 1848, as *Andremo a Parigi*.

Vianesi, Auguste-Charles-Leonard-François (*b* Livorno, 2 Nov. 1837; *d* New York, 4 Nov. 1908). Italian, later French, conductor and composer. Studied Livorno with his father Giuseppe. Went to Paris in 1857 with a letter of introduction to Rossini from Pasta. London, D.L., 1858-9. Moscow 1863-4, St Petersburg 1867-9; Paris, T.I, 1873 and O., 1887-91. London C.G., 1870-80; conducted the first London performances of *Lohengrin, Tannhäuser, Il Guarany, Le Roi de Lahore*, and other works, as well as the French and Italian repertory. N.Y., Met., 1883-4, 1891-2, conducted *Faust* at the opening performance of the house. New Orleans 1899-1900. Taught singing in New York from 1892.

Viardot-Garcia, Pauline (Michèle-Ferdinande) (*b* Paris 18 July 1821; *d* Paris, 18 May 1910). French mezzo-soprano and composer of Spanish birth. Daughter of Manuel Garcia, and younger sister of Malibran. Studied singing with her mother and brother Manuel, and piano with various teachers including Liszt. Début (in concert) Brussels 13 Dec. 1833 with her brother-in-law, the violinist De Bériot; stage début London, H.M's., May 1839, as Desdemona (Rossini). Real success dates from her Paris début, in same role, at the T.I. later that year, under the management of Louis Viardot, whom she married in 1840. Created Fidès in *Le Prophète* (1849) at Meyerbeer's request, and sang the role more than 200 times. The same year met Gounod, and was largely instrumental in getting his *Sapho* produced at the Paris O.; created the title role. London, C.G., 1848-51, 1854-5. Largely owing to her efforts, *Les Huguenots* was produced at C.G., in 1848; she sang Valentine. She was the first London Azucena and a greatly admired Donna Anna and Rachel. In 1859 she sang the title role in Gluck's *Orfeo* in the famous Paris revival in Berlioz's arrangement, and in 1861 she sang the title role in *Alceste*; she was also the first to sing Leonore in *Fidelio* in French (1860). In 1859 she sang in excerpts from *Les Troyens* at Baden-Baden, and the following year (privately) she sang Isolde in Act 2 of *Tristan* at Wagner's request, with the composer singing Tristan. She continued to appear during the 1860s, in Stuttgart 1864-5, Baden-Baden 1864-

6, finally Weimar in March 1870 as Orfeo. She settled first in Baden-Baden, then in Paris, where she composed, wrote poetry and plays, and painted.

For many years she was the constant companion of *Turgenev, and a close friend of Schumann. Her circle also included Alfred de Musset, George Sand, and Chopin. In 1872 she sang Delilah (at a private audition) for Saint-Saëns and a select audience; and in the following year she sponsored the first performance of Massenet's oratorio *Marie Magdeleine* at the Paris Odéon, in which she herself sang the title role. Her voice extended from c' to f'''. She sang several operettas, some to librettos by Turgenev, including *Cendrillon* (revived Newport, 1971), *Trop de femmes* (1867), *Le Dernier sorcier* (1867), and *L'Ogre* (1868). Turgenev's *Lettres à Madame Viardot* were published in Paris in 1907. Her daughter Louise Héritte Viardot wrote about her mother in *Memories and Adventures* (1913).

Her pupils included Desirée Artôt, Teresa Arkel, Organi, Marianne Brandt, and her daughter, **Louise** (-Pauline-Marie) (*b* Paris, 14 Dec. 1841; *d* Heidelberg, 17 Jan. 1918), a contralto, who married Héritte de La Tour and taught in St Petersburg, Frankfurt, and Heidelberg; she wrote a comic opera, *Lindoro*, produced in Weimar in 1879. Pauline's son, **Paul** (*b* Courtanavel, 20 July 1857; *d* Algiers, 11 Dec. 1941) was a violinist, and conducted at the Paris Opera from 1893.

Bibl: A. Fitzlyon: *The Price of Genius – A Life of Pauline Viardot* (1964).

Vibrato (*It* vibrated). A fluctuation of pitch and intensity in the voice, admirable when used judiciously to keep the note 'alive' but often abused; in the latter case, the word 'wobble' has almost become a technical term. Used as a direction by some composers in the Romantic period.

Vicenza. Town in Veneto, Italy. The Accademia Olimpica was founded in 1555 by leading figures in the arts and society including Palladio, who designed the T. Olimpico (designs completed by Vincenzo Scamozzi), which opened in 1585 and is still standing. Regular operatic performances began in the T. Castelli in 1656. The T. Eretenio opened in 1784 with the première of Cimarosa's *L'Olimpiade*. A new theatre, built by Pamato in 1828 and named after him, was later taken over by the city and renamed the Politeama Comunale. In 1901 it was renamed the T. Verdi. It was destroyed during the Second World War.

Vickers, Jon (orig. Jonathan Stewart) (*b* Prince Albert, Saskatchewan, 29 Oct. 1926). Canadian tenor. Studied Toronto with George Lambert. Début Toronto, Canadian O.C., 1954, Duke of Mantua; Canadian O.C., 1954-6; Stratford Festival, Ontario, Male Chorus (*Lucretia*) 1956; London, C.G., since 1957, quickly establishing himself as fine dramatic tenor in such roles as Don José, Aeneas, Don Carlos, and later Radamès, Florestan, Siegmund; Bayreuth 1958, 1964 Siegmund, Parsifal; San Francisco, 1959-60, 1963-4, 1966, 1969-70; N.Y., Met. since 1959; Vienna S.O., Salzburg Easter and summer festivals, especially as Otello, Tristan, and Siegmund. Repertory also includes Grimes, Hermann (*Queen of Spades*), Jason in *Medée*. One of the finest English-language heroic tenors, vocally and physically, of the post-war period. A deeply moving singing-actor with a highly individual voice. (R)

Vida Breve, La (Brief Life). Opera in 2 acts by Falla; text by Carlos Fernandez Shaw. Prod. (in French) Nice, 1 Apr. 1913 with Lilliane Grenville, David, Devries, Edouard Cotreuil, cond. Miranne; N. Y., Met., 6 Mar. 1926 with Bori, Howard, Alcock, Tokatyan, d'Angelo, cond. Serafin; Edinburgh 9 Sept. 1958 with De los Angeles, Gomez, Del Pozo, Martinez, Duis, cond. Toldrá.

Salud (sop.) loves Paco (ten.), who is secretly about to marry another. At the wedding she curses him, but is overcome by her love and dies brokenhearted at his feet.

Vidal, Paul Antonin (*b* Toulouse, 16 June. 1863; *d* Paris, 9 Apr. 1931). French conductor and composer. Studied Toulouse, and Paris with Massenet. Prix de Rome 1883. Assistant chorus director, O., 1889, chief conductor 1906 (conducted performances from 1894). Conducted premières of many works. With Georges Marty, founded the Concerts de l'O. (1895-7). Music Director, O.C., 1914-19. Also an important teacher, especially at the Conservatoire, also at evening classes in poor districts of Paris. His own most successful opera was the *fantaisie lyrique, Eros* (1892). The *drame lyrique, Guernica* (1895), and *La Burgonde* (1898) were unsuccessful. He also wrote a *drame, Ramsès*, for the Egyptian T. at the 1900 Exhibition. His elder brother **Joseph Bernard** (*b* Toulouse, 15 Nov. 1859; *d* Paris, 18 Dec. 1924) was a conductor and composer, especially of operettas (*Le Mariage d'Yvette*, 1896).

Vienna (Ger., Wien). Capital of Austria. The first operas heard in Vienna were given during the reign of Ferdinand III – Bonacossi's *Ariadna abbandonata* (1641) and Cavalli's *Egisto* (1643). During the reign of Leopold I (1658-1705), opera became firmly established as a Court entertainment. The Emperor, himself a poet and a composer, contributed some of the music for the splendid production of Cesti's *Il pomo d'oro* (1666 or 1667), written for his marriage to the Infanta Margherita. To house the elaborate production, the architect Burnacini designed a theatre in the main square of the

Imperial Palace, the Hofburg, which was the predecessor of the Burgtheater. In Joseph I's reign (1705-11), Giuseppe Galli-Bibiena was appointed chief theatre architect; he built two theatres, where the splendid productions of the court composer, Johann Josef Fux, were staged. Charles VI continued the Royal patronage of opera, and increased the Court Orchestra from 107 to 134 musicians, but insisted that the production of opera should remain a Royal monopoly, despite the demand for a theatre for the ordinary people. This resulted in the building of the T. am Kärntnerthor in 1708.

The reign of Maria Theresa (1740-80) saw the erection of the Theater bei der Hofburg, which opened on 14 May 1748 with Gluck's *Semiramide riconosciuta*. In 1754 Gluck was appointed Court Kapellmeister, and between then and 1770 ten of his operas received their first performances in Vienna, including *Orfeo, Alceste*, and *Paride ed Elena*. After Gluck's departure for Paris the Burgtheater gradually yielded its position of Court Opera to the Theater am Kärntnerthor; the former, however, staged the premières of *Die Entführung aus dem Serail, Figaro, Così fan tutte*, and Cimarosa's *Il matrimonio segreto*. But Emanuel Schikaneder challenged the monopoly of the court theatres by producing *Die Zauberflöte*, for which he wrote the libretto, at his own Theater auf der Wieden in 1791. Meanwhile Salieri had been appointed Court conductor, and opera after opera by him was produced at the Kärntnerthor T. In 1801 Schikaneder moved to the new Theater an der Wien, where he produced *Fidelio* in 1805.

After the Napoleonic wars, Rossini became the most popular composer in Vienna; and in 1821 an Italian, *Barbaia, was appointed manager of the Kärntnerthor and the T. an der Wien. During his régime he produced the première of *Euryanthe* and introduced the subscription system for opera to Vienna. Between 1823 and 1842 only three now long-forgotten operas received Vienna premières; but in 1842 Donizetti was appointed Court composer and conductor, and wrote *Linda di Chamounix* and *Maria di Rohan* for the Kärntnerthor. Except for Lortzing's *Der Waffenschmied* (1846) and Flotow's *Martha* (1847), there were no important Vienna premières during the next 30 years or so. The Vienna audiences, however, made the acquaintance of Verdi and Wagner, the latter conducting the local première of *Lohengrin* in 1861, which he was hearing himself for the first time in a theatre.

It had been decided in 1857 to rebuild the centre of Vienna, and part of the plans included the building of a new opera house, the Oper am Ring, which was designed by Eduard von der Null and August Siccard von Siccardsburg, and which cost £600,000. Its seating capacity was 2,260, and it opened on 25 May 1869 with *Don Giovanni*. The first director was J. F. von Herbeck (1870-5), who mounted Goldmark's *Die Königin von Saba* and introduced Götz's *Der widerspänstigen Zähmung*, Schumann's *Genoveva*, and *Aida* to Vienna. He was succeeded by Franz Jauner (1875-80), who brought Richter to Vienna as music director, staged *The Ring* and *Samson et Dalila*, and assembled a company that included Materna, Wilt, Papier, Reichmann, and Scaria. William Jahn, who followed Jauner, was himself a conductor. He retained Richter, however, and from 1880 to 1896 they both directed the destinies of the theatre; the ensemble included Materna, Winkelmann, Reichmann, Scaria (the four creators of Kundry, Parsifal, Amfortas, and Gurnemanz at Bayreuth in 1881), Toni Schläger, Lola Beeth, Ernest van Dyck, and Marie Renard (the last two, superb Massenet interpreters who had created Werther and Charlotte (1892)).

From 1897 to 1907, the Opera enjoyed its greatest triumphs under the direction of Gustav *Mahler. He was succeeded by Weingartner (1907-11) and Hans Gregor (1911-18). The famous Mahler singers, including Gutheil-Schoder, Mildenburg, Kurz, Weidt, Kittel, Schmedes, Slezak, Maikl, Demuth, and Mayr, continued as members of the ensemble. Weingartner's régime was generally undistinguished; Gregor's was more successful, and included the first Viennese performances of *Rosenkavalier*, *Pelléas*, *La fanciulla del West*, *Parsifal*, works by Korngold and Pfitzner, and the engagements of Jeritza, Lotte Lehmann, and Piccaver.

In 1918 the Hofoper became the Staatsoper, and the music and artistic director was Franz Schalk, who held the position until 1929, for four of these years (1920-4) in association with Strauss. There were few world premières (*Die Frau ohne Schatten* was an exception), but many first Vienna performances, including the Puccini *Trittico*, *Turandot*, and *Boris*. Luise Helletsgruber, Felice Hüni-Mihacsek, Maria Rajdl, Elisabeth Schumann, Alfred Jerger, Emil Schipper, and Josef von Manowarda joined the company. Schalk was succeeded by Clemens Krauss (1929-34), Weingartner (1934-6), and Bruno Walter (1936-8). Angerer, Németh, Anday, Novotná, Kern, Ursuleac, Rünger, the Konetzni sisters, Olszewska, Wildbrunn, Kappel, Schwarz, Dermota, Kiepura, Tauber, Voelker, Schorr, Rode, and the conductors Karl Alwin and Josef Krips joined the company during these years. When the *Anschluss* came in 1938, many of the leading artists left Austria, including Walter, Lehmann, Schumann, Tauber, Piccaver, Schorr, Kipnis, and List.

After a period of artistic and administrative chaos, Karl Böhm was appointed director in 1943 and attempted to rebuild the ensemble. He began with a Strauss cycle, and produced *Capriccio;* the composer himself attended a performance of *Ariadne auf Naxos* on his eightieth birthday. On 30 June 1944 Böhm conducted *Götterdämmerung*, the last performance in the old house; in Sept. 1944 the house remained closed on the orders of Goering; and on 12 Mar. 1945, seven years to the day after Hitler had entered Vienna, the Opera House was destroyed by bombs.

Opera began again on 1 May 1945 at the Volksoper with *Figaro* conducted by Krips. In June Franz Salmhofer was appointed director, and in October the old Theater an der Wien was reopened with *Fidelio*. For the next ten years the company played in two houses. With Böhm, Krips, and Krauss as its chief conductors, and an ensemble that included Gueden, H. Konetzni, Jurinac, Reining, Schwarzkopf, Lipp, Seefried, Welitsch, Dermota, Lorenz, Hotter, Kunz, Klein, Patzak, Schoeffler, and Weber, it quickly regained its pre-1938 prestige and made guest appearances all over Europe. In 1954 Böhm was again appointed director to prepare for the reopening of the rebuilt opera house (cap. 2,200), which opened on 5 Nov. 1955 with *Fidelio*. Böhm resigned after much public criticism in March 1956 and was succeeded by Karajan, with Egon Seefehlner, who had been Böhm's deputy director, as Secretary General. Karajan concluded an agreement with La Scala, Milan, for joint productions by both houses, and leading Italian and Austrian/German singers found themselves under contract to both houses. Karajan gradually assumed the role of conductor-producer, and became the most powerful figure at the Vienna Opera since Mahler. The ensemble of the Karajan régime, which lasted until 1964, included, in addition to the leading Scala singers, Christa Ludwig, Birgit Nilsson, Lucia Popp, Leonie Rysanek, Walter Berry, and Eberhard Waechter. Seefehlner was succeeded by Albert Moser, who later moved to the Volksoper, and was succeeded by Walter Erich Schaefer. He was succeeded in the summer of 1963 by Egon Hilbert. Disagreements between Karajan and Hilbert, whose artistic aims were quite different, led to the former's resignation in May 1964. Hilbert remained sole director until his death in 1969, when he was succeeded by Heinrich Reif-Gintl, whose connections with the house went back to 1923. He appointed Horst Stein as First Conductor, a new position in Vienna. Reif-Gintl retired in June 1972 and was followed by Rudolf Gamsjäger, who had been General Secretary of the Musikverein since 1945. Gamsjäger's contract expired in 1976 and was not renewed, and he was succeeded by Seefehlner, one of whose first actions was to announce the return of Karajan and a Strauss festival for 1977.

The Volksoper, which housed performances by the State Opera during the period 1945-55, was opened in December 1898 in Währinger Strasse, a not very fashionable district of the city; it was originally known as the Kaiser-jubiläums Stadttheater and began life as a theatre. In 1903 Rainer Simons was appointed director and made plans to turn it into a popular opera theatre with the name of Volksoper. It opened as such on 15 Sept. 1904 with *Der Freischütz* under Zemlinsky; the same composers's *Preciosa* had been produced a year earlier. Rainer's directorship lasted until 1917 and included the premières of Kienzl's *Der Kuhreigen* and *Das Testament*, and the first performances in Vienna of *Manon Lescaut, Tosca, Salome, Königskinder*, and *Ariane et Barbe-Bleue*. Among the singers who began their careers in the house were Jeritza, Schipper, and Manowarda. Rainer was followed by Raoul Mader, who resigned in 1919; he was succeeded by Weingartner, who remained until 1924, giving the first Austrian performance of Holbrooke's *The Children of Don*, and revivals of *Masaniello* and *Louise*. Among the new singers was Ursuleac. Weingartner was followed by Stiedry, Hugo Gruder-Guntram, and Hermann Frischler in quick succession. This period included the première of Schoenberg's *Die glückliche Hand*, performances by the Prague National Theatre, the first Vienna *Arlecchino*, and the débuts of Anny Konetzni, Emanuel List, and Ludwig Weber.

The house was closed 1928-9, and reopened in November 1929 as the Neues Wiener Schauspielhaus. Between then and 1938 occasional operas and operettas were staged, including the famous Reinhardt production of *La Belle Hélène* in Korngold's arrangement in 1932. Maria Reining began her career there in 1930, as did Hilde Gueden, under the name of Hulda Gerin, in 1938 in Benatzky's *Herzen in Schnee*. In 1938-44 the theatre was renamed the Opernhaus der Stadt Wien and came under the direction of the bass Anton Baumann (1938-41) and Oskar Jölli (1941-4), with Robert Kolisko as chief conductor. A popular repertory was given and a number of well-known singers made their débuts in Vienna, including Welitsch, Gertrud Grob (later known as Grob-Prandl), Josef Gostic, and Alois Pernerstofer.

Although sharing the post-war seasons of the State Opera with the Theater an der Wien until 1955, the Volksoper began to build up its operetta repertory, and the Johann Strauss revival can be said to have begun there. Salmhofer was appointed director in 1955, with Marcel Prawy, who introduced the American musical to Vienna with *Kiss Me Kate*, as Dramaturg and chief producer. In September 1963 Salmhofer was succeeded by Moser, and during the next ten years the Volksoper expanded its repertory, giving premières of

works by Salmhofer, Stolz, and others, as well as revivals of *I masnadieri, Feuersnot, La Fille du régiment, Fra Diavolo*, and first local performances of *Il campiello, The Excursions of Mr Brouček, Mahagonny, Porgy and Bess*, and *West Side Story*. Karl Dönch was appointed director in September 1973; the house underwent extensive modernization, including the removal of what had become known as Hitler's box. (See also *Burgtheater, Kärnterthortheater, Theater auf der Wieden, Theater an der Wien*.)

Bibl: A. Bauer: *150 Jahre Theater an der Wien (1801-1951)* (1952); A. Bauer: *Das Theater in der Josefstadt ...* (1957); E. Pirchan and others: *300 Jahre Wiener Operntheater* (1953); H. Kralik: *The Vienna Opera* (1963); M. Prawy: *The Vienna Opera* (1970).

Vieuille, Félix (*b* Saugéon, 15 Oct. 1872; *d* Saugéon, 28 Feb. 1953). French bass. Studied Paris Conservatoire. Début Aix-les-Bains 1897, Leporello. Leading bass, Paris, O.C., 1898-1928, where he created Arkel (*Pelléas*), Father (*Louise*), Barbe-Bleue (*Ariane et Barbe-Bleue*), Sultan (*Mârouf*), Eumée (*Pénélope*), Macduff (Bloch's *Macbeth*), and many other parts. N.Y., Manhattan O., 1908-9. (R) His nephew **Jean Vieuille** (1902-1964) was bass-baritone at the O.C., 1928-58. (R)

Viglione-Borghese, Domenico (*b* Mondovì, 13 July 1877; *d* Milan, 26 Oct. 1957). Italian baritone. Studied Pesaro, then Milan with Cotogni. Début Lodi 1899, Herald (*Lohengrin*). Gave up career for commerce; while in San Francisco was recommended by Caruso to Tetrazzini, opposite whom he sang as Rigoletto, Enrico, Figaro, etc. Second Italian début Parma 1907, Amonasro. Established himself as the finest interpreter of Rance (*La fanciulla*) – Puccini called him 'Il principe degli sceriffi' ('the prince of sheriffs'). Had a repertory of more than 70 roles. Continued to sing until 1940. (R)

Vignas (orig. Viñas), **Francisco** (*b* Moyá, Barcelona, 27 Mar. 1863; *d* Barcelona, 14 July 1933). Spanish tenor. Studied Barcelona and Paris. Début Barcelona, 1888, Lohengrin. London 1893, Shaftesbury T., Turiddu in first perf. in England of *Cavalleria rusticana*; C.G., 1893, 1895, 1901 Fritz, Turiddu, Lohengrin, Tannhäuser, and Verdi roles; N.Y., Met., 1893-7. Last appearance, Madrid, 1917, after which taught in Barcelona. A powerful, heroic singer, who during his prime was thought to be the equal of *Gayarre. Married the mezzo soprano **Giulia Novelli** (1860-1932) who created Loretta in Franchetti's Asrael and Anacoana in his *Cristoforo Colombo*. (R)

Villabella, Miguel (*b* Bilbao, 20 Dec. 1892; *d* Paris, 28 June 1954). Spanish tenor. Voice discovered by Fugère; studied Paris with

Isnardon. Début Poitiers, 1918, Cavaradossi. Paris, O.C., 1920-40; O., from 1928. Retired from stage 1940 and taught in Paris. (R)

Village Romeo and Juliet, A. Opera in prologue and 3 acts by Delius; text by composer, after the story by Gottfried Keller in his *Leute von Seldwyla* (i, 1856; ii, 1874). Prod. (in German) Berlin, K.O., 21 Feb. 1907, with Lola Artôt de Padilla, Merkel, Egener, cond. Cassirer; London, C.G., 22 Feb. 1910, with Vincent, Terry, Hyde, Dearth, cond. Beecham; Washington, Kennedy Center, 26 Apr. 1972, with Wells, Stewart, Reardon, cond. Gallaway. The intermezzo before the final scene, *The Walk to the Paradise Garden,* is well known as a concert piece.

The theme is the love of two children of quarrelling farmers. Sali (treble, later ten.) and Vrenchen (girl sop., later sop.) leave their fathers, Manz (bar.) and Marti (bass), encouraged by the mysterious Dark Fiddler (bar.), and from the fair in the Paradise Garden wander to the river and die together in a barge that sinks as it floats downstream.

Another opera on *Leute von Seldwyla* is Zemlinsky's *Kleider machen leute* (1910).

Villi, Le. Opera in 1 act by Puccini, text by Fontana after a popular folk legend (and perhaps suggested by Adam's ballet Giselle). Prod. Milan T.d.V., 31 May 1884 with Caponetti, Antonio d'Andrade, cond. G. Panizza; Manchester 24 Sept. 1897, with Rousney, Beaumont, Lord. cond., N.Y. Met. 17 Dec. 1908 with Alda, Bonci, Amato, cond. Toscanini. Puccini's first opera.

Robert (ten.), betrothed to Anna (sop.), goes to seek his fortune. Plunging into vice, he forgets Anna, who dies brokenhearted. When Robert returns to find Anna, he is confronted by her ghost, and witches dance round him until he drops dead at their feet.

Another opera on the subject by Loder (*The Night Dancers,* 1846).

Vilnius. See *Lithuania.*

Vinay, Ramón (*b* Chillan, 31 Aug. 1912). Chilean tenor, orig. baritone. Studied Mexico. Début Mexico 1938, Count Luna; tenor début 1943, Don José. N.Y., C.C., 1945-6; 1948; Met., 1946-61; London, C.G., 1950, Otello with Scala Co., and in Wagner 1953-60. Bayreuth 1952-7. Coached as Otello by Toscanini, with whom he sang and recorded the role. His voice always retained its dark baritone-like colour; his acting was filled with pathos and nobility, and reached a standard rare among operatic artists. In 1962 he resumed baritone roles, singing Telramund at Bayreuth, and Iago, Flastaff, Scarpia, Bartolo (Rossini). Farewell Santiago, Sept. 1969, singing last act of *Otello;* continued to produce opera until 1972. (R)

Vinci, Leonardo (*b* Strongoli, 1690; *d* Naples, 27 May 1730). Italian composer. The success of his first opera, *Lo cecato fauzo* (Neapolitan dialect), was followed by similar pieces; later he turned to opera seria. Prompted by Farinelli's gifts, Vinci differentiated even more sharply the central section of the aria, and so elaborated the contrasts between sections as to influence the development of sonata form. He was the most vigorous of Scarlatti's successors.

Violetta. The Lady of the Camelias (sop.), heroine of Verdi's *La traviata.*

Vi ravviso. Count Rodolfo's (bass) aria in Act 1 of Bellini's *La sonnambula* in which he greets the village he last saw as a young man.

Visconti, Luchino (*b* Milan, 2 Nov. 1906; *d* Rome, 17 Mar. 1976). Italian producer and designer. Originally a film and theatre producer, turned to opera in 1954 after seeing Callas's *Norma.* Worked with Callas at Milan, Sc., producing for her *La vestale, La sonnambula, La traviata, Anna Bolena,* and *Iphigénie en Tauride.* Designed and produced C.G.'s *Don Carlos,* and Spoleto's *Macbeth, Duca d'Alba,* and *Manon Lescaut.* Returned to C.G., to produce *Il trovatore,* a 'black and white' *Traviata,* and an *art nouveau Rosenkavalier.* He accepted all grand opera's conventions and seized on opera's dramatic spirit, re-creating it in visual terms to match the music. His colours, lighting, and groupings all made for the most satisfying of stage pictures. There is an opera on his ancestor by Amadei (1869).

Vishnevskaya, Galina (Pavlovna) (*b* Leningrad, 25 Oct. 1926). Russian soprano. Studied Leningrad with V. Garina. Début Leningrad, 1950, Polenka (Strelnikov's *Kholopka*). Moscow, B., 1952-74. N.Y., Met., 1961-2, 1975, Aida, 1977 Tosca. Butterfly, Tosca; San Francisco, 1975, Lisa (*Queen of Spades*). London, C.G., 1962, Aida. Repertory also includes Leonore (*Fidelio*), Tatyana, Marguerite, Katerina Izmaylova. Married to the cellist Rostropovich, who began to conduct her performances from 1969. They left the U.S.S.R. in 1974. Has a rich, lyric-dramatic soprano voice and is a highly emotional and dramatic performer. (R)

Vision fugitive. Herod's (bar.) aria in Act 2 of Massenet's *Hérodiade,* in which he sings of the vision of Salome that haunts him day and night.

Vissi d'arte. Tosca's (sop.) aria in Act 2 of Puccini's opera, lamenting the unjustness of her fate.

Vitale, Edoardo (*b* Naples, 29 Nov. 1872; *d* Rome, 12 Dec. 1937). Italian conductor. Début aged 14 as an operetta conductor; studied Rome, Santa Cecilia. Conducted first Rome

Götterdämmerung 1897, and first Bologna *Walküre* same year, establishing himself as a Wagner conductor. Milan, Sc., 1908-10; conducted first performances in Italy of *Medée, Boris Godunov*, and *Elektra*. Rome, T.C., 1913-26 as music and artistic director. Conducted many premières, including Refice's *Cecilia*. He married the soprano Lina *Pasini. Their son, **Riccardo Vitale** (*b* Rome 1903) was the artistic director of Rome Opera, 1958-62.

Vivaldi, Antonio (*b* Venice, *c*1675; *d* Vienna, [buried 28] July 1741). Italian composer. Though esteemed principally as an instrumental composer, especially for his violin music, Vivaldi also wrote some 44 operas. Many of these were hastily assembled in a few days for a production which Vivaldi himself would organize and supervise down to the last detail. Some show the vivid illustrative gift that is familiar to concert-goers from *The Seasons* and other violin concertos – for instance, the storm in *La fida ninfa* (1732) is paralleled in the *Tempesta di mare* violin concerto (Op. 8, No. 5). But as the eminent Vivaldi scholar Marc Pincherle admits, 'there is probably more waste material in the operas, which the unlucky composer had to do. . . in haste and confusion'. A few arias, some bold strokes of characterization, a number of striking instrumental pictorial effects – these continue to impress the curious who investigate Vivaldi's operas. The works satisfied the elaborate and restricting conventions of Venetian opera, with its demand for mythological or historical plots deployed against elaborate scenic effects; and it is the passing of the culture this genre so intricately reflects that has proved fatal to Vivaldi's operas.
Bibl: W. Kolneder: *Antonio Vivaldi* (1970).

Voce di donna. La Cieca's (con.) prayer in Act 1 of Ponchielli's *La gioconda.*

Voelker, Franz (*b* Neu-Isenburg, 31 Mar. 1899; *d* Darmstadt, 5 Dec. 1965). German tenor. Engaged by Clemens Krauss for Frankfurt Opera without any proper vocal training; successful début 1926 as Florestan. Frankfurt 1926-35; Vienna, S.O., 1931-6, 1939-40, 1949-50; Berlin, S.O., 1933-43; Munich, 1936-7, 1945-52. London, C.G., 1934, 1937 Florestan, Siegmund; Bayreuth 1933-42 Siegmund, Lohengrin, Erik, Parsifal; Salzburg 1931-4, 1939, Belmonte, Florestan, Emperor, Menelaus, Max. One of the finest Siegmunds and Lohengrins of the inter-war years. Later in his career a successful Otello. After retiring from stage taught in Stuttgart; one of his pupils was his son, the baritone Georg Voelker. (R)

Vogl, Heinrich (*b* Au, 15 Jan. 1845; *d* Munich, 21 Apr. 1900). German tenor. Studied Munich with Lachner and Karl Jenke. Début Munich 1865, Max. Succeeded Schnorr von Carolsfeld

as leading Tristan. Created Loge and Siegmund. Bayreuth 1876-97, Loge, Siegmund, Parsifal, Tristan. Vienna 1884-5. London H.M.'s, 1882; first London Loge and Siegfried. N.Y. Met., 1890. Also composed an opera, *Der Fremdling*, prod. Munich 1899, in which he sang the leading role. Married the soprano **Therese Thoma** (*b* Tutzing, 12 Nov. 1845; *d* Munich 29 Sept. 1921), who for some years was the only Isolde in Germany. She created Sieglinde and was the first London Brünnhilde (1882).

Vogler, Georg Joseph (known as Abt, or Abbé, Vogler) (*b* Würzburg, 15 June 1749; *d* Darmstadt, 6 May 1814). German pianist, organist, composer, and teacher. His nine operas were generally unsuccessful (*La Kermesse* (1783) did not even complete its première), with the exception of the last of them, *Samori* (1804). Weber, who became his pupil, prepared the vocal score before the première.

Voi, che sapete. The canzonetta written and sung by Cherubino (sop.) to the Countess in Act 2 of Mozart's *Figaro.*

Voi lo sapete, O mamma. Santuzza's (sop.) account to Mamma Lucia of her betrayal by Turiddu in Mascagni's *Cavalleria rusticana.*

Voix Humaine, La (The Human Voice). *Tragédie lyrique* in one act by Poulenc; text by Cocteau. Prod. Paris, O.C., 6 Feb. 1959 with Duval, cond. Prêtre; N.Y. Carnegie Hall, 23 Feb. 1960 with Duval, cond. Prêtre; Edinburgh, King's T., 30 Aug. 1960 with Duval, cond. Pritchard. This is a 45 minute 'concerto' for soprano voice and orchestra – a one-sided telephone conversation between a jilted young woman and her lover.

Volo di Notte (Night Flight). Opera in 1 act by Dallapiccola; text by composer after St Exupéry's novel *Vol de Nuit* (1931). Prod. Florence, P., 18 May 1940, with Fiorenza Danco, Pauli, Melandri, Valentino, Guicciardi, cond. Previtali; Glasgow, King's T., by Scottish O., 29 May 1963, with Collier, Sarti, Andrew, Raymond Nilsson, Garrard, McCue, cond. Gibson; Stanford University 1 Mar. 1962. Successfully given in many European theatres since the war.
The opera is set in the control room of an airport. It tells of the anxieties and relationships of Rivière (bass-bar.), the flight controller, the radio-telephonist (ten.), and Sgra. Fabien (sop.), wife of one of the pilots, whose arrival on a night flight is anxiously awaited.

Voltaire (orig. François Marie Arouet) (*b* Paris, 24 Nov. 1694; *d* Paris, 30 May 1778). French writer. Operas on his works are as follows:
Gertrude: Grétry (1766).
Samson (1732): Rameau, with Voltaire as librettist, (unprod); Mercadante (1831); Champein (early 19th cent.).

Zaïre (1732); Nasolini (1797); Queiroz (1800); Portugal (1802); Federici (1803); Winter (1805); Lavina (1809); Garcia (1825); Bellini (1829); Gardini (1829); Mercadante (1831; libretto written for Bellini); Manni (1845); Ernst II of Saxe-Coburg-Gotha (1846); Lefèbvre (1887); La Nux (1890).

Alzire (1736); Zingarelli (1794); Portugal (1810); Verdi (1845).

Mahomet (1742): Rossini (1820).

Mérope (1743): Graun (1756, text by Frederick II); Zandomeneghi (1871).

Zadig (1748): Catrufo (1818); Dupérier (1938).

Sémiramis (1748): Bianchi (*La Vendetta di Nino*, 1790); Catel (1802); Rossini (1823).

L'Orphelin de la Chine (1755): Winter (*Tamerlan*, 1802).

Candide (1756): Knipper (comp. 1926-7); Bernstein (1958).

Tancrède (1760): Rossini (1813).

Ce qui plaît aux dames (1764): Duni (*La Fée Urgéle*, 1765); Schulz (1780-1); Fortia de Piles (1784); Arquier (1804); Catrufo (1805); Blangini (1812).

Olympie (1764): Kalkbrenner (1798); Mosel (1813); Spontini (1819).

Les Scythes (1767): Mayr (1800); Mercadante (1823).

Charlot (1767): Stuntz (*Heinrich IV zu Givry*, 1820).

L'Ingénu (1767): Grétry (*Le Huron*, 1768).

La Bégueule (1772): Monsigny (*La Belle Arsène*, 1773).

Also operas *Une Matinée de Voltaire* by Solié (1800) and *Voltaire* by F. Müller (before 1845).

La Pucelle: Langlé (1791).

Von. For names with this prefix, see following word.

Von der Osten. See *Plaschke von der Osten.*

Von Heute auf Morgen (From Day to Day), Opera in 1 act by Schoenberg; text by Max Blonda (composer's wife). Prod. Frankfurt 1 Feb. 1930 with Gentner-Fischer, Friedrich, Töplitz, Ziegler. cond. Steinberg; London, Royal Festival Hall, 13 Nov 1963 (concert perf.) with Harper, Schmidt, Schachtschneider, Olsen, cond. Dorati. Schoenberg's only comic opera (the first 12-note opera, and long the only comic one), it describes the wiles of a witty and determined woman in keeping her husband.

Vorobyov, Yakov (Stepanovich) (*b*? 1766; *d* St Petersburg, 19 June 1809). Russian bass. Studied St Petersburg with Marochetti, Sapienza, and Martín y Soler. Début 1787, quickly becoming leading Russian buffo bass. Appointed Inspector of the Imperial O., St Petersburg, 1803. His wife, **Avdota Vorobyova,** (d. 1836) was also a singer at St Petersburg from 1787. Their daughter, **Anna Yakovlevna Vorobyova-Petrova** (1816-1901), was a leading Russian contralto; she created Vanya in *A Life for the Tsar*. 1836 She married Osip *Petrov.

Vorspiel (*Ger* *prelude).

Votto, Antonino (*b* Piacenza, 30 Oct. 1896). Italian conductor. Studied Naples. Originally répétiteur at La Scala under Toscanini, then asst. cond. there 1924-9; regular cond. there 1948-70. London, C.G., 1924-5, 1933; Chicago 1960-1, 1970 (R)

Vroons, Frans (orig. Franciscus) (*b* Amsterdam, 28 Apr. 1911). Dutch tenor. Studied Amsterdam and Paris. Début Amsterdam 1938, Don Curzio (*Figaro*). Netherlands Opera 1941-71(assistant director, producer, director of opera school 1956-71). London, C.G., 1948-50, Don José; N.Y., City O.; San Francisco 1951. Pelléas, Hoffmann, and Grimes were among his best roles. Retired 1971; teaches in Amsterdam. (R)

Vyvyan, Jennifer (*b* Broadstairs, 13 Mar. 1925; *d* London, 28 Mar. 1974). English soprano. Studied R.A.M. and with Roy Henderson. Gly. Chorus. Jenny Diver in E.O.G.'s prod. of *The Beggar's Opera* (1947). Studied in Switzerland with Fernando Carpi 1950. London, S.W., 1952, Donna Anna, and Constanze; C.G., 1953, where she created Penelope Rich in Britten's *Gloriana*; Gly. 1954, Electra (*Idomeneo*). Also created Governess in Britten's *Turn of the Screw* (1954), Tytania in *A Midsummer Night's Dream* (1960), Mrs. Julian in *Owen Wingrave*, Countess Serendin in Williamson's *The Violins of St Jacques*, and various roles in his *Lady Peter's Journey*. An accomplished Handel singer. (R)

W

Wach' auf. The chorus sung in Hans Sachs's honour, to a modernization of words with which the historical Sachs greeted Luther and the Reformation, in Act 3, scene 2 of Wagner's *Die Meistersinger von Nürnberg.*

Wachtel, Theodor (*b* Hamburg, 10 Mar. 1823; *d* Frankfurt, 14 Nov. 1893). German tenor. Studied Hamburg with Julie Grandjean and Vienna with Eckhardt. Début Hamburg 1847. Schwerin 1848–51; Berlin 1863–8. London, C.G., 1862, 1864–5; 1870, and H.M.'s, 1879. U.S.A. 1871–2, 1875–6. First London Vasco da Gama and Alessandro Stradella. Particularly admired as Arnold and Manrico. One of his most famous roles in Germany was the title role in Adam's *Le Postillon de Longjumeau,* which he sang more than 1,000 times: he was particularly suited for this not only by his chest high C, but also his professional use of the whip (he had started life as a stable boy). His three sons, Theodor (1841–71), August, and Ferdinand were all tenors.

Wachter, Ernst (*b* Mulhouse, 19 May 1872; *d* Leipzig, Aug. 1931). German bass. Studied Leipzig with Goldberg. Début Dresden, 1894, Ferrando in *Trovatore;* Dresden, H., 1894–1912; Leipzig 1915–19; Bayreuth 1896–9, Fasolt, Hunding, Gurnemanz. (R)

Waechter, Eberhard (*b* Vienna, 8 July 1929). Austrian baritone. Studied Vienna with Elisabeth Rado. Début Vienna, V.O., 1953 Silvio; Vienna, S.O., since 1954. London, C.G., 1956, Count Almaviva; 1959, Amfortas, Renato. Salzburg since 1956. Bayreuth 1957–9, 1962–3, Amfortas, Wolfram. Chicago and Dallas 1960; N.Y., Met., 1961. One of the most polished artists of the 1950s and 1960s. (R)

Waffenschmied, Der (The Armourer). Opera in 3 acts by Lortzing; text by composer, after Ziegler's *Liebhaber und Nebenbuhler in einer Person* (1790). Prod. Vienna, W., 31 May 1846; Milwaukee 7 Dec. 1853.

In Worms, in the 16th century, the Graf von Liebenau (bar.) has fallen in love with Marie (sop.), daughter of the armourer Stadinger (bass). He woos her both in his own person and disguised as an apprentice smith, Conrad. When she tells the Count that she loves Conrad, he is triumphant until rejected in both guises by Stadinger, who wants her to marry the Count's servant Georg (ten.). When Georg refuses, Marie is given to Conrad, and all is revealed.

Other operas on the subject are by Kauer (1798) and Weigl (*Il rivale di se stesso,* 1808).

Wagner, Albert (*b* Leipzig, 2 Mar. 1799; *d* Berlin, 31 Oct. 1874). German singer and producer. Elder brother of Richard. Appeared in opera in Würzburg and Bernburg and for a period produced opera in Berlin.

Wagner, Cosima (*b* Bellaggio, 24 Dec. 1837; *d* Bayreuth, 1 Apr. 1930). Daughter of Liszt; married first Hans von Bülow (1857) and then Wagner (1870), with whom she worked to establish Bayreuth. After Wagner's death she maintained an autocratic rule over Bayreuth until her own death.
Bibl: R. du Moulin Eckart: *Cosima Wagner* (2 vols., 1929, 1931).

Wagner (Jachmann), **Johanna** (*b* Seelze, nr Hanover, 13 Oct. 1826; *d* Würzburg, 16 Oct. 1894). German soprano. Adopted niece of Richard Wagner. Début, Bällenstadt 1841, Urbain. Naumburg, 1843; Dresden 1844, created Elisabeth in *Tannhäuser,* 1845. Studied Paris with Bordogni and Viardot, 1846–8. Berlin 1850–61, after which she lost her singing voice but followed a successful career on the straight stage. Her voice returned in the 1870s and she sang the alto part in the performance of the Choral Symphony at Bayreuth in 1872, and Schwertleite and 1st Norn in the first Bayreuth *Ring,* 1876. Engaged for C.G., 1852, but prevented from appearing through a law-suit brought by Lumley. H.M.'s 1856, scoring great success as Tancredi, Lucrezia Borgia, and Romeo (Bellini). Taught at Munich 1882–4. Her son Hans Jachmann wrote *Wagner and his first Elisabeth* (1926); according to him, Brünnhilde was written for her.

Wagner, (Wilhelm) **Richard** (*b* Leipzig, 22 May 1813; *d* Venice, 13 Feb. 1883). German composer. Wagner's early musical studies were casual and frequently disrupted. His first important influences were the music of Beethoven and the singing of Wilhelmine Schröder-Devrient, but his serious training as a composer dates from 1828; in 1831 he enrolled as a music student at Leipzig University. Various works date from this period, including the Symphony in C. In 1833 he became chorus master at Würzburg, where his theatrical experience was founded and where he began work on *Die Feen* (prod. 1888). He moved to Magdeburg as conductor in 1834, and here his next opera, *Das Liebesverbot,* was unsuccessfully given in 1836. In this year he married Minna Planer, who arranged his transfer to Königsberg. He remained for a year before moving to Riga. *Rienzi* was written at Riga, whence Wagner, in debt not for the first time, fled to London. Going on to Paris, he completed *Rienzi,* began work on the libretto of *Der fliegende Holländer,* and became acquainted with the stories of Lohengrin and Tannhäuser. He moved to Dresden in 1842 for the production there of *Rienzi*. In the same year he visited Berlin to investigate chances of a production of *Holländer*, which took place in 1843.

Die Feen and *Das Liebesverbot* have seldom been revived. They show little of Wagner's mature genius, though their nature clearly marks him as a committed composer of German opera in the Weber-Marschner succession. *Rienzi* is more ambitious in a Meyerbeer manner; but even *Der fliegende Holländer*, the first of his operas to stay in the repertory, retains many Weberian touches alongside passages that indicate an altogether larger mind. It is also notable for the introduction of an important Romantic *idée fixe* that came to possess Wagner, Redemption through Love.

Tannhäuser was completed in the spring of 1845 (when Wagner began work on an unfinished opera, *Die Sarazenin*, and on the text of *Meistersinger*), and performed with some success that October. It marks an advance over *Holländer*: the characterization is hardly subtler, but there is a major increase in the continuity of thought over a larger time-span. There are also more imposing effects, finer choruses and arias, richer orchestration, and a consistency of imagination that makes such lapses from it as the hymn-tune religiosity of the pilgrims seem secondary. A later revision (1861) for the Paris production commanded by the Emperor Napoleon extended the opening Bacchanale and the subsequent scene for Venus and Tannhaüser — very much in the light of *Tristan*, then behind Wagner.

1848 found Wagner in the middle of revolutionary activities; in the following year a warrant was out for his arrest, and he fled to Zürich. But banishment increased his fame, which Liszt and others were busy fanning; meanwhile he occupied his time chiefly with prose works. In 1850 Liszt celebrated Goethe's anniversary with the première of *Lohengrin* at Weimar. Less evenly inspired than *Tannhaüser*, it rises at its best to far greater heights. If much of Act 1 is beneath *Tannhäuser*, the conception of Ortrud and Telramund and the opening of Act 2 are considerably superior, while the Grail music of the opening can rank with Wagner's finest ideas. *Lohengrin* is still, however, a singers' work, and this exercises on its design an influence which it was part of Wagner's life's work to shake off from opera.

This manner survived as far as sketches for *Siegfrieds Tod*, the first stage in the long, complex planning of *Der Ring des Nibelungen*, upon which Wagner was now engaged. This was commissioned from Weimar in 1851, when Wagner announced his wish to write a prefatory work, *Der junge Siegfried*; but later that year he was thinking in terms of three dramas with a 3-act *Vorspiel*. This was too

much for Liszt's resources at Weimar, but Wagner went ahead to outline and write much of the text for *Der Ring* as we now know it in 1852.

In 1853 Liszt produced *Holländer* at Weimar and there was a successful Wagner Festival in Zürich; his growing fame also led to an invitation to London, where Queen Victoria and the Prince Consort defied *The Times* by admiring selections from *Lohengrin* and *Tannhäuser*. Back in Zürich, he worked on *Siegfried* and gave some thought to *Tristan*, moving in 1857 to a quieter house provided by his friends, the Wesendonk family. Wagner's entanglement with Frau Wesendonk is celebrated in five songs to her poems, influenced by the current work on *Tristan*. It is not possible to summarize his many marital and financial difficulties; the tide of his affairs reached its lowest ebb in Paris in 1861, where *Tannhäuser* was forced off the stage, and in the two years that followed.

Finally, rescue came from King Ludwig II of Bavaria, a fervent admirer of Wagner and soon to be his greatest benefactor. Meanwhile the unhappy marriage to Minna had disintegrated. She died in 1860, but Wagner had already taken up with Liszt's daughter (and Hans von Bülow's wife), Cosima.

Tristan und Isolde was produced in Munich in 1865, and poorly received. Its stature now, a century later, is unquestioned. Music was never the same again after this pressing of chromaticism to and beyond the limits of tonality. Wagner's Schopenhauerian studies influence its pessimistic philosophy, and musical continuity is achieved to a pitch that led the opera to be called one long love-duet. The orchestra assumes new prominence and eloquence, in part due to the development of **Leitmotiv* into a fully expressive language. There is in the treatment of the hero and heroine not so much straightforward characterization as the discovery of an infinite number of psychological undertones in their situation. Wagner here reveals himself as a poet of the subconscious.

Exiled for political reasons from Munich, Wagner found his way to Triebschen, near Lucerne. In his six years here, he completed *Meistersinger, Siegfried,* and most of *Götterdämmerung*. In 1870 he and Cosima were married. Ludwig had lost faith in Wagner personally over Cosima, but remained loyal to him as an artist.

In 1868 *Die Meistersinger von Nürnberg* was produced in Munich. Wagner here celebrates the virtues of a bourgeois normality to which his whole life ran counter. There is personal malice in the portrait of the town-clerk Beckmesser, enemy of the new and strange in art (a celebrated tilt at the anti-Wagnerian critic Hanslick); but the central figure is neither he nor the lovers Walther and Eva, but the wise cobbler-poet Hans Sachs. The score is less neurotically intense, no less rich than that of *Tristan,* and the discursive method Wagner had perfected proves adaptable to this new purpose. There are more set pieces than in *Tristan,* but they scarcely halt the action. And in the provincial town, its guilds and its quarrels, Wagner finds his most comforting vein of poetry. *Meistersinger* is an opera that persuades the listener of the goodness not of gods or heroes or ideals, but simple man. Not only does the work dramatize the contest between the old and the new in art, in the persons of the Mastersingers challenged in their loyalties by Walther: it also declares the possibility of an ordered society being maintained by the intelligent action, and personal sacrifice, of the good man, as Sachs renounces his own hopes in favour of the achievement of the greater good.

Das Rheingold followed at Munich in 1869; but Ludwig was entitled to this and the whole cycle. A long-cherished plan for a festival theatre was now realized through his generosity. In 1871 the Wagners settled near *Bayreuth for the purpose; and in the following April the foundation stone was laid. Liszt, visiting Bayreuth, was excited by the sketches of *Parsifal.* Wagner moved to a new house, 'Wahnfried', provided by the King, and elaborate preparations for the festival culminated in the opening of the theatre in 1876 with the complete *Der Ring des Nibelungen* – which thus also became the first major artistic enterprise of a united Germany.

The fact that the composition of *Der Ring* was spread over more than 20 years colours it surprisingly little, so constant was Wagner's vision. His *Leitmotiv* system advances markedly from simple tags in *Rheingold* to a dense, expressive network of allusions in *Götterdämmerung* that speaks directly to the sensibilities. It is a unified work of art (the last successful attempt at a great dramatic cycle), a cosmic drama of vast ambition and hardly less achievement. Like so much that is concerned with Wagner, it is too huge, too subtle and rich in its statements and implications, to be summarized. Yet it is in a sense a summary of many disparate strands in the German experience, a residue of mythic and national feeling that also has a vast amount for the rest of the world. Such a scheme as that of *Der Ring* demands a versatility of invention of which Wagner was now fully master. He genuinely achieves his aim of 'unending melody'; yet it is the weaving of small fragments of *Leitmotiv* into an elaborate pattern that characterizes the score. The harmony, less advanced than *Tristan's,* has a fluidity that never loses its sense of expressive direction. This, he believed, was the road to the future; but it was more truly the end of a road.

Wagner had now achieved much of the impossible he set out to do. He was at last comfortably provided for, famous, and in control of a theatre built as temple for his art, which he envisaged as a rite of profound social value in which all men could share. The sacred nature of Bayreuth was further emphasized by the provision that *Parsifal* should never be staged elsewhere.

Certainly it is in the ritual atmosphere which Bayreuth still retains that *Parsifal* continues to make its best effect. The work is described as a 'sacred festival drama', and its religious atmosphere has caused distress among both sincere Christians who deplored Wagner's own habits and beliefs, and non-believers who are stifled by its odour of sanctity. Wagner, it is true, conceived Montsalvat in terms closer to the theatre he knew than the organized religious life he did not. But though the work uses the Christian metaphor, including the representation of Holy Communion, it is not strictly a Christian work, so much as about the importance and value for man of seeking and achieving a structure of belief. *Parsifal* manages to enshrine an extraordinary complex of sexual and spiritual truths, not least in the concept of Kundry as an ambiguous Virgin-Venus figure, temptress and redemptress together. *Parsifal* (1882) is even further advanced harmonically than *Tristan,* taking its musical language well into Schoenbergian territory.

In the autumn of 1882, Wagner and his family left for Venice. Here he died the following February. His body was taken to Bayreuth and buried in the garden of Wahnfried. Cosima survived him, an autocrat in her husband's artistic kingdom, until 1930, when she was laid beside him.

Bibl: E. Newman: *The Life of Richard Wagner* (4 vols., 1933–47); C. von Westernhagen: *Richard Wagner* (1956); R. Wagner: *My Life* (1911); C. Wagner: *Die Tagebücher* (Vol. 1, 1976, trans. 1978).

Wagner, Siegfried (*b* Triebschen, nr Lucerne, 6 June 1869; *d* Bayreuth, 4 Aug. 1930). German composer and conductor. Son of Richard Wagner and Cosima von Bülow. Studied with Humperdinck and Kniese. Conducted at Bayreuth and elsewhere in Germany from 1896. Artistic director, Bayreuth 1908–30, producer from 1901. Twelve of his 15 operas were staged, *Der Bärenhäuter* (1899), *Der Kobold* (Hamburg 1904), and *Der Schmied von Marienburg* (Rostock 1923) being the most successful. He married Winifred Williams (*b* England, 1894). (R)

Wagner, Wieland (*b* Bayreuth, 5 Jan. 1917; *d* Munich, 17 Oct. 1966). German producer and designer. Son of above and grandson of Richard. Studied privately for a short period with Roller in 1934. His first designs were for his father's opera *Der Bärenhäuter,* Lübeck 1936; this was followed by designs for *Parsifal* at Bayreuth 1937, and for two more of his father's operas in Antwerp and Düsseldorf 1937 and 1938. Exempted from military service by Hitler on the grounds that he was to 'preserve and perpetuate the family name', Wieland designed the 1943 Bayreuth *Meistersinger* and produced *Walküre* and *Siegfried* in Nuremberg. Produced complete *Ring*, *Freischütz*, and Siegfried's *An allem ist Hütchen schuld* at Altenburg, 1943–4. Studied Wagner scores with Kurt Overhoff at Strauss's home in Garmisch, 1947.

Cleared by the de-Nazification court, he assumed, with his brother Wolfgang, the artistic and business administration of postwar Bayreuth. Together they completely revolutionized the style of Wagner production, abandoning pageantry and naturalism in favour of a more abstract approach designed to emphasize the works' mythic characteristics. Less use was accordingly made of scenery, more of suggestive (and masterly) lighting. Wieland also produced regularly in Stuttgart, and occasionally in other German cities. His productions of *Fidelio, Carmen, Orphée,* and *Aida* aroused as much controversy as those of his grandfather's operas; his productions of *Salome, Elektra, Wozzeck,* and *Lulu,* however (generally with Anja Silja, with whom he had made a close artistic and personal relationship) were enthusiastically received. Wieland's style in his own words was to 'replace the production ideas of a century ago, now grown sterile, by a creative intellectual approach which goes back to the origins of the work itself. Every new production is a step on the way to an unknown goal.'
Bibl: G. Skelton: *Wieland Wagner, The Positive Sceptic* (1971).

Wagner, Wolfgang (*b* Bayreuth, 30 Aug. 1919). German producer, designer, and administrator. Brother of above. Worked as musical assistant Bayreuth 1942. Responsible for the business and administration side of the Bayreuth Festivals from 1951. Produced and designed all the works in the Bayreuth canon at least once.

Wagner-Régeny, Rudolf (*b* Szász-Régen, 28 Aug. 1903; *d* Berlin, 18 Sept. 1969). Hungarian, later German, composer. His operas include *Der Günstling* (Dresden 1935), *Die Bürger von Calais* (Berlin 1939), and *Johanna Balk* (Vienna 1941), all with librettos by Neher; *Prometheus,* Kassel 1959; *Dar Bergwerk zu Falun,* Salzburg 1961.

Wagner Tuba. An instrument invented by Wagner to bridge the gap between the horns, which he regarded as lyrical and romantic, and the trombones, which he regarded as solemn, dignified, and heroic. The tone is brusquer than that of either instrument, with a certain dark

masculinity that admirably suits the music of Hunding in *The Ring.* The quartet used in *The Ring* consists of two tenors in B♭ and two basses in F. They are played by the 5th-8th horns.

Wagner-Vereeniging. See *Amsterdam.*

Wahn! Wahn! Hans Sachs's (bar.) monologue at the beginning of Act 3 of Wagner's *Meistersinger,* in which he muses on the follies of the world.

Wakhevitch, Georges (orig. Georgy Vakhevich) (*b* Odessa, 18 Aug. 1897). Russian designer. Studied Paris. Has worked in most leading European houses. London, C.G., *Boris* (1949), and subsequently *Hoffmann, Otello, Carmélites.* His settings are rich in colour, solid, and traditional.

Waldmann, Maria (*b* Vienna, 1842; *d* Ferrara, 6 Nov. 1920). Austrian mezzo-soprano. Studied Vienna with Passy-Cornet and Milan with Lamperti. Début Pressburg, 1865, Pierotto (*Linda di Chamounix*). After engagements in Wiesbaden, Amsterdam, and Trieste, engaged for Moscow, Italian O., 1869-70. Milan, Sc., 1871-2, Maffeo Orsini, Preziosilla, Aennchen, Zerlina, and Amneris in first Italian *Aida.* Cairo 1873-6. One of Verdi's preferred singers; sang in the first and subsequent performances of his Requiem (London 1875). Retired from stage in 1876 to marry Count Galeazzo Massari. Her correspondence with Verdi and his wife continued until the composer's death and is published in the *Carteggi Verdiani.*

Walker, Edyth (*b* Hopewell, N.Y., 27 Mar. 1867; *d* New York, 19 Feb. 1950). American mezzo-soprano. Studied Dresden with Orgeni, Eichenberger, and Von Schreiner; Berlin with Brandt. Début Berlin, 1894, Fidès. Vienna 1895-1903. N.Y., Met., 1903-6, Hamburg 1906-12; Munich 1912-15. London, C.G., 1900, 1908, 1910 (first London Elektra). Bayreuth, 1908, Kundry and Ortrud. Also much admired as Isolde. Farewell, 1918, Elberfeld, in *Ring.* After retiring she taught at the American Conservatory at Fontainebleau, 1933-6, and then in New York, where her pupils included Irene Dalis and Blanche Thebom. (R)

Walküre, Die. See *Ring des Nibelungen, Der.*

Wallace, Ian (*b* London, 10 July 1919). English bass. Début London, Cambridge T., 1946, Schaunard (*Bohème*). New London Opera Co., 1946-9; Glyndebourne 1948-56, also at S.W. and with the E.O.G. and the London Opera Society; Parma and Venice. S.W. 1960, Don Magnifico. Established himself as one of the leading English buffo singers; his most successful roles are Bartolo and Don Magnifico. (R)
Bibl: I. Wallace: *Promise Me You'll Sing Mud* (1975).

Wallace, (William) **Vincent** (*b* Waterford, 11 Mar. 1812; *d* Vieuzos, 12 Oct. 1865). Irish composer. Studied with his father, a bandmaster, and with W. S. Conran and Haydn Corri. Played in the Theatre Royal, Dublin, then emigrated to Tasmania. Later moved to Australia and made a name as a violin virtuoso. Many adventurous travels then ensued, including visits to India and Chile. In Mexico City in 1841 he conducted the Italian opera season, moving on to New York to give concerts and then returning by way of Europe to England. Soon after his return he wrote *Maritana* (1845), to a text by Edward Fitzball, which was an immediate success. Wallace's travels gave him a musical sophistication: he was able to introduce into *Maritana* effects ranging from the direct use of gipsy music and Spanish colouring to a feeling for the style of Meyerbeer and Italian opera. *Maritana* originally ran for 50 nights, and was quickly taken up by European and American theatres.

His next opera, *Matilda of Hungary* (1847), was a failure; its successor, in a manner closer to grand opera than *Maritana*, was *Lurline*, commissioned for Paris in 1848 and announced by C.G., but not given in London until 1860. Though it did not match the success of *Maritana*, *Lurline* won a considerable following, especially for its grandiose scenes and vigorous effects in a manner then unknown in English opera. After many more travels, concluded in time for *Lurline*'s London production, Wallace settled in London and wrote three more ambitious grand operas, *The Amber Witch* (1861), *Love's Triumph* (1862), and *The Desert Flower* (1864): these were unsuccessful, and others, and some operettas, were not performed.

Bibl: A. Pougin: *William Vincent Wallace* (1866).

Wallberg, Heinz (*b* Herringen, 16 Mar. 1923). German conductor. Studied Dortmund and Cologne. Engagements in Münster, Trier, Hagen, and Hamburg; music director Augsburg 1954. Bremen 1955-61; Wiesbaden 1961-74. Guest appearances elsewhere in Europe, including London C.G., 1962, *Rosenkavalier*. (R)

Wallerstein, Lothar (*b* Prague, 6 Nov. 1882; *d* New Orleans, 13 Nov. 1949). Czech, later American, conductor and producer. Répétiteur Dresden 1909; cond. and prod. Poznań 1910-14. Chief prod. Breslau 1918-22. Duisberg 1922-4; Frankfurt 1924-6; Vienna 1927-38, where he produced 65 operas including *Wozzeck*; Salzburg Festivals 1926-37. Guest producer at Milan, Sc., and Buenos Aires, Colón. Founded Opera School in The Hague 1939; joined N.Y., Met., 1941, remaining there until 1946 when he returned to Europe. Edited versions of *Idomeneo, Don Carlos,* and other operas.

Wallmann, Margherita (*b* Vienna, 22 June 1904). Austrian producer. Began career as ballet dancer in Munich and Vienna. Choreographer Salzburg Festival, 1931-7. Forced to give up dancing after an accident. Invited by Bruno Walter to produce *Orfeo* at Salzburg in 1933. Spent war years in U.S.A. and Argentina, working at Buenos Aires, C. Has produced opera at the world's leading opera house, and since 1952 has established herself in Italy (especially at Sc.), where her many new productions have included world premières of Milhaud's *David,* Poulenc's *Dialogues des Carmélites,* Pizzetti's *Assassinio nella cattedrale* and *Il calzare d'argento,* the first performances in Italy of Strauss's *Liebe der Danae* and Berlioz's *Les Troyens,* as well as revivals of *Norma, Medée, Alceste,* and many other works. London, C.G., *Aida* 1957, *Carmélites* 1958. Paris, O., 1958 *Ballo in maschera, Troyens* and *Don Carlos.* Chicago, 1959 *Carmen*; N.Y. Met., 1964 *Lucia di Lammermoor.* Her productions, generally traditional, are marked by fluidity of movement and excellent handling of crowd scenes.

Bibl: M. Wallmann: *Les balcons du ciel* (1976).

Wally, La. Opera in 4 acts by Catalani; text by Illica, after Wilhelmine von Hillern's novel *Die Geyer-Wally* (1875, dram. 1880). Prod. Milan, Sc., 20 Jan. 1892, with Darclée (to whom the score is dedicated), Stehle, Guerrini, Suagnes, Pessina, cond. Mascheroni; N.Y., Met., 6 Jan. 1909, with Destinn, L'Huilier, Martin, Amato, Rossi, cond. Toscanini; Manchester 27 Mar. 1919.

Catalani's last, and best, opera describes how La Wally (sop.) is drawn still closer to her lover Hagenbach (ten.) when her suitor Gellner (bar.) tries to kill him; the lovers perish in an avalanche. Toscanini admired the opera so much that he named his daughter Wally.

Walter (orig. Schlesinger), **Bruno** (*b* Berlin, 15 Sept. 1876; *d* Los Angeles, 17 Feb. 1962). German, later American, conductor. Studied Berlin, with Ehrlich, Bussler, and Radeke. Répétiteur Cologne 1893-4, where he conducted his first opera, *Der Waffenschmied.* Conductor Hamburg 1894-6; Breslau 1896-7; Pressburg 1897-8; Riga 1899-1900; Berlin 1900-1; Vienna 1901-12 (first as Mahler's assistant). Generalmusikdirector Munich 1913-22; conducted premières of Korngold's *Violanta* and *Der Ring des Polykrates,* Pfitzner's *Palestrina,* and Schreker's *Das Spielwerk.* Berlin, Stä, O., 1925-9; Generalmusikdirektor Vienna 1936-8. Salzburg 1922-37. London, C.G., 1910 (*The Wreckers*) and 1924-31 (Wagner, Strauss, and Mozart). N.Y., Met., 1941-6, 1951, 1955-7, 1958-9. Also in Milan, Florence, Chicago. One of the great opera conductors of this century; his readings were characterized by a warmly humane, lyrical approach. (R)

Bibl: B. Walter: *Theme and Variations* (1946).

Walters, Jess (*b* New York, 1906). American baritone. Studied New York with Giuffrida. Début N.Y., New Opera Co., 1941, Macbeth. After appearances with various American companies, including New Orleans and the City Center, engaged London. C.G., 1947 and from 1948 to 1959 a leading baritone. Netherlands Opera 1960-4. (R)

Walther von Stolzing. A Franconian knight (ten.), hero of Wagner's *Die Meistersinger von Nürnberg.*

Walton, (Sir) **William** (Turner) (*b* Oldham, 29 Mar. 1902). English composer. Walton did not turn to opera until *Troilus and Cressida* (1954), a work cast in traditional Romantic opera vein, setting the story of Chaucer's lovers. It includes some lively characterization of Cressida's uncle, Pandarus. This was followed by the 1-act *The Bear* (1967), a vigorous Romantic comedy after Chekhov using only three characters.

Waltz, Gustavus (*b* ?; *d* ? London, *c*1753). German bass singer and cook. He is said to have served Handel in both capacities, appearing, for instance, as Polypheme in *Acis and Galatea* in 1732. Handel's celebrated comment that Gluck knew 'no more of contrapunta than my cook Waltz' has some of its sting drawn if we remember that Waltz must have been a fine musician.

Wanderer, The. The guise in which Wotan (bass-bar.) appears in Wagner's *Siegfried.*

Wandering Scholar, The. Chamber opera in 1 act by Holst; text by Clifford Bax, founded on an incident in Helen Waddell's *The Wandering Scholars* (1928). Originally entitled *The Tale of the Wandering Scholar*; rev. Britten (1951), edited Britten and Imogen Holst (1968). Prod. Liverpool, David Lewis T., 31 Jan. 1934, with Pryce, Eastwood, Maher, J. Ward, cond. Wallace; Toronto, Royal Conservatoire of Music, 25 Mar. 1966; N.Y., State Univ., 1 Aug. 1968.

Father Philippe (bass) visits Alison (sop.) in the absence of her husband Louis (bar.), but is interrupted by the Scholar, Pierre (ten.). They refuse him food and drink and he leaves, but returns with Louis, and tells him a pointed tale that leads to the discovery of unexpected food and drink and then the priest hidden under a heap of straw.

Another opera on the subject is by Bell (1935).

War and Peace. Opera in 5 acts (1st version: 13 scenes with choral prologue; 2nd version: 11 scenes) by Prokofiev; text by composer and M. Mendelson-Prokofieva, after Tolstoy's novel (1869). Prod. (1st version) Leningrad, Maly T., 12 June 1946, with Lavrova, Petrov, Chishko, Zhuravlenko, Andrukovich, Golovina, Butyagin, cond. Samosud; (2nd version) Leningrad, Maly T., 31 Mar. 1955, with Lavrova, Shaposhnikov, Glebov, Matusov, Andrukovich, Golovina, Butyagin, Modestov, cond. Grikurov; London, Col., 11 Oct. 1972, with Barstow, McDonnell, Collins, Shilling, Woollam, Brecknock, Bailey, Myers, cond. Lloyd-Jones; U.S., N.B.C. TV, 13 Jan. 1957; Boston, 8 May 1974, with Saunders, Neill, Carlson, Gramm, cond. Caldwell. Chosen to open the Sydney O.H., 5 Aug. 1974. The long, episodic score has undergone various revisions, but was finally cast in 13 scenes, the first seven concentrating on Peace, the last six on War. Choosing dramatic key moments from Tolstoy with great skill, the composer manages to reflect private and public destinies against a background of Russia under threat.

Ward, David (*b* Dumbarton, 3 July, 1922). Scottish bass. Studied London R.C.M. with Clive Carey and Munich with Hotter. Joined Sadler's Wells chorus 1952; first solo role Old Bard in *Immortal Hour,* 1953. Principal bass S.W., 1953-9; created Hardy in Berkeley's *Nelson*; Bluebeard in first S.W. *Duke Bluebeard's Castle* and Count Walter in first S.W. *Luisa Miller.* His first Dutchman in 1958 indicated that the Wagner repertory was to be his speciality; London, C.G., since 1960 in major Wagner and Verdi roles, Morosus in first British *Schweigsame Frau,* Golaud, Ivan Khovansky, etc. Bayreuth 1960-2, Fasolt, Titurel, Nightwatchman. Guest appearances U.S.A., Germany, Italy, and Buenos Aires, where in 1957 he sang Wotan in five *Ring* cycles. Has a bass voice of beautiful quality and sensitivity. (R)

Warot, Victor (Alexandre Jean) (*b* Verviers, 18 Sept. 1834; *d* Bois-Colombe, Apr. 1906). Belgian tenor. Studied with his father and in Paris with Giulio Alary. Début Paris, O.C., 1858 in Limnander de Nieuwenhove's *Les Monténégrins.* Paris, O., 1861-8; Brussels, M., 1868-9, 1870-4, the first Brussels Erik and Tannhäuser. Continued to sing in France and Belgium until 1888, after which he taught at the Paris Conservatoire: here his pupils included Bréval, Clément, Gautier, Hatto, and Pacary. Wrote *Brévaire du chanteur,* 1901.

Warren (orig. Warenoff), **Leonard** (*b* New York, 21 Apr. 1911; *d* New York, 4 Mar. 1960). American baritone. Studied N.Y. with Sidney Dietsch, Milan with Picozzi, and again N.Y. with De Luca. Won N.Y. Met. Auditions of Air, 1938. Début N.Y., Met., 1939, Paolo (*Boccanegra*); remained member of company until his death, and became leading Verdi baritone of his day. Milan, Sc., 1953 Rigoletto and Iago; toured U.S.S.R. 1958; also sang with success in Chicago, San Francisco, Buenos Aires, and Mexico. Died on stage of Met. during perf. of *Forza del destino.* (R)

Warsaw (Pol., Warszawa). Capital of Poland. In 1628 an Italian opera *Galatea* (by Sante Orlandi?) was given at Court on the initiative of Prince Władysław Zygmunt. When he was crowned Władysław IV, he formed an Italian company (1634-48) with Margherita Cattaneo as prima donna and including a few young Poles. In 1637 the Mantuan architect Bartolomeo Bolzoni built a provisional wooden theatre (cap. 1,000); and for his wedding celebrations Władysław built a permanent theatre in the castle (1637). When Augustus II was crowned in 1697, he formed a company under J. C. Schmidt and Jacek Różycki; in 1700 a French company under Deschallières spent five days in the city. Other companies made visits. In 1725 the Operalnia (Opera T.) was opened. Augustus III, crowned in 1733, provided large subsidies, and twice-weekly performances were given by a company with an orchestra of over 100.

A more systematic encouragement of opera came with the reign (1764-95) of Stanisław August Poniatowski. In 1765 the first public theatre was opened, with Karol Tomatis (1739-1806) as director: under him French and Italian companies played until 1767. In 1772 the Operalnia was demolished. In 1772 a company under Joseph Kurtz-Bernardon performed in the Radziwiłł Palace; the directorship passed in 1776 to Franciszek Ryx (1732-99), who gave the first opera seria with Italian singers and in 1778 gave the first Polish opera, *Nędza Uszczęśliwiona* (Sorrow Turned to Joy) by Macfej Kamieński (1734-1821). The T. Narodowy (National T.) was opened in 1779 (reconstructed 1791, cap. *c* 800) with *Le Tonnelier* (sung in Polish) by Nicolas-Médard Audinot (1732-1801). Operas by Sacchini and Duni followed. Ryx's directorship saw the début in 1778 of 'the father of the Polish theatre', Wojciech Bogusławski (1757-1829), whose activities included directing the theatre 1782-4 and 1799-1814. French and Italian operas were given, later some Mozart (from 1783), in Polish with Polish singers. Opera was also staged in the Royal Lazienki Garden, in the T. w Pomarańczarni (opened 1788), and in the open-air Amfiteatr on an island (also known as the T. na Wyspie) (1790). After Bogusławski, the most important figure in the early 19th cent. was Józef Elsner (1769-1854), who wrote and conducted original operas at the theatre. In 1810 Karol Kurpiński (1785-1857) was appointed to the opera; he became director 1823 and introduced a predominantly French and Italian repertory. With the revolution of 1830, *La Muette de Portici* was introduced, but dropped when the revolution failed. In 1833, the Teatr Wielki (Grand T.), built by Corazzi, was opened; here the opera company, separating from the drama company, reached a high artistic standard under Kurpiński, later (1840-52) under the

conductorship of Tomasz Nidecki and (1853-74) Giovanni (Jan) Quattrini.

A major event was the first Warsaw production of *Halka* in 1858: Moniuszko was immediately appointed director of the opera, and introduced many new Polish works, including (after a period of inactivity following the 1863 revolution) his *Straszny Dwór* (The Haunted Castle, 1865). Cesare Trombini was music director 1874-81: works he introduced included *Lohengrin* (1879). Emil Młynarski was director 1898-1903 and 1919-29, introducing works by Szymanowski and many modern operas. A great feature of the period between the 1890s and 1914 were the seasons of Italian opera with the greatest international artists, including Battistini who sang every year in Warsaw from 1894 to 1912 and made many of his recordings there. At the T. Nowości (opened 1901) operetta was cultivated under the energetic guidance of Ludwik Śliwiński. Financial difficulties forced the T. Wielki to interrupt its work repeatedly during the 1930s. The theatres closed in 1939, and the T. Wielki was damaged by fire; then in 1944 bombs destroyed all but Corazzi's fine façade. The theatre re-opened in Nov. 1965. After the war, opera was resumed in 1945, first in an ex-cinema, then in the Roma Hall, which was re-fitted in 1953 (cap. 1,000) and in which opera quickly re-established itself. There are also two chamber opera companies (one attached to the T. Wielki); these give occasional performances of chamber opera and ballet. A State Operetta Co. was founded in 1949.

Bibl: J. Karski (ed.): *Teatr Wielki in Warszawe* (1965).

Wartel, Pierre-François (*b* Versailles, 3 Apr. 1806; *d* Paris, 3 Aug. 1882). French tenor. Studied Paris with Nourrit and Banderali. Début Paris, O., 1831 as a comprimario. Created Don Gasparo in *La Favorite* (1840). After leaving stage taught in Paris; his pupils included Christine Nilsson and Trebelli. His wife, **Atale Thérèse Annette** (orig. Adrien) (1814-65), was a pianist and composer, and their son, **Louis Emile Wartel** (1834-?), was a bass who sang at the T.L., 1857-70.

Washington. Capital of U.S.A. Like most American cities, Washington relied until after World War II on visiting companies for its opera, and short seasons were given by the Hammerstein, Metropolitan, and San Carlo companies. In 1965 the Opera Society of Washington was founded, and since 1971 it has performed at the Kennedy Center for the Performing Arts (cap. 2,200). This opened in Sept. that year with the world première of Ginastera's *Beatrice Cenci*, which had been specially commissioned for the occassion. Ian Strasfogel was director of the organization 1956-75, and George London since 1975, with

Paul Calloway as music director 1957-67. Many works in recent years have received their American premières in Washington, including Cavalli's *L'Ormindo*, Monteverdi's *Il ritorno d'Ulisse*, Haydn's *L'infedeltà delusa*, Verdi's *Attila*, Berlioz's *Beatrice and Benedict*, and Delius's *Koanga* and *A Village Romeo and Juliet*. Other outstanding events have included Stravinsky conducting his *Oedipus Rex* and *The Nightingale; The Magic Flute* in the Auden-Kallman translation; and the world première of Ginastera's *Bomarzo*.

Watson (orig. McLamore), **Claire** (*b* New York, 3 Feb. 1927). American soprano. Studied N.Y. with Elisabeth Schumann and Sergius Kagen, and Vienna with Klemperer. Début Graz, 1951, Desdemona. Frankfurt 1956-8; Munich since 1958, where she sang Countess Almaviva at reopening of Cuvilliés T., (1958) and Eva at reopening of National T., (1963). London, C.G., 1958-63, 1964, 1970, 1972 (with Munich Company); Gly., 1959; Salzburg Festival 1966-8, guest appearances Vienna, Rome, Milan, Buenos Aires, San Francisco, Chicago. Retired from stage 1976. Repertory included Donna Elvira, Sieglinde, Eva, Elisabeth de Valois, Desdemona, Marschallin, Ariadne, Countess (*Capriccio*), Tatyana, Ellen Orford. A versatile and highly gifted performer, with impressive musicianship, sincerity, and personal charm on stage. (R)

Weber. German family of musicians.

(1) **Fridolin** (1733-1779), uncle of the composer Carl Maria von Weber, married Marie Cäcilia Stamm of Mannheim, by whom he had four daughters, all singers:

(2) **Josepha** (*b* Zell, 1759; *d* Vienna, 29 Dec. 1819). German soprano, for whom Mozart wrote Queen of Night in *Zauberflöte* and the bravura aria, K.580, to be sung in Paisiello's *Barbiere di Siviglia;* married Franz de Paula Hofer, violinist in Schikaneder's theatre in 1788, and after his death the bass, Friedrich Sebastian Mayer, in 1797.

(3) **Aloysia** (*b* Zell, 1761; *d* Salzburg, 1839). German soprano. Mozart's first love, who jilted him in 1778. She married the actor Josef Lange, and as A. Lange sang in Vienna; Mozart wrote eight concert arias for her, and she created Mme Herz in *Der Schauspieldirektor.*

(4) **Constanze** (*b* Zell, 1762; *d* Salzburg, 6 Mar. 1842). Mozart's wife; not a professional singer.

(5) **Sophie** (*b* 1763; *d* Salzburg, 1846). German soprano. In 1803 married the tenor and composer Jakob Haibl, who was a member of Schikaneder's company. Present at Mozart's deathbed and wrote a moving account of the composer's last hours.

Weber, Bernhard Anselm (*b* Mannheim, 18 Apr. 1764; *d* Berlin, 23 Mar. 1821). German composer, conductor, and pianist. No relation to Carl Maria von Weber. After studying with Vogler, held a conducting appointment in Hanover (1787); then toured with Vogler as a virtuoso. In 1792 became joint musical director (with Bernhard Wessely) of Berlin National-theater; first director 1796. Illness reduced his activities after 1818, and he had to give way to Spontini in 1820. His own stage works include, as well as operas, Singspiels and melodramas. Was most celebrated as a conductor, in particular as a champion of Gluck.

Weber, Carl Maria (Friedrich Ernst) **von** (*b* Eutin, ?18 Nov. 1786; *d* London, 5 June 1826). German composer, conductor, pianist, and critic. Studied with various teachers on his youthful travels, including Heuschkel and Michael Haydn, later Abbé Vogler. His first opera was a childish essay, later destroyed. In 1800 came *Das Waldmädchen,* of which only fragments survive: this was later reworked as *Silvana* (1810). Meanwhile he had written *Peter Schmoll und seine Nachbarn* (1803), which shows his continued interest in Romantic subjects and includes some original and charming music alongside much that is inexperienced. In 1804, not yet 18, he was appointed music director at Breslau: he instituted sweeping reforms anticipating those he was to pursue in Prague and Dresden, but largely through youth and inexperience failed to win sufficient support for them. While in Breslau, he began an opera, *Rübezahl,* of which three numbers survive. During a later (non-musical) post in Stuttgart he wrote *Silvana*: though still showing many signs of inexperience, it also reveals an instinct for the theatre, and includes some woodlande and chivalric music which gives a foretaste of *Der Freischütz* and *Euryanthe.* Its title-role is silent, and the problems of writing an opera for a dumb heroine are ingeniously tackled if not wholly successfully overcome. In Mannheim in 1810 he first read the story of *Der Freischütz,* and even planned an opera on it; the project fell through when the librettist defaulted. However, he did write the 1-act *Abu Hassan,* a brilliant little work, witty and tuneful in his freshest vein.

In 1816, in one of the reviews he had begun writing, Weber referred in connexion with Hoffmann's *Undine* to 'the kind of opera all Germans want – a self-contained work of art in which all elements, contributed by the arts in co-operation, disappear and re-emerge to create a new world'. All his mature life, as Kapellmeister, critic, and composer, was dedicated to the aim of developing German opera along the lines of what Wagner was to call a **Gesamtkunstwerk.* Appointed to Prague as opera director in 1813, he set about reforming operatic practice there, recruiting singers for their capacity as members of an ensemble rather than as stars, revising rehearsal schedules, re-forming the orchestra, and taking a practical interest in all theatrical matters from the scenery to the library catalogue. His *Spielplan* consisted of works that were the theoretical and creative basis of German Romantic opera, mostly French operas by Cherubini, Spontini, Isouard, Boieldieu, Dalayrac, Méhul, Grétry, Catel, and others. He also prepared the way with essays on each opera he was to perform. He had no time for original opera composition himself, though he contemplated *Tannhäuser*, to a text by Brentano.

In 1816 Weber resigned and was appointed Royal Saxon Kapellmeister in Dresden. Here his reforms were still more searching, and included the development of an elaborate rehearsal schedule for each work that began with a reading of the text so as to impress the drama upon the singers; he also re-formed the chorus, re-seated the orchestra, made important developments with scenery and lighting, and again planned his repertory so as to provide a background for the art of German opera, in competition to the Italian opera also flourishing in Dresden under Morlacchi. In 1821 he went to Berlin to conduct his own contribution to German Romantic opera, *Der Freischütz*. The work triumphed; and especially when seen in comparison with Spontini's *Olympie* (also being staged in Berlin), it came at once to represent a kind of opera that had immediate relevance to German life and popular music. The plot, the characters, the legend, the music, all closely based on the daily country life of Germany, caught the imagination of the people in times when nationalism was emerging as a powerful force. Basically a Singspiel, *Der Freischütz* transcends the old form by its imaginative strength: some of the numbers, such as the Huntsmen's Chorus and Bridesmaids' Chorus, were to become almost folksongs; the Wolf's Glen Scene, with its ingenious mixture of speech, song, and loosely contructed musical numbers, cleverly related to the powers of evil by use of *Leitmotiv*, remained an unsurpassed example of Romantic horror in music.

The success of *Der Freischütz* led Barbaia to invite him to write another similar work for Vienna; but Weber was anxious to move onto a different plane, and turned to a grand opera with *Euryanthe* (1823). Despite inept writing by the librettist, Helmina von Chézy, he succeeded in constructing an opera, virtually continuous and without spoken dialogue, that anticipates much in Wagner and is itself a masterpiece. Exaggerated distrust of the libretto long inhibited the work's success, but it has increasingly come to be seen as an opera of extraordinary beauty and originality, far in advance of *Der Freischütz* (even in its orchestration, characteristically subtle and functional) and anticipating much in Wagner's *Lohengrin* and beyond.

Weber did not build further upon this new creative achievement because of the rapid advance of his tuberculosis. Though invited to write an opera for Covent Garden, he was obliged to fall in with the suggestions of his English librettist, James Robinson Planché, who pressed upon him the kind of pantomime that was current English musical taste. *Oberon* (1826) is consequently constructed in separate numbers, though of greater subtlety and delicacy than anything in Weber's other operas, setting a standard and providing an idiom for fairy music as *Der Freischütz* has for the music of the forest's sunniest and darkest sides. However, it was, Weber sadly acknowledged, not what he meant by a German opera; and he planned to rewrite it, using recitative, in a more suitable manner. He did not live to do so, for having journeyed to London to conduct the première, his health finally gave way, and he died in Sir George Smart's house the day before he was hoping to return to Germany.

A projected comedy, *Die drei Pintos*, left unfinished in 1821, was first entrusted to Meyerbeer; later it was given to Mahler, who completed it with music from other of Weber's works, scored it, and conducted it in 1888.

Weber was also one of the most important critics of his day, and his essays and reviews are valuable for the insight they show into the problems of Romantic opera and for their accounts of contemporary works.
Bibl: J. Warrack: *Carl Maria von Weber* (2/1976).

Weber, Ludwig. (*b* Vienna, 29 July 1899; *d* Vienna, 9 Dec. 1974). Austrian bass. Studied Vienna with Alfred Boruttau. Début Vienna, V.O., 1920, Fiorello. Barmen-Elberfeld 1925–7; Düsseldorf 1927–30; Cologne 1930–32; Munich 1932–45; Vienna 1945–60. London, C.G., 1936–9, 1947, 1950–1; Bayreuth 1951–60. One of the finest Wagner basses of the century. Hagen and Gurnemanz were among his greatest roles, and his Rocco (*Fidelio*) and Daland have rarely been equalled in our day. Also a sympathetic Boris, which he sang at Covent Garden in 1951. His repertory included Wozzeck, Baron Ochs, Barak, Kecal, Kaspar, and Méphistophélès. From 1961 he was a professor at the Mozarteum in Salzburg. (R)

Webster, (Sir) **David** (Lumsden) (*b* Dundee, 3 July 1903; *d* London, 11 May 1971). British administrator. Produced several operas as a student at Liverpool University; then entered the commercial world. Chairman of Liverpool Philharmonic Society, 1940–45. General administrator to the newly-formed Covent Garden Opera Trust, 1945–70, successfully established the Royal O. House in the period following World War II as the permanent home

of the Sadler's Wells (subsequently Royal) Ballet and the C.G. (subsequently Royal) O. Largely responsible for launching several British singers, including Sutherland, Vickers, and Geraint Evans, on successful international careers. Knighted 1961; K.C.V.O. 1970.
Bibl: M. Haltrecht: *The Reluctant Showman* (1975).

Weidemann, Friedrich (*b* Ratzeburg, 1 Jan. 1871; *d* Vienna, 30 Jan. 1919). German baritone. Studied Hamburg with Vilmar and Berlin with Muschler. Début Brieg (Silesia) 1896. After engagements in Essen, Hamburg, and Riga, engaged by Mahler for Vienna 1903, where he remained until his death. First Vienna Orestes, Faninal, and Golaud. Salzburg 1906, Almaviva. London, C.G., 1910, Kurwenal, and first London Orestes. (R)

Weidt, Lucie (*b* Opava, ? 1876; *d* Vienna, 28 July 1940). Austrian soprano. Daughter of conductor and composer Heinrich Weidt (1828–1901). Studied Vienna with Rosa Papier. Début Leipzig 1900; Vienna 1902–27; N.Y., Met., 1910–11. Created Nurse in *Die Frau ohne Schatten*, and was first Vienna Lisa, Marschallin, and Kundry, and first Kundry at Milan, Sc. One of the famous members of Mahler's Vienna ensemble. After retiring taught in Vienna. (R)

Weigl, Joseph (*b* Kismarton (Eisenstadt), 28 Mar. 1766; *d* Vienna, 3 Feb. 1846). Austrian composer. The son of an Esterház cellist, and godson of Haydn, he studied with Gassmann and Witzig, later with Albrechtsberger and Salieri. He wrote his first opera *Die unnützige Vorsicht* (1783) aged 16; this was produced on Gluck's recommendation and won him the favour of the Emperor Joseph. From 1791 he was Salieri's assistant at the Vienna Court T., from 1792 composer to the O. Among many invitations he received were to Dresden as director of opera (Morlacchi was actually appointed) and to Milan to compose operas in 1807–8 and 1815–16.

Weigl long retained Royal favour, as well as public following. Many of his works were in popular Singspiel style; some were Italian; others were a more ambitious mixture of genres that reached towards grand opera and continuously composed opera. *La principessa d'Amalfi* (1794) is a reconciliation of Italian and Viennese opera; his most famous work, however, which long endured on German stages, was *Die Schweizerfamilie* (1809), whose melodic charm and dramatic fluency were much admired.

Weil, Hermann (*b* Karlsruhe, 29 May 1876; *d* Blue Mountain Lake, 6 July 1949). German baritone. Studied Karlsruhe with Mottl, Frankfurt with Adolf Dippel. Began career as répétiteur at Karlsruhe, 1900: Début Freiburg

1901, Wolfram. N.Y., Met., 1911–17, Lexington O. H., 1919; U.S.A. German O. C., 1923–4. London, C.G., 1913; Bayreuth 1903–12, 1924–5, Amfortas, Gunther, Sachs; Vienna 1920–3. A much admired Sachs and Kurwenal. Had repertory of more than 100 roles. Forced to emigrate from Germany in 1931; settled in N.Y., where he taught. (R)

Weill, Kurt (*b* Dessau, 2 Mar. 1900; *d* New York, 3 Apr. 1950). German composer. Studied Berlin with Krasselt and Humperdinck, and worked as Korrepetitor in Dessau 1919, director of opera in Lüdenscheid 1920; studied further, Berlin with Busoni. His first stage works were with various librettists, and included *Der Protagonist* (with Georg Kaiser, 1926), *Royal Palace* (with Iwan Goll, 1927), and *Der Zar lässt sich photographieren* (with Kaiser, 1928; he later planned a setting of *Moby Dick* with Kaiser). His collaboration with Bertolt Brecht began with the 'Songspiel' *Mahagonny* (1927). His interest in artistic topicality was early signified (and largely misunderstood) in *Die Dreigroschenoper* (1928), which transposed *The Beggar's Opera* of 1728 to the Berlin of two centuries later. Together with Brecht, many of whose artistic aims he shared, Weill widened his range and effect in the moral and political operas *Aufstieg und Fall der Stadt Mahagonny* (1930), *Der Jasager* (1930), and *Die Bürgschaft* (1932). *Die sieben Todsünden* (The Seven Deadly Sins, 1933) is a ballet with singing; in them we find the fullest expression of his style – popular and up-to-the-minute but uncompromising, basically Romantic, pointing with brilliant and wounding musical symbols the message of the text, direct in appeal but bearing a deeply felt political message. Forced out of Hitler's Germany, Weill settled in America in 1935, where he wrote some musical comedy and light opera: *Street Scene* (1949) and *Down in the Valley* (1948) have been especially successful.

Weimar. Town in Thuringia, Germany. In 1772 the Duchess Anna Amalia summoned the composer Seyler to work in the castle theatre, and Singspiels by Benda, Neefe, and Schweitzer were given. Goethe came in 1775, and directed the Liebhabertheater; the Duchess provided music for his Singspiels *Erwin und Elmire* (1776) and *Das Jahrmarktfest* (1776). The Hoftheater opened in 1784; it burned down in 1826, and was reconstructed. The town had a particularly distinguished operatic period between 1847 and 1858 when Liszt was chief Kapellmeister and Bülow one of the conductors. It was the scene of the premières of *Lohengrin* (1850), Schubert's *Alfonso und Estrella* (1854), and *Der Barbier von Bagdad* (1858), as well as the second performances of Berlioz's *Benvenuto Cellini* and Schumann's *Genoveva*. Liszt was succeeded by Eduard

Lassen, who produced the première of *Samson et Dalila* (1877) and gave the first performances following the Munich première of *Tristan* (1874) and the first prod. in Germany of *Mignon* (1868). In 1893 *Hänsel und Gretel* received its première at Weimar and in the same year *Werther* its first performance in Germany. At this time the first conductor was Richard Strauss, whose *Guntram* had its première there in 1894. The present Deutsches National theater, formerly Hoftheater (cap. 2,000), was opened in 1907.

Weinberger, Jaromír (*b* Prague, 8 Jan. 1896; *d* St Petersburg, Fla., 8 Aug. 1967). Czech composer. Studied Prague with Křička and Karel, then with Novák and briefly (but significantly) with Reger. *Švanda dudák* (Shvanda the Bagpiper, 1927) followed the Smetana tradition with great commercial, if less artistic, success: it has been translated into at least 17 languages. His other operas, which include a setting of Schiller's *Wallenstein* to a text by Max Brod, *Valdštejn* (1937), have not approached this success.

Weingartner, Felix (Paul) **von** (*b* Zara, 2 June 1863; *d* Winterthur, 7 May 1942). Austrian conductor and composer. Studied Graz, Leipzig, and Weimar with Liszt. At Weimar his first opera, *Sakuntala*, was produced in 1884. Kapellmeister, Königsberg 1884–5; Danzig 1885–7; Hamburg 1887–9; Mannheim 1889–91; Berlin 1891–8; Vienna (succeeding Mahler) 1908–11; Hamburg 1912–14; Darmstadt 1915–19; Vienna, V.O., 1919–24, and S.O., 1935–6; Boston 1912–13; London, C.G., 1939. Wrote seven other operas, and edited versions of *Oberon*, *Der fliegende Holländer*, and Méhul's *Joseph*. One of the great conductors of his day, still invoked as an exemplar to his successors. (R)

Weiss, W. H. (Willoughby Hunter) (*b* Liverpool, 2 Apr. 1820; *d* London, 24 Oct. 1867). English bass. Studied with George Smart and Balfe. Début Dublin 1842, Oroveso; London, Prince's T., 1842, Count Rodolfo. Appeared with Pyne-Harrison and other English companies, singing in premières of many English works. His wife **Georgina Weiss** (1826–80) was a soprano who often sang with her husband – début D.L. 1847.

Welche Wonne, welche Lust. Blonde's (sop.) aria in Act 2 of Mozart's *Die Entführung aus dem Serail,* in which she delightedly receives the news of Belmonte's plans for escape.

Welitsch (orig. Velichkova), **Ljuba** (*b* Borisovo, 10 July 1913). Bulgarian soprano. Studied Sofia with G. Zlater-Cherkin, and Vienna with Lierhammer. Début Sofia, 1934, small role in *Louise.* Graz 1936–41; Hamburg 1941–3; Vienna, V.O., 1940, 1941–4; S.O., 1943, 1946–64. London, C.G., 1947 with Vienna Co., Salome, Donna Anna; 1948–52 Salome

Musetta, Aida, Lisa, Tosca; Gly., at Edinburgh Festival, 1948–9, Donna Anna, Amelia. N.Y., Met., 1948–52. Her most famous role was Salome, which she first sang at a special performance for Strauss's 80th birthday in Vienna in June 1944; sang the part in English in the notorious Dali-Brook prod. at C.G., 1949. Her operatic appearances decreased after 1955, though she made several films; but she continued to appear in character roles at the Vienna V., including the Duchess of Krakenthorp in *La Fille du régiment,* in which part she returned to the Met., 1972. A highly temperamental and dramatic singer: her Tosca, Aida, Musetta, Donna Anna, and Amelia were all strikingly individual performances as memorable as her silvery and often sensuous voice. (R)

Wellesz, Egon (Joseph) (*b* Vienna, 21 Oct. 1885; *d* Oxford, 9 Nov. 1974). Austrian composer and musicologist. Studied musicology with Guido Adler, counterpoint with Schoenberg. Five of Wellesz's operas were written in the years between 1918 and 1931, and are a result of the researches into Baroque opera he pursued during the war. This, coupled with his interest in expressing not his own destiny but 'those things which betoken the link between the material and the spiritual world' drew him to myths, in modern interpretations that would stress their continuing validity. Musically the influences include Baroque opera, Schoenberg, and medieval music, unified by a scholarly and compassionate mind. *Incognita* (1951) dates from his years as Reader in Byzantine Music at Oxford, where he eventually settled after leaving Austria in 1938.

Bibl: E. Wellesz: *Essays on Opera* (1951).

Welsh National Opera. Launched in Apr. 1946 in Cardiff, largely thanks to the efforts of Dr. W. H. Smith, with performances of *Faust, Cavalleria rusticana,* and *Pagliacci.* By 1956 the company, which was giving regular seasons in Wales and a number of cities in southern England, had a repertory of 13 works, including Arwel Hughes's *Menna,* which was sung in Welsh that year at the National Eisteddfod; by 1966 this had increased to 34, and by 1976 to over 50. Works using the excellent amateur chorus, including *Nabucco, Lombardi, Vêpres siciliennes, Mosè, Guillaume Tell, Mefistofele,* and *Lohengrin,* were often performed, and were given by the company during its London seasons at S.W., 1955–7 and 1961–2. Idloes Owen was music director, 1946-52, Leo Quayle 1952–3, Frederick Berend 1953–5, Vilem Tausky 1955–6, Warwick Braithwaite 1956–61, Charles Groves 1961–3, and Bryan Balkwill 1963–8. The appointment of James Lockhart as music director in 1968 and of Michael Geliot as director of productions the following year contributed to a more adventurous musical and visual policy. The chorus began to include professionals from 1968. New productions included the first staging by a British company of *Lulu*. Other additions to the repertory included *Simon Boccanegra, Falstaff, Idomeneo, Billy Budd, Don Carlos,* and *Fliegende Holländer.* Lockhart was succeeded in 1973 by Richard Armstrong, and the repertory was further expanded to include Hoddinnott's *Beach at Falesá, La Grande Duchesse de Gérolstein, Jenůfa, Otello,* and *Elektra.* The company has appeared in Switzerland and Spain. Welsh-born artists appearing with the company have included Anne Howells, Gwyneth Jones, Margaret Price, Elizabeth Vaughan, Geraint Evans, Delme Bryn-Jones, and Ryland Davies.

Werther. Opera in 4 acts by Massenet; text by Blau, Millet and Hartmann, after Goethe's novel *Die Leiden des jungen Werthers* (1774). Prod. Vienna, O., 16 Feb. 1892 with Renard, Forster, Van Dyck, Neidl, cond. Massenet; Chicago, 29 Mar. 1894, by Met. Opera N.Y., with Eames, Arnoldson, J. de Reszke, Martapoura, cond. Mancinelli; London, C.G., 11 June 1894, with Eames, Arnoldson, Jean De Reszke, Albers, cond. Mancinelli.

Werther (ten.) loves Charlotte (mezzo), who returns his love although betrothed to his friend Albert (bar.). He leaves her, returning to find Charlotte married. She urges him to leave her again, but on hearing that he has asked Albert for his pistols, rushes through a snowstorm to him to find that he has shot himself.

Other operas on the subject are by Aspa, Benvenuti, Puccita (1804), Gentili (1864), and Randegger. Parody by W. Müller (1830).

Westrup, (Sir) **Jack** (Allan) (*b* London, 26 July 1904; *d* Headley, 21 Apr. 1975). English musicologist. One of the founder members of the *Oxford University Opera Club, for which he prepared editions of *Orfeo* (1925) and *L'incoronazione di Poppea* (1927). As Professor of Music (1947–71), conducted the Club's productions. His literary works include translations for these productions, and valuable studies of Handel and Purcell.

Wettergren, Gertrud (Pålson) (*b* Eslöve, 17 Feb. 1897). Swedish contralto. Studied Stockholm with Capiani and Gillis Brett. Début Stockholm, 1922, Cherubino. Stockholm, Royal O., 1922–52, where she created roles in operas by Atterberg and Rosenberg, and was the first Stockholm Rubria in Boito's *Nerone*, also Grete in *Der ferne Klang*, Konchakovna, Eboli, Khivria, Kostelnička, Marfa, Mrs Peachum, Mother in *The Consul*; N.Y., Met, 1935–8; London, C.G., 1936, 1939. One of the outstanding Swedish singers of the inter-war years. Much admired as Carmen and in Verdi and Wagner. (R)
Bibl: G. Wettergren: *Mitt öddes Stjärnu* (1949).

Wexford. Town in Eire. An autumn festival has taken place since 1951, when Balfe's *The Rose of Castile* was given. The festival was founded by Dr. T.J. Walsh, who remained director until 1966; he was succeeded by Brian Dickie (1966-74) and Thomson Smillie (1974-8). Opera is given in the picturesque little T. Royal, and the repertory has included the revival of many neglected but attractive works, including *Aroldo, I due foscari,* Rossini's *Otello,* Cavalli's *Eritrea,* Mayr's *Medea in Corinto, Oberon,* Prokofiev's *The Gambler,* and a number of French works. The festival also has a reputation for giving an early chance to singers who have gone on to make distinguished careers, including Mirella Freni, Jeannette Pilou, Ugo Benelli, and Christiane Éda-Pierre.

Weyse, Christoph Ernst Friedrich (*b* Altona, 5 Mar. 1774; *d* Copenhagen, 8 Oct. 1842). Danish composer of German birth. After studying in Copenhagen with J.A.P. Schulz, he became well known as a pianist and organist, and as a composer especially of religious music and songs. His Singspiels contain examples of his individual fusion of simple, naïve song style with a more sophisticated Lieder manner. They comprise *Sovedrikken* (The Sleeping Draught, 1809), *Faruk* (1812), *Ludlams Hule* (1816), all to texts by Oehlenschläger, *Floribella* (1825), *Festen paa Kenilworth* (text by Hans Andersen after Scott, 1836), and a light opera, *Et Eventyr i Rosenborg Have* (An Adventure in Rosenborg Gardens, 1827).

When I am laid in earth. Dido's (sop.) lament at the end of Purcell's *Dido and Aeneas.*

Whitehill, Clarence (*b* Marengo, Iowa, 5 Nov. 1871; *d* New York, 18 Dec. 1932). American bass-baritone. Studied Chicago with L.A. Phelps, Paris with Giraudet and Sbriglia. Début Brussels, M., 1898, Capulet. Paris, O.C., 1899, under name of Eugen Clarence (first American singer to appear there). Returned to U.S.A. 1900 and sang with Savage C., then after a further period of study in Frankfurt with Stockhausen, made German début Lübeck 1901 as Lothario. Urged by Cosima Wagner to study with Kniese in Bayreuth; sang there 1904, 1908–9 as Wolfram, Amfortas, Gunther. Cologne 1903–9, N.Y., Met., 1909–10 and 1914–32; Chicago 1911–16, 1919. London, C.G., 1905–10, Wotan in the famous English *Ring*, 1914, 1922 with B.N.O.C. First Met. Father in *Louise,* Althair in *Aegyptische Helena,* and a famous Sachs and Golaud. At the Met. sang 308 performances of 26 roles. Neville Cardus called him 'an artist of rare dignity with a superb and humane voice equalled only in Wagner by Schorr'. (R)

Widdop, Walter (*b* Norland, nr Halifax, 19 Apr. 1892; *d* London, 6 Sept. 1949). English tenor.

Studied with Dinh Gilly. Début B.N.O.C., 1923, Radamès. London, C.G., 1923, 1928–33, 1935, 1937–8. Also sang in Barcelona, Amsterdam, and Germany. A fine Siegmund and Tristan (he sang the latter opposite Flagstad). He sang Lohengrin's Farewell at the R.A.H., London, the night before he died. (R)

Wiedemann, Hermann (*b* ?, 1879; *d* Berlin, 2 July 1944). German baritone. Début Elberfeld 1905. Brno 1906–10; Hamburg 1910–14; Berlin, H., 1914–16; Vienna 1916–44; Salzburg Festival 1922–5, 1929–32, 1934–7, 1939, 1941, Guglielmo, Faninal, Beckmesser. London, C.G., 1913, 1938, Faninal, Beckmesser. Buenos Aires, C. Repertory also included Alberich, Donner, and roles in Italian opera. (R)

Wiegand, (Josef Anton) **Heinrich** (*b* Fränkisch Crumbach, 9 Sept. 1842; *d* Frankfurt 28 May 1899). German bass. Studied Paris. Début Zurich 1870. Frankfurt 1873–77 as leading bass. Toured U.S.A. 1877 with Adams-Pappenheim C.; Leipzig 1878–82; Vienna 1882–4; Hamburg 1884–90. London, H.M.'s., 1882, first London Hunding, Hagen; C.G., 1892 in the Wagner performances under Mahler. Bayreuth 1886, 1888, 1889, 1891, Gurnemanz, Mark, Landgrave, Pogner.

Wiesbaden. Town in Hesse, Germany. Opera first given in 1765. In 1810 the town's theatre was named the Herzoglich-Nassauisches-Hoftheater; regular performances were given by a company from Mainz until the middle of the 19th cent. In 1866 the theatre was renamed the Königliche Hoftheater. The present Grosses Haus (cap. 1,325) opened in Oct. 1894. Klemperer was music director 1923–27 with Carl Hagemann as General-intendant; together they pursued a progressive policy, continued by Paul Bekker and Joseph Rosenstock until 1932. Staged premières of Milhaud's *L'Abandon d'Ariane* and *La Deliverance de Thesée,* and Křenek's triple bill, *Schwergewicht, Der Diktator,* and *Das geheime Königreich.* Carl von Schirach was intendant 1933–43 and Karl Elmendorff music director, 1932–45. Wartime damage was minimal, and the house reopened in Sept. 1947; Heinrich Köhler-Heiffrich (1949-52), Friedrich Schramm (1952–62), Claus Helmut Drese (1962–68), Alfred Erich Sistig (1968–75), and Peter Ebert (1975-7) have since been the Generalintendants, and Wolfgang Sawallisch (1957–9), Heinz Wallberg (1961–74), and Siegfried Köhler (from 1974) music directors. The annual Wiesbaden May Festival dates back to 1896, and became well-established under Bekker in the 1920s. Since 1950 it has become the show-case in the West for companies from Eastern Europe, and since 1963 there have been performances by ensembles from Prague, Warsaw, Sofia, Budapest, Bratislava, Bucharest, Belgrade, Zagreb, Halle, Leipzig, Dresden, and Moscow.

Wildbrunn (orig. Wehrenpfennig), **Helene** (*b* Vienna, 8 Apr. 1882; *d* Vienna, 11 April 1972). Austrian soprano, formerly contralto. Studied Vienna with Rosa Papier. Début Vienna V.O, 1906 under her original name in small roles. Dortmund 1907–14, Ortrud, Fricka, Amneris, Delilah, etc; Stuttgart 1914–18, when her voice changed to soprano. Berlin, S.O., 1916–25 and Deutsche Oper 1926–9; Vienna S.O., 1919–32. London, C.G., 1927, Leonore (*Fidelio*). Milan, Sc., 1922, Kundry; Buenos Aires, T.C., 1922, Brünnhilde, Kundry, Marschallin. Notable Isolde and Brünnhilde. Taught Vienna Academy of Music 1932–50. (R)

Wildschütz, Der (The Poacher). Opera in 3 acts by Lortzing; text by composer, after Kotzebue's comedy *Der Rehbock.* Prod. Leipzig 31 Dec. 1842, with Günther, Lanz, Krüger, Düringer, Kindermann, Schmidt, Berthold, Wallmann; Brooklyn, 25 Mar. 1859, with Hübner, Heyde, Siedenberg, Lehmann, Graf, Fortner, Quint; London, D.L., 3 July 1895.

Baculus (buffo bass), a schoolmaster on the estate of the Count of Eberbach (bar.), has accidentally shot a buck. His betrothed, Gretchen (sop.), is willing to intercede for him, but he is reluctant and a young student offers to go instead: this is really Baroness Freimann (sop.), the Count's sister, who accompanied by her maid Nanette (sop.) sets off to keep an eye on her own betrothed, the Count's brother Baron Kronthal (ten.). The Count is much taken with 'Gretchen', and the Baron bribes Baculus with 5,000 thalers to give her up; meanwhile, 'Gretchen' is rescued from the situation by being allowed to spend the night in the room of the Countess (con.) (whose unremitting Greek quotations are a satire on the recent success of Mendelssohn's *Antigone* music and the ensuing mania in Berlin for all things Greek). The unravelling of these confusions still leaves Baculus guilty of poaching and of having sold his betrothed; but he is forgiven by all.

Willan, Healey (*b* Balham, 12 Oct. 1880; *d* Toronto, 16 Feb. 1968). English composer. In addition to the church and organ music for which he was most famous, Willan also wrote incidental music for about twenty plays, arranged five ballad operas from folk material, and composed two original operas. *Transit Through Fire* (1942), with text by John Coulter, was the first opera to be commissioned by the Canadian Broadcasting Corporation. A second radio commission followed in 1946 for *Deirdre,* again with text by Coulter. This, with its ancient story and richly Romantic music, is in the Wagnerian style of half a century earlier, but it was a successful work and in a slightly revised version for the stage has been given in Toronto by both the O. School of the University of Toronto (1965) and the Canadian O.C. (1966), and at the summer festival at Banff (1972).

Willer, Luise (*b* Seeshaupt, 1888; *d* Munich 27 Apr. 1970). German contralto. Studied Munich with Maria Hepner. Chorister Munich, N., 1906–10, soloist 1910–55. Début Annius (*Clemenza di Tito*). London, C.G., 1926, 1931 Erda, Fricka, Waltraute, Brangaene; Salzburg 1930, 1942–3. Farewell appearance Munich 1955 as Erda in *Siegfried*. Possessed a large, rich, and true contralto voice. (R)

William Ratcliff. Opera in 3 acts by Cui; text by A. Pleshcheyev, after Heine's ballad (1823). Prod. St Petersburg, M., 26 Feb. 1869. Cui's most famous opera. Other operas on the subject are by Pizzi (1889), Bavrinecz (1895), Mascagni (1895), Leroux (1906), Dopper (1909), and Andreae (1914).

Williamson, Malcolm (*b* Sydney, 21 Nov. 1931). Australian composer. Studied Sydney with Eugene Goossens, London with Elisabeth Lutyens. His operas, which show his fluent, eclectic, highly professional gift, include *Our Man in Havana* (1963), *English Eccentrics* (1964), *The Happy Prince* (1965), *Julius Caesar Jones* (1966), *The Violins of St Jacques* (1966), *Dunstan and the Devil* (1967), *The Growing Castle* (1968), and *Lucky Peter's Journey* (1969). He was made Master of the Queen's Music, 1975.

William Tell. See *Guillaume Tell.*

Willow Song. See *Salce, salce.*

Wilno. See *Poland.*

Wilson, (Sir) **Steuart** (*b* Bristol, 21 July 1889; *d* 18 Dec. 1966). English tenor and administrator. Studied with Jean de Reszke and George Henschel. Sang Tamino in *The Magic Flute* at Cambridge in 1910. Sang in occasional performances with B.N.O.C., Old Vic, at Glastonbury, and in Bristol in the opera festivals organized by Napier Miles. Deputy general administrator, C.G., 1949–55. (R)
Bibl: M. Stewart: *English Singer* (1970).

Wilt (orig. Liebenthaler), **Marie** (*b* Vienna, 30 Jan. 1883; *d* Vienna, 24 Sept. 1891). Austrian soprano. Début Graz 1865, Donna Anna. Vienna 1867–77. London, C.G., as Norma (under the name Maria Vilda), 1866–7, 1874–5. Leipzig 1878, Brünnhilde. Sang Donna Elvira in Vienna on the opening night of the Vienna Opera 1869; was the first Aida there 1874; created Sulamith in *Die Königin von Saba* (1875); and sang Donna Anna there in the centenary performances of *Don Giovanni* 1884. Hanslick said 'she delighted the ear, but had not a vestige of dramatic talent or education'.

Windgassen, Wolfgang (*b* Annemasse, 26 June 1914; *d* Stuttgart, 8 Sept. 1974). German tenor. Studied with his father, the tenor Fritz Windgassen (1883–1963) and in Stuttgart with Maria Ranzow and Alfons Fischer; his mother, Vally von der Osten, was the sister of the more famous Eva von der Osten. Début Pforzheim 1941, Alvaro. Stuttgart 1945–74, singing first the Italian repertory, then Tamino, Max, Hoffmann, and Florestan. Sang his first Siegmund in 1950; Bayreuth 1951–71, Parsifal, Siegmund, Siegfried, Loge, Lohengrin, Tannhäuser, Erik, Walther, and Tristan; established himself as the leading *Heldentenor* in the postwar opera. London, C.G., 1955–66; N.Y., Met., 1957, San Francisco 1970. Began to produce opera in 1970 and was director of opera at Stuttgart 1972–4. Repertory also included Adolar in *Euryanthe*, Rienzi, Emperor in *Frau ohne Schatten*, and Otello. Voice light for a Heldentenor by pre-war standards; he always sang with great sensitivity and musicality. Married to the soprano Lore Wissmann (*b* 1922). (R)
Bibl: B. Wessling: *Wolfgang Windgassen* (1967).

Winkelmann (also Winckelmann), **Hermann** (*b* Brunswick, 8 Mar. 1849; *d* Vienna, 18 Jan. 1912). German tenor. Studied Hanover. Début Sonderhausen 1875, Manrico. After engagements in Altenburg, Darmstadt, and Hamburg, where he created title role in Rubinstein's *Nero* (1879), sang Lohengrin and Tannhäuser in Vienna with such success that Richter recommended him to Wagner. Created Parsifal, Bayreuth, 1882, singing the title there until 1888, and was also heard there as Walther and Tannhäuser. London, D.L., 1882, Lohengrin and Tannhäuser, and first London Walther and Tristan. U.S.A. 1884 in Wagner Festival concerts. Vienna 1883–1906, first Vienna Tristan and Otello. His admirers formed themselves into the 'Hermann League', and performances were often disturbed by vociferous outbursts of applause. (R)

Winter, Peter von (*b* Mannheim, bapt. 28 Aug. 1754; *d* Munich, 17 Oct. 1825). German composer. Studied with Vogler, but principally self-taught. Music director Mannheim, then moved with the Court to Munich; assistant Kapellmeister 1794, Kapellmeister 1798. Began as a composer of Singspiel and light magic opera, developed a more adventurous style in the early years of the 19th cent., absorbing Romantic tendencies in *Der Sturm* (1798) and in the 'Ossian' opera *Colmal* (1809). By far his most famous work – and the most successful German opera between *Die Zauberflöte* and *Der Freischütz* – was *Das unterbrochene Opferfest* (1796). An eclectic who absorbed much from Mozart as well as from opera seria and opera buffa, and from opera comique, Winter contributed some original handling of chorus and orchestra to opera; his fluent reconciliation of different genres of opera won him a following in his own day.

Witherspoon, Herbert (*b* Buffalo, 21 July 1873; *d* New York, 10 May 1935). American bass and administrator. Studied music with Stoeckel, Parker, and McDowell, and singing with Hall and Treumann; later Paris with Capoul and Bouhy, London with Wood, and Milan with Lamperti. Début Newhaven, Conn., 1895 in concert; stage début N.Y., 1898, Castle Square Opera Co., Ramfis. N.Y., Met., 1908–16; roles included Pogner, Titurel, Donner, Fasolt, King Mark, Landgrave, Gurnemanz, Heinrich, Sarastro, Pizarro, Petruchio in first Met. *Widerspänstigen Zähmung*. Artistic director, Chicago Opera, 1930; chosen to succeed Gatti-Casazza as general manager of Met., but died in his office at the opera house before his first season opened. (R)

Witte, Erich (*b* Bremen, 19 Mar. 1911). German tenor and producer. Début Bremen 1932. Wiesbaden 1937–8; N.Y., Met., 1938–9; Breslau 1940–42; Berlin, S.O., 1945–60; Bayreuth, 1943, 1952-5. Originally a Spieltenor, later became a dramatic tenor singing Otello, Florestan, etc. His Loge was much admired in Bayreuth and London, and his Peter Grimes in Germany. Prod. *Meistersinger*, C.G., also singing Walther. Oberspielleiter Frankfurt 1961–4; Berlin, S.O., since 1964, singer and producer. (R)

Wittich, Marie (*b* Giessen, 27 May 1868; *d* Dresden, 4 Aug. 1931). German soprano. Studied Würzburg. Début Magdeburg 1882 (aged 14) as Azucena. After engagements in Düsseldorf, Basle, and Schwerin, engaged Dresden 1889–1914, created Salome in 1905. London, C.G., 1905–6; Bayreuth 1901–10, Sieglinde, Kundry, and Isolde.

Wittrisch, Marcel (*b* Antwerp, 1 Oct. 1901; *d* Stuttgart, 2 June 1955). German tenor. Studied Munich, Leipzig, and Milan. Début Halle, 1925, Konrad (*Hans Heiling*). Brunswick 1927–9; Berlin, S.O., 1929–43. London, C.G., 1931 as Tamino and Eisenstein. Bayreuth 1937, Lohengrin; Stuttgart, 1950–55. Also made name in operetta, especially Lehár. (R)

Wixell, Ingvar (*b* Luleå, 1931). Swedish baritone. Studied Stockholm with Dagmar Gustafsson. Début Gåvle 1952. Stockholm Royal Opera since 1956. London, C.G., 1960 with Stockholm company in *Alcina*, 1972 Boccanegra, 1973 Scarpia, 1977 Belcore and Mandryka. Chicago 1967; San Francisco 1972 Count Almaviva, Scarpia; N.Y., Met., 1973–4, Rigoletto, Scarpia, Boccanegra. Frequent guest in Berlin and Stuttgart. A true Verdi baritone, with a powerful stage personality. (R)

Wolf, Hugo (*b* Windischgraz, 13 Mar. 1860; *d* Vienna, 22 Feb. 1903). Austrian composer. His only completed opera, *Der Corregidor* (1895), a setting of Alarcón's *The Three-Cornered Hat*, has great charm but little dramatic force, being in effect hardly more than a Wolf *Lieder* cycle in costume. Another opera, *Manuel Venegas*, was unfinished.

Wolf-Ferrari, Ermanno (*b* Venice, 12 Jan. 1876; *d* Venice, 21 Jan. 1948). Italian composer of German-Italian parentage. Original intention to be a painter changed by a visit to Bayreuth. Studied Munich with Rheinberger. His first opera, *La Cenerentola*, was prod. Venice 1901. His first success was with *Le donne curiose* (Munich 1903); this was followed in 1906 by *I quatro rusteghi*. Both these were based on Goldoni, as were also *Gli amanti sposi* (Venice 1925), *La vedova scaltra* (Rome 1931), and *Il campiello* (Milan 1936). It was in these comic operas that Wolf-Ferrari excelled, with his elegant style, light touch, and skilful use of the orchestra. He wrote kindly for the voice in these and in the trifle *Il segreto di Susanna* (Munich 1909), *L'amore medico*, after Molière (Dresden 1915), and *La dama boba*, set on a comedy by Lope de Vega (Milan 1939). He made one successful incursion into verismo, *I gioielli della Madonna* (Berlin 1911); but his nearest attempt at music drama, *Sly* (Milan 1927), was less successful. Made an edition of *Idomeneo* (Munich 1931).

Wolff, Albert (Louis) (*b* Paris, 19 Jan. 1884; *d* Paris, 20 Feb. 1970). French conductor and composer. Studied Paris Conservatoire. Chorus master, Paris, O.C., 1908, conductor there from 1911. Conducted premières of Laparra's *La Jota*, *Angélique*, *Julien*, *Madame Bovary*, *Les Mamelles de Tirésias*. Music director, O.C., 1921–4, theatre director 1945–6. N.Y., Met., 1919–21, where his opera *L'Oiseau Bleu* was produced 1919; London, C.G., 1937, *Pelléas*. Also conducted French repertory for several seasons at Buenos Aires, Colón. (R)

Wolff, Fritz (*b* Munich, 28 Oct. 1894; *d* Munich, 18 Jan. 1957). German tenor. Studied Würzburg with Heinrich König. Début Bayreuth 1925, Loge. Bayreuth 1925–41; Hagen, 1925–6; Chemnitz 1926–8. Berlin 1930–43; London, C.G., 1929–33, 1937–8; Cleveland 1934–5. A much admired Lohengrin, Loge, Parsifal, and Walther. From 1946 until his death he taught in Munich. (R)

Wolfram. A minstrel knight (bar.) and friend of Tannhäuser, in Wagner's opera.

Wood, (Sir) Henry J. (*b* London, 3 Mar. 1869; *d* Hitchin, Herts., 19 Aug. 1944). English conductor. Studied London, R.A.M., with Prout and Garcia. First conducted with the Arthur Rouseby Opera Co. 1889; helped Sullivan pre-

pare *Ivanhoe* 1890; C.R. 1891; Burns-Crotty Co. 1892; London, Olympic T., Lago's 1892 season, when he conducted the English première of *Eugene Onegin*. Music adviser for the Mottl-Wagner concerts, 1894; conducted Stanford's *Shamus O'Brien* 1896, after which he devoted his life to concert work. (R)
Bibl: R. Pound: *Sir Henry Wood* (1969).

Wotan. The ruler of the gods (bass-bar.) in Wagner's *Ring der Nibelungen*.

Wotan's Farewell. The title commonly given to the closing scene of Wagner's *Die Walküre* in which Wotan (bass-bar.) takes leave of Brünnhilde as she lies encircled by fire on her rock.

Wozzeck. Opera in 3 acts by Berg; text by composer, after Büchner's play (1836). Prod. Berlin, S.O., 14 Dec 1925, with Johannsen, Scheele-Müller, Henke, Soot, Leo Schützendorf, Abendroth, cond. Kleiber; Philadelphia 19 Mar 1931, with Roselle, Eustis, Korell, Leonoff, Ivantzoff, Steschenko, cond. Stokowski; London, C.G., 22 Jan. 1952, with Goltz, Sinclair, Hannesson, P. Jones, Rothmüller, Dalberg, cond. Kleiber.

Wozzeck (bar.), an ordinary soldier, is lectured by the Captain (ten.), who despises him. Gathering sticks with his friend Andres (ten.), Wozzeck is alarmed by strange sounds and visions. Wozzeck's mistress Marie (sop.) flirts from her window with a passing Drum Major. Wozzeck is examined by a half-crazed Doctor (bass) who is using him for experiments. The Drum Major (ten.) seduces Marie.

Wozzeck becomes suspicious of Marie. The Captain taunts him with suggestions of her infidelity and Wozzeck accuses her. He finds her dancing with the Drum Major. The Drum Major boasts of his success, and when Wozzeck refuses to drink with him, beats him.

The repentant Marie is reading the Bible. As they walk by a pond, the distraught Wozzeck stabs her. Later, drinking in a tavern, he is seen to have blood on his hands, and rushes away. Wading into the pond to find the knife, he drowns. Their child is playing with his hobbyhorse, and does not understand when the other children tell him that his mother is dead.

Wranitzky (orig. Vranický: other forms common), **Paul** (orig. Pavel) (*b* Nová Říše, 30 Dec. 1756; *d* Vienna, 28 Sept. 1808). Austrian composer of Moravian origin. Much admired by Haydn, the best known of his numerous works was the opera *Oberon, König der Elfen* (1789), with a libretto by Giesecke from the Wieland poem later used as a source for Weber's *Oberon*. This was the first important fairy opera. His brother **Anton** (*b* 13 June 1761; *d* 6 Aug. 1820) was also a composer, and had two daughters who became singers – **Anna Katherina** (married name Kraus) (1801–51) and **Karoline** (married name Seidler) (1794–1872), who was the first Agathe.

Wreckers, The. Opera in 3 acts by Ethel Smyth; text by 'H.B. Laforestier' (Harry Brewster). Prod. Leipzig 11 Nov. 1906, cond. Nikisch; London, H.M.'s., 22 June 1909, with Sapio, Amsden, Seiter, Coates, James, Winckworth, Byndon-Ayres, cond. Beecham; Newport Festival, 3 Aug. 1972.

The scene is an 18th cent. Cornish village that lives by wrecking. Thirza (mezzo), the young wife of the preacher and headman Pascoe (bass-bar.), is in love with Mark (ten.), who in turn is loved by the lighthouse-keeper's daughter Avis (sop.). Thirza and Mark light a bonfire to warn ships to keep clear of the rocky coast, but Pascoe is discovered near it by the suspicious villagers. Mark admits that it was he who lit it, and Thirza joins him in their death by drowning.

Wrocław (Ger., Breslau). Town in Poland. In the late 17th cent. works by Johann Hallmann were given in which musical interludes and accompaniments played a part. The first operatic performances were organized by Daniel Treu (1695–1749), who organized a company in 1725 that gave successful performances at the Ballhaus of *Orlando furioso* by Antonio Bioni (1698–1739). Bioni had further successes in the city, which he dominated musically, before leaving in 1734. Operas given included Treu's own *Astarte* (1725), *Coriolano* (1726), *Ulisse e Telemacco* (1726) and *Don Chischiotte* (1727), and works by F.B. Conti, Albinoni, Porta, and Astorga (41 operas between 1725 and 1734). In 1782 the Opernhaus opened: here the repertory included much Mozart. In 1800 Vincenz Tuczek became director, with Joseph Schnabel as leader of the orchestra; when, on the Abbé Vogler's recommendation, the 17-year-old C.M. von Weber became music director in 1804, friction ensued, but outstanding performances were given of *Titus, Alceste,* and Weber's own *Peter Schmoll*. Weber started substantial reforms, but during his absence through an accident they were undone, and he resigned (1806). Under Gottlob Bierey (1772–1840) opera flourished 1808–28; the company was enlarged, new singers were brought in, and new works staged. Important Wagner performances were given in 1852–88.

When the city became Polish after the Second World War, the Opera Dolnośląska (Lower Silesian Opera) from 1945 gave Polish works, especially Moniuszko, as well as French and Italian, and later made a speciality of Czech opera. 1951 saw an important première in *Bunt Zaków* (The Revolt of the Goliards) by Tadeusz Szeligowski (1896–1963).

Wüllner, Franz (*b* Münster, 28 Jan. 1832; *d* Braunfels, 7 Sept. 1902). German conductor and composer. His first wholly operatic appointment, at the Munich Court T. as

Bülow's successor in 1869, brought him face to face with the difficulties surrounding the production of *Das Rheingold*. His successful handling of this and of *Die Walküre* led to his appointment as Court Kapellmeister in chief in 1870. Dresden 1877; deprived of his post 1882. Prepared a new version of Weber's *Oberon*. His son **Ludwig** (1858-1938) was a baritone who sang at Meiningen (1889–95) and then devoted himself to the concert platform.

Wunderlich, Fritz (*b* Kusel, 26 Sept. 1930; *d* Heidelberg, 17 Sept. 1966). German tenor. Son of a conductor and violinist; studied Freiburg, and directed his own dance-band to finance his studies. Début in student perf. Tamino 1954. Stuttgart 1955–8, Frankfurt 1958–60; Munich 1960-66: created Christoph in Egk's *Die Verlobung in San Domingo;* also created Tiresias in Orff's *Oedipus der Tyrann.* Salzburg 1959–66. London, C.G., 1965, Don Ottavio; Edinburgh Festival, 1966, Tamino. Repertory also included Henry Morosus, Lensky, and title-role in *Palestrina*. One of the finest tenors of post-war Germany, especially distinguished in Mozart roles. (R)

Wuppertal. Town in Rhineland-Westphalia, Germany. Opera is given in the new opera house (cap. 870) opened in 1956 with *Mathis der Maler.* Under Grischa Barfuss, Intendant 1958–64, and with Hans-Georg Ratjen as music director and Georg Reinhardt as designer, the company became one of the most progressive in Germany, maintaining a high standard. Its productions of operas by Monteverdi, Hindemith, and Busoni won high praise. Janos Kulka was music director 1964–76 and Kurt Horres director of opera 1964–9.

Würzburg. Town in Bavaria, Germany. After performances had been given in Sälen and Schloss Marienburg, a permanent theatre was built in 1804. Wagner was invited to become chorus master by his brother Albert, who was stage-manager and a singer there, which he did 1833–4. The old house was destroyed in March 1945 and the present theatre (cap. 750) opened in Dec. 1966 with *Meistersinger.*

X

Xenia. The Tsar's daughter (sop.) in Mussorgsky's *Boris Godunov.*

Xerxes. See *Serse.*

Xyndas, Spyridon (*b* Corfu, ?1812; *d* Athens, 12 Nov. 1896). Greek composer. Studied Corfu, then Naples, both with Mantzaros. Wrote various Italian and Greek operas; his most famous work was *O ypopsifios vouleftis* (The Parliamentary Candidate, 1867); the first opera written to a Greek libretto, this was a political satire.

Y

Yakutsk. The first moves towards the foundation of a national opera were made, as in many other Asian Soviet republics, on the basis of folk dramas with musical accompaniments. In 1940 Mark Zhirkov (1892–1951) wrote new music for one of these, and then collaborated with Genrikh Litinsky (*b* 1901) on the first Yakuti opera, *Nürgun Bo'otur* (1947). Other national operas include *Lo'okut i Nürgusun* (1959) by the Armenian Grant Grigoryan (1919–1962); *Pesn o Manchary* (The Song of the Manchary, 1967) by Edward Alexeyev (*b* 1937) and German Komrakov (*b* 1937); and *Krasny Shaman* (The Handsome Shaman, 1967) by Litinsky.

Yamadori. A Japanese prince (bar., though sometimes sung by a ten.) who is a suitor for Butterfly's hand in Puccini's *Madama Butterfly*.

Yaroslavna. Prince Igor's wife (sop.) in Borodin's opera.

Yeats, William Butler (*b* Dublin, 13 June 1865; *d* Menton, 28 Jan. 1939). Irish poet and dramatist. Operas on his works are as follows:
The Countess Cathleen (1892): Egk (*Irische Legende*, 1954).
The Land of Heart's Desire (1894): F. Hart (1914).
The Shadowy Waters (1900): Kalomiris (1951); Swain (unfin.).
The Only Jealousy of Emer (1919): Harrison (1949).
Purgatory (1939): Weisgall (1961): Crosse (1966).

Yeletsky. See *Eletsky.*

Yermolenko-Yuzhina, see *Ermolenko-Yuzhina*

Yniold. Golaud's young son (soprano, though sometimes sung by treble) in Debussy's *Pelléas et Mélisande.*

Yolanta. Opera in 1 act (9 scenes) by Tchaikovsky; text by Modest Tchaikovsky, after Henrik Hertz's story *Kong Renés Datter* (trans. Zvantsev), after Hans Andersen. Prod. St Petersburg, M., 18 Dec. 1892, with Serebryakov, Yakovlev, N. Figner, Chernov, Karelin, Frey, M. Figner, Kamenskaya, Runge, Dolina, cond. Nápravník; Scarborough-on-Hudson, Garden T., 10 Sept 1933; London, St Pancras T.H., 20 Mar. 1968, with Barstow, De Peyer, Welsby, Raffell, N. Noble, cond. Lloyd-Jones.

Yolanta (sop.), daughter of King René of Provence (bass), has had knowledge of her blindness kept from her, and the penalty for

anyone revealing her disability to her is death. Ebn-Hakia (bar.), a Moorish doctor, tells the King that only if she knows of her blindness and wills its removal can he cure her. Into her garden comes Robert, Duke of Burgundy (bass-bar.), with Count Vaudémont (ten.), who discovers Yolanta's blindness and falls in love with her, as she with him. They are interrupted, and the King declares that Vaudémont must die unless she gains her sight. This ruse succeeds in curing her; Robert, who was engaged to Yolanta but loved another, is released from his bond and she is betrothed to Vaudémont.

Other operas on the subject are by Edwards (1893) and Behrend (1919). King René of Provence is also the subject of an opera by Hérold (1824).

Young (also Youngs), (Basil) **Alexander** (*b* London, 18 Oct. 1920). British tenor. Studied London, R.C.M., and with Pollmann. Gly. 1948–9; first solo role, Scaramuccio (*Ariadne auf Naxos*), Edinburgh Festival, 1950. London, C.G., 1955–6, 1962, 1965–7, 1970 Vašek, Matteo, Monostatos, Gonzalve, Lysander; S.W., Eisenstein, Ramiro, Count Ory, Almaviva, Tom Rakewell, Orpheus (Gluck – first tenor interpreter in England), Orfeo (Monteverdi), Belmonte, Tamino, Jupiter (*Semele*); created Charles Darnay (*Tale of Two Cities*), Prince Philippe (*Dinner Engagement*), Poristchin (*Diary of a Madman*); sang in *The Government Inspector*, Wat Tyler (B.B.C.), *Bassarids* (B.B.C.). San Francisco 1965; Scottish Opera, Norwegian Opera, Wexford. Sang David in Nielsen's *Saul and David* for E.B.U. Broadcast, Copenhagen. Specially associated with *The Rake's Progress*, which he recorded under Stravinsky and sang in Europe and U.S.A. (R)

Young, Cecilia (*b* London, prob. 1711; *d* London, 6 Oct. 1789). English soprano. Made a mark as early as 1730 at D.L., and by 1735 was in Handel's company. Married Arne in 1737, and sang in his works in Dublin, but separated from him about 1755. Ill health dogged her, but Burney could find that, at her best, 'her voice, shape and singing were superior to those of any female singer in the country'. The Arnes' separation was caused by their quarrel over the apprenticeship of **Polly Young** (*b* London, *c* 1749; *d* London, 20 Sept. 1799), who sang at King's and C.G., and in Italy with her husband Barthélemon in his works.

Young Lord, The. See *Junge Lord, Der.*

Ysaÿe, Eugène (-Auguste) (*b* Liège, 16 July 1858; *d* Brussels, 12 May 1931). Belgian violinist and composer. Conducted C.G., 1907 (*Fidelio*). Though famous as a violinist and composer for his instrument, Ysaÿe composed an opera to his own text in Walloon, *Piér li houïeu* (Peter the Miner, 1931). He hoped to conduct the work himself, but collapsed at the

553

first rehearsal and only heard one performance before his death.

Yugoslavia. Of the states of modern Yugoslavia, opera has principally flourished in Croatia, Serbia, and Slovenia, though in recent times other states and their towns have made considerable advances.

Croatia. Even during the period of Habsburg hegemony, attempts were made to develop a Croatian tradition. Vatroslav *Lisinski wrote the first Croatian opera in *Ljubav i zloba,* later producing a more mature work in *Porin.* In 1870 Ivan *Zajc reorganized the Zagreb Oper and gave a new artistic lead. His *Nikola Šubić Zrinjski* (1876), in Croatian, is the first Croatian national Romantic opera; but his repertory in Zagreb was dependent upon French and German works supplementing the basic Italian repertory, together with some new Czech and Russian works. His principal successor as a Croatian composer of opera was Blagoje Bersa (1873–1904), with *Oganje* (Fire, 1911). Josip Hatze (1879–1959) wrote a 1 act *verismo* opera *Povratak* (The Return, 1911), also *Adel i Mara* (1932). Antun Dobronić (1878–1955) wrote many operas, some in original and experimental forms. Other Croatian composers include Jakov *Gotovac, whose *Ero s onogo svijeta* (Ero from the other world, or Ero the Joker, 1935) has won international success. Croatia's operatic life, which is centred on Zagreb, continues to be rich and enterprising.

Serbia. In 1831 Prince Miloš summoned Josif Šlezinger (1794–1870) to Kragujevac, then capital of Serbia. Šlezinger composed music for plays, the most important of which was *Tsar Dušan's Wedding* (1840), described in contemporary accounts as 'in the manner of an Italian opera'. A form of Serbian Singspiel also began to gain in popularity and to earn more serious attention from musicians. Davorin Jenko (1835–1914) worked in Belgrade, adding music of his own to operas performed at the National T.; he also wrote *Vračara* (The Fortune-Teller, 1882), and the more musically elaborate *Pribislav and Božana* (1894). The first opera performed was the Czech Vilem Blodek's *V studni* (In the Well); many Czechs, working in Serbia, exercised a stimulating influence on local musical life. The first important Serbian opera composer was Stanislav Binički (1872–1942), who conducted the first operas at the National Theatre and in 1920 became director of the newly founded permanent ensemble. His *Na uranku* (The Mayday Feast, 1903) is in *verismo* manner. Isidor Bajić (1878–1915) wrote *Knez Ivo od Semberije* (Prince Ivo of Semberia 1911), in which some use is made of *Leitmotiv*. Petar Krstić (1877–1957) wrote some Singspiel works, including *Snežana i sedam patuljaka* (Snow-White and the Seven Dwarfs, 1912); his most famous opera was *Zulumćar* (The Tyrant, 1928), a comparatively modest work musically. Petar Stojanović (1877–1957) wrote some operas and operettas. A stronger individual talent was shown by Petar Konjović (1883–1970), influenced by Russian and Czech opera, especially Mussorgsky and Janáček, though his *Vilin veo* (The Fairy's Veil, 1917) is a Weberian fairy opera. His *Knez od Zete* (The Prince of Zeta, 1929) and *Koštana* (1931) are more original. Serbian opera is now securely established, with a number of younger composers writing works.

Slovenia. The proximity of Slovenia to Italy has influenced the development of opera. The first Italian opera was staged in Ljubljana as early as 1652. A theatre was built in the city in 1765 (cap. 800). The first Slovenian opera composer was Jacob Zupan (1734–1810), with *Belin* (1780). Franz Pollini (1762–1846) wrote an opera buffa, *La casetta nei boschi.* In the middle of the 18th cent. German companies began paying visits, and Mozart's works were first heard. J.B. Novak (1756–1833) wrote *Figaro* (1790); other Slovenian composers were Jurij Mihevec (1805–82) and Gašpar Mašek (1794–1873), later Risto Savin (pseudonym of Frideric Širca, 1859–1948), with *Lepa Vida* (Fair Vida). In general, the tradition has been less nationalistic than in Croatia and Serbia.

See also *Belgrade, Dubrovnik, Novi Sad, Rijeka, Split, Zagreb.*

Z

Zaccaria. The High Priest of Israel (bass) in Verdi's *Nabucco*.

Zaccaria, Nicola (*b* Athens, 9 Mar. 1923). Greek bass. Studied Athens. Début Athens, 1949, Raimondo. Milan, Sc., 1953–74. London, C.G., 1957, 1959, Oroveso, Creon (*Medée*); Dallas, Vienna, etc. Created 3rd Tempter (*Assassinio nella cattedrale*); repertory also includes Zaccaria, Silva, Conte Rodolfo, and Sarastro. (R)

Zádor, Dezső (Desider) (*b* Horna Krupa, 8 Mar. 1873; *d* Berlin 24 April 1931). Hungarian baritone. Studied Budapest with Adele Passy-Cornet and Vienna. Début Czernowitz, 1898, Almaviva; Elberfeld 1898–1901; Prague 1901–6; Berlin, K., 1906–11; Dresden, 1911–16; Budapest (also conductor) 1916–19; Berlin, Stä. O., 1920–24; London, C.G., 1906–8, 1910, Alberich, Father in *Hänsel und Gretel*. Towards end of career confined himself to bass roles; sang Valentine in one of the earliest recordings of *Faust* (Berlin 1908), which reveals a beautiful and flexible voice. (R) Married the contralto Emma Bassth (1888–?).

Zafred, Mario (*b* Trieste, 2 Mar. 1922). Italian composer and critic. Studied Rome with Pizzetti, and in Paris. Critic of *Unità* (Rome) 1949–56. Artistic director Trieste, T. Giuseppe Verdi 1966, and Rome T. dell'Opera, 1968. His operas include *Hamlet* (Rome 1961) and *Wallenstein* (Rome 1965) and are very much in the vein of contemporary Soviet composers, in line with his own political philosophy.

Zagreb (Ger. Agram). Town in Croatia, Yugoslavia. The first centre of operatic life was at the palace of Count Amadea, who introduced a German company in 1797. For 37 years opera was performed there. In 1834 the first public theatre was built and was in use until 1895. It is interesting to note that a theatre journal was already in circulation in 1815. From 1841 regular visits of German companies were organized by the German Opera and Dramatic Society, but performances in Croatian began about the same time, and in 1846 Lisinski's *Ljubav i zloba* (Love and Malice) was given its first performance (by amateurs). In 1861 official blessing was given to a policy of fostering Croatian opera, and the period of German domination thus ended. When Zajc, one of the first composers to write in the Croatian language, returned from Vienna in 1870, he reorganized the Zagreb Opera and Operetta Theatres, the latter having been founded in 1863. At the end of the 19th cent. the Croatian theatre encountered difficulties from the Magyar Government, which closed the theatre in 1889. Performances continued in the open air in summer and in 1895 the present theatre, by Hellmer and Fellner, was opened, with the first Croatian national opera, Zagc's *Nikola Šubić Zrinjski*, only to close again in 1902. It reopened in 1909 and has maintained regular performances except during the two wars. The company has toured abroad and made several recordings, but has been weakened by the loss to foreign companies of singers and conductors such as Sena Jurinac, Zinka Milanov, Vladimir Ruždjak, Nada Puttar, Josip Gostić, Rudolf Francl, Marijana Radev, Tomislav Neralić, Dragica Martinis, Berislav Klobučar, and Mladen Bašić. Opera is given at the National T., operetta at the Comedy T. The producer Vlado Habunek has also worked at C.G., with the designer Božidar Ražica.

Zaïde. Opera in 2 acts, unfinished, by Mozart; text by Schachtner. Prod. Frankfurt 27 Jan. 1866, when the dialogue was rewritten and completed by Gollmick and an overture and finale added by Anton André. London, Toynbee Hall, 10 Jan. 1953, by City O.C., with S. Barrett, cond. Dempster; Tanglewood 8 Aug. 1955, with Cardillo, Lussier, Boatwright, Zulick, cond. Sarah Caldwell.

Zaïde (sop.), the favourite of the Sultan (ten.), pities his captive Gomatz (ten.), and secretly provides him with money for escape. Allazim, a renegade in the Sultan's service, helps them to escape, but they are captured. The Sultan remains tyrannical. It is not known how the plot might have finished. The work includes a comic slavemaster, Osmin, and anticipates not only *Die Entführung*, but also *Die Zauberflöte* in details such as Gomatz falling in love with Zaïde's portrait.

Zajc, Ivan (*b* Rijeka, 21 Jan. 1832; *d* Zagreb, 17 Dec. 1914). Yugoslav (Croatian) composer. Studied with his father, later Milan with Lauro Rossi. After working in Italy and in Vienna, he returned home in 1870 and became director of the Zagreb Conservatory and conductor at the theatre. He was an important founder of Croatian opera, and was the first composer to set Croatian texts (as well as Italian and German). His most important work is *Nikola Šubić Zrinjski* (1876), to a text by Hugo Badalić based on Körner's drama *Zriny* (1814). Based on the manner of Verdi's Risorgimento operas, the work includes some charming Oriental music (of which Zajc had a good knowledge) and some rousing tunes mostly built on the short phrases that were part of his idiom, and is well scored, especially for woodwind.
Bibl: H. Pettan: *Popis Skladbi Ivana Zajca* (1956).

Zamboni, Luigi (*b* Bologna, 1767; *d* Florence, 28 Feb. 1837). Italian bass. Début Ravenna 1791 in Cimarosa's *Fanatico in Berlina*. Became one of the leading buffo basses of the day; created Rossini's Figaro (1816) and appeared in operas by Fioravanti, Paisiello, Pavesi, etc. Retired 1825.

Zamboni, Maria (*b* Peschiera, 25 July 1895; *d* Verona, 25 Mar. 1976). Italian soprano. Studied Parma with Silva. Début Piacenza, 1921, Marguerite. Rome, T. Costanzi, 1922–6, and T.R., 1929–30, where she created Maria in Pizzetti's *Lo straniero*. Milan, Sc., 1924–7, 1929–31, where she created Liù and also sang Eurydice, Elsa, Eva, Mimì and Manon. Buenos Aires, Colón, 1924; career continued until 1934. (R)

Zampa. Opera in 3 acts by Hérold; text by Mélisville. Prod. Paris, O.C., 3 May 1831, with Casimir, Boulanger, Chollet, Féréol, Moreau-Cinta; London, Hm., 19 Apr. 1833; Boston 26 July 1833, with St Clair, Amédée, Hurteaux.

At the head of his pirate band, Zampa invades the island of Castel Lugano and forces Camilla, daughter of the Count, to abandon her betrothed Alfonso for him. As they celebrate this new betrothal, Zampa places a ring on the finger of the statue of his former bride Alice: the fingers close over the ring threateningly. Zampa remains unmoved by all pleas to release Camilla, and reveals that he is the Count of Monza, and thus Alfonso's brother. Zampa sends Alfonso to prison and orders the statue to be thrown into the sea, while Camilla claims sanctuary at the altar; Zampa tears her away from the altar but is dragged beneath the waves by the cold hand of the statue. Camilla is joined to Alfonso.

Zandonai, Riccardo (*b* Sacco, 28 May 1883; *d* Pesaro, 5 June 1944). Italian composer. Studied Pesaro with Mascagni. Basically an operatic composer; seized on by Ricordi as a successor to Puccini in the *verismo* tradition. *Il grillo del focolare* (1908) was well received, but his wider fame dates from *Conchita* (1911) and still more from *Francesca da Rimini* (1914). Of the six works that followed, the most popular have been *Giulietta e Romeo* (1922) and especially *I cavalieri di Ekebù* (1925). His wife was Tarapunia Tarquin (1883–1976), who created the title role in *Conchita*, and also sang Carmen, Salome, and Santuzza.

Zandt, Marie van (*b* New York, 8 Oct. 1858; *d* Cannes, 31 Dec. 1919). American soprano. Studied with her mother, the soprano Jennie van Zandt, and in Milan with Lamperti. Début Turin 1879, Zerlina; Paris, O.C., 1880–5, where she created Lakmé, which was specially written for her by Delibes. N.Y., Met., 1891–2 and 1896. London, H.M.'s 1880; Gaiety T., 1885 (Lakmé); C.G., 1889. Her success as Lakmé caused jealousy among her French colleagues at the O.C., who accused her (falsely) of

appearing on stage drunk.

Zanelli (orig. Morales), **Renato** (*b* Valparaiso, 1 Apr. 1892; *d* Santiago, 25 Mar. 1935). Chilean tenor, orig. baritone. Studied Chile with Angelo Querze. Début Santiago 1916, Valentine. N.Y., Met., 1919–23 in Italian repertory as baritone. Went to Italy, and after further study in Milan with Dante Lari and Fernando Tanara, made tenor début Naples, S.C., 1924 as Raoul. London, C.G., 1928–1930 Otello. Rome, T.R., 1928–32 Tristan, Siegmund, Alvaro, also creating title-role in Pizzetti's *Lo straniero*; Milan, Sc., 1930–32 Lo Straniero and Tristan. Career cut short by ill-health in 1933, though he sang Otello once in Santiago in 1935 a few weeks before his death. One of the great Otellos of the century; was studying the Wagner Heldentenor repertory in German with view to singing Tristan at Covent Garden. (R) His brother **Carlo Morelli** (1897–1970) was a baritone who sang with success in Italy, and at the N.Y., Met., 1935–40, and elsewhere in the U.S.A. until 1949. (R)

Zanten, Cornelie van (*b* Dordrecht, 2 Aug. 1855; *d* The Hague, 10 Jan. 1946). Dutch soprano. Studied Cologne, and Milan with Lamperti. Début Turin, 1875, Leonore (*Favorite*). Breslau 1880–82; Kassel 1882–3; Amsterdam from 1884. Toured U.S.A. 1886–7 with Theodore Thomas's National Opera Co. Sang in *Ring* in Russia. Repertory included Fidès, Sextus, Orfeo, Azucena, Amneris, and Ortrud. After leaving stage taught in Amsterdam; her pupils included Julia Culp and Urlus.

Zareska, Eugenia (*b* Rava Ruska, 9 Nov. 1910). Ukrainian, later British, mezzo-soprano. Studied Lwów Conservatory with Didur, Vienna with Mildenburg, and Milan. Début Milan Sc. 1941, Dorabella. London, Cambridge T., 1947, Rosina; C.G., 1948–9, 1952–3, 1957–8 Cherubino, Carmen; Glyndebourne 1948. Has appeared at Aix and Florence Festivals, and in 1949 sang the Gräfin Geschwitz in Berg's *Lulu* at the Venice Festival. (R)

Zar und Zimmermann (Tsar and Carpenter). Opera in 3 acts by Lortzing; text by composer, after the play by Mélesville, Merle, and De Boirie (1818). Prod. Leipzig 22 Dec. 1837, with Günther, Frau Lortzing, A. Lortzing, Richter, Berthold; N.Y. 9 Dec. 1851, with Arming, Müller, Oehrlein, Beutler; London, Gaiety T., 15 Apr. 1871, with B. Cole, A. Tremaine, Lyall, Santley, Cook, cond. Meyer Lutz.

Peter the Great (bar.) is working in the Saardam shipyards under the name of Peter Michaelov so as to learn trades he cannot in Russia. He befriends a deserter, Peter Ivanov (ten.), in love with Marie (sop.), daughter of the Burgomaster Van Bett (bass). Asked by the English to discover if Peter the Great is indeed in the shipyard, Van Bett identifies the wrong

Peter; the English Ambassador Lord Syndham (bass) and the Russian Ambassador Admiral Lefort (bass) are taken in, though the French Ambassador, the Marquis de Châteauneuf (ten.), recognizes the real Tsar. After a festival, Van Bett prepares to send Peter Ivanov home with an anthem (whose rehearsal provides an entertaining number). Meanwhile the real Tsar slips away. See also *Peter the Great*.

Zarzuela. A type of Spanish opera, mingling dialogue with music, usually popular in nature. The word derives from *zarza*, a bramble: at the Palace of La Zarzuela, near Madrid, which took its name from the surrounding brambles, festive entertainments known as *Fiestas de zarzuela* were given in the 17th cent. The earliest was Lope de Vega's *La selva sin amor* (The Forest without Love, 1629), and the earliest known composer was Juan Hidalgo (*Los celos hacen estrellas*, ?1644). Hidalgo also composed music for Calderón's *Ni amor se libra de Amor* (*c*1640) and *Celos aun del aire matan* (1662). At this stage, the zarzuela resembled the French *ballet de cour*, with the formality of mythological subjects occasionally relieved by the introduction of popular songs. With the Italian domination of opera in the succeeding century, zarzuela was rare, though it was kept alive as a relief from the unwelcome foreign formality of opera seria. Nevertheless, it was itself formal enough to prompt a reaction in the form of *tonadilla.

By the early to mid–19th cent. a revival of zarzuela was under way with the growth of nationalism. Great popularity attached to *El novio y el concierto* (1839), with music by an Italian, Basilio Basili, parodying Italian operatic mannerisms. The fashion grew to the point at which the T. de la Zarzuela was opened in Madrid in 1856, followed by the T. Apolo (1873). Prominent composers of this period included Francisco Barbieri (1823–94: *Jugar con fuego*, 1851; *Pan y toros*, 1864, in which Goya makes an appearance) and Pascual Arrieta (1823–94: *Marina*, 1871). Different categories of zarzuela developed, principally *zarzuela grande*, normally in 3 acts and close to Romantic opera in style, and the *género chico* or *zarzuelita*, in 1 act and normally satirical in content. Important composers of later 19th cent. zarzuela included Ruperto Chapí y Lorente (1851–1909), M. Fernández Caballero (1835–1906), Tomás Bretón y Hernández (1850–1923), Joaquín Valverde (1846–1910), Amadeo Vives (1871–1932), Gerónimo Giménez (1854–1923), Jesús Guridi (1886–1961), Jacinto Guererro (1895–1951), Francisco Alonso (*b* 1887), and Federico Moreno-Torroba (*b* 1891).
Bibl: G. Chase: *The Music of Spain* (R/1959).

Zauberflöte, Die (The Magic Flute). Opera in 2 acts by Mozart; text by Emanuel Schikaneder,

after the story *Lulu* in Wieland's collection of Oriental fairy tales *Dschinnistan* (1786). Prod. Vienna, W., 30 Sept. 1791, with Hofer, Gottlieb, Gerl, Schack, Nouseul, Schikaneder, Winter, cond. Mozart; London, Hm., 6 June 1811 with Griglietti, Bertinotti-Radicati, Cauvini, Sgra. Cauvini, Righi, Naldi, Rovedino, cond. Weichsell (leader) and Pucilta (continuo); N.Y., P.O.H., 17 Apr. 1833, with Mrs Wallack, Mrs Austin, Mrs Sharpe, John Jones, Placide, Horn. There is an opera *Mozarts Zauberflöte* (1820) by Riotte.

Tamino (ten.) is saved from a serpent by three attendants of the Queen of Night, but having fainted believes his rescuer to be the bird-catcher Papageno (bar.). For not admitting the truth, Papageno is punished by the attendants, who produce a picture of Pamina with which Tamino falls in love. Her mother, the Queen of Night (sop.), arrives to tell Tamino of Pamina's capture by Sarastro. For their rescue mission, Tamino is provided with a magic flute, Papageno with magic bells. Pamina (sop.) is guarded in Sarastro's palace by the evil Moor, Monostatos (ten.), who flees, mistaking Papageno for the Devil. Tamino learns that Sarastro is a wise priest, and that it is the Queen who is evil. Papageno and Pamina are caught trying to escape by Monostatos and his slaves, but the magic bells set the capturers dancing helplessly. Tamino and Pamina meet and fall in love; they are made ready for initiation ordeals.

Sarastro (bass) obtains the consent of the priests for Tamino to undergo initiation to their brotherhood. In the vaults, Tamino and Papageno are under a vow of silence which the latter finds intolerable. Tamino refuses to flee when urged by the Queen's attendants. Monostatos tries to kiss Pamina, who is told by the Queen to kill Sarastro; she asks mercy for her mother and is told by Sarastro that in a holy place there is no hatred. Papageno is provided with a feast, and Tamino resists the temptation to speak to a hurt and bewildered Pamina, who thereupon longs for death. Sarastro reassures the lovers. Papageno wishes for a wife, and an old woman (sop.) who had previously brought him water presents herself. As Papageno reluctantly accepts, she turns into a beautiful girl, Papagena, but disappears immediately. Pamina's suicide is forestalled by three boys. The lovers pass together through fire and water, protected by the flute. The dejected Papageno tries to hang himself but on the boys' advice he uses the magic bells to bring Papagena back. The Queen, her attendants, and Monostatos make a last attempt to destroy Sarastro and rescue Pamina, but flee before the noise of thunder. Tamino and Pamina are united, and all join in praise of Isis and Osiris.

Zauberoper (*Ger* magic opera). A form of

opera, distinguished only by its greater substance from *Zauberposse* (above), popular in Vienna in the late 18th and early 19th cent., which a fairy story was told with sumptuous scenic effects, ribald comedy, and music by a distinguished composer. One of the earliest examples was Wranitzky's setting of the Oberon story (1789) and the latest Weber's (1826). Its greatest example, entirely transcending the form through its moral substance, is Mozart's *Die Zauberflöte*.

Zauberposse. A version of the popular Viennese musical form *Posse, in which magic and the supernatural played a leading part.

Zazà. Opera in 4 acts by Leoncavallo; text by composer, after the play by Simon and Berton. Prod. Milan, T.L., 10 Nov. 1900, with Storchio, Garbin, Sammarco, cond. Toscanini; San Francisco 27 Nov. 1903; London, Coronet T., 30 Apr. 1909.

After *Pagliacci* Leoncavallo's most successful opera, it tells of the affair between the Parisian music-hall singer Zazà (sop.) and Milio Dufresne (ten.), a married man about town, and of Zazà's return to her lover Cascart (bar.).

Zbruyeva, Evgeniya (Ivanovna) (*b* Moscow, 5 Jan. 1868; *d* Moscow, 20 Jan. 1936). Russian contralto. Illegitimate daughter of the composer P.P. Bulakhov. Studied Moscow with Lavrovskaya. Début Moscow, B., 1894, Vanya. Moscow 1894–1905; St Petersburg, M., 1905–17. Appearances in Germany and France 1907–12. Taught St Petersburg 1915–17, Moscow 1917–36. Sang Marfa with Shalyapin, St Petersburg 1911. Her other most famous roles included Lel, Hänsel, Erda, and Konchakovna. (R)

Zdenka. Arabella's sister (sop.) in Strauss's *Arabella*.

Zeani (orig. Zahan), **Virginia** (*b* Solovastru, 21 Oct. 1928). Romanian soprano. Studied Bucharest with Anghel and Lipkowska and Milan with Pertile. Début Bologna, 1948, Violetta. London, Stoll, 1953, Violetta; 1957, Lucia (first in London since 1925); C.G., 1959. Milan, Sc., 1956 Cleopatra (Handel), and subsequently; created Blanche in *Carmélites*, 1957; Rome since 1955; N.Y., Met., 1966. Sang in major revivals of neglected works of Rossini (Desdemona in *Otello*); Donizetti (inc. title-role in *Maria di Rohan*), and Verdi (title-role in *Alzira*). After successes in bel canto repertory began to sing more dramatic roles, including Manon Lescaut, Tosca, Aida, etc. Repertory also includes the four soprano roles in *Hoffmann*. Married to bass Nicola *Rossi-Lemeni. (R)

Zeffirelli, Franco (orig. Gian Franco Corsi) (*b* Florence, 12 Feb. 1923). Italian producer and designer. After working for the straight stage

and films, Zeffirelli turned to opera in 1948. He produced and designed several works for Sc., Milan, notably *Il Turco in Italia, Cenerentola,* and *Don Pasquale.* He gave new life to Italian Romantic opera with his production of *Lucia di Lammermoor* at C.G., in 1959, and later that year turned his attention to *verismo* with his *Cavalleria rusticana* and *Pagliacci.* His production of Verdi's *Falstaff* was thought by some to be fussy and un-Shakespearian. He has also produced opera in the U.S.A., notably at Dallas, San Francisco, and Chicago.

Zeffiretti lusinghieri. Ilia's (sop.) aria in Act 3, scene 1, of Mozart's *Idomeneo.*

Zeller, Carl (Johann Adam) (*b* St Peter in der Au, 19 June 1842; *d* Baden, nr Vienna, 17 Aug. 1898). Austrian composer. Studied with the village teacher and organist, later with Sechter. After practising law, entered the Ministry of Education and Culture in 1873. His greatest success, which revived enthusiasm for Viennese operetta in the 1890s, was *Der Vogelhändler* (1894). Its lively melodic charm won it a wider following than most of his other works, though *Der Obersteiger* (1894) achieved some popularity.

Zémire et Azor. *Comédie-ballet* in 4 acts by Grétry; text by Marmontel, after La Chaussée's comedy *Amour par amour* (1742). Prod. Fontainebleau (Court) 9 Nov. 1771, with Clavibal; London, D.L., 5 Dec. 1776; N.Y., 1 June 1787, cond. M. Huni. This version of the *Beauty and the Beast* fairy tale was also set by Baumgarten (1775), Neefe (1776), Tozzi (1791), Spohr (1819), Garcia (1827), and Chukhadjian (1891); sequel by Umlauff, *Der Ring der Liebe* (1786).

Zemlinsky, Alexander von (*b* Vienna, 4 Oct. 1872; *d* Larchmont, N.Y., 16 Mar. 1942). Austrian, later American, conductor and composer. Studied Vienna. Conductor Vienna, Karl T., V.O., 1906, Court O., 1908; Mannheim 1909–11; Prague, Deutsche Oper, 1911–27; Berlin 1927–32 collaborating with Klemperer at the Kroll; Vienna 1933–8. His six operas were all produced with moderate success in Germany and Austria. He was the teacher of Schoenberg, who married his sister. Other pupils were Bodanzky, Peter Hermann Adler, and Korngold.

Zenatello, Giovanni (*b* Verona, 22 Feb. 1876; *d* New York 11 Feb. 1949). Italian tenor, formerly baritone. Studied Verona. Début Belluno, 1898, Silvio. Tenor début Naples, T. Mercadante, 1899, Canio (having sung Silvio at previous performance). Milan, Sc., 1903–7, creating Pinkerton and leading tenor roles in *Siberia, Figlio di Jorio, Gloria,* and *Germania.* London, C.G., 1905–6, 1908–9, 1926; first London Loris (*Fedora*), the first C.G. Chénier, and a much-admired Otello, which he sang more than 300 times. N.Y., Manhattan O., 1907–10; Met. tour (replacing Caruso) 1909; Chicago 1911–13; Boston Opera 1910–17. Instrumental in launching the *Verona Arena project. Married mezzo-soprano Maria *Gay (1913). Final appearance, Sept. 1933, Canio in N.Y.; thereafter devoted his time to teaching. Pupils included Lily Pons and Nino Martini. Also heard Callas at an audition and arranged her engagement for Verona in 1947 as La Gioconda; this launched her international career. (R)

Zeno, Apostolo (b Venice, 11 Dec. 1668; d Venice, 11 Nov. 1750). Italian librettist. By profession an historian and critic, and editor of an important journal, he regarded libretto-writing as incidental to his career. He was, however, Caesarean Poet 1718–29, a post that demanded the provision of librettos among its other formal duties; he was succeeded in this by Metastasio. He is important as a crucial founder of opera seria. His version of opera restricts the cast to eight characters (more often six), restricts the action to one main plot (perhaps with an amorous sub-plot) in three to five acts, arranges for each scene to end with an exit aria, and is written for noble characters of exemplary moral behaviour whose predicament culminates in a triumphal scene resolving all. His scholarly bent ensured that the sources and background to his plots were carefully set out in his prefaces: authors upon whom he drew include Thucydides, Herodotus, Plutarch, and Livy, as well as Racine and Corneille. Though he was a poor versifier, he was expert at providing his composers with scenes of action, of confrontation, and of forceful emotion. The many composers who used his librettos included Araia, Ariosti, Bononcini, Cherubini, Ciampi, Duni, Fux, Galuppi, Guglielmi, Handel, Hasse, Pergolesi, Porpora, Sacchini, Scarlatti, Traetta, Vivaldi, and Zingarelli.

Zerbinetta. The leader of the Harlequinade (sop.) in Strauss's *Ariadne auf Naxos.*

Zerlina. (1) The peasant girl (sop.) betrothed to Masetto in Mozart's *Don Giovanni.* (2) An innkeeper's daughter (sop.), heroine of Auber's *Fra Diavolo.*

Zerr, Anna (b Baden-Baden, 26 July 1822; d Winterbach, 14 Nov. 1881). German soprano. Studied with Bordogni. Début Karlsruhe 1839, singing there until 1846. Vienna, Kä., 1846–52 where she created title-role in *Martha.* London, 1851–2 Queen of Night, Lucia, Rosa in first London performance of Spohr's *Faust* and Catherine in Jullien's *Pietro il Grande.* Disliked by Chorley, who likened her to 'a pea-hen masquerading as a lark'. Deprived of her title of Court Singer in Vienna because she sang in a Benefit for Hungarian refugees. Went to U.S.A., where she remained until 1857; she then married and retired from the stage.

Zigeunerbaron, Der (The Gipsy Baron). Operetta in 3 acts by Johann Strauss; text by Schnitzer, altered from a libretto by Jókai on his story *Saffi.* Prod. Vienna, W., 24 Oct. 1885, with Collin, Hartmann, Reisser, Streitmann, Girardi, cond. J. Strauss; N.Y., Casino T., 15 Feb. 1886, with Hall, Fritch, St John, Castle, Wilson, Fitzgerald, cond. Williams; London, Rudolf Steiner T., 12 Feb. 1935, by amateurs.

The complicated plot tells of Sandor Barinkay (ten.) who comes to claim his ancestral lands only to find them overrun by gipsies. He falls in love with one of them, Saffi (sop.), who turns out to be a princess.

Zilli (orig. Fiappo), **Emma** (b Fagnana, Udine, 11 Nov. 1864; d Havana, Jan. 1901). Italian soprano. Studied piano with her mother Lucia Carlini and only began to study singing after her marriage to the painter Giacomo Zilli in 1882. Début Ferrara 1887, Paolina in *Poliuto.* Appeared throughout Italy, Spain, Poland, Hungary, etc. Milan, Sc., 1889, Camille (*Zampa*); Created Alice in *Falstaff* 1893. London, C.G., 1894 Alice. Admired by Puccini and successful as Manon Lescaut and Fidelia in *Edgar.* An exciting singing-actress. Contracted yellow fever during a tour of South America, where she died in 1901.

Zilliani, Alessandro (b Busseto, 3 June 1907; d Milan, 18 Feb. 1977). Italian tenor. Studied Milan with Alfredo Cecchi. Début Milan, T.d.V., 1928 Pinkerton. Milan, Sc., 1932–6, 1938–9, 1945–6; Rome, T.R., 1930–34, 1936–9, 1941–2, 1946–7 and most Italian houses; created leading tenor roles in operas by Wolf-Ferrari (*Vedova scaltra*), Mascagni (*Pinotta*), Peragallo, Pannain, Pedrollo, and others. Calaf in first Italian perf. of Busoni's *Turandot* (1940). San Francisco 1938. Guest appearances in Germany during Second World War in opera and operetta. Married soprano Mafalda *Favero. (R)

Zimin, Sergey (Ivanovich) (b Orekhovo-Zuyevo, 3 July 1875; d Moscow, 26 Aug. 1942). Russian impresario. Studied singing, then in 1904 began organizing opera seasons in his own name in Moscow, opening with *May Night* at the Aquarium T. He made out of this enterprise one of the finest companies in Russia, gathering excellent singers (many from the recently disbanded Mamontov company, Nov. 1908), directors, and designers. The company performed at the Solodovnikov Theatre which was taken out of Zimin's hands in the revolution, though he continued working in opera as an adviser and producer, including 1919-20 at the Maly T. and 1924-42 at the Bolshoy. In its day, the Zimin T. did much to advance the

works of Russian composers, giving the première of *The Golden Cockerel*, the first Moscow *Khovanshchina*, and a series of all Tchaikovsky's operas from 1904 until 1917. It also gave the first Russian *Rienzi* and *Meistersinger*. Artists who worked with the company included the singers Yermolenko-Yuzhina, Matveyev, Shevelyov, and Osipov, with as guests Shalyapin, Sobinov, and Battistini, the conductors Ippolitov-Ivanov and Emil Cooper, and the producers Pyotr Olenin (chief producer 1907-15) and Komissarzhevsky (chief producer 1915-19).
Bibl: S. Zimin: *History of the S. I. Zimin Opera Company* (MS).

Zimmermann, Bernd-Alois (*b* Bliesheim, 20 Mar. 1918; *d* Cologne, 10 Aug. 1970). German composer. Studied Cologne with Lemacher and Jarnach. His opera *Die Soldaten* (1960, after R. Lenz) aroused considerable controversy, and was successful in several countries.

Zimmermann, Erich (*b* Meissen, 29 Nov. 1892; *d* Berlin, 24 Feb. 1968). German tenor. Studied Dresden. Début there 1918. Munich 1925–30, Vienna 1931–4; Berlin, S.O., 1934–44; Bayreuth 1925–44. London, C.G., 1934, 1937–9, 1950. One of the outstanding Mimes and Davids of the inter-war years. (R)

Zingarelli, Niccolò Antonio (*b* Naples, 4 Apr. 1752; *d* Torre del Greco, 5 May 1837). Italian composer. Studied Naples with Fenaroli, Speranza, Anfossi, and Sacchini. His first opera, *I quattro pazzi* (1768) was produced while he was still a student, and shortly afterwards *Montezuma* (1781) was produced at Esterház and commended by Haydn. His greatest triumphs were in Milan, where he wrote popular works at incredible speed for Sc. Returned to Milan after an unsuccessful venture in Paris and concentrated on comic opera, which spread his fame to Germany, before a church appointment turned his attention toward sacred music. In Rome from 1804, he composed comic operas, including the popular *Berenice* (1811), his last opera. His resistance to Napoleon caused him to be arrested and taken to Paris, where the Emperor, an admirer of his music, released him and granted him a pension.

Zingarelli was the last major composer of opera seria, and most of his operas are on the conventional mythological subjects. The fluency of his technique enabled him to turn out large numbers of works that efficiently served the demands of the singers of the day, but this also encouraged him to write too much, too fast. He was a skilful orchestrator, and his tragic heroines are especially well drawn; but there is too much that is hasty or trivial in his work to encourage modern revival.

His best-known opera, *Giulietta e Romeo* (1796), loosely based on Shakespeare through with a happy ending, survived in repertories until the 1830s, largely through its adoption by Malibran.

Zíték, Vilem (*b* Prague, 9 Sept. 1890; *d* Prague, 16 Aug. 1956). Czech bass. Studied Prague Pivoda School. Début Prague, April 1911, singing secondary roles until 1914 when he sang Gremin. Leading bass in Prague until his retirement in 1947, singing more than 3,000 performances, in the Czech, Russian, Italian, and German repertories. Went to Italy 1925 for further study, and was engaged by Toscanini for Milan, Sc., 1927–8 as Fasolt and Hunding, returned 1929–31 as Gessler, Commendatore, Fafner, and Hunding; also Turin, Florence, Paris, where he sang Mozart roles under Bruno Walter. His most famous roles were Beneš in *Dalibor*, Kecal, the Water Goblin in *Rusalka*, Barach in *The Devil's Wall*, and Mozart's Figaro. (R)

Zola, Emile (*b* 2 Paris, Apr. 1840; *d* Paris, 29 Sept. 1902). French author and dramatist. Zola's wide human interests included a belief in the powers of the musical stage to express real and important issues; he collaborated on several operas with Alfred *Bruneau (or wrote texts later used by him): these were *Le Rêve* (1891), *L'Attaque du moulin* (1893), *Messidor* (1897), *L'Ouragan* (1901), *L'Enfant-Roi* (1905), *Naïs Micoulin* (1907), and *Les Quatre journées* (1916). Other operas on his works are as follows:
Nana (1880): Gurlitt (1933).
Germinal (1885): Kaan z Albéstů (comp. 1902-8).
L'Attaque du moulin (1893): K. Weis (*Útok na mlýn*, 1912).

Zöllner, Heinrich (*b* Leipzig, 4 July 1854; *d* Freiburg, 8 May 1941). German conductor and composer. Studied Leipzig with Reinecke, Jadassohn, and Richter. Kapellmeister of new Flemish Opera, Antwerp, 1907–14. His ten operas include *Faust* (1887) and, his most successful work, *Die versunkene Glocke* (1899), frequently revived up to 1939.

Zottmayr, Georg (*b* Munich, 24 Jan. 1869; *d* Dresden, 11 Dec. 1941). German bass. The son of **Ludwig Zottmayr**, who was leading bass at Munich Opera and created King Mark. Studied Munich and began career as concert singer. Vienna, 1906, 1909; Prague, Deutsches T., 1908–10; Dresden 1910–192?, leading bass, especially renowned for his Wagner roles, and as Sarastro, Stadinger in *Waffenschmied*, and Hermit in *Freischütz*. (R)

Zukunftmusik (*Ger* music of the future). The term coined by Wagner for his music in suggesting that he had discovered and opened up a new means of composition: it was much used in the polemics surrounding him.

Zumpe, Hermann (*b* Taubenheim, 9 Apr. 1850; *d* Munich, 4 Sept. 1903). German conductor and composer. Studied Leipzig. Helped Wagner to prepare first *Ring*, Bayreuth 1873–6. Appointments in Salzburg, Würzburg, Magdeburg, Frankfurt, Hamburg (1884–6), Stuttgart (1891–5), Schwerin (1897) and Munich (1900–3), where he conducted the first Wagner performances at the newly opened Prinzregententheater. London, C.G., 1898. He composed a number of operas and operettas.

Zumsteeg, Johann Rudolf (*b* Sachsenflur, 10 Jan. 1760; *d* Stuttgart, 27 Jan. 1802). German composer. Though well known as a song composer, he also wrote a number of successful operas which showed an early interest in subjects that were to absorb the Romantics, including the exotic, the chivalric, and the fantastic (*Die Geisterinsel*, 1798).

Zurich. Town in Switzerland. Opera is given at the Stadttheater, first opened in 1833. The present theatre (cap. 1,200) dates from 1891. It was at Zurich that the first legitimate stage performance of *Parsifal* outside Bayreuth was given in 1903 (Swiss copyright having then expired, though this was hotly disputed by Cosima Wagner). Hans Zimmermann directed the theatre 1937–56, establishing the June Festival and staging the premières of *Lulu, Mathis der Maler,* and *Jeanne d'Arc au bûcher,* During Zimmermann's régime, Strauss and Wagner performances reached a very high standard with productions by Rudolf Hartmann, Karl Schmid-Bloss, and Oskar Wälterlin, under the musical direction of Ackermann, Knappertsbusch, Furtwängler, and with outstanding singers. The permanent Zurich company during this period included Lisa della Casa, Else Cavelti, Ira Malaniuk, Andreas Boehm, Franz Lechleitner, and Heinz Rehfuss. In 1955 Hans Rosbaud was appointed music director, after conducting the first stage performance of *Moses und Aron.* Succeeded by Christian Vöchting (1858–1967) and Ferdinand Leitner (from 1969). Zimmermann was succeeded by Karl Heinz Krahl (1956–9) and Herbert Graf (1959–62). Hermann Juch followed Graf (1964–74), and Carl Helmut Drese was appointed director in 1975. The Opera Centre attached to the Opera House was the training ground for Gwyneth Jones, Katherine Pring, and Edith Mathis.
Bibl: M. Hürlimann and H. Olt: *Theater in Zürich – 125 Jahre Stadttheater* (1959)

Zylis-Gara, Teresa (*b* Landvarov, nr. Wilno, 23 Jan. 1935). Polish soprano. Studied Łódź with Olga Olghina. Début Kraków, 1956, Halka. After winning voice competition in Munich, 1960, engaged at Oberhausen, Dortmund, Düsseldorf-Duisburg 1965–70; particularly successful as Poppea, Cio-Cio-San, Anna Bolena, and Violetta. Gly. 1965, Octavian, 1967, Donna Elvira; London, C.G., 1968–9, 1976–7 Violetta, Donna Elvira; Salzburg 1968–70; San Francisco 1968; N.Y., Met., since 1969 Countess, Fiordiligi, Elvira, Violetta, Marguerite, Desdemona, Mimì, Tosca, Marschallin. Highly gifted and committed artist whose achievements have sometimes been under-rated. (R)